HANDBOOK OF INTERNATIONAL ECONOMICS

VOLUME III

HANDBOOKS
IN
ECONOMICS

3

Series Editors

KENNETH J. ARROW
MICHAEL D. INTRILIGATOR

ELSEVIER
AMSTERDAM · LAUSANNE · NEW YORK · OXFORD · SHANNON · TOKYO

EHEHEHEHEHEHEHEHEHEHEHEHEHEHEHEHEHEHEHE

HANDBOOK OF INTERNATIONAL ECONOMICS

VOLUME III

Edited by

GENE M. GROSSMAN
Princeton University

and

KENNETH ROGOFF
Princeton University

1995
ELSEVIER
AMSTERDAM · LAUSANNE · NEW YORK · OXFORD · SHANNON · TOKYO

ELSEVIER SCIENCE B.V.
Sara Burgerhartstraat 25
P.O. Box 211, 1000 AE Amsterdam, The Netherlands

ISBN for this volume: 0 444 81547 3

INTRODUCTION TO THE SERIES

The aim of the *Handbooks in Economics* series is to produce Handbooks for various branches of economics, each of which is a definitive source, reference, and teaching supplement for use by professional researchers and advanced graduate students. Each Handbook provides self-contained surveys of the current state of a branch of economics in the form of chapters prepared by leading specialists on various aspects of this branch of economics. These surveys summarize not only received results but also newer developments, from recent journal articles and discussion papers. Some original material is also included, but the main goal is to provide comprehensive and accessible surveys. The Handbooks are intended to provide not only useful reference volumes for professional collections but also possible supplementary readings for advanced courses for graduate students in economics.

CONTENTS OF THE HANDBOOK

VOLUME I

VOLUME III

PART 1: INTERNATIONAL TRADE THEORY AND POLICY

PREFACE TO THE HANDBOOK

Preface

The first *Handbook of International Economics*, edited by Ronald W. Jones and Peter B. Kenen, was published in two volumes in 1984 and 1985. These volumes surveyed the existing state of the art in research on "real" and "monetary" aspects of international economics. Of course, the field has evolved enormously over the past decade, and many areas that are central to modern research were barely touched upon in the original Handbook. On the macroeconomic side, topics such as the intertemporal approach to the current account, sovereign default, and speculative attacks received virtually no consideration. More fundamentally, the macroeconomics papers in the first Handbook were largely based on aggregative Keynesian models; models with microfoundations appeared only in a couple of isolated sections. On the trade side, formal models of international trade with imperfect competition were still in their infancy in 1985, whereas today they form the basis for much of modern trade theory. Fueled by theoretical developments, research on topics such as strategic trade policy, trade and growth, and economic integration has burgeoned in the past decade.

Even some topics that were covered in the first Handbook, such as the empirical evidence bearing on purchasing power parity or the Heckscher–Ohlin model, have undergone such a profound rethinking that it is necessary to revisit them here. Similarly, on topics such as the political economy of trade policy and international monetary policy coordination, thinking has evolved considerably beyond the treatments in the first edition.

The first *Handbook of International Economics* segregated work on trade flows and trade policies – the so-called "real" side of the international field – from work on macroeconomic interdependence and international financial markets. Over the past twenty years, as trade economists have placed more emphasis on dynamics, and as finance economists have placed more emphasis on microfoundations, the distinctions between the fields have become somewhat blurred. The chapter on growth, for example, could easily have been categorized as trade or finance. It is hard to discuss purchasing power parity without discussing the microeconomic factors that determine the long-run determinants of the real exchange rate. In recognition of the cross-fertilization that exists across the two subfields, we have chosen to publish this second edition of the *Handbook of International Economics* in one volume.

Nevertheless, the reader will observe that we have still attempted to maintain the traditional dichotomy between trade and open-economy macroeconomics as an organizing device. Roughly speaking, the first eight chapters listed in the table of contents cover trade issues, and the second eight cover open-economy macroeconomics. The trade section includes topics such as the determinants of trade patterns, the efficacy of strategic trade policy, and the game-theoretic interactions between governments seeking cooperation in their trade policies. The finance part of the book covers the determinants of exchange rates (real and nominal) and the current account, sovereign debt, global capital market integration, and the international transmission of business cycles.

There is no secret formula that explains our exact choice of topics, though we have intentionally placed greater emphasis on substantive research that employs modern analytical tools, and have paid less attention to topics where the literature is largely narrative. Undoubtedly, one can find other reasonable ways to parse the subject, and some topics omitted here might have found their way into the volume had other editors been in charge. Certain chapters – such as those on monopolistic competition in trade, trade and growth, and strategic trade policy on the micro side, and those on the behavior of nominal exchange rates, the intertemporal approach to the current account, and sovereign debt on the macro side – were obvious candidates, because so much research has been done in these areas since the publications of the first two volumes of the Handbook. Others, like those on international rules and institutions for cooperative trade policy and the strategic aspects of international economic policy are perhaps more idiosyncratic choices, but their inclusion reflects our view that interesting progress has been made and that an assessment of progress to date might be helpful in pointing the way to further research.

It is perhaps worth taking a moment to explain our thinking about a few of the omissions. We considered including a separate chapter on the determinants of direct foreign investment and the role of multinational corporations in trade. This has certainly been a fertile research area, but much of the modeling builds directly on the approaches to trade in differentiated products that are described in the chapter on positive developments in the theory of trade. It was our feeling that repetition could be avoided and continuity of thought maintained by coupling the discussion of multinationals with that on trade with imperfect competition. Much research effort has also been devoted to the construction of computable equilibrium models for use in evaluating trade policies. We decided not to include a chapter defined solely in terms of the research tool that was used, but rather to request a discussion of these models from the authors of the chapter on strategic trade policy and regional integration, since it is in the evaluation of these two types of policies that many of the computable models have been applied. On the finance side, a number of central issues relating to the economics of European Monetary Union are covered in the chapters on fixed exchange rate systems and on strategic international macroeconomic policy. But our volume does not encompass the vast historical and institutional literature relating to EMU that has appeared in the past decade. This is not to deny the importance of this largely narrative literature, but one must recognize that the field of international economics is vast, and some limits have to be placed on a project of this scope. Our decision to focus on the more technical material is certainly in keeping with the general approach used in the Handbooks for other fields.

Trade

As we have already asserted, the most important development in recent years on the microeconomic side of the field has undoubtedly been the incorporation of imperfect competition into the theory of international trade and into empirical investigations of trade flows and trade policies. This "revolution" began with the attempts by Kelvin Lancaster and Paul Krugman to provide a theoretical explanation for the great deal of intra-industry trade described by Herbert Grubel and Peter Lloyd, and with James Brander's attempt to account for the mutual penetration by oligopolisitic competitors into one another's markets. Some of the early modeling efforts of this sort were covered in Elhanan Helpman's chapter in the first volume of the Handbook, but the topic was too new and the understanding too sketchy to warrant star billing for imperfect competition in that volume. In contrast, models featuring imperfect competition play a central role in nearly every chapter of the first part of this volume.

This volume begins with an overview by Paul Krugman of recent developments in the positive theory of international trade. Krugman picks up where Helpman left off, by examining richer and more complete models of trade in differentiated products under conditions of monopolistic competition and models of trade that results from the international rivalry between large, oligopolistic competitors. He also surveys the new literature on the role of multinational corporations in international trade, a literature that was hardly touched upon in Roy Ruffin's treatment of international factor movements in volume one of the Handbook. This literature has made great strides in recent years by recognizing that multinationals typically have ownership rights to intangible assets which often afford them some degree of monopoly power in a local or global market.

The first volume of the Handbook included two chapters focusing on dynamic models of trade and growth. Ron Findlay discussed trade issues that arise in the context of economic development, while Alasdair Smith covered the causes and consequences of capital accumulation in an open economy. Neither of these authors could discuss the long-run effects of trade on growth, because the engines of growth were all exogenous in the research they reviewed. But since that time, the incorporation of imperfect competition into trade models has allowed the development of a dynamic theory in which firms create new technologies in pursuit of monopoly profits. This literature and a related one on technological progress that stems from learning-by-doing are reviewed in the chapter by Gene Grossman and Elhanan Helpman.

Imperfect competition also features prominently in several of this volume's chapters on trade policy. A major research undertaking in the period since the writing of the first Handbook has been the study of the strategic motives that may exist for interventionist trade policies. James Brander reviews the literature on trade policy that alters the nature of oligopolistic competition, beginning with the now well-known Brander-Spencer argument for export subsidies and import tariffs and continuing through the more recent analyses of situations where firms or governments are imperfectly informed. Richard Baldwin and Tony Venables cover recent research on regional economic integration, research that has been inspired by events in Europe and North America. They argue that many of the new insights regarding the effects of customs unions and free trade agreements concern the production shifting and agglomeration of economic activity that can occur when discriminatory trade liberalization takes place in an environment of imperfect competition and increasing-returns technologies. Finally, Robert Feenstra devotes much of his chapter on estimating the effects of trade policy to explaining the new econometric approaches that have been developed to evaluate how trade policy operates in imperfectly competitive market environments.

The first Handbook volume contained an excellent survey by Alan Deardorff of empirical tests of positive trade theories. However, the survey was written before Edward Leamer and various of his co-authors and students had completed their excellent recent re-evaluations of the empirical strengths and shortcomings of the Heckscher–Ohlin model. This alone would have been reason enough to include an update chapter on the empirical evidence bearing on international trade theories. But the decade since the first Handbook has also seen the beginnings of a literature evaluating the empirical support for trade models incorporating economies of scale and imperfect competition, and these studies too are described in the chapter by Leamer and James Levinsohn.

Finally, there are two chapters in the first part of this volume that take up subjects that were touched upon in Robert Baldwin's chapter in the first Handbook volume on trade policies in developed countries. Baldwin devoted some space to the political–economic determinants of trade policies. Since his writing, a considerable amount of additional research has been devoted to the task of explaining why we observe the (seemingly suboptimal) trade policies that we do. Dani Rodrik surveys the recent literature on the political economy of trade policy and provides a very valuable evaluation of what the literature has achieved and what it has as yet failed to accomplish. Baldwin also touched upon some of the rules and institutions of modern trade, such as antidumping and countervailing duty laws and the directions of potential reform of the GATT. However, at that time, little formal analysis had been done to explain why international institutions are structured the way they are and how effective they are in fostering cooperation. Robert Staiger describes some of the recent efforts that have been made in this regard, and indicates a number of areas where further research is likely to be highly productive.

Open-economy macroeconomics

On the finance side, research over the past decade has been fueled both by issues – increasing world capital market integration, the developing-country debt crisis, European Monetary Union – and by the incorporation of microfoundations into macroeconomic models. The first Handbook contained papers by Peter Kenen, and by John Helliwell and Tim Padmore on the international transmission of business cycles. These chapters, however, were based on a Keynesian perspective. Marianne Baxter's chapter in the present Handbook looks at newer models of international transmission based on dynamic stochastic optimizing models; she also considers the implications of various capital market structures for how disturbances are transmitted internationally. Except for brief discussions by Michael Mussa and Jacob Frenkel, and by Maurice Obstfeld and Alan Stockman, the papers in the first Handbook barely touched on the implications of intertemporal optimization for the current account (despite the fact that research on this new approach was already well underway at the time). The chapter by Obstfeld and Kenneth Rogoff in this volume illustrates how current account imbalances can be viewed as intertemporal trade. Their analysis also suggests a very different empirical approach to understanding current account imbalances than the earlier trade equation approach, discussed in Morris Goldstein and Mohsin Khan's contribution to the first Handbook.

In the 1985 volume, a great deal of attention was devoted to the optimal choice of exchange rate regime, both in the chapter by Richard Marston on stabilization and in the one by Stan Black on alternative international monetary arrangements. In many respects, the Marston and Black surveys are still relevant today. However, as global capital markets have deepened, the resources available to private creditors have come to swamp the intervention funds available to central banks, as illustrated by the spectacular breakdown of the European Monetary System in 1993. Today, the stabilization issues surrounding fixed versus flexible exchange rate systems seem secondary to policymakers who have come to realize that there are limits to how "fixed" any fixed exchange rate system can be. Lars Svensson and Peter Garber survey the recent literature on speculative attacks on fixed exchange rate regimes and on evolving target-zone alternatives to fixed rates.

In their chapter on strategic international macroeconomic policy, Torsten Persson and Guido Tabellini provide a new perspective on many of the policy coordination issues considered by Richard Cooper in the first edition. Their approach emphasizes the importance of institutions as a foundation for macro policy, as well as the interplay between domestic authorities' credibility vis-à-vis the private sector, and the strategic interactions between governments of different countries. Persson and Tabellini also use analytical methods to try to capture some of the issues Cooper raised in his more narrative approach.

The finance side of international finance was covered in the first Handbook in a theoretical chapter by William Branson and Dale Henderson, and in an empirical chapter by Richard Levich. Here, in her chapter on international finance, Karen Lewis combines theoretical and empirical methods to analyze some key empirical puzzles, including the home bias anomoly, and the seemingly perverse behaviour of the forward rate discount. Levich's chapter in the original Handbook also covered empirical research on exchange rates and on purchasing power parity. The discussion of these issues has been greatly expanded in the present Handbook. Kenneth Froot and Rogoff consider the explosion of new research on purchasing power parity, where new time series methods and expanded data sets have yielded some very important insights. Jeffrey Frankel and Andrew Rose not only assess the empirical literature on nominal exchange rates, but also consider empirical research using expectations survey data and market micro-structure data. Finally, Jonathan Eaton and Raquel Fernandez look at the large literature on sovereign debt spawned by the developing-country debt crisis of the 1980s. Their chapter illustrates one area where there has clearly been a very constructive interplay between theory and policy.

Acknowledgements

We owe a debt of gratitude to several individuals and organizations who helped make this volume possible. Mike Intriligator convinced us of the potential usefulness of the project, and he and series co-editor Ken Arrow gave us comments on our draft list of chapters. We also received useful comments on this list and comforting moral support from the editors of the first two volumes of the *Handbook of International Economics*, Ron Jones and Peter Kenen. The International Finance Section, the Center of International Studies at Princeton, and the Woodrow Wilson School of Public and International Affairs jointly sponsored a conference held at Princeton University in March 1994, at which first drafts were presented and discussed. This conference proved invaluable not only for improving the individual papers, but for coordinating topics across chapters and for helping authors frame their papers in the context of a larger project. At the conference, in addition to the chapter authors, James Anderson, Andy

Atkeson, David Backus, Lael Brainard, Rich Clarida, Donald Davis, Avinash Dixit, Penny Goldberg, Patrick Kehoe, and Peter Kenen, served as commentators and provided valuable comments that helped to improve the chapters. Carsten Kowalczyk and Daniel Trefler each prepared thoughtful reports in response to our request for further external input. Last, but not least, Michelle Browna, Ruth Miller, and Amy Valis helped to run the pre-publication conference and Sherri Ellington performed a yeoman's job in assembling and editing the final manuscript for submission to the publisher.

GENE M. GROSSMAN
KENNETH ROGOFF
Princeton University

CONTENTS OF VOLUME III

Chapter 26

International Trade Theory: The Evidence   1339

EDWARD E. LEAMER and JAMES LEVINSOHN

Chapter 36

The Operation and Collapse of Fixed Exchange Rate Regimes

PETER M. GARBER and LARS E.O. SVENSSON

Chapter 39

Sovereign Debt   2031

JONATHAN EATON and RAQUEL FERNANDEZ

PART 1

INTERNATIONAL TRADE THEORY
AND POLICY

Chapter 24

INCREASING RETURNS, IMPERFECT COMPETITION AND THE POSITIVE THEORY OF INTERNATIONAL TRADE

PAUL KRUGMAN*

MIT, Cambridge

Contents

*I would like to thank Don Davis and Gene Grossman for extremely helpful comments. Don Davis, in addition to providing invaluable help in revising an early draft, did the yeoman service of presenting that draft in my absence.

Handbook of International Economics, vol. III, Edited by G. Grossman and K. Rogoff
© *Elsevier Science B.V., 1995*

0. Introduction

This chapter is an awkward one to write, because it is in effect squeezed between an illustrious predecessor and the topics covered in other chapters. On one side, I need not retrace the ground covered by Elhanan Helpman's ground-breaking survey in the original *Handbook of International Economics* (written in 1982). On the other side, it is probably fair to say that most of the innovative work on increasing returns and imperfect competition in international trade theory since the late 1980s has focussed on dynamic issues, especially technological change – and these issues are covered in Chapter 2 and other chapters in this volume.

Why, then, write this chapter? For three reasons. First, Helpman's survey turns out to have come a few years too soon. Perhaps inevitably given the state of the field at that time, the general impression conveyed in that chapter was of a collection of highly disparate and messy approaches, standing both in contrast and in opposition to the impressive unity and clarity of constant-returns, perfect-competition trade theory. And yet within only a few years after Helpman's survey, it had become clear (largely due to his own work) that the new ideas were not such a grab-bag after all. On the contrary, many of the insights of increasing returns trade theory could be understood in terms of a quite simple common framework, in which trade has the effect of moving the world economy toward the "integrated economy" that would exist if national boundaries could be eliminated. The integrated-economy approach also suggested considerable continuity between the new elements in trade theory and the older tradition. Furthermore, the framework provided a "grammar" that could be used to discuss topics that went well beyond the standard analysis of trade in final goods, such as the effects of trade in intermediate goods and the role of multinational firms in the world economy.

One purpose of this chapter, then, is to present a compact restatement of this integrated economy approach. In effect, the first part of the chapter is a *Reader's Digest* version of Helpman and Krugman (1985).

At the same time, since Helpman wrote his survey there have been a number of developments in the theory of trade (and direct investment) under imperfect competition that cannot be represented using the integrated economy approach, typically because they rely on some kind of persistent market segmentation that trade does not fully eliminate. These developments include, most notably, analyses of the effects of the size of the domestic market, and of price discrimination; they also have a bearing on recent thinking about multinational enterprise. So a second purpose of this chapter is to summarize some of these post-1982 developments.

Finally, the years that have passed since the original Helpman survey offer us a chance to gain some perspective. Now that the "new trade theory" has grown middle-aged along with its founders, we can try to ask what it accomplished and what it left undone.

This chapter, then, is in three parts: a restatement of the integrated-economy approach to trade theory, a survey of other developments that cannot be treated within that approach, and a brief reconsideration of the achievements and limits of the now not-so-new "new trade theory".

1. The integrated-economy approach to international trade

1.1. Samuelson's angel

It is common in expositions of international trade theory to start by imagining two isolated countries, which then are allowed to begin trade with each other. The integrated economy approach goes in the reverse direction, starting from a unified economy, then breaking it up.

Perhaps the first suggestion of using this approach to think about international trade came in a parable used by Paul Samuelson to explain the concept of factor price equalization. Here's the parable: Once upon a time, all the factors of production in the world were part of a single economy, able to work freely with each other. This integrated world economy had reached an equilibrium, with all the things that go with such an equilibrium: goods prices, factor prices, resource allocations, and so on.

And then down came an angel. (Although Samuelson does not say so, this is obviously the angel from the Tower of Babel story; presumably the factors of production had dared to challenge heaven, and were being punished for their presumption.) The angel smote each unit of each factor of production on the forehead, labelling it as belonging to a particular nation; and thenceforth factors could only work with other factors from the same country.

But how much damage had the angel done? Well, perhaps none. Provided that the angel had not divided the factors of production too unevenly between the nations, it might still be possible through specialization and trade to achieve exactly the same global output and consumption as before. In that case, trade would have the effect of "reproducing the international economy"; and one could indeed describe such a restoration of the integrated economy (which would involve, among other things, equalization of factor prices) as the purpose of international trade.

Samuelson's angel story can be given a very convenient representation in a two-factor, two-good, two-country, constant returns world. Consider Figure 1.1, which was originally suggested by several authors in the 1960s but whose dissemination is due to Dixit and Norman (1980). The box in Figure 1.1 represents the resources of the world economy as a whole, with the height of the box representing the world supply of capital, the width the world supply of labor. In the pre-angel, integrated economy there will be full employment of both factors; we represent the

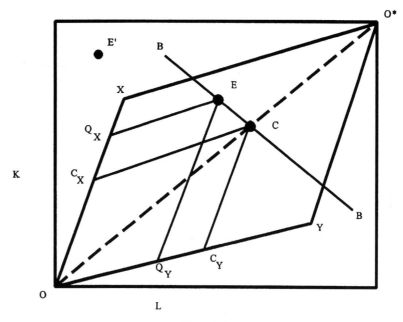

Figure 1.1.

resources devoted to the capital-intensive industry by OX, those devoted to the labor-intensive industry by OY. The two vectors must, of course, sum to the world factor endowment – that is, the completed parallelogram just fits into the box.

Now let the angel come down, and divide the factors of production into two nationalities, Home and Foreign. Let us measure Home endowments from the southwest corner of the box, O, and Foreign endowments from the northeast corner, O^*. Then the angel's punishment can be represented by a single point which, measured from O, shows the Home endowment, and which shows the Foreign endowment measured from O^*. Point E is one example of a world endowment point; E' is another.

Did the angel do any harm? In order to reproduce the integrated-economy outcome, it must be possible to use the same production techniques (i.e. capital–labor ratios) that were used in the integrated economy to produce the same outputs, while fully employing the resources of each country. It is immediately obvious that this is possible if the endowment point is, like point E, within the parallelogram OXO^*Y. Indeed, we can determine the required resource allocation simply by completing parallelograms. Let Home devote resources OQ_X to production of X, OQ_Y to production of Y; and let Foreign correspondingly devote resources Q_XX and Q_YY to the two industries. That will precisely replicate the integrated economy production, while fully employing both countries' resources. It is also immediately apparent that this is an equilibrium, one in which both countries have the same factor prices as in the integrated economy (and therefore the same as each other). In this case, then, the angel's action was a warning, not an actual punishment.

It is conversely clear that if the endowment point lies outside the parallelogram, at a point such as E', there is no way to replicate the integrated economy. Among other things, factor prices will therefore not be equalized. It then becomes a fairly nasty business to determine the details of the pattern of specialization.

Returning to the case in which the integrated economy is reproduced, we have seen how the pattern of resource allocation and production is determined. Can anything more be said? Let us make one more assumption: that everyone has the same homothetic preferences. Then everyone in the economy will consume the two goods in the same ratio. But this means that the factor services embodied in each individual's consumption must also be in the same ratio – and this ratio must be the same as the world ratio of capital to labor. Geometrically, the factor services embodied in each country's consumption must lie on the diagonal OO^*.

Where on this diagonal does the consumption point lie? At that point at which income equals spending for each country. But all income takes the form of factor earnings. Suppose that E is the endowment point. Then draw a line (BB) with a slope $-w/r$, where w is the wage rate and r the rental rate on capital in the integrated equilibrium, passing through E. All combinations of factor services on that line have the same value, and the factors embodied in Home consumption must therefore be at the point where BB crosses the diagonal, C.

Once we have determined this consumption point, several things become obvious. First, since E represents the factor services embodied in Home production and C the factors embodied in Home consumption, EC is Home's net trade in factor services. Second, we can read off Home's consumption of each good (or more precisely, the resources used to produce its consumption of each good) by completing parallelograms: OC_X is consumption of X, OC_Y is consumption of Y. And therefore the pattern of trade in goods can also be seen: Home exports $OQ_X - OC_X$, imports $OC_Y - OQ_Y$.

The end result, of course, is to give yet another statement of the Heckscher–Ohlin theorem that the capital-abundant country Home exports the capital-intensive good X. Here, however, we view the theorem in a different light: the point of trade in this case is to reproduce the integrated economy by trading embodied factor services; trade in commodities is simply a means to that end.

One convenient aspect of this diagram is that it can readily be adapted to situations in which there are more than two goods. Suppose, for example, that there are three goods. Then the situation is as represented in Figure 1.2. Here we let OX be the vector of resources that the integrated economy would employ in producing the most capital-intensive good, XY the resources in the good of intermediate capital intensity, and YO^* the resources in the most labor-intensive good. Clearly, the integrated economy can be reproduced as long as the endowment point lies within the hexagonal area traced out by these vectors. The actual pattern of production and trade is

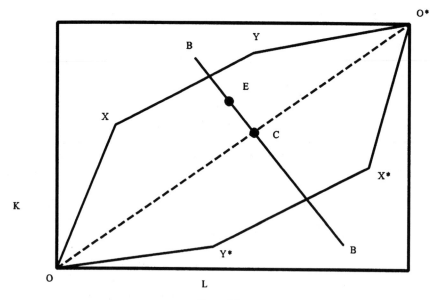

Figure 1.2.

indeterminate, since there are many ways to fully employ the resources of each country. However, the Heckscher–Ohlin principle is still honored in the sense that the net trade in embodied factor services must still be *EC*. That is, the capital-abundant country is a net exporter of the embodied services of capital, a net importer of the services of labor.

   The most useful thing about this approach, however, is that it can be applied to models in which returns to scale are not constant, and in which differences in factor proportions are not the only motive for trade.

1.2. Differentiated products

During the course of the 1970s several industrial organization theorists, notably Dixit and Stiglitz (1977) and Lancaster (1975) offered ways to give the old tradition of Chamberlinian monopolistic competition solid microfoundations, and to embed monopolistic competition in differentiated products within general equilibrium models. These new models depended on very special and essentially implausible assumptions about tastes and technology, but they were quickly recognized as useful devices for thinking about a variety of issues involving increasing returns and imperfect competition. In particular, towards the end of that decade several international trade theorists realized that the new models of monopolistic competition offered a particularly clean way to think about trade based on economies of scale rather than comparative advantage. These initial developments, and the issues associated with the choice of alternative ways of modeling product differentiation, were covered in the 1982 Helpman survey and need not be reviewed here.

At first it seemed that the various models of trade with monopolistic competition were essentially inconsistent both with the more traditional factor-proportions approach and with each other. I think that it is fair to say that this would have appeared to be the case even to most readers of Helpman's survey, although Helpman (1981) made a major effort to unify the new approaches with the older tradition. By thinking in terms of the integrated-economy approach, however, it becomes easy to embed trade in differentiated products within a factor proportions model. Indeed, one does not even need to redraw the diagram!

Let's change the story of Samuelson's angel slightly. We now imagine that one of the industries in the pre-angel world – say industry X – was characterized by Chamberlinian monopolistic competition. That is, there were many firms in that industry, each a little monopolist producing a distinct product with a technology that exhibited internal economies of scale – but free entry into the industry had driven firms to the tangency position in which no economic profits were being earned. (The zero-profit assumption implies that all income is still factor income.) We need not specify the details of how products were differentiated – whether individuals loved variety, as in Dixit–Stiglitz models, or whether each individual consumed a preferred variety, as in Lancastrian models – except to assume that all varieties were symmetric.

Now let the angel come down, and divide the world into nations. What must be done to reproduce the integrated economy? As before, the pre-angel output of each industry must be allocated among countries in such a way as to fully employ all factors of production using pre-angel techniques. But what does it mean to allocate the production of an industry that consists of many differentiated products? It could mean allocating a certain share of the production of each variety to each country. This, however, would not reproduce the integrated economy, because production of each variety would take place at a smaller, and thus less efficient scale. To reproduce the integrated economy, then, one must allocate each *variety* of X to only one country. If there are 100 X varieties, and Home gets 57 percent of the world X production, then it must produce all of the pre-angel output of 57 varieties, while Foreign produces the other 43. (It is indeterminate which varieties are produced in which country, but it doesn't matter, because the varieties are by assumption symmetric.)

We can still use Figure 1.1 to describe the aggregate outcome. If the endowment point is E, Home will still devote resources OQ_X to the production of X, and consume a volume of X products that required OC_X to produce. We must now, however, reinterpret the quantity $OQ_X - OC_X$. It no longer represents Home's total exports of X. The reason is that X is now not a homogeneous good but a group of differentiated products, and the varieties produced in Foreign are different from those in Home. As a result, Home consumers will spend some of their income on X-varieties produced in Foreign (either because individuals have a taste for variety, or because there is a dispersion of tastes). That is, Home will import as well as export X. We must therefore reinterpret $OQ_X - OC_X$ as Home's *net* exports of X.

The overall pattern of trade can be schematically represented by Figure 1.3, where the length of arrows represents the value of trade. Home is a net exporter of the monopolistically competitive good X and an importer of Y; this pattern of *inter-industry* trade can be viewed as the comparative advantage component of the trade flow. However, there is additional trade over and above this interindustry trade, because Home and Foreign produce different varieties of X; this two-way trade within the X industry constitutes the *intraindustry* component of international trade.

The essential reason for this intraindustry trade is the existence of economies of scale. That is, if varieties of X were produced under constant returns, it would be possible to reproduce the integrated economy by dividing the production of each variety between the countries, and there would be no need to engage in intraindustry trade to satisfy consumers' taste for variety; it is increasing returns that prevent each country from producing the full range. Thus in this model we can make a simple distinction: interindustry trade – which allows countries to trade embodied factor services – is the result of comparative advantage; intraindustry trade – which allows countries to retain the integrated economy scale of production – is the result of increasing returns.

As one might expect, the relative importance of these two kinds of trade depends on the difference in the countries' factor abundances. Imagine sliding the endowment point E back and forth along the line BB (which amounts to varying the resources of the countries while keeping their relative economic size constant). If E is moved down to the diagonal OO^*, there will be no net trade in factor services, and hence no interindustry trade. However, trade will not vanish, because the two countries will

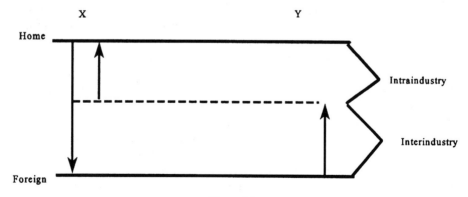

Figure 1.3.

still be producing different varieties of X. Thus all trade will be intraindustry. Conversely, move E to the edge of the parallelogram. Then Foreign will produce no X, and there will be only interindustry trade. So countries with similar resources will tend to engage primarily in intraindustry trade, countries with very different resources will tend to engage primarily in interindustry trade.

By using the integrated economy approach, then, we are able to accomplish several things. First, we can show that the details of particular monopolistic competition models of trade, such as the form of product differentiation, do not matter when it comes to the description of the motives for and pattern of trade. Second, we can very easily offer a picture of trade in which both economies of scale and comparative advantage are motives for trade. Finally, this approach makes the role of increasing returns seem less a departure from, than a natural extension of the grand tradition in trade theory: both trade in embodied factors and specialization to achieve scale economies are ways in which the trading world "tries" to reproduce the integrated economy.

1.3. External economies

Until the monopolistic competition models of trade emerged in the late 1970s, nearly all thinking about increasing returns in trade took the form of models in which economies of scale were purely external to firms. While the tradition of such models had some influence, however, it was limited, probably for three reasons. First, the disembodied, abstract nature of pure external economies may have seemed unsatisfactory: how would you recognize such external effects if you saw them? Second, external-economy models of trade typically seemed to yield a bewildering variety of equilibria, leaving the modeler with a taxonomy rather than a clear set of insights. Finally, much of the traditional literature on external-economy models regarded the effect of external economies as being one of modifying or distorting the pattern of specialization away from that implied by resource abundance; given the dominance of comparative advantage thinking, most international economists instinctively tended to regard any such effects as probably minor.

The 1982 Helpman survey offered a major clarification of the role of external economies in trade – indeed, it offered an interpretation of equilibrium in an externality-ridden world that was later to be rediscovered with considerable fanfare in the "new growth" literature [Romer (1986)]. Nonetheless, the integrated economy approach allows us to add some further insights.

External economies are by no means always, or even usually, consistent with the integrated-economy approach. There are, however, some cases in which external economies are consistent with that approach, and those cases do offer some interesting intuition into the possible role of external economies in the world economy.

1.3.1. The pattern of trade

Consider an integrated economy that produces *three* goods, one of which is subject to industry-specific external economies. That is, production of X takes place under constant returns from the point of view of the individual firm, but the efficiency of each atomistic firm is an increasing function of total industry output. Despite these external economies, there will normally be a competitive equilibrium in this integrated economy. (If the external effects are very strong, there may be multiple equilibria even in the integrated economy; we disregard this possibility.) Associated with this integrated economy equilibrium will be resource allocations to all three industries as well as goods and factor prices.

Now once again we invoke Samuelson's angel. As before, the angel divides factors between two nations. He or she must also, however, make a critical decision about the extent of the punishment: do external benefits spill over between the nations? If there is full international spillover of externalities – if factors of production in each country derive the same external benefits from X production abroad as at home – then all that is needed to reproduce the external benefits of the integrated economy is that total world X production be the same as integrated economy X production – which is the same criterion that applies in the absence of externalities. That is, factor price equalization and trade can be represented as in Figure 1.2, with the presence of external economies making no difference as long as E lies within the hexagon.

But suppose that the angel's rules are stricter, and that external benefits accrue only from production that takes place in the same country. Then the integrated-economy outcome can be reproduced only if we add another criterion to those of matching integrated economy resource allocation and full employment: *all of the industry that is subject to external economies must be concentrated in one country.*

Figure 1.4 shows what this criterion implies. In the figure, OX represents the resources that the integrated economy would have devoted to the production of the good subject to external economies; XY and YO^* represent the resources devoted to two constant-returns sectors. (It is, of course, not necessary that the external-economy sector be the most capital-intensive; it is straightforward to see how the diagram changes if it is of intermediate capital intensity.) In order to reproduce the integrated economy, we must concentrate the X industry either in Home or in Foreign; the other two industries can then be allocated between the countries to fully employ their resources. This means, then, that the integrated economy can be reproduced as long as the endowment point lies inside either of the solid parallelograms in the figure. (These parallelograms are shown here as overlapping, but they need not be.)

The choice of words here is deliberate: provided that E lies in the right region, the integrated economy *can* be reproduced. That is, there then exists an equilibrium that reproduces it. There may also be other equilibria which do not. This point is easier to make in a two-good, one factor model: it is a familiar result there that there may be both an equal-wage equilibrium in which the increasing returns industry is concen-

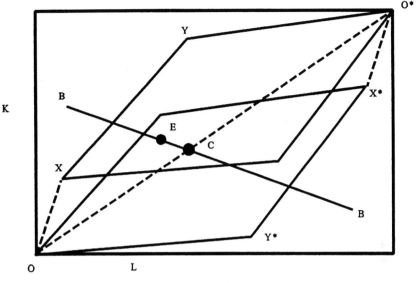

Figure 1.4.

trated in the larger country, and an unequal-wage equilibrium in which the smaller country is specialized in the increasing-returns sector [see, for example, the analysis in Ethier (1982a)]. The former equilibrium reproduces the integrated economy, while the latter does not. Thus it is something of a cheat in this case to focus only on equilibria that reproduce integrated economy; but we will nonetheless do so.

Suppose, then, that the endowment point lies within one or both of the parallelograms, and that we consider only equilibria that reproduce the integrated economy. We can then say several useful things about international trade.

First, even if the countries have identical factor abundances – if E lies on the diagonal line OO^* – X production will be concentrated in only one country, and there will therefore be international trade. Thus in an external-economy model, as in the monopolistic competition models, international trade will occur as a result of increasing returns even if there is no comparative advantage.

Second, the pattern of production and trade may be indeterminate. Suppose that E, as drawn, lies in the overlap between the two parallelograms. Then there are two patterns of production (and hence trade) that reproduce the integrated economy: one in which X is concentrated in Home, one in which it is concentrated in Foreign.

Third, although there may be indeterminacy, the factor proportions theory continues to hold in the sense that the capital-abundant country is a net exporter of capital services embodied in goods. In Figure 1.4, as in earlier figures, EC represents the net trade in factor services. Thus this approach suggests the happy interpretation that increasing returns add an overlay of additional specialization and trade to the trade required to embody the necessary movement of factor services, adding to comparative advantage rather than modifying or distorting it (although we no longer have the simple distinction between intra- and inter-industry trade).

1.3.2. The gains from trade

Much of the traditional literature on external economies in trade seemed to imply that such external economies created a conflict of interest between countries; that there could be a more or less zero-sum battle over who got the external benefits of increasing-returns industries. And even in Helpman's 1982 survey he seemed to suggest that welfare might decline if your country saw its increasing-returns sectors shrink as a result of trade. The particular version of external-economy trade described here suggests, however, an alternative and more benign view.

First, even when the pattern of trade is indeterminate – where either country might end up with the X industry – as long as the integrated economy is reproduced it doesn't matter for either country's welfare, since the owners of factors in either case are exactly as well off as they were pre-angel.

But are countries better off with trade than they would be in its absence? It is possible to establish a sufficient criterion for such gains: a country gains from trade if the *world* output of the external-economy good with trade is larger than that country's *individual* output of that good would be in the absence of trade. This seems a fairly weak test, and therefore suggests a more optimistic view about the welfare effects of trade under external economies than the older literature.

The criterion may be justified by an argument developed in Helpman and Krugman (1985), and illustrated in Figure 1.5. In that figure, the curve II represents the unit isoquant for some good before trade; we suppose that the initial factor prices are represented by ww, so that V represents the initial unit factor inputs.

The opening of trade will have two effects. First, factor prices may change. Second, if this good is subject to external effects, the unit isoquant may shift. Suppose first that the good is not subject to external effects. Then the iso-value line of the inputs used to produce a unit of the good after trade will be a line with a slope different from ww, say $w'w'$. Obviously, V must lie above that line. That means, however, that the *post-trade* income of the inputs used to produce the *pre-trade* output of a good is always more than enough to purchase that pre-trade output. But if this is true for all goods, then post-trade income is always more than enough to purchase pre-trade consumption – which means that the country's choice has been expanded, and that it gains from trade.

If a good is subject to external effects, the unit isoquant may shift. What matters for the price of the good is the isoquant *in the country in which the good is produced*. As long as that isoquant shifts inward – as in the illustrated isoquant $I'I'$ – then V is still certain to lie above the iso-value line, which is now shown as $w''w''$. That is, it remains true, indeed is true a fortiori, that after trade the pre-trade inputs can more

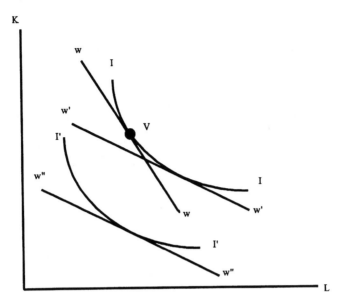

Figure 1.5.

than afford to buy their previous production. But the unit isoquant for the producing country will indeed be inside our autarky isoquant as long as that country's output is larger than ours would have been in the absence of trade.

We are therefore able to justify our criterion for gains from trade: a country gains as long as the *world* output of each external-economy good, wherever it may be located, exceeds our autarky output. The gains from trade, like trade itself, arise both from comparative advantage – reflected here in a change in factor prices – and from the additional external economies achieved through geographic concentration of industries, reflected in the inward shift in the unit isoquant.

All of this suggests a rather benign view of trade under external economies. According to this view, it is a good thing for the world that there be a Silicon Valley, that is, that the semiconductor industry be concentrated *somewhere*; it really doesn't matter where. The conclusion is, of course, sensitive to the model, but it at least serves as a corrective to the assumption that country-specific external economies always imply a struggle over who gets the good sectors.

1.4. Intermediate goods, traded and nontraded

In some of the early papers on increasing returns in trade, Ethier (1979, 1982b) argued that intraindustry trade in practice consists largely of trade not in differentiated final goods but in differentiated inputs, and that the possibility of such trade in effect gives rise to international (as opposed to national) external economies. As we have just seen, even in the case of purely national external economies the welfare gains from these external effects may be effectively globalized. Nonetheless, Ethier's point appears to be largely if not completely correct about actual intraindustry trade, and in any case the implications of trade in differentiated intermediate goods – or its absence – are a subject of considerable interest.

Imagine a world economy in which there are two sectors X and Y, and in which X is a monopolistically competitive, differentiated-product industry. The varieties of X do not, however, enter into final consumption. Instead, they are used as inputs into the production of Y.

What effect does this have on the model? If both goods are costlessly tradeable, the fact that one of the industries is an intermediate good makes little difference. Indeed, we can still apply Figure 1.1: trade will reproduce the integrated economy as long as the endowment point lies within the parallelogram, and the volumes of both intra- and inter-industry trade will be exactly as in the case of two final goods.

Matters become very different, however, if differentiated intermediate goods are made nontradeable.

Nontraded final goods can be introduced into the integrated-economy framework with little difficulty. Essentially, factor-price equalization can still occur for a non-trivial set of endowments as long as there are at least as many tradeable sectors as factors of production. The region of endowments leading to factor price equalization is, however, smaller the larger the share of expenditure on nontradeables.

The case of nontraded intermediates poses additional issues. Suppose that an upstream industry provides many differentiated inputs to a downstream sector; that each of those inputs is produced subject to scale economies; and that the inputs cannot be traded (or indeed have transport costs). Then the integrated economy can only be reproduced if *all* of the intermediate varieties and the good whose production uses them are concentrated in the same country! This obviously rules out reproducing the integrated economy in the two-industry case just described.

We can still make use of the integrated-economy approach, however, if we introduce some extra industries. Suppose, in particular, that there are *four* industries: N, X, Y, Z. Industry N produces differentiated and nontradeable inputs used in the production of X; Y and Z are constant-returns. In Figure 1.6, we let ON, NX, XY, and YO^* represent the integrated-economy vectors of resource use in each industry. (Again, the factor-intensity rankings are arbitrary.)

In order to reproduce the integrated economy, the "industrial complex" consisting of the N and X industries must be concentrated in one country. The Y and Z industries can then be allocated between the countries. On reflection, the implication is apparent: trade can reproduce the integrated economy as long as the endowment point lies either in the parallelogram defined by Y and Z after putting the N–X complex in Home, or in that defined after placing N–X in Foreign. Thus the region of such endowment points is the shaded area in the figure.

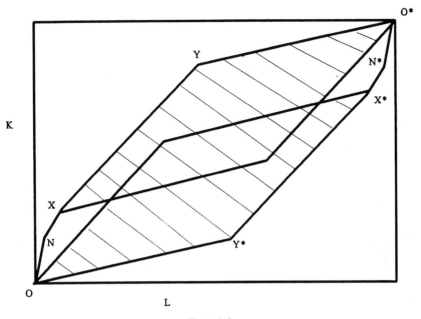

Figure 1.6.

This looks familiar. It is, in fact, essentially the same result as that shown in Figure 1.4, where the X industry was subject to pure national external economies. All of the other implications of that model carry over as well: trade due to both increasing returns and comparative advantage, determinate net trade in factor services but possibly indeterminate trade in goods, and (with some care) the proposition that all countries benefit from the establishment of an industrial concentration somewhere, no matter where. The reassuring implication is that the insights from external economy stories continue to apply when the externalities result from market-size effects rather than purely disembodied spillovers.

1.5. Multinational enterprise

A final application of the integrated economy approach is to the role of multinational enterprise in the world economy. Multinationals fit awkwardly into perfect-competition trade theory. After all, the whole subject is concerned with the way that the boundaries of firms may cut across the boundaries of nations; yet in a perfectly competitive, constant-returns model firms are essentially invisible. As a result, attempts to introduce multinationals into trade models before 1980 often involved ad hoc assumptions, such as the idea that firms in a certain industry possessed some kind of internationally mobile specific capital. (The fact that the expansion of multinational firms is often described as "foreign direct investment", and tracked via balance of payments statistics, may have helped confuse the picture.)

Within the integrated-economy approach, however, it is possible to offer a quite simple way of thinking about the nature and role of multinational firms.[1] This analysis [due originally to Helpman (1984b)] is, as we will see shortly, quite obviously incomplete as a story about real-world multinational enterprise; but at least it offers a reasonable first cut.

Return one last time to the pre-angel integrated economy. Let us again suppose that there are two industries, X and Y, with X consisting of many differentiated products. However, we now suppose that the X industry involves two stages of production for each variety. These might involve two stages in a physical production process (that is, the upstream stage might involve a variety-specific intermediate good, as opposed to the general-purpose intermediates discussed above); or one part of the process might involve intangible services, such as home-office activities. Without necessarily committing ourselves to the latter interpretation, let us call one activity "headquarters" and the other "production". In Figure 1.7, the vector OH represents integrated-economy inputs to headquarters, HX inputs to production of X, and XO^* inputs to Y.

In contrast to the three-industry models described before, however, we now assume that for some reason it is difficult to sell headquarters services to producers of X via arms-length transactions. The reasons may involve any of the variety of explanations invoked by industrial-organization theorists to explain vertical integration; the obvious candidate is some version of the bilateral monopoly problem, if firms must make specific investments. The details do not matter, as long as we assume that in the integrated economy each headquarters and its corresponding production unit are under common management.

Now let the angel descend one last time. He or she again divides productive factors into nations, establishing an endowment point. But there is now a further choice in the degree of punishment: can activities in different nations be under common management? If so, multinational enterprise is allowed.

Consider what happens if multinational enterprise is *not* allowed. In that case each

---

[1]The general idea of the model described here is that multinational enterprise arises from the combination of two things: industrial-organization motives to place two or more activities under common ownership and management, and comparative-advantage reasons to place those activities in separate countries. Obviously this story need not be told in an integrated-economy framework, although it is convenient to do so. A paper very much in the same spirit as Helpman (1984) was simultaneously and independently published by Markusen (1984); Ethier (1986) refers to the general idea that both papers embody as the Markusen–Helpman model, and I will follow his usage. Ethier's own contribution focussed on the reasons for integration of activities under common ownership – the "internalization" issue that is simply assumed by Helpman and Markusen – rather than on the reasons for geographic separation of activities.

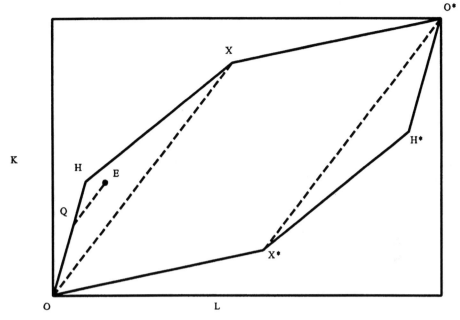

Figure 1.7.

X factory and its headquarters must be in the same country. Thus there is an X industry, whose integrated economy inputs are OX, which can be allocated between the countries (by locating some headquarters/factory combinations in each). The integrated economy can be reproduced only if the endowment point lies in the parallelogram OXO^*X^*.

If it is possible to have geographically separate operations under common control, however, the region of integrated-economy reproduction is expanded to the full hexagon $OHXO^*H^*X^*$.

Suppose that the endowment point lies in one of the "flanges" that are added by the possibility of multinational enterprise, say at point E. Then the precise structure of production – how many headquarters are located in Home – is indeterminate, although as usual the net trade in embodied factor services is determinate. It is possible to tie down the extent of multinational operation with one more assumption: that the world economy makes do with as little direct investment as possible. (This assumption may be justified by assuming that there is some small cost to operating across national boundaries, a cost small enough that the assumption of a reproduced integrated economy remains a close approximation.) Then the Home endowment will be employed by a combination of stand-alone headquarters and integrated operations, with resources OQ devoted to the former and QE to the latter.

An important point about world equilibrium with multinationals is that trade in physical commodities will in general not be balanced. In the case shown in Figure 1.7, Home will run a persistent trade deficit. This deficit will, of course, be offset by the invisible exports of headquarters services, but one could well imagine that these exports would in practice be misreported or even ignored.

How satisfactory is this as a model of multinational enterprise? It is certainly better than trying to represent such enterprise as a movement of some kind of physical capital. Even casual observation, however, suggests that a model along these lines is very incomplete as a description of the actual extent of multinational enterprise. In the model, direct investment (by which I here mean the control of a foreign production unit by a domestic headquarters) goes in only one direction, reflecting comparative advantage. In reality, direct investment is like trade in manufactured goods: it mostly takes place among similar nations, and often reflects two-way flows within the same industry. This suggests that the integrated-economy approach is a bit less successful here than elsewhere; I will return to the issue of multinational enterprise below.

1.6. The integrated-economy approach: Concluding remarks

The parable of Samuelson's angel turns out to be a way to gain insight into a surprisingly wide range of issues in international trade: not only the original Heckscher–Ohlin–Samuelson propositions, but intraindustry trade, external economies, nontraded and intermediate goods, and even multinational enterprise. As is often the case in theory, a great simplification follows from changing the question. Instead of asking "What is the effect of unifying two economies?", we ask "What must a divided economy do to neutralize the effects of that division?". The answer, in general, is that the pieces of the integrated economy must trade factor services, explicitly or implicitly through trade in goods; and that activities which are efficient only if carried on at a single location must be concentrated in only one country. From that answer follows the result that trade reflects both comparative advantage (differences in factor endowments) and increasing returns, internal or external.

There are also two obvious limitations to the approach. One is that as a practical matter it is very clear that international transactions do *not* reproduce the integrated economy; I will return to this issue in the third part of the chapter. First, however, let us turn to the other limitation, which is that there are a number of important issues involving trade under conditions of increasing returns and imperfect competition that inherently involve market segmentation and the failure to achieve a fully integrated economy.

2. Market segmentation

2.1. The home market effect

During the 1960s and 1970s, a time when formal trade theory was almost entirely dominated by models with constant returns and perfect competition, there was a sort of "counter-culture" in international trade that claimed that other forces explained trade patterns. Perhaps the most influential work in this counter-tradition was Steffan Burenstam Linder's 1961 *An Essay on Trade and Transformation*, which argued among other things that countries tend to export goods for which they have large domestic *demand* rather than conventional supply-based comparative advantage. The mis-named "Linder hypothesis" (his family name is Burenstam Linder) seemed intuitively plausible to many observers, and generated a large if inconclusive empirical literature. The analytical underpinnings of the hypothesis, however, remained unclear. Burenstam Linder himself seems to have had in mind a process of induced innovation, in which ideas for new products are suggested by the environment. With the development of the new models of international trade, however, it became apparent that a version of the hypothesis could be given a much more mundane justification, resting on the interaction of scale economies and transport costs. [The approach described here was introduced in Krugman (1980).]

Consider a world in which labor is the only factor of production, and in which a constant share of expenditure falls on each of two industries: a constant-returns sector Y, and a Dixit–Stiglitz-type monopolistically-competitive sector X consisting of many differentiated products in which there is a constant elasticity of substitution ρ between any two varieties. Suppose also that there are two countries Home and Foreign, with labor forces L and L^*. Unlike in the integrated-economy approach, however, we suppose that there are costs of transportation between these two economies: while the constant returns good may be shipped costlessly, when a variety of the differentiated products is shipped only $\gamma < 1$ units arrive for each unit sent. (This assumption was described by Samuelson as the "iceberg" transportation model, in which goods simply melt in transit. It has two advantages as a modeling trick. First, it eliminates the need to introduce transportation as an additional sector. Second, it implies that the elasticity of demand with respect to a firm's f.o.b. price is the same as that with respect to its c.i.f. price, eliminating many potential complications.)

It turns out that in this model there is a "home market effect": the country with the larger economy tends to be a net exporter in the monopolistically-competitive sector. In particular, if L/L^* is sufficiently large all X production will be concentrated in Home.

The argument proceeds as follows. First, we note that as long as both countries produce the constant-returns good, wages will be equal. Let w be the common wage rate.

Next, let us *posit* that all production of X is concentrated in Home, and check to see whether this is in fact an equilibrium. Let μ be the share of expenditure that falls on X, and n be the number of firms that would earn zero profits if all X were produced in Home. Then each firm will have a total value of sales (including sales of goods that melt away in transit) equal to

$$S = \mu w[L + L^*]/n$$

Now consider an individual firm that begins production in Foreign. Since it will have the same marginal cost and face the same elasticity of demand as existing firms (remember the iceberg assumption), it will want to charge the same f.o.b. price as those firms. But if it charges the same f.o.b. price as the typical firm in Home, its c.i.f. price will be only γ times as high to local consumers, but $1/\gamma$ times as high to consumers abroad. But that means that the value of its sales will be[2]

$$S^* = \mu w[L\gamma^{\rho-1} + L^*\gamma^{1-\rho}]/n$$

Now the existing Home firms are, by assumption, earning zero profits. It therefore follows that this entering firm will be profitable if $S^* > S$, unprofitable if $S^* < S$.

Is concentration of all X production in Home an equilibrium? It is if, given such a concentration, an individual firm cannot enter profitably in Foreign. That is, concentration of production in Home is an equilibrium if $S^* < S$, or

$$L\gamma^{\rho-1} + L^*\gamma^{1-\rho} < L + L^*$$

On rearrangement, this yields the criterion for concentration of production,

$$\frac{L}{L^*} > \gamma^{1-\rho}$$

where the right hand side of the inequality exceeds one.

What is the intuition behind this result? Roughly, we can think of the logic as follows. Due to economies of scale, each good is produced in only one location, and sold to consumers in both. If the cost of production is the same, then the deciding factor in location is transport costs; total transportation costs are lower if production takes place in the country with the larger market.

If transport costs are high (corresponding to a low γ) or if the two countries are close in size, full concentration of the increasing-returns industry in the larger country will no longer occur. It is, however, possible to show that the larger country will still be a net exporter in this industry.

Aside from offering a relatively down-to-earth rationale for the Linder hypothesis,

---

[2]Bear in mind that a 1 percent increase in the price will reduce the *volume* of sales by ρ percent, but will reduce the *value* of sales by only $\rho - 1$ percent.

the analysis of the home market effect has played a significant role in recent developments in economic geography, our next topic.

2.2. The "new economic geography"

In the last few years there has been a movement toward applying concepts from the theory of international trade to the analysis of the location of population and industry *within* countries; or more precisely, within economic units characterized by a high degree of labor mobility. This is not exactly a new idea: Ohlin's 1933 book was, after all, entitled *Interregional and International Trade*, and concluded with the declaration that international trade theory is simply international location theory. In practice, however, international trade theorists have worked almost completely without reference to the ideas of location theorists and regional scientists.

This surprising lack of communication may have had much to do with the fact that regional analysis, by sheer force of empirical compulsion, has always taken the role of economies of scale both internal and external very seriously; as long as trade theory was dominated by a constant-returns tradition, the fields had little to say to each other. It is, however, surprising that trade theorists took so long to apply the tools of the new trade theory to economic geography.

During the 1980s, several urban economists, notably Fujita (1988), used the assumption of a monopolistically competitive sector producing nontraded intermediate goods to give a micro foundation to the agglomeration economies that are a necessary part of any theory of city formation. These models essentially exploited the same point made in the discussion of intermediate goods above: market-size effects on a monopolistically-competitive intermediate goods sector can have essentially the same implications as a pure external economy. These market-size externalities could then be inserted into a well-developed literature of which international economists have been oddly ignorant, that of urban systems models along the lines of Henderson (1974).

There is an older tradition in regional economics that also emphasizes market-size effects, but in a more specifically geographical context. Krugman (1991) is a simple model that attempts to capture the spirit of classic writings on economic geography such as Pred (1966) that emphasize cumulative processes of regional growth based on forward and backward linkages – but does so within a formal framework that draws on the insights and technical tricks of the new trade theory. It imagines an economy with two symmetric regions, east and west, two sectors, agriculture and manufacturing, and two factors of production, workers and farmers. Manufactures is a Dixit–Stiglitz sector, with iceberg transport costs to ship manufactured goods between regions. We now suppose, however, that workers (but not farmers) are mobile between regions, and will move to whichever region offers them a higher real wage.

The key question is whether equilibrium will involve workers equally divided between the two regions, or will involve concentration of workers in one or the other region. It turns out that one can represent the issue in terms of a tension between one "centrifugal" force pushing toward dispersal of workers and two "centripetal" forces encouraging them to concentrate. The centrifugal force is the assumed immobility of farmers; if there were no economies of scale, workers would of course have an incentive to move toward locations where they are a relatively scarce factor. Working against this are two forces. First, whichever region has a larger population of workers will also offer a larger market for manufactured goods – and thus the home market effect will operate. Second, workers will, other things equal, receive a higher real wage if they are located close to the suppliers of manufactured goods.

These two centripetal forces can be identified with the "linkages" that played a large role in pre-1970 discussion of development economics, with the home market effect representing a backward linkage and the desire to be close to suppliers a forward linkage. And it is possible to develop a simple criterion for the sustainability of an equilibrium with concentrated manufacturing that depends in an intuitively sensible way on the levels of scale economies and transport costs, together with the share of manufacturing in expenditure.

The framework developed in that model is extremely special and unrealistic. Nonetheless, it has the useful feature of being relatively tractable in an area that has long seemed very resistant to formal modeling. And rather than displacing the traditional insights in that field, this effort at modeling seems to confirm their usefulness, even while helping clarify them. Indeed, one of the pleasant surprises of applying the methods of new trade theory to location issues is that they appear both to validate and to unify a number of seemingly disparate traditions in economic geography. The relationship to the "cumulative process" analysis of Pred and others has already been mentioned. There is another tradition in geography which attempts to explain location decisions in terms of plausible but ad hoc "market potential functions", a method created by analogy with physics, and exemplified by the work of Harris (1954). In Krugman (forthcoming) it is shown that models of economic geography based on new trade theory modeling tricks do imply the existence of market potential functions that are a little more complex than but bear a clear resemblance to those used in the geography literature.

Perhaps most interestingly, the new economic geography models appear to offer a way to integrate trade theory with two classic traditions in location theory: the land-rent theory of von Thünen and the central-place theory of Christaller (1933) and Lösch (1940). Krugman (1993) shows via simulation experiments with a dynamic, multi-region version of the model that a random initial spatial allocation of manufacturing tends to group itself into a multiple concentrations more or less evenly spaced across the landscape – a vindication of Lösch, whose central-place model had never been justified in terms of a fully specified description of individual behavior. Fujita (1994) has shown in models where all labor is mobile both how an urban center can be sustained and how a hierarchy of urban centers can emerge – a vindication of Christaller's vision of an urban system.

There have also been several papers that attempt to link the new economic geography back more directly to international trade issues per se. Venables (1993) has put forward a model in which vertical linkages between industries whose products are tradeable only at a cost create a tension between forces of specialization and of dispersion; in effect, intermediate goods play the same role that factor mobility plays in the more geographically oriented literature. Krugman and Livas (forthcoming) offer a model in which there is an interaction between trade policy and agglomeration: protectionism, by increasing the importance of domestic forward and backward linkages, raises the likelihood that a domestic agglomeration will be sustainable.

The verdict on the importance of the new economic geography is still not in. It will be obvious that I personally am very excited by it, and am inclined to messianic visions – not only of a grand union between trade and location theory, but of a linkage with current research on "self-organizing systems" in physics, chemistry, biology, and other fields. On the other hand, in fairness it should be reported that many geographers feel that the new literature is only telling them what they already knew, with a few technical gimmicks – and that the current trend among geographers proper is, if anything, away from quantitative modeling and toward a more literary and impressionistic approach.

2.3. Multinational enterprise, again

Transport costs that segment markets are also central to post-Helpman efforts to model multinational enterprise. As pointed out above, models in which firms place operations in different countries for comparative advantage reasons are unsatisfactory as a complete explanation for the actual pattern of foreign direct investment. An alternative view is that firms go multinational in order to improve their access to markets – that is, to avoid transportation costs or other barriers to trade in their products.

Brainard (1992) and Horstmann and Markusen (1992) have recently offered models of multinational enterprise in which the decision of firms to go multinational reflects a tradeoff between the loss of economies of scale associated with multiple plants and the reduction in transport costs they can achieve by producing locally for each market. These models are fairly general: factor proportions as well as transport costs may motivate overseas production, and firms can make a tradeoff between fixed and variable costs. The essence of the idea can, however, be conveyed in a simplified example.

Consider a world in which labor is the only factor of production, and in which there are two equal-sized countries. Assume that there is only one final-goods industry, and that this industry is characterized by Dixit–Stiglitz preferences, with an elasticity of substitution ρ between varieties. But now make the following additional assumptions:

(i) To produce each variety requires a fixed cost F_1 to operate a "headquarters", and a second fixed cost F_2 to operate each "factory"; there is also a constant marginal cost c per unit of final output.

(ii) While the services of each headquarters can be shipped costlessly to any factories that a firm operates, it is costly to ship final goods. Specifically, of every unit of final good shipped internationally, only γ units arrive.

Clearly, in this setup each firm faces a choice between two strategies. It may choose to have only one factory, and export its variety to the other country; or it may incur the extra fixed cost to open a second factory, and supply each market from local production. Obviously this choice will depend on the parameters of the model.

As in the case of the home market effect, it is easiest to develop intuition about this model by positing an equilibrium of one form or the other, then checking to see whether an individual firm will have an incentive to follow the posited strategy. Suppose, then, that all firms engage in local production. Then there will in effect be a world economy in which each good is produced with a fixed labor input $F_1 + 2F_2$, and with a constant marginal labor requirement c. Firms will enter until profits are eliminated, and there will be a symmetric equilibrium with the same number of headquarters in each country; denote this number by n. Each firm will then have sales of

$$S = 2wL/n$$

with half of its sales in each country. The operating surplus of each firm – the excess of sales over the non-fixed part of its costs – will be proportional to its total sales, and equal to its fixed costs:

$$OS = S/\rho = F_1 + 2F_2$$

But is this the most profitable strategy for each individual firm? Suppose that a single firm decides to opt for producing all its output in the headquarters country. It will now face a higher marginal cost of delivering output to the other country; it is straightforward to show that its operating surplus will fall to

$$OS' = OS(1 + \gamma^{\rho-1})/2$$

But the firm will also save on fixed costs, eliminating F_2 for the second factory. Thus the firm will find it optimal to close one plant unless

$$OS - OS' = (1 - \gamma^{\rho-1})(F_1 + 2F_2)/2 > F_2$$

or

$$1 - \gamma^{\rho-1} > \frac{2}{(F_1/F_2) + 2}$$

This, then, is the criterion for sustainability of an equilibrium in which all firms are multinational. It will tend to be satisfied, in particular, if F_2/F_1 is small, that is, if the fixed costs of opening an additional plant are not too large – or, to put it differently, if economies of scale are primarily at the level of the firm, not that of the individual plant. It will also tend to be satisfied if γ is small, that is, if transportation costs are high.

If the equilibrium does take the form of multi-plant operation, the integration of the two countries will take the following form: each country has n headquarters; each headquarters controls a plant in each country; there is no trade in final products, but there is implicit exchange of headquarter services. That is, the equilibrium will involve *intraindustry* direct foreign investment between similar countries, which is in fact characteristic of much direct investment.

Of course this model has the somewhat unsatisfactory feature that all trade is in implicit services, and that there is no trade in goods at all. It is not too hard, however, to remedy this feature by adding additional sectors and/or intermediate goods.

It may be interesting to note that the two approaches to modeling multinational enterprise described in this chapter appear to offer opposite answers to one of the traditional questions in the informal literature on direct investment: are trade and direct investment complements or substitutes? If firms go multinational in order to take advantage of cost differences – which is the underlying motive in the Markusen–Helpman model – then by so doing they will tend to create international trade. And conversely we would expect that factors that tend to increase international trade in any case, such as reductions in transportation cost, will encourage firms to separate operations geographically and thus to become multinational.

If, on the other hand, firms go multinational in order to get better access to local markets, by so doing they will replace conventional international trade. And barriers to trade, both natural and artificial, will promote such market-oriented internationalization of operations.

In the real world, there is no question that both motives are operating. Japanese electronics firms who move assembly operations to Thailand are engaging in comparative-advantage direct investment; Japanese auto firms who establish plants in the United States or the UK are engaging in market-access direct investment.

It may also be worth pointing out that in all theories of multinational enterprise it is assumed that there exist motives for placing different operations that can in principle be geographically separated under common control. The nature of these motives is, however, left fairly unspecified. The fact is that despite some deep insights by industrial organization theorists, there is still no generally accepted theory of the boundaries of the firm – certainly no theory that is operational in the sense that it can be used to predict the effects of technological or resource changes on those boundaries.

Because of these limitations, the existing models of multinational enterprise are less helpful than we would like in interpreting, or still less predicting, the effects of changes in the world economy on the extent of multinational enterprise.

2.4. Price discrimination

The models discussed in this section up to this point share many of the same features: they are general-equilibrium monopolistic-competition models, based on the two tricks of Dixit–Stiglitz preferences and iceberg transport costs. There is one more strand in the literature on trade with segmented markets, however, which needs to be discussed: that of price discrimination as a cause of trade. The models in this area are characteristically quite different, based on partial equilibrium analysis and homogeneous products.

International economists have long had to take account of the possible role of price discrimination in international trade, if only because anti-dumping legislation is of so much practical importance. Price discrimination between national markets is possible, of course, only if the markets are segmented by transport costs or other barriers. Traditional analyses of dumping, however, treated the price-discriminating firm as a pure monopolist at home, and often as a pure price-taker in export markets.

Brander (1981) first suggested modeling price discrimination in a framework in which two firms are able to sell in both of two markets, and came up with a surprising conclusion: that the firms would each sell into the other's market, possibly generating two-way trade in identical products. The point was elaborated, together with a welfare analysis, in Brander and Krugman (1983).

The basic point of the analysis may be made with a partial-equilibrium, linear example. Consider two symmetric firms producing the same good, each initially a domestic monopolist, each with the linear cost function

$$C = F + cX$$

and facing the linear demand curve

$$P = A - BX$$

Suppose initially that there is no possibility of exporting the good. Then each firm will behave as a monopolist, charging the optimal monopoly markup $(A - c)/2$.

Now suppose that the possibility of trade is opened up, but only at a cost; specifically, suppose that goods can be shipped from one market to the other only at a unit transportation cost t. If this cost is not too high – specifically, if $t < (a - c)/2$ – then each firm will have what appears to be a profitable opportunity to "dump" output in the other's market. After all, if a firm can sell a unit of its good in the other market, even after absorbing the transport cost it will still receive a price above marginal cost. It refrains from selling additional units in its own market, of course, because it is aware that to do so would drive down the price of inframarginal units; but export sales will drive down the price of someone else's inframarginal units, not its own.

But does this temptation to absorb transportation costs and sell in the other country's market persist in equilibrium? The answer depends on the nature of competition. In the Brander analysis firms are assumed to engage in an extended version of Cournot quantity competition. Each firm chooses *two* quantities: its level of shipments to the domestic and export markets respectively. And each firm takes the other firm's shipments to those markets as given. In this case the firms can be seen as playing two separate Cournot games, one in each market.

Since these markets are symmetric, it suffices to consider one country's market. In Figure 2.1, X is the domestic firm's delivery to its own market, Y the foreign firm's exports to that market. The price in that market is determined by the demand curve

$$P = A - B(X + Y)$$

The two lines are the reaction functions of the two firms. They are derived by maximizing each firm's operating surplus in the local market, taking the other's deliveries as given. The domestic firm maximizes

$$\Pi = (P - c)X = [a - B(X + Y) - c]X$$

implying the reaction function

$$X = \frac{A - c}{2B} - \frac{Y}{2}$$

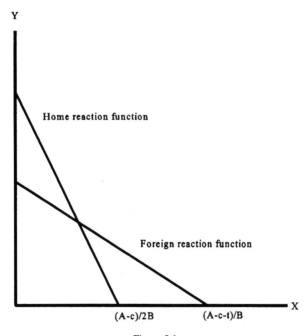

Figure 2.1.

The foreign firm, which must incur a transport cost to sell in this market, maximizes

$$\Pi^* = (P - c - t)X$$

implying the reaction function

$$Y = \frac{A - c - t}{2B} - \frac{X}{2}$$

Now recall that Y represents sales by the foreign firm in the domestic market. If these reaction functions intersect at a positive value of Y, then equilibrium will involve exports by the foreign firm to the home market – and since the markets are symmetric, exports by the home firm to the foreign market. That is, there will be two-way trade in an identical product. As the figure makes clear, this will take place as long as

$$t < \frac{A - c}{2}$$

that is, as long as the transportation cost is less than the pre-trade monopoly markup.

This model of trade due to "reciprocal dumping" is interesting in several respects. Aside from the seemingly paradoxical result of two-way trade in the same good, it is a model in which the usual roles of market structure and economies of scale are reversed. That is, in most models of trade with increasing returns and imperfect competition, the driving force behind trade is the increasing returns; imperfect competition is a necessary result of those increasing returns, but not a motivating factor. Indeed, the monopolistic-competition model is as close to perfect competition as one can get with marginal cost below average. In the reciprocal-dumping model, however, trade is essentially driven by imperfect competition – it is precisely because price is above marginal cost that each firm is tempted to raid the other's market.

How reasonable is the reciprocal dumping story? Theoretical criticism has focussed on the assumption of multimarket Cournot competition. After all, in practice oligopolistic firms seem as a rule to set prices rather than auction off predetermined quantities. The standard justification for Cournot competition in the industrial organization literature is to imagine firms that are price-setters, but are subject to short-run capacity constraints [Kreps and Scheinkman (1983)]; in a single market this ends up producing de facto quantity competition in terms of capacity choice. But even a firm that is able to price-discriminate between domestic and foreign markets is likely to face only a single, global capacity constraint. Ben-Zvi and Helpman (1992) have examined what happens to the Brander–Krugman model when the firms engage in price rather than quantity competition, with a prior competition in setting *overall* capacity. It turns out that the two-way trade in the product disappears; the result is instead one of limit pricing, in which each firm sets a price equal to marginal cost plus transportation costs.

As an empirical matter, two-way international trade in literally identical products is surely rare. On the other hand, the practice of "basing point pricing", in which firms absorb transport costs, has been historically important in interregional trade within the United States, and has led to substantial cross-hauling of such products as cement and steel. Basing point pricing arises in the context of imperfect collusion, rather than a noncooperative game. Nonetheless, it is essentially driven by the desire of firms to raid their rivals' market areas in order to take advantage of prices above marginal cost, and is thus at least a cousin of the reciprocal dumping story about trade.

2.5. Concluding remarks

The literature on segmented markets in international trade has two main virtues. First, it helps us recognize that access to markets may matter. This point will seem hardly worth mentioning to anyone who has looked either at the pattern of actual trade flows, which fall off sharply with distance, or at surveys of businesses, who invariably mention proximity to markets as a prime determinant of location. But many models of international trade, including the integrated-economy framework applied to imperfect competition and scale economies, treat transportion and transaction costs across space as nuisances to be assumed away or sterilized by introducing a rigid distinction between traded and nontraded goods. The segmented market literature reminds us that in some cases, far from being an intellectual nuisance, the costs of doing business across space may be an important explanatory variable.

Second, the segmented-market literature offers a useful set of modeling tricks for handling the effects of such costs. In particular, the combination of Dixit–Stiglitz monopolistic competition with Samuelson's iceberg transport costs – which involves a kind of layering of implausible but convenient assumptions – has turned out to be a remarkably flexible tool of analysis, allowing us to think coherently about market-size and market-access effects in a wide variety of contexts.

3. Unresolved issues and future concerns

This final section of the chapter considers a number of issues that the literature on increasing returns and imperfect competition in trade has either not addressed effectively or not addressed at all, but that seem of considerable importance. I consider these issues under two headings: issues regarding the pattern of specialization and trade, and those regarding more fundamental micro foundations.

3.1. Trade issues per se

3.1.1. Failure to reproduce the integrated economy

Focussing on trade that reproduces an integrated economy turns out to be a tremendously powerful simplifying and unifying device, and did much to make the literature on increasing returns and imperfect competition seem like a natural next step in the development of trade theory rather than a set of disparate alternative approaches. Unfortunately, casual observation suggests pretty strongly that trade does *not* reproduce the integrated economy. Wage rates of equivalent labor are certainly not equalized.

While transportation costs are one reason for a breakdown in factor-price equalization, few economists think that they are the main explanation of this incomplete integration. Rather, most of us are inclined to blame one or both of two causes: differences in factor endowments which are too large to allow factor price equalization, and differences in production functions between countries. These may be summarized by saying that the world economy is either out of the parallelogram, or completely outside the box.

There is no fundamental conceptual difficulty in introducing either wide endowment disparities or technological differences into models with increasing returns and either monopolistic competition or external economies. What is lacking, however, is any systematic treatment of the patterns of specialization that might result, or of the likely empirical counterparts of such deviations from the canonical assumptions. This criticism admittedly applies equally to constant-returns trade theory; indeed, many international economists seem remarkably relaxed about relying on Heckscher–Ohlin models to analyze some issues, Ricardian models to analyze others (in particular, the trade foundations of international macroeconomic models are generally more or less Ricardian).

There has been some movement toward modeling that combines factor proportions with technological differences. Davis (1992) has offered an influential critique of the interpretation of intraindustry trade as scale-economy-based, proposing instead that it is due to exogenous technological differences. But it would be useful if there were a more systematic treatment of what happens when the integrated-economy approach doesn't work.

3.1.2. Multilateral trade

The great bulk of the theoretical literature on international trade, old and new, focusses on trade between two countries. In the real world, however, there are many countries, and practical policy debates in international economics often depend on the interpretation of multilateral trade data. Two important recent examples are the dispute over the degree of closure of Japan's market, in which many authors tried to compare Japan's actual volume of trade with the predicted volume given an empirical model of multilateral trade [see, for example, Lawrence (1987)]; and the more recent literature in which essentially the same method is used to ask whether East Asia is becoming an implicit trading bloc (see Frankel 1993).

In both literatures the essential empirical tool was some version of the "gravity" equation, which relates the trade between any pair of countries to their populations, incomes, and the distance between them. But some trade theorists have complained that such analysis is irrelevant, because the gravity equations do not arise from any well-specified model of multilateral trade.

At first sight, monopolistic competition models of trade seem to offer a justification for using gravity-type regressions. Helpman and Krugman (1985) consider the case of a world in which *all* tradeable industries consist of differentiated products. If tastes are identical and homothetic, and – crucially – if those goods that can be traded have zero transport costs, then the value of exports from any country j to some other country k will be

$$T_{jk} = \tau \frac{Y_j Y_k}{Y_W}$$

where Y_j is the GDP of country j, Y_W is gross world product, and τ is the share of tradeables in expenditure. This looks like a classic gravity equation: trade between two countries, other things equal, is proportional to the product of the incomes of those two countries. And this analysis helps to suggest why gravity equations work as well as they do. Unfortunately, empirical gravity equations invariably include not only the incomes of j and k but some measure of the distance between the countries – and distance always shows up as a crucial determinant of trade flows. That is, the empirical evidence, reflected in the empirical models, clearly shows that transportation costs (perhaps in the form of invisible transaction costs) play a crucial role in the pattern of multilateral trade.[3]

The problem, however, is that the apparent rationale for a simple gravity equation breaks down when transport costs are important. Even in a one-industry world, the trade between two countries should depend not only on their incomes and the distance between them but on the sizes and distances of other economies. Consider, for example, two small equal-size economies. If they were located on Mars, able to trade with each other but separated from all other economies by near-prohibitive transport costs, half of each country's spending on tradeables should consist of imports from

---

[3]An important practical issue is what we mean by "transport costs". Measured shipping costs are quite small for most goods that can be shipped at all; yet trade falls off quite strongly with distance. This suggests that transportation costs in our models are a proxy for more subtle transaction costs involving the difficulty of maintaining personal contact, or perhaps differences in culture that are correlated with physical distance. In any case, one wonders how badly misleading it is to represent these as a proportional melting of goods in transit!

the other. That is, the value of trade between the two should be equal to $\tau Y/2$, where Y is each country's income. On the other hand, if the two countries were located in the middle of Europe, close to much larger countries offering competing products, then each would spend only a small fraction of its income on imports from the other. Thus the trade between them would be much less, even if the distance between the two were the same.

Matters become much worse when we consider that there are many sectors, differing both in the importance of scale economies and in the level of transport cost. Now the pattern of trade may be influenced by home market effects; sectors characterized by large economies of scale, for example, will tend to be produced not only by countries that are themselves large (Germany) but by those that are located close to large external markets (Belgium) – and predicting the pattern and volume of trade becomes yet more complex.

Or so it appears. Perhaps, like so many issues in economic theory, this issue is much less complex than it seems when looked at the right way. The point is that there is not now a careful, generally accepted analysis of the pattern of multilateral trade when transport costs matter – as they clearly do – which allows us to assess observed patterns with any assurance. This is not a critique of the gravity-equation based literature. The fact is that such equations work very well, and it is entirely reasonable to use an ad hoc approach that seems to work until someone comes along with a more rigorous approach. What is clear is that the lack of a good analysis of multilateral trade in the presence of transport costs is a major gap in trade theory.

3.2. Deeper issues

Ohlin concluded his 1933 book by declaring that international trade theory is nothing but international location theory. The new economic geography is in a way an attempt to prove his point, but he was surely only partly right: if there is an overriding conclusion from the last 15 years of research it is that international trade theory is also international industrial organization. And therefore any weaknesses in our understanding of industrial organization are also weaknesses in our study of international economics.

Where is our theory of industrial organization most inadequate? The answer, surely, is in the attempt to explain the nature and boundaries of the firm. Why are some activities carried out within hierarchical organizations, while others are carried out through arms-length transactions? There is a rigorous literature demonstrating that the simple view that vertical integration is a response to market imperfections is not a sufficient answer, because it does not explain why individuals do not write contracts to deal with these imperfections. This result is, however, essentially negative; efforts to explain, given this result, why some transactions characteristically take place via markets and others within command structures are at best suggestive. Indeed, there is even a dispute over whether the conventional distinction between transactions carried out within and between firms is truly valid. Some theorists, such as Michael Jensen, claim that individuals are the only true economic actors, and that the economy is simply a web of contracts; calling some dense parts of that web firms is no more than a conceptual and legal convenience. On the other hand, such theorists as Oliver Hart have argued that the distinction between within-firm and market transactions is indeed a fundamental one, and that ownership of productive assets is not just a particular form of contract but a crucial issue.

What is noteworthy, however, is that the theory of trade under conditions of increasing returns and imperfect competition is at present blithely insensitive to these conceptual problems. Consider even the simplest monopolistic-competition model of trade. Why do we assume that each firm produces only a single variety, rather than imagine a firm or alliance of firms producing many varieties and taking their interdependence into account in pricing decisions? Or for that matter why don't firms use two-part tariffs to allow customers to pay marginal cost? The answer is that we have implicit notions that there are diseconomies to grouping many products into a single firm, and that the transactions costs of nonlinear pricing schemes are too high. In this case these implicit assumptions seem reasonable, but the models are actually less rigorous than they first appear.

More seriously, when there are external economies, is it right to assume that firms behave atomistically – or should we assume that someone will try to internalize the externality? (Interestingly and contrastingly, in Henderson (1974)-type urban models the standard closure is to envision "city corporations" that compete precisely by internalizing the external economies of agglomeration.) Again, the assumption that firms remain small and take external effects as given represents some implicit theorizing.

Where the failure to have a real theory of the boundaries of the firm becomes truly serious, however, is of course in the analysis of multinational firms. While Ethier and others have tried to establish microfoundations for the internalization decision, these efforts are, like those in the industrial organization literature generally, interesting and suggestive rather than fully satisfactory. Why, exactly, did United Fruit want to own Central American banana plantations (and often the republics in which they were located), while many US sellers of personal computer clones seem reconciled simply to contract with their Korean or Taiwanese suppliers? The answer is not at all obvious from the international economics literature.

What makes this an important issue is, in particular, the fact that firms in today's international economy are in the process of experimenting both with new boundaries and with novel forms of organization. During the late 1980s Japanese electronics manufacturers managed, with a little help from fast-talking Americans, to persuade themselves that they needed to own major Hollywood film studios. Were they, despite current appearances, right? More to the point, what can our theory say about the issue? At the same time, there is a great deal of buzz in the business strategy area about international corporate alliances – a form of interaction that is neither arms'-length market transactions nor extension of the boundaries of the firm in the usual sense. How does this fit into our analysis?

These are deep questions, and not specifically international in nature. Nonetheless, international as well as general industrial organization must eventually confront them.

4. Concluding remarks

I do not want to end this survey on a negative note. The previous section was, in effect, a catalogue of problems with what has become the standard analysis of trade under increasing returns and imperfect competition. In spite of these problems, however, the most remarkable thing to someone who was trained in international trade theory before 1980 – or even to someone who read the 1982 Helpman survey – is how comprehensible the roles of increasing returns and imperfect competition have turned out to be. Before the new models appeared, traditional trade theorists believed that to introduce these factors into the theory would be to plunge into an impenetrable thicket of conceptual difficulties. When it turned out that coherent models could be written down, the expectation was that they would be too diffuse a set of mutually contradictory approaches to offer more than isolated insights. Instead, the field has turned out to be characterized by a surprising degree both of cohesion and of continuity with the older traditions of international trade theory.

References

Ben-Zvi, S. and E. Helpman (1992), "Oligopoly in segmented markets", in: G. Grossman, ed., Imperfect competition and international trade (MIT Press, Cambridge, MA) 31–53.

Brainard, L. (1992), "A simple theory of multinational corporations and trade with a trade-off between proximity and concentration", mimeo (MIT Press, Cambridge, MA).

Brander, J. (1981), "Intra-industry trade in identical commodities", Journal of International Economics 11:1–14.

Brander, J. and P. Krugman (1983), "A 'reciprocal dumping' model of international trade", Journal of International Economics 15:313–323.

Burenstam Linder, S. (1961), An essay on trade and transformation (Wiley, New York).

Christaller, W. (1933), Central places in southern Germany [English translation by C.W. Baskin (1966) (Prentice-Hall, Englewood Cliffs)].

Davis, D. (1992), "Intra-industry trade: A Heckscher–Ohlin–Ricardo approach", in: Essays in the theory of international trade and economic growth, Ph.D. thesis, Columbia University.

Dixit, A. and V. Norman (1980), Theory of international trade (Cambridge University Press, Cambridge, UK).

Dixit, A. and J. Stiglitz (1977), "Monopolistic competition and optimum product diversity", American Economic Review 67:297–308.

Ethier, W. (1979), "Internationally decreasing costs and world trade", Journal of International Economics 9:1–24.

Ethier, W. (1982a), "Decreasing costs in international trade and Frank Graham's argument for protection", Econometrica 50:1243–1268.

Ethier, W. (1982b), "National and international returns to scale in the modern theory of international trade", American Economic Review 72:950–959.

Ethier, W. (1986), "The multinational firm", Quarterly Journal of Economics 101:805–834.

Frankel, J. (1993), "Is Japan creating a yen bloc in East Asia and the Pacific?", in: J. Frankel and M. Kahler, eds., Regionalism and rivalry: Japan and the U.S. in Pacific Asia (University of Chicago Press, Chicago).

Fujita, M. (1988), Urban economic theory (Oxford University Press, Oxford).

Fujita, M. (1994), Monopolistic competition and urban hierarchies, mimeo, University of Pennsylvania.

Harris, C.D. (1954), "The market as a factor in the localization of industry in the U.S.", Annals of the Association of American Geographers 44:315–348.

Helpman, E. (1981), "International trade in the presence of product differentiation, economies of scale, and imperfect competition: A Chamberlin–Heckscher–Ohlin approach", Journal of International Economics 11:305–340.

Helpman, E. (1984a), "Increasing returns, imperfect markets, and trade theory", in: R. Jones and P. Kenen, eds., Handbook of international economics, vol. 1 (North-Holland, Amsterdam).

Helpman, E. (1984b), "A simple theory of trade with multinational corporations", Journal of Political Economy 92:451–472.

Helpman, E. and P. Krugman (1985), Market structure and foreign trade (MIT Press, Cambridge, MA).

Henderson, J.V. (1974), "On the sizes and types of cities", American Economic Review 64:640–656.

Horstmann, I. and J. Markusen (1992), "Endogenous market structures in international trade", Journal of International Economics 32:109–129.

Kreps, D. and J. Scheinkman (1983), "Quantity precommitment and Bertrand competition yield Cournot outcomes", Bell Journal of Economics 12:326–337.

Krugman, P. (1980), "Scale economies, product differentiation, and the pattern of trade", American Economic Review 70:950–959.

Krugman, P. (1991), "Increasing returns and economic geography", Journal of Political Economy 99:183–199.

Krugman, P. (1993), "On the number and location of cities", European Economic Review 37:293–298.

Krugman, P. (1995) Development, geography, and economic theory (MIT Press, Cambridge, MA), forthcoming.

Krugman, P. and R. Livas-Elizondo (1995), "Trade policy and the third world metropolis", Journal of Political Economy, forthcoming.

Lancaster, K. (1975), "Socially optimal product differentiation", American Economic Review 65:567–585.

Lawrence, R. (1987), "Japan: Closed markets or minds?", Brookings Papers on Economic Activity 2:517–554.

Lösch, A. (1940), The economics of location [English translation (1954) (Yale University Press, New Haven)].

Markusen, J. (1984), "Multinationals, multi-plant economies, and the gains from trade", Journal of International Economics 16:205–226.

Pred, A. (1966), The spatial dynamics of U.S. urban-industrial growth, 1800–1914 (MIT Press, Cambridge, MA).

Romer, P. (1986), "Increasing returns and long-run growth", Journal of Political Economy 94:1002–1037.

Venables, A. (1993), "Equilibrium locations of vertically linked industries", mimeo, London School of Economics.

Chapter 25

TECHNOLOGY AND TRADE

GENE M. GROSSMAN

Princeton University

and

ELHANAN HELPMAN*

Tel Aviv University and CIAR

Contents

*We thank Jim Anderson, Pranab Bardhan, John Black, Jon Eaton, and Jim Markusen for their comments and suggestions, and the National Science Foundation and the U.S.–Israel Binational Science Foundation for financial support. Grossman also thanks the John S. Guggenheim Memorial Foundation, the Sumitomo Bank Fund, the Daiwa Bank Fund, and the Center of International Studies at Princeton University.

Handbook of International Economics, vol. III, Edited by G. Grossman and K. Rogoff

0. Introduction

Ever since David Ricardo published his *Principles of Political Economy,* cross-country differences in technology have featured prominently in economists' explanations of the international pattern of specialization and trade.[1] Yet, until quite recently, the formal trade-theory literature has focused almost exclusively on the *effects* of technological disparities without delving much into their *causes.*

This focus – which undoubtedly has produced many useful insights – is nonetheless somewhat surprising. After all, informal commentators see the integration of the world economy as having an important influence on the pace and direction of technological change. Indeed, allusions to "globalization" pervade popular discussions of recent technological developments, where trade is seen variously as a "highway of learning" and a "handmaiden of growth". Global integration presumably affects both the private incentives for and the social benefits from investments in technology. On the positive side, integration expands the size of the market and so the potential profit opportunities available to a firm that succeeds in inventing a new product or process. Also, because knowledge is the quintessential public good, a country that integrates itself into the world economy often can benefit from learning that takes place outside its borders. On the negative side, firms sometimes cite international competition as one of the major risks associated with investments in high technology and as an element in the case for greater government involvement in the development of new technologies.

The prolonged absence of a formal literature on the determinants of national productivity levels and on the relationship between trade and technological progress cannot be ascribed to lack of interest. Rather, trade theorists lacked the tools needed to deal with these issues. Since most of the costs of developing a new technology occur before production begins and do not vary with the intended scale of output, innovation normally gives rise to dynamic scale economies. And since firms typically cover the costs of their up-front investments by exploiting market power generated by their inventions, innovation

---

[1]In his famous wine-and-cloth example, Ricardo gave no explicit reasons for the difference in comparative costs between Portugal and England. Many believe that Ricardo thought exclusively in terms of differences in soil, climate and national character, rather than in terms of cross-country differences in knowledge. But Ricardo clearly was aware that differences in production capabilities could account for comparative advantage. He even discussed a case where the discovery of a new production process for wine making in England might flip the international pattern of specialization and trade [Ricardo, (1951–55, pp. 137–138)]. Other classical writers, including John Stuart Mill, Torrens, Malthus, and Cairns, regularly pointed to technological disparity in addition to other factors as a potential source of comparative advantage. Bloomfield (1978) examines the views of the nineteenth-century British authors on the role of technology in trade.

gives rise to imperfect competition. Not until scale economies and imperfect competition had been incorporated into static trade theory (a development that is reviewed in Chapter 24 of this volume) could dynamic theories of the relationship between trade and technology evolve.

The modelling efforts that we survey in this chapter have been motivated by a number of important concerns. Some of these concerns remain the same as in earlier work on trade and growth [which was reviewed by Ronald Findlay (1984) in the first volume of the *Handbook of International Economics*]. For example, many authors continue to be interested in the link between the nature of differences in countries' technological capabilities and the pattern of world trade. Recent research has asked: How will an across-the-board technological gap between rich and poor countries be reflected in global trade structure? And how will the invention of new goods in the industrialized "North" affect the number and type of goods that are produced by the less developed "South"? Also, attention still focuses on the age-old question of how technological developments in one country or region affect living standards abroad. Should a country be happy to see technological progress in its trade partners, or should it disparage the consequent "loss of competitiveness"? Is trade typically beneficial to all parties in a world of unequal (and changing) technological capabilities or might some be losers in the long run?

However, many of the questions posed in the recent literature – while long of interest to trade economists and often made the subject of their informal writings – could not be addressed in a formal and rigorous way using the static models of old. At the most general level, there is the question: How does trade affect a country's (and the world's) growth rate? Will every country grow faster if it chooses to be open to international trade? Or does the answer depend on the nature of its natural endowments, its initial conditions, or something else? One wonders also whether, over time, trade will tend to shrink the enormous disparities that exist between countries' productivity and income levels, or whether the differences should be expected to persist or even grow. In other words, are there mechanisms unleashed by international integration that serve to close the technological gaps between nations? Or are technological processes better seen as cumulative, so that trade might reinforce the initial gaps?

These positive questions suggest some normative ones, which have also been addressed in the research we describe. What is the relationship between the national growth rate and welfare in an open economy? What policies are likely to promote productivity growth and national welfare? Should a country's trade stance depend on its stage of technological development, with lagging countries perhaps needing some form of protection until the technological gap between themselves and their trade partners has been narrowed or closed? Can temporary policies have long-lasting, beneficial effects? And how do the trade and technology policies in one country impact upon its trade partners?

As always, the answers to such questions depend upon the particular assumptions that are made about the economic environment. The literature has explored a wide variety of assumptions, in models that are not always readily comparable. One clear distinction concerns the driving force behind technological progress. Many recent (and older) writings investigate technical gains that stem from *learning by doing*; that is, the mere repetition of certain productive activities, which may allow firms and industries to find new and better ways of doing things. Another body of research focuses more on *research and development*; that is, on investments in activities undertaken with the primary or sole objective of discovering new technologies. Besides this fundamental distinction there are other, more subtle ones. Technological improvements may be targeted at intermediate goods or at final goods. Newly discovered products may be better than older varieties or merely different from them. Investments in knowledge may generate widespread benefits or benefits that are fully appropriable by the investor. If spillovers do occur, they may take place across firms in an industry, across industries in a country, or across national borders, and so on. One of our goals in this chapter is to provide a unified and synthetic treatment of the various models, so that their common elements can be appreciated and their essential distinguishing features understood. In this way, the different answers they give to the above-mentioned questions can be linked to differences in primitive assumptions. Hopefully, this will pave the way for empirical work aimed at identifying the more realistic of the alternative assumptions.

We have divided the chapter into four sections. The first one reviews the literature that takes technology as exogenous and examines the implications of productivity differences for trade patterns and the effects of technical change on outputs and welfare. This sets the stage for Sections 2 and 3, both of which treat dynamic models in which the evolution of technology is endogenous. In Section 2, technological progress is viewed as an accidental by-product of production activities, while in Section 3 it results from deliberate investment. The various sub-sections explore the implications of alternative assumptions about the form of industrial innovation and the nature of technological spillovers. The last section contains a melange of topics not covered elsewhere, including a discussion of the effects of trade and industrial policies, of trade based on imitation in a setting of imperfectly-protected intellectual property rights, and of direct foreign investment and international licensing as vehicles for technology transfer.

1. Exogenous technology

In what follows we will largely be concerned with how the international trading environment affects the pace and direction of technological change. In our view, the trade pattern should properly be regarded as a dynamic phenomenon, responding continuously to the ebbs and flows of accumulating knowledge. Moreover, foreign market opportunities and international competition have an important influence on the course of technological progress. Yet even if one adopts this perspective on world trade, it is necessary to understand fully how technology differences shape the pattern of global specialization before proceeding to the full dynamic process. This is because, in the short run, history dictates a relatively fixed distribution of knowledge, and the resource allocations effected by this momentary distribution weigh heavily in the determination of subsequent technological developments.

We begin this section with a review of the familiar Ricardian model, including extensions that allow for a continuum of goods. We then show how, by adding structure to the model, it can shed light on some commonly observed trade dynamics. After a brief mention of several elaborations that allow for more than one factor of production, we conclude the section with a discussion of the effects of exogenous technological progress on national welfare levels.

1.1. The Ricardian model

The Ricardian model provides the simplest framework in which one can examine how national differences in technological capabilities give rise to specialization and trade. We review this venerable model in order to introduce notation and to recall some results for later use.

In the simplest Ricardian setting, there are two countries, two goods, and a single factor of production. With only one productive factor, the composition of countries' endowments are bound to be identical. This leaves tastes and technology as the only dimensions along which countries may differ. (We ignore government policies and institutional disparities for the time being.) Technologies are characterized by constant returns to scale, and so can be fully described by a single number. In the home country, a_i units of labor are needed to produce one unit of good i, $i = x, y$. Unit labor coefficients for the foreign country are similar, but are distinguished by an asterisk. Then the model predicts – as is very well known – that comparative advantage alone determines the pattern of trade. That is, in a competitive equilibrium with freely transportable goods but immobile labor, the home country exports good x if and only if $a_x/a_y < a_x^*/a_y^*$. This can be seen in Figure 1.1, which also shows the different types of equilibria that are possible.

Assume for concreteness that $a_x/a_y < a_x^*/a_y^*$. Then both countries will specialize in the production of good y (and therefore world output of good x is nil) if $p_x/p_y < a_x/a_y$, where p_i denotes the price of good i. This is because the cost of producing good i at home is wa_i, where w is the home wage rate, and production of a good is profitable if and only if its unit cost does not exceed the

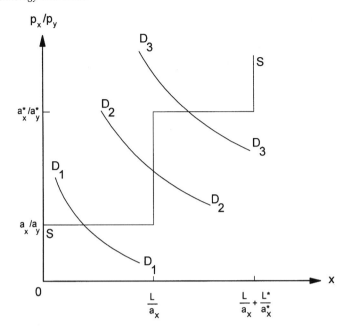

Figure 1.1.

price. Thus, if $p_x/p_y < a_x/a_y$, production of good x is not profitable at home and, a fortiori, not profitable abroad. By similar reasoning both countries will specialize in the production of good x if $p_x/p_y > a_x^*/a_y^*$, in which case the world supply of this goods equals $L/a_x + L^*/a_x^*$, where L and L^* are the home and foreign labor supplies, respectively. If $a_x^*/a_y^* > p_x/p_y > a_x/a_y$, the home country produces only good x (with output equal to L/a_x) and the foreign country produces none of it. Finally, if the relative price happens to equal the relative input requirements in one of the countries, then production of both goods will be (marginally) profitable in that country, and the supply of good x there will be infinitely price elastic within the range of outputs that can feasibly be produced. Taking all of this into account, the figure shows SS, the world supply curve for good x.

World demand for good x can take any of the three positions labelled D_1D_1, D_2D_2, or D_3D_3. In the first and last of these, the share of world income spent on one or the other of the two goods is relatively high. Then one of the countries remains incompletely specialized in the free-trade equilibrium, while the other is active only in the sector in which it is relatively more productive. The free-trade relative price equals the relative input requirement of the country that

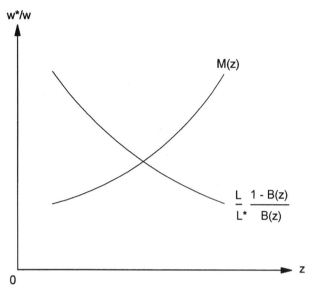

Figure 1.2.

remains incompletely specialized. Clearly, this country exports the good in which it enjoys a comparative advantage, because that good is consumed by its trade partner but not produced there.

The other type of equilibrium arises when a moderate share of world income is spent on both goods, so that world demand is as depicted by D_2D_2. Then both countries specialize in their production. The pattern of trade is immediate in this case.

The model can readily be extended to include more goods.[2] It is simplest, in fact, to allow for a continuum of goods, as in Dornbusch et al. (1977). Let the goods be indexed by $z \in [0,1]$ and let $a(z)$ and $a^*(z)$ be the unit labor requirements for producing good z in the home and foreign countries, respectively. Order the goods so that $M(z) \equiv a(z)/a^*(z)$ is increasing in z, as shown in Figure 1.2. This means that for any two goods z' and z'', if $z' < z''$ the home country has the greater relative technological advantage in producing z'. Then, for any pair of wage rates in the two countries, the unit cost of producing good

---

[2]It is also straightforward to expand the number of countries. With only two goods, all of the countries with the greatest comparative technological advantage in sector x (i.e. those with the smallest values of a_x/a_y) produce and export this good, while the remaining countries produce and export good y [see Becker (1952)]. If all countries have different relative input requirements, then at most one of them can be incompletely specialized in the free-trade equilibrium. The identity of the marginal country producing each good is determined by demand conditions. The model with more than two countries *and* goods is somewhat more complicated [see Jones (1961)].

z at home is less than the cost of producing that same good abroad if and only if $wa(z) < w^*a^*(z)$, or $M(z) < w^*/w$. Once we have determined the equilibrium relative wage, we will also know which goods are produced by each country; the home country produces all and only those goods for which $M(z) \leq w^*/w$.

To determine the relative wage we must specify the demand conditions. The simplest case is one in which all consumers have identical Cobb–Douglas preferences, spending the constant share $b(z)$ of their income on good z.[3] If the home country produces all of the goods with an index less than z, the share of world income devoted to its (aggregate) output is $B(z) \equiv \int_0^z b(s)\,ds$. This must match the value of its output, which, in a competitive equilibrium, equals its total wage bill. Thus $B(z)(wL + w^*L^*) = wL$, or

$$\frac{w^*}{w} = \frac{L}{L^*}\frac{1 - B(z)}{B(z)} \tag{1.1}$$

We plot the right-hand side of (1.1) in Figure 1.2, and find the equilibrium wage at the intersection with the $M(z)$ curve. The equilibrium features a "chain" of comparative advantage, with the home country producing all of those goods for which its *relative* technological advantage is the greatest.

This simple continuum model gives sharp predictions about the static pattern of trade. It has been used extensively to study a number of important issues, including the gains from trade, the effects of technological progress, the interaction between monetary disturbances and international specialization, and the effects of environmental regulations on trade. We will illustrate some of these applications in Sections 1.2. and 1.5.

1.2. Technology gaps

In the general Ricardian model, the pattern of relative technological capabilities is entirely arbitrary. As a consequence, the model has nothing to say about the *type of goods* in which a country with certain characteristics might be expected to export. To fully address this issue, it is necessary to endogenize the accumulation of technical know how, as we intend to do in the sections that follow. But even within the present paradigm it is possible to put more structure on the nature of technological differences across countries, in order to make the model consistent with observed patterns of trade.

For example, it is commonly noted that the more advanced countries typically produce and export the more technologically sophisticated goods. Krugman (1986) describes a model of "technology gaps" that has this feature. Suppose there is a "best-practice" labor requirement for producing good z, $\tilde{a}(z)$,

---

[3] Wilson (1980) treats the case with non-homothetic and non-identical demands.

that evolves according to $\tilde{a}(z) = e^{-g(z)t}$. Goods are ordered so that $g(z)$ is an increasing function of z. Then we can interpret z as a measure of the technological intensity of a good, because goods with higher indexes experience more rapid technological progress. Now suppose that both home and foreign producers lag behind the technological frontier, but by differing amounts. Let γ and γ^* be the respective technological lags. This means, for example, that a home firm can produce a unit of good z at time t with $a(z) = e^{-g(z)(t-\gamma)}$ units of labor. According to this formulation, the foreign country, which we take to be more "advanced" (i.e. $\gamma^* < \gamma$), has an absolute advantage in producing *all* goods. But its comparative advantage lies in the more sophisticated goods, because the technological gap matters relatively least for the goods that experience the slowest technological progress. So the more technologically advanced country indeed produces and exports the more knowledge-intensive goods.

1.3. Product cycles

It has also been observed by Vernon (1966) and others that the North produces and exports the majority of newly invented goods. The South, meanwhile, specializes in goods that have been around for longer. This trade pattern emerges in Krugman's (1979) model of the "product life cycle", which emphasizes the slow diffusion of technologies from North to South.

Let consumers have the utility function $u = [\int_0^\infty c(z)^\alpha \, dz]^{1/\alpha}$, $0 < \alpha < 1$, that is defined over all existing *and potential* goods. Here $c(z)$ is consumption of good z. At time t there are n_t goods available and every pair of these has a constant elasticity of substitution $\sigma \equiv 1/(1 - \alpha)$. Now suppose that all innovation takes place in the North. At every moment Northern producers somehow acquire the additional knowledge needed to produce a certain number of new goods. Firms in the South, meanwhile, learn the methods of producing these goods only after a (random) adoption lag. This sequence of innovation in the North and diffusion to the South gives rise to a particular pattern of trade when the South has a cost advantage due to lower wages: the North enjoys comparative advantage in relatively new goods (those technologies that the South has not yet learned to produce), while the South has comparative advantage in older products whose technologies it has already mastered.

The static equilibrium can be described as follows. Let n_N denote the number of goods that can only be produced in the North (at a moment in time) and let n_S denote the number of goods that can be produced in both the North and the South. With perfect competition, the price of a good produced in country j is aw_j, $j = S, N$, where w_j is the country's wage rate. Using the assumed CES utility function, we can derive the relative demands for typical goods produced in the North and the South, $c_N/c_S = (w_N/w_S)^{-\sigma}$. Then, if the North manufactures all of the goods and only those goods that solely its producers know how to produce, labor-market clearing in each country entails $n_j c_j = L_j$, $j = S, N$. We can solve for the equilibrium relative wage that is implied by this hypothesis, namely $w_N/w_S = (n_N/n_S)^{1/\sigma}(L_N/L_S)^{-1/\sigma}$. For a range of values of n_N/n_S and L_N/L_S, the implied relative wage exceeds one, which is all that we need to support the pattern of specialization that we have assumed. Krugman (1979) notes that the long-run relative wage of the North varies positively with its rate of new product development, but negatively with the rate of technological diffusion to the South. Yet, as Helpman (1993) points out, the North must benefit in welfare terms from an increase in the rate of technology transfer, at least if the initial diffusion rate is small.

1.4. Many factors of production

When there is more than a single factor of production and countries differ in their relative factor endowments, general propositions about the relationship between technology and the pattern of trade are harder to come by. As Jones (1965, 1970) has shown, technological differences must be gauged not only in terms of the sectorial advantages of one country vis-à-vis its trade partners, but also in terms of the *factor bias* of the technological superiority. For example, a country that has a capital-saving technological superiority in the labor-intensive production sector may find itself importing the labor-intensive good, even if it is relatively well endowed with labor compared to its trade partner.

Markusen and Svensson (1985) have examined the implications of (small) Hicks-neutral technological differences between two countries that have similar factor endowments and tastes. Let the technology for producing good z at home be $F_z(V_z)$, where V_z is the vector of inputs used in producing good z and $F_z(\cdot)$ is homogeneous of degree one. Suppose that the foreign technology differs slightly (i.e. by an arbitrary vector of *infinitesimal* deviations), and is given by $A_z F_z(V_z^*)$. Then it can be shown that $\sum_z A_z p_z m_z > 0$, where p_z is the price of good z and m_z is the home country's imports of this good. In other words, each country exports *on average* the goods in which it enjoys the relatively largest productivity advantages.

Small, Hicks-neutral technological differences also feature prominently in a recent paper by Davis (1994). Suppose there are two factors of production and two industries with differing factor intensities. The first industry produces a single good while the second produces a pair of goods that are imperfect substitutes. Then if the home country holds a small technological advantage in producing one of the two outputs of the second industry, it must produce all of the world's output of this good in any trade equilibrium with factor price equalization. It is likely that the other country will produce much or all of the other product of the second industry, especially if the two goods enter demand relatively symmetrically and the countries are of nearly equal size. In this case, small technological differences give rise to *intra-industry trade* in a world of perfect competition and constant returns to scale.

1.5. Technical progress and national welfare

Models of trade with exogenous technological differences can be used to study the effects of technical progress in one country on national welfare there and abroad. This line of inquiry dates back at least to Hicks (1953), who introduced the useful distinction between "export-biased" and "import-biased" technological change.

The basic ideas can be illustrated most readily in the simplest Ricardian model with two goods. Suppose first that the home country is incompletely specialized, while the foreign country specializes in producing good x. Import-biased technical progress reduces the labor requirement in the home country's import-competing sector. Take the foreign wage rate as numeraire (i.e. $w^* = 1$). Then the price of good x must remain fixed at $p_x = a_x^*$. Since $p_x = wa_x$, the home wage rate rises in proportion to the fall in the input requirement; i.e. $\hat{w} = -\hat{a}_x$, where a circumflex indicates a proportional change. So the price of good y, which equals its unit cost of production wa_y, rises in response to the import-biased technological progress. In short, the home country's terms of trade improve. It follows that the home country must benefit from this form of technological progress, while its trade partner must be harmed by the change.

Now consider export-biased technical progress. For this purpose, it is best to focus on an initial equilibrium with specialization in both countries. It is necessary to take a particular form for consumer utility in order to evaluate the welfare changes. We assume for this purpose that $u = (c_x^\alpha + c_y^\alpha)^{1/\alpha}$; i.e. consumers perceive a constant elasticity of substitution $\sigma \equiv 1/(1 - \alpha)$ between the two goods. With these preferences, the share of individual (and world) income devoted to good x is $b_x = p_x^{1-\sigma}/(p_x^{1-\sigma} + p_y^{1-\sigma})$. For concreteness, suppose that the foreign country produces good x, and again take its wage as numeraire. Then $p_x = a_x^*$ is unaffected by the productivity gain in the home country. Since the share b_x of world spending goes to good x, equilibrium requires $(wL + L^*)b_x = p_x L^*/a_x^*$. We can use these equations to calculate the equilibrium change in the home country's wage rate and, from that, the change in p_y.[4]

---

[4]From the equilibrium requirement we calculate $\hat{b}_x + (1 - b_x)\hat{w} = 0$, where we have used the fact that the share of spending devoted to good y equals the share of the home country in world income, in view of the complete specialization by both countries. Also, from the definition of b_x and the fact that $p_y = wa_y$, we find that $\hat{b}_x = (1 - b_x)(\sigma - 1)(\hat{w} + \hat{a}_y)$. These two equations enable

Stability of world markets requires the price of good y to fall in response to an exogenous increase in its supply. Thus, the home country suffers a deterioration of its terms of trade in response to its export-biased technological progress. This movement in the terms of trade offsets the direct gain from the productivity increase. The question that arises is: Can a country that sees its production methods improve actually be harmed by the technological advancement? In our example the change in real income is given by $\hat{u} = \hat{w} - b_x \hat{p}_x - b_y \hat{p}_y$. It is straightforward to show that "immiserizing growth" can indeed occur in a stable equilibrium, and does so if and only if $\sigma < b_x$. Intuitively, the home country's terms of trade deteriorate most when the two goods are poor substitutes, while the home residents benefit least as consumers from the fall in the relative price of good y when good x comprises the bulk of their consumption basket.[5]

The effects of technological divergence and convergence across countries can be captured in Krugman's (1986) model of technology gaps. Suppose that the adoption lag shrinks in the country that already has the shorter lag, thereby widening this country's technological lead. Such technical change is export biased, because the fall in production costs is proportionally greatest in the most knowledge-intensive sectors, where the country already holds its comparative advantage. Using a diagram like Figure 1.2, we can see that the relative wage of the advanced country must rise while the range of goods that it produces expands. But then the relative wage increase must be proportionally smaller than the productivity gain in the original marginal sector, and a fortiori in the other sectors with even greater knowledge intensities. As a result, the lagging country sees its terms of trade improve (the prices of all goods originally produced by the leading country fall relative to the prices of all goods originally produced by the lagging country) and its welfare rise. The advanced country also must gain in this case, because its real wage rises in terms of the products it originally produced (since productivity has improved), in terms of the products that it ultimately imports (since the relative wage gap widens), and in terms of the goods that it begins to produce (since these goods would have become cheaper in terms of the advanced country's labor had the other country continued to produce them, and the shift in production to the new low-cost location reduces their price even more).

Now consider technological "catch-up" by the less advanced country. Such learning is import biased; i.e. it reduces costs the most for the goods that the lagging country initially imports, including those that are at the margin of competitiveness between the two countries. The range of goods produced in the

us to solve the proportional rate of change of the wage rate and the price of good y in response to an exogenous change in a_y.

[5]Bhagwati (1958a,b) coined the term immiserizing growth and explained how it could arise in the face of adverse movements in the terms of trade. The equations derived in the previous footnote can be used to derive the condition for immiserizing growth given in the text.

lagging country expands while its relative wage rises. The lagging country's welfare must improve, because its real wage rises in terms of all goods. But the advanced country may suffer from the narrowing of its technological lead. The goods that it formerly produced but now imports are cheaper relative to its own wage rate (or else the location of production would not have changed), but the goods that it imports before and after the narrowing of the gap are more expensive due to the adverse movement in its terms of trade.

Finally, Findlay and Grubert (1959) have studied the terms-of-trade effects of technological progress in a world of two goods and two factors of production. Hicks-neutral technological progress in a country's import-competing sector must improve its terms of trade, while the same form of technological progress in the export sector has just the opposite effect. This is because, at constant prices, Hicks-neutral advancement always expands relative output in the sector that experiences the productivity gain, and so the price of this good must fall to restore a stable, global equilibrium. In contrast, capital-using technological progress in a capital-intensive export industry may improve the terms of trade, while labor-using progress in a labor-intensive import-competing industry may cause the terms of trade to deteriorate. In these two cases, the factor bias in the technological change works against the direct effect of the productivity gain by making relatively more scarce the factor used intensively in the advancing sector's production. If the induced change in relative factor prices is large enough, the relative output of the advancing sector may fall at constant prices even though its technology has improved. Then the relative price will move in favor of the advancing sector.

It is apparent from our review that models with exogenous differences in technological capabilities have much to offer trade theory. These models provide clear insights into important policy issues at relatively low cost in terms of technical complexity. Still, they are rather limited in what they can teach us, because they fail to identify the primitive sources of national competitiveness. We turn now to the recent developments in the theory that allow us to address issues having to do with the endogenous creation of comparative advantage

2. Learning by doing

While technological progress sometimes happens serendipitously, more often it is a consequence of economic activity. Two modes of learning seem most prevalent in commercial enterprises. Some learning occurs as a by-product of activities undertaken for other purposes. In particular, firms often discover better ways of doing things in the course of producing output or installing capital. Other learning is the result of more deliberate efforts to create knowledge. This section focuses on the relationship between international trade and incidental learning, while the next treats purposive investments in the acquisition of knowledge.

Where a learning curve applies to a single plant or firm, the distinction between learning by doing and more formal R&D activities may not be so important. In both cases the firm recognizes a cost of creating knowledge, which it weighs against the potential benefits of a new or improved technique or product. But where the benefits that derive from experience spill across firms – as when knowledgeable workers move between rival producers or when the expertise accumulated by a company can be gleaned by inspecting its products – the evolution of technology may reflect decisions taken with quite different objectives in mind. In this section we focus on learning that occurs not only "by doing", but also "by accident".

Once we recognize that firms may gain knowledge from the experience of others, a question that arises is: What is the set of others from which a given firm learns? There are at least two dimensions to this question. First, does a firm in a given industry acquire technical information from the activities of local firms in other industries? Second, does it gain such information from the activities of firms in its own industry operating in other countries? These are empirical matters that obviously may vary with the particular context one has in mind.[6]

It is useful to begin with a unified perspective from which the various special cases can be analyzed and compared. To this end, suppose again that all outputs are produced by labor alone and that production everywhere exhibits constant returns to scale. But now suppose that the labor necessary to produce a unit of good i in some country depends not only on the *intrinsic* productivity of the country's labor in producing that good, but also on the *accumulated knowledge* available there for manufacturing the product. In particular, let the production function take the form

$$Z_i = A_i(\cdot)\frac{L_i}{a_i}, \qquad (2.1)$$

where L_i denotes the labor used in producing good i, $1/a_i$ measures intrinsic productivity, and $A_i(\cdot)$ is the relevant index of technical know how. In the models that we will consider in this section, knowledge accumulates in the course of manufacturing output. The most general specification would make A_i a function of the experience in each country at producing every one of the different goods. Rather than treat this general case, we will highlight various special cases in which spillovers are limited in some way, for example to firms operating in a

---

[6]As an example, Irwin and Klenow (1994) have investigated the existence and geographic scope of knowledge spillovers from learning by doing in the semi conductor industry. They find that firms indeed learn from the experience of others, and that learning spills over as much across borders as it does between firms located in the same country.

given industry or cluster of industries, or to firms operating in a given country. This will allow us to isolate the specific implications of each new assumption.

2.1. Complete international spillovers

To begin with, suppose that technical information flows readily across international borders. In the most extreme case, the experience of home producers contributes as much to the knowledge base abroad as it does to that at home. We take learning to be external to any individual firm but specific to its industry and proportional to cumulative industry output. Then, with two countries, $A_i = A_i^* = \delta_i(Q_i + Q_i^*)$, where $Q_i(t) \equiv \int_\infty^t Z_i(s) \, \mathrm{d}s$ is cumulative output of good i at home and $Q_i^*(t) \equiv \int_\infty^t Z_i^*(s) \, \mathrm{d}s$ is cumulative output of the good abroad.

In this case, the relative labor requirement for producing a unit of good i at home versus abroad equals a_i/a_i^* at every moment in time. Evidently, learning neither strengthens nor weakens the forces of intrinsic comparative advantage. Intuitively, when producers in both countries share access to the same body of technical information, the accumulation of knowledge does not affect their relative abilities to produce any good. The trade pattern must be determined by other considerations.

This conclusion applies to a broader set of circumstances. For example, if countries have similar intrinsic abilities but different endowments of several factors of production, then Heckscher–Ohlin-like considerations dictate the pattern of trade. Our dynamic result mirrors Ethier's (1982a) finding that trade patterns are determined by traditional, comparative cost considerations when there are static increasing returns to scale emanating from international external economies.

Although technological progress has no bearing on comparative advantage when spillovers are global in their scope, trade may affect national rates of productivity and output growth in the short and long run. To illustrate this, we develop an example where, for certain parameter values and initial conditions, trade causes growth to slow in one or both trading economies. To this end, consider once again a world economy with two goods, x and y, in which consumers have the CES preferences $u = (c_x^\alpha + c_y^\alpha)^{1/\alpha}$. Recall that $\sigma = 1/(1 - \alpha)$ is the elasticity of substitution and suppose that $\sigma > 1$. In autarky, each country eventually specializes in producing one good or the other (at least, asymptotically), where the sector of eventual concentration depends on intrinsic abilities and initial conditions. Take, for instance, the home country. Its relative autarky outputs, x/y, must satisfy relative demands, $(p_x/p_y)^{-\sigma}$, at the prevailing relative prices, $p_x/p_y = Sa_x/a_y$. Here $S \equiv A_y/A_x$ denotes the ratio of the stocks of knowledge capital in the two industries. Using the production functions for x and y analogous to (2.1), we can solve for the momentary employment level in each industry. Then we can calculate output levels in each sector and so the additions to experience and to the stocks of knowledge. We find that

$$\hat{S} = \frac{L}{1 + (Sa_x/a_y)^{1-\sigma}} \left[\frac{\delta_y}{a_y} - \frac{\delta_x}{a_x} (Sa_x/a_y)^{1-\sigma} \right]. \tag{2.2}$$

The dynamics represented by eq. (2.2) are globally unstable when $\sigma > 1$. So S tends to infinity or zero as the initial ratio of knowledge stocks exceeds or falls short of $(\delta_x/\delta_y)^{1/(\sigma-1)}(a_y/a_x)^{\sigma/(\sigma-1)}$. If S approaches zero, the fraction of the labor force employed in sector y does likewise, while if S approaches infinity, the fraction of the labor force employed in sector y approaches one. The long-run autarky growth rate of output is $L\delta_x/a_x$ in the former case and $L\delta_y/a_y$ in the latter.

Now suppose that the two countries trade. For concreteness, assume that the home country has comparative advantage in producing good x. This means, as we have seen, that its relative intrinsic productivity in this sector exceeds that in the foreign country. Also, let the initial equilibrium involve complete specialization in both countries. Then as long as both countries remain completely specialized, $\hat{A}_x = \delta_x L/a_x$ and $\hat{A}_y = \delta_y L^*/a_y^*$. So $\hat{S} = \delta_y L^*/a_y^* - \delta_x L/a_x$, which may be positive or negative. If it is positive, then eventually the home country will find it profitable to begin producing good y, whereupon relative productivity in that sector will accelerate further. On the other hand, if $\hat{S}$ is negative, then eventually the foreign country will find it profitable to produce good x, and the relative productivity of sector y will decline more rapidly. In the long run, both countries specialize in producing whichever good *initially* experiences the more rapid productivity growth.

Notice that trade may lead one or both countries to specialize in a good different from the one in which it specialized in autarky. Suppose this is true of the home country, which specialized, say, in producing good x in autarky but ultimately switches to producing good y after the opening of trade. Then, since $\delta_x L/a_x > \delta_y(L/a_y + L^*/a_y^*)$ is required for a switch to take place, trade effects an acceleration of this country's growth rate.[7] If the foreign country also happens to specialize in producing good x in autarky and if $\delta_x L^*/a_x^* > \delta_y(L/a_y + L^*/a_y^*)$, then this country will experience a slowdown in growth as a result of trade. Here, *comparative* advantage determines the initial pattern of specialization when trade begins, but then *absolute* productivity and the size of each country determine how rapidly experience accumulates in each sector. If the country that has comparative advantage in the sector with the lesser long-run growth prospects happens to be larger or more intrinsically productive, trade can tilt its equilibrium growth path in the "wrong" direction [see Yanagawa (1993)].

---

[7]If both countries specialize in producing good i, world output of this good amounts to $A_i(L/a_i + L^*/a_i^*)$. Then $\delta_i(L/a_i + L^*/a_i^*)$ gives the proportional rate of productivity and output growth.

On the other hand, if the countries ultimately specialize in producing the same good with trade as they did in autarky, or if the two sectors do not differ greatly in their growth potential (e.g. if $\delta_x[L/a_x + L^*/a_x^*] = \delta_y[L/a_y + L^*/a_y^*]$), then trade must boost the long-run growth rate in each country. This is because the long-run trade equilibrium has both countries concentrating their production in the same industry, and knowledge accumulates more rapidly when the experiences of two sets of producers contribute to learning instead of just one. Even so, one of the countries may suffer a deceleration of its growth in the short or medium run. Suppose, for example, that both countries produce good x in autarky and that both also will produce this good (which, say, has greater growth potential) in the long-run trade equilibrium. The foreign country may nonetheless experience a period where it specializes in the production of good y, as a result of its comparative advantage in producing that good. In the event, the opening of trade may have an adverse impact on its growth rate during the initial phase of the trading era.

2.2. National spillovers

Most of the literature, beginning with Bardhan (1970), assumes that companies learn more from the experiences of other domestic producers than they do from firms located abroad. To understand the implications of having learning spillovers that are limited in their geographic reach, we consider the extreme case of national learning; that is, we posit industry-specific knowledge stocks that accumulate in proportion to *local* industry activity alone. With the same notation as before, $A_i = \delta_i Q_i$ and $A_i^* = \delta_i Q_i^*$.

Krugman (1987) studies a world economy with two countries and a continuum of industries. He takes preferences to be Cobb–Douglas, so that the initial equilibrium is determined as in Figure 1.2. Then, if industries are arranged in order of decreasing relative productivity advantage for the home country at time 0, the home country initially produces all goods with indexes below some critical number. Over time, learning by doing makes the home producers even more productive in each of the goods initially manufactured at home, while foreign producers gain no experience in these sectors. Therefore, the relative productivity advantage of the home country in each of these industries grows over time. Similarly, foreign firms gain experience and knowledge in producing the range of goods initially manufactured abroad, while home firms learn nothing in these industries. This widens the foreign relative productivity advantage of its export sectors. In short, the analog to the $M(z)$ schedule in Figure 1.2 becomes steeper over time, and the initial pattern of trade gets "locked in". Since the initial pattern of specialization depends not only on intrinsic ability but also on the initial stocks of industry knowledge in each country, *history matters* for the determination of the long-run trade pattern.

Lucas (1988) treats a similar model, but with two goods, CES preferences, and a continuum of small countries. Suppose all countries have the same labor force L and the same intrinsic abilities $1/a_x$ and $1/a_y$, but they differ in their initial stocks of knowledge capital. Then those with the highest ratios A_x/A_y at time 0 initially produce good x and the remaining countries initially produce good y. Will any country have an incentive to switch as time passes? To answer this question, we note that productivity grows at the rate $\delta_x L/a_x$ in each country that produces good x. World output of this good expands at this same rate, assuming that no country changes its sector of specialization. Similarly, productivity grows at the rate $\delta_y L/a_y$ in the typical country producing good y, and aggregate output of this good grows at the same rate under our working hypothesis. Let's assume for concreteness that $\delta_x/a_x > \delta_y/a_y$, so that the relative output of good x is increasing over time and its relative price is falling. Then, if any country will switch its industry of specialization, it must be the marginal country that produces good x. But competitive producers will switch from producing good x to producing good y in this country only if the rate of price decline exceeds the rate at which productivity expands in sector x (since productivity in sector y is stagnant so long as none of this good is being produced). The relative price of good x falls at the rate $L(\delta_x/a_x - \delta_y/a_y)/\sigma$.[8] With $\sigma > 1$, this never exceeds the rate of productivity growth. So, again, the initial pattern of trade gets locked into place.

It can readily be shown that the countries that specialize in producing good x in the trade equilibrium experience faster real income growth than those that specialize in producing good y.[9] This raises the possibility that some countries might wish to use trade or industrial policies to alter their patterns of specialization. Indeed a small country that specializes in the slower-growing sector in the absence of any policy intervention but that is close to the margin of competitiveness in the faster-growing sector would gain from any policy that induced its producers to switch over to the other good. The short-run income loss for such a country would be small, while the policy would generate a permanent boost to its productivity growth. Moreover, the government intervention would only be needed for a short time, until the country had collected enough experience in its new area of specialization to overcome its initial comparative disadvantage in this sector. Policy here can correct the inefficiency that results

---

[8]The CES preferences give rise to a constant elasticity of demand, so relative price movements are related to relative quantity changes according to $\hat{Z}_y - \hat{Z}_y = \sigma(\hat{p}_x - \hat{p}_y)$. The expression in the text follows from the fact that aggregate output of good j grows at rate $\hat{Z}_j = L\delta_j/a_j$, for $j = x, y$.

[9]Matsuyama (1992) makes a similar point in a model with specific factors in each sector, where countries remain incompletely specialized.

from producers' failure to account for the externalities associated with their production decisions.[10]

Krugman (1987) makes a slightly different point about policy in his analysis of two large countries trading a continuum of goods. Each country then has an incentive to subsidize production of a few goods near the margin of competitiveness, so that it can gain experience and take over production of these goods. By doing so, it expands the range of products it manufactures, increases demand for its labor, and betters its terms of trade. Again, the requisite subsidy need be in place for only a short time, as producers soon will accumulate the knowledge to make up for any deficiency in intrinsic ability or initial experience. The incentive to slice off new sectors a few at a time continues for a while (Krugman refers to this as the "narrow moving band"), but eventually the wage differential between the countries becomes sufficiently large that the social cost of capturing the next industry exceeds the benefit.

2.3. Inter-industry spillovers

Firms sometimes enjoy learning spillovers from the experiences of other firms producing entirely different goods. Moreover, the activities undertaken in certain industries may be especially conducive to generating ideas with widespread potential for improving productivity, while those performed in others may be more mundane and thus contribute little to the accumulation of knowledge. Boldrin and Sheinkman (1988) and Grossman and Helpman (1990b) have examined the implications of intersectoral learning by doing, where various industries do not contribute equally to the creation of knowledge.

Let us again examine an extreme case, this time assuming that learning takes place only in the course of producing good x. Let the knowledge so generated bolster productivity equally in each of two sectors. In particular, take $A_i = \delta Q_x$, for $i = x, y$. Suppose, moreover, that each industry uses a non-accumulable specific input, in addition to labor, so that there are strictly decreasing returns to labor in any one activity at every moment in time. This will allow a long-run equilibrium with active production in both sectors. We denote the production functions for goods x and y by $A_x F_x(L_x)$ and $A_y F_y(L_y)$, respectively. The functions $F_x(\cdot)$ and $F_y(\cdot)$ may differ across countries, if the countries happen to have different stocks of the sector-specific factors.

Consider again a world economy with a continuum of small countries. At every moment in time, competition drives each country to produce where the

---

[10]Bardhan (1970) studied the time pattern of the optimal subsidy to production in a small country that benefits from learning by doing in only one sector and that initially produces both goods, because it has two inputs and the sectors have different factor intensities.

ratio of the marginal products of labor in the two industries, F'_y/F'_x, equals the world relative price of good x. Then knowledge accumulates at the rate $F_x(L_x)$, and output and productivity grow in each sector at this rate. Since only experience in sector x generates technological progress, growth proceeds faster the greater are the resources devoted to this activity in the trade equilibrium. Evidently, countries with a natural comparative advantage in producing good x will grow faster than those with endowments suitable for producing good y. Moreover, if a country happens to accumulate more of the factor specific to industry y or if it somehow experiences an exogenous productivity improvement in this sector, its growth will slow and its aggregate welfare may fall [see Grossman and Helpman (1990b) and Matsuyama (1992) for further discussion].

2.4. Industry clusters

Posner (1961) was the first to note that "clusters" of industries might migrate together to particular nations. This dynamic process would occur, he argued, if learning by doing generated knowledge spillovers within but not between the clusters and if these spillovers were limited in their geographic reach. We will illustrate here how clustering might happen, without providing a general analysis.

Suppose that there are two distinct industry clusters, each comprising two goods. Let consumers worldwide devote constant and equal shares of their spending to each of the total of four goods. In the home country, one unit of labor can produce A_{ij} units of good i in cluster j at a given moment in time. The corresponding (time-varying) productivity parameters for the foreign country are denoted by A^*_{ij}. We assume that the home country initially has an absolute advantage in producing the first good in each cluster ($A_{1j} > A^*_{1j}$ for $j = 1, 2$) and that the foreign country has an absolute advantage in producing the second good in each cluster ($A^*_{2j} > A_{2j}$ for $j = 1, 2$). But we also suppose that $A_{11} > A^*_{21}$ and $A^*_{22} > A_{12}$; i.e. the home country's initial productivity advantage in the first good of cluster 1 exceeds the foreign country's productivity advantage in the second good of that same cluster, whereas the opposite is true for cluster 2. Finally, we assume that productivity improves with national experience in producing any good in a cluster; i.e. $dA_{ij}/dt = X_j$ and $dA^*_{ij}/dt = X^*_j$, where $X_j = \sum_i X_{ij}$ and $X^*_j = \sum_i X^*_{ij}$ are aggregate home output and aggregate foreign output in cluster j, respectively.

Let the two countries have the same labor force L. Then the initial equilibrium has the home country producing the first good in each cluster and the foreign country producing the second good in each cluster, in accordance with the dictates of (initial) comparative advantage. In this equilibrium, the wage rates in the two countries are equal.[11] Home output in cluster 1 amounts to $X_1 = X_{11} = A_{11}L/2$, which exceeds foreign output in that cluster, $X_1^* = X_{21}^* = A_{21}^*L/2$. So home productivity in manufacturing the two goods of cluster 1 initially grows faster than does foreign productivity. Similarly, foreign productivity grows faster in cluster 2, as the foreign country produces a greater quantity of output there. It is this differential in national productivity growth rates that gives rise to the possibility of industry clustering.

In our example, eventually either A_{21} catches up with A_{21}^*, or else A_{12}^* catches up with A_{12}. That is, either the rapid home productivity growth in cluster 1 eliminates the foreign country's initial productivity advantage in producing the second good in this cluster, or else the rapid foreign productivity growth in cluster 2 eliminates its initial disadvantage in producing the first good of that cluster. Suppose, for concreteness, that the former event happens first. Then, at the moment that the two productivity parameters become equalized ($A_{21} = A_{21}^*$), the home country commences production of the second good in cluster 1 and the home wage begins to rise above the foreign wage.[12] There ensues a period during which $w/w^* = A_{21}/A_{21}^*$ and both countries produce the second good of cluster 1. During this period, the home country's market share in this good increases over time. During this period, also, the foreign country sees a (continued) narrowing of its relative cost disadvantage in producing the first good of cluster 2. This narrowing occurs now for two reasons. First, the foreign country continues to produce more output in cluster 2, so its productivity grows faster than that in the home country. Second, the rising relative wage of the home country enhances foreign relative competitiveness in all industries, given the productivity levels. Eventually, there comes a time when $w/w^* = A_{12}/A_{12}^*$, whereupon firms in the foreign country find it profitable to begin production of the first good of cluster 2.[13] Thereafter, the wage gap between the countries narrows while the foreign country's share of world production of good X_{12} grows, until in the long run the wage rates are again equalized and each country specializes in producing both of the goods in one of the two industry clusters.

The explanation for the clustering of goods here is apparent. If a country initially produces a large quantity of any one good in a cluster, then the learning

---

[11]When the home country produces all of world output of exactly two goods, the share of world spending devoted to its product is one half. World spending on home goods thus amounts to $(wL + w^*L^*)/2$, where w and w^* are the home and foreign wage rates, respectively. This must equal the value of home output, wL, which implies $w = w^*$ in view of the fact that $L = L^*$.

[12]If the home wage did not rise above the foreign wage, the home country would immediately have a cost advantage in producing three of the goods. But with three quarters of world spending devoted to its goods and the value of spending on home goods equal to the value of output, we could not have $w = w^*$.

[13]Before this happens, there may or may not occur a period during which the home country produces all of world output of the second good in cluster 1 and the relative wage between countries remains constant for a time.

spillovers from this activity will tend to confer a dynamic comparative advantage in other industries in the same cluster, even if productivity in those other industries initially is low. In our example, the large initial outputs resulted from an assumed pattern of absolute productivity differentials. But a similar dynamic would arise if, for example, demands for the various goods were asymmetric. Then, a country that has an initial comparative advantage in producing the most popular good or goods in a cluster would tend, over time, to gain competitive advantage in producing the remaining, less-popular goods.

2.5. Bounded learning

In all of the settings we have examined thus far, indefinite productivity growth has been possible due to unbounded opportunities for learning by doing. Yet, as Young (1991) points out, the empirical evidence points to strongly diminishing returns to this type of learning, at least where any particular manufacturing process is concerned. Diminishing returns set in, presumably, because fresh insights are more difficult to come by once a given activity has been repeated a large number of times.[14] But Young (1991) and Stokey (1991) have shown that productivity growth may be sustained in the long run, despite the boundedness of opportunities for learning in every sector, provided that there are sufficient spillovers of knowledge from each activity to some others with greater long-run potential for contributing to well-being.

In order to illustrate their point, we introduce two new forms for consumers' preferences. These are

$$u = c_0^{1-\mu} \left[\sum_{i=1}^{\infty} \lambda^i c_i \right]^{\mu}, \quad \lambda > 1, \quad \mu > 1/2, \tag{2.3}$$

and

$$u = c_0 \left[\sum_{i=1}^{\infty} \lambda^i \log(1 + c_i) \right], \quad \lambda > 1, \tag{2.4}$$

where c_0 is consumption of a numeraire good 0 and c_i is consumption of good i. If consumers have the first of these two utility functions, they view all products except the numeraire good as perfect substitutes, but see products with higher indexes as contributing greater utility per unit of consumption. If they have the second set of preferences, they again see products with higher indexes

---

[14]Bardhan (1970, pp. 112–113) also recognized the possibility that opportunities for learning by doing might be bounded. He examined the implications of this for the time path of the optimal production subsidy.

as more desirable, but view the non-numeraire goods as imperfect substitutes while showing a taste for diversity in consumption. In either case, technological progress may take the form of improvements in the techniques for producing a given set of goods or the replacement of some goods by others of higher "quality".

We now suppose that the opportunities for learning by doing are bounded for any product but that spillovers take place from one industry to another. In particular, the act of producing any "generation" of product contributes information that improves firms' abilities to produce that generation *and the next*. More formally, we assume that one unit of labor can produce one unit of the numeraire good and A_i units of good i, where $Q_{i-1} = 0$ implies $A_i = 0$ and $Q_{i-1} > 0$ implies

$$A_i = A_0 + \beta \min(Q_{i-1}, \bar{A} - A_0) + (1 - \beta) \min(Q_i, \bar{A} - A_0).$$

This means that goods must be introduced in order; i.e. the production of good i remains infeasible until some positive amount of good $i - 1$ has been produced. Once the production of a good becomes possible, labor productivity starts at A_0 and improves with experience in producing either the good before it on the quality ladder or the good itself. When the productivity level reaches $\bar{A}$, the opportunities for learning about the good are exhausted.

Consider first a closed economy in which households have the preferences given by (2.3). We will show that, with certain parameter restrictions, there exists a steady-state equilibrium in which utility grows indefinitely and new goods replace older ones at regular intervals. We do this by construction. Suppose that, at some moment, the economy produces the numeraire good and good i, and that experience in producing good $i - 1$ had accumulated to Q_s before production of that good had ceased. Assuming that there exists a periodic steady state, good i should also be replaced by good $i + 1$ when cumulative experience in the former reaches Q_s. Consumers begin to buy good $i + 1$ at the moment when its price falls to a level only λ times as great as that of good i. This requires, in a competitive market, that the productivity of labor in producing good i be only λ times as great as that in producing good $i + 1$. In other words, we need $A_0 + Q_s = \lambda(A_0 + \beta Q_s)$, for good $i + 1$ to become competitive at precisely the right moment. The solution to this equation gives a positive value for $Q_s = (\lambda - 1)A_0/(1 - \lambda\beta)$, provided that $\beta < 1/\lambda$. We also require that good $i + 2$ not be competitive at the moment after good $i + 1$ is introduced. Consumers will not purchase good $i + 2$ at this moment if its price exceeds λ times the price of good $i + 1$; i.e. if $A_0 + \beta Q_s > \lambda A_0$. Given the value of Q_s that we have already determined, this inequality is satisfied for $\beta > 1/(1 + \lambda)$. Finally, the steady state we have described can obtain only if good $i + 1$ has been introduced before learning in good i has been exhausted; that is, if $Q_s < \bar{A} - A_0$.

Under the parameter restrictions just described, a periodic steady state exists. In the steady state, the wage rate remains fixed at one. Households spend a fraction $1 - \mu$ of their income of L on purchases of the numeraire good and the fraction $1 - \mu$ of the labor force is employed producing this good to meet their demands. The remaining fraction μ of the labor force produces a "current generation" of knowledge-intensive products. Each generation is replaced by the next as soon as experience in the current product provides enough technical information to make its successor economically viable. As in Young (1991) and Stokey (1991), knowledge spillovers from one industry to the next sustain productivity growth in the long run.

Now let us reintroduce trade between two countries that are in every way identical except that the home country initially is less advanced in its production of the non-numeraire good. We assume that the foreign country has accumulated experience in producing good i^*, while the home country has only produced goods up to i, $i < i^*$. We will establish that, in the steady state of the trade equilibrium, the (lagging) home country specializes in producing the numeraire good while the (advanced) foreign country produces a succession of knowledge-intensive products introduced at regular intervals. Thus trade retards growth in the country that begins behind.

Again we proceed by construction. If the home country produces the numeraire good, then its wage rate must equal one. Moreover, if this country specializes in producing the numeraire and the foreign country produces none of it, then total output of this good and the total wage bill amount to L. Since a fraction $1 - \mu$ of world spending is devoted to the numeraire good, the matching of revenues and costs implies $L = (1 - \mu)(L + w^*L^*)$, or $w^* = \mu/(1 - \mu)$ whenever $L = L^*$. Note that this gives $w^* > 1$ when $\mu > 1/2$; i.e. when there is sufficient demand for the non-numeraire good. In the event that $w^* > 1$, the foreign country indeed is uncompetitive in producing the numeraire good.

We know also that the knowledge available for producing good i at home is at most $A_0 + Q_s$, while that available for producing good i^* abroad is at least $A_0 + \beta Q_s$. Recognizing that the wage rate in the foreign country is higher than that at home, consumers will nonetheless prefer the foreign good of generation i^* to the home good of generation i if $\lambda^{i^*}(A_0 + \beta Q_s)/w^* > \lambda^i(A_0 + Q_s)$, or

$$\lambda^{i-i^*-1} > \frac{\mu}{1 - \mu} \ . \tag{2.5}$$

If inequality (2.5) is not satisfied at time 0, then the home country produces some knowledge-intensive goods at first. But since it also produces all of the world's output of the numeraire good, it must devote less labor to the sector with learning than its trade partner and so its experience accumulates less rapidly. Over time, the technological gap between the two countries widens and eventually it becomes so wide that an inequality like (2.5) is satisfied. Then the home country terminates its production in the knowledge-intensive sector forever. The conclusion is much the same as in Young (1991): trade causes the more advanced country to specialize in producing the goods that generate the most learning and accelerates productivity growth in that country. Meanwhile, the lagging country finds itself specializing in goods where learning opportunities are fewer (or, as here, absent), and so its growth slows.[15] The more advanced country must gain from trade, but the less advanced country may gain or lose.

The equilibria described so far have the unrealistic feature that the switch from one generation of good to the next occurs quite abruptly. The alternative preferences given by (2.4) generate a more gradual transition. For certain parameter values there exists a steady state in which the economy passes through a succession of phases in which: (i) only generation i of the knowledge-intensive good is produced; (ii) generations i and $i+1$ are produced; (iii) learning by doing becomes exhausted in the production of good i; and (iv) production of good i ends and only good $i + 1$ is produced.

We construct such an equilibrium for a closed economy. The country devotes $L/2$ units of labor to producing the numeraire good and the remaining $L/2$ units to the set of sectors where learning is possible. The prices of the knowledge-intensive goods of generations i and $i + 1$ are A_i and A_{i+1}, respectively. Altogether, half of aggregate income of L is spent on one or both of these goods. If consumption of both of these goods occurs at some moment in time, then maximization of (2.4) implies that the quantities purchased of each one must satisfy

$$\frac{C_i}{A_i} = \frac{1}{1 + \lambda} \left(\frac{1}{A_{i+1}} - \frac{\lambda}{A_i} + \frac{L}{2} \right) \tag{2.6}$$

and

$$\frac{C_{i+1}}{A_{i+1}} = \frac{1}{1 + \lambda} \left(\frac{\lambda}{A_i} - \frac{1}{A_{i+1}} + \frac{\lambda L}{2} \right). \tag{2.7}$$

When the expression in (2.6) or (2.7) gives a negative value for consumption of one good or the other, then in fact none of that good is consumed and spending of $L/2$ falls entirely on the other product.

We can define Q_b as the level of cumulative experience in producing good i at the moment when good $i + 1$ is first introduced, and Q_h as the cumulative experience in producing good $i+1$ when production of good i ceases.[16] It is easy

---

[15] Here, as in Young (1991), an initially lagging country that is larger than its trade partner can sometimes overcome its technological disadvantage and eventually capture the technologically progressive industry.

[16] The first of these is found by substituting for A_i in terms of Q_i, using $Q_{i-1} = \bar{A} - A_0$ and $A_{i+1} = A_0 + \beta Q_i$, and solving (2.7) for the value of Q_i that makes $C_{i+1} = 0$. The second is found by substituting for A_i and A_{i+1} in terms of Q_{i+1}, using $A_i = \bar{A}$, and solving (2.6) for the value of Q_{i+1} that makes $C_i = 0$.

to show that parameter values exist for which $Q_h < Q_b$ (so that the replacement of each generation by the next takes place smoothly) and also $Q_b < \bar{A} - A_0$ (so that each product exhausts its learning potential before it exits the market).

What are the effects of trade when consumers have the alternative preferences? They are the same as before. A country that begins with a technological lead will widen its lead over time, and eventually (if not immediately) take over the world's production in the sector with learning. The other country will find that trade slows its productivity growth, perhaps only moderately at first, but to zero in the long run. The initially lagging country might gain from trade, because it can import the leading country's advanced goods, but gains from trade are in no way ensured.

2.6. Technological leapfrogging

Up to this point we have dealt with situations in which national learning by doing means that an initial technological lead is self-reinforcing (see, however, footnote 15). Brezis et al. (1993) identify circumstances under which *leapfrogging* may occur; that is, a country that begins technologically behind may eventually surpass its trade partner, only to be overtaken again in a subsequent phase of the periodic steady state. This happens because new and superior technologies, which arrive exogenously in their model, may be adopted by the lagging country even though they are not profitable in the leading country.

To see how this works, let preferences be given by (2.3) and consider a closed economy. At first, only goods with indexes up to and including j can be produced, with one unit of labor yielding one unit of the numeraire or A_i units of good i, where $A_i = A_0 + \min(Q_i, \bar{A} - A_0)$ for $i \leq j$. Here, all spillovers are confined to the industry in which they are generated and the opportunities for learning by doing are bounded for every product. We assume that the knowledge stock for good j (and perhaps for all goods before it) has already reached its maximum of $\bar{A}$ at time 0.

Now let the technology for good $j + 1$ suddenly become available, although of course no producer has had any experience in using it. The technologies for producing goods $j + 2$, $j + 3$, and so on, will arrive subsequently, at regular (but perhaps long) intervals of time. At the moment when it first becomes feasible to produce good $j + 1$, the price of this good is $1/A_0$, while that of good j is $1/\bar{A}$. Consumers buy the new good only if $\lambda > \bar{A}/A_0$. Otherwise, the new and superior product never is introduced into the market, and productivity growth does not pick up until some even more desirable product arrives on the scene.

But now let there be two countries and trade. At the outset, the home country produces good j with labor productivity $1/\bar{A}$, while the foreign country has no experience in this industry. Then, if the countries are not too different in size, the foreign country initially specializes in producing the numeraire good while the home country produces only good j. With this pattern of specialization, the foreign wage equals one and equality of foreign labor income and spending on the numeraire good implies that $w = \mu L^*/(1 - \mu)L$. The hypothesized pattern of specialization is realized for $\bar{A}/A_0 > \mu L^*/(1 - \mu)L > 1$.

What happens when the technology for producing good $j + 1$ comes along? If the new generation of good is sufficiently better than the current generation ($\lambda > \bar{A}/A_0$), then producing with the new technology would be profitable in either country. The model does not tell us which country would adopt it first, but as soon as one gains a small edge in experience the pattern of trade gets locked in. A more interesting equilibrium can arise if the superiority of the new generation is not so large ($\lambda < \bar{A}/A_0$). Then producers in the home country, who must pay w to their labor no matter which technology they use, will be unable to produce good $j + 1$ at a profit in competition with good j. On the other hand, production with the new technology may be profitable in the foreign country. There, the wage rate initially equals one, so the new good can be offered at a competitive price of $1/A_0$. Consumers will have positive demand for the good at this price provided that $\bar{A}/A_0 < w\lambda = \lambda \mu L^*/(1 - \mu)L$. In the event, the new technology will be adopted by the foreign (lagging) country. As soon as this happens, the wage rate in the home country falls, so that the quality adjusted price of its knowledge-intensive good of generation j, $w\lambda/\bar{A}$, matches that of the foreign country's good of generation $j + 1$. With $w = \bar{A}/\lambda A_0 > 1$, the home country still specializes in the production of good j while the foreign country produces the numeraire good and good $j + 1$.[17]

Over time, the foreign country gains experience at producing good $j + 1$. As it does so, its productivity rises and the price of its product falls. Demand for good j produced by the home country declines. The home wage must fall, so that consumers are still willing to buy this good. Eventually, the home wage falls to $w = 1$. In the next instant, the home country takes over production of the numeraire good, and the foreign country specializes in the production of good $j+1$. From then on, w^* rises, until learning by doing in the $j+1$st good ends when $A_{j+1} = \bar{A}$. Finally the world economy enters a stationary period which persists until the technology for good $j + 2$ arrives, whereupon it is adopted in the home country. The countries alternate the lead position in the knowledge-intensive sector indefinitely.

Essentially the same pattern emerges if preferences are given by (2.4), except that the location of production of the numeraire good switches only gradually, rather than abruptly, from country to country. (We leave this case as an exercise

---

[17]The foreign country's output of good $j + 1$ at the moment of its introduction to the market is the solution to the equation $\mu(L^* + wL) = \bar{A}L/\lambda \bar{A}_0 + Z_{j+1}/A_0$. The left-hand side of this equation is total spending on non-numeraire goods, while the right-hand side gives the value of output of goods j and $j + 1$ at the market-clearing prices.

for the interested reader.) Indeed, leapfrogging can arise anytime learning by doing is bounded for a given product and specific to the product and country. Then, if the eventual superiority of a new technology is not enormous, existing producers will pass over that technology in favor of the one in which they are already experienced. No single firm in the experienced country will find it profitable to change, in view of its inability to internalize the externalities from learning. But firms in the lagging country may be able to adopt the new technology, even though they lack experience in using it, because they initially face a lower wage. When they do so, their productivity improves over time and eventually the superiority of the new technology spells the demise of the old. In short, the lagging country, by dint of its *lack* of experience with the existing technology, always enjoys a *comparative* advantage in any new one that may happen along.

This concludes our discussion of learning that occurs as an accidental by-product of manufacturing activities. We have seen that the traditional forces of comparative advantage dominate long-run outcomes whenever knowledge spillovers are global in scope. In contrast, when knowledge spillovers are confined to a single country or region, the vagaries of history can influence the trade patterns even in the long run. National spillovers introduce a positive feedback that tends to reinforce any existing pattern of specialization and trade.

3. Innovation

Accidental discoveries undoubtedly play an important role in the advance of technology. But firms also invest vast resources in order to generate productivity improvements; in the advanced industrial economies, private spending on research and development typically exceeds two percent of industrial value added, and this number has been growing steadily in recent years. In this section we discuss the relationship between trade and technological progress when new technologies are the result of intentional investments.

Deliberate investments in knowledge require an environment where intellectual property rights are protected. Without such protection, investors cannot appropriate the fruits of their labor. In some cases, the legal system provides the needed protection, as when governments grant patents for original ideas. In other cases the protection comes more or less automatically, because imitation is costly and trade secrets can be preserved. A patent or trade secret typically gives an innovator the ability to exercise monopoly power in the product market. That is, a firm with proprietary access to an innovative technology usually can price above marginal cost without losing all of its sales. And the more unique and superior the innovator's technology, the greater will be the monopoly power and the larger the reward [see Arrow (1962)]. This explains why imperfect competition features prominently in the various models we shall discuss below.

3.1. Economies due to increasing specialization

It is useful to begin our discussion of endogenous innovation with a model that has many parallels with our treatment of learning by doing. The model is one where productivity gains stem from increasing specialization of the production process. The particular formalization is due to Ethier (1982a).

Consider an industry in which output is manufactured from an assortment of intermediate inputs, with a greater number of inputs associated with more specialization and refinement of each stage of production. In this setting, it is reasonable to suppose that total factor productivity will vary with the degree of specialization. A CES production function can be used to capture this idea. We suppose

$$X = \left[\int_0^n z(j)^\alpha \, dj \right]^{1/\alpha} , \quad 0 < \alpha < 1 , \tag{3.1}$$

where X denotes final industry output, $z(j)$ represents the input of intermediate good j, and n is the number of intermediates employed. We treat n as a continuous variable for convenience.

Given the number of intermediates in use, the technology represented by (3.1) exhibits constant returns to scale. We assume that each producer takes the set of available intermediates as given. Since each has an incentive to use some of every available input (that is, to specialize the production process as finely as possible), the number of intermediates in use is effectively beyond its control. Thus each producer of final goods perceives constant returns in production. The producers behave competitively, pricing their output equal to perceived marginal cost.

Now suppose that every intermediate input is used in equal quantity z, as will be the case when the intermediates carry the same price. Then $X = A(\cdot)Z$, where $Z = nz$ is the aggregate quantity of intermediates and $A = n^{(1-\alpha)/\alpha}$ is an index of the state of technology.[18] This reduced-form production function has the same form as (2.1), which we used to study learning by doing. The difference, however, is that whereas the index of the state of technology in (2.1) measured the accumulated experience in manufacturing the final good, here it depends upon the number of available intermediate inputs. This number will

---

[18]Whenever all intermediates are produced with the same constant returns to scale production function, it is meaningful to define an aggregate measure Z, where Z too can be produced with constant returns to scale.

reflect cumulative investment in R&D, if intermediates must be invented before they can be produced.

We proceed to determine the flow of profits that accrue to a new invention. Inventors are granted indefinite patents and produce their differentiated input with one unit of labor per unit of output. With the number of intermediate inputs given at a moment in time, each patent holder faces a demand with an elasticity approximately equal to $1/(1 - \alpha)$.[19] The firm equates marginal cost with marginal revenue, which calls for a mark-up pricing rule,

$$p_z = \frac{1}{\alpha} w. \tag{3.2}$$

This yields an equilibrium profit flow of

$$\pi = (1 - \alpha) \frac{p_z Z}{n}. \tag{3.3}$$

Here, profits per variety are inversely proportional to the number of competitors and directly proportional to aggregate spending on intermediates. Aggregate spending matches the value of final output, because producers of final goods earn zero profits.[20]

The incentive to innovate is given by the present value of the profit stream. If Z is constant, n grows at a constant rate g, and the prices of intermediates grow at a common, constant rate, then the present value of profits from any time t onward equals $\pi(t)/(r + g)$, where r is the real interest rate in terms of intermediates. It follows that the incentive to innovate varies directly with the extent of product differentiation (as reflected in the parameter $1/\alpha$) and inversely with the number of available intermediates, the rate of introduction of new intermediates, and the real rate of interest.

Having derived a measure of the incentive to innovate, we need to introduce a cost of innovation and examine how private benefits and costs interact to determine the evolution of industry output. The simplest way to treat the innovation cost is to assume that there exists a deterministic production function relating R&D inputs, which we take to include labor and a stock of knowledge capital, to research output, which includes a flow of blueprints and perhaps additions to the knowledge stock. We assume that there are constant returns to labor in research, so that $\dot{n} = A_I(K_n)L_I$, where $\dot{n}$ is the flow of newly invented products, L_I is the labor employed in R&D, and $A_I(\cdot)$ measures the productivity of labor in the research lab. Research productivity varies with the stock of knowledge

---

[19] The approximation neglects terms of order $1/n$; it becomes precise as the number of competing differentiated products grows large. For further details, see Helpman and Krugman (1985, pp. 118–119) or Dixit and Stiglitz (1993).

[20] Equations (3.2) and (3.3) apply at each moment in time. We omit the time variables in order to simplify the notation.

capital K_n, which represents the accumulated scientific and engineering wisdom in society. We treat general knowledge as a free public good. Then the cost of inventing a new product is $w/A_I(K_n)$.

With free entry into R&D and an active research sector, the value of a blueprint matches the cost of inventing a new product. Using the present discounted value of profits for the value of a blueprint, we have (after rearranging terms)

$$\frac{(1 - \alpha)Z}{\alpha n} A_I(K_n) = r + g. \tag{3.4}$$

The left-hand side of (3.4) gives the profit rate for a firm producing a differentiated product (i.e. the ratio of profits to the value of the blueprint) while the right-hand side gives the real effective cost of capital. The latter includes not only the interest cost, but also the rate at which the blueprint value depreciates in view of the ongoing entry of new competitors.

Equation (3.4) has important implications for the long-run dynamics of an economy with costly innovation and free entry into R&D. Suppose that the stock of knowledge ceases to grow, or that its contribution to research productivity peters out. Then, if n grows continually, the profit rate on the left-hand side of (3.4) must eventually fall below the effective cost of capital. At this point, there is insufficient incentive for conducting research [see Judd (1985)]. Evidently, ongoing innovation requires sustained increases in research productivity. The analogy with our earlier discussion of bounded learning by doing is clear: If opportunities for learning are bounded or the learning process runs into diminishing returns, then the engine of technological progress must eventually grind to a halt.

Although the formal structure of our model is similar to that for learning by doing, the underlying economics are different. Whereas bounded learning by doing in manufacturing seems a plausible and even compelling assumption, it is easy to imagine that knowledge useful for conducting research might continue to accumulate forever. In industrial research, almost every new invention builds on some that came before it and many industrial research projects generate knowledge beyond what was intended for the specific application. If creative ideas are in limitless supply, so too may be the opportunities to improve upon research productivity.

Let us suppose, then, that an unbounded potential exists for learning about how better to invent new products. We assume that each research project generates some additional knowledge that is potentially useful to subsequent inventors and that this knowledge enters rapidly into the public domain. In particular, we take K_n to be proportional to the number of research projects previously undertaken (so there are no diminishing returns to learning) and A_I to be proportional to K_n; then we can write $A_I(K_n) = n/a_I$. In the event, the profit rate does not decline with an increase in the number of available products, because as the expansion of variety reduces the profitability of a new product, the expansion of knowledge reduces the cost of inventing it as well.

It is possible now to have ongoing innovation in the steady state. The long-run rate of innovation satisfies

$$\frac{(1-\alpha)Z}{\alpha a_I} = r + g. \tag{3.5}$$

To close the model, we must specify how the equilibrium output of intermediate goods and the real rate of interest are determined. Take for the moment the case where the industry under examination comprises the entirety of the domestic economy. Then all labor must be employed either in manufacturing intermediate goods or in conducting industrial research. (Recall that final goods are produced from intermediates alone.) Total employment in manufacturing matches the aggregate output of intermediates, while employment in R&D is a_I/n times the number of new products invented per unit of time. Thus, equilibrium in the labor market requires

$$a_I g + Z = L, \tag{3.6}$$

where L once again represents the aggregate labor force. Finally, suppose that households maximize the discounted value of the log of consumption and that they can borrow and lend on a frictionless credit market. Then the real interest rate in terms of intermediates will be constant and equal to the subjective discount rate ρ.[21]

It is now straightforward to solve for the long-run rate of innovation in a closed economy of the type just described. Combining (3.5) and (3.6), we have $g = (1 - \alpha)L/a_I - \alpha\rho$. The innovation rate is larger the less substitutable are the specialized inputs, the greater is the stock of resources suitable for conducting R&D, the more productive are these resources in the research lab, and the lower is the subjective discount rate. Moreover, the "long run" is achieved immediately, with a constant rate of innovation g at every moment in time [see Grossman and Helpman (1991a, ch. 3)].

We now have the building blocks needed to examine how trade evolves in a world economy with endogenous technological progress. The answer, it turns out, depends upon the nature of the stock of general knowledge capital. We will distinguish two cases, one where knowledge spillovers are *local* in scope, so that only national R&D contributes knowledge that is useful in subsequent research, and another where the spillovers are *global* in scope, so that knowledge

---

[21] When households maximize $\int_t^\infty e^{-\rho(s-t)} \log[c(s)]ds$ subject to an intertemporal budget constraint, the first-order condition implies $\dot{c}/c + \dot{p}_x/p_x = r + \dot{p}_z/p_z - \rho$, where p_x is the price of final output. In every momentary equilibrium we must have $c = X$ and $p_x X = p_z Z$. Then, since Z is constant in the steady state, the real interest rate in terms of intermediates, r, is equal to ρ.

generated in any country augments research productivity worldwide.[22] This distinction is reminiscent of the one we made in our earlier discussion of learning by doing, and many of the implications of it will be the same. There are two new points to emphasize, however. First, whereas trade had no direct effect on productivity in the model of learning by doing, here access to foreign-made intermediate goods raises productivity in manufacturing even in the absence of international knowledge spillovers. Productivity in manufacturing depends on the range of intermediates used in production, irrespective of the sources of those various inputs. Second, it may well be that foreign trade itself influences the degree to which knowledge spills across international borders. Knowledge may be transmitted, for example, when exporters describe the best uses of their products or when importers report the needs of their customers. The role of trade as a conduit for knowledge has been explored in Grossman and Helpman (1991c).

3.2. International knowledge stocks

We begin with the case where knowledge spillovers are global in scope. For simplicity we assume that dissemination is immediate, so that researchers worldwide draw on a common stock of general knowledge. Denoting this public input again by K_n, we suppose that K_n is proportional to the cumulative number of research projects previously undertaken in all countries combined. We also assume that countries have the same production technologies, with one unit of labor required per unit of intermediate and a_I/K_n units of labor required for each invention.

Now consider a world economy that produces only the single final good, X. In the steady state, each country produces and exports a constant fraction of the total number of input varieties. This fraction matches the country's share in the world supply of labor. All countries import the differentiated varieties invented and produced abroad and all experience the same rate of productivity growth in their final-goods sectors. Productivity growth in final manufacturing is proportional to the rate of expansion in the total number of input varieties,

---

[22]Grossman and Helpman (1990a) describe an intermediate case where knowledge capital diseminates globally, but international transmission involves longer lags than transmission within a country. Some such intermediate case is probably closest to the truth, inasmuch as Coe and Helpman (1994), Eaton and Kortum (1994), and Bernstein and Mohnen (1994) present evidence of the existence of international spillovers from R&D activity, while Jaffe et al. (1993) provide evidence that the extent of knowledge spillovers from R&D falls (at least for some time) with geographic distance from the source. Lichtenberg (1992) explicitly rejects the hypothesis of complete and instantaneous international R&D spillovers, while Eaton and Kortum (1994) find that technology diffusion is considerably more rapid within than between countries. Still, the extreme cases that we consider are pedagogically useful for bringing out the forces at work.

with a factor of proportionality of $(1 - \alpha)/\alpha$. In each country, and in the world as a whole, the number of produced inputs expands in the long run at the rate $g = (1 - \alpha) \sum_j L^j/a_I - \alpha\rho$, which is larger than the rate of innovation experienced by any country in autarky. So integration boosts not only manufacturing productivity at a moment in time (by expanding the range of intermediate inputs available to a producer of final goods) but also the long-run rate of productivity growth (by providing access to the general knowledge generated abroad). There are both (welfare) gains from trade and a positive effect of trade on the rate of technological progress in every country.

While the above model highlights the importance of trade in differentiated inputs, it allows limited scope for interindustry trade. Besides trading intermediates, a country may import some final goods. But inasmuch as the assembly of final goods requires no primary resources here, such trade has no meaningful effects. To consider the determinants of the *pattern of trade*, we must further elaborate the general equilibrium structure of our model. To this end, suppose that two primary factors – say, unskilled labor and human capital – are used in manufacturing the various inputs into the production of final good X. Suppose also that there is a second final good Y that is produced directly with these same primary inputs, also with constant returns to scale but with no prospect for technological progress. Finally, suppose that human capital and unskilled labor are also used in R&D and that the three activities employing the primary resources vary in their factor-intensity requirements. How will the pattern of trade evolve over time?

In the short run (i.e. shortly after trade begins), history may afford some particular country an initial advantage in producing intermediates. That is, a country may have invented a disproportionate number of intermediates before trade commenced, in which case it would become an immediate net exporter of these goods. But any competitive advantages due to prior experience are bound to be short lived; initial conditions play no role in determining the ultimate pattern of trade when general knowledge is a global public good [see Grossman and Helpman (1991a, ch. 7)].

Suppose there are two countries, A and B. Figure 3.1 portrays the long-run equilibrium when intermediate goods must be produced where they are invented and when consumers allocate a constant fraction of their spending to the technology-intensive good X. The dimensions of the box represent the world endowment of the two factors of production. The origin for country A is at the lower left corner, and the vector $O^A E$ represents its factor endowment. That of country B is represented by EO^B, which culminates in its origin at the upper right corner. The figure depicts the case where country A has the relatively larger endowment of human capital compared to its endowment of unskilled labor.

We use the familiar procedure of constructing a long-run trade equilibrium by

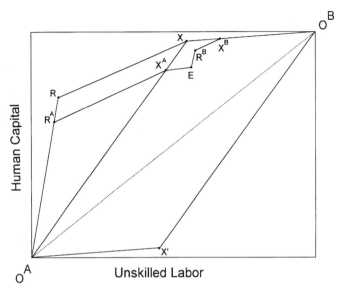

Figure 3.1.

showing that it is possible to allocate resources in each country so as to mimic the steady-state outputs of a hypothetical integrated equilibrium with no international borders. Assume that, in the integrated equilibrium, the vector $O^A R$ of resources would be used in inventing new intermediate inputs, the vector RX would be used in manufacturing the existing assortment of these goods, and the vector XO^B would be used in producing the traditional good Y. Clearly, the figure depicts the case where R&D is the most human-capital-intensive activity and the production of the final good Y is the least so. In the long-run equilibrium with trade, country A can employ the vector $O^A R^A$ in its R&D labs, the vector $R^A X^A$ in manufacturing the varieties of intermediates that it has previously developed, and the vector $X^A E$ in the traditional manufacturing sector. Country B can employ the resources ER^B in R&D, $R^B X^B$ in producing intermediates, and $X^B O^B$ in producing good Y. The important thing to notice is that the ratio of $O^A R^A$ to $R^A X^A$ is the same as the ratio of ER^B to $R^B X^B$, which is the same as the ratio of $O^A R$ to RX; in other words, the ratio in country A of the size of its research sector to the size of its sector manufacturing intermediates is the same as for country B, which in turn is the same as for the world as a whole. This means that, when equal quantities of each intermediate are produced, the number of different intermediates produced in each country is in exact proportion to the number of intermediates being invented there per unit time. The latter condition is a requirement of a steady-state equilibrium in which intermediates must be produced where they are invented and the allocation of resources among sectors in each country is constant over time.[23]

In the long-run equilibrium depicted by the figure, aggregate outputs of intermediate goods are constant in each country, as are outputs of the traditional good Y. So too are the fractions of the total number of intermediate goods emanating from each country, which implies that the rate of innovation g is eventually the same in both places. Now suppose for concreteness that assembly of good X from intermediates takes place where the good is consumed, as it would for example if X were nontradable (or if the intermediates were in fact final goods and X were only a fictitious good representing a subutility index). Then intraindustry trade in intermediates would coexist with a predictable long-run pattern of interindustry trade. In particular, the country with an abundance of the factor used intensively in the high-technology sector (that is, in research and production of intermediates together) becomes a net exporter of intermediate goods. The other country balances its long-run deficit in the high-technology sector by exporting the unskilled-labor-intensive, traditional good.[24]

We find that factor abundance alone determines the steady-state pattern of intersectoral trade. This is like the result for static trade models with monopolistic competition, except that here it applies only as a long-run proposition. A human-capital rich country may begin as a net importer of intermediates, if historically it has not been very active in inventing new products. But once it becomes integrated into the world economy, its natural comparative advantage will eventually take hold. The country will specialize disproportionately in the R&D activity, and over time will develop the capacity to produce a disproportionate share of the differentiated products.

What is the effect of trade on a country's technological progress in this setting? Consider first the case where factor compositions are everywhere the same (i.e. the point E in Figure 3.1 lies on the diagonal of the box). In this case, trade accelerates every country's long-run rate of innovation, just as it does when there is only one final good and one primary factor. When relative factor endowments are the same, so too are long-run factor rewards and the long-run division of resources among sectors. Then countries do not engage in interindustry trade in the long run, although they do trade their unique varieties of the intermediate

---

[23]Figure 3.1 is constructed under the assumption that the relative factor endowments in the two countries do not differ too greatly (i.e. point E lies inside the parallelogram $O^A X O^B X'$), which enables a long-run equilibrium with factor price equalization. For endowments outside the parallelogram, long-run factor prices must differ and at least one of the countries must specialize in production.

[24]Our discussion presumes that no country imports in both sectors (on net) in the steady state. It is in fact possible in our model that a country might run a long-run trade surplus in order to service debt acquired along the equilibrium path. If the overall deficit were large enough, and its factor composition not too different from that abroad, the country could even have a net surplus in both sectors.

goods. With knowledge spillovers that are global in reach, the knowledge stock grows faster in a larger world economy than any single, smaller economy with similarly allocated resources. It follows that the pace of innovation must increase as a result of the scale economies associated with producing knowledge [see Rivera-Batiz and Romer (1991)].

Now consider a world where countries differ in their factor composition. Continuity implies that innovation must accelerate if the differences in factor abundance are small. But what if these differences are larger, though still not so large as to eliminate the possibility of a long-run equilibrium with factor price equalization? With factor price equalization, trade is like an enlargement of the economy. The human-capital-poor country finds itself a part of a larger world economy that is relatively better endowed with human capital. Since an increase in the endowment of human capital causes an expansion of the relative size of the world research sector, this country experiences an increased rate of innovation in its high-technology sector.[25]

The conclusion differs for the human-capital-rich country. On the one hand, this country too enjoys the benefits of a larger world economy. On the other hand, its relative endowment of human capital in autarky exceeds the human-capital-to-labor ratio for the integrated world economy. Depending on the elasticities of substitution between human capital and unskilled labor in the three activities, the overall size of the world R&D sector may be larger or smaller than the size of its own sector in autarky [see Grossman and Helpman (1991a, ch. 9)]. If these elasticities are small, then the human-capital-rich country may see its rate of innovation slowed as the (long-run) result of an opening of trade and knowledge flows.

3.3. National knowledge stocks

We saw in our discussion of learning by doing that new factors enter into the determination of the trade pattern when knowledge spillovers are local rather than global in reach. Global learning means shared experience and so only the traditional forces of comparative advantage can shape the pattern of international trade. But local learning means distinct national experience, which introduces a role for history in determining the trade pattern. We will see that a similar conclusion is warranted when technology results from deliberate investment. In this case, global knowledge means similar research capability and so traditional forces determine whether a country is competitive in the research lab. Then

---

[25]Note, however, that trade causes this country to specialize relatively more than in autarky in the production of traditional goods. So while trade must increase the country's rate of technological progress in industry X, it may slow its average rate of technological progress, when sectoral productivity gains are weighted by initial or final GDP shares.

a country that has an appropriate resource base can overcome any initial disadvantage in the knowledge-intensive sector by specializing relatively in R&D. But initial disadvantages may have long-lasting effects if a lack of local research experience means low research productivity.

A simple model helps to reveal the novel features of a world economy with local knowledge capital. Let there again be two countries, A and B, and a single primary factor of production. As before, a traditional consumer good is manufactured with constant returns to scale. Also, a high-technology product is assembled from differentiated inputs and research generates the blueprints for intermediates. But now suppose the knowledge capital that determines national research productivity accumulates in proportion to local R&D activity. It takes a_I/K_n^j units of labor to invent a new intermediate in country j. Finally, with knowledge capital proportional to cumulative R&D experience, we choose units so that $K_n^j = n^j$.

Suppose first that the countries are of equal size ($L^A = L^B$) and also that $(1 - b_x)/b_x \geq L^j/(L^j + \rho)$, where b_x is the fraction of spending devoted to good X and ρ is the subjective discount rate (equal to the long-run real interest rate). The inequality guarantees that both countries must produce some traditional output in order to satisfy world demand for good Y. If both countries do (always) produce the traditional good in common, then competitive pricing ensures that their wage rates will be equalized all along the equilibrium path.

Now consider the incentive that exists in each country to engage in R&D. With wage rates always the same, the prices of intermediates produced in both countries are the same. So the instantaneous profits earned by a producer of an intermediate good are the same. And the value of a blueprint, which equals the present value of the profit flow, is also the same, assuming that the real interest rate is the same (as it will be if international borrowing and lending takes place). This means that the R&D activity will be more profitable in the country that has the lower cost of innovation. But the cost of an invention in country j equals wa_I/K_n^j, and w and a_I are common to the two countries. It follows that R&D is more profitable in whichever country happens to have the larger knowledge stock; i.e. in the country that has the greater prior experience in R&D.

Suppose it is country A that begins with more research experience. Then initially this country's researchers have a competitive advantage in the research lab, and they perform all of the world's R&D at time 0. But then additional knowledge accumulates in country A, while in the absence of international knowledge spillovers, the knowledge stock remains unchanged in country B. Country A's competitive lead in R&D widens and there is even greater reason for this country to conduct all of the world's research in the next period. In other words, the initial lead is self-reinforcing. Eventually country A will come to dominate production in the high-technology sector [see Grossman and Helpman (1991a, ch. 8) for further details].

This example illustrates several points. First, an accident of history can have long-lasting implications for trade when there is a national component to the knowledge capital stock. In the example, the two countries are identical except for their initial conditions, and yet there is the clear prediction that the initial technological leader must come to dominate the world market in high-technology goods.[26] Second, trade can reduce the rate of innovation and growth in a country that begins with a technological disadvantage. Here, the initially lagging country would continue to innovate (indeed, at the same pace as the leader) if it were isolated from competition with its more advanced trade partner. Yet, as soon as it opens itself to trade, competitive forces drive its resources out of the R&D activity. But third, the rate of innovation (or even the growth rate of national output) can be a misleading gauge of aggregate welfare. In our example, residents of both countries experience the same wage trajectory and have access to the same investment opportunities. With free international trade, they can buy the same goods at the same prices. It follows that a unit of labor enjoys the same lifetime utility regardless of where the worker happens to reside. Not only do residents of both countries enjoy the same welfare levels in this example, but both gain from trade, even though all innovation happens to take place in only one of the countries.

While our example is one where an initial technological disadvantage has no adverse welfare consequences, this need not always be the case. Consider, for instance, what happens when one country starts with greater knowledge and $(1 - b_x)/b_x < L^j/(L^j + \rho)$. Then it may be that both countries conduct R&D for a while, but again the initial leader will widen its knowledge advantage over time and eventually come to dominate the world market for the differentiated inputs [see Grossman and Helpman (1991a, ch. 8)]. Moreover, the demand for the high-technology product is sufficiently great under this parameter restriction that the country producing the preponderance of intermediates comes to enjoy a higher wage than its trade partner. In this case an initial national advantage in research productivity translates into a higher national standard of living. Indeed, the country that begins as the technological laggard might even suffer from trade as compared to its welfare along the autarky equilibrium path.[27]

In both of the cases just described, a country that initially lags behind in the technology race can never catch up. While prior experience generally does

---

[26]Markusen (1991) derives a similar result in a two-period model.

[27]The possibility of losses from trade arises because the autarky equilibrium is distorted (no compensation for the spillovers to the general knowledge stock) and the effect of trade on the initial lagging country is to exacerbate the distortion. The situation is similar to that with national increasing returns to scale, where a country that specializes in the constant-returns sector may lose from trade. [See Ethier (1982b) and Helpman (1984a)].

provide an edge in a world of national knowledge stocks, the prospects for late-comers are not always so bleak. For one thing, a natural comparative advantage in R&D – arising, for example, from an abundance of human capital – can give an inexperienced country a cost advantage that may offset its disadvantage due to a lack of accumulated knowledge. Even if a country does not have any nat-ural comparative advantage in performing R&D, it may be able to overcome an initial lack of research experience if it happens to be a large country. The benefit of size when there are national knowledge stocks is similar to that which arises when there are national increasing returns to scale in production [Help-man, (1984a)] or national knowledge associated with learning by doing. It arises because R&D, as we have conceived of it, is an activity with dynamic increasing returns to scale.

To see this point, consider further the case where there is a single factor of production and identical input coefficients in manufacturing in the two countries. Again assume that one of the countries has an initially larger national knowledge base. For the lagging country to be competitive in R&D, its wage rate would have to be lower than that in the leading country. But with a lower wage, its cost of producing traditional manufactures would also be lower, and so its firms would capture all of the world's market for this competitively-priced good. The satisfaction of world demand for traditional goods would absorb a portion of its labor supply, leaving only a residual supply for inventing and producing intermediate goods. Still, if the country were large enough, that residual might be bigger than the entirety of the labor force of its trade partner. In the event, the initial laggard could conduct more research activity than its smaller rival and thereby overcome its knowledge deficiency.

Our examples show that initial conditions and, indirectly, country size influ-ence the long-run pattern of trade when spillovers from research activity are confined within a nation's borders. What about the effects of trade on techno-logical progress under these conditions? We have seen already that trade may slow a country's rate of innovation, if the country has an initial disadvantage in research productivity and if there is another production sector into which its resources might be driven. Feenstra (1990) shows that country size, too, can intervene in the relationship between trade and technological progress. Suppose there is only one final-goods sector in each country, which uses intermediates invented in the research lab. Now all of a country's labor must be used either in developing new technologies or in producing previously invented goods. In-novative firms can sell to a larger market with trade than without. This alone serves to enhance the profitability of R&D. But global competition means that firms must compete with a larger number of rivals than in autarky. This tends to reduce the incentive for R&D. In the small country, where product development is less rapid than in the larger country, profits erode much faster with trade than without. The net effect of trade is to reduce the incentive to innovate and to slow the long-run rate of technological progress. In contrast, the enlarged-market effect dominates for the larger country. Firms there find a greater incentive to innovate in a world with international trade and trade accelerates technological progress all along the equilibrium path, though not in the very longest of runs.[28]

3.4. Process innovation and quality ladders

So far, we have equated innovation with the development of new varieties of a horizontally differentiated product. Of course, firms also invest in developing new products that are of higher quality than similar goods available on the market, and in lowering the cost of producing existing goods. Many of our conclusions about the relationship between trade and technological progress apply also to these alternative forms of innovation.

We describe a model with building blocks drawn from Aghion and Howitt (1992) and Segerstrom et al. (1990).[29] In this model, a final good X again is assembled from intermediate inputs. This time, however, the number of inputs is taken as fixed. Research investments are intended to improve the quality of the various inputs. Alternatively, these investments can be seen as attempts to reduce their production cost. With either interpretation, a successful innovation reduces the primary resource cost of manufacturing the final good.

To make matters simple, suppose that final production uses a continuum of inputs and that the assembly technology has a symmetric, Cobb–Douglas form. Then we can write

$$\log X = \int_0^1 \log[\hat{z}(j)] \, dj, \tag{3.7}$$

after arbitrarily setting the measure of different inputs to one. Here $\hat{z}(j)$ represents the *effective* quantity of input j, adjusting for the different qualities of the inputs used.[30] An input that has been improved m times from its initial condition provides λ^m times as many input services as the basic version of the product, where $\lambda - 1 > 0$ represents the percentage quality increment associated with each improvement.

For every input j there is a state-of-the-art product at every moment in time. The state of the art is the highest quality version of the input whose technology

---

[28] In the very long run, the large country – with its faster pace of product development – comes to dominate the world economy. Therefore the long-run equilibrium in this country with trade is virtually the same as the long-run equilibrium without trade.

[29] The particular formulation follows Grossman and Helpman (1991b).

[30] We use the "quality ladders" interpretation of innovation in the text. Only the wording would need to be changed to describe process innovation.

is known. This product, and all earlier vintages, can be produced by their inventors with one unit of labor per unit of output. Assuming that the producers of intermediates engage in Bertrand (price) competition, only state-of-the-art products are sold in equilibrium. These are priced at $p_z = \lambda w$, in view of the fact that the competitor with the ability to produce the second highest quality has a marginal production cost of w and a product that is only $1/\lambda$ times as good.

Since only state-of-the-art inputs are used in equilibrium, the effective quantity of input j is $\lambda^{m(j)}z$, where $m(j)$ is the number of times input j has been improved and z is the common physical amount used of every input. The inputs are employed in equal quantities, because they all carry the same price. Then, (3.7) implies $X = \lambda^{\bar{m}}Z$, where $\bar{m} = \int_0^1 m(j)\,\mathrm{d}j$ is the number of times that the average intermediate input has been improved, and Z is the volume of intermediates employed in final production. This production function again has the form $X = A(\cdot)Z$, but the technology indicator this time reflects the average number of successful innovations.

Now assume that R&D is a risky investment. A would-be innovator who devotes ℓ units of labor to research for a time period of length $\mathrm{d}t$ succeeds in developing the next generation of some particular, targeted product with probability $(\ell/a_I)\,\mathrm{d}t$. Let $\bar{\iota}$ denote the average (across intermediates) instantaneous probability of a research success and let $\bar{\ell}$ denote the average employment in R&D. Then $\bar{m}(t) = \int_0^t \bar{\iota}(\tau)\,\mathrm{d}\tau = (1/a_I)\int_0^t \bar{\ell}(\tau)\,\mathrm{d}\tau$. In other words, the productivity of the economy once again depends upon the cumulative investment in R&D. Also, $\mathrm{d}\bar{m}/\mathrm{d}t = \bar{\iota} = \bar{\ell}/a_I$. So, in a steady state with constant employment in manufacturing and R&D, the rate of innovation and the rate of growth of final output are both proportional to total employment in the research activity. We see that the links between R&D investment, technological progress, and aggregate growth are quite similar to those in the model of horizontal product differentiation.

Two equations describe the long-run equilibrium for a closed economy that produces only the single, final good. The first equates the cost of R&D to the expected return. The second ensures full employment of labor, in view of the demands by research labs and manufacturers of state-of-the-art intermediate goods. These two equations have exactly the same form as (3.5) and (3.6), which applied to the model of increasing specialization, except that $1/\lambda$ here takes the place of α there, and ι here takes the place of g there. Evidently the two models share the same reduced form [see Grossman and Helpman (1991b)].

The model of quality ladders (or process innovation) can be elaborated to address trade issues. Assume, for example, that there are two countries, each capable of generating quality innovations and producing state-of-the-art inputs. Suppose, to begin with, that there is only the single, final consumption good. Then all trade is intraindustry trade. At a moment in time, firms from each country hold the technological lead for some subset of the intermediates, because these firms were the last to succeed in improving the particular products. The technological leaders capture the entire world market and so must export their state-of-the-art products to the trading partner. Notice that the pattern of trade fluctuates over time, as an extant home-country leader for one input will be displaced by a successful innovator abroad, while a home innovator will capture the market for a good that was formerly imported. Despite this turbulence at the product level, the aggregates trade flows are stable in the steady state. The equilibrium investment in R&D in each country is just enough to generate balanced trade at equal wages. In the long run, country j holds the technological lead for a constant fraction $L^j/\Sigma_i L^i$ of the intermediate goods.

How does this trade affect the long-run rate of innovation in each country? The answer is that, just as in the model of horizontal product differentiation with international knowledge stocks, each country enjoys a faster rate of technological progress with trade than without.[31] Trade stimulates technological progress, because the instantaneous probability of a research breakthrough is greater when two countries' would-be inventors are attempting to achieve it than when only one set of researchers is doing so. In other words, the research activity again is characterized by a dynamic scale economy and international trade again enlarges the size of the relevant economy. In the model of horizontal product differentiation, international knowledge spillovers were necessary for world trade to generate a scale economy in research. But here such international spillovers are an inherent feature of the environment. They occur naturally whenever one country succeeds in making the mth improvement of some input i, whereupon researchers there *and abroad* cease their efforts to make that discovery and begin to pursue instead the $(m + 1)$st improvement.

If there are instead two final-goods sectors, the determinants of the pattern of interindustry trade also are the same as before. Suppose, for example, that state-of-the-art inputs are produced with unskilled labor and human capital, and that these factors are also used to conduct R&D and to produce a traditional, consumption good Y. Again, let R&D be the most human-capital-intensive activity and production of the traditional good, the least so. Then the country that has a relative abundance of human capital will specialize relatively in R&D. Firms located in this country will win a disproportionate share of the technology races and so come to hold leadership positions in a disproportionate share of the intermediate input markets. The human-capital-rich country becomes a net exporter of the technology-intensive intermediates in the steady state, and a net importer of the technologically-unsophisticated, traditional good. As in the

---

[31] In the trade equilibrium, the average instantaneous probability of a research success in a given industry equals $(1 - 1/\lambda)\Sigma_j L^j/a_I - \rho/\lambda$. This exceeds the average success probability in autarky, which is $(1 - 1/\lambda)L^j/a_I - \rho/\lambda$ in country j.

previous cases with international knowledge spillovers, the initial conditions have no bearing on the long-run trade pattern [see Grossman and Helpman (1991a, ch. 7), and Dinopoulos et al. (1993)].

Taylor (1993) gains further insights by relaxing the assumption that all intermediate inputs are symmetric in terms of their prospects for technological advancement, their unit labor requirements, and their contribution to final production. He shows how comparative advantage in innovation interacts with comparative advantage in production to determine the long-run pattern of trade. Only if the ranking of goods by the two countries' relative labor productivity in manufacturing matches the ranking by their relative labor productivity in innovation does the long-run pattern of trade conform to the simple predictions of the Dornbusch et al. (1977) Ricardian model.

In summary, we have found quite a few analogs between the theory of trade and growth that emerges when technological progress results in investments in R&D and the theory that emerges when such progress is a consequence of learning by doing. In each case, considerations of natural comparative advantage determine the long-run trade pattern if externalities in the learning process spread rapidly around the globe, but size and initial conditions may also be important if the extent of spillovers varies with distance from (or the nationality of) the source. When knowledge spillovers are localized – be they spillovers from learning by doing or spillovers from research discoveries – a small country or one that begins at a technological disadvantage may find that trade slows its technological progress, as competitive forces drive its resources into more traditional, slower-growing activities. Trade may even be harmful for such a country, as it may exacerbate the inefficiencies associated with the existence of externalities and (perhaps) imperfect competition. On the other hand, when the learning process is characterized by dynamic scale economies, the scope for gains from international integration and trade may be many times larger than is suggested by static models of trade. It seems that the answers to many of the questions that motivated the recent research hinge on the nature and extent of technological spillovers, about which the empirical evidence is just beginning to accumulate.

4. Further topics

In this closing section we take up three issues that have not been treated elsewhere in this chapter. First we consider how trade and industrial policies affect long-run rates of innovation and national welfare. Next we examine how imperfect protection of intellectual property rights can generate a product cycle in trade between the North and the South. Lastly, we discuss the relationship between endogenous innovation and the incentives for foreign direct investment and the international licensing of technology.

4.1. Trade and industrial policies

Grossman and Helpman (1991a, ch. 6) study the efficacy of trade policies and R&D subsidies in a small, open, innovating economy. In their model, R&D gives rise to new varieties of *nontraded*, differentiated, intermediate goods.[32] The intermediates are combined with human capital to produce one final good, and with unskilled labor to produce a second, final good. Both final goods are traded at exogenously given world prices. Human capital is needed to perform R&D while human capital and unskilled labor are used in manufacturing the intermediates. In this setting, consider a tariff that protects the import-competing sector in a country that is relatively abundant in unskilled labor. Protection causes the human-capital-intensive manufacturing sector to expand, which bids up the return to human capital. This raises the cost of innovation and thus reduces R&D activity in the new, steady-state equilibrium. In contrast, a subsidy to exports of the labor-intensive final good has just the opposite effects. The wage rate rises, the return to human capital falls, and innovation accelerates, as the R&D sector absorbs some of the human capital released by the contracting, import-competing sector. Evidently, the effects of trade policy on long-run innovation depend on whether the favored sector is a substitute or complement for R&D in the general equilibrium production structure.

Trade policies sometimes can provide second-best welfare benefits in economies with endogenous innovation, although policy prescriptions may be far from obvious. For example, a policy that spurs innovation can nonetheless reduce aggregate welfare in the model we have described, if the policy also causes the output of intermediate goods to fall. Similarly, a policy that retards productivity growth can be beneficial, if it promotes greater output of intermediates. The ambiguity reflects the two market distortions that often will be present in an innovating economy. Not only does the market fail to give appropriate incentives for innovation – insofar as private agents generate externalities in the course of creating knowledge – but also there is underproduction of those goods that are sold at prices in excess of their marginal production costs. Ideally, two policy instruments are needed to target these two market distortions.

Rodriguez (1993) and Rodrik (1993) identify another potential use of policy in a small, open economy similar to the one examined by Grossman and Helpman.

---

[32] Grossman and Helpman also allow for the case where the intermediates are vertically differentiated and innovation involves quality upgrading.

They assume, contrary to Grossman and Helpman, that the two final-goods in-dustries rely on intermediate inputs to different extents. This modification of the model creates the possibility of multiple equilibria. If the manufacturers of the final good that uses intermediates intensively decide to produce a great volume of output, they will have much derived demand for intermediates. This makes entry into the intermediate-goods sector profitable. The resulting economies of specialization raise productivity for the final-goods producers and thus justify their great output. On the other hand, if the producers of the final good that uses intermediates intensively decide to manufacture on a smaller scale, then there is less demand for the inputs and fewer varieties will be developed. In the event, productivity will be lower, and again the producers' decisions will be justified. In such a setting, government policy (including trade policy) often can be used to eliminate the "bad" equilibrium and thereby ensure coordination on the Pareto-superior outcome.[33]

In a world of large trading economies, the policies of one country can affect innovative activity in the others. Grossman and Helpman (1991a, ch. 10) and Ofer (1991) study the international transmission of policy effects. Both examine world economies with two large countries, with Grossman and Helpman assum-ing that innovation serves to improve the qualities of a fixed set of goods and Ofer assuming that it expands the variety of differentiated products. In both cases, there are two final goods, one assembled from intermediate inputs and the other from human capital and unskilled labor, and in both cases R&D is assumed to be the most human-capital-intensive activity, while the production of traditional final goods is assumed to be the least so. In these settings, if one country introduces a small, permanent subsidy to R&D the steady-state rate of productivity growth will fall in its trade partner. In other words, when a country promotes its research sector, it typically does so at least partly at the expense of innovation abroad. In the quality-ladders model, this occurs because trade in fi-nal goods equalizes factor prices, and the R&D subsidy raises the cost of human capital in both countries. The resulting increase in innovation costs means a de-cline in the incentive for research in the country where private agents bear the full, unsubsidized cost of R&D. In the model with horizontal product differen-tiation, the transmission mechanism is somewhat different. There, the increase in innovation in the subsidizing country raises the real effective cost of capital to firms contemplating research abroad. Both Grossman and Helpman (1991a, ch. 10) and Ofer (1991) find that the negative effect on innovation in the trade partner country is never so large as to more than offset the positive effect in the subsidizing country. In each of these cases, a subsidy to R&D in one country

---

[33]Murphy et al. (1989), Krugman (1991), and Cicconi and Matsuyama (1993) also study multiple equilibria that can arise when there are increasing returns to scale and imperfect competition. Of these, only Krugman examines an open economy, and he does not explicitly mention the potential use of policy in selecting among equilibria.

leads to an acceleration of aggregate innovation in the world economy. But in Grossman and Helpman (1990a), where countries are assumed to differ in their productivity in the research lab, a different result is possible. A subsidy to R&D in the country that has a comparative disadvantage in this activity actually can lead to a decline in the overall rate of productivity growth in the world economy.

Grossman and Helpman (1991a, ch. 10) also consider the effects of production subsidies and trade policies. A country that subsidizes production of knowledge-intensive intermediates with the aim of boosting profitability and thereby spurring innovation may be surprised to find that the subsidy actually reduces national and global innovation rates. The direct effect of a subsidy to firms producing intermediates is to raise their demand for primary factors. Not all of these increased demands can be met with resources released from the traditional manufacturing sector, because traditional manufacturing uses relatively little human capital compared to what is needed to produce intermediates. This means that some of the expanded employment of human capital in the intermediate-goods sector must come at the expense of R&D activity. The reallocation of resources is effected by a rise in the return to human capital, which causes the R&D labs to release the resources demanded by the subsidized producers.

Trade policies generate more complicated responses. Of course an import tariff or an export subsidy combines a production subsidy with a consumption tax. Consider the effects of uniform protection of the high-technology manufacturing sector; that is, an equal rate tariff on all intermediates purchased from abroad combined with an equal rate subsidy on all foreign sales of domestically-produced intermediates. The production subsidy alone would impede innovation, as we have just noted, but the consumption tax has the opposite effect. It reduces demand for intermediates in the policy-active country and so tends to free resources for use in other activities. Taken together, the effect of the production subsidy and consumption tax on R&D investment depends on the net trade position of the policy-active country. If the country that protects its intermediate producers is one that exports these high-tech products on net, then the subsidy component of the trade policy is more important, and R&D activity declines. On the other hand, if the country is a net importer of intermediates, the tax component dominates, and R&D activity expands. Since the long-run net trade position in high-technology products tends to go hand in hand with comparative advantage in R&D, protection of the high-technology sector is likely to spur global innovation if and only if the protection is enacted by the country with comparative *disadvantage* in research.[34]

---

[34]The result must be qualified slightly, inasmuch as a country with comparative disadvantage in R&D may nonetheless become a net exporter of high-technology products in the steady state. This could happen if the country borrowed heavily along the path to the steady state, in which case it

In leaving this section, we emphasize that our discussion has focused on the response of innovation rates, not aggregate welfare. A complete normative analysis would need to account for the terms-of-trade effects of policy in goods and asset markets, and for the transitional effects of policy in addition to those that persist in the steady state. No such complete analysis has yet been performed for a large, open, innovating, economy.

4.2. Intellectual property rights and North–South trade

We have noted that some protection of intellectual property rights is a sine qua non for private investment in new technologies. Yet even where patents and copyrights are strictly enforced, such protection is rarely perfect. There are tremendous incentives for followers to imitate the technological leaders and little prospect that the legal authorities will be able to prevent all forms of reverse engineering and "inventing around the patent".

Imitation plays an especially important role in some trade between the North and the South. This is true for several reasons. First, firms in the South have shown only limited ability to develop innovative products of their own. Second, several of the governments of less developed nations have been somewhat lax in their enforcement of foreign intellectual property rights. Finally, the low wage rates of the South make it an especially attractive place for copying some kinds of products, because successful imitators can expect to earn substantial profits in their competition against innovators who bear higher labor costs.

The pattern of product innovation in the North and imitation in the South gives rise to a product cycle in international trade. We described such trade in Section 1.3, where we reviewed Krugman's (1979) model of exogenous product innovation and technology transfer. Grossman and Helpman (1991a, ch. 11) have extended Krugman's model to incorporate endogenous innovation and imitation based on profitability considerations. They have used the extended model to study how North–South trade affects the long-run rate of technological progress.[35]

Recall that Krugman posited a common CES utility function, $u = [\int_0^\infty c(j)^\alpha \, dj]^{1/\alpha}$, for Northern and Southern households. He assumed that a unit of any good could be produced anywhere with one unit of labor once its technology becomes known. We maintain these assumptions here, but also assume that Northern researchers can increase the stock of known products by dn by devoting a_I/K_N units of labor to product development for a time dt.

---

would need to run trade surplus in order to service its debt. In the event, the country might run positive trade surpluses in both sectors in the long run.

[35] See also Segerstrom et al. (1990) and Grossman and Helpman (1991a, ch. 12), who study models of endogenous quality improvement with imitation in the South.

Here K_N is the stock of knowledge in the North, assumed to be equal to the cumulative number of Northern research projects, n, by appeal once more to the existence of learning externalities. In the South, a firm can copy dn_S products previously developed by the North by devoting a_M/K_S units of labor to reverse engineering for a time dt. The Southern knowledge stock K_S might depend on the cumulative Southern experience at imitation or on that experience plus the Northern experience at innovation, depending on whether or not there are international spillovers of knowledge. For simplicity, we suppose here that there are no such spillovers, and specify $K_S = n_S$, where n_S is the number of imitation projects previously completed in the South. Finally, we suppose that a Northern innovator and Southern imitator who share the ability to produce the same differentiated product engage in price competition. This means that only the low-cost producer can make positive sales and positive profits in any duopoly equilibrium.

In the North, firms with the unique ability to produce a good that has not yet been copied practice mark-up pricing. They charge the monopoly price $p_N = w_N/\alpha$, where w_N is the Northern wage and also the unit production cost there. In the South, successful imitators charge either the unconstrained monopoly price, $p_S = w_S/\alpha$, or the limit price, $p_S = w_N$, whichever is less. Here we will suppose that the monopoly price prevails. Then, if x_i denotes the sales of a firm producing in region i, the flow of profits for a typical firm there is $\pi_i = (1 - \alpha)w_i x_i/\alpha$. Labor market equilibrium requires $x_N = (L_N - a_I g)/n_N$ and $x_S = (L_S - a_M g_S)/n_S$, where L_i is the labor supply in region i, n_i is the number of products manufactured there, $g = \dot{n}/n$ is the rate of product innovation and $g_S = \dot{n}_S/n_S$ is the rate of increase in the technological capacity of the South.

The profit flow for a Southern imitator lasts forever. In a steady state in which each country produces a constant fraction of the total number of products, we must have $g_S = g$. Then the requirement that the return on investment equals the effective cost of capital in the South implies

$$\frac{1 - \alpha}{\alpha}\left(\frac{L_S}{a_M} - g\right) = \rho + g \tag{4.1}$$

where ρ once again is the subjective discount rate. This equation, describing labor and financial market equilibrium in the South, appears as the horizontal line SS in Figure 4.1. A Northern firm, on the other hand, faces not only the prospect of a falling patent value due to ongoing innovation, but also the constant risk that a Southern entrepreneur will target its product for imitation and so end its monopoly profit stream. The latter risk raises the effective cost of capital to a Northern firm, so that equality of the rate of return and the effective capital cost implies

$$\frac{1 - \alpha}{\alpha}\left(\frac{L_N}{a_I} - g\right)\frac{n}{n_N} = \rho + g + m \tag{4.2}$$

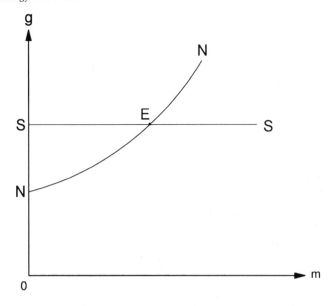

Figure 4.1.

where $m = \dot{n}_S/n_N$ is the rate of product imitation (fraction of Northern products copied per unit time) and also the instantaneous risk of loss of monopoly power for a Northern producer (assuming, as we do, that Southern imitators choose their targets with equal likelihood).

In the long run, the fraction of goods produced in the North approaches the constant $g/(g + m)$. Using this fact and (4.2), we can plot the equation representing Northern labor and financial market clearing as the upward sloping NN curve in Figure 4.1. The intersection of NN and SS at E gives the steady-states rates of innovation and imitation.

From the figure it is immediate that product-cycle trade boosts the long-run rate of product innovation in the North. The autarky innovation rate corresponds to the point where the NN curve hits the vertical axis, because $m = 0$ in the absence of Southern imitation. Since the NN curve is upward sloping, E must lie above and to the right of this autarky point. Intuitively, Southern imitation has two distinct effects on the incentive to innovate in the North. First, with imitation, each innovator faces an eventual end to monopoly profits. This most obvious implication of the imperfect protection of intellectual property rights serves to reduce the incentive to innovate by raising the effective cost of capital on the right-hand side of (4.2). But second, with imitation, some of the products originally invented in the North are later manufactured by the

South. This frees up Northern labor to produce more of the remaining products (and also to conduct more R&D). As a result, each Northern firm earns greater monopoly profits during its stay in the market, even though that stay is more limited. It turns out that the second effect dominates in the model of horizontal product differentiation with CES utility, and so imperfect protection of intellectual property rights by the South actually serves to encourage technological progress.[36]

The figure can also be used to gauge the effects of region size on steady-state rates of imitation and innovation. An increase in the size of the North causes the NN curve to shift upward, reducing the rate of imitation, but leaving the rate of innovation unchanged.[37] An increase in the size of the South shifts the SS curve upward, increasing both the long-run rate of innovation and the long-run rate of imitation. It can be shown, moreover, that the relative wage of the North rises when L_N increases, while the relative wage of the South rises when L_S increases. These results are the opposite of those derived by Krugman, who took the rates of innovation and technology transfer to be exogenous and implicitly assumed that product development and reverse engineering require no resources.

Several authors have studied whether the South benefits in welfare terms from protecting foreign intellectual property rights, and whether a failure to protect these rights would damage the North. Chin and Grossman (1990) developed a partial-equilibrium, duopoly model in which a Northern firm engages in cost-reducing R&D while recognizing that its Southern competitor might or might not be able to copy its improvements, depending on the property rights regime. In this setting, the North always suffers from a failure of the South to protect intellectual property rights, while the South typically gains from allowing copying.[38] Deardorff (1992) established similar results for product innovation. In his partial-equilibrium setting, there are many potential new products that offer differing amounts of surplus and bear differing R&D costs. Although more new products are introduced when property rights are protected, the South's gain from this typically is dwarfed by its loss of consumer surplus due to monopoly pricing. Interestingly, Deardorff shows that as patent protection is extended to

---

[36]This result is not general, however. In a model of Northern quality improvements with Southern imitation of the current state-of-the-art, North–South trade can reduce the long-run rate of technological progress. [See Grossman and Helpman (1991a, ch. 12)].

[37]This result relies on the assumption that there are no knowledge spillovers from North to South and that the equilibrium wage gap is such that Southern firms charge monopoly prices rather than limit prices. If either of these assumptions is reversed, an increase in L_N boosts the long-run rate of innovation, g.

[38]In this partial equilibrium setting, a lack of enforcement of intellectual property rights always reduces the incentives to innovate in the North. The South could be harmed by the reduction in technological progress, but only if its share in world consumption of the product is very large.

a larger and larger portion of the world, the effect on aggregate world welfare of extending protection further eventually becomes negative.

A case where the South might wish to protect Northern intellectual property rights has been described by Diwan and Rodrik (1991). In their model, the North and South have different preferences over the direction that technological progress should take (e.g. the types of goods that should be invented). Then, patent protection in the South can induce Northern innovators to invent products more to the Southern consumers' liking, whereas a lack of such protection would lead to very undesirable products from the South's point of view.

The analysis in Helpman (1993) is closest in spirit to what we have described here. He considers a general equilibrium in which new goods are invented and manufactured with labor in the North and old goods are manufactured with labor in the South. All consumers have CES preferences, so that Northern producers of goods whose technologies have not yet been mastered in the South practice mark-up pricing. Technology transfer to the South takes place at an exogenous rate $m = \dot{n}_S/n_N$ and requires no Southern resources. Helpman treats the rate of imitation as a policy parameter reflecting the strictness of the South's property rights regime, and he supposes that all Southern firms are able to produce any good whose technology diffuses there, so that old goods are sold competitively. In this setting, a tightening of the intellectual property rights regime as reflected in a fall in m spurs Northern innovation upon impact, but slows the rate of innovation in the long run. If the world economy is in a steady state before m falls, the equilibrium shift in the time profile of new product development harms the South, as does the reallocation of production from the low cost to the high cost producer and the adverse movement in the South's terms of trade. In short, the South must lose from an exogenous fall in m. As for the North, the change in the time profile of product availability and the reallocation of production from North to South contribute to a welfare loss, but there are offsetting effects due to an adjustment of the savings rate and a favorable movement in the terms of trade. Still, the North must lose from a decline in m if the rate of imitation is initially low.

4.3. Direct foreign investment and international licensing

We have recognized that some types of knowledge may flow across international borders as an inevitable consequence of the public-good nature of information. We have also noted that some knowledge may flow from one country to another due to the intentional actions of would-be imitators. But we have not examined the incentives that innovators themselves have to transfer knowledge and technologies abroad.

Technology transfer by innovating firms can take one of two forms. An innovator can establish a wholly or partly-owned offshore subsidiary, and thereby maintain full control over the use of its proprietary technology. Or it can license the technology in an arms-length transaction with a foreign firm, and rely on the enforcement of contractual terms to limit the diffusion of its intellectual property. Much has been written about the incentives firms have to engage in one or both of these types of activities. It is beyond the scope of this chapter to review this literature thoroughly; instead we briefly comment on a few themes and then point to some issues that the literature has hardly addressed.

There are two obvious reasons why a firm might wish to take its technology abroad. First, production costs might be lower there. Second, the firm might be able to avoid some of the costs of serving the foreign market, such as transportation charges and tariff levies. Markusen (1984) and Helpman (1984b) have developed models of direct foreign investment based on the first of these considerations, while Horstmann and Markusen (1992) and Brainard (1993) provide modern treatments of the second.[39] As Horstmann and Markusen show quite clearly, multinational firms are most likely to emerge when the fixed costs of adding a plant or maintaining a subsidiary are small, compared with the size of transport costs, trade barriers, and the fixed costs of operating a firm. It should be noted that technology plays an important role in these models of the multinational corporation in at least two respects. First, a theory of multinational investment must explain not only why a firm would wish to locate some of its activities offshore, but also why the firm would be able to compete with locally owned establishments in performing these activities despite the disadvantages that derive from unfamiliarity with local customs, language, business practices, etc. Proprietary access to a unique technology provides just such an explanation. Second, research and development is exactly the sort of firm-level fixed cost that generates economies of multi-plant production.

Licensing provides an alternative means to the same ends. By licensing its technology to a local firm, an innovator can reap the benefits of lower production costs, or gain access to a protected market, without suffering the penalties of operating in an unfamiliar business environment.[40] But licensing has its own costs and risks. First, since it is impossible to write a complete contract specifying every possible contingency that may arise, a patent holder may find itself unable to respond as flexibly to unforeseen events when it is locked into a contractual

---

[39]The recent literature on the role of multinational corporations in international trade is reviewed by Krugman in Chapter 24 of this Handbook.

[40]Feenstra and Judd (1982) have formulated a static model of monopolistic competition and trade in which the fixed cost of entry is interpreted to be an R&D charge and firms can sell their technologies developed in one country to producers in the other in order to take advantage of lower production costs there. This model is analogous, in many ways, to Helpman's (1984b) model of direct foreign investment.

licensing arrangement as when it is operating its own manufacturing facility [see Ethier (1986)]. Second, an innovative firm may be unable to prevent all forms of opportunistic behavior by a licensee after its technology has been transferred; the licensee might, for example, use the technology in markets other than the one specified in the agreement or it might use the knowledge it gains from the agreement as a springboard for developing a different or better technology of its own. Finally, the innovative firm may be unable to credibly commit to forego opportunities of its own. If a potential licensee expects that the licensor will eventually enter the market itself either by opening a local subsidiary or with exports, its willingness to pay for the license will be diminished relative to the case where it expects to enjoy a monopoly. Part of the incidence of any anticipated dissipation of profits will fall on the innovator that is looking to rent out its technology [see Grossman and Helpman (1991a, ch. 7)].

An additional risk associated with both direct foreign investment and licensing is that they might speed up the process of imitation and diffusion. It may be that learning spillovers are more prevalent when production takes place locally than when goods are imported from a foreign manufacturing base. Then the innovating firm must weigh the profit gains associated with having lower production costs against the potential losses from losing its monopoly position more rapidly. Ethier and Markusen (1991) study this aspect of a firm's decision problem.

Many papers in the literature on direct foreign investment and licensing focus on a firm's choice of how best to exploit its technological advantage once that advantage has already been developed. In contrast, there have been very few papers that have addressed the important question of how opportunities for direct investment and licensing affect the pace and pattern of technological progress. For this, the static models – which have served well for investigating firms' optimal decisions at a point in time – will not suffice.

Grossman and Helpman (1991a, ch. 7) have introduced direct foreign investment and international licensing into a dynamic model; namely, the two-country model of endogenous innovation with international knowledge spillovers that was described in Section 3.1. They have shown that (costless) foreign investment or (costless) international licensing of technologies can enlarge the set of divisions of the world factor endowment that give rise to factor price equalization. In their analysis, some firms that develop new technologies in the human-capital-rich country may find it profitable to manufacture their newly-invented products (either themselves, or by entering a licensing agreement) in the unskilled-labor-rich country. Then the long-run pattern of trade may involve the human-capital-rich country as a net importer of high-technology products, as subsidiaries of innovating firms export their finished products back home. This, of course, is similar to the predictions about the trade pattern in static models of multinational corporations; [see, for example, Helpman and Krugman (1985, chs. 12, 13)].

The incentives for exploiting technological advantage through foreign production are especially great in the context of North–South trade. In fact, Vernon's (1966) seminal discussion of product-cycle trade envisioned not the production of old goods by indigenous Southern producers, but rather the eventual shifting of production by innovative Northern firms to their subsidiaries in the South. Lai (1992) attempts to capture the original Vernon notion in a variant of Grossman and Helpman's (1991a, ch. 11) model of the product cycle. He allows innovators to transfer their production activities to the South costlessly once the technology becomes "standardized". This happens randomly and exogenously, he assumes, some time after the new technology has been introduced. In a similar vein, Liu (1992) introduces the possibility of technology licensing into the same Grossman and Helpman model. Licensing too is treated as costless, except that the technology must be adopted for use in the South before production can begin there. Adoption involves a fixed cost per product that varies with the stock of knowledge in the South.

These treatments of foreign subsidiaries and licensing pacts (including our own!) are too simple, however. They neglect the above mentioned risks associated with these types of activities, such as the risk of faster loss of monopoly power, the risk of opportunistic behavior on the part of licensees, and the risk that contingencies will arise that are not foreshadowed in the licensing agreement. The dynamic models must be extended to incorporate these and other realistic aspects of the different modes of technology transfer (some of which have been dealt with in the static literature), before a convincing answer can be given to the question of how such transfers affect the incentives for innovation.

Another topic deserving further attention is how policies affect the transfer of technology. Should governments in the North take actions to impede the transfer of technology as is often suggested in the public policy debates, or would this have adverse consequences for the rate at which new technologies are developed? And what can the South do to encourage technology transfer to indigenous agents without causing the Northern innovators to take their business elsewhere? To answer these questions we will need models that pay closer attention to how knowledge is transmitted within and between firms.

References

Aghion P. and P. Howitt (1992), "A model of growth through creative destruction", Econometrica, 60:323–351.

Arrow, K.J. (1962), "Economic welfare and the allocation of resources for inventions", in: R.R. Nelson, ed., The rate and direction of inventive activity (Princeton University Press, Princeton) 609–626.

Bardhan, P.K. (1970), Economic growth, development, and foreign trade (Wiley, New York).

Becker, G. (1952), "A note on multi-country trade", American Economic Review, 42:558–568.

Bernstein, J.I. and P. Mohnen (1994), "International r&d spillovers between U.S. and Japanese r&d intensive sectors", National Bureau of Economic Research Working Paper No. 4682.

Bhagwati, J.N. (1958a), "International trade and economic expansion", American Economic Review, 48:941–953.

Bhagwati, J.N. (1958b), "Immiserizing growth: A geometrical note", Review of Economic Studies, 25:201–205.

Bloomfield, A.I. (1978), "The impact of growth and technology on trade in nineteenth-century British thought", History of Political Economy, 10:608–635.

Boldrin, M. and J.A. Sheinkman (1988), "Learning by doing, international trade and growth: A note", in: SFI Studies in the Sciences of Complexity (Addison–Wesley, Reading MA).

Brainard, S.L. (1993), "A simple theory of multinational corporations and trade with a trade-off between proximity and concentration", National Bureau of Economic Research Working Paper No. 4269.

Bresiz, E.S., P.R. Krugman, and D. Tsiddon (1993), "Leapfrogging in international competition: A theory of cycles in national technological leadership", American Economic Review, 83:1211–1219.

Chin, J. and G.M. Grossman (1990), "International property rights and north–south trade", in: R.W. Jones and A.O. Krueger, eds., The political economy of international trade (Basil Blackwell, Cambridge, MA) 90–107.

Cicconi, A. and K. Matsuyama (1993), "Start-up costs and pecuniary externalities as barriers to economic development", Institute for Empirical Macroeconomics Discussion Paper No. 83, Federal Reserve Bank of Minneapolis.

Coe, D.T. and E. Helpman (1994), "International r&d spillovers", National Bureau of Economic Research Working Paper No. 4444; forthcoming in: European Economic Review.

Davis, D.R. (1994), "Intra-industry trade: A Heckscher–Ohlin–Ricardo approach", mimeo, Harvard University.

Deardorff, A.V. (1992), "Welfare effects of global patent protection", Economica, 59:35–51.

Dinopoulos, E., J.F. Oehmke, and P.S. Segerstrom (1993), "High-technology-industry trade and investment: The role of factor endowments", Journal of International Economics, 34:49–71.

Diwan, I. and D. Rodrik (1991), "Patents, appropriate technology, and north–south trade", Journal of International Economics, 30:27–47.

Dixit, A.K. and J.E. Stiglitz (1993), "Monopolistic competition and optimum product diversity: Reply", American Economic Review, 83:302–304.

Dornbush, R., S. Fischer, and P.A. Samuelson (1977), Comparative advantage, trade and payments in a Ricardian model with a continuum of goods", American Economic Review, 67:823–839.

Eaton, J. and S. Kortum (1994), "International patenting and technology diffusion", mimeo, Boston University.

Ethier, W.J. (1982a), National and international returns to scale in the modern theory of international trade", American Economic Review, 72:389–405.

Ethier, W.J. (1982b), "Decreasing cost in international trade and Frank Graham's argument for protection", Econometrica, 50:1243–1268.

Ethier, W.J. (1986), "The multinational firm", Quarterly Journal of Economics, 80:805–833.

Ethier, W.J. and J.R. Markusen (1991), "Multinational firms, technology diffusion and trade", National Bureau of Economic Research Working Paper No. 3825.

Feenstra, R. (1990), "Trade and uneven growth", National Bureau of Economic Research Working Paper No. 3276.

Feenstra, R. and K. Judd (1982), "Tariffs, technology transfer and welfare", Journal of Political Economy, 90:1142–1165.

Findlay, R. (1984), "Growth and development in trade models", in: R.W. Jones and P.B. Kenen, eds., Handbook of international economics, vol. 1 (North-Holland, Amsterdam) 185–236.

Findlay, R. and H. Grubert (1959), "Factor intensities, technological progress and the terms of trade", Oxford Economic Papers, 11:111–121.

Grossman, G.M. and E. Helpman (1990a), "Comparative advantage and long-run growth", American Economic Review, 80:796–815.

Grossman, G.M., and E. Helpman (1990b), "Trade, innovation and growth", American Economic Review, 80 (Papers and Proceedings): 86–91.

Grossman, G.M. and E. Helpman (1991a), Innovation and growth in the global economy (MIT Press, Cambridge, MA).

Grossman, G.M. and E. Helpman (1991b), "Quality ladders in the theory of growth", Review of Economic Studies, 58:43–61.

Grossman, G.M. and E. Helpman (1991c), "Trade, knowledge spillovers and growth", European Economic Review, 35:517–526.

Helpman, E. (1984a), "Increasing returns, imperfect markets, and trade theory", in: R.W. Jones and P.B. Kenen, eds., Handbook of international economics, vol. 1 (North-Holland, Amsterdam) 325–365.

Helpman, E. (1984b), "A simple theory of international trade with multinational corporations", Journal of Political Economy, 92:451–472.

Helpman, E. (1993), "Innovation, imitation and intellectual property rights", Econometrica, 61:1247–1280.

Helpman, E. and P.R. Krugman (1985), Market structure and foreign trade (MIT Press, Cambridge, MA).

Hicks, J.R. (1953), "An inaugural lecture", Oxford Economic Papers, 5:117–135.

Horstmann, I.J. and J.R. Markusen (1992), "Endogenous market structures in international trade", Journal of International Economics, 32:109–129.

Irwin, D.A. and P.J. Klenow (1994), "Learning by doing spillovers in the semiconductor industry", Journal of Political Economy, 102: 1200–1227.

Jaffe, A., M. Trajtenberg and R. Henderson (1993), "Geographic localization of knowledge spillovers as evidenced by patent citations", Quarterly Journal of Economics, 108:577–598.

Jones, R.W. (1961), "Comparative advantage and the theory of tariffs: A multi-country, multi-commodity model", Review of Economic Studies, 28:161–175.

Jones, R.W. (1965), "The structure of simple general equilibrium models", Journal of Political Economy, 73:557–572.

Jones, R.W. (1970), "The role of technology in the theory of international trade", in: R. Vernon, ed., The technology factor in international trade (National Bureau of Economic Research, New York) 73–92.

Judd, K.L. (1985), "On the performance of patents", Econometrica, 53:567–586.

Krugman, P.R. (1979), "A model of innovation, technology transfer, and the world distribution of income", Journal of Political Economy, 87:253–266.

Krugman, P.R. (1986), "A 'technology gap' model of international trade", in: K. Jungenfelt and D. Hague, eds., Structural adjustment in developed open economics (Macmillan Press, London) 35–49.

Krugman, P.R. (1987), "The narrow moving band, the Dutch disease, and the competitive consequences of Mrs. Thatcher: Notes on trade in the presence of dynamic scale economics", Journal of Development Economics, 27:41–55.

Krugman, P.R. (1991), "History vs. expectations", Quarterly Journal of Economics, 106:651–667.

Lai, E. (1992), "International intellectual property rights protection and the rate of product innovation", mimeo, Vanderbilt University.

Lichtenberg, F. (1992), "R&D investments and international productivity differences", in: H. Siebert, ed., Economic growth in the world economy: Symposium 1992 (Tubingen, J.C.B. Mohr).

Liu, X. (1992), "Technology trade, endogenous growth and welfare", mimeo, University of Pittsburgh.

Lucas, R.E. Jr. (1988), "On the mechanics of economic development", Journal of Monetary Economics, 22:3–42.

Markusen, J.R. (1984), "Multinationals, multi-plant economies, and the gains from trade", Journal of International Economics, 14:205–226.

Markusen, J.R. (1991), "First mover advantages, blockaded entry, and the economics of uneven development", in: E. Helpman and A. Razin, eds., International trade and trade policy (MIT Press, Cambridge, MA) 245–269.

Markusen, J.R. and L.E.O. Svensson (1985), "Trade in goods and factors with international differences in technology", International Economic Review, 26:175–192.

Matsuyama, K. (1992), "Agricultural productivity, comparative advantage and economic growth", Journal of Economic Theory, 58:317–334.

Murphy, K.M., A. Shleifer, and R.W. Vishny, (1989), "Industrialization and the big push", Journal of Political Economy, 97:1003–1026.

Ofer, G. (1991), "International effects of trade policy", MA dissertation, Tel-Aviv University (Hebrew).

Posner, M.V. (1961), "International trade and technological progress", Oxford Economic Papers, 13:323–341.

Ricardo, D. (1951–1955), in: P. Sraffa, ed., The works and correspondence of David Ricardo (Cambridge).

Rivera-Batiz, L.A. and P.M. Romer (1991), International trade with endogenous technological change", European Economic Review, 35:715–721.

Rodriguez, A. (1993), "The division of labor and economic development", mimeo, Stanford University.

Rodrik, D. (1993), "Do low-income countries have a high-wage option?", National Bureau of Economic Research Working Paper No. 4451.

Segerstorm, P.S., T.C.A. Anant, and E. Dinopoulos (1990), "A Schumpeterian model of product life cycle", American Economic Review, 80:1077–1091.

Stokey, N. (1991), "Human capital, product quality, and growth", Quarterly Journal of Economics, 425:587–616.

Taylor, M.S. (1993), "Quality ladders and Ricardian trade", Journal of International Economics, 34:225–243.

Vernon, R. (1966), "International investment and international trade in the product cycle", Quarterly Journal of Economics, 80:190–207.

Wilson, C.A. (1980), "On the general structure of Ricardian models with a continuum of goods: Application to growth, tariff theory, and technical change", Econometrica, 48:1675–1702.

Yanagawa, N. (1993), "Economic development in a world with many countries", mimeo, Keio University.

Young, A. (1991), "Learning by doing and the dynamic effects of international trade", Quarterly Journal of Economics, 105:369–405.

Chapter 26

INTERNATIONAL TRADE THEORY: THE EVIDENCE

EDWARD E. LEAMER

UCLA and National Bureau of Economic Research

and

JAMES LEVINSOHN*

University of Michigan and National Bureau of Economic Research

Contents

*We would like to thank Robert Feenstra, Bob Staiger, and Dan Trefler for suggestions. Special thanks to Alan Deardorff and Gene Grossman for their very detailed comments and suggestions.

Handbook of International Economics, vol. III, Edited by G. Grossman and K. Rogoff
© *Elsevier Science B.V., 1995*

1. Introduction

International microeconomics is primarily a theoretical enterprise that seems little affected by empirical results. "How can this be?", we ask ourselves. After all, trade flows have been measured with greater accuracy over longer periods of time than most other economic phenomena. One might have guessed that these rich trade data bases would have yielded findings that materially affected the way that international economists think. But with a few notable exceptions, they have not. Some might argue that we don't really have very much useful data. Rather, we have reams of noisy data drawn from extremely complex non-experimental settings that are very imperfectly understood so we shouldn't be expecting very much from these data.

We can hardly review the empirical work in international economics with such a defeatist premise, and we prefer to think that the fault lies elsewhere. First of all, the data have not really been very accessible. Fortunately, technological change is making the dissemination of large data bases much less costly. To assist in that dissemination, we have listed in the Appendix some of the most important data sources.

Our review is premised, however, on the idea that we have not done the job right. If we examined the data correctly, and reported the findings persuasively, then data would have a much more substantial impact. Thus in the midst of the summaries of methods and findings, we will insert many comments and ideas about why the results have ended up to be fairly unimportant. There are two main messages we hope to convey.

The first message is: "Don't take trade theory too seriously". In practice, this means "Estimate, don't test". Estimate the speed of arbitrage, don't test if arbitrage is perfect and instantaneous. Understand that theorems are neither true nor false. They are sometimes useful and sometimes misleading. If we approach a data base with the contrary attitude, hoping to determine the verity or falsity of a theorem, we may statistically "reject" the theory, but leave it completely unharmed nonetheless. After all, we already knew it wasn't literally true.

"Estimate, don't test" is important advice, but it can be taken too far when empirical analysis is done without benefit of a clear theoretical framework. Our second piece of advice points in the opposite direction: "Don't treat the theory too casually". In practice this means: "Work hard to make a clear and close link between the theory and the data". We are convinced from several notable failures that it is important to have clear linkages between the theory and the data if empirical results are to have any hope of having a lasting impact. High partial correlations by themselves are not enough. We need a good story.

Our failures in linking theory with data, either too closely or too loosely, come in part from our excessive specialization. Some economists imagine the data (theorists), some imagine how to analyze imagined data (econometric theorists), some collect the data (usually government statisticians), and others analyze the data (applied econometricians). It seems healthier to us if we collectively make more of an effort to bridge the gaps between these distinct functions. Better communication between theorists and data analysts would be helpful. For example, we think it would be extremely valuable if international trade theorists attempted to connect aspects of their theories to observable phenomenon by indicating what data would shake their faith in the usefulness of the theory that they present.

Of course, not all useful theory is linkable to observable phenomena. Proofs of the static gains of trade fall into the unrefutable category yet these are some of the most important results in all of economics. But this extraordinary success of theory without data should not be taken as a license for the creation of an unlimited array of theories that are completely without any possible connection to observables. On a case by case basis, we need to ask what function the theory is serving, beyond mathematical amusement.

For instance, when the Law of Comparative Advantage is expressed in terms of a comparison of price vectors in autarky and trade, and when autarky prices are completely unobservable, we must ask what this theory is all about. When a theory is completely dependent on the number of goods and the number of factors being equal, we need to be told how to count factors and goods. When it is demonstrated that a production frontier has flats of dimension equal to the number of goods minus the number of factors, we need to know what observable phenomenon would make us think the real world closely approximates this abstract model.

While it would be helpful for theorists to think about data, it would also be helpful for data analysts to develop more of a "feel" for theory. Many data analysts do not understand that theories are designed to serve a single limited purpose. The proper function of empirical work is not to test the validity of the theory but to determine if the theory is working adequately in its limited domain. International trade in lumber might be well characterized by a factor endowments-based model, while an endogenous growth model might better explain trade patterns in computer memory chips, and a model of monopolistic competition might best characterize international trade in varieties of furniture.

Data analysts need to understand also that distinct theories that are intended for use in different limited domains cannot properly be mixed together in a multiple regression in the absence of a generalizing theory that covers multiple domains. Frequently in the literature we review, empirical work takes a grab-bag approach with variables intended to capture features of different theories thrown together in a multiple regression. But the theories may have no content outside their own domains, and may bear no meaningful relationship with the conditional correlations that come rolling out of multiple regression packages. Many of the empirical studies on international trade and monopolistic competition reviewed in Section 4 are examples of this grab-bag approach.

With these guiding principles in mind, we turn to reviewing the recent empirical literature on "testing" trade theories and "estimating" the relative importance of different sources of comparative advantage. In our review, we have placed heavier emphasis on newer work and refer the reader to Deardorff (1984) for a review of older work. We have also tried to go beyond just reviewing the literature and, on several occasions, suggest possibly fruitful but as yet unexplored research topics and strategies. This review is organized around the sources of comparative advantage ordered by intellectual chronology: technological differences in Section 2, factor proportions in Section 3, competitive strategies in Section 4, demand biases in Section 5 and distance in Section 6. The Appendix provides a brief discussion of some of the data sources often used in the empirical international trade literature as well as possibly useful but less well exploited data sources.

2. Empirical studies of the Ricardian and Ricardo–Viner models

The Ricardian and the Ricardo–Viner models point to technological differences as the source of international comparative advantage. A simple Ricardian model has one input, labor, which is assumed to be mobile across the two sectors of the economy, but internationally immobile. The Ricardo–Viner model introduces into the model two additional factors which are sector-specific. This gives curvature to the production possibilities curve and also allows international commerce to affect the distribution of income. Although there is little or no direct empirical support for these simple models, there is nonetheless growing awareness that technological differences are a natural consequence of economic isolation and play a role in the integration process following an economic liberalization.

2.1. The Ricardian model

In 1817, David Ricardo developed the now familiar model with two countries, two goods, and a single input, labor. Ricardo demonstrated the remarkable result that both countries can gain from trade if their (constant) labor input ratios differed, even if one country had an absolute advantage in both goods.

The intellectual power of the model lies in its simplicity, but this same simplicity causes great difficulties when one tries to translate the theory into predictions that might be worth exploring in real data sets. The real skill in doing empirical work is the wise separation of those aspects of a theory that have empirical content from those that do not. Below we discuss three Ricardian propositions that might or might not fall into the "empirically relevant" category.

Except when labor input requirements are identical across countries, there exist gains from trade. This proposition has been the focus of much theoretical analysis. Using revealed preference arguments, theorists such as Ohyama (1972) and Dixit and Norman (1986) have shown that this proposition is quite general, and the proposition is not restricted to just the Ricardian model. Though obviously important and theoretically robust, the existence of gains from exchange is fundamentally a premise of economics, not a testable implication of a particular model. Some studies use the competitive paradigm as a foundation for measuring the gains from trade, some studies have connected growth with openness, but none has connected static gains from trade with openness.

The observed terms of trade are bounded between the comparative labor cost ratios of the two countries. The existence of gains from market exchanges is a theoretically sturdy result, derivable from widely differing kinds of assumptions. But the Ricardian link between comparative cost ratios and the terms of trade is quite fragile, hardly surviving even the generalization to the multi-good case. Moreover, any serious attempt to study the determinants of relative product prices would surely allow for other inputs including physical and human capital. We are inclined therefore to think of this result as a mathematical toy. It is great fun to have it in our play-pens but it has little to do with economics outside the play-pen.

A country exports the commodity in which it has a comparative labor cost advantage and imports the commodity in which it has a comparative disadvantage. The Ricardian link between trade patterns and relative labor costs is much too sharp to be found in any real data set. A weaker but also theoretically fuzzy link was uncovered by some of the first studies of comparative advantage by MacDougall (1951) and Balassa (1963). These studies are reviewed in Deardorff (1984). We are unaware of any recent work testing or estimating the applicability of the Ricardian model.

Aside from the three propositions just listed, the Ricardian model is an important reminder that technological differences can be a source of comparative advantage. However, the Ricardian one-factor model is a very poor setting in which to study the impacts of technologies on trade flows, because the one-factor model is just too simple. Below, we discuss how technological differences have been incorporated into empirical studies of the Heckscher–Ohlin model, thereby capturing the content of the Ricardian model but not the detail.

2.2. *The Ricardo–Viner model*

The Ricardo–Viner model has one mobile factor, typically labor, that is used economy-wide and a set of sector-specific factors. The sector-specific factors can be interpreted as technological inputs, in which case the Ricardian model and the Ricardo–Viner model are very similar, differing only in an assumption about the constancy of the marginal productivity of labor. In a dynamic model, the sector-specific factors can be allowed to be mobile over time, thereby producing in the long run a Heckscher–Ohlin equilibrium. This transformation has been examined in theoretical papers by Neary (1978) and Mussa (1974).

A dynamic version of a multi-factor Ricardo–Viner model is a natural theoretical foundation for a study of a panel data set with observations of trade flows or production levels over time. The empirical work of which we are aware is almost exclusively cross-sectional, with separate models estimated for each time period. Though the Ricardo–Viner model has been much neglected empirically, we expect it to be employed extensively when analysts turn to the study of panel data. [1]

3. The Heckscher–Ohlin model

The Heckscher–Ohlin model has served as the backbone of traditional trade theory for almost 60 years. This model identifies a mapping from exogenously given factor supplies and exogenously given external product prices (determined in the international market place) into internal factor prices, output levels and consumption levels, the difference between these last two items being international trade. Although the two sets of exogenous variables and the three sets of endogenous variables can be used to form six sets of partial derivatives, four of these have been selected for special attention, theoretically and empirically. The Rybczynski theorem connects output levels with factor supplies; the Stolper–Samuelson theorem connects factor prices with product prices; the Factor Price Equalization theorem connects factor prices with factor supplies; and the Heckscher–Ohlin theorem connects trade with factor supplies. Each of these has been subjected to some empirical examination which we review in this section. [The relationship between consumption levels and product prices has been extensively studied in a largely separate literature, e.g. Deaton (1992)]. The other general equilibrium relationship – between either output levels or

---

[1]Grossman and Levinsohn (1989) find evidence suggesting that capital is sector-specific. While this is consistent with the Ricardo–Viner model, it is also consistent with other models in which capital is sector specific. Kohli (1993) also finds results consistent with a Ricardo–Viner model.

trade on the one hand and product prices on the other – has not been examined empirically, possibly because the only price variability allowed in the simple static models comes from trade barriers, which are not enormously variable across countries and which are extremely difficult to measure. Interest in dynamic models is likely to generate increased attention to the relationship between output levels (or commodity composition of trade) and product prices.

3.1. The Rybcyzinski theorem

The Rybcyzinski theorem relates changes in endowments to changes in the pattern of production. In particular:

The 2×2 Rybczynski theorem: Holding product prices fixed, an increase in the quantity of one factor will give rise to a more than proportional increase in the output of the good which uses that factor intensively and a reduction of the output of the other good.

According to the two-factor two-good Rybczynski theorem, the positive derivative is no surprise; the negative derivative is a surprise. At least one negative derivative for each factor occurs also for higher dimensional models.

It isn't altogether clear how one should approach the Rybczynski theorem empirically. The result seems to allow four different levels of interpretation:

(1) Total current factor supplies matter. History does not.
(2) The relationship between outputs and factor supplies is homothetic.
(3) The relationship is linear.
(4) At least one Rybczynski derivative is negative.

Cross-section studies by their very nature take as given the lack of historical persistence. This seems unfortunate since real output levels have a high degree of persistence over time. We expect that increased interest in dynamics is likely to have a large effect on empirical analysis of this result and many other ones as well.

Homotheticity is an important property and deserves to be examined carefully since scale effects in these output functions would suggest either increasing returns to scale or non-competitive behavior, both of which leave scope for ameliorative government trade interventions which can only cause inefficiencies in an H–O model.

Linearity is highly specific to the model with equal numbers of factors and goods, and does not seem worth taking seriously.

The negative derivative might seem like a curiosum, but we think that it is actually a very important property. What is really at stake here is not the Rybczynski theorem but rather its travelling companion, the Factor Price Equalization theorem. These results together imply that factor supply changes, such as waves of migrants, do not have much affect on factor prices because the potential affect on factor prices is dissipated by product mix changes in favor of the products that use the accumulating factor intensely. If one cannot find much association between product mix and factor supplies, one suspects that the factor price equalization theorem is not operating properly either. A negative derivative is precisely the kind of extreme result that would tend to lend credence to the FPE theorem.

Data bases for studying the Rybczynski theorem are difficult to come by. Natural experiments that might be worth looking at include the inflow of over half a million immigrants from the former Soviet Union to Israel, a country with a population of only about 5 million, and the reallocation of relative factor endowments in recently unified Germany. Since the Rybczynski theorem is a result about the pattern of production, empirical work directly addressing the theorem requires production data. The OECD has a fairly complete data base on production (and other variables) at the 3-digit ISIC level. Regressions explaining these production levels as functions of national factor endowments can be found in Leamer (1993a) and Harrigan (1993). Using a panel of 20 countries over 15 years and country specific fixed effects, typical estimated regressions reported by Harrigan are:

Iron and steel:

$$y = 0.824 \text{ capital} - 2.311 \text{ skilled labor} - 0.590 \text{ unskilled labor}$$

Printing and publishing:

$$y = 0.570 \text{ capital} + 1.089 \text{ skilled labor} - 0.529 \text{ unskilled labor}$$

with *t*-statistics (in absolute value) between 2 and 3.5 for each estimated coefficient. Land is excluded from the fixed effects regressions since it does not vary over time within a country. From results like these, Harrigan infers that capital is a source of comparative advantage in these industries, while skilled labor is a source of comparative advantage in printing and publishing, but not in iron and steel. Unskilled labor is a source of comparative disadvantage in both. (Notice the negative coefficients!) Most of his results are similarly sensible. He finds that the coefficients on capital are generally robust to different specifications while those on labor are not. These results are not that different from Leamer (1984b) findings for trade flows.

Rybczynski derivatives for two-digit manufacturing sectors in U.S. SMSA's have been estimated by Leamer (1987) who finds that labor supplies, if treated as exogenous and immobile across cities, do seem to have an impact on the SMSA output composition. Leamer also finds that while the smaller SMSA's as a group have their full share of most of the manufacturing sectors, individual small

SMSA's tend to have more concentrated product mixes than large SMSA's. This suggests indivisibilities, not agglomeration effects. In the econometric language, the discovery is heteroscedasticity, not nonlinearities.

3.2. The Stolper–Samuelson theorem

The Stolper–Samuelson theorem describes a mapping from prices determined externally in international markets to prices determined internally in local markets. The result applies if the external markets determine prices of commodities and the internal markets determine prices of factors, but the framework applies also when some factors are traded internationally and some goods are not. For empirical studies, it isn't usually obvious which markets are global and which are local. Capital, for example, is sometimes thought to be traded in global markets, but Feldstein and Horioka (1980) have argued that there is a strong "home bias" of savings. (See the chapter in this volume by Rogoff and Obstfeld for a discussion of the evidence on this.) Because of the impact that distance has on costs, most commodity prices have important local components of variability as well as global components.

The Stolper–Samuelson theorem was originally developed in a model with two traded goods and two non-traded factors.

The 2×2 Stolper Samuelson theorem: An increase in the relative price of a good yields an increase in the real return to the factor used intensively in that good and a decrease in the real return to the other factor.

Just as is the case with the two-good Ricardian model, "two-ness" is not an aspect of the model that is sensibly transferred into the empirical arena. To get to the real message of the result, we must accordingly read between the lines, and express results that are not dependent on two-ness. Here are some possible interpretations:

Winners and losers corollary: When a relative price changes, there is at least one winner and at least one loser.

Factor–Industry detachment corollary: External price changes have an effect on the return to a factor regardless of the industry in which the factor happens to be employed.

Scarce factor corollary 1: A scarce factor is helped by trade barriers; an abundant factor is hurt.

Scarce factor corollary 2: If a factor is "scarce enough" it will be helped by trade barriers.

The winners and losers corollary was really the main message of the original Stolper–Samuelson paper. Contrary to widely held opinion, free trade is not good for everyone. This winners and losers corollary is true in higher dimensional models with equal numbers of goods and factors [Ethier (1984)] and, if properly stated, is true for uneven models also [see Deardorff (1994)]. The Factor–Industry Detachment corollary is a direct consequence of the assumption of an integrated internal factor market, but it is worth stating the result explicitly since it contrasts with the prediction of a specific-factors model which finds some support in research reviewed below.

The first Scarce Factor corollary is not true in higher dimensional cases, but the second is true [see Leamer (1994)].

These corollaries can be said to be implicit but there is another important message that is communicated by its absence from the above list of interpretations:

Price Signal–Price Response corollary: Global "shocks" are communicated to local markets through price changes, not quantity changes. The response to this price signal is a price response, not a quantity response.

This Price Signal corollary is substantially at odds with a number of studies by labor economists and others who have attempted to estimate the impact of globalization on U.S. wages and U.S. employment levels taking as the measure of globalization the increase in the quantity of imports or the increase in the U.S. external deficit. This is discussed in more detail below. Also, see the chapter in this volume by Robert Feenstra.

These results have been used as a theoretical foundation for two different kinds of empirical exercises. Some studies examine the validity of these results, and other studies use the framework to estimate the impact of external events on internal factor markets. We review each of these in turn.

3.3. Political coalitions and the Stolper–Samuelson theorem:

The validity of the Stolper–Samuelson framework has been examined using a "revealed preference approach" by Magee (1980) and by Rogowski (1987). Magee noted that the Stolper–Samuelson theorem implies that:

(1) Capital and labor in a given industry will oppose each other on the issue of protection (or free trade) for that industry;

(2) For the country as a whole, each factor will favor either free trade or protection, but not both; and

(3) The position taken by capital or labor in an industry on the issue of protection will be independent of whether the industry is export or import competing.

These three implications are tested by using data on the lobbying position of labor unions (proxying labor) and on the lobbying position of manufacturers' trade associations (proxying capital) taken from their Congressional testimony with regard to the Trade Reform Act of 1973. A stark but representative result is given by the following table.

Table 3.1
Positions taken by capital and labor:
Twenty-two industries in 1973

Position of Capital	Position of Labor	
	Protectionist	Free Trade
Protectionist	14	1
Free trade	1	5

Source: Magee(1980).

If the Stolper–Samuelson theorem were correct, positions toward free trade should not depend on the factor's industry of employment, and capital and labor should always be in opposition to one another. In terms of Table 3.1, all industries would be in one of the off-diagonal cells. But in only 2 of the 21 industries (petroleum and tobacco) do management and labor have opposing positions. Magee argues that his results are much more supportive of a specific-factors model. Magee's other tests are also broadly supportive of this view.

Unlike Magee's results, Rogowski's are very supportive of the Stolper–Samuelson theorem. Rogowski uses the Stolper–Samuelson framework ingeniously to discuss the political coalitions that have formed historically among land owners, capitalists and laborers, including the German "marriage of iron and rye", U.S. and Latin American populism, and Asian socialism. Perhaps the difference between Magee's negative findings and Rogowski's positive ones comes from the time frame that is implicit in their data. Magee's industrial attitudes data seem inherently short-run, whereas party affiliation studied by Rogowski is a much longer run phenomenon. May we conclude that the Ricardo–Viner model is useful for the short run, and the Heckscher–Ohlin model is useful for the long run?

3.4. Product prices and wages:

One possible source of increased income inequality in the United States and elsewhere is increased competition from low-wage developing countries. The Stolper–Samuelson theorem and the Factor Price Equalization theorem establish one foundation for a study of the impacts of international competition on wages. These results together imply that changes in the international marketplace are communicated through relative price changes and only through relative price changes.

In this section we first review work that is explicitly based on the Stolper–Samuelson theorem and that attempts empirically to estimate the link between product prices and factor prices. Next we review work based on a partial equilibrium model which links changes in import prices to wages (and employment) by sector. Later, in the discussion of the Factor Price Equalization, we will discuss attempts to link quantity measures of global shocks (like the level of imports) to wages.

A. General equilibrium approaches.

Unfortunately, it doesn't take much disaggregation to get to a Stolper–Samuelson system that will overwhelm any real data set. But in a highly aggregated system, O'Rourke and Williamson (1992) find substantial support for Ohlin's hypothesis that equalization of commodity prices in the U.S. and Europe was a major source of factor price convergence in the last half of the nineteenth century. Chipman (1977) attempts to tackle the high-dimensional case, mapping external prices into internal German prices, but this paper seems to get bogged down in the econometric treatment of the data deficiency. Leamer (1994) and Leamer (1993a) attack the dimensionality problem indirectly. Instead of estimating the Stolper–Samuelson derivatives, he estimates the Rybczynski derivatives using cross country comparisons of output mix and factor supplies. Then, by appealing to the duality theorem, these Rybczynski derivatives are treated as Stolper–Samuelson derivatives.[2]

Baldwin and Cain (1994) exploit the general equilibrium nature of the Heckscher–Ohlin model to investigate possible influences on the returns to skilled labor, unskilled labor, and capital. Letting p_j denote the proportional change in the price of industry j's product, w_i the proportional change in the return to factor i, and θ_{ij} the distributive share of the ith factor in the production of the jth good (where $\sum \theta_{ij} = 1$), Baldwin and Cain make use of the fact that in the Heckscher–Ohlin model, $p_j = \sum \theta_{ij} w_i$. They estimate the following stochastic version:[3]

$$p_j = w_{\text{un}} \theta_{\text{un}j} + w_{sk} \theta_{skj} + w_k \theta_{kj} + e_j,$$

[2]Lawrence and Slaughter (1980) assert and Deardorff and Hakura (1993) conjecture that the duality result cannot be applied in models with more goods than factors, but Leamer (1994) shows how, in such a model, the dimensionality of price variability is restricted to the dimensionality of the factor space. For price variability so restricted the Stolper–Samuelson derivatives are well defined and the Samuelson duality theorem still applies.

[3]This same equation serves as a foundation for Leamer's (1994) reexamination of Lawrence and Slaughter's (1993) contention that globalization has not much affected wages.

where θ_{unj}, θ_{skj}, and θ_{kj} are the factor shares of unskilled labor, skilled labor, and capital for the jth industry while the analogous w's are the estimates of the proportional changes in the respective factor returns. The w's are estimated. Baldwin and Cain then examine whether the estimated w's are different in sign from the actual changes and whether these relationships are changing over the 1967–1992 time span. They note that,

> Should the regressions over a particular time period yield estimates of proportional changes in wages that correspond in sign with the actual changes over the period, one can conclude that the observed factor price changes are consistent with price changes that could have been brought about by changes in relative factor endowments domestically or in other factors affecting domestic or foreign prices besides technological change. One could then examine related data on domestic endowment changes and on other non-technological factors that can affect domestic and foreign prices as well as data on terms of trade improvements, shifts in the output of skilled labor-intensive goods relative to unskilled-labor intensive goods, and changes in the use of skilled versus unskilled labor in industries in an effort to narrow down the likely causes of the observed factor price changes.

Baldwin and Cain's results suggest that foreign competition has not been a big influence on the increased wage gap between skilled and unskilled workers in the U.S.

B. Partial equilibrium approaches.

Many other studies of globalization and wages have taken a partial equilibrium perspective connecting price changes in an industry with wage and employment changes in the same industry. These studies are substantively in conflict with the Stolper–Samuelson framework since they do not estimate spill-overs of the price change in one industry on wages in another industry. Among the first of these studies was Grossman (1987) who estimates the impact of international competition, proxied by industry-level import price indexes, on wages and employment in nine U.S. manufacturing industries.

The basic problem confronting Grossman and several of those who have tackled this problem since is decomposing the many influences on domestic wages in a sensible and theoretically consistent way. Grossman specifies a simple structural model and then estimates the reduced form equations that result from solving out for wages in terms of the exogenous variables. His estimating equation for industry i is given by:

$$\log w_{it} = \beta_0 + \beta_1 \text{ trend} + \beta_2 \log K_{it}^{\text{agg}} + \beta_3 \log L_t^{\text{agg}} + \beta_4 \log P_t^{e}$$
$$+ \beta_5 \log(P_{it}^*(1 + \tau_{it})) + \beta_7 \log Q_t + \varepsilon_t,$$

where w_{it} is the wage in industry i in year t, K^{agg} and L^{agg} are aggregate capital and labor, P^{e} is the price of energy, P_{it}^* is the import price index for industry i, and Q is GNP. The coefficient β_5 measures how much import prices affect domestic wages in that industry. This regression is run separately for each of the nine industries, and a similar regression is run with employment instead of wages as the dependent variable. Grossman finds that the elasticities of domestic wages with respect to import prices are very small and often statistically insignificantly different from zero. Using simulations based on his estimated coefficients, he shows that in only two of the nine industries do wages fall by more than ten cents an hour due to increases in import competition over his sample period. While Grossman does not provide confidence intervals, ignoring co-variance terms it appears that he would be unable to reject the hypothesis that import competition had no effect on wages in any of the industries studied. Wages moved around, but import competition played a negligible role in this phenomenon. Grossman takes this as evidence of "a fairly high degree of labor mobility out of declining sectors, at least in the long run (i.e. after eighteen months)". This high degree of mobility is an essential feature of the Stolper–Samuelson theorem. What is lacking, however, is a treatment of the other essential feature: cross-industry elasticities.

Grossman found that the employment effects of import competition were more substantial (but again imprecisely estimated) than the wage effects. What this implies for a theorem based on full-employment is unclear. With only a few industries examined, one does not know whether workers switched into expanding sectors or became unemployed.

Revenga (1992) followed up on Grossman's original methodology. Sticking with the reduced form estimation approach, Revenga added two twists. First, she suggested that for a large country like the United States, import prices may be endogenously determined and hence not orthogonal to the disturbance term in the estimating regression. She adopted standard instrumental variables methods to address this concern. Her selected instruments were exchange rates and foreign production costs. She also adopted a panel data approach, essentially "stacking" industries and allowing for an industry fixed effect. Revenga found that, depending on the chosen specification, employment elasticities are somewhat larger than Grossman's while wage elasticities remain very small. Correcting for the endogeneity of import prices results in larger elasticities. Still, many of her key parameters are not precisely estimated. Finally, the panel treatment she adopted is questionable, since in terms of the underlying model, it seems to imply that all industries have the same production function up to an affine transformation. Revenga's results, though, are consistent with the message of Grossman's original study. Labor appears fairly mobile.

Grossman and Levinsohn (1989) look at the effect of changes in import prices on the return to capital. They are unable to adopt the methods used in studying the effects of import competition on labor since the price of capital, given by its stock market value, is determined on a very efficient and forward-looking market. Only unanticipated "news" about the import competition, again proxied by an industry-specific import price index, will affect the price of capital, as expected shocks have already been capitalized. Grossman and Levinsohn face the task of decomposing the change in an equity price into news about several components. They estimate the effect of import competition on the return to capital in a given industry for six import-competing industries. They find that they can reject the assumption of perfect capital mobility at the 95 percent significance level for five of the six industries studied. They show that the magnitude of the estimated coefficient on import price news is similar to what results from a static model with perfectly immobile industry capital stocks. Finally, for five of the six industries, a one standard deviation shock to the expected import price creates substantial capital gains and losses for shareholders.[4] These gains and losses are on the order of 1.4 to 3.0 percent quarterly. Hence, while Grossman and Levinsohn start out with the notion of estimating Stolper–Samuelson derivatives, their estimates also reflect (favorably) on the appropriability of a specific factors model.

3.5. The Factor Price Equalization theorem

Labels are important since they can influence the conversation in important but unfelt ways. For example, when we call trade barriers "protection" and estimators "unbiased", our critical attitudes can diminish. Likewise when we name a result the "Factor Price Equalization" theorem, it is unsurprising that most of us have the impression that it deals with the international equalization of factor prices. Indeed it does, but only as a corollary. A more accurate name for conveying the true meaning of the result would be the Factor Price Insensitivity theorem, which contrasts in important ways with FPE.

Factor Price Insensitivity theorem (FPI): Within a country, factor prices are altogether insensitive to changes in factor supplies, holding product prices fixed.

Factor Price Equalization theorem (FPE): Factor prices are the same in different countries.

Another way of stating the Factor Price Insensitivity theorem is that the demand for labor in an open economy is infinitely elastic. This requires that factor supply variation is too small to take the country into a different cone of spe-

---

[4]A related paper is Brander (1991). In that paper, Brander applies standard event study analysis to examine stock market reaction to the U.S.–Canada free trade agreement.

cialization. Factor price equalization is a corollary requiring the additional and unlikely trio of assumptions: identical technologies, identical product mixes and no factor intensity reversals.

In addition to deflecting our attention away from the empirically more relevant FPI theorem, the traditional way of expressing FPE hides its real message. The message isn't that factor prices are equalized, or even that they are insensitive to variation in factor supplies. The message is the mechanism, namely variation in the mix of output. There might well be other mechanisms to achieve the same results, but both FPE and FPI rely on changes in the composition of output, and these results should be judged to be empirically invalid if there is no evidence that the mix of output depends on factor supplies.

Furthermore, like any other arbitrage condition, both FPI and FPE are conditions that necessarily take some time to hold, if they hold at all. Although the theories make no explicit reference to time, we all understand what is really being asserted: arbitrage works rapidly enough so that in the vast vibrating real economy we can "see" the force of arbitrage at work.

To be explicit, a dynamic version of FPI might be called Factor Price Adjustment, a version of Samuelson's Le' Chatelier principle applied over time and also over space:

Factor Price Adjustment (FPA). The initial factor price response to an increase in a factor supply is reduced over time as the economy shifts its output mix toward sectors that employ this factor most intensively. The more open a country is to international commerce, the greater will be the opportunities for adjustment in the output mix and the less will be the factor price response at any point in time.

Expressed differently, this is saying that the derived demand for labor is more elastic in the long run than in the short run, and more elastic for an open economy than for a closed one.

A dynamic version of FPE, suggested by Samuelson (1971) in an attempt to give FPE some empirical content is

Factor Price Convergence (FPC). As barriers to international commerce diminish, factor prices converge.

Trade in goods substitutes for trade in factors. With free trade in goods, factor prices are equalized. Hence, as trade in goods becomes more free, there is a tendency for factor price differentials across trading partners to be reduced. This leads to factor price convergence. This result is related to the Stolper–Samuelson theorem which we discuss above. Indeed, the Stolper–Samuelson theorem is usually combined with a theory of global price determination to establish FPC.

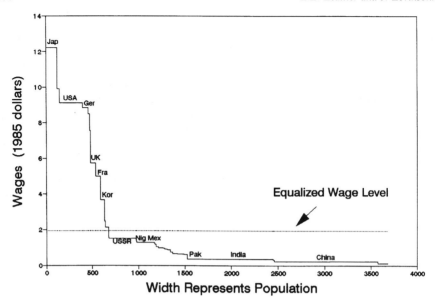

Figure 3.1. Industrial wages and population, 1989.

3.6. Empirical studies of FPE

Given the policy importance of these results, it is surprising how little study there has been of FPI, FPE, FPC and FPA. Perhaps FPE is so obviously violated that economists feel it doesn't merit close scrutiny. After all, neither Heckscher nor Ohlin thought the result was empirically valid. Ohlin (1933) asserted: "Complete equality of factor prices is ... almost unthinkable and certainly highly improbable". In a very useful survey of FPE and associated literature, Rassekh and Thompson (1993) include similar quotations from Samuelson, Caves, Bhagwati, and Travis. If the force of authority isn't adequate, take a look at Figure 3.1 from Leamer (1993b) which illustrates the vast differences in wages around the globe. Each country in this figure is represented by a rectangle with height equal to wages and width equal to population, thus with area roughly proportional to GDP.

But merely to dismiss FPE as empirically invalid is a dangerous attitude that is not evident in the frequent studies of other equally invalid arbitrage conditions such as purchasing power parity. Careful study of FPE seems desirable for two reasons. First we need to know just how badly violated is this arbitrage condition. Much of the apparent differences in wages can be explained by differences in benefits, and vacations and work conditions and, most importantly, differences in skill, and it seems wise to find out how much; [see e.g. Krueger (1968)]. More importantly, the real question isn't whether FPE is true or not. Trust us, it isn't true. The real question is what causes the violations that we observe. Is it increasing returns to scale, or technological differences, or multiple cones, or inertia, or what? Again, estimate, don't test.

We are inclined to think that factor price disparities come from three sources: differences in product mix (the multi-cone model), technological differences, and inertia. The inertia and multi-cone explanation have not received adequate attention empirically, especially in comparison with the technological explanation. The technological difference explanation harkens back to Leontief's favorite explanation of his non-paradox: in productivity equivalent units, the U.S. was labor abundant. Dollar, Baumol, and Wolff (1988) point out that a country's productivity advantages in one sector tend to be matched by productivity in other sectors, and convergence of total factor productivity over time seems to affect all sectors about the same. More recently, Trefler [see Trefler (1993) and Trefler (1994)] has made a lot of mileage out of the assumption that there are technological differences across countries, which in the H–O model implies that the ratio of the factor return to factor productivity ought to be equal for a given factor across countries. Factor productivity is not observed and is inferred by assuming that the Heckscher–Ohlin–Vanek model explains trade exactly when factors are measured in productivity equivalents. In Trefler (1993), he asks, what productivity adjustment ought to be made to a factor if the H–O–V model were to fit exactly. He then examines whether these inferred productivity adjustments are consistent with observed relative factor prices.

Trefler finds evidence of neutral technological differences, although he reports that for labor there is a systematic predictive bias such that wages in the poorest countries are under-predicted while those in the richest are over-predicted. The gist of Trefler's results are well illustrated in the figures below (generated from data reported by Trefler).

If factor price equalization held exactly for these factors, then all points would lie on the diagonal line.[5] Trefler investigates reasons why the data might not fit the theory exactly, but the lasting impression is that FPE finds significant support in the data once productivity differentials have been incorporated into the analysis. Incidentally, Trefler is rejecting FPE as it is originally stated, but he is not rejecting FPI. Indeed he has presented implicitly a model in which FPE is false but FPI is valid. By the way, this finding is only the first step. Before we can place much faith in the hypothesis of systematic technological differences, we

---

[5]For the case of capital, the price of capital is the investment price index from the Penn World Tables.

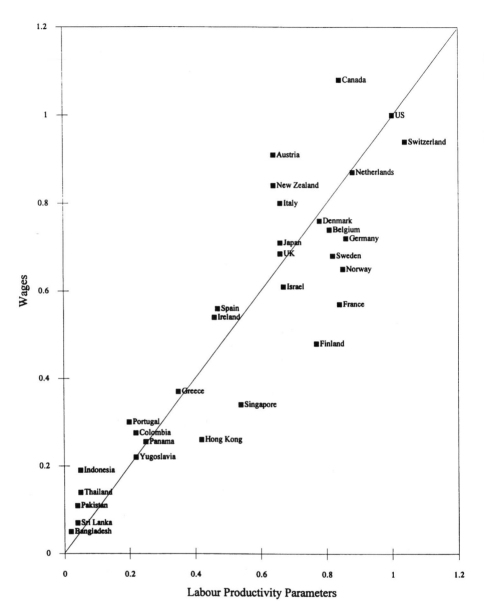

Figure 3.2.

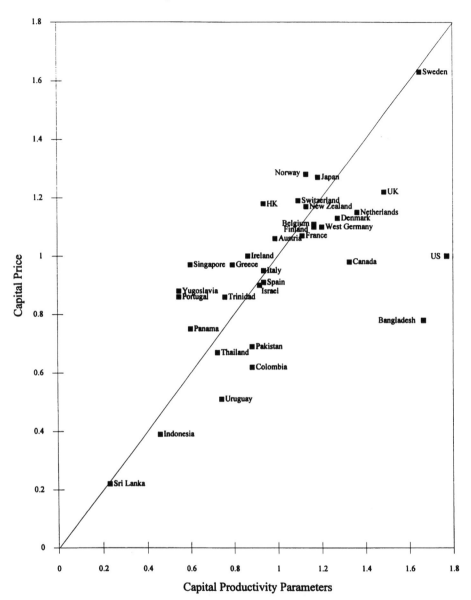

Figure 3.3.

will need a lot more work to determine exactly the source of these differences. Is it infrastructure? Is it organizational forms? Or what?

3.7. Empirical studies of Factor Price Insensitivity and Factor Price Adjustment[6]

The formal theory of Factor Price Insensitivity makes explicit reference to variations of factor supplies only within a cone of diversification. Thus if FPI were taken literally, an important empirical task would be to determine the edges of the cones, beyond which factor prices and output composition change. In fact, few empirical workers will take FPI that seriously. Most will be interested in the speed and process by which arbitrage takes place, as described by the Factor Price Adjustment theorem. How much potential impact of a migrant flow on wages is dissipated by changes in the composition of output? How fast does this occur?

The great waves of migration that moved large numbers of workers from low-wage regions to high-wage regions form severe tests of Factor Price Insensitivity. Results are surveyed in Hatton and Williamson (1992). Did the Irish migration into Britain between the 1820s and the 1850s suppress real wages? Indeed it did. [Williamson (1990)]. What about the repeated waves of migrants into the United States in the 19th and 20th century? The answer to this question seems sufficiently unclear empirically that historians have succumbed to the seduction of CGE models [e.g. O'Rourke and Williamson (1992)]. What about the recent waves of migrants into U.S. cities? Borjas, Freeman, and Katz (1991) finds no discernible effect of migrants on the cross-city variation of wage rates in the United States. Card (1990) finds that the very large Mariel migration from Cuba had no impact on wages in Miami.

These studies by labor economists generally are concerned with the effect of the migrant flow on wages, but not the mechanism, which as we have argued is the essence of all the theorems on factor price determination discussed here. To support these results, we need to uncover a response to a migrant flow in the composition of output; we need to find evidence of the Rybczynski theorem. For example, why has apparel employment plummeted almost everywhere in this country, except in Los Angeles, where it is now practically the only industry that is experiencing growth? Isn't this the FPA theorem at work, with output responding to the Mexican migration? More on this above in our review of the Rybczynski theorem.

---

[6]The recent great burst of academic interest in "convergence" has used the scale economies of the endogenous growth literature as an intellectual foundation, but has until recently altogether neglected the fact that countries are economically interconnected by flows of commodities, physical and knowledge capital and labor.

Hatton and Williamson (1992, p. 54) summarize the ambiguity that this literature leaves:

> We need to learn much more about these global market forces, and the complex interdependence between capital, labor and commodity markets is likely to be central to any comprehensive explanation that emerges.

3.8. Quantity signal and price response approaches.

The FPI theorem establishes conditions under which external or internal quantity shocks have no affect on wages. According to this result, if the relevant product prices do not change, then wages will not change even if there is international migration, or internal factor accumulation, or changes in the external deficit or increased imports. Conversely, there may be little or no change in these quantities, and if product price changes are substantial, the Stolper–Samuelson theorem indicates that there will be a substantial wage response. In great conflict with the foregoing remarks, many studies having an informal theoretical basis proceed as if external shocks are transmitted by quantity signals, and sometimes only by quantity signals. For example, partial equilibrium equations are often estimated with wages or employment levels in an industry as the dependent variable, and with a measure of the quantity of imports in that industry as an explanatory variable. Informal general equilibrium treatments such as Freeman and Lawrence (1991) and Katz and Murphy (1992) compute the "net factor content" of trade and act as if this net factor flow were equivalent to an internal change in the factor supply. This is dangerously confusing. In a model in which Factor Price Insensitivity holds, factor supply changes have no affect on wages, so why bother with the calculation? Deardorff and Staiger (1988) offer one answer: changes in the factor content of trade may serve as a proxy for the product price changes that are the real route by which globalization is affecting wages. This relationship between changes in product prices and the factor content of trade clearly depends on technologies and tastes. Using log-linear technologies and preferences, Deardorff and Staiger are able to derive a simple expression linking changes in wages to changes in the factor content of trade, but more generally only correlation-type results are possible. This is intriguing, but not a full justification for the calculations because other sources of variation in the factor content of trade would leave wages unaffected. These include capital flows that alter the external deficit, and also changes in the factor supplies.

The Deardorff and Staiger argument requires all goods to be produced, and the factor content calculations are all the more suspect if one uses the multicone model and if the price changes occur only for commodities that are not produced at home. Wood (1994b) makes this point in a way by showing how much greater are the labor-service imports of the developed countries if the factor content calculation uses developing-country input intensities instead of developed.

Our conclusion: DANGER, PELIGRO

Other recent studies in labor economics that address the general issue of trade and employment include Bound and Johnson (1992), Lawrence and Slaughter (1980) and Murphy and Welch (1991, 1992). For more on wages and trade, see the review article by Deardorff and Hakura (1993).

3.9. The Heckscher–Ohlin theorem

International trade is the difference between production and consumption. Although there has been a very substantial amount of empirical study of the commodity composition of international trade, very little of policy relevance hinges on the nature of consumption. Most of the theoretical and policy action of the general equilibrium model is on the production side, not the consumption side. Thus the study of patterns of international trade is really an indirect way to study the production side of the model: the Rybczynski theorem, the Stolper–Samuelson theorem, and the Factor Price Insensitivity theorem. To accomplish this indirect study, it is traditional theoretically, and often empirically, to neutralize the consumption side by assuming identical, homothetic tastes. This makes trade behave pretty much the same as production.

The studies of the Heckscher–Ohlin model form a good case study illustrating what may happen if one tries to do empirical work without a clearly articulated theory. Time and again we will see that unsupported and even erroneous conclusions have been drawn from data sets studied without a theoretical basis.

A matrix of equations that characterize the production side of the $n \times n$ version of the Heckscher–Ohlin model is

$$Q = A^{-1}V \tag{3.1}$$

where Q is the vector of outputs, V is the vector of factor supplies, A is the input–output matrix with elements equal to the amount of a factor used to produce a unit of a good. This is just the inverted form of the factor market equilibrium conditions equating the supply of factors V to the demand for factors AQ.

The consumption side of the model is neutralized by the assumption of identical homothetic tastes. Then, in the absence of barriers to trade, all individuals face the same commodity prices, and they consume in the same proportions:

$$C = sC_w = sA^{-1}V_w \tag{3.2}$$

where C is the consumption vector, C_w is the world consumption vector, V_w is the vector of world factor supplies, and s is the consumption share. Thus, trade is

$$T = Q - C = A^{-1}V - sA^{-1}V_w = A^{-1}(V - sV_w). \tag{3.3}$$

The consumption share s will depend on the level of output and also on the size of the trade balance, $B = \pi'T$, where π is the vector of external prices which in the absence of trade barriers would equal the internal prices p. Premultiplying (3.3) by the vector of prices π and then rearranging produces the consumption share:

$$s = \frac{\pi'A^{-1}V - B}{\pi'A^{-1}V_w} = \frac{\text{GNP} - B}{\text{GNP}_w}. \tag{3.4}$$

This is often called the Heckscher–Ohlin–Vanek model referring to Vanek's [see Vanek (1968)] use of the assumption of homothetic tastes. Using this H–O–V model, trade given by eq. (3.3) and production given by eq. (3.1), are identical except that production takes as an input the total factor supplies, but trade uses the net factor supplies, adjusted for implicit factor consumption. For a small country with an exogenously determined level of the trade balance B proportional to GDP, the consumption share (3.4) and consequently the trade vector (3.3) are both approximately homothetic linear functions of the endowments. The more basic Heckscher–Ohlin proposition retains homotheticity but makes no reference to linearity and merely asserts that trade arises because of the unequal distribution of resources across countries. A pure H–O model thus implies that if the ratios of resources were the same in all countries then there would be no trade. Several of the assumptions listed above can be altered without affecting this basic H–O proposition. These assumptions only introduce nonlinearities in the relationship between trade and factor supplies.

Incidentally, one rather awkward assumption that cries out for change is that of equal numbers of commodities and factors. After all, we really don't know how to count either.

3.10. Factor content studies

The first and by far the most influential study of trade patterns using the Heckscher–Ohlin model was done by Leontief (1953), who found that U.S. imports in 1947 were more capital intensive relative to labor than U.S. exports. This empirical "paradox" sparked a search of great breadth and intensity for a theory that could explain it. Among the explanations were labor skills, trade barriers, natural resource abundance, capital-biased consumption, and technological differences.

Surprise! The Leontief finding is compatible with the U.S. being capital abundant as shown in Leamer (1980). This is a good illustration of the need for a clear conceptual framework when empirical work is being carried out since in its absence substantial mistakes can be made.

One suspicious step in Leontief's calculation is that he separately computes the factor content of exports and imports, whereas the H–O–V theory relates to net exports.[7] From (3.3), the H–O–V theory implies that the factor content of trade satisfies the relationship $F = AT = V - sV_w$. From this set of equations we can separate the capital and labor content of trade: $F_K = X_K - M_K = K - sK_w$, $F_L = X_L - M_L = L - sL_w$, where X and M refer to exports and imports respectively. Leamer (1980) shows that the Leontief finding, that exports are less capital intensive than imports, $X_K/X_L < M_K/M_L$, is compatible with capital abundance, $K/L > K_w/L_w$.

A correct way to use the H–O–V theory to infer the relative abundance of factors from the factor content of trade refers to the factor content adjusted for the trade imbalance, $F^A = AT - V_w B/GNP_w$. Using (3.3) and (3.4) for country i, this adjusted factor content is $F_i^A = AT_i - V_w B_i/GNP_w = V_i - (GNP_i/GNP_w)V_w$. Dividing the kth element of each side by $(V_{wk})/(GNP_i/GNP_w)$ produces

$$Z_{ik} = (F_{ik}^A/V_{wk})/(GNP_i/GNP_w) = (V_{ik}/V_{wk})/(GNP_i/GNP_w) - 1 \qquad (3.5)$$

The ratio of the resource share (V_{ik}/V_{wk}) to the GNP share (GNP_i/GNP_w) of the right-hand side of this expression is a measure of the abundance of factor k. On the left-hand side of this expression is the exported share of the domestic supply adjusted for the trade imbalance. Thus the theory suggests there are two ways to measure factor abundance: directly by $(V_{ik}/V_{wk})/(GNP_i/GNP_w) - 1$ or through the adjusted factor content of trade Z_{ik}. Measures of the adjusted factor content of trade Z_{ik} for the United States, the United Kingdom and Japan in 1967 using U.S. factor intensities are reported in Table 3.2.

The qualitative content of eq. (3.5) has been studied in at least two ways: by examining the signs of the numbers Z_{ik} or their rank ordering. A Leontief type of study selects a country i and compares the numbers Z_{ik} for different factors k, say capital and labor. If $Z_K > Z_L$ where K and L refer to capital and labor, then trade reveals that the country is capital abundant compared to labor. Indeed, that is the Leamer (1980) comment on Leontief: if you do the calculation right, then the U.S. is revealed to be relatively capital abundant. This is true also for the 1967 data reported in Table 3.2 since the U.S. capital number of 0.08 percent exceeds the overall labor number of −0.25 percent. According to the data in Table 3.2, the United States is most abundant in arable land and most scarce in forest land.

---

[7]Note, though, that the H–O–V model did not appear until about 15 years *after* Leontief's study.

Table 3.2
Ratio of adjusted net trade in a factor to its
national endowment (times 100)

	U.S.	U.K.	Japan
Capital	0.08	−12.86	−5.47
Labor	−0.25	0.63	0.10
Prof/Tech	0.23	1.77	0.44
Manager	−0.11	2.04	0.48
Clerical	−0.19	1.37	0.33
Sales	−1.10	1.30	−0.05
Service	−0.68	1.32	−0.03
Agriculture	1.54	−18.57	−1.54
Production	−0.34	1.11	1.18
Land			
Arable	19.45	−313.42	−341.42
Forest	−23.82	−2573.99	−268.58
Pasture	−1.63	−91.89	−1998.58

Source: Bowen, Leamer, and Sveikauskus (1987)

It is also possible to make comparisons across countries. The United Kingdom is more scarce in capital than Japan which is more scarce in capital than the United States. The United Kingdom is most abundant in labor, overall. Japan is scarcest in arable land.

A test of the H–O theorem compares the numbers in Table 3.2 with direct measures of factor abundance. Tests of this form are what Bowen, Leamer, and Sviekauskaus (1987) call rank tests since they compare the rank order of factor abundance measured directly and measured through the factor content of trade.

It is also possible to perform "sign" tests that compare the signs of the left and right of eq. (3.5). This was first done by Brecher and Choudhri (1982) who mention that a feature of Leontief's data is that the net export of labor services is positive, even after adjusting for the trade imbalance. Using the right-hand side of (3.5) this implies that the U.S. per capita GNP is less than world per capita GNP, which is impossible to square with the facts. Another way to describe sign tests is that they compare the resource abundance of one factor with an average of all the other factors, since the GNP ratio is an earnings weighted average of all the factor abundance ratios. By examining the signs in Table 3.2 we infer that the United States was abundant in capital, professional workers and arable land and scarce in unskilled labor. Both the United Kingdom and Japan were scarce in capital and land and abundant in labor. Sign tests would compare these signs with the corresponding signs of direct measures of the factor abundance.

Bowen, Leamer, and Sviekauskaus (1987) in a study of 1967 data on 27 countries and 12 factors find about thirty five percent violations of the signs implied by (3.5) and about fifty percent violations of the ranks. This seems disappointing, but what did you expect? In the absence of a clearly stated alternative theory, it seems impossible to determine just how many violations are enough to cast substantial doubt on the theory.

Beginning with Leamer and Bowen (1981), Leamer has often made the observation that the Heckscher–Ohlin model links three separately observable phenomena: trade, resource supplies and technological input coefficients. A full test of the theory accordingly must begin with separate measures of all three of these concepts and must explore the extent to which the observed data violate the H–O restrictions.

Bowen, Leamer and Sveikauskus use measurements of all three concepts and link their work to a carefully formulated model, namely the H–O–V model as captured by eq. (3.5) which determines the adjusted factor content of trade as a function of resource supplies. Recognizing the impossibility of testing a theory without an alternative, these authors generalize the H–O–V model to allow (a) non-homothetic tastes characterized by linear Engel curves, (b) technological differences among countries that affect all technological coefficients proportionately and (c) various kinds of measurement errors. Hence, they do posit some alternative hypotheses. (They do not, though, consider a fixed factor model as an altogether different alternative.) In the words of Bowen, Leamer, and Sviekauskaus (1987)

> The data suggest errors in measurement in both trade and national factor supplies, and favor the hypothesis of neutral technological differences across countries. However, the form of the technological differences favored by the data involves a number of implausible estimates, including some in which factors yield strictly negative outputs. Thus, ... The Heckscher–Ohlin model does poorly, but we do not have anything that does better.

Brecher and Choudhri (1988) test the H–O–V model by exploiting the model's prediction that the amount of a factor embodied in a dollar of domestic expenditure should be the same for any pair of countries. In order to give the model a fighting chance, Brecher and Choudhri examine data from the United States and Canada – a country-pair for which the model's assumptions of identical tastes and technologies, free trade, and common factor prices might be expected to be fairly reasonable. The implications of the H–O–V model examined by Brecher and Choudhri do not find support in the data.

Trefler (1994) revisits Bowen, Leamer, and Sveikauskus and arrives at very different conclusions. Using basically the same variables and tests as Bowen, Leamer, and Sveikauskaus (BLS), but with data from 1983, Trefler first replicates BLS's test of the Heckscher–Ohlin–Vanek theorem. Like BLS, he finds that "it performs miserably". Trefler closely examines where the theory fits especially poorly and finds that deviations from theoretical predictions follow pronounced patterns. In particular, he finds that:

(1) these deviations are correlated with country size;

(2) rich (poor) countries are scarce (abundant) in almost all factors; and

(3) the ratio of net factor service trade to its theoretical prediction has a very small variance across countries.

Like BLS, Trefler posits modifications to the H–O–V model and asks whether the modified theory better fits the data. Trefler shows that one of the alternatives considered by BLS (neutral international technology differences) is very important when trying to explain why the standard H–O–V model performs so poorly. After correcting an error in their calculations, he finds that the H–O–V model with neutral technological differences "performs remarkably well". Trefler's preferred specification allows for home bias in consumption as well as neutral technological differences.

Hufbauer (1970) is a notable early study that employs measurements of trade, resource supplies, and technological input coefficients using only two-dimensional data. Some typical results are reported in Table 3.3.

Table 3.3
Captial per person

	Abundance	Exports	Imports
Canada	8,850	17,529	11,051
United States	7,950	11,441	13,139
Norway	6,100	16,693	10,476
Sweden	5,400	12,873	11,373
Netherlands	4,750	11,768	11,706
Korea	850	8,004	14,900
India	500	7,339	12,019
Pakistan	500	5,725	12,371

Source: Hufbauer (1970)

The countries in this list are ordered by measures of their capital per person, with Canada being the most abundant in capital and Pakistan the least abundant. The capital per person in exports is compared with the capital per person in imports in the next two columns. It should be noted that the U.S. data display the "Leontief paradox" that imports are more capital intensive than exports. But this is not true for the other countries at the top of the list. Hufbauer reports that the capital per person overall (first column) has a correlation of 0.625 with the capital per person in exports (second column) and a correlation of −0.353 with capital per person in imports (third column). This is regarded to be confirmatory of the H–O model: capital abundant countries tend to have capital intensive exports and labor intensive imports.

There are four comments that can be made about this study. First, the study uses measures of all three concepts: factor supplies, trade and technological input intensities. As we have already mentioned, a full test of the H–O model must surely make reference to all of these. Second, Hufbauer's analysis does not refer explicitly to any model. It separates imports from exports, which got Leontief in trouble. Third, we find it curious that the capital per person in exports varies greatly across countries in contrast to the capital per person in imports. We would not have expected this result based on our understanding of the H–O model. What might account for it? Perhaps the model with more goods than factors can help. In the H–O model with many goods and two inputs, countries can concentrate production on just two of the goods and import all the rest. The two produced goods have similar capital intensities. In other words, countries have a diversified import structure but a concentrated export structure. Fourth, competing models and/or factors that might explain trade are "tested" by comparing the size of the correlations that they produce. Hufbauer's list of theories is noticeably inclusive: factor proportions, human skills, scale economies, stage of production, technological gap, product cycle and preference similarity.

3.11. Cross-commodity comparisons

The Heckscher–Ohlin theorem has often been studied empirically with cross-commodity comparisons implicitly based on the assumption that the export performance "should" depend on the characteristics of the industry. Simple correlations were rather common early in the literature, but these gave way to multiple correlations in the 1970's.

For example, Keesing (1966) reports some simple correlations of export performance (U.S. exports) / (Group of 14 countries exports) with skill intensities that are reported in Table 3.4.

Table 3.4
Simple correlations of labor share and export performance

Skill groups	46 industries	35 industries
Scientists and engineers	0.49	0.72
Technicians and draftsmen	0.37	0.55
Other professionals	0.41	0.58
Managers	0.16	0.06
Machinists	0.22	0.37
Other skilled manual workers	0.11	0.21
Clerical and sales	0.35	0.44
Unskilled and semi-skilled	−0.45	−0.64

Note: The column with 35 industries excludes natural resources industries.
Source: Keesing (1966)

These results are suggestive of human capital abundance in the United States because the largest positive correlations occur at the highest skill levels and because the unskilled labor share is actually negatively correlated with export performance.

A typical multiple regression from Baldwin (1971) is given in Table 3.5.

Table 3.5
A sample Baldwin regression dependent variable is (adjusted) net exports by the U.S.

Independent variable	Parameter estimate	t-statistic
K/L	−1.37	−4.35
Percent labor in:		
Eng. and science	7011	2.13
Other professional	−1473	−0.69
Clerical and sales	71	0.06
Craftsmen/foremen	1578	1.96
Operatives	−248	−0.79
Non-farm labor	−761	−0.80
Farm labor	845	3.81
Scale index	−421	−1.25
Unionization index	343	1.11

Note: R^2 for this regression is 0.44
Source: Baldwin (1971)

One thing that might be concluded from this regression is that the negative sign on the capital intensity variable suggests the Leontief paradox that the United States does not export goods that are capital intensive.

More recently, Wright (1990) has used cross-industry regressions for 1879, 1899, 1909, 1914, 1928, and 1940 to track the sources of American industrial success. This study adds an interesting twist by running the cross-industry regression for multiple time periods and searching for patterns of change over time. For example, Wright finds that the capital to labor ratio is an important source of comparative advantage in the early periods, but that its coefficient becomes negative (connoting a comparative disadvantage) by 1940. Natural resources, on the other hand, do not contribute to export success in the late nineteenth century, but become increasingly important during the twentieth.[8]

It is difficult to interpret these findings without answering, implicitly or explicitly, the following difficult questions:

(1) How should the export performance variable be scaled? Keesing scales by the exports of a comparison group of fourteen countries. Baldwin uses the unscaled data, which seems a bit uncomfortable since all of his explanatory variables are scaled.

[8]A related study is Stern and Maskus (1981).

(2) Is it more appropriate to use simple correlations or multiple regressions?

(3) How should the "importance" of a resource be inferred? By the size of the simple correlation? By the t-statistic in the multiple regressions?

(4) Is it legitimate to exclude the natural resource industries?

(5) Is it legitimate to include measures like the indices of scale and unionization?

(6) What economic phenomena are generating the disturbance term in these regressions and what stochastic properties should be assumed? Regressions never fit exactly and a careful discussion of why is essential. For example, without knowing what economic phenomena the disturbance term is capturing, it is impossible to evaluate the reasonableness of orthogonality assumptions.

These questions can only be answered with reference to a clear theoretical framework.

Leamer has argued in several papers, [Leamer and Bowen (1981), Leamer (1984b) and Leamer (1987)], that cross-industry regressions generally have an unclear theoretical foundation. In deciding the kind of equation to estimate, the first important question is how to scale the dependent variable in a way that makes the cross industry comparisons sensible. The absolute level of output or trade does not seem to be a very sensible dependent variable because some commodity groups form large shares of output and consumption whereas others form small shares. If no attempt is made to control for scale, any explanatory variable that is correlated with the size of the commodity group will pick up the scale effect. To put this another way, without some way to correct for the relative sizes of different commodity groups, the estimates will be highly sensitive to the level of aggregation. The scale effect has traditionally been controlled by dividing the dependent variable by some measure of market size. The ideal candidate would seem to be total world output. What seems to lie behind this normalization is the intuitive notion that a country's share of world output can be expected to depend on the input mix of the commodity: Thus countries that are abundant in capital "ought" to have larger shares of capital intensive industries than of labor intensive industries. But what seems intuitively clear is not always true. To explore this formally, let us focus on the production side of the Heckscher–Ohlin model with equal numbers of factors and goods and with sufficient similarity of endowment supplies that all countries have the same factor prices and use the same input mixes.

Equation (3.1) then identifies a set of relationships between outputs, factor intensities and factor supplies. If data are collected for a single country only, then the endowment vector V is necessarily constant and (3.1) explains the level of production of each commodity as a function of the factor intensities A. (This is the type of regression discussed in the above section on the Rybczynski theorem.) This equation suggests that the "correct" variables to include in the equation are elements of the inverse of A, not elements of A. Usually, however, the dependent variable is not selected to be the level of output which can vary enormously if data are in monetary units and oddly if data are in other units. It is traditional to normalize by a variable that represents the "size" of the commodity in world markets such as the level of the world's output of the commodity. By Cramer's rule, the share of the country output of commodity one is

$$Q_1/Q_{1w} = \det[V, A_2, A_3, ..., A_N]/\det[V_w, A_2, A_3, ..., A_N]$$

where A_j refers to a column of the matrix A, Q_{1w} is the world output of commodity one and V_w is the world's vector of factor endowments. *Note that this formula indicates that the share of world output of commodity one does not depend on A_1, the input mix in industry one.*[9] This model thus suggests that it is entirely inappropriate to regress output shares on characteristics of industries.

Many cross-industry regression studies in the literature have not used the world shares as the dependent variable. Typically, the dependent variable is the "trade-dependence ratio" equal to the level of net exports as a share of domestic consumption. Exactly the same comment applies if the model (3.1)–(3.4) is used. Using Cramer's rule we can solve for the trade dependence ratio for the first commodity as:

$$T_1/C_1 = \det(V - sV_w, A_2, A_3, ..., A_n)/\det(sV_w, A_2, A_3, ..., A_n)$$

The same result thus applies: *the trade dependence ratio in industry one is altogether unrelated to the characteristics of that industry.* This suggests something of a puzzle, though, for some of these regressions actually fit the data reasonably well. What is going on here?

Another comment on cross-commodity regressions is offered by Leamer and Bowen (1981). It has been a tradition to regress trade on factor intensities and to assume that the signs of the coefficients reveal the relative abundance of factors. For example, a country that is relatively well endowed with capital is expected to have a positive coefficient on the capital variable when trade is regressed on a set of factor intensities. But as Leamer and Bowen (1981) observe, there is no assurance that this is true. The regression vector formed when the unscaled trade data T are regressed on the input intensities A is $(AA')^{-1}A'T = (AA')^{-1}(V - sV_w)$, which has the same sign as $(V - sV_w)$ only under special circumstances.

Bowen and Sviekauskaus (1992), though, argue that while this is certainly true in theory, in practice this concern is not very important. They run several cross-industry regressions and show that the signs of the estimated coefficients usually match the sign on the revealed factor abundance when data on technologies are used. They note that the regression approach works well, but that it is

---

[9]Leamer (1984a)

important to correct the trade data for trade imbalances. The general message from Bowen and Sveikauskas is that while the cross-industry approach may not be theoretically correct (as would be the case if factor complementarities were strong), in practice the problem is not severe.

Although the H–O–V framework seems theoretically incompatible with multiple regression, it can be used to justify the calculation of simple correlations. If trade is balanced, the theory predicts that the sign of the simple correlation between the trade vector and a set of input intensities is the same as the sign of the excess factor supply $V - sV_w$. For example, a country that is well endowed in capital will have trade positively correlated with capital intensity. By this type of reasoning, the simple correlations in Table 3.4 suggest that the U.S. was relatively abundant in all the skilled labor categories and relatively scarce in unskilled labor.

More than just the sign, it is natural to suspect that the simple correlation between trade and factor intensity is highest for the factor that is most "important", scientists and engineers in Table 3.5, for example. Although the absolute value of the predicted correlation is indeed high if the supply of the resource is unusual, it is also high if the input intensities are highly variable across industries.

Petri (1991) relaxes the assumption of factor price equalization and simultaneously makes a very strong set of assumptions on the demand side of the model to derive a relationship between import (or export) shares relative to total consumption and $A'w + b$ where A is the standard input-output matrix, w a vector of factor prices, and b is a vector of tariff equivalents. The demand side assumptions amount to assuming that all goods are differentiated by country of origin *and* that the choice among varieties of one product (what's a product?) does not depend on the choice among varieties of the other products. This is a strong form of separability. Petri linearly regresses import penetration and export shares for 49 manufacturing industries in Japan in 1985 on a series of proxies for comparative advantage, market structure, and protection. The extensive use of proxies makes it difficult to know just what to make of the results, but Petri does provide a theoretical justification for cross-commodity regressions by relaxing the FPE assumption and adding strong assumptions on the demand side.

3.12. Studies of the Heckscher–Ohlin model based on cross country comparisons

Cross-country comparisons are another way to study the validity of the Heckscher–Ohlin theorem. Studies of this type hold fixed the commodity and use the country as the experimental unit. Normally the tool of analysis is multiple regression, with some measure of trade performance as the dependent variable and various characteristics of countries as the explanatory variable. Chenery (1960), Chenery and Taylor (1968), Chenery and Syrquin (1975), were some of the earliest studies of this type, although these studies did not deal with details of the structure of trade but rather with more aggregate features of the economy like the ratio of gross imports to GNP. Leamer (1974) was one of the first to study commodity composition questions, contrasting the performance of three groups of variables as predictors of imports disaggregated by commodity; these groups are resistance (tariffs and distance), stage of development (GNP and population) and resource supplies (capital, labor, education and R&D). Leamer finds that the development group is generally most important in helping to predict import patterns.

The theory underlying many of these cross-section regressions is casual at best. This contrasts with Leamer (1984b) which takes eq. (3.3), the H–O–V model $T = A^{-1}(V - sV_w)$, as the clearly stated foundation for running regressions of net exports on factor supplies. One function of such an estimation exercise implicitly is to infer the value of A^{-1} and to study how this changes over time. The question that is implicitly addressed is: "What resource supplies determine comparative advantage?"

Some typical results from Leamer (1984b) are reported in Table 3.6. These are beta-values from regressions of four commodity aggregates on 11 resource supplies. The data refer to trade and resource supplies of 60 countries in 1975.[10]

Based on these beta-values, comparative advantage in cereals is associated with abundance of highly skilled labor, land of type 3 and oil. Comparative advantage in the three manufactures is associated with supply of the moderately skilled workers and capital, and is negatively related to the supply of land.

3.13. Multi-cone models

The foregoing discussion is based entirely on the one-cone model in which countries produce the same mix of products and factor price equalization holds. When data from developing countries are combined with data from developed countries, the possibility of multiple cones of diversification needs to be explicitly considered. This is not an easy task empirically because the theoretical model with multiple cones has as its basic feature something which is not present

---

[10] A beta coefficient is equal to the estimated coefficient times the ratio of the standard error of the explanatory variable to the standard error of the dependent variable. A beta coefficient answers the question: if the explanatory variable changes by one standard error, by how many standard errors does the dependent variable change?

Table 3.6
Beta values of net export regressions

	Cereals	Labor Intensive Manufactures	Capital Intensive Manufactures	Machinery
CAPITAL	−0.17	0.08	0.78	0.49
LABOR1	0.74	−1.13	−1.80	−0.39
LABOR2	−0.55	0.93	0.85	0.18
LABOR3	−0.15	0.08	0.37	0.02
LAND1	0.09	−0.04	−0.03	−0.01
LAND2	0.03	0.02	−0.01	0.00
LAND3	0.26	−0.04	−0.15	−0.06
LAND4	0.05	−0.15	−0.10	−0.11
COAL	0.03	−0.14	−0.09	−0.02
MINERALS	0.00	−0.03	−0.03	−0.01
OIL	0.72	−0.24	−0.60	−0.21

Note: LABOR1 is professional/technical; LABOR2 is literate but non-professional; LABOR3 is illiterate. For the LAND definitions, see Leamer (1984).
Source: Leamer (1984)

in any data set: namely the complete absence of output of some products. This theoretical feature needs to be "softened" in some way before data are examined. Leamer (1994) does this somewhat casually by including non-linearities in the Heckscher–Ohlin and Rybczynski functions. Trefler (1994) also has a multi-cone feature in his technological differences.

Incidentally, in deference to the one-cone model it has been the tradition in this literature to take the dependent variable to be net exports. Most analysts must worry that something is lost by not studying imports and exports separately. The multi-cone model is a natural theory on which to base such a study.

The multi-cone model may also serve as a casual foundation for the cross-industry regressions about which we have been so critical. As Baldwin and Hilton (1983) observe, production cost is the inner product of factor prices and input intensities.[11] In the one-cone model, both factor prices and input intensities are identical, and production costs do not vary across countries. But in the multi-cone model, factor price differences across countries can give one location a cost advantage over another. The cross industry regressions of trade performance on input intensities can then be interpreted as a regression of market share on cost advantage. This has a great deal of appeal, but don't forget that pooling data across different industries implicitly assumes that the same demand conditions apply in all.

[11] See also Petri (1991).

3.14. Cross-country comparisons of production functions

We have discussed in several instances inferences drawn from trade data concerning technological differences among countries. This seems like such an important possibility that it calls for more direct international comparisons of production functions. It is interesting that there is a very old literature on the comparison of production functions that seems not to have been followed up. Minhas (1962), drawing heavily on Arrow, Chenery, and Solow (1961), makes use of the CES production function to examine both the empirical importance of factor intensity reversals and international differences in technology using factor data on only labor and capital. Minhas claims to find factor intensity reversals and also differences in technologies, though Leontief (1953) mounts a spirited counterattack.

3.15. Summing up

The voluminous and complex literature on testing and/or estimating Heckscher–Ohlin models may appear to have left the framework battered and beaten, but nonetheless it remains entirely healthy. Some of the attacks are irrelevant because they used inappropriate methods. The more serious attacks using appropriate methods require us to enrich the simple one-cone model, not to discard it. ["Give it a chance". in the words of Adrian Wood. See Wood (1994a)]. The model needs to include especially technological differences, home bias, and multiple cones of diversification. After allowing for these factors, there appears to be a substantial effect of relative factor abundance on the commodity composition of trade. Of course, not all of international trade can be explained without reference to economies of scale and product differentiation, subjects to which we now turn.

4. Models with monopolistic competition

The intellectual life cycle of a trade theory typically begins with an elegant theory and only in adulthood (or senility) is the theory examined empirically. The intellectual life of the theory of international trade with monopolistic competition is an exception to this pattern. Empirical work came *first*. Grubel and Lloyd (1975) noted that when inspecting trade flows, a significant amount of international trade was within industry classifications. Their work did not include a formal theory. In terms of evidence, though, their data appendix gave measures of intra-industry trade for a broad array of two-digit industries.

The index of intra-industry trade they used, since coined the Grubel–Lloyd index is given by:

$$IIT_{ijk} = \frac{2 \min (X_{ijk}, X_{ikj})}{(X_{ijk} + X_{ikj})},$$

where i indexes the industry, and j and k index countries. Exports of i from j to k are denoted by X_{ijk}. This index has the appealing property that it varies from zero (no intra-industry trade) to one (all intra-industry trade). Some of the first empirical work dealt with whether the existence of intra-industry trade, as evidenced by the Grubel–Lloyd index, is really inconsistent with more traditional endowments-based motivations for trade. Grubel and Lloyd themselves noted that goods that are homogeneous with respect to production and consumption may still be differentiated by either location or by time. The former gives rise to border trade while the latter gives rise to seasonal trade. Trade in these goods will be measured as intra-industry trade even though such trade is not really inconsistent with an endowments-based story.

Finger (1975) has argued that intra-industry trade is a figment of the data classification. At the highest level of aggregation (one commodity), this is tautologically true. Regardless, the phenomenon (real or data-induced) stimulated much empirical work. This work did not take the theory "seriously" since there was, in the late 1970's, no formal theory. Instead, this work searches for correlates and partial correlates of an index of intra-industry trade.

A representative empirical study of this sort is Loertscher and Wolter (1980). They note that the following hypotheses *seem warranted* (our italics.) Intra-industry trade between countries should be intense if:

(1) the average of their level of development is high;
(2) the difference in their levels of development is relatively small;
(3) the average of their GDP's is large;
(4) the difference in their GDP's is small;
(5) barriers to trade are low. Intra-industry trade in an industry should be intense if:
(6) the potential for product differentiation is high and market entry in narrow product lines is impeded by significant barriers;
(7) transactions costs are low;
(8) the definition of an industry is comprehensive.

Loertscher and Wolter then construct proxies for each of these phenomena. For example, per capita GDP proxies for level of development, a distance variable and customs union dummy variable proxy for barriers to trade, and the number of 4-digit classifications within a 3-digit classification proxies for how comprehensive an industry definition is. Using these proxies, Loertscher and Wolter run ordinary least squares multiple regressions with these regressors using a cross-section of 3-digit SITC data from OECD countries. The indepen-

Table 4.1
Country- and industry-specific determinants of intra-industry trade
OECD countries, cross-section 1972/73 averages

	Sign of Estimate	t^2 value
Country-specific variables		
Development stage differential	(−)	47.95
Average development stage	(+)	1.68
Market size differential	(−)	82.71
Average market size	(+)	108.71
Distance	(−)	44.52
Customs union dummy	(+)	64.89
Language group dummy	(+)	6.43
Border trade dummy	(+)	20.41
Cultural group dummy	(−)	0.01
Industry specific variables		
Product differentiation	(+)	0.45
Scale economies	(−)	91.23
Transactions costs	(−)	3.71
Level of aggregation	(+)	3.05
Product group	(+)	5.56

Adjusted $R^2 = 0.072$, and 6975 degrees of freedom.
Source: Loertscher and Wolter (1980)

dent variable is one of two arbitrary but reasonable indexes of intra-industry trade. (They do not use the Grubel–Lloyd index.) Their results are reproduced in Table 4.1. Some of the signs of the coefficients make intuitive sense were they simple correlation coefficients. For example, the regression indicates that countries that are closer to their trading partners and that have similar incomes experience more intra-industry trade. Other coefficients, such as that on scale economies, are counter-intuitive.

Loertscher and Wolter note that

> The equation presented (in the above table) is the best fit estimate of both linear and logarithmic formulations of the exogenous variables, chosen from those equations which yielded a maximum number of significant coefficients.

This kind of specification searching is characteristic of the empirical literature on monopolistic competition. [See, for example, Caves and Jones (1981), and Balassa (1986a)]. There are several important problems with this approach.

First, authors in this literature frequently tell a fairly convincing story about why, for example, scale economies might be positively correlated with intra-industry trade. They also can tell a similarly convincing story about why a customs union dummy variable might be positively correlated with intra-industry trade and a market size differential negatively correlated. These stories argue for empirical work that computes simple correlations. What none of the authors do, though, is tell a convincing story about why, for example, in the presence of a customs union and scale economies, increasing the size differential between trading partners will also increase intra-industry trade. Yet it is these partial correlations, conditional on the other included regressors, that these studies always estimate.

Second, the "kitchen-sink" attitude toward the choice of variables makes the list of possibilities very long and the extensive data-mining that is used to prune this long list makes the final estimates highly suspect. Even after all the mining, the R^2 typically is very small. With an R^2 as small as the one reported in Table 4.1, the *signs* of the (precisely estimated) coefficients are not very robust to measurement error adjustments. See Klepper and Leamer (1984) for relevant bounds tests.

Third, it is often difficult to find an observable that closely measures the hypothetical construct stipulated by the theory. For example, Loertscher and Wolter measured "the potential for large scale production" by value added per establishment. But it is not obvious what this has to do with the fixed costs and differentiated products that are the bases for models of intra-industry trade.

Fourth, in many of these studies, the variation in the data is cross-industry, yet we believe that studies that combine data from many industries are suspect, since the theoretical underpinnings of these studies are often quite weak. Economists would (or at least, should) distrust estimates of a price elasticity of demand based on observations of price and quantity collected from many industries. Some of this distrust ought to carry over to the cross-industry studies patterns of trade.

Clearly, here is a setting that could stand a good dose of economic theory. Krugman's theoretical paper on monopolistic competition and international trade [Krugman (1979) and the ensuing work by Helpman and Krugman (1985)], represent a step in the right direction, but these simple models do not really help much in studying the impact of scale economies and product differentiation on trade. Most empirical work continued to compute correlates of indexes of intra-industry trade with each trying to medal a competition for the highest R^2. Balassa (1986b) took the gold medal with an $R^2 = 0.999$ using cross-industry U.S. data and 15 regressors. We note that one regressor which always shows up very significantly in these studies is distance. (We expand on this in Section 6 below.)

One of the first studies that attempted to make a formal link between theory and data was Helpman (1987). In this paper, Helpman examines three hypotheses that emerge from theoretical models of monopolistic competition using OECD data spanning 1956 to 1981. Helpman's first empirical test concerns the volume of trade in a model in which all trade is, by assumption, intra-industry trade. Neglecting a correction for trade imbalances (which does not change any of the empirical results), Helpman defines an index of size similarity for a group (I) of trading partners. This index is given by:

$$\text{SIMILARITY}_I = 1 - \sum_{j \in I}(s_j)^2$$

where s_j is country j's share of group I's GDP. If all GDP originates from a single country, this index takes on the value 0. It is maximized when all countries are equal in size. Total intra-group trade (which by assumption is also intra-industry trade) is defined as

$$V_I = \sum_{i \neq j} X_{ij}$$

where X_{ij} is the value of exports from i to j. Helpman's theoretical model implies that trade increases with SIMILARITY:

$$\frac{V_I}{\text{GNP}_I} = \frac{\text{GNP}_I}{\text{GNP}_{\text{world}}} * \text{SIMILIARTY}.$$

Helpman computes the right-hand and left-hand side of this equation for the OECD for each of the 26 years in his sample. He graphs these and finds that the theory is supported in that both the volume of trade and the measure of size similarity increased over time together.

What is being summarized in this complicated way are two simple facts. First, trade has recently increased more rapidly than GDP for the OECD countries. Second, the U.S. share of OECD GDP has fallen substantially, and thus the U.S. size is more similar to other OECD countries. While these facts are compatible with a model of monopolistic competition, they are also compatible with many other models, specifically any model with an "Armington" demand side in which goods are differentiated by country of origin. But even a standard H–O model with homogeneous commodities produces the result that the trade volume is low if most of the world's GDP originates in a single country.

Helpman's first "test" is based on a structural equation from a model in which all trade is intra-industry. His other "tests" are based on a model in which some trade is intra-industry and some trade is endowments-based. The hypotheses that he studies concern the share of total trade that is intra-industry trade. While he does not derive a structural equation from the theory, he reports that his theory "suggests" (the same word as Loertscher and Wolter!!) that: "The share of intra-industry trade in bilateral trade flows should be larger for countries with similar incomes per capita". Helpman calculates bilateral intra-industry trade as the Grubel–Lloyd index given above. For each year from 1970–1981, this measure of intra-industry trade is regressed on:

$$X_1 = \ln | (\text{GDP}_i/\text{POP}_i) - (\text{GDP}_j/\text{POP}_j) |,$$

$$X_2 = \min(\ln(\text{GDP}_i), \ln(\text{GDP}_j)),$$
$$X_3 = \max(\ln(\text{GDP}_i), \ln(\text{GDP}_j)),$$

The inclusion of X_1 as a regressor is robust to several theoretical specifications, while the min and max GDP variables are less so. The intuition behind including the difference in per-capita GDP's is fairly straightforward. This variable is proxying for differences in relative factor endowments and the proxy is exact when there are only two factors. If two countries have identical relative endowments, there is no role for endowments based (Heckscher–Ohlin) trade, and all trade is intra-industry trade. Hence theory suggests that the coefficient on X_1 is negative. Helpman runs this regression separately for each of the 12 years of his data and finds that the coefficient on X_1 is negative although the precision of the estimate declines steadily over the sample years. By the end of the sample, the R^2 has fallen from 0.266 to 0.039. The coefficient on X_2 is positive and usually precisely estimated while that on X_3 is negative and less precisely estimated. The signs are those suggested by the theories of monopolistic competition that Helpman considers.

A second set of regressions reported by Helpman separates GDP size from GDP similarity and confirms that both seem to contribute positively to intra-industry trade.

Helpman, like Loertscher and Wolter, concludes that the theory finds some support in the data. But there is clearly a lot that needs to be done. We need to know how much of the results are due to tastes and how much to monopolistic competition. It would also be interesting to know which industries are "Heckscher–Ohlin" and which are "Chamberlinian". How much of trade is due to economies of scale and how much to factor supply differences? What does this imply about policy?

Hummels and Levinsohn (1993, 1994) follow up on Helpman's paper. They use country-pairs, instead of the entire OECD, as their unit of observation, and instead of estimating each year as a separate regression, they employ standard panel data econometric techniques (fixed and random effects for country pairs). They report two main results.

First, the model in which all trade is, by assumption, intra-industry trade and trade volume within a group depends on the size similarity of the countries comprising the group finds support for both an OECD data set (like in Helpman's) and for a data set in which a model of monopolistic competition is ex ante inappropriate. The latter data set comprises a random selection of developed and developing countries distributed across the globe. Hummels and Levinsohn conclude that perhaps something other than monopolistic competition is generating the empirical success of the estimating equation.

Second, the estimating equation in which the share of trade that is intra-industry trade is explained by the differences in log per capita GDP is less robust to standard panel data estimation. Hummels and Levinsohn use OECD data from 1962 to 1983. Organizing the data so that each country pair in a given year constitutes an observation, they first (successfully) replicate Helpman's tests. They then demonstrate that when fixed (or random) effects estimators are used, thereby accounting for non-independence in the residual within country pairs but over time, and when one instruments for the endogeneity of GDP, the results disappear and the theory finds little support in the data. They conclude by noting that most of the variation in intra-industry trade is explained by factors idiosyncratic to country pairs. Residual analysis also leads them to suspect that distance and multinational corporations may be empirically important variables that do not enter the theory.

Harrigan (1992) also estimates an equation purporting to explain bilateral trade volumes in a model of monopolistic competition. He conducts a residual analysis to examine which countries are outliers. He finds that, within the OECD, the European Union countries engage in more trade than is predicted by the model, while the U.S. and Japan engage in much less than is predicted by the model.

In Helpman, Hummels and Levinsohn, and Harrigan, it is unclear why countries like the U.S. and Japan are often outliers, with much less intra-industry trade than the model predicts, while bordering EC countries often have the most intra-industry trade. Their methods do not separately identify the often empirically collinear effects of customs unions and distance. For example, do Belgium and the Netherlands have a lot of intra-industry trade because they are close to one another or because of special trade policies?

These recent studies demonstrate a tension in this literature. The authors refrain from tossing in whatever regressors seem like they *ought* to matter. Yet, when one examines why the estimating equation does not fit the data very well, one is tempted to move in that direction. These studies are helpful, though, for they are beginning to demonstrate where the theory, taken seriously, needs amendments. With modified theory, new empirical work will surely follow.

Models with monopolistic competition motivating intra-industry trade *and* factor endowments motivating traditional trade have also been most recently examined. One study [Harrigan (1993)] focuses on what such a model implies about trade in intermediate goods. Another [Brainard (1993a,b)] focuses on what the model implies about multinational corporations. Each are briefly discussed in turn.

Harrigan begins by noting that an implication of the Helpman and Krugman (1985) model, in which some trade is intra-industry and the rest is endowments-based, is that gross import volumes do not depend on the importing country's relative factor endowments, although net industry trade balances are influenced by factor endowments. This result, though, is only correct when the differentiated products are for final consumption by variety-loving consumers. If the

differentiated products are used as intermediate inputs by final goods producers, the volume of gross imports will depend on the industrial structure of the
importing country. Taking his theory carefully into account, Harrigan finds that
his model – in which the bilateral volume of trade in manufactures depends on
the structure of the importing country's industrial sector – is rejected by the
data. Instead, simpler models of monopolistic competition in final goods such
as the above mentioned papers by Helpman, Levinsohn and Hummels, and
Harrigan better explain the data.

Brainard notes that different theories of international trade have different
implications for how multinational corporations behave. She writes that "the
same tests on intra-industry trade ratios and total volumes that were used to
demonstrate that a substantial part of trade is explained by factor and income
similarities rather than differences" [Brainard (1993a, p. 1)] can be applied to
tests of multinational trade. In particular, she asks whether a factor proportions
view of the world can explain the location patterns of U.S. multinational firms.
In the factor proportions model, multinational firms arise because factor price
equalization does not obtain. The factor price differences arise due to large variations in relative factor endowments. Firms move to take advantage of the lower
factor prices abroad and then re-export to their home country. An alternative
to the factor-proportions model posits locational advantages in terms of proximity to customers. This advantage to multi-nationalization is balanced against
the benefits of scale economies that are realized when all production is in the
home country. This model, in contrast to the factor proportions model, implies
that the firms will not export back to their home countries. Using industry-level
data on inter-affiliate sales by U.S. multinationals, Brainard investigates these
hypotheses. She finds that (p. 25) "Overall, the evidence suggests that only a
small part of multinational activity into and out of the U.S. in the late 1980's
can be explained by factor proportions differences". Rather, the same variables
measuring similarity among trading partners [similarity in per capita GDP as in
Helpman (1987), for example] that have been used in empirical studies of intra-
industry trade also explain the volume of inter-affiliate trade reasonably well.
She also finds that trade flows and multinational sales differ in their response
to trade barriers and transport costs.

5. Demand-side explanations for international trade

International trade is determined by both international patterns of production
and consumption. Most of the theoretical literature in international economics
concentrates on the production side and often uses assumptions that neutralize demand as a determinant of the composition of trade. From a theoretical
vantage point, the studies of the effect of demand on trade are somewhat self-

limiting. After all, one could impose assumptions that neutralized differences in technologies or endowments and tautologically explain all trade flows as reflecting differences in tastes. Still, while differences in tastes might not be all that theoretically exciting, they might nonetheless be empirically important.

Linder (1961) was one of the first to argue that demand played a role in determining trade patterns. While Linder did not have a formal model, he had a compelling story. Linder argued that countries with similar demand structures would develop similar sets of goods, first for home consumption and later for export. The resulting trade would look like intra-industry trade. If per-capita income, though, is a good gauge for demand, countries with similar and sufficiently high incomes will engage in a lot of (intra-industry) trade. This is usually interpreted to mean that the intensity of bilateral trade decreases with differences in per capita income. The Heckscher–Ohlin model, on the other hand, "suggests" the reverse association because countries with substantially different per capita incomes are "likely" to have different resource endowments, offer different baskets of goods for trade and therefore become trading partners.

Most of the theoretical work in traditional trade theory deals with the commodity composition of trade, not the partner composition. The Linder hypothesis has traditionally been interpreted in terms of its implications for partner composition by including a measure of similarity of per capita GNP's in "gravity equations" that explain bilateral trade. For an example of work in this vein that builds a rigorous economic model, as opposed to just a compelling story, see Bergstrand (1985).

An interesting example of a gravity model is estimated by Hoftyzer (1984) who attempts to explain the 1970 bilateral trade of each of eleven importers using data for fifty eight exporters. The Linder hypothesis is interpreted to mean that the dissimilarity of countries as measured by the difference in per capita incomes will lower the intensity of trade. In other words, the coefficient on differences in per capita income between trading partners should be negative. Hoftyzer finds otherwise, in the sense that the estimated coefficient is positive for most countries. This contrasts with some more supportive results by other authors, which Hoftyzer argues are due to their failure to control for border effects and membership in free trade associations and their failure to consider other functional forms, as he does by means of a Box–Cox analysis.

Even though the theoretical foundation is murky, the findings of Hoftyzer seem to us to be unsettling to the Linder viewpoint. According to Hoftyzer, trade may seem intense between similar countries, but that can be explained by the fact that they are neighbors and/or members of free trade associations. Moreover whatever relationship does exist, it is probably not log-linear. The idea that distance between trading partners may matter for bilateral trading patterns is taken up in the next section.

A different approach to investigating the effects of demand on trade is adopted by Hunter and Markusen (1988). Hunter and Markusen note that if one allows completely general preferences, then one can always estimate taste parameters consistent with any pattern of trade. Therefore, the research is forced to impose some structure on the problem. Hunter and Markusen adopt the Linear Expenditure System (LES) while maintaining the assumption of identical preferences across countries. They relax, though, the assumption of homotheticity. In this way, per capita income plays a role in determining the pattern of trade. Hunter and Markusen estimate the LES using data on eleven types of expenditures and deflators culled from the Penn World Tables. They then pose the following thought experiment. Suppose all countries had identical relative endowments and technologies, hence removing the basis for inter-industry trade. Based solely on differences in per-capita income, how much trade would take place? Their answer to this counter-factual is about 14 percent of observed trade.

6. International trade and distance between partners

What about proximity as a source of comparative advantage? At one level of consciousness, economists have long been aware of the impact of distance on the patterns of international commerce. Some of the earliest empirical studies in international trade were Beckerman (1956) with his studies of intra-European trade flows, and Poyhonen (1963), Tinbergen (1962) and Linnemann (1966) who estimated "gravity" models.

A gravity model is a typically log-linear relationship expressing bilateral trade between a pair of countries as a function of the two countries' income levels, populations, and distance. Typically included also are an adjacency dummy, a common language dummy, and dummies for commercial preferences such as the EEC and the British Commonwealth. Tariffs and transportation costs are sometimes explicitly included, but data on these variables are sometimes difficult to obtain. These gravity models are usually estimated for total trade, but Frankel (1991) does some disaggregation and Leamer (1993a) studies 3-digit ISIC data from OECD countries. These and many subsequent studies have found a distance elasticity of about −0.6.

These estimates of gravity models have been both singularly successful and singularly unsuccessful. They have produced some of the clearest and most robust empirical findings in economics. But, paradoxically, they have had virtually no affect on the subject of international economics.[12] Textbooks continue to be written and courses designed without any explicit reference to distance, but with

---

[12] A possible exception is the rebirth of interest in economic geography which is discussed briefly below.

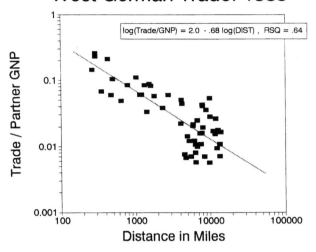

Figure 6.1.

the very strange implicit assumption that countries are both infinitely far apart and infinitely close, the former referring to factors and the latter to commodities.

Why don't trade economists "admit" the effect of distance into their thinking? How can this obvious conflict between fact and theory continue? These questions have several possible answers. One is that human beings are not disposed toward processing numbers, and empirical results will remain unpersuasive if not accompanied by a graph. As a step toward remedying this potential problem, we include Figure 6.1 from Leamer (1993a), which is a scatter diagram illustrating the relationship between distance and West Germany's volume of bilateral trade in 1985.

On the vertical axis is total trade (exports plus imports) scaled by partner GDP. On the horizontal is the distance to the partner's geographic center. Both scales are logarithmic. The figure shows, clear as day, that distance matters, and it matters a lot!

Another possible explanation for their limited influence is that gravity models and international economics have separate intellectual domains. Gravity models are usually concerned with the total trade between pairs of countries, whereas the subject of international economics is concerned with the trade of a country vis-à-vis the world, and has little to say about the choice of its trading partners. While there is some truth to this, there is more intellectual overlap than is apparent. Geographic size and geographic isolation can affect both the total trade of a country and also the composition of that trade. Countries like the

United States that form large geographic areas have much of their economic mass far from their borders, and they are accordingly much less dependent on trade than smaller countries. Small Asian countries that are far from the economic mass in either Europe or North America specialize in products that travel well over long distances. In contrast, the countries of Europe have a mutual comparative advantage over Asia in the European marketplace in those commodities that do not travel well. To give a hint what these commodities are, Table 6.1 contains the percent of trade in 2-digit ISIC categories that occurs between adjacent countries. At the top of the list are wood and paper products which do not travel well. Near the bottom are wearing apparel and footwear, which do travel relatively well.

A third possible explanation for the lack of influence is the very weak link

Table 6.1
Percent of trade between adjacent countries
OECD countries

	1970	1985	Ratio
TOTAL	30.6	27.6	0.90
Wood	32.7	42.4	1.30
Printing and publishing	40.4	41.0	1.02
Paper and paper products	35.9	37.7	1.05
Furniture	50.9	37.3	0.73
Transport equipment	41.1	36.8	0.90
Misc. petroleum products	45.8	35.7	0.78
Glass and glass products	37.1	34.4	0.93
Other non-metallic minerals	39.5	33.9	0.86
Metal scrap	31.8	33.2	1.04
Other food	31.7	32.5	1.03
Fabricated metal products	34.6	32.3	0.94
Rubber products	34.1	31.9	0.94
Plastic products	32.4	30.1	0.93
Non-ferrous metal basic ind.	26.7	28.9	1.09
Industrial chemicals	27.9	27.8	1.00
Iron and steel basic ind.	33.2	26.1	0.79
Textiles	30.3	25.3	0.84
Food manufacturing	19.6	23.5	1.20
Beverage	26.9	23.2	0.86
Other chemicals	24.7	23.1	0.93
Petroleum refineries	18.2	22.9	1.26
Machinery except electric	27.7	21.8	0.79
Tobacco	22.2	20.0	0.90
Pottery, china, and earthware	21.9	19.0	0.86
Elec. machinery	25.2	18.9	0.75
Wearing apparel	28.6	18.8	0.66
Leather	26.5	16.9	0.64
Footwear	17.7	16.4	0.93
Prof., scientific, and measuring	23.4	16.4	0.70
Other manufacturing industries	14.8	12.4	0.84

Note: Includes only trade flows with at least one OECD partner.

between theory and the empirical work. The gravity models are strictly descriptive. They lack a theoretical underpinning so that once the facts are out, it is not clear what to make of them.[13] In addition, they do not link clearly with any issues: For example, the basic proposition that free trade is beneficial doesn't seem obviously at risk if distance is added to the model, so why bother? But the clarity of the empirical findings and the absence of distance in the standard theory creates a degree of professional tension that needs to be remedied by a much closer association of the descriptive gravity models with the theory and with the issues of international economics. Furthermore, once we admit distance between countries into our theories, it begs the question: what about the role of distance within them?

The impact of the EEC on trade was one source of issues on which gravity models were first focussed [e.g. Aitken (1973)]. More recently, interest in regional trading blocs is generating a new flurry of gravity models offered by Frankel and others [e.g. Frankel and Wei 1993), Frankel, Stein, and Wei (1994), Frankel and Wei (1994), Leamer (1993), and Losada (1993)]. At the theory level, Krugman (1991) has made an effort to bring to the attention of international economists the substantial body of work by economic geographers. This work, though, typically focuses on issues such as path dependence and agglomeration economies – issues that may be more important to where a firm locates than to which countries it trades with. Krugman's work on geography is somewhat more subtle than the "look at a map" notion of distance that we are thinking about. Rauch (1990) has included geographic area as a determinant of trade dependence in a theory supported by evidence. Trefler (1994), in a very promising development, has successfully allowed for "home bias" in a Heckscher–Ohlin based study of net trade in factor services, a' la Bowen, Leamer, and Sviekauskaus (1987). Although Trefler doesn't do so, it seems appropriate to link home bias with distance. Hummels and Levinsohn (1993) also experiment with distance as an explanation for why a Helpman–Krugman model of intra-industry trade and endowments-based trade fits the data so poorly. They too find that distance matters very much.

Finally, it seem appropriate to mention that the effect of distance on trade patterns is not diminishing over time. Contrary to popular impression, the world is not getting dramatically smaller. You can see this a bit in the figures in the last column of Table 6.1, which reports the 1985 adjacency shares divided by the 1970 adjacency shares. The share of trade between adjacent countries did decline overall from 30.6 to 27.6 percent, but there are plenty of commodities for which the adjacency share increased. More to the point, Leamer's (1993) estimated distance elasticities in 1985 are not dramatically smaller than the 1970

---

[13] An attempt to give a theoretical foundation by Anderson (1979) is formally fruitful but seems too complex to be part of our everyday toolkit.

elasticity. How can this be so? We know that there has been a large increase in trade across the Pacific and the Atlantic? Why isn't this picked up by a declining effect of distance in the gravity models? The answer is that the gravity models account for economic size as well as for distance. This model predicts that the smallest amount of world trade occurs when most of the world's GDP originates in one country (e.g. the U.S.). As the U.S. share of world GDP has declined, this implies an increase in the volume of trade relative to world GDP, even though the effect of distance remains exactly the same. Indeed the increased trade across the oceans is almost fully explainable by the increase in the economic sizes of Europe and Asia. Thus, dispersion of economic mass is the answer, not a shrinking globe.[14]

Appendix: Data sources

In this appendix, we discuss some important sources for the sort of data international microeconomists might find helpful. While a complete compendium of actual and potential data sources is beyond the scope of this review, hopefully researchers will find even a brief review somewhat useful. Incidentally, Maskus (1991) is a very useful source of information on measurement problems with international data.

The most used data source on international trade flows is probably the United Nations Trade Data Tapes. This data base provides bilateral trade flows at the 4 and/or 5 digit SITC level. There are a few minor problems with this data and one major problem. The minor problems include the use of SITC industry codes, while much other international data uses the ISIC industry codes, and the fact that imports reported by one country for a particular good frequently do not match the exports reported by the partner country for the same good. (There are concordances to deal with the former problem.) The more major problem is that the United Nations makes these data prohibitively expensive for most academic users. While prices vary depending on the restrictions attached to the use of the data and the amount of data ordered, one can easily spend over $100,000 on this data! A potentially very helpful solution to this problem is being provided by Statistics Canada. This agency has recompiled the U.N. trade data tapes, reconciled the import versus export inconsistencies, and aggregated commodities into about 600 groups (by SITC code). The entire world bilateral trade flows for 1980 to 1992 are available on CD-ROM from Statistics Canada for prices ranging from about $1750 to under $8000, with the actual price depending on how many users have access to the data (LAN connections) and whether one is an academic user (this carries a 50 percent discount). (These

---

[14]But see Boisso and Ferrantino (1993) for a contrary opinion that reports very large and declining distance elasticities.

prices are as of 1994 and are sure to change, but the general point is that the U.N. trade data are becoming much more available at a fraction of the U.N.'s price.) For more information, fax Statistics Canada at (613) 951-0117.

The Statistical Yearbook of the United Nations is available on CD-ROM. This data base is a comprehensive description of the world economy. The U.N. Publications telephone number in the U.S. is (800) 253-9646.

Highly detailed information regarding the current structure of U.S. trade, by commodity and by partner, as well as a host of other information, is distributed on CD-ROM by the U.S. Department of Commerce for an extraordinarily nominal fee. For more information on this National Trade Data Base call the help line at (202) 377-1986.

The OECD STAN DATABASE has production, value added, gross fixed capital formation, laborers engaged, labor compensation and exports and imports for 49 two-digit ISIC sectors from 1970–1991 available on diskette for $290. Information on ordering this data set is available by calling (33-1) 49 10 42 65 in Paris.

Data on endowments are available from several sources. Labor data is available from either the International Labor Office (ILO) publication *Yearbook of Labor Statistics* or from the World Bank's World Tables. (The latter are available on diskette, tel: (202) 473-1155.) Land endowments are available from the Food and Agricultural Organization (FAO) publication *Production Yearbook*. Capital stock data are not as readily obtained, but one series used by many researchers is that contained in the Penn World Tables. This data base is available free over the internet. (Details on how to explore the internet for trade data are provided below.)

Input–output tables for the United States are made available by the Commerce Department and are found in the *Survey of Current Business*. They are also available on diskette.

Data on trade and labor by industry for the United States are also found in the National Bureau of Economic Research (NBER) Trade and Immigration data set. This data set contains trade, employment and output data for 450 U.S. manufacturing industries by 4-digit SIC code from 1958–86. Variables include employment, unionization, import, exports, firm size, industry concentration as well as many other related data. This data set is free and is available on the internet. Most economics gophers can point one to this data. (A specific address is given below.)

Data on tariffs and non-tariff barriers are compiled by the GATT and UNCTAD. UNCTAD produces the TNT data base. This data base provides nominal tariff rates by harmonized tariff code as well as non-tariff measures. The nontariff measure available is a weighted coverage ratio, where the weights used are trade values. This data is available from UNCTAD in Geneva for a few thousand dollars.

The U.S. Bureau of Labor Statistics maintains a fairly comprehensive data base on import and export price indexes for U.S. industries by SIC code. These data are free in hard copy or available on diskette for a nominal fee. The data are used in many of the studies investigating the effects of import competition on domestic wages and employment.

One very rich data set that has not been exploited much (if at all) by trade economists is the U.S. Census' Annual Survey of Manufacturers. This annual data set comprises detailed plant-level information on tens of thousands of U.S. manufacturing plants. Recent empirical work in Industrial Organization and in Labor economics has made fruitful use of these data, and international economists would probably also find them very useful. The data, though, are not especially easy to use, since one has to obtain approval from the Census Bureau and all work must be conducted at their facility in Suitland, Maryland (although a new branch will soon open in Boston).

There are many other data sources that the empirical researcher in international trade may find useful. One way to search these resources is via one of the economics gophers on the internet. There are several, but a good starting point is Hal Varian's gopher. The address is: http://gopher.econ.lsa.umich.edu.

References

Aitken, N.D. (1973), "The effect of the EEC and EFTA on European trade: A temporal cross-section analysis", American Economic Review, 63:881–892.

Arrow, K., B.M.H. Chenery, and R. Solow (1961), "Capital-labor substitution and economic efficiency", Review of Economics and Statistics, 43:225–251.

Balassa, B. (1963), "An empirical demonstration of classical comparative cost theory", Review of Economics and Statistics, 45.

Balassa, B. (1986a), "Comparative advantage in manufactured goods: A reappraisal", Review of Economics and Statistics, 68(2):315–319.

Balassa, B. (1986b), "The determinants of intra-industry specialization in U.S. trade", Oxford Economic Papers, 38(2):220–233.

Baldwin, R. and G. Cain (1994), "Trade and U.S. relative wages: Preliminary results", University of Wisconsin Working Paper.

Baldwin, R.E. (1971), "Determinants of the commodity structure of U.S. trade", American Economic Review, 61:126–146.

Baldwin, R.E. and R.S. Hilton (1983), "A technique for indicating comparative costs and predicting changes in trade ratios", Review of Economics and Statistics, 105–110.

Beckerman, W. (1956), "Distance and the pattern of intra-European trade", Review of Economics and Statistics, 38.

Bergstrand, J.H. (1985), "The gravity equation in international trade: Some microeconomic foundations and empirical evidence", Review of Economics and Statistics, 67(3):474–481.

Boisso, D. and M. Ferrantino (1993), "Is the world getting smaller? A gravity export model for the whole planet, 1950–1988", Richard B. Johnson Center for Economic Studies, SMU, Working Paper No. 9225.

Borjas, G., R. Freeman, and L. Katz (1991), "On the labor market effects of immigration and trade", NBER Working Paper 3761.

Bound, J. and G. Johnson. (1992), "Changes in the structure of wages during the 1980's : An evaluation of alternative explanations", American Economic Review, 82:371–392.

Bowen, H.P., E.E. Leamer, and L. Sviekauskaus (1987), "Multicountry, multifactor tests of the factor abundance theory", American Economic Review, 77(5):791–801.

Bowen, H.P. and L. Sviekauskaus. (1992), "Multicountry, multifactor of the factor abundance theory", Quarterly Journal of Economics, 107(2):599–620.

Brainard, L.S. (1993a), "An empirical assessment of the factor proportions explanations of multinational sales", mimeo.

Brainard, L.S. (1993b), "An empirical assessment of the proximity/concentration tradeoff between multinational sales and trade", mimeo.

Brander, A. (1991), "Election polls, free trade, and the stock market: Evidence from the 1988 Canadian general election", Canadian Journal of Economics, 24:827–843.

Brecher, R.A. and E.U. Choudhri (1988), "The factor content of consumption in Canada and the United States : A two-country test of the Heckscher–Ohlin–Vanek model", in: R.C. Feenstra, ed., Empirical methods for international trade. (MIT Press, Cambridge, MA).

Brecher, R.A. and E.U. Choudhri (1982), "The Leontief paradox, continued", Journal of Political Economy, 90(4):820–823.

Card, D. (1990), "The impact of the Mariel boatlift on the Miami labor market", Industrial and Labor Relations Review, 43:245–257.

Caves, R.E. and R.W. Jones (1981), World trade and payments. (Little Brown, Boston).

Chenery, H.B. (1960), "Patterns of industrial growth", American Economic Review, I, 624–654.

Chenery, H.B. and M. Syrquin (1975), Patterns of development, 1950–1970 (Oxford University Press, Oxford).

Chenery, H.B. and L. Taylor (1968), "Development patterns: Among countries and over time", Review of Economics and Statistics, 50(4):391–416.

Chipman, J.S. (1977), "Towards the construction of an optimal aggregative model of international trade: West Germany, 1963–1975", Annals of Economic and Social Measurement, 5:535–554.

Deardorff, A. (1984), "Testing trade theories and predicting trade flows", in: R.W. Kenen and P.B. Jones, eds., Handbook of international economics, vol 1. (North-Holland, Amsterdam).

Deardorff, A. (1994), "An overview of the Stolper–Samuelson theorem", in: A.V. Deardorff, and R.M. Stern, eds., The Stolper–Samuelson theorem: A golden jubilee. (The University of Michigan Press, Ann Arbor).

Deardorff, A. and R. Staiger (1988), "An interpretation of the factor content of trade", Journal of International Economics, 24:93–107.

Deardorff, A.V. and D. Hakura (1993), "Trade and wages: What are the questions?", mimeo.

Deaton, A. (1992), Understanding consumption. (Claredon Press, Oxford).

Dixit, A. and V. Norman (1986), "The gains from trade without lump-sum compensation", Journal of International Economics, 21(1):111–122.

Dollar, D., W. Baumol, and E. Wolff (1988), "The factor price equalization model and industry labor productivity: An empirical test across countries", in: R. Feenstra, ed., Empirical methods for international trade. (MIT Press Cambridge, MA).

Ethier, W.J. (1984), "Higher dimensional issues in trade theory", in: R.W. Kenen, and P.B. Jones, eds., Handbook of international economics, vol. 1. (North-Holland, Amsterdam).

Feldstein, M. and C. Horioka (1980), "Domestic savings and international capital flows", Economic Journal, 90:314–329.

Finger, J.M. (1975), "A new view of the product cycle theory", Weltwirtshaftliches Archiv, 79–99.

Frankel, J. (1991), "Is a Yen bloc forming in Pacific Asia", in: R. Brien, ed., Finance and the international economy. (Oxford University Press, Oxford).

Frankel, J., E. Stein, and S. Wei (1994), "Trading blocs: The natural, the unnatural and the supernatural", Journal of Development Economics.

Frankel, J. and S. Wei (1993), "Trade blocks and currency blocks", NBER Working Paper No. 4335.

Frankel, J. and S. Wei (1994), "Is there a currency bloc on the Pacific", in: A. Wignall and S. Grenville eds., Exchange rates, international trade, and monetary policy. (Reserve Bank of Australia, Sydney).

Freeman, R.B. and F.K. Lawrence (1991), "Industrial wage and employment determination in an open economy", in: M.A. John, and R.B. Freeman, eds., Immigration, trade and the labor market (University of Chicago Press, Chicago).

Grossman, G.M. (1987), "The employment and wage effects of import competition in the U.S.", Journal of International Economic Integration, 2, 1–23.

Grossman, G.M. and J.A. Levinsohn (1989), "Import competition and the stock market return to capital", American Economic Review, 198:1065–1087.

Grubel, H.G. and P.J. Lloyd (1975), Intra industry trade. (Macmillan, UK).

Harrigan, J. (1992), "Openness to trade in manufactures in the OECD", mimeo.

Harrigan, J. (1993), "The volume of trade in differentiated intermediate goods: Theory and evidence", Forthcoming in 1995 in Journal of International Economics.

Hatton, T. and J.G. Williamson (1992), "International migration and world development: A historical perspective", DAE Working Paper 41.

Helpman, E. (1987), "Imperfect competition and international trade: Evidence from fourteen industrialised countries", Journal of the Japanese and International Economies, 1.

Helpman, E. and P.R. Krugman (1985), Market structure and foreign trade: Increasing returns, imperfect competition, and the international economy (MIT Press, Cambridge, MA).

Hoftyzer, J. (1984), "A further analysis of the Linder trade thesis", Quarterly Review of Economics and Business, 24(2), 57–90.

Hufbauer, G.C. (1970), "The impact of national characteristics and technology on the commodity composition of trade in manufactured goods", in: R. Vernon, ed., The technology factor in international trade (Columbia University Press, New York).

Hummels, D. and J. Levinsohn (1993), "Product differentiation as a source of comparative advantage?", American Economic Review, 83:445–489.

Hummels, D. and J. Levinsohn (1994), "Monopolistic competition and international trade: Reconsidering the evidence", Forthcoming in Quarterly Journal of Economics.

Hunter, L. and J. Markusen (1988), "Per capita income as a determinant of trade", in: R.C. Feenstra, ed., Empirical methods for international trade. (MIT Press, Cambridge, MA).

Katz, L. and K.M. Murphy (1992), "Changes in relative wages, 1963–1987: Supply and demand factors", Quarterly Journal of Economics, 107:35–78.

Keesing, D.B. (1966), "Labor skills and comparative advantage", American Economic Review, 56(2):249–258.

Klepper, S. and E.E. Leamer (1984), "Consistent sets of estimates for regression with all variables measured with error", Econometrica, 52:163–183.

Kohli, U. (1991), Technology, duality, and foreign trade, (The University of Michigan Press, Ann Arbor).

Kohli, U. (1993), "U.S. technology and the specific factors model", Journal of International Economics, 34:115–136.

Krueger, A.O. (1968), "Factor endowments and per capita income differences among countries", Economic Journal, 78(311):641–659.

Krugman, P. (1979), "Increasing returns, monopolistic competition, and international trade". Journal of International Economics, 9(4):469–479.

Krugman, P.R. (1991), Geography and trade. (MIT Press, Cambridge, MA).

Lawrence, R.Z. and M.J. Slaughter (1980), "Trade and U.S. wages: Great sucking sound or small hiccup?", J.F.K. School, Harvard University, Faculty Research Working Paper Series.

Leamer, E. (1994), "Two-ness and the Stolper–Samuelson theorem", in: A.V. Deardorff and R.M. Stern, eds., The Stolper–Samuelson theorem: A golden jubilee (The University of Michigan Press, Ann Arbor).

Leamer, E.E. (1974), "The commodity composition of international trade in manufactures: An empirical analysis", Oxford Economic Papers, 26(3):350–374.

Leamer, E.E. (1980), "The Leontief paradox reconsidered", Journal of Political Economy, 88:495–503.

Leamer, E.E. (1984a), "Cross-section estimation of the effects of trade barriers", in: R.C. Feenstra, ed., Empirical methods for international trade (MIT Press, Cambridge, MA).

Leamer, E.E. (1984b), Sources of comparative advantage, theory and evidence (MIT Press, Cambridge, MA).

Leamer, E.E. (1987), "Theory and evidence of immigrant enclaves", mimeo.

Leamer, E.E. (1993a), "U.S. manufacturing and an emerging Mexico", North American Journal of Economics and Finance, 4, 51–89.

Leamer, E.E. (1993b), "Wage effects of a U.S.–Mexican free trade agreement", in: P.M. Garber, ed., The Mexico–U.S. free trade agreement, pp. 57–125. (MIT Press, Cambridge, MA).

Leamer, E.E. (1994), "Trade, wages and revolving door ideas", Working Paper No. 4716, April.

Leamer, E.E. and H.P. Bowen (1981), "Cross-section tests of the Heckscher–Ohlin theorem: Comment", American Economic Review, 71:1040–1043.

Leontief, W.W. (1953), "Domestic production and foreign trade: The American capital position re-examined", Proceedings of the American Philosophical Society, 97, 332–349.

Linder, S.B. (1961), An essay on trade and transformation (Wiley, New York).

Linnemann, H. (1966), An econometric study of international trade flows. (North-Holland, Amsterdam).

Loertscher, R. and F. Wolter (1980), "Determinants of intra-industry trade: Among countries and across countries", Weltwirtshaftliches Archiv, 116:280–293.

Losada, F. (1993), "Partners, neighbors, and distant cousins: Explaining bilateral trade flows in Latin America", Dissertation Paper.

MacDougall, G.D.A. (1951), "British and American exports: A study suggested by the theory of comparative costs, part I", Economic Journal, 61.

Magee, S.P. (1980), "Three simple tests of the Stolper–Samuelson theorem", in: P. Oppenheimer, ed., Issues in International Economics, pp. 138–151. (Oriel Press, Stocksfield, London).

Maskus, K. (1991), "Comparing international trade data and product and national characteristics data for the analysis of trade models", in P. Hooper and J. D. Richardson, eds., International economic transactions: Issues in measurement and empirical research, pp. 17–60. (University of Chicago Press, Chicago).

Minhas, B.S. (1962), "The homohypallagic production function, factor-intensity reversals, and the Heckscher–Ohlin theorem", Journal of Political Economy, 70:138–156.

Murphy, K.M. and F. Welch (1991), "The role of international trade in wage differentials", in: H.K. Marvin ed., Workers and their wages: Changing trade patterns in the U.S., pp. 39–69. (American Enterprise Institute Press, Washington, DC).

Murphy, K.M. and F. Welch (1992), "The structure of wages", Quarterly Journal of Economics, 107:285–326.

Mussa, M. (1974), "Tariffs and the distribution of income: The importance of factor specificity, substitutability and intensity in the short and long run", Journal of Political Economy, 82:1191–1204.

Neary, J.P. (1978), "Short-run capital specificity and the pure theory of international trade", Economic Journal, 88:488–510.

Ohlin, B. (1933), Interregional and international trade. (Harvard University Press, Cambridge).

Ohyama, M. (1972), "Trade and welfare in general equilibrium", Keio Economic Studies, 9:37–73.

O'Rourke, K. and J.G. Williamson (1992), "Were Heckscher and Ohlin right? Putting the factor-price-equalization theorem back into history", Harvard Institue of Economic Research Discussion Paper 1593.

Petri, R.A. (1991), "Market structure, comparative advantage, and Japanese trade", in: P.R. Krugman, ed., Trade with Japan: Has the door opened wider? (University of Chicago Press, Chicago).

Poyhonen, P. (1963), "A tentative model for the volume of trade between countries", Weltwirtshaftliches Archiv, 90:93–99.

Rassekh, F. and H. Thompson (1993), "Factor price equalization: Theory and evidence", Journal of International Economic Integration, 8(1), 1–32.

Rauch, J. (1990), "Comparative advantage, geographic advantage, and the volume of trade", NBER Working Paper No. 3512.

Revenga, A.L. (1992), "Exporting jobs: The impact of import competition and employment and wages in U.S. manufacturing", Quarterly Journal of Economics, 107:255–284.

Rogowski, R. (1987), "Political cleavages and changing exposure to trade", American Political Science Review, 81:1121–1137.

Samuelson, P.A. (1971), "An exact Hume–Ricardo–Marshall model of international trade", Journal of International Economics, 1:1–18.

Stern, R.M. and Maskus, K.E. (1981), "Determinants of U.S. foreign trade 1958-1976", Journal of International Economics, 11:207–224.

Tinbergen, J. (1962), Shaping the world economy: Suggestions for an international economic policy. (New York).

Trefler, D. (1993), "International factor price differences: Leontief was right!", Journal of Political Economy, 101(6):961–987.

Trefler, D. (1994), "The case of the missing trade and other HOV mysteries", University of Toronto, mimeo.

Vanek (1968), "The factor proportions theory: The N-factor case", Kyklos, 21(4):749–756.

Wood, A. (1994a), "Give Heckscher and Ohlin a chance!", Weltwirtschaftliches Archiv.

Wood, A. (1994b), North-South trade, employment and inequality: Changing fortunes in a skill-driven world. (Clarendon Press, Oxford).

Wright, G. (1990), "The origins of American industrial success, 1879–1940", American Economic Review, 80(4):650–668.

Chapter 27

STRATEGIC TRADE POLICY

JAMES A. BRANDER*

University of British Columbia

Contents

*I am grateful to Gene Grossman for inviting me to write this chapter and for his very helpful comments. In addition, I am very much indebted to Kyle Bagwell, Clive Chapple, David Collie, Murray Frank, Keith Head, Jota Ishikawa, Larry Qiu, Michael Rauscher, John Ries, Barbara Spencer, and Scott Taylor for their help. I also thank Avinash Dixit and Tony Venables (my two discussants), and other participants at the March 1994 Handbook Conference held at Princeton University.

Handbook of International Economics, vol. III, Edited by G. Grossman and K. Rogoff
© *Elsevier Science B.V., 1995*

1. Introduction

The meaning of the term "strategic trade policy" is not completely self-evident, and different researchers have used the term in slightly different ways. In this chapter I define strategic trade policy to be trade policy that conditions or alters a strategic relationship between firms. This definition implies that the existence of a strategic relationship between firms is a necessary precondition for the application of strategic trade policy.

By a strategic relationship I mean that firms must have a mutually recognized strategic interdependence. More formally, the payoffs (profits) of one firm must be directly affected by the individual strategy choices of other firms, and this must be understood by the firms themselves. Strategic trade policies would therefore not arise under perfect competition, nor under pure monopoly unless potential entry were an important consideration. Monopolistic competition may or may not incorporate strategic interaction depending on how it is interpreted and modelled, but typically does not [as, for example, in Krugman (1980)]. Accordingly, strategic trade policy as defined here amounts to the study of trade policy in the presence of oligopoly.

The analysis of strategic trade policy is part of a broader research agenda that has been very active since the beginning of the 1980s. Over this period, international trade economists have sought to incorporate oligopoly and other forms of imperfect competition into the formal analysis of international trade and trade policy so as to make contact with important empirical regularities and policy concerns. Traditional trade theory based on perfect competition did not effectively explain phenomena such as intra-industry trade and the high volume of trade between similar countries. Furthermore, such models failed to successfully incorporate some important policy-relevant considerations, such as firm-level increasing returns to scale, learning-by-doing, R&D, and inter-firm strategic rivalries. Convincing treatment of these topics requires imperfect competition. Oligopoly turned out to have particularly interesting implications because it allows trade policy to take on an additional role not present under other market structures. This leads to the central game-theoretic insight of strategic trade policy: intervention to alter the strategic interaction between oligopolistic firms can itself be an important basis for trade policy.

As is often the case in economics, the academic use of the term strategic trade policy differs from the way the term is used in political debate, where it has at least two other distinct meanings. First, strategic trade policy sometimes refers to trade policy that has direct military implications. Secondly, the term strategic is sometimes used simply as a synonym for important; thus strategic trade policy is trade policy targeted toward industries that are thought to be important for some reason. Neither of these definitions is considered further, although an industry that is strategic by one of these definitions might also be strategic in the game theoretic sense used here.

The focus in this chapter will be normative, in that governments will be assumed to maximize some measure of national economic welfare, rather than having their behavior determined by more fundamental individual actions such as voting or lobbying. Political economy is covered in Chapter 28 of this volume. As implied by the definition of strategic trade policy given above, this chapter does not cover trade policy in the presence of monopolistic competition. Building on the positive analysis of trade under monopolistic competition in Helpman and Krugman (1985) and elsewhere, analysis of some associated trade policy issues can be found in Venables (1987) and Lancaster (1991). This chapter also does not cover the substantial literature on pure strategic interactions between governments [started by Johnson (1954)] in which firm-level behavior is either perfectly competitive or suppressed entirely. Much of the material in this area (up to the mid-1980s) is reviewed in McMillan (1986).

Strategic trade policy is such a heavily surveyed field that I will not attempt to provide a full list of earlier surveys, as any such attempt would surely be incomplete and I have no wish to invite the wrath of excluded authors. Widely cited earlier overviews include Dixit (1987), Krugman (1987), and Helpman and Krugman (1989). This chapter begins its coverage of trade policy where the previous volumes of the Handbook of International Economics left off in 1984, so there is some overlap with other published surveys. However, in addition to offering my best attempt at a clear, accurate, and interesting exposition of the main ideas, this chapter seeks to provide significant value added, or at least product differentiation, in several dimensions.

First, I have the obvious opportunity to include more recent material than is discussed in earlier surveys. While this chapter does not come anywhere close to citing all relevant published work, I believe that it is a more complete guide to the literature, at least within the fairly narrow definition of the topic adopted here, than is available in previous surveys. Secondly, there is somewhat more emphasis on the game theoretic structure of strategic trade policy than in most other surveys. Finally, while existing surveys cover a range of levels from highly technical to completely descriptive, my objective is to provide a sufficiently detailed algebraic treatment that a first-year graduate student with little specific knowledge of trade theory or game theory can develop some skill in the technical formulation and analysis of strategic trade policy models. Due to space constraints, however, some material is dealt with purely descriptively.

Section 2 is devoted to the basic game theoretic structure of strategic trade policy. Section 3 sets out what I refer to as the "third-market" model, in which rival oligopolistic exporters from two countries compete only in a third market. The basic strategic export subsidies model is developed in this context, along with some of the more important qualifications and extensions. Section 4 presents the reciprocal-markets model, in which oligopolistic firms in two countries compete in those two countries. In this context, strategic rent-shifting tariffs, subsidies and other instruments are considered. Section 5 reviews some of the major calibrated simulations of strategic trade policy, and Section 6 contains final reflections and concluding remarks.

2. The game theoretic structure of strategic trade policy

The study of strategic trade policy is fundamentally an application of non-cooperative game theory and therefore uses the Nash equilibrium [as first defined by Nash (1950)] as the central equilibrium concept. [A good general reference on game theory is Fudenberg and Tirole (1991).] It is useful to formally define the Nash equilibrium here. Consider a game with n players in which each player i selects strategy s^i from strategy set S^i so as to independently and noncooperatively maximize payoff function $\pi^i(s^1, s^2, \ldots, s^n)$. Let $s^e = (s^{1e}, s^{2e}, \ldots, s^{ne})$ be a feasible vector of strategies, one selected by each player. This vector of strategies is defined to be a Nash equilibrium if, for every player i and every possible strategy choice s^i,

$$\pi^i(s^e) \geq \pi^i(s^e(-i), s^i) \tag{2.1}$$

where $s^e(-i)$ is a vector consisting of the strategies of all players except player i. An equivalent statement is that the Nash equilibrium arises when all players choose strategies such that each player's strategy maximizes that player's payoff, given the strategies chosen by other players.

The Nash equilibrium can be viewed as a rationality concept. If I am a rational participant in a strategic game, in selecting my strategy, I should try to anticipate what strategies my rivals will play and select my best strategy accordingly. I should also recognize that they are trying to anticipate my behavior, and that they know that I am trying to anticipate their behavior. But they know I recognize this, and I know they know, etc. If the Nash equilibrium is unique, it is a consistent solution to this infinite regress problem. Thus the Nash equilibrium has the "no surprises" property that each player plays the strategy anticipated by the other players. The Nash equilibrium is very general in the sense that the strategies can be defined in many ways. A strategy might be a single move such as a one-shot price or quantity decision by a firm, or it might be a complex rule describing some sort of contingent behavior.

The Nash consistency property alone is not sufficient to fully capture the notion of rationality, especially in games with a sequential structure. Consider the following game. A multinational firm is considering building a new plant in a potential host country. There is no other feasible location for the plant. If the firm builds the plant, the firm and the host country would receive net benefits of 10 each. However, the firm would like a subsidy of 5 from the government, raising the firm's benefit by 5 (to 15) and lowering domestic welfare by 5. First the government decides whether to give the firm a subsidy, then the firm decides whether to build the plant. Figure 2.1 illustrates this game in extensive form. The numbers at the bottom of the game tree indicate the payoffs to the government and to the firm, respectively, following from each possible combination of actions.

The payoffs are assumed to be common knowledge (i.e. each player knows them and knows that the other player knows them, etc.). Prior to actually taking their actions, the government and the firm simultaneously decide on their overall strategies.

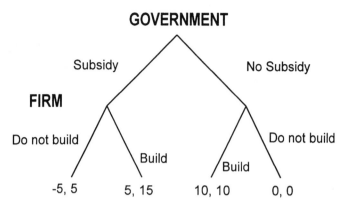

Figure 2.1. *A sequential game.* The first number shows the payoff to government (domestic welfare) and the second shows the payoff to the firm.

There are two Nash equilibria in this game. In one Nash equilibrium, the government's strategy is: "offer no subsidy", and the firm's strategy is: "build the plant whether or not we get the subsidy". The other Nash equilibrium is for the government's strategy to be: "provide a subsidy" for the firm's strategy to be "build the plant if we get a subsidy and do not build the plant if we do not get a subsidy".

The second of these two Nash equilibria seems odd. How can not building the plant be part of the firm's equilibrium strategy when the firm would always prefer to build? The answer is that in this Nash equilibrium the firm is never actually called upon to forego the plant, because the part of the game under which this threat arises is not played as part of the equilibrium. It is an "out-of-equilibrium" threat, and there is nothing in the Nash equilibrium concept that restricts or disciplines the nature of such threats. Careful inspection shows that the strategies proposed for this equilibrium satisfy condition (2.1). Taking the proposed strategy of the other player as given, neither player has an incentive to deviate.

But giving a subsidy seems irrational in this context, as the government should realize that the firm will always build. However, our intuition about why this is irrational goes beyond the Nash equilibrium and incorporates the idea that even out-of-equilibrium threats should be credible in the sense that a player should actually be willing to carry out a threat if called upon to do so. This requirement seems necessary for sequential rationality. It is equivalent to subgame perfection [first proposed by Selten[1] (1965)], which means that an equilibrium strategy for the full game must have the property that each component of the strategy in every subgame

---

[1] John Nash and Reinhard Selten were co-winners, along with John Harsanyi, of the 1994 Nobel Prize in Economics for their pioneering work in game theory and its economic applications. Nash's main contribution was the Nash equilibrium and Selten was honored largely for the development of subgame perfection and other 'refinement' concepts.

(including out-of-equilibrium subgames) must itself be a Nash equilibrium in the subgame. This condition can be imposed by backward induction. Starting at the end of each branch of the game tree, we work backwards, asking what each player would do if that part of the game were reached. We assume that earlier players correctly anticipate the outcomes of lower level subgames as we move up the game tree. Any surviving Nash equilibria will be subgame perfect. In the example discussed above, the only remaining Nash equilibrium is that no subsidy is given and the firm builds anyway.

Now consider a game with two firms and a domestic government. The government's payoffs are, as before, taken to be equal to domestic welfare. The government may undertake some trade policy intervention or it may choose not to intervene. To illustrate the point as simply as possible, assume that this is a discrete binary choice, with no discretionary degrees of intervention available. The government moves before the firms. If it intervenes it changes the payoffs to the firms arising from the various possible combinations of actions by the firms. The firms then simultaneously choose their actions. An example of such a game is illustrated in Figure 2.2. The government may choose to intervene or not to intervene. If it does not intervene, then the right hand matrix shows the payoffs to the firms and the government as a function of the strategies chosen by the firms. Firm x may play $x1$ or $x2$ and firm y can play $y1$ or $y2$. In each cell of the payoff matrix, the first number is the payoff to firm x, the second number is the payoff to firm y, and the third number is the payoff to the government (i.e. domestic welfare). If the government chooses to intervene then the payoffs are given by the left-hand matrix. If firm x were a domestic firm and firm y were a foreign firm, then these strategies might be "low output" and "high output", and the intervention might be something like a subsidy to firm x or a tariff on firm y.

This game can be solved by backward induction, insuring that the solution is

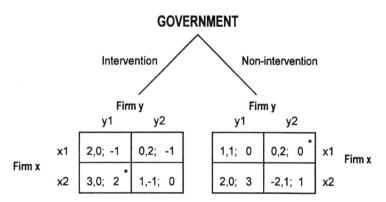

Figure 2.2. *The general structure of strategic trade policy.* In each cell, the first number shows the payoff to firm *A*, the second number shows the payoff to firm *B*, and the third number is domestic welfare (the government's payoff).

subgame perfect. If firms find themselves in the right-hand matrix (i.e. where no government intervention has occurred), the solution will be the upper right cell (marked by an asterisk). This is easily seen as $y2$ is a dominant strategy for firm y: if firm x chooses $x1$, then the choice of $y2$ yields 2 rather than 1 to firm y; and if firm x chooses $x2$, then $y2$ yields 1 rather than 0 to firm y. As firm y should certainly choose $y2$, the best firm x can do is to choose $x1$, obtaining 0 rather than the loss of 2 it would suffer if it chose $x2$. The government's payoff would be 0 at the solution.

If, on the other hand, firms were in the subgame represented by the left-hand payoff matrix, $x2$ would be a dominant strategy for firm x, and firm y would accordingly choose $y1$ so as to avoid a loss, yielding the lower left cell (also indicated by an asterisk) as the solution. The payoffs would be 3 for firm x, 0 for firm y, and 2 for the domestic government. Working backwards up Figure 2.2, it then follows that the government would choose intervention, as its payoff would be 2 rather than 0. This is a subgame perfect (or sequentially rational) Nash equilibrium in the 3-player game. Note that the backward induction process presumes that the government correctly anticipates how firms would react to each of its choices.

There are several points to make about this diagram. First, every cell in the left hand payoff matrix has a lower domestic welfare payoff than the corresponding cell in the right hand matrix. This means that government action is costly in a direct sense: conditional on any given strategy combination by the two firms, national welfare would be lower as a result of government action. The national benefit comes about entirely because of the government's ability to alter the strategic interaction between the two firms, leading them to make different strategic choices than they would in the absence of government policy. This strategic effect in this case more than offsets the direct inefficiency of the policy.

The second point to emphasize is the potential generality of this reasoning. This game is similar to the matrix in Krugman (1987) designed to illustrate the reasoning behind the strategic export subsidies analyzed in Brander and Spencer (1985). However, there is nothing in principle that restricts the reasoning to export subsidies as a policy tool, or to any of the other specifics assumed in Krugman (1987) or Brander and Spencer (1985). One could imagine that the policy tool in question might be tariffs, quotas, voluntary export restraints, R&D subsidies or any one of a wide range of policy instruments that can alter the payoffs of oligopolistic firms. Furthermore, we have assumed nothing in particular about where the firms are located, who owns them, or whether the firms' choice variable is price, quantity, an entry decision, R&D, or something else. More firms or more governments could be added, more complicated dynamic or sequential structures could be constructed, and risk and incomplete information could be introduced.

It is not completely obvious that all of these variations could give rise to a payoff structure of the type used in the example. However, the basic insight that strategic interaction between firms creates an opportunity for government action to modify the terms of that interaction is very robust. The precise nature of the implied policy action is, however, very sensitive to the specifics of the underlying model structure.

One necessary assumption is that the government can credibly commit to its policy choice before the firms make their choices. In the game given here, if the government could not commit to its policy and was in a position to renege on its policy action, it would have an ex post incentive to do so. Once firm x has chosen $x2$ and firm y has chosen $y1$, the government would like to withdraw its policy and get to the lower left corner of the right hand matrix, where national welfare (its payoff) is 3 instead of 2. Rational firms would anticipate this. Firm y would then choose $y2$, and firm x would select $x1$, reverting to the non-interventionist equilibrium. Strategic trade policies require some degree of precommitment by governments, as reflected by the assumption that the government moves first in the game tree. Most observers find it plausible that governments often have some sort of commitment advantage, but it is important to be alert for circumstances in which the asymmetry may run in the other direction.

3. Profit-shifting export subsidies in a "third-market" model

3.1. Export subsidies under Cournot duopoly

In the examples given so far, firms' payoffs have been arbitrarily specified as convenient numbers. It is, of course, necessary to model the underlying structure that gives rise to these payoffs. In short, we need to pay some attention to the theory of oligopoly itself. A valuable review of oligopoly theory can be found in Shapiro (1989) and a standard graduate-level textbook is Tirole (1988).

3.1.1. The Cournot model

Much of the analysis of strategic profit-shifting makes use of the Cournot (1838) model of oligopolistic behavior, which can be set out as follows. Assume there are n firms producing a homogeneous product, and consider a representative firm, called firm x, whose profit is denoted π and whose output is denoted x. The other $n - 1$ firms produce aggregate output Y and a representative other firm produces output y. The profit of firm x is

$$\pi(x; Y) = xp(x + Y) - C(x) , \tag{3.1}$$

where p is the price or inverse demand function (assumed to be downward-sloping) and C is cost. Firms make independent simultaneous one-shot decisions over output levels. Each firm seeks to maximize its own profit. Using a subscript x to denote a derivative taken with respect to x, the first order condition associated with maximization of (3.1) is

$$\pi_x = xp' + p - C_x = 0 , \tag{3.2}$$

with associated second order condition

$$\pi_{xx} < 0, \tag{3.3}$$

where, in this case, $\pi_{xx} = 2p' + xp'' - C_{xx}$. First order condition (3.2) makes it clear that a Cournot equilibrium is a Nash equilibrium in outputs, as (3.2) is implied by (2.1) for the case in which each player's strategy set is simply the set of possible output quantities it might produce in a one-shot simultaneous-move game. The Cournot equilibrium therefore has the same "no surprises" rationality property that any Nash equilibrium has. First order condition (3.2) could be solved in principle for the profit-maximizing choice of x for any given set of output choices by the other firms. This resulting implicit function is the reaction function or best-response function.[2] The common intersection of the n best-response functions (one for each firm) is the Cournot equilibrium.

3.1.2. Strategic substitutes

An additional regularity condition that turns out to be central to the characterization of the Cournot equilibrium is the following.

$$\pi_{xy} < 0, \tag{3.4}$$

where $\pi_{xy} = p' + xp''$. This condition obviously holds for all nonconvex demand curves (including linear demand), but it can be violated if demand is very convex. Condition (3.4) is linked to many properties of the Cournot model. It means that each firm's marginal revenue declines as the output of any other firm rises. It is the so-called Hahn stability condition for certain proposed dynamic adjustment mechanisms. (Note, however, that the pure Cournot model is a one-shot static game with no real-time dynamics. Any proposed dynamic adjustment is an extension to the model.) Presuming that second order conditions are globally satisfied, global satisfaction of (3.4) in this context is also the Gale–Nikaido condition for uniqueness of the Cournot equilibrium. Condition (3.4) also ensures that various comparative static properties of the model are "well-behaved". [See Dixit (1986)].

Most importantly, however, condition (3.4) means that strategy variables x and y are strategic substitutes as defined by Bulow, Geanakopolous, and Klemperer (1985). If $\pi_{xy} < 0$, this means that the marginal value, π_x, of increasing firm x's strategy variable decreases when the strategy variable of a rival increases. This implies that an

---

[2]Note that the response or reaction embodied in the best-response function is purely notional. The reaction function is useful for considering how a firm "thinks through" its strategy selection. It does not, however, capture any real-time action and reaction. In a simultaneous move "one-shot" game, players do not have an opportunity to react to rivals' moves. In the Cournot model, firms make simultaneous output choices, before observing the output choices of rivals, then these output levels are simultaneously revealed, prices adjust to clear the market, payoffs are made, and the game ends.

increase in y would reduce the best-response value of x (i.e. the best-response function for firm x is downward-sloping). If, on the other hand, $\pi_{xy} > 0$, then strategy variables x and y would be "strategic complements" for firm x in the sense that an increase in y would raise the best-response value of x. The best-response function for firm x would be upward-sloping in such a case.

3.1.3. The third-market model

Brander and Spencer (1985) incorporated an international Cournot duopoly into a "third-market" model to provide a striking demonstration of strategic trade policy. A third-market model is one in which one or more firms from a domestic country and one or more firms from a foreign country compete only in a third market. These firms therefore produce only for export. This simplification turns out to be very useful in allowing the strategic effects of certain trade policies to be seen in pure form, and third-market models have therefore been extensively used in the literature. In a third-market model, a domestic government can do nothing to directly hinder a foreign firm (i.e. there is no scope for import tariffs or quotas), and the natural policy to consider is an export subsidy, whose direct effect is to help a domestic firm vis-à-vis its foreign rival.

The sequential structure of the model consists of two stages. In stage 1 the domestic government sets a subsidy level of s per unit. In stage 2, the domestic and foreign firms simultaneously choose output (or export) levels for the third market. Using backward induction to focus on sequentially rational Nash equilibria for the full game, we consider the second stage of the game first.

3.1.4. Stage 2: Equilibrium outputs and comparative statics

There is a single factor of production in each country, referred to as labor. Labor can be used in the oligopoly sector or it can be used to produce a numeraire good with price 1. Consumers in the foreign and domestic countries consume only the numeraire good. The numeraire good is produced under competitive conditions with constant returns to scale, and labor has the same productivity in the numeraire sector in all countries. Units are selected so that one unit of labor produces one unit of the numeraire good. Assuming that labor is paid its marginal product, the wage is one. In the domestic country, labor input F is required as a fixed input for production of the oligopoly good, and variable input requirements are c units of labor input per unit of output. F and c are therefore simply fixed and variable cost for the domestic oligopolist. Using an asterisk to denote (most) variables associated with the foreign country, foreign fixed cost is denoted F^* and foreign marginal cost is denoted c^*. There is one domestic firm and one foreign firm. The domestic firm produces quantity x and the foreign firm produces quantity y. Profit functions π and π^* for the domestic and foreign firms can therefore be written, respectively, as

$$\pi(x, y; s) = xp(x + y) - cx + sx - F , \qquad (3.5)$$

$$\pi^*(x, y; s) = yp(x + y) - c^*y - F^* , \qquad (3.6)$$

with associated first order conditions

$$\pi_x = xp' + p - c + s = 0; \quad \pi_y^* = yp' + p - c^* = 0 . \qquad (3.7)$$

Conditions (3.3) and (3.4) are also assumed to hold for each firm. By stage 2, subsidy s has been predetermined in stage 1 and is therefore treated as exogenous. Thus the solution to the first order conditions will yield x and y as functions of subsidy s. The comparative static effects dx/ds and dy/ds can be obtained by totally differentiating first order conditions (3.7) with respect to x, y, and s as follows.

$$\pi_{xx} \, dx + \pi_{xy} \, dy + \pi_{xs} \, ds = 0 . \qquad (3.8)$$

$$\pi_{yx}^* \, dx + \pi_{yy}^* \, dy + \pi_{ys}^* \, ds = 0 . \qquad (3.9)$$

Dividing (3.7) and (3.8) through by ds and using matrix notation yields

$$\begin{bmatrix} \pi_{xx} & \pi_{xy} \\ \pi_{yx}^* & \pi_{yy}^* \end{bmatrix} \begin{bmatrix} dx/ds \\ dy/ds \end{bmatrix} = \begin{bmatrix} -\pi_{xs} \\ -\pi_{ys}^* \end{bmatrix} \qquad (3.10)$$

Noting that $\pi_{xs} = 1$ and $\pi_{ys}^* = 0$ [from (3.7)], these equations can be solved using Cramer's rule to yield

$$dx/ds = -\pi_{yy}^*/D > 0; \quad dy/ds = \pi_{yx}^*/D < 0 , \qquad (3.11)$$

where D is the determinant of the left-hand matrix in (3.10). This determinant is $\pi_{xx}\pi_{yy}^* - \pi_{xy}\pi_{yx}^*$. From (3.4), $\pi_{xy}(=p' + xp'') < 0$, so $\pi_{xx}(=2p' + xp'')$ is also negative and larger in absolute value than π_{xy}. A similar pattern applies to π_{yy}^* and π_{yx}^*, implying that D must be positive.

Naturally enough, introducing or increasing an export subsidy to the domestic firm causes the output of the domestic firm to rise and output of the foreign firm to fall. As shown in Figure 3.1, increasing an export subsidy shifts out the best-response function of the domestic firm, because its lower effective cost makes it want to export more for any given export level by the rival. Because x and y are strategic substitutes, as reflected in the downward-sloping best-response functions, we see that the foreign firm is induced to reduce its equilibrium output. It also follows that total quantity rises, price falls, profits of the domestic firm rise, and profits of the foreign firm fall as the domestic export subsidy increases.

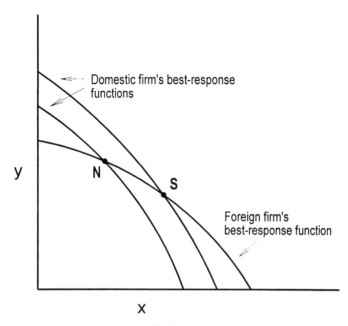

Figure 3.1. *The effects of a domestic export subsidy in a Cournot industry.* An increase in the domestic subsidy causes the output best-response function of the domestic firm to shift out, allowing the domestic firm to increase its market share as the Cournot equilibrium moves from *N* to *S*.

3.1.5. Stage 1: The optimal subsidy

We now consider the first stage, when the domestic government sets a subsidy, fully aware of how that subsidy will affect the second-stage values of x and y. The government wishes to maximize domestic welfare, which in this case is equivalent to consumption of the numeraire good, which in turn is equal to net domestic income. Assume that the country's initial endowment of labor is L and that all domestic profits accrue to domestic residents. Then net income is simply $L + \pi - sx$. (The "behind-the-scenes" trade flow is that the numeraire good is exported from the third market to the domestic country in exchange for x.) L is a fixed endowment that can ignored, so incremental domestic welfare, denoted W, is just net profits.

$$W(s) = \pi(x(s), y(s); s) - sx(s) . \tag{3.12}$$

At this point it is necessary to clarify some notation. When considering simple functions such as $z = z(x, y)$, the expressions dz/dx and z_x are used interchangeably to denote the partial derivative of z with respect to x. The notation $\partial z/\partial x$ is not used. However, in the case of composite functions such as $\pi(x(s), y(s), s)$ it is necessary to distinguish between partial and total derivatives. In such a case, subscript notation such as π_s is used to represent just the pure partial derivative $\partial \pi / \partial s$, while $d\pi / ds$ represents the total derivative.

$$d\pi / ds = \pi_x \, dx/ds + \pi_y \, dy/ds + \pi_s .$$ (3.13)

The derivative of W [from (3.12)] with respect to s is given by $dW/ds = d\pi/ds - x - s \, dx/ds$. Substituting (3.13) into this expression and noting that $\pi_s (=\partial \pi / \partial s) = x$ yields

$$dW/ds = \pi_x \, dx/ds + \pi_y \, dy/ds - s \, dx/ds .$$ (3.14)

Noting further that $\pi_x = 0$ by first order condition (3.7) yields

$$dW/ds = \pi_y \, dy/ds - s \, dx/ds .$$ (3.15)

It is clear from (3.15) that dW/ds is unambiguously positive at $s = 0$ since, from (3.5), $\pi_y = xp'$ is negative (noting that p' is negative) and, from (3.11), dy/ds is also negative. The optimal subsidy can be obtained by setting dW/ds to zero and rearranging.

$$s^0 = \pi_y (dy/ds)/(dx/ds) > 0 .$$ (3.16)

It is useful to link the formula given by (3.16) for the optimal subsidy to the strategic substitutes condition given by (3.4). Substituting for dx/ds and dy/ds from (3.11) into (3.16) yields

$$s^0 = -\pi_y \pi_{yx}^* / \pi_{yy}^* .$$ (3.17)

The denominator of (3.17) must be negative by second order conditions, and $\pi_y (=xp')$ is negative, essentially because x and y, as homogeneous products, are necessarily gross substitutes in the inverse demand function. Thus the sign of s^0 is implied by the sign of π_{yx}^*. If, as assumed here, x and y are strategic substitutes, then π_{yx}^* is negative, and the optimal subsidy is positive. If x and y were strategic complements $(\pi_{yx}^* > 0)$, then the optimal policy would be to tax exports. In such a case, the tax would be a facilitating device (i.e. facilitating a more collusive outcome) rather than a profit-shifting device.

The optimal subsidy can be viewed in more concrete form if a specific demand function is assumed. In the case of linear demand of the form $p = a - Q$, where $Q = x + y$, expression (3.16) [or (3.17)] reduces to

$$s^0 = a/4 - c/2 + c^*/4 .$$ (3.18)

Linear demand implies that x and y are strategic substitutes, so s^0 must be positive. [Combinations of a, c and c^* that would apparently make s^0 negative in (3.18) are inconsistent with positive domestic output.] Note that the optimal subsidy is increasing in the relative cost advantage of the domestic firm. Firms that "need" help to compete with foreign rivals are the least attractive targets for strategic assistance from a welfare-maximizing government's point of view. [Further analysis of firm asymmetries in the strategic subsidies model can be found in De Meza (1986) and Neary (1994).]

3.1.6. Profit-shifting

Expression (3.16) implies the noteworthy result that there is a domestic rationale for offering the domestic firm an export subsidy, even though the subsidy payment itself is just a transfer. The key point is that gross profits to the firm rise by more than the amount of the subsidy, implying a net gain to the domestic economy. The net benefit comes about because the subsidy has the effect of committing the domestic firm to a more aggressive best-response function (as shown in Figure 3.1) which in turn induces the foreign firm to produce less. The optimal domestic subsidy moves the domestic firm to the Stackelberg leader output level, while the foreign firm produces the Stackelberg follower output. In effect, the government is able to convert its first-mover advantage into an equivalent advantage for the domestic firm.

This model fits the structure of Figure 2.2. The domestic government has an incentive to take a prior policy action that alters the strategic interaction between firms. In this case, the subsidy policy implies a terms of trade loss for the domestic country, but there is a profit-shifting effect that more than offsets this terms of trade effect. The subsidy acts to shift profits from the foreign firm to the domestic firm. Profit-shifting can therefore be viewed as a rationale for trade policy intervention that is quite distinct from terms of trade effects and rationalization (or scale) effects.

3.2. Extensions of the Cournot strategic subsidies model

The strategic subsidies model presented in Section 3.1 abstracts from many things that we know to be important. However, quite a few extensions, generalizations, and qualifications can be readily established.

3.2.1. Two active governments: A prisoner's dilemma

Perhaps the first point to observe is that allowing the foreign government to be active simultaneously with the domestic government does not affect the structure of the analysis. In such a case, the foreign firm's profit function given by (3.6) must have s^*y added to it, where s^* is the foreign subsidy. Output levels x and y then depend on both s and s^*, but comparative static effects dx/ds and dy/ds have exactly the form given in (3.11). Effects dx/ds^* and dy/ds^* have symmetric structures. In the stage 1 game, we allow governments to simultaneously choose subsidy levels s and s^*. The welfare function, W^*, of the foreign government is the analog of the domestic welfare function given by (3.12). The derivative dW/ds has the form given in (3.15) and dW/ds^* has an analogous form. Simultaneous solution of the two first order conditions $dW/ds = 0$ and $dW^*/ds^* = 0$ then yields the solution values of s and s^*, which are given by (3.16), and an analogous expression for s^*. Thus the qualitative properties of the solution are as before. Provided x and y are strategic substitutes, both governments provide positive subsidies. Under symmetry, this government-level game has the general form of a prisoner's dilemma, as both producing countries are worse off at the strategic subsidy equilibrium than they would be under free trade, but each has a unilateral incentive to intervene.

3.2.2. The opportunity cost of public funds

In the preceding analysis subsidy dollars and profit dollars have been treated as equivalent. As implied by welfare function (3.12) the government is indifferent about pure transfers from the domestic treasury to the firm's shareholders (or vice versa). In practice, however, raising subsidy revenue imposes distortionary costs on the economy, implying that the opportunity cost of a dollar of public funds would exceed 1. [The discussion in, for example, Ballard et al. (1985) suggests an opportunity cost in the range of 1.17 to 1.56 per dollar raised.] In this case the welfare function would be written as

$$W = \pi - \delta sx, \tag{3.11'}$$

where $\delta > 1$. This case has been analyzed by Neary (1994) following similar work by Gruenspecht (1988). Proceeding from (3.11') yields the following expression.

$$dW/ds = xp' \, dy/ds - (\delta - 1)x - \delta s \, dx/ds. \tag{3.15'}$$

If we consider the value of dW/ds at $s = 0$, the third term disappears, but it is no longer obvious that dW/ds is positive. The first term is positive, as in (3.15), but the second term is negative and may more than offset the first term. Thus, as expected, if δ is sufficiently high, the implied policy is a tax rather than a subsidy.

Two other important concessions to reality lead to essentially the same formulation. First, if the domestic government simply puts less weight on shareholders' welfare than on taxpayers' welfare for income distributional or other reasons, then (3.11') would apply. In addition, if some of the domestic firm's shareholders are foreign rather than domestic residents, then presumably the share of profits received by foreigners would not count in domestic welfare. In this case the relative weight on profits should be less than the weight on (domestically funded) subsidies, as implied by (3.11'). This point is examined by Lee (1990), and Dick (1993) carries out some related empirical analysis.

3.2.3. Multiple domestic and foreign firms

The analysis so far has been carried out for the case of duopoly, where strategic interactions arise most starkly, but there is always some concern that results obtained for a duopoly might be diluted if the number of firms were to increase. The effect of exogenously increasing the number of firms has been examined by Dixit (1984). Dixit actually carries out the analysis in a reciprocal-markets model (as described in Section 4), but the argument is simplest in a third-market model. With n domestic Cournot firms and n^* foreign Cournot firms, the effect of a domestic subsidy on the ith domestic firm's profit is

$$\mathrm{d}\pi^i/\mathrm{d}s = (\mathrm{d}\pi^i/\mathrm{d}x^i)x_s^i + (n-1)(\mathrm{d}\pi^i/\mathrm{d}x^j)x_s^j + n^*(\mathrm{d}\pi^i/\mathrm{d}y)y_s + \pi_s^i, \qquad (3.19)$$

where x^j is the output of a representative domestic rival and y is the output of a representative foreign rival.

Comparing this with expression (3.13) indicates a new consideration, corresponding to the second term of expression (3.19). Specifically, a domestic subsidy now has the effect of increasing the output of domestic rivals. This effect tends to reduce the profit of the ith domestic firm and is an additional cost of a domestic subsidy. If n were large and n^* were negligible, then a subsidy would certainly be damaging to the national interest, as domestic firms would compete excessively from the national point of view. National welfare would be enhanced by imposing an export tax, moving domestic firms closer to the cartel output. (This is just the standard terms of trade argument for intervention.) Conversely, as the number of foreign firms grows relative to the number of domestic firms, a subsidy to the domestic firms becomes more attractive.

3.2.4. Multiple oligopolies

One striking aspect of the early examples of strategic trade policy is their apparent abstraction from traditional general equilibrium considerations. Indeed, the basic ideas have frequently been presented in a purely partial equilibrium setting, although alert readers will have noticed that the economic environment considered in Section 3.1 is a full, albeit highly simplified, general equilibrium model. The assumptions that there is a single factor of production, that the rest of the economy can be aggregated into a single numeraire sector, and that utility is linear in income serve, however, to eliminate many of the usual general equilibrium issues from consideration.

Dixit and Grossman (1986) relax the assumption that there is only one oligopoly in an otherwise undistorted numeraire economy. They assume that there are several Cournot oligopoly industries, with one domestic and one foreign firm each, all with sales only in third markets. They also assume two factors of production, "workers" and "scientists", rather than just one. Scientists are specific to the oligopolistic sector. In the extreme version of the model, production in the oligopoly sector uses a fixed proportions technology, so aggregate output in the sector is constrained to be proportional to the (fixed) supply of scientists. It is clear that such a structure will greatly diminish any value of strategic subsidies, for an expansion of one duopoly firm and the associated profit-shifting benefit must come at the cost of contraction by another duopoly firm and an associated profit-shifting loss. Gains can come only from shifting output toward those firms with the most attractive profit-shifting opportunities and away from those with less attractive opportunities, implying a subsidy for some firms and a tax for others.

If the domestic government were constrained to offer a uniform subsidy and the oligopoly sector were symmetric, then a subsidy would have no benefit and free trade would be optimal. If, more realistically, there are some substitution possibilities between scientists and workers in the oligopoly sector, then the aggregate incentive for a subsidy is restored, although in weakened form. Thus a partial-equilibrium analysis that focuses on just one industry at a time might give an excessively favorable view of strategic intervention.

Dixit and Grossman consider "scientists" to be the scarce resource, but any other input with similar properties would do. Scientists are, however, of particular interest. In practice, there is substantial mobility of scientists across countries, which has led to a long-standing concern with the "brain drain" problem. For an interesting analysis and calibration of strategic trade policy in the presence of internationally mobile scientists see Ulph and Winters (1994) who find, among other things, that R&D subsidies to the high-tech sector are attractive precisely because they attract scientists and engineers from other countries, which has nationally beneficial profit-shifting and terms of trade effects.

3.3. Strategic subsidies and industry conduct

3.3.1. Conjectural variations and conduct parameters

Section 3.2 considered various worthwhile and intuitively plausible extensions and qualifications of the Cournot version of the third-market model. Another important class of extension is to consider oligopoly models other than the Cournot model. A very influential analysis of this type was undertaken by Eaton and Grossman (1986), who replaced the Cournot model with the so-called conjectural variation model. The conjectural variation language has fallen out of favor because of certain associated logical difficulties, but the technical apparatus of the model remains useful. Industry output is Q and the output of the firm in question (called firm x) is x. Output of all other firms is Y, so $X = x + Y$. Suppose we think of industry output as a function of own output. In the absence of subsidies or fixed costs, we can then write

$$\pi(x) = xp(Q(x)) - cx . \tag{3.20}$$

Mechanically writing down a first order condition arising from maximization of (3.29) yields

$$d\pi/dx = p + xp'\, dQ/dx - c = 0, \tag{3.21}$$

where dQ/dx is the covariation of industry output with own output. We can write $dQ/dx = dx/dx + [dY/dx]_v = 1 + \lambda$, where $\lambda = [dY/dx]_v$. The term $[dY/dx]_v$ was referred to as the "conjectural variation" because it reflects the conjecture that firm x makes concerning how other firms' output would co-vary with its own output. First order condition (3.21) can then be written as

$$d\pi/dx = p + xp'(1 + \lambda) - c = 0. \tag{3.22}$$

A Cournot game is a simultaneous-move one-shot game in which outputs are the strategy variables. To say that firms choose outputs simultaneously means that each firm must choose its output before observing the output of its rivals. Before actually playing its output, a firm can consider the consequence of choosing some output other than the Cournot level. It must recognize, however, that even if it surprised other firms by playing some such deviation, by the time other firms observed this deviation, it would be too late for them to change their outputs in response. A consistent interpretation of the Cournot model is that firms commit to output levels, and prices then adjust to clear the market. A firm contemplating a deviation from the Cournot output level would imagine that prices would adjust when outputs were brought to the market, but quantities would not. Therefore, $\lambda = 0$ is the "correct" conjectural variation for the Cournot model. Note that with $\lambda = 0$, (3.22) coincides with (3.2) as required.

A Bertrand game is a simultaneous-move one-shot game in which prices are the strategy variables. The Bertrand model can be thought of as a model in which firms simultaneously commit to price levels, then quantities adjust to clear the market. If one firm contemplates choosing a price other than its Bertrand equilibrium price, it must recognize that if it played this deviant strategy as its part of the simultaneous price announcements made by all firms, then other firms could not, by the definition of the game, adjust their prices. This implies that the output levels of both the deviant firm and the other firms must adjust from their Bertrand equilibrium levels so as to clear the market. In this case, therefore, the firm should anticipate a non-zero covariation between other firms' output and its own. For a Bertrand game, the "correct" conjectural variation in quantities is something other than zero. In fact, with homogenous products, λ takes on the value -1, and we can see from (3.22) that this yields $p = c$, as required by the homogenous product Bertrand model.

From this reasoning, λ may be called a "conduct parameter" and may be regarded as a representation of the effective degree of competitiveness in the industry. λ indexes the range of possible conduct in the industry, from cutthroat competition to full collusion. (If there are n identical firms, then $\lambda = n - 1$ will yield the cartel or monopoly outcome.) This conduct parameter (or conjectural variation) formulation is not a true game form, as strategy spaces are not clearly identified for all values of λ, but it can be a very useful model in empirical applications, because λ can be readily estimated or calibrated, as discussed in Section 5.

3.3.2. Product differentiation

For the Cournot model, the assumption of homogeneous (rather than differentiated) products allows simpler notation and improved clarity. Note, however, that everything that has been done so far can be readily extended to the case of differentiated products. With product differentiation, let $p(x, y)$ represent the price of good x, and let $r(x, y)$ be the price of good y. Assume that price is declining in own output and in the rival's output (i.e. that goods are substitutes). Therefore $\pi_y(=xp_y) < 0$. For the Cournot model, provided that we require $\pi_{xy} < 0$ (strategic substitutes), then comparative static effects and trade policy implications apply exactly as already derived. For the duopoly version of the conduct parameter formulation we would rewrite (3.22) as

$$\pi_x = p + xp_x + xp_y\lambda - c = 0.\tag{3.22'}$$

Under Bertrand competition, the case of product differentiation is more analytically convenient than the homogeneous product case. The homogeneous product case is logically consistent, but demand and profit are discontinuous at the equilibrium price, as a slight increase in price by one firm would cause its sales and price to drop to zero. Any analysis making use of derivatives therefore becomes cumbersome to carry out.

   Accordingly, to analyze the effects of market conduct other than Cournot on the strategic export subsidies argument, Eaton and Grossman (1986) use a differentiated product version of the conduct parameter model. [See also Cheng (1988).] Eaton and Grossman considered ad valorem subsidies, but the structure of their results is unaffected if we continue to use specific subsidies. Except for introducing a conduct parameter and reinterpreting the model as allowing product differentiation, the structure is identical to the duopoly model of Section 3.1. The domestic firm's profit can be written as $\pi(x, y(x))$ and foreign profit can be written $\pi^*(x(y), y)$. The associated first order conditions for domestic and foreign firms can then be written as

$$d\pi/dx = \pi_x + \pi_y\lambda = 0,\tag{3.23}$$

$$d\pi^*/dy = \pi_y^* + \pi_x^*\lambda^* = 0,\tag{3.24}$$

where subscripts denote partial derivatives and λ^* is used to denote the foreign firm's conduct parameter.

3.3.3. Optimal subsidies and taxes

As before, expression (3.14) shows the welfare effect of a change in s, where dx/ds and dy/ds are the actual comparative static effects of s on equilibrium outputs x and y. As just noted, with product differentiation, $\pi_y = xp_y$. Then, from (3.23), $\pi_x = -xp_y\lambda$. Substituting these values for π_x and π_y into (3.14) and defining $\gamma = (dy/ds)/(dx/ds)$ then gives the expression

$$dW/ds = (\gamma - \lambda)xp_y\, dx/ds - s\, dx/ds . \tag{3.25}$$

Setting (3.25) to zero and solving for the optimal subsidy yields

$$s^0 = (\gamma - \lambda)xp_y . \tag{3.26}$$

Under Cournot competition, $\lambda = 0$, and this reduces to the Brander–Spencer optimal subsidy for the Cournot model. If, on the other hand, competition is of the Bertrand type, then λ is negative and the optimal "subsidy" turns out to be negative. The domestic government would have an incentive to tax exports, exactly the reverse of the Brander–Spencer result. If market conduct happened to be such that $\lambda = \gamma$, then free trade would be optimal. Expression (3.26) embodies a remarkable result, for the policy conclusion of the strategic subsidies model is seen to be exactly reversed by assuming Bertrand rather than Cournot competition.

3.3.4. A generic strategic model

Consider a "generic" strategic model in which there are two rival firms, firm A and firm B, with strategy variables or activities A and B respectively. The firms choose A and B simultaneously. At this point A and B could be anything, possibly outputs, possibly prices, possibly R&D, or possibly something else. We imagine that activity A might be subsidized or taxed at rate s per unit. We can write the profit of firm A as $\pi(A, B; s)$. Its first order condition is $\pi_A = 0$, and its second order condition is $\pi_{AA} < 0$. The other firm, whose profit is denoted $\pi^*(A, B)$, has comparable first and second order conditions. This structure is exactly parallel to that developed in Section 3.1, except that here we have A and B instead of x and y. It follows immediately that the expression for the optimal subsidy has exactly the same form as (3.17).

$$s^0 = -\pi_B \pi_{BA}^* / \pi_{BB}^* . \tag{3.17'}$$

The denominator must be negative. Therefore, whether there is an incentive to tax or subsidize activity A depends on the sign of π_B and the sign of π_{BA}^*. If $\pi_B < 0$, then an increase in the rival's strategy variable lowers the profit of firm A. In this case I will refer to activity B as "unfriendly" to firm A. If $\pi_B > 0$, then B is "friendly". As is now familiar, if $\pi_{BA}^* < 0$, then A and B are strategic substitutes (for firm B), and if $\pi_{BA}^* > 0$, then A and B are strategic complements (for firm B). If A and B are outputs of identical or similar products, we have the case of Section 3.1. If strategy variables *A* and *B* are prices, we have the Bertrand case as just considered, where *A* and *B* will normally be strategic complements, and *B* will be friendly. The implied policy is that higher prices should bring forth higher subsidies. Because higher prices are associated with lower export demand, this implies an export tax.

Diagrammatically, the Bertrand model implies that price best-response functions of both firms are upward-sloping. A domestic export tax commits the domestic firm to a higher gross price for any given price chosen by the rival, so the domestic firm's price best-response function shifts up. This is illustrated in Figure 3.2 for the case of differentiated products. By committing the domestic firm to a less aggressive best-response function, the domestic government induces the foreign firm to charge a higher price, which in turn benefits the domestic country.

In the Cournot case, the domestic firm would like to threaten production of the Stackelberg output level (which is higher than the Cournot level), if only it could persuade its rival that this threat were credible. Note that because output increases are "unfriendly", we view the possibility of producing the Stackelberg level of output as a "threat". A subsidy makes this threat credible. In the Bertrand case, by way of contrast, the domestic firm would like to charge a higher price than the standard Bertrand level, if only its rival would take such a price as credible. In this case, because price increases are "friendly", we might view this as a "promise" rather than a threat. An export tax makes this promise credible.

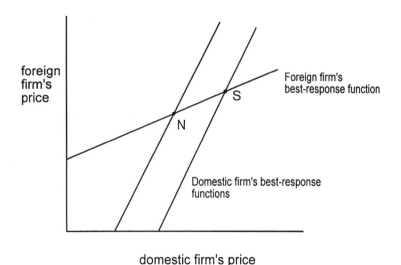

domestic firm's price

Figure 3.2. *The effects of an export tax in a Bertrand industry.* An increase in a domestic export tax causes the price best-response function of the domestic firm to shift out, inducing an equilibrium price increase for both firms as the equilibrium moves from *N* to *S*.

The Bertrand model is not necessarily any less plausible than the Cournot model as an approximation to actual conduct. Because it is hard to know in practice which of the two models (if either) is appropriate in a given case, the Eaton–Grossman analysis implies that even finding the sign or direction of the optimal policy might be difficult.

3.3.5. R&D subsidies

So far, our model of firm behavior is rather spartan in that only output and price decisions have been considered. Many of the industries of greatest policy interest are those where R&D and sunk investments play a prominent role. Furthermore, GATT explicitly forbids export subsidies, but this ban does not extend to R&D subsidies. Possibly for this reason R&D and investment subsidies seem more important empirically than export and production subsidies.

From expression (3.17') it is possible to immediately infer the implied policy toward R&D by determining whether R&D levels are strategic substitutes and by determining whether R&D is friendly or unfriendly. We would normally expect cost-reducing R&D to be unfriendly in the absence of R&D spillovers, as more R&D means lower production costs, and this can only make rivals worse off. The strategic substitutability or complementarity is less obvious and requires a detailed modelling effort. The first model of strategic R&D subsidies was a three stage third-market model considered by Spencer and Brander (1983). In stage 1 governments consider setting subsidies; in stage 2, firms simultaneously select R&D levels; and in stage 3 firms play a Cournot output game. R&D is assumed to have a deterministic cost-reducing effect. Third stage outputs are functions of second stage R&D levels, implying that the firms themselves use R&D strategically to influence the third stage game. This induces firms to overinvest in R&D relative to cost-minimizing levels. Despite this effect, if only an R&D subsidy is available (i.e. in the absence of export or output subsidies) R&D levels still turn out to be strategic substitutes and the implied policy is an R&D subsidy.

Bagwell and Staiger (1994) consider a similar model, except that they allow the effects of R&D to be explicitly stochastic, making the model both more difficult and more realistic as a representation of real R&D. In light of the Eaton–Grossman policy reversal results described in Section 3.3.2, Bagwell and Staiger consider both Cournot and Bertrand output market competition. Strikingly, for the case in which R&D simply reduces the mean but does not change the variance of the cost distribution, they find that R&D choices are strategic substitutes regardless of the nature of downstream competition. This suggests that R&D subsidies might be more robust than export subsidies as strategic policy tools.

Bagwell and Staiger also incorporate the firm numbers effect discussed in Section 3.2.3 taking into account the potential restraining effect of R&D taxes on domestic firms who would otherwise compete excessively with one another. As before, whether a tax or subsidy is required depends on relative numbers of foreign and domestic firms and on various model parameters. Note, however, that any positive R&D spillovers between domestic firms would favor subsidization. Bagwell and Staiger also show that the incentive to tax or subsidize depends on the structure of uncertainty. In particular, if R&D changes the variance as well as the mean of the cost distribution, then additional strategic considerations arise.

3.4. Timing

An intriguing but under-appreciated aspect of strategic trade policy analysis is the crucial importance of timing in decisions. In the games considered so far, governments are assumed to move before firms. But, as argued persuasively by Carmichael (1987), some interventions may have the reverse order. For example, Carmichael quotes Congressional testimony from a former Chairman of the United States Export–Import Bank that exporting firms (such as Boeing) credibly set their prices before the Exim Bank decides on whether and to what extent to subsidize foreign purchases.

3.4.1. Firms move first

In an effort to analyze the implications of this order of moves, Carmichael considers a third-market model in which foreign and domestic duopolistic firms sell differentiated products. Firms play a Bertrand (price-setting) game, and set prices before the government sets a subsidy or tax rate. Gruenspecht (1988) considers a variation of this model in which government revenue has an opportunity cost exceeding one. The basic insight of these papers can be illustrated most simply using a linear demand structure. The model is a two-stage game. In stage 1 the domestic and foreign firms set prices p and r respectively, then in stage 2 the domestic government sets a per-unit subsidy s, taking producer prices p and r as predetermined and therefore fixed. Thus consumers face a net price of $p - s$ for the domestic good. Consumption demand for domestic exports, x, and foreign exports, y, is therefore written as

$$x = a - (p - s) - br; \quad y = a - r - b(p - s),\qquad(3.27)$$

where $b < 1$. The second stage objective function maximized by the domestic government is [as given by (3.11′)], $W = \pi - \delta sx$, where $\delta \geq 1$, reflecting a possible distortionary cost of raising government revenue. The domestic firm receives gross price p for its product, s of which comes from the domestic treasury. Domestic welfare can then be written $W = px - cx - F - \delta sx$, where, as before, c and F are marginal and fixed cost. Substituting from (3.27) for x and rearranging then yields

$$W = (p - c - \delta s)(a - (p - s) - br) - F.\qquad(3.28)$$

Taking p and r as given, the domestic government's welfare-maximizing choice of s is characterized by first order condition $dW/ds = 0$, which implies the following solution for s.

$$s = p(1 + \delta)/2\delta - c/2\delta - a/2 + br/2 . \tag{3.29}$$

If there is no distortionary cost of raising government revenue, so profit dollars and subsidy dollars are both given weight 1, then $\delta = 1$, and we see from (3.29) that $ds/dp = 1$. This is the case considered Carmichael (1987). It implies that the government would exactly offset stage 1 price increases by the domestic firm with higher subsidies, on a dollar for dollar basis. In essence, given any particular price set by the foreign rival, there is only one profit and welfare maximizing net consumer price for good x. If the domestic firm sets its producer price above this level, a welfare-maximizing government must use its subsidy to restore this net consumer price. Such a government is trapped by its own good intentions.

In this setting, the domestic firm would choose an infinitely high price in stage 1, as this would guarantee an infinite profit. To eliminate this possibility, Carmichael imposes an "eligibility" requirement that limits the maximum mark-up. Gruenspecht's analysis allows $\delta > 1$, in which case we can see from (3.29) that $ds/dp = (1 + \delta)/2\delta < 1$. In this more realistic version, the domestic firm adopts a finite mark-up above the Bertrand level and the domestic government provides a partially offsetting subsidy. These results offer a striking contrast to the Bertrand version of the export subsidy game discussed in Section 3.3.3, where the optimal domestic policy is to tax exports. By having the government move after rather than prior to firms, the optimal tax switches to a subsidy.

3.4.2. Non-intervention as a strategic choice

One interesting feature of Carmichael (1987) is that the subsidy program as a whole is of no value. If the government could simply abolish the program altogether, it would lose nothing by doing so. With the program in place, however, and anticipated by firms, a positive subsidy becomes optimal because of the actions taken by firms prior to the subsidy decision. This suggests that we need to consider the government's prior decision to implement the subsidy program, as distinct from its later decision to select a particular subsidy level.

Because the subsidy is set after firms have made their strategy decisions, the Carmichael–Gruenspecht (CG) model does not fit the general game structure of Figure 2.2, and one might argue that the CG subsidy is not really a strategic trade policy at all, at least as I have defined the term. However, in this case, it is really the decision to implement a subsidy program in the first place that is the strategic trade policy, as this decision certainly affects the strategic rivalry between firms.

The importance of distinguishing between the implementation and design of a policy program, and the level of the policy instrument arises explicitly in papers by Cooper and Riezman (1989), Arvan (1991), and Shivakumar (1993), where governments decide in the first stage what policy instrument they will use, then subsequently decide on the level of the instrument. Hwang and Shulman (1994) confront this issue most directly. They consider a three stage third-market duopoly model. In the first stage (which occurs before the resolution of some uncertainty) a foreign and domestic government simultaneously decide whether to use a subsidy instrument, a strict export quantity control or, most significantly, whether to commit to non-intervention. Following this decision, uncertainty is resolved and, in stage 2, if a government committed itself to use either a subsidy or a strict quantity control, it sets the level of this instrument. If, on the other hand, it committed itself to non-intervention, then it has no further choices to make. In the third stage, firms play a duopoly game. Hwang and Schulman consider duopoly of the Bertrand, Cournot, and Stackelberg types.

It is apparent that non-intervention could arise in one of two ways, either by a stage 1 commitment to non-intervention, or by a stage 1 commitment to a policy instrument followed by a situation in which the optimal subsidy happened to be zero or the optimal quantity control equalled the non-intervention level. The main finding is that by introducing non-intervention as a distinct stage 1 policy choice, non-intervention is much more likely to arise than if the policy regime and the level of the policy instrument are chosen simultaneously. In essence, separating the policy decision into two steps yields a very different game than when these two steps are compressed into a single simultaneous decision. Under the sequential two-step process, a government is able to take into account the effect of its stage 1 decision on its stage 2 optimal instrument level and, more importantly, on its rival's stage 2 decision as well.

This general point can be demonstrated very easily using a somewhat simplified algebraic structure. Let government payoffs in the two countries be denoted W and W^*. Suppose that the policy regime choice is represented by ρ and ρ^*, respectively, for the home and foreign governments, and that the stage 2 instruments are denoted s and s^*. To allow a simple demonstration of the point, assume that ρ is a continuous variable rather than being discrete. If decisions over ρ and s are made simultaneously, then the domestic country faces the problem of maximizing $W(\rho, s; \rho^*, s^*)$, and the associated Nash first order conditions are simply

$$W_\rho = 0 ; \quad W_s = 0 . \tag{3.30}$$

If, on the other hand, decisions over ρ and s are made sequentially, then second stage solutions for s and s^* must be treated as functions of ρ and ρ^*. Thus the objective function of the domestic firm must be written $W(\rho, s(\rho, \rho^*); \rho^*, s^*(\rho, \rho^*))$. The first stage first order condition is then

$$dW/d\rho = W_\rho + W_s \, ds/d\rho + W_{s^*} \, ds^*/d\rho = 0 , \tag{3.31}$$

and the second stage first order condition will be $W_s = 0$. Substituting $W_s = 0$ into

(3.31) (i.e. using the envelope theorem) still leaves $dW/d\rho = W_\rho + W_{s*} \, ds*/d\rho = 0$. This differs from the first order condition given in (3.30) because of the additional strategic effect represented by the term $W_{s*} \, ds*/d\rho$. In the Cournot version of the Hwang–Schulman example, this term is the analog of the idea that if one government can commit itself to non-intervention at stage 1, then it reduces the optimal stage 2 subsidy chosen by the other country. This is an additional advantage of non-intervention that does not arise when the regime choice and the subsidy level choice are compressed into a single step. Thus the sequential structure of the game is very important in determining policy incentives.

3.5. Dynamics

Most of the work discussed so far involves games in which each player gets to move just once. Single-move games may have a sequential structure as, for example, when a government moves before firms or when one firm moves before another, but such games have no interactive dynamics. A slightly more sophisticated environment allows for multiple moves, as when firms choose R&D levels followed by output levels. In such a case, firms' strategy choices include the capacity to reciprocally condition output decisions on the R&D decisions of rivals. Thus firms react to each other to a limited extent. Even this game, however, is still a "one-shot" game in that firms have only one R&D decision and one output decision to make.

Single-move and one-shot games do not seem to be a very good description of ongoing commercial or government-to-government rivalries. Perhaps the simplest truly dynamic interaction is a pure repeated game between firms, with a government having a single policy move to make at the beginning of the game. Such a game is considered by Davidson (1984) who considers how tariffs affect the ability of foreign and domestic firms to maintain partial collusion using trigger strategies in an infinitely repeated game.

In a related paper, Rotemberg and Saloner (1989) make the interesting point that the imposition of quotas can significantly weaken the ability of foreign and domestic firms to maintain tacit collusion in an infinitely repeated game. In such a game, firms can support collusive or partially collusive outcomes by selecting trigger strategies that require firms to punish rivals by producing high levels of output (or selecting low prices) if rivals defect from the collusive output or price. If, however, quotas are imposed on foreign firms at the free-trade level of imports (or below), then foreign firms can no longer credibly commit to raising output levels in the domestic market in the event of excessive production by domestic firms. Thus domestic firms no longer face as strong an incentive to restrain their output, because foreign rivals cannot punish them. Therefore, firms are able to sustain a lower level of tacit collusion and the industry may become more competitive as a result of quotas.

The next natural step is consideration of repeated government policy decisions.

Collie (1993) considers an infinitely repeated version of the Brander–Spencer (1985) export subsidies model in which, each period, competing governments set subsidy levels and Cournot duopoly firms select output levels. In keeping with the "folk theorem" of repeated games [see, for example, Fudenberg and Tirole (1991, p. 152)], Collie finds that a wide range of alternative outcomes can be supported by infinite horizon trigger strategies. In particular, free trade can be supported if the countries are sufficiently similar and discount rates are sufficiently low. It would follow easily that governments could sometimes also support the jointly optimal solution in which both would impose taxes. The repeated one-shot solution with subsidies is, of course, also a subgame-perfect Nash equilibrium. The basic structure of these results will presumably apply to any full information infinitely repeated game.

More complex (and realistic) dynamic games would allow for repeated price, output, or other decisions against the background of an evolving state variable (like the R&D stock or capital stock of the firms). Note, however, that any game with a repeated game structure exogenously imposes important aspects of timing. Essentially, within a given "period" the analyst always decides whether players move simultaneously or whether one moves before the other, or whether players alternate moves. This choice is often rather arbitrary.

Probably the most descriptively accurate type of game to consider is the "game of timing". In a game of timing, time is normally treated as a continuous variable. There is some interval, possibly open-ended, within which players can make moves. Thus, for example, a government could set or change a tariff at any time. Timing is therefore endogenous. Typically, making a new move is assumed to be costly and, in addition, players may discount the future. Relatively few dynamic models of this type have been studied in the strategic trade policy literature as such models tend to give rise to considerable computational difficulty.

A partial step in this direction is provided by Dockner and Huang (1990) who examine a trade policy model in which oligopolistic firms interact in differential game fashion, but a government trade policy is set exogenously at the beginning of the game. Another example is Cheng (1987), who examines a dynamic version of the model developed by Spencer and Brander (1983) (and obtains similar results to theirs). Cheng also considers the possibility of technological spillovers between firms, which of course strengthens the case for export or R&D subsidies. Another interesting example is given by Driskill and McAfferty (1989) who provide a differential game version of the Eaton–Grossman (1986) model. Brainard (1994) considers a model in which trade policy influences the timing of possible exit by a domestic firm.

3.6. Asymmetric information

One of the major objections to the theory of strategic trade policy is that it presumes too much knowledge on the part of governments. To implement an optimal tax or subsidy, a government must have a good idea of cost, demand, and the nature of conduct in the industry. We might reasonably believe, however, that governments would be less well-informed about such things than the firms themselves. It therefore seems both inevitable and desirable that the role of asymmetric information be formally investigated in strategic trade policy models.

Perhaps the first observation to make is that firms would have an incentive to mislead governments if they could. Recall the formula given by (3.18) for the optimal domestic export subsidy for a third-market Cournot duopoly model with linear demand.

$$s = a/4 - c/2 + c*/4 . \qquad (3.18)$$

The optimal subsidy increases as domestic cost c falls. If c is not directly observable to the domestic government then, as pointed out by Wong (1991), the domestic firm would have an incentive to persuade the government that its marginal cost is lower than it actually is.

The domestic government might, of course, anticipate the domestic firm's incentive to misrepresent its costs. A formal analysis of this problem is contained in Qiu (1994). Qiu assumes that the domestic firm is one of only two possible types: high-cost or low-cost. The domestic firm knows its own costs, but neither the domestic government nor the foreign firm can observe the firm's type, although each knows the distribution from which the type is drawn. The foreign firm's cost is common knowledge. The domestic government may set a menu of per unit and lump-sum subsidies (or taxes), or it may adopt a uniform subsidy program that would apply to all firms.

This structure is familiar from the large literature on informational asymmetries. However, one interesting innovation is that the model contains both screening and signalling. Screening (an action by the uninformed party) is in this case carried out by the domestic government, but signalling (an action by the informed party) also occurs in the sense that the domestic firm signals its type to the foreign firm via its selection from the menu proposed by the domestic government.

A central question in screening and signalling models is whether the solution is a separating equilibrium, in which different types of domestic firm would opt for different subsidy programs, or whether it is a pooling equilibrium, in which all types would choose the same program. In this case, Qiu shows that a domestic government will (for the Cournot duopoly case) choose a menu of subsidy programs that induces separation by firms. Furthermore, the resulting allocation is the same as the allocation that would occur if the government had full information ex ante about the firm's costs. Interestingly, however, Qiu also considers the case of Bertrand competition and finds that the domestic government would then prefer a uniform subsidy program, leading to a pooling equilibrium. The allocation in this case differs from the full information allocation.

The basic intuition of these results is as follows. A separating equilibrium induces greater variance in the foreign firm's strategy variable (output or price) than a pooling equilibrium. Under separation, the foreign firm infers the true cost of the domestic firm before making its strategy selection and adjusts its output or price accordingly. Under pooling, the foreign firm selects price or quantity on the basis of expected cost and therefore its strategy selection does not vary with the domestic firm's type. The welfare effects of inducing variance in the foreign firm's strategy are opposite in the Cournot and Bertrand models. Under Cournot competition, the domestic country gains under separation relative to pooling when the domestic firm proves to be low cost, because this revelation inhibits the foreign firm's output. The domestic country loses from separation relative to pooling when the domestic firm has high costs because the foreign firm produces more than it would under pooling. However, in the low cost case potential profits are higher, so the gains from getting an advantage in this case outweigh the losses from being disadvantaged by separation when costs are high. Thus separation is preferred.

Under Bertrand competition, however, the gains from separation come in the high cost case because the foreign firm charges a higher price, knowing that the domestic firm's price reaction function is in a less aggressive (i.e. higher-priced) position. The losses from separation come in the low cost case as the foreign firm charges a lower price than it would under pooling. Thus, with Bertrand competition, the gains from separation come when the stakes are low and the losses when the stakes are high, so pooling is preferred. As before, this policy reversal is based on whether the strategy variables are strategic substitutes (as in the Cournot model) or strategic complements (as in the Bertrand model).

Brainard and Martimort (1992) consider the same basic economic environment as Qiu in that they too introduce cost-based informational asymmetries into the third market export subsidies model. However, there are several important differences. In Qiu (1994) subsidies have the added advantage of providing a means by which the domestic firm can credibly reveal its costs to the foreign rival when it is advantageous to do so. Brainard and Martimort assume that the foreign firm observes the cost level of the domestic firm, so only the domestic government is uninformed. Thus the signalling benefit of a subsidy is absent, and Brainard and Martimort obtain the result that the government's lack of information weakens the commitment value of a subsidy and reduces the optimal subsidy relative to what it would be under full information.

Collie and Hviid (1993) consider the complementary case, in which the domestic firm and the domestic government know the domestic firm's costs, but the foreign firm does not. In this case [as in Qiu (1994)] the domestic government has a stronger incentive to use an export subsidy because the government's willingness to use a subsidy signals to the foreign firm that the domestic firm is a low-cost firm, inhibiting the foreign rival and providing benefits to the domestic firm over and above the direct value of the subsidy.

The analysis of the effects of informational asymmetries on strategic trade policy is still in its early stages. However, as is clear from the papers just discussed, the analysis will draw heavily from the large existing body of work on principal-agent models. (In essence, the domestic government is a principal and the domestic firm is an agent.) Furthermore, the application of the agency framework to strategic trade policy will be similar in some respects to its application to regulation, which also comprises a large literature. One problem that strategic trade policy will inherit from the general theory of agency is that the range of possible outcomes will be expanded depending on alternative plausible specifications of the information structure and the equilibrium concepts that may be invoked. When this range of possibilities is multiplied by the range of alternative market structures and alternative dynamic specifications, the set of models to be understood expands significantly.

Nevertheless, such models do need to be understood. The existence of informational asymmetries seems both indisputable and important, and we know that markets with even small informational asymmetries may be qualitatively different from markets with symmetric information. It is quite possible that some robust general insights will emerge. For example, the contrasts between Brainard and Martimort (1992), Collie and Hviid (1993) and Qiu (1994) highlight the possible importance of government policy in facilitating strategic information revelation.

3.7. Entry

So far the number of firms has been taken as exogenous, with firms allowed to earn positive above-normal profits. Indeed, shifting these above-normal profits from one firm to another is a central aspect of strategic trade policy. It is, however, important to consider endogenous entry in response to profitable opportunities. At one extreme, the cost structure in a given market might be such that only a few (or perhaps only one) firm can exist successfully. The one (or few) firms who do establish themselves might be very profitable, but potential entrants would expect to make losses. Thus, even though entry is free, supra-normal profits would exist and strategic trade policy models of the type considered previously would apply. Papers by Brander and Spencer (1981), Dixit and Kyle (1985), and Bagwell and Staiger (1992) explicitly consider the use of strategic trade policy to influence entry in markets of this type.

Another possibility is that cost indivisibilities might be small enough relative to overall demand that entry occurs until the excess profits of the marginal firm are driven to precisely zero. This assumption is often combined with the assumption of symmetry among firms. Then, if a marginal firm earns zero profits, all firms earn zero profits. In such a model, strategic profit-shifting effects disappear, as there are no profits to shift. Often the term "free entry" is taken to mean this case, in which profits are entirely absent. It is important to recognize, however, that this is an extreme case in which results may be artifacts of the symmetry assumption. More descriptively accurate models would allow for asymmetries among firms so that infra-marginal firms might earn pure profits even if marginal firms earned precisely zero profits. In such models, free entry would not necessarily eliminate profit-shifting effects. Most of the analysis of zero-profit free entry models has been carried out in the context of the reciprocal-markets model as described in Sections 4.5 and 4.6.

4. Strategic trade policy in the reciprocal-markets model

4.1. Market segmentation and the reciprocal-markets model

The third-market model considered in Section 3 is a very efficient model structure for examining many strategic policy issues. There are, however, additional issues to consider that require a more complete trading structure. Aside from the third-market model, the other environment that has been most extensively used in the analysis of strategic trade policy is what I refer to as the "reciprocal-markets" model, the basic structure of which is set out in Brander (1981).

There are two countries, typically but not necessarily with identical demand and cost conditions. One country is referred to as the domestic country and the other as the foreign country. Within each country, two (or more) goods are consumed. At least one of these goods is produced by oligopolistic firms, some domestic and some foreign. A key assumption of the reciprocal-markets model is that markets are assumed to be segmented in the sense that oligopolistic firms make separate strategic decisions concerning foreign and domestic markets. If output is the choice variable, then firms choose distinct output levels for each market, rather than throwing all their output on a unified or integrated world market and relying on arbitrage to distribute it to different locations. Market segmentation implies that prices in the two countries are treated as independent variables, as under price discrimination. If, however, domestic and foreign countries are symmetric, prices will be the same in both markets and no arbitrage opportunities will exist, despite market segmentation.

4.2. Profit-shifting in a reciprocal-markets model with Cournot oligopoly

Brander and Spencer (1984a,b) use Cournot duopoly and related reciprocal-markets models to investigate the possible use of tariffs to shift profits from a foreign firm (or firms) to domestic claimants. This section presents the Cournot oligopoly case with n domestic firms and n^* foreign firms. The sequence of events is that governments set tariffs in stage 1 and firms choose outputs in stage 2. There are two goods, one produced by Cournot oligopolists producing a homogeneous output. The other good is a competitive numeraire good produced with constant returns to scale in labor, which is the only factor of production. Let x denote domestic sales by a representative domestic firm, while y denotes domestic sales by a foreign firm. Correspondingly, using asterisks to denote variables associated with the foreign country, sales of a domestic firm in the foreign country are denoted x^*, and sales of a foreign firm in the foreign country are denoted y^*. The n domestic firms are identical, as are the n^* foreign firms. Total sales in the two countries are denoted Q and Q^* respectively.

$$Q = nx + n^*y ; \quad Q^* = nx^* + n^*y^* . \tag{4.1}$$

As in Section 3, marginal costs c and c^* are constant, and there are possible fixed costs F and F^*. Domestic and foreign consumer prices are denoted p and p^*, and specific import tariffs set by the domestic and foreign governments are denoted t and t^*. Profits of representative home and foreign firms can then be written

$$\pi = xp(Q) - cx + x^*p^*(Q^*) - (c + t^*)x^* - F , \tag{4.2}$$

$$\pi^* = yp(Q) - (c^* + t)y + y^*p^*(Q^*) - c^*y^* - F^* . \tag{4.3}$$

Because of market segmentation and because of the constancy of marginal cost, we can proceed by examining just one national market. The Cournot oligopoly first order conditions for representative domestic and foreign firms are simply the application of first order conditions (3.2) to this particular context.

$$\pi_x = xp' + p - c = 0 ; \quad \pi_y^* = yp' + p - c^* - t = 0 . \tag{4.4}$$

Note that x^* and y^* do not appear in these first order conditions. Similarly, x and y would not enter the first order conditions associated with the foreign market. At a technical level, this is why we can consider the two national markets separately. Conditions (3.3) (second order conditions) and (3.4) (strategic substitutes) are assumed to hold for all firms.

The solution of the first order conditions will yield x and y as functions of t and t^*. This solution will normally have the property that firms will sell in both home and export markets, implying that intra-industry trade occurs, as shown by Brander (1981).

As in Section 3.1, comparative static effects dx/dt and dy/dt can be obtained by totally differentiating (4.4) with respect to t and the outputs of all firms. Due to the assumption that all firms in a given country are symmetric, this differential system can be written as follows.

$$(n(xp'' + p') + p') \, dx + n^* \pi_{xy} \, dy + \pi_{xt} \, dt = 0 . \tag{4.5}$$

$$n \pi_{yx}^* \, dx + (n^*(yp'' + p') + p') \, dy + \pi_{yt}^* \, dt = 0 . \tag{4.6}$$

Dividing through by dt and expressing the system in matrix form yields

$$\begin{bmatrix} n(xp'' + p') + p' & n^* \pi_{xy} \\ n \pi_{yx}^* & n^*(yp'' + p') + p' \end{bmatrix} \begin{bmatrix} dx/dy \\ dy/dt \end{bmatrix} = \begin{bmatrix} -\pi_{xt} \\ -\pi_{yt}^* \end{bmatrix} . \tag{4.7}$$

Noting that $\pi_{xt} = 0$ and $\pi_{yt}^* = -1$ [from (4.4)], and letting D represent the determinant of the left-hand matrix in (4.7), which is positive by (3.3) and (3.4), the following comparative static effects can be obtained.

$$dx/dt = -n^*\pi_{xy}/D > 0 \; ; \quad dy/dt = (n(xp'' + p') + p')/D < 0 \,, \tag{4.8}$$

where the numerators of these expressions are signed using condition (3.4) (i.e. using the assumption that outputs are strategic substitutes). As expected, a tariff on imports reduces domestic sales of foreign firms and increases domestic sales of domestic firms.

If there were just one foreign firm and one domestic firm, these effects could be shown in a best-response function diagram similar to Figure 3.1, except that it is the foreign best-response function that would be shifted. For any given output by the domestic firm, the foreign firm would want to produce less because the tariff raises its effective marginal cost. Therefore, the foreign reaction function would shift in.

With general numbers of firms, it follows easily that a domestic tariff causes foreign profits to fall, domestic profits to rise, and overall price to rise ($dp/dt > 0$) and quantity to fall ($dQ/dt = n \, dx/dt + n^* \, dy/dt < 0$). The situation in the foreign country is symmetric, implying that aggregate profits of each firm depend on the tariff levels set by both governments. For the case of linear demand given by $p = a - Q$, comparative static effects can be very readily calculated. In this case $p'' = 0$, $p' = -1$, $D = n + n^* + 1$, and $\pi_{xy} = \pi_{yx}^* = -1$. Expression (4.8) becomes

$$dx/dt = n^*/(n + n^* + 1) \; ; \quad dy/dt = -(n + 1)/(n + n^* + 1) \,, \tag{4.8'}$$

and $dp/dt = -dQ/dt$, where $dQ/dt = -n^*/(n + n^* + 1)$.

We now turn to the decision problem faced by the domestic government. Assume that domestic utility derives from utility function

$$u(Q) + m \,. \tag{4.9}$$

This utility function, sometimes referred to as "quasi-linear" or "transferrable", is more general than the utility function used in Section 3, as two goods are now consumed in the domestic country, but it retains the key feature that utility is linear in the numeraire good and hence linear in income. This implies that changes in domestic welfare can, as in Section 3, be represented exactly by conventional surplus measures (i.e. by changes in profit, consumer surplus, and government net revenues). Accordingly, domestic welfare W associated with domestic tariff t and foreign tariff t^* is given by

$$W(t, t^*) = u(Q(t)) - pQ(t) + R(t) + n\pi(t, t^*) \,, \tag{4.10}$$

where $R(t)$ represents tariff revenue n^*ty. Domestic welfare depends on the foreign tariff only through the effect of the foreign tariff on the profits of domestic firms, which are assumed to count fully in domestic welfare. Domestic welfare is maximized by setting the derivative dW/dt to zero.

$$dW/dt = u' \, dQ/dt - p \, dQ/dt - Q \, dp/dt + dR/dt + n \, d\pi/dt = 0. \tag{4.11}$$

Noting that $u' = p$, that $d\pi/dt = (p - c) \, dx/dt + x \, dp/dt$, and that $Q - nx = n^*y$ yields

$$dW/dt = -n^*y \, dp/dt + n(p - c) \, dx/dt + dR/dt = 0. \tag{4.12}$$

The first term reflects the loss in consumer surplus associated with paying more for imports, the second term represents the marginal surplus associated with the expansion of domestic production and the third term reflects increased tariff revenue. Both the second and third terms contain profits shifted from the foreign firm to domestic claimants. Substituting $dR/dt = n^*y + tn^* \, dy/dt$ into (4.12), solving for t, and letting subscripts denote comparative static derivatives gives an expression for the optimal tariff.

$$t^0 + (y(p_t - 1))/y_t - (n/n^*)(p - c)x_t/y_t. \tag{4.13}$$

The simplest case to consider is the case of pure foreign monopoly, in which $n = 0$, $n^* = 1$, and $Q = y$. In this case, $dQ/dt = 1/\pi^*_{yy}$. If we let $V = yp''/p'$ (the relative convexity of demand), we find that $\pi^*_{yy} = p'(2 + V)$, so $p_t = p'y_t = 1/(2 + V)$ and we can write the optimal tariff (on a foreign monopoly) as

$$t^{0m} = -p'y(V + 1). \tag{4.14}$$

Thus, under simple foreign monopoly, the optimum tariff may be negative, zero, or positive, depending on whether V is less than, equals, or exceeds -1. In the case of linear demand, $V = 0$, and the optimal profit-shifting tariff is definitely positive as obtained by Katrak (1977) and Svedberg (1979). More generally, the condition $V + 1 > 0$ is equivalent to the condition that the marginal revenue curve be steeper than the inverse demand curve, which is certainly the standard case. However, it is possible, if demand is highly convex, that marginal revenue may be less steep than (inverse) demand and, correspondingly, that an import subsidy might be optimal. [See Brander and Spencer (1984a).] In the oligopoly case, the presence of domestic rivals means that foreign profits can be shifted to the domestic firms as well as to the domestic treasury. It is still possible that the optimal ''tariff'' could be negative (i.e. a subsidy) if demand is very convex, but a profit-shifting tariff is typically implied.

The incentives faced by the foreign government are exactly the same as those faced by the domestic government, as reflected in its objective function, W^*.

$$W^*(t, t^*) = u^*(Q^*) - p^*Q^* + t^*x^* + \pi^*(t, t^*). \tag{4.15}$$

Maximizing W^* with respect to t^* yields a first order condition similar to condition (4.11). Simultaneous satisfaction of (4.11) and (4.15) typically leads to a Nash equilibrium in which both governments use tariffs. This non-cooperative equilibrium in which both governments use tariffs is normally welfare-inferior to the free trade regime where neither uses tariffs.

4.3. Tariffs and subsidies

Section 4.2 considers the case in which government policy is limited to an import tariff (cum subsidy) instrument. Export subsidies or subsidies for local sales could also be considered, as in Dixit (1984). Let s and s^* denote domestic and foreign export subsidies, and let σ and σ^* be subsidies on local sales. (A general production subsidy for the domestic firm is implied if $s = \sigma$.) The effective marginal cost of a domestic firm in its home market would be $c - \sigma$, and its effective marginal cost of export would be $c + t^* - s$. Similar modifications apply to foreign marginal cost. Equation (4.7) would become

$$
\begin{bmatrix} n(xp'' + p') + p' & n^*\pi_{xy} \\ n\pi^*_{yx} & n^*(yp'' + p') + p' \end{bmatrix} \begin{bmatrix} dx \\ dy \end{bmatrix}
$$
$$
= \begin{bmatrix} -\pi_{xt} & -\pi_{x\sigma} & -\pi_{xs^*} \\ -\pi^*_{yt} & -\pi^*_{y\sigma} & -\pi^*_{ys^*} \end{bmatrix} \begin{bmatrix} dt \\ d\sigma \\ ds^* \end{bmatrix}. \tag{4.16}
$$

Following characterization of these comparative statics, and corresponding comparative statics for the foreign market, one can then characterize nationally optimal import tariffs, export subsidies, and local sales subsidies for each government, as in Dixit (1984, 1988b). Allowing for a subsidy on local sales shifts the emphasis of the analysis away from trade policy, because a government has an incentive to use such a subsidy simply to offset the output-restricting effect of oligopoly. Even in the absence of trade, this apparent incentive to subsidize monopolies and oligopolies always exits. Such policies seem of limited practical significance, suggesting that the case in which subsidies on local sales are constrained to be zero is perhaps of more interest.

   With or without local subsidies, this structure allows for derivation of simultaneous "countervailing" effects. Thus, for example, an export subsidy adopted by the foreign government could be "countervailed" by a simultaneously chosen domestic import tariff. The reader may find it useful to carry out these calculations for the case of linear demand. The interesting point about these countervailing effects is that they do not eliminate incentives to use active strategic trade policy, and the policy equilibrium normally implies positive subsidies and tariffs.

   Using the term "countervailing" to describe simultaneous selection of export subsidies and possibly offsetting tariffs is perhaps misleading. In practice the term countervailing carries the presumption that the export subsidy is applied first, then possibly offset by a tariff that is applied later. Collie (1991) considers a model of this type that is otherwise very similar to Dixit (1988b). For concreteness, say that the foreign government moves first, selecting an export subsidy. The domestic country subsequently selects an optimal tariff. Like Dixit, Collie finds that the domestic country would normally adopt a partially but not fully countervailing tariff. In contrast to Dixit (1988b), however, Collie finds that the extent of countervailing is sufficient in most cases to eliminate the foreign country's incentive to use an export subsidy.

This contrast is based purely on timing and is very similar to the contrasts discussed in Section 3.4.2. It is not clear whether the assumption that governments move simultaneously or the assumption that one moves before the other is preferable as governments can, in practice, choose new policies at any time. Spencer (1988) analyzes countervailing of capital or investment subsidies and emphasizes that the institutional structure of GATT and other trade agreements can be invoked for specifying timing in particular applications.

4.4. Comparison of the reciprocal-markets model and the third-market model

Most of the issues addressed by the third-market model are subsumed when considering export subsidies in the reciprocal-markets model, albeit with somewhat less clarity. There would, however, be some additional points of interest in combining the two models into a three country model with the oligopoly good being produced in two countries and consumed in all three. One could, for example, address the interaction of strategic trade policy and regional trade arrangements in such a model, but that takes us beyond the scope of this chapter.

The extensions applied to the third-market model can also be applied here. Specifically, allowing for public funds to have an opportunity cost exceeding 1 (as in Section 3.2.2) is straightforward and implies that tariffs become relatively more attractive and subsidies relatively less attractive. Allowing for consideration of R&D and investment, and allowing for market conduct other than Cournot (such as Bertrand competition) have similar interesting consequences. Very similar issues relating to timing, possible dynamics, and informational asymmetries also arise, although these areas are far from fully explored. There are, moreover, certain issues that have much more significance with reciprocal markets than in a third-market model. One of these issues is the role of home market protection in the presence of learning-by-doing, which is taken up as a calibration exercise in Section 5.2. Other issues include entry, the comparison of segmented and integrated markets, and the comparison of different trade policy instruments, particularly quotas and tariffs.

4.5. Entry

As mentioned in Section 3.7, it is important to consider the effects of free entry in response to profitable opportunities. The analysis already developed applies to situations where indivisibilities are sufficiently large so as allow positive profits for incumbents while preventing further entry.

At the other extreme, it is also worth considering the case in which free entry drives the profit of marginal firms to precisely zero. Most of the associated analysis has been carried out under the assumption of symmetry, in which all firms earn precisely zero profits. Brander and Krugman (1983) consider a reciprocal-markets Cournot model in which firms have declining average costs arising from a fixed cost and constant marginal costs. Entry occurs in both countries until all firms earn zero profits, giving rise to intra-industry trade arises even in the presence of positive transport costs. Despite the apparently unnecessary transport costs that are incurred, free trade is welfare superior to autarky. The central insight is that the zero-profit assumption holds producer surplus at zero, so welfare (which then arises purely from consumer surplus) is monotonically and inversely related to price. Trade increases the level of effective competition, forcing price to fall and exit to occur until surviving firms have increased output and moved down their average cost curves sufficiently to avoid losses at the new lower price. Thus welfare benefits come from rationalization of production.

Venables (1985) considers a similar reciprocal-markets model (with positive transport costs), introducing consideration of tariffs and subsidies. Venables finds that despite the absence of profit-shifting effects, both governments have incentives to use import tariffs and export subsidies. Consider first a tariff imposed by the domestic country. On impact, as the tariff is introduced, if no entry and exit took place and individual firms did not adjust outputs, the domestic price of imports would rise and consumers would switch to domestically produced output. This would bid up the price of domestically produced output and force down the price of foreign output until foreign imports and domestic output would sell for the same price. At this configuration, domestic firms would make profits and foreign firms would make losses. In order for equilibrium to be restored, firms would adjust outputs and, in addition, entry would occur in the domestic economy and exit would occur in the foreign country until the zero-profit condition was re-established.

This effective movement of firms from the foreign country to the domestic country is advantageous to the domestic country because, in the presence of positive transport costs, each firm sells more at home than it exports. Total sales in the domestic market rise, implying that consumer price in the domestic market must fall. Since consumer surplus rises and producer surplus is constant at zero, the domestic country gains. Thus the effect of domestic "protection" is pro-competitive in the domestic market because it induces entry. In addition, the domestic country becomes a net exporter of the imperfectly competitive good and experiences a terms-of-trade improvement due to the tariff, which is a second source of gains. The foreign country experiences exactly opposite effects, leading to a welfare loss. More surprisingly, an optimally chosen export subsidy also leads to gains for the domestic country. An export subsidy has a relocation effect similar to the effect of a tariff. The resulting benefit to the domestic economy is sufficient to ensure gains, even though the domestic economy earns no tariff revenue and subsidizes consumption abroad.

4.6. Comparison of segmented and integrated markets

Horstmann and Markusen (1986) investigate the effects of (zero-profit) free entry using a model structure similar to Venables (1985) except that international markets are assumed to be integrated rather than segmented. Firms do not make separate decisions about the two markets, but simply bring all their output to the unified world market. In analyzing this case, there are various effects that arise from either a tariff or a subsidy, and the relative importance of various effects is sensitive to functional forms for demand and cost. However, for most cases considered by Horstmann and Markusen, tariff or subsidy interventions are welfare-reducing for the country attempting them because they induce inefficient entry, driving firms up their average cost curves.

Markusen and Venables (1988) provide a systematic attempt to link strategic trade policy implications to the nature of entry and to whether markets are segmented or unified. As is consistent with the previous papers by Venables (1985) and Horstmann and Markusen (1986), this synthesis shows that tariffs or subsidies improve welfare more (or reduce it less) if markets are segmented rather than unified, and that free entry tends to reduce the attractiveness of tariff or subsidy interventions.

The assumption that markets are segmented rather than integrated is a central aspect of the reciprocal-markets model. For example, in contrast to Brander's (1981) demonstration of intra-industry trade in a simple Cournot reciprocal-markets model, Markusen (1981) uses an otherwise very similar model except that markets are integrated rather than segmented and obtains the result that no intra-industry trade occurs.

In richer models of firm behavior, it is possible that some decisions might be made on a world-wide basis (i.e. under an integrated markets perception) while others might be made on a market-by-market or segmented basis. Venables (1990) considers such a model in which oligopolistic firms in two countries may compete with each other in either Cournot or Bertrand fashion. Firms make a two-stage decision. In stage 1 firms simultaneously decide on world-wide capacity. In the second stage firms decide on market-specific quantities or prices. Venables argues that this structure is more realistic than simple Cournot or Bertrand models. In his analysis, consideration of a prior worldwide capacity stage significantly changes implied trade volumes, but leaves intact the strategic trade policy incentives to subsidize exports and tax imports. There are, however, alternative ways to characterize the distinction between capacity and price and/or quantity decisions in a multi-market setting. [See, in particular, Ben-Zvi and Helpman (1992).]

4.7. Choice of trade policy instruments

A classic question in the theory of international trade policy concerns the relative effects of tariffs and quotas or, more generally, the effects of a variety of possible policy instruments. In perfectly competitive models of trade, tariffs and quotas are normally equivalent, in the sense that the effect of a tariff can be duplicated by an appropriately chosen quota. As Bhagwati (1965) noted, however, this need not be true under imperfect competition. Accordingly, we might expect some interesting comparisons between tariffs and quotas as strategic trade policy tools (i.e. in international oligopoly settings). More generally, we might expect the analysis of quotas under oligopoly to offer additional insights over and above the insights obtained from the analysis of tariffs and subsidies. Quite a few papers have addressed aspects of this question, including Itoh and Ono (1984), Harris (1985), Hwang and Mai (1988), Cooper and Riezman (1989), Krishna (1989), Levinsohn (1989), Das and Donnenfeld (1989), Ries (1993a,b), Anis and Ross (1992) and Ishikawa (1994), among others.

Perhaps the central difference between tariffs and quotas as policy instruments relates to their effects on foreign firms. Any tariff on foreign firms reduces their profits, and a subsidy to domestic firms also tends to reduce the profits of foreign firms. With quotas, on the other hand, there is a much greater possibility that the foreign firms might benefit, particularly if the quota is implemented as a voluntary export restraint (VER), meaning that foreign firms keep any quota rents rather than having to buy quota licenses. In effect, a VER acts as a device that facilitates a more collusive outcome for foreign firms. This implies that a VER is less likely to be in the interest of a domestic welfare-maximizing government.

In the case where there are several foreign firms, it is fairly clear that a quota set below the free trade level of imports has the primary effect of moving the foreign firms closer to the jointly optimal (collusive) output level, and is therefore a facilitating device for collusion. A very restrictive quota could reduce output sufficiently far below the jointly optimal output level that the foreign firms could suffer reduced profits, but there is a substantial range for the quota within which both foreign firms and the domestic firm (or firms) can gain.

A more surprising facilitating effect is demonstrated by Krishna (1989) who considers the case of an international Bertrand duopoly with one foreign and one domestic firm producing slightly differentiated products. She examines the effect of a VER imposed at the free trade level. In a perfectly competitive market, a VER at the free trade level would have no effect. In this Bertrand duopoly case, however, the VER alters the strategic relationship between the two firms, and this may have an important effect on market outcomes.

In order to see whether the free trade prices still constitute a Nash equilibrium after the imposition of a VER at the free trade level, we must ask whether each firm is still doing the best it can given its rival's price. The free trade prices are denoted $p0$ and $r0$ for the domestic and foreign firm respectively. Consider the home firm first.

Taking the rival's price, $r0$, as given, the domestic firm now finds it more attractive to raise its price than before. Prior to the VER, the domestic firm would imagine that if it raised its price, while the rival held price fixed, then it (the domestic firm) would sell less and the foreign firm would sell more. However, with the VER in place, the foreign firm cannot sell more, so the domestic firm suffers fewer lost sales from its price increase than it otherwise would. Thus the VER increases the domestic firm's incentive to raise its price. Letting $p1$ represent the domestic firm's post-VER best-response to foreign price $r0$, it follows that $p1 > p0$.

This argument shows that if the foreign firm kept its price at the free trade level, the domestic firm would raise its price. The foreign firm will not keep its price at the free trade level, however. For example, if it anticipated that the domestic firm would raise its price, then its corresponding best response would also involve a higher price, for its price best-response function is upward-sloping. Thus we can see that a VER imposed at the free trade import level creates incentives for both firms to raise prices.

The actual solution is fairly complicated, because the domestic firm's best-response function turns out to be discontinuous. The solution is illustrated in Figure 4.1, which shows post-VER reaction functions for the two firms. The foreign firm's best-response function is continuous but kinked, as shown. The kink occurs at the initial free trade equilibrium price, reflecting the fact that beyond this point, the foreign firm is constrained by the VER. The domestic firm's best-response function is discontinuous. At the free-trade foreign price, $r0$, the domestic best response is price $p1$. This price is really just a best response to the VER fixed quantity and remains the same for

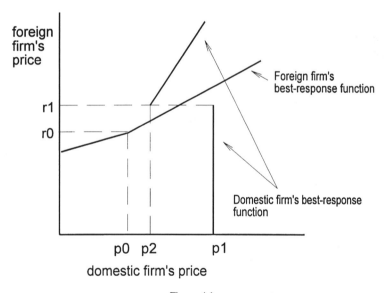

Figure 4.1.

any foreign price for which the VER is binding. However, as we consider increases in the foreign price, at some price the VER ceases to be binding. At this point, the best-response of the domestic firm is given by its old pre-VER best-response function, implying a discrete fall in its price. At this pivotal foreign price, the domestic firm switches from a conciliatory to an aggressive price response.

The "hole" in the domestic firm's best-response function occurs just where the rival's best-response function passes through, as shown in the diagram. Thus there is no single pair of prices (or "pure strategy") that constitutes a Nash equilibrium. The only Nash equilibrium is a "mixed strategy" in which the domestic firm charges price $p1$ with some probability and price $p2$ with some probability. The foreign firm must charge price $r1$. All three of these prices exceed the corresponding free trade prices. Thus Krishna (1989) obtains the striking result that, in this simple Bertrand duopoly model, a VER is unambiguously a "facilitating device" that raises prices and profits at consumers' expense, even if the VER is imposed at the free trade level of imports. [This is in contrast to the dynamic effect of quotas under tacit collusion analyzed by Rotemberg and Saloner (1989) as discussed in Section 3.5.] Note that in Krisha (1989), the VER has important effects even though, on average, the VER is not binding at the solution.

The value of Krisha (1989) is not so much that it is likely to be a literal description of an actual outcome. The paper's important contribution is that it focuses attention on the idea that a VER (and, by extension, any trade policy instrument) can have important effects through the effects on imperfectly competitive rivalries between firms. A closely related possibility is that a VER might lead to a change in the mode of rivalry between firms, as in Harris (1985), who assumes that the imposition of a VER at the free-trade level converts a Bertrand rivalry to a structure in which the domestic firm becomes a Stackelberg price leader. Once again, such a VER acts as a facilitating device.

In addition to the choice between tariffs and quotas, there are many other closely related issues. Even if attention is restricted just to tariffs, there is the question of whether ad valorem or specific tariffs should be chosen. As shown in Brander and Spencer (1984b), under imperfect competition, specific and ad valorem tariffs are not equivalent and their relative attractiveness depends on the functional form of demand and other very specific aspects of the model. More generally, we might consider tariffs with specific and ad valorem components (or more general non-linear tariffs). Various other possible policies could also be used to shift rents under oligopoly, including price controls [De Meza (1979)] discretionary anti-dumping policies [Prusa (1992)], content protection [Krishna and Itoh (1988)], government procurement policies [Branco (1994)] and even trade related intellectual property rights or TRIPS [Taylor (1993)]. More generic domestic policies such as competition policy, environmental policy, and the setting of industrial standards can also be used to influence the strategic structure of international rivalries.

There is a long-standing literature in international trade theory seeking to establish how to efficiently target instruments to distortions. [See, in particular, Bhagwati (1971).] Thus, for example, either an export subsidy or a production subsidy may appear attractive in dealing with a particular distortion, but one instrument may be more efficient than the other. This issue applies in strategic trade policy just as it does in the analysis of trade policy more generally. Krishna and Thursby (1991) seek to establish some general principles in applying instruments to distortions under oligopoly.

4.8. Additional issues

The preceding material in this chapter ignores some worthwhile topics in strategic trade policy that should at least be acknowledged. One such topic concerns labor market rents. Much of the work on strategic trade policy focuses on profits earned by firms in imperfectly competitive product markets, usually against a background of undistorted labor markets. This emphasis might be misplaced, in that deviations from perfect competition in labor markets seem at least comparable in significance to product market deviations. Also, when industrial policy advocates encourage "high value added production" they seem to place more weight on high-wage jobs than on high-income shareholders. Evidence presented by Katz and Summers (1989) suggests that much of the rent at stake in international trade policy games accrues to workers. Analysis of strategic trade policy in the presence of active unions is contained in Brander and Spencer (1988), Mezzetti and Dinopolous (1991), and Fung (1995).

It is also important to consider the effects of strategic trade policies when firms have a vertically integrated multinational structure, as in Spencer and Jones (1991, 1992) and Rodrik and Yoon (1989), and to understand the effects of trade policies when firms are not simple profit-maximizers. For example, Fung (1992) considers the effects of trade policies on the so-called "J-firm" (for Japan) in which the firm is viewed as a coalition of shareholders and workers. We might also wish to relax the assumption that the structure of firms is exogenous and ask how strategic trade policy might affect the multinational structure of firm operations, as in Levinsohn (1989), Horstmann and Markusen (1992), and Flam (1994). Trade policy might also affect the internal organization of the firm, as in Friedman and Fung (1996). Another lively recent topic in international trade theory, particularly in empirical work, is the effect of trade policy on product quality. Das and Donnenfeld (1989) provide a theoretical analysis of product quality in a strategic trade policy model.

5. Calibration of strategic trade policy models

Any attempt to implement an informed strategic trade policy would require significant industry-specific empirical knowledge. For some questions of interest there may be insufficient data to support statistical estimation of an appropriate model. An alternative way of undertaking empirically-based quantification of economic models is the calibration method pioneered by Shoven and Whalley (1972) and first applied to trade models incorporating imperfect competition by Harris and Cox (1984).

One starts with a model containing general parameters that are to be replaced with specific values. Instead of using multiple observations to estimate these parameter values statistically, parameter values are taken from external sources, subject only to the constraint that the final selected parameter values be consistent with a single base case observation (or perhaps a small number of observations). External sources may include previous econometric work, engineering studies, and the analyst's judgement. Typically the first set of parameter values obtained will not be consistent with the one (or few) observations available, so one or more of the parameter values are modified using a combination of judgement and formal methods until consistency is obtained. It is in this sense that the model is calibrated to the data. A special case of this method is to obtain outside estimates for all parameters but one, then assign this free parameter precisely the value necessary to make the model consistent with the data. Once the model has been calibrated, it can then be used to consider policy experiments such as tariff and subsidy changes.

We should really take account of the fact that outside parameter estimates have uncertainty associated with them. Without this step, some observers have argued that calibration exercises should be viewed essentially as simulations in that they simply show how a given theoretical structure works under the assumption of particular parameter values. The main reason for emphasizing calibration exercises in this chapter is for the light they shed on the theoretical structure of strategic trade policy, rather than because of their empirical significance.

5.1. Calibration of a strategic trade policy model for the U.S. automobile industry

Dixit (1988a) uses a calibration technique to assess the effects of strategic trade policies on the U.S. automobile industry. His underlying model is a reciprocal-markets model with Japanese and American producers where firm conduct is characterized by a conduct parameter model. He focuses on just the U.S. market. Concern about the rising level of Japanese import penetration in the U.S. market led U.S. policy-makers in 1981 to impose a voluntary export restraint (VER) on Japanese imports. Dixit calibrates the model for 1979, 1980, and 1983, then, armed with a calibrated version of the model, evaluates different trade polices. He is primarily interested in how actual U.S. trade policies compared with optimal policies.

The basic logic of Dixit's approach can be seen by taking a first order condition for a representative firm, as given by expression (3.22), then solving for the conduct parameter, λ. We can rewrite (3.22) as

$$\lambda = -1 - (p - c)/xp' , \tag{5.1}$$

or, equivalently, as

$$\lambda = [(p - c)/p][\eta/ms] - 1, \tag{5.2}$$

where η is the (positive) elasticity of market demand and ms is the market share of this firm. This first order condition forms the core of the model. Typically we have information on price, quantity, and market share that we can take as known. However, the elasticity of demand, marginal cost, and the conduct parameter itself are less likely to be available as data. If we make an attempt to measure marginal cost and to get some estimate of the elasticity of demand, then from (5.2) we can determine what the conduct parameter λ must be in order to fit the data. Alternatively, looking at formulation (5.2) we might assume that the Cournot model is correct, so λ must equal 0, and let η be determined by the data, as is done, for example, in Klepper (1994).

Dixit generalizes the model of Section 3.3.1 slightly by assuming that cars made in the U.S. are differentiated from cars produced in Japan. However, all U.S. cars are homogeneous, as are all Japanese cars. There are n American firms and n^* Japanese firms. Demand is linear. With differentiated products, (5.2) does not apply exactly, but we can write the first order condition of a representative American firm as

$$p - c + x\phi = 0, \tag{5.3}$$

where, in a Cournot model, $\phi = dp/dx$, the slope of U.S. inverse demand for U.S. cars. If the auto industry is not Cournot, then ϕ will differ from this slope. For example, under Bertrand competition, $\phi = 0$. As in the homogeneous product case, market information can be used to calibrate ϕ. Dixit finds that the U.S. industry is more competitive than implied by a Cournot model but less competitive than a Bertrand model would imply.

Dixit considers the case in which only a tariff is available as well as the case in which both a tariff on Japanese imports and a U.S. production subsidy are available. He finds that a considerably higher tariff than was actually in place on Japanese cars would have been welfare-improving for the U.S., whether or not a production subsidy was applied. For the 1979 base case, the actual tariff on an imported Japanese car was $100 on a price of about $4000, while the optimal tariff would have been $570 in the absence of a subsidy and $408 in combination with an optimal subsidy of $611. The total U.S. welfare benefit from this combined optimal tariff and subsidy would have been $309 million, which is small compared to total U.S. surplus in the industry of $33 billion.

In the base calculations, wages paid to workers are treated as (opportunity) costs. It is likely, however, that some portion of wages is a rent or payment above opportunity cost to auto workers. Taking account of such rents, optimal policy would require an even greater reduction in Japanese imports. Thus, for 1979, with labor rents taken to be about $1000 per car (corresponding to half the wage bill), the optimum tariff with no subsidy would increase to \$812. Dixit also considers the effect of deadweight taxation costs as a modification to the base case (i.e. without labor rents). Assuming that the deadweight cost of raising government revenue is a modest 20 percent, Dixit finds that the optimum tariff with no subsidy rises to \$791 from its base value of \$570. The joint tariff-subsidy optimum would imply a tariff of \$922 and a tax (or negative subsidy) of \$487.

As recognized by Dixit, there are several aspects of this analysis to be concerned about. Perhaps the biggest concern derives from the calibration of the conduct parameter, as it is essentially treated as a residual. Any error in the data, in model specification, or in outside parameter estimates would be incorporated in the all-important conduct parameter. One possible manifestation of this problem is that measured conduct was markedly different in each of three years studied (1979, 1980 and 1983). Also, despite the apparent volatility of conduct, the policy simulations assume that market conduct (as reflected by the conduct parameter) would be unaffected by policy changes.

In addition, it is hard to take on faith that marginal cost is constant, that demand in the industry is linear, or that the only meaningful product differentiation in the industry is between U.S. and Japanese producers. Similarly, it is not clear how to implement the maintained assumption of symmetric producers in an industry where the firms differ substantially in size. Dixit adopts the standard practice of selecting the number of symmetric firms that would give the same Herfindal index as given by the actual data, but this could easily be a source of error. It is not even clear how to count firms, as one could reasonably take either corporations (like General Motors) or divisions (like Chevrolet) as the basic decision-making unit. Dixit makes a valiant attempt to address most of these issues through sensitivity analysis, but one must remain cautious about the empirical significance of the results.

The need for such caution is reinforced by a paper by Krishna, Hogan, and Swagel (1994) (denoted KHS). Like Dixit, KHS evaluate the U.S. automobile market, focusing on U.S. and Japanese producers, and they consider the period 1979–85, which includes the three years considered by Dixit. The major difference in the analysis is that KHS wish to allow product differentiation within the U.S. and Japanese auto industries. Accordingly, KHS assume a demand structure that can readily handle such product differentiation. Specifically, demand for automobiles is assumed to derive from a (sub) utility function of the form βS^{α} where S is a nested constant elasticity of substitution (CES) function with two CES subaggregates (one for Japanese cars and one for U.S. cars). This gives rise to nonlinear (and highly convex) demand curves for individual varieties. KHS use the same cost data as Dixit and very similar quantity data. Strikingly, however, KHS find that industry conduct for U.S. producers is more competitive than implied by Bertrand competition (and therefore much more competitive than implied by Cournot behavior) in contrast to Dixit's finding that behavior is between Cournot and Bertrand.

This result is not difficult to explain. With homogenous products in the U.S.

industry, as assumed by Dixit, Bertrand behavior implies marginal cost pricing. Therefore, any excess of price over marginal cost indicates that behavior is less competitive than Bertrand. However, with differentiated products in the U.S. industry, as assumed by KHS, Bertrand competition implies a positive markup of price over marginal cost. Therefore, price may exceed marginal cost and still be consistent with conduct that is more competitive than Bertrand competition, as found by KHS.

In addition, KHS find that the optimal U.S. policy is to subsidize (rather than tax) Japanese imports. This finding is explained by the assumption of highly convex demand, which tends to make an import subsidy optimal under imperfect competition because the gains in consumer surplus from lower prices are large relative to the subsidy cost. [This is shown by expression (4.14) for the monopoly case.]

By changing just one of the major components in Dixit's analysis (the demand structure) KHS obtain qualitatively different results. While the KHS analysis is more sophisticated, there is very little basis for confidence that the KHS analysis is closer to being correct. In particular, while there is little doubt that product differentiation is important in the industry, it is not clear that the functional forms used for demand in KHS are good approximations to actual demand. KHS themselves emphasize that perhaps the major conclusion to be drawn from their work is that results obtained from calibrated models of oligopoly are worryingly sensitive to untested assumptions about model structure.

5.2. Calibration of the 16K RAM computer chip market

Baldwin and Krugman (1988) undertake a strategic trade policy calibration in a market where learning-by-doing is very important, the international market for 16 Kilobyte (16K) Random Access Memory (RAM) computer chips. The 16K RAM chip was first shipped in 1976, became a significant market presence in 1978 (21 million units shipped), reached its peak in 1982 (263 million units shipped), then suffered a sharp loss in market as it was superseded by 64K and 256K RAM chips. Prices followed a dramatic decline, starting at $46 per unit in 1976, falling to $8.53 in 1978, to $2.06 in 1981, and to under a dollar by 1984. This price decline was associated with a decline in production cost, as plant yields tend to rise dramatically with experience. Like the auto industry, the market for RAM chips attracted substantial attention from U.S. policy-makers, in part because of rising penetration by Japanese manufacturers in the market.

Krugman (1984) made an influential contribution to strategic trade policy by proposing that import protection may act as a form of export promotion if the industry in question is subject to significant learning-by-doing or other dynamic economies. More generally, any incentives to apply strategic trade policies might be enhanced by the presence of learning-by-doing of the type that appears to be so important in the production of RAM chips. [See Gatsios (1989) and Neary (1994) for an analysis of subsidies in the presence of learning-by-doing and Head (1994) for an analysis of learning-by-doing in the 19th century steel rail industry, showing that learning-by-doing was as important for trade policy a century ago as it is today. See also Dinopolous, Sappington, and Lewis (1994) for an analysis of strategic trade policy in a model where a domestic firm's rate of learning-by-doing is unobserved by the domestic government.]

Baldwin and Krugman (1988) (denoted BK) construct a calibrated oligopoly model of the 16K RAM market to examine the effects of Japanese home market protection on market outcomes and welfare. The following description follows the version of this model in Helpman and Krugman (1989). BK assume that costs at time t for a representative RAM producer can be written as

$$C(t) = x(t)c[k(t)] , \tag{5.4}$$

where $x(t)$ is output at time t, $k(t)$ is cumulative output up to time t, and $c' < 0$, indicating that the marginal cost of production decreases with cumulative output. Note that cumulative output can be written as $k(t) = \int_0^t x(z)\,dz$. Modelling dynamic oligopoly can be difficult, but BK make two common simplifying assumptions. First, they assume that rivalry between firms is of the open loop variety – as if firms simultaneously choose and commit to their output paths as functions of time at the beginning of game. Secondly, BK assume that the life of the product is sufficiently short that discounting can be ignored, which greatly simplifies the required algebra. Given this structure, the effective marginal cost at time t, denoted $\mu(t)$, can be written as

$$\mu(t) = c(k(t)) + \int_t^T x(z)c'(k(z))\,dz . \tag{5.5}$$

The first term on the right-hand side of (5.5) is just current marginal production cost at time t. The second term reflects the impact of an extra unit of current production at time t on future production costs. This second term is negative for all $t < T$, as higher current production reduces future costs. Thus, except at the last moment of time, when $\mu = c$, marginal production cost c always exceeds effective marginal cost μ.

Marginal production cost $c(k(t))$ declines over time, but so does the future value of the learning effect. Taking the derivative of (5.5) with respect to t and recalling that $x(t) = dk/dt$ yields

$$d\mu/dt = c'(k(t))\,dk/dt - x(t)c'(k(t)) = 0 . \tag{5.6}$$

Thus effective marginal cost is constant over time and must be equal to $c(T)$. This constancy of effective marginal cost simplifies the model, as we can characterize the maximizing decision of a representative firm by the instantaneous condition that $MR = \mu = c(T)$, where MR is current marginal revenue. This leads to a first order condition for a representative American firm much like (5.1), except that c is replaced by μ.

BK are interested in both U.S. and Japanese markets and therefore use a reciprocal-markets model structure (i.e. with segmented markets). They allow for the possibility that conduct might differ in the two countries. They also allow for the possibility that the conduct of Japanese firms operating in either country might differ from the conduct of American firms in that country. Let American conduct in the American market be represented by conduct parameter, λ_u. Then we can rewrite (5.2) for a representative U.S. firm operating in the U.S. market in the following way.

$$\lambda_u = [(p - \mu)/p][\eta/ms_u] - 1 , \tag{5.7}$$

where ms_u is the market share of a representative U.S. firm in the U.S. market. There is a corresponding condition for Japanese firms in the U.S., for American firms in Japan, and for Japanese firms in Japan. Furthermore, BK want to allow for the alleged Japanese trade barriers against U.S. firms and therefore include a tariff equivalent in the market conduct condition for U.S. firms operating in Japan. Using asterisks to represent variables associated with the Japanese market, the condition representing U.S. market conduct in Japan can be written as

$$\lambda_u^* = [(p^* - (\mu + \theta))/p^*][\eta^*/ms_j] - 1 , \tag{5.8}$$

where θ is measure of Japanese trade barriers expressed as a tariff equivalent, and ms_j is the share of a representative U.S. firm in the Japanese market.

Conditions (5.7) and (5.8), and the two corresponding conditions for Japanese firms can be calibrated to actual data much as in Section 5.1. Ideally, we would observe prices, quantities, demand elasticities, effective marginal costs, and Japanese protection, then calculate the conduct parameters required to calibrate the model to actual data. The additional difficulty in this case is that it is very hard to "observe" effective marginal cost, μ. To estimate this parameter, BK assume that marginal production cost $c[k(t)]$ has the form $c = Bk^{1-\beta}$, and assume, based on engineering information, that $\beta = 0.28$, which implies very substantial learning economies. They also assume free entry in the strong form that revenue over the product life cycle must equal full cost for each firm. All American firms are assumed to be symmetric to each other, as are Japanese firms. As in Dixit (1988a), BK allow the number of "firm-equivalents" to equal the number of symmetric firms that would generate the actual Herfindahl index. These assumptions allow μ to be calculated from just market prices and quantities (revenues), adjusting properly for transportation costs.

BK also assume that (inverse) demand in the U.S. is of the form $P = AQ^{-\alpha}$, where Q is total U.S. sales, and that Japanese demand has the same functional form. They obtain outside estimates of the elasticity of demand (taking it to be 1.8 for the U.S. market), and are then able to solve an expression like (5.7) for conduct parameter λ_u. U.S. firms are found to have conduct parameters in the U.S. market that are considerably less competitive than Cournot ($\lambda_u = 4.76$). Japanese firms are found to have conduct parameters of about 2.8 in Japan and 8.3 in the U.S. However, expression (5.8) cannot be solved for the U.S. firms' conduct parameter in Japan because the Japanese tariff-equivalent trade barrier cannot be observed. BK therefore assume that American conduct in Japan is the same as in the U.S., i.e. that $\lambda_u = \lambda_j = 4.76$, then use (5.7) to estimate effective Japanese trade barriers. They conclude that Japanese trade barriers were equivalent to a tariff of about 26 percent.

Having carried out this elegant but somewhat heroic calibration exercise, BK are then able to conduct policy experiments to determine the effects of different trade policy regimes on production, trade flows, and, using surplus measures of the type set out in Section 3, on welfare. The main hypothetical policy of interest is the "free trade" case, in which there are no Japanese trade barriers. BK also consider a "trade war" case in which tariffs in each country are set at 100 percent, which is enough to choke off all trade between the two countries. As in Section 5.1, the effects of trade policy variations on U.S. welfare are modest. A trade war would, however, have imposed significant damage on Japan. The main costs of Japanese protection arise from induced proliferation of firms in what is essentially a natural monopoly, which drives firms up their cumulative average cost curves and causes prices to rise.

Most interesting is the comparison of Japanese protection (the base case) with free trade. BK conclude that Japan was a net loser from protection, as consumers paid higher prices and obtained less consumer surplus than they would have under free trade. (Japanese firms are confined by the zero-profit assumption to earn zero surplus in either regime.) However, the policy had a major effect on the pattern of world protection in that no Japanese industry would have emerged (in their model) under free trade. Thus the Japanese policy was "successful" in the sense that it allowed a robust Japanese industry to emerge. Even if we take the view that this calibration exercise tells us more about the theoretical structure of trade models with learning-by-doing than it does about actual empirical magnitudes in the computer chip industry, the finding that a modest level of protection can have very significant effects on the pattern of production and trade is very striking.

5.3. Smith–Venables calibrations of EC industries

In addition to the papers discussed in Sections 5.1 and 5.2, a substantial number of additional strategic trade policy calibration exercises have been carried out. Several of these are contained in Krugman and Smith (1994). Perhaps the most systematic set of industry calibrations are those done by Alisdair Smith and Tony Venables in a series of papers including Smith and Venables (1988), Smith (1994) and Venables (1994). These studies focus on major industries in the European Community, with particular emphasis on the automobile industry. The basic logic of the analysis in these papers is much as in Dixit (1988a), but like Krishna et al. (1994), a more sophisticated demand structure is assumed so as to allow for the substantial product heterogeneity that exists in these markets.

Many of these markets have implicit barriers to trade that are difficult to measure directly. Given the difficulty created by unobserved trade barriers and the difficulty in observing the degree of product differentiation, Smith and Venables are unable to calibrate conduct parameters. Instead they assume a particular form of rivalry and use this to help solve for trade barrier equivalents and the degree of product differentiation. They are able to repeat the exercise for different assumptions about firm rivalry (and many other things) and are therefore able to distinguish between results that are sensitive and those that are robust.

My interpretation of the basic conclusions is as follows. First, given the existence of oligopoly and the possibility of using strategic trade policies, only by great coincidence would the optimal policy for a given country be free trade, and, as in Baldwin and Krugman (1988), the effects of such policies on trade flows and production magnitudes are large. However, the magnitude of welfare changes is small. In the nine industries considered in Venables (1994), in only one does an optimal tariff yield gains in excess of 2.5 percent of the base value of consumption. Export subsidies are even less significant in their welfare effects. Also, the details of policy effects are sensitive to assumed model structure. Policy has a bigger impact under Cournot rather than Bertrand rivalry, as we might expect, because firm profits are higher under Cournot rivalry. If, however, we invoke a (zero profit) free entry assumption this comparison is reversed in many cases (as profit-shifting effects disappear). Without free entry, policy effects are greater under segmented markets than under unified markets. Venables (1994) argues that the implied optimal strategic trade policies are not as sensitive to model specifics as we might anticipate from the theoretical literature, and that there are relatively few "sign reversals" where changing some parameter changes the optimal policy from tariff or tax to subsidy. Thus this work appears useful in narrowing down the range of plausible effects. However, as noted by Venables (1994), the calibration methodology is not robust enough, nor are the implied gains large enough, to suggest using calibration exercises as a basis for implementing actual policies.

6. Concluding remarks

Having worked through the many details in this chapter (or having skipped straight to the conclusion), a reader might reasonably ask three questions. First, is strategic trade policy something that a competent government might actually be able to carry out? Secondly, what are the main results and major intellectual contributions of the strategic trade policy literature; and finally, what are the most promising lines of enquiry for further research?

6.1. The practice of strategic trade policy

Most contributors to the analysis of strategic trade policy would view any government attempt to apply strategic trade policy as something of a Pandora's box. As already discussed, the informational requirements for application of strategic trade policies are high. Also, although beyond the scope of this chapter, distortions arising from political economy considerations such as lobbying and other forms of transfer-seeking are a major concern. It seems natural to expect that strategic trade policy can only expand the scope for socially wasteful transfer-seeking [as modeled, for example, in Moore and Suranovic (1993)]. Even if free trade does not emerge as an optimal policy in normative strategic trade policy models, once political economy considerations are taken into account, perhaps it is the best we can do.

It is, however, important not to overstate the case against strategic trade policy activism. The informational requirements are high, but not impossibly high. Most of the relevant pieces of information that a well-meaning government needs are potentially observable, or at least can be reasonably estimated. Spencer (1986), for example, undertakes a coherent examination of how strategic trade policy targeting might be linked to observables. Political systems in some countries might be particularly prone to political economy distortions, but this is not true in all countries. Rodrik (1993) provides a comparison of the consequences of trade policy targeting in four selected countries and concludes that results are mixed, not uniformly bad.

Even if the prospects for forward-looking normative application of strategic policy are poor, using a strategic trade policy lens can aid the retrospective understanding of some trade policy interventions. For example, it has been persuasively asserted that interventionist policies in countries like Japan, Korea and France have had important effects in allowing industries and individual firms in those countries to develop a strong international presence. (Welfare effects are more ambiguous.) Perhaps more interestingly, one could speculate that the pattern of U.S. high technology production and exports is due in large part to three important interventions. Most importantly, U.S. policy has provided very substantial R&D subsidies to many industries through its heavily subsidized and very productive university research sector. In combination with local agglomeration effects, such as those in evidence at "Silicon Valley" near Stanford University, such R&D subsidies have apparently had a large impact. Secondly, the publicly funded defence and space exploration sectors have provided protected markets for U.S. firms not unlike those considered in Krugman (1984). Finally, the Export-Import Bank of the U.S. has, among other things, provided direct export subsidies to very successful high-technology industries, including aircraft production.

Strategic trade policy allows us to understand how apparently modest interventions in these areas could have large effects. If a comparatively small subsidy determines whether a foreign or domestic firm enters a given industry, and there is a significant learning curve, then a large long-run impact can arise. Thus strategic trade policy helps us understand how the history of trade and industrial policies (even if not given those names) has had a major role in influencing the current international pattern of specialization and trade. More detailed discussion of cases in which such policies have allegedly had a major impact can be found in Cohen and Zysman (1987) and Tyson (1993).

6.2. Main results and intellectual contributions of strategic trade policy research

The central contribution of strategic trade policy is that it allows trade theory to address some of the practical concerns that dominate the debate over actual trade policy. Earlier trade policy models based on perfect competition gave more clear answers to policy questions, but were vulnerable to the critique that they either ignored or provided unsatisfactory treatment of major concerns, such as increasing returns, learning-by-doing, R&D, and inter-firm strategic rivalries. Furthermore, many of those actively seeking to influence trade policy represent firms. Economists may assume that all firms earn precisely normal profits, but many private sector decision-makers believe that firms may make losses or (above-normal) profits for systematic reasons (i.e. for reasons beyond simple exogenous randomness or "luck") and that government policies have an important impact on those outcomes. Explicit consideration of profits is therefore important.

Reasonable consideration of all these issues is possible using oligopoly as the underlying industry structure. Even if the conclusion is that some proposed intervention is unwarranted, at least we have a reasonable basis for making that statement. In contrast, an assertion about non-intervention based on the assumption that the auto industry or the aircraft industry is perfectly competitive seems less convincing.

Perhaps the most robust finding in the analysis of strategic trade policy is that imperfect competition of the oligopoly type almost always creates apparent unilateral incentives for intervention. When strategic trade policy models were first presented, it was often suggested that some important "correction" of the models would eliminate the apparent role for such policies. Perhaps some appropriate characterization of government-level or firm-level rationality, or some plausible informational asymmetry, or entry, or international arbitrage, or general equilibrium effects, or some other powerful force would sweep away the foundations of strategic trade policy. This research agenda provided very valuable scrutiny of the theory of strategic trade policy, but no philosopher's stone that would transmute the normative analysis of strategic trade policy into free trade was found.

This apparent robustness of strategic trade policy incentives is, however, tempered by another important and fairly robust finding. Specifically, even nationally successful strategic trade policies typically have a beggar-thy-neighbor aspect. Thus countries that would otherwise compete with each other at the level of strategic trade policy have an incentive to make agreements that would ameliorate or prevent such rivalries. It should be noted, however, that imperfectly competitive goods tend to be underprovided from the overall world point of view. Therefore, other things equal, policies that subsidize such goods actually tend to enhance overall efficiency. On the other hand, policies that restrict such outputs tend to exacerbate the underlying imperfectly competitive distortion. In any case, decentralized strategic trade policies will not, except by remarkable coincidence, achieve outcomes that approach the world-level normative ideal, suggesting that international trade policy coordination should act as an important restraint on nationally-determined strategic trade policies.

Furthermore, models underlying strategic trade policy imply that the gains from trade are larger than in traditional models. Thus the stakes from getting multilateral agreements right are higher. Strategic trade policy provides valuable insight into the potential design of multilateral trade regimes and, in particular, provides a foundation for understanding how to treat such things as R&D subsidies, capital subsidies, and related policies at the level of international coordination.

One general finding emphasized in the paper is that the design of nationally optimal policy is sensitive to model structure and parameters. This is true of all economic policy, but policy directions seem more fragile in the presence of international oligopoly than in, for example, traditional trade theory based on perfect competition. To a large extent, this sensitivity reflects the nature of oligopoly theory (and real oligopoly conduct). Comparable policy sensitivity arises in the study of regulation, competition policy, and other areas where oligopoly market structures are seriously considered. We cannot always expect simple policy prescriptions in the presence of complex distortions. The task is to focus on simple, powerful, and potentially observable criteria for distinguishing between important general cases.

One such criterion for oligopoly is whether competition between firms is based on strategies that are strategic substitutes or strategic complements. An implication of this approach is that policies that directly promote R&D, investment, or learning-by-doing are likely to be more robust than policies that operate directly on output market variables, as investment-like strategies appear to be natural strategic substitutes in most cases. Two other general findings are that strategic trade policies will of course be more attractive if an industry earns substantial above normal profits and, less obviously, that market segmentation increases the apparent incentives for intervention in the presence of above-normal profits. We also have a good idea of how the relative importance of foreign and domestic competition, comparative foreign and domestic costs, and distortionary taxation affect trade policy incentives.

6.3. Future directions in strategic trade policy research

It is always difficult to predict the direction of any research area, so perhaps I can start by discussing the recent past. The concern that strategic trade policy generates many possibilities has, very naturally, led to substantial emphasis on empirical work so as to determine which possibilities are relevant in particular cases. Over the past few years relative effort has shifted toward empirical work, much of which is reviewed in Chapter 31 of this volume. [See also the edited volumes by Feenstra (1988, 1989).] The cost of computing power continues to fall, good data is increasingly available (especially on CD-ROM), and there are many econometric techniques yet to apply and interesting questions yet to address. Accordingly, it seems likely that the econometric analysis of strategic trade policy will continue to be a very active and fruitful area.

As for theoretical topics, many important gaps are left to be filled, and whole new directions are yet to be explored. In the category of gaps, it is important to analyze industries where free entry drives profits of marginal firms to zero but allows positive profits for inframarginal firms. Such cases require giving up analytically convenient symmetry assumptions and may require extensive use of specific functional forms, but seem worthwhile even so. In addition, the impact of informational asymmetries in strategic trade policy certainly has not been investigated as fully as it might be. Also, while regional trading arrangements are covered elsewhere in this volume, it is worth noting that the analysis of regional and multilateral arrangements in the presence of oligopoly is an active and promising area.

Perhaps the biggest area of incompleteness in strategic trade policy (as in many areas of economics) is the heavy reliance on simple one-shot or static models of both oligopoly and government policy formulation. We know that long-term interactions at the industry and government level are the rule rather than the exception and that they may differ significantly from short-term interactions, especially if we allow for full endogeneity in the timing of moves. However, the appropriate differential game versions of strategic interaction with rational, calculating players seem intractable at this stage. Furthermore, even if we could solve such models effectively, I am not sure that we would believe the results.

We might reasonably believe that players can find a Nash equilibrium in a simple one-shot game. Student subjects seem to do it pretty well, and presumably expert decision-makers in firms and governments are no less capable. Expecting real players to incorporate a sequential rationality requirement such as subgame perfection in simple games is asking a lot more, and experimental subjects have a much harder time with this refinement. Still, as a modelling strategy it seems better to require credible threats than to ignore the issue. However, once we consider requiring players to undertake rational strategic calculations in long and complicated differential games, especially if information is incomplete, we have passed the boundary of reasonable suspension of disbelief. Very few economists can calculate fully rational solutions to differential games of even moderate complexity; actual participants in games would not even try. Furthermore, there is little reason to believe that the relevant environments are stable enough to allow players using the method of trial and error to approach fully maximizing solutions. In light of this, much of the work in current game theory deals with games in which players have limited powers of calculation and use explicit learning strategies in sensible but heuristic ways to guide long-run strategic behavior. Application of such methods to strategic trade policy seems a challenging but potentially fruitful line of enquiry.

Among the most important consequences of any trade policy, strategic or otherwise, arise from its effects on economic growth. The static "one-shot" gains or losses from trade policy changes that are estimated in strategic trade policy models are larger than in traditional trade policy models, but still seem to be of modest size. It is possible that the effect of trade policy on growth might be more important still. This question is, however, not likely to yield a general answer, for we already know that there is apparently no theoretical presumption that the growth effects of trade policy necessarily dominate static distortions. For example, Grossman and Helpman (1991, ch. 6) examine a dynamic model in which a policy that slows growth but reduces an ongoing monopoly distortion may be desirable. This shows that the "growth rate" effect may be less significant than the conventional monopoly distortion effect that shows up in static models. In recent years much progress has been made in incorporating richer theories of the firm into models of trade and growth, as reviewed in Chapter 2 of this volume, but there is much yet to be done in understanding the interaction between strategic trade policy and economic growth. In this general area, as elsewhere in the analysis of strategic trade policy, the questions of greatest policy interest will have a particularly strong empirical component.

Finally, as the world becomes increasingly crowded, the interaction between trade policies and environmental policies will become more important. I would predict that much of the actual trade policy debate over the next decade or two will deal with environmental and resource use issues. Accordingly, since many of the relevant industries are of the oligopoly type, it will be important to integrate resource and environmental concerns into models of strategic trade policy. Relevant early work includes Barrett (1994), Brander and Taylor (1995), Kennedy (1994), and Rauscher (1994), but much remains to be done.

References

Anis, A.H. and T.W. Ross (1992), "Imperfect competition and pareto-improving strategic trade policy", Journal of International Economics 33:363–371.

Arvan, L. (1991), "Flexibility versus commitment in strategic trade policy under uncertainty: A model of endogenous policy leadership", Journal of International Economics 31:341–355.

Bagwell, K. and R.W. Staiger (1992), "The sensitivity of strategic and corrective R&D policy in battles for monopoly", International Economic Review 33:795–816.

Bagwell, K. and R.W. Staiger (1994), "The sensitivity of strategic & corrective R&D policy in oligopolistic industries", Journal of International Economics 36:133–150.

Baldwin, R. and P. Krugman (1988), "Market access and competition: A simulation study of 16K random access memories", in: R. Feenstra, ed., Empirical research in industrial trade (MIT Press, Cambridge, MA).

Ballard, C.L., J.B. Shoven, and J. Whalley (1985), "General equilibrium computations of the marginal welfare costs of taxes in the United States", American Economic Review 75:128–138.

Barrett, S. (1994), "Strategic environmental policy and international trade", Journal of Public Economics 54:325–338.

Ben-Zvi, S. and E. Helpman (1992), "Oligopoly and segmented markets", in: G. Grossman, ed., Imperfect competition and international trade (MIT Press, Cambridge, MA).

Bhagwati, J.N. (1965), "On the equivalence of tariffs and quotas", in: R.E. Baldwin, ed., Trade, growth and the balance of payments: Essays in honor of Gottfried Haberler (North-Holland, Amsterdam).

Bhagwati, J.N. (1971), "The generalized theory of distortions and welfare", in: Bhagwati et al., eds., Trade, balance of payments and growth (North-Holland, Amsterdam).

Brainard, L. (1994), "Last one out wins: Trade policy in an international exit game", International Economic Review 35:151–172.

Brainard, L. and D. Martimort (1992), "Strategic trade policy with incompletely informed policymakers", National Bureau of Economic Research Working Paper No. 4069.

Branco, F. (1994), "Favoring domestic firms in procurement contracts", Journal of International Economics 37:65–80.

Brander, J.A. (1981), "Intra-industry trade in identical products", Journal of International Economics 11:1–14.

Brander, J.A. and P.R. Krugman (1983), "A reciprocal dumping model of international trade", Journal of International Economics 15:313–389.

Brander, J.A. and B.J. Spencer (1981), "Tariffs and the extraction of foreign monopoly rents under potential entry", Canadian Journal of Economics 14:371–389.

Brander, J.A. and B.J. Spencer (1984a), "Tariff protection and imperfect competition", in: H. Kierzkowski, ed., Monopolistic competition and international trade (Clarendon Press, Oxford).

Brander, J.A. and B.J. Spencer (1984b), "Trade warfare: Tariffs and cartels", Journal of International Economics 16:227–242.

Brander, J.A. and B.J. Spencer (1985), "Export subsidies and market share rivalry", Journal of International Economics 18:83–100.

Brander, J.A. and B.J. Spencer (1988), "Unionized oligopoly and international trade policy", Journal of International Economics 24:217–234.

Brander, J.A. and M.S. Taylor (1995), "International trade and open access renewable resources: The small open economy case", NBER Working Paper 5021 (NBER, Cambridge, MA).

Carmichael, C. 1987, "The control of export credit subsidies and its welfare consequences", Journal of International Economics 23:1–19.

Cheng, L. (1987), "Optimal trade and technology policies: Dynamic linkages", International Economic Review 28:757–776.

Cheng, L. (1988), "Assisting domestic industries under international oligopoly", American Economic Review 78:291–314.

Cohen, S.S. and J. Zysman (1987), Manufacturing matters: The myth of the post-industrial economy (Basic Books, New York).

Collie, D. (1991), "Export subsidies and countervailing tariffs", Journal of International Economics 31:309–324.

Collie, D. (1993), "Profit-shifting export subsidies and the sustainability of free trade", Scottish Journal of Political Economy 40:408–419.

Collie, D. and M. Hviid (1993), "Export subsidies as signals of competitiveness", Scandanavian Journal of Economics 95:327–339.

Cooper, R. and R. Riezman (1989), "Uncertainty and the choice of trade policy in oligopolistic industries", Review of Economic Studies 56:129–140.

Cournot, A. (1838), Recherches sur les principes mathematiques de la theorie des richesses. [English translation in: N. Bacon, ed., 1897, Researches into the mathematical principles of the theory of wealth (Macmillian, New York)].

Das, S.P. and S. Donnenfeld (1989), "Oligopolistic competition and international trade: Quantity and quality restrictions", Journal of International Economics 27:299–318.

Davidson, C. (1984), "Cartel stability and trade policy", Journal of International Economics 17:219–237.

De Meza, D. (1979), "Commercial policy toward multinationals: Reservations on Katrak", Oxford Economic Papers 31:334–337.

De Meza, D. (1986), "Export subsidies and high productivity: Cause or effect?", Canadian Journal of Economics 19:347–350.

Dick, A.R. (1992), "Strategic trade policy and welfare: The empirical consequences of cross-ownership", Journal of International Economics 35:227–249.

Dinopoulos, E., T.R. Lewis, and D. Sappington (1995), "Optimal industrial targeting with unknown learning-by-doing", Journal of International Economics, forthcoming.

Dixit, A.K. (1984), "International trade policy for oligopolistic industries", Economic Journal, 94 supplement, 1–16.

Dixit, A.K. (1986), "Comparative statics for oligopoly", International Economic Review 27:107–122.

Dixit, A.K. (1987), "Strategic aspects of trade policy", in: T. Bewley, ed., Advances in economic theory (Cambridge University Press, Cambridge) 329–362.

Dixit, A.K. (1988a), "Optimal trade and industrial policy for the U.S. automobile industry", in: R. Feenstra, ed., Empirical methods for industrial trade (MIT Press, Cambridge, MA).

Dixit, A.K. (1988b), "Anti-dumping and countervailing duties under oligopoly", European Economic Review 32:55–68.

Dixit, A.K. and G.M. Grossman (1986), "Targeted export promotion with several oligopolistic industries", Journal of International Economics 21:233–250.

Dixit, A.K. and A.S. Kyle (1985), "The use of protection and subsidies for entry promotion and deterrence", American Economic Review 75:139–152.

Dockner, E.J. and A.A. Huang (1990), "Tariffs and quotas under dynamic duopolistic competition", Journal of International Economics 29:147–160.

Driskill, R. and S. McCafferty (1989), "Dynamic duopoly with output adjustment costs in international markets: Taking the conjectures out of conjectural variations", in: R.C. Feenstra, ed., Trade policies for international competitiveness (University of Chicago Press, Chicago).

Eaton, J. and G.M. Grossman (1986), "Optimal trade and industrial policy under oligopoly", Quarterly Journal of Economics 101:383–406.

Feenstra, R.C. ed. (1988), Empirical methods for industrial trade (MIT Press, Cambridge, MA).

Feenstra, R.C., ed. (1989), Trade policies for international competitiveness (University of Chicago Press, Chicago).

Flam, H. (1994), "EC members fighting about surplus: VERs, FDI and Japanese cars", Journal of International Economics 36:117–132.

Friedman, D. and K.C. Fung (1996), "International trade and the internal organization of firms: An evolutionary approach", Journal of International Economics, forthcoming.

Fudenburg, D. and J. Tirole (1991), Game theory (MIT Press, Cambridge, MA).

Fung, K.C. (1992), "Some international properties of Japanese firms", Journal of the Japanese and International Economies 6:163–175.

Fung, K.C. (1995), "Rent shifting and rent-sharing: A reexamination of the strategic industrial policy problem", Canadian Journal of Economics, forthcoming.

Gatsios, K. (1989), "Imperfect competition and international trade", in: F.H. Hahn, ed., The economics of missing markets, information, and games (Oxford University Press, Oxford).

Gatsios, K. (1990), "Preferential tariffs and the most favoured nation principle", Journal of International Economics 28:365–373.

Grossman, G. and E. Helpman (1991), Innovation and growth in the global economy (MIT Press, Cambridge, MA).

Gruenspecht, H.K. (1988), "Export subsidies for differentiated products", Journal of International Economics 24:331–344.

Harris, R. (1985), "Why voluntary export restraints are 'voluntary'", Canadian Journal of Economics 18:799–809.

Harris, R.G. (1989), "Innis lecture: The new protectionism revisited", Canadian Journal of Economics 22:751–778.

Harris, R.G. and D. Cox (1985), Trade, industrial policy, and manufacturing (Ontario Economic Council, Toronto).

Helpman, E. and P. Krugman (1985), Market structure and foreign trade: Increasing returns, imperfect competition, and the international economy (MIT Press, Cambridge, MA).

Helpman, E. and P. Krugman (1989), Trade policy and market structure (MIT Press, Cambridge, MA).

Head, K. (1994), "Infant industry protection in the steel rail industry", Journal of International Economics, 37:141–166.

Horstmann, I.J. and J.R. Markusen (1986), "Up the average cost curve: Inefficient entry and the new protectionism", Journal of International Economics 20:225–247.

Horstmann, I.J. and J.R. Markusen (1992), "Endogenous market structures in international trade", Journal of International Economics 32:109–130.

Hwang, H. and C. Mai (1988), "On the equivalence of tariffs and quotas under duopoly: A conjectural variation approach", Journal of International Economics 24:373–380.

Hwang, H.-S. and C.T. Schulman (1992), "Strategic non-intervention and the choice of trade policy for international oligopoly", Journal of International Economics 34:73–93.

Ishikawa, J. (1994), "Ranking alternative trade-restricting policies under international duopoly", Japan and the World Economy 6:157–169.

Itoh, M. and Y. Ono (1984), "Tariffs vs. quotas under duopoly of heterogeneous goods", Journal of International Economics 17:359–374.

Johnson, H.G. (1954), "Optimum tariffs and retaliation", Review of Economic Studies 21:142–153.

Lee, S. (1973), "International equity markets and trade policy", Journal of International Economics 29:173–184.

Katrak, H. (1977), "Multinational monopolies and commercial policy", Oxford Economic Papers 29:283–291.

Katz, L.F. and L.H. Summers (1989), "Can interindustry wage differentials justify strategic trade policy", in: R. Feenstra, ed., Trade policies for international competitiveness (University of Chicago Press, Chicago).

Kennedy, P.W. (1994), "Equilibrium pollution taxes in open economies with imperfect competition", Journal of Environmental Economics and Management 27:49–63.

Klepper, G. (1994), "Industrial policy in the transport aircraft industry", in: P.R. Krugman and A. Smith, eds., Empirical studies of strategic trade policy (University of Chicago Press, Chicago).

Krishna, K. (1987), "Tariffs vs. quotas with endogenous quality", Journal of International Economics 23:9–112.

Krishna, K. (1989), "Trade restrictions as facilitating practices", Journal of International Economics 26:251–270.

Krishna, K., K. Hogan, and P. Swagel (1994), "The nonoptimality of optimal trade policies: The U.S. automobile industry revisited, 1979–1985", in: P.R. Krugman and A. Smith, eds., Empirical studies of strategic trade policy (University of Chicago Press, Chicago).

Krishna, K. and M. Itoh (1988), "Content protection and oligopolistic interaction", Review of Economic Studies 55:107–125.

Krishna, K. and M.C. Thursby (1991), "Optimal policies with strategic distortions", Journal of International Economics 31:291–308.

Krugman, P.R. (1980), "Scale economies, product differentiation, and the pattern of trade", American Economic Review 70:950–959.

Krugman, P.R. (1984), "Import protection as export promotion: International competition in the presence of oligopoly and economies of scale", in: H. Kierzkowski, ed., Monopolistic competition and international trade (Clarendon Press, Oxford).

Krugman, P.R., ed. (1986), Strategic trade policy and the new international economics (MIT Press, Cambridge, MA).

Krugman, P.R. (1987), "Is free trade passé?", Journal of Economic Perspectives 1:131–144.

Krugman, P.R. and A. Smith, eds. (1994), Empirical studies of strategic trade policy (University of Chicago Press, Chicago).

Lancaster, K. (1991), "The product variety case for protection", Journal of International Economics 31:1–26.

Levinsohn, J.A. (1989), "Strategic trade policy when firms can invest abroad: When are tariffs and quotas equivalent?", Journal of International Economics 27:129–148.

Markusen, J.R. (1981), "Trade and the gains from trade with imperfect competition", Journal of International Economics 11:531–551.

Markusen, J.R. and A.J. Venables (1988), "Trade policy with increasing returns and imperfect competition: Contradictory results from competing assumptions", Journal of International Economics 24:299–316.

McMillan, J. (1986), Game theory in international economics (Harwood, London).

Mezzetti, C. and E. Dinopolous (1991), "Domestic unionization and import competition", Journal of International Economics 31:79–100.

Moore, M. and S. Suranovic (1992), "Lobbying and Cournot-Nash competition: Implications for strategic trade policy", Journal of International Economics 35:367–376.

Nash, J. (1950), "Equilibrium points in n-person games", Proceedings of the National Academy of Sciences 36:48–49.

Neary, J.P. (1994), "Cost asymmetries in international subsidy games: Should governments help winners or losers?", Journal of International Economics, 37:197–218.

Prusa, T.J. (1992), "Why are so many anti-dumping petitions withdrawn", Journal of International Economics 33:1–20.

Qiu, L.D. (1994), "Optimal strategic trade policy under asymmetric information", Journal of International Economics 36:333–354.

Rauscher, M. (1994), "On ecological dumping", Oxford Economic Papers 46:822–840.

Ries, J. (1993a), "Windfall profit and vertical relationships: Who gained in the Japanese auto industry from VERs?", Journal of Industrial Economics 41:259–27.

Ries, J. (1993b), "Voluntary export restraints, profits and quality adjustment", Canadian Journal of Economics 2:706–724.

Rodrik, D. (1993), "Taking trade policy seriously: Export subsidization as a case study in policy effectiveness", National Bureau of Economic Research Working Paper No. 4567.

Rodrik, D. and C. Yoon (1989), "Strategic trade policy when firms compete against vertically integrated rivals", National Bureau of Economic Research Working Paper No. 2919.

Rotemberg, J. and G. Saloner (1989) "Tariffs vs. quotas with implicit collusion", Canadian Journal of Economics 22:237–244.

Selten, R. (1965), "Spieltheoretische behandlung eines oligopolmodells mit Nachfragetragheit", Zeitschrift für die gesant Staatswissenschaft 121:301–24. [English translation by R. Selten (1975), "Reexamination of the perfectness concept for equilibrium points in extensive games", International Journal of Game Theory 4:25–55.]

Shapiro, C. (1989), "Theories of oligopoly behaviour", in: R. Schmalensee, and R. Willig, eds., Handbook of industrial organization, vol. 1 (North-Holland, Amsterdam) 329–410.

Shivakumar, R. (1992), "Strategic trade policy: Choosing between export subsidies and export quotas under uncertainty", Journal of International Economics 35:169–183.

Shoven, J. and J. Whalley (1972), "A general equilibrium calculation of the effects of differential taxation of income from capital in the U.S.", Journal of Public Economics 1:281–321.

Smith, A. (1994), "Strategic trade policy in the European car market", in: P.R. Krugman and A. Smith, eds., Empirical studies of strategic trade policy (University of Chicago Press, Chicago).

Smith, A. and A.J. Venables (1988), "Completing the internal market in the European Community: Some industry simulations", European Economic Review 32:1501–1525.

Spencer, B.J. (1986), "What should strategic trade policy target?", in: P.R. Krugman, ed., Strategic trade policy and the new international economics (MIT Press, Cambridge, MA) 69–89.

Spencer, B.J. (1988), "Capital subsidies and countervailing duties in oligopolistic industries", Journal of International Economics 25:45–70.

Spencer, B.J. and J.A. Brander (1983), "International R&D rivalry and industrial strategy", Review of Economic Studies 50:707–722.

Spencer, B.J. and R.W. Jones (1991), "Vertical foreclosure and international trade policy", Review of Economic Studies 58:153–170.

Spencer, B.J. and R.W. Jones (1992), "Trade and protection in vertically related markets", Journal of International Economics 32:31–56.

Svedberg, P. (1979), "Optimal tariff policy on imports from multinationals", Economic Record 55:64–67.

Taylor, M.S. (1992), "TRIPS, trade, and technology transfer", Canadian Journal of Economics 26:625–637.

Tirole, J. (1988), The theory of industrial organization (MIT Press, Cambridge, MA).

Tyson, L. (1992), Who's bashing whom: Trade conflicts in high technology industries (Institute for International Economics, Washington, DC).

Ulph, D. and L.A. Winters (1994), "Strategic manpower policy and international trade", in: P.R. Krugman and A. Smith, eds., Empirical studies of strategic trade policy (University of Chicago Press, Chicago).

Venables, A.J. (1985), "Trade and trade policy with imperfect competition: The case of identical products and free entry", Journal of International Economics 19:1–19.

Venables, A.J. (1987), "Trade and trade policy with differentiated products", Economic Journal 97:700–717.

Venables, A.J. (1990), "International capacity choice and national market games", Journal of International Economics 29:23–42.

Venables, A.J. (1994), "Trade policy under imperfect competition: A numerical assessment", in: P.R. Krugman and A. Smith, eds., Empirical studies of strategic trade policy (University of Chicago Press, Chicago).

Wong, K-y. (1991), "Incentive compatible immiserizing export subsidies", mimeo, University of Washington.

Chapter 28

POLITICAL ECONOMY OF TRADE POLICY

DANI RODRIK*

Columbia University, CEPR, and NBER

Contents

*I am indebted to Kym Anderson, Bob Baldwin, Dick Baldwin, Jim Cassing, Rob Feenstra, Arye Hillman, Steve Magee, Wolfgang Mayer, Doug Nelson, Sharyn O'Halloran, Edward John Ray, Ray Riezman, Ron Rogowski, Guido Tabellini, Mariano Tommasi, and especially Gene Grossman for their help in the preparation of this paper.

Handbook of International Economics, vol. III, Edited by G. Grossman and K. Rogoff
© *Elsevier Science B.V., 1995*

1. Introduction

Perhaps no other area of economics displays such a gap between what policy makers practice and what economists preach as does international trade. The superiority of free trade is one of the profession's most cherished beliefs, yet international trade is rarely free. Partly as a consequence, a large and distinguished literature has developed over the years on the political economy of trade policy. This literature has been well surveyed in a number of recent contributions, including Nelson (1989), Hillman (1989), Magee, Brock and Young (1989), Riezman and Wilson (1993a), Mayer (1991), Magee (1994), and Ray (1990).

This chapter overlaps with these existing surveys, but also differs from them in being more specifically focussed on the questions to which the literature should be providing answers. In other words, I will review the literature from the perspective of what I take to be the interesting questions, and evaluate it by how well it measures against this yardstick. This kind of approach necessarily makes for a more critical perspective on the literature than is common. In particular, I will suggest that the political economy literature has lost sight of the very questions that have motivated it. My purpose in taking this approach is not to belittle the contributions made by the researchers in the area, who include some of the profession's best minds. The questions at issue are tough ones, and I hope that the difficulty of providing satisfactory answers will come across in my discussion. Rather, my primary goal is to refocus attention on these fundamental questions, and in doing so suggest interesting avenues of research for the next generation of political economy work.

To set the stage, I begin by setting out a general framework to assess the distributional consequences of trade policy (Section 2). Using this framework as the background, the next section provides a guided tour of the leading approaches to formalizing the political economy of trade policy (Section 3). I then turn to the questions of interest: Why is international trade not free? (Section 4). Why are trade policies universally biased against trade? (Section 5). What are the determinants of the variation in protection levels across industries, countries, and time? (Section 6). In the penultimate section, I discuss the economic consequences of viewing trade policy endogenously (Section 7). A final section provides a brief summary and concludes the chapter (Section 8).

2. General considerations

As illustrated in Figure 2.1, in principle a political-economy model of trade policy must have four elements. First, it must contain a description of individual preferences over the domain of policy choices available to policymakers (box A). This is of

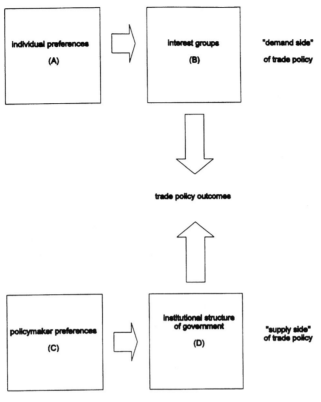

Figure 2.1.

course the easiest part of the exercise, insofar as much of trade theory is devoted to analyzing the consequences of trade policy for individuals who derive their incomes from different factors of production or sectors. Given an underlying economic model of the Heckscher–Ohlin or Ricardo–Viner type, and the presumption that preferences for policy depend only on self-interest, one can deduce individuals's policy rankings on the basis of their factor endowments or sector-specific skills. Second, the model must contain a description of how these individual preferences are aggregated and channeled, through pressure groups, political parties, or grass-roots movements, into "political demands" for a particular policy or another (box B). This step is considerably harder, as it involves a characterization of the modes of political organization as well as of the forms that political influence takes (lobbying, campaign contributions, voter registration, etc.). As we shall see, most models treat this component implicitly rather than explicitly.

The next two components have to do with the "supply side" of trade policy. Here, the model must first characterize policymakers' preferences (box C): do politicians do what they do because they want to get re-elected? because they want to transfer resources to favored groups? because they have partisan preferences? or simply because they are interested in maximizing social welfare? To know how these preferences play out and eventually interact with the demands for trade policy, the model then has to specify the institutional setting in which policy takes place (box D): is it Congress or the executive that sets tariffs? is the electoral system proportional representation or first-past-the-post? are there international treaty obligations that rule out certain forms of trade interventions?

A satisfactory treatment of all of these issues is naturally a very tall order.[1] None of the existing models claims to provide a complete political-economic model, and appropriately so, since the end result would likely be intractable. The established practice is to take short cuts, and to leave implicit some of the elements discussed above. The success of a model must then be judged not only by the insights it provides, but also by the plausibility of the implicit stories that fill in the gap between what is explicitly modeled and what is left out.

2.1. A general framework

We begin by describing a general model of a small open economy, to serve as a backdrop to the specific models that will be discussed below. For simplicity, we assume all goods (but no factors) are tradeable. On the demand side, we take individual preferences to be identical and homothetic (as most of the models also do). Each individual's indirect utility function can be written as $V(p)I^h$, where p is a vector of domestic prices and I^h is the individual's income. We will allow (some) domestic prices to differ from world prices p_i^* due to trade interventions. Since we will focus on perfectly-competitive settings for the most part, these interventions can be thought of as price policies (tariffs, export subsidies) as well as quantitative restrictions (quotas).

On the supply side, we could use either a specific-factors framework or the Heckscher–Ohlin framework. In the former case, let there be m sectors, indexed by i, with each sector using one mobile factor (labor) and one sector-specific factor with a constant-returns to scale technology. The returns to the specific factors can be captured by restricted profit functions of the form $\pi_i(p_i, w)$, where w is the wage. An individual's income can now be expressed as

$$I^h = s_L^h wL + \sum_i s_i^h \pi_i(p_i, w) + \sigma^h \sum_i (p_i - p_i^*)m_i, \quad \forall h \qquad (2.1)$$

---

[1] And one might add, as did Dick Baldwin in his comments on this chapter, that this framework leaves out some important features that may need to be included: trade policies are often chosen simultaneously with other policies, so this interdependence may need to be taken into account; there is as well interdependence with foreign countries' trade policies; we need dynamic elements to understand how trade policy evolves over time; etc.

where L is the economy's aggregate labor endowment, p_i^* are the world prices, m_i are net imports, and s_L^h, s_i^h and σ^h are the individual's shares in the labor endowment, industry profits (or quasi-rents to specific factors) and net government revenue, respectively. The model is completed by the full-employment condition for labor

$$L + \sum_i \frac{\partial \pi_i(p_i, w)}{\partial w} = 0 \tag{2.2}$$

and by the resource-balance constraints

$$m_i = -\frac{\partial V(\boldsymbol{p})}{\partial p_i} V(\boldsymbol{p})^{-1} \sum_h I^h - \frac{\partial \pi_i(p_i, w)}{\partial p_i}, \quad \forall i. \tag{2.3}$$

Note that we have used Hotelling's lemma and Roy's identity (which are the derivative properties of the profit and indirect utility functions) to state labor demand and commodity supplies and demands in terms of these functions.

In the Heckscher–Ohlin case, we have two goods and two factors, and the supply side of the economy can be summarized by using a revenue function of the form $R(p_1, p_2, K, L)$. An individual's income can now be expressed as

$$I^h = s_L^h wL + s_K^h rK + \sigma^h \sum_i (p_i - p_i^*)m_i \tag{2.4}$$

where s_L^h and s_K^h are the individual's ownership shares in the economy's aggregate endowments of labor and capital, respectively. As long as both goods are produced, factor prices are determined by equality between unit costs and output prices in each sector. Letting $\theta(w, r)$ and $\phi(w, r)$ stand for the unit-cost functions for goods one and two, respectively:

$$\theta(w, r) = p_1$$
$$\phi(w, r) = p_2 \tag{2.5}$$

Resource-balance constraints are in turn given by

$$m_i = -\frac{\partial V(p_1, p_2)}{\partial p_i} V(p_1, p_2)^{-1} \sum_h I^h - \frac{\partial R(p_1, p_2, K, L)}{\partial p_i}, \quad i = 1, 2. \tag{2.6}$$

Note that the model can determine only the *relative* price p_1/p_2, so that we are free to take either price as the numeraire and set it equal to any constant.

Now consider the decision problem of a social planner who does not care about income distribution. His problem is to choose trade policies (or equivalently, domestic prices) to maximize the aggregate real income of the economy. This can be achieved by solving the following problem:

$$\max_{p} W^* \equiv V(p) \sum_{h} I^h .$$
(2.7)

Let good k be the numeraire and set $p_k = p_k^*$. Then it is straightforward to show that the solution to this problem in both the specific-factors and Heckscher–Ohlin settings consists of:

$$t_i \equiv \frac{p_i - p_i^*}{p_i^*} = 0, \quad \forall i .$$
(2.8)

This simply expresses the optimality of free trade in an economy free of distortions and in which distributional objectives can be carried out through lump-sum transfers or other policies.

The specific-factors and Heckscher–Ohlin models both imply that trade policy has stark distributional consequences. In the specific-factors model, these consequences are particularly strong for owners of specific factors, and can be deduced from the ownership pattern of individuals across the specific factors employed in import-competing and exporting sectors [see eq. (2.1)]. Since $\partial \pi_k(p_k, w)/\partial p_k > 0$, an import tariff or export subsidy in sector k increases the return to the specific factor in that sector, while harming returns to other specific factors through the induced increase in wages. In the Heckscher–Ohlin model, the distributional implications work along factor (rather than industry) lines and are described by the Stolper–Samuelson theorem. An import tariff raises the real return to the economy's scarce factor and reduces the real return to the abundant factor. An individual who is specialized in the scarce factor (relative to the "representative" individual) would be better off [see eq. (2.4)].

Neither the specific-factors nor the Heckscher–Ohlin models can account for the large share of world trade that is intra-industry. And since intra-industry trade can have distributional implications that are considerably less stark than either of these, we close this section by considering briefly a model with differentiated products and increasing returns to scale (IRS).

Consider an economy with two sectors and two factors (labor and capital). Let sector one produce differentiated goods under IRS. In a symmetric equilibrium, each variety is produced by a different firm at an identical level and at price p_1, and free entry drives excess profits to zero. The second sector produces a homogeneous good under standard conditions. We assume consumers have a preference for variety along Spence–Dixit–Stiglitz lines and are (as before) identical in their preferences. Their indirect utility function can then be expressed as a variation of the one we have so far used, as $\gamma(n)V(p_1, p_2)I^h$, where n denotes the number of varieties available for consumption and $\gamma'(n) > 0.$[2] Each individual's income level is the same as that expressed in eq. (2.4).

In this economy free trade will have some redistributive consequences along Stolper–Samuelson lines as long as its relative factor endowments differ from that of the rest of the world. However, the presence of IRS generates a motive for trade distinct from factor-endowments considerations. Consequently, there will exist trade – intra-industry trade – even if there are no differences in relative factor endowments across countries. Moreover, what is particularly important from the political-economy standpoint is that this intra-industry trade will make *everyone* better off: it will increase the number of varieties available for consumption (n) without reducing anyone's real income ($V(.)I^h$). Therefore, as long as intra-industry trade dominates factor-endowments-based trade, no individual will prefer autarky to free trade [see Helpman and Krugman (1985, pp. 190–195)]. However, this does not mean that trade is distributionally neutral. Trade, and trade policy, will continue to have redistributive consequences as long as the home economy differs in its relative factor endowments from its trading partners.

3. A typology of models

Political-economy models generally take the specific-factors or Heckscher–Ohlin settings described above, and modify it in one or both of the following ways: (i) the objective function maximized by the policymaker is taken to show a preference for certain distributional outcomes, and hence to differ from that of the social planner (W^*); and (ii) individuals or lobbying groups are assumed to be able to take actions to shape the policymaker's preferences. We now turn to discuss the leading models in the literature, emphasizing these two dimensions.

3.1. The tariff-formation function approach

The most direct way in which trade policy can be endogenized is to link the level of a particular trade policy instrument, say a tariff, to the amount of lobbying resources deployed by contending organized groups. This approach was first used by Findlay and Wellisz (1982). In its simplest version, the model consists of a two-sector economy where one of the sectors uses only labor under constant returns to scale, while the other one (which is also the politically-active sector) employs labor and

---

[2]This formulation assumes either that imported varieties sell at the same price as domestically-produced varieties (free trade), or that no imported varieties are consumed (autarky). So, implicitly we are restricting attention to comparisons of autarky to free trade only.

sector-specific capital [Rodrik (1986)]. As long as the first sector is active, the constant marginal product of labor there fixes the economy-wide wage (say at unity). The tariff-formation function consists of a relationship of the form $t = t(L^I)$, where L^I is the amount of labor used by the politically active sector in the lobbying process. The endogenous level of lobbying (and hence of trade protection) is given by the solution to the following problem:

$$\max_{L^I} \pi(p^*(1 + t(L^I)), 1) - L^I .$$ (3.1)

This story assumes that owners of the specific factor can perfectly coordinate their lobbying behavior and costlessly prevent free riding.

The Findlay and Wellisz (1982) model has two industry lobbies in a sector-specific factors setting, each deciding how much labor to devote to the lobbying activity. The resulting tariff level is expressed as $t = t(L_1^I, L_2^I)$, with L_1^I and L_2^I standing for the amount of labor devoted to lobbying activities by each of the sector-specific factors. The tariff is increasing in the import-competing industry's lobbying, and decreasing in the other industry's lobbying. There is diminishing returns to lobbying. A Nash equilibrium in the two groups' lobbying strategies determines the tariff. Feenstra and Bhagwati (1982) allow both labor and capital to be used in lobbying activities, but they focus on a case where only a single industry is politically active. While popular, the lobbying function approach has been criticized for treating the supply side of protection as a black box: the preferences of the politicians are not explicitly stated.

3.2. The political support function approach

In this approach, the policy maker is assumed to be partial to political influence from an organized interest group representing a particular industry (as before), but is also assumed to care about the efficiency consequences of restricting trade. The policymaker maximizes a function which trades off the gains from protection to this industry against the losses to the general population. Letting p stand for the relative price of the organized industry, Hillman (1989) writes the political-support function as follows:

$$W^{PS} \equiv M(\pi(p) - \pi(p^*), p - p^*) .$$ (3.2)

The first argument captures the political-support motive in favor of the industry whose profit function is included in the maximand, while the second represents the efficiency loss (hence $M_1 > 0$ and $M_2 \leq 0$ for $p \geq p^*$). Note that both industry profits and overall welfare enter the political-support function not in levels but in deviations from the free-trade benchmark. The first-order condition for maximizing W^{PS} is given by:

$$M_1 \pi_p + M_2 = 0 .$$ (3.3)

Since $M_1 > 0$ and $\pi_p > 0$, an interior solution to this problem always requires that a positive level of protection be provided to the industry concerned ($p > p^*$). This framework has been applied to numerous issues, including declining-industry protection [Hillman (1982)] and bilateral exchange of trade "concessions" [Hillman and Moser (1995)].

Van Long and Vousden (1991) provide a generalization in which political support depends explicitly on the income levels of different groups in a sector-specific factors economy. These authors distinguish between three groups in a two-good economy: owners of the specific factor in sector one, owners of the specific factor in sector two, and owners of the mobile factor (labor). Letting $h = 1, 2, 3$ denote representative individuals from each one of these groups, respectively,

$$I^1 = \pi_1(p, w) + \sigma^1(p - p^*)m_1$$
$$I^2 = \pi_2(1, w) + \sigma^2(p - p^*)m_1 \qquad (3.4)$$
$$I^3 = wL + \sigma^3(p - p^*)m_1$$

where good 2 is taken to be the numeraire (so that p is the relative price of good 1). The political-support function used by Van Long and Vousden (1991) then becomes:

$$\tilde{W}^{PS} \equiv \sum_h a_h V(p) I^h = V(p) \sum_h a_h I^h \qquad (3.5)$$

where a_h are exogenous weights reflecting the politician's preferences over the three groups. Van Long and Vousden recognize explicitly that the shares of the three groups in tariff revenue (σ^h) need not be constant, and will depend in general on the equilibrium prices. This approach can be viewed as the mirror image of the lobbying function approach: it makes explicit the objective function of the policymakers while leaving obscure the actions taken by influential groups to extract the desired behavior from them.

3.3. Median-voter approach

This approach was pioneered by Mayer (1984), who considered a direct-democracy model where the tariff level is determined by voting among the population. Using a Heckscher–Ohlin model, Mayer showed that each factor owner has an optimal tariff rate (possibly negative) whose value is uniquely determined by the individual's factor ownership. Let the exportable (good 2) be the numeraire with $p_2 = p_2^* = 1$ and $p_1 = p = p_1^*(1 + t) = p^*(1 + t)$. Assuming that tariff revenue is distributed in proportion to each person's share in factor income, individual h's optimal tariff rate is found by maximizing $V(p)I^h$ with respect to p. This yields:

$$t^h = -\frac{I}{p^* \partial m_1 / \partial p} \frac{\partial \phi^h / \partial p}{\phi^h} \tag{3.6}$$

where I is aggregate income, ϕ^h is individual h's share in aggregate income, and $\partial m_1 / \partial p < 0$. In the Heckscher–Ohlin model $\partial \phi^h / \partial p > 0$ if individual h is relatively well endowed in the factor that is used intensively in the importable, and the strength of the effect is larger the more "specialized" the individual is in that factor. Consequently, such an individual's most preferred tariff will be strictly positive. Note also that the more open the economy to imports, and the more price sensitive is import demand, the lower the individually desirable tariff (or export subsidy).

As long as voters differ only along a single dimension (say, in their relative capital-labor endowment), the median-voter theorem can be applied to determine the tariff rate that would emerge from voting. If there are no costs to voting, the median eligible voter's decision is the outcome of majority voting. Therefore, under majority voting the endogenous level of trade policy is determined *as if* a policy maker maximized the utility of the median voter:

$$W^{MV} \equiv V(p)I^m \tag{3.7}$$

where m denotes the median individual. Mayer (1984) also considers the specific factors case, to show that if there exists voting costs, a small industry is likely to gain protection because other interests may find voting against the proposed tariff increase is not worthwhile.[3]

This model is exemplary in that it is a fully-specified political-economic model, with no black boxes. The assumption of direct democracy greatly simplifies the institutional setting, obviating much of the detail normally needed. The downside, of course, is the lack of realism: in practice, trade policy is rarely determined by majority voting.

3.4. The campaign contributions approach (Magee–Brock–Young)

In the models mentioned so far, the transfer of resources from special-interest groups to politicians does not play any direct role. Models by Magee, Brock, and Young (MBY, 1989, chs. 3 and 9) and Grossman and Helpman (1994) have explicitly addressed the role of political contributions. In MBY, lobbies make campaign

---

[3]Mayer assumes that only individuals whose real income gain from a tariff or subsidy exceeds the voting cost will choose to vote. However, this is problematic. The gain from the policy must be multiplied by the probability that the voter in question will be pivotal, which is near zero. (I am grateful to Gene Grossman for bringing this point to my attention.) This is another manifestation of the "voting paradox", a paradox which can be resolved only by assuming that voting is motivated by other than pure self interest.

contributions to increase the probability that their favored political party wins at the polls. In Grossman and Helpman, campaign contributions are made to influence the policy stance of the incumbent government.

The MBY model adds two lobbies and two political parties (or candidates) to the standard 2×2 Heckscher–Ohlin model. One of the parties is assumed to be pro-trade, while the other is pro-protection. Each lobby represents one factor of production (capital or labor), and makes contributions to one of the two parties. (In equilibrium, it does not pay to split contributions.) Each party's election probability is increasing in the campaign contributions it receives but decreasing in the level of the policy intervention it commits itself to.

Formally, assume good 1 is capital-intensive and let q be the probability that the pro-capital party is elected. Denote by C_K and C_L the campaign contributions made respectively by the capitalist lobby to the pro-capital party and by the labor lobby to the pro-labor party. Magee et al. express q as $q(C_K, C_L, p_1 - p_1^*, p_2 - p_2^*)$, where $q(.)$ is increasing in own contributions and in the pro-labor distortion $(p_2 - p_2^*)$ and decreasing in the contributions received by the other party and in the pro-capital distortion $(p_1 - p_1^*)$. The pro-capital party selects p_1 to maximize $q(.)$, while the pro-labor party selects p_2 to maximize $1 - q(.)$. As for lobbies, they maximize the expected incomes of the factors they represent, net of campaign contributions. Letting $\{r_K, w_K\}$ represent the factor returns when the pro-capital party is in power and $\{r_L, w_L\}$ the factor returns when the pro-labor party is in power, the relevant maximands are

$$\max_{C_K} \ [qr_K + (1-q)r_L]K - C_K$$

$$\max_{C_L} \ [qw_K + (1-q)w_L]L - C_L \tag{3.8}$$

The assumed strategic interactions are as follows: the two parties play Nash against each other, as do the two lobbies. But the parties are assumed to be Stackelberg leaders over the lobbies which contribute to them. This is equivalent to having parties move (that is, select their policies) in the first stage of a two-stage sub-game perfect equilibrium, with the lobbies moving in the second stage. The implication is that lobbies' contributions are intended to affect election outcomes but not party platforms. The model generates equilibrium levels of p_1 and p_2, i.e. an import tariff and an export subsidy. However, the framework is too complex to yield reduced-form solutions, short of making specific parametric assumptions.

The MBY model has been vigorously criticized by Austen-Smith (1991), both for its artificial restriction on the parties' platforms (either pro-export or pro-protection) and for its use of probabilistic voting without a rational-choice foundation. Mayer and Li (1994) have reworked the MBY framework tackling both criticisms. They provide better microfoundations for the MBY assumption that campaign contributions enhance electoral strength by modeling uncertainty explicitly. The full justification for the MBY model requires two-sided uncertainty: voters must not know exactly the policy preferences of the two parties, and parties in turn must be uncertain about some aspect of the voters' preferences. Mayer and Li also allow the parties to choose any policy they want. The result of these refinements is to weaken some of the MBY findings: it is no longer certain that the two lobbies will never contribute to the same party, for example.

3.5. The political contributions approach (Grossman–Helpman)

The Grossman and Helpman (1994) model does not allow explicit competition among politicians. Instead, there exists a single incumbent who maximizes a weighted sum of total political contributions and aggregate welfare:

$$W^{\mathrm{GH}} = a \sum_h V(p, I^h) + \sum_h \lambda^h(p) \tag{3.9}$$

where a (>0) is the relative weight placed on aggregate welfare, and $\lambda^h(p)$ represents the contributions. (I^h refers to individual incomes *before* political contributions.) The underlying economic model is that of a small open economy, where the wage is fixed to unity due to the presence of a numeraire sector which uses labor alone. There exist n additional sectors which use labor plus a specific factor. Some of these specific factors are represented by lobby groups. Each lobby presents the incumbent with a contribution schedule, mapping the policy vector (restricted to trade taxes and subsidies) into a contribution level.[4] Letting H_i stand for the set of individuals who own some of the specific factor used in sector i,[5] the lobby representing sector i makes contributions amounting to $\Lambda_i(p)$, where

$$\Lambda_i(p) = \sum_{h \in H_i} \lambda^h(p). \tag{3.10}$$

Grossman and Helpman restrict individual preferences to the form $V(p, I^h) = I^h - \delta(p)$. Each lobby wants to maximize its membership's utility (net of contributions). Therefore the lobbies' problem consists of selecting $\Lambda_i(p)$ to maximize

$$v^i \equiv \sum_{h \in H_i} [I^h - \delta(p)] - \Lambda_i(p). \tag{3.11}$$

The incumbent government takes these contribution schedules as given and maximizes W^{GH} (eq. 3.9) accordingly. Note that lobbies commit to their contributions

---

[4] Riezman and Wilson (1993a) call this an ''inverse tariff formation function'', except that its form is determined endogenously. Indeed, the determination of the form that this function will take represents the analytical core of the Grossman and Helpman paper.

[5] Individuals are assumed to own at most one type of factor.

before policies are selected. In contrast to MBY, then, political contributions are intended to directly influence the policies selected by the policy maker.[6]

An equilibrium consists of a set of contribution functions $\{A_i(\boldsymbol{p})\}$ such that each of these maximizes the joint welfare of the lobby's membership given the schedules of other lobbies *and* the anticipated decision rule of the government, plus a vector of domestic prices which maximizes W^{GH}. Grossman and Helpman (1994) rely on results from Bernheim and Whinston's (1986) work on common agency to show that the equilibrium tariffs (or export subsidies) take the following form (provided the contribution schedules are differentiable around the equilibrium point):

$$\frac{t_i}{1+t_i} = \frac{\zeta_{iL} - \alpha_L}{a + \alpha_L} \frac{x_i}{m_i \varepsilon_i} \tag{3.12}$$

where ζ_{iL} is an (exogenous) indicator that equals one if industry i is represented by a lobby (and zero otherwise), α_L is the (exogenous) share of the population that is represented by lobbies, x_i is the domestic output in sector i, and ε_i is the import demand or export supply elasticity (defined as a positive number for the former and a negative number for the latter).[7] The protection received by a sector is higher when it is organized, when its output is high relative to competing imports, and when the price responsiveness of the corresponding trade flows is low.

This model is applied to a two-country setting in Grossman and Helpman (1993a) and to analyze the political viability of a free-trade agreement in Grossman and Helpman (1993b). The great advantage of the Grossman–Helpman framework is that it allows the endogenous derivation from first principles of the campaign contribution schedules of competing lobbies in a fairly general framework. Moreover, it does so without sacrificing tractability. On the other hand, the model is subject to the criticism that only a small part of lobbying activity in real politics takes the form of financial contributions.[8]

---

[6]Whether political contributions are made to influence candidates' choices (as in Grossman–Helpman) or to increase the likelihood that a candidate of the desired ideology wins office (as in MBY) is an unsettled issue in the literature on campaign contributions. Bronars and Lott (1994) find that retiring Congressmen who experience large reductions in donations do not change how they vote in their last term, interpreting this as evidence in favor of the second hypothesis. See Magleby and Nelson (1990) for a good introduction to the literature on campaign contributions in the U.S.

[7]This is the formula for a small country. In the case of a large country, there is an additional term capturing the optimum tariff motive.

[8]The following critique of MBY by Austen-Smith (1991, p. 84) is equally relevant to the Grossman–Helpman model: "...lobbying activity is predominantly not financial, but rather to do with information transmission. Specifically, lobbying activity involves the efforts of individuals and groups to influence individual legislators' decisions through various forms of persuasion: for example, direct mail campaigns, face-to-face discussion about the policy consequences of a bill, providing information on the distribution of constituency support with respect to an issue, etc., etc. On the other hand, as remarked earlier, campaign contributions cannot be used legally in this way. While interest groups can give resources to support the electoral campaigns of favored candidates, they cannot do so in direct exchange for policy decisions or make donations explicitly conditional on a legislator promising to vote one way or another if elected".

4. Why is international trade not free?

The *raison d'être* for the literature on the political economy of trade policy is the need to provide an answer to the question posed by this section's title. How well does the literature fare in this regard? At one level, quite well. Each of the family of models reviewed above provides a particular story about how organized groups or individual voters can take political action to reinforce or alleviate the income-distributional consequences of trade flows. While the manner in which political influence is exercised differs across models, the conclusion in common is: trade is not free because politically-influential groups can be made better off by policy interventions in trade.

At a deeper level, however, this shared bottom-line is problematic, or at least incomplete. The reason has to do with the well-known argument that trade policy is a highly inefficient tool for redistributing income [see Dixit (1985), for a broad treatment]. Saying that trade policy exists because it serves to transfer income to favored groups is a bit like saying Sir Edmund Hillary climbed Mt. Everest because he wanted to get some mountain air. There was surely an easier way of accomplishing that objective!

To be more concrete, consider the case of garment workers in the United States. Let us assume that these workers are politically influential (in the relevant sense), and that transferring income to them is the politically efficient thing to do. Assume, moreover, that the political equilibrium requires the garment workers' lifetime wealth to be higher than what it would have been under unfettered market competition by $$x$. Now consider the following five ways of achieving this transfer: (i) a lump-sum grant of $$x$ to every worker employed in the garment industry *presently*; (ii) the same lump-sum grant, but to future as well as present garment workers; (iii) a permanent employment subsidy to the garment industry which increases workers' lifetime wealth by $$x$; (iv) a permanent production subsidy to the garment industry; and (v) a permanent tariff on imported foreign garments. By construction, garment workers should be indifferent among these possibilities. The rest of society, however, progressively becomes worse off as we move from option (i) to option (v).

The puzzle then is why the worst of these options – trade intervention – should emerge in political equilibrium. This apparently perverse outcome is not only puzzling, but also goes against the expectation, most clearly articulated by Becker (1983, 1985), that pressure groups will favor more efficient means of transferring income to themselves. The models discussed above are largely silent on this issue, since they explicitly rule out recourse to other policies besides trade policy. Put differently, the existing literature is largely a literature on the political economy of *redistribution*, and not of trade policy proper.[9] The links with trade policy arise only

---

[9] In the preface to their book, Magee et al. write: "the theory [developed here] describes any government policy motivated by special interests" (1989, p. xvii). This is of course precisely the problem.

in the special case wherein policymakers are assumed to have access to no other instruments beside trade interventions.[10]

This is not to say that the existing models cannot be manipulated to generate examples in which trade policy is used in equilibrium even when a choice of alternative, more direct instruments is available. I will mention such examples below. The point is that the leading models are not primarily aimed at addressing this question. Therefore, there continues to exist a serious gap in our understanding of what makes trade policy so politically efficient, as it must be judged to be by revealed preference, when considerably more direct means of redistributing income certainly exist.

The existing work suggests two broad avenues for reconciling the political efficiency of trade policy with its economic inefficiency for redistributive purposes. First, it is possible that tariff-equilibria are preferred because they entail less cost to relevant political actors, in part because their economic inefficiency may make them harder to use. Second, tariff-equilibria may emerge as preferred outcomes in models with incomplete information because of informational reasons. I will take up each type of explanation in turn.

4.1. Tariffs as a means of reducing costly redistribution

Return for a moment to the discussion above about alternative forms of transferring income to garment workers. What allowed us to rank these policies in terms of payoffs to relevant parties (garment workers and the rest of society) was that they were each calibrated so as to transfer a fixed amount of income (x) to garment workers. But in a political-economy framework, this is an inappropriate comparison. After all, the amount of income that in equilibrium garment workers manage to extract from the rest of society is really *endogenous*. Depending on the policies that are available, and the rules of the game, the distributive gains to workers will change, as will the associated costs – lobbying, campaign contributions – incurred both by workers in the pursuit of these gains and by others in the attempt to avoid the transfers. Consequently, the preferences of the relevant actors for specific types of redistributive policies cannot be known ex ante, and will depend in general on the features of the model at hand. Nor can the social desirability of one type of policy be easily ranked against that of another, once the endogeneity of the process generating these policies is recognized [Rodrik (1987)].[11]

---

[10]Moreover many models of political economy contain an inconsistency: They allow tariff revenue to be distributed in lump-sum fashion back to the population. Unless the distribution is undertaken in the form of poll subsidies (an equal amount for every individual), this is inconsistent with the maintained assumption in the same papers that only tariffs can be used to redistribute income.

[11]This complication was recognized by Becker, although in passing. He notes the "tendency for the political sector to use the most efficient methods available to redistribute to beneficiaries", but then adds: "a satisfactory analysis of the choice of methods must consider whether the influence function itself depends on the methods used" (1985, p. 338).

The earliest paper that I am aware of which gives concrete form to this line of reasoning is Rodrik (1986). The paper undertakes a comparison of two policy regimes, one in which a politically-powerful industry can lobby only for production subsidies and another in which it can lobby only for import tariffs. The crucial difference between the two policies is that production subsidies can be in principle firm-specific, while import tariffs are not. In view of the free-rider problem associated with lobbying for tariffs, then, the endogenous policy equilibrium involves a higher level of transfers to firms when production subsidies are the only instrument available. This added redistribution can be large enough to offset the by-product distortion of tariffs on the consumption side. Hence, citizens acting behind a Rawlsian veil of ignorance, not knowing their later position in society, may well choose a tariff regime over a subsidy regime.

Wilson (1990) has provided a more elegant model, with the same flavor. In his words, ''a move to relatively inefficient forms of income transfers may reduce the total excess burden in the economy, because the greater inefficiency induces the politicians to lower their use of transfers'' (1990, p. 242).

The model has two candidates competing to win office, with the probability of winning increasing in own contributions and decreasing in the rival's. The higher the level of contributions a candidate receives the higher the transfer he will have to make when in office. But these transfers are costly to the politician due to their dead-weight loss. If the two candidates behave in Nash fashion in pursuit of contributions, in equilibrium there is excess contributions and excess transfers compared to what could have been achieved if they had colluded. So restricting the efficiency of transfers alleviates this particular problem, reduces the transfers in equilibrium, and could even make both politicians better off (since politicians are assumed to also care about deadweight loss). In particular, the political equilibrium with tariffs is more efficient than the one with production subsidies.

In a similar vein, Grossman and Helpman (1994, Section 6) show in their model that lobbies would not necessarily prefer the government to use more efficient means of transferring income to them. The reason is that when competition between lobbies is intense, each lobby is making a large contribution, yet at the same time its effect on policy outcomes is being cancelled by the equally large contributions of other lobbies. So lobbies may support institutions that constrain governments to transfer income as inefficiently as possible (i.e. through trade policy), thus inducing lower contributions by each of the lobbies. As in Wilson (1990), the counter-intuitive result is the consequence of wasteful competition among lobbies that cannot coordinate their actions. Put differently, more efficient transfers allow the incumbent to play off lobbies against each other more easily, and to collect more contributions (1990, p. 33).

As a final example of this kind of logic, consider the paper by Staiger and Tabellini (1987). In the Staiger–Tabellini framework, trade policy is the consequence of a benevolent government's incentive to provide ''surprise'' protection to workers adversely affected by a fall in world prices. Since, workers cannot be systematically surprised, however, the time-consistent equilibrium involves excessive protection (in the sense that the government may have preferred to commit itself to providing no protection at all). In this context, a switch from a more "efficient" policy tool (production subsidy) to a less "efficient" one (import tariff) can make the government better off: the less efficient policy alleviates the time-inconsistency problem by making it less beneficial to surprise the workers.

In each of the above models, the comparison involves equilibria of different "policy regimes", where each regime is characterized by the use of a specific policy (tariffs or production subsidies, say). What is often left vague is the political mechanism that governs the *choice* of one regime over another. One can think of this choice as being made in the first stage of a two-stage political economy model. This appears to be the implicit view in the previous papers, but the decision-making process for this first stage is not well specified in any one of them. The main contribution of the type of reasoning represented by these papers is to suggest that tariff equilibria do not necessarily generate more deadweight loss than equilibria in which more direct redistributive policies are used, once the political determination of the magnitude of policy interventions is accounted for.

4.2. Tariffs as informationally efficient policies

Most of the models discussed so far are complete-information models where uncertainty or asymmetric information plays no role. In particular, politicians are assumed to be perfectly informed about the characteristics of pressure groups and the latter in turn to have full information about the economy-wide consequences of policy choices. In practice, of course, neither of these assumptions is tenable. Some effort has gone recently into modelling the consequences of relaxing them, with a particular eye towards generating a rationale for the use of inefficient redistributive polices such as trade policy.

Magee, Brock, and Young (1989) propose the principle of "optimal obfuscation" as an explanation for the existence of trade restrictions. They argue that indirect policies present a political advantage precisely because their effects are less likely to be observed by those who bear the costs. Their formalization, however, is incomplete and presents more questions than it answers. In particular, as Austen-Smith (1991, p. 82) has argued, "rational maximizers without complete information may nevertheless be able to infer sufficient information from the behavior of others to make the 'correct' decision". A satisfactory model dealing with this issue must incorporate explicit uncertainty and be built on information-theoretic foundations.

A recent paper by Coate and Morris (1993), although not concerned directly with trade policy, represents an important beginning in that direction. They construct a model in which voters have uncertainty both as to the motive of the politician (well-meaning or redistributive), and as to the efficiency of the indirect transfer. With regard to the latter, there exists some states of the world in which the less direct transfer is also the more efficient one. They show that under these conditions inefficient transfers will sometimes be made. The reason is that politicians care about their reputations, and redistributive politicians will sometimes rather maintain their reputation (of not being redistributive) than make the efficient transfer (which will be recognized directly for what it is). In other words, "the reputational penalty for using the [inefficient] policy to make transfers is likely to be less than that for making direct transfers" [Coate and Morris (1993, p. 25)].

One important contribution of the Coate–Morris paper is its demonstration that both types of uncertainty are needed for inefficient transfers to be made in equilibrium: if all politicians were alike, then their type could be readily discerned from their behavior. So uncertainty about the efficiency of the indirect transfer is not sufficient. But note also that their model has only partial applicability to the issues at hand. Trade restrictions are economically efficient only for a large country and for "optimum tariff" reasons; it is hard to believe that there would exist much uncertainty in practice about the legitimacy of this motive.[12] (Remember that the indirect redistributive policy must be efficient in *some* states of the world, and that the state of the world is not observed by voters.)

Feenstra and Lewis (1991a) consider the role of asymmetric information from the perspective of a benevolent government. Suppose the government wants, following a fall in the world price of importables, to make sure that no one loses. Suppose further that the government can observe nothing about the domestic economy, and therefore that it can neither target lump-sum transfers, nor ensure that the taxes needed to finance a production subsidy on import-competing producers are designed appropriately to leave no individual worse off. Under these conditions, an import tariff is an informationally efficient policy because the tariff necessarily and automatically benefits those that lose out, while leaving no one worse-off relative to the initial situation. In particular, a tariff equivalent to the decline of import prices will leave everyone in the economy as well off as before, while generating some government revenue which can be redistributed. The tariff policy does not require the government to have any information about individual production and consumption levels. Feenstra and Lewis show that the optimal, incentive-compatible policy in this case is actually a non-linear tariff, with larger producers of the import-competing good being protected by lower tariffs.

---

[12] Perhaps infant-industry protection fits the Coate–Morris argument best. While trade policy is rarely first- or even second-best for purposes of infant-industry promotion (Baldwin 1969), it was widely believed until recently that its use is economically justified under certain conditions.

4.3. Other explanations

In a series of papers, Mayer and Riezman (1987, 1989, 1990) have considered the choice between tariffs and more direct redistributive policies in Mayer (1984)-type models. In Mayer and Riezman (1987), they show that where voter preferences are based only on differences in factor ownership, production subsidies are preferred by the median voter to tariffs (as expected). In Mayer and Riezman (1989), they allow voters to differ on other dimensions besides factor ownership, namely in consumption preferences and in their treatment under income taxes. With multidimensional voting of this type, there is of course no unique equilibrium. We need an agenda setter to determine equilibrium, but with that included, the more inefficient tariffs can certainly arise as a possible equilibrium. Finally, Mayer and Riezman (1990) provide additional reasons for why tariffs may be preferred by certain voters in the same kind of framework: if income taxes are progressive, the cost of financing subsidies will be focussed on richer individuals, while the cost of the tariff is more broadly distributed among the population, leading to some individuals preferring tariffs; a tariff regime may be less risky ex ante, since the range of ex post optimal tariffs is smaller than in the case of subsidies, resulting in risk-averse voters preferring the former.

4.4. The choice among alternative trade policy instruments

There also exists a related literature that analyzes the political choice between tariffs and other trade policy instruments (mainly VERs). Hillman (1990) discusses how non-tariff barriers such as VERs and trigger price mechanisms can be viewed as arrangements that benefit producers in both exporting and importing countries at the expense of consumers. Hillman and Ursprung (1988) model how VERs can be preferred to import tariffs by both domestic and foreign producers, and therefore can emerge in a political equilibrium where each industry makes campaign contributions to their respective domestic politicians. Feenstra and Lewis (1991b) provide a model in which VERs are an efficient response to the following problem: when domestic political pressures are not directly observed by trade partners, each country may have an incentive to exaggerate the political pressure at home, so as to jack up its protection; therefore, "the transfer of quota rents [through VERs] can play a useful role in ensuring that countries do not exaggerate the political pressure for protection" (p. 1304).

4.5. Summary and evaluation

The collective effect of these papers is to weaken considerably the presumption that direct redistributive policies should be politically more efficient than trade interventions. However, the reader would be fully justified if s/he is left feeling uneasy about how well the literature has tackled the task at hand. The results discussed above tend to be too narrow and specific to account for what is essentially a universal phenomenon: the preference of political systems to use trade interventions to generate or sustain distributional outcomes. Of course, trade policy is not the only, or even the most important, mechanism of redistribution used by governments. But practically all governments apparently use it for that purpose. A sufficiently general and convincing explanation for this phenomenon has yet to be formulated.

Part of the problem is that the literature has largely relegated the preference for trade policies to a side show. The papers discussed in this section represent a tiny minority within the literature on the political economy of trade policy, and even in some of these the question of policy choice is an afterthought. This is also reflected in the small role attached to the question in existing surveys. In Hillman (1989), for example, the chapter entitled "Political choice of the means of protection" focusses its analytical core on the choice between tariffs and quotas, and not on the choice between these and more efficient distributive policies. In Magee, Brock, and Young (1989), the preference for trade policies over other policies is not discussed until the very last chapter. Clearly, the literature needs a shift in focus.

5. Why are trade policies biased against trade?

Let us assume for a second that the existing literature provides a satisfactory explanation for the prevalent use of trade policies for distributive purposes. We now confront a second, equally important puzzle: why are trade policies almost always biased against trade, rather than in favor of it? That is, why is trade policy systematically used to transfer resources to import-competing sectors and factors rather than to export-oriented sectors and factors? That there exists a systematic bias should be obvious: there is no country that I am aware of where the *net* effect of commercial policies is to expand rather than contract trade.[13] This is also reflected in the fact that multilateral (as well as bilateral) trade negotiations typically focus on eliminating barriers to trade rather than artificial inducements thereon. The few case studies that focus on the political activities of export-oriented interests take it for granted that the focal point around which such interests coalesce is free trade, *not* export subsidization [see Destler and Odell (1987) and Milner (1988)]. It is not clear

---

[13]In his discussion of the Trade Act of 1974, Baldwin (1976, p. 36) notes that there were few industries that testified strongly in favor of liberalization, in stark contrast to the many demands for less liberalization.

why this should be so, when the analogous benchmark for import-competing interests is protection.[14]

On this puzzle we get very little help from the literature. Consider the leading models. The tariff-formation function approach à la Findlay and Wellisz (1982) essentially assumes the problem away by stipulating that sectoral interests lobby for tariffs but not export subsidies. The political-support function approach à la Hillman (1982) generates the asymmetry by assuming that the policymaker desires support from import-competing interests but not from exporting ones. The other leading approaches do not introduce artificial asymmetries, and therefore generate no presumption that the equilibrium trade policy is a tariff rather than an export subsidy (although their language often suggests otherwise). In Mayer (1984), for example, the equilibrium trade policy would consist of an export subsidy when the median voter is relatively well endowed with the economy's abundant factor.[15]

Let us look at this question more closely using the Grossman and Helpman (1994) framework. As shown in eq. (3.12), the level of support (import tariff or export subsidy) received by an industry depends in this framework on a number of features, including whether the industry is organized or not and the size of its trade elasticity. Leaving aside artificial asymmetries along these two dimensions, the model predicts that industries with high levels of output relative to their respective trade volumes receive more protection. To see what this implies, let us consider the case of a single import-competing and a single exporting industry. Since trade must be balanced, the question of which industry gets more protection then boils down to which industry has the higher level of output. And if comparative advantage carries any force, countries will tend to specialize in their export sectors; that is, they will have larger export sectors than import-competing sectors. The unfortunate implication is that we should observe a bias towards export subsidies, and not import tariffs! Indeed, Levy (1993a) has shown that in a symmetric, two-country Grossman–Helpman world the effect of lobbying is to encourage net trade promotion.[16] Hence, the Grossman–

---

[14]It could be argued that one reason for the anti-trade bias is that direct export subsidization, unlike import tariffs, has long been illegal under the GATT. However, quantitative restrictions for manufactured goods have also been GATT-illegal (save for developing countries and under proscribed conditions), yet countries have found imaginative ways of using them without sanction. Governments have been significantly more prone to flout international obligations on import restrictions than on export inducements. In addition, one may ask why the prohibition on export subsidization was agreed to by governments in the first place (when no such prohibition on import tariffs would have been feasible).

[15]Sometimes appeal is made to Corden's "conservative social welfare function" to explain why there is a bias towards trade restrictions. According to this idea, "any significant absolute reductions in real incomes of any section of the community should be avoided" [Corden (1974, pp. 107–108)]. However, there is no reason to believe that over the long run export interests receive negative shocks with lower frequency (or lesser force) than do import-competing interests. And if they do not, why should there be a universal bias towards import restrictions?

[16]Levy (1993a, p. 17) provides a good discussion of what would need to hold for anti-trade bias to exist. Judging that none of these requirements is satisfactory, he gets out of the conundrum by simply assuming that export subsidies are ruled out.

Helpman framework not only does not help out with the puzzle, it actually makes it worse.

The starting point for any explanation for the systematic bias in favor of trade restrictions is likely to be a bit of history: revenue-hungry rulers in countries with poor administrative capabilities know that trade is an excellent tax handle. Trade taxes therefore typically contribute a very large share of government revenue in any nation's early history. In the United States, for example, tariffs provided on average more than 50 percent of government revenue from 1870 to 1914 [Baack and Ray (1983)]. Prior to the Civil War, this ratio actually stood at 90 percent! [Hansen (1990)]. Not surprisingly, then, the sharp drop in the average U.S. tariff rate at the start of World War I coincides with the introduction of the income tax in 1913.

Cross-country evidence is also consistent with the hypothesis that poorer countries rely more heavily on trade taxes. As shown in Table 5.1, there is a robust negative relationship between per capita income and the share of trade taxes in total tax revenue: an increase in per capita income of $1,000 is associated with a reduction in 3.7 percentage points in the share of taxes that originate from foreign trade.

Viewed from this perspective, the political-economy puzzle becomes why the bias against trade remains even when governments develop alternative, more efficient sources of tax revenue.[17] That is, the puzzle about anti-trade bias turns into a puzzle about persistence. It is well known that the OECD countries have moved to non-tariff barriers just as they were reducing their reliance on import tariffs. Of course, one can

Table 5.1
Relationship between trade taxes and per capita income

	Dependent variable:		
	All trade taxes as a share of total tax revenue (1984–86 average)	Import duties as a share of total tax revenue (1984–86 average)	Export taxes as a share of total tax revenue (1984–86 average)
Constant	0.353*	0.279*	0.065*
Per capita GDP (1985)	−0.037	−0.030*	−0.011**
$\bar{R}^2$	0.18	0.12	0.07
Number of countries	77	77	77

Source: Tax data have been supplied by the Fiscal Affairs Department, IMF. Per capita GDP is from the Heston–Summers data set.
Notes: * Significant at the 1 percent level; ** significant at the 5 percent level.

[17] By the same token, explaining the bias against trade by appealing to revenue considerations – export subsidies cost money while import tariffs raise revenue – is unsatisfactory. Most advanced industrial economies have well-developed tax systems which render trade taxes unnecessary. As for developing economies, the most popular forms of protection – quantitative restrictions – do not raise revenue for the treasury. Similarly, many pro-export policies (such as export targets or export performance requirements, which have been used widely in East Asia) do not require the expenditure of fiscal resources.

appeal to the terms-of-trade benefits of trade restrictions for large countries. But this explanation would be implausible, not the least because governments have been so quick to transfer rents created by quantitative restrictions to foreign exporters through VERs. Moreover, there is corroborating historical evidence that it is difficult to take protection away once it has been given: Gardner and Kimbrough (1989) show that the average U.S. tariff follows close to a random walk in the pre-1913 period (that is, any increase in the tariff was essentially permanent).

There are practically no models in the literature that deal with this issue of persistence, and very few that can account for it.[18] Two exceptions are Fernandez and Rodrik (1991) and Brainard and Verdier (1993). The first of these papers shows that there is a natural status-quo bias to policymaking whenever some of the gainers (or losers) from reform cannot be identified ex ante. Many reforms that are politically sustainable ex post will not be adopted ex ante. Fernandez and Rodrik (1991) show that the bias exists even when individuals are risk neutral, rational and forward-looking.

To see how the argument works, consider a democracy where a majority vote is needed before trade reform can be adopted. Let the economy have 100 voters and suppose that the reform in question will increase the incomes of 51 individuals by $5 each and decrease the incomes of the rest by $1 each, leaving a net gain of $(5 \times 51) - (1 \times 49) = \$206$. In the absence of uncertainty, the majority of the population would vote in favor and the reform would be adopted. We assume that all these consequences of reform are common knowledge. Now suppose that while 49 individuals know for sure that they will gain, the remaining 51 are in the dark as to which among them will gain and which will lose; however, since aggregate consequences are common knowledge, individuals in the latter group know that two of them will eventually benefit while 49 will lose out. (Such uncertainty may arise from, say, incomplete information at the individual level about the skills needed to succeed in the post-reform environment.) This renders individuals in the second group identical ex ante, with an expected benefit from reform of $[(5 \times 2) - (1 \times 49)]/51 = -\$0.76$ each. Hence the individuals in the uncertain group will reject reform, blocking its adoption.

Conversely, uncertainty of this kind can lead to reforms that will prove unpopular ex post (and hence be reversed) to be adopted ex ante. The bias towards the status quo derives from the following asymmetry: due to the uncertainty about the consequences of the reform, some reforms that will be ex post unsustainable are adopted, while some that would have been sustainable are not. Both of these types of "error" leave the polity in the status-quo position (as the former cases are eventually followed by a return to the status quo).

---

[18]One can of course assume that the policymaker is simply loath to have any sector of the economy incur a real income loss. Corden (1974, p. 107) has coined the term "conservative social welfare function" to describe the objective function of a policymaker acting in this fashion.

Brainard and Verdier (1993) use a dynamic version of the Grossman–Helpman (1994) framework to show that industries that have high protection today are more likely to have high protection tomorrow as well. The reason is that current protection makes these industries adjust (contract) less, with the result that output will be higher in the future than in the absence of the protection. The higher future output in turn translates in the Grossman–Helpman framework into greater future protection.

To sum up, to date very little attention has been paid to explaining why trade policies are systematically biased against trade. What I have argued here is that a two-part explanation for this bias holds the greatest promise. First, the initial conditions: since trade is a convenient tax handle, most governments inherit trade taxes originally put in place for revenue motives. Second, persistence and status-quo bias: once protection is awarded, it is difficult to take it away. However, more work is needed on this last point.

6. Protection across industries, countries, and time

What are the determinants of protection levels across different industries, among countries, or over time? These questions, and particularly the first one, have been the subject of a large body of empirical literature. The typical approach in the empirical work has been to regress some measure of protection on a number of economic and political variables.[19] While the relevance of the included independent variables is typically motivated by appealing loosely to the theoretical literature, the links between the empirical and theoretical work have never been too strong in this area. Regression analysis often takes the kitchen-sink approach, with a large number of "relevant" variables – some obviously endogenous – thrown in on the right-hand side. None of the leading approaches discussed earlier has been subjected to direct empirical test. On the other hand, nor are some of the empirical regularities uncovered by the econometric work adequately explained by existing theory (see below).

There exist quite a few surveys of the empirical literature on the political economy of trade policy [Ray (1990); Marks and McArthur (1990); Anderson and Baldwin (1987)]. Therefore, I will only summarize some of the main conclusions coming out of this literature and relate these to theory.

---

[19] In addition to econometric work, on which I will focus, there is a large body of case studies. For some recent U.S. examples, see Nelson (1994) on the auto industry, Moore (1994) on steel, Orden (1994) on agriculture in the context of NAFTA, and Irwin (1994) on semiconductors.

6.1. Protection across industries

The cross-industry determinants of levels of protection within a country have been analyzed in a regression framework by a large number of authors. The studies to date have focussed on advanced industrial countries (mainly the U.S.), and have used many different indicators of trade protection, including nominal and effective tariffs, non-tariff coverage ratios, and exemptions from multilateral trade liberalization. To summarize the key findings of this literature, the protection received by an industry is higher when:

- it is a labor-intensive, low-skill, low-wage industry [Caves (1976); Saunders (1980); Anderson (1980); Ray (1981); Marvel and Ray (1983); Baldwin (1985); Anderson and Baldwin (1987); Ray (1991); Finger and Harrison (1994)];
- it has high import penetration [Anderson (1980); Finger and Harrison (1994)], has experienced an *increase* in import penetration [Trefler (1993)], or has been in decline [Marvel and Ray (1983); Ray (1991)];
- it produces consumer goods rather than intermediate goods [Baack and Ray (1983); Marvel and Ray (1983); Ray (1991)];
- its production is regionally concentrated [Pincus (1975); Caves (1976); Godek (1985)], except for in the case of non-tariff barriers [Ray (1981)];
- it engages in little intra-industry trade [Ray (1991); Marvel and Ray (1987)];
- its customers are not highly concentrated [Pincus (1975); Trefler (1993)].

High levels of concentration in the affected industry itself is apparently not always conducive to protection: some studies find a negative relationship between seller concentration and protection [Anderson and Baldwin (1987); Finger, Hall, and Nelson (1982)], while many others find a positive relationship [Pincus (1975); Saunders (1980); Marvel and Ray (1983); Godek (1985); Trefler (1993)]. Another noteworthy finding is that tariffs and non-tariff barriers are complements [Ray (1981); Ray and Marvel (1984); Godek (1985)]. We note that the studies listed here are not directly comparable for a number of reasons: they use different measures of protection, cover different countries and time periods, and include different sets of right-hand side variables.

One recent paper in this tradition that is particularly noteworthy is Trefler (1993). This paper is novel in that it considers the joint determination of import penetration levels with non-tariff protection. The argument is that there is a two-way dependence between these two: an increase in import penetration stimulates demands for NTBs, while an increase in NTBs naturally restrict imports. The correct procedure, therefore, is to undertake a simultaneous estimation of the import-penetration and NTB equations. Once the endogeneity of NTBs is taken into account, Trefler shows that the restrictive effect of NTBs on U.S. trade is much greater than what is usually estimated in single-equation trade models. He finds that the 1983 average import penetration in U.S. manufactures would rise from 13.8 to 15.4 percent, which is equivalent to an increase in actual imports of $49.5 billion under conservative estimates. With regard to the NTB equation, Trefler finds that the level of NTB coverage is positively and significantly correlated not with the level of import penetration but with the *change* in it.

These empirical regularities overlap only imperfectly with the results of the theoretical literature. The finding that advanced industrial countries protect mainly their labor-intensive sectors is essentially a consequence of the fact these are their import-competing sectors. As discussed above, the theoretical literature does not provide any robust reason as to why protection should be biased in favor of sectors with comparative *dis*advantage.

The finding with respect to import-penetration levels (or the changes therein) is also poorly explained. The Grossman–Helpman model in fact yields the opposite presumption, namely that sectors with high import penetration should get low protection.[20,21] Hillman (1982) and van Long and Vousden (1991) use the political-support function approach to explain why declining industries get more protection: when the world price of an import-competing sector drops, the policymaker wants the rest of society to share the cost, so she raises the tariff. Note that the logic in this story is not essentially political, but has to do with risk-sharing. The same outcome obtains in Staiger and Tabellini (1987) as well, where the government does not have an explicitly political motive, and simply wants to redistribute income from groups with low marginal utility of income at the margin – those adversely affected by trade – to those with high marginal utility.[22]

Regarding the nature of the industry's output (consumer versus intermediate good) and its market structure, there is again a dearth of theoretical research. It is of course reasonable that intermediate-good industries will have a comparatively hard time receiving protection, as long as consumer interests are less well organized and represented than producer interests. But almost all theoretical models of political economy exclude intermediate goods and focus on consumer goods [see however last

---

[20] As Grossman and Helpman (1994) point out in a footnote (footnote 16), however, the result can be reversed if sectors with high import penetration have very low elasticities of import demand (so that the efficiency cost of protecting them is low). Since existing empirical work does not control for sectoral differences in import demand elasticities, and add ''extraneous'' variables to the regressions, Grossman and Helpman argue that their theoretical results cannot be directly compared with the empirical findings. This is a good illustration of the gulf that currently separates empirical and theoretical work in the area of political economy of trade policy.

[21] Brainard and Verdier (1993) use the Grossman–Helpman framework to address the issue of senescent industry protection, but they simply assume that the industry starts to lobby only after it experiences a reduction in its world price. So they cannot address the question of whether the industry receives more or less protection after it is hit with the shock.

[22] In his discussion on why declining industries get preferential treatment, Baldwin (1989) refers in passing to the work of psychologists Kahneman and Tversky (1979, 1984) on how individuals place greater weight on a loss than a gain of an equivalent amount.

section of Grossman and Helpman (1994)]. On industry structure, it is perhaps disappointing that the empirical literature is not more clearcut on the political advantages of high concentration, in view of the strong presumption that free-rider effects should be important in lobbying. Here too, however, theoretical contributions are scant. In Rodrik (1987), there is an unambiguous negative relationship between the numbers of firm in an industry and the amount of tariff protection it receives. Hillman (1991) has undertaken a more complete analysis using a model where owner-managers have to choose how much to invest in internal monitoring of their production activity and how much to lobby in favor of a tariff. He finds that the relationship between concentration and the level of protection is ambiguous in general.[23]

Finally, on intra-industry trade, it stands to reason that pressures for protection are diluted in industries where two-way trade is significant. Krugman's original work on international trade with monopolistic competition was motivated at least in part by the observation that the huge expansion of intra-OECD trade in the postwar period has apparently taken place without large distributive effects, and hence with few political-economy repercussions [Krugman (1981)]. And one interpretation of the disproportionate barriers facing Japanese exports in importing countries is that these are the consequence of Japan's much lower share of intra-industry trade relative to other developed countries.[24] Interestingly, the relationship between intra-industry trade and the political economy of trade policy has not been formally modelled. The only exception seems to be a paper by Levy (1993b), who does so in the context of the debate between bilateralism and multilateralism. Levy models a world with both intra-industry trade and Heckscher–Ohlin trade. An expansion of the former benefits everyone, while an expansion of the latter has redistributive effects along Stolper–Samuelson lines. He shows that the option of integrating with a similar economy ("bilateralism") may foreclose the option of multilateral free trade, when the median voter stands to lose from Heckscher–Ohlin trade.

6.2. Protection across countries or institutional contexts

There is great variation among countries in their average levels of protection. Developing countries, in particular, have much higher levels of protection than the advanced industrial countries – although recently this has begun to change in the case of Latin American countries. Among the industrial countries, the small European countries have tended to be more open (at least when agriculture is excluded) than the

---

[23] An alternative approach is to consider whether an industry is able to maintain cooperative lobbying activities using trigger strategies in a dynamic setting. [See Riezman and Wilson (1993a) on this].

[24] Only 58 percent of Japan's trade was intra-industry in 1990, compared to 83 percent in the U.S., 73 percent in Germany, and 79 percent in Great Britain [Bergsten and Noland (1993), p. 66].

larger economies. The empirical literature on the determinants of cross-country protection is not large. In fact, I found only few systematic studies on the subject.

Magee et al. (1989, ch. 16) find that average tariff rates tend to decrease across countries as capital–labor ratios increase. This is a reflection of the fact that rich countries have lower protection than poor countries. As noted above, there is a solid revenue reason for why this should be so, independent of political economy. In addition, developing countries have been until recently under the influence of infant-industry reasoning. Once these motives are taken into account, it is unclear whether political circumstances provide additional explanatory power for the observed tendency of poor countries to be more protectionist.

Anderson (1993) has analyzed a related asymmetry concerning rich and poor countries: poor countries tend to tax agriculture while rich countries subsidize it. Anderson's main argument is that a tax on agriculture in a developing country results in a relatively small cost for farmers but a big gain for industrialists, while an agricultural subsidy in a developed country entails big gains for farmers but small costs to industrialists. This asymmetry is the consequence of a number of structural differences: in a developing country, agricultural production is a larger share of GDP, uses less capital and industrial inputs, and is a bigger part of domestic consumption. Anderson uses a CGE model with parameters reflecting archetypal developing and developed countries to demonstrate the asymmetric distributional implications of taxing/subsidizing agriculture.

The cross-national variation in average protection levels among advanced industrial countries is examined in Mansfield and Busch (1993). Their sample is small – 14 countries pooled over two years, 1983 and 1986 – but the results are interesting. They find that non-tariff barriers are higher in countries that are larger in size (in terms of either GDP or imports), have higher unemployment rates, have larger number of parliamentary constituencies, and use proportional representation (PR) as their electoral system.

The last two findings deserve special comment, as they are concrete indication that the institutional context of government matters. Following Rogowski (1987), Mansfield and Busch argue that the number of constituencies is an inverse measure of the "insulation" of the executive from narrow interest groups. The reason is that the smaller the average size of the constituency the more likely that a single group can exercise political power: "When automakers or dairy farmers entirely dominate twenty small constituencies and are a powerful minority in fifty more, their voice will certainly be heard in the nation's councils" [Rogowski (1987), p. 208]. This expectation is borne out in the results. The presence of a PR system in turn is taken to indicate that the executive possesses greater "autonomy" as list-system PR tends to lead to strong parties: "[p]ressure groups are restrained where campaign resources or the legal control of nominations are centralized in the hands of party leaders" [Rogowski (1987), p. 209]. The Mansfield–Busch finding that PR systems are associated with higher NTBs, however, contradicts this line of reasoning.

Theoretical and empirical work relating institutional contexts to trade policy outcomes is in its infancy but should be a promising area of research. Cross-national studies necessarily confront variability in institutional context. Single-country studies do not necessarily do so, although different trade policy "tracks" exhibiting different institutional realities may well co-exist within a single political entity. Finger, Hall, and Nelson (1982), in particular, have made this argument for the United States. They distinguish between a "technical" track and a "political" track en route to protection. In the case of anti-dumping proceedings, for example, the determination of whether there has been dumping is a largely technical one, whereas the determination of injury is more political. The rules for the former determination are more clearly specified, while the rules for the latter are more subjective and open to interpretation. Consistent with this hypothesis, Finger et al. find that in less-than-fair value (LFV) pricing determinations, political factors such as industry concentration and size of industry either do not play a role or enter with the "wrong" sign (concentration), while technical factors play an important role. In the case of injury determinations, size of employment enters positively and significantly, while technical factors play a much smaller role. Hence, just as in the Rogowski–Mansfield–Busch line of analysis, different rules of the game produce different outcomes.[25]

6.3. Protection over time

Some of the trends in trade policy over time have already been noted. Notably, countries have tended to reduce their levels of trade restrictions, and, at least among developed countries, there has been a shift away from tariffs in the direction of non-tariff barriers. The former is probably best explained by the development of alternative tax instruments as countries develop, and by the falling out of favor of import-substitution and infant-industry arguments. As for the shift towards NTBs, this is usually explained by reference to successive rounds of agreements under the GATT, which by cutting and binding tariffs have left governments little discretion over their tariff levels. So governments that want to protect have little choice but to resort to NTBs. Note that this argument, as stated, is incomplete. That multilateral agreements under GATT restrict freedom of action for tariffs but not for all kinds of NTBs is common knowledge to all parties concerned. Why governments still have the incentive to negotiate agreements that they know they and others will be able to flout by resorting to NTBs is not so easily explained.

In this sub-section I focus on the following two questions: (i) what do we know about the determinants of short-term fluctuations in levels of trade protection? (ii) what explains the drastic reversals in trade policy we occasionally observe?

---

[25]See also Hall and Nelson (1992) on how legislative and administered protection routes may provide different incentives to lobbying industries.

With regard to the time-series correlates of protection, there exists a number of studies for the United States. That the average tariff level tends to rise in recessions is a robust finding in this literature [Ray (1987); Hansen (1990); O'Halloran (1994)]. In the most careful empirical study to date of the historical experience of the U.S. with tariffs, Bohara and Kaempfer (1991) find that U.S. tariffs are Granger-caused by unemployment, real GNP, the price level, but not the trade balance. Presumably the reason tariffs tend to increase in recessions is the Keynesian motive of switching demand to home products. Note, however, that the practice predates Keynes.[26] In addition, historically Republicans have tended to raise tariffs while Democrats have reduced them [O'Halloran (1994); Magee, Brock, and Young (1989), ch. 13].[27] O'Halloran (1994) emphasizes the importance of political parties taking distinct positions on the tariff issue and implementing them when elected. She takes this to indicate that parties are more than pure aggregators of social pressures, thus reflecting the importance of political institutions.

One interesting time-series study outside the U.S. context is Rama's (1993) work on Uruguay. In this study, Rama goes through historical government records to count the annual number of statutes relating to foreign trade over the 1925–1983 period. He distinguishes between regulations imposed to the benefit of a single firm or industry and regulations that seem more broadly public-spirited, with the first presumably indicating rent-seeking activities. These series are then scaled by aggregate output or exports. Rama regresses this measure of rent-seeking on its lagged value and a series of dummies that represent sub-periods with different political and trade-policy regimes. He finds that sub-periods with policy activism – either in the direction of import substitution or export promotion – are also ones in which rent-seeking activity is largest. This is a notable paper in that it is one of the few attempts to seriously quantify rent-seeking in the trade policy arena, and to delineate its relationship to the government's policy stance.

Finally, let us turn to cases of sharp reversal in trade policy. Such cases pose problems of explanation because the distributional consequences of trade – the basis for trade politics – are unlikely to change very rapidly. Cassing and Hillman (1986) provide a model in which small changes in external conditions can have drastic effects on trade policy: the reason is that declines in economic and political standing are related and can amplify each other's effects. Other explanations are related to

---

[26]Cassing, McKeown and Ochs (1986) provide an alternative explanation that does not depend on the Keynesian motive. They argue that "old" industries with fixed capacities benefit from increases in demand for their product disproportionately at the bottom of the business cycle.

[27]As Ray (1987) points out, the Heckscher–Ohlin–Samuelson model can explain the switch in the Democrats' and Republicans' favored trade policy stances in the post-World War II period. Let the Democratic Party represent farmers and labor, and the Republican party represent business (capital). Prior to World War I, the U.S. was relatively poor in capital and rich in labor and land. This led the Republicans to prefer protection and Democrats to prefer free trade. As the underlying pattern of comparative advantage changes, so do party stances. By the 1970s, Democrats – representing labor – are on the anti-trade side and Republicans on the pro-trade side.

changes in the institutional background. A significant instance is provided by the experience of the United States since the passage of the Reciprocal Trade Act of 1934. Following this act, which delegated Congressional authority over tariff-setting to the President, U.S. tariff levels declined significantly. It has been suggested that this particular institutional innovation – delegation – was chiefly responsible for the subsequent move towards free trade, as the President is presumed to be less susceptible to pressure from narrow pressure groups [Pincus (1986); Baldwin (1991)].

O'Halloran (1994) has provided a more nuanced argument about the role of delegation, in which "Congress meticulously designs procedures to ensure that the actions taken by the president are in line with legislators' preferences" (1994, pp. 5–6). In this view, delegation to the executive is a willful action aimed at getting desirable outcomes. O'Halloran shows that Congress delegates less authority to the president of an opposing party, with the consequence that divided government is associated with higher levels of protection. Once again, these considerations highlight the role played by the institutional setting in determining trade policy outcomes.

More recently, a growing number of developing countries have accomplished a dramatic turn-around by abandoning their protectionist trade regimes in favor of more open trade policies (Bolivia and Mexico since 1985, Argentina since 1987, Brazil since 1988, Peru since 1990). What makes this change in course difficult to explain is that it has taken place in the most unfavorable economic circumstances: these countries were all mired in deep macroeconomic crises with high inflation and stagnant or falling output at the time that they decided to open up. A small literature has emerged trying to explain the puzzle. Many of the explanations center on the political benefits of a deep economic crisis in enabling policy reform. Drazen and Grilli (1993) focus on a "war of attrition" between two social groups and show that a negative shock (a "crisis") leads to an earlier resolution of the conflict. In Rodrik (1994), I explain the reforms by arguing that a deep economic crisis relegates distributional considerations to second place behind economy-wide concerns, and therefore allows an agenda-setting government to sneak in trade policy reforms alongside macroeconomic reforms.

7. Consequences of viewing trade policy from political-economy lenses

This chapter has so far focussed on the contribution that the political-economy perspective can make to our understanding of the actual conduct of trade policy. But there is an additional payoff. Political-economy models can actually enhance the sophistication of our *economic* analysis as well, by providing a fuller account of the likely consequences of policy. In addition, they can be an important input to the design of appropriate institutions and regimes in the trade policy area. Consequently, they can be invaluable for normative analysis as well as positive analysis [Rodrik (1993)]. I conclude this essay by giving some illustrations.

Trefler's (1993) empirical analysis of non-tariff barriers in the U.S., discussed earlier, provides an excellent example of how political-economy analysis enriches our understanding of the economic consequences of trade policy. Trefler notes that the level of imports and of NTBs are both endogenous and influence each other. A single-equation framework that regressed import quantities on NTBs would be subject to simultaneous-equation bias, as import penetration has consequences in turn for NTB levels thanks to political forces. In fact, he finds that the simultaneous-equation estimate of the restrictiveness of NTBs on U.S. imports is 10 times larger than the single-equation estimate. Hence, viewing NTBs as endogenous rather than exogenous corrects the previous literature's conclusion that the effect of trade restrictions on import quantities has been small.[28,29]

As an additional example, consider the paper by Brainard and Verdier (1993). As this paper shows, taking into account the endogeneity of protection gives us a more complete understanding of the process of inter-sectoral resource flows. The easier it is for industries to obtain protection in response to a fall in their price, the slower is the rate of adjustment, and the higher is the long run capacity in the sector experiencing the adverse shock. So, the "specificity" of factors to an industry becomes endogenous through the political process. Our economic models would not give a full account short of taking this endogeneity into account.

One can go one step further. Economic behavior is distorted not only by the actual imposition of trade restrictions, but by the *prospect* of their imposition as well – even if the prospect never becomes reality. So, even Trefler's estimates are biased downwards to the extent that foreign exporters are reducing their sales in the U.S. market to moderate the likelihood that they will bring protection on themselves. Leidy (1993) provides a useful broad discussion of this issue. As he puts it,

> the *prospect* of protection, as it is institutionalized in the policy formation process and the rules for administered protection, can induce real changes in economic activity independent of whether actual barriers have been imposed. Import-competing and exporting firms may be able to manage the prospect of protection under existing rules by modifying decisions pertaining to foreign direct investment, output, employment, exports, capital expenditures, and the like.... The mere absence of current barriers to trade in some sectors, therefore, is not sufficient to

---

[28]Trefler estimates that if U.S. manufacturing NTBs were eliminated, the average import penetration would rise from 13.8 to 15.4 percent, which is an increase of $49.5 billion under conservative assumptions.

[29]In a similar vein, Devereux and Chen (1993) argue that the observed correlation between growth and openness across countries may be an artifact of the endogeneity of trade policy. As the urban industrial sector experiences growth due to technical progress, a political-support maximizing government will want to share the wealth by providing the rural sector with some of the gains as well. The government will consequently respond to growth by reducing the protection of industry.

assume, as is typically done in pure trade theory, that firm conduct and trade is free of policy-induced distortions [Leidy (1993), p. 2].

Bhagwati and Srinivasan's (1976) work on endogenous "market disruption" is the first paper that formalized this idea in a particular instance: if the exporting industry does not internalize the risk of protection in the importing country, it is desirable to impose an export tax on it. Leidy (1993) reviews other papers in this tradition. Winters (1994) provides evidence that the European Union's practice of "import surveillance" (the collection of detailed statistics on particular imports either prior to or immediately after their importation) can lead to reduced imports.

A consistent theme in the political-economy literature is that trade policies can have unanticipated effects unless their political consequences are taken into account. Krueger's (1974) paper on rent-seeking is of course the foremost source on this. A recent application is Sturzenegger (1993), which shows that the rent-shifting benefits of strategic trade policy can be undone completely if the policy leads to rent-seeking that competes with R&D activity for resources. Largely in view of such considerations, Krugman (1993) has argued that free trade remains a good rule of thumb, even if not the optimal policy in an imperfectly-competitive world. However, more work remains to be done on this – to demonstrate in particular the circumstances under which free trade is a politically sustainable policy.

All these considerations suggest that it is important to have a good idea of political economy consequences when advocating policies or designing institutions. The literature on this is not very large. Aside from the papers mentioned above, we can cite Richardson (1993), Riezman and Wilson (1993b), and Panagariya and Rodrik (1993). Richardson (1993) focusses on the differing implications of a customs union and a free trade area for trade diversion in a model where tariff levels are determined endogenously: he shows that an FTA has the added benefit that tariff levels are likely to decline endogenously. Riezman and Wilson (1993b) discuss the consequences for tariff levels of various kinds of political reforms such as ceilings on political contributions, and argue that these restrictions can be easily offset by behavioral adjustments on the part of politicians and lobbyists. Panagariya and Rodrik (1993) consider whether a uniform tariff rule may be desirable as a way of diminishing sectoral pressure for protection.

One important advantage of this line of research is to place on a more solid analytical footing the loose and informal political-economy arguments often deployed in favor of one policy regime or another. As pointed out in Rodrik (1993), the political arguments in favor of, say, uniformity in tariff schedules or shock therapy in trade reform do not have to rest on hand-waving. It is necessary to construct rigorous models to demonstrate the logical soundness of such propositions, no matter how intuitive they may seem.

An analogy with macroeconomic policy is useful here. Thanks in part to the research on time consistency, much of the literature on fiscal and monetary policy has long focussed on the design of rule-based regimes and institutions which would enhance price stability without damaging real activity. Think of the work on central-bank independence or optimum currency zones, for example. In trade policy, we have an analogous set of questions. In particular, we would like to know what kind of multilateral, bilateral, or unilateral rules ("regimes") are: (a) politically feasible, and (b) most conducive to the emergence of desirable trade policies. What is the best way to structure interest-group participation in the policy-making process? Do constitutional restrictions on certain types of trade policies (export taxes? VERs?) make sense? When is delegation of trade policy to the executive feasible, and does it always help in reducing protection? Should trade policy be carried out in a centralized or de-centralized manner? Are regional arrangements desirable as a complement (or substitute) to multilateral institutions? What kind of "safeguard" measures should a multilateral regime sanction to sustain relatively free trade? All these questions are political in nature, and it is natural to turn to the political economy literature for assistance. So far, there has been little work on such issues, but my guess is that this is an area very well worth exploring.[30]

8. Concluding remarks

Economists have always been aware that the determinants of trade policy are deep down political. There is a long and distinguished literature that attests to this awareness. However, I have indicated here a number of areas where more progress is needed. First, we do not fully understand the apparent political advantage of trade policy in redistributing income over more direct policy instruments. Second, we lack a good explanation of the universal preference for trade-restricting policies over trade-promoting ones. Third, the theoretical and empirical literatures dealing with the determinants of protection levels across industries, countries, and time need to be better integrated. Finally, there is plenty of room for sketching out the implications of hard-headed political-economy analysis for normative economics.

References

Anderson, K. (1980), "The political market for government assistance to Australian manufacturing industries", The Economic Record 56:132–44.
Anderson, K. (1993), "Lobbying incentives and the pattern of protection in rich and poor countries", Centre for Economic Policy Research Discussion Paper No. 789.
Anderson, K. and R.E. Baldwin (1987), "The political market for protection in industrial countries", in A.M. El-Agraa, ed., Protection, cooperation, integration and development (Macmillan, New York).

[30]Where international institutions are concerned, the research that is needed would integrate the approaches discussed in this paper with those discussed by Staiger in his chapter in this volume.

Austen-Smith, D. (1991), "Rational consumers and irrational voters", Economics & Politics 3:73–92.

Baack, B.D. and E.J. Ray (1983), "The political economy of tariff policy: A case study of the United States", Explorations in Economic History 20:73–93.

Baldwin, R.E. (1969), "The case against infant-industry promotion", Journal of Political Economy 77:295–305.

Baldwin, R.E. (1976), "The political economy of postwar U.S. trade policy", The Bulletin, No. 4, New York University Graduate School of Business Administration.

Baldwin, R.E. (1989), "The political economy of free trade", Journal of Economic Perspectives 3:119–135.

Baldwin, R.E. (1991), "The political-economy perspective on trade policy", in A. Hillman, ed., Markets and politicians: Politicized economic choice (Kluwer Academic Publishers, Boston).

Becker, G. (1983), "A theory of competition among pressure groups for political influence", Quarterly Journal of Economics 98:371–400.

Becker, G. (1985), "Public policies, pressure groups and deadweight costs", Journal of Public Economics 28:329–347.

Bergsten, C.F. and M. Noland (1993), Reconcilable differences? United-States-Japan economic conflict (Institute for International Economics, Washington, DC).

Bernheim, B.D. and M.D. Whinston (1986), "Menu auctions, resource allocation, and economic influence", Quarterly Journal of Economics 101:1–31.

Bhagwati, J.N. and T.N. Srinivasan (1976), "Optimal trade policy and compensation under endogenous uncertainty", Journal of International Economics 6:317–336.

Bohara, A.K. and W.H. Kaempfer (1991), "A test of tariff endogeneity in the United States", American Economic Review 81:952–960.

Brainard, S.L. and T. Verdier (1993), "The political economy of declining industries: Senescent industry collapse revisited", National Bureau of Economic Research Working Paper No. 4606.

Bronars, S.G. and J.R. Lott, Jr. (1994), "Do campaign donations alter how politicians vote?", unpublished manuscript, University of Pennsylvania.

Cassing, J. and A. Hillman (1986), "Shifting comparative advantage and senescent industry collapse", American Economic Review 76:516–523.

Cassing, J., T.J. McKeown, and J. Ochs (1986), "The political economy of the tariff cycle", American Political Science Review 80:843–862.

Caves, R.E. (1976), "Economic models of political choice: Canada's tariff structure", Canadian Journal of Economics 9:278–300.

Coate S. and S. Morris (1993), "On the form of transfers to special interests", unpublished paper, University of Pennsylvania.

Corden, W.M. (1974), Trade policy and economic welfare (Oxford University Press, Oxford).

Destler, I.M. and J. Odell (1987), Anti-protection: Changing forces in United States trade politics (Institute for International Economics, Washington, DC).

Devereux, J. and L.L. Chen (1993), "The external terms of trade, growth and endogenous trade liberalization", unpublished paper, University of Miami.

Dixit, A.K. (1985), "Tax policy in open economies", in: A.J. Auerbach and M. Feldstein, eds., Handbook of public economics, vol. I (North-Holland, Amsterdam).

Drazen, A. and V. Grilli (1993), "The benefit of crises for economic reforms, American Economic Review 83:598–607.

Feenstra, R.C. and J.N. Bhagwati (1982), "Tariff seeking and the efficient tariff", in: J.N. Bhagwati, ed., Import competition and response (The University of Chicago Press, Chicago and London).

Feenstra, R.C. and T.R. Lewis (1991a), "Distributing the gains from trade with incomplete information", Economics & Politics 3:21–40.

Feenstra, R.C. and T.R. Lewis (1991b), "Negotiated trade restrictions with political pressure", Quarterly Journal of Economics 106:1287–1307.

Fernandez, R. and D. Rodrik (1991), "Resistance to reform: Status-quo bias in the presence of individual-specific uncertainty", American Economic Review 81:1146–1155.

Finger, J.M., H.K. Hall, and D. Nelson (1982), "The political economy of administered protection", American Economic Review 72:452–466.

Finger, M. and A. Harrison (1994), "The MFA paradox: More protection and more trade?", unpublished paper, The World Bank.

Gardner, G.W. and K.P. Kimbrough (1989), "The behavior of U.S. tariff rates", American Economic Review 79:211–218.

Godek, P.E. (1985), "Industry structure and redistribution through trade restrictions", The Journal of Law and Economics 28:687–703.

Grossman, G.M. and E. Helpman (1993a), "Trade wars and trade talks", National Bureau of Economic Research Working Paper No. 4280.

Grossman, G.M. and E. Helpman (1993b), "The politics of free trade agreements", National Bureau of Economic Research Working Paper No. 4597.

Grossman, G.M. and E. Helpman (1994), "Protection for sale", American Economic Review 84:833–850.

Hall, H.K. and D. Nelson (1992), "Institutional structure in the political economy of protection: Legislated v. administered protection", Economics & Politics 4:61–77.

Hansen, J.M. (1990), "Taxation and the political economy of the tariff", International Organization 44:527–552.

Helpman, E. and P. Krugman (1985), Market structure and foreign trade (MIT Press, Cambridge, MA).

Hillman, A.L. (1989), The political economy of protection (Harwood Academic Publishers, Chur).

Hillman, A.L. (1990), "Protectionist policy as the regulation of international industry", Public Choice 67:101–110.

Hillman, A.L. (1991), "Protection, politics and market structure', in: E. Helpman and A. Razin, eds., International trade and trade policy (MIT Press, Cambridge, MA).

Hillman A.L. and P. Moser (1995), "Trade liberalization as politically optimal exchange of market access", in: M. Canzoneri, W. Ethier, and V. Grilli, eds., The new transatlantic economy (Cambridge University Press, London and New York).

Hillman A.L. and H.W. Ursprung (1988), "Domestic politics, foreign interests, and international trade policy", American Economic Review 78:729–745.

Irwin, D.A. (1994), "Trade politics and the semiconductor industry", National Bureau of Economic Research Working Paper No. 4745.

Kahneman, D. and A. Tversky (1979), "Prospect theory: An analysis of decision under risk", Econometrica 47:263–291.

Kahneman, D. and A. Tversky (1984), "Choices, values, and frames", American Psychologist 4:341–350.

Krueger, A.O. (1974), "The political economy of the rent-seeking society", American Economic Review 64:291–303.

Krugman, P. (1981), "Intraindustry specialization and the gains from trade", Journal of Political Economy 89:959–973.

Krugman, P. (1993), "The narrow and broad arguments for free trade", American Economic Review 83:362–366.

Leidy, M.P. (1993), "Trade policy and indirect rent seeking: A synthesis of recent work", unpublished paper, University of Michigan.

Levy, P.I. (1993a), "Lobbying and international cooperation in tariff setting", unpublished paper, Stanford University.

Levy, P.I. (1993b), "A political-economic analysis of free trade agreements", unpublished paper, Stanford University.

Magee, S.P. (1994), "Endogenous protection: A survey", in: D.C. Mueller, ed., Handbook of public choice (Basil Blackwell, Cambridge, MA).

Magee, S.P., W.A. Brock, and L. Young (1989), Black hole tariffs and endogenous policy theory (Cambridge University Press, Cambridge and New York).

Magleby, D.B. and C.J. Nelson (1990), The money chase: Congressional campaign finance reform (The Brookings Institution, Washington, DC).

Mansfield, E.D. and M.L. Busch (1993), "The political economy of non-tariff barriers: A cross-national analysis", unpublished manuscript, Columbia University.

Marks, S.V. and J. McArthur (1990), "Empirical analyses of the determinants of protection: A survey and some new results", in: J.S. Odell and T.D. Willett, eds., International trade policies: Gains from exchange between economics and political science (The University of Michigan Press, Ann Arbor).

Marvel., H.P. and E.J. Ray (1983), "The Kennedy Round: Evidence on the regulation of trade in the U.S.", American Economic Review 73:190–197.

Marvel, H.P. and E.J. Ray (1987), "Intra-industry trade: Sources and effects on protection", Journal of Political Economy 95:1278–1291.

Mayer, W. (1984), "Endogenous tariff formation", American Economic Review 74:970–985.

Mayer, W. (1991), "The political economy of trade policy formulation", unpublished paper.

Mayer, W. and J. Li (1994), "Interest groups, electoral competition, and probabilistic voting for trade policies", Economics & Politics 6:59–77.

Mayer, W. and R. Riezman (1987), "Endogenous choice of trade policy instruments", Journal of International Economics 23:377–381.

Mayer, W. and R. Riezman (1989), "Tariff formation in a multidimensional voting model", Economics & Politics 1:61–79.

Mayer, W. and R. Riezman (1990), "Voter preferences for trade policy instruments", Economics & Politics 2:259–273.

Milner, H.V. (1988), Resisting protectionism: Global industries and the politics of international trade (Princeton University Press, Princeton, NJ).

Moore, M.O. (1994), "Steel protection in the 1980s: The waning influence of big steel?", National Bureau of Economic Research Working Paper No. 4760.

Nelson, D. (1988), "Endogenous tariff theory: A critical survey", American Journal of Political Science 32:796–837.

Nelson, D. (1994), "The political economy of U.S. automobile protection", National Bureau of Economic Research Working Paper No. 4746.

O'Halloran, S. (1994), Politics, process, and American trade policy, book manuscript (University of Michigan Press).

Orden, D. (1994), "Agricultural interest groups and the North American Free Trade Agreement", National Bureau of Economic Research Working Paper No. 4790.

Panagariya, A. and D. Rodrik (1993), "Political economy arguments for a uniform tariff", International Economic Review 34:685–704.

Pincus, J.J. (1975), "Pressure groups and the pattern of tariffs", Journal of Political Economy 83:757–778.

Pincus, J.J. (1986), "Why have U.S. tariffs fallen since 1930", in: R.H. Snape, ed., Issues in world trade policy (St. Martin's Press, New York).

Rama, M. (1993), "Endogenous trade policy: A time-series approach", unpublished paper, The World Bank.

Ray, E.J. (1981), "The determinants of tariff and non-tariff trade restrictions in the United States", Journal of Political Economy 89:105–121.

Ray, E.J. (1987), "Changing patterns of protectionism: The fall in tariffs and the rise in non-tariff barriers", Northwestern Journal of International Law & Business 8:285–327.

Ray, E.J. (1990), "Empirical research on the political economy of trade", in: C.A. Carter, A.F. McCalla, and J. Sharples, eds., Imperfect competition and political economy (Vestview Press, Boulder).

Ray, E.J. (1991), "Protection of manufactures in the United States", in: D. Greenaway, ed., Global protectionism: Is the U.S. playing on a level field? (Macmillan, London).

Ray, E.J. and H.P. Marvel (1984), "The pattern of protection in the industrialized world", Review of Economics and Statistics 66:452–58.

Richardson, M. (1993), "Endogenous protection and trade diversion", Journal of International Economics 34:309–324.

Riezman, R. and J.D. Wilson (1993a), "Politics and trade policy", unpublished paper, The University of Iowa.

Riezman, R. and J.D. Wilson (1993b), "Political reform and trade policy", unpublished paper, The University of Iowa.

Rodrik, D. (1986), "Tariffs, subsidies, and welfare with endogenous policy", Journal of International Economics 21:285–296.

Rodrik, D. (1987), "Policy targeting with endogenous distortion: Theory of optimum subsidy revisited", Quarterly Journal of Economics 102:903–910.

Rodrik, D. (1993), "The positive economics of policy reform", American Economic Review 83:356–361.

Rodrik, D. (1994), "The rush to free trade in the developing world: Why so late? why now? will it last?", in: S. Haggard and S. Webb, eds., Voting for reform: The politics of adjustment in new democracies (Oxford University Press, New York).

Rogowski, R. (1987), "Trade and the variety of domestic institutions", International Organization 41:203–223.

Saunders, R.S. (1980), "The political economy of effective protection in Canada's manufacturing sector", Canadian Journal of Economics 13:340–348.

Staiger, R. and G. Tabellini (1987), "Discretionary trade policy and excessive protection", American Economic Review 77:340–348.

Sturzenegger, F. (1993), "The fallacy of strategic trade policy", unpublished paper, University of California, Los Angeles.

Trefler, D. (1993), "Trade liberalization and the theory of endogenous protection", Journal of Political Economy 101:138–160.

Van Long, N. and N. Vousden (1991), "Protectionist responses and declining industries", Journal of International Economics 30:87–103.

Wilson, J.D. (1990), "Are efficiency improvements in government transfer policies self-defeating in equilibrium?", Economics & Politics 2:241–258.

Winters, L.A. (1994), "Import surveillance as a strategic trade policy", in: P. Krugman and A. Smith, eds., Empirical studies of strategic trade policy (The University of Chicago Press, Chicago and London).

Chapter 29

INTERNATIONAL RULES AND INSTITUTIONS FOR TRADE POLICY

ROBERT W. STAIGER*

The University of Wisconsin-Madison

Contents

*I am grateful to Lael Brainard and Jim Brander who as my discussants at the Handbook Conference provided extremely detailed and helpful comments on an earlier draft, to Gene Grossman for providing an additional set of very helpful comments, and to Kyle Bagwell, Alan Deardorff, Dale Henderson, Catherine Mann, participants in the Handbook Conference, and participants in the International Finance Workshop at the Federal Reserve Board and the NBER Conference on International Trade Rules and Institutions for helpful comments and discussion. I gratefully acknowledge financial support from the National Science Foundation.

Handbook of International Economics, vol. III, Edited by G. Grossman and K. Rogoff
© *Elsevier Science B.V., 1995*

1. Introduction

What are the potential benefits from establishing international rules for the conduct of trade policy and how should these rules be designed? The answers to these questions are central to the evolution of national trade policies in the post-war era, a period characterized by sustained *reciprocal* trade liberalization. An elaborate system of international rules has evolved to facilitate this process, both at the multilateral level as embodied in the General Agreement on Tariffs and Trade (GATT), and at the regional and bilateral levels as well. These rules, which are as much about the way countries *enforce* their mutual commitments to reduce trade barriers and the permissible *exceptions* from these commitments as they are about the commitments themselves, reflect the relevant margins over which modern trade intervention is shaped.

Yet the theory of trade policy has traditionally had little to say about these rules and the issues that underlie them. Traditional economic analysis has focused primarily on the unilateral incentives that countries have to intervene in trade, and sometimes on the "retaliatory" outcomes that would emerge from the unfettered pursuit of such incentives across countries, without exploring the nature of the rules and institutions that countries might establish to mitigate these incentives. Recently, there has been increasing attention paid to formal economic analysis of these issues. This chapter will review and synthesize several of the currents of this growing literature.

My focus in reviewing the literature will be on its implications for the design of international institutions relating to reciprocal trade liberalization.[1] North (1994, p. 360) defines institutions as

> ...the humanly devised constraints that structure human interaction. They are made up of formal constraints (e.g. rules, laws, constitutions), informal constraints (e.g. norms of behavior, conventions, self-imposed codes-of-conduct), and their enforcement characteristics. Together, they define the incentive structure of societies and specifically economies.

I will restrict my attention to formal constraints and their enforcement characteristics, acknowledging that there may be important informal constraints that I am neglecting.

---

[1] I am restricting my attention in this chapter to *international* institutions relating to reciprocal trade liberalization, and to a literature concerned with them, although in so doing I am ignoring the potential role played by *national* institutions, e.g. the U.S. Constitution [see Jackson (1989), ch. 3] or domestic trade adjustment assistance programs (see Fung and Staiger, forthcoming), in this context.

Effectively, I am restricting my focus to international trade agreements, and will review a literature that relates to their design and operation.[2]

The specific objectives of this chapter are threefold: To describe the basic structure of international trade agreements as they exist in practice; to explore theoretically the normative consequences of actual and alternative trade agreements; and to offer some theoretically-based explanation for the structure of trade agreements that we observe. I will attempt to achieve the first objective by focusing on the important features of GATT.[3] While GATT is far from the only explicit international trade agreement to which countries subject their trade policies, it represents the most important and well-developed set of *multilateral* trading rules, and has served as the standard over the post-war period by which multilateral trading practices are judged.[4] Moreover, the broad features of GATT are, with some exceptions, common to many *regional* trade agreements.[5] I will attempt to achieve the latter two objectives by reviewing a body of literature and drawing out its implications as they relate to these issues.

The remainder of this chapter is organized as follows. The next section describes the nature of international trade agreements as they exist in practice and some of the major themes that characterize the behavior of trade intervention in their presence. Section 3 then discusses why and in what circumstances countries might wish to enter into international trade agreements. The next four sections review a literature that is related to the collection of rules and institutions that define an international trade agreement: Section 4 is devoted to issues of enforcement, Section 5 to exploring the process of multilateral and bilateral liberalization, Section 6 to safeguard measures and managed trade, and Section 7 to countervailing duty and antidumping laws. The final section concludes by discussing some of the major gaps in this literature and possible directions for future research.

2. The structure of international trade agreements

International trade agreements codify attempts by countries to mutually restrain the degree of trade intervention from what might otherwise obtain. Generally, they

---

[2]My emphasis in this chapter is on understanding and evaluating the nature and operation of the rules that define an international trade agreement rather than the particular pattern of concessions that emerge from negotiation [on the latter, see for example Baldwin and Clarke (1987)].

[3]While the Uruguay Round of GATT negotiations has resulted in an agreement that calls for the creation of a World Trade Organization (WTO) to replace GATT, I will describe the features of GATT rather than the WTO both because GATT is familiar while the WTO has yet to be tested and because many of the broad features of GATT that I will emphasize will be shared by the WTO.

[4]It is not my purpose here to trace the history of international agreements in trade policy matters, though this history certainly precedes GATT [see, for example, Jackson (1969), ch. 2].

[5]The most-favored nation (MFN) rule of GATT is one attribute that is generally absent from regional trade agreements, although the United States included an MFN clause in each of the bilateral tariff-reduction agreements it negotiated between 1934 and 1939 under the Reciprocal Trade Agreements Act of 1930 [Winters (1990)].

include three basic elements: Substantive obligations (e.g. elimination of quotas, tariff commitments); permissible exceptions to those obligations (e.g. general escape clauses, provisions for the imposition of antidumping duties); and enforcement mechanisms (e.g. dispute settlement procedures, provisions for retaliation). Through the provisions of a trade agreement countries therefore typically agree to mutually restrain both their "baseline" levels of trade intervention and their use of "special protection", with the effectiveness of these restraints determined ultimately by the strength of the enforcement mechanisms in place. As such, where international trade agreements operate, a country's trade intervention can be understood to reflect its baseline commitments, its current use of exceptions, and the operation and effectiveness of enforcement procedures.

In this section I will attempt to provide an overview of the important features of trade rules and institutions that typify international trade agreements. As mentioned above, I will do this by describing the key features of GATT. I will then sketch in broad terms the nature of trade liberalization among industrialized economies under the rules of GATT that have motivated the literature I am addressing.[6] There is a great deal of complexity in the system of rules that has developed under GATT, and I could not possibly address all the details here [authoritative references on GATT rules and procedures include Dam (1970), Hudec (1975), and Jackson (1969, 1989)]. Instead, my purpose is first to sketch at the broadest level the basic elements of GATT, and then to distill a few broad themes in the ways that trade liberalization has occurred under GATT rules. My description of GATT follows Jackson (1969, 1989). Bhagwati (1988, 1991) provides a more detailed elaboration of the way in which trade liberalization has proceeded under GATT.

2.1. The structure of GATT

Broadly speaking, a description of GATT can be organized under three main headings: Organizational structure and procedural rules; substantive obligations; and exceptions to those obligations.

2.1.1. Organizational structure and procedural rules

GATT's organizational structure and procedural rules themselves raise interesting and important institutional questions. They dictate such issues as how countries can amend the agreement, the rules of membership and voting, the role of the Secretariat

---

[6] I confine my discussion here to the rules as applied to industrialized countries, since many of the rules that I discuss do not apply to developing economies as a result of GATT's Article XVIII.

and the structure and purpose of committees, and the provisions for dispute resolution and enforcement of GATT obligations. Many of these issues are especially interesting because GATT was never supposed to be an international organization, and so made no provisions for several of the institutional features that would be necessary to make the agreement operational.[7] Nevertheless I will focus only on the last of these, that is, on the provisions for dispute resolution and enforcement of GATT obligations.

Ultimately, as with any international trade agreement, GATT obligations will only be honored if the incentives created by the agreement are compatible with the desired behavior. That is, since no external enforcement mechanism exists to punish GATT violations, meaningful GATT commitments must be self-enforcing, with violations deterred primarily by the credible threat of subsequent retaliation. This points to provisions for dispute resolution and enforcement of GATT obligations as essential to the workings of GATT. Dam (1970) provides a concise statement of the need to view international trade agreements as necessarily self-enforcing:

> The best guarantee that a commitment of any kind will be kept (particularly in an international setting where courts are of limited importance and, even more important, marshals and jails are nonexistent) is that the parties continue to view adherence to their agreement as in their mutual interest....
>
> Thus, the GATT system, unlike most legal systems,..., is not designed to exclude self-help in the form of retaliation. Rather, retaliation, subjected to established procedures and kept within prescribed bounds, is made the heart of the GATT system. [Dam (1970 pp. 80–81)]

While dispute settlement procedures are spread throughout GATT, the key provisions are contained in Articles XXII and XXIII. These provisions typically are invoked on the grounds of "nullification or impairment" of benefits expected under the agreement and do not require a violation of the legal obligations under GATT. Nullification or impairment has been interpreted to include actions taken by one country "...which harmed the trade of another, and which 'could not reasonably have been anticipated' by the other at the time it negotiated for a concession" [Jackson (1989, p. 95)].[8] The procedure for settling disputes proceeds through three

---

[7]As originally conceived, GATT was drafted as a trade agreement and was designed to include only those clauses that were normally found in trade agreements and deemed to be essential to protect the value of tariff concessions. The proposed International Trade Organization (ITO) was supposed to have furnished the necessary organizational and secretariat support for GATT, but the ITO never came into being [see Jackson (1969, pp. 42–53)].

[8]The ambiguity of this phrase led to efforts to define three conditions for *prima facie* nullification or impairment: The breach of an obligation; the use of a domestic subsidy to inhibit imports in certain cases; and the use of quantitative restrictions. The burden of proof that no nullification or impairment occurred then falls on the country which breached or took such actions [see Jackson (1989, p. 95)].

stages: Consultation between or among the parties in the dispute; investigation, ruling and recommendation by a GATT panel; and as a last resort, authorization for one or more countries to suspend GATT obligations against another, i.e. retaliation. In practice, the greatest emphasis has been placed on consultation and negotiation rather than on retaliation, although a number of GATT disputes have resulted in unauthorized retaliation, and other disputes between GATT members have occurred outside GATT procedures entirely [see Kovenock and Thursby (1992)].[9]

This observation points to a basic tension in the GATT dispute settlement procedures between what Jackson (1989, pp. 92–93) has called "rule integrity" and "negotiation/conciliation". That is, GATT dispute settlement procedures seem to acknowledge the essential role of retaliatory threats in preventing unilateral deviations from the agreement but at the same time display an aversion to actually allowing those threats to be carried out. This tension is reflected in the view of legal scholars as to the role and purpose of dispute settlement procedures in a well-functioning GATT system. Again I will quote from Dam (1970), although similar views can be found elsewhere, e.g. Jackson (1989) and Hudec (1993):

> ...The principal tariff function of the GATT, beyond the sponsoring of rounds of tariff negotiations, are therefore (1) to prevent contracting parties from upsetting the balance of advantages by unilateral withdrawals of concessions, (2) to maintain the general level of liberalization already achieved by assuring that retaliatory action by other contracting parties is not greater than necessary to reestablish the balance of advantages and does not set off further rounds of retaliatory actions, and (3) to establish procedures for original withdrawals of concessions and for subsequent retaliatory withdrawals so that disputes among contracting parties do not destroy confidence in the GATT system. [Dam (1970, p. 80)]

As enumerated by Dam, function (1) amounts to preventing violations of the agreement, function (2) amounts to containing the retaliation required to carry out function (1), and function (3) amounts to achieving functions (1) and (2) without losing credibility of the entire GATT system!

In part this tension may reflect several different and not necessarily consistent purposes that the dispute settlement procedures of GATT were designed to serve [Jackson (1969, p. 169)]. These purposes included securing compliance with GATT obligations through the threat of punitive sanctions, but there was also a view that these procedures should be used primarily to maintain the balance between obliga-

---

[9]While a major accomplishment of the WTO as proposed under the Uruguay Round Agreement is to strengthen dispute settlement procedures by, for example, streamlining the process and preventing blockage and delay of panel reports, it is not clear that such changes will result in greater reliance on actual retaliation [see, for example, Jackson (1989, p. 110)].

tions and benefits in a changing environment.[10] This suggests that several categories of disputes were envisioned, each requiring a different kind of response. Indeed, during the original drafting of GATT's dispute settlement procedures statements were made suggesting the need for "more rigorous retorsion" in circumstances where the offending action was "abusive" [Jackson (1969, p. 169)]. In any event, as I will discuss below, both sides of this tension have been picked up in the economics literature that has focused on the role of dispute settlement procedures in international trade agreements.

2.1.2. Substantive obligations

Jackson (1969, p. 194) groups the substantive obligations contained in GATT into three categories: Tariff commitments (Articles II and XXVIII bis.); most-favored-nation (MFN) treatment (Article I); and a series of other commitments that together represent a "code of conduct" regarding non-tariff barriers (Articles III, VII through XI, and XV through XVII). At the broadest level these provisions amount to an obligation to concentrate national protective measures into the form of tariffs (and possibly subsidies), to apply them on an MFN basis, and to honor any tariff ceilings that are agreed to as "concessions" in a GATT negotiation.

With regard to tariff commitments and MFN treatment, several points should be noted. Tariff commitments made under GATT are in the form of "bindings", with the actual tariff not to exceed the bound duty rate. MFN treatment requires further that goods of any member country be given no less favorable treatment than goods of any other country, so that tariff concessions granted to one country must be extended to all member countries. There are also specific obligations that accompany a tariff binding that are meant to insure that the binding can not be undone by other governmental measures, such as non-tariff charges, new subsidies, or new methods of classifying or valuing goods. Tariff bindings can be altered through time, however,

---

[10]Jackson (1969, p. 170) quotes a statement made by a draftsmen of GATT's Article XXIII, which I reproduce here:

We shall achieve, under the Charter, if our negotiations are successful, a careful balance of the interests of the contracting States. This balance rests upon certain assumptions as to the character of the underlying situation in the years to come. And it involves a mutuality of obligations and benefits. If, with the passage of time, the underlying situation should change or the benefits accorded any member should be impaired, the balance would be destroyed. It is the purpose of Article 35 [corresponding to GATT Article XXIII] to restore this balance by providing for compensatory adjustment in the obligations which the Member has assumed. This adjustment will not be made unless the Member has asked that it be made. And it is then the function of the Organization to insure that compensatory action will not be carried out to such a level that the balance would be tipped the other way. What we have really provided, in the last analysis, is not that retaliation shall be invited or sanctions invoked, but that a balance of interests once established, shall be maintained. [U.N. Doc. EPCT/A/PV.6 at 5 (1947)]

and indeed, GATT provides for its members to sponsor "rounds" of negotiations to lower the general level of tariff bindings "from time to time".[11]

The remaining substantive obligations of GATT, which amount to a "code of conduct" regarding non-tariff barriers, include provisions for national treatment of all goods once they have cleared customs, a basic prohibition against quotas, restrictions on the behavior of state trading and monopolies, limits on the use of certain subsidies, standards for customs administration, and limits on the use of exchange controls. These obligations apply generally, and are not limited to products that have been the subject of negotiated tariff agreements. As such, they differ from the specific obligations on non-tariff measures that accompany a tariff binding and which are meant merely to assure that the value of negotiated tariff concessions is not undone by non-tariff measures. Instead, these obligations amount to a broad determination that protection afforded by MFN tariffs is preferable – possibly in part because it is thought more amenable to negotiated liberalization – to a system of non-tariff barriers.[12] This is evident in the broader structure of GATT itself which, while requiring of its members a code of conduct with regard to the use of non-tariff barriers, does not place restrictions on the use of MFN tariffs except for those restrictions ("bindings") that members may voluntarily negotiate.[13]

2.1.3. Exceptions

While the substantive obligations of GATT represent an attempt at the international level to restrain the incentives for trade intervention that may exist at the national level, countries are not held rigidly to these obligations. Instead, GATT provides for various exceptions that can be invoked in certain circumstances. Jackson (1969, p. 536) describes three kinds of exceptions in GATT: "Universal" exceptions, that can

---

[11]Under Article XXVIII, GATT members can also renegotiate their tariff bindings every three years, but are obligated to keep the overall tariff levels from rising as a result of such renegotiations. Interestingly, Article XXVIII bis., which provides for the periodic rounds of trade-liberalizing negotiations that have become synonymous with GATT, was not included in the original GATT agreement, and was added only after it became clear that the proposed ITO, which was to have sponsored such negotiations, would never come into force [Jackson (1969, pp. 220–221)].

[12]The question of whether "tariffication" (or more generally limiting the choice of instruments) is enforceable, and if so whether it is desirable, is an interesting and important question, but not one which I will consider in this chapter. Copeland (1990) assumes that tariffication is not enforceable and that countries will set non-tariff barriers non-cooperatively, but shows that there are still gains from negotiating tariff agreements in this setting. Copeland (1989) shows that, if countries can limit themselves to two instruments (tariffs and quotas), then negotiations on either tariffs or quotas alone, leaving the other instrument to be set non-cooperatively, leads to essentially equivalent outcomes. Under the assumption that countries can limit themselves to the use of one (common) instrument, Webb (1984) and Bagwell and Staiger (1990) show that tariffication can facilitate trade liberalization.

[13]GATT's creation was accompanied by an initial round of tariff negotiations at Geneva in 1947, but these initial tariff reductions were not seen as a quid pro quo for original membership. In fact, there is no legal obligation in GATT for members to enter into tariff negotiations.

apply to any GATT obligation; "particular" exceptions, that can only apply to certain GATT obligations; and "tacit" exceptions, which refer to GATT obligations that can be avoided without consequence.

Important universal exceptions include the following: General waivers (Article XXV), as well as departures from GATT obligations authorized under the dispute settlement procedures in cases of "nullification and impairment", each of which requires specific GATT approval; escape clause actions (Article XIX), which require notification to GATT; and exceptions for health, welfare, and national security reasons (Articles XX and XXI), which require no such notification. Important particular exceptions include exceptions from tariff bindings in the case of antidumping duties and countervailing duties (Article VI), opportunities for renegotiation and modification of tariff schedules (Article XXVIII), and exceptions from MFN treatment in the case of free trade areas and customs unions (Article XXIV).[14] Examples of tacit exceptions can be found with reference to tariff surcharges and "residual" quotas originally imposed in connection with balance-of-payments difficulties.

The large number and variety of permissible exceptions suggests that GATT "obligations" are not what they might appear, and indeed they are not. Dam (1970) observes:

> The goal of achieving and maintaining a relatively low tariff level has resulted in a system that contrasts sharply with the international law of treaties and the domestic law of contracts in the world's major legal systems. Public international law and domestic contract law tend to view agreements as binding even when one of the parties no longer regards continued performance of the agreement to be in its interest (although the two bodies of law give some recognition to the principle of *rebus sic stantibus*, under which an agreement is not held binding if the circumstances have fundamentally changed in a way that was not anticipated by the parties at the time of the making of the agreement). This indicates that, with many obvious exceptions, domestic contract law and public international law are more concerned with assuring that commitments made are carried out than with promoting the making of agreements in the first place.
>
> The GATT has a special interest in seeing that as many agreements for the reduction of tariffs as possible are made. Enforcement of bindings is important in the GATT insofar as such enforcement gives contracting parties the confidence necessary to rely upon tariff concessions offered by other contracting parties. But because of the economic nature of tariff concessions and the domestic political sensitivity inherently involved in trade issues, a system that made withdrawals of concessions impossible would tend to discourage the making of concessions in the

---

[14]GATT Articles XII, XIV and XVIII also provide exceptions to the prohibitions on quantitative restrictions for balance-of-payments purposes.

first place. It is better, for example, that 100 commitments should be made and that 10 should be withdrawn than that only 50 commitments should be made and that all of them should be kept. [Dam (1970, p. 80)]

Still, while numerous, the exceptions provided for in GATT are not without some (at least potentially) disciplining structure. Particular exceptions, for example from tariff bindings in the case of antidumping duties and countervailing duties and from MFN treatment in the case of free trade areas and customs unions, are to be used only in relatively narrowly defined circumstances, or, as in the case of renegotiation of tariff schedules, are to be accomplished without increasing the overall level of protection. The universal exceptions embodied in GATT waivers and those authorized under dispute settlement procedures must receive GATT approval, and so must at some level be deemed in the general interest.[15] In contrast, escape clause actions, which allow a temporary response to "changed circumstances", are less disciplined by GATT in that they do not require GATT approval but only notification. Finally, it is only over exceptions for non-economic reasons (health, welfare, security) that countries are given relatively complete autonomy (no notification is required).[16] In a sense, the effectiveness of GATT as an institution hinges upon its ability to strike the appropriate balance between requiring adherence to a rigid set of rules and disciplines and at the same time providing for sufficient flexibility so that countries see it in their own interests to abide by these rules in a changing and uncertain environment.

2.2. Trade liberalization under GATT

As noted above, the original focus of GATT was on the "tariffication" of existing non-tariff trade barriers and on reducing tariff levels on a multilateral MFN basis. This focus was gradually overtaken by other issues which took on increasing importance as the process of multilateral liberalization matured over the eight Rounds of GATT negotiations that have occurred since 1947. But the first five Rounds, undertaken between 1947 and 1961, were devoted almost exclusively to reducing the level of tariffs, and tariff reduction has continued to be an important objective up through the most recently completed (Uruguay) Round. The success with which countries have been able to negotiate reciprocal tariff reductions under GATT has been remarkable, first for the depth of the tariff reductions achieved through this process (world tariffs have been reduced by 90 percent, from an average ad valorem rate of 40 percent in 1947 to 4 percent in 1994) but also for the extended period of time over which the process has occurred.

---

[15]Although what is perceived to be in the "general interest" may correspond to that which does not thwart the national interests of a powerful member. For example, the agriculture waiver granted to the United States essentially "legitimized" prior actions otherwise in violation of GATT.

[16]In this case, the practical protection against abuse must rely on the claim of nullification and impairment in the context of dispute settlement procedures.

However, accompanying the success in reducing baseline tariff levels has been the rising importance of various kinds of exceptions and the increasing prominence of enforcement difficulties. Among the most important and potentially troublesome exceptions have been the following: Exceptions from MFN treatment associated with the formation of regional trading blocs; exceptions for "special protection" associated with safeguards actions; and exceptions for antidumping and countervailing duty actions. These exceptions have played an important role in shaping the pattern of protection under GATT. The increasing prominence of enforcement difficulties has been crystallized with the controversy surrounding the United States use of "Section 301" procedures. Since these developments have served to motivate the literature I will survey below, I will elaborate briefly on each.

Regionalism: Exceptions to the MFN principle afforded to pairs or groups of countries who wish to liberalize on a reciprocal basis more quickly than the pace set by multilateral negotiations, and who are willing to completely eliminate tariffs on "substantially all" of their trade, have allowed the formation of a number of free trade areas and customs unions. The most visible episodes of regional bloc formation falling within this exception include: (i) the formation of the original European Community with the Treaty of Rome in 1957; the subsequent enlargement to its present twelve-member size, and the further elimination of its remaining internal barriers to become the European Union of today; and (ii) the signing of the U.S.–Canada free trade agreement and its extension to include Mexico. These regional initiatives raise a number of important questions regarding their interpretation and role in the broader efforts to liberalize trade on a multilateral basis.

Managed trade: The rise in special protection that has accompanied the gradual reduction in baseline tariffs has served to alter the rate of expansion of imports and exports from what might have occurred absent such intervention.[17] This form of protection, which has been little constrained by the safeguards provisions in GATT, is epitomized by the growing use of Voluntary Export Restraints (VERs), Voluntary Import Expansions (VIEs), Orderly Market Arrangements (OMAs), and tariffs that are designed to suit the needs of a particular sector. The prominent use of these instruments has given rise to the term "managed trade" to describe an environment in which relatively low levels of baseline protection are combined with the use of special protection to dampen underlying changes in trade flows and trade balances. An important question is whether the use of special protection and the forms that it has taken can be understood within the context of the broader trade agreements within which it arose.

---

[17]The increasing relative importance of special protection has been widely noted, and attempts to quantify this trend include Page (1979) and Bergsten and Cline (1983). Trefler (1993) estimates the effects of non-tariff barriers on U.S. imports in 1983 and concludes that these effects are very large.

Unfair trade laws: Whereas safeguard actions carry with them no implication of wrong-doing, antidumping and countervailing duty procedures are intended to be used against "unfair" trading practices of foreign exporters and their governments, respectively. Antidumping duties can be imposed when foreign firms are found to be "dumping", that is, exporting at a price below either the home-market selling price or the cost of production. Countervailing duties can be imposed to offset foreign government subsidies. The increasing frequency with which these so-called "unfair trade" laws have been invoked, and the belief shared by many that the multilateral rules governing their use are ineffectual, brings into question the purpose to which these laws are being put and the effects that they have on trade.

Aggressive unilateralism: Finally, a growing frustration on the part of the United States that the dispute settlement procedures of GATT were not sufficient to enforce its rights within the agreement, and that policies in important areas of trade and investment which fell outside any agreement were left completely undisciplined, led to the inclusion of Section 301 in the 1974 Trade Act and to its subsequent amendments. Section 301 provides the authority and procedures for the President to enforce unilaterally the perceived U.S. rights under international trade agreements where such agreements exist, and to respond to certain "unfair" foreign practices where agreements do not exist.[18] Associated with the rise of this so-called "aggressive unilateralism" are important questions relating to the role served by multilateral dispute settlement procedures and the consequences of adopting alternative enforcement methods.

2.3. What is the role of GATT?

It is one thing to describe the reciprocal liberalization that has occurred under GATT during the past 50 years, but there is still the question, what has been the role of GATT in promoting and maintaining this process? One possible answer is that GATT represents a codification of the post-war effort to achieve a liberal multilateral trading environment. Under this interpretation, GATT is simply an explicit record of how countries attempt to liberalize trade in a way that is self-enforcing, and GATT's existence plays no independent role in making this liberalization possible. But there are other possibilities.

At a minimum GATT probably serves a coordination function, providing countries with a forum for communication and a means for seeking out and implementing efficient equilibria. Beyond that, there is some evidence [see Jackson (1989, pp.

---

[18]In 1984 the EC adopted a new commercial policy instrument that shares several common elements with Section 301, although there are also significant differences [see Jackson (1989, pp. 107–109)].

88–91)] that GATT legal precedent often affects GATT deliberations and the outcomes of dispute settlement procedures. It is also possible that the existence of an explicit dispute settlement procedure in GATT instills in countries a sense of "international obligation" [Hudec (1990), Jackson (1989), Kovenock and Thursby (1992)] to the agreement which makes the act of violating the agreement costly, independent of any future response from trading partners that a violation might trigger, and thereby strengthens enforcement capabilities associated with the agreement. Finally, GATT may serve a possible information-dissemination role, either in providing objective information to countries directly involved in a dispute [Hungerford (1991)] or in coordinating multilateral punishments [Maggi (1994)].

Which, if any, of these institutional roles GATT plays is an important issue that has only just begun to be explored. But even if it plays no such role, GATT is still worth studying as an explicit representation of the most detailed and well-developed effort to liberalize trade on a multilateral basis in the post-war world. In what follows, I will attempt to bring out those features of liberalization under GATT that the literature seems well-equipped to explain, and also highlight some features that are more difficult to interpret.

3. Strategic interaction and the benefits from international trade agreements

In this section I will postpone consideration of the design of international trade agreements, and instead ask under what conditions the benefits of entering into such agreements might exist. An answer to this question requires a definition of what is meant by an international trade agreement. For the purposes of this chapter I will define an international trade agreement as a collection of rules regarding the conduct of trade policy, compliance to which requires some form of enforcement mechanism, that is, where unilateral incentives to violate the rules of the agreement are kept in check by the desire to avoid punishments that are themselves specified in the agreement. Whether these punishments rely on external enforcement mechanisms or are carried out by parties to the agreement and must themselves be incentive compatible is for the moment not important: Below I will discuss a number of papers focusing on the issue of enforcement that take the latter view, and other papers that assume instead the existence of an external enforcement mechanism in order to focus on different dimensions of trade agreements. What this definition does preclude is consideration of the gains that might come from simple (or "pure") coordination of trade policies across countries, as could arise for example in a one-shot tariff game when there are multiple Nash equilibria, since in such instances the coordinated outcome is free of incentive problems in the usual sense.[19] However, the definition of

---

[19]This is not to say that I will ignore coordination problems completely, since the issue of coordination will arise in attempts to implement international trade agreements as I have defined them when there are multiple equilibria. But I will not consider pure coordination problems.

international trade agreements that I adopt is consistent with the institutional structure I have outlined above and does represent a view that permeates the literature that I discuss below.[20]

There are two environments within which the effects of adhering to international trade agreements of the sort I have just defined have been explored in the economics literature. One environment is characterized by the presence of governments (i) whose private agents make decisions that, at least collectively at the national level, have a perceptible impact on trading partners, (ii) who have the capability and unilateral incentive to manipulate these private sector decisions through trade policy intervention for their international "beggar-thy-neighbor" effects, and (iii) who look mutually to international trade agreements as a way to mitigate these unilateral incentives. The other environment is characterized by the presence of governments that are unable on their own to commit to announced trade policy decisions, and who look to international trade agreements as a way to enhance the credibility of their trade policy choices with respect to the private sector. In the former case, it is the strategic interaction across governments in their trade policy choices that gives rise to the possibility of beneficial international agreements. In the latter case, it is the strategic interaction between a government and the private sector that makes international agreements look potentially attractive. Common to both environments is the notion that an international trade agreement can serve to alter the incentives of policy makers with regard to the use of trade policy instruments, and that the agreement could be designed in such a way that policy makers would have incentives to enter into it.

These environments can be illustrated at a general level with the aid of a simple two-country three-stage game structure. Indexing countries by $j \in \{1, 2\}$ and goods by $i \in \{1, \ldots, M\}$, let $\bar{x}_j$ denote the $1 \times M$ vector of country j's production, $\bar{y}_j$ the $1 \times M$ vector of country j's consumption, and $\bar{\tau}_j$ the $1 \times M$ vector of country j's trade taxes. Let $W^j(\bar{\tau}_j, \bar{\tau}_{ij})$ denote country j's objective function, assumed globally concave in $\bar{\tau}_j$ and depending also on $\bar{\tau}_{ij}$, the $1 \times M$ vector of trade taxes set by j's trading partner.[21]

The first environment described above, in which strategic interaction across governments in their trade policy choices becomes the focus of the international trade agreement, is represented by the following timing of moves in this three-stage game: First governments choose trade taxes; then production decisions are made; and finally consumption occurs. In this environment two extreme situations can be compared,

---

[20]By equating international trade agreements with regimes in which enforcement mechanisms are required, I do not mean that I will restrict my attention only to a body of literature that is concerned with enforcement of trade agreements, but rather that I will restrict my attention to a literature that illuminates various aspects of trade agreements that share this structure. Also, I focus on the economic aspects of international trade agreements, and ignore potentially important aspects associated with political/national security issues.

[21]By country j's objective function I mean the objective function of the government of country j when setting trade policy, which may or may not correspond to social welfare. Similarly, I am examining the potential gains from the introduction of international rules evaluated with reference to government objective functions.

one corresponding to the absence of an international trade agreement, and the other to the presence of a trade agreement that achieves perfect cooperation. Under the first regime, governments set trade taxes simultaneously to maximize their individual objective functions. Under the second regime, governments set trade taxes jointly to maximize a weighted sum of their objective functions. In each case, I wish to consider the subgame perfect equilibrium of the associated three-stage game.[22]

The question of whether there are potential gains from an international trade agreement in this environment can then be posed by asking whether the equilibrium absent such an agreement is Pareto efficient. If it is, then there can be no Pareto gains from a trade agreement. If it is not, then such gains may be possible.[23] Denote by $\bar{\tau}_j^N$ and $\bar{\tau}_{\backslash j}^N$ the $1 \times M$ vector of tariffs selected by country j and j's trading partner, respectively, in the subgame perfect equilibrium of the three-stage game when no trade agreement is present, defined by $\partial W^j(\bar{\tau}_j^N, \bar{\tau}_{\backslash j}^N)/\partial \bar{\tau}_j = \bar{0}$ for $j \in \{1, 2\}$. Then the necessary and sufficient conditions for this equilibrium to be Pareto optimal are simply $\partial W^j(\bar{\tau}_j^N, \bar{\tau}_{\backslash j}^N)/\partial \bar{\tau}_{\backslash j} = \bar{0}$ for $j \in \{1, 2\}$. These conditions say that the trade tax equilibrium absent an international trade agreement will be Pareto efficient if and only if each country's equilibrium trade tax choices impose at the margin no externalities on its trading partner.[24] Thus, in this first environment, the gains that come with an international trade agreement stem from internalizing the externalities that each country would impose on its trading partners in the absence of such an agreement through its equilibrium trade tax choices. One mechanism through which these externalities could be transmitted is the terms-of-trade effects of trade policy intervention. This is the mechanism that arises in all of the formal economic modeling of international trade agreements in this environment of which I am aware, and it is the mechanism present in each of the formal models of this environment reviewed below.[25]

---

[22]For purposes of discussion at this point, I will assume that such an equilibrium exists and is unique, and that the equilibrium trade taxes are non-prohibitive. Non-uniqueness would introduce additional coordination issues of the kind I am not concerned with here, while the possibility of prohibitive equilibrium tariffs would unnecessarily complicate the conditions for Pareto optimality discussed below.

[23]Posing this question becomes more complicated when there are more than two countries in the world and gains from agreements among a subset of countries are considered.

[24]Throughout this discussion I assume that international income transfers are feasible in the context of an international trade agreement. Where such transfers are not feasible, the scope for Pareto improving trade agreements can be reduced if there is no mechanism by which each country can be compensated for its tariff reductions. In the two country case considered above, this issue arises when countries are asymmetric [see, for example, Johnson (1953–54) or Kennan and Riezman (1988)]. On the general importance of international income transfers in reaching efficient outcomes in trade policy negotiations [see Kowalczyk and Sjostrom (1994)].

[25]This is true both of models that assume trade taxes are set to maximize national welfare as, for example, in Dixit (1987) and of models in which trade taxes are chosen with political objectives in mind as, for example, in Grossman and Helpman (1993). This is not to say that terms-of-trade effects, or more generally world price effects, are the only possible mechanism through which these externalities can be transmitted [see Robinson (1947), for a discussion of employment effects as a possible transmission mechanism]. But terms-of-trade effects are the only mechanisms that have been studied in a formal economic model of international trade agreements. [See, for example, Yarbrough and Yarbrough (1992) for a broader interdisciplinary approach to this issue.]

The second environment described above, in which the important strategic interaction is between a government and its private agents, can be represented by a different timing of moves in the three stage game: First production decisions are made; then governments set trade taxes; and finally consumption decisions are made. Under this timing and in the absence of an international trade agreement, governments may face constraints in their ability to set desired tariffs due to their inability to commit prior to the decisions of producers. In this case, the role and potential impact of an international trade agreement depends in part on whether or not the timing of moves is altered with the introduction of such an agreement. If it is not, then an agreement can be counter-productive, a point made by Kehoe (1989) in the context of a two-country two-period optimal capital/labor taxation problem. Intuitively, when government commitment with regard to the private sector is infeasible, the tax competition between governments absent an agreement may constrain their ability to act opportunistically relative to the private sector, and may thus serve as a partial commitment device that is lost under an agreement.[26] If the timing is altered by the agreement, and in particular if a trade agreement allows governments to move first, before producers, then whatever partial commitment might have been provided by government behavior absent the agreement is now obviated by the provision of full commitment under the agreement, and any gains from the agreement within the first environment outlined above would be realized as well. A second literature that I discuss below has considered formally the benefits of government commitment in trade policy, and has appealed informally to the potential role that international trade agreements could play in providing this commitment, i.e. in altering the timing of government decisions relative to the private sector.

3.1. Strategic interaction across governments

Of the two environments noted above, the one for which the role and design of international trade agreements has been most thoroughly developed in the literature is that of strategic interactions across governments. Here, international agreements can be designed to mitigate the unilateral incentives of each country to pursue beggar-thy-neighbor trade policies. This basic point was made by Scitovszky (1942), who described how the pursuit of unilateral interests could lead to an escalating tariff war and emphasized the need for enforcement mechanisms in any attempt to escape from the resulting dilemma. Imagining a first round of tariff retaliation triggered by the

---

[26]A somewhat related point is made by McLaren (1994), who shows that a small country can be made worse off under an anticipated free trade agreement with a large country than it would be in an anticipated tariff war. This possibility occurs when future production requires irreversible investment in the present. In this setting, producers in the small country, correctly anticipating a free trade agreement with the large country, make irreversible investments tying their production to the large country market, thereby robbing the small country of its flexibility at the bargaining stage of the free trade agreement.

"rational behavior of a single country trying to maximize its national welfare" through beggar-thy-neighbor tariff setting, Scitovszky continued:

> When tariff walls have been erected all around, those who started the process will find some of their initial advantage gone; but they are also likely to find that they can improve their position by raising tariffs further, even if initially they made full use of their monopolistic position. As tariff walls rise, conferences on international trade may be called to arrest the process, which is obviously harmful to all concerned. Yet as long as it remains in the individual interests of each country separately to raise tariffs, such collective attempts are bound to be ineffectual if not backed by international sanctions... [Scitovszky (1942, p. 377)].

In this section I will review the basic unilateral incentives to pursue beggar-thy-neighbor trade policies which, if pursued by all countries, can lead to a situation analogous to the Prisoner's Dilemma in which each is made worse off.[27] I will do so in a simple partial equilibrium tariff-setting framework which builds on the framework developed in Bagwell and Staiger (1990, 1993a, 1993b).[28] I consider a domestic (no *) and foreign (*) country, each endowed with 3/2 units of a locally abundant good and 1/2 unit of a locally scarce good, and each wishing to consume both goods symmetrically through trade. I will refer to the domestic (foreign) locally abundant good as good 1 (good 2). I take the demand functions in the two countries to be symmetric across products and countries, and assume that the demand for product i is independent of the price of product $j \neq i$. Specifically, the demand functions for product $i \in \{1, 2\}$ are given by $C(P^i) = \alpha - P^i$ and $C(P^{i*}) = \alpha - P^{i*}$ where $\alpha > 0$, P^i is the price of good i in the domestic country and P^{i*} is the corresponding price in the foreign country. Given the symmetry between the two countries, for any product i I will simply speak of "the exporting country" and "the importing country". Accordingly, let P^i_x denote the price of good i in the exporting country and P^i_m give the price of good i in the importing country, with τ^i_m representing the (specific) import tariff levied on good i. It follows that $P^i_m = P^i_x + \tau^i_m$ for each good i provided that τ^i_m is non-prohibitive. The structure of the basic model is completed with the market clearing condition for each product i: $2 = \alpha - P^i_x + \alpha - (P^i_x + \tau^i_m)$. Solving for equilibrium prices $\hat{P}^i_x$ and $\hat{P}^i_m$ and the equilibrium import volume of good i, denoted by $\hat{M}^i(\tau^i_m)$, and imposing symmetric tariffs across

---

[27]Strictly speaking, the Prisoner's Dilemma refers to a simultaneous move two-person static game where each player has just two strategies to choose from (cooperate or defect). The (stage) games I consider below are similar in nature to the Prisoner's Dilemma in that mutual cooperation would be better for all than mutual non-cooperation, but defecting when everyone else cooperates would be better still.

[28]Johnson (1953–54) was the first to illustrate the tariff reaction curves and Nash equilibrium of a tariff war in a formal setting, adopting a standard two-good two-country general equilibrium trade model for this purpose [see Dixit (1987) for a recent general equilibrium treatment]. I adopt a simple partial equilibrium trade model for clarity of exposition, but the basic points I will illustrate depend only on the properties of the model reminiscent of a Prisoner's Dilemma, and would be shared by any trade model possessing these general properties.

products, yields expressions for market-clearing export prices, import prices, and import volume for each good: $\hat{P}_x(\tau_m) = (\alpha - 1) - \tau_m/2$; $\hat{P}_m(\tau_m) = (\alpha - 1) + \tau_m/2$; $\hat{M}(\tau_m) = 1/2 - \tau_m/2.$[29] These expressions hold for tariffs in the range $\tau_m \in [0, 1]$ with $\tau_m = 1$ the prohibitive tariff level. For $\tau_m \geq 1$, the tariff is prohibitive ($\hat{M}(\tau_m) = 0$), $\hat{P}_x(\tau_m) = \alpha - 3/2$, and $\hat{P}_m(\tau_m) = \alpha - 1/2$.

I can now define the government objective function. I will assume that each government sets tariffs to maximize the sum of producer surplus, consumer surplus, and tariff revenue, with a weight γ on the producer surplus generated in its import-competing sector. If $\gamma = 1$, then the governments simply maximize social surplus with their tariff choices. I interpret $\gamma > 1$ as a reflection of political economy considerations. Such an objective function will emerge in a lobbying context where the import-competing industry lobbies the government with a schedule of payments associated with different tariff levels and the government then chooses tariffs to maximize a weighted sum of social surplus and lobbying contributions, provided that the lobby is "small" relative to the whole economy. Under this interpretation, the government's weight on lobbying contributions is $\gamma - 1$ [see Grossman and Helpman (1993) for this interpretation and its generalization to a multiple-lobby setting].[30] The domestic country's welfare function is

$$W(\tau_m, \tau_m^*) = \int_{\hat{P}_m(\tau_m)}^{\alpha} C(P)\,\mathrm{d}P + \int_{\hat{P}_x(\tau_m^*)}^{\alpha} C(P)\,\mathrm{d}P + \gamma \int_0^{\hat{P}_m(\tau_m)} 1/2\,\mathrm{d}P$$

$$+ \int_0^{\hat{P}_x(\tau_m^*)} 3/2\,\mathrm{d}P + \tau_m \hat{M}(\tau_m)\,,$$

where τ_m is the import tariff levied by the domestic country and τ_m^* is the import tariff imposed by the foreign country. The welfare of the foreign country is defined in an exactly symmetric fashion.

Consider now the incentive of a government to impose a tariff. With primes denoting derivatives, the effects on government welfare of a small increase in the tariff for $\tau_m \in [0, 1)$ are given by $\partial W(\tau_m, \tau_m^*)/\partial \tau_m = \hat{M}(\tau_m)[1 - \hat{P}_m'(\tau_m)] + \tau_m \hat{M}'(\tau_m) + [(\gamma - 1)/2]\hat{P}_m'(\tau_m)$. Three features are noteworthy. First, the marginal effect of an import tariff for the domestic country is completely independent of the trade policy of the foreign country. This arises because I have assumed that demands are independent and have ruled out export taxes; it will imply that each country's optimal tariff is independent of the tariff choice of its trading partner. While in general this independence will not hold, there is no presumption as to the sign that the dependence would take [see, for example, Dixit (1987)]. Thus, the independent case seems a reasonable one to consider. Second, $\hat{P}_m'(\tau_m) < 1$, which simply reflects the

[29]Here and throughout the rest of the chapter I use "hats" to refer to equilibrium values.

[30]Under this interpretation, the government's welfare function would also contain an additive constant term to adjust for its equilibrium share of the surplus from its relationship with the lobby [see Grossman and Helpman (1993)].

fact that the government has the power to affect world prices through tariff policy. Consequently, a small import tariff would improve government welfare even if the government were concerned only with social welfare (even if $\gamma = 1$). Third, even absent terms-of-trade effects (i.e. even if $\hat{P}'_m(\tau_m) = 1$), the government would find it beneficial to impose a small import tariff as long as political economy motives are present (that is, provided $\gamma > 1$). Finally, it is easily shown that $\partial W(\tau_m, \tau_m^*)/\partial \tau_m = \gamma/4 - 3\tau_m/4$ for $\tau_m \in [0, 1)$. It follows that $W(\tau_m, \tau_m^*)$ is concave in τ_m over the range of non-prohibitive tariffs. Thus, for any fixed τ_m^*, the government's optimal response is $\tau_m = \gamma/3$ provided that $\gamma/3 < 1$, which requires the parameter restriction $\gamma < 3$ that I maintain for the remainder of the discussion.[31]

Now suppose that both governments simultaneously select an import tariff, with each government seeking to maximize its own welfare in a one-shot game. Since each government's best-response tariff is independent of the tariff imposed by the other country, the Nash equilibrium of this tariff game occurs when each government selects the import tariff given by $\hat{\tau}^N = \gamma/3$. It is easily verified that $W(\tau, \tau)$ is strictly decreasing in τ for $\tau \in ((\gamma - 1)/2, \gamma/3]$, and so the tariff game has the structure reminiscent of a Prisoner's Dilemma: both governments are better off when tariffs are set symmetrically at $\tilde{\tau} \equiv (\gamma - 1)/2$ and are monotonically made better off with any symmetric movement towards $\tilde{\tau}$, but in the Nash equilibrium they are led by the unilateral pursuit of beggar-thy-neighbor terms-of-trade effects to impose the higher tariff $\hat{\tau}^N$ and experience the consequent lower welfare.

Figure 3.1 illustrates this situation by depicting for the domestic country the social surplus from importing in the top left panel, the social surplus from exporting in the top right panel, and the politically weighted $(\gamma - 1)$ import-competing producer surplus in the top center panel, for the case where $\gamma \in (1, 3)$. Under symmetric tariffs set at $\tilde{\tau}$, these gains would be given by the area under the import demand curve and the tariff revenue $(m_1 m_2 m_3 + m_2 m_3 m_4 m_5)$, the area above the export supply curve $(x_1 x_2 x_3)$, and the political benefit $(l_0 l_1)$, respectively. Under the unilaterally optimal tariff $\hat{\tau}^N$, the additional social gains from importing are given by the additional net tariff revenue collected from abroad minus the additional dead-weight loss imposed on the domestic country $(m_4 m_6 m_7 m_8 - m_3 m_5 m_6 m_9)$, while the additional political benefits are given by $(l_1 l_2)$. Facing the unilaterally optimal tariff abroad, the reduction in the social gains from exporting are given by the additional net import taxes paid by exporters and the additional dead-weight loss imposed on the domestic country $(x_2 x_6 x_4 x_5 + x_3 x_4 x_6)$. Taken together, when both governments raise their tariffs from $\tilde{\tau}$ to $\hat{\tau}^N$, the losses in each country's export market outweigh the sum of the gains in its import market and its political market, with the net loss for each government

---

[31] If $\gamma \geq 3$, then the government's optimal tariff is driven by political considerations to be prohibitive, and there will be no gains from trade (as perceived by the government), and no role for international trade agreements.

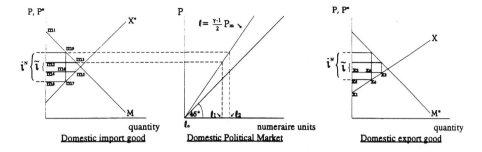

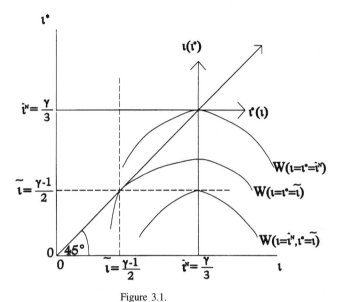

Figure 3.1.

amounting to the sum of the additional dead-weight loss across sectors minus the additional political benefits $(m_3 m_5 m_6 m_9 + x_3 x_4 x_6 - l_1 l_2)$.

The lower panel of Figure 3.1 depicts the domestic and foreign tariff reaction curves, with domestic indifference curves reflecting the relative government welfare rankings associated with reciprocal tariffs set at $\tilde{\tau}$, unilateral optimal tariff setting, and Nash equilibrium tariffs in the tariff game. Provided that the governments perceive any gains from trade (i.e. provided that $\gamma < 3$), there will clearly be a role for an international trade agreement that internalizes the externalities that each country would impose on the other and restricts tariffs to $\tilde{\tau}$.

3.2. Strategic interaction between a government and its private sector

As described above, the second environment where the potential benefits of international trade agreements have been noted is one where the credibility of announced trade policy plans is in question. Often a government may be confronted with trade policy decisions that require commitment to a course of action that it might be tempted to reverse at a later date. When such dynamically- (or "time-")inconsistent policies are optimal, effective government intervention may hinge on a government's ability to make a credible commitment to announced policies. Where domestic institutions allow a high degree of discretion in trade policy, making credible commitments may be difficult unless international rules can provide the needed credibility.

The idea that policy discretion might provide governments with an incentive to surprise the private sector, that this incentive to surprise could undermine the credibility of optimal government policies, and that adherence to policy rules might restore credibility and therefore lead to preferred outcomes, was introduced in the seminal paper by Kydland and Prescott (1977), and quickly had a major influence in macroeconomics and public finance [see Persson and Tabellini (1990), for a survey of the theoretical literature on the issue of rules versus discretion in these fields]. Ironically, despite the fact that the practical relevance of these ideas is probably more important for international trade policy, their impact on the international trade literature was virtually non-existent until relatively recently.

The pervasive importance of the issues raised by Kydland and Prescott in the context of trade intervention can be appreciated intuitively by observing that a necessary condition for an economic policy to be time-inconsistent is that the government pursuing the policy find itself in a second best (or worse) situation. But with trade intervention this condition will virtually always be met: If a government is forced to rely on trade intervention to achieve its policy goals, this is because it lacks other less distortionary instruments. This is the central conclusion to emerge from the literature on distortions and trade policy intervention [see, for example, Corden (1984)]. In such an environment, unexpected trade policy actions can enlarge the set of policy instruments at the government's disposal, allowing it to move closer to the first best. This provides the government with an incentive to attempt to surprise the private sector with unexpected policies whenever it has sufficient discretion to do so. That is, with a sufficient degree of discretion, the optimal trade policy is bound to lack credibility, because it is almost surely time-inconsistent. When this is the case, and when domestic institutions are too weak to provide the desired commitment, international trade agreements could serve as a possible commitment device in interactions between a government and the private sector, and restore the credibility of the optimal trade policy.

This general theme or some variation on it runs through a number of papers in the international trade literature. I will illustrate the basic point by describing the results of Staiger and Tabellini (1987), who consider the credibility issues arising from the use of tariffs as a redistributive tool.[32] They explore the use of tariffs to redistribute income from workers with low marginal utility of income to those with high marginal utility of income subsequent to a terms-of-trade shock. Specifically, workers can change sectors in response to a random terms-of-trade shock which lowers the world price of the imported good, but as a consequence of relocating a worker's marginal productivity falls by the fraction $1 - \lambda$. In this setting, a terms-of-trade shock can create a wage differential across sectors in the economy, with injured sector workers receiving in equilibrium a wage amounting only to the fraction λ of the favored sector wage as long any workers actually leave the injured sector. Under such circumstances, a government might be tempted to use trade policy to reduce the wage differential between the two sectors.[33]

However, the wage differential will tend to persist even if the government intervenes with a trade policy designed to soften the terms-of-trade shock, provided that the intervention is fully anticipated by workers: Such intervention only serves to reduce the number of workers leaving the injured sector, with the wage differential unaffected as long as some exit from the injured sector occurs.[34] This property underlies the equilibrium combinations of sectoral wage differential W^y/W^x and ad valorem tariff $1 + \tau$ available to the government as depicted in Figure 3.2 by the locus *abc*, for the case in which the import-competing sector y faces injury from a terms-of-trade shock that lowers the world price of y by the fraction ϵ. Given the large tariff and associated distortions that must be introduced into the economy in order to achieve any redistributional effects (corresponding to the long horizontal portion of the locus *abc* in Figure 3.2), the optimal trade policy response to such a terms-of-trade shock will be free trade for a wide range of parameters. And under a system of "rules" and the implied timing of moves in the game between the government and the private sector (first the government sets tariff policy, then supply side decisions are made, and finally consumption decisions are determined), the optimal trade policy response to the terms-of-trade shock can be implemented.

But when free trade is the optimal response, it will not be time-consistent. Thus, absent rules, i.e. if the government is endowed with sufficient policy discretion so that its tariff choice comes after supply side decisions are made, the optimal tariff policy

---

[32]Other papers focussing on credibility problems associated with the use of trade policy instruments include Carmichael (1987), Gruenspecht (1988), Lapan (1988), Staiger and Tabellini (1989, 1991, forthcoming), Maskin and Newbery (1990), Matsuyama (1990), Tornell (1991), Devereux (1993), Brainard (1994), Mayer (1994), and Goldberg (1995).

[33]Eaton and Grossman (1985) show that such a policy can be optimal ex ante, in the sense that it can achieve some beneficial risk-sharing between risk averse individuals when insurance markets are incomplete. [See Dixit (1989), however, for a challenge to this view.]

[34]With heterogeneous moving costs across workers, the sectoral allocation decisions of workers would not completely undo the redistributive impacts of anticipated tariffs, but would still diminish them, and the incentive to provide surprise protection and associated credibility problems are still present (see Staiger and Tabellini, forthcoming).

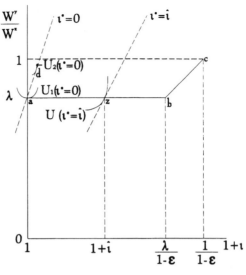

Figure 3.2.

can not be implemented. The problem is that while small amounts of anticipated protection can not affect the distribution of income, small amounts of *un*anticipated protection can do so, since labor cannot reallocate to offset the wage effects of such protection. This provides the government with an incentive to surprise the private sector with unannounced protection.

Figure 3.2 illustrates this incentive to surprise together with the time-consistent solution. A family of government indifference curves defined over the sectoral wage differential and tariff exists for each level of the tariff expected by the private sector, τ^e (since this determines the intersectoral allocation of labor). Consider the government's tariff choice facing a private sector that anticipates free trade. The government indifference curve corresponding to $\tau^e = 0$ and passing through point a on the equilibrium locus abc is flat at $\tau = 0$ and upward sloping for $\tau > 0$ in a neighborhood of a, reflecting the tradeoff between the benefits of redistributing income toward injured-sector workers and the distortionary costs of the tariff. However, with the labor allocation (and production plans) from the first stage based on $\tau^e = 0$ taken as a bygone when the government sets tariffs in the second stage, the locus of feasible points as perceived by the government is given not by abc but by the upward sloping dashed line labeled as $\tau^e = 0$: As noted above, the government can increase W^y/W^x towards unity by imposing a small *un*anticipated tariff. This gives the government an incentive to surprise a private sector that was anticipating free trade by imposing an unexpected tariff that would move the economy to a point such as d in Figure 3.2, where a government indifference curve is tangent to the $\tau^e = 0$ locus. Of course, anticipating these government incentives, the private sector will not expect free trade in equilibrium, and a point such as *d* in Figure 3.2 cannot be an equilibrium outcome of the game. The (time-consistent) equilibrium outcome will occur at a point such as *z* on the *abc* locus in Figure 3.2, where the tariff is fully anticipated and the government has no further incentive to surprise.

The "discretionary" outcome is clearly inferior to the "rules" outcome of laissez faire, because under the former regime the government's tariff policy distorts production and consumption decisions while achieving no distributional benefits. Hence, if an international trade agreement can supply a government with such trade policy rules where the government would lack them otherwise, then the agreement can serve a valuable function.

4. Enforcement of international trade rules

In this section I review the literature on enforcement issues that arise with international trade agreements. This literature begins with the view that international trade agreements must be self-enforcing, and proceeds to examine the possible role played by international dispute settlement procedures such as those in Articles XXII and XXIII of GATT. I will proceed by first laying out the basic limits imposed by the restriction that an agreement must be self-enforcing, and will then discuss and interpret a number of papers that have attempted to shed light on the role of international dispute settlement procedures in this context.

4.1. Repeated interaction and enforcement

Whether the economic benefits of international trade agreements stem from their potential to limit the temptation to pursue beggar-thy-neighbor trade policies or their potential to broaden the range of trade policies that are credible with respect to each country's private sector, the temptations for unilateral trade policy choices do not simply go away once an agreement is in place. Instead, international agreements must be constructed so that these temptations remain in check.

Consider, for example, the beggar-thy-neighbor trade policies which underlie Figure 3.1. It is clear from the situation depicted in Figure 3.1 that each country could gain if both agreed to adhere to an international rule that "bound" tariffs at $\bar{\tau}$. But it is equally clear that each country would have a unilateral incentive to cheat on such an agreement, and move to its tariff reaction curve. This raises a crucial question that confronts governments when they attempt to implement a trade agreement in this situation: By what mechanism is the tariff binding to be enforced? Since countries trade repeatedly through time, a natural possibility is to use the threat of future punishments to deter violations of an agreement. As noted in Section 2 above, in a general sense, this is precisely what countries do in practice: Such enforcement procedures are codified in national law, e.g. Section 301 of the 1974 Trade Act in the United States, and in international agreements, e.g, the dispute settlement procedures in GATT. I will turn to the possible design of these enforcement mechanisms and the literature concerned with them in a moment. Here I simply illustrate that the effectiveness of enforcement mechanisms may be limited by the severity of credible (e.g. subgame perfect) threats and that, when this is the case, governments may find that their ability to implement international trade agreements is constrained by their temptation to cheat. Indeed, when enforcement issues are important it will be the incentive constraints that determine the equilibrium trade barriers.

To illustrate this basic point, I consider an infinitely repeated tariff game along the lines of Bagwell and Staiger (1993a), which is defined by the infinite repetition of the one-shot tariff game described in Section 3.1. In each period the countries observe all previous import tariff selections and simultaneously choose import tariffs. Let $\delta \in (0, 1)$ denote the discount factor between periods.[35] For illustrative purposes, I consider subgame perfect equilibria in which (i) symmetric stationary tariffs no lower than $\tilde{\tau}$ are selected along the equilibrium path, meaning that in equilibrium the two countries select the same import tariff in each period, and (ii) if a deviation from this common tariff occurs, then in the next period and forever thereafter the countries revert to the Nash equilibrium tariffs of the one-shot tariff game given by $\hat{\tau}^N$.[36]

In this repeated tariff game, countries have the possibility of supporting a "cooperative" tariff τ^c, with $\tau^c < \hat{\tau}^N$, since any attempt to raise the current-period tariff will under the agreement lead in all future periods to a retaliatory (one-shot Nash) tariff from the trading partner.[37] Intuitively, an agreement to bind tariffs at τ^c can be enforced if the one-time incentive to cheat is sufficiently small relative to the discounted future value of avoiding the "trade war" that would be triggered as a consequence. Put differently, for enforcement to present a relevant constraint on the

---

[35]The infinitely repeated tariff game with discounting at rate δ can equivalently be thought of as a repeated tariff game with a constant hazard rate that the game will continue. In the latter case, $\delta = he^{-rL}$ where h is the hazard rate, r is the pure interest component of the discount factor, and L is the period length. In the former case, h would be one. Repeated tariff games with a fixed and finite termination, on the other hand, may preclude opportunities for self-enforcing cooperation as a subgame-perfect equilibrium, although see Dixit (1987) for the case in which there are multiple static Nash equilibria, and Jensen and Thursby (1984) who consider incomplete information and also alternative equilibrium concepts.

[36]Subgame perfection allows more severe punishments than the infinite Nash reversion that I adopt here [see Abreu (1986, 1988)], and with more severe punishments comes greater liberalization. Here I adopt infinite Nash reversion to illustrate the main ideas, but more severe punishments could easily be accommodated. For example, if export taxes were introduced into the model set out above [see, Bagwell and Staiger (1990)], then autarky could be supported as a Nash equilibrium, and infinite reversion to autarky would provide an optimal punishment in the sense of Abreu. Also, see Furusawa (1994) for a treatment of asymmetries across countries.

[37]Throughout the remainder of the chapter I will refer to tariffs stemming from international trade agreements as "cooperative" tariffs, whether or not the international agreements are modeled as cooperative games (i.e. requiring an external enforcement mechanism) or non-cooperative games (i.e. self-enforcing) as in the present example [see Friedman (1986), Ch 1].

feasible trade agreements in this setting, there must be significant one-time gains in defecting from $\tilde{\tau}$, and the cost of future punishments must be discounted heavily. In fact, for a given rate of time preference, these two conditions are related, and reflect a common underlying factor: The length of each period in the repeated tariff game must be sufficiently long. The period length, in turn, can be thought of as reflecting the length of time it takes to observe the trade policies of one's trading partner and respond.[38,39]

To formalize this intuition, I first examine the temptation a country has to cheat. Given the symmetry of the model, I will do so from the domestic country's perspective. For a fixed cooperative tariff $\tau^c < \hat{\tau}^N$, and given the class of subgame perfect equilibria I consider, if a country deviates and selects $\tau \neq \tau^c$, then it will deviate to its best-response one-shot Nash tariff, $\hat{\tau}^N$.[40] Thus, the domestic country's gain in cheating is $\Omega(\tau^c) \equiv W(\hat{\tau}^N, \tau^c) - W(\tau^c, \tau^c)$. When a country cheats, however, it triggers a "trade war", the cost of which must also be considered. The one-period value to the domestic country in avoiding a trade war and sustaining the cooperative tariff is $\omega(\tau^c) \equiv W(\tau^c, \tau^c) - W(\hat{\tau}^N, \hat{\tau}^N)$. Then the cost to the domestic country associated with cheating is $V(\delta, \tau^c) \equiv \delta \cdot \omega(\tau^c)/(1 - \delta)$, since once a country defects and selects a high import tariff, cooperative tariffs are thereafter replaced by the higher one-shot Nash tariffs. This allows the domestic government's incentive constraint, which requires that the benefit of cheating be no greater than the discounted future value of cooperation that would be forfeited as a consequence, to be written as $\Omega(\tau^c) \leq V(\delta, \tau^c)$. An identical (redundant) incentive constraint holds for the foreign country. Any cooperative tariff τ^c that satisfies this incentive constraint can be supported in a subgame perfect equilibrium of the repeated tariff game.

---

[38]This statement is correct within a setting of perfect monitoring, i.e. where the period's tariff choices become common knowledge at the end of each period. For important qualifications on the role of interest rates, information lags, and response times in a setting of imperfect monitoring, see Abreu, Milgrom and Pearce (1991).

[39]In this regard, there is ample historical and anecdotal evidence that response times in trade disputes are often lengthy, and sometimes exceedingly so. A detailed historical account of a number of major trade wars can be found in Conybeare (1987). A recent and instructive example is that of the Chicken War [see also Talbot (1978)]. This trade war between the United States and the European Community (EC) effectively began in July 1962 when EC regulations associated with the implementation of the Common Agricultural Policy brought to a halt the rapid increases in U.S. exports of frozen chickens into the EC market. For the next year the United States was involved with the EC in a debate over the degree of discrimination against U.S. chicken exports. The United States then requested compensation from the EC under an agreement reached as part of the Dillon Round, but failed to come to agreement with the EC over the amount of compensation it should receive. Finally, in September 1963, both sides agreed to submit the dispute to a special GATT tribunal. The tribunal found U.S. complaints to be justified and authorized the United States to withdraw concessions by an equivalent amount, which the United States subsequently did on January 7, 1964, 18 months after the original EC actions had taken effect.

[40]Note that the choice of defection tariff, while generally a move to one's tariff reaction curve, is made trivial in the particular model I am considering by the lack of slope in the tariff reaction curves. More generally, a government's defection tariff would depend on the equilibrium tariff of its trading partner.

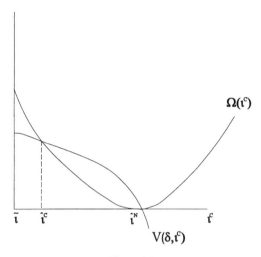

Figure 4.1.

Now consider the "most-cooperative" tariff, $\hat{\tau}^c$, which I define as the smallest tariff equal to or above $\tilde{\tau}$ that satisfies the incentive constraint. The determination of the most-cooperative tariff can be simply illustrated by Figure 4.1, which depicts $\Omega(\tau^c)$ and $V(\delta, \tau^c)$ as a function of τ^c. Observe in Figure 4.1 that $\Omega(\tau^c)$ is monotonically decreasing in τ^c for $\tau^c < \hat{\tau}^N$, and is flat and equal to zero at $\hat{\tau}^N$. This reflects the fact that a government gains less in deviating from a cooperative tariff τ^c the closer is that tariff to the one-shot Nash tariff $\hat{\tau}^N$, and gains nothing in deviating at (or around) $\hat{\tau}^N$. On the other hand, Figure 4.1 depicts $V(\delta, \tau^c)$ as equal to zero at $\hat{\tau}^N$, monotonically decreasing in τ^c for $\tau^c > \tilde{\tau}$, and flat at $\tau^c = \tilde{\tau}$. This reflects the fact that the gains from avoiding a trade war decline to zero as the tariffs stipulated in the agreement rise from $\tilde{\tau}$ and approach the level that would be chosen in a trade war anyway, and that, at $\tilde{\tau}$, a small symmetric increase in cooperative tariffs would have no impact on government welfare (this is just the first-order condition that defines $\tilde{\tau}$). Since the government incentive constraint requires that $V(\delta, \tau^c)$ be no less than $\Omega(\tau^c)$, Figure 4.1 implies that the range of tariffs $\tau^c \in [\hat{\tau}^c, \hat{\tau}^N]$ are supportable as subgame perfect equilibrium tariffs, with the most-cooperative tariff $\hat{\tau}^c$ defined where the incentive constraint holds with equality.[41]

---

[41]In the formal model provided in the text, $\Omega(\tau^c)$ will be convex while $V(\delta, \tau^c)$ will be concave, as depicted in Figure 4.1. Thus, the two curves will intersect at most once over the range $\tau^c \in [\tilde{\tau}, \hat{\tau}^N)$. More generally, if the two curves intersect in multiple places, then $\hat{\tau}^c$ will correspond to the lowest such intersection (provided that $\Omega(\tau^c)$ lies above $V(\delta, \tau^c)$ at $\tilde{\tau}$). Also, consideration of alternative punishments with more or less severity would act to shift $V(\delta, \tau^c)$ up or down in Figure 4.1 accordingly.

4.2. Dispute settlement procedures

I now turn to the literature that is directly related to the role and design of dispute settlement procedures. This literature takes as its starting point the presumption that enforcement issues place a binding constraint on international trade agreements, and models trade agreements as repeated games played between or among countries, as in the case of the determination of $\hat{\tau}^c$ illustrated in Figure 4.1. It then asks what the role of an explicit dispute settlement procedure might be in facilitating liberalization under the agreement.

One view is that dispute settlement procedures simply serve to codify the kinds of trigger strategies supporting the most-cooperative tariff illustrated in Figure 4.1, and thereby help to eliminate the well-known coordination problems that could otherwise plague countries in their attempts to choose among the multiplicity of cooperative tariffs supported by such strategies, i.e. any tariff between $\hat{\tau}^N$ and $\hat{\tau}^c$ in Figure 4.1. It seems plausible that dispute settlement procedures do provide such a coordination device, but as discussed in Section 2 it seems less plausible that this is all they do. Surely this view abstracts from many complications that are likely to be important in the actual workings of any mechanism for enforcement of international agreements. Moreover, even a minimal dispute settlement procedure that simply codified the rules of enforcement is likely to change as additional complications are considered. The literature highlights a number of these complications, and considers how dispute settlement procedures might look in their presence.

While an interpretation of the model underlying Figure 4.1 is that trade policies are perfectly and costlessly observable with a (one period) lag, in practice this perfect, costless observability is unlikely. Dispute settlement procedures may therefore play an important role in gathering and disseminating information. A first attempt to capture this information role is contained in Hungerford (1991), who depicts the central enforcement problem faced by countries attempting to sustain international trade agreements as one of monitoring. In a setting adopted from Green and Porter's (1984) analysis of industry cartel behavior when price information is imperfect, Hungerford considers a two-country world in which movements in the terms of trade cannot readily be assigned to their underlying causes. These causes may either be random and unobserved shocks to supply and demand, or the beggar-thy-neighbor use of unobserved non-tariff barriers by one's trading partner. Tariffs, on the other hand, are taken to be observable, and are set at (externally enforced) GATT-bound levels.

Hungerford's point is essentially this. One way for countries to reduce their non-tariff barriers below the one-shot Nash levels in this setting is to accept the unobservability of non-tariff barriers and to condition retaliation on movements in observable variables which (imperfectly) reflect information about these non-tariff barriers.[42] One such variable might be the level of

---

[42] An alternative would be for countries simply to enter into trade agreements covering only those trade policy instruments which they can observe, e.g. tariffs (see Copeland, 1990).

exports.[43] If this approach to enforcement were adopted, and if tariffs were the designated instrument of retaliation, the role of a dispute settlement procedure would be minimal, simply providing a coordination device for selecting punishment strategies and granting exceptions from GATT tariff bindings to carry out the agreed-upon punishments. Consider first this minimal version of a dispute settlement procedure. The punishment strategies are analogous to those suggested by Green and Porter for collusive firms, and will lead to the analogous outcome: Countries agree to switch temporarily from their GATT-bound tariff levels to one-shot Nash tariffs (engage in trade wars of a pre-specified duration) when either country's exports fall unexpectedly below a cut-off level as a way to mitigate each country's incentives to secretly defect from the agreed-upon non-tariff barrier choices. The non-tariff barriers are themselves set at the lowest non-negative level that maintains incentive compatibility under these strategies.

Now consider an alternative depiction of dispute settlement procedures that captures some of the aversion to retaliation that, as described in Section 2, seems to characterize actual procedures. While the minimal procedure outlined above might correspond roughly to the "rule integrity" forces operating in actual dispute settlement procedures, Hungerford attempts to capture the counterbalancing "negotia-tion/conciliation" forces by adding the requirement that a costly and imperfectly-informative (but instantaneous) investigation must take place as a prerequisite to retaliation. This tends to reduce the frequency of trade wars, a change which on the surface might appear to be for the better since trade wars are never triggered by a defection from agreed-upon low levels of non-tariff barriers anyway, always caused instead by random shocks to supply and demand.

And indeed, if the investigation required by the dispute settlement procedure could perfectly discern whether or not a defection had taken place, and if retaliation could be conditioned on this information, then the fact that information gathering is costly might justify the use of such investigations periodically: The information gathered

---

[43]While Hungerford (1991) focusses on movements in the terms of trade to trigger punishments, Riezman (1991) has shown that no trigger strategy equilibrium can exist when terms-of-trade movements are the trigger. Intuitively, at the equilibrium, each country must be deterred from deviating to a slightly higher trade barrier by the increased likelihood that a punishment phase will be triggered as a result. Under a terms-of-trade trigger, to keep the incentives of each country in check, punishments must be triggered whenever *either* country's terms of trade drops below a critical level. In other words, countries must adopt a terms-of-trade *band* around the no-intervention no-shock terms of trade, and must revert to a punishment phase whenever the terms of trade falls outside this band. But a slightly higher trade barrier then has an ambiguous effect on the likelihood that a punishment phase will be triggered, since it will increase the likelihood that a country's terms of trade falls above the upper limit of the band, but will decrease the likelihood that a country's terms of trade will fall below the lower limit. Riezman shows that each country can not simultaneously perceive that the likelihood of a punishment phase is increased by a small increase in its trade barrier, and thus that no trigger-strategy equilibrium can exist under terms-of-trade triggers. For this reason, I describe Hungerford's results on dispute settlement procedures under an export-trigger interpretation (which does not suffer from this problem provided that offer curves are elastic over the relevant range).

could be used to avoid otherwise costly trade wars without undercutting the incentives to keep non-tariff barriers low. That is, each time a trade war would have erupted under the minimal dispute settlement procedures outlined above, this alternative dispute settlement procedure would launch a costly investigation instead, to reveal whether or not defections from the agreed-upon non-tariff barrier levels had occurred. A trade war would only erupt if indeed a defection had occurred. Since defections never do occur in equilibrium, the benefits of such a dispute settlement procedure would be the complete elimination of costly trade wars (without interfering with the incentive effects of the threat of trade wars), and these benefits would have to be weighed against the cost of periodic investigations.[44]

But if the information gathering functions of the dispute settlement procedure are weak as Hungerford assumes (in fact, under Hungerford's depiction, they are essentially uninformative), the trade wars themselves are necessary if unfortunate episodes required to maintain rule integrity, as it is the periodic outbreak of such wars that *prevents* countries from cheating on the agreement. Consequently, institutions that interfere with their occurrence and do no more will be counter-productive. Thus, in this case, there will be a tradeoff between allowing low-tariff episodes to be interrupted periodically by costly trade wars and the ability to maintain low levels of non-tariff barriers. This is a crucial point, since it provides a formalization of the tension that has been noted in the design and workings of actual dispute settlement procedures. That is, the rule integrity and negotiation/conciliation forces operating in such procedures may work at cross purposes, and especially so if the latter do not serve an important information gathering role.

Ludema (1990) also explores the apparent aversion to retaliation exhibited by dispute settlement procedures. He considers the emphasis that has been observed on *negotiated* settlements of the dispute that are agreeable to both sides. Ludema models the dispute settlement procedure as providing a forum for renegotiation after a dispute erupts. Formally, ascertaining the effect of such a dispute settlement procedure amounts to comparing the most-cooperative tariff in an infinitely repeated tariff game across two different scenarios: One in which threatened punishments need be subgame perfect (a minimal dispute settlement procedure which serves only to coordinate countries on the equilibrium punishments, and does so at the outset of the agreement) and the other in which threatened punishments must be "renegotiation-proof", i.e. they must be expected to arise from the renegotiation process that occurs as a result of a dispute settlement procedure that provides on-going communication channels. Ludema chooses a definition of renegotiation-proof equilibria due to Pearce (1987), which requires that a punishment equilibrium be Pareto optimal on the set of subgame perfect equilibria that rely on no punishments worse than themselves. Not surprisingly, by providing a forum for renegotiation once a dispute has begun, the

---

[44]There is still the important question of why an international (as opposed to domestic) institution would be required to carry out this information gathering function.

dispute procedure diminishes the deterrent effect of threatened punishments, and so dispute settlement procedures as envisioned by Ludema can only impede the maintenance of low tariff levels. In terms of Figure 4.1, the renegotiation channels provided by a dispute settlement procedure would shift $V(\delta, \tau^c)$ down. But the result should be thought of not as a case against maintaining dispute settlement procedures, but rather as an inevitable consequence of the communication channels that must exist if a dispute settlement procedure is to perform its other, presumably cooperation-enhancing, functions (e.g. monitoring).

A possibly trade-liberalizing role for dispute settlement procedures is considered by Kovenock and Thursby (1992). They view a workable dispute settlement procedure as necessary to induce countries to feel an "international obligation" to upholding the agreement, a point often emphasized by legal scholars [such as Hudec (1990) and Jackson (1989)] and somewhat related to Dam's (1970) function (3), as enumerated above. That is, according to Kovenock and Thursby, the existence of a dispute settlement procedure can endow countries with a sense of "obligation" to the agreement, and this in turn can relax the incentive constraints that restrict the degree of tariff liberalization attainable. For example, if violating such an international obligation imposed a fixed "psychic" cost on the violator in the period of defection and in all subsequent periods, and if this cost were in addition to all costs of changes in future actions that were induced by the defection, then a dispute settlement procedure would have the effect of inducing a downward shift of $\Omega(\tau_c)$ and an upward shift of $V(\delta, \tau^c)$ in Figure 4.1, resulting in a lower sustainable tariff level.

The notion of international obligation, and the role that dispute settlement procedures may play in instilling such a sense of obligation in parties to an international agreement, may well be an important dimension of the benefits of a "well-working" dispute settlement procedure. A difficulty with this approach is that what is meant by "well-working" becomes somewhat tautological (whatever instills countries with this sense of international obligation). Still, it does point to one reason why dispute settlement procedures that are generally approved of by all parties to the agreement may facilitate trade liberalization under the agreement. This seems to provide a possible starting point for evaluating alternative enforcement mechanisms, such as unilateral retaliation occurring outside the dispute settlement procedures of the agreement, as has occurred for example when the United States has retaliated under its "Section 301" authority without abiding by GATT dispute settlement procedures [see, for example, McMillan (1990), Bayard and Elliott (1992) and Finger and Fung (1993)].

Finally, while the debate on the implications of ignoring GATT dispute settlement procedures and relying instead on alternative enforcement mechanisms is often framed in the context of multilateral versus unilateral or bilateral approaches to dispute resolution [see for example Bhagwati (1991) on "aggressive unilateralism"], the papers reviewed thus far have not formally considered the possibly unique advantages of a multilateral dispute settlement procedure over a bilateral procedure.

Indeed, since these papers all adopt a two-country setting, they can make no distinction between the two. This distinction is the focus of a recent paper by Maggi (1994).

Maggi identifies two broad categories of gains from a multilateral enforcement mechanism over a web of bilateral mechanisms. The first gain arises in the presence of local "imbalances of power", defined by Maggi as a situation where different countries stand to lose different amounts from a trade war, with the more "powerful" countries standing to lose less. In such circumstances, the exchange of enforcement power that can be achieved under a multilateral dispute settlement procedure can serve to support lower tariffs than would be possible under purely bilateral procedures. Specifically, in a multilateral enforcement mechanism, each country can serve as a third-party enforcer of low tariffs in bilateral relationships where it is "strong" in exchange for receiving third-party enforcement from others in bilateral relationships where it is "weak". Purely bilateral enforcement mechanisms cannot effect this "exchange" of enforcement power.[45] A second kind of gain from multilateral enforcement mechanisms identified by Maggi is associated with the "aggregation" of enforcement power: Since tariffs levied by different governments on the same imported product tend to be strategic complements [see, also, Bagwell and Staiger (1993b)], a multilateral enforcement mechanism that has many governments joining in the punishments can lead to proportionately more severe punishments than would be forthcoming under bilateral enforcement procedures.

When either local imbalances of power or strategic tariff complementarities are present, Maggi shows that a multilateral dispute settlement procedure is necessary to achieve the gains from exchange and aggregation of enforcement power. Hence, the monitoring function of the dispute settlement procedure is once again emphasized, but now it is the dissemination of information to third parties that is the crucial service provided by the dispute settlement procedure.[46]

In summary, the literature I have reviewed in this section has been motivated by the opposing forces that work to shape dispute settlement procedures in practice. These contradictory forces present a substantial challenge for developing a coherent picture of the role of dispute settlement procedures in international trade agreements, but such a picture is a necessary precursor to a serious evaluation of the costs and benefits of alternative enforcement mechanisms. At the same time, the literature illustrates the subtle issues involved in the design of dispute settlement procedures and suggests that, as a practical matter, enforcement capabilities are likely to be

---

[45]This point is reminiscent of the pooling of incentive constraints analyzed by Bernheim and Whinston (1990) in the case of collusive firms competing across distinct markets.

[46]Whether such third-party sanctions play an important role in actual multilateral dispute settlement procedures such as GATT's is less clear. Certainly the role for *explicit* third-party sanctions is not large, although Article XXIII provides for the possibility of effectively expelling a notoriously offending country from GATT [see Jackson (1969, pp. 186–187)] and more subtle forms of third-party pressure are evident in practice [see Maggi (1994)].

imperfect. As a result, the nature and performance of international trade agreements are likely to reflect the limitations imposed by weak enforcement capabilities, a theme that recurs in much of the literature on other dimensions of trade rules to which I now turn.

5. The process of reciprocal trade liberalization

A striking feature of the multilateral trade liberalization that has occurred since 1947 is just how long it has taken. While the extent of liberalization achieved is certainly remarkable for the depth in the reduction of trade barriers, the process by which this liberalization has occurred through eight "rounds" of negotiation over a fifty year period is no less remarkable for its gradualism. There are two dimensions of this observation that pose a challenge to the literature on international trade agreements that I have reviewed thus far. The first is that the rounds of negotiations themselves often take many years to complete. The second is that there have been so many rounds, or steps, in the liberalization process stretching out over so many decades. Neither of these features could be explained well within the picture of international trade agreements emerging from Figure 4.1, which would suggest that the liberalization from a high-tariff outcome such as $\hat{\tau}^N$ to the most-cooperative outcome $\hat{\tau}^c$ could be achieved in one great leap and without delay.

Understanding the reasons for delays in the process of negotiation and for gradualism in the process of reciprocal liberalization is important for several reasons. First, such an understanding may help to illuminate the pros and cons of various paths to liberalization, such as regional versus multilateral initiatives, and the implications of each for the other. Second, understanding the success of post-war liberalization may require an understanding of the process by which that success was achieved. The GATT process of on-going rounds of liberalization has been credited with generating the momentum for this success, and has led to an informal "bicycle" theory of GATT: Unless you keep pedaling, you will fall off [for a recent statement of this view, see Bhagwati (1988, p. 41)]. And third, by understanding the reasons for delays in the negotiation process and the gradual nature of trade liberalization, changes in the institutional structure may suggest themselves that would help to reduce delays and hasten liberalization where desirable.

Of related but independent interest is the role that MFN has played in the process of multilateral trade negotiations. Asymmetries across countries are likely to lead to different bargaining outcomes in the presence of MFN as compared to the outcomes that would arise in its absence, both in terms of efficiency properties and in terms of distributional consequences. An important question is whether these differences are desirable.

In this section I will discuss a literature that relates to these issues. I will begin with the literature on trade bargaining under MFN. Next I will discuss delays in trade negotiations, and then consider gradualism in the liberalization process itself. After that, I will turn to the bicycle theory, and discuss the importance of the process by which liberalization has proceeded for the success that has been achieved. Finally, I will conclude this section by considering how regional liberalization initiatives which are able to outpace the multilateral liberalization process may affect the degree of multilateral liberalization attainable.

5.1. Trade bargaining and MFN

Abiding by the principle of MFN is a central obligation under GATT, but the economic case for such a principle is far from clear.[47] Against the potential benefits of MFN that come from avoiding the transactions costs and "trade diverting" effects associated with the ability to offer preferential treatment to selected trading partners are the potential costs associated with "free riding" on the reciprocal agreements of others [Viner (1924, 1931, 1936)]. The free-rider issue has been explored with formal bargaining models in several recent papers.

Caplin and Krishna (1988) formally illustrate the free-rider problem associated with MFN in a static model of simultaneous bilateral bargains. MFN's requirement that each country in a bilateral bargain lower its tariffs to other countries not involved in the bargain creates an externality which is not internalized in the bilateral bargaining process. Consequently, a simultaneous round of bilateral bargains under MFN may be less effective at lowering tariffs than would be the case if MFN treatment were not required. Caplin and Krishna also explore the role of MFN in a three-country dynamic (sequential) bargaining context based on Rubinstein (1982), in which one country makes tariff-cutting proposals alternately to the second and third countries until an agreement is reached (which in equilibrium occurs immediately). Their results suggest that MFN may have important effects on the distribution of bargaining power across countries.

This theme is picked up by Ludema (1991), who constructs a three-country, non-cooperative, dynamic bargaining game in which the choice between bilateral and multilateral tariff reductions is endogenous. In Ludema's model, when one country makes a proposal to the other two, they respond simultaneously to the proposal with acceptance or rejection. If both countries accept, agreement is reached and the negotiations end. If both reject, negotiations continue with the next proposer selected

---

[47]The MFN clause in trade agreements has a long and interesting history which pre-dates GATT. See Jackson (1969, pp. 249–255) on the history of MFN leading up to its inclusion in GATT. Also, while a distinction can be made between conditional and *un*conditional MFN (the former requiring the granting of some reciprocal privilege as a condition for MFN treatment), I will focus throughout on unconditional MFN as has the literature that I review.

at random. But if one country accepts and the other rejects, the initial acceptance is taken to be on an *ad referendum* basis, and the accepting country is allowed to reconsider its position given that the third country has rejected. Ludema establishes that bargaining in this setting under MFN will yield tariff agreements which are Pareto efficient on the set of MFN tariffs, and in this sense the free-rider problem often associated with MFN does not arise. Intuitively, Ludema shows that any rational proposal made by one country must leave the other two countries indifferent between accepting the proposal and rejecting it and continuing negotiations. If, faced with such a proposal, one of the two remaining countries attempted to "free ride" on the MFN tariff concessions of the others by rejecting the proposal in the hope that its acceptance by the other country would lead to a bilateral agreement between that country and the proposer, the remaining country would then choose to reject (since it was just indifferent between rejection and acceptance of the full multilateral agreement at the *ad referendum* stage) and negotiations would continue. As a consequence, the MFN externality provides no advantage for free-riders in this setting. This does not mean that MFN has no efficiency costs, since the negotiated tariff equilibrium under MFN may not be Pareto efficient on the wider set of tariffs that include discriminatory tariffs. But it does suggest that the efficiency costs of MFN may be smaller than is commonly perceived.[48] On the other hand, like Caplin and Krishna (1988), Ludema does associate distributional effects with MFN, in that he finds that all countries gain from negotiations under MFN but not necessarily in its absence.

All in all, by formalizing and evaluating the free-rider issues associated with MFN, this literature has raised doubts about the importance of these effects, suggesting that the efficiency cost of MFN may not be large. On the other hand, the benefits of MFN have not yet been adequately captured in a formal model, and so a convincing rationale for MFN is still lacking. As Caplin and Krishna observe:

> There is a simple observation which illustrates the difficulties in providing a general bargaining-theoretic rationale for MFN. There is a grand utility possibility frontier available to countries using all the commercial trading instruments at their disposal, such as tariffs. If we view the bargaining process as yielding efficient outcomes, as for example with the Nash bargaining solution, then MFN simply limits the tools available to different countries, shifting in the utility possibility frontier. Hence the most positive aspects of MFN can only be illustrated when the bargaining process absent-MFN yields inefficient outcomes. [Caplin and Krishna (1988, pp. 281–282)].

This seems to point in a fruitful direction for future work in this important area.

---

[48]A similar point is made by Maggi (1994), who argues that the efficiency costs of imposing MFN in a multilateral bargaining context may be small.

5.2. Negotiation delay

I will consider next the literature on negotiation delay. While there is a large literature focused on delays in negotiations generally [see, for example, a recent review of this literature by Kennan and Wilson (1993)], the literature explaining delays in the process of trade negotiation is still in its infancy.[49] Bac and Raff (1994) appear to be the first to consider formally the role of bilateral incomplete information in generating delays in the completion of trade talks. Each country's private information concerns whether it is a "tough" type (refusing to make any tariff concessions of its own, but benefiting from any tariff concessions made by its trading partner) or a "soft" type (willing to make unilateral tariff concessions but also benefiting from any tariff concessions made by its trading partner). Countries enter into negotiations aware that any outcome of the negotiations must be self-enforcing in an infinitely repeated tariff game with subgame perfect punishments. It may benefit a soft-type country to attempt to masquerade during the negotiations as a tough type by "holding out", in the hope of extracting unilateral concessions from the other country. Bac and Raf show that soft-type countries may adopt these delaying tactics in a mixed strategy equilibrium, and that drawn-out negotiations may be necessary to complete the process of Bayesian updating that must ultimately lead one side to concede and an agreement to be reached. Thus, as in the larger literature on bargaining delays, drawn out trade negotiations may generate an unavoidable cost of private information as a result of the learning that must occur before agreement can be reached.

Whether there is more to be said in the context of delays in international trade negotiations than has already been said in the general bargaining literature is not clear. To generate further insights, it may well be necessary for researchers to introduce detailed institutional structure in order to capture what is unique in this problem to trade negotiations.[50]

5.3. Gradualism

I now turn to the literature concerned with gradualism of the reciprocal trade liberalization process itself. By this I mean the literature that seeks to explain why reciprocal trade liberalization seems to proceed in a long series of steps. While the general issue of gradualism in the reform process is a topic that has received a great

---

[49]Agreements are reached immediately in Caplin and Krishna (1988) and Ludema (1991). Matsuyama (1990) considers reasons for delay in trade liberalization, but my focus here is on delay in negotiation.

[50]Nevertheless, there are other insights from the bargaining literature that seem to have special significance in international trade applications. One example would be the relevance for the issue of multilateral versus bilateral approaches to trade liberalization of the findings of Mailath and Postlewaite (1990) that the length of delay in bargaining increases with the number of privately informed parties to the negotiation.

deal of attention as a result of the many recent attempts at unilateral macroeconomic and structural reform, it is an issue of special significance in the case of *reciprocal* trade liberalization, where at the multilateral level reciprocal reform has been proceeding with the same basic goal for 50 years.[51] It is hard to think of an example of a coherent *unilateral* economic reform program, trade or otherwise, that has exhibited gradualism to this extreme.

Nevertheless, a good place to begin is with the literature on gradualism in unilateral trade reforms, since the optimal pace of unilateral trade liberalization is likely to affect the pace of reciprocal trade liberalization as well. Mussa (1984) argues that adjustment costs by themselves are *not* a reason for gradualism in the reform process. That is, workers or other factors of production who face adjustment costs may choose to make their sectoral reallocation decisions slowly over time, but that does not imply that the reform itself should proceed slowly. Mussa shows that the optimal reform will be instantaneous in the presence of adjustment costs unless other market distortions are present, or unless the government chooses gradual reform to minimize its distributional consequences. Dewatripont and Roland (1992) and Brainard and Verdier (1994) study cases of unilateral trade liberalization in the presence of specific market imperfections, and provide reasons to expect that such reforms may proceed gradually. Dewatripont and Roland show how dynamic adverse selection can lead to gradualism in the reform process when a government lacks the ability to commit with regard to its private sector not to use information revealed in a partial reform for the design of later reforms. Brainard and Verdier examine the implications for the speed of unilateral trade liberalization of introducing political economy concerns into a model of quadratic (labor) adjustment costs.

As noted, the considerations that determine the optimal pace of unilateral trade liberalization are likely to affect the pace of reciprocal trade liberalization as well. But when trade liberalization requires reciprocal agreement between or among governments, there are likely to be additional reasons for gradualism. Two papers that focus on gradualism in reciprocal trade liberalization point to strategic interaction across governments as a potentially important additional explanation. These are the papers by Devereux (1993) and Staiger (forthcoming). Both papers focus on non-stationarities in the government incentive constraints that are triggered by initial liberalization, and lead to the possibility of further incentive compatible liberalization at some point in the future.

Devereux explores the relationship between trade liberalization and economic growth in a setting where production technologies exhibit learning-by-doing and governments set tariffs in an infinitely repeated game. Although his focus is on the relationship between trade liberalization and growth, the model he develops exhibits gradualism in the trade liberalization process. That is, the government incentive

---

[51] Other long episodes of reciprocal trade liberalization in the context of regional agreements are noted in Dam (1970, pp. 282–283).

constraints that define the most-cooperative tariffs in every period are gradually relaxed over time by the effects of learning-by-doing in the model, provided only that the initial liberalization starts the process off by moving resources into each economy's export sector. Essentially, as the learning-by-doing in each economy's export sector outpaces the rate of (domestic) technological advance in its import-competing sector, the two economies become increasingly dependent on one another, and (i) the payoff from unilateral defection declines ($\Omega(\tau^c)$ is now time-dependent and shifts downward over time in Figure 4.1) and (ii) the gains associated with avoiding a trade war rise ($\omega(\tau^c)$ is now time-dependent and increases over time, so that $V(\delta, \tau^c)$ shifts up over time in Figure 4.1). This allows the most-cooperative tariff $\hat{\tau}^c$ to fall over time as learning proceeds.

A gradual process of trade liberalization can also arise if two changes are introduced to the model underlying Figure 4.1 (the following builds on Staiger, forthcoming). First, allow rent-earning workers in the import-competing sector with sector-specific skills to relocate in response to changing tariff levels. Second, allow the sector-specific skills of workers who have exited the import-competing sector to depreciate over time. The key point to observe is that the presence of resources in an import-competing sector that are (or could be) earning rents from their sector-specific skills will exacerbate the government incentive constraints associated with low cooperative tariffs and limit the degree of attainable trade liberalization. Intuitively, by being able to transform into rents a portion of what otherwise would be dead-weight loss under a tariff hike, the presence of such resources makes deviation from a low cooperative tariff to a high tariff more desirable for the deviating country, and makes punishments under reciprocally high tariffs less painful. But this in turn suggests that an initial round of liberalization might eventually feed back upon itself and pave the way for further liberalization, as the workers who initially leave the import-competing sector eventually see their import-sector-specific skills depreciate over time through lack of use.

The basic point can be illustrated with reference to Figure 4.1. If import-competing resources employed outside the import-competing sector face some probability each period of losing their sector-specific skills, then the amount of resources left in the economy with the potential to collect rents in the import-competing sector will eventually be diminished by the previous round's liberalization ($\hat{\tau}^c_{-1}$) and the exit from the import-competing sector that it causes. As a consequence, the one-time payoff associated with defection from the low cooperative tariff τ^c will be given by the function $\Omega(\tau^c, \hat{\tau}^c_{-1})$. This function is decreasing in τ^c over the relevant range as in Figure 4.1 but increasing in $\hat{\tau}^c_{-1}$, the equilibrium most-cooperative tariff achieved in the previous round. Similarly, the one period stake in maintaining cooperation at τ^c will be given by the function $\omega(\tau^c, \hat{\tau}^c_{-1})$, which is decreasing in both τ^c and $\hat{\tau}^c_{-1}$. The discounted value of maintaining a cooperative trading relationship into the infinite future, suppressing (in notation only) dependence on the future path of equilibrium cooperative tariffs, will then be given by the function $V(\delta, \tau^c, \hat{\tau}^c_{-1})$ which is decreasing in both τ^c and $\hat{\tau}^c_{-1}$.[52] Hence, as a round is completed and the resulting tariff cuts yield a cooperative tariff $\hat{\tau}^c$ that causes current incentive constraints to bind $(\Omega(\hat{\tau}^c, \hat{\tau}^c_{-1}) = V(\delta, \hat{\tau}^c, \hat{\tau}^c_{-1}))$, a process is set in motion that will eventually diminish the rents that could be earned by a return to high tariffs, causing $\Omega(\tau^c, \hat{\tau}^c_{-1})$ to shift down and $V(\delta, \tau^c, \hat{\tau}^c_{-1})$ to shift up, and permitting a further round of liberalization to go forward at some point in the future.

5.4. The bicycle theory

That the process of liberalization can gather momentum and sew the seeds of further liberalization is encouraging for the prospects of reciprocal trade liberalization, but there is also a more ominous side: Anything that interrupts the expected future *progress* of the liberalization process may impact negatively on the ability to sustain the liberalization that has already been achieved. This notion embodies the core feature of what has become informally known as the "bicycle" theory of GATT. It emerges naturally when reciprocal liberalization is viewed from the perspective of a self-enforcing agreement. This point can be seen with reference to the augmented version of Figure 4.1 just discussed, by observing that the position of $V(\delta, \tau^c, \hat{\tau}^c_{-1})$ incorporates the entire anticipated equilibrium path of tariff liberalization. If an unanticipated event were to postpone or disrupt the expected path of future liberalization, then the discounted value of maintaining the integrity of the agreement into the future would have to be recalculated with this less favorable liberalization path taken into account. This implies that $V(\delta, \tau^c, \hat{\tau}^c_{-1})$ would shift down in Figure 4.1, and the current tariff level $\hat{\tau}^c$ achieved in the last round of liberalization could no longer be sustained (see Staiger, forthcoming, for an elaboration on this point). Hence, according to this view, past GATT successes become hostage to the continuation of the process that made those successes possible.

5.5. Regionalism and its implications for multilateral liberalization

In light of the delay and gradualism reflected in historical experience with general multilateral liberalization, it is natural that smaller groups of countries may find it both feasible and in their mutual interest to proceed with liberalization at a faster pace than the multilateral trading system at large. This requires a fundamental exception to the principle of MFN, and the conditions under which such an exception will be granted for purposes of forming a regional trade arrangement are spelled out in

---

[52]The function $V(\delta, \tau^c, \tau^c_{-1})$ will be decreasing in τ^c for two reasons. First, $V(\delta, \tau^c, \hat{\tau}^c_{-1})$ will be decreasing in τ^c for the same reason that $V(\delta, \tau^c)$ was in the original stationary model underlying Figure 4.1. And second, the equilibrium path of future tariffs will be higher if τ^c is higher, and this indirect effect will also make $V(\delta, \tau^c, \hat{\tau}^c_{-1})$ decreasing in τ^c.

Article XXIV of GATT. The chapter by Richard Baldwin and Tony Venables in this Handbook treats the many dimensions of regional integration in detail. Here I focus narrowly on one question: What are the implications of regional trade agreements for the operation of multilateral trade agreements?

From a historical perspective, it appears that the formation of regional trade agreements can provide an impetus to further liberalization at the multilateral level, at least judging from GATT's response to the formation and later broadening of the European Community: The future prospect of an integrated European Community market devoid of internal barriers but with common external tariffs was seen as a major factor leading to the Kennedy and Tokyo Rounds of GATT negotiations (see, for example, Bergsten, 1991). However, the impact of regional agreements on liberalization at the multilateral level has recently received renewed interest as countries have begun to turn with increasing frequency to regional trade agreements. The continued integration of the European Community culminating in EC92, and the integration of North America beginning with the U.S.–Canada Free Trade Agreement and continuing with the addition of Mexico under the North American Free Trade Agreement, are but the most prominent examples of regional trade liberalization that have occurred over the past decade. In contrast with the earlier episodes of regional integration, associated with these recent efforts to liberalize at the regional level has been a growing concern that continued efforts to liberalize at the multilateral level could be undermined as a consequence.

There are several ways to evaluate the basis for this concern. One possibility might be to ask how the internal political support for multilateral trade liberalization would be affected by regional integration. A second might be to ask how regional integration might affect the bargaining outcomes of multilateral trade negotiations. A third might be to consider the impact of regional integration on enforcement issues at the multilateral level. A complete answer might attempt to address all of these questions together, since they are unlikely to be independent. However, useful insights can be obtained by examining each of these questions in isolation, which is what the literature to date has done.

Levy (1994) considers the first question, that is, whether opportunities to negotiate bilateral trade agreements might undermine political support for broader multilateral liberalization. He establishes, in a median-voter model, that such an "undermining" result is, in fact, *not* possible if trade occurs in a standard $2 \times 2 \times 2$ Heckscher-Ohlin setting. However, in the presence of trade based in part on increasing returns and product variety, bilateral agreements between sufficiently similar countries *can* undermine political support for multilateral liberalization. The intuition for this result can be seen by considering the political implications of a bilateral agreement between two identically endowed countries when, absent such an agreement, political support in these two countries for multilateral liberalization would be "marginal", i.e. the median voters would be just slightly better off under multilateral free trade than under the status quo trading arrangements. If, in the absence of such a bilateral free trade area, the median voters in each of the two countries would only marginally prefer multilateral liberalization to the status quo, then their marginal support must reflect the near balance of two effects of multilateral liberalization on the welfare of the median voter. These are the redistributive Stolper-Samuelson effects and scale-economy/variety effects. Since the scale-economy/variety effects of multilateral liberalization are generally beneficial to all voters, including the median voter, the redistributive effects of the relative price changes that would come about from multilateral liberalization must work *against* the median voters in the two countries if they are in fact just marginally supportive of the move to multilateral free trade. But then a bilateral agreement between these two identically-endowed countries would allow them to achieve a portion of the "politically easy" scale-economy/variety gains without having to suffer any of the "politically difficult" redistributive effects that come from relative price movements triggered by broader multilateral liberalization in a dissimilar world. Such a bilateral agreement would surely improve the welfare of each country's median voter over the status quo, but would also tip the scales against political support in these two countries for further multilateral liberalization, since the median voters in each country would no longer care to suffer the redistributive effects of multilateral trade liberalization in order to enjoy the remaining scale effects. Levy shows that this "undermining" is most likely to occur when the countries combining into regional trading areas are quite similar.

The impact of regional agreements on multilateral trade negotiations has been studied by Ludema (1993) in a three-country, dynamic, non-cooperative bargaining model. Neutralizing any efficiency effects of regional agreements by maintaining the assumption of costless international transfers, Ludema shows that the *distribution* of the gains from trade can be influenced by regional agreements.[53] Ludema also draws a distinction between the bargaining advantages associated with the formation of a free trade area (whose member countries drop internal barriers to trade but maintain independent external trade policies) and those associated with a customs union (whose members also agree to adopt a common external trade policy). In effect, the formation of a customs union provides a bargaining advantage to its member countries as a result of the strategic commitment afforded by its common external trade policy. Free trade agreements, on the other hand, need not actually be formed to have an impact on bargaining outcomes: The proposer can make credible threats to sign bilateral agreements in the event that its multilateral offer is rejected.

Finally, I turn to the impact of regional integration on the enforceability of multilateral agreements. This issue has been addressed in the context of free trade agreements by Bagwell and Staiger (1993a), and in the context of customs unions by Bagwell and Staiger (1993b) and Bond and Syropoulos (1993). To interpret the

---

[53]Maggi (1994) establishes the possibility of efficiency gains from multilateral trade bargaining over what could be achieved with a web of bilateral trade bargains in the absence of costless international transfers.

findings of these papers, it is helpful to identify two principal effects of regional agreements: A *trade diversion effect*, whereby intra-member trade volume rises at the expense of trade between member and non-member countries; and a *market power effect*, which occurs if the member countries adopt a common external tariff policy (i.e. form a customs union) that enables them to impose higher (credible) tariffs on their multilateral trading partners should such punitive tariff action be desired.

Bond and Syropoulos (1993) compare the level of self-enforcing tariffs sustainable in an infinitely repeated tariff game when there are different (stationary) patterns of customs union formation. Their central finding is that the effectiveness of multilateral trade agreements is likely to suffer as a result of the (symmetric) formation of customs unions, i.e. the most-cooperative multilateral tariff $\hat{\tau}^c$ must rise with the formation of customs unions. In essence, they argue that both the one-time payoff from defection and the discounted value of maintaining future cooperation ($\Omega(\tau^c)$ and $V(\delta, \tau^c)$, respectively, in Figure 4.1) will rise with the formation of customs unions owing to the market power effect; they find, however, in simulations of their model that $\Omega(\tau^c)$ rises proportionately more than $V(\delta, \tau^c)$.[54]

Bagwell and Staiger (1993a,b) adopt a somewhat different focus. They view the period of *transition*, during which a regional agreement is negotiated and then implemented, as a crucial feature of the formation of regional trade arrangements, and explore how the process of regional bloc formation can alter the prior balance of incentives that supported the most-cooperative multilateral tariff level $\hat{\tau}^c$. Consider first the formation of a free trade agreement, which entails trade diversion away from multilateral trading partners at the end of the transition period. As the transition begins, the current temptation to cheat on the wider multilateral agreement remains basically as before ($\Omega(\tau^c)$ in Figure 4.1 remains in place), since multilateral trade patterns are at this point still the same. But the cost of a future trade war triggered by cheating on the multilateral agreement now seems less ominous ($V(\delta, \tau^c)$ shifts down in Figure 4.1) owing to the expected future trade diversion and reduced reliance on multilateral trading partners. Hence, as the transition associated with the formation of free trade agreements begins, the effectiveness of the multilateral trade agreement will deteriorate ($\hat{\tau}^c$ rises in Figure 4.1). By the end of the transition, however, the expected trade diversion will have occurred ($\Omega(\tau^c)$ will fall in Figure 4.1), and the imbalance between current and expected future multilateral trading relationships that arose during the transition will once again subside, allowing multilateral trade barriers to return to more normal levels as well ($\hat{\tau}^c$ falls back down in Figure 4.1). Thus, the effectiveness of multilateral trade agreements *worsens* during the transition period to a fully implemented free trade agreement, but improves again once the transition period is over.

In an analogous way, the market power effect of customs union formation leads to

---

[54]They also consider the effects of size asymmetries on tariff liberalization, and find that, in a two bloc world, liberalization is more difficult the greater the difference in bloc size.

the opposite prediction for the performance of multilateral trade agreements as this kind of regional bloc is formed: Prospects for multilateral tariff liberalization *improve* during the transition period to a fully implemented customs union, but worsen again once the transition period is over. Intuitively, as the transition period begins, non-member countries are less apt to take a confrontational stance in trade disputes with member countries of the emerging customs union, as the risks of a possible trade war with such countries now pose a greater deterrent to confrontation than they once did. Eventually, however, as the impact of the emerging customs unions on the degree of market power becomes felt, the "honeymoon" period for multilateral liberalization ends, and a less favorable balance between current and expected future conditions reemerges.

6. Safeguards and managed trade

If the extended decline in multilateral tariff levels represents one major feature of post-war trade policy, the move toward "special" protection which has accompanied it represents a second. As noted in Section 2, the possibility of temporary reversions to high protection or on occasion even permanent reversal of previous tariff reductions was anticipated to be a part of the natural process of liberalization, and was viewed as an inevitable consequence of low levels of baseline protection envisioned by GATT. But while the safeguards included in GATT were meant to keep the inevitable deviations from rigid tariff bindings within GATT rules, in practice the growing use of VERs, VIEs, OMAs, and tariff programs that are tailor made to suit the needs of particular sectors signals a failure of the rules to contain these actions, and has given rise to the term "managed trade".

There are several dimensions on which the so-called "grey-area" measures that form the tools of managed trade might be said to have spilled over the confines placed on them by GATT rules. A first dimension is simply the frequency and intensity with which they have been used. Recent estimates by Trefler (1993), for example, suggest that the non-tariff barriers in place for the United States manufacturing sector in 1983 reduced U.S. manufacturing imports by 24 percent, calling into question the "special" nature of the protection that takes this form. A second dimension is the duration of many of these grey-area measures. While for the most part safeguard actions are viewed as temporary measures within GATT, a number of instances of extended protection, e.g. textiles and the Multi-Fiber Arrangement, have clearly surpassed any reasonable definition of temporary. A third dimension is the form that these measures have taken, often providing for the "target" country to share in administration and rent-collecting actions associated with the measure.[55] In

---

[55]There is also the fact that these measures are often quantitative in nature, and therefore go against GATT's emphasis on "tariffication". See note 12 for a discussion of some of the literature relevant to this issue.

this section I will discuss a number of papers which bear on each of these dimensions.

6.1. Frequency and intensity

What does it mean for countries to utilize the tools of special protection "too" frequently and aggressively? Two possible interpretations are suggested by the literature, and both can ultimately be traced to weak enforcement mechanisms. These interpretations correspond to the two environments described in Section 3 where adherence to international rules could be beneficial, and in each case weak enforcement of the rules limits their potential usefulness.

Where the central strategic interaction is across governments, Bagwell and Staiger (1990) have built on the work of Rotemberg and Saloner (1986) to show that weak international enforcement mechanisms will lead to episodes of special protection when trade volumes surge, as a way to cope with the temporary incentive problems that accompany such trade swings. More specifically, a period of high trade volume will tend to be associated with an especially high payoff in pursuing unilaterally preferred trade policies in that period. In terms of the incentives depicted in Figure 4.1, this will correspond to an upward shift in $\Omega(\tau^c)$. If this high trade volume is perceived as transitory, corresponding to a temporary "surge" with expected future trade volumes left unaltered, then the expected future cost of a trade war will be unaltered ($V(\delta, \tau^c)$ will not shift in Figure 4.1). Where the desire to avoid a trade war is sufficiently strong so that enforcement was not an issue prior to the surge ($V(\delta, \tau^c)$ is greater than $\Omega(\tau^c)$ at $\bar{\tau}$), no tariff response may be needed. However, if enforcement is sufficiently weak ($V(\delta, \tau^c)$ is sufficiently low in Figure 4.1), the tariff binding that was supportable prior to the surge in trade volume can no longer be sustained. This does not imply that the international trade agreement need break down. Instead, countries can agree to use special protection during periods of exceptionally high trade volume to mitigate the unilateral incentives to defect.[56] The frequency and intensity of use of special protection according to this view is then determined as the minimum required to maintain the incentive compatibility of the overall agreement in the presence of volatile trade swings. Generally, the weaker the enforcement mechanism, the greater the dependence on special protection necessary to maintain the integrity of the agreement.[57]

A second interpretation of the too-frequent use of special protection is associated with the literature on time-consistent trade policy and the possible role of international rules in providing governments with greater credibility in their use of trade policies in responding to injured sectors. Where these rules are weak and domestic institutions

---

[56] For some empirical evidence relating to this interpretation, see Dick (1994).

[57] Maggi's (1994) findings on the role of multilateral enforcement mechanisms in the presence of local imbalances of power (e.g. bilateral trade imbalances) also suggest an interpretation of VIEs as a mechanism for reducing local imbalances of power when multilateral enforcement mechanisms are weak.

inadequate to provide the needed commitment, special protection is likely to be over-utilized relative to a government's optimal but time-inconsistent plan [see, for example, Staiger and Tabellini (1987), Matsuyama (1990), Brainard (1994), and Mayer (1994)]. But while these papers all suggest that GATT rules could be helpful as a commitment device when confronting injured sectors, it is in precisely these situations that GATT commitments can be suspended under the safeguards provisions of the agreement.[58] There would appear to be a tradeoff between flexibility and rigidity in such circumstances that, as indicated above, may be an important element of the design of international trade agreements when enforcement mechanisms are weak, but may also serve to undercut or at least severely limit the effectiveness of international agreements in providing the kind of commitment benefits suggested by the literature.[59] If this is the case, then GATT rules may provide little in the way of commitment when countries face import surges, and over-utilization of special protection may be the rule rather than the exception.

6.2. Duration

Matsuyama (1990) is concerned with the credibility of temporary protection in a situation where the government would find it optimal to offer such protection if the "temporary breathing space" were used by the protected industry to make adjustments that prepared it to face import competition without the benefit of protection in the future. One interpretation of the reduced-form payoffs in his model is that the government has distributional concerns and would be willing to offer temporary protection to an injured sector if such protection allowed adjustment to import competition to occur in a way that reduced the resulting distributional consequences, e.g. minimized sectoral unemployment.

The structure of the game played between a government and an import-competing industry in Matsuyama is as follows: In the first period, the government chooses whether or not to liberalize the (pre-existing) tariff. If it chooses to liberalize, the game ends. But if it chooses to protect for the period, then the industry chooses whether to "prepare" for liberalization next period or not. This structure repeats itself in all subsequent periods until the game ends; i.e. until the government chooses to liberalize. The general credibility issue arising here is in regard to the temporary nature of the protection afforded. If the government finds that it is in its interest to offer "temporary" protection today so that the industry can use today to prepare for trade liberalization tomorrow, and if tomorrow comes and the industry has *not* chosen

---

[58]Empirical evidence that GATT rules do serve this function more generally, and that escape clause actions do not benefit from this disciplining role, is presented in Staiger and Tabellini (forthcoming), though Rodrik (1993) provides some evidence to the contrary.

[59]The literature on strategic delegation [see, for example, Katz (1991)] may suggest promising avenues for research in this area.

to prepare, what ensures that the government will not renew the "temporary" protection tomorrow, especially since it will then find itself tomorrow in exactly the same position as today? And if the industry can be sure that "temporary" protection will be renewed tomorrow if it chooses not to prepare today, then it will never choose to prepare, and the government's "temporary" protection program cannot be temporary.

Matsuyama examines the set of Nash outcomes to this game under a number of equilibrium refinements that imply successively more stringent "credibility" criteria. He finds that the optimal one-period protection plan – give the industry one period to prepare and then liberalize – will not be renegotiation-proof in either the sense of Farrell and Maskin (1989) or Pearce (1987). The interpretation of the possible effects of rules in this context would be that, through adherence to them, a government might be able to relax some of the equilibrium refinements that rule out the optimal protective policy as an equilibrium outcome. However, if international enforcement mechanisms are weak, so too would be the effect of international rules on reducing the length of "temporary" protection.

6.3. Form

Managed trade is often characterized by a distinctive form of intervention. Frequently, the protective measures are negotiated, and often the agreement calls for sharing of administration and rent-collecting functions by the countries involved. Several papers have addressed the question of what role such forms of protection, as opposed to a more standard unilaterally-imposed tariff, could play in facilitating or hindering the operation of broader international trade agreements. While institutional efforts have been made to reign in these forms of special protection (the safeguards provisions of the Uruguay Round GATT agreement explicitly proscribe the former grey area measures) the literature suggests reasons for at least some caution in determining how far to go in this regard, in that eliminating completely the ability of countries to use these forms of protection might actually interfere with the operation of the broader trade agreements to which they are a perceived threat.

Feenstra and Lewis (1991) explore whether the rent-sharing aspects of managed trade might serve some role in facilitating trade agreements between countries facing private political pressure. In a setting where countries must negotiate a long-term trade agreement that specifies a trade policy "safeguard" action under all future contingencies of political pressure, and where that political pressure will be privately observed, Feenstra and Lewis derive the optimal incentive-compatible trade policies. They interpret the form of the optimal policy to be a tariff-quota. The rent-sharing aspect of such negotiated protection serves the role of maintaining incentive compatibility of the agreement, as a government will then have incentive to announce truthfully its privately observed political pressure. That is, the truthful reporting of political pressure is ensured by transferring some of the rents from special protection to foreigners. Bagwell and Staiger (1990), Ono (1991), and Eaton and Ono (1992) also find that the distribution of rents created by special protection will generally be an important factor in maintaining incentive compatibility of trade agreements, though the incentive compatibility issues analyzed by these authors arise in the context of enforcement rather than truth-telling.

7. Antidumping law and countervailing duties

While antidumping and countervailing duty laws are typically referred to as "unfair trade" laws, the practices they are meant to address (dumping by foreign firms and subsidies by foreign governments, respectively) are not generally proscribed by GATT.[60] As Jackson (1969) notes:

> ...The GATT approach was to leave these dumping and subsidy measures generally legal, but to arm importing nations with an exception to GATT obligations to enable them to defend against these practices by antidumping and countervailing duties. [Jackson (1969, p. 403)].

In the case of dumping, this approach evidently reflects the fact that such behavior is a phenomenon of private firms, not governments, and proscribing it is therefore beyond the scope of traditional government obligations under GATT [see Jackson (1969, p. 402)]. In the case of subsidies, this approach reflects the view, as expressed in the preamble of the GATT Subsidies Code, that such policies can have a legitimate role to play in promoting national objectives. Therefore, the role of international trade agreements where subsidies are concerned is generally not to attempt to control their use directly, but simply to keep to a minimum their trade effects. Antidumping and countervailing duty provisions have as a result found their way into many trade agreements to counteract actions which are out of reach of direct disciplines.

Article VI of GATT lays out conditions under which antidumping and countervailing duty actions can be taken with the intent of preventing their misuse. Characterizing and understanding the potential for misusing these provisions, as well as the potential for unintended effects of the provisions even when they are used in the circumstances for which they were intended, has been the focus of a growing literature that I discuss briefly below. However, before turning to this literature, I briefly discuss the prior question of whether efforts to counteract the effects of foreign subsidies or foreign dumping make sense from an economic perspective. That is, while the intended role of GATT's Article VI and provisions like it in other trade

---

[60]There is no general proscription against dumping in GATT, while that against subsidies is limited to export subsidies on non-primary products for developed countries [see Jackson (1969, p. 377), and Hufbauer and Erb (1984, ch. 2)].

agreements may be to keep in check the potential for misusing antidumping and countervailing duty actions, why should an international trade agreement allow these kinds of actions to be taken in the first place?[61]

7.1. The response to dumping and export subsidies

Because the antidumping and countervailing duty provisions of an international agreement such as GATT specify conditions under which exceptions can be made to certain obligations under the agreement, one approach to evaluating the place of these provisions in a broader trade agreement is to view them as additional "safeguards", similar to a general escape clause but available only under particular circumstances.[62] From this perspective, two central questions arise: How do these provisions differ from those associated with general escape clause actions?; and to the extent that they do differ, do the circumstances under which these provisions are made available warrant special exceptions to obligations under an international trade agreement beyond what are available from a general escape clause?

As to the first question, there are several important differences between antidumping and countervailing duty provisions and the escape clause found in GATT and other trade agreements. First and most obvious is the fact that antidumping and countervailing duty actions are not available to a country unless foreign firms are found to have dumped or foreign governments subsidized products for export.[63] On the other hand, if such actions are found, the degree of injury to the domestic industry and the causal link from imports necessary to elicit antidumping or countervailing duty remedies is low as compared to the injury threshold for escape clause actions [see, for example, Jackson (1989, pp. 149–165)]. Against this must be weighed the differences in actual remedies under each provision. While escape clause remedies are typically imposed against imports from all sources and are intended to be used only temporarily and to the extent necessary to remedy the injury, remedies under antidumping and countervailing duty law are intended to counter the amount of dumping or subsidization found, and thus apply to selected countries at levels and

---

[61]See Dixit (1988) for an interesting analysis of the role of antidumping and countervailing duties in a setting where foreign government policies are set exogenously, and Collie (1991) for an extension of Dixit's results on countervailing duties to a setting where foreign government policies are responsive to domestic policy choices. Gruenspecht (1988) observes that mutual antidumping enforcement across countries can lead to a Prisoner's Dilemma situation. However, none of these papers address the general role of antidumping and countervailing duty provisions in the context of international trade agreements.

[62]Prusa and Hansen (forthcoming) describe this view in their analysis of the industry-level choice between filing an antidumping or countervailing duty petition versus an escape clause petition.

[63]Recall that dumping is defined as exporting products at export prices "below fair value", i.e. either below the prices of comparable products for sale in the domestic market of the exporting country or below costs of production. The definition of a subsidy is a "bounty" or "grant" offered to producers, although coming to agreement on what constitutes a subsidy in practice is an issue fraught with difficulty [see, for example, Hufbauer and Erb (1984)].

durations dictated by the foreign practices that the remedies are supposed to counteract. While the selective coverage of antidumping and countervailing duty actions diminishes their overall protective effect, the level and duration of the remedies involved combined with the low injury threshold required to secure these remedies evidently is sufficient to make them overwhelmingly the preferred "safe-guard" action. This relative popularity is borne out in practice by the degree of utilization of each kind of remedy. Messerlin (1990) reports, for example, that of the 2,348 notifications to GATT of restrictions imposed between 1979 and 1988, over 75 percent were antidumping actions and another 18 percent were countervailing duty actions, with safeguards actions accounting for only 3 percent of the total. It seems safe to conclude that the conditions for granting exceptions to international obligations are significantly more attractive when dumping or foreign subsidies can be asserted.

This leads to the second question raised above: Is there a basis for granting countries exceptions from their obligations under an international trade agreement more readily when dumping or foreign subsidies are involved? A satisfactory answer to this question requires attention to the underlying issues of why these foreign practices occur and what are their likely effects on other countries. Reviewing the literature on why firms dump or why governments subsidize their export sectors is beyond the scope of this chapter, and the specific question posed above has not been formally analyzed within the context of this literature.[64] Thus, a formal answer must await further work. What can be said, however, is this: While a given fall in the price of foreign exports may well have the same impact on the domestic economy regardless of whether it is caused by a foreign government subsidy, a foreign firm that is dumping, or a change in the foreign firm's cost structure, this is *not* enough to conclude that the nature of the response to such a price shock within the broader context of an international trade agreement should be independent of the causes of that shock. Drawing this conclusion would ignore the strategic dimension of the problem, i.e. that the nature of the government response to foreign price changes may affect the nature of the foreign price changes themselves in a manner which depends on their underlying causes.[65]

---

[64]Recent papers exploring the circumstances under which firms might engage in dumping include Ethier (1982), Brander and Krugman (1983), Pinto (1986), Gruenspecht (1988), Bagwell and Staiger (1989), Berck and Perloff (1990), Staiger and Wolak (1992), Weinstein (1992), Anderson (1992, 1993), and Clarida (1993). The voluminous literature on strategic trade policy (see the chapter by James Brander in this Handbook) and political economy (see the chapter by Dani Rodrik in this Handbook) is relevant for understanding why governments might subsidize their export sectors, as is the literature on informational barriers to entry [see, for example, Grossman and Horn (1988), Bagwell and Staiger (1989), and Bagwell (1991)].

[65]Certainly outside the context of a trade agreement such a conclusion would be false [see, for example, Collie (1991), on the implications of strategic interactions across governments for the optimal countervailing duty response to a foreign government's export subsidy policy].

7.2. The uses and effects of antidumping and countervailing duty actions

To the extent that antidumping and countervailing duty provisions do have a place in international trade agreements, the role of these provisions has been to place restrictions on the use of such actions. In this section I will discuss some of the literature that relates to the possible need for international constraints in this regard and the nature of the unintended effects and outright misuse of antidumping and countervailing duty actions that could occur in the absence of effective constraints. Three kinds of potential problems with the use of antidumping and countervailing duty law have been discussed in the economics literature: Measurement bias; unintended effects of "legitimate" use; and abuse. I will briefly discuss each in turn.

The measurement problems associated with administering these laws have received an enormous amount of attention [see, for example, the papers in Boltuck and Litan (1991)]. This literature has focussed primarily on the way that dumping and subsidy margins have been calculated by the administrating authorities, and has detailed numerous difficulties with these procedures. A consistent finding is that there are strong biases in the methodologies adopted for dumping margin and subsidy calculations that predispose the authority to find a positive margin or subsidy. Many authors conclude that international rules regarding the acceptable procedures in calculating dumping and subsidy margins must be tightened if protectionist biases in the administering of these laws are to be avoided.

A number of papers have focussed on the unintended effects of enforcement of antidumping and countervailing duty laws that can arise even when the kinds of measurement issues pointed out above are absent and when the laws are being put to the purposes for which they seem to be designed. Gruenspecht (1988) explores the implications of mutual antidumping enforcement in a two-country two-period duopoly model in which dumping is defined as exporting at a price below marginal cost and the technology exhibits firm-specific learning-by-doing. The dynamic economies of scale can give rise to dumping in the first period, as firms attempt to capture a larger share of the second-period profits via lower second-period costs. Here, unilateral antidumping enforcement can serve as a rent-shifting device, but mutual antidumping enforcement simply helps firms restrain their first-period output and raise first-period price, and in so doing raises second period prices and costs as well. A situation analogous to the Prisoner's Dilemma can result from mutual antidumping enforcement, with implications for the potential benefits of the restraining effects of international rules. Anderson (1993) makes a different point with regard to the unintended effects of antidumping law. Noting that the remedies available under antidumping law have in practice included "grey area" measures such as VERs, and that export licenses under a VER (which have rents associated with them) are often allocated on the basis of historical market shares, Anderson shows that stronger antidumping enforcement, by raising the probability of future VERs, can actually encourage dumping, as exporting firms are led to price more aggressively in order to secure a stake in the possibility of future VER-generated rents. Bagwell and Staiger (1989) reach a similar conclusion in a different context with regard to antidumping and countervailing duty law: In a setting where foreign firms view dumping as a way to break informational barriers to entry in an export market, domestic enforcement of antidumping and countervailing duty laws can encourage foreign export subsidies, as foreign firms refrain from dumping and foreign governments are induced to offer export subsidies instead (despite the countervailing duties imposed by importing countries) in order to break the informational barrier to entry. Finally, when a foreign monopolist dumps in order to reduce the cost of holding excess capacity in periods of slack demand, antidumping laws can restrict trade even when they are not being utilized, because the foreign monopolist will choose a smaller capacity in the presence of antidumping enforcement [see Staiger and Wolak (1992)].

I now come to the third kind of problem associated with these laws, namely that of abuse. Prusa (1992) has argued that antidumping petitions that are withdrawn by the domestic industry before a final determination, and that fail therefore to secure an antidumping duty, nevertheless may restrict post-investigation trade flows by as much as if antidumping duties had actually been imposed. Essentially, he argues that domestic firms can use the threat of antidumping duties, together with the protection from domestic antitrust laws afforded when an antidumping proceeding is in progress, to bargain with foreign firms over domestic market share, and that the antidumping petition is withdrawn by the domestic industry if and when an acceptable bargain is struck.[66] Staiger and Wolak (1991) focus on the possible effects of antidumping law on trade flows and prices *during* the investigation process. They argue that domestic firms may make strategic use of an on-going antidumping investigation into the pricing and sales practices of their foreign competitors in order to prevent the occurrence of price wars that otherwise might be triggered by temporary downturns in demand and capacity utilization. Their results suggest that domestic firms may value the competition-dampening effects of an on-going antidumping investigation for its own sake, and may initiate such petitions when capacity utilization is low with no expectation that they would actually result in duties or other remedies.[67]

Taken together, these papers suggest some of the many ways that restrictions on the use of antidumping and countervailing duty law might be beneficial. But a more complete understanding of the appropriate role, if any, that these laws should play in the broader context of international trade agreements appears still to be needed.

---

[66]Prusa (1991) provides some empirical support for this view.
[67]Evidence of this is provided in Staiger and Wolak (1994).

8. Conclusion

I conclude this chapter with four observations on possible directions for future research on trade rules and institutions. First, while there would appear to be many potentially fruitful ways to build on the research reviewed above, there are important dimensions of international trade agreements that seem to be almost completely unrepresented in the formal economics literature. Some of these areas have only recently become the subjects of serious trade discussions (for example, intellectual property rights, services, and investment). Others are noteworthy for their long omission from international trade agreements despite their obvious importance (for example, agriculture). Each of these areas presents distinct challenges for the design of international trade agreements, and formal economic analysis of the issues involved is needed. Moreover, the general topic of the sequence in which issues should be incorporated into international trade agreements seems an important and fruitful area to explore. Second, the important interaction between domestic and international rules and institutions as they relate to trade policy is a feature that needs to be introduced into the formal analysis reviewed above. Third, the degree to which governments can increase their credibility with the private sector by entering into international trade agreements that operate under the kinds of constraints discussed above is still an open question, and one that seems particularly important for improving our understanding of the benefits international trade agreements are capable of delivering. And finally, the different approaches to international rules and institutions for trade and for macroeconomic policy, both in their actual design (for example, contrast the approaches of the International Monetary Fund and World Bank with GATT) and in the academic literature concerned with them [contrast the literature reviewed here with that reviewed in the chapter by Torten Persson and Guido Tabellini in this Handbook and in Canzoneri and Henderson (1991)] suggests that each literature could learn from the other about the distinctive nature of the problems faced by policy-makers in these two arenas.

References

Abreu, D. (1986), "Extremal equilibria of oligopolistic supergames", Journal of Economic Theory 39:191–225.

Abreu, D. (1988), "On the theory of infinitely repeated games with discounting", Econometrica 56:383–396.

Abreu, D., P. Milgrom, and D. Pearce (1991), "Information and timing in repeated partnerships", Econometrica 59:1713–1733.

Anderson, J.E. (1992), "Domino dumping I: Competitive exporters", American Economic Review 82:65–83.

Anderson, J.E. (1993), "Domino dumping II: Anti-dumping", Journal of International Economics 35:133–150.

Bac, M. and H. Raff (1994), "A theory of trade concessions", mimeo, Indiana University.

Bagwell, K. (1991), "Optimal export policy for a new-product monopoly", American Economic Review 81:1156–1169.

Bagwell, K. and R.W. Staiger (1989), "The role of export subsidies when product quality is unknown", Journal of International Economics 27:69–89.

Bagwell, K. and R.W. Staiger (1990), "A theory of managed trade", American Economic Review 80, 779–795.

Bagwell, K. and R.W. Staiger (1993a), "Multilateral tariff cooperation during the formation of free trade areas", National Bureau of Economic Research Working Paper No. 4364.

Bagwell, K. and R.W. Staiger (1993b), "Multilateral tariff cooperation during the formation of customs unions", National Bureau of Economic Research Working Paper No. 4543.

Baldwin, R.E. and R.N. Clarke (1987), "Game-modeling multilateral trade negotiations", Journal of Policy Modeling 9:257–284.

Bayard, T.O. and K.A. Elliott (1992), "'Aggressive unilateralism' and Section 301: Market opening or market closing?", The World Economy 15:685–705.

Berck, P. and J.M. Perloff (1990), "Dynamic dumping", International Journal of Industrial Organization 8:225–243.

Bergsten, F.C. (1991), "Commentary: The move toward free trade zones", in: Policy implications of trade and currency zones (Federal Reserve Bank of Kansas City, Jackson Hole, WY).

Bergsten, F.C. and W.R. Cline (1983), "Trade policy in the 1980's: An overview", in: W.R.Cline, ed., Trade policy in the 1980's (MIT Press, Cambridge, MA).

Bernheim, B.D. and Whinston, M.D. (1990), "Multimarket contact and collusive behavior", Rand Journal of Economics 21:1–26.

Bhagwati, J. (1988), Protectionism (MIT Press, Cambridge, MA).

Bhagwati, J. (1991), The world trading system at risk (Princeton University Press, Princeton, NJ).

Bond E.W. and C. Syropoulos (1993), "Trading blocs and the sustainability of inter-regional cooperation", manuscript, University of Pennsylvania.

Brainard, S.L. (1994), "Last one out wins: Trade policy in an international exit game", International Economic Review 35:151–172.

Brainard, S.L. and T. Verdier (1993), "The political economy of declining industries: Senescent industry collapse revisited", National Bureau of Economic Research Working Paper No. 4606.

Brander, J.A. and P. Krugman (1983), "A 'reciprocal dumping' model of international trade", Journal of International Economics 15:313–321.

Boltuck, R. and R.E. Litan (1991), Down in the dumps: Administration of the unfair trade laws (Brookings Institute, Washington, DC).

Canzoneri, M.B. and D.W. Henderson (1991), Monetary policy in interdependent economies: A game-theoretic approach (MIT Press, Cambridge, MA).

Caplin, A. and K. Krishna (1988), "Tariffs and the most-favored-nation clause: A game theoretic approach", Seoul Journal of Economics 1:267–289.

Carmichael, C. (1987), "The control of export credit subsidies and its welfare consequences", Journal of International Economics 23:1–19.

Clarida, R.H. (1993), "Entry, dumping, and shakeout, American Economic Review 83:180–202.

Collie, D. (1991), "Export subsidies and countervailing duties", Journal of International Economics 31:309–324.

Conybeare, J.A.C. (1987), Trade wars: The theory and practice of international commercial rivalry (Columbia University Press, New York).

Copeland, B.R. (1989), "Tariffs and quotas: Retaliation and negotiation with two instruments of protection", Journal of International Economics 26:179–188.

Copeland, B.R. (1990), "Strategic interaction among nations: Negotiable and non-negotiable trade barriers", Canadian Journal of Economics 23:84–108.

Corden, W.M. (1984), "The normative theory of international trade", in: R.W. Jones and P.B. Kenen, eds., Handbook of international economics, volume 1 (North-Holland, Amsterdam).

Dam, K.W. (1970), The GATT: Law and international economic organization (University of Chicago Press, Chicago).

Devereux, M.B. (1992), "Growth, specialization, and trade liberalization", mimeo, Queens University.

Devereux, M.B. (1993), "Sustaining free trade in repeated games without government commitment", mimeo, Queens University.

Dewatripont, M. and G. Roland (1992), "Economic reform and dynamic political constraints", Review of Economic Studies 59:703–730.

Dick, A.R. (1994), "Explaining managed trade: Non-cooperative politics or cooperative economics?", mimeo, University of California, Los Angeles.

Dixit, A. (1987), "Strategic aspects of trade policy", in: Trewman F. Bewley, ed., Advances in economic theory: Fifth world congress (Cambridge University Press, New York).

Dixit, A. (1988), "Antidumping and countervailing duties under oligopoly", European Economic Review 32:55–68.

Dixit, A. (1989), "Trade and insurance with imperfectly observed outcomes", Quarterly Journal of Economics 104:195–203.

Eaton, J. and Y. Ono (1992), "Tariff wars, retaliation, and managed trade", mimeo, Boston University.

Eaton, J. and G.M. Grossman (1985), "Tariffs as insurance: Optimal commercial policy when domestic markets are incomplete", Canadian Journal of Economics 18:258–272.

Ethier, W.J. (1982), "Dumping", Journal of Political Economy 90:487–506.

Farrell, J. and E. Maskin (1989), "Renegotiation in repeated games", Games and Economic Behavior 1:327–360.

Feenstra, R.C. and T.R. Lewis (1991), "Negotiated trade restrictions with private political pressure", Quarterly Journal of Economics, November.

Finger, J.M. and K.C. Fung (1993), "Can competition policy control '301'?", mimeo, The World Bank.

Friedman, J. (1986), Game theory with applications to economics (Oxford University Press, New York).

Fung, K.C. and R.W. Staiger, "Trade liberalization and trade adjustment assistance", in: M. Canzoneri, W. Ethier, and V. Grilli, eds., The new transatlantic economy, forthcoming.

Furusawa, T. (1994), "The negotiation of sustainable tariffs", in: Three essays in the new international trade theory, Ph.D. Dissertation, The University of Wisconsin.

Goldberg, P. (1995), "Strategic export promotion in the absence of government precommitment", International Economic Review 36:407–426.

Green, E.J. and R.H. Porter (1984), "Noncooperative collusion under imperfect price information," Econometrica 52:87–100.

Grossman, G.M. and H. Horn (1988), "Infant-industry protection reconsidered: The case of informational barriers to entry", Quarterly Journal of Economics 103:767–787.

Grossman, G.M. and E. Helpman (1993), "Trade wars and trade talks", National Bureau of Economic Research Working Paper No. 4280.

Gruenspecht, H.K. (1988), "Dumping and dynamic competition", Journal of International Economics 25:225–248.

Hudec, R.E. (1975), The GATT legal system and world trade diplomacy, 2nd ed. (Butterworth, Salem, NH).

Hudec, R.E. (1990), "Dispute settlement", in: Jeffrey Schott, ed., Completing the Uruguay round, (Institute for International Economics, Washington, DC).

Hudec, R.E. (1993), Enforcing International Trade Law: The evolution of the modern GATT legal system. (Butterworth, Salem, NH).

Hufbauer, G.C. and J.S. Erb (1984), Subsidies in international trade (MIT Press, Cambridge, MA).

Hungerford, T.L. (1991), "GATT: A cooperative equilibrium in a noncooperative trading regime?", Journal of International Economics 31:357–369.

Jackson, J. (1969), World trade and the law of GATT (Bobbs-Merrill Co, Inc., New York).

Jackson, J. (1989), The world trading system (MIT Press, Cambridge, MA).

Jensen, R. and M. Thursby (1984), "Free trade: Two non-cooperative equilibrium approaches", Ohio State University Working Paper No. 58.

Johnson, H.G. (1953), "Optimum tariffs and retaliation", Review of Economic Studies 21:142–153.

Katz, M. (1991), "Game-playing agents: Unobservable contracts as precommitments", Rand Journal of Economics 22:307–328.

Kehoe, P. (1989), "Policy cooperation among benevolent governments may be undesirable", Review of Economic Studies 56:289–296.

Kennan, J. and R. Riezman (1988), "Do big countries win tariff wars?", International Economic Review 29:81–85.

Kennan, J. and R.B. Wilson (1993), "Bargaining with private information", Journal of Economic Literature 31:45–104.

Kovenock, D. and M. Thursby (1992), "GATT, dispute settlement and cooperation", Economics and Politics 4:151–170.

Kowalczyk, C. and T. Sjostrom (1994), "Bringing GATT into the core", Economica 61:301–317.

Kydland, F.E. and E.C. Prescott (1977), "Rules rather than discretion: The inconsistency of optimal plans", Journal of Political Economy 85:473–491.

Lapan, H.E. (1988), "The optimal tariff, production lags and time consistency", American Economic Review 78:395–401.

Levy, P.I. (1994), "A political-economic analysis of free trade agreements", in: Political economy and free trade agreements, Ph.D. Dissertation, Stanford University.

Ludema, R.D. (1990), "Optimal international trade agreements and dispute settlement procedures", working paper, University of Western Ontario.

Ludema, R.D. (1991), "International trade bargaining and the most-favored nation clause", Economics and Politics 3:1–20.

Ludema, R.D. (1993), "On the value of preferential trade agreements in multilateral negotiations", mimeo, University of Western Ontario.

Maggi, G. (1994), "The role of multilateral institutions in international trade cooperation", in: Essays on trade policy and international institutions under incomplete information, Ph.D. Dissertation, Stanford University.

Mailath, G. and A. Postlewaite (1990), "Asymmetric information bargaining problems with many agents", Review of Economic Studies 57:351–367.

Maskin, E. and D. Newbery (1990), "Disadvantageous oil tariffs and dynamic consistency", American Economic Review 80:143–156.

Matsuyama, K. (1990), "Perfect equilibria in a trade liberalization game", American Economic Review 80:480–492.

Mayer, W. (1994), "Optimal pursuit of safeguard actions over time", in: A.V. Deardorff and R.M. Stern, eds., Analytical and negotiating issues in the global trading system (University of Michigan Press, Ann Arbor, MI).

McLaren, J. (1994), "Size, sunk costs, and Judge Bowker's objection to free trade", mimeo, Columbia University.

McMillan, J. (1990), "The economics of Section 301: A game-theoretic guide", Economics and Politics 2:45–57.

Messerlin, P.A. (1990), "Antidumping", in: J.J. Schott, ed., Completing the uruguay round, (Institute for International Economics, Washington, DC).

Mussa, M. (1984), "The adjustment process and the timing of trade liberalization", National Bureau of Economic Research Working Paper No. 1458.

North, D.C. (1994), "Economic performance through time", American Economic Review 84:359–398.

Ono, Y. (1991), "Orderly-marketing arrangements in the context of the GATT regime", Economics and Politics 3:151–162.

Page, S.A.B. (1979), "The management of international trade", in: R. Major, ed., Britain's trade and exchange rate policy (Heinemann, London).

Pearce, D.G. (1987), "Renegotiation-proof equilibria: Collective rationality and intertemporal cooperation", Cowles Foundation Discussion Paper No. 855.

Persson,T. and G. Tabellini (1990), Macroeconomic policy, credibility and politics (Harwood, London).

Pinto, B. (1986), "Repeated games and the reciprocal dumping model of trade", Journal of International Economics 20:357–366.

Prusa, T. J. (1991), "The selection of antidumping cases for withdrawal", in: R.E. Baldwin, ed., Empirical studies of commercial policy (University of Chicago Press, Chicago).

Prusa, T.J. (1992), "Why are so many antidumping petitions withdrawn?", Journal of International Economics 33:1–20.

Prusa, T.J. and W.L. Hansen, "The road most travelled: The rise of title VII protection", The World Economy, forthcoming.

Riezman, R. (1991), "Dynamic tariffs with asymmetric information", Journal of International Economics 30:267–283.

Robinson, J. (1947), "Beggar-my-neighbor remedies for unemployment", in: Essays on the theory of employment, 2nd Edition (Basil Blackwell, Oxford). [Reprinted as Chapter 17 of Readings in the theory of international trade (George Allen and Unwin, London) 1950.]

Rodrik, D. (1993), "Taking trade policy seriously: Export subsidization as a case study in policy effectiveness", National Bureau of Economic Research Working Paper No. 4567.

Rotemberg, J.J. and G. Saloner (1986), "A supergame-theoretic model of price wars during booms", American Economic Review 76:390–407.

Rubinstein, A. (1982), "Perfect equilibrium in a bargaining model", Econometrica 50:97–109.

Scitovszky, T. (1942), "A reconsideration of the theory of tariffs", Review of Economic Studies 9. [Reprinted as Chapter 16 of Readings in the theory of international trade (George Allen and Unwin, London) 1950.]

Staiger, R.W., "A theory of gradual trade liberalization", forthcoming in: Deardorff, A., Levinsohn, J., and Stern, R., eds., New directions in trade theory (University of Michigan Press, Ann Arbor).

Staiger, R.W. and G. Tabellini (1987), "Discretionary trade policy and excessive protection", American Economic Review 77:823–837.

Staiger, R.W. and G. Tabellini (1989), "Rules and discretion in trade policy", European Economic Review 33:1265–1277.

Staiger, R.W. and G. Tabellini (1991), "Rules versus discretion in trade policy: An empirical analysis", in: R.E. Baldwin, ed., Empirical studies of commercial policy (University of Chicago Press, Chicago and London).

Staiger, R.W. and G. Tabellini, "Does commitment matter in trade policy?", Economics and Politics, forthcoming.

Staiger, R.W. and F.A. Wolak (1992), "The effect of domestic antidumping law in the presence of foreign monopoly", Journal of International Economics 32:265–287.

Staiger, R.W. and F.A. Wolak (1991), "Strategic use of antidumping law to enforce international collusion", mimeo, Stanford University.

Staiger, R.W. and F.A. Wolak (1994), "Measuring industry specific protection: Antidumping in the United States", Brookings Papers on Economic Activity: Microeconomics, 51–118.

Talbot, R.B. (1978), The chicken war: An international trade conflict (Iowa State University Press, Ames, IA).

Tornell, A. (1991), "On the ineffectiveness of made-to-measure protectionist programs", in: E. Helpman and A. Razin, eds., International trade and trade policy (MIT Press, Cambridge, MA).

Trefler, D. (1993), "Trade liberalization and the theory of endogenous protection: An econometric study of U.S. import policy", Journal of Political Economy 101:138–160.

Viner, J. (1924), "The most-favored-nation clause in american commercial treaties", Journal of Political Economy. [Reprinted as Chapter 1 of International economics (The Free Press, Glencoe, IL) 1951.]

Viner, J. (1931), The most-favored-nation clause, index (Sevnska Handelsbanken, Stockholm). [Reprinted as Chapter 5 of International economics (The Free Press, Glencoe, IL) 1951.]

Viner, J. (1936), "Comments on the improvement of commercial relations between nations", in: The improvement of commercial relations between nations and the problem of monetary stabilization (Carnegie Endowment-International Chamber of Commerce Joint Committee, Paris).

Webb, M. (1984), "A theoretical note on quota-reduction negotiations", Oxford Economic Papers 36:288–290.

Weinstein, D.E. (1992), "Competition and unilateral dumping", Journal of International Economics 32:379–388.

Winters, A.L. (1990), "The road to uruguay", in: David Greenaway, ed., Policy forum: Multilateralism and bilateralism in trade policy: Editorial note, Economic Journal 100:1288–1303.

Yarbrough, B.V. and R.M. Yarbrough (1992), Cooperation and governance in international trade: The strategic organizational approach (Princeton University Press, Princeton, NJ).

Chapter 30

ESTIMATING THE EFFECTS OF TRADE POLICY

ROBERT C. FEENSTRA

University of California, Davis, and National Bureau of Economic Research

Contents

Handbook of International Economics, vol. III, Edited by G. Grossman and K. Rogoff
© *Elsevier Science B.V., 1995*

1. Introduction

Governments of all countries routinely intervene in trade across borders, through the use of tariffs, quotas, and other non-tariff barriers, in ways that they would not do within their borders. Reductions in these trade restrictions are regularly achieved through international negotiations, but even as one set of trade barriers are lowered, there remain barriers in other sectors waiting to be addressed. An important part of this ongoing policy process is the measurement of the costs of trade restrictions. Beginning with the deadweight loss calculations of Johnson (1960), each new round of tariff negotiations has seen an attempt to measure the gains to the countries involved. The small size of gains for industrial countries has been adjusted upwards by more recent estimates, that incorporate economies of scale, while the developing countries are typically estimated to receive larger gains.[1]

In a way, those involved in the initial calculations of the gains from tariff removal had it easy: everyone knew that the gains were positive, and only the magnitude remained to be determined. This iron-clad rule has been challenged by the recent theories of imperfect competition and trade, which suggest various ways that a country may gain through the use of "strategic" trade policy. Krugman (1987) has argued that the presumption in favor of free trade is still a reasonable rule of thumb, though not a guarantee, under these circumstances. This conclusion is reinforced by computable models of imperfect competition and trade, in which the ambiguity of the theoretical results is resolved by introducing a minimum amount of data. These models often show that the scope for strategic policy is very limited.[2] It can be questioned, however, whether the results from these computable models are really convincing. They share with the deadweight loss calculations the reliance on elasticity assumptions, but add onto this another layer of assumptions on the conduct of firms, which are not verified from any empirical evidence. While the qualitative conclusions may not be guaranteed from the start, there is enough structure forced on the models that the data could never refute the theory.

In this chapter we shall examine how imperfect competition affects the gains and losses from trade policies, but focus on empirical models that estimate the impact of trade policies, with minimum structure imposed on the data. Like Krugman, we will conclude that there is little support for national gains due to strategic trade policies, but unlike the computable models, the data has an opportunity to accept or reject the hypotheses being considered. In their chapter in this volume, Leamer and Levinsohn adopt the principle of "estimate, don't test" as a desirable methodology for

---

[1] Some of these studies are summarized in Lindert (1991, Table D.1, p. 607).

[2] The theoretical arguments for strategic trade policies and reviewed and the computable models are discussed in Chapter 27 in this volume, by James Brander.

evaluating trade theory. The analogous message of this chapter for the evaluation of trade policy is "estimate, don't calculate". This message applies equally well to the analysis of trade policies under perfect competition, and recent developments in that context will also be reviewed.

We begin in Section 2 by decomposing the welfare effects of trade policy under imperfect competition into four possible channels: (i) a deadweight loss from distorting consumption and production decisions; (ii) a possible gain from improving the terms of trade; (iii) a gain or loss due to changes in the scale of firms; and, (iv) a gain or loss from shifting profits between countries. These channels are listed in decreasing order from the greatest to the least amount of available empirical evidence, and our discussion of each will vary accordingly. Two others channels by which trade policy affects social or individual welfare – through changes in wages and changes in product variety – are not examined in the theoretical model, but will be discussed at the end of the chapter.

Deadweight losses and the terms of trade will be the focus of our analysis in Section 3, where tariffs are considered. An important insight of the imperfect competition models is that "no country is small": a tariff can be expected to lower the price at which the foreign firms are willing to sell their products, so that the tariff has a beneficial terms of trade effect. We find that this prediction has received indirect empirical support from studies of exchange rates, but that the magnitude of the terms of trade impact differs a great deal across industries. It follows that we cannot presume that tariffs will lead to a terms of trade gain in most industries, so that this channel does not amount to an argument for strategic trade policy. On the contrary, the use of tariffs in the form of antidumping duties has been found to lead to a terms of trade loss, due to collusion between firms, even in cases where the duties are not imposed.

Attention is shifted to import quotas in Section 4, and their effect on product quality. In many industries, quotas have led to an increase in the quality of imports purchased, which is an optimal response by consumers and firms. We argue that this upgrading imposes an additional deadweight loss, over and above the loss from a tariff of the same average magnitude. We introduce an index number method that can be used to measure this loss, and which applies more generally to any non-uniform trade barriers over multiple goods. The effects of the "voluntary" export restraint on Japanese auto sales to the U.S. are also considered. Extensive modeling of the automobile industry has led to estimates of how the price-cost margins, and profits of firms, have responded to quotas. These studies provide indirect evidence on the hypothesis of Bhagwati (1965), Harris (1985) and Krishna (1989), that quotas lead to more collusive market conduct.

In Section 5 the effects of trade policy on the markups of firms, and thereby on their output and profits, is considered. Recent studies for developing countries have demonstrated that trade liberalization can lead to substantial reductions in price-cost margins, at least in those industries that are imperfectly competitive. Corresponding to these reductions in margins will be an increase in firm-level output, which leads to welfare gains if there are economies of scale. Conversely, in industrial countries it is more common to treat import competition as a potential source of unemployment, with private (if not social) losses. The evidence linking import competition, wages and employment for the United States is reviewed in Section 6, and the impact of changes in product variety is also considered. In Section 7 we describe an ongoing project to provide international data, and present conclusions.

2. General framework

In order to organize our subsequent discussion, we first show how the welfare effects of trade policy under imperfect competition can be decomposed into separate components. We shall slightly extend the framework of Rodrik (1988), and treat imports and domestically produced goods as imperfect substitutes. Let the index i denote goods $i = 1, \ldots, I$, each of which is available in an import and domestic variety. Imports are sold at the international price p_i^* and the domestic price p_i, where $(p_i - p_i^*)$ is a wedge reflecting tariffs or quotas. Domestically produced goods are exported and sold domestically at the price q_i, where for convenience we ignore export taxes or subsidies. We let C_i denote the consumption of each import good, and let D_i denote the consumption of the domestically produced variety. The overall level of expenditure needed to obtain the level of utility U can be written as a function $E(p, q, U)$, depending on the price vectors $p = (p_1, \ldots, p_I)$ and $q = (q_1, \ldots, q_I)$. The derivatives of the expenditure function with respect to prices equal the levels of consumption:

$$\partial E / \partial p_i = C_i \text{ and } \partial E / \partial q_i = D_i, \quad i = 1, \ldots, I. \tag{2.1}$$

We will suppose that each domestically produced good is sold by n_i firms, where the output each firm is denoted by y_i, and industry output is $Y_i \equiv n_i y_i$. The total costs for each firm in industry i are denoted by $\phi_i(y_i, w)$, where w is the vector of wages. Under increasing return to scale, average costs exceed marginal costs, so that $\phi_i / y_i > \phi_{iy} \equiv \partial \phi_i / \partial y_i$. Denote the endowment of each factor of production by v_j, $j = 1, \ldots, J$. Under full employment, the endowment equals the total demand for each factor, which is obtained by differentiating the cost function with respect to wages, and summing across firms and industries:

$$v_j = \sum_i n_i (\partial \phi_i / \partial w_j), \quad j = 1, \ldots, J. \tag{2.2}$$

Under any system of import tariffs and quotas, the level of home utility can be determined by setting expenditure E equal to the value of income from all sources:

$$E(p, q, U) = \sum_i [q_i - (\phi_i / y_i)] Y_i + \sum_j w_j v_j + \sum_i (p_i - p_i^*) C_i. \tag{2.3}$$

The first term on the right of (2.3) is profits earned across the industries, which would equal zero under free entry. The second term is the value of factor income. The third term is total tariff revenues or quota rents, if these are redistributed to consumers. If the quota rents are instead captured by foreigners, as occurs under a "voluntary" export restraint (VER), then these rents will not appear in the third term in (2.3) because $p_i = p_i^*$.

Let U^0 be the level of welfare obtained under free trade, with expenditure equal to income in (2.3). Our goal is to compare the level of welfare obtained under free trade with that obtained under some trade policies. Rather than directly compare utilities, it is convenient to ask how much income the consumers need to give up (or be compensated) in the presence of the trade policies, to obtain the same level of utility U^0 as under free trade. This income is computed by taking the difference between total income received under the trade policies, and consumer expenditure $E(p, q, U^0)$ at the free trade utility U^0:

$$B(p, q, p^*, U^0) = \left\{ \sum_i [q_i - (\phi_i/y_i)]Y_i + \sum_j w_j v_j + \sum_i (p_i - p_i^*)C_i \right\}$$
$$- E(p, q, U^0), \tag{2.4}$$

where p^* is the vector of world prices for imported goods. The right side of (2.4) is just the difference between the right and left sides of (2.3), except that we compute consumer expenditure at the free trade utility level U^0. If (2.4) is positive, it represents the gains due to the trade policies, while if (2.4) is negative then it represents the losses, so that B can be interpreted as a measure of welfare or "benefits". In addition, B can be interpreted as the balance of trade surplus (deficit if negative) obtained with the utility level U^0 in the presence of the trade policies.

2.1. Welfare effects

To determine the effect of any small change in trade policy, let U^0 now denote the utility level at any initial equilibrium with tariffs and quotas, satisfying (2.3). Then the change in welfare due to a small change in trade policy can be obtained by totally differentiating (2.4), holding U^0 fixed. Making use of (2.1) and (2.2), the resulting change in welfare can be written as,

$$dB = \sum_i (p_i - p_i^*) \, dC_i + \sum_i [(Y_i - D_i) \, dq_i - C_i \, dp_i^*]$$
$$+ \sum_i [(\phi_i/y_i) - \phi_{iy}]n_i \, dy_i + \sum_i [q_i - (\phi_i/y_i)] \, dY_i. \tag{2.5}$$

The first term on the right of (2.5) is the deadweight loss caused by the change in import volume. The second summation is the terms of trade effect, on both exports $(Y_i - D_i)$ and imports C_i. The third term is the difference between average and marginal costs (which is positive), multiplied by the change in industry outputs due to changes in *firm* outputs, reflecting the potential for raising welfare through greater use of economies of scale.[3] The final term on the right of (2.5) is the change in profits caused by a change in industry outputs. This term disappears if profits were equal to zero initially, as under free entry.

We should also mention two other channels by which trade policy affects welfare, that are ignored in (2.5). The first is changes in employment in the presence of wage distortions across industries. In this case, an expansion of employment in the highest-wage industries increases welfare: in terms of eq. (2.5), the average costs of production exceed the social opportunity costs of withdrawing workers from other industries. Katz and Summers (1989a,b) have argued that wage distortions across industries justify the use of trade policy, as will be discussed in Section 6. The second is changes in the number or range of differentiated products available. While we have treated the import and domestic variety as imperfect substitutes, we have not allowed for changes in the range of these varieties available, as would occur under monopolistic competition. The welfare impact of changes in domestic variety requires a comparison of marginal costs and benefits, but the impact of an increase (decrease) in *import* variety is always positive (negative). The welfare effects of changes in product variety has received little empirical attention,[4] though it is an important area for further research, as also discussed in Section 6.

2.2. Mode of market conduct

So far, we have not specified the form of industry pricing. In some cases in this chapter we will concentrate on perfectly competitive pricing, and in other cases allow for oligopoly pricing. These can be nested by using a general form of the pricing relation, which is written for the domestic firms as:

$$q_i[1 - (\theta_i/\eta_i)] = \phi_{iy}(y_i, w), \tag{2.6}$$

where $\eta_i \equiv -\partial \ln D_i / \partial \ln q_i$ denotes the elasticity of demand for the domestic good, and θ_i denotes the firm's "mode of market conduct": $\theta_i = 0$ under perfect competition, and $\theta_i > 0$ under oligopoly. For example if we assume Cournot–Nash pricing, then θ_i equals the share $(1/n_i)$ of an individual firm. More generally, θ_i reflects the

---

[3]The fact that social welfare depends on changes in firm-level output to exploit economies of scale has been emphasized by Horstmann and Markusen (1986). In particular, an increase in industry output by the entry of firms will not add to welfare through economies of scale, but might instead reflect inefficient entry.

[4]An exception is Feenstra (1988b), who estimates the welfare impact of new American varieties following a U.S. tariff on compact trucks from Japan. This tariff increased the number of American models available, but each of these models were very similar to existing Japanese models in characteristics, so that the domestic models added very little to consumer welfare. Romer (1994) also examines the welfare cost of trade restrictions with changing product variety.

strategies played by domestic firms, as well as their size-distribution. Methods for estimating the market conduct have been developed as part af the "new empirical industrial organization", surveyed by Bresnahan (1989). While we will not discuss these methods until Section 5, it will be clear that some of the empirical techniques dealt with before then provide information on the market conduct parameter.

The analogous pricing relation for the foreign firms is:

$$p_i^*[1 - (\theta_i^*/\eta_i^*)] = \phi_{ix}^*(x_i^*, w^*), \tag{2.7}$$

where x_i^* denotes the exports (or output) of each foreign firm, with total exports $X_i^* \geq C_i$; $\phi_i^*(x_i^*, w^*)$ are foreign costs; $\eta_i^* \equiv -\partial \ln C_i/\partial \ln p_i$ denotes the elasticity of demand for imports; and θ_i^* denotes the foreign firms' "mode of market conduct". Finally, if there is free entry of firms, prices will equal average cost, so that,

$$q_i = \phi_i(y_i, w)/y_i, \tag{2.8}$$

and

$$p_i^* = \phi_i^*(x_i^*, w^*)/x_i^*, \tag{2.9}$$

for the domestic and importing firms, respectively.

3. Tariffs

In this section and the next, we focus on the first two terms in (2.5) – the deadweight loss and terms of trade effect – while ignoring the welfare effect of changes in domestic output and profits, which will be considered in Section 5. Initially, we will consider an ad valorem tariff of τ applied to a single good, and suppose that the prices of all other goods are held constant. Then dropping the subscript i, the first two terms in (2.5) can be written as:

$$\frac{dB}{d\tau} = (p - p^*)\frac{dC}{d\tau} - C\frac{dp^*}{d\tau}, \tag{3.1}$$

where C denotes imports of the good in question, and p and p^* are scalars.

Let p^0 denote the initial, free trade price of the good. By integrating (3.1) over the tariff levels between 0 and t, we can obtain an expression for the total change in welfare due to the tariff:

$$\Delta B = \int_0^t (p - p^*)\frac{dC}{d\tau}\,d\tau - \int_0^t C\frac{dp^*}{d\tau}\,d\tau \tag{3.2a}$$

$$= \int_0^t (p - p^0)\frac{dC}{d\tau}\,d\tau + (p^0 - p^*)C. \tag{3.2b}$$

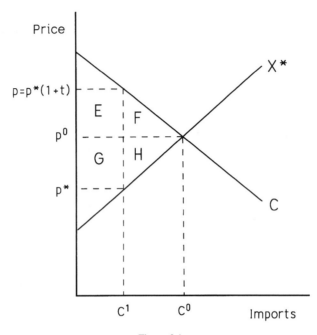

Figure 3.1.

This derivation can be understood by referring to Figure 3.1, where we show the domestic import demand curve C and the foreign export supply curve X^*. The effect of the tariff is to lower the international price from p^0 to p^*, and raise the domestic price from p^0 to $p = p^*(1 + t)$. The first term on the right of (3.2a) is the deadweight loss, equaling areas $F + H$ in Figure 3.1, and the second term is the terms of trade gain, equaling areas $G + H$. Alternatively, we can cancel area H in both these terms, and obtain (3.2b), where the first term on the right is the deadweight loss F, and the second term is the terms of trade gain G.

If the demand curve is linear, then the deadweight loss F can be written as $\frac{1}{2}(p - p^0)(C^0 - C^1)$, where C^1 is expenditure on imports at the domestic price $p = p^*(1 + t)$. To measure this cost we need estimates of the change in imports due to the tariffs, as well as the change in the domestic price of the importable. If international prices are fixed, then the change in the domestic price is just the (specific) tariff. The drop in imports is frequently obtained by multiplying the (ad valorem) tariff by a "reasonable" import demand elasticity. As simple as this triangle formula is, it is frequently used in policy analysis (e.g. Hufbauer and Elliott, 1994).

Despite the attractiveness of using a simple formula to measure the deadweight loss, this approach has several limitations. The most obvious is that it is extremely sensitive to the projected change in imports, so that the deadweight loss has a standard error that is proportional to that of the demand elasticity used, which is most often not reported in this context. Furthermore, studies such as Leamer (1988a,b, 1990) have directly estimated the impact of tariff and non-tariff barriers on imports, and found that this impact is very small or even of the "wrong" sign. This leads us to question whether the use of "reasonable" import demand elasticities to measure the loss in (3.2) is supported by the data at all.

Leamer suggests that the unusual magnitudes obtained from direct estimation of the effects of tariffs on imports may be due to a simultaneity problem: high tariffs may be applied to those industries with high imports. In this case, a regression of imports on tariffs could not be expected to uncover the import demand elasticity. Instead, the elasticity should be obtained by explicitly recognizing the endogeneity of tariffs and non-tariff barriers, and modeling these with another equation motivated from a political-economy framework. This is the approach taken by Trefler (1993), with dramatic results: when trade protection for the U.S. in 1983 is modeled endogenously, its estimated impact on imports is 10 times larger than obtained by treating it as exogenous. While additional work would be desirable to see how this estimate extends to other samples, these results illustrate the usefulness of an estimation approach rather than the rote calculation of deadweight loss triangles.

3.1. Trade distortion index

A second limitation of the triangle formula arises when non-uniform tariffs are applied over multiple industries. In this case, a common empirical practice is to average the tariff rates, and then compute a deadweight loss triangle for this average. The problem with this approach is that the average tariff is computed by adding up tariff revenue over all the goods being considered, and then dividing by total expenditure on imports. For example, applying this method to the U.S. yields an average tariff level of 3.7 percent in manufacturing. However, this method of computing the average tariff is completely wrong for making any welfare inference. The reason is that a prohibitive tariff would lead to zero tariff revenue, and therefore not be counted at all in the average. A valid averaging procedure, however, can be obtained from the balance of trade function in (2.4), and is referred to as a "trade restrictiveness index" by Anderson and Neary (1992, 1994a,b) and Anderson (1994a,b).[5]

To develop their index, let τ_i denote the ad valorem tariff on good i. Suppose that international prices are fixed at p_i^0, so that domestic prices of the imports are $p_i = p_i^0(1 + \tau_i)$, or the vector p. Letting U^0 be the level of utility obtained with free trade, then $B(p, q, p^0, U^0)$ is interpreted as welfare under the tariffs. Now consider obtaining the same level of welfare under a uniform import tariff at the rate T, so that

---

[5]The early results of Leamer (1974) anticipate some features of the trade restrictiveness index.

domestic prices are $p_i^0(1 + T)$, or the vector $p^0(1 + T)$. Then the "trade restrictiveness index" is defined as the value of T that results in the same level of welfare as
the individual tariffs τ_i,

$$B[p^0(1 + T), q, p^0, U^0] = B(p, q, p^0, U^0). \tag{3.3}$$

In order to determine the index corresponding to any pattern of individual tariffs,
we would need to solve for T from (3.3), as could be done with a computable general
equilibrium (CGE) model. However, some insight into the properties of this index
can be obtained by differentiating (3.3) with respect to T and τ_i, holding world prices
constant. This exercise yields,

$$\sum_i \frac{\partial B}{\partial p_i} p_i^0 \, d\tau_i = \sum_i \frac{\partial B}{\partial p_i} p_i^0 \, dT. \tag{3.4}$$

For fixed world prices, the derivative of B with respect to domestic prices is given by
the first term in (3.1), or $\partial B / \partial p_i = (p_i - p_i^0) \partial C_i / \partial p_i$, which is interpreted as the
marginal deadweight loss of the tariff. Assuming that the import demand curves are
linear, we can integrate (3.4) over values of the individual tariffs from 0 to t_i,
$i = 1, \ldots, I$, and for the trade restrictiveness index between 0 and T. Performing this
exercise, we obtain,

$$T = \left[\frac{\sum_i (\partial C_i / \partial p_i)(p_i^0 t_i)^2}{\sum_i (\partial C_i / \partial p_i)(p_i^0)^2} \right]^{1/2}. \tag{3.5}$$

The trade restrictiveness index is therefore a weighted average of the squared
values of individual tariffs t_i, where the weights reflect the change in import
expenditures caused by a one percent change in the price: $(\partial C_i / \partial p_i)(p_i^0)^2 = p_i^0(\partial C_i / \partial \ln p_i)$, evaluated at the free trade prices p_i^0. Using these weights, prohibitively high
tariffs will still receive positive weight in the index.[6] Having the squared value of
individual tariffs appear in (3.5) means that the restrictiveness index will depend on
both the weighted average level of the tariffs, and their variance, where both these
measures are sometimes used by policy analysts.[7] This reflects the general result that
increases in the dispersion of tariff rates will raise their deadweight loss.

Given an estimate of the trade restrictiveness index T, the deadweight loss of these
tariffs could be obtained by using a triangle formula, applied to the change in the
Hicksian aggregate of imports between the price p^0 and $p^0(1 + T)$. The problem,
however, is that this hypothetical change in aggregate imports is not the same as the

---

[6]More generally, Anderson (1994a) shows that import expenditures in the *tariff-ridden* equilibrium are
the appropriate weights to use if and only if the balance of payments function has a constant elasticity of
substitution form.

[7]Letting $\bar{t}$ denote the weighted mean of the individual tariffs, and V denote the coefficient of variation
(ratio of the weighted standard deviation to the mean), it is readily shown that $T = \bar{t}(V^2 + 1)^{1/2}$.

observed change due to the actual tariffs, and would therefore need to be calculated using some elasticity for the Hicksian aggregate, multiplied by T. This leads us to the same limitation discussed above, namely, that the use of a "reasonable" elasticity for the Hicksian aggregate would not be based on the drop in imports in the data. The same reliance on elasticity parameters occurs in the calculation of the trade restrictiveness index itself (to obtain $\partial C_i / \partial p_i$ for the individual imports i). Thus, while this index solves the problem of how to aggregate tariffs over multiple goods, it does not really meet our criterion of "estimate, don't calculate". In Section 4.1 we will discuss an alternative method for measuring the deadweight loss from trade barriers applied over multiple goods, which goes some distance toward meeting this criterion. These two methods for measuring the deadweight loss are noted in the first row of Table 3.1, where we shall keep a running list of trade policy issues and the available estimation methods.

3.2. Terms of trade

Returning to the case of a tariff on a single good, let us now consider the possible terms of trade effect. In competitive models, the tariff results in a terms of trade gain only if the reduction in import demand is large enough to lower the world price, as illustrated in Figure 3.1. Since any country is but a fraction of the world market, there has been a tendency to treat the terms of trade as fixed in policy analysis. However, the imperfect competition literature suggests that tariffs will result in terms of trade gains regardless of the buyer's size, since foreign exporters will generally not allow consumer prices in the importing country to rise by the full amount of the tariff. This behavior simply reflects profit-maximization by the foreign exporters, and we refer to it as "incomplete pass-through" of the tariffs. This result was first noted by Katrak (1977), De Meza (1979) and Svedberg (1979) for a monopoly model, while Brander and Spencer (1984) further developed it in a monopoly and oligopoly context, and Gros (1987) extended it to a monopolistic competition framework. We shall illustrate the result for the simple case of a foreign monopolist facing a linear demand curve in the home country.

In Figure 3.2, the foreign firm faces the home demand curve of C, and has constant marginal costs of production of ϕ_x^*. The profit-maximizing price and imports are p^0, C^0, where marginal revenue equals marginal cost. If a *specific* tariff of s is applied, then the marginal costs of selling in the home market rise by the amount s, leading to a fall in sales from C^0 to C^1, and an increase in the domestic price from p^0 to p. However, because the demand curve is only half as steep as the marginal revenue curve, the increase in price is only one-half as much as the rise in marginal costs: it follows that the net price received by the foreign firm has fallen, $p^* = (p - s) < p^0$, which is a terms of trade gain for the importing country. Generalizing this result, the

Table 3.1
Trade policy issues and estimation methods

Trade Policy Issue	Estimation Method (section)	Results
Deadweight loss of tariffs or quotas over multiple goods	Trade distortion index (3.1) Index number method (4.1)	Index number method imposes less structure on the data, but there is little experience with its use.
Terms of trade impact of tariffs	Pass-through regression of tariffs (3.2), or of exchange rates (3.3)	Strong evidence that pass-through is less than unity, though its size differs substantially across industries.
Effects of antidumping duties	Comparison of import prices or quantities at various stages of dumping actions (3.4)	Strong evidence that the dumping actions reduce imports, even when duties are not applied.
Effects of trade barriers on imports, and measures of "openness"	Regressions of imports on factor endowments and trade barriers (3 and 4)	Simultaneity between trade barriers and imports must be taken into account; measures of "openness" are sensitive to the structural model. Both Japan and the U.S. import "too little".
Quality upgrading under quotas	Comparison of unit-value and exact price index (4.1), and hedonic regression (4.2)	Strong evidence from various industries of upgrading, which has an additional deadweight loss.
Effects of the VER on Japanese autos in the U.S.	Hedonic regression; joint estimation of demand and cost functions (4.2)	Very large rents or profits created for Japanese, European, and U.S. producers. Overall negative impact for the U.S., though equivalent tariff could have raised welfare.
Changes in markups of firms when trade liberalization occurs	Hall method incorporating imperfect competition into TFP measures (5.1)	Weak evidence that markups have fallen for some developing countries. Invalid to correlate tariffs with TFP to assess "infant industry" protection.
Effects of import competition on employment and wages	Regressions of import shares or prices on employment and wages (6.1 and 6.2)	Simultaneity of import prices or shares must be taken into account. Weak evidence that import competition lowers employment and wages, but tariffs do not raise union wages.

terms of trade gain will occur whenever the demand curve is flatter than the marginal revenue curve.

The welfare gain for the importing country equals $G - F$ in Figure 3.2, where these areas have the same interpretation as in the competitive case illustrated in Figure 3.1. To maximize the gains, the home country should apply a tariff until the derivative in (3.1) equals zero. Writing the change in import demand as $\partial C / \partial \tau = (\partial C /$

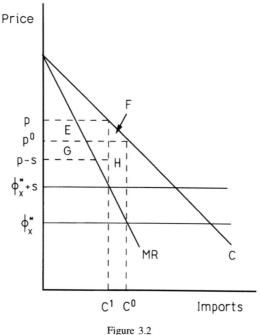

Figure 3.2

$\partial p)(\partial p/\partial \tau)$, the optimal ad valorem tariff τ^* can be readily solved as:

$$\tau^* = \left(\frac{1}{\eta^*}\right)\left[\left(\frac{\partial \ln p}{\partial \ln(1 + \tau)}\right)^{-1} - 1\right], \tag{3.6}$$

where η^* is the elasticity of import demand, and $\partial \ln p/\partial \ln(1 + \tau)$ is the response of the tariff-inclusive price to changes in the tariff, or the "pass-through elasticity". If the pass-through elasticity is less than one, then the foreign firms are absorbing part of the tariff by lowering their selling price, and the optimal tariff is positive. This expression for the optimal tariff contrasts with the more conventional "inverse of the foreign supply elasticity" formula, which is not a helpful way to think about the optimal tariff when the foreign firm is imperfectly competitive, and has no supply curve (but just points of optimal supply).

There have only been a few cases where the pass-though elasticity has been estimated for tariffs, but a large number of cases where this elasticity has been estimated for changes in exchange rates, in what is called "pricing to market" behavior (Krugman, 1987). To see the connection between these, suppose that the import is provided by a single foreign firm with output equal to import demand, $x^* = C$. Write the marginal costs of the foreign firm as $\phi_x^* = v^*(C)w^*e$, where

$v^{*\prime} > (<)0$ denotes rising (falling) marginal costs, w^* is an aggregate of foreign factor prices, and e denotes the (actual or expected) exchange rate to convert the foreign costs into the domestic currency.[8] An appreciation of the exporter's currency corresponds to a rise in e. The first-order condition (2.9) is now written as:

$$\frac{p}{(1+\tau)}\left[1-\left(\frac{\theta^*}{\eta^*}\right)\right] = v^*(C)w^*e, \tag{3.7}$$

where $p/(1+\tau)$ is the import price net of the tariff, and θ^* denotes the mode of market conduct. Assuming that the domestic and import varieties of the good in question are weakly separable from other goods in the expenditure function, then import demand C and the elasticity η^* depend on the prices p and q of the import and domestic goods, as well as consumer expenditure E on just these goods. Then multiplying both sides of (3.7) by the tariff factor $(1+\tau)$, the tariff-inclusive price of the importable can be solved from (3.7) as an implicit function:

$$p = \psi^*[w^*e(1+\tau), q, E, \theta^*]. \tag{3.8}$$

It is immediate from (3.7) that changes in the tariff, $d\ln(1+\tau)$, and changes in the expected exchange rate, $d\ln e$, should have *equivalent* effects on the domestic price: Feenstra (1989) refers to this as "symmetric" pass-through of tariffs and exchange rates. The pass-through elasticity can be solved from (3.7) as:

$$\frac{\partial\ln p}{\partial\ln e} = \frac{\partial\ln p}{\partial\ln(1+\tau)} = \left[1+\left(\frac{\theta^*}{\eta^*-\theta^*}\right)\frac{\partial\ln\eta^*}{\partial\ln p} + \eta^*\left(\frac{Cv^{*\prime}}{v^*}\right)\right]^{-1}, \tag{3.9}$$

where $\partial\ln\eta^*/\partial\ln p$ is the change in the demand elasticity η^* with respect to a change in the import price. This term reflects changes in the price-cost margins charged by firms. For demand curves that are less convex than a constant-elasticity curve, the elasticity η^* increases with price, $\partial\ln\eta^*/\partial\ln p > 0$. This means that exporters lower their markups as their currency appreciates, so the pass-through elasticity is less than unity. However, it is evident from (3.5) that rising marginal costs ($v^{*\prime} > 0$) will *also* make the pass-through less than unity. Thus, the empirical finding of incomplete pass-through is consistent with either imperfectly competitive pricing, or rising marginal costs under perfect competition. When foreign firms are exporting to multiple markets, as discussed below, we will be able to control for changes in marginal cost due to changes in output or other reasons: in this case, a pass-through elasticity less than unity will be interpreted as evidence of imperfect competition, or "pricing to market" behavior.

Feenstra (1989) tests for equal pass-through of tariffs and exchange rates for U.S.

---

[8]We will not make a distinction between actual and expected exchange rates, though this can be introduced into the model, and has been investigated empirically by Froot and Klemperer (1989) and Feinberg and Kaplan (1992).

imports of heavyweight motorcycles and compact trucks from Japan. The former was subject to a tariff between April 1983 and October 1987, declining from 45 to 10 percent, while the latter has had a 25 percent tariff imposed since August 1980. A log-linear form for (3.8) is used,

$$\ln p_t = \alpha_0 + \alpha \ln(w_t^* e_t) + \beta \ln(1 + \tau_t) + \sum_i \gamma_i \ln q_{it} + \delta \ln E_t + \varepsilon_t, \qquad (3.10)$$

where p_t is the annual price of Japanese cycles or trucks, q_{it} refers to the price of various competing varieties, and ε_t is a random error. The expected exchange rate e_t is modeled as a weighted average of past spot rates (though a forward rate could also be used). Several of the regressors in (3.10) are endogenous, including the prices q_{it} and expenditure E_t, so the regression is estimated with instrumental variables.

Symmetric pass-through of exchange rates and tariffs is tested as the equality of α and β. For compact trucks the estimated coefficients (standard errors) were 0.63 (0.08) and 0.57 (0.14), respectively, while for heavyweight cycles the two estimates were 0.89 (0.22) and 1.13 (0.16). The hypothesis that these two coefficients are equal for each product is accepted, and when this hypothesis is imposed, the estimated coefficients are 0.58 (0.06) for trucks and 1.08 (0.15) for motorcycles. The pass-through of less than unity for compact trucks means that the tariff led to a terms of trade gain, but this apparently did not occur for motorcycles, where the pass-through is insignificantly different from unity. Feenstra argues that the difference in the pass-through in these two industries reflects the different market shares of Japanese imports: in trucks, the Japanese imports faced significant competition from American compact models that were newly developed; whereas in heavyweight cycles, the only competitor was Harley-Davidson, which had a relatively small market share.

3.3. Exchange rate pass-through

Many other studies have estimated the pass-through of exchange rates rather than tariffs. Knetter (1989, 1993) and Gagnon and Knetter (1992) use panel data for industry exports to several destination markets. Marginal costs to destination market k are written as $v^*(x_t^*)w_t^* e_{kt}$, depending on total exports x_t from each firm, and the exchange rate e_{kt} between the source country and destination market k. In this case foreign marginal costs, $v^*(x_t^*)w_t^*$, can be estimated as a fixed-effect for each period. Letting $\omega_t \equiv \ln[v^*(x_t^*)w_t^*]$ denote this fixed-effect, the estimating equation becomes:

$$\ln p_{kt} = \lambda_k + \omega_t + \alpha_k \ln e_{kt} + \delta_k \ln E_{kt} + \varepsilon_{kt}, \qquad (3.11)$$

where p_{kt} is the price of the export in the destination market currency, λ_k is a fixed effect across destination markets, and E_{kt} is consumer expenditure in that market. The aggregate price of competing goods is used as a deflator for all the variables in

(3.11), so it does not appear explicitly.[9] The advantage of this formulation over (3.10) is that we are able to control for any changes in foreign marginal costs using the fixed effect ω_t. For example, the prices of imported intermediate inputs would depend on the exchange rate, which would affect the degree of pass-through unless controlled for.[10] By estimating foreign marginal costs as a fixed effect, the pass-through coefficient α_k reflects *only* changes in price-cost margins, so that $\alpha_k < 1$ is evidence of imperfect competition.

Knetter (1989, 1993) finds incomplete pass-through over a wide range of manufactured goods, for exporters from several countries. Generally, exporters from the Germany, Japan or the U.K. are found to have lower pass-through coefficients than exporters from the United States (high pass-through for U.S. exporters was also found by Mann, 1986). However, this pattern appears to be primarily due to differences *across* industries. In the industries for which comparable export data were available for these four countries, no significant difference in the pass-through behavior of the exporters could be found.[11] Knetter concludes that industry effects appear to be more important than either source or destination-market effects in explaining differences in pass-through behavior.

The mode of market conduct parameter θ^* appearing in (3.9) will influence the degree of pass-through.[12] Feinberg (1986, 1989a, 1991) tests the related hypothesis that market concentration affects the pass-through of exchange rates to *domestic* prices. In terms of our framework, assuming for simplicity that output y goes entirely to domestic demand (i.e. there are no exports), the first-order condition (2.6) can be solved to determine the equilibrium level of domestic prices,

$$q = \psi[w, p, E, \theta] . \tag{3.12}$$

Analogous to the determination of import prices in (3.9), domestic prices depend on the mode of market conduct, as well as on the import prices themselves. This is one route by which changes in exchange rates will influence domestic prices, and a second route is the use of imported intermediate inputs, which affects the factor price aggregate w in (3.12). Feinberg finds that the impact of exchange rates on domestic prices is higher for those industries depending more heavily on imported inter-

---

[9]In general, the function ψ^* in (3.8) is homogeous of degree one in $[w^*e(1 + \tau), q, E]$. It follows that one price can be used as a deflator for all other variables appearing on the right and left of (3.11).

[10]Harrison (1992) finds that the pass-through behavior of European and Japanese steel exporters to the U.S. was heavily affected by their use of imported intermediate inputs, and also by changes in U.S. trade policy.

[11]An exception is automobiles, where Gagnon, and Knetter (1992) find that Japanese producers have the lowest pass-through coefficient, followed by German producers and then American. They suggest that this may be due to differences in the models exported by each country. Feenstra, Gagnon, and Knetter (1993) relate the pass-through behavior in autos to the share held by exporters in their destination markets.

[12]For example, if a market is highly competitive so that θ^* is close to zero, and marginal costs are constant or controlled for, then the pass-through in (3.9) will be close to unity. More generally, we expect that pass-through will depend on the degree of product differentiation, as found by Yang (1993).

mediates, or producing goods that are close substitutes for imports, and lower for capital-intensive and concentrated industries. The estimating equation should be viewed as a reduced form of (3.9) and (3.12), where domestic prices are solved in terms of the variables $[w^*e(1 + \tau), w, E, \theta^*, \theta]$. More recently, Ceglowski (1991) and Feinberg (1993) have simultaneously estimated (3.9) and (3.12), and Feinberg finds that the indirect effect of exchange rates on U.S. prices – through the import prices – dominates the direct effect through imported intermediates.

The general conclusion to be drawn from these studies of exchange rates and international prices is that pass-through is less than unity for many manufactured products, but its magnitude differs a great deal across industries. This conclusion is indicated in the second row of Table 3.1. Even without relying on complete symmetry of pass-through between tariffs and exchange rates (as would not occur with imported intermediates, for example), these results indicate we should not have any presumption about the extent of terms of trade gain due to tariffs, but must treat each industry on a case-by-case basis. Moreover, it should be emphasized that the terms of trade is but one component of the welfare effects discussed in Section 2, and evidence of a large terms of trade gain does not necessarily mean that a tariff in that industry is desirable. For example, in the cases of U.S. import of compact trucks and heavyweight motorcycles, the tariff on motorcycles was temporary (lasting four years) and allowed Harley-Davidson to recover its profitability, while the tariff on compact trucks is still in effect. For this reason alone, the tariff on cycles might be judged superior to that on trucks, even though it did not yield a terms of trade gain.

3.4. Antidumping duties

In recent years there has been a surge in cases of alleged dumping, which is defined in U.S. law as foreign products exported to the U.S. at prices below "fair value", i.e. either below the prices of comparable goods sold in the exporter's home market, or below the cost of production. In cases where it is determined that dumping has occurred, antidumping duties can be applied. Researchers have recently turned their attention to these cases to understand both the reasons for their frequency (Baldwin and Steagall, 1993; Hansen and Prusa, 1993), and the welfare effects.

One explanation for the frequency of cases is related to the incomplete pass-through of exchange rates. If foreign currencies appreciate, and foreign exporters raise their prices (in the importer's currency) by less than the appreciation, then it is quite possible that the import price will be less than the foreign cost or price of comparable goods, when these are converted at the current exchange rate. Thus, the appreciation of foreign currencies makes the finding of "less than fair value" more likely. On the other hand, the imposition of a dumping duty also requires that imports cause "material injury" to the domestic industry, which is less likely when foreign currencies are appreciating. Feinberg (1989b) finds that the first of these effects dominates, and the frequency of dumping complaints in the U.S. (particularly those against Japan) increases with the appreciation of foreign currencies.

A second explanation for the frequency of cases is that filers expect some benefit even before a case is concluded. Prusa (1992) was the first to recognize that antidumping petitions can be *withdrawn* prior to their resolution, in which case the domestic and foreign firms are permitted to jointly determine the selling price for imports (typically negotiated through the Department of Commerce). Cases can also be *suspended* prior to their termination, in exchange for a promise by the foreign firms to stop dumping. We expect that both these actions would lead to an increase in import prices, and a terms of trade loss. In addition, the *investigation* of "less than fair value" may also lead exporting firms to increase their prices, to lower the probability of a positive finding. Harrison (1991) and Staiger and Wolak (1994) examine the impact of these various "non-duty" channels on imports, and find that the impact is substantial. In particular, Staiger and Wolak find that suspended agreements lead to a reduction in imports (with an implied increase in price) similar in magnitude to cases were duties are applied. Furthermore, the impacts of investigations themselves are substantial, providing about one-half the reduction in imports that would occur from duties.

Thus, we see that the application of anti-dumping law has increased collusion between domestic and foreign firms and reduced imports, even when duties are not levied. This conclusion in indicated in Table 3.1, and shows how rather than imperfect competition leading to a strategic use of trade policy, the antidumping policy itself has led to an enhancement of collusive behavior. Without any tariff revenue collected in this case, the importing country very likely suffers a welfare loss.[13]

4. Quotas

For nearly all quotas used in the United States, the rents are earned by the foreign exporters in the form of higher prices, as under "voluntary" export restraints (VERs).[14] In terms of eq (2.5), the domestic and international prices of imports are equal ($p_i = p_i^*$), and the importer faces an increase in this price, which is a terms of trade loss. With the competitive foreign supply curve X^* in Figure 3.1, a quota at the level C^1 would increase the (domestic and international) price of imports to p, resulting in quota rents of $E + G$. Relative to free trade, the cost to the importing

---

[13]Unless the domestic firm obtains an sufficient increase in profits at the expense of the foreign firm – a case that has not been investigated empirically.

[14]One exception to this is U.S. dairy imports, where the quota rents are shared between U.S. and foreign firms. In addition, Krishna and Tan (1993) have recently argued that some sharing of rents occurs for U.S. imports of textiles from Hong Kong, and other countries as well, despite the fact that exporters from Hong Kong can sell their quotas on an open market (Hamilton, 1986).

country equals the areas $E + F$. Calculations of these losses for the principal U.S. quotas are summarized in Feenstra (1992).

While the fact that foreign exporters earn the quota rents means that they might gain from the trade restriction, this result is not assured. In Figure 3.1, where competitive foreign exporters have the supply curve X^*, the foreign gain due to a quota at C^1 equals $E - H$, where H is a deadweight loss for the foreign producers. This gain will be negative if the quota is sufficiently restrictive. In the case of a monopolistic foreign supplier, the impact of the quota at C^1 on foreign profits is measured by $E - H$ in Figure 3.2, which is necessarily negative since profits were maximized initially. In contrast, under oligopoly a quota at near the free trade level can raise the profits of foreign exporters, and possibly also of domestic firms, due to more collusive market conduct. This is demonstrated by Harris (1985) and Krishna (1989), extending the analysis of Bhagwati (1965). Indirect evidence of the impact of quotas on market conduct will be presented in Section 4.2. The *converse* hypothesis – that trade liberalization will lead to less collusive pricing – has recently been confirmed for several developing countries, as we shall discuss in Section 5.1.

In comparison with tariffs, estimation of the welfare costs of quotas is more difficult for two reasons. First, the amount by which the quota raises the domestic price – or the price-equivalent of the quota – is not directly observed, but must be estimated. One common method for doing so is just the reverse of what we described in Section 3 for calculating the drop in imports under a tariff: take the difference between the quota level and some projected (free trade) imports as the drop in quantity, and multiply this (percentage) drop by a "reasonable" import demand elasticity, to obtain the increase in price due to the quota. This method suffers from the same problems discussed for the tariff case: the estimated price increase is very sensitive to both the projected imports and the demand elasticity that are used, and would have a standard error depending on both of these. In order to directly estimate the impact of the quota on price, an alternative method is to compare the price in the quota-restrained market to that in some similar market that does not have the quota. This method will be described for the automobile industry, in Section 4.2.

In order to estimate the impact of quotas on import quantity, the method used by Leamer (1988a,b, 1990) and Trefler (1993) is to specify a structural model of imports, the Hecksher–Ohlin–Vanek (HOV) model, and then investigate how tariffs, quotas, and other non-tariff barriers affect the import levels. Leamer uses this approach to develop measures of the "openness" of the industries and countries in his sample. The advantage of these measures is that they consistently estimate the impact of the trade barriers and their standard errors. The disadvantage, however, is that they are very sensitive to the structural model used to estimate the import equations. This disadvantage is seen most clearly by considering studies that also use the HOV model, but *do not* include data on trade barriers. For example, Lawrence (1987) and Saxonhouse (1989) are both interested in the question of whether Japan imports "too little" as compared with other countries, and both use the HOV model extended to allow for intra-industry trade to specify the import equations. But without having explicit data on trade barriers, the hypothesis of importing "too little" is evaluated by the residuals in the estimated import equations, and these authors are simply not able to agree on the statistical and economic significance of these residuals. This controversy appears to be resolved by Harrigan (1991), whose results support the conclusion that Japan does indeed import "too little", but then, so does the United States! This conclusion is listed in Table 3.1.

A second feature not often considered in the welfare costs is the possibility that the quota leads to *quality upgrading*. This upgrading can refer to either a shift in demand towards higher priced import varieties (i.e. a change in product mix), or to the addition of improved characteristics on each variety. Using the terms suggested by Helpman and Krugman (1985), the first case fits the "love of variety" approach used to describe consumer preferences under monopolistic competition, since we use a utility function defined over all varieties; whereas the second case fits the "ideal variety" approach. In both cases, we will argue that the quality change leads to an additional deadweight loss due to the quota. These two cases are discussed in the following sections, the first dealing with an index number method to measure the upgrading and its welfare loss, and the second focusing on hedonic methods applied to U.S. imports of automobiles.

4.1. Quality upgrading and welfare loss

To illustrate the change in product mix, let the subscript i now denote varieties of some differentiated import good, where p_i is the price of each variety. We will suppose that these imports are weakly separable from all other goods in the overall utility function, and let $U(C)$ denote the sub-utility function corresponding to these imports, where $C \equiv (C_1, \ldots, C_I)$ is the import vector. In the case where the imports are intermediate goods, then $U(C)$ is interpreted as a production function, and we shall suppose in general that it is homogeneous of degree one. The corresponding expenditure function can then be written as $E(p, U) = e(p)U$, where $p = (p_1, \ldots, p_I)$, and $e(p)$ is the expenditure function to obtain one unit of utility. We will treat each import variety as sold under perfect competition with a fixed marginal cost of v_i^*, though many of the results below can be generalized to imperfect competition.[15]

Each foreign firm faces an import quota on their sales to the domestic market, and also collects the quota rents (as under a VER). While this quota restricts the *total* sales to the domestic market – denoted by $\bar{C}$ – it can be expected to also change the *relative* sales of the various import varieties. To see this, suppose that each firm can produce several possible import varieties. Then to maximize the rents obtained, each

---

[15]Rodriguez (1979) considers the competitive case, while Falvey (1979), Das and Donnenfeld (1987, 1989) and Krishna (1987) allow for imperfect competition.

firm would ensure that they earn the *same* quota premium s from each variety exported (if this were not true, then the firm would export more of the variety with the highest quota premium, and thereby lower its price and premium). Thus, import prices after the quota will equal marginal cost plus the quota premium, or $v_i^* + s$.[16] Relative to their free trade values, import prices have risen by $(v_i^* + s)/v_i^* = 1 + (s/v_i^*)$, so that the *higher-priced* import varieties have the *lowest* percentage increase in price. It follows that demand will shift towards the higher-priced import varieties.

This shift in the relative composition of imports is sometimes called an increase (or upgrading) in import "quality". The definition of "quality" implicitly being used in this case is the *total utility per unit of the import*, or $U(C)/\bar{C}$. Since expenditure equals $E(p, U) = e(p)U$, this definition of quality can be rewritten as $U(C)/\bar{C} = [E(p, U)/\bar{C}]/e(p) \equiv UV/e(p)$, where $UV \equiv E(p, U)/\bar{C}$ denotes the *unit-value* of imports (which is simply the average price). Thus, we see that quality equals the ratio of the unit-value to the unit-expenditure function $e(p)$. The quota will increase the unit-value for two reasons: because the price of each variety increases, and because demand shifts towards the higher-priced varieties, thereby pulling up the average. However, the quota will increase the unit-expenditure only due to the first reason – the price increase for each variety. Thus, the quota can be expected to increase the unit-value more than the price index, and therefore raise this measure of quality (Falvey, 1979).

To empirically test for the change in quality due to a quota, we construct the ratio of quality in two years $t - 1$ and t:

$$\frac{UV_t/e(p_t)}{UV_{t-1}/e(p_{t-1})} = \left(\frac{UV_t}{UV_{t-1}}\right)/\pi(p_t, p_{t-1}, C_t, C_{t-1}), \tag{4.1}$$

where $\pi(p_t, p_{t-1}, C_t, C_{t-1}) = e(p_t)/e(p_{t-1})$ denotes an *exact* price index that can be constructed using data on import prices and quantities, and equals the ratio of the unit-expenditure functions. The idea behind an exact price index is that it measures the ratio of unit-expenditure functions, even when the functions themselves are not fully known. For example, if the unit-expenditure function is a quadratic function of prices, then a Fisher-Ideal price index can be used to measure the ratio (where the Fisher-Ideal is a geometric mean of the Paasche and Laspeyres indexes).[17] The change in import quality between two years is measured by taking the natural log of (4.1),

$$\ln\left(\frac{UV_t/e(p_t)}{UV_{t-1}/e(p_{t-1})}\right) = \ln\left(\frac{UV_t}{UV_{t-1}}\right) - \ln \pi(p_t, p_{t-1}, C_t, C_{t-1}). \tag{4.1'}$$

Thus, an increase in import quality occurs when the unit-values rise by a greater

---

[16] The quota premium can vary across foreign firms, depending on the amount they are allowed to export, but we shall not take this into account.

[17] A complete exposition of exact price indexes is Diewert (1976), which is not easy reading, but is well worth the effort.

percentage amount than an exact price index. The impact of the quota on quality is evaluated by letting $t - 1$ and t denote years before and after the quota comes into effect, and comparing the change in quality during this period with other years when trade policy did not change.

This method has been applied to U.S. imports of footwear and steel. In footwear, Aw and Roberts (1986) evaluate the 1977–81 quota with Korea and Taiwan. Upgrading of the import bundle was observed in most quota categories throughout this period, and accounted for 12 percent of the observed rise in the unit-value of footwear imports. For steel, Boorstein and Feenstra (1991) measure quality upgrading due to the VER negotiated with Japan and the European Community in 1969. Comparing that year with 1968, the unit-value rose by 15 percent, but nearly half of this increase (7 percent) was due to an increase in import quality, or a shift towards higher-priced varieties of steel. Some of this upgrading was reversed in 1971, when the agreement broke down, but when it was renewed during 1972–73 quality again rose by a modest amount (3 percent). The agreement lapsed in 1974, and in subsequent years the change in import quality was erratic, and quite small. The evidence from these and other industries strongly supports the hypothesis of upgrading under quotas, as indicated in Table 3.1.

It could be expected that the change in import composition – or quality – due to the quota would have a deadweight loss over and above the cost of an ''equivalent'' tariff. One reason to expect this is from our discussion of the trade distortion index, in Section 2.1. There we argued that when the *percentage* tariffs across products differed, the deadweight loss would depend on both the mean and the variance of these rates. The same observation applies to a quota. Even when the quota premium (denoted by s) is equal in *dollar* terms across products, when expressed as a percentage of marginal cost (i.e. s/v_i^*) the premium is highest on the lower-priced products. This explains the shift in import composition, and will result in an additional deadweight loss. For example, Anderson (1991) applies the trade distortion index to evaluate U.S. quotas on cheese, and finds that the shift in import composition due to the quotas accounts for 16 percent of the total deadweight cost.[18]

Anderson's methods requires that the trade surplus function in (2.4) and (3.3) be calculated. An alternative way to measure the additional deadweight loss of the quota using index numbers is developed by Boorstein and Feenstra (1991), and is illustrated in Figure 4.1. There we show the case of two import varieties C_1, and C_2, where the free trade price (equal to marginal cost) of the first exceeds the second, $p_1^0 \equiv v_1^* > p_2^0 \equiv v_2^*$. Under free trade, consumption is at C^0 where utility of U^0 is obtained. A

---

[18]Anderson and Neary (1994b) apply the trade restrictiveness index to U.S. quotas on textiles under the Multi-Fibre Arrangement, while Anderson, Bannister, and Neary (1995) apply it to evaluate Mexican agricultural policy.

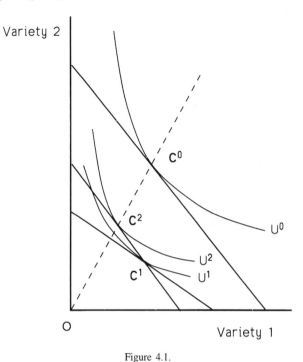

Variety 2

C^0

U^0

C^2

U^2

C^1 U^1

O   Variety 1

Figure 4.1.

quota on these two goods, with the quota premium of s, will lead to a greater percentage increase in the price of variety 1. For fixed total expenditure, the budget line shifts inward and rotates counter-clockwise, so at the new consumption point of C^1 there is greater *relative* demand for variety 1: this illustrates the shift in import composition, or quality upgrading.

Utility under the quota is U^1, but higher utility could be obtained from an ad valorem tariff of $\bar{\tau}$, with tariff revenue equal to the quota rents at the point C^1. By setting the revenue equal to rents at this consumption point, the ad valorem tariff $\bar{\tau}$ is what would typically be calculated as the price-equivalent to the quota. Applying this tariff, however, leads to a parallel inward shift of the original budget line, to the point where C^1 is still affordable (since revenue equals rents at that point). The optimal choice for the consumer on this budget line is C^2, with utility of U^2. Thus, higher utility of U^2 is available than with the quota, and the difference $(U^2 - U^1)$ can be interpreted as the *extra deadweight loss* due to the quality upgrading.

While Figure 4.1 is probably familiar to the reader, it is not generally recognized that the difference $(U^2 - U^1)/U^0$ can be easily calculated with available data. To see this, note that the ratio U^1/U^0 can be measured by an *exact quantity index* between the free trade and quota-induced consumption points C^0 and C^1.[19] Since we kept total expenditure fixed when comparing free trade and the quota, the exact quantity index equal the inverse of the exact price index. Thus, utility under a quota, relative to free trade, is $U^1/U^0 = \pi(p^0, p^1, C^0, C^1)^{-1}$, where p^1 denotes the quota-inclusive prices and p^0 the free-trade prices.

Turning to the ratio U^2/U^0, it can be measured by the inverse of the increase in prices from p^0 to $p^2 = p^0(1 + \bar{\tau})$, relative to any fixed consumption point. Choosing the quota-induced consumption point C^1, we obtain $U^2/U^0 = (\Sigma_i\ p_i^2 C_i^1 / \Sigma_i\ p_i^0 C_i^1)^{-1}$. However, since the budget lines under the tariff and quota both pass though the point C^1 (reflecting the fact that the tariff revenue equals the quota rents), we have that $\Sigma_i\ p_i^2 C_i^1 = \Sigma_i\ p_i^1 C_i^1$. It follows that $U^2/U^0 = (\Sigma_i\ p_i^1 C_i^1 / \Sigma_i\ p_i^0 C_i^1)^{-1}$, which is precisely the inverse of the *Paasche price index* between the free trade and quota-induced points. Thus, we have shown that the extra deadweight loss equals,

$$\frac{(U^2 - U^1)}{U^0} = \left(\frac{\Sigma_i\ p_i^1 C_i^1}{\Sigma_i\ p_i^0 C_i^1}\right)^{-1} - \pi(p^0, p^1, C^0, C^1)^{-1}, \tag{4.2}$$

which is the inverse of a Paasche price index minus the inverse of the exact. If the data are consistent with utility maximization, then the Paasche index understates the true rise in prices, so that (4.2) is positive.

Boorstein and Feenstra (1991) have applied this formula to the quota on U.S. steel imports during 1969–74, and obtain a deadweight loss due to quality upgrading of about 1 percent of import expenditure during these years. Based on the 1970 expenditure, this is a welfare cost of about $15 million. It should be stressed that this cost is *additional* to the conventional deadweight loss triangle that would be calculated using the price-equivalent tariff $\bar{\tau}$. This tariff has been estimated at about 7 percent, which can lead to a deadweight loss triangle between 0.5–1 percent of import expenditure, depending on what estimate is used for the change in imports. Thus, the extra deadweight loss due to the quality upgrading is at least as high as the conventional deadweight loss triangle, and possibly larger.[20]

It is worth noting that the formula in (4.2) can also be derived using the trade surplus function from (2.4), as in Boorstein and Feenstra (1991). In that case, a tariff and quota leading to the same increase in the import price index are compared. The difference between the trade surplus with these two instruments, relative to initial import expenditure, is given by (4.2). In general, this index number method is an alternative to the trade distortion index for evaluating the welfare loss due to a non-uniform tariff structures.[21] In comparison with the trade distortion index, this method seems to impose less structure on the data. Whereas the trade distortion index is typically calculated from a CGE model, and relies on the elasticity parameters used, the index number comparison in (4.2) simply reflects the extent of substitution between products in the data. This is clear from Figure 4.1, where the distance $(U^2 - U^1)/U^0$ depends on how much the consumption point C^1 differs from C^2. In addition to the application we have described in steel, this index number method has also been applied to quality upgrading in autos (see below), but not for any other industries; further work is necessary to determine its general usefulness.

4.2. U.S. automobile imports

One of the most extensively studied quotas in the United States is the "voluntary" export restraint (VER) on Japanese automobiles, that began in 1981 and expired only recently. For this trade policy we have estimates of the price impact of the VER, its effect on product quality, and its impact on the profits of U.S. producers, as will be reviewed in this section.

The appropriate concept of quality for automobiles is the utility obtained from its characteristics. Empirically, the market equilibrium locus between prices and characteristics is estimated using a *hedonic regression* (Griliches, 1971), which is a linear regression of prices (usually in logs) on characteristics. The estimated coefficients in this regression are generally interpreted as the marginal value that consumers place on the characteristics, which in equilibrium also equals the marginal cost to firms.[22] Then quality can be measured by a weighted average of the characteristics, using their estimated coefficients as weights. It has been shown in various theoretical models, under either perfect or imperfect competition, that a quota may cause an increase in product characteristics, though this result is not guaranteed (Rodriguez, 1979; Das and Donnenfeld, 1987, 1989; Krishna, 1987).

Using a hedonic regression, Feenstra (1988a) estimates both the price the quality change in Japanese automobiles exported to the U.S. under the VER over 1981–85.

---

[21]In general applications, it would be important to include products not subject to the trade barriers in the calculation, so that substitution towards them is taken into account. Then the formula in (4.2) would measure both the conventional deadweight loss triangle, and the extra loss due to upgrading.

[22]Rosen (1974) establishes this result under perfect competition, while Feenstra (1993) discusses the noncompetitive case.

The regression is specified as:

$$p_{it} = s_t + \exp(\alpha_t + \beta' z_{it}) + \varepsilon_{it},\tag{4.3}$$

where z_{it} is a vector of characteristics for each car model i in year t, such as weight, width, height, and horsepower, and s_t is the price effect of the VER in year t. Note that the VER is modeled as leading to a *specific* (dollar) price increase, whereas the coefficient α_t allows for any other *percentage* change in prices (due to inflation, for example). When both s_t and α_t are estimated, multicollinearity between them leads to very high standard errors. Feenstra solves this problem by pooling the auto data in (4.3) with data for imports of Japanese compact trucks to the U.S. Trucks were not subject to the VER, but did have a tariff of 25 percent imposed since 1980. The hedonic regression for trucks omitted the specific price terms s_t, and allowed for different coefficients on the characteristics, while imposing the same coefficients on the percentage price changes α_t (after correcting for the impact of the ad valorem tariff). In this way, the increase in the quality-adjusted prices of both Japanese cars and trucks that would have occurred *without* trade barriers are treated as identical, and the remaining impact of the VER in cars is estimated by α_t. Rather precise estimates of this price impact are obtained, ranging from $434 in 1981 to $1,096 in 1984 (with standard errors of $250 and $267, respectively).

Using the coefficient estimates from (4.3), the quality of each car is measured by $\exp(\alpha_{1980} + \beta' z_{it})$. The increase in product quality accounted for a substantial portion of the nominal prices increases in Japanese auto imports during the VER. For example, in the first year of the VER quality rose by 7 percent on average over the models, which was one-third of the average price increase. Over the entire 1980–85 period, quality upgrading accounted for fully one-half of the increase in prices. We expect this upgrading to have a deadweight loss for two reasons: due to the changing composition of imports (as consumers substituted towards luxury models), and also because consumers would attach a *declining* shadow value to the extra characteristics added onto each model. Using a more general version of (4.2), Feenstra (1993) shows that the deadweight loss of the upgrading is surprisingly large, between one-quarter and one-third of the quality increase itself, or about $500 in 1985. Combining the transfer of quota rents and the deadweight loss due to upgrading, we obtain $1,500 over the 1.8 million autos imported, for a welfare loss to the U.S. of $2.7 billion annually (not including the conventional deadweight loss).

Dinopoulos and Kreinin (1988) have also used hedonic regressions and several other methods to estimate the increase in the prices of European cars exported to the U.S., and find that these prices increased by about one-third, with a further cost to the U.S. of $3.4 billion annually. Unless the European firms had strongly increasing marginal costs for their sales to the U.S., which seems unlikely, these price increases support the hypothesis of a change in market conduct. That is, if initially the

European producers were engaged in Bertrand competition in prices with the Japanese firms, then the presence of the VER would cause them to instead treat Japanese quantities as fixed (since the VER specified the total sales of each company), with a corresponding increase in price. This seems like the most plausible explanation for the increase in the European prices found by Dinopoulos and Kreinin, though a direct estimate of the mode of market conduct is not made.[23]

In order to estimate the effect of the VER on profits of auto producers, it is necessary to jointly estimate demand and costs. Bresnahan (1981) provided the first, fully-specified estimates of the oligopoly equilibrium in the U.S. automobile market where each consumer has an ideal auto variety on a line of characteristics. Later work by Goldberg (1995) and Berry, Levinsohn, and Pakes (1995) has generalized the demand side of this model while jointly estimating the cost side, and these authors calculate the impact of various trade policies. There is some disagreement concerning which years the VER was most binding. Goldberg finds that in 1983 and 1984 the VER was binding with a price impact of about $1,000 (similar to that found by Feenstra 1988a). The quota was increased in 1985, and Goldberg finds that it was not binding in that year or 1986, though it becomes binding again in 1987. In contrast, Berry, Levinsohn and Pakes obtain estimates of the price impact of the VER that are insignificant in 1981–83, and then rise steadily in subsequent years.

However, these authors are in agreement on the overall conclusions for trade policy: the quota was much worse than a equivalent tariff, that would have led to the same reduction in Japanese imports. Both studies find a substantial increase in American and European prices due to the VER, again offering indirect evidence of the change in market conduct. Berry, Levinsohn, and Pakes estimate that European producers increased their profits by about $1 billion annually in 1987–89, while the profits of U.S. producers increased by $3–5 billion annually. This gain for American firms illustrates the ''profit-shifting'' effects of trade policy, and would not be present in a competitive model. The profits of Japanese producers fall only slightly, because the quota rents nearly offset the reduction in profits through lost sales. Over the entire 1984–1990 period, these authors estimate that the VER increased U.S. profits by $16 billion, but created a loss for U.S. consumers of $18 billion, for a cumulative net loss to the U.S. of $2 billion. In contrast, the revenue raised from an equivalent tariff is estimated at $14.5 billion, so that the U.S. welfare gain from this tariff would have been $12.5 billion. Thus, this industry appears to be an instance were strategic trade policy – in the form of a tariff – could have worked, but this was not the policy that was actually used.

---

[23]For a later year, 1987, Feenstra and Levinsohn (1995) have found that European producers appear to use quantity as their strategic variable, while American producers use price (and the strategic variable of Japanese producers cannot be distinguished).

5. Estimating markups

In the previous sections, we have ignored the potential change in the output of domestic firms due to trade policy. This appears as the third term on the right side of (2.5), where a change in the output of domestic firms is multiplied by the difference between average and marginal cost: an expansion in the output of firms with increasing returns provides a welfare gain. There is some indirect evidence that increasing returns serve as a source of comparative advantage, which suggests welfare gains (Tybout, 1993). Rather than directly test the effect of trade policy on industry output, however, an alternative method has been to estimate the impact of policy on the price-cost margins charged by firms.

Under freedom of entry and zero profits, the price-cost margins and the output levels can be related by dividing conditions (2.6) and (2.8), to obtain:

$$\lambda_i \equiv \frac{\phi_i(y_i, w)/y_i}{\phi_{iy}(y_i, w)} = \left[1 - \left(\frac{\theta_i}{\eta_i} \right) \right]^{-1} \equiv \mu_i . \tag{5.1}$$

The left-hand side of (5.1) is the ratio of average to marginal costs, which is sometimes called the degree of increasing returns to scale, and we shall denote it by λ_i. The right-hand side is the ratio of price to marginal cost, or the degree of monopoly power, and is denoted by μ_i. It is normally assumed that the degree of increasing returns to scale *falls* as output increases. In that case, there will be a *negative* relationship between firm output and the price-cost ratio μ_i: an increase in output is associated with a fall in this ratio, and conversely. Thus, trade policies that lead to a fall in markups can be expected to have a beneficial welfare effect, through the expansion of firm outputs.[24] Effects of this type have been captured in a CGE model of Cameroon by Devarajan and Rodrik (1991), who calculate the welfare gains from trade liberalization as between one and two percent of national income. The question we address in this section is how one could econometrically estimate the impact of liberalization on markups.

5.1. Hall method

One method for estimating markups has been suggested by Hall (1988), and relies on the same data that could be used to estimate productivity in an industry. Levinsohn (1993) and Harrison (1994a) have applied this method to panel data sets on firms in developing countries, facing trade liberalization; Levinsohn considers the 1984 trade

---

[24]This is sometimes referred to as a "rationalization" of the domestic industry. Brown and Stern (1989) note that rationalization may fail to occur due to differential effects on factor prices, and provide simulation results for U.S.–Canada trade.

liberalization in Turkey, while Harrison considers the 1985 reform in Cote d'Ivoire. Their applications are described as follows.

Let the production function for a domestic firm denoted by i be specified as $y_{it} = A_{it} f(L_{it}, K_{it})$, where L_{it} and K_{it} denote the labor and capital inputs (materials can also be added), and A_{it} is a productivity parameter. We shall suppose that this function is homogeneous of degree λ_i, which is the degree of increasing returns to scale. Firms will hire inputs until their marginal-revenue product equals their wage, or using the price-cost margin μ_{it} from (5.1) along with (2.6):

$$(q_{it}/\mu_{it}) \frac{\partial f_{it}}{\partial L_{it}} = w_t, \text{ and } (q_{it}/\mu_{it}) \frac{\partial f_{it}}{\partial K_{it}} = r_t. \tag{5.2}$$

Then totally differentiating the production function, and using (5.2), we obtain,

$$\frac{dy_{it}}{y_{it}} = \mu_{it} \left[\alpha_{it} \left(\frac{dL_{it}}{L_{it}} \right) + \beta_{it} \left(\frac{dK_{it}}{K_{it}} \right) \right] + \frac{dA_{it}}{A_{it}}, \tag{5.3}$$

where $\alpha_{it} \equiv w_t L_{it} / q_{it} y_{it}$ denotes the share of labor in total revenue, and $\beta_{it} \equiv r_t K_{it} / q_{it} y_{it}$ denotes the share of capital. Thus, (5.3) states that the growth in output is a weighted average of the growth in inputs, where the weights are $\mu_{it} \alpha_{it}$ and $\mu_{it} \beta_{it}$. It is readily confirmed that these weights sum to λ_i, the degree of increasing returns to scale of the production function.

This formulation can be contrasted with the conventional measurement of productivity under perfect competition, where *total factor productivity* (TFP) is defined as,

$$\text{TFP}_{it} \equiv \frac{dy_{it}}{y_{it}} - \left[\alpha_{it} \left(\frac{dL_{it}}{L_{it}} \right) + (1 - \alpha_{it}) \left(\frac{dK_{it}}{K_{it}} \right) \right]. \tag{5.4}$$

In words, TFP (also called the "Solow residual") is defined as the difference between the growth in output and a weighted average of the growth in inputs, where the weights sum to unity by construction. Under this weighting scheme, any portion of revenue not paid to labor – such as pure profits – is attributed to capital. This scheme gives too little weight to the growth in labor input as compared to (5.3), $\alpha_{it} < \mu_{it} \alpha_{it}$. The reason for this is that under oligopolistic conduct, firms will restrict their output and hire less inputs than under perfect competition. It follows that the marginal physical product of labor *exceeds* its real wage. The weight α_{it} in (5.4) is essentially using the real wage (w_t/q_{it}) to proxy for the marginal physical product of labor, so it gives too little weight to the labor input.

In order to see how conventionally measured TFP in (5.4) can mismeasure the true productivity shock dA_{it}/A_{it}, we can combine (5.3) and (5.4) to obtain:

$$\text{TFP}_{it} = (\mu_{it} - 1)\alpha_{it} \left(\frac{dL_{it}}{L_{it}} - \frac{dK_{it}}{K_{it}} \right) + (\lambda_i - 1) \left(\frac{dK_{it}}{K_{it}} \right) + \frac{dA_{it}}{A_{it}}, \tag{5.5}$$

where we have used $\lambda_i = \mu_{it}(\alpha_{it} + \beta_{it})$. The first term on the right side of (5.5) reflects changes in the labor-capital ratio, and arises due to the mismeasurement of the weight on labor. The second term reflects increasing returns to scale in the production function. In studies of developing countries, it is quite common to correlate total factor productivity with trade volumes, to determine whether firms exposed to international competition are more efficient.[25] From (5.5), it is apparent that variation in TFP – across industries or over time – could be caused by *either* productivity shocks dA_{it}/A_{it}, by changes in markups, by changes in the labor-capital ratio, or by changes in the capital input under increasing returns to scale, so that changes in conventionally measured TFP must be interpreted with great caution.[26]

One example of an attempt to relate protection to TFP performance is Krueger and Tuncer (1982), who argue that there is little connection between these two variables for a cross-section of Turkish industries. They conclude, therefore, that there is little support for the idea of "infant industry" protection. In contrast, Harrison (1994b) finds that the same data show a *positive* correlation between tariffs or non-tariff barriers and TFP. From (5.5), the correlation could be explained by either higher markups and/or higher input growth in protected industries, both of which are plausible. The presence of these effects means that conventional TFP measures do not estimate the true productivity shock dA_{it}/A_{it}, so that a simple comparison of TFP with tariffs is not a valid test for "infant industry" protection.

In order to properly determine the effects of trade policy on productivity, then, it is necessary to also estimate its effects on markups μ_{it}. The markups can be estimated by rewriting (5.3) in discrete form as,

$$\Delta \ln y_{it} = \mu_{it}\bar{\alpha}_{it}[\Delta \ln L_{it} - \Delta \ln K_{it}] + \lambda_i \Delta \ln K_{it} + \gamma_t + \varepsilon_{it}, \tag{5.6}$$

where the productivity changes are specified as $\Delta \ln A_{it} = \gamma_t + \varepsilon_{it}$, and $\bar{\alpha}_t$ refers to an average of the labor shares in years $t - 1$ and t. It is not feasible to allow the markup μ_{it} to vary in all years, so it is generally restricted to be constant over some intervals, while possibly changing discretely at a major break. In addition, μ_{it} and λ_i are typically restricted to be equal across firms (though this can be relaxed).

It should be expected that the labor and capital inputs in (5.6) are affected by the changes in productivity ε_{it}, so that instrumental variables must be used in the estimation. Appropriate instruments should be correlated with demand for factors but not with productivity shocks. Examples include variables shifting product demand international prices and exchange rates, and sectoral or economy-wide factor prices. Instruments of this type are used by Harrison (1994a) in her study of trade liberalization in Cote d'Ivoire. She finds declining markups due to trade reform for a

---

[25] A theoretical justification for this hypothesis, based on imperfect monitoring of managerial effort, is developed in Horn, Lang, and Lundgren (1995).

[26] Note that this difficulty would not arise when productivity is measured by directly estimating the production function (for example, Aw and Hwang, 1993), without relying on real wages to measure marginal physical products.

number of industries, although the changes in the markups are not statistically significant. Harrison also finds that correcting the measurement of TFP for changes in markups, and allowing for non-constant returns to scale, leads to a positive and substantial effect of trade reform on productivity.

Levinsohn (1993) exploits the panel nature of the data set to estimate an annual productivity shock γ_t (common across firms), assuming that remaining shocks ε_{it} are not forecast by firms, and therefore uncorrelated with factor demand. He finds evidence of decreased markups due to liberalization in Turkey when comparing the years 1984 with 1985–86, for those industries that were imperfectly competitive initially and had declining levels of protection. In contrast, for the two industries where protection increased, markups were also found to increase. Thus, the results for both Turkey and (to a weaker extent) Cote d'Ivoire are consistent with the hypothesis of declining markups due to trade liberalization, as indicated in Table 3.1.

5.2. Other methods

Our discussion of price-cost margins has taken for granted that these cannot be directly measured from firm or industry data. The reason is that accounting data on costs cannot generally be relied upon to obtain a marginal cost measure, used to compute the price-cost margins. Instead, marginal cost must be estimated, which was implicitly done in the Hall method. The joint estimation of marginal cost and marginal revenue, together with a market conduct parameter, is the starting point of the "new empirical industrial economics", as surveyed by Bresnahan (1989), which is highly recommended for reading. Some of these methods have already been mentioned in our discussion of the automobile industry (Section 4.2).

Aw (1992, 1993) has taken the approach of this literature to estimate the markup conduct of textiles exporters from Hong Kong. She specifies a functional form for the demand curve, from which marginal revenue is calculated. Then the first-order condition (2.6) is estimated jointly with the demand curve, which yields an estimate of the market conduct parameter θ_{it}. Not surprisingly, Aw finds that the textile exporters act in a perfectly competitive manner. Schembri (1989) takes a similar approach to estimate the markups of a major Canadian export industry, which are then used to simulate the pass-through behavior. The incomplete pass-through that he finds provides additional evidence of the exercise of market power by exporters, as was discussed in Section 3.

6. Wages and employment

So far, the only form of imperfect competition we have considered is that exercised by firms. However, it is realistic to suppose that unions will also exercise some monopoly power in the labor market, with the result that workers with the same skills in various industries may earn different wages. In principle, this might justify some type of trade policy. Katz and Summers (1989a,b) have argued that such wage distortions are pervasive in industrial countries, with more capital-intensive industries paying higher wages, even after correcting for characteristics of workers, union activity, etc. This means that the high-wage industries are producing too little: in terms of eq. (2.5), the average costs of production exceed the social opportunity costs of withdrawing workers from other industries, so that a rise in output is welfare increasing. Based on this wage evidence, they argue that trade subsidies to the capital-intensive industries, which in the United States are the export industries, would be in the national interest.

The recommendation of Katz and Summers is highly controversial, to say the least. One response is that the wage distortions they identify may be endogenous, so that the application of wage subsidies could lead to even *greater* differences in the wages paid across industries. Possible evidence supporting this idea is provided by Gaston and Trefler (1994a), in their study of wage premia and protection in U.S. manufacturing. They find a strong positive correlation between exports and wage premia across industries. If this correlation also applies in a time-series context, it suggests that an expansion of exports would increase the premia, so it is unlikely that there would be any gain from applying an export subsidy.

In any case, it is unlikely that trade policy as practiced in the U.S. is directed at resolving inefficiencies due to wage distortions. Instead, this policy seems to have an equity rationale. Under Article XIX of the General Agreement on Tariffs and Trade (GATT), the use of tariffs and quotas is limited to cases where there is evidence of harm in the importing industry. In the United States, these rules are legislated in Section 201 of the Trade Act of 1974, under which trade protection can be granted if "increased imports of an article are a substantial cause of serious injury, or threat thereof, to the domestic industry". The following criteria can be used to determine if the industry has suffered "serious injury": "the significant idling of productive facilities in the industry, the inability of a significant number of firms to operate at a reasonable level of profit, and significant unemployment or underemployment within the industry". All of these criterion are related to a drop in income faced by some factors of production in the industry.

One reason to base trade policy on a change in factor income is to achieve the following equity goal: that all individuals gain from increases in trade, so that "Pareto gains" are achieved. This equity goal is *not* related to income distribution in the usual sense, since workers in import-competing industries (such as autos) may be more highly paid then elsewhere in the economy. If Pareto gains are specified as a goal, however, then these workers should be compensated for reductions in their income due to import competition. There is considerable evidence that workers forced to change industries experience a large drop in their income, due to the loss of their firm-specific skills (Bale, 1976, Hamermesh, 1987). The question is then how to best compensate these workers. The idea of "lump-sum" transfers, under which individuals are each fully compensated for their losses, is highly impractical, since the government would not know the losses faced by each person. Recently, policies that require less information have been explored in theoretical models.[27] This work is very recent, however, and there is no consensus as to how compensation should be achieved, or if it is always feasible.

6.1. Import prices versus shares

Thus, the provisions of Section 201 can be viewed as one method of achieving compensation, in a world where the best policy is not known. This legislation restricts the use of tariffs or quotas to cases where import competition is a "substantial cause" of unemployment or other injury, which is defined as a "cause that is important and not less than any other cause". In order to implement this rule, there must be some basis to judge the importance of various causes of injury within an industry. One method is to compare changes in the share of expenditure within an industry going to imports, with changes in overall expenditure, and grant protection only if the former is greater. For example, in the report of the U.S. International Trade Commission (USITC, 1980, A-70) to evaluate the industry request for a tariff in automobiles, it was found that the import share rose from 25 percent in Jan.–June 1979 to 30 percent in July–Dec., and 35 percent in Jan.–June 1980. However, over the same period U.S. consumption of autos fell by about 20 percent, so that a majority of ITC commissioners determined that import competition was *not* the principal cause of unemployment. As a result, protection was not granted under Section 201, but instead, the VER with Japan was negotiated.

As simple as the above calculation is, the use of import shares to determine the effects of trade on unemployment extends to many studies, as surveyed in Deardorff and Hakura (1994). For example. Krueger (1980a,b) uses the import share in a decomposition of the sources of unemployment for the United States, as do Berman, Bound and Griliches (1994) more recently, while Freeman and Katz (1991) have used import volumes as an explanatory variable in regressions explaining employment and wages. The use of import shares has been criticized by Grossman (1982, 1986, 1987), however, who argues that the import share is *endogenous* and may change due to many underlying causes. Grossman's argument can be briefly summarized as follows.

---

[27] See Dixit and Norman (1986) and the papers in the May 1994 *Journal of International Economics*. A particularly dramatic example of an attempt to achieve Pareto gains from trade is in the union of East and West Germany, where the political goal was that no citizen should lose from this union; in particular, wages in the East and West should be equalized. To offset the resulting high costs in East Germany, Akerlof et al. (1991) argue that wage subsidies should be applied there. There is a remarkable affinity between this recommendation and the theoretical policies of Dixit and Norman (1986), where factor subsidies (or taxes) play a significant role.

Suppose that real expenditure for industry i is denoted by (E_i/q_i), and that the import share is m_i, so that $Y_i = (1 - m_i)(E_i/q_i)$ equals domestic output. If a_i workers are needed per unit of output, then employment in the industry is:

$$L_i \equiv a_i(1 - m_i)(E_i/q_i) \,. \tag{5.7}$$

According to this expression, changes in employment can be decomposed into changes in real expenditure, changes in the import share, and changes in technology a_i. However, it would be incorrect to attribute any *causality* to these relations. For example, if the import share rises by 10 percentage points, so that employment falls by 10 percent, it would be incorrect to conclude that the fall in employment is caused by import competition. Instead, it might be that a fall in productivity within the domestic industry, or a rise in wages, has caused both the decline in employment and the rise in imports. The point to recognize is that the import share m_i, or import quantities, are endogenous variables, which should be taken into account when estimating their effects on employment or wages.

To correctly assess the impact of import competition on employment, Grossman (1986, 1987) recommends that *import prices* rather than shares be used to measure international competition. He derives a log-linear relation between industry wages or employment, and exogenous variables including the prices of inputs, international price and exchange rate, tariffs, industry output, and possibly industry wages. In one application, Grossman (1986) estimates the impact of import competition – measured by the international price – on employment and wages in the U.S. steel industry. It is found that job losses due to import competition depend primarily on the appreciation of the dollar after 1979. In the period 1979–83, the job losses due to appreciation are comparable to those due to a secular decline in employment, picked up by a time trend in the regression.[28] Over the longer period 1976–83, however, the job losses due to appreciation are an order of magnitude smaller than those due to the secular decline. Based on these results, Grossman concludes that whether import competition is considered the most important cause of injury depends on the time period used, and on whether exchange rate effects qualify as "injury caused by imports".[29]

Grossman (1987) applies the same methods to a wider group of U.S. industries over 1969–79, but finds a significant effect of import competition on employment in only one of the nine industries, and a significant effect of import competition on wages in only two. A greater impact of import competition on employment and

---

[28]This secular decline reflects technological and product changes in purchasing industries (such as smaller cars), labor-saving technological change in steel, or growth in other sectors than would pull resources out of the steel industry.

[29]Despite this, on June 12, 1984, the ITC concluded that import protection was justified in the steel industry under Section 201.

wages is obtained by Revenga (1992). Her data applies to a wide sample of U.S. industries, with the advantage that she has a better measure of the import prices than used by Grossman, though the disadvantage that she pools data across the different industries. Revenga treats the *import prices as endogenous*, which is to be expected from our discussion of pricing under imperfect competition in Section 3: the import price in (3.8) depends on domestic prices, and therefore depends on domestic productivity, wages, etc. Using industry-specific indexes of exchange rates and foreign costs, she finds a significant impact of import prices on both employment and wages: a 10 percent reduction in import prices reduced employment by 3.5–3.9 percent, and reduces wages by about 1 percent. According to these estimates, the reduction in import prices due to dollar appreciation over 1980–85 reduced employment by 6.5–7.5 percent. In addition, Revenga (1990) re-estimates the relation between import volumes and wages reported in Freeman and Katz (1991), using instrumental variables. She finds that the revised estimates reinforce the findings of Freeman and Katz, that industry wages respond significantly to import prices.

From the results of Grossman and Revenga, we conclude there is weak evidence that import competition lowers wages. Surprisingly, however, the converse hypothesis does not appear to hold empirically: tariffs or non-tariff barriers need not raise wages. In particular, Gaston and Trefler (1994a) find a *negative* relationship between tariffs and wages. They suggest that this may be due to a willingness of unions to accept lower wages in exchange for employment guarantees, when protection is granted. This hypothesis is confirmed in later work (Gaston and Trefler, 1994b), where the negative correlation between tariffs and wages is found to occur only for a union sample, while non-union wages are insignificantly related to tariffs. Gaston and Trefler argue that this is consistent with optimizing behavior on the part of unions, if they use tariff protection as an opportunity to increase employment rather than wages. This is demonstrated in the theoretical model of Grossman (1984), for example, where workers with less seniority would be more willing to accept lower wages in exchange for employment guarantees. The negative correlation between wages and tariffs found by Gaston and Trefler deserves further empirical study.[30]

6.2. Product variety

We have argued above that the problem with using import shares to measure competition is that they are endogenous; yet, Revenga also finds that the prices need to be treated this way. It follows that either import shares or prices could be used to measure international competition in a regression framework, provided that in-

---

[30]Quite different results for Canada are reported by Fung and Huizinga (1991), who find that tariffs increase union wages at the expense of non-union wages.

strumental variables are used in the estimation.[31] The question then arises as to which variable is preferred. While this question can only be settled by further research, there is one reason to believe that import *shares* will be the preferred variable when products are differentiated. In that case, an increase in the variety of imports available will shift demand away from domestic varieties, and reduce output and employment. It is doubtful, however, that this impact would be reflected in an import price index, but it would be reflected in import shares or volumes, which are then a better measure of international competition.

There is indirect evidence that changes in the range of product varieties has had an important impact on trade. This evidence comes from the estimation of import demand. Since the work of Houthakker and Magee (1969), it has been known that the estimated income elasticity of demand for U.S. imports exceeds unity, and also exceeds the foreign income elasticity of demand for U.S. exports.[32] One explanation for the high income elasticity is that it is a *spurious* result of omitting new product varieties from indexes of U.S. import prices [see Helkie and Hooper (1988); Hooper (1989); and Krugman (1989)]. According to this argument, over the past several decades the U.S. has experienced an expansion in the range of new imports from rapidly growing, developing countries, but no corresponding decrease in import prices. Then the rising share of imports is (incorrectly) attributed to a high income elasticity in the import demand equation.

To precisely determine the connection between import prices and product variety, suppose that all import varieties within some industry enter into a constant elasticity of substitution utility or production function. Let the elasticity of substitution be denoted by σ, and let $\pi(p_{t-1}, p_t, C_{t-1}, C_t)$ denote the exact price index for imports. This index will decline as new product varieties become available, because the new varieties lower the cost of obtaining any level of utility or output. In contrast, a conventionally measured price index – denoted by $P(p_{t-1}, p_t, C_{t-1}, C_t)$ – would not reflect the presence of new product varieties. Let the set I_t denote the varieties that are available in period t, and let $I \subseteq (I_t \cap I_{t-1})$, $I \neq \emptyset$, denote any non-empty subset of the product varieties available in *both* periods. Then Feenstra (1994) shows that the exact index is related to the conventional index by:

$$\pi(p_{t-1}, p_t, C_{t-1}, C_t) = P(p_{t-1}, p_t, C_{t-1}, C_t)(\lambda_t/\lambda_{t-1})^{1/(\sigma-1)}, \qquad (5.8)$$

---

[31]In the context of Section 201 protection, Pindyck and Rotemberg (1987) specify a regression equation that explains injury in terms of variables shifting domestic supply and demand, along with import volume, which is treated as endogenous; their approach is an alternative to the regression specified by Grossman (1986, 1987).

[32]This result applies more generally when comparing the income elasticity of demand for imports into industrial countries, with the developed country's income elasticity of import demand, as discussed in the survey by Goldstein and Khan (1985).

where

$$\lambda_r \equiv \sum_{i \in I} p_{ir} x_{ir} \Big/ \sum_{i \in I_r} p_{ir} x_{ir}, \text{ for } r = t - 1, t \,.$$

This result states that the exact price index $\pi(p_{t-1}, p_t, C_{t-1}, C_t)$ equals the conventional price index $P(p_{t-1}, p_t, C_{t-1}, C_t)$ times the additional term $(\lambda_t / \lambda_{t-1})^{1/(\sigma-1)}$. To interpret this term, note that λ_t equals the fraction of expenditure in period t on the goods $i \in I$ relative to the entire set $i \in I_t$. Alternatively, λ_t measures *one minus the share of expenditure in period t on the new product varieties.* If these new varieties have a substantial share of expenditure, then λ_t will be small, and this will tend to make the exact index $\pi(p_{t-1}, p_t, C_{t-1}, C_t)$ significantly lower than the index $P(p_{t-1}, p_t, C_{t-1}, C_t)$. In other words, the introduction of new product varieties will *lower* the exact price index. The term λ_{t-1} equals *one minus the share of expenditure in period t − 1 on the product varieties that are not available in t.* Thus, if there are many disappearing varieties between the two periods, this will tend to make λ_{t-1} small, and *raise* the exact price index.

It is clear from (5.8) that increases in the share of differentiated imports from new suppliers will lower the exact price index, which will reduce employment in the domestic import-competing industry. This reduction in the effective price due to new product varieties would not be reflected in a conventional price index. Thus, for industries where product differentiation is important, it is desirable to include import shares (either over all countries or just the new suppliers) as measures of import competition, where these shares must be treated as endogenous.

7. Conclusions

In this chapter, we have attempted to show how the evaluation of trade policy, which has traditionally been based on models of competitive industries, can be extended to incorporate imperfect competition. Our major conclusions have been summarized in Table 3.1. For tariffs, the key insight is that imperfectly competitive foreign firms will generally choose to pass-through only a portion of the tariff, resulting in a terms of trade gain for the importing country. Most empirical studies of incomplete pass-through have focused on exchange rates rather than tariffs, though we expect that there is at least a partial symmetry between these effects. These studies of exchange rate pass-through provide an indication of imperfectly competitive market conduct. However, because the magnitude of pass-through differs substantially across industries, the possibility of a terms of trade gain cannot be used as a general argument for strategic trade policy.

Indeed, rather than imperfect competition forming the basis for national gains due to trade policy, the actual policies that have been used have sometimes led to losses from enhanced collusion. This has occurred due to the application of anti-dumping policies, for example. It has also occurred in the one case where strategic trade policy in the form of tariffs might have led to a welfare gain: U.S. automobile imports. The VER that was actually used led to an increase in profits for American firms, but not by enough to offset the loss to consumers, so that the United States suffered a net welfare loss.

The quality upgrading that occurred under the VER in autos, as measured by the change in product characteristics, has also been observed in a number of other industries, where it is measured by a change in the composition of imports. We have suggested that the first measure of quality-upgrading fits the "ideal variety" approach to modeling consumer preferences under monopolistic competition, whereas the second measure fits the "love of variety" approach. In either case, an additional deadweight loss due to the quality change can be estimated using index number techniques. We have argued that this technique imposes less structure on the data than the "trade distortion index" of Anderson and Neary (1992, 1994a,b), though both methods can be used to measure the impact of any non-uniform trade policy over multiple goods.

Direct estimates of the markups charged by firms have been made for several developing countries, drawing on methods from the "new empirical industrial organization". It has been confirmed that trade liberalization tends to reduce the markups charged by firms. Again, these empirical results lend no support to a strategic role for trade policy, and on the contrary, suggest that the application of tariffs may enhance collusion with corresponding welfare losses. The one instance we have found where protection may reduce the distortions caused by imperfect competition comes from a surprising source: the reduction in union wages under protection. The negative correlation between wages and tariffs observed for the U.S. is consistent with unions accepting employment gains rather than wage increases as a result of protection. Further work is needed to determine the generality of this result.

We conclude by mentioning a future source of data on trade patterns and trade policy. The National Science Foundation is currently funding a project to collect large data sets on trade – some of which have been used in the studies reported in this chapter – and make them widely available on CD-ROM. This project will be completed by late 1996, and the data will be described in a working paper of the National Bureau of Economic Research, and also will be announced in the February 1997 *Journal of International Economics*. If you are unaware of how to obtain this data after that date, please contact me by e-mail at rcfeenstra@ucdavis.edu.

References

Akerlof, G.A., A.K. Rose, J.L. Yellan, and H. Hessenius (1991), "East Germany in from the cold: The economic aftermath of currency union", Brookings Papers on Economic Activity 1:1–87.

Anderson, J.E. (1991), "The coefficient of trade utilization: The cheese case", in: R.E. Baldwin, ed., Empirical studies of commercial policy (Univ. of Chicago Press and National Bureau of Economic Research, Chicago) 221–244.

Anderson, J.E. (1994a), "Tariff index theory", Review of International Economics, forthcoming.

Anderson, J.E. (1994b), "Trade restrictiveness benchmarks", mimeo, Boston College.

Anderson, J.E., G.J. Bannister, and J.P. Neary (1995), "Domestic distortions and international trade", International Economic Review, 36(1):139–158.

Anderson, J.E. and J.P. Neary (1992), "A new approach to evaluating trade policy", Center for Economic Policy Research Discussion Paper No. 683, London.

Anderson, J.E. and J.P. Neary (1994a), "Measuring the restrictiveness of trade policy", The World Bank Review 8:151–170.

Anderson, J.E. and J.P. Neary (1994b), "The trade restrictiveness of the Multi-fibre arrangement", The World Bank Review 8:171–190.

Aw, B.Y. (1992), "An empirical model of mark-ups in a quality-differentiated export market", Journal of International Economics 33:327–344.

Aw, B.Y. (1993), "Price discrimination and markups in export markets", Journal of Development Economics 42:315–337.

Aw, B.Y. and A.R. Hwang (1993), "Productivity and the export market: A firm-level analysis", mimeo, Pennsylvania State and Academia Sinica, Taiwan.

Aw, B.Y. and M.J. Roberts (1986), "Measuring quality changes in quota constrained import markets: The case of U.S. footwear", Journal of International Economics 21:45–60.

Baldwin, R.E. and J.W. Steagall (1993), "An analysis of ITC decisions in antidumping, countervailing duty and safeguard cases", mimeo, Univ. of Wisconsin.

Bale, M.D. (1976), "Estimates of trade-displacement costs for U.S. workers", Journal of International Economics 6:245–250.

Bhagwati, J.N. (1965), "On the equivalence of tariffs and quotas", in: R.E. Baldwin et al., eds., Trade, growth and the balance of payments: Essays in honor of G. Haberler (Rand McNally, Chicago) 52–67.

Berman, E., J. Bound, and Z. Griliches (1994), "Changes in the demand for skilled labor within U.S. manufacturing: Evidence from the annual survey of manufacturing", Quarterly Journal of Economics 109:367–398.

Berry, S., J. Levinsohn, and A. Pakes (1995), "Voluntary export restraints on automobiles: Evaluating a strategic trade policy", Econometrica, forthcoming.

Boorstein, R. and R.C. Feenstra (1991), "Quality upgrading and its welfare cost in U.S. steel import, 1969–74", in: E. Helpman and A. Razin, eds., International trade and trade policy (MIT Press, Cambridge, MA) 167–186.

Brander, J.A. and B.J. Spencer (1984), "Trade warfare: Tariffs and cartels", Journal of International Economics 16:227–242.

Bresnahan, T.F. (1981), "Departures from marginal cost pricing in the American automobile industry: Estimates for 1977–1978", Journal of Econometrics 11:201–227.

Bresnahan, T.F. (1989), "Empirical studies of industries with market power", in: R. Schmalansee and R.D. Willig, eds., Handbook of industrial organization, vol. 2 (North-Holland, Amsterdam) 1011–1057.

Brown, D.K. and R.M. Stern (1989), "U.S.–Canada bilateral tariff elimination: The role of product differentiation and market structure", in: R.C. Feenstra, ed., Trade policies for international competitiveness (University of Chicago and National Bureau of Economic Research, Chicago) 217–245.

Ceglowski, J. (1991), "Dollar import prices and domestic prices in the 1980's: A simultaneous approach", mimeo, Bryn Mawr College.

Das, S.P. and S. Donnenfeld (1987), "Trade policy and its impact on the quality of imports: A welfare analysis", Journal of International Economics 23:77–96.

Das, S.P. and S. Donnenfeld (1989), "Oligopolistic competition and international trade: Quantity and quality restrictions", Journal of International Economics 27:299–318.

Deardorff, A.V. and D. Hakura (1994), "Trade and wages: What are the questions?", in: J. Bhagwati and M.H. Kosters, eds., Trade and wages (American Enterprise Institute, Washington, D.C.) 76–107.

De Meza, D. (1979), "Commercial policy towards multinational monopolies – Reservations on Katrak", Oxford Economic Papers 31:334–337.

Devarajan, S. and D. Rodrik (1991), "Pro-competitive effects of trade reform: Results from a CGE model of Cameroon", European Economic Review 35:1157–1184.

Diewert, W.E. (1976), "Exact and superlative index numbers", Journal of Econometrics 4:115–145.

Dinopoulos, E. and M. Kreinin (1988), "Effects of the U.S.–Japan VER on European prices and on U.S. welfare", The Review of Economics and Statistics 70:484–491.

Dixit, A.K. and V. Norman (1986), "Gains from trade without lump-sum compensation", Journal of International Economics 21:111–122.

Falvey, R.E. (1979), "The composition of trade within import-restricted product categories", Journal of Political Economy 87:1105–1114.

Feenstra, R.C. (1988a), "Quality change under trade restraints in U.S. autos", Quarterly Journal of Economics 103:131–146.

Feenstra, R.C. (1988b), "Gains from trade in differentiated products: Japanese compact trucks", in: R.C. Feenstra, ed., Empirical methods for international trade (MIT Press, Cambridge, MA) 119–136.

Feenstra, R.C. (1989), "Symmetric pass-through of tariffs and exchange rates under imperfect competition: An empirical test", Journal of International Economics 27:25–45.

Feenstra, R.C. (1992), "How costly is protectionism?", Journal of Economic Perspectives 6:159–178.

Feenstra, R.C. (1993), "Measuring the welfare effect of quality change: Theory and application to Japanese autos", National Bureau of Economic Research Working Paper No. 4401.

Feenstra, R.C. (1994), "New product varieties and the measurement of international prices", American Economic Review 84:157–177.

Feenstra, R.C., Knetter, M.M. and J.E. Gagnon (1993), "Market share and exchange rate pass-through in world automobile trade", National Bureau of Economic Research Working Paper No. 4399.

Feenstra, R.C. and J. Levinsohn (1995), "Estimating markups and market conduct with multidimensional product attributes", Review of Economic Studies, 62:19–52.

Feinberg, R.M. (1986), "The interaction of market power and exchange rate effects on German domestic prices", Journal of Industrial Economics 35:61–70.

Feinberg, R.M. (1989a), "The effects of foreign exchange movements on U.S. domestic prices", Review of Economics and Statistics 71:505–511.

Feinberg, R.M. (1989b), "Exchange rates and 'unfair trade'", Review of Economics and Statistics 71:704–707.

Feinberg, R.M. (1991), "The choice of exchange rate index and domestic price passthrough", Journal of Industrial Economics 39:409–420.

Feinberg, R.M. (1993), "A simultaneous model of exchange-rate passthrough into prices of imperfectly substitutable domestic and import goods", mimeo, The American University.

Feinberg, R.M. and S. Kaplan (1992), "The response of domestic prices to expected exchange rates", Journal of Business 65:267–280.

Freeman, R.B. and L. Katz (1991), "Industrial wage and employment determination in an open economy", in: J.M. Abowd and R.B. Freeman, eds., Immigration, trade, and the labor market (University of Chicago and National Bureau of Economic Research, Chicago) 235–260.

Froot, K.A. and P.D. Klemperer (1989), "Exchange rate pass-through when market share matters", American Economic Review 79:637–654.

Fung, K.C. and H. Huizinga (1991), "Trade protection and wages in Canada", mimeo, University of California, Santa Cruz.

Gaston, N. and D. Trefler (1994a), "Protection, trade, and wages: Evidence for U.S. manufacturing", Industrial and Labor Relations Review 47:574–593.

Gaston, N. and D. Trefler (1994b), "Union wages sensitivity to trade and protection: Theory and evidence", mimeo, Tulane University and University of Toronto.

Gagnon, J. and M. Knetter (1992), "Markup adjustment and exchange rate fluctuations: Evidence from panel data on automobile exports", National Bureau of Economic Research Working Paper No. 4123.

Goldberg, P.K. (1995), "Product differentiation and oligopoly in international markets: The case of the U.S. automobile industry", Econometrica, forthcoming.

Goldstein, M. and M.S. Khan (1985), "Income and price effects in foreign trade", in: R.W. Jones and P.B. Kenen, eds., Handbook of international economics, vol. 2 (North-Holland, Amsterdam).

Griliches, Z. (1971), "Hedonic price indexes for automobiles: An econometric analysis of quality change", in: Z. Griliches, ed., Price indexes and quality change (Harvard University Press, Cambridge, MA) 55–87.

Gros, D. (1987), "A note on the optimal tariff, retaliation and the welfare loss from tariff wars in a framework with intra-industry trade", Journal of International Economics 23:357–367.

Grossman, G. (1982), "Comment", in: J.N. Bhagwati, Import competition and response (University of Chicago Press and NBER, Chicago) 396–399.

Grossman, G. (1984), "International competition and the unionized sector", Canadian Journal of Economics 17:541–556.

Grossman, G. (1986), "Imports as a cause of injury: The case of the U.S. steel industry", Journal of International Economics 20:201–223.

Grossman, G. (1987), "The employment and wage effects of import competition", Journal of International Economic Integration 2:1–23.

Hall, R. (1988), "The relation between price and marginal cost in U.S. industry", Journal of Political Economy 96:921–947.

Hamilton, C. (1986), "An assessment of voluntary restraints on Hong Kong exports to Europe and the U.S.", Economica 53:339–350.

Hamermesh, D. (1987), "The costs of worker displacement", Quarterly Journal of Economics 102:51–75.

Hansen, W.L. and T.J. Prusa (1993), "The road most traveled: The rise of Title VII protection", mimeo, State University of New York at Stony Brook.

Harrigan, J. (1991), Openness to trade in manufactures in the OECD, University of Pittsburgh, Department of Economics Working Paper No. 272.

Harris, R.G. (1985), "Why voluntary export restraints are 'voluntary'", Canadian Journal of Economics 18:799–809.

Harrison, A. (1991), The new trade protection: Price effects of antidumping and countervailing measures in the United States, The World Bank, Trade Policy Division Working Paper No. 808.

Harrison, A. (1992), "Imperfect explanations for imperfect pass-through: Market power and exchange rates in the U.S. steel industry", mimeo, The World Bank.

Harrison, A. (1994a), "Productivity, imperfect competition and trade reform", Journal of International Economics 36(1/2):53–74.

Harrison, A. (1994b), "An empirical test of the infant industry argument: Comment", American Economic Review 84:1090–1095.

Helkie, W.H. and P. Hooper (1988), "An empirical analysis of the external deficit, 1980–86", in: R.C. Bryant, G. Holtham, and P. Hooper, eds., External deficits and the dollar: The pit and the pendulum (The Brookings Institution, Washington, D.C.) 10–56.

Helpman, E. and P. Krugman (1985), Market structure and foreign trade (MIT Press, Cambridge, MA).

Hooper, P. (1989), Exchange rates and U.S. external adjustment in the short run and the long run, Board of Governors, International Finance Discussion Paper No. 346.

Horn, H., H. Lang and S. Lundgren (1995), "Managerial effort incentives, X-inefficiency, and international trade", European Economic Review 39:117–138.

Horstmann, I.J. and J.R. Markusen (1986), "Up the average cost curve: Inefficient entry and the new protectionism", Journal of International Economics 20:225–247.

Houthakker, H.S. and S.P. Magee (1969), "Income and price elasticities in world trade", The Review of Economics and Statistics 51:111–125.

Hufbauer, G.C. and K.A. Elliott (1994), Measuring the costs of protection in the United States (Institute for International Economics, Washington, D.C.).

Johnson, H.G. (1960), "The cost of protection and the scientific tariff", Journal of Political Economy 68:327–345.

Katrak, H. (1977), "Multi-national monopolies and commercial policy", Oxford Economic Papers 29:283–291.

Katz, L.F. and L.H. Summers (1989a), "Can interindustry wage differentials justify strategic trade policy?", in: R.C. Feenstra, ed., Trade policies for international competitiveness (University of Chicago and National Bureau of Economic Research, Chicago) 85–116.

Katz, L.F. and L.H. Summer (1989b), "Industry rents: Evidence and implications", Brookings Papers on Economic Activity: Microeconomics, 209–290.

Knetter, M.M. (1989), "Price discrimination by U.S. and German exporters", American Economic Review 79:198–210.

Knetter, M.M. (1993), "International comparisons of pricing-to-market behavior", American Economic Review 83:473–486.

Knetter, M.M. and J.E. Gagnon (1992), Markup adjustment and exchange rate fluctuations: Evidence from panel data on automobile exports, National Bureau of Economic Research Working Paper No. 4123.

Krishna, K. (1987), "Tariffs versus quotas with endogenous quality", Journal of International Economics 23:97–117.

Krishna, K. (1989), "Trade restrictions as facilitating practices", Journal of International Economics 26:251–270.

Krishna, K. and L.H. Tan (1993), "On the importance and extent of rent sharing in the multi-fibre arrangement: Evidence from U.S.–Hong Kong trade in apparel", mimeo, Pennsylvania State University.

Krueger, A.O. (1980a), "Protectionist pressures, imports and employment in the United States", Scandinavian Journal of Economics 82:133–146.

Krueger, A.O. (1980b), "Restructuring for import competition from developing countries, I: Labor displacement and economic redeployment in the United States", Journal of Policy Modeling 2:165–184.

Krueger, A.O. and B. Tuncer (1982), "An empirical test of the infant industry argument", American Economic Review 72:1142–1152.

Krugman, P.R. (1987), "Pricing to market when the exchange rate changes", in: S.W. Arndt and J.D. Richardson, eds., Real-financial linkages among open economies (MIT Press, Cambridge, MA) 49–70.

Krugman, P. (1989), "Differences in income elasticities and trends in real exchange rates", European Economic Review 33:1031–1054.

Lawrence, R. (1987), "Imports in Japan: Closed markets or minds?", Brookings Papers on Economic Activity, 517–554.

Leamer, E.E. (1974), "Nominal tariff averages with estimated weights", Southern Economic Journal 41:34–46.

Leamer, E.E. (1988a), "Cross-section estimation of the effects of trade barriers", in: R.C. Feenstra, ed., Empirical methods for international trade (MIT Press, Cambridge, MA) 52–82.

Leamer, E.E. (1988b), "Measures of openness", in: R.E. Baldwin, ed., Trade policy issues and empirical analysis (University of Chicago Press and National Bureau of Economic Research, Chicago) 147–200.

Leamer, E.E. (1990), "The structure and effects of barriers in 1983", in: R.W. Jones and A.O. Krueger, eds., The political economy of international trade (Basil Blackwell, Oxford) 224–260.

Levinsohn, J. (1993), "Testing the imports-as-market-discipline hypothesis", Journal of International Economics 35(1/2):1–22.

Lindert, P.H. (1991), International economics, 9th edition (Irwin, Boston).

Mann, C.L. (1986), "Prices, profit margins, and exchange rates", Federal Reserve Bulletin, June, 366–379.

Pindyck, R.S. and J.J. Rotemberg (1987), "Are imports to blame? Attribution of injury under the 1974 Trade Act", Journal of Law and Economics 30:101–122.

Prusa, T. (1992), "Why are so many antidumping petitions withdrawn?", Journal of International Economics 33:1–20.

Revenga, A.L. (1990), "Wage determination in an open economy: International trade and U.S. manufacturing wages", mimeo, Harvard University.

Revenga, A.L. (1992), "Exporting jobs? The impact of import competition on employment and wages in U.S. manufacturing', Quarterly Journal of Economics 107:255–284.

Rodriguez, C.A. (1979), "The quality of imports and the differential welfare effects of tariffs, quotas and quality controls as protective devices", Canadian Journal of Economics 12:439–449.

Rodrik, D. (1988), "Imperfect competition, scale economics, and trade policy in developing countries", in: R.E. Baldwin, ed., Trade policy issues and empirical analysis (University of Chicago and National Bureau of Economic Research, Chicago) 109–137.

Romer, P. (1994), "New goods, old theory, and the welfare costs of trade restrictions", Journal of Development Economics 43:5–38.

Rosen, S. (1974), "Hedonic prices and implicit markets: Product differentiation in pure competition", Journal of Political Economy 82:34–55.

Saxonhouse, G.R. (1989), "Differentiated products, economies of scale, and access to the Japanese market", in: R.C. Feenstra, ed., Trade policies for international competitiveness (University of Chicago and National Bureau of Economic Research, Chicago) 145–174.

Schembri, L. (1989), "Export prices and exchange rates: An industry approach", in: R.C. Feenstra, ed., Trade policies for international competitiveness (University of Chicago and National Bureau of Economic Research, Chicago) 185–206.

Staiger, R. and F. Wolak (1994), "Measuring industry specific protection: Antidumping in the United States", Brookings Papers on Economic Activity: Microeconomics, 51–118.

Svedberg, P. (1979), "Optimal tariff policy on imports from multinationals", The Economic Record, March, 64–67.

Trefler, D. (1993), "Trade liberalization and the theory of endogenous protection: An econometric study of U.S. import policy", Journal of Political Economy 101:138–160.

Tybout, J.R. (1993), Increasing returns as a source of comparative advantage: The evidence, Working Paper No. 93–01, Georgetown University.

U.S. International Trade Commission (1980), Certain motor vehicles and certain chassis and bodies therefor, U.S. International Trade Commission Publication 1110, Washington, D.C.

Yang, J. (1993), "Exchange rate pass-through in U.S. manufacturing industries", mimeo, Vanderbilt University.

Chapter 31

REGIONAL ECONOMIC INTEGRATION

RICHARD E. BALDWIN

Graduate Institute of International Studies, Geneva

and

ANTHONY J. VENABLES*

London School of Economics

Contents

*The authors would like to thank participants in the Handbook Conference, Princeton, and in the European Research Workshop in International Trade, Castelgandolfo, for valuable comments. Particular thanks go to Gene Grossman, Peter Neary, Victor Norman, Patricia Rice and Ken Rogoff for their detailed comments.

Handbook of International Economics, vol. III, Edited by G. Grossman and K. Rogoff.
© *Elsevier Science B.V., 1995*

1. Introduction

Europe and North America, which together account for two thirds of world trade, have both liberalized their regional trade substantially more than they have liberalized trade with the rest of the world. As a result of initiatives in these two areas alone, 40 percent of world trade is now directly affected by regional integration agreements. Given this, the importance of regional economic integration is self evident. This chapter deals with two main questions concerning these regional trade arrangements. How does regional integration affect the integrating countries? And what does it mean for the global trading system as a whole?

A large number of theoretical and empirical studies have addressed the first question, and we spend most of the chapter presenting the analysis and findings of these studies. While the second question may be just as important, it is much harder to formalize and has therefore evoked less systematic thinking, and we devote less space to it. Before turning to the studies we begin by giving a brief description of various types of regional integration agreements, and by outlining those that operate in North America and Europe.

1.1. Regional integration agreements.

Geographically discriminatory trade policy is the defining characteristic of a regional integration agreement (RIA). Traditionally, three types of RIAs are distinguished. A free trade area (FTA) is an RIA formed by removing tariffs on trade among member nations and leaving members with autonomy in setting their tariffs on trade with non-member countries. A customs union (CU) applies a common tariff structure to trade with non-members. A common market (CM) permits free movement of factors of production, as well as goods and services, between member states.[1]

At present some 35 RIA's exist with a range and variety of rules far richer than these traditional distinctions.[2] Some function rather poorly or have not been fully implemented (particularly many among less developed countries).[3] Others vary in the range of product coverage (for example, the inclusion or exclusion of services), in the extent to which they address non-tariff barriers (due, for example, to differing

---

[1]Another frequently used term is preferential trading arrangement, sometimes used synonymously with RIA, and sometimes to denote a region with reduced, but not necessarily zero, tariffs.

[2]More than 80 preferential trade agreements have been notified to the GATT as required by Article XXIV. Some of these are components of European and North American RIAs. De Torre and Kelly (1992) list 17 nonNAFTA RIAs in the Western Hemisphere, eight in Africa and eight in Asia–Pacific and the Middle East.

[3]De Torre and Kelly (1992) and Schott (1989) study the reasons for this.

national product standards or discriminatory government procurement policies), and in their handling of contingent protection (for example, anti-dumping actions). To deal with this range of issues, modern RIAs often involve thousands of pages of text and are accompanied by administrative, political, and judicial institutions.

Space limitations prevent us from describing all but the two largest RIAs, namely those in North America and Europe.[4] Post war integration in North America began with the 1965 Canada–US agreement that created free trade in the automobile sector.[5] In 1988 the Canada–US FTA removed tariff and many non-tariff barriers to bilateral trade in most industrial goods and liberalized rules covering foreign investment. It did not forbid contingent protection measures but did establish a separate adjudication procedure for bilateral dumping and subsidy cases. In 1993 the Canada–US FTA evolved into the North American FTA (NAFTA), with the addition of Mexico. This agreement provides for free trade in most industrial goods, albeit with long phase out periods for certain "sensitive" sectors, and also liberalizes restrictions on direct investment. NAFTA does not rule out contingent protection and the special Canada–US contingent protection procedures were not extended to US–Mexico trade disputes.

European integration started earlier and has proceeded much further than that in North America.[6] The European Community (EC) completed its common market in 1968. By that date, contingent protection measures on intra-EC trade were forbidden and free capital and labour mobility were instituted.[7] In addition to covering industrial products, this common market removed duties and quotas on intra-EC food trade, replacing them with a complex system of subsidies, price supports and external trade barriers known as the Common Agricultural Policy. A separate group of West European nations formed the European Free Trade Area (EFTA), which is an FTA for industrial goods that was completed in 1968. The EC and all EFTA countries signed bilateral FTAs in 1974, implicitly forming a duty-free zone for industrial goods covering most of Western Europe. The membership of the EC was enlarged in 1974, 1981 and 1986 and now includes 12 countries with a combined population of 350 million people.

In 1986 the EC's Single European Act proposed the establishment of the "Single Market" by calling for removal of all intra-EC barriers to the movement of goods, services, people and capital by 1992. We refer to this programme as EC92 and note that it still has not been fully implemented. EC92 promised mutual recognition of product, health and safety regulations, and unrestricted rights of establishment of EC firms, financial institutions and other service providers. The Single European Act also

---

[4]See De Melo and Panagariya (1993), Anderson and Blackhurst (1993) and De Torre and Kelly (1992) for details on other RIAs.

[5]See Hufbauer and Schott (1992) on North American integration.

[6]See Baldwin (1994) and Molle (1990) for a brief history of European integration and for details of arrangements and institutions in place.

[7]The EC changed its name from European Economic Community (EEC) to European Community (EC) to European Union (EU). We use EC throughout this chapter.

centralized economic decision making on matters concerning the Single Market, and doubled EC funds available for intra-regional transfers. The 1992 European Economic Area (EEA) agreement extended EC92 to the EFTA countries,[8] although it did not apply to food trade; EEA members now account for about half of world trade and a third of world GDP. The EC has recently signed agreements with ten Central and Eastern European countries. These "Europe Agreements" call for free trade in industrial goods (with long phase out of barriers for certain sensitive sectors). They include evolutionary clauses that will lead to deeper integration including eventual EC membership.[9]

RIAs are inconsistent with the GATT's most favored nation (MFN) principle. However, GATT Article XXIV specifically allows RIAs unless they violate certain conditions. FTAs are allowed under the GATT unless they fail to eliminate barriers on "substantially all the trade" among members. There is the additional requirement that external tariffs "shall not on the whole be higher or more restrictive" than prior to the CU. Judgement on whether a particular RIA violates these conditions requires a unanimous conclusion of a GATT working party. None of the 50 or so such working parties formed over the last three decades has reached unanimity, so no RIA has been ruled inconsistent with the GATT.[10]

Our objective in this chapter is to review and evaluate some of the voluminous literature, theoretical and applied, on the economic effects of RIAs. To do this we organise these effects into three types: allocation effects, accumulation effects and location effects. The first (addressed in Section 2) consists of RIAs' impact on the static allocation of resources, in settings with both perfect and imperfect competition. The second, (accumulation, considered in Section 3) encompasses RIAs' impact on the accumulation of productive factors and covers both medium and long run growth effects. The third (location, described in Section 4) studies the impact of an RIA on the spatial allocation of resources; this analysis draws on the recent "economic geography" literature. These sections are primarily theoretical. In Section 5, we turn to a discussion of the methods and results of empirical evaluations of RIAs, concentrating on NAFTA and the EC. Section 6 deals with further issues, including the structure of RIAs and the implications of RIAs for the world trading system.

1.2. A framework for welfare analysis

At many points in the succeeding analysis we shall discuss the welfare effects of RIAs. For this, it is useful to have a framework that categorizes the possible sources of welfare change in an open economy. Suppose that the welfare of the representative

---

[8]With the exception of Switzerland which voted in a referendum to remain outside the EEA.

[9]See Baldwin (1994) for analysis of current and possible future trading arrangements between the EC and Eastern Europe.

[10]See Roessler (1993) and Finger (1993) for further details and analysis.

consumer in a country at a moment in time can be represented by an indirect utility function $V(p + t, n, E)$, where p is the vector of border prices, t is a vector of trade costs including the tariff equivalent of import barriers, n is a vector of the number of product varieties available in each industry, and the scalar E is total spending on consumption.[11] Expenditure is equal to the sum of factor income, profits, and rent from trade barriers that accrues to domestic agents (including the government), minus investment; that is,

$$E = wL + rK + X[(p + t) - a(w, r, x)] + \alpha tm - I . \qquad (1.1)$$

Total factor income is $wL + rK$, where L and K are the country's supply of labour and capital and w and r are factor prices. The third term on the right hand side is total profit. It is the inner product of the economy's production vector X and the gap between domestic prices and average costs, $a(w, r, x)$, where average cost in each sector depends on factor prices and production per firm in that sector, x. Domestically accruing trade rents amount to αtm, where m is the net import vector (positive elements indicates imports) and α is a diagonal matrix that measures the proportion of the wedge t that creates income for domestic agents; $\alpha = 1$ for a tariff or other barrier with domestically captured rent (DCR) and $\alpha = 0$ for a barrier where no trade rent is captured domestically (nonDCR).[12] Finally, I denotes investment.

Totally differentiating $V(p + t, n, E)$ and dividing through by the marginal utility of expenditure we find (see Appendix A)[13]:

$$\begin{aligned} dV/V_E = {} & \alpha t\, dm - m\, d[t - \alpha t] - m\, dp \\ & + [p + t - a]\, dX - Xa_x\, dx + (V_n/V_E)\, dn \\ & + (\tilde{r}/\rho - 1)\, dI . \end{aligned} \qquad (1.2)$$

We shall refer back to the terms in this expression throughout the chapter. The three terms in the first row represent welfare effects that appear in models with perfect competition; the first term is the "trade volume" effect, and arises when there are changes in volumes of trade subject to the wedge created by DCR trade barriers, αt. The second is the "trade cost" effect, measuring the change in costs generated by changes in the nonDCR elements of trade barriers. The third is the "terms of trade" effect. The three terms in the second row are relevant in models that allow for increasing returns to scale and imperfect competition; the first term is the "output" effect, arising if there is a change in output in industries where price differs from average cost; the second is the "scale" effect, which gives the value of changes in

---

[11]The interpretation of n is developed more fully in Section 2.2.

[12]For example, t_i may represent real trade costs or a quota or VER under which foreigners capture the quota rents.

[13]We use calculus here and elsewhere although RIAs are non-marginal changes. As usual, the mean value theorem for derivatives indicates how non-marginal changes can be incorporated.

average costs induced by changes in firm scale; the third term gives "variety" effects which may arise when the number of differentiated consumer products changes. The term in the third row depends upon the accumulation of factors. A change in investment is instantaneously costly, but augments the capital stock with social rate of return $\tilde{r}$. Discounting this at social discount rate ρ gives present value $\tilde{r}/\rho$, and a change in investment has a first-order welfare effect if this ratio differs from one.

2. Allocation effects

The first question we address is, how does the formation of an RIA change the static allocation of resources in participating economies, and in particular, what can be said about the welfare implications of these changes? Section 2.1 provides a brief survey of the effects of integration under perfect competition [as given in the first row of eq. (1.2)]. Section 2.2 studies effects under imperfect competition, and evaluates their welfare implications by incorporating also the terms in the second row of eq. (1.2).

2.1. Perfect competition and constant returns

Modern regional integration theory began with Viner (1950) under the name of "customs union theory". His lucid, but informal, reasoning is full of insights and anticipates many of the post-war theoretical and policy debates. Viner's most famous result – that the welfare impact of customs union formation is ambiguous – triggered a flood of papers. Most of these assumed perfect competition and constant returns, and many merely contributed to the debate about what Viner really meant.[14] The most useful of them illuminated special cases where total welfare effects can be signed despite the fundamental second-best nature of RIAs. We devote relatively little space to this literature since econometric and simulation studies (see Section 5) have shown these effects to be quantitatively small and good surveys already exist [see for example Lipsey (1960), Krauss (1972), Pomfret (1986) and Kowalczyk (1992)].[15]

2.1.1. National welfare for a small country

We consider first a small country that has fixed border prices, so that only the first two terms in eq. (1.2), the trade volume and trade cost effects, are relevant. The traditional literature dealt with tariffs, i.e. DCR barriers ($\alpha = 1$), implying no trade-cost effects. The welfare effects of integration then collapse to $t \, dm$, the sum of tariff wedges multiplied by changes in the volumes of trade. As pointed out by Meade

---

[14]See Kowalczyk (1992) for summaries of the literature on "what Viner really meant".
[15]See O'Brien (1976) for a review of pre-Vinerian literature.

(1955 p. 35), this says that necessary and sufficient condition for a welfare gain in a small country is that the tariff weighted change in a nation's trade volume should increase.

The term $t\,dm$ illustrates the fundamental ambiguity in evaluating the welfare effects of an RIA. Even if all elements of t are non-negative[16] some elements of dm, the changes in trade volume, are likely to be positive and others negative. One approach to resolving this ambiguity is to identify sufficient conditions for gain. For example, some empirical literature (see Section 5.2) assumes no export barriers and equality of all elements of t. In this case, a nation gains from integration if and only if the RIA raises its aggregate import volume. Another special case is discussed by Ethier and Horn (1984). When initial tariffs on intra-RIA trade, but not extra-RIA trade, are in the neighbourhood of zero, an increase in tariff revenues on external trade is a necessary and sufficient condition for welfare gain.

We may also note that a small country should prefer unilateral trade liberalization to membership of an RIA [Johnson (1965), Cooper and Massell (1965)]. Since, with constant border prices, the welfare change reduces to $t\,dm$, optimal policy puts all elements of t equal to zero. Changes in other countries' trade barriers then have no effect on domestic welfare, so no benefit is derived from partner country tariff reductions. This result holds only in the case of a small country; more generally, the possibility that border prices may change means that unilateral trade liberalization and membership of an RIA cannot be ranked in terms of their implications for aggregate welfare.

An alternative way of expressing trade volume effects are the much used concepts of trade creation (the sum of increased imports from RIA and non-RIA nations) and trade diversion (reduced imports from non-RIA nations).[17] Trade diversion occurs when discriminatory tariff liberalization leads private agents to import from a supplier that is not the lowest cost source, thereby reducing home welfare by raising the nation's cost of consuming such goods. Clearly trade diversion can arise from discriminatory, but not MFN, tariff reductions. Of course, if bilateral tariffs are reduced only on imports from countries that already are the lowest-cost supplier, trade diversion does not occur. This observation motivated the claim by Lipsey (1957) that RIAs are likely to be beneficial if the RIA partners initially account for large shares of each other's imports, as would be the case if they were low cost producers.

Recent integration in Western Europe has not involved removal of DCR barriers (tariffs on intra-West European trade were eliminated by 1975), but instead the removal of non-tariff barriers. The removal of such barriers is also an important part of NAFTA and many other RIAs. Since most non-tariff barriers do not produce rents for the domestic economy, the nonDCR case – where α is zero – is relevant,

---

[16]Positive elements of t are import tariffs or export taxes.

[17]See Kowalczyk (1992) for the many other definitions of trade creation and diversion.

although it was largely ignored in the early CU literature. When $\alpha = 0$, only the second term in eq. (1.2), $-m \, \mathrm{d}t$, remains, which implies another simple rule. If all barriers are nonDCR, then a nation gains from any RIA that lowers its average (trade-weighted) tariff equivalent trade barriers. Notice that the extent of trade creation and trade diversion are irrelevant in this case.

2.1.2. Large country and regional welfare results

If countries in the RIA are "large", then changes in their trade will induce changes in world prices with consequent effects on welfare reflected in the term $-m \, \mathrm{d}p$ in eq. (1.2). This is a potential further source of gain – if imports from the rest of the world fall, then RIA terms of trade are likely to improve. Terms of trade changes may occur on both the internal trade of a member of the RIA and on its external trade. However, terms of trade changes on internal trade have equal and opposite effects on member countries, so we can abstract from them if we focus only on the sum of the welfare of RIA members.[18]

We can investigate these effects by considering a three country model in which countries 1 and 2 form the RIA and country 3 remains outside. Subscripts denote country specific variables, and we distinguish imports according to source and destination, using m_{ij} and t_{ij} to denote the vector of imports of country j from i, and the associated tariff vector. We can then derive the combined welfare effect from eq. (1.2) (with $\alpha = 1$, and adding for countries 1 and 2) as:

$$\mathrm{d}V_1/V_{E_1} + \mathrm{d}V_2/\mathrm{d}V_{E_2} = (t_{21} \, \mathrm{d}m_{21} + t_{12} \, \mathrm{d}m_{12}) + (t_{31} \, \mathrm{d}m_{31} + t_{32} \, \mathrm{d}m_{32})$$
$$- (m_{31} + m_{32}) \, \mathrm{d}p \, . \tag{2.1}$$

The first and second terms on the right-hand side give trade volume effects on internal and external trade respectively, while the third gives terms of trade effects, applying only to external trade. Terms of trade effects arise because of changes in trade volumes, and are related to optimal tariffs, denoted $\tilde{t}_{ij}$, by the equation $\tilde{t}_{ij} \, \mathrm{d}m_{ij} = m_{ij} \, \mathrm{d}p$.[19] We can therefore rewrite (2.1) as

$$\mathrm{d}V_1/V_{E_1} + \mathrm{d}V_2/V_{E_2} = t_{21} \, \mathrm{d}m_{21} + t_{12} \, \mathrm{d}m_{12} + [t_{31} - \tilde{t}_{31}] \, \mathrm{d}m_{31} + [t_{32} - \tilde{t}_{32}] \, \mathrm{d}m_{32} \, .$$
$$\tag{2.2}$$

This says that aggregate welfare change for RIA members comes from changes in

---

[18]This will be a legitimate welfare criterion if transfers between member countries are being used to equate social marginal utilities of income.

[19]The optimal tariff requires that, for all $\mathrm{d}p$, $\tilde{t}M_p \, \mathrm{d}p = m \, \mathrm{d}p$, where M_p is the matrix of partial derivatives of country 3 excess demand functions [Dixit and Norman (1980)]. Writing $\mathrm{d}m = M_p \, \mathrm{d}p$ gives the equation of the text.

internal and external trade volumes, where the former are multiplied by tariff rates, and the latter by deviations of tariffs from their optimal values.

Inspection of eq. (2.2) reveals that free internal trade is the optimal policy for the RIA if, as its internal trade policy is changed, the external trade of the RIA remains constant (i.e. $dm_{31} = dm_{32} = 0$). This is the Meade–Ohyama–Kemp–Wan theorem. Meade (1955 p. 98) showed that if all external trade barriers are "fixed and unchanging" quantitative restrictions, then an RIA must increase the sum of the economic welfare of member nations. Ohyama (1972), and Kemp and Wan (1976) rediscovered and extended Meade's result, by showing that a sufficiently intricate change in the CU's external tariffs could be used to freeze external trade, so that standard gains from trade arguments could be applied to trade within the RIA.

More generally, eq. (2.2) captures the same fundamental ambiguity about the effects of an RIA as we noted in the small-country case. Some elements of the vectors dm_{ij} will be positive and others negative. It is tempting to say that an RIA brings expansion of intra-RIA trade and contraction of external trade, but this is not true in general. In a multi-good general equilibrium model the pattern of changes dm_{ij} induced by an RIA will be complex, and it is possible that complementarities between goods traded internally and externally may lead to increases in some elements of the external trade vector. Some researchers have responded to this ambiguity by building low dimension models in which explicit expressions for these quantity changes can be derived. These have ranged from simple partial equilibrium models focusing on imports of a single good, to the three-good three-country models surveyed by Lloyd (1982). While these models are of some value in pointing to the importance of key relationships, the general message they deliver is that assessment of the costs and benefits of RIAs depends on detailed knowledge of the pattern of trade flows, of trade distortions, and of the quantity responses likely to follow from an RIA. We discuss the attempts that have been made to assess these magnitudes in Section 5.

2.2. Market structure, scale economies and imperfect competition

Much of the recent literature on RIAs has focused on environments that are imperfectly competitive. While this is a focus shared by much recent trade theory (see Paul Krugman's chapter in this volume), it is particularly important for the analysis of RIAs for two reasons. The first is that integration in Europe has occurred between economies with similar structures and large volumes of intra-industry trade, and European developments have motivated a good deal of the recent research. The second is the possibility that there is an interaction between market structure and gains from integration. Certainly the "pro-competitive" effects of regional integration have figured prominently in the European debate.

We want to know how an RIA affects an imperfectly competitive industry with firms located both within and outside the RIA. How does the total volume of production in the industry change, and how is competition between firms and the scale of operation of firms affected? The theoretical literature on RIAs does not provide a unified treatment of imperfect competition, although imperfect competition has been assumed in many numerical simulations.[20] These studies suggest that the welfare effects of an RIA may be many times larger if industries are imperfectly, rather than perfectly, competitive. In order to understand the forces at work, we specialise the framework of Section 1 into a simple model of trade and imperfect competition, variants and extensions of which are employed throughout the rest of the chapter. A particularly simple version of this core model – the large-group case – is used to analyse the effects of an RIA on production volumes (Section 2.2.1). To look at competition and firm scale, we need to pay more attention to game-theoretic interactions between firms, as we do in Sections 2.2.2 and 2.2.3.

Our core model of trade and imperfect competition has N economies, each with two sectors. The X sector has imperfectly competitive firms producing differentiated goods with increasing returns to scale technologies, while the Z sector has perfect competition, constant returns to scale and produces a homogeneous good that is costlessly tradeable and serves as numeraire. There is a single factor of production, labour, and the quantity of country j's labour endowment is denoted L_j. Free trade in Z makes wages invariant to X-sector trade policy changes, and units are chosen so that wages are unity.

To capture product differentiation in a tractable manner, we specialise the indirect utility function of Section 1 to the form proposed by Dixit and Stiglitz (1977). That is, the representative consumer in country j has indirect utility function $v_j(P_j, 1, E_j)$ where 1 is the price of Z sector output, E_j is consumption expenditure, and P_j is a price index of X industry varieties supplied to market j. The price index takes the following CES form:

$$P_j^{1-\sigma} = \sum_{k=1}^{N} [n_k(p_{kj}\tau_{kj})^{1-\sigma}], \quad \sigma > 1, \tag{2.3}$$

where n_k is the number of varieties supplied by country k, and $p_{kj}\tau_{kj}$ is the price at which they are sold in country j; the latter is the product of the producer price, p_{kj}, and the trade cost factor incurred in selling products from k in j, τ_{kj}. Notice that we have assumed that all products from a particular source are symmetric.

Consumer demands can be derived in two stages. Let total expenditure in country j on X sector products be $E_j^X(P_j, E_j)$; we shall denote the elasticity of this expenditure with respect to the price index by $1 - \eta$, and assume that η is constant. Consumption

---

[20] Analytical work on RIAs with imperfect competition was initiated by Corden (1972), and further studies include Ethier and Horn (1984), Venables (1987) and Haaland and Wooton (1992).

of a single product variety is denoted c_{kj} and expenditure on this variety is

$$
p_{kj}\tau_{kj}c_{kj} = E_j^X(P_j, E_j)\left(\frac{p_{kj}\tau_{kj}}{P_j}\right)^{1-\sigma}
\tag{2.4}
$$

(This and following results are derived in more detail in Appendix B.) We often make the simplifying assumption that trade costs τ_{kj} are "iceberg" costs. That is, a proportion $(\tau_{kj} - 1)/\tau_{kj}$ of goods "melt" in transit, so output, x_{kj}, exceeds consumption according to $x_{kj} = \tau_{kj}c_{kj}$. Equation (2.4) then gives producer revenue as well as consumer expenditure for each product.

Each firm produces a single product variety. The profit of a typical country j firm in the X sector is

$$
\pi_j = \sum_{k=1}^{N} p_{jk}x_{jk} - x_j b_j - f_j, \quad x_j \equiv \sum_{k=1}^{N} x_{jk}.
\tag{2.5}
$$

where technology has fixed cost f_j and constant marginal cost b_j. We assume that firms compete in each market separately, so they play what has been termed a "segmented market" game [see for example Helpman and Krugman (1989)]. This gives a first order condition for profit maximisation,

$$
p_{jk} = (1 + \lambda(s_{jk}))b_j
\tag{2.6}
$$

where $\lambda(s_{jk})$ is the price-marginal-cost mark up. This mark-up depends on s_{jk} which is the value share of a country-j firm's sales in country k's market. The exact form of the function λ depends on the nature of strategic interaction between firms. For a Nash equilibrium in prices, it is given by

$$
\lambda(s_{jk}) = 1/(\sigma(1 - s_{jk}) + \eta s_{jk} - 1).
\tag{2.7}
$$

Equation (2.7) captures the different sources of a firm's market power. If market shares are negligible the mark-up depends only on σ, the elasticity of demand for a single variety, holding the price index constant. The other extreme case is monopoly, where $s_{jk} = 1$, and the mark-up is determined by the elasticity of the industry aggregate demand curve, η. Generally the mark up is a weighted average of these two elasticities. We assume $\sigma > \eta$, so that the mark-up is an increasing and strictly convex function of the firm's share in the relevant market.

The numbers of firms operating in each country, n_k, are, in long-run equilibrium, determined by entry and exit in response to profits. We treat the n_k as continuous variables, so long-run industry equilibrium obtains when profits are equal to zero. Using (2.5) and (2.6), the zero profit condition is:

$$
\sum_{k=1}^{N} \lambda(s_{jk})x_{jk} = f_j/b_j.
\tag{2.8}
$$

2.2.1. Production shifting in the "large-group case"

The formation of an RIA tends to shift production of the liberalized good into the liberalizing region. We refer to this as "production shifting". To investigate this effect we consider a three-country world where an RIA forms between countries 1 and 2. We look first at the effect of the RIA on the profitability of firms in the different countries, and then at the production shifting which occurs as numbers of firms change in response to profit levels. We study the determinants of the magnitude of this effect, and its welfare implications.

It is convenient to specialize our core model still further (for the moment) with what is known as the large-group assumption. That is, we assume that each firm ignores the effects of its actions on the industry as a whole. Formally, this is equivalent to the assumption that each firm acts as if its market shares, s_{jk}, were zero. Inspection of (2.7) shows that under this approximation all mark-ups, λ, are equal to $1/(\sigma - 1)$, so country-j firms set producer prices of $b_j\sigma/(\sigma - 1)$ in all markets. This simplifies the model in two important ways. First, equilibrium firm scale now depends only on parameters of technology and demand. We denote equilibrium scale by $\bar{x}$; eq. (2.8) implies that $\bar{x} = (\sigma - 1)f_j/b_j$. Second, with iceberg trade costs, demand functions [eqs. (2.4)] can be expressed in the form

$$
p_k x_{kj} = E_j^X \frac{\theta_{kj}}{\sum_{i=1}^{N} n_i \theta_{ij}}, \quad \theta_{ij} \equiv \frac{p_i x_{ij}}{p_j x_{jj}} = \left(\frac{b_i \tau_{ij}}{b_j}\right)^{1-\sigma}.
\tag{2.9}
$$

This says that the value of a firms' sales in a particular market depend only on total expenditure in that market, E_j^X, the number of firms in each country, n_i, and these firms' relative costs of supplying the market. Relative costs – including trade costs – are summarised by the numbers θ_{ij}, which measure the ratio of an importing firm's sales to a home firm's sales. Clearly $\theta_{jj} = 1$. Trade liberalization raises θ_{ij} from zero at autarky, to unity for free trade, if the trading countries happen to have the same production costs.

Pulling this together, we can see what determines the number of firms and volume of output in each country. For simplicity let the two RIA countries be symmetric, and write $\theta_{12} = \theta_{21} = \theta$, and $\theta_{i3} = \theta_{3i} = \theta^*$, $i = 1, 2$. We can then derive the following equations for the total sales of a representative country 1 firm (equal to those of a country 2 firm), and country 3 firm:

$$
x_1 = \frac{1}{p_1}\left[\frac{E_1^X}{n_1 + \theta n_2 + \theta^* n_3} + \frac{E_2^X \theta}{\theta n_1 + n_2 + \theta^* n_3} + \frac{E_3^X \theta^*}{\theta^* n_1 + \theta^* n_2 + n_3}\right]
\tag{2.10}
$$

$$
x_3 = \frac{1}{p_3}\left[\frac{E_1^X \theta^*}{n_1 + \theta n_2 + \theta^* n_3} + \frac{E_2^X \theta^*}{\theta n_1 + n_2 + \theta^* n_3} + \frac{E_3^X}{\theta^* n_1 + \theta^* n_2 + n_3}\right].
\tag{2.11}
$$

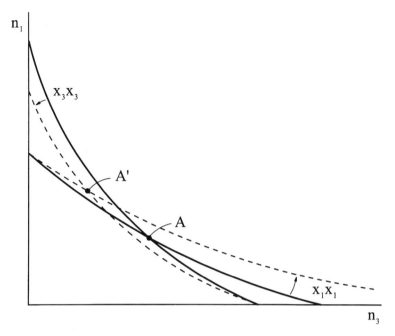

Figure 2.1.

Industry equilibrium in each country occurs when $x_i = \bar{x}$. If $x_i > (<)\bar{x}$, then profits are positive (negative).

We illustrate these relationships in Figure 2.1, which uses the further assumption that expenditures on X are constant.[21] Axes are n_3 and n_1 ($=n_2$). The heavy-lined curve labelled $x_1 x_1$ gives combinations of n_1 ($=n_2$) and n_3 at which the industry is in equilibrium in countries 1 and 2. The curve $x_3 x_3$ depicts the similar locus for country 3 firms. The curves are drawn as downward sloping, because an increase in the number of firms in country 3 reduces profits of firms in 1 and 2, and vice versa. (In the limiting case of no trade with country 3, $\theta^* = 0$, so that $x_1 x_1$ is horizontal and $x_3 x_3$ vertical.) To the northeast of each curve, the relevant firms are operating at scales that give negative profits, and to the southwest firms have positive profits. The curves need not intersect in the positive quadrant – if they do not do so some country will be specialized in the Z industry. If they do, as we shall assume here, then stability (under a process of entry and exit in response to positive and negative profits) requires that they intersect in the direction illustrated.

Point A is the initial (pre-RIA) equilibrium. The RIA increases θ, shifting the curves to positions illustrated by the dashed curves. Holding constant the numbers of

---

[21] This will be true if income effects are zero and $\eta = 1$.

firms, we see that firms in the RIA now have expanded production and make positive profits (A is below the new $x_1 x_1$) while firms in country 3 have reduced sales and make negative profits (A is above the new $x_3 x_3$). This occurs because of the cost advantage that RIA firms now have in their RIA partner country, relative to non-RIA firms. Allowing entry and exit to occur restores all profit levels to zero and moves the new equilibrium to A' in Figure 2.1; a number of country 3 firms exit, and firms enter in countries 1 and 2. This is "production shifting", into the RIA. The magnitude of production shifting will be greater the higher is θ^*, since this makes the gradients of $x_1 x_1$ and $x_3 x_3$ more similar. Intuitively, higher θ^* means lower trade barriers between the RIA and country 3, this rendering the industry more "footloose".

The welfare effects of these changes can be found by referring back to eq. (1.2). Producer prices are constant in our example, so the only first-row effects present are trade volume effects if barriers are DCR, or trade cost effects if they are non-DCR. Turning to the second row, in industry equilibrium price equals average cost, and firm scale is unchanged by the experiment. The only second row effect is therefore a variety effect occurring as the location of firms changes. This arises because more varieties are now produced in each economy in the RIA and these avoid trade costs, which reduces the price index P_j for RIA member countries and raises it for non-members.[22] This means that production shifting increases welfare in RIA countries and reduces it in country 3.[23]

This "large-group case" has the virtue of simplicity and helps us to identify an important mechanism – production shifting – that plays a role in understanding the allocation (and later the accumulation and location) effects of regional integration. However, its simplifying assumption of constant mark-ups rules out scale effects in the long run. Since scale effects have proved to be important in studies of NAFTA and EC92, we turn now to a less restrictive version of the core model in which scale changes may occur.

2.2.2. The pro-competitive effect: Scale and cost implications

Allowing for oligopolistic interaction between firms in the industry makes price cost mark-ups endogenous. Policy changes may then alter profits earned per unit sold, in which case maintaining zero profits (covering fixed costs) will require changes in firm scale. For example, a lowering of the average mark-up requires that there be an increase in long run output per firm, which in turn reduces average costs of production. Simulation studies reported in Section 5 show that these reductions in average cost may be quantitatively significant; in this section we use our core model to investigate the forces at work.

---

[22]Helpman and Krugman (1989) refer to this welfare gain as a "home market effect".
[23]If expenditures E_i^X change then this will change the total number of firms bringing further variety effects.

The mechanism through which an RIA changes price cost mark-ups is often referred to as the pro-competitive effect of integration. Many observers have argued informally that integration leads to an erosion of firms' dominant positions in their home markets. While the argument seems intuitive, care is required in its development. Loss of profits on domestic sales may be associated with higher profits on export sales. In general the net effect on firm size is ambiguous, and the analytics have not been fully worked out in the literature.

To develop the argument, we note that the zero profit condition [eq. (2.8)] can be rearranged to give an explicit expression for firm scale:

$$\sum_{k=1}^{N} x_{jk} = \frac{(f_j/b_j - \text{cov}[x_{jk}, \lambda(s_{jk})])}{\mathscr{E}\lambda(s_{jk})}. \tag{2.12}$$

Here cov and $\mathscr{E}$ denote the covariance operator and the unweighted average over all markets.[24]

Equation (2.12) reveals the two distinct channels by which integration may alter firm scale: the average mark-up may change and so may the covariance of sales and mark-ups. To see how this operates, consider a symmetric experiment in which similar economies all engage in trade liberalisation. This will reduce the dispersion of market shares, s_{jk}, as firms gain exports and lose home market sales. Since λ is strictly convex, a reduction in dispersion lowers the mean, $\mathscr{E}\lambda(s_{jk})$.[25] In other words, equalisation of market shares has the effect of reducing average mark-ups, because extreme concentrations of market power are diminished. Furthermore, since firms' market shares are high where their sales are high, there is positive covariance, $\text{cov}[x_{jk}, \lambda(s_{jk})]$, which also declines as dispersion falls. This captures the fact that the liberalisation reduces sales at home (where a firm's market share and mark-up is high) and increases sales in export markets (where the mark-up is lower). These two channels – the diminution of market power, and the redistribution of sales towards markets with low mark-ups – both mean that equilibrium firm scale must increase.

Regional as opposed to global integration will normally amplify these effects. Production shifting increases the number of firms in the RIA, which reduces further the home market shares of firms in RIA countries, and leads to lower overall dispersion of market shares and of sales, and lower covariance. In such asymmetric cases, the exact effects of liberalisation are difficult to characterise.[26] But both the theoretical arguments given above and simulation studies suggest that the pro-competitive effects may be substantial, leading to significant increases in firm scale.

---

[24] If the λ are independent of market shares, as in the large group case, the covariance term is zero and firm scale is independent of market shares.

[25] This is clearly true for a mean preserving reduction in the spread. It will also be true for other reductions although the analysis is more complicated.

[26] Asymmetries in country size mean that initial $\text{cov}[x_{jk}, \lambda(s_{jk})]$ need not be positive; if a firm has small shares where it sells the most (as might be the case for a small country located near a large country) covariance may be negative, and integration will raise the covariance towards zero. This creates the perverse effect found in a study of Norway by Orvedal (1992).

The possibility that an RIA will have pro-competitive effects on price cost mark-ups means that two additional welfare effects come into play in eq. (1.2). In the first row of eq. (1.2), we have trade-volume and trade-cost effects as before, and in addition terms of trade effects as prices change. If marginal costs are constant, then changing market shares will increase producer prices charged on intra-RIA imports, and decrease import prices from the rest of the world; however, if marginal costs depend on scale, these effects could easily be swamped by scale induced cost and price changes. More importantly, we now have the scale effects identified in the second row. Pro-competitive effects of integration bring about an expansion of firms in RIA countries, thereby reducing average production costs. Of course, a reduction in average costs is spread over all the firms' output, non-traded as well as traded, which means that the effect may be quantitatively important.

2.2.3. Market segmentation and integration

So far, the policy change we have studied involves the removal of tariffs or other trade barriers between RIA countries. But European experience suggests that the removal of tariffs is not sufficient to achieve a "single market". There is extensive evidence of wide price differentials between European countries even for goods that can be traded at low cost. Flam and Nordstrom (1994), for instance, demonstrate this fact for automobile prices, and argue that firms have discretion in setting different prices in different countries. Despite the removal of tariffs, firms appear to have retained an ability to segment markets, that is, to price discriminate between countries, and thereby maintain dominant positions in their domestic markets. The EC92 policy measures can be viewed as an attempt to reduce the extent of segmentation and move towards a single "integrated" market in Europe.

One way to explore the distinction between segmented and integrated markets is to investigate different representations of the competition between firms. Comparison of trade and welfare levels in a variety of oligopoly games provides a way of assessing the costs and benefits of more or less "integrated" outcomes; the first part of this section is devoted to such comparisons. However, merely comparing the outcomes of different games leaves the analysis incomplete, as it leaves open the more difficult questions of how different degrees of market segmentation or integration could arise. Ultimately we wish to know what policy instruments might be used to change the degree of market integration.

The essence of segmentation is that firms have discretion to exercise market power in each segment of the market independently. For example, the equilibrium characterized in eqs. (2.6) and (2.7) has firms competing in each national market separately. That is, each firm is able to choose a value of its strategic variable in each market, Nash equilibria are found market by market, and the price cost mark up, λ, depends on the firm's share in the particular market, s_{jk}. Suppose in contrast that national boundaries were of no significance for competition between firms. Firms would then choose a single value of their strategic variable, which would apply RIA-wide. For example, in the case of price competition, a single price would be chosen, which we here assume to be the producer price (the "mill pricing" assumption of location theory)[27]. The implication of this alternative assumption is that the relevant market share in the mark-up relationship, λ, becomes the share of the firm in the RIA as a whole, which we denote $\mathscr{E}[s_{jk}]$. The difference between this "integrated" outcome and the segmented outcome is immediate. With market integration firms have lower prices in markets where they were formerly dominant and higher prices in markets where they previously had small market shares. This typically means a reduction in price in home markets and an increase in prices in export markets which, paradoxically, reduces trade volumes. The loss of market power associated with integration reduces firms' profits, and hence increases equilibrium firm scale, as can be seen from (2.12). The price cost mark-up is given by $\lambda(\mathscr{E}[s_{jk}])$, and no longer varies across markets, and the covariance between λ and x_{jk} goes to zero. If $\text{cov}[x_{jk}, \lambda(s_{jk})]$ is positive and $\lambda(s_{jk})$ is convex this brings an increase in firm scale and hence a fall in average costs and a welfare gain. Empirical estimates of these effects in the context of EC92 are reported in Section 5.

This reasoning suggests that substantial welfare gains might be achieved by the equilibrium "switching" from segmented to integrated market behaviour. But the comparison raises several questions. The first is, are either of these alternatives appropriate equilibrium concepts to use for modelling multi-market interaction between firms? Segmented market equilibrium has become the benchmark in the theory of trade under oligopolistic competition (from the early work on "reciprocal dumping" [Brander (1991), Brander and Krugman (1983)] onwards), but it is far from compelling. Segmentation implies that when marginal cost curves are flat, the games played by firms in each market are completely independent of one another. It seems implausible that two firms would compete in a number of different markets yet recognise no interaction between the various competitions. At the other extreme, the integrated market hypothesis has firms choosing a single decision variable at the RIA-wide level; it seems implausible that firms should not have access to some country-specific instruments.

A more satisfactory approach would recognise that some variables are set at the national level (perhaps price, or sales volume) while others are set at a world or RIA-wide level [e.g. R&D in Brander and Spencer (1983)] capacity [Ben-Zvi and Helpman (1992), Venables (1990a,b)]. In the case of a two-stage game with world capacity choice followed by national price competition, equilibrium has trade and welfare levels intermediate between the segmented and the integrated outcomes. The general point here is that it is possible to characterise equilibrium in a variety of

---

[27]The quantity competition analogue is choice of a single level of output, with this distributed across markets such that producer prices are the same in all markets.

different ways, with different degrees of cross market interaction and consequently different price cost mark-ups and equilibrium firm sizes.

Accepting that it is possible to specify oligopoly games that capture more or less integrated outcomes, and that the distinction is important for firms' scale and average costs, the remaining question is, how might policy be used to induce a movement to a "more integrated" equilibrium? To answer this, the different concepts we have discussed need to be embedded in a larger game. The larger game might be one in which there are alternative opportunities for arbitrage across markets [see Horn et al. (1994)], or one in which firms choose whether or not to install capacities in production or distribution systems [Norman and Venables (1994)]. In such a framework, changes in trade costs might change the game so that the resulting equilibrium might be more or less integrated. Our understanding of these issues remains incomplete, and study of the way in which policy, such as RIA formation, may change the degree of market integration remains an area requiring further research.

3. Accumulation effects

The potential growth effects of RIAs often seem to be uppermost in the minds of policy makers, yet they have received relatively little attention in the academic literature. An RIA will affect growth if it changes the return on investment – in physical, human, or knowledge capital – and hence spurs accumulation. These changes may be transient, as will be the case if increased accumulation reduces the return to the accumulated stock, or may be permanent if diminishing returns to accumulation are not encountered. In this section we discuss first the transient, or medium-run growth implications of an RIA, and then turn to the permanent, or long-run effects.

3.1. Medium-term effects: Investment creation and diversion

The potential for investment diversion and investment creation has played an important role in the public debates on RIAs, especially in North America and Europe. In Mexico, many hoped NAFTA would attract foreign investment to the country and indeed a surge in such investment did occur when NAFTA became a serious possibility. Spain and Portugal experienced similar investment booms once their accession to the EC seemed certain. In EFTA nations, the possibility of investment diversion has been important in the debate over EC membership. The countries fear that local firms will invest in the EC instead of at home in order to get inside the Single Market. Indeed CEPR (1992) shows that a substantial outflow of direct investment has occurred from these countries in recent years.

Regional integration will usually affect factor prices, including the rate of return on capital, in member and non-member nations. For example, consider again the "core model" of Section 2 and assume that both sectors use capital as well as labor, with the imperfectly competitive X sector being the relatively more capital intensive. In this case, the production-shifting effect identified in the preceding section will raise the demand for capital in member nations and lower it in non-member nations. If capital is perfectly mobile internationally, this will generate pure "investment diversion", whereby capital flows to the RIA countries from the rest of the world. These capital flows will raise GDP in the RIA and lower it elsewhere, but to the extent that capital owners remit their earnings, these GDP changes will not be matched by changes in GNP. Alternatively, if capital is completely immobile internationally, capital stock adjustments will occur through domestic accumulation.[28] This will show up as a higher saving and investment rate in member countries, and investment-led growth in both GDP and GNP.

Regardless of the source of any increased investment, if capital faces diminishing returns, the rate of return will eventually return to its normal level. Nevertheless, the additional capital will generate permanent changes in output and income, over and above allocation effects described before. The magnitude of these changes can be described by an output multiplier [Baldwin (1989)]. We illustrate by adopting Cobb–Douglas national production functions of the form, $AK^{(\varepsilon + \phi)}L^{\gamma}$, where allocation effects are summarised by changes in A, ε measures the private return to capital, and $\varepsilon + \phi$ the social return. The parameter ϕ reflects the gap between social and private rates of return that may exist due to external economies of scale of other types of spillovers. If we suppose that steady-state capital stocks are determined by the equality of the private rate of return to the (constant) subjective discount rate, then each one percent increase in A will raise the steady-state capital stock by $1/(1 - \varepsilon - \phi)$ percent. Then GDP will rise by $1/(1 - \varepsilon - \phi)$ percent as well. This is what Baldwin (1989) termed the output multiplier. Econometric estimates of aggregate $\varepsilon + \phi$, suggest values of the multiplier in the range 1.24 to 2.36, with 1.8 as the median estimated value.

Note that the output multiplier need not exceed unity or even be positive. If an RIA's main impact is on labor-intensive sectors then the policy change could lower the rate of return on capital, changing the sign of effects in the preceding discussion. Evidence from empirical evaluations of RIAs suggest that this has not been the case for NAFTA and EC92, and that the output multiplier indeed exceeds unity (see Section 5.3).

The output multiplier tells us that allocation effects will underestimate long-run income gains from integration, but the extra steady state income generates greater lifetime welfare only if there exists a wedge between the private and social return to

---

[28]Feldstein and Bacchetta (1991) argue that international capital flows are not large enough to have macro-economic effects. See also Obstfeld and Rogoff, Chapter 34 of this volume.

capital. A number of econometric studies find that a wedge does exist, for instance Hall (1988), Caballero and Lyons (1990) and De Long and Summers (1991). Using a Cobb–Douglas production function, Baldwin (1992) derives an explicit formula that relates the welfare gain from integration to the wedge between the social and private returns to capital.

3.2. Long run growth effects

The new growth theory investigates circumstances under which capital (physical, human or knowledge) may not be subject to diminishing returns, which makes continuing growth possible. In such settings the rate of growth is determined endogenously and a policy change that alters the return to accumulation may have permanent growth effects. The impact of trade in such models has been studied extensively by Grossman and Helpman (1991) (see also their chapter in this volume). But we know of no such formal analysis of the long-run growth effects of discriminatory trade liberalization. The literature on trade and growth does however suggest some mechanisms through which an RIA might influence long-run growth.

The first possible mechanism arises if there are technological spillovers which are limited in their geographic reach. An RIA might promote the volume of spillovers between members – either as a consequence of increased trade volumes or because of policies designed to encourage scientific interchange, as have been pursued in the EC. This may change the international location of knowledge-producing activities, and thus growth rates and income levels (see Section 3.3 of Chapter 2 in this volume).

The second mechanism can arise if an RIA directly affects the efficiency of sectors that produce accumulable factors. For example, if the knowledge-creation sector is imperfectly competitive and integration has a pro-competitive effect, then integration may have long-run growth effects similar to those that Baldwin (1993) derived in the two country case. Similarly, integration might raise efficiency in producing capital goods and reduce their relative prices. Capital market integration might have similar effects, if it serves to reduce the wedge between returns to borrowers and lenders or improve the efficiency of the capital market in other ways. Application of these ideas to RIAs remains to be fully developed.

4. Location effects

There is a long standing concern that regional integration may be associated with increased inequality between regions. In Europe, there is a striking inverse relationship between per capita income and proximity to the geographical core of the EC. Concerns with continuing regional inequalities have led to a dramatic expansion of EC expenditures on regional policy, which now amount to approximately 0.3 percent of EC GDP or more than one quarter of the budget of the European Commission. Ben-David (1993) argues that integration has reduced income differentials between countries, but using European regional data as well as national, Quah (1994) finds that the picture is more complex, with a widening of regional inequalities occurring in some countries. The idea that "cumulative causation" may generate inequalities in regional development goes back to Perroux (1955), Myrdal (1957) and Hirschman (1958). These ideas have received renewed attention from economists following recent work by Krugman (1991a,b). In this section, we draw on this new literature to investigate ways in which integration may alter the distribution of economic activity within an RIA and thereby influence regional inequalities.

In a perfectly competitive world, the expectation is that regional integration would reduce intra-RIA factor price differences. The strongest statement of this prediction comes in the form of the factor price equalization theorem. If each country's endowment lies inside the same cone of diversification, then integration, by equalizing goods prices, will equalize factor prices. This will not occur if endowments lie outside cones of diversification, but integration may increase the number of internationally traded goods or factors and thereby increase the size (and possibly dimension) of the cones of diversification, increasing the "likelihood" that a given country's endowment vector lies inside the cone. The suggestion then is that integration should lead to equalization, or at least convergence, of factor returns within the union.

Imperfect competition and scale economies can modify, or even reverse, the traditional thinking. Scale economies mean that firms have to make discrete location decisions (they will not locate some productive capacity in every country or region). These decisions will depend on the balance between production costs and the trade costs that must be incurred in supplying different markets. This balance changes as trade barriers are reduced, and it is possible that industry will be drawn into high wage locations, thereby increasing inter-regional wage differences. In Section 4.1 we investigate this possibility using the "large-group" model developed in Section 2.2.1. Section 4.2 extends the analysis to situations in which forces for agglomeration are present. Integration may then trigger a process of cumulative causation, in which economic activity comes to be concentrated in particular areas. Regional inequalities – in both industrial structure and income levels – then result from integration.

4.1. Location of firms

To understand the effects of integration on the intra-RIA location of an imperfectly competitive industry, we consider integration between two economies with different size markets. The idea is that a country with a large market may be a "central" region, with easy access to many customers; the other country is "peripheral", having relatively few local consumers. For example, one might think of Spain as a small market, Germany as a large one, and European integration as reducing the cost of trade between the two. How do these changes in trade costs affect the location of industry, and hence the demand for labour and relative wages? We can see that there is a potential ambiguity here. On the one hand, firms in the small country benefit more from reduction in trade costs than do firms in the large, because more of their output is exported. But on the other hand, there are relatively many firms in the large economy, each of which increases exports to the small, so firms in the small economy suffer more from import growth.

To analyse this situation we use the large group model of Section 2.2.1. In order to highlight intra-union issues we shall set external trade barriers prohibitively high $(\theta^* = 0)$ and concentrate on the two economies in the RIA. The first question is, what happens to the sales of firms in each country as trade barriers are reduced? The total sales of a country 1 firm are, from (2.9):

$$ x_1 = \frac{1}{p_1} \left[\frac{E_1^X}{n_1 + \theta_{21} n_2} + \frac{E_2^X \theta_{12}}{\theta_{12} n_1 + n_2} \right]. \tag{4.1} $$

As before, θ_{ij} measures the ratio of an importing firm's sales to a domestic firm's sales, and this ratio increases with integration. Now suppose for simplicity that $p_1 = p_2$, so that $\theta_{21} = \theta_{12} = \theta$, and also that expenditures E_2^X and E_2^X are constant.[29] Furthermore, let the number of firms be set at their autarky levels, so that n_1 and n_2 are determined from $n_i p_i \bar{x} = E_i^X$, where $\bar{x}$ is the equilibrium firm scale. Using this equation in (4.1), we can rearrange terms to get:

$$ \frac{x_1}{\bar{x}} = \frac{E_1^X}{E_1^X + \theta E_2^X} + \frac{E_2^X \theta}{\theta E_1^X + E_2^X} = 1 + \frac{(1 - \theta)\theta E_2^X (E_1^X - E_2^X)}{(E_1^X + \theta E_2^X)(\theta E_1^X + E_2^X)}. \tag{4.2} $$

We see that the autarky number of firms satisfies the requirements for an equilibrium $(x_1 = \bar{x})$ not only when $\theta = 0$, but also at free trade, when $\theta = 1$. However, the equation makes clear that at all intermediate values of θ, x_1 is greater or less than its equilibrium value, $\bar{x}$, according to whether expenditure in country 1 is greater or less than expenditure in country 2. This implies that if numbers of firms are held constant, then sales per firm in the small economy must be a U-shaped function of trade costs, falling then rising during a process of integration. The U-shape arises because, as we have noted, there are two forces at work. Firms in the small economy benefit more from the reduction in trade costs, because much of their output is exported; but they also stand to lose, as there are many firms in the large economy, all of which increase their exports to the small.

In the preceding thought experiment the numbers of firms were held constant and

---

[29]Trade in the Z sector equalizes wages and hence X sector costs, income effects are ignored, and $\eta = 1$.

profits were non-zero, except at autarky and free trade. Now we allow entry and exit of firms to keep profits at zero ($x_i = \bar{x}$, $i = 1, 2$). As would be expected in view of the preceding discussion, reducing trade barriers causes movement of firms from the small economy to the large, this continuing until $\theta = 1$, at which point location is indeterminate. It follows that the larger economy must be a net exporter of the imperfectly competitive industry's products, [as in Krugman (1980)].

This relocation of industry to the "centre" will be offset if factor scarcities cause changes in relative factor prices in the two economies. We can see this most starkly if we suppose that labor used in the X industry is a specific factor, national supplies of which are proportional to market size. Full employment of this specific factor means that the number of firms in each economy must stay constant. Then the wage rate must change to ensure that this is an equilibrium, i.e. to give $x_i = \bar{x}$ and zero profits in each economy. These equilibrium wages are depicted in Figure 4.1. The horizontal axis in the figure is the iceberg trade cost, τ, and the vertical axis gives wages, assumed to be the only element of costs. The figure is constructed with $E_2^X > E_1^X$, and the curves w_1 and w_2 are the equilibrium wages.

When trade costs are high, wages are similar in the two countries. When these costs are reduced, the large market becomes the more attractive location, as we have seen,

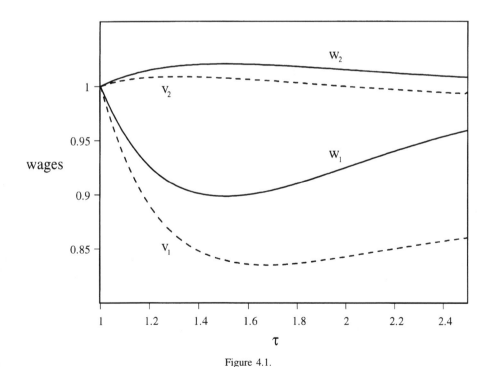

Figure 4.1.

so in order to hold firms in each location there must be a fall in wages in location 1 and a rise in wages in location 2. But as trade costs fall further, location becomes increasingly sensitive to differences in production costs. At low enough trade costs, smaller wage differences are required to maintain employment in the small economy and, in the limit, factor price equalisation takes over. Curves w_1 and w_2 give wages in terms of the numeraire. We can look at welfare by adjusting these wages by the consumer prices indices. Curves v_1 and v_2 illustrate one possible outcome.[30] The small economy gains relatively more from complete integration – it gets access to many more varieties without bearing trade costs. However, there are values for τ at which trade liberalization brings real wage reductions to the large region (when τ is very low) and to the small (when τ is quite high).

Figure 4.1 was constructed under extreme assumptions about labour supply to the industry under study, but nevertheless is indicative of more general conclusions [see Krugman and Venables (1990), who also look at different forms of competition]. Firms in an imperfectly competitive industry will, during a process of integration, be drawn towards ''central'' areas of the region, because having good access to consumers becomes *more* not less important to firms as the costs of market access decline. If wages change little (the rest of the economy releases or absorbs labour with little change in the wage) then this process will lead to a divergence of industrial structure. But if changing industrial employment does impact on wages, then integration will lead to divergence of relative wages up to a point, and convergence thereafter. Which side of this turning point actual economies are on is an empirical matter, about which little is known.

4.2. Linkages and agglomeration

In the model described above, as in most conventional economic models, an increase in the number of firms at a particular location reduces the return to firms at that location. This tends to generate an outcome in which firms are geographically dispersed. If instead, an increase in the number of firms at a location were to raise the return to other firms, then agglomeration would occur. Dispersed outcomes would be unstable and firms would tend to concentrate in a few locations, although the model might not predict which ones (there may be multiple equilibria). It turns out that the level of trade costs is an important determinant of whether agglomeration will occur. Of course, regional integration can change these trade costs. We investigate in the remainder of this section the causes and consequences of agglomeration.

Agglomeration requires that there are positive ''linkages'' between the activities of

---

[30] The real wage lines, v_1 and v_2, are constructed with the assumption that the X industry accounts for 1/3 of national income. Both nominal and real wages are expressed relative to their values when trade costs are zero.

agents at the same location. These linkages could be technological externalities with a limited spatial range, or pecuniary externalities which can arise in an imperfectly competitive industry. It is convenient to distinguish "demand linkages" and "cost linkages". If an increase in the number of firms at a location raises profits of other firms at that location via an increase in demand for output, then we say there is a demand linkage; if it increases profits via a reduction in the cost of inputs, this is a cost linkage. We can see how these operate by using the two-country model of location set out in the preceding sub-section. Equilibrium numbers of firms in each economy are determined by the zero profit conditions [eq. (4.1) with $x_1 = \bar{x}$, and the country 2 analogue]. Evidently, the right hand sides of these equations depend on the number of firms at each location, n_1 and n_2, directly. There is a demand linkage if expenditures, E_1^X and E_2^X, depend on numbers of firms, and a cost linkage if costs (and hence prices and θ_{12} and θ_{21}) do.

Although "linkages" of some form are necessary for agglomeration to occur, they are not sufficient. For example, if there is a fixed amount of final consumer demand at each location, then at very high levels of trade costs there will be no agglomeration – firms will locate close to final consumers. At lower levels of trade costs being close to final consumers is less important and agglomeration becomes possible. At what level of trade costs does industrial location switch from being dispersed to agglomerated? To answer this question, suppose that the two economies are identical in technology, preferences and endowments, so that a symmetric equilibrium exists in which industry is equally dispersed between the two countries. If the forces leading to agglomeration dominate, this equilibrium will be unstable. That is, the relocation of a firm from country 2 to country 1 will reduce profits in 2 and raise them in 1. This suggests that we can find the point at which symmetry is broken and the system "self organizes" into an asymmetric equilibrium, by examining the stability of the symmetric equilibrium, i.e. by asking whether relocating a firm from 2 to 1 reduces or raises profits in each location. A marginal reallocation of firms from 2 to 1, denoted dn, where $dn \equiv dn_1 = -dn_2$, induces changes in endogenous variables $dE^X \equiv dE_1^X = -dE_2^X$, $dp \equiv dp_1 = -dp_2$, and $dx \equiv dx_1 = -dx_2$. Denoting the right hand side of (4.1) by R and totally differentiating gives

$$p\frac{dx}{dn} = \frac{\partial R}{\partial n} + \frac{\partial R}{\partial E^X}\frac{dE^X}{dn} + \left[\frac{\partial R}{\partial \theta}\frac{\partial \theta}{\partial p} - x\right]\frac{dp}{dn}. \tag{4.3}$$

Now evaluating the partial derivatives at the symmetric equilibrium and choosing units such that $p = 1$ at this equilibrium, we find,[31]

$$\frac{n}{x}\frac{dx}{dn} = \left(\frac{1-\theta}{1+\theta}\right)^2\left[-1 + \left(\frac{1+\theta}{1-\theta}\right)\frac{n}{E^X}\frac{dE^X}{dn} - \left(\frac{4\theta\sigma}{(1-\theta)^2} + 1\right)n\frac{dp}{dn}\right]. \tag{4.4}$$

[31]The calculations are contained in Appendix C.

The left-hand sides of eqs. (4.3) and (4.4) give the change in output, and hence the sign of the change in profits. The right-hand sides contain three distinct terms. The first is the direct effect of changes in n; as expected this is negative, a force for stability. The second is the demand linkage; if $dE^X/dn > 0$, then this is a positive term tending to destabilize the symmetric equilibrium. The final term is a price effect; if $dp/dn < 0$ (a cost linkage meaning that more firms cause a reduction in costs) then the term is positive, again tending to destabilize the equilibrium.

Symmetry is broken and agglomeration occurs if the right hand side of (4.4) is positive. The role of trade barriers is immediate. The coefficients on the linkage terms inside the square brackets in (4.4) are strictly increasing in θ, and they approach infinity at free trade, where $\theta = 1$. Integration raises θ, and so it may destroy the stability of the symmetric equilibrium. In this event, integration induces agglomeration. We turn to examples of this in the next two sections.

4.2.1. Labour mobility

Integration may change both the barriers to, and the incentives for, labour migration. In a perfectly competitive economy, the expectation is that migration will reduce differences in factor prices, but Krugman (1991a) demonstrated how, with imperfect competition, it could lead to agglomeration of activity and divergence of income levels. The argument follows straightforwardly from what we have already seen. In Section 4.1 we saw how the interaction between a reduction in trade costs and firms' location decisions could cause divergence of wage levels between regions, with regions with the larger markets capturing higher wages. If migration is possible, then workers might move from the small region to the large. As they do so, they take their expenditure with them, thereby increasing the difference between market sizes. Migration may therefore increase the wage gap between locations, this encouraging further migration and possibly leading to an outcome in which all mobile factors are concentrated in a few locations.

In terms of the analysis of Section 4.2, migration generates a demand linkage; the movement of firms is associated with a movement of workers and their expenditure, so $dE^X/dn > 0$. The linkage is not necessarily destabilising, but will tend to be so the lower are trade costs (higher is θ) and the larger is the share of mobile firms in the economy [which raises the elasticity $(dE^X/dn)(n/E^X)$; see Krugman (1991a) for the details]. Clearly, the importance of this argument depends on the extent to which workers are willing to move between countries or regions. While labour mobility within some countries is high [for example the United States, see Blanchard and Katz (1993)], there is no evidence that mass migration has been part of recent RIAs.

4.2.2. Integration and industrial agglomeration

Labour mobility creates a positive demand linkage between industrial location and the location of final expenditure, but not a cost linkage. Other mechanisms for industrial agglomeration have been suggested, most of them dating back to Marshall (1920), who identified three distinct reasons for agglomeration. The first is the possibility of labour market pooling – a cost linkage that could arise if firms benefit from the existence of a localized pool of skilled workers. The second is the existence of technological spillovers – a cost linkage which, if spatially limited, may give rise to agglomeration. The third is intermediate inputs, which – combined with economies of scale – may generate both a cost and a demand linkage. Porter (1990) has also emphasised the importance of these mechanisms in determining industrial location.

The intermediate input story has been addressed by a number of authors [for example Faini (1984)], and can be developed with a minor modification of our core model of location of an imperfectly competitive industry. Suppose that the X industry now uses its own output as an input in production [Venables (1993), Krugman and Venables (1993)]. Each firm in the industry faces an average cost function $a(w_j, P_j, x_j)$, where P_j is the price index for products of the industry, which are now used as a composite input.[32] This modification of the model generates both cost and demand linkages. We have already seen that the price index depends on the location of firms [eq. (2.3)], and that the more firms there are in a location the lower is the location's price index. This implies the existence of a cost linkage. The demand linkage arises because products are used now by both consumers and other firms. Formally, expenditure in location j on the industry output is given by:

$$E_j^X = E_j^X(c) + n_j x_j \frac{\partial a(w_j, P_j, x_j)}{\partial P_j} \tag{4.5}$$

where $E_j^X(c)$ is consumer expenditure, and the second term is the value of intermediate demand.

Equilibrium configurations are illustrated in Figures 4.2a–c. These figures are similar to Figure 2.1, but have the numbers of firms in each of the RIA countries on the axes. Figure 4.2a describes the case when trade costs are high. Combinations of n_1 and n_2 consistent with zero profits in each country are given by the lines $x_1 x_1$ and $x_2 x_2$. The equilibrium is at point A, where production is divided equally between the two economies. Arrows indicate a hypothetical out-of-equilibrium adjustment process in which entry (exit) occurs in each country in response to positive (negative) profits. As should be clear, the equilibrium at A is stable. Figure 4.2c depicts the situation that arises with low trade costs. The crucial difference is that the direction of intersection of the zero profit contours is reversed, which happens when the trade costs fall below the critical level determined by eqs. (4.3) and (4.4). The equilibrium at A is unstable, and there are instead two stable equilibria at the points labelled B. Agglomeration occurs – although there is nothing in the theory to say at which location. Finally, Figure 4.2b illustrates a case of intermediate trade costs. The

---

[32]This assumes that the price index for intermediates can be constructed in exactly the same way as the price index for consumption.

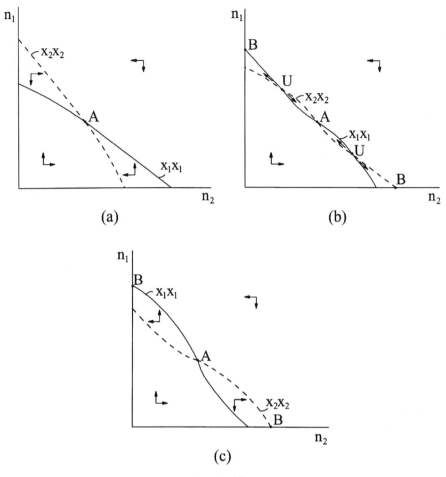

Figure 4.2.

symmetric equilibrium at A is stable, as are asymmetric equilibria at the points labelled B; in between the stable equilibria are unstable equilibria at the points labelled U.

This example illustrates how trade liberalization may unravel a symmetric equilibrium and cause agglomeration of activity even in the absence of labour mobility or of any externalities. Its applicability depends, amongst other things, on the structure of the input-output matrix. Depending on this structure, linkages could be important at an industry wide level, or at the level of particular tightly linked groups of industries. In the former case, the forces of agglomeration affect industry as a whole, and the theory suggests that integration could be associated with a substantial widening of wage differences between countries. In the latter case, integration would be associated not with aggregate wage differences, but with concentration of particular industries in particular locations [Krugman and Venables (1993)]. In the European context, each country might be expected to give up a presence in some industries, so that the economic geography of Europe would become more regionally specialised, like that of the United States. In this case the potential gains from integration are relatively large, as integration permits the benefits from agglomeration to be achieved. However, adjustment costs and political frictions may also be high, as integration might give rise to the need for substantial relocation of activities between countries in the RIA.

5. Empirical evaluations.

In this section we review some of the empirical evaluations of RIAs that have been undertaken. No review of this literature can hope to be exhaustive, and we concentrate on four topics. These are (i) trade creation and diversion in the EC; (ii) the growth effects of RIAs; (iii) the NAFTA, and (iv) EC92. As well as being topics of interest in their own right, the discussion serves to illustrate different methods that can be employed to establish the effects of RIAs; in surveying the first two topics we look at econometric approaches, while in covering the last two we review computable equilibrium techniques. We begin with a few comments on the range of different methods available to a researcher studying the effects of regional integration.

5.1. Methodologies for empirical evaluations.

The task of a researcher undertaking an empirical evaluation of an RIA is to establish the effect of the policy change on some set of endogenous variables. The difficulty arises from the need to disentangle the effect of the RIA from other changes in the economy. Many different techniques have been employed, ranging from single equation regressions to large-scale computable general equilibrium models. François and Shiells (1994) classify these approaches by comparing them to an ideal evaluation, where one would specify a complete world model based on micro-economic theory, estimate all of the parameters simultaneously on internationally comparable data, and then use the estimated model to evaluate the RIA. In practise, computational and data limitations rule out such an ideal approach, thereby forcing a trade-off between theory and econometrics. The two major types of evaluations – involving econometric techniques and computable equilibrium (CE) methods – come down on opposite sides of this trade-off. Econometric evaluations typically manage to estimate all parameters by positing very simple models and/or by focusing on only a few endogenous variables. CE evaluations typically work with models that are more rigorously based on theory, but force the researchers to choose parameters using ad hoc methods. The most common method is the "calibration" technique, which involves taking some parameter estimates from diverse econometric studies, setting the values of other parameters (for which estimates are unavailable) in accordance with the researcher's prior beliefs, and choosing the remaining parameter values so that the model exactly fits the data for some base year.

Both approaches have strengths and weaknesses. Econometric evaluations have an advantage in that they can be appraised with standard statistical criteria. Their drawback is that they cannot capture the complicated interplay of effects which may be important for massive policy changes such as NAFTA or EC92. CE evaluations allow for more interactions among endogenous variables, but neither the models nor their results can be judged statistically. Moreover, CE models face two trade-offs between transparency and complexity. First, it is hard to understand what is driving the results in very complex models and this can be a problem even with medium-sized CE models, as we shall see below. Second, to implement large complex models the researcher is compelled to make a number of essentially arbitrary choices regarding data, parameter values and functional forms. These are often too numerous to report and yet they may affect the results. We turn now to discuss each approach in more detail.

5.2. Econometric evaluations

Econometric approaches have been used to study the effects of RIAs on a wide range of variables. Researchers have tested for the impact of an RIA on variables such as firm size and price-cost margins [Sleuwaegen and Yamawaki (1988) and Muller and Owen (1985)], intra-regional trade [Jacquemin and Sapir (1988)], or the stock market [Thompson (1994)]. In this section we review only studies that examine trade creation and trade diversion, and the growth effects of integration.

5.2.1. Trade creation and diversion in the EC

Following in the Vinerian tradition, the earliest evaluations focused on imports to member countries, the object being to identify trade creation and diversion. The main application was to the formation of the EC and the UK's accession to it. The earliest studies used a technique known as residual imputation. This approach uses an estimated model to construct what imports would have been without the RIA (the counterfactual or anti-monde) and calculates the impact of the RIA as the difference between actual and constructed imports for a post-RIA year. A wide range of import equations and econometric techniques has been used to construct what imports would have been without the EC. The earliest studies used only pre-RIA data and very simple bilateral import models. For instance, they constructed bilateral imports from partner and non-partner nations using the pre-RIA time trends [Clavaux (1969), EFTA (1972)], or pre-RIA shares in apparent consumption [Truman (1969)].

The residual imputation method attributes both random shocks and any effects excluded from the model to the impact of the RIA. To avoid this, more recent studies have incorporated the effects of the RIA into the specification of the model and estimated the model using pre-RIA and post-RIA data. In some cases the impact of the policy on trade flows is captured through the use of dummy variables. Aitken (1973) and Aitken and Lowry (1973) used gravity models, Balassa (1974) estimated income elasticities of demand for imports, while Resnik and Truman (1973), and Winters (1984, 1985) estimated systems of import demand equations.

Mayes (1978), Winters (1987) and Balassa (1975) provide detailed surveys of the results in the literature on trade creation and diversion, and we limit ourselves to discussing the main conclusions. The consensus finding is that the EC increased members' imports from one another more than it decreased their imports from non-members, i.e. trade creation exceeded trade diversion. To understand the small amount of trade diversion, we note that much of Europe's trade took place among eventual EC members even prior to the formation of the EC. Thus EC nations must already have been each others' lowest-cost suppliers for many goods.[33] In such cases, the scope for trade diversion is limited. Agriculture does not fit into this story, and indeed Thorbecke (1975) shows that trade diversion in food was quite important, particularly as many countries experienced external tariff increases as part of the Common Agricultural Policy. However, looking at trade as a whole, trade creation was found to be positive, and generally many times larger than trade diversion.

Changes in trade volumes weighted by corresponding tariffs provide a first order approximation to welfare change generated by "trade volume effects" (see Section 2.1). Most studies did not explicitly derive welfare implications (though many implicitly took creation exceeding diversion as an indicator of gain). Those that did found the effects to be extremely small. Winters (1987), for instance, found that the UK accession to the EC generated a welfare gain from the trade volume effect equal to 0.11 percent of UK GDP. The reason for the small size of the gains is that the estimated volume of trade creation is small – approximately 1 percent of GDP – as are initial trade barriers.

5.2.2. Growth regressions

A more recent type of econometric evaluation focuses on the growth effects of RIAs. These studies typically estimate simple linear growth models using a variety of independent variables, including dummies or proxies for regional integration. The parameters are estimated on cross-country data or time-series data for a single nation. Some studies draw their conclusions from the sign and significance of the RIA proxy.

---

[33] See Anderson and Norheim (1993).

Others use their estimated coefficients and the actual changes in their RIA proxies to quantify the growth effect. This literature is far from mature and new conclusions may emerge, but the existing studies tentatively suggest that some RIAs have had a positive impact on growth, at least in Europe.

Coe and Moghadam (1993), using French time-series data, test for cointegration among non-farm GDP, labour, physical capital, cumulated R&D spending, and an integration proxy defined as the ratio of intra-EC trade to GDP. On the basis of their estimates they conclude that 0.3 percentage points of the French annual growth rate from 1984–1991 was attributable to EC integration. Using EC time-series data, Italianer (1994) estimates a linear regression relating the rate of income growth to a set of variables that includes an RIA proxy, defined as intra-EC trade as a share of total EC trade. He finds that his RIA proxy is positively and statistically significantly related to the growth rate. In contrast, De Melo, Montenegro and Panagariya (1992) find that RIAs have no growth effects. Using OLS on cross-country data, they estimate a linear regression of income growth rates, with dummies for six RIAs (EU, EFTA, two Latin American RIAs and two African RIAs) among the right-hand side variables. They find that only the coefficient on the RIA dummy for the South African Customs Union is positive and significant.

Clearly, further refinements of this literature are necessary before firm conclusions can be drawn. Three shortcomings of the literature are worth noting. First, OLS is an inappropriate estimation method since many of the regressors are endogenous; the correlation between the included and omitted variables biases the estimates. Second, these regressions cannot capture the investment creation effects discussed in Section 3, since they include measures of capital formation as well as proxies for the RIA. Finally, the regressions cannot establish causality. It could be that purely domestic factors drive growth and exports separately, so that the coefficients on the RIA proxies and dummies reflect only a spurious correlation.

5.3. Computable equilibrium evaluations

CE models have made two distinct contributions to the evaluation of RIAs. First, they have been used to provide estimates of the effects of actual or proposed RIAs. However, since even the most sophisticated models cannot capture the full impact of complicated RIAs, the results give only a partial estimate of the true impact of an RIA. But secondly, they have also helped us to understand theoretical interactions in models that are too complicated to study analytically. Indeed this "theory with numbers" interpretation is the basis of much of the received wisdom on the relative importance of different effects of RIAs.

CE models and their results vary widely, but it is helpful to think of three generations of models, corresponding to the three rows into which we classified welfare effects in eq. (1.2). The first generation of models assumes perfect competition and ignores dynamics. A good example of such a model is the Michigan model [Deardorff and Stern (1986)]. The model is large – it has 34 countries and 29 sectors – and the modellers assume that each industry produces a homogeneous good under perfect competition and constant returns to scale. Intra-industry trade is difficult to explain under such assumptions, yet it is important in the data. To match the models to the data, an ad hoc assumption about preferences is introduced. This so-called Armington assumption is that goods in each sector are perfect substitutes if they are produced in the same nations, but imperfect substitutes if they are produced in different nations. National supplies of the factors, labour and capital, are assumed to be fixed.

Second-generation models allow for increasing returns and imperfect competition in some of the industrial sectors. The first example of such a model is that developed by Harris and Cox (1984). Typically, the description of the imperfectly competitive sectors has been similar to the "core model" developed in Section 2.2 of this chapter, involving product differentiation and monopolistic competition. These models can provide estimates of the output, scale and variety effects discussed above, but, as we shall see, results are sensitive to the assumed form of competition between firms and the pricing rules that follow.

Third generation models [e.g. Harrison, Rutherford and Tarr (1994)] incorporate some simple accumulation effects by allowing capital stocks to change, (usually in an imperfectly competitive setting). Typically this is done by having capital stocks adjust to ensure equality of rates of returns and discount rates, although occasionally an assumption of a constant savings to income ratio has been used. Third generation models capture the medium term dynamics – investment creation and diversion – of Section 3.1, but not continuing, endogenous growth.

Differences between these models are best seen by comparing their applications, and to this we now turn.

5.3.1. Evaluations of NAFTA

Excellent surveys of the results of NAFTA evaluations are available in U.S. International Trade Commission (1992), Francois (1993) and Francois and Shields (1994). These surveys review a broad range of studies and summarize results on issues including employment, wages, migration and trade effects. To illustrate the main findings, Table 5.1 presents the real income changes predicted from the median estimate of all the studies surveyed in U.S. International Trade Commission (1992) and from some of the scenarios presented in three of the individual studies. These are Bachrach and Mizrahi (1992), Brown, Deardorff and Stern (1992), and Roland-Horst, Reinert and Shiells (1992), which we abbreviate as BM, BDS and RRS. The three are representative of the range of the ITC-survey studies. BM present first and third generation models, which we refer to as BM-I, BM-III. BDS have second and third generation variants, BDS-II and BDS-III respectively. RRS is a second generation

Table 5.1
Aggregate impact of NAFTA as percent of GDP

	Median	I BM-I	II BDS-II	II RRS	III BM-III	III BDS-III
Mexico	2.59	0.32	1.6	3.4	4.6	5.0
Canada	3.26	n.a.	0.71	10.6	n.a.	0.7
USA	0.16	0.02	0.01	2.1	0.4	0.3

Notes: 1. Column 1 presents the median of all results surveyed in ITC (1992). 2. BM is Bachrach and Mizrahi (1992). Scenario ''I'' looks at a US–Mexico FTA with a first-generation model. Scenario ''III'' performs the same experiment with endogenous capital stocks. 3. BDS is Brown, Deardorff, and Stern (1992). Scenario ''II'' considers tariffs and NTB removal among NAFTA members with a second-generation model. Scenario ''III'' is the same as ''II'' plus an exogenous inflow of capital into Mexico. 4. RRS is Roland-Horst, Reinert and Shiells (1992), which looks at the removal of tariffs and NTBs in a second-generation model.

model. Roman numerals I, II and III in the column headings of Table 5.1 are our classification of models by generation.

The first point to note about the models' predictions is that all participating countries are expected to gain from NAFTA. Furthermore, the median predicted gains for Mexico and Canada, at 2.5 and 3.3 percent of GDP, are quite sizeable. RRS and Hinjosa and Robinson (1992) attribute much of the Mexican and Canadian gains to the removal of non-tariff barriers. Prospective gains for the US are estimated to be very much smaller, reflecting both the much smaller share of US GDP directly affected by the policy change and the lower initial trade barriers.

A second point to note is the magnitude of the difference between the estimates produced by the various studies. Comparing second generation models with first, we see estimated gains more than fives times as large. This is because, as the theory sections showed, allowing for scale economies creates additional mechanisms through which an RIA can affect welfare. Theory does not say that aggregate gains are necessarily greater in an imperfectly competitive framework, but it is not surprising that CE simulations give this result.

The difference between the two second generation models is equally striking, and can be attributed to the different approaches that the researchers take to modelling imperfect competition.

BDS assume monopolistic competition in which markets are integrated and firms are Bertrand competitors. This generates small changes in mark-ups, and very modest scale effects; firms in their imperfectly competitive sectors typically expand by less than 1 percent. The version of RRS reported in Table 5.1 uses a different pricing rule, which assumes that firms price at average cost, and that the number of firms in the industry remains fixed. The theoretical justification of such a rule is unclear, but its implications are immediate. Any expansion in industry output translates automatically into a scale effect, thereby generating larger reductions in average costs and welfare gains.[34]

Most of the studies surveyed by the U.S. International Trade Commission (1992) find that NAFTA would raise the return to capital in all three countries when capital stocks are held constant, suggesting that NAFTA might generate investment creation. Comparison of third generation with earlier generation variants of the same model (BM-I and III, BDS-II and III) indicate possible income growth associated with an increased capital stock. (The numbers reported are for GDP growth and, for the reasons discussed in Section 3, do not have a direct welfare interpretation). For example, endogenizing the capital stock in the BM model increases the projected change in US and Mexican GDP by factors of 20 and 15 respectively. The BDS studies also suggest that accumulation effects might be important. They simulate the impact of an exogenous 10 percent rise in Mexico's capital stock, which more than triples the impact of NAFTA on Mexico's output, compared to the case in which the capital stock is held constant. Although it is suggestive, this experiment raises more questions than it answers. BDS find that the increase in capital stock leads to a higher rate of return, an effect they attribute to the presence of increasing returns to scale.

The difference between the results obtained in these studies alerts us to the sensitivity of results to changes in the structure of the model. For example, in second generation models the description of imperfect competition is probably the dominant factor in determining the magnitude of effects. Conclusions will in general depend on the assumed form of competition, on the extent of product differentiation, on the degree of concentration in the industry (and hence also the selected level of industrial aggregation), and on the degree of unexploited economies of scale. Good data on these things are typically not available. Clearly, it is important that these inputs to the model and to the calibration procedure be chosen carefully and reported in full. It is also helpful if sensitivity analysis can be conducted, in order to establish the force of the researcher's assumptions.

5.3.2. Evaluations of EC92

EC92 was a complex set of policy measures aimed at removing non-tariff barriers to trade in the EC, and creating a "single market". Some of the measures are described in Section 1.1, and a full description is contained in Emerson et al. (1988).

The first studies of EC92 used partial equilibrium rather than aggregate models, and explored the effects of the policy on particular industries using second generation modelling approaches. Smith and Venables (1988) investigate the programme's possible pro-competitive effects in a model similar to that of Section 2.2 of this

---

[34]RRS refer to this as a "contestable market form of monopolistic competition". They also consider a case of Nash equilibrium in quantities, with free entry, which gives somewhat smaller welfare effects.

chapter. They look at two different representations of the EC92 policy change. The first is a reduction in intra-EC trade costs, the reduction being set (somewhat arbitrarily) at 2.5 percent of the value of intra-EC trade. This generates predictions of substantial increases in trade volumes, generating the pro-competitive effects analysed in Section 2.2.2 above. There are predicted increases in firm scale and, in moderately concentrated industries, average costs are estimated to fall by 1–2 percent. The second experiment adds to the first a switch from market segmentation to integration. Results then vary substantially across industries, but the model typically predicts average cost reductions several times larger than in the first experiment. Welfare gains range from a value of less than 1 percent of output in relatively unconcentrated industries, to about 5 percent in highly concentrated. When gains are decomposed into different elements the main source of potential gain appears to be scale induced reductions in average costs [Gasiorek, Smith and Venables (1992)].

Aggregate evaluations of EC92 are surveyed in Flam (1992) and Baldwin and Venables (1994), so we limit ourselves here to three representative studies. These are Haaland and Norman (1992), Harrison, Rutherford and Tarr (1994), and Baldwin, Forslid and Haaland (1994), which we abbreviate respectively as HN, HRT and BFH. All three have at their core second generation models, and the authors describe industries and the policy change in a manner similar to Smith and Venables (1988).[35] BFH is a third generation extension of HN, and HRT was constructed to allow comparison of first, second and third generation effects in the same model.

Results from these studies are contained in Table 5.2, which suggest a number of points. First, the EC is expected to gain from the policy change, but the prospective gains are typically rather modest. This is partly because the only distortions are imperfect competition and external tariffs; there are no tariffs on internal trade and

Table 5.2
Aggregate impact of EC92 as percent of GDP

	Median	II HN-a	II HN-b	III BFH	I HRT-I	II HRT-II	III HRT-III
EC	0.52	0.40	0.64	0.80	0.50	1.18	2.60
EFTA	n.a.	−0.15	−0.22	−0.24	n.a.	n.a.	n.a.

Notes: 1. Column is the median estimate of five studies surveyed by Baldwin and Venables (1994). 2. HN is Haaland and Norman (1992). Scenario "a" is a 2.5 percent reduction in intra-EU trade costs assuming segmented markets, scenario "b" is trade cost reduction with integrated markets. 3. BFH is Baldwin, Forslid and Haaland (1994), and is identical to HN-b except capital stocks are endogenous. 4. HRT is Harrison, Rutherford and Tarr (1994). The I, II and III scenarios are the first, second and third generation versions of their model. All look at lower trade costs and assume integrated markets.

[35]HRT discuss alternative representations of integration and explore the effects of changing the degree of substitutability between domestic and foreign varieties of differentiated product.

hence no "trade creation". More importantly, it is because the models look only at changes in manufacturing industry, which accounts for approximately one third of EC GDP. The focus of the models on manufacturing means that they possibly understate the overall effect of the EC92 programme, which had important reforms aimed at service trade and financial market liberalization. The studies also report welfare change country by country, and in general there are predicted gains for all countries. The estimates suggest that the largest gains will be realised by smaller countries which are the most open to intra-EC trade.

A second point to notice is that several of the studies estimate the welfare effect of EC92 on EFTA, and these estimates turn out to be negative, though small. The projected loss is the result of "production shifting", as described in Section 2.2.2. Sectors affected by the policy see expanded output in the EC and contracted output in countries heavily dependent on sales in the EC market. BFH and HN evaluate additional experiments (not reported in the table) including the possible effects of the European Economic Area agreement which extends EC92 to most EFTA countries. They see this as bringing gains to EFTA and slightly increased benefits to the EC as well.

A third set of observations concerns the sources of difference between results. The range of differences are not as large as in the NAFTA studies, which may be attributed to the similar basic structure of the various models. The difference between HN-a and HN-b lies in the nature of the experiment – the former does not include a switch to market integration and the latter does, giving, as we would expect, a further welfare gain. The move to a third generation model (BFH) increases the predicted effect on income further, through an output multiplier, although, as noted before, this cannot be construed as a welfare gain. The HRT experiments use first, second, and third generation models, and confirm the view that by incorporating additional effects one does indeed raise the estimated net effect of the policy. Again, we should stress that this need not be the case. For example, the output multipliers associated with accumulation effects could be less than unity, but estimates of these multipliers are in the range $1.2 - 2.2$, reflecting the fact that traded goods tend to be capital intensive. The RIA stimulates production of these goods and raises the demand for capital.

5.3.3. Concluding comments on computable equilibrium evaluations

Computable equilibrium methods have perhaps become the predominant research approach to assessing RIAs. The studies of NAFTA and EC92 discussed here illustrate the wide range of possible effects that can be captured in such models and the range of predictions that can be generated. It is important to think of these models as playing two distinct roles; namely, policy analysis and "theory with numbers".

For ex ante policy analysis the researcher is bound to use computable equilibrium techniques, but the limitations of the technique must be recognised. The fundamental problem with the CE method is that there is no satisfactory way of subjecting the model to tests that could determine its validity. One response a researcher might make to this problem is to undertake sensitivity analysis – that is, to conduct simulations for a wide range of values of key parameters and present the policy maker with a range of estimates. The difficulty with this is that there may be a very large number of "key parameters" (however these are identified). Furthermore, sensitivity analysis is needed not just with respect to parameters, but also with respect to other aspects of the model such as functional form and, more fundamentally, behavioural relationships such as the form of imperfect competition. An alternative response to the problem is to increase the extent to which CE models are confronted with data. Although econometric estimation of complete systems may be infeasible given the complexity of such models, greater use can be made of econometric estimation of parts of the model. For example, models of particular sectors can be estimated empirically (including estimates of competitive behaviour), and then used as components of the full model. The models can also be confronted with data by using them for ex post, as well as ex ante evaluations of policy change, in order to compare the predictions of the model with actual outcomes.

The second role of computable equilibrium models is as a complement to theoretical research – the "theory with numbers" approach. Theoretical research reveals channels through which RIAs may be expected to change economic variables, but often fails to give a sense of the quantitative importance of effects, and may leave ambiguities about net effects (as we have seen repeatedly in this chapter). Computable equilibrium techniques provide a way of assessing orders of magnitudes of the effects predicted by theory, and of indicating the way in which ambiguities may be resolved. This is perhaps the most important contribution that CE techniques can make. But in order to make this contribution the models need to be made transparent, and researchers must resist the temptation to construct ever larger and more complex "black boxes".

6. Regionalism and world trading arrangements

Up to this point, we have studied individual RIAs, taking the form of the RIAs as given. In this section, we examine regionalism in a broader context and consider two sorts of questions. First, what are the economic differences between different sorts of RIA? Second, what are the implications of regionalism for the world trading system as a whole? Is regionalism bad for global welfare, and how will regionalism affect multilateral tariff setting?

6.1. The structure of RIAs

Customs unions and free trade areas: In an FTA each member sets its own external tariffs, whereas a CU sets a common external tariff schedule. This difference has two main economic implications. The first is that an FTA requires the enforcement of rules of origin; in order to prevent imports from all coming in through the country with the lowest external tariff, free internal trade is permitted only for goods which can be proved to originate in the FTA, and not for re-exports. Rules of origin are frequently complex and sometimes arbitrary [see Hoekman (1994)]. For instance, while the basic provisions of the Polish-EC FTA take up 13 pages, rules of origin occupy over 60 pages. Enforcing these rules has administrative costs, which in the case of EFTA have been estimated to be around 3 percent of the value of intraEFTA and EFTA-EU trade [Herin (1986)]. These are nonDCR barriers, which may serve to support segmentation of markets, and may also be used to disguise protection of intermediate goods producers [Krueger (1993)], all suggesting that the welfare costs of such rules may be substantial.

The second main difference is that a CU requires joint decision making on trade policy whereas an FTA does not. EC trade policy, for instance, is proposed by the supranational European Commission and approved by the EC heads of government in the Council of Europe; tariff revenue accrues to the EC. This requires that nations surrender autonomy both in multilateral trade talks and in the application of antidumping measures and other forms of contingent protection, and it implies that members may end up with external trade barriers that are not nationally optimal from an economic or political perspective. For example, Richardson (1993) argues that members of an FTA may be able to avoid some of the costs of trade diversion (importing from high cost partner countries) by reducing their external tariffs. This autonomy is lost in a CU, and the loss is probably an important reason why most real-world RIAs are FTAs instead of CUs.

Joint decision making, however, has some benefits. When FTA members choose their external trade policy independently, two types of pecuniary externalities may arise. First, there may be an incentive for FTA countries to compete for tariff revenue. Low tariffs on a good will attract imports of that good and bring revenue. This can occur even with when imports are subject to rules of origin, because the sales of FTA firms will be diverted to high tariff countries, raising imports in a low tariff country [Richardson (1995)]. Second, an import tariff set by one country will, if it decreases the world price of the product, affect all countries in the FTA, with these other countries gaining or losing according to whether they import or export the good. The arguments of revenue competition and the common impact of world price changes suggest both that there are gains from setting a common external tariff, and that, if countries in the CU have similar external trade patterns, then a CUs joint welfare maximising external tariff is likely to exceed those set by an FTA.

Examples of this are given in simulations by Kennan and Riezman (1990).

Hub and Spoke FTAs: The relationships between countries in an RIA and between intersecting RIAs are much more complex than we have analyzed so far. For instance, both the EC and the US are at the centre of systems of bilateral FTAs. The 1993 Europe Agreements between the EC and former Eastern bloc countries form bilateral

RIAs between the EC and these countries, without addressing trade barriers between Eastern countries.[36] In addition to NAFTA membership the US has a bilateral FTA with Israel.[37] Such arrangements are known as "hub and spoke" RIAs, and were first analysed by Wonnacott (1975). Kowalcyzk and Wonnacott (1992) suggest that the benefits to the hub nation are likely to be greater than benefits to the spoke nations in a world of perfect competition. Their basic point is simple. Consider a three country world forming a hub and spoke system, with country 1 as the hub. This arrangement may lead to trade diversion for countries 2 and 3, but not for 1. If the example is extended to allow for more countries to be linked to the hub, each new spoke will lead to more trade creation for the hub. The welfare implications for existing spoke economies depend upon the whether the exports of the new spoke are complements or substitutes to those of old members. If they are substitutes, existing spoke nations may be harmed by an erosion of their degree of preference in the hub market. If they are complements, the initial members will also tend to gain.

A further argument suggesting that benefits to the hub will be relatively large is given by Krugman (1993a). The flavour of his argument can be appreciated with reference back to Section 4.1. With imperfect competition, we saw that industrial location will, given some non-prohibitive level of trade costs, tend to be skewed towards the location with the large market. In a hub and spoke system (where, for simplicity, all countries have the same size market) firms located in the hub will have better access to consumers than firms located in spokes, this creating exactly the same market access effect and causing the hub to have relatively more industry, and possibly also relatively higher wages, than the spokes.

6.2. Regionalism and the multilateral trading system

Is regionalism bad for global welfare? There are two aspects to this question. First, what are the implications for global welfare of countries lowering tariffs among themselves while holding their external barriers constant? Second, will the fact that countries are in an RIA lead them to set higher external trade barriers, perhaps causing trade wars and a breakdown of the multilateral trading system?

The former question is easily answered. If the RIA is small and there is perfect competition, then the agreement has no effect on welfare outside the region. But if the RIA causes terms of trade changes or, in an imperfectly competitive setting, production shifting, then we may expect a negative impact on the rest of the world. This expectation is confirmed in the studies of the effects of EC92 on EFTA reported in Section 5.3.2.

---

[36]For discussion of present and future trading arrangement in Europe, see Baldwin (1994).

[37]The US also has "Friendship, Commerce and Navigation" treaties with 47 countries. These treaties set out rules to govern bilateral trade and investment. [See Schott (1989) for further discussion].

The latter question is more difficult to answer as it requires a positive theory of tariff setting by RIAs. A simple, if unsatisfactory, approach is to suppose that external tariffs are set to maximise a country's or region's welfare. Then, parties to an FTA may have an incentive to cut their tariffs to capture revenue, as discussed in Section 6.1. A CU in contrast, might set a relatively high external tariff, because it can internalise the benefits of terms of trade improvements. This argument has been pursued by Krugman (1991c) who considers a world divided into a number of symmetric trading blocs or CUs, which are assumed to engage in a tariff-setting game. Krugman investigates how the equilibrium tariff depends on the number of CUs into which the world is divided. It turns out that the fewer CUs there are, the higher is the equilibrium tariff (except in the limit where the world is a single CU with no external trade policy). Although a reduction in the number of CUs means higher tariffs, it means also that less trade is subject to tariffs, and this generates a U-shaped relationship between welfare and the number of CUs. Krugman's numerical examples indicate that world welfare is minimised when there are three CUs. However, his conclusion rests on there being a considerable amount of trade diversion, (which is inevitable if blocs are symmetric). If CUs form instead along the lines of "natural trading blocs" – i.e. between countries that already conduct most of their trade with one another – then trade diversion will be small relative to trade creation. This reduces the likelihood that world welfare will be reduced by a move to fewer blocs [Krugman (1991d, 1993b)].

This line of reasoning depends on CUs setting tariffs to maximise instantaneous welfare – an assumption that is unsatisfactory for at least three reasons. First, as previously noted, CUs are constrained by Article XXIV of the GATT not to set external tariffs "higher or more restrictive" than those prevailing prior to the CU. Second, tariff setting may be better described by a repeated game than a one-shot Nash equilibrium [Bond and Syropoulos (1993), Bagwell and Staiger (1993)]. If so, cooperation (in this context, low tariffs) may be supported by the credible threat of punishing those who deviate, providing that short run benefits from deviation are outweighed by the long run costs of the punishment. Bond and Syropoulos (1993) investigate this problem. It may be that membership of a large CU may raise a country's incentive to deviate (more of the gains from terms of trade improvement are internalised) and also reduce the cost of punishment (since intra-RIA trade would be unaffected by punishment). This suggests that cooperation might become more difficult to support in a world of large trading blocs, offering support for the idea that regionalism might be dangerous for multilateralism.

The third criticism is that tariffs may be determined not by considerations of maximising aggregate national welfare, but rather as the outcome of political-economic interactions within countries and between countries in the CU. If each country in a CU has some sectors it wishes to protect and others it cares little about, then log-rolling might occur and protection may be the outcome of majority decision taking by RIA governments [Winters (1994)]. However, formal analysis of these issues is in its infancy.

7. Concluding comments

The resurgence of regionalism has elicited a great deal of theoretical and empirical research. This chapter has attempted to survey and synthesise the main contributions to this literature. Perhaps the most important conclusion to be drawn is that – despite theoretical ambiguities – RIAs seem to have generated welfare gains for the participants, with small, but possibly negative spillovers onto the rest of the world.

As we pointed out in the introduction, RIAs directly account for a large share of world trade, and it seems likely that this share will continue to grow. The study of RIAs should remain an important research topic for economists, and our survey has identified many areas where research is still needed. What determines cross market interaction between firms, and what is meant by a "single market"? What are the effects of RIAs on long-run growth? Will RIAs serve to promote convergence or divergence of members' income levels? Above all, better empirical evaluations are needed. The varied integration programmes undertaken throughout the world in the last few years provide a great opportunity for ex post evaluation of the effects of RIAs.

Appendices

Appendix A

Using (2.1) in the indirect utility function and totally differentiating gives:

$$
\frac{dV}{V_E} = \left[\frac{V_p}{V_E} + X \right] d(p + t) + \frac{V_n}{V_E} dn + [L - Xa_w] dw + [K - Xa_r] dr
$$
$$
+ [p + t - a] dX - Xa_x dx + \alpha t \, dm + m \, d(\alpha t) - dI + r \, dK . \qquad (A.1)
$$

By Roy's identity $V_p/V_E + X = -m$, and by Shephard's lemma and factor market clearing $L = Xa_w$ and $K = Xa_r$. We suppose that dI generates a permanent change in the capital stock yielding a social rate of return $\tilde{r}$ and discounted at rate ρ so write $r \, dK = (\tilde{r}/\rho) \, dI$. Using this and rearranging (A.1) gives (1.2) of the text.

Appendix B

Distinguishing individual product varieties by superscripts, eq. (2.3) takes the form:

$$
P_j^{1-\sigma} = \sum_{k=1}^{N} \left[\sum_{i=1}^{n_k} (p_{kj}^i \tau_{kj})^{1-\sigma} \right], \quad \sigma > 1 . \qquad (B.1)
$$

By Roy's identity, with the marginal utility of income set at unity,

$$c_{kj} = -\frac{\partial V(P_j, 1, E_j)}{\partial P_j} \cdot \frac{\partial P_j}{\partial(p_{kj}^i \tau_{kj})} = (p_{kj}^i \tau_{kj})^{-\sigma} P_j^{\sigma-1} E_j^X(P_j, E_j). \tag{B.2}$$

To find the Nash equilibrium in prices (Bertrand) we need to know the changes in c_{kj}^i when a firm's own price p_{kj}^i changes. Differentiating the price index with respect to a single price gives,

$$\frac{\partial P_j}{\partial(p_{kj}^i \tau_{kj})} \cdot \frac{p_{kj}^i \tau_{kj}}{P_j} = \left(\frac{p_{kj} \tau_{kj}}{P_j}\right)^{1-\sigma} = s_{jk} \tag{B.3}$$

where the derivative is evaluated at a point where all supplies from a particular source are the same, superscripts have consequently been dropped, and where the final equality comes from using (B.2). Differentiating the demand function (B.2) and using (B.3) gives,

$$\frac{\partial c_{kj}^i}{\partial(p_{kj}^i \tau_{kj})} \cdot \frac{p_{kj}^i \tau_{kj}}{c_{kj}^i} = (\sigma - \eta)s_{jk} - \sigma \equiv -\varepsilon \tag{B.4}$$

where ε is the perceived elasticity of demand. The first order condition for profit maximisation is $p_{kj}(1 - 1/\varepsilon) = b_k$, which gives eqs. (2.6) and (2.7) of the text.

The Nash equilibrium in quantities (Cournot) is found by working with the demand system in primal not dual form, and with the quantity index Y_j dual to P_j,

$$Y_j^{(\sigma-1)/\sigma} = \sum_{k=1}^{N} \left[\sum_{i=1}^{n_k} (c_{kj}^i)^{(\sigma-1)/\sigma} \right], \quad \sigma > 1. \tag{B.5}$$

Changing a single quantity, holding others constant gives perceived elasticity of demand $\tilde{\varepsilon}$,

$$1/\tilde{\varepsilon} = 1/\sigma - (1/\sigma - 1/\eta)s_{jk}. \tag{B.6}$$

The mark-up, $\tilde{\lambda}(s_{jk})$, is given by

$$\tilde{\lambda}(s_{jk}) = \frac{1 + s_{jk}(\sigma - \eta)/\eta}{\sigma - 1 - s_{jk}(\sigma - \eta)/\eta} \tag{B.7}$$

which is an increasing and convex function of s_{jk}.

Appendix C

Totally differentiating (4.1) around a symmetric equilibrium gives:

$$x \, dp + p \, dx = \left(\frac{1 - \theta}{1 + \theta}\right)^2 \left[\left(\frac{1 + \theta}{1 - \theta}\right) \frac{dE}{n} - E \frac{dn}{n^2} + \frac{2E}{n(1 - \theta)^2} \, d\theta\right]. \tag{C.1}$$

Totally differentiating (2.9) and noting the proportionality of prices to marginal costs gives:

$$d\theta = 2\theta(1 - \sigma) \, dp \, . \tag{C.2}$$

Choosing units such that $p = 1$, which implies that $nx = E$, and using this and (C.2) in (C.1) gives eq. (4.4) in the text.

References

Aitken, N. (1973), "The effect of the EEC and EFTA on European trade: A temporal cross-section analysis", American Economic Review, 63:881–892.

Aitken, N. and W. Lowry (1973), "A cross-sectional study of the effects of LAFTA and CACM on Latin American trade", Journal of Common Market Studies 11:326–336.

Anderson, K. and R. Blackhurst (1993), Regional integration and the global trading system (St.Martin's Press, New York).

Anderson, K. and H. Norheim (1993), "From imperial to regional trade preferences: Its effect on Europe's intra-and extra-regional trade", Weltwirtschaftliches Archiv 129:8–102.

Bachrach, C. and L. Mizrahi (1992), "The economic impact of a free trade agreement between the United States and Mexico: A CGE analysis", in: Economy-wide modelling of the economic implications of a FTA with Mexico and a NAFTA with Mexico and Canada, U.S. International Trade Commission Publication No. 2508.

Bagwell, K. and R.W. Staiger (1993), "Multilateral tariff cooperation during the formation of regional free trade areas", National Bureau of Economic Research Discussion Paper No. 4364.

Balassa, B. (1974), "Trade creation and trade diversion in the European Common Market: An appraisal of the evidence", Manchester School of Economic and Social Studies 42:93–135.

Balassa, B. (1975), "Economic integration among developing countries", Journal of Common Market Studies 14:37–55.

Baldwin, R. (1989), "The growth effects of 1992", Economic Policy: A European Forum 9:247–281.

Baldwin, R. (1992), "Measurable dynamic gains from trade", Journal of Political Economy 100:162–174.

Baldwin, R. (1993), "On the growth effects of import competition", mimeo, Graduate Institute of International Studies, Geneva.

Baldwin, R. (1994), Towards an integrated Europe (Centre for Economic Policy Research, London).

Baldwin, R. and A.J. Venables (1994), "Methodologies for an aggregate ex post evaluation of the completion of the Internal Market", mimeo, Graduate Institute of International Studies, Geneva.

Baldwin, R., R. Forslid, and J. Haaland (1994), "Investment diversion and investment creation: A simulation study of the EU's single market programme", mimeo, Graduate Institute of International Studies, Geneva.

Ben-David, D. (1993), "Equalizing exchange; trade liberalization and income convergence", Quarterly Journal of Economics 108:653–680.

Ben-Zvi, S. and E. Helpman (1988), "Oligopoly in segmented markets", in: G. Grossman, ed., Imperfect competition and international trade (MIT Press, Cambridge, MA).

Blanchard, O. and L. Katz (1992), "Regional evolutions", Brookings Papers on Economic Activity 1:1–61.

Bond, E. and C. Syropoulos (1993), "Trading blocs and the sustainability of inter-regional cooperation", mimeo, Penn State University Department of Economics.

Brander, J. (1981), "Intra-industry trade in identical commodities", Journal of International Economics 11:1–14.

Brander, J. and P.R. Krugman (1983), "A 'reciprocal dumping' model of international trade", Journal of International Economics 15:313–321.

Brander, J. and B. Spencer (1983), "International R&D rivalry and industrial strategy", Review of Economic Studies 50:707–722.

Brown, D.K. (1992), "Properties of computable general equilibrium trade models with monopolistic competition and foreign direct investment", in: Economy-wide modelling of the economic implications of a FTA with Mexico and a NAFTA with Mexico and Canada, U.S. International Trade Commission Publication No. 2508.

Brown, D.K., A.V. Deardorff and R.M. Stern (1992), "A North American free trade agreement: Analytic issues and a computational assessment", The World Economy 15:15–29.

Caballero, R.J. and R.K. Lyons (1990), "Internal versus external economies in European industry", European Economic Review 34:805–826.

Centre for Economic Policy Research (1992), Is bigger better: The economics of EC enlargement (Centre for Economic Policy Research, London).

Clavaux, F. (1969), "The import elasticity as a yardstick for measuring trade creation", Economia Internazionale 22:606–612.

Coe, D. and R. Moghadam (1993), "Capital and trade as engines of growth in France: An application of Johansen's cointegration methodology", International Monetary Fund Staff Papers 40:542–566.

Cooper, C.A. and B.F. Massell (1965), "A new look at customs union theory", Economic Journal 75:742–747.

Corden, M.W. (1972), "Economies of scale and customs union theory", Journal of Political Economy 80:456–475.

Cox, D. and R. Harris (1985), "Trade liberalisation and industrial organization: Some estimates for Canada", Journal of Political Economy 93:115–145.

Deardorff, A.V. and R.M. Stern (1986), The Michigan model of world production and trade (MIT Press, Cambridge MA).

De Long, J.B. and L.H. Summers (1991), "Equipment investment and economic growth", Quarterly Journal of Economics 106:445–502.

De Melo, J., C. Montenegro, and A. Panagariya (1993), "L'integration regionale hier et aujourd'hui", Revue d'Economie du Developpement, 0(2):7–49.

De Melo, J. and A. Panagariya, eds. (1993), New dimensions in regional integration (Cambridge University Press, Cambridge, UK).

De Melo, J., A. Panagariya, and D. Rodrik (1992), "The new regionalism: A country perspective", Centre for Economic Policy Research Discussion Paper No. 715.

De Torre, A. and M.R. Kelly (1992), "Regional trade arrangements", International Monetary Fund Occasional Papers, No. 93.

Dixit, A.K and J.E. Stiglitz (1977), "Monopolistic competition and optimum product diversity", American Economic Review 67:297–308.

Dixit, A.K. and V. Norman (1980), Theory of international trade (Cambridge University Press, Cambridge, UK).

EFTA (1972), The Trade Effects of EFTA and the EEC, 1959–1967, EFTA Secretariat, Geneva.

Emerson, M. et al. (1988), The economics of 1992: The E.C. Commission's assessment of the effects of completing the internal market (Oxford University Press, Oxford, UK).

Ethier, W. and H. Horn (1984), "A new look at economic integration", in: H. Kierszkowski, ed., Monopolistic competition and international trade (Oxford University Press, Oxford).

Ethier, W., E. Helpman, and P. Neary, eds. (1992), Theory, policy and dynamics in international trade: Essays in honor of Ronald W. Jones (Cambridge University Press, Cambridge, UK).

Faini, R. (1984), "Increasing returns, non-traded inputs and regional developments, Economic Journal 94:308–323.

Feldstein, M. and P. Bacchetta (1991), "National savings and international investment", in: D. Dernheim and J. Shoven, eds., National savings and economic performance (University of Chicago Press, Chicago).

Finger, J.M. (1993), Antidumping: How it works and who gets hurt (University of Michigan Press, Ann Arbor).

Flam, H. (1992), "Product markets and 1992: Full integration, large gains?", Journal of Economic Perspectives 6:7–30.

Flam, H. and H. Nordstrom (1994), "Why do car prices differ before tax between European countries?", working paper, Institute for International Economic Studies, Stockholm.

Francois, J.F. (1993), "Assessing the effects of NAFTA: Economy-wide models of North American trade liberalization", in: E. Echeverri-Carroll, ed., NAFTA and trade liberalization in the Americas (University of Texas Press, Austin).

Francois, J.F. and C.R. Shiells (1994), "AGE models of North American free trade: An introduction", in: J.F. Francois and C.R. Shiells, eds., Modelling trade policy: Applied general equilibrium assessments of North American free trade (Cambridge University Press, Cambridge, UK).

Gasiorek, M., A. Smith, and A.J. Venables (1992), "Trade and welfare: A general equilibrium model", in: L. Winters, ed., Trade flows and trade policy after 1992 (Cambridge University Press, Cambridge, UK).

Grossman, G. and E. Helpman (1991), Innovation and growth in the world economy (MIT Press, Cambridge, MA).

Haaland, J. and I. Wooton (1992), "Market integration, competition and welfare", in: L.A. Winters ed., Trade flows and trade policy after '1992' (Cambridge University Press, Cambridge, UK).

Haaland, J. and V. Norman (1992), "Global production effects of European integration", in L.A. Winters, ed., Trade Flows and Trade Policy After '1992' (Cambridge University Press, Cambridge, UK).

Harris, R.G. and D. Cox (1984), Trade, industrial policy and Canadian manufacturing (Ontario Economic Council, Toronto).

Harrison, G.W., T.F. Rutherford, and D.G. Tarr (1994), "Product standards, imperfect competition and the completion of the market in the European community", World Bank Mimeo No. 6.

Helpman, E. and P.R. Krugman (1989), Trade policy and market structure (MIT Press, Cambridge, MA and London).

Helpman, E. and A. Razin, eds. (1991), International trade and trade policy (MIT Press, Cambridge, MA).

Herin, J. (1986), "Rules of origin and differences between tariff levels in EFTA and the EC", European Free Trade Association Occassional Paper No. 13.

Hinjosa, R. and S. Robinson (1991), "Alternative scenarios of US–Mexican integration: A computable general equilibrium approach", University of California Working Paper No. 609.

Hirschman, A.O. (1958), The strategy of economic development (Yale University Press, New Haven, CT).

Hoekman, B. (1993), "Conceptual and political economy issues in liberalising international transaction in services", Aussenwirtschaft, 48:203–234.

Horn, H., H. Lang, and S. Lundgren (1994), "International integration of oligopolistic markets with interrelated demands", mimeo, Institute for International Economic Studies, Stockholm.

Hufbauer, G.C. and J.J. Schott (1992), North American free trade: Issues and recommendations, assisted by L. Lee et al. (Institute for International Economics, Washington, DC).

Italianer, A. (1994), "Whither the gains from European economic integration?", Revue Economique, forthcoming.

Jacquemin, A. and A. Sapir (1989), "International trade and integration of the European community: An econometric analysis", in: A. Jacqemin and A. Sapir, eds., The European internal market: Trade and competition, Selected Readings (Oxford University Press, Oxford).

Johnson, H.G. (1965), "An economic theory of protectionism, tariff bargaining and formation of customs unions", Journal of Political Economy 73:256–283.

Kemp, M. and H.Y. Wan (1976), "An elementary proposition concerning the formation of customs unions", Journal of International Economics 6:95–97.

Kennan, J. and R. Riezman (1990), "Optimal tariff equilibria with customs unions", Canadian Journal of Economics 23:70–83.

Kowalczyk, C. (1992), "Paradoxes in integration theory", Open Economies Review 3:51–59.

Kowalczyk, C. (1993), "Integration in goods and factors: The role of flows and revenue", Regional Science and Urban Economics 23:355–367.

Kowalczyk, C. and R. Wonnacott (1992), "Hubs and spokes, and free trade in the Americas", Darmouth Working Paper No. 92–14.

Krauss, M.B. (1972), "Recent developments in customs union theory: An interpretative survey", Journal of Economic Literature 10:413–436.

Krueger, A.O. (1993), "Free trade agreements as protectionist devices: Rules of origin", National Bureau of Economic Research Working Paper No. 4352.

Krugman, P.R. (1980), "Scale economies, product differentiation and the pattern of trade", American Economic Review 70:950–959.

Krugman, P.R. (1991a), "Increasing returns and economic geography", Journal of Political Economy 99:483–499.

Krugman, P.R. (1991b), Geography and trade (MIT Press, Cambridge, MA).

Krugman, P.R. (1991c), "Is bilateralism bad?", in: E. Helpman and A. Razin, eds., International trade and trade policy (MIT Press, Cambridge MA).

Krugman, P.R. (1991d), "The move to free trade zones", Federal Reserve Bank of Kansas City Review 76:5–25.

Krugman, P.R. (1993a), "The hub effect: Or, threeness in interregional trade", in: W.J. Ethier, E. Helpman, and J.P. Neary, eds., Theory, policy and dynamics in international trade: Essays in honor of Ronald W. Jones (Cambridge University Press, Cambridge, UK).

Krugman, P.R. (1993b), "Regionalism versus multilateralism; analytical notes", in: J. De Melo and A. Panagariya, eds., New dimensions in regional integration (Cambridge University Press, Cambridge, UK).

Krugman, P.R. and A.J. Venables (1990), "Integration and the competitiveness of peripheral industry", in: C. Bliss and J. de Macedo, eds., Unity with diversity in the European community (Centre for Economic Policy Research/Cambridge University Press, Cambridge, UK).

Krugman, P.R. and A.J. Venables (1993), "Integration, specialization and adjustment", National Bureau of Economic Research Working Paper No. 4559.

Lipsey, R.G. (1957), "The theory of customs unions: Trade diversion and welfare", Economica 24:40–46.

Lipsey, R.G. (1960), "The theory of customs unions: A general survey", Economic Journal 70:496–513.

Lloyd, P.J. (1982), "3×3 Theory of customs unions", Journal of International Economics 12:41–63.

Marshall, A. (1920), Principles of economics (Macmillan, London).

Mayes, D.G. (1978), "The effect of economic integration on trade", Journal of Common Market Studies 17:1–25.

Meade, J.E. (1955), The theory of customs unions (North-Holland, Amsterdam).

Molle, W. (1990), The economics of European integration: Theory, practice, policy (Dartmouth, Aldershot).

Muller, J. and N. Owen (1985), "The effect of trade on plant size", in: J. Schwalback and Bohn Sigma, eds., Industry structure and performance (Edition Sigma, Berlin) 41–60.

Myrdal, G. (1957), Economic theory and underdeveloped regions (Duckworth, London).

Norman, V.D. and A.J. Venables (1994), "Export commitment and market segmentation", mimeo, London School of Economics.

O'Brien, D.P. (1976), "Customs unions: Trade creation and trade diversion in historical perspective", History of Political Economy 8:540–563.

Ohyama, M. (1972), "Trade and welfare in general equilibrium", Keio Economic Studies 9:37–73.

Orvedal, L. (1992), "Norway, Sweden and the EC 1992: Three industry simulations", mimeo, Norwegian School of Economics and Business Administration, Bergen.

Pelkman, J., H. Wallace, and A. Winters (1988), The European domestic market (Chatham House, London).

Perroux, F. (1955), "Note sur la notion de 'pole de croissance'", Economie Applique 8:93–103.

Pomfret, R. (1986), "The theory of preferential trading arrangements", Weltwirtschaftliches Archiv 12:439–465.

Porter, M.E. (1990), The competitive advantage of Nations (Free Press, New York).

Quah, D. (1994), "Convergence across Europe", mimeo, London School of Economics.

Resnik, S.A. and E.M. Truman (1973), "An empirical examination of bilateral trade in Western Europe", Journal of International Economics 3:305–335.

Richardson, M. (1993), "Endogenous protection and trade diversion", Journal of International Economics 34:309–324.

Richardson, M. (1995), "Tariff revenue competition in a free trade area", European Economic Review, forthcoming.

Roessler, F. (1993), "The relationship between regional integration agreements and the multilateral trade order'', in: K. Anderson and R. Blackhurst, eds., Regional integration and the global trading system (Harvester-Wheatsheaf, London).

Roland-Horst, D.W., K.A. Reinert, and C.R. Shiells (1992), "North American trade liberalization and the role of nontariff barriers", in: Economy-wide modelling of the economic implications of a FTA with Mexico and a NAFTA with Mexico and Canada, U.S. International Trade Commission Publication No. 2508.

Schott, J.J. (1989), "More free trade areas?", in: J.J. Schott, ed., Free trade areas and U.S. trade policy (Institute for International Economics, Washington, DC).

Sleuwaegen, L. and H. Yamawaki (1988), "The formation of the European Common Market and changes in market structure and performance", European Economic Review 32:1451–1475.

Smith, A. and A.J. Venables (1988), "Completing the internal market in the European Community: Some industry simulations", European Economic Review 32:1501–1525.

Thompson, A.J. (1994), "Trade liberalization, comparative advantage and scale economies: Stockmarket evidence from Canada", Journal of International Economics 37:1–27.

Thorbecke, E. (1973), "Sector analysis and models of agriculture in developing countries", Food Research Institute Studies 12:73–89.

Truman, E.M. (1969), "The European Economic Community: Trade creation and trade diversion", Yale Economic Essays 9:201–257.

U.S. International Trade Commission (1992), "Economy-wide modelling of the economic implications of a FTA with Mexico and a NAFTA with Mexico and Canada", U.S. International Trade Commission Publication No. 2508.

Venables, A.J. (1987), "Customs union, tariff reform and imperfect competition", European Economic Review 31:103–110.

Venables, A.J. (1990a), "International capacity choice and national market games", Journal of International Economics 29:23–42.

Venables, A.J. (1990b), "The economic integration of oligopolistic markets", European Economic Review 34:753–769.

Venables, A.J. (1993), "Equilibrium locations of vertically linked industries", Centre for Economic Policy Research Discussion Paper No. 802.

Viner, J. (1950), The customs union issue (Carnegie Endowment for International Peace, New York).

Winters, L.A. (1984), "Separability and the specification of foreign trade functions", Journal of International Economics 17:239–263.

Winters, L.A. (1985), "Separability and the modelling of international economic integration: U.K. exports to five industrial countries", European Economic Review 27:335–353.

Winters, L.A. (1987), "Britain in Europe: A survey of quantitative trade studies", Journal of Common Market Studies 25:315–335.

Winters, L.A. ed. (1992), Trade flows and trade policies after '1992' (Cambridge University Press, Cambridge, UK).

Winters, L.A. (1994), "The EC and protection: The political economy", European Economic Review 38:596–603.

Wonnacott, R.J. (1975), "Industrial strategy: A Canadian substitute for trade liberalization?", Canadian Journal of Economics 8:536–547.

Wonnacott, P. and R.J. Wonnacott (1981), "Is unilateral tariff reduction preferable to a customs union? The curious case of the missing foreign tariffs", American Economic Review 71:704–714.

Wonnacott, P. and R.J. Wonnacott (1982), "Free trade between the United States and Canada: Fifteen years later", Canadian Public Policy, Supplement, 8:412–427.

PART 2

OPEN ECONOMY MACROECONOMICS
AND INTERNATIONAL FINANCE

Chapter 32

PERSPECTIVES ON PPP AND LONG-RUN REAL EXCHANGE RATES

KENNETH A. FROOT

Harvard and NBER

and

KENNETH ROGOFF*

Princeton University

Contents

*The authors are grateful to Marianne Baxter, Jose De Gregorio, Rudiger Dornbusch, Hali Edison, Jeffrey Frankel, Gene Grossman, Karen Lewis, Richard Marston, John Rogers and Julio Rotemberg for helpful comments, and to Michael Kim and Paul O'Connell for research assistance.

Handbook of International Economics, vol. III, Edited by G. Grossman and K. Rogoff

1. Introduction

This paper overviews what we know – and what we don't know – about the long-run determinants of purchasing power parity. A decade ago, when the papers for the first edition of the *Handbook of International Economics* were written, PPP seemed like a fairly dull research topic. On the one hand, the advent of floating exchange rates made it obvious to even the most stubborn defenders of purchasing power parity that PPP is not a short-run relationship; price level movements do not begin to offset exchange rate swings on a monthly or even annual basis. On the other hand, there were neither sufficient time spans of floating rate data nor adequate econometric techniques for testing the validity of PPP as a long-run relationship. Fortunately, the past decade has witnessed a tremendous degree of progress in the area and, in spite of some mis-steps and research tangents, several important results have emerged.

First, a broad body of evidence suggests that the real exchange rate is not a random walk, and that shocks to the real exchange rate damp out over time, albeit very slowly. Consensus estimates put the half-life of deviations from PPP at about 4 years for exchange rates among major industrialized countries. Second, there is some evidence that real exchange rates tend to be higher in rich countries than in poor countries, and that relatively fast-growing countries experience real-exchange rate appreciations. But the empirical evidence in favor of a "Balassa–Samuelson" effect is weaker than commonly believed, especially when comparing real exchange rates across industrialized countries over the post-Bretton Woods period.

Section 2 of the paper reviews the huge time series literature testing simple PPP. This area has proven fruitful ground for applying modern methods for dealing with nonstationary and near-nonstationary time series. Our organization traces out the evolution of the literature, from naive static tests of PPP, to modern unit-root approaches for testing whether real exchange rates are stationary, to cointegration techniques, the most recent phase of PPP testing. As we shall see, cointegration approaches have sometimes created as much confusion as clarity on the issue of PPP. It appears that this approach is plagued by small-sample bias when applied to floating exchange rates, often yielding nonsensical results.

Because convergence to PPP is relatively slow, it is not easy to empirically distinguish between a random-walk real exchange rate and a stationary real exchange rate that reverts very slowly. This is particularly problematic when looking at highly volatile floating exchange rates, where the noise can easily mask slow convergence toward long-run equilibrium. One of the major innovations has been to look at longer historical data sets, incorporating fixed as well as floating rate periods. There are some obvious problems in mixing regimes, though these have been addressed to some extent recently. One issue that has not been looked at in the literature is the problem of selection bias, which we discuss in Section 2.3.6.

In Section 2.5 we discuss research on more disaggregated price data, including a nearly two-hundred year data set on commodity prices in England and France during the seventeenth and eighteenth centuries. Aside from providing an extremely long data set, this historical data offers some perspective on the behavior of cross-country relative prices in more modern times.

In Section 3 of the paper, we look at some possible medium- to long-run determinants of the real exchange rate, particularly the supply-side determinants emphasized in the popular Balassa–Samuelson model. We also consider some evidence that positive demand shocks, such as unexpected increases in government spending, lead to medium-run appreciations of the real exchange rate. Finally, we consider "pricing-to-market" theories. The conclusions offer some possible directions for future research.

2. Evolving tests of simple PPP

In this section, we examine simple PPP – Cassel's (1922) notion that exchange rates should tend to equalize relative price levels in different countries.[1] While this notion appears simple enough, many subtleties arise in trying to implement it. In Subsection 2.1, we begin by briefly reviewing the basic motivation underlying PPP and some alternative definitions. Following that, we turn in the next three subsections to the very large recent literature on testing for PPP. We distinguish three different stages of PPP tests:

(1) older tests in which the null hypothesis is that PPP holds (Section 2.2)

(2) more recent theories and time series tests in which the null hypothesis is that PPP deviations are completely permanent (Section 2.3); and

(3) even more recent cointegration tests in which the null hypothesis is that deviations away from *any* linear combination of prices and exchanges rates is permanent (Section 2.4).

We show how each stage reflects reactions to prior empirical results as well as to advances in theoretical modeling and econometric technique. Finally, in Section 2.5, we consider tests based on more disaggregated price data.

2.1. Definitions and basic concepts

The starting point for most derivations of PPP is *the law of one price*, which states that for any good i,

---

[1] See Dornbusch (1987) for a historical treatment of the PPP doctrine.

$$p_t(i) = p_t^*(i) + s_t \tag{2.1}$$

where $p_t(i)$ is the log of the time-t domestic-currency price of good i, $p_t^*(i)$ is the analogous foreign-currency price, and s_t is the log of the time-t domestic-currency price of foreign exchange. The premise underlying the law of one price is a simple goods-market arbitrage argument: abstracting from tariffs and transportation costs, unfettered trade in goods should ensure identical prices across countries. In practice, the "law" of one price holds mainly in the breech, as we shall later see. Still, it provides a very useful reference point.

If the law of price holds for every individual good, then it follows immediately that it must hold for any identical basket of goods.[2] Most empirical tests, however, do not attempt to compare identical baskets, but use different countries' CPIs and WPIs instead. In general, these have weights and mixes of goods that vary across countries. [In principle, it is possible to construct international price indices for identical baskets of goods and, starting in the 1950s, there have been a few attempts to do so. These culminate in the influential work of Summers and Heston (1991), discussed later in Section 3.]

Absolute consumption-based PPP requires:

$$p_t(\text{CPI}) = p_t^*(\text{CPI}) + s_t \tag{2.2}$$

where CPI denotes the basket of goods used in forming the consumption price index. Clearly, even if the law of one price holds, there is no reason why condition (2.2) should hold, unless the two countries have identical consumption baskets. In order to allow for a constant price differential between baskets, the bulk of the empirical literature focuses on testing *relative consumption-based PPP*:

$$\Delta p_t(\text{CPI}) = \Delta p_t^*(\text{CPI}) + \Delta s_t \tag{2.3}$$

which requires that *changes* in relative price levels be offset by changes in the exchange rate. Indeed, much of the post World War I debate over re-establishing pre-war parities, which provided the genesis of PPP theory, implicitly referred to relative PPP. Of course, among low inflation economies, there is little more reason to believe that (2.3) will hold than (2.2), since real shocks can lead to changes in the relative prices of different goods baskets. Across countries with very different inflation rates, however, one might expect condition (2.3) to hold even when (2.2) does not.

Indeed, much of economists' faith in PPP derives from a belief that over most of the past century, price level movements have been dominated by monetary factors. If price index movements are dominated by monetary shocks, and if

---

[2] Even if the law of one price fails for individual goods, it is possible that the deviations roughly cancel out when averaged across a basket of goods.

money is neutral in the long run, then it won't matter if the two baskets being compared are not the same; relative PPP should still hold (approximately). Of course, economists like to use PPP as a frame of reference not just for hyperinflationary economies, but for any pair of economies. Most of this section will be concerned with straightforward tests of PPP, but later in Section 3, we shall consider various adjustments that have been proposed to try to give PPP more meaning for low-inflation economies.

2.2. Stage one: Simple purchasing power parity as the null hypothesis

In Cassel's (1922) view, PPP was seen as a central tendency of the exchange rate, subject to temporary offset, and not a continuously-holding equivalence. Much of the work on PPP through the 1970s [see Officer's classic (1976a) survey] recognizes the importance of temporary disturbances to PPP, in principle. But early formal empirical analyses were limited by the absence of statistical and theoretical tools for distinguishing between short-run and long-run real effects. Thus, typically, the early studies at best only allowed for a disturbance term, and did not specifically allow for any dynamics of adjustment to PPP.

Without doubt, the most positive results in stage-one tests came from data on high inflation economies. Frenkel (1978) ran regressions of the form

$$s_t = \alpha + \beta(p_t - p_t^*) + \varepsilon_t \tag{2.4}$$

for a number of hyperinflationary economies. He was not so much interested in the properties of the error term, as in whether the slope coefficient was one. Frenkel indeed found estimates of β quite close to one and, based on these estimates, argued that PPP should be an important building block of any model of exchange rate determination.

Outside of hyperinflations, however, most stage-one tests produced strong rejections of PPP. (Today, of course, it is well known that stationarity of the residuals in eq. (2.4) is required for standard hypothesis testing, a condition that will fail if some types of shocks to the real exchange rate are permanent.) Frenkel (1981) reports that PPP performed poorly for industrialized countries during the 1970s, with β estimates typically far from one (some country-pairs actually yield negative coefficients while for others β estimates exceeded 2.0). Frenkel suggested that the failure of PPP might be attributable to some combination of temporary real shocks and sticky goods prices, implicitly arguing that PPP still holds in the long run even though short-run factors get in the way of finding $\beta = 1$. However, Frenkel made no attempt to model the short-run bias in the coefficients.

Aside from failing to allow for dynamic adjustment, another obvious problem with eq. (2.4) is that exchange rates and prices are simultaneously determined, and there is no compelling reason to put exchange rates on the left-hand side, rather than visa-versa. Indeed, many authors [e.g. Isard (1977) and Giovannini (1988)] ran the reverse regression, projecting relative prices on the exchange rate.

Krugman (1978) was an attempt to explicitly address the endogeneity problem [see also Frenkel (1981)]. Krugman offered a flex-price model which had the domestic monetary authorities offsetting the effects of real shocks by expanding the money supply and thereby raising the price level. Krugman showed that in this case the endogeneity of the price level introduces a downward bias in OLS estimates of β in eq. (2.4). To control for this bias, Krugman (1978) and Frenkel (1981) re-estimated the equation using instrumental variables.[3] Their methodology succeeded in that it yielded coefficients closer to one than under OLS, though one could still soundly reject purchasing power parity. The endogeneity issue can, of course, also be cast as a left-out regressor problem. That is, the bias in the key coefficient β can be removed by conditioning the regression on the real exogenous factors that affect both exchange rates and prices and which, according to some model, explain deviations from PPP. We will look at some of these factors later in Section 3.

A fundamental flaw in the econometrics of stage-one tests was the failure to take explicitly into account the possible nonstationarity of relative prices and exchange rates. Today it is well known that if there is a unit root in the error term to eq. (2.4), then standard hypothesis tests of the proposition $\beta = 1$ are invalid. Both the stage-two and stage-three tests we consider next are explicitly designed to deal with this problem. Overall, the main lesson from stage-one tests was that PPP does not hold continuously, but the results provided no perspective on whether PPP might be valid as a long-run proposition.

2.3. Stage two: The real exchange rate as a random walk

Stage-one tests' disappointing results and flawed hypothesis testing led to an alternative approach. In stage-two tests, the null hypothesis becomes that the real exchange rate follows a random walk, with the alternative hypothesis being that PPP holds *in the long run*. These tests stand those from stage-one tests on their head: they impose – rather than estimate – the hypothesis that $\beta = 1$, and test – rather than impose – the hypothesis that the (log of the) real exchange rate

$$q_t \equiv s_t - p_t + p_t^* \tag{2.5}$$

is stationary. Examples of early stage-two tests include Darby (1983), Adler and Lehman (1983), Hakkio (1984), Frenkel (1986), Huizinga (1987) and Meese and

---

[3]Krugman (1978) used a time trend as an instrument, whereas Frenkel (1981) used a time polynomial as well as lagged exchange rates and price levels.

Rogoff (1988). As we shall see, the main problem with stage-two tests is low power. Given the phenomenal volatility of floating exchange rates, it can be very hard to distinguish between slow mean reversion and a random walk real exchange rate, especially if one relies only on post-Bretton Woods data. Much of the evolution of stage-two testing has revolved around finding longer or broader data sets, and implementing more powerful unit roots tests.

Leaving aside the problem of low power, how plausible is the null that the real exchange rate follows a random walk? Roll (1979) argued that a random walk is a sensible null hypothesis because real exchange-rate changes, like changes in asset prices, should not be predictable if foreign exchange markets are efficient. Of course, this analogy is inappropriate, since real exchange rates are not traded assets and therefore not subject to the usual efficient capital markets logic. Indeed, there is no reason why even the nominal exchange rate – which is a market variable – should follow a random walk in the presence of nominal interest differentials or risk premia.

Certainly it is possible to find rationales for random walk, or near random walk, exchange rate behavior that are more defensible than Roll's. In Section 3 below, we will discuss the Balassa–Samuelson model, in which cross-country sectoral differences in productivity growth can lead to real CPI exchange rate changes. If productivity differential shocks are permanent, sectoral productivity shocks can induce a unit root in the real exchange rate. We also discuss Rogoff's (1992) model, in which intertemporal smoothing of traded goods consumption can lead to smoothing of the *intra*temporal price of traded and nontraded goods. This in turn implies a unit root in the real exchange rate, even when productivity shocks are temporary. Obstfeld and Rogoff (1995) offer a model in which any shock (even a monetary one) that effects a wealth transfer across countries will lead to a potentially long-lasting change in relative work effort, and therefore the real exchange rate.[4] Space considerations prevent us from presenting these and other related rationales for random walk real exchange rates in any detail. For our purposes here, though, it is enough to note that there are a variety of simple yet reasonable models that can generate highly persistent deviations from PPP.

2.3.1. Econometric techniques to test for random walk real exchange rates

Once the null hypothesis posits that the real exchange rate follows a random walk (or more generally has a "unit root" component),[5] it becomes necessary

---

[4]There is a substantial empirical literature on the effects of wealth re-distributions on the long-run equilibrium exchange rate; [see for example, Krugman (1990), and Bayoumi, Clark, Symansky and Taylor (1994)]. For further discussion of the effects of wealth transfers on the long-run equilibrium exchange rate, see Baxter's, and Obstfeld and Rogoff's chapters in this Handbook.

[5]If the real exchange rate has one unit root, then its first difference must be stationary though not necessarily serially uncorrelated as in the random walk model.

to negotiate a number of important econometric subtleties. Most importantly, conventional confidence intervals calculated under the null of a stationary real exchange rate are no longer appropriate and, as Dickey and Fuller (1979) emphasized, the correct confidence intervals should be wider.

The modern literature uses three main techniques for distinguishing the real exchange rate from a random walk.[6] The first, and most commonly used, is the Dickey–Fuller and augmented Dickey–Fuller tests. These involve a regression of the real exchange rate, q_t, on a constant, a time trend, q_{t-1}, and lagged changes in q_{t-1}:

$$q_t = \alpha_0 + \alpha_1 t + \alpha_2 q_{t-1} + \Phi(L)\Delta q_{t-1} + \varepsilon_t \qquad (2.6)$$

where L is the lag operator, $\Phi(L)$ is a pth order polynomial in L, with coefficients $\phi_1, \phi_2, \ldots \phi_p$, and ε_t is white noise. Under the null hypothesis that q_t has a unit root, $\alpha_2 = 1$. Under the alternative hypothesis that PPP holds in the long run, $\alpha_1 = 0$ and $\alpha_2 < 1$.[7] The distribution of the OLS estimates for eq. (2.6) is nonstandard under the random walk null, with the appropriate confidence intervals reported by Dickey and Fuller (1979). An example of a study applying the Dickey–Fuller test to floating real exchange rates is Meese–Rogoff (1988), who are unable to reject the unit root hypothesis for monthly dollar/pound, dollar/yen, and dollar/DM floating exchange rate data.

Equation (2.6) can also be used to calculate Phillips (1987) Z test, which allows for conditional heteroskedasticity of the residual. Perron (1989) extends these tests to allow for one-time changes in the constant and the trend by including dummy variables. However, in introducing break points, data snooping biases can make the resulting test statistics difficult to interpret [see Christiano (1992)].

The second commonly-used technique is that of variance ratios. The idea here is that under the null hypothesis of a random walk, the variance of the real exchange rate should grow linearly over time. This implies that the statistic

$$k(i) = \frac{T}{T-i+1} \cdot \mathrm{var}\left[(1-L)\,q_t\right] i/\mathrm{var}\left[\left(1-L^i\right) q_t\right], \quad i = 2, 3, \ldots T-1$$

$$(2.7)$$

should be one for all i. For a stationary series, on the other hand, the k statistic converges to zero as k increases.[8]

---

[6]See also Breuer (1994) for an excellent survey of econometric problems in testing for unit roots in real exchange rates. Some of the very early efforts to test the random walk real exchange rate hypothesis, including Darby (1983), and Adler and Lehman (1983), did not use modern root testing methodologies, but nevertheless illustrated the difficulties in rejecting the random walk model.

[7]Some of the studies below test only $\alpha_2 < 1$, and do not jointly apply the restriction $\alpha_0 = 0$. Also, many studies look only at the straight Dickey–Fuller test and do not augment the regression with the lagged changes. There is no problem with this simplification as long as the residuals are not autocorrelated.

[8]Poterba and Summers (1986) show that the variance ratio is a function of the processes' autocorrelation coefficients 1 through i.

A third technique is that of fractional integration, which encompasses a broader class of stationary processes under the alternative hypothesis. A fractionally integrated process allows the real exchange rate to evolve according to:

$$\Phi(L)(1 - L)^d q_t = \chi(L)\varepsilon_t, \tag{2.8}$$

where $\Phi(L)$ and $\chi(L)$ are polynomial lag operators with roots outside the unit circle and ε_t is white noise. If the parameter $d = 0$, then the real exchange rate is confined to the class of stationary ARMA processes described by $\Phi(L)$ and $\chi(L)$. If $d = 1$ and $\Phi(L) = \chi(L) = 1$, then the real exchange rate follows a random walk. The advantage of this class of processes is that it allows for fractional integration, $0 < d < 1$. Because fractionally integrated processes are stationary, but have autocovariance functions that die off more slowly than ARMA processes, encompassing them under the alternative hypothesis may enhance one's chances of rejecting the random walk null. [See Diebold, Husted and Rush (1991) for citations and a discussion of estimation techniques.]

2.3.2. Results for post-Bretton Woods data

The basic result in the empirical literature is that if one applies unit roots tests to bilateral industrialized-country monthly data, it is difficult to reject the null of a unit root for currencies that float against each other. [See, for example, Meese and Rogoff (1988) or Mark (1990).] An exception is Huizinga (1987), who constructed variance ratios to argue in favor of *positive* autocorrelation in U.S. dollar real exchange rates for horizons under two years. However, Huizinga's results may be attributable to the long, large swings in the dollar between the mid-1970s and mid-1980s.

For currency pairs that are fixed (or formally stabilized), the evidence is more mixed. In Mark's (1990) tests for the 1973–1988 period, the intra-European exchange rates come closest to rejecting a random walk, although it is only for the Belgium/Germany currency pair that a random walk can be rejected at the 5 percent confidence level. Chowdhury and Sdogati (1993) look at the 1979–1990 period, during which time the EMS was in place. They strongly reject the random walk for bilateral rates of various European currencies against the Deutsche mark, but not for European exchange rates against the U.S. dollar. The apparent systematic differences in the behavior of the real exchange rate for various floating versus fixed exchange rates has been noted and explored by a number of authors [see, for example, Mussa (1986) and the Frankel and Rose chapter in this Handbook].

2.3.3. Power against persistent alternatives

The major concern with the early stage-two tests of the random walk hypothesis is that they lack sufficient power to reject. Because slow, albeit positive, rates of reversion toward PPP are plausible in many models, random walk tests may provide little information against relevant alternative hypotheses.

To see how important the issue of power is, and to gain a sense of how much data is needed to reject plausible alternatives, it is useful to calibrate a simple autoregression, as done by Frankel (1986, 1990). The results of this analysis show that the post-Bretton Woods sample period is far too short to reliably reject the random walk hypothesis.

Suppose that PPP indeed holds over the long run, and that deviations from PPP follow an AR(1) process (on monthly data), with serial correlation coefficient ρ and error variance σ^2. That is

$$q_t - \overline{q} = \rho(q_{t-1} - \overline{q}) + \varepsilon_t \tag{2.9}$$

where $0 \leq \rho < 1$, $\overline{q}$ is the long-run equilibrium real exchange rate and ε is a white noise error term with variance σ^2. Suppose that the autoregression is run on a panel data set with T observations and N independent bilateral exchange rates, each governed by the same stochastic process.

In these circumstances, the variance of the OLS estimate of ρ is given by[9]

$$\text{var}(\hat{\rho} - \rho) = \sigma^2 / [NT \cdot \text{var}(q - \overline{q})] \tag{2.10}$$

where $\text{var}(q - \overline{q}) = \sigma^2/(1 - \rho^2)$. Thus, we find that the standard error of the OLS estimate converges to[10]

$$\text{plim}\,[\text{std}\,(\rho - \overline{\rho})] = \left[\frac{1 - \rho^2}{NT}\right]^{1/2} \tag{2.11}$$

How many years of data does expression (2.11) imply one needs to be able to reject the random walk process when the real exchange rate is governed by the stationary process (2.9)? Suppose for a moment that the true half-life of PPP deviations is 36 months (3 years). This translates into a true value of the AR coefficient in monthly data of $\rho = 0.981 = 0.5^{1/36}$.

Assuming 18 years of data ($T = 216$) on a single exchange rate ($N = 1$), eq. (2.11) then implies that the standard error of the OLS estimate of ρ is approximately $0.0132 = [(1 - 0.981^2)/216]^{1/2}$. With this degree of imprecision, the true value of ρ ($= 0.981$) is only approximately 1.44 [$= (1 - 0.981)/0.0132)$] standard errors away from one. Thus 18 years of data are not likely to be sufficient for rejecting the random walk null – and this calculation uses conventional stationary real exchange rate standard errors, rather than Dickey–Fuller standard errors.

[9]This example assumes for simplicity that the mean of the log real exchange rate, $\overline{q}$, is known. Estimation of the mean can induce finite sample bias in the estimated autoregressive coefficient, but this nuance is not central to our example here.

[10]Note that by using the asymptotic standard error, we avoid small sample problems which introduce non-normality into the distribution of the t-statistic for ρ.

How many years of data would it take to reject $\rho = 1$ at a 5 percent confidence interval for a single currency using the large-sample Dickey–Fuller critical t value of 2.89? Solving the condition

$$2.89^2 = T(1 - \rho)^2/(1 - \rho^2)$$

implies $T = 864$ months, or 72 years! Obviously, with a longer half life (i.e. a larger value of ρ), even more data would be required. Indeed, the preceding calculation understates the problem, since we have employed asymptotic standard errors in making these calculations.

Two approaches to dealing with the power problem have been tried in the literature; one is to look at a number of currencies simultaneously (allow for $N > 1$), and the other is to look at long-horizon data sets encompassing both pre- and post-Bretton Woods data.[11]

2.3.4. Tests using cross sections of currencies

With 18 years of data, simultaneously testing $N = 4$ *independent*, identically-distributed currencies would expand the data set sufficiently to reject (since $18 \cdot 4 = 72$). Hakkio (1984) was the first to suggest using cross-section data to gain power; he employed GLS to allow for cross-exchange rate correlation in the residuals in four exchange rates against the dollar. Despite the enhanced power of his test, Hakkio was unable to reject the random walk model.

Abuaf and Jorion (1990) perform similar tests, running autoregressions in levels using GLS for ten countries's currencies against the US dollar over the period 1973–1987. The longer time series and the larger cross-section does generate more power, but nevertheless permits only the weakest of rejections of the random walk hypothesis – at the 10 percent significance level using one-sided tests. These results roughly fit our calibration above: with 14.5 years of data and (say) 5 independent bilateral exchange rates, we have the equivalent of 72 years of data. Thus, even with this size cross-section, one would expect rejections to be marginal. It would be interesting to see if adding more recent data to their sample would lead to more decisive rejections.

In an interesting recent study, Cumby (1993) makes clever use of the *Economists'* "Hamburger Standard", which each year reports the dollar price of McDonald's Big Mac hamburgers in up to 25 countries. Although only about 7 years (1987–1993) of data are available, Cumby finds that the large cross-section yields enough power to detect substantial reversion toward the law of one price. In

---

[11]Some improvement in power can be achieved simply by avoiding inefficient test specifications. Abuaf and Jorion (1990), for example, note that the early tests performed by Adler and Lehman (1983) – which estimated autoregressions of real exchange rate *changes* – were likely to be much less powerful than similar tests performed on the levels of the real exchange rate. Cheung and Lai (1993c) apply a more powerful version of the Dickey–Fuller test due to Elliot, Rothenberg and Stock (1992).

fact, deviations from Big Mac parity exhibit remarkably little persistence, with only 30 percent of the deviation in one year persisting to the next. This fact seems striking given that a large fraction of the 'goods' embodied in a Big Mac, including local infrastructure costs and labor, are essentially nontraded.

How can Cumby's finding of relatively rapid convergence to "hamburger PPP" be reconciled with most other studies of PPP, which find relatively slow rates of convergence? One factor may be that relatively few of the currency pairs in Cumby's sample were actually floating against one another. As we have already seen, convergence appears easier to detect in fixed rate than in floating rate data. Second, peso problems may lead to understated standard errors: the Big Mac sample includes a number of relatively high inflation countries – Argentina, Brazil, Hungary, Malaysia, Mexico, Russia and Thailand – whose currencies are generally pegged except for the occasional large realignment.[12] Finally, McDonald's own pricing policies may produce a more rapid rate of convergence in Big Mac prices than in broader aggregate price indexes.

2.3.5. Tests using longer time series

The second approach to improving power is to extend the sample period. Frankel (1986), for example, uses 116 years (1869–1984) of data for the dollar/pound real exchange rate. (Other, earlier, long-horizon studies such as Lee (1976), did not incorporate modern unit root methodology.) Frankel finds that a simple first-order autoregression yields a coefficient of 0.86, which implies that PPP deviations have an annual decay rate of 14 percent and a half life of 4.6 years. His rejection of the unit root null is significant at the 5 percent level, using Dickey–Fuller confidence intervals. Another early attempt to use long samples to test convergence towards PPP is Edison (1987), who looks at dollar/pound data for the years 1890–1978. Edison uses an error-correction mechanism [see also Papell (1994)], regressing the change in the log of the nominal exchange rate, Δs_t, on the contemporaneous change in the log of relative prices, $\Delta(p-p^*)_t$, and the lagged real exchange rate, $(s-p-p)_{t-1}$:

$$\Delta s_t = \alpha_0 + \alpha_1 [\Delta(p-p^*)_t] + \alpha_2 (s-p-p)_{t-1} \tag{2.12}$$

Edison estimates $\alpha_2 = 0.09$, i.e. that the nominal exchange rate decays towards PPP at a statistically-significant 9 percent per year, implying a half life of roughly 7.3 years. In a similar exercise, Johnson (1990) uses 120 years of Canadian dollar/U.S. dollar exchange rate data. He, too, is able to reject the random walk hypothesis, and finds a half life for PPP deviations of 3.1 years.

Abuaf and Jorion (1990) use time series data from 1901–1972 for eight currencies. Their point estimates suggest a half-life of PPP deviations of 3.3 years, and they are easily able to reject a random walk. Both their results and Frankel's are

---

[12]See Karen Lewis's chapter in this Handbook for a discussion of the peso problem.

consistent with the simple model calibrated above. Glen (1992) uses variance ratios to test for mean reversion in the real exchange rate for 9 bilateral exchange rates over the 1900–87 period. Glen, too, finds strong evidence of mean reversion.

It must be emphasized that in addition to extending the sample, the long-sample studies discussed above all combine relatively low variance pre-Bretton Woods exchange rate data with the highly volatile post-Bretton Woods data. For the simple first-order AR process specified in (2.9), the variance of the real exchange rate does not affect the power of the test. If, however, the real exchange rate is better described by a richer ARMA process, and if there are different parameters governing fixed versus floating rates, the test results may be heavily affected by the inclusion of fixed rate periods. Thus these papers leave unresolved the question of whether mean reversion would be detected in 100 years of floating rate data. [Wars may also affect PPP dynamics; see Rogers (1994).]

Lothian and Taylor (1994) is an interesting attempt to cast some light on this issue. Their data set consists of almost two centuries of data for the dollar/pound (1791–1990) and franc/pound (1803–1990) real exchange rates. Using only the post-Bretton Woods portion of the data, they are not able to reject the random walk hypothesis for either exchange rate. But when the entire sample is used, the random walk null is easily rejected for either rate. (They estimate half lives of 4.7 years for the dollar/pound and 2.7 years for the franc/pound.) Moreover, using a simple Chow test to compare first-order AR coefficients before and after Bretton Woods, they find that one cannot reject the hypothesis of no structural change. In fact, if one estimates a simple AR (1) model on the pre-Bretton Woods data, it outperforms a random walk model on post-Bretton Woods data at one- to five-year horizons. Thus Lothian and Taylor conclude that there is no evidence for the view that the inclusion of fixed-rate periods biases unit roots tests of the real exchange rate.

Of course, there is at least one striking difference between fixed and floating regimes: Under fixed rates, deviations from PPP must be eliminated by domestic price level movements. The error correction specification (2.12) is ideally suited to measure the degree to which reversion toward PPP occurs through the nominal exchange rate versus through prices. Under floating rates, both Edison (1987) and Johnson (1990) cannot reject the hypothesis that all of the reversion towards PPP is due to exchange rate movements.

Finally, we note two recent studies that have allowed for the possibility that long-run real exchange rate data is better characterized by fractionally integrated processes rather than by the usual ARMA models. Diebold, Husted and Rush (1991) look at a novel data set that encompasses over a hundred years of gold-standard data, and find that little power is added by allowing for fractional integration. They are able to strongly reject the random walk model, but in most cases their estimates suggest that a simple ARMA model best describes real exchange rates.

Cheung and Lai (1993a) arrive at a somewhat different conclusion using a similar technique. Using a shorter time sample (1914–72) than DHR, they are unable to reject a random walk model against fractional and ARMA alternatives. However, they estimate the parameter d in eq. (2.8) to be about 0.5, suggesting evidence of fractional integration in real exchange rates. They also show that the power of fractionally-integrated alternatives to reject a random walk when the true process has $d = 0.5$ is considerably greater than that of standard ARMA alternatives.

2.3.6. A caveat: Sample selection or "survivorship" bias in long-horizon tests of PPP

One interesting question that has not previously been raised in the long-sample PPP literature is whether "survivorship" bias might exaggerate the extent to which PPP holds in the long run. Specifically, the countries for which very long-run PPP series are easily available tend to be those few who have continuously been among the world's wealthiest nations. Countries that grew very fast from a low level (e.g. Japan), and countries that were once rich but are no longer so (e.g. Argentina) have not been studied as extensively. But these are precisely the countries for which one might expect the relative price of nontraded goods to have changed most dramatically (see our discussion of the Balassa–Samuelson effect in Section 3), and for which tests of long-run PPP are most likely to fail.

To intuitively gauge the importance of this sample-selection effect, we consider data for the Argentine peso against the US dollar and the British pound over the period 1913–1988. The Argentine CPI and nominal exchange rate data

Table 2.1
Augmented Dickey–Fuller Regressions on Argentine/American and Argentine/British CPI Real Exchange Rates

$$q \equiv s - p + p^*$$
$$q_t = \alpha_o + \alpha_1 q_{t-1} + \phi_1 (1 - L) q_{t-1} + \varepsilon_t$$

Sample Period	Peso/dollar 1913–1988	Peso/pound 1913–1988
N	74	74
α_0	−0.931	−1.466
t-stat (against $\alpha_0 = 0$)	−3.21	−3.14
α_1	0.808	0.764
t-stat (against $\alpha_1 = 1$)	−3.20	−3.12
1% critical value	−3.52	−3.52
10% critical value	−2.59	−2.59
ϕ_1	0.256	0.06
R^2	0.152	0.122
DW	1.92	1.98
σ_q	0.203	0.220

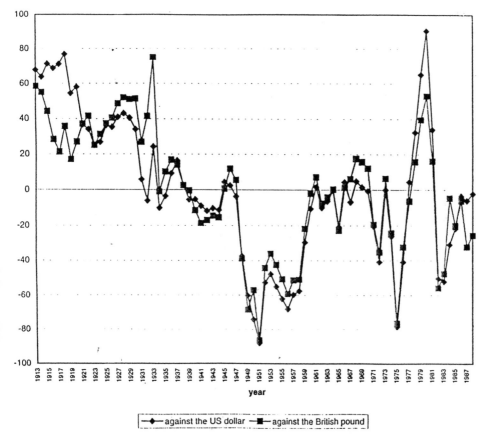

Figure 2.1. Real value of the Argentine peso, 1913–1988 (log percentage deviations from period average).

come from Cavallo (1986), except for the post-1980 data which is from *International Financial Statistics*.

As Figure 2.1 shows, with the exception of the well-known massive overvaluation of the peso during the early 1980s, there is a steady decline of the peso over the period. The real peso has fallen by roughly 80 percent (in log terms) since the beginning of the century, a rate of decline of almost 1 percent per year. This trend is highly statistically significant, as Table 2.1 illustrates.[13] Moreover, the strong rejections of a unit root that emerge in the pound/dollar data are

[13] As the table also illustrates, however, the time trend is not significant under the alternative hypothesis of a stationary real exchange rate.

absent here. Even with seventy-five years of data, it is not possible to reject the hypothesis that the detrended peso/dollar or peso/pound exchange rates follow a random walk.

Although only suggestive, these results indicate that one must be cautious in interpreting results from long-run PPP tests, as the tendency towards long-run PPP may not apply to countries whose incomes relative to the rest of the world have undergone sharp changes.

2.4. Stage three tests: Cointegration

At first glance, PPP testing would seem to provide the perfect context for Engle and Granger's (1987) work on cointegration.[14] The techniques are designed to test for long-run equilibrium relationships, for which the adjustment mechanism remains unspecified. Cointegration tests are thus liberated from stage-one concerns about endogeneity and left-out variables. Moreover – and, as we shall see, more controversially – cointegration tests hold forth the promise of testing weaker versions of PPP, since they require only that *some* linear combination of exchange rates and prices be stationary. In other words, stage-two tests ask whether the real exchange rate $q_t \equiv s_t - p_t - p_t^*$ is stationary. Stage-three tests ask only whether

$$s_t - \mu p_t + \mu^* p_t^* \tag{2.13}$$

is stationary for *any* constant μ and μ^*. Any incremental power from stage-three tests over stage-two tests must therefore come from relaxing the symmetry and proportionality restrictions that $\mu = \mu^* = 1$. In the discussion below, we will distinguish between *trivariate* tests that place no restrictions on the coefficients in (2.13), and *bivariate* tests that impose the symmetry restriction $\mu = -\mu^*$.[15]

Why might μ not equal one? Consider the following model used by Taylor (1988), Fisher and Park (1991), and Cheung and Lai (1993a,b). First, assume that PPP holds exactly for traded goods so that

$$s_t = p_t^T - p_t^{*T} \tag{2.14}$$

where p_t^T is the time t (log) home price of traded goods. Second, assume that the overall price index consists of a weighted average of traded and nontraded goods prices:

$$p_t = \gamma p_t^T + (1 - \gamma) p_t^N \tag{2.15}$$

where p_t^N is the time t home price of nontraded goods, for which PPP does not

---

[14] For a review of the cointegraton literature and its applications to macroeconomcs, see Campbell and Perron (1991).

[15] A stage-two test, which imposes $\mu = -\mu^* = 1$, may simply be thought of as the univariate case in this categorization.

necessarily obtain. The price index abroad is similar to (2.15), with weights γ^* and $1 - \gamma^*$. Finally, the price of nontraded goods is assumed to be proportional (in the limit) to the price of traded goods:

$$p_t^N = \alpha_0 + \phi p_t^T + \varepsilon_t \tag{2.16}$$

$$p_t^{*N} = \alpha_0 + \phi p_t^{*T} + \varepsilon_t^* \tag{2.17}$$

where the residuals ε and ε^* are stationary. Given eqs. (2.14) – (2.17), a regression of the form

$$s_t = \mu p_t + \mu^* p_t^* + \varepsilon_t' \tag{2.18}$$

yields coefficients[16]

$$\mu = \frac{1}{\gamma + \phi(1 - \gamma)} \tag{2.19}$$

$$\mu^* = \frac{1}{\gamma + \phi^*(1 - \gamma^*)} \tag{2.20}$$

One possible explanation of why the slope coefficients in eqs. (2.16) and (2.17) might not equal one is simply that there is a trend in the relative prices of traded and nontraded goods. Another explanation, offered by Taylor (1988), Fisher and Park (1991), and Cheung and Lai (1993a,b) is that errors in measuring nontraded goods prices can imply ϕ, $\phi^* \neq 1$. But can measurement error interfere with the proportionality of p_t^N and p_t^T? One possibility is to think of p^N as an index of nontraded goods prices that is subject to either "fixed-weight" or "new goods" bias. (For simplicity assume that no such bias exists in the traded-goods price index.) Fixed-weight bias results when fixed-weight price indices confront changing relative prices. Bryant and Cecchetti (1993) show how these effects can generate permanent upward index movements when relative prices change, and therefore bias measured inflation upward. A second source of bias comes from the introduction of new goods, which one can think of having high implicit prices prior to their introduction.

Thus, in principle, it is possible to think of plausible reasons why one might want to allow for $\mu \neq \mu^* \neq 1$ in eq. (2.13). We turn next to giving a brief overview of cointegration methods.

2.4.1. Techniques and potential applications to real exchange rates

Cointegration techniques ask whether a group of nonstationary variables can be combined to produce a stationary variable. If so, the nonstationary variables are said to be cointegrated. More precisely, consider the $N \times K$ matrix X_t,

---

[16]We are implicitly assuming that the home and foreign price indices are not themselves cointegrated. If they are, one can impose the assumption $\mu = \mu^*$ in the cointegrating regression.

which consists of all the dependent and independent variables in the system. Suppose, for example, that individually, the variables are integrated of order one (i.e. are stationary in first differences, as is the case with exchange rates and prices).[17] Then if there exists a linear combination of the data, given by the $1 \times N$ vector $B(i)$, such that $B(i)X_t$ is stationary, then we say that X_t is cointegrated. Denoting the matrix of all vectors that yield stationary results by B, the rank of B $(r < N)$ gives the number of cointegrating vectors.

Early applications of cointegration methods to testing PPP were based on a three-step procedure. In the first stage, one tests the exchange rate and the two domestic price series for unit roots, using the augmented Dickey–Fuller test as in eq. (2.6) above. For the bivariate case, of course, there are only two series, the exchange rate and relative prices.

Assuming that one cannot reject the random walk hypothesis for any of the variables, the second stage is to estimate the cointegrating regression (2.18) using OLS. For the bivariate case one imposes $\mu = -\mu^*$. (If one can reject the unit root hypothesis for at least one variable, but cannot for at least one other variable, one cannot reject the no-cointegration null.)

Cointegration of prices and exchange rates implies that the error term in eq. (2.18), ε_t, is stationary. Thus, the third step is to use the OLS residuals from (2.18) to run the Dickey–Fuller regression (2.6), but with the time trend omitted, and to test the hypothesis that $\alpha_2 = 1$. Using this approach, prices and exchange rates are *not* cointegrated under the null hypothesis, whereas they are cointegrated under the alternative hypothesis $\alpha_2 < 1$.[18]

The three-step method is inherently inefficient in part because it requires choosing, somewhat arbitrarily, a single right-hand side variable. More recent PPP tests have been able to avoid this inefficiency, using a technique due to Johansen (1991). Johansen proposed a one-step full-information maximum-likelihood estimator for estimating the coefficients in specifications such as eq. (2.18), and simultaneously testing for the presence of a unit root. Unlike the method above, the ML estimates are not influenced by which variable is on the left-hand side of the single equation regression. The parameter estimates are thus more efficient, and the Johansen test for cointegration thus more powerful than a two-step test.[19] Horvath and Watson (1993) extend the

---

[17]Ogaki and Park (1990) distinguish between "deterministic" and "stochastic" cointegration. The former is satisfied if a linear combination of X_t is stationary around a deterministic trend, whereas the latter requires that the linear combination of X_t contain no trend. Our definition is essentially one of deterministic cointegration.

[18]Fisher and Park (1991) employ a test proposed by Park that takes cointegration to be the null hypothesis and no cointegration to be the alternative. In essence, this test is constructed by adding a time polynomial to the right-hand side of eq. (2.6), and testing its significance.

[19]Cheung and Lai (1993c) provide evidence for the Johansen test's higher power.

Johansen methodology to allow for constraints that represent long-run equilibrium conditions; this effectively transforms the Johansen test into a stage-two procedure.[20]

2.4.2. Empirical results of cointegrating tests of PPP

A plethora of studies have applied cointegration methods to testing PPP. A partial list includes Edison and Klovland (1987), Corbae and Ouliaris (1988), Enders (1988), Kim (1990), Mark (1990), Fisher and Park (1991), Cheung and Lai (1993a), and Kugler and Lenz (1993). Surveys of this material include Giovannetti (1992) and Breuer (1994).

These studies reveal several systematic features of the data. First, it is easier to reject the no-cointegration null across pairs of currencies that are fixed than across pairs that are floating. This finding is consistent with the stage-two results discussed in section (2.3). Second, one finds that tests based on CPI price levels tend to reject less frequently than tests based on WPIs. One explanation for this finding is that consumer price indices have a higher nontraded goods component than wholesale prices, which tend to weight manufactured goods more heavily.[21]

A third common finding is that for post-Bretton Woods floating exchange rates, rejections of the no-cointegration null occur more frequently for trivariate systems (where p and p^* enter separately) than for bivariate systems (where they enter as $p - p^*$), or for stage-two tests (where the coefficient on $p - p^*$ is constrained to be one).[22] Weakening the proportionality and symmetry restrictions therefore makes the residuals appear more stationary.

At first glance, these results seem to provide a strong endorsement for stage-three tests (cointegration) over stage-two tests, since they are generally more successful in rejecting the random walk hypothesis. The problem, unfortunately, is that the estimates of μ and μ^* vary wildly across the various studies based on modern floating rate data, and the magnitudes are often rather implausible. Cheung and Lai, for example, find coefficients that range from 1.03 to 25.4 for CPIs, and 0.3 to 11.4 for WPIs, with most of the coefficients coming in above 1. Imposing the symmetry restriction (looking at the bivariate case instead of the trivariate case) reduces this range only slightly.

Rationalizing these extreme empirical estimates of μ is difficult, to say the

---

[20]For an application of the Horvath and Watson procedure, see Edison, Gagnon, and Melick (1994).

[21]Keynes (1932) sharply criticized Churchill's Exchequer for using WPIs when making PPP calculations to evaluate Britain's decision to return to its pre-World War I gold parity. Keynes argued WPIs were misleading as index of the real exchange rate because they did not sufficiently reflect nontraded goods prices. McKinnon (1971) also argues that PPP should hold to a much greater extent for WPIs than for CPIs.

[22]See, for example, Cheung and Lai (1993a), Mark (1990), and Kugler and Lenz (1993).

least. How large a bias, for example, can be rationalized by the model embodied in eqs. (2.14) – (2.17)? Bryant and Cecchetti (1993) attempt to measure the size of the "weighting bias" by comparing CPI-index inflation with the rate of inflation that emerges as a common component across goods included in the CPI index. They estimate that weighting bias leads to an overstatement of inflation of about 0.6 percent per annum for the CPI and about 0.35 percent per annum for the personal consumption expenditure deflator. Lebow, Roberts and Stockton (1992) attempt to estimate the size of the new goods bias, and find that it leads to an overstatement of inflation by at most 0.5 percent per annum. Thus, taken together, these two sources of measurement error bias might raise consumer price inflation by roughly 1 percent per year. Then, if inflation averages 5 percent, these effects might raise ϕ from 1 to 1.2, implying that $\mu = 0.83$. This of course, assumes that there is no similar bias in the traded goods index, which would push μ back towards one.

Nor can a trend rise in nontraded relative to traded goods prices explain values of μ far from one. Assuming that both monetary factors and productivity differentials are trend stationary, the coefficient in eq. (2.16) turns out to be $\phi = (\lambda_m + \lambda_a)/\lambda_m$, where λ_m and λ_a are the rates of money growth, and traded relative to nontraded goods productivity growth respectively. Thus if we take inflation to 5 percent and the trend traded/nontraded goods productivity growth differential to be 2 percent, then $\phi = 1.4$, and $\mu = 0.71$.

Clearly, it is very difficult to interpret the results of cointegration tests when estimates of the cointegrating vector have no apparent economic meaning.[23] One possible explanation for the wide-ranging coefficient estimates is small-sample bias. Banerjee et al. (1986) show that in finite samples, cointegrating regressions can result in substantial bias, and that the severity of this bias is related to R^2 – they suggest that regressions with $R^2 < 0.95$ are likely to lead to substantial bias. The problem of low R^2 is, of course, especially likely to plague exchange rate regressions over floating rate data.

Indeed, cointegration tests seem to yield much more reliable results when estimated over long sample periods, rather than just over post-Bretton Woods data. Kim (1990), for example, uses WPI and CPI real exchange rates for the US against five countries – Canada, France, Italy, Japan and the United Kingdom – during the 1900–1987 period. He is always able to reject no cointegration, and he finds coefficients that are strikingly close to one in all cases but for that of Canada.[24]

---

[23] See also Hakkio and Rush (1991) and Breuer (1994) for critiques of unit root and cointegration tests of PPP.

[24] Kim runs the cointegrating regression (2.13) for the CPI and WPI respectively, and finds ϕ coefficients of 0.99 and 0.98 (France), 0.99 and 0.98 (Italy), 1.00 and 0.98 (Japan), 0.96 and 1.00 (United Kingdom), and 0.73 and 0.55 (Canada). The R^2 are high in all these regressions (averaging around 0.96) except for Canada, in accordance with the theoretical results of Banerjee et al. (1986).

2.4.3. Summary: What have we learned from stage-three tests?

There have been a plethora of papers applying cointegration testing to PPP, but on the whole it is not clear that technique has yet provided a net benefit over earlier stage-two tests; indeed, it may have produced some misleading results due to small sample bias. Over longer time periods, and for fixed rates, the bias becomes less serious. Thus far, however, the results from cointegration tests on long-horizon data have not produced any insights not available from stage-two tests.[25]

2.5. Tests using disaggregated price data

In order to gain a deeper understanding of why PPP fails, a number of studies have attempted to look at a central building block of PPP, the law of one price.

In his classic (1977) paper, Isard looks for, and finds, deviations from PPP where one would least expect them – in highly disaggregated traded goods price indices. He reports large and persistent deviations from the law of one price in U.S. and German export transactions prices for various 2 though 5 digit SITC categories (e.g. pumps, internal combustion engines, etc.) and in U.S. export unit values in 7-digit A and B groupings when compared to similar unit values from Canada, Germany and Japan. Isard goes on to demonstrate a positive correlation between contemporaneous dollar exchange rates and relative dollar prices.[26] He speculates that this correlation might disappear at longer horizons, but (as with other stage-one tests) does not formalize or test this conjecture explicitly.

Giovannini's (1988) paper is similar in spirit. He finds deviations from PPP not only among disaggregated traded goods, but even among basic "commodity" manufactured goods, such as ball bearings, screws, nuts and bolts. Giovannini's data (which come from the Bank of Japan) compare Japanese domestic and export prices (on shipments bound for the US) during the floating rate period. In line with Isard's results, Giovannini finds large and persistent deviations from the law of one price that are strongly correlated with the nominal exchange rate.[27]

---

[25] Johansen and Julius (1992) argue that deviations from PPP and deviations from uncovered interest parity may be cointegrated, so that it is important to analyze both simultaneously. This presumes, of course, that deviations from PPP have a unit root component.

[26] Of course, such correlations can be trusted only to the extent that the exchange rate and relative prices are stationary.

[27] Isard and Giovannini both suggest that sticky nominal prices may account for the exchange rate/relative price correlation. See Frankel and Rose's paper in this Handbook for a detailed discussion of the effects of nominal exchange rate movements on the real economy.

2.5.1. Disaggregated price data for the modern floating rate period

Several recent studies that employ disaggregated data have investigated the extent to which departures from PPP are caused mainly by the presence of nontraded goods versus deviations from the law of one price in traded goods. To see this dichotimization, suppose the real exchange rate is $q_t \equiv s_t - p_t + p_t^*$ as defined in eq. (2.5), and the price index in each country is a weighted average of traded and nontraded goods prices $p_t = \gamma p_t^T + (1 - \gamma)p_t^N$ as in eq. (2.15). Combining these two expressions, we can write

$$q_t = (s_t - p_t^T + p_t^{*T}) - (\gamma - 1)(p_t^T - p_t^N) - (\gamma^* - 1)(p_t^{*T} - p_t^{*N}) \qquad (2.21)$$

so that real exchange rate depends on deviations from the law of one price in traded goods, as well as on the relative price of traded and nontraded goods within each country.

One study that addresses this issue is Engel (1993). Engel examines a multi-country data set of individual prices, including goods of varying degrees of tradedness. Engel finds that monthly fluctuations from the law of one price for individual traded goods across countries are very large in comparison with fluctuations in relative prices within a country. Even for apparently homogenous traded goods such as bananas, the deviations from the law of one price can be large and volatile. Rogers and Jenkins (1995) extend this result in two ways. First, they sort out traded and nontraded components of the CPI and find that, on average, 81 percent of the variance in the real CPI exchange rate is explained by changes in the relative price of traded goods (which they measure using food prices).

Both of these studies seem to support the view that deviations from the law of one price in traded goods – the first term on the right-hand side of eq. (2.21) – dominate short-term real exchange rate fluctuations. One important qualification to these results is that they are based on retail (CPI) data, and even the "traded" goods embody substantial nontraded inputs. The retail price of bananas includes not only the traded goods input, but local shipping, rent and overhead for the retailer, and labor. Indeed, for many seemingly highly-traded goods, these indirect costs can far outweigh direct traded-goods costs.

Engel and Rogers (1994) provide some further perspective on this issue. Their analysis is based on CPI data for both U.S. and Canadian cities for 14 categories of consumer prices. They find that the variability in the price of a good in two different locations within a country depends on the distance (and the squared distance) between locations, as in gravity models of trade. However, they find that holding other variables (including distance) constant, the variability in prices between two U.S. or two Canadian cities is much less than between a Canadian and a U.S. city. Crossing the U.S.–Canadian border adds as much to the variability of prices as adding (a minimum) of 2500 miles between cities within a country.

Engel and Rogers interpret their finding as strong evidence that prices are sticky in local currency, and that changes in the exchange rate lead to deviations in the law of one price. While their evidence is striking, retail goods generally contain substantial nontraded components, and these components may be much larger across countries than within countries. For example, labor may be much more mobile between New York and Los Angeles than between cross-border neighbors such as Buffalo and Toronto.

Rogers and Jenkins (1993) look at the persistence of deviations from PPP for each component of the CPI across 11 OECD countries as well as across 54 disaggregated goods between the US and Canada. For each good (or index component) i, they test whether deviations in the law of one price

$$q_t(i) = s_t - p_t(i) + p_t^*(i) \tag{2.22}$$

follow a random walk, using the augmented Dickey–Fuller test in eq. (2.6) without a time trend. (Thus, this is a stage-two-type test.) Interestingly, for highly nontraded index components (such as rent), Rogers and Jenkins are unable to reject a random walk for any of the 39 country pairs. They occasionally reject, however, when food prices are used as the index. When looking at more disaggregated individual goods prices between the U.S. and Canada over samples which run from the mid-1970s to 1990, they find similar results:

(1) it is not possible to reject a random walk in the relative price of haircuts (a nontraded good); and

(2) rejection rates are considerably higher for potatoes, eggs, etc. (which are taken to be traded goods).

While disaggregation appears quite informative, the papers by Engel and by Rogers and Jenkins all use relatively short sample periods. They may have enough data to detect statistical differences in relative-price variances, but not enough to provide much power to detect differences in persistence.

2.5.2. Tests using disaggregated price data and longer times series samples

In order to obtain a longer time series of disaggregated price data and to gain some perspective on the behavior of prices during recent periods, we consider data from the period 1630–1789 in England and France for three commodities: wheat, charcoal and butter.[28] All prices are in terms of silver (implicitly we assume that the law of one price holds for silver.)

---

[28] The main data sources are Beveridge (1939), Hauser (1936), and Jastram (1981). For further discussion of the data, see Froot, Kim and Rogoff (1995), who look at deviations from the law of one price for a seven-hundred year data set for England and Holland.

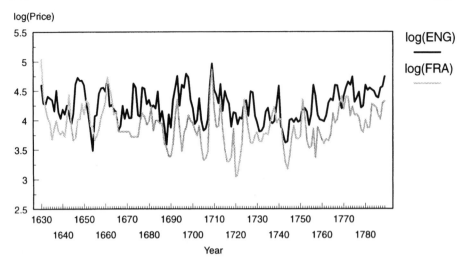

Figure 2.2. Log wheat price, 1630–1789. Price in grams of silver per hectoliter of wheat.

The individual and relative (log) prices are graphed in Figures 2.2–2.4, which reveal several striking aspects of the data. First, note the high volatility of goods prices within a country and of relative prices for the same good across countries. Deviations in PPP for wheat are the most volatile, with a standard deviation of 30 percent per annum. Relative butter and charcoal prices follow, with annual standard deviations of 17 and 12 percent respectively.

The second striking fact is the appearance of trends in individual commodity prices. The log price of wheat, measured in hectoliters per gram of silver and depicted in Figure 2.2, shows little or no trend between 1630 and 1789, averaging about 4.08 during the sample. Indeed, as Froot, Kim and Rogoff (1995) note, this level is strikingly near today's relative price of 4.00.[29] Over a time span this long – almost four centuries – it might be fair to assume that the absence of a relative price trend suggests roughly equal growth rates in wheat and silver productivity.

For charcoal prices, shown in Figure 2.3, there is a slight upward trend over the sample. In addition, charcoal is on average 25 percent more expensive in France than in England over the sample. The price differential probably reflects endowments (England had a greater domestic supply), though the price differential is, of course, bounded by customs charges and transportation costs.

Figure 2.4 depicts the (log) price of butter, measured in kilograms of butter per gram of silver, for the years 1717 to 1789. Butter is probably the least traded of the three goods in our sample, since there was no refrigeration during this period. Note that in contrast to charcoal, butter's price was initially 2.7

---

[29]This is based on a price $3.40 per American bushel of wheat and $5.45 per troy ounce of silver.

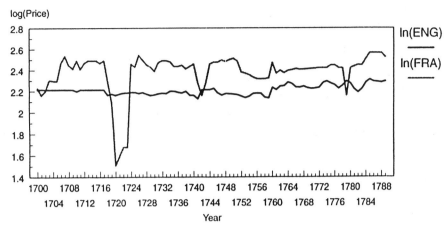

Figure 2.3. Log charcoal prices, 1700–1789. Price in grams of silver per hectoliter of charcoal.

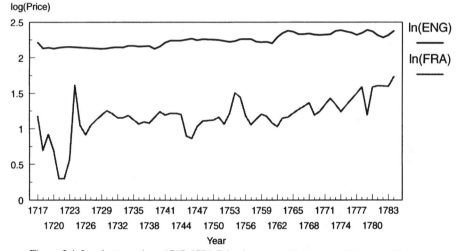

Figure 2.4. Log butter prices, 1717–1784. Price in grams of silver per kilogram of butter.

times higher in England than in France, though this ratio drops to 1.8 by the end of the period. (One possible explanation is that France's industrialization during the mid and latter parts of the 18th century drove up nontraded prices relative to England, where by 1717 the industrial revolution was already in full swing.) In contrast to wheat and charcoal, the (silver) price of butter trended upward during the period. If one thinks of dairy products as being more labor intensive than grains and charcoal, this fact is consistent with the Baumol–Bowen hypothesis, discussed in Section 3. Indeed, the price of butter relative to silver has continued to rise and stands today at roughly five times the price

Table 2.2

Augmented Dickey–Fuller regressions on English/French relative prices

$$q(i) = s - p(i) + p^*(i)$$
$$q_t(i) = \alpha_0 + \alpha_1 q_{t-1}(i) + \phi_1(1-L)q_{t-1}(i) + \epsilon_t(i)$$

Sample Period	Wheat 1632–1789	Charcoal 1702–1789	Butter 1719–1784
N	158	74	41
α_1	0.445	0.303	0.737
t-stat	−7.09	−8.95	−2.05
1% critical value	−3.47	−3.52	−3.60
ϕ_1	0.103	0.10	0.08
R^2	0.262	0.533	0.112
DW	2.02	1.43	1.75
σ_q	0.293	0.119	0.172

at the beginning of the eighteenth century. Put differently, if the relative price of butter to silver had remained constant since the early 17th century, butter would today cost approximately $0.43 per pound.

The third striking feature of the relative prices – especially wheat – is the strong appearance of stationarity. To check this more formally, we ran unit root tests on the English/French relative price of wheat, charcoal and butter. The results reported in Table 2.2 above are based on the augmented Dickey–Fuller specification (2.6), except that the time trend has been omitted (including a time trend does not affect the results). For wheat and charcoal, one can reject the unit root null at the 1 percent level. The autoregressive coefficient for the relative price of wheat is 0.445, implying a half life for PPP deviations of roughly one year. For charcoal, the autoregressive coefficient is only 0.303, implying a half life of only seven months.

Interestingly, we cannot reject the random-walk hypothesis for the relative price of butter, despite the relatively long time span. The estimated autoregressive coefficient is 0.74, an implied half-life of 2 years. This result that the half life of PPP deviations for butter is greater than for other commodities accords with our intuition, as butter is more likely to be nontraded than wheat or charcoal over this period. Of course, our calculations in section 2.3.3 suggest that seventy-five years may not be enough data to reliably reject nonstationarity.

3. Structural models of deviations from PPP

Until now, all the evidence we have looked at has been based on price and exchange rate data. In this section, we discuss a number of studies that attempt to explain empirically deviations from PPP in terms of more fundamental factors such as productivity, government spending, and strategic pricing decisions by firms. Our focus is on medium- to long-term movements; Frankel and Rose deal with short-term fluctuations elsewhere in this volume. We begin by reviewing some of the key theoretical issues, and then turn to the empirical evidence.

3.1. Productivity, government spending and the relative price of nontradeables

Of the many models that have been put forth to explain long-term deviations in consumption-based PPP, the most popular and enduring one is due to Balassa (1964) and Samuelson (1964). They posited that, after adjusting for exchange rates, CPIs in rich countries will be high relative to those in poor countries, and that CPIs in fast-growing countries will rise relative to CPIs in slow-growing countries. We will formalize their analysis shortly, but the main idea is as follows.

Balassa and Samuelson argue that technological progress has historically been faster in the traded goods sector than in the nontraded goods sector (perhaps because traded goods are weighted towards high-innovation agricultural or manufacturing goods) *and*, crucially, that this traded-goods productivity bias is more pronounced in high-income countries. As a consequence, CPI levels tend to be higher in wealthy countries. Why? A rise in productivity in the traded goods sector will bid up wages in the entire economy; producers of nontraded goods will only be able to meet the higher wages if there is a rise in the relative price of nontraded goods.

To take an example, consider the fact that nontraded goods are cheaper in India than in Switzerland. Although Switzerland's absolute level of productivity is higher than that of India, the productivity in its nontraded-goods sector relative to its traded-goods sector is lower.

It is important to distinguish the Balassa–Samuelson effect from the related "Baumol–Bowen" effect. Baumol and Bowen (1966) argued that within a country, there is a broad tendency for the prices of service intensive goods (education, health care, auto repair, banking, etc.) to rise over time. Historically, productivity growth in services has tended to be much slower than in more capital intensive manufacturing industries. This argument is obviously closely parallel to a key building block of the Balassa–Samuelson model, since there is a heavy overlap between nontradeables and service-intensive goods. Note, however, that the presence of a Baumol–Bowen effect is not necessarily sufficient to imply a Balassa–Samuelson effect.[30]

---

[30] Will there ever be a service productivity revolution to turn the Baumol–Bowen effect on its head? The possibility cannot be dismissed. Banking services have become vastly more efficient in recent years, with innovations ranging from ATMs to derivative securities; it seems plausible that the information revolution may someday lead to a long pause, if not a reversal, of the trend differential in productivity growth.

It is arguable whether one should expect to detect a Balassa–Samuelson effect in really long-run data. Even though technology can differ across countries for extended periods, the free flow of ideas together with human and physical capital produces a tendency towards long-run convergence of incomes. Of course, in the final analysis, the effect of income growth on PPP is an empirical question. Before looking at the empirical evidence, however, we examine more closely the theoretical underpinnings of the model; readers whose main interest is in the empirical material may wish to skip to the next subsection.

3.2. A small country model of the Balassa–Samuelson effect

In this section, we derive the central equation of the Balassa–Samuelson relationship between the real (CPI) exchange rate and the productivity differential between traded and nontraded goods.[31] One important point, generally overlooked in the literature, is that even balanced growth across the two sectors can lead to a rise in the relative price of nontradeables if nontraded goods are relatively labor intensive.

Consider the case of a small, open economy, that produces both traded and nontraded goods. The sectoral production functions are

$$Y_t^T = A_t^T (L_t^T)^{\theta^T} (K_t^T)^{1-\theta^T} \tag{3.1}$$

$$Y_t^N = A_t^N (L_t^N)^{\theta^N} (K_t^N)^{1-\theta^N} \tag{3.2}$$

where Y^T (Y^N) denote domestic output of the traded and nontraded good respectively, and K^I, L^I, and A^I are capital, labor and productivity in sector I. Let us initially assume that capital is mobile both internationally and across the two sectors internally. Assuming perfect competition in both sectors, profit maximization implies

$$R = (1 - \theta^T) A^T (K^T/L^T)^{-\theta^T} \tag{3.3}$$

$$R = P^N (1 - \theta^N) A^N (K^N/L^N)^{-\theta^N} \tag{3.4}$$

$$W = \theta^T A^T (K^T/L^T)^{1-\theta^T} \tag{3.5}$$

$$W = P^N \theta^N A^N (K^N/L^N)^{1-\theta^N} \tag{3.6}$$

where R is the rental rate on capital (determined in world markets), W is the wage rate (measured in tradeables) and P^N is the relative price of nontradeables. Since we assume no adjustment costs, it is convenient to omit time subscripts.

---

[31]The analysis here is based on Froot and Rogoff (1991b); [see also Rogoff (1992)].

The key result is that with perfect capital mobility, the relative price of non-tradeables P^N is governed entirely by the production side of the economy. Equations (3.3)–(3.6) involve four equations in four variables, K^T/L^T, K^N/L^N, W, and P, which can be solved recursively as follows: Given the constant returns to scale production functions (3.1) and (3.2), eq. (3.3) implies a unique level of K^T/L^T consistent with the world rate of return on capital R. Given K^T/L^T, eq. (3.5) determines the economy-wide wage rate W. The remaining two equations (3.4) and (3.6) then determine K^N/L^N and P.

By log-differentiating eqs.(3.3)–(3.6), one can obtain a (slight) generalization of the classic Balassa–Samuelson hypothesis:

$$\widehat{p} = (\theta^N/\theta^T)\widehat{a}^T - \widehat{a}^N \tag{3.7}$$

where $\widehat{x} \equiv d \log x$. If both sectors have the same degree of capital intensity – if $\theta^N = \theta^T$ – then the percentage change in the relative price of traded goods is simply equal to $\widehat{a}^T - \widehat{a}^N$, the productivity growth differential between the traded and nontraded sectors. If, however $\theta^N > \theta^T$ (one generally thinks of nontraded goods as being more labor intensive), then even balanced productivity growth $(\widehat{a}^T = \widehat{a}^N)$ will lead to an appreciation of the relative price of traded goods.[32]

Note that in the small open economy with perfect factor mobility, demand factors do not affect P^N, they only affect a country's consumption basket.[33] This is not the case for an economy fully (or partially) shut off from world capital markets, since R is no longer tied down by world markets. (The same is true, of course, for a large economy.) In this case, eqs. (3.3)–(3.6) must be supplemented by the demand side of the model.[34]

Demand factors can also be important in the small-country case *in the short run* if labor and/or capital cannot be transferred instantly across sectors.[35] Froot and Rogoff (1991) show that in this case, government spending will tend to raise the relative price of nontradeables, if the spending falls disproportionately on nontraded goods, relative to private expenditure shares. Rogoff (1992) shows that the model also implies that temporary shocks to traded goods productivity can have *permanent* effects on P^N. The reason is that private agents can use international capital markets to smooth their consumption of traded goods. As a result the relative *intratemporal* price of traded and nontraded goods is smoothed.

---

[32] De Gregorio and Wolf (1994) extend this model to allow for changes in the terms of trade (the relative price of importables and exportables).

[33] For further discussion, see Obstfeld and Rogoff (1995), ch. 4.

[34] This is a short-run result. In a representative agent model with constant discount rate β, the long-run interest rate is again tied down, and other demand factors do not enter into the determination of P^N.

[35] Demand factors will matter in the long run provided there is some fixed factor (e.g. land) which can be transferred across sectors.

Having discussed the basic theory underpinning the Balassa–Samuelson approach, we are now ready to examine the empirical literature.

3.3. Long-term productivity differentials and the real exchange rate

Balassa was the first to formally test the proposition that richer countries have higher real exchange rates; Balassa (1964), for example, reports the following regression for a cross-section of twelve industrial countries for the year 1960:[36]

$$(P/SP^*)_i = \alpha + \beta(GNP/POP)_i$$
$$0.49 \quad 0.51 \ (8.33) \tag{3.8}$$

where P/SP^* is the inverse of the level of the real exchange rate, GNP/POP is GNP/ population, and t statistics are in parentheses; the regression has 10 degrees of freedom. Balassa (1973) presents similar results, again finding that richer countries have higher (exchange-rate adjusted) price levels. Officer (1976b) surveys a host of follow-up studies that, on the whole, yielded much more negative results. Officer argued that Balassa's results are extremely sensitive to the year chosen and to the countries included in the regression. Note that eq. (3.8) is a test of *absolute* purchasing power parity; some of the data sources used for early absolute PPP comparison include Gilbert and Kravis (1954), Gilbert et al. (1958), and Kravis et al. (1975).

The most recent effort to construct absolute comparisons of PPP is Summers and Heston (1991), who construct absolute PPP data for a broad range of countries. Generally, their data reveal striking differences in price levels between poor countries as a group and rich countries as a group. Once divided into two groups, the within-group correlations between income and price level are much less apparent (see their figure on p. 336).

The preceding studies dealt with the cross-sectional implications of Balassa–Samuelson. Hsieh (1982) was the first to look at time series implications. His study focused on Japanese and German real exchange rates vis-à-vis the United States for the years 1954–1976. Hsieh's central regressions were of the form:

$$p_t - s_t - p_t^* = \beta_0 + \beta_1 \left[a_t^T - a_t^N \right] - \beta_2 \left[a_t^{*T} - a_t^{*N} \right]$$
$$+ \beta_3 \left[w_t - s_t - w_t^* + a_t^T - a_t^{*T} \right] \tag{3.9}$$

where w is the (log) nominal wage rate. Hsieh found that the productivity differential variables were significant and of the correct sign for both real exchange rates, and that his OLS regression results were robust both to correcting for serial correlation and to using instrumental variables techniques. It should be

---

[36]Balassa does not provide the standard error on α or R^2; the correlation coefficient is 0.92.

noted that the variable $\left[w_t - s_t - w_t^* + a_t^T - a_t^{*T}\right]$, which includes nominal wage differentials, is extremely highly correlated with the lagged real exchange rate. Thus Hsieh's results may be sensitive to whether or not this "error correction" term is included.

Marston (1987) and Edison and Klovland (1987) also present evidence suggestive of a Balassa–Samuelson effect. Edison and Klovland examine time series data on the real exchange between the British pound and the Norwegian krone for the years 1874–1971. This long time period allows them to detect significant evidence of a productivity differential effect using as proxies both the real output differential and a measure of the commodity/service productivity ratio differential.

Marston (1987) looks at the yen/dollar real exchange rate over the period 1973–1983, and calculates traded-nontraded goods productivity differentials using OECD data that disaggregates the economy into ten subsectors. It is worthwhile to digress briefly to explain his aggregation approach. He designates two sectors as traded: manufacturing; and agricultural, hunting, fishing and forestry. Six sectors are deemed nontraded: construction; wholesale and retail trade; restaurants and hotels; transport, storage and communication; finance, insurance, real estate; business services, community, social and personal services; and government services. Marston excludes the mining and quarrying sector, because it is energy intensive and therefore was very sensitive to OPEC pricing policies over the period. For the same reason, he excludes the electricity, gas and water sector.

Using sectoral employment data, Marston calculates labor productivity differentials between traded and nontraded goods, and argues that these variables provide an extremely plausible explanation of the long-run trend real appreciation of the yen against the dollar.

The evidence of later studies is somewhat mixed. Froot and Rogoff (1991a,b) look at a cross-section of 22 OECD countries for the years 1950–1989. They find that the correlation between productivity differentials and the real exchange rate is weak at best, both for their full sample and for various subsamples.

Asea and Mendoza (1994), take a different approach; their analysis is based on a dynamic two-country general equilibrium model. They take sectoral OECD data to calculate relative traded goods prices for fourteen OECD countries over the period 1975–1985. They first regress the relative price of nontraded goods for each country against traded-nontraded productivity differentials, and then regress cross-country real exchange rates against the relative price of nontraded goods (they try both actual and estimated). Asea and Mendoza conclude that although the productivity differentials between traded and nontraded goods are extremely significant in explaining changes in the relative price of nontraded goods within each country, changes in nontraded goods prices account for only a small and insignificant part of real exchange-rate changes across countries (using either CPI or GDP deflators). Thus while the data reveal evidence of a Baumol–Bowen effect, the Balassa–Samuelson effect is more difficult to detect.

De Gregorio, Giovannini, and Wolf (1994a) similarly conclude that differences in productivity growth across traded and nontraded goods help explain the relative price of nontraded goods. (However, they reach somewhat more positive conclusions than Asea and Mendoza concerning the ability of productivity differentials to explain changes across countries in the real exchange rate; we will discuss their results in more detail shortly.)

Note that if two countries have different weights on services in their consumption baskets, then the Baumol–Bowen effect alone can produce significant trend movements in CPI real exchange rates, even in the absence of a Balassa–Samuelson effect. Suppose, for example, that two countries have identical technologies at all times, but that one country has a higher share of services in the CPI. Then the presence of a Baumol–Bowen effect is sufficient to yield a trend in the CPI real exchange rate. If the Baumol–Bowen effect is indeed important – the evidence in both Asea and Mendoza, and in De Gregorio, Giovannini, and Wolf strongly suggests that it is – then one must have convergence in *tastes*, not just technologies, for the real exchange rate to converge in the long run.

3.4. Demand factors and the real exchange rate

A striking feature of the Balassa–Samuelson model developed in Section 3.2 is that the real exchange rate depends entirely on supply factors; demand factors do not enter. This property of the model depends on several assumptions:

(1) the country is small and cannot affect the world interest rate;

(2) capital is mobile internationally;

(3) both capital and labor are instantaneously mobile across sectors internally;

(4) there are constant returns to scale in the mobile factors (i.e. there is no third factor in production such as land which is immobile across sectors).

If, for example, capital and labor are mobile across sectors in the long run but not in the short run, demand factors can have a short-run impact on the real exchange rate. The possibility that demand factors may matter, at least in the short run, has been explored empirically by Froot and Rogoff (1991a,b), Rogoff (1992) and by De Gregorio, Giovannini, and Wolf (1994a).[37]

Froot and Rogoff (1991a) look at alternative explanations for the significant shifts in real exchange rates over the EMS period. Between 1986 and 1991,

---

[37] Ahmed (1987) also looks empirically at the effects of government spending on the real exchange rate. His model, however, focuses on home-produced versus foreign goods (the terms of trade), as opposed to traded versus nontraded. He assumes that government spending falls more heavily on foreign goods than does spending by domestic consumers, and he finds support for this hypothesis on historical data for Great Britain.

for example, Italy's CPI inflation rate exceeded Germany's by more than 15 percent, while the lira/mark exchange rate remained fixed. Froot and Rogoff explore to what extent relative growth in Italian government spending might account for this phenomenon. In their model, it is assumed that government spending falls disproportionately on nontraded goods, thereby bidding up their relative price. They regress the real CPI exchange rate against various measures of productivity differentials and government spending (as a ratio to GNP). The government spending variable consistently enters with correct sign in all the individual country regressions and is strongly significant in the pooled time series cross-section regressions. Neither productivity differentials or government spending enters significantly.

Froot and Rogoff suggest that government spending effects, because they are transitory, may be difficult to pick up in highly volatile floating exchange rate data. To pursue this conjecture, Froot and Rogoff (1991b) look at data for twenty-two OECD countries for the period 1950–1989, a sample which includes both fixed and floating rate data. They also modify their earlier model to allow for gradual factor adjustment across sectors, implying that the effects of government spending will only be temporary. Overall, they find that the government spending differential consistently enters pooled regressions significantly and with the correct sign, both over the full sample and over separate fixed and floating rate periods. Though factor mobility causes the effect to die out over the long run, the half life appears quite long – more than five years.

Rogoff (1992) estimates a related model on quarterly data for the yen/dollar rate over the period 1975–1990. Although government spending appears to be highly correlated with the real exchange rate, it does not enter significantly into the regressions once one controls for shocks to the world price of oil.

De Gregorio, Giovannini, and Wolf (1994a) present a cross-country panel regression that attempts to sort of the importance of demand and supply factors. Their model is closely related to the model presented in Section 3.1. Like Asea and Mendoza (1994), they use the OECD intersectoral data base to construct measures of productivity growth in the traded and nontraded goods sectors. The version they use covers fourteen countries[38] and twenty sectors; the data include both real and nominal output permitting construction of sectoral price deflators as well as detailed input data allowing derivation of total factor productivity levels.[39] Their method for classifying sectors between traded and nontraded is somewhat different than Marston's, though yielding broadly similar results. De Gregorio, Giovannini, and Wolf calculate total exports of each sector across all fourteen OECD countries and take the ratio to total production. They define

---

[38] Australia, Belgium, Canada, Denmark, Finland, France, Germany, Italy, Japan, the Netherlands, Norway, Sweden, the United Kingdom, and the United States.

[39] Stockman and Tesar (1995) have previously used this same data set in their work on international real business cycles.

a sector as tradeable if more than ten percent is exported. This leads them to classify as tradeables all of manufacturing, agriculture and mining; they also classify transportation services as tradeable. All other services, comprising 50–60 percent of GNP are classified as nontradeable. De Gregorio, Giovannini, and Wolf then calculate total factor productivity using Solow residuals.[40] They also test for the effect of government spending on the relative price of nontradeables.

Their results are very interesting and instructive. De Gregorio, Giovannini, and Wolf's central regression is of the form:[41]

$$\left(p^N - p^T\right)_{i,t} = \alpha_i + \beta_1 \left[\left(\theta^N/\theta^T\right) a^T - a^N\right]_{i,t} + \beta_2 g_{i,t} + \beta_3 y_{i,t} \tag{3.10}$$

where g is real government spending (excluding government investment) over real GDP, y is real per capita income, i subscripts denote country and t subscripts denote time. Note that the weight on tradeable goods productivity growth a^T is greater than the weight on a^N if $\theta^N > \theta^T$, which is very plausible. As we discussed in Section 3.1, balanced productivity growth is likely to raise the relative price of nontradeables in the small open economy. Because the rate of return on capital is tied down by international capital mobility, productivity growth raises the wage/rental ratio, and therefore raises the relative price of the labor-intensive good.[42] In constructing g, the share of government spending in GNP, De Gregorio, Giovannini, and Wolf use separate deflators to convert nominal government spending to nominal GDP.[43] Otherwise, because government spending has a higher share of nontraded goods than overall GDP, changes in the relative price of nontradeables will affect the ratio even if quantities are constant. (The OECD data permits this adjustment.)

Pooling data for all fourteen countries over the full 1971–1985 sample period (they have 210 observations), De Gregorio, Giovannini, and Wolf obtain

$$\left(p^N - p^T\right)_{i,t} = \alpha_i + \beta_1 \left[\left(\theta^N/\theta^T\right) a^T - a^N\right]_{i,t} + \beta_2 g_{i,t} + \beta_3 y_{i,t}$$
$$\underset{(0.018)}{0.234} \qquad\qquad\qquad \underset{(0.119)}{1.974} \quad \underset{(0.030)}{0.281}$$

---

[40]De Gregorio et al. use of total factor productivity, which controls for capital inputs, contrasts with Marston's use of labor productivity. (Asea and Mendoza also use total factor productivity.) It is not obvious, however, that the total factor productivity is necessarily superior, since data on capital inputs is notoriously unreliable.

[41]They also consider a variant of their empirical model where the lagged rate of change of nontraded goods prices enters into the regression; this modification does not substantially affect the results.

[42]Strictly speaking, the coefficient in eq. (3.10) is correct for the case of perfect factor mobility. When factors are immobile across sectors, the weights depend on shares in aggregate demand; [see Rogoff (1992)].

[43]Froot and Rogoff (1991b) also attempt to control for this effect by using CPI and WPI data to construct separate deflators for government spending and GNP, but their data are much cruder.

where standard errors are in parentheses. The productivity, government spending and income variables are all highly significant and of the theoretically predicted signs.

Although their model is not explicitly dynamic, De Gregorio, Giovannini, and Wolf attempt to see whether demand factors matter in the long run by averaging data for each country over time, and running a regression for the cross-section data. They find that over the long run, the productivity differentials remain extremely significant whereas the effects of demand factors (government spending and income) become less important. It would be interesting to explore this issue further by estimating a model that explicitly accounts for dynamic adjustment. (Asea and Mendoza (1994) and Rogers (1994) both represent useful efforts in this direction.)

Recently, De Gregorio and Wolf (1994) have extended this analysis to incorporate term of trade shocks (shocks to the relative price of home exports versus home imports). They find that the terms of trade are important empirically, though productivity and government spending differentials continue to be important. Relative incomes, however, become insignificant when terms of trade shocks are included. They conclude that the income variable in the above regression may be proxying for terms of trade shocks.

3.5. Pricing to market

Most of our discussion in this section has focused on deviations from the law of one price due to the presence of nontraded goods. We have paid relatively little attention to the factors that may cause deviations from the law of one price in traded goods (except to note that one must be careful to recognize that many goods that appear to be highly "traded" in fact have a large nontraded component). The empirical evidence, including Isard (1977), Giovannini (1988) and Engel (1993), strongly suggests that deviations from the law of one price in traded goods are important in practice and that the short-run size and direction of these departures appears to track closely nominal exchange rate movements. One obvious explanation is that of short-term price rigidities, due, say, to menu costs in changing prices. Frankel and Rose, as well as Garber and Svensson deal with price rigidities elsewhere in this volume, discussing how short-term nominal rigidities can affect the transmission of real and monetary disturbances.

Another theory of why there can be deviations from the law of one price in traded goods is the "pricing to market" theory of Krugman (1987) and Dornbusch (1987). This literature is also covered by Feenstra elsewhere in this Handbook, so our discussion here is brief. In the pricing to market framework, oligopolistic suppliers are able to charge different prices for the same good in different countries; thus the prices of BMWs can differ between Germany and the United States. If the BMWs are truly tradeable, why isn't this gap closed by goods market arbitrage? The theory posits that there are important cases where companies can separately license the sale of goods at home and abroad. Of course, the ability to price discriminate across markets may be very limited in practice. In electronics, for example, there exists an active "gray market" in which goods are purchased in low-price countries for immediate resale in countries where the manufacturer is attempting to charge a higher price.[44]

In addition to potentially explaining longer-run deviations from the law of one price, "pricing to market" theories also have implications for the transmission of monetary disturbances if there are nominal rigidities. The Dornbusch–Krugman models assume that in the short-run, costs are set in nominal terms in the currency of the supplier. Then, if there is an exogenous appreciation in the home country's nominal exchange rate (the pricing to market literature is partial equilibrium), the real cost of supplying goods for foreign sale rises. If demand were unit elastic, the markup of price over cost would not be affected [see Marston, (1990)], but the markup over cost on foreign goods will fall if the foreign price elasticity of demand is greater than unity. (This would generally be the case for a monopolist with non-zero marginal cost of production.) Indeed, much of the empirical literature focuses on short-run transmission effects.

Kasa (1992) questions the price discrimination story as the underlying rationale for pricing to market. Why do studies such as Knetter (1989) find relatively similar effects of exchange rates on markups across industries, if price discrimination is central?[45] Kasa argues that pricing to market is better rationalized using an adjustment cost framework, where either the firm faces some kind of adjustment cost in changing prices or, as in Froot and Klemperer (1989), consumers face fixed costs in switching between products. Froot and Klemperer point out that if their adjustment cost story is correct, then changes in exchange rates that are expected to be temporary should lead to much greater fluctuations in markups than deviations that are expected to be permanent. They present some evidence that is suggestive of their theory, under the assumption that private agents generally viewed the mid-1980s run up in the dollar as temporary.

A number of studies, including Knetter (1989), find that pricing to market is more pronounced for German and Japanese exporters than it is for American exporters. Recently, some explanations for this stylized fact have been unearthed. Knetter (1993) finds that pricing to market behavior seems more similar across countries if one controls for industry effects; U.S. exporters tend to be concentrated in industries where, globally, pricing to market behavior is less pronounced. Rangan and Lawrence (1993) argue that part of the reason

---

[44] The main defense against the "gray market" is for manufacturers to refuse to honor the warranty except in the original country of sale. This strategy is obviously more likely to be successful in the case of autos than for, say, VCRs.

[45] Elsewhere in this volume, Feenstra argues that the differences in "pass-through" of exchange-rate changes across industries are in fact quite large.

U.S. pricing to market behavior seems less pronounced is that many U.S. firms sell their products abroad to subsidiaries, and that the pricing to market behavior takes place at the subsidiary level.

Ghosh and Wolf (1994) try to discriminate between menu costs and pricing to market theories. Their data set consists of cover prices of the magazine *The Economist* for eleven European countries and the United States for the years 1973–1990. They argue that importance of lagged exchange rate changes on relative price changes (across countries) supports the view that deviations from the law of one price must be driven at least partly by menu costs. As we have argued above, however, the pricing to market and menu cost theories of PPP deviations are not mutually exclusive.

Finally, in an interesting recent paper, Feenstra and Kendall (1994) argue that changes in price markups across countries over time may have a permanent component and that, empirically, this effect may in some cases be as important as the Balassa–Samuelson effect in explaining deviations from the law of one price. The existence of a permanent component, of course, essentially requires that firms be able to maintain segmentation across the markets indefinitely.

4. Conclusions

Over the past ten years, research on purchasing power parity has enjoyed a rebirth, partly due to innovations in econometrics, and even more to the development of new data sets that allow researchers to investigate both longer and more disaggregated time series. The main positive result is that there does seem to be long-run convergence to PPP, though further work on the issue of survivorship bias would be valuable. Also, the most convincing evidence on long-run convergence to PPP still comes from data sets that employ at least some fixed-rate data. Perhaps by the time of the next Handbook, there will be more years of floating-rate data from more countries and perhaps, if these are combined with more powerful econometric techniques, we will have a clearer picture of whether and how fast exchange rates converge to PPP under floating rates.[46]

There has also been a considerable amount of progress in recent years in analyzing the effect of productivity and government spending shocks on real exchange rates. Most of the empirical literature, however, does not explicitly take dynamics into account. As we have seen in the simple PPP literature, dynamics can be quite central, so further progress on understanding the dynamic effects of various real shocks might potentially prove fruitful.

---

[46]Since this survey was written, Frankel and Rose (1995), and Wei and Parsley (1995), have attempted to demonstrate mean reversion using only post-1973 data. Wei and Parsley look at tradeable goods prices for a cross-section of 14 OECD countries. Frankel and Rose use CPI data for a broader cross-section, including some high-inflation countries. Interestingly, both studies find half lives for PPP deviations very close to the 4-year consensus estimate noted here.

References

Abuaf, N. and P. Jorion (1990), "Purchasing power parity in the long run", Journal of Finance 45:157–174.

Adler, M. and B. Lehman (1983), "Deviations from purchasing power parity in the long run", Journal of Finance 39:1471–1487.

Ahmed, S. (1987), "Government spending, the balance of trade and terms of trade in British history", Journal of Monetary Economics 20:195–220.

Asea, P.K. and E. Mendoza (1994), "The Balassa–Samuelson model: A general equilibrium appraisal", Review of International Economics, 2:244–267.

Balassa, B. (1964), "The purchasing power parity doctrine: A reappraisal", The Journal of Political Economy 72:584–596.

Balassa, B. (1973), "Just how misleading are official exchange rate conversions: A comment", Economic Journal 83:1258–1267.

Banerjee, A., J. Dolado, D. Hendry, and G. Smith (1986), "Exploring equilibrium relationships in econometrics through static models: some Monte Carlo evidence", Oxford Bulletin of Economics and Statistics 48:253–277.

Baumol, W. (1993), "Social wants and dismal science: The curious case of climbing costs on health and teaching", mimeo, Princeton University.

Baumol, W. and W. Bowen (1966), Performing arts: The economic dilemma (The Twentieth Century Fund, New York).

Bayoumi, T., P. Clark, S. Symansky, and M. Taylor (1994), "Robustness of equilibrium exchange rate calculations to alternative assumptions and methodologies", in: J. Williamson, ed., Estimating equilibrium exchange rates (Institute for International Economics, Washington DC).

Beveridge, W. (1939), Prices and wages in England: From the twelfth to the nineteenth century, vol. 1 (Longman, Greens and Co., London).

Breuer, J. (1994), "Purchasing power parity: A survey of and challenge to recent literature", in: J. Williamson, ed., Estimating equilibrium exchange rates (Institute for International Economics, Washington DC).

Bryant, M. and S. Cecchetti (1993), "The consumer price index as a measure of inflation", Economic Review of the Federal Reserve Bank of Cleveland Q4:15–24.

Campbell, J. and R. Clarida (1987), "The dollar and real interest rates: An empirical investigation", in: K. Brunner and A. Meltzer, eds., Carnegie–Rochester Series on Public Policy 27:103–140.

Campbell, J. and P. Perron (1991), "Pitfalls and opportunities: What every macroeconomist should know about unit roots", in: S. Fischer and O. Blanchard, eds., NBER macroeconomics annual (MIT Press, Cambridge, MA).

Cassel, G. (1921), The world's money problems (E.P. Dutton and Co., New York).

Cassel, G. (1922), Money and foreign exchange after 1914 (Macmillan, New York).

Cavallo, D. (1986), "Estadisticas de la evolucion economica de Argentina, 1913–1984", Estudios 9:103–184.

Cheung, Y. and K. Lai (1993a), "Long-run purchasing power parity during the recent float", Journal of International Economics 34:181–192.

Cheung, Y. and K. Lai (1993b), "A fractional cointegration analysis of purchasing power parity", Journal of Business and Economic Statistics 11:103–112.

Cheung, Y. and K. Lai (1993c), "Mean reversion in real exchange rates", mimeo, UCLA.

Chowdhury, A. and F. Sdogati (1993), "Purchasing power parity in the major EMS countries: The role of price and exchange rate adjustment", Journal of Macroeconomics 15:25–45.

Christiano, L. (1992), "Searching for a break in GNP", Journal of Business and Economic Statistics 10:237–500.

Corbae, D. and S. Ouliaris (1988), "Cointegration and tests of purchasing power parity", Review of Economics and Statistics 70:508–521.

Cumby, R. (1993), "Forecasting exchange rates on the hamburger standard: what you see is what you get with McParity", mimeo, Stern School of Business.

Cumby, R. and J. Huizinga (1991), "The predictability of real exchange rate changes in the short and long run", Japan and the World Economy 3:17–38.

Darby, M. (1983), "Movements in purchasing power parity: The short and long runs", in: M. Darby and J. Lothian, eds., The international transmission of inflation (University of Chicago Press, Chicago).

Davutyan, N. and J. Pippenger (1985), "Purchasing power parity did not collapse during the 1970's", American Economic Review 75:1151–1158.

Diebold, F., S. Husted, and M. Rush (1991), "Real exchange rates under the gold standard", Journal of Political Economy 99:1252–1271.

De Gregorio, J., A. Giovannini, and H. Wolf (1994a), "International evidence on tradables and nontradables inflation", European Economic Review, 38:1225–1244.

De Gregorio, J., A. Giovannini and H. Wolf (1994b), "The behavior of nontradeable goods prices in Europe: Evidence and interpretation", Review of International Economics, 2:284–305.

De Gregorio, J., and H. Wolf (1994), "Terms of trade, productivity, and the real exchange rate", National Bureau of Economic Research Working Paper No. 4807.

Dickey, D. and W. Fuller (1979), "Distribution of the estimators for autoregressive time series with a unit root", Journal of the American Statistical Association 74:427–431.

Dornbusch, R. (1976), "Expectations and exchange rate dynamics", Journal of Political Economy 84:1161–1176.

Dornbusch, R. (1987), "Purchasing power parity", in: J. Eatwell, M. Migare, and P. Newman, eds., The New Palgrave Dictionary (Stockton Press, New York).

Edison, H. (1987), "Purchasing power parity in the long run: A test of the dollar/pound exchange rate (1890–78)", Journal of Money, Credit, and Banking 19:376–387.

Edison, H., J. Gagnon, and W. Melick (1994), Understanding the empirical literature on purchasing power parity: the post-Bretton Woods era (Division of International Finance, Board of Governors of the Federal Reserve System, Washington, DC).

Edison, H. and J.T. Klovland (1987), "A quantitative reassessment of the purchasing power parity hypothesis: Evidence from Norway and the United Kingdom", Journal of Applied Econometrics 2:309–333.

Elliot, G., Rothenberg, T., and J. Stock (1992), "Efficient tests for an autoregressive root", National Bureau of Economic Research Technical Working Paper No. 130.

Enders, W. (1988), "Arima and cointegration tests of PPP under fixed and flexible exchange rate regimes", Review of Economics and Statistics 70:504–508.

Engel, C. (1993), "Is real exchange rate variability caused by relative price changes? An empirical investigation", Journal of Monetary Economics 32:35–50.

Engel, C. and J. Rogers (1994), "How wide is the border?", National Bureau of Economic Research Working Paper No. 4829.

Engle, R. and C. Granger (1987), "Cointegration and error correction: Representation, estimation, and testing", Econometrica 55:251–276.

Feenstra, R., and J. Kendall (1994), "Pass-through of exchange rates and purchasing power parity", National Bureau of Economic Research Working Paper No. 4842.

Feldstein, M. (1993), "The dollar and the trade deficit", National Bureau of Economic Research Working Paper No. 4325.

Fisher, E. and J. Park (1991), "Testing purchasing power parity under the null hypothesis of co-integration", The Economic Journal 101:1476–1484.

Flynn, N. and J. Boucher (1993), "Tests of long run purchasing power parity using alternative methodologies", Journal of Macroeconomics 15:109–122.

Frankel, J. (1986), "International capital mobility and crowding out in the U.S. economy: Imperfect integration of financial markets or goods markets?", in: R. Hafer, ed., How open is the US economy (Lexington Books, Lexington).

Frankel, J. (1990), "Zen and the art of modern macroeconomics: The search for perfect nothingness", in: W. Haraf and T. Willett, eds., Monetary policy for a volatile global economy. (American Enterprise Institute, Washington, DC).

Frankel, J. and A. Rose (1995), "A panel project on purchasing power parity: Mean reversion within and between countries", National Bureau of Economic Research Working Paper No. 5006.

Frenkel, J. (1978), "Quantifying international capital mobility in the 1980s", in: D. Bernheim and J. Shoven, eds., National saving and economic performance (University of Chicago Press, Chicago) 227–260.

Frenkel, J. (1981), "The collapse of purchasing power parity during the 1970s", European Economic Review 16:145–165.

Friedman, M. (1957), "The case for flexible exchange rates", in: Essays in positive economics (University of Chicago Press, Chicago).

Froot, K. and P. Klemperer (1989), "Exchange-rate pass through when market share matters", American Economic Review 79:637–654.

Froot, K. and K. Rogoff (1991a), "The EMS, the EMU, and the transition to a common currency", in: S. Fisher and O. Blanchard, eds., National bureau of economic research macroeconomics annual (MIT Press, Cambridge, MA) 269–317.

Froot, K. and K. Rogoff (1991b), "Government consumption and the real exchange rate: The empirical evidence", mimeo, Harvard Business School.

Froot, K., Kim, M., and K. Rogoff (1995), "The law of one price over seven hundred years", mimeo, Princeton University.

Ghosh, A. and H. Wolf (1994), "Pricing in international markets: Lessons from the Economist", National Bureau of Economic Research Paper No. 4806.

Gilbert, M. and Associates (1958), Comparative national price products and price levels: A study of western Europe and the United States (Organization for European Economic Cooperation, Paris).

Gilbert, M., and I. Kravis (1954), An international comparison of national products and the purchasing power of currencies: A study of the United States, the United Kingdom, France, Germany, and Italy (Organization for European Economic Cooperation, Paris).

Giovannetti, G. (1992), "A survey of recent empirical tests of the purchasing power parity hypothesis", Banca Nazionale del Lavoro Quarterly Review 180:81–101.

Giovannini, A. (1988), "Exchange rates and traded goods prices", Journal of International Economics 24:45–68.

Glen, J. (1992), "Real exchange rates in the short, medium, and long run", Journal of International Economics 33:147–166.

Grilli, V. and G. Kaminsky (1991), "Nominal exchange rate regimes and the real exchange rate: Evidence from the United States and Great Britain, 1885–1986", Journal of Monetary Economics 27:191–212.

Hakkio, C. (1984), "A reexamination of purchasing power parity", Journal of International Economics 17:265–277.

Hakkio, C.S. and M. Rush (1991), "Cointegration: How short is the long run?", Journal of International Money and Finance 10:571–581.

Hauser, H. (1936), Recherches et document sur l'histoires des prix en France de 1500 a 1800 (Slatkive, Geneva).

Horvath, M. and M. Watson (1993), "Testing for cointegration when some of the cointegrating vectors are known", Federal Reserve Bank of Chicago Working Paper No. 93–15.

Hsieh, D. (1982), "The determination of the real exchange rate: The productivity approach", Journal of International Economics 12:355–362.

Huizinga, J. (1987), "An empirical investigation of the long-run behavior of real exchange rates", in: K. Brunner and A. Meltzer, eds., Carnegie–Rochester Series on Public Policy 27:149–215.

Isard, P. (1977), "How far can we push the law of one price?", American Economic Review 67:942–948.

Jastram, R. (1981), Silver: The restless metal (Wiley, New York).

Johansen, S. (1988), "Statistical analysis of cointegration vectors", Journal of Economic Dynamics and Control 12:231–254.

Johansen, S. (1991), "Estimation and hypothesis testing of cointegration vectors in gaussian vector autoregressive models", Econometrica 59:1551–1581.

Johansen, S. and K. Juselius (1992), "Testing structural hypotheses in a multivariate cointegration analysis of the PPP and the UIP for U.K.", Journal of Econometrics 53:211–244.

Johnson, D.R. (1990), "Co-integration, error correction, and purchasing power parity between Canada and the United States", Canadian Journal of Economics 23:839–855.

Johnson, P. (1991), "Aggregate price indices, cointegration, and tests of the purchasing power parity hypothesis", Economics Letters 36.

Kasa, K. (1992), "Adjustment costs and pricing to market: Theory and evidence", Journal of International Economics 32:1–30.

Keynes, J. (1932), Essays in persuasion (Harcourt Brace, New York).

Kim, H. (1990), "Purchasing power parity in the long run: A cointegration approach", Journal of Money, Credit, and Banking 22:491–503.

Knetter, M. (1989), "Price discrimination by U.S. and German exporters", American Economic Review 79:198–210.

Knetter, M. (1993), "International comparisons of pricing to market behavior", American Economic Review 83:473–486.

Kravis, Irving B. (1975), A system of international comparisons of gross product and purchasing power, Phase 1 (Johns Hopkins University Press, Baltimore).

Kravis, I. and R. Lipsey (1988), "National price levels and the prices of tradeables and nontradeables", American Economic Review 78:474–478.

Krugman, P. (1978), "Purchasing power parity and exchange rates", Journal of International Economics 8:397–407.

Krugman, P. (1987), "Pricing to market when the exchange rate changes", in: S. Arndt and J.D. Richardson, eds., Real-financial linkages among open economies (MIT Press, Cambridge, MA).

Krugman, P. (1990), "Equilibrium exchange rates", in: W. Branson, J. Frenkel, and M. Goldstein, eds., International monetary policy coordination and exchange rates (The University of Chicago Press, Chicago).

Kugler, P. and C. Lenz (1993), "Multivariate cointegration analysis and the long run validity of PPP", Review of Economics and Statistics 75:180–184.

Lastrapes, W. (1992), "Sources of fluctuations in real and nominal exchange rates", Review of Economics and Statistics 74:530–539.

Lebow, D., J. Roberts, and D. Stockton (1992), "Economic performance under price stability", Board of Governors of the Federal Reserve System Working Paper No. 125.

Lee, M. (1974), Purchasing power parity (Marcel Dekker, New York).

Lothian, J. and M. Taylor (1994), Real exchange rate behavior: The recent float from the perspective of the past two centuries (International Monetary Fund, Washington DC), Journal of Political Economy, forthcoming.

Mark, N. (1990), "Real exchange rates in the long run: An empirical investigation", Journal of International Economics 28:115–136.

Marston, R. (1987), "Real exchange rates and productivity growth in the United States and Japan", in: S. Arndt and J.D. Richardson, eds., Real-financial linkages among open economies (MIT Press, Cambridge, MA).

Marston, R. (1990), "Pricing to market in Japanese manufacturing", Journal of International Economics 29:217–236.

McKinnon, R. (1971), "Monetary theory and control flexibility in the foreign exchanges", Princeton University, Essays in International Finance 84.

McKinnon, R.I. (1984), An international standard for monetary stabilization (Institute for International Economics, Washington, DC).

McNown, R. and M. Wallace (1989), "National price levels, purchasing power parity, and cointegration: A test of four high inflation economies", Journal of International Money and Finance 8:533–546.

Meese, R. and K. Rogoff (1983), "Empirical exchange rate models of the seventies: do they fit out of sample?", Journal of International Economics 14:3–24.

Meese, R. and K. Rogoff (1988), "Was it real? The exchange rate interest differential relation over the modern floating exchange rate period", Journal of Finance 43:933–948.

Mussa, M. (1986), "Nominal exchange rate regimes and the behavior of real exchange rates: Evidence and implications", in: K. Brunner and A. Meltzer, eds., Carnegie–Rochester Series on Public Policy 25:117–214.

Obstfeld, M. and K. Rogoff (1995), "Exchange rate dynamics redux", Journal of Political Economy 102, forthcoming.

Obstfeld, M. and K. Rogoff (1996), Foundations of international macroeconomics, (MIT Press, Cambridge, MA) forthcoming.

Officer, L. (1976a), "The purchasing power parity theory of exchange rates: A review article", International Monetary Fund Staff Papers 23:1–60.

Officer, L. (1976b), "The productivity bias in purchasing power parity: An econometric investigation", International Monetary Fund Staff Papers 10:545–579.

Ogaki, M. and J. Park (1991), "Inference in cointegrated models using VAR prewhitening to estimate short-run dynamics", University of Rochester Center for Economic Research Working Paper No. 281.

Papell, D. (1994), "Exchange rates and prices: An empirical analysis", International Economic Review 35:397–410.

Perron, P. (1988), "Trends and random walks in macroeconomic time series: Further evidence from a new approach", Journal of Economic Dynamics and Control 12:277–302.

Perron, P. (1989), "The great crash, the oil price shock, and the unit root hypothesis", Econometrica 57:1361–1401.

Phillips, P. (1987a), "Time series regression with a unit root", Econometrica 55:297–332.

Phillips, P. (1987b), "Asymptotic expansions in nonstationary vector autoregressions", Econometric Theory 3:45–68.

Poterba, J. and L. Summers (1986), "The persistence and volatility of stock market fluctuations", American Economic Review 76:1142–1151.

Rangan, S. and R. Lawrence (1993), "The responses of US firms to exchange rate fluctuations: Piercing the corporate veil", Brookings Papers on Economic Activity 2:341–369.

Rogers, J.H. (1995), "Real shocks and real exchanges in really long-term data", Journal of International Economics 26, forthcoming.

Rogers, J.H. and M.A. Jenkins (1993), "Haircuts or hysteresis? Sources of movements in real exchange rates", mimeo, Pennsylvania State University.

Rogoff, K. (1992), "Traded goods consumption smoothing and the random walk behavior of the real exchange rate", Bank of Japan Monetary and Economic Studies 10:1–29.

Roll, R. (1979), "Violations of purchasing power parity and their implications for efficient international commodity markets", in: M. Sarnat and G. Szego, eds., International finance and trade (Ballinger, Cambridge, MA).

Samuelson, P.A. (1964), "Theoretical notes on trade problems", Review of Economics and Statistics 46:145–164.

Stockman, A. and L. Tesar (1995), "Tastes in a two-country model of the business cycle: Explaining international comovement", American Economic Review, 85:168–185.

Summers, R. and A. Heston (1991), "The Penn world table (Mark 5): An expanded set of international comparisons, 1950–88", Quarterly Journal of Economics 106:327–368.

Taylor, M.P. (1988), "An empirical examination of long-run purchasing power parity using cointegration techniques", Applied Economics 20:1369–1381.

Taylor, M. and P. McMahon (1988), "Long run purchasing power parity in the 1920s", European Economic Review 32:179–197.

Wei, S. and D. Parsley (1995), "Purchasing power disparity during the floating rate period: Exchange rate volatility, trade barriers and other culprits", mimeo, Harvard University.

Chapter 33

EMPIRICAL RESEARCH ON NOMINAL EXCHANGE RATES

JEFFREY A. FRANKEL

Institute for International Economics

and

ANDREW K. ROSE*

University of California, Berkeley

Contents

*Frankel is Professor of Economics at the University of California, Berkeley, Director of the NBER's program in International Finance and Macroeconomics, and Senior Fellow at the Institute for International Economics; Rose is Associate Professor of Business at the University of California, Berkeley, Research Associate, NBER, and Research Fellow, CEPR. For comments, we thank: Michael Dooley, Charles Engel, Robert Flood, Peter Garber, Charles Goodhart, Karen Lewis, Richard Lyons, Maurice Obstfeld, Ken Rogoff, and participants at the Handbook of International Economics Conference at Princeton.

Handbook of International Economics, vol. III, Edited by G. Grossman and K. Rogoff
© *Elsevier Science B.V., 1995*

0. Introduction

This paper is intended to be a selective critical survey and interpretation of recent exchange rate research. We focus on empirical results for exchange rates among major industrialized countries.

In the decade since the publication of the first two volumes of *The Handbook of International Economics*, there have been three main strands of empirical research in international finance. The first and largest has been concerned with the determination of floating exchange rates; the second has addressed the issue of foreign exchange market efficiency and uncovered interest parity; the most recent has dealt with the characteristics of explicitly managed exchanged rates. In this chapter, we review the first topic. (The second and third topics are covered in this Handbook in the chapters by Lewis, and Garber and Svensson, respectively.) We begin by surveying the work on exchange rate determination in floating rate regimes, and then consider evidence across exchange rate regimes. After a brief examination of the issue of speculative bubbles, our chapter finishes with a discussion of some relatively new directions in exchange rate research that focus on the micro-structure of foreign exchange markets.

1. Floating exchange rates

1.1. Overview

Most of the large industrialized economies floated their exchange rate in early 1973, after the demise of the post-war Bretton Woods system of fixed exchange rates. While there had been extensive academic disputes on the relative merits of fixed and floating exchange rates, this discussion had been carried on at a largely hypothetical level. The generalized floating regime provided economists with the empirical data set required to resolve such academic disputes, as well as raising more immediate policy issues. Much of the international finance literature produced in the decade after the move to generalized floating focused on the development and estimation of empirical models of floating exchange rates.

By the early 1980s however, some early apparent empirical successes in the literature had been overturned and key empirical findings began to turn negative, a state of affairs that continues through the present day. The most profound negative result was produced by Meese and Rogoff (1983a,b), who compared the predictive abilities of a variety of exchange rate models. Their key result was that no existing structural exchange rate model could reliably out-predict the naive alternative of a random walk at short- and medium-run horizons, even when aided by actual future values of the regressors. This extremely negative finding has never been entirely convincingly overturned despite many attempts. The simple random walk model of the exchange rate has become the standard benchmark for empirical exchange rate performance, no matter how uninteresting it is per se. (Indeed, a number of researchers have professed to view the random walk "model" as being intrinsically interesting.)

Many of the most important empirical regularities remain what they were 15 years ago. Mussa (1979) made the following points, among others: (1) the log of the spot rate is approximately a random walk; (2) most changes in exchange rates are unexpected; (3) countries with high inflation rates tend to depreciate, and at approximately the inflation differential in the long run; and (4) actual exchange rate movements appear to overshoot movements in smoothly adjusting equilibrium exchange rates. The recent literature on floating rates is quite consistent with these propositions.

Nevertheless, some progress has been made. Above and beyond the issue of the determination and prediction of floating exchange rates, there have been a number of smaller streams of research in the area. One looks across exchange rate regimes; another focuses on survey evidence of exchange rate expectations; a third promising new area is the microeconomic modelling of foreign exchange markets. One of our objectives in this chapter is to provide a road map to these areas; we survey each in turn.

There are already a number of existing surveys. MacDonald (1990) and MacDonald and Taylor (1989, 1992, 1993b) offer particularly comprehensive reviews of the literature, focussing primarily on exchange rate determination and prediction. More selective perspectives are offered by Dornbusch (1987), Boughton (1988), Kenen (1988), Mussa (1989), Meese (1990), and Krugman (1993).

1.2. Models with fundamentals

1.2.1. Empirical equations of exchange rate determination

The standard workhorse of international finance is the monetary model of the exchange rate. The model starts with the reasonable statement that, as the exchange rate is the relative price of foreign and domestic money, it should be determined by the relative supply and demand for these moneys. The typical model stems from three equations. The first is money-market equilibrium:

$$m_t - p_t = \beta y_t - \alpha i_t + \varepsilon_t \tag{1.1}$$

where: m_t denotes the stock of money at time t; p denotes the price level; y denotes real income (all three in natural logarithm form); i denotes the nominal interest rate; ε denotes a shock to money demand; and α and β are positive structural parameters. It is traditional to assume that there is a comparable equation for the foreign country, and that domestic and foreign elasticities are equal.[1] Subtracting the foreign analog (where an asterisk denotes a foreign value) yields:

$$(p - p^*)_t = (m - m^*)_t - \beta(y - y^*)_t + \alpha(i - i^*)_t - (\varepsilon - \varepsilon^*)_t . \qquad (1.2)$$

1.2.1.1. The monetary model with flexible prices

The other two conditions enter as different substitutions for two of the terms in this equation. One can model (and replace) the relative price term by assuming that prices are either flexible or sticky. Similarly, one can model the interest rate differential as either simply satisfying uncovered interest parity, or as incorporating some adjustment for risk. The simplest monetary model assumes flexible prices; thus, in the absence of transportation costs and other distortions, purchasing power parity (PPP) holds, at least up to a disturbance:

$$(p - p^*)_t = e_t + \nu_t \qquad (1.3)$$

where e denotes the (log) spot domestic price of a unit of foreign exchange, and ν is a stationary disturbance. The solution for the exchange rate is then immediate:

$$e_t = (m - m^*)_t - \beta(y - y^*)_t + \alpha(i - i^*)_t - (\varepsilon - \varepsilon^*)_t - \nu_t . \qquad (1.4)$$

Finally, it is typically assumed that domestic and foreign assets are perfect substitutes, except possibly for an exogenously-varying time premium, so that the interest rate differential equals the expected depreciation rate plus a possible risk premium, ρ_t. Thus a modified form of uncovered interest parity [UIP] holds:

$$(i - i^*)_t - \rho_t = E_t(e_{t+1} - e_t) \qquad (1.5)$$

where E_t denotes the expectations operator conditional on information available at time t. The simple flexible-price monetary "fundamental" can be defined as:

$$f_t \equiv (m - m^*)_t - \beta(y - y^*)_t - (\varepsilon - \varepsilon^*)_t - \nu_t + \rho_t . \qquad (1.6)$$

Substituting in the modified UIP condition, the exchange rate equation then becomes:

$$e_t = f_t + \alpha E_t(e_{t+1} - e_t) . \qquad (1.7)$$

This expression was first derived by Mussa (1976). A very similar equation can be derived from the currency substitution model (e.g. Calvo and Rodriguez, 1977). Stockman (1980) and Lucas (1982) gave the simple monetary model more respectability by replacing the ad hoc money demand equations with money-in-the-utility-function and cash-in-advance assumptions, respectively. Early and influential empiri-

---

[1]Though Haynes and Stone (1981) object to this practice.

cal studies included Frenkel (1976, 1978), Bilson (1978), and Hodrick (1978) and other papers gathered in Frenkel and Johnson (1978).

After initial claims of success, the empirical failures of the simple monetary model became swiftly apparent. The coefficient estimates (of α and β) and empirical fit of such models were never particularly good, except perhaps under hyperinflation conditions. Also, high volatility of real exchange rates, and the highly positive correlation of nominal and real exchange rates, became obvious enough to warrant explicit treatment. Finally, the models turned out to forecast poorly out-of-sample. Some of these problems can be easily illustrated using actual data. Figure 1.1 contains time-series plots of bilateral Japanese–American data from 1960 though 1992; Figure 1.2 has the analogs for the UK vis-à-vis Germany. Each figure portrays three variables: the nominal exchange rate (graphed with a thin solid line); the real exchange rate (graphed with plus marks); and "monetary fundamentals" (graphed with small circles). The real exchange rate is the nominal exchange rate adjusted using Consumer Price Indices; monetary fundamentals are a (scaled) standard measure of flexible-price monetary fundamentals, namely the ratios of domestic and foreign money supplies over the ratio of domestic and foreign levels of real output (that is, $[(M_{\mathrm{UK}}/M_{\mathrm{G}})/(Y_{\mathrm{UK}}/Y_{\mathrm{G}})]$ for the British–German case, and analogously for the Japanese–U.S. case, where capital letters denote the levels of the variables).

The graphs show a number of features which are pervasive in bilateral data. First, both the nominal exchange rate and fundamentals appear to be non-stationary, while

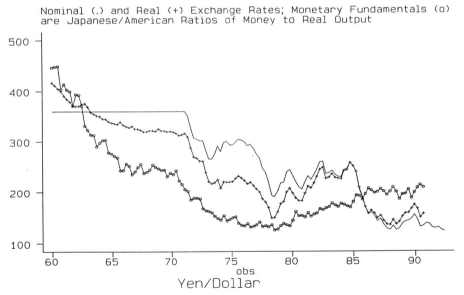

Figure 1.1.

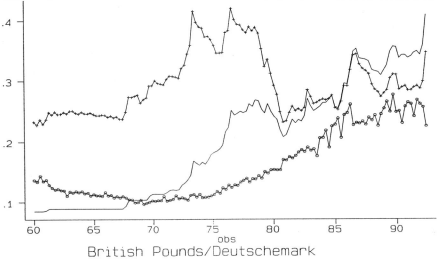

Figure 1.2.

it is less clear that the real exchange rate is (except perhaps for a trend in the real yen/dollar rate). Second is the important comparison across regimes. Nominal exchange rates were fixed explicitly at the beginning of the sample under the Bretton Woods regime, and the pound/mark rate was also stabilized during the period 1990–92, when Britain was in the Exchange Rate Mechanism of the European Monetary System. In each case (1960–72 for the yen/dollar rate in Figure 1.1, and 1960–69 and 1990–92 for the pound/mark rate in Figure 2.2), nominal exchange rate stabilization is reflected in a corresponding stabilization of the real exchange rate, but surprisingly did not require a corresponding stabilization in macroeconomic fundamentals.

A third stylized fact is that the relationship between the monetary fundamentals and the nominal exchange rate does not appear to be close in the short-run, though they may share longer-run trends. Given that both sets of data are typical for industrialized countries, the finding of poor coefficient estimates and goodness-of-fit in flexible-price monetary models is unsurprising. Finally, the correlation between nominal and real exchange rates is considerable at high frequencies, though it appears to fall at lower frequencies. This apparent contradiction to the assumption of flexible prices leads naturally to the subject of price stickiness.

1.2.1.2. Price stickiness and overshooting

An alternative to making the PPP assumption is explicitly to model goods–market prices as being sticky, at least in the short run. The classic theoretical paper was

Dornbusch's (1976b) contribution which demonstrated that in the short run, nominal exchange rates may "overshoot" their long-run levels.[2] This was followed by Frankel (1979), Mussa (1979), and Buiter and Miller (1982).[3] Price-stickiness can be easily incorporated into the empirical structural models of exchange rates.

A simple, yet strong, statement that captures the essence of the Dornbusch model is a statement of proportionality between the real exchange rate and the contemporaneous real interest differential. Start by subtracting expectations of the inflation differential from the statement of uncovered interest parity:

$$(i - i^*)_t - E_t[(p_{t+1} - p_t) - (p^*_{t+1} - p^*_t)] = E_t(e_{t+1} - e_t) - E_t[(p_{t+1} - p_t)$$
$$- (p^*_{t+1} - p^*_t)] + \rho_t$$

or

$$r_t - r^*_t = E_t(q_{t+1} - q_t) + \rho_t, \tag{1.8}$$

where: r_t and r^*_t are the ex ante expected real interest rates, defined by $r_t \equiv i_t - E_t(p_{t+1} - p_t)$, and q_t is the real exchange rate, defined as $e_t - p_t + p^*_t$. Equation (1.8) states that for both countries' assets to be willingly held, a difference in real interest rates across countries must be matched by an expectation of real depreciation.

A second assumption used is that the real exchange rate is expected to revert toward a long run equilibrium value, $\bar{q}_t$.

$$E_t(q_{t+1} - q_t) = -\theta(q_t - \bar{q}_t). \tag{1.9}$$

Combining equations and solving, we obtain a proportionality between the level of the real exchange rate and the real interest differential:[4]

$$q_t - \bar{q}_t = -(1/\theta)[r_t - r^*_t] + \rho_t. \tag{1.10}$$

Recent tests have focused on this equation per se.

Early tests of the overshooting model tended to focus on models more like Dornbusch (1976b), that is, fleshed out in a form more complete than the simple proportionality between the real exchange rate and the real interest differential. The more complete model allows for price stickiness in a standard way. Substitute a

---

[2]Forerunners included Mundell (1964), Niehans (1975) and Dornbusch (1976a).

[3]Extensions, such as full system estimation with an allowance for cross-equation constraints, included Driskill (1981), Driskill, Mark and Sheffrin (1992) and Papell (1988, 1989, 1993).

[4]Initially, attention focused on short-term real interest rates. Short-term rates are implicit in eq. (1.10) here, as is appropriate if the expected regression of the real exchange rate in eq. (1.9) is assumed to follow a first-order autoregressive process, which in turn is the rational expectation if price adjustment follows a first-order autoregressive process. An alternative approach using long-term differentials was inaugurated by Isard (1983). Assume a version of eq. (1.9) in which some long span of time, say $1/\theta$ years, is considered sufficiently long for q_t to return to equilibrium (with no position taken on the specific time path). If such an equation is combined with a version of eq. (1.8) expressed with correspondingly long-term interest rates, the result is a version of eq. (1.10) suitable for use with real interest rates of term $1/\theta$.

Phillips-curve equation where the flexible-price model assumed continuous purchasing power:

$$p_{t+1} - p_t = \mu(y - y^{LR})_t + g_t + E_t(\hat{p}_{t+1} - \hat{p}_t)$$
$$y_t - y^{LR} = \gamma + \theta' q_t + \phi' r_t$$
$$\Rightarrow p_{t+1} - p_t = \theta q_t + \phi r_t + g_t + E_t(\hat{p}_{t+1} - \hat{p}_t) \tag{1.11}$$

where: y^{LR} is the long-run level of output; g is a well-behaved shock to goods market equilibrium; and $\hat{p}_t$ is defined as the price level that would prevail at time t if prices were flexible and goods markets cleared:[5]

$$\theta(e + p^* - \hat{p})_t + \phi r_t + g_t = 0.$$

Equation (1.11) gives the system its long-run equilibrium $(\bar{q}_t)$, and its dynamics (which are correctly incorporated in θ, if investors are rational). Substituting eq. (1.10) and conventional money demand functions like eq. (1.1) yields a complete equation of exchange rate determination. This is essentially the flexible-price monetary model with the addition of extra terms representing the real interest differential, the risk premium ρ_t [if any] and variation in the long-run equilibrium exchange rate $\bar{q}_t$ [if any]. These extra terms can be measured in a variety of ways, allowing for estimation of the exchange rate equation.

At first, empirical tests of exchange rate models with price stickiness met with success, particularly for the mark/dollar rate.[6] Subsequently, however, results began to fall apart, even in-sample: e.g. Frankel (1983a,b) and Backus (1984). More importantly, the models caved in to the same Meese and Rogoff onslaught that effectively did in the flexible-price models (i.e. unsuccessful tests of out-of-sample predictive performance).

Recent research has focused on eq. (1.10) – the simple testable implication of the model relating the real exchange rate to the contemporaneous real interest differential – using increasingly sophisticated time-series econometrics. The third in the series of papers by Meese and Rogoff (1988) used the Engle–Granger test for co-integration, and failed to find evidence of such a relationship. Similarly, Campbell and Clarida (1987) found that very little of the variation in the real exchange rate could be explained by variation in the real interest differential. Many authors have noted that a possible reason for such results is the existence of a missing variable, which would enter as a determinant of either a time-varying long-run real exchange rate or a risk premium. Another possibility is weak power in the tests, since failure to find statistically significant evidence of co-integration never entitles one to claim that such a relationship does not exist.

---

[5]Obstfeld and Rogoff (1984) and Engel and Frankel (1984b) provide a detailed discussion of the $\hat{p}$ term.
[6]E.g. Frankel (1979).

A number of subsequent studies have used increasingly powerful econometric firepower (e.g. the Johansen procedure), and have also included other variables. Blundell-Wignall and Browne (1991) find evidence of co-integration between the real exchange rate and real interest differential when a measure of the cumulated current account is included; Edison and Pauls (1992) find less evidence. Throop (1992) claims strong results, including out-of-sample predictive ability, when allowing for several other variables: a lagged effect of the real interest differential, the budget deficit, the real price of oil, and a measure of the relative price of non-traded goods. Baxter (1994) finds evidence of a relationship between real exchange rates and real interest rates by looking at lower-frequency data than earlier studies.

1.2.1.3. Portfolio balance models and sterilized intervention

The portfolio-balance model is a third approach to modelling exchange rates, beyond the flexible-price and sticky-price monetary models. Tobin's portfolio-balance model was internationalized by Kouri (1976), Branson (1977), Girton and Henderson (1977) and Allen and Kenen (1980), among others. The literature was ably surveyed by Branson and Henderson (1985).

Relative to the monetary models of exchange rate determination, the key modification made by the portfolio-balance theorists is the assumption that domestic and foreign securities are not perfect substitutes. The result is that a risk premium intrudes on the uncovered interest parity condition, and supplies of bonds and other non-monetary assets intrude on the equation of exchange rate determination. The exchange rate is determined by the supply and demand for all foreign and domestic assets, not just the supply and demand for money as in the monetary approach. The resulting models are of particular use when one wants to consider the possible effects of sterilized intervention by the monetary authorities or of current account imbalances. Intervention represents a change in the supplies of assets, and thus in the portfolio balance model works to change the exchange rate accordingly: a purchase of foreign assets drives up the price of foreign exchange. In the "small-country portfolio-balance model" where international capital flows are assumed to be denominated solely in foreign currency, current account balances represent a change in asset supplies. A surplus raises the supply of foreign assets and thus reduces their price, which is an appreciation of the domestic currency. In more realistic models where the portfolio behavior of both domestic and foreign residents is relevant for market equilibrium, current account balances represent a change in asset demands, if the foreigners have a preference for their own assets. A surplus raises the net wealth-weighted worldwide demand for domestic assets, and thus again leads to an appreciation of the domestic currency.

Early empirical tests of the portfolio-balance model, such as Branson, Halttunen and Masson (1977, 1979), were not particularly successful, even in-sample. The outlook did not much improve when researchers did a more careful job of measuring asset supplies [e.g. Frankel (1983b), Backus (1984), and Golub (1989)].

This line of research took a new direction in the 1980s. Early work had modelled international asset demands as arbitrary functions of expected returns. Subsequently, portfolio-balance modelers made the assumption that investors diversified their portfolios optimally, in the manner dictated by expected utility maximization. A typical implication in these models was that the degree of substitutability between domestic and foreign assets depended inversely on the degree of risk-aversion and the exchange rate variance (or variance-covariance matrix, when there are more than two currencies in the portfolio). The relevant empirical tests are surveyed in the chapter by Lewis in this volume.[7]

As noted, one of the major motivations for considering the portfolio-balance approach is that it enables one to consider the possible effects of sterilized intervention, that is, intervention that is not allowed to affect money supplies, and thus has no effect on the fundamentals dictated by monetary exchange rate models. Several studies published in the aftermath of the 1983 Jurgensen Report by research departments of G-7 central banks on intervention surveyed the empirical literature that existed at that time [Tryon (1983), Henderson (1984), Henderson and Sampson (1983), and Henderson, Danker, Haas, Symansky, Tryon (1987)]. The early studies mostly consisted of various tests of the portfolio-balance model, using quarterly data on asset supplies. Estimated effects were generally small and statistically insignificant, if even of the correct sign. This was especially true when the quantity of intervention was calculated in the theoretically correct fashion (i.e. cumulative, combined with government deficits and any other components of the net supplies of assets denominated in the currencies in question).[8]

Several developments reinvigorated this subject of research toward the end of the 1980s: the advent of the "signaling" hypothesis, the increased availability of daily data, and the widely perceived success of concerted intervention by the G-7 in the period beginning with the 1985 Plaza Agreement to bring down the value of the dollar. Studies such as Dominguez (1990, 1992) seemed to show an effect when actual daily intervention data were used. The more recent literature has been comprehensively and ably surveyed by Edison (1993).

The current conventional wisdom (e.g. Obstfeld 1990) is that – precisely because international financial markets are well-developed, highly integrated, and subject to diversification – central bank purchases or sales of foreign exchange are unlikely to be large enough to have much of an effect on the exchange rate. The possible exception is non-sterilized intervention that affects money supplies. If the effect is contemporaneous, it is simply a variety of monetary policy. However, the effects on future money also matter. Some years ago Mussa (1981), among others, suggested the "signaling" hypothesis: sterilized intervention may be effective if it signals future changes in monetary policy. This channel requires, first, that intervention is reported

---

[7]E.g. Frankel (1982), Black and Salemi (1988), Lewis (1988), and Engel and Rodriguez (1989).
[8]E.g. Dooley and Isard (1982a, 1983), Frankel (1982) or Rogoff (1984).

to market participants, and second that they interpret it as conveying information on future monetary policy that is actually validated on average by the monetary authorities. Klein (1993) offers evidence relevant to the first proposition; Kaminsky and Lewis (1993), Klein and Rosengren (1991) and Lewis (1990, 1993) offer much more ambiguous evidence relevant to the second. Dominguez and Frankel (1993a,b) have found evidence of intervention effects through both the signaling channel and the traditional portfolio channel.[9] Catte, Galli, and Rebecchini (1994) and Eijffinger and Gruijters (1991) claim even stronger evidence of effects of daily intervention.

A persuasive, but less-noticed, train of thought within the portfolio-balance model has been pursued by Dooley and Isard (1982b, 1987, 1991), as well as Krugman (1985) and Bovenberg (1989), who view the cumulated current account deficit as an important determinant of the exchange rate because *political risk* puts a limit on the extent to which international investors wish to lend to a particular country, rather than because *exchange risk* puts a limit on the extent to which investors wish to hold assets denominated in a particular currency. Dooley, Isard and Taylor (1993) claim some supporting empirical findings.

1.2.2. Anticipated vs unanticipated effects: The "news"

Volatility of foreign exchange rates is sufficiently high to be worthy of study by applied researchers. Standard asset-pricing models rationalize volatility in terms of revisions of expectations arising out of new information, that is, in terms of "news". In this sub-section, we review recent developments in this literature.

From the time when expectations were first introduced into the asset-market approach to exchange rate determination, it has been recognized that unexpected events have a qualitatively different effect on the exchange rate from anticipated developments.[10] Specifically, the exchange rate should change discontinuously in response to new pieces of unanticipated relevant information, and not otherwise. Anticipated discrete changes are ruled out, since they would represent an unexploited profit opportunity. Only gradual changes are possible in the absence of news. Such gradual changes can occur, for example, in step with the price level or the stock of foreign assets, which typically move gradually over time.[11] (For the time being, we are ruling out speculative bubbles and the bursting thereof, which would constitute a sudden change without an exogenous cause. They are considered further below.)

---

[9]Dominguez and Frankel (1993a,b) use survey data to measure investors' expectations, as discussed in Section 5 below, and newspaper accounts to distinguish between public reports of intervention and true intervention.

[10]Black (1973) was an early introduction of rational expectations and test of anticipated vs. unanticipated effects of news reports.

[11]Obstfeld and Stockman (1985) provide a survey. For the efficient markets hypothesis to hold, gradual appreciation or depreciation must be offset by sufficient differences in interest rates, so that domestic and foreign assets are equally attractive at the margin.

1.2.2.1. Statistical innovations

Dornbusch (1978; 1980, pp. 157–163) and Frenkel (1981, pp. 686–693) suggested the term "news" to call attention to the sort of unanticipated developments that should affect the exchange rate discretely. Their empirical work used *statistical innovations* (from ARIMA processes) in interest differentials and other macro-economic variables to model expectations and thereby derive measures of news.[12] This approach tends to produce more significant effects on the exchange rate than using similar macroeconomic variables that have not been converted to statistical innovations. Dornbusch found that unexpected current account improvements result in dollar appreciations, as did Branson (1983) in a VAR study motivated by the portfolio-balance model. Dornbusch found that business cycle effects were also of the right sign, but insignificant. The money supply effects were mixed. Edwards (1982, 1983) found positive effects of innovations in the domestic/foreign money supply ratio on the price of foreign exchange, as would be predicted by most monetary models. MacDonald (1983), however, found that an unanticipated increase in the German money supply led to an appreciation of the Deutschemark, suggesting anticipations of future tightening.

To distinguish between the flexible-price and sticky-price versions of monetary models, one can look at interest rate innovations. On the one hand, Frenkel found positive effects of innovations in interest rates on the price of foreign exchange, suggesting that they capture inflation expectations, as called for in his flexible-price monetarist model. Copeland (1989, p. 225), on the other hand, found that an unanticipated increase in the German interest rate led to an appreciation of the Deutschemark, as in the overshooting model.

More recently, Eichenbaum and Evans (1993) have sought to isolate changes in the U.S. money policy that can be specifically identified as unanticipated, exogenous, or deliberate, using three alternative methods: statistical innovations in a measure of non-borrowed reserves; innovations in the federal funds rate; and deliberate policy shifts recorded from history using the minutes of the Federal Reserve's Open Market Committee. They find similar results with all three measures: monetary contractions lead to dollar appreciations. At the same time, there are also positive effects on interest rates, suggesting to Eichenbaum and Evans a rejection of the popular real business cycle model (the modern successor to the flexible-price monetary model), and support for a "liquidity effect" as in the overshooting model. The surprising aspect of their findings is that, in violation of rational expectations, there is a two-year lag before the peak effect is felt in the market. Grilli and Roubini (1993) have recently extended the Eichenbaum–Evans approach to include monetary policy in other major industrialized countries. Clarida and Galli (1994) undertake a VAR decomposition of exchange rate variation into nominal shocks and real shocks. They

---

[12] For current account balances and business cycle developments, Dornbusch used deviations from OECD forecasts.

interpret the results as consistent with the Eichenbaum–Evans finding, and therefore with the sticky-price textbook model with lags. However, it should be stressed that the Eichenbaum–Evans results have not yet been subjected to a thorough sensitivity analysis (e.g. out-of-sample forecasting tests).

Even though the Dornbusch–Frenkel approach of using fundamentals that have been converted to statistical innovations tends to produce more satisfactory results than the earlier studies, the improvement is distinctly limited. In the first place, market anticipations are not measured accurately. To use an ARIMA or VAR process as a measure of what agents expect, is to ascribe to them simultaneously not enough information, and too much. It does not ascribe to them enough information, because it leaves out all the thousands of bits of information that market investors use, beyond a few simple macroeconomic times series. It ascribes to them too much information (even under the assumption that agents are rational and thus use all available information), because it assumes that they know the parameters of the statistical process from the beginning of the sample period. A second problem with early implementations of the methodology is that they typically measure the news with *final* money supply numbers *after revisions by government agencies*, ignoring that these are not generally the same as numbers first announced, and that even first announcements generally take place days, weeks, or months after the period to which they pertain.

1.2.2.2. Announcement effects

Both of the measurement problems inherent in the statistical approach can be solved, albeit not without work. By compiling actual *announcements* of official statistics from press releases, wire service stories, or newspapers, one can measure information as it actually becomes available to the market.[13] One major advantage of such announcement data is that one can pinpoint the day, and often the time of day, when the announcement was made. One can then observe the exchange rate immediately before and after the announcement, to see the effect. The advantage of such precise timing is that one can hope to isolate the impact of one particular bit of information. Empirical results show that effects typically diffuse rapidly in a stream of other information that the researcher is not able to observe, so that statistical significance disappears when exchange rate changes are measured a day or two late, let alone over months (as in standard tests of exchange rate determination). By seeking to isolate the impact of the announcement, one might hope to explain a large fraction of the variation in the exchange rate over short intervals. However, in practice, even when the effects are highly significant statistically, the goodness-of-fit statistics are usually disappointing.

The use of data from surveys on the forecasts of market participants is a way of addressing the problem that agents form their expectations based on a far wider set of

---

[13]The analogous stock-market tests are called event studies.

data than anything the econometrician can ever hope to measure. The survey data have become a standard basis from which to measure the unanticipated component of announcements; Money Market Services, International ("MMS") provides the most popular survey. The timing of the MMS surveys is almost perfect for research purposes, since MMS and other financial services collect their surveys in order to see what market participants expect the datum in question to be, typically a couple of days before the scheduled announcement date. The use of survey data is discussed at greater length in Section 4 below.

Engel and Frankel (1984a) examined the reaction of the mark/dollar rate to announcements regarding the preceding week's M1 in the early 1980s. Positive U.S. money surprises were associated with appreciations of the dollar at the same time that they were associated with increases in interest rates, leading the authors to conclude that: (1) during this period the Federal Reserve was expected to correct any deviations of the money supply from its target path; and (2) expectations of monetary contraction tend to raise real interest rates and cause the currency to appreciate, as in the Dornbusch overshooting model. Cornell (1982), Frankel and Hardouvelis (1985), and Tandon and Urich (1987) found the same patterns in other exchange rates: U.S. money surprises are followed by significant changes in the U.S. interest rate that are negatively correlated with the price of foreign exchange.

Ito and Roley (1987) looked at the reactions in the yen/dollar rate both to macroeconomic announcements in the United States and to those in Japan. They found that U.S. money announcements had the greatest effect.

The money announcements lost much of their impact later in the 1980s, after the Fed began to put less emphasis on its M1 targets. A number of authors have found strong announcement effects for other variables, however. Hardouvelis (1988) finds significant dollar appreciations associated with news of increases in the trade balance, decreases in inflation, and improvements in the business cycle.[14] A general pattern throughout is that the reaction in the price of foreign exchange is in the opposite direction as the reaction in interest rates, which tends to support the view that these are changes in real interest rates, and that they work on the exchange rate in the manner of the Dornbusch overshooting model. Beck (1993) finds that government announcements of unexpectedly large budget deficits cause the dollar to appreciate against foreign currencies, and argues that this is evidence against debt neutrality, and in favor of the Dornbusch overshooting model.

1.3. Forecast analysis

Fitting exchange rates to contemporary observable variables, in-sample, is one thing. Forecasting out of sample is quite another, as many applied researchers have found.

---

[14]Hogan, Melvin, and Roberts (1991) find the same trade balance effect.

1.3.1. Forecasting with fundamentals

In a now-classic study, Meese and Rogoff (1983a) compared the out-of-sample forecast precision of a variety of different exchange rate models. Using monthly data for three bilateral dollar exchange rates (as well as an effective dollar exchange rate), Meese and Rogoff compared forecasting performance by both structural and non-structural exchange rate models, as well as by contemporaneous spot and forward rates. The non-structural models included both univariate models and vector-autoregressions. The structural models included variants of both flexible- and sticky-price monetary models. It had been widely recognized [e.g. Meese and Singleton (1982)] that exchange rates could in some sense be modelled well by an autoregression with one unit root. But Meese and Rogoff (1983a,b) showed the important result that a simple martingale process forecasts as well as more complex structural models – up to a year in advance – *even providing to the structural models ex post information on future fundamentals such as money and output.* Meese and Rogoff (1983a) found these results using a variety of different estimation techniques. They corroborated their results in Meese and Rogoff (1983b) using grid-search techniques in place of actual estimation, a procedure that is immune to the usual endemic estimation problems such as simultaneity bias. Their work permanently shifted the focus of empirical exchange rate work from in-sample fitting to prediction analysis.

Some authors have pursued more sophisticated econometric estimation techniques in attempts to overturn such results. For instance, Meese and Rose (1991) used a variety of non-linear and non-parametric techniques in the context of structural exchange rate models. They found little evidence of either "time-deformation" or significant non-linearities in the functional forms linking exchange rates to fundamentals which could explain the poor performance of linear exchange rate models.

Not all performance tests on structural exchange rate models have come out completely negative. Woo (1985) estimated a flexible-price version of the monetary model for the dollar/Deutschemark and found that the model worked well in the sense that maximum likelihood estimation lead to plausible and stable parameter estimates which did not reject tests of cross-equation restrictions and which out-forecast a random walk model a year ahead. The use of a lagged endogenous variable was crucial; Woo justifies it by appealing to slow adjustment of money demand. Similarly, Somanath (1986) also found that a monetary model with a lagged endogenous variable forecasts better than either a monetary model by itself or the lagged endogenous variable by itself (i.e. better than the random walk). Finn (1986), and MacDonald and Taylor (1993a, 1994) also claimed some predictive power for the monetary model. Schinasi and Swamy (1989) found that the sticky-price monetary model outperforms the random walk when allowance is made for both a lagged endogenous variable and time-varying coefficients. Related results are reported in Wolff (1987).

A number of authors have found that structural models appear to dominate the random walk's forecasting ability at relatively long prediction horizons, a result consistent with the visual impression of common trends in exchange rates and fundamentals given by Figures 1.1 and 1.2. They include Meese and Rogoff (1983b); Mark (1994); Chinn (1991); and Chinn and Meese (1992). However, the Meese and Rogoff analysis at short horizons has never been convincingly overturned or explained. It continues to exert a pessimistic effect on the field of empirical exchange rate modelling in particular and international finance in general.

1.3.2. Forecasting without fundamentals

The triumph at short and medium horizons of the naive random-walk "model" of exchange rates (if only by default) over fundamental-based models, first discovered by Meese and Rogoff, lead to a burst of research on the univariate characteristics of nominal exchange rates. It still remains distressing that a model as simplistic as a martingale appears to perform empirically as well as extremely sophisticated alternatives, which sometimes involve complicated estimation strategies.

Engel and Hamilton (1990) use a two-state Markov switching univariate model, and find that the movements of three bilateral American dollar rates are characterized by long swings (although the exchange markets seem not to realize this in the sense that the model does not help to explain deviations from uncovered interest parity). They also find that the forecasts of this model are somewhat better than those of the pure random walk. However, Engel (1992) analyzes eighteen exchange rates, including eleven non-dollar rates, and finds that the Markov-switching models does not have superior forecast precision to that of a simple random walk, even though it performs better inside the sample. This has become a standard finding; a number of authors have found models which perform well in-sample (e.g. compared with a simple martingale) but which break down in out-of-sample prediction analysis. For instance, Diebold and Nason (1990) use a general non-parametric estimator on a number of different exchange rates. They find that univariate models fit the data much better in-sample with their estimator than, e.g. a simple random walk, but that the non-parametric estimator does not produce forecasts superior to those of a random walk.[15]

Baillie and Bollerslev (1989) find co-integration in a set of American dollar exchange rates; that is, the dollar/yen exchange appears to be co-integrated with e.g. the dollar/DM rate. This finding is quite plausible (and not especially striking) in the context of standard structural exchange rate models, since all bilateral dollar exchange rates can be expected to react similarly to American-specific shocks, for example. However, Diebold, Gardeazabal and Yilmaz (1994) point out that co-integration of bilateral rates implies that, *univariate* dollar/yen exchange rate

---

[15]Small-sample problems – learning and the "peso problem" – are relevant here; e.g. one might explain Engel and Hamilton in this vein. Other references include Lewis (1989).

forecasts, for example, should be out-performed by incorporating information from the dollar/pound rate (since co-integration implies predictability from the co-integrating relationship). It is therefore all the more striking that Diebold et al. find no evidence of predictability and co-integration, using the data set of Baillie and Bollerslev. They claim that there is little evidence of common shocks to the movements in dollar exchange rates.

1.4. Summary

Studies such as Backus (1984), Meese and Rogoff (1983a,b, 1988) and Campbell and Clarida (1987) are typical of the empirical literature that seeks to explain or forecast the monthly or quarterly exchange rate with traditional observable macroeconomic fundamentals, whether based on the monetary or portfolio-balance models. The dispiriting conclusion is that relatively little explanatory power is found, and the models contain little forecasting ability compared to very simple alternatives. Existing structural models have little in their favor beyond theoretical coherence. Positive results, when they are found, are often either fragile, or unconvincing in that they rely on implausible theoretical or empirical models. For these reasons, we, like much of the profession, are doubtful of the value of further time-series modelling of exchange rates at high or medium frequencies using macroeconomic models.

2. Evidence from across fixed and floating regimes

It is widely known that real and nominal exchange rates are highly correlated, and that the shocks common to both are highly persistent [e.g. Mark (1990)]. These correlations are visible in Figures 1.1 and 1.2. To many, the fact that real exchange rate variability went up when nominal variability did after 1973 (also visible in the Figures), suggests that nominal prices are sticky and that monetary disturbances therefore cause both nominal and real exchange rate changes, as in the Dornbusch model. Others, such as Stockman (1987, 1988), argue that real exchange rate variability is caused by shifts to tastes and technology, and would have gone up after 1973 regardless of the exchange rate regime, which is endogenously chosen in any case. (Real exchange rate variability is surveyed in the chapter of this volume by Froot and Rogoff; regime choice is surveyed by Garber and Svensson.) A small recent literature has considered evidence across exchange rate regimes. We now survey this work.

The evidence discussed in Section 1 above shows that it is difficult to model exchange rate movements in many respects. Nevertheless, exchange rates have one striking empirical feature with which any plausible theory must be consistent: systematically differing volatility. In particular, exchange rates that are officially stabilized show not only low nominal variability, which one would expect virtually by definition, but low real variability as well, compared to those that are allowed to float more or less freely. In the past decade, a number of empirical papers have characterized or exploited these and other regime-specific differences in volatility.

Mussa (1986, 1990) convincingly demonstrated that nominal and real exchange rate volatility moved closely together, both being substantially lower during regimes of fixed rates. Persuasive examples include the Canadian experiment with floating in the 1950s, and changes in Ireland's exchange rate regime from a pound to a Deutschemark peg. Eichengreen (1988) provides similar evidence from the interwar period. Mussa reasoned that nominal exchange rate regime-specific differences in real exchange rate volatility could be caused for a variety of reasons, including bubbles, sticky prices, systematically varying macroeconomic shocks, or regime-specific differences in policy behavior.

The subsequent literature has corroborated Mussa's findings regarding real exchange rate volatility, and examined differences in macroeconomic behavior to discover the source of the finding. For instance, Baxter and Stockman (1989) looked at the behavior of a variety of macroeconomic variables across different types of exchange rate regimes, arguing, as had Mussa, that most theories of the open economy imply economic behavior which varies systematically with the nominal exchange rate regime. Baxter and Stockman examined a number of real macro-economic variables (including consumption, output, and trade flows, de-trended in two ways) over forty industrialized and developing countries. While non-theoretical in nature, their results are striking and intuitive. The only systematic regime-specific pattern in the data is higher volatility of the real exchange rate in regimes of floating rates. By way of contrast, the volatility of, for example, output and consumption does not appear to vary systematically with the exchange rate regime.

A similar tactic has been used by Flood and Rose (1993) to study monetary models of exchange rate determination (with both flexible and sticky prices). They rewrite the structural form of the simple monetary model with flexible prices as

$$e_t - \alpha(i - i^*)_t \approx (m - m^*)_t - \beta(y - y^*)_t - (\varepsilon - \varepsilon^*)_t, \qquad (1.4')$$

and note that both the left- and the right-hand side variables can be measured or estimated. Their analysis hinges on the fact that the volatility of the left-hand side variable during a regime of floating is between three and nine times as volatile as during a fixed exchange rate regime. However, the right-hand side has approximately comparable volatility in fixed and flexible exchange rate regimes. (Both facts are consistent with Figures 1.1 through 1.2.) The more general point is that the volatility of macroeconomic variables such as money, output, and prices (appropriately parameterized) does not vary much across exchange rate regimes, certainly not enough to rationalize the large cross-regime differences in exchange rate volatility. Since few macroeconomic variables have regime-specific volatility, they interpret this to mean that macroeconomic variables cannot be very important determinants of exchange rate volatility. This point transcends the narrow confines of the flexible-price monetary model, since different macroeconomic theories of exchange rate determination (e.g. models with sticky prices) merely change the right-hand side of eq. (1.4′) from one set of macroeconomic components to another. There appears to be a growing general consensus for this conclusion; it is the rule rather than the exception that large movements in exchange rates occur in the absence of plausible or detectable macroeconomic events.[16]

The strength of this work is that it characterizes a wide range of currencies and exchange arrangements, and does not rely on sensitive statistical techniques. The evidence convincingly shows that the nominal exchange rate regime is systematically and substantially associated with differences in real exchange rate volatility. This evidence is inconsistent with a large class of models which predict "nominal exchange rate neutrality". This insight is deceptively simple, yet empirically potent. It is quite general, since many theories of the open economy imply that the behavior of such variables as, e.g. money, inflation, and output vary with the exchange rate regime. Differences in economic behavior are especially plausible since the exchange rate regime is chosen by the monetary authorities deliberately.

Instead of looking across regimes of fixed and floating exchange rate regimes, one can also look across regimes of tranquility and turbulence. Hyperinflations represent one of the most interesting types of economic turbulence from the viewpoint of an exchange rate analyst. Monetary theories of exchange rates work substantially better in hyperinflations than in periods of low inflation, in that they can explain the trend in the nominal exchange rate. The classic work is by Frenkel (1976, 1980). The impression that variation in the real exchange rate is lower in hyperinflations than in normal times is not correct, however.[17]

To sum up, there are substantial differences in nominal and real exchange rate behavior across exchange rate regimes which do not appear in observable macro-economic variables. There are two possible reasons for this. The first is that *unobservable* macroeconomic shocks affect the exchange rate. The second is that bubbles, defined as exchange rate movements that are unrelated to fundamentals, are the cause of regime-varying exchange rate volatility.

3. Speculative bubbles

Sections 1 and 2 suggest that the case for macroeconomic determinants of exchange rates is in a sorry state. With the exception of some significance in tests of statistical

---

[16]In a similar vein, Rose (1993) finds that the width of the officially announced band, where one exists, has a significant effect on exchange rate volatility, even in the absence of a change in the variability of macroeconomic fundamentals.

[17]See, e.g. Davutyan and Pippenger (1985) and Krugman (1978).

innovations and announcements at very short horizons, and some hazy predictive power at long horizons, there is little support for the standard macroeconomic models. Negative findings such as Meese and Rogoff (1983a,b), Campbell and Clarida (1987), and Flood and Rose (1993) suggest more than a failure of specific models of exchange rate determination or typical econometric difficulties. Instead, such results indicate that no model based on such standard fundamentals like money supplies, real income, interest rates, inflation rates and current account balances will ever succeed in explaining or predicting a high percentage of the variation in the exchange rate, at least at short- or medium-term frequencies.

As noted, two broad possibilities remain. The "equilibrium theory" of exchange rates asserts that real exchange rate movements have their roots in real fundamental determinants such as productivity shocks and changes in tastes, even if these factors are unobservable to the econometrician. The alternative theory is that speculative bubbles exist which affect nominal and real exchange rates. A number of pieces of evidence point us away from the equilibrium theory.

First, the observed pattern of co-movement of exchange rates and interest rates, documented in Section 1, contradicts the equilibrium view.[18] Second, direct evidence on goods prices such as Engel (1993), covered in the chapter by Froot and Rogoff, suggests price stickiness. Third, and most convincingly, the cross-regime evidence reviewed in Section 2 shows little support for the conclusion that exchange rate variability is caused by shocks to tastes and technology. No macroeconomic variable other than the exchange rate demonstrates regime-varying volatility; there is little indirect confirmation of regime-varying unobservable shocks from other parts of the economy.

The alternative is the possibility of speculative bubbles, i.e. exchange rate movements that are not based in fundamentals, but rather are based in self-confirming expectations. We now turn to this possibility.

In the theoretical literature, a rational speculative bubble is simply the additional indeterminate term that appears in the solution to a differential or difference equation representing a rational-expectations equilibrium to eq. (1.7). These bubbles arise both in monetary models [e.g. Mussa (1976) or Dornbusch (1976b)] and portfolio-balance models [e.g. Rodriguez (1980)], although Obstfeld and Rogoff (1983) have sought to rule out bubbles on a priori grounds.

If we could be confident of the fundamentals part of the equation, we could test for the presence of the additional bubble term in (1.7). Flood and Garber (1980) introduced a test for a deterministic speculative bubble, that is, one that never bursts once it gets started. Rational speculative bubbles were made stochastic by Blanchard (1979) and Dornbusch (1982). Several researchers have sought to introduce tests for stochastic bubbles in the foreign exchange market, to see if variability is higher than

---

[18]E.g. Engel and Frankel (1984a), Hardouvelis (1988), and Eichenbaum and Evans (1993), Baxter (1984), and Clarida and Galli (1994).

can be explained by macroeconomic fundamentals. These tests are closely related to so-called volatility tests, and are surveyed in Frankel and Meese (1987). They have in common that their usefulness is sharply limited by the prerequisite that one already knows how to model fundamentals.

Meese (1986) uses a conventional monetary approach to define fundamentals and a Hausman-style specification test to test for bubbles; he finds some evidence of exchange rate bubbles.[19] Evans (1986) has produced evidence of bubbles in the pound/dollar exchange rate in the early 1980s, based upon a non-parametric test for systematic deviations from uncovered interest parity. Evans' work is distinguished by its careful treatment of the issue of potential data mining, which is accounted for by simulation analysis of different aspects of his test procedure. However, Flood and Hodrick (1990) argue that there is an observational equivalence between expectations of process-switching and bubbles. This problem, in addition to the fact that any test for bubbles is based upon a posited model of fundamentals (an especially important problem in the exchange rate context, given the serious specification difficulties which plague structural exchange rate models) lead Flood and Hodrick to contend that there is little convincing evidence of bubbles in exchange rates.

It is unfortunate but true that these tests cannot help us choose between the bubble hypothesis and the hypothesis of unknown or unobservable fundamentals as maintained by the equilibrium theorists. Nevertheless, the fact that exchange rate variation cannot be explained with any existing model of fundamentals is certainly intuitively consistent with the existence of bubbles, especially when coupled with the cross-regime evidence.

However, if one is to conclude that speculative bubbles are important in exchange rate determination, this still leaves us with a rather unsatisfying conclusion. Rational speculative bubbles are completely indeterminate. It would be nice if economists could say something more specific about what gets bubbles started or what causes them to burst, and perhaps also why large bubbles appear to exist in floating rather than fixed exchange rate regimes. This leads us to the subject of the microstructure of the foreign exchange market, and the possibility of endogenous speculative bubbles.

4. Evidence on the micro-structure of the foreign exchange market

To repeat a central fact of life, there is remarkably little evidence that macroeconomic variables have consistent strong effects on floating exchange rates, except during extraordinary circumstances such as hyperinflations. Such negative findings have led the profession to a certain degree of pessimism vis-à-vis exchange rate research.

We are somewhat more optimistic about the course of future research in international finance, in part because of the prospect of new developments that

---

[19]A related test, in the context of the German hyperinflation, is Casella (1989).

analyze the market for foreign exchange primarily from a microeconomic perspective. This "market microstructure" approach represents a radical departure from the traditional modelling strategy of treating foreign exchange rates as a macroeconomic relative price. The microeconomic approach to the foreign exchanges is at least potentially consistent with well-known regularities in the data. For example, the volume of transactions in foreign exchange markets is very large. The April 1992 surveys conducted by the Federal Reserve, Bank of England and Bank of Japan found that daily trading totaled $623 billion in New York, London and Tokyo combined, up from $430 billion a day in April 1989. (The global total, including other locations as well, is considerably higher.) It is difficult to rationalize the well-known high gross (but low net) volume of trading on foreign exchange markets without some microeconomic modelling, particularly attention to heterogeneity in the forecasts of market participants. It is far too early to say whether this research agenda will be successful; but the beginnings look promising.

4.1. The formation of expectations

Expectations of future exchange rate changes are a key determinant of asset demands, and therefore of the current exchange rate. The expectations variable is relatively straightforward in the conventional monetary models: in theoretical terms it is determined by the rational expectations assumption, while in empirical terms it is typically measured by the forward discount or interest differential. The standard empirical implementation of rational expectations methodology infers ex ante expectations of investors from ex post changes in the exchange rate. (This is a particularly attractive way to measure investors' forecasts in the portfolio-balance model, where expectations cannot be measured from the forward market because of a possible exchange risk premium.) However, we may wish to consider a possible failure of the rational expectations methodology, for example due to learning, or peso problems arising from infrequent sudden changes in the exchange rate, as are likely in models like those with speculative bubbles. In this case, we need direct measures of expectations.

4.1.1. Are expectations stabilizing or destabilizing? Survey data

One of the things we would like to know about expectations is whether they are stabilizing or destabilizing. Expectations can be described as stabilizing when the effect of an appreciation today – relative to some long-run path or mean – is to induce market participants to forecast depreciation in the future. If investors act on such expectations, they will seek to sell the currency, thereby dampening the original appreciation. This is the stabilizing speculation that Friedman (1953) argued would thrive under floating rates. Expectations can be described as destabilizing, on the other hand, when the effect of an appreciation is to induce market participants to forecast more appreciation in the future. If investors act on such expectations, they will seek to buy the currency, thereby exaggerating the original appreciation. This "bandwagon behavior" can create speculative bubbles. The question then becomes whether expectations are in fact formed in a stabilizing or destabilizing manner. (This question is independent of the perennial question of whether expectations are rational, covered in Lewis's chapter.)

The forward rate cannot be used to measure expectations if one does not feel able a priori to rule out the importance of risk. A new data source has been used to shed light on such questions: the results of surveys of market participants conducted by financial services firms.[20] Much of the new literature on survey data has been surveyed by Takagi (1991).

Frankel and Froot (1987a) found that investors tended to react to current appreciations by expecting future depreciations, consistent with either regressive expectations, adaptive expectations, or distributed-lag expectations, at horizons of one year, six months, or three months. In other words, expectations appeared to be stabilizing.[21] Subsequent studies, however, indicated that investors at shorter horizons of one week to one month tend to extrapolate recent trends: Frankel and Froot (1987b, 1990a), Froot and Ito (1989) and Ito (1994). Expectations at these short horizons appear destabilizing. Since most trading in the foreign exchange market is known to consist of taking and unwinding positions at horizons measured in hours rather than months or years, these findings have potentially serious implications.

Most of the survey services that furnish data for these tests are conducted at either the short horizons or the long horizons, but not both. This raises the possibility that different types of market participants form expectations in different ways, and that some are more heavily represented at the short horizons (call them speculators) and others at the long horizons (call them investors). The distinction between speculators and investors is one of several motivations for departing from the assumption that all participants share the same expectations, which until recently was universally made in the field, and to focus on heterogeneity.

---

[20]These data have also been used for other purposes. One purpose is testing rational expectations: Dominguez (1986); MacDonald (1990); Liu and Maddala (1992); Chinn and Frankel (1994). Another purpose is studying the behavior of the risk premium: Froot and Frankel (1989); MacDonald and Torrance (1988b, 1990); Cavaglia, Nieuwland, Verschoor, and Wolff (1993); Cavaglia, Verschoor, and Wolff (1993a); Frankel and Chinn (1993). The earlier part of this literature has been surveyed by Froot and Thaler (1990) and Hodrick (1988). The survey data have also been used in studies of announcement effects and foreign exchange intervention, discussed in Sections 1.2.2.2 and 1.2.1.3 of this paper, respectively.
[21]Also Cavaglia, Verschoor and Wolff (1993b).

4.1.2. Heterogeneous expectations

Some of these articles acknowledge that survey respondents exhibit diverse opinions, even though a measure of central tendency (usually the median) is typically used to measure "the" expectation. More recent papers have explicitly pursued the heterogeneity of expectations, in two ways. One approach is to look for different patterns of expectation formation among different classes of actors. The other approach looks for a relationship between the dispersion of opinion and other microstructure variables of interest, such as the volume of trade in the market.

Ito (1990) and MacDonald (1992) have access to disaggregated data on survey responses. Ito examines systematic differences in the behavior of Japanese respondents, distinguished by function such as banker, trader, corporate economist, etc. He finds evidence of "wishful thinking": Japanese exporters forecast a depreciation of the yen, and importers an appreciation. MacDonald looks at differences in the behavior of corporate respondents residing in seven major countries. He finds more evidence of extrapolative behavior among German respondents than in other countries.

The brute fact of expectations heterogeneity, regardless of the cause, has implications for the foreign exchange market. A high dispersion of expectations should lead to a high volume of trade. Indeed, in the absence of some sort of heterogeneity, it is hard to see why investors trade at all. Frankel and Froot (1990b) look at dispersion in the survey data, and find that it is related to a measure of the volume of trade as well as to market volatility.

4.1.3. Technical analysis

Frankel and Froot (1986, 1990a,b) reported that "technical analysis" became increasingly prevalent in the exchange rate forecasting business during the first half of the 1980s. Similarly, Taylor and Allen (1992) conducted a questionnaire survey on the use of technical analysis in the London foreign exchange in 1988. At least 90 percent of respondents reported placing some weight on technical analysis, with the proportion rising steadily with the shortness of the horizon. These short-horizon technical analysts bear a striking resemblance to the infamous destabilizing speculators of classical financial mythology.

Schulmeister (1987) offered a description of the various rules of technical analysis that are in widest use, and calculated that all of the rules would have made money over the period 1973–86. Goodman (1979) also found that the forecasts of technical analysis performed relatively well as did Levich and Thomas (1993), although Blake, Beenstock, and Brasse (1986) found the reverse.

Most of the rules of technical analysis seem to fit into the category of destabilizing behavior, such as the "momentum" models that call for buying when the current price exceeds the price that held, for example, five days ago. The rules are clearly more complicated than simple extrapolation, however, and in some cases may not be destabilizing at all.[22] De Grauwe and Decupere (1992) find significant evidence of psychological barriers at round numbers in the yen/dollar market: exchange rates tend to resist movements towards numbers such as 130 or 140 yen to the dollar, but to accelerate away from them once the barriers have been crossed. Garber and Spencer (1994) argue that the use of dynamic hedging programs by portfolio managers has been destabilizing in recent episodes.

Krugman and Miller (1993) show that the existence of stop-loss orders can induce excess volatility in the sense that it increases the instantaneous variance of the exchange rate, but the declaration of a target zone by the monetary authority can eliminate this effect. The use of stop-loss orders, as well as the specific trigger points at which they are activated, are taken as exogenous in the text of the paper. But the Krugman–Miller appendix derives stop-loss behavior in a model in which portfolio-managers are supervised under a "drawdown" rule: when the value of a manager's portfolio sinks by a certain proportion relative to its previous high, the firm takes away the funds, which in effect makes the manager very risk-averse to future losses which near that proportion. Work like this may allow for much more progress in the future.

4.1.4. Models of chartists, fundamentalists and noise traders

A number of researchers have deviated from the rational expectations paradigm to sketch what might be called theories of endogenous speculative bubbles. They typically start from the proposition that market participants' forecasts are drawn from competing views, including for example both technical analysis and economic fundamentals. From there they attempt to build models of exchange rate determination.

Relevant studies include Goodhart (1988), Frankel and Froot (1986, 1990a), Cutler, Poterba and Summers (1991), De Long, Shleifer, Summers and Waldmann (1990) and Goldberg and Frydman (1993a,b).[23] In such models, changes in the weights assigned by the market to the competing models can themselves alter asset demands and give rise to changes in the exchange rate. DeGrauwe and Dewachter (1990) show that the interaction of chartists and fundamentalists can give rise to an exchange rate process characterized by chaos: a process that is essentially unpredictable, despite the fact that the underlying model is deterministic.

This area of research is quite small. However, it is potentially important, since it is the part of the market microstructure work that is concerned with some of the most

---

[22]Allen and Taylor (1989).
[23]The implications of a mixture of noise traders and regressive expectations for the question of systematic differences in rates of return on currencies are considered in Evans and Lewis (1992).

central issues of international finance, such as excess volatility and exchange rate determination. We hope for further developments.

4.2. Trading

The tremendous level and growth in the volume of trading, particularly in the New York, London and Tokyo foreign exchange markets, has been documented in statistics collected by central banks every three years. An important question is: Who does all this trading? Typically, a high fraction of these transactions are reported to take place among banks; a relatively small percent involve importers, exporters or other non-financial companies.[24] Traders at most banks take large positions for a few hours, but limit their overnight and weekend positions sharply, or close them out altogether.[25] Recently, new players such as hedge funds and other institutional investors have become more important.[26] Much of the work on market microstructure has analyzed the process and characteristics of trading on foreign exchange markets; we now survey that literature.

4.2.1. The nature of trading and volatility

The market micro-structure literature has been successful in uncovering a number of trading regularities in the data. For instance there is evidence of "time deformation".

4.2.1.1. Time-varying volatility, trading volume, and location
Many econometricians have observed that exchange rate volatilities change over time. The ARCH model (AutoRegressive Conditional Heteroskedasticity) has become a very popular way of addressing time-varying variances. Bollerslev, Chou and Kroner (1992) offer a general survey. The pattern of time-varying variances matters for the *statistical properties* of econometric tests of all sorts of propositions, such as those covered in this survey. The pattern matters particularly when *investor behavior* is thought to depend on perceived uncertainty, as in the literature on time-varying risk premiums surveyed by Frankel (1988) and the chapter by Lewis. Here we consider only the evidence relevant to microstructure.

Goodhart and Giugale (1993) and Wasserfallen and Zimmerman (1985) have observed systematic patterns to intra-day volatility. They find that volatility is smaller during intervals when trading volume is known to be smaller, such as over the weekend and over the lunch hour, and is especially large during the first hour of

---

[24]E.g. Frankel and Froot (1990b).

[25]Fieleke (1981).

[26]Hedge funds manage portfolios for a small number of relatively large individual investors. They deal heavily in derivatives, but the implication of the name is the reverse of the truth: they speculate rather than hedge. On the topic of the new institutional investors, see International Monetary Fund (1993).

Monday trading for each currency in its own market (i.e. in the domestic country), even when markets in other time zones have opened earlier. Such findings suggest either that residents have a comparative advantage at processing news regarding their own currencies, or else that trading is in some sense largely unrelated to news, perhaps even that trading activity per se generates volatility.

Engle, Ito and Lin (1990, 1992) examine intra-day yen/dollar volatility in four markets: Europe, New York, Pacific and Tokyo. They find that upswings in volatility in one market are passed on as higher volatility to the next market, an ARCH pattern that they describe by analogy with a global meteor shower and interpret as evidence of information processing. Baillie and Bollerslev (1991) also find evidence of the meteor shower in hourly data on four exchange rates. In each case they also find evidence of increased volatility occurring around the opening and closing of each of the three major world markets, London, New York and Tokyo. Harvey and Huang (1992) find in the Chicago and London futures markets that volatility is sharply higher on Friday openings.

Goodhart and Demos (1990) seek to infer trading volume from quote frequency on the Reuters screen, and note that activity declines just before the weekend. Such studies often find a correlation of intra-day patterns in volatility and trading activity (e.g. high at the opening and closings of markets). The question becomes whether high volume and volatility reflect the efficient processing of information regarding fundamentals, or something else (such as noise trading). Batten and Bhar (1993) explore the observed statistical relationship between trading volume and price changes, in yen futures markets in three locations. They find, contrary to their expectations, that the relationship does not depend on the size of the market, and they suspect an asymmetry in the role of information flows emanating from the U.S. and Japan.

Jorion (1994) seeks to test one important microstructure theory. The theory says that the correlation between trading volume and volatility should be positive when the source of trading volume is disagreement (heterogeneity of beliefs), but the correlation should be negative when volume is determined by the number of traders, due to averaging over larger numbers (liquidity) should reduce variability. He finds support for the theory, in that the variance is observed to depend negatively on a time trend intended to reflect the growing number of traders, and otherwise to depend positively on volume. He uses options prices to obtain an implicit measure of the anticipated component of the variance, rather than the usual ARCH approach.

4.2.1.2. The bid–ask spread, volatility and volume

Jorion also looks at the bid–ask spread, the standard measure of transactions costs. He confirms earlier findings (Glassman, 1987 and Bessembinder, 1993) that the spread widens before weekends and holidays, supporting the liquidity effect. He also confirms earlier findings that the bid–ask spread depends positively on the variance, but negatively on volume. He and Wei (1994) use the option-implied volatility for this purpose. Glassman (1987), Boothe (1988), Bollerslev and Domowitz (1993), Bollerslev and Melvin (1994), and Lee (1994), use GARCH models of the variance in their tests of the effect on the bid–ask spread.

The presumption here is that information is processed efficiently. At a time when beliefs are particularly heterogenous and therefore trading volume is particularly high, the presumption is that the market is responding to a rapid generation of information.

Hsieh and Kleidon (1994) cast some doubt on the proposition that information is processed efficiently. Their point of departure is a model by Admati and Pfleiderer. It features a crucial distinction between well-informed traders and liquidity traders. Some of the liquidity traders have some discretion as to when they trade, and so seek to trade at a time when high volume drives down the cost of transaction. (This is the liquidity effect on the bid–ask spread.) Hsieh and Kleidon confirm the correlation of volume and volatility that others have found and that the Admati–Pfleiderer model is designed to explain: there is a bunching of volume and volatility at both the open and the close in the foreign exchange market.

A deeper look uncovers serious problems, however. First, the bid–ask spread is observed to go *up*, not down, at the open and close, contradicting the notion that liquidity traders are deliberately bunching at these times to save on transactions costs. Second, at the close in London, when volume and volatility are high in that market, *there is no detectible simultaneous effect in the open New York market.* This seems to contradict existing models of asymmetric information, which presuppose a common knowledge of economic structure despite the existence of idiosyncratic information. If volatility is high in London because information relevant to the pound/dollar rate is coming out, then why shouldn't the same effect show up in the pound/dollar rate in the New York market?

Hsieh and Kleidon think that the answer lies in models where information is aggregated imperfectly and inventories are important. They take at their word traders who explain that at morning open, they need to get a "feel" for the market by trading, thus explaining the combination of high trading volume, high volatility and high spreads in the morning. Towards evening close, traders are anxious to unload excess inventories, explaining the reappearance of the heightened volume, volatility and spreads.

4.2.2. The behavior of market-makers

In equity markets, research into microstructure has explored such questions as whether the existence and behavior of "market-makers" responsible for market clearing makes a difference. Several researchers have begun to extend this exploration of microstructure to the foreign exchange market.

The foreign exchange market is a "decentralized, quote-driven dealership market" [Lyons (1993)]. In other words, it is a phone-and-computer network over which dealers (both traders at banks, who can take open positions, and brokers who do not)1 quote bid and offer prices, and then consummate transactions. These communications are purely bilateral, so that the prices and quantities traded are not transparent as they are in other financial markets.

Lyons (1991) is a first cut at a microstructural perspective. It models customer order flow as the source of information asymmetry among dealers. The configuration of the market can lead to an externality in the processing of information. To the extent that dealers have market power and are risk averse, their trading behavior will not result in prices that reveal all information fully. The main result is that the greater the market power and risk-aversion of dealers, the less revealing are prices.

Lyons (1993) investigates these issues using a data set on five days in the life of a single market-maker, containing the time-stamped transaction prices and quantities in the New York mark/dollar market.[27] Earlier high-frequency data, e.g. Goodhart's 13 weeks of "indicative quotes" obtained from the Reuters screen, did not include actual order flow or transaction prices.[28] Lyons finds evidence of two different channels whereby trading volume generates movements in the bid and offer rates quoted by individual dealers: the inventory-control channel; and the information channel. Inventory costs create incentives for market-makers to change prices so as to control their positions. However, if some traders have better information than others, it is also rational for market-makers to adjust their own beliefs, and price quotes, in response to order flow.

Lyons (1994) uses the same data set to test an additional effect on the transactions price: the effect of the quantity traded. He seeks to shed light on two competing theories of why trading volume is sometimes very high. What he calls the "event uncertainty" view is that high trading volume indicates that information is being processed rapidly. What he calls the "Hot Potato" theory is that high trading volume indicates that little information is being processed. Rather, "liquidity-trader" customers are placing orders with their traders, who then unload their over-extended positions on other traders, who continue to pass the exposure like a hot potato (consistent with the Admati–Pfleiderer model of discretionary liquidity traders tested

---

[27]More specifically, the data set consists of time-stamped inter-dealer quotes and trades, the market-maker's indirect (brokered) trades, and the time-stamped prices and quantities for transactions mediated by a broker.

[28]Goodhart and Figliuoli (1991). Goodhart, Ito and Payne (1994) suggest that a good deal of skepticism is warranted regarding such "indicative quotes", i.e. the bid and ask quotes that are posted to all potential customers. Traders usually set better prices when they transact with each other. Goodhart, Ito and Payne use data from a new trading system, the Reuters 2000-2, to compare actual transactions prices *via this new electronic broker* with the indicative quotes ("FXFX"). They find that movements in the two are very close, so that for some purposes either series can be used. But the behavior of the margin between the highest bid price and the lowest ask price, known in the UK as the "touch", in the Reuters 2000-2 data is quite different from the behavior of the spread between the FXFX bid and ask quotes. In the first case the two prices are both firm and they are normally input by different banks; in the second the quotes are both indicative and they are always from the same bank. In other words, one should not mistake the publicly posted bid and ask prices for the prices at which foreign exchange traders trade with each other. Fortunately, Lyons' (1993, 1994) data set constitutes direct observation of trader behavior. It shows that actual median interdealer spreads are smaller still, as compared to Goodhart's sort of spreads.

by Hsieh and Kleidon). The evidence supports the Hot Potato view: the quantity traded has a significant effect only when the time between transactions is long. When the time between transactions is short, the quantity traded has no significant effect on the trader's prices, suggesting that the trader views these orders as coming from liquidity traders rather than informed traders.

4.3. An early assessment of the market micro-structure literature

The foreign exchange research on market microstructure is newborn. It has a long way to go before it can claim to produce a model of exchange rate determination. After realistic models of dealer behavior are constructed, the desirable next step is to let such dealers interact in the market place, in order to derive a central tendency to the torrent of bid and offer quotes and transaction prices in which each individual deals. That central tendency would be what in macroeconomic models we call "the" market-clearing exchange rate. Then the interaction among dealers needs to be imbedded in the larger universe of borrowers, lenders, importers and exporters, who play a role in the foreign exchange market, so that economic fundamentals can ultimately be brought back in. Such a strategy might lead to models of endogenous speculative bubbles that could account for some of the problematic empirical findings reviewed in this survey.

This said, the market microstructure literature is a long way from achieving these goals. Much has been learned about volatility, volume, and bid–ask spreads, from the studies described in Section 4.2; little as yet about central issues like the sources and persistence of heterogeneous beliefs, excess volatility, and exchange rate determination. The macroeconomic literature on exchange rates has not provided the right answers. But we believe it does have the right questions. Research like that described in Sections 4.1 and 4.2 might turn out to point the right direction.

5. Conclusion: endogenous speculative bubbles?

Although the evidence of Meese and Rogoff and others on the failure of the standard models based on monetary fundamentals to predict at short horizons still holds, there is more reason at longer horizons to pay attention to some of the models, such as the Dornbusch overshooting theory. Three independent strands of research are consistent with the hypothesis that the exchange rate may move in the direction suggested by the Dornbusch model, but in an inertia-laden manner that is inconsistent with the standard rational expectations approach. The hypothesis can be described as "overshooting the overshooting equilibrium".

The three strands are as follows.

(1) Tests of bias in the forward market show a persistent pattern whereby the

exchange rate not only on average fails to move in line with the predictions of the forward discount or interest differential, but actually moves in the *opposite* direction (at short horizons that are tested). Neither those who interpret the forward discount bias as a risk premium nor those who interpret it as a systematic prediction error have been able to explain convincingly why the correlation with the forward discount should be negative.

(2) Some researchers claim an ability for fundamentals models to pick the *direction* of movement, relative to the current spot rate, especially at longer horizons. As noted in Section 1.3.1 above, Woo (1986), Somanath (1986), Mark (1992) and a number of others claim, essentially, that a convex combination of the monetary model and the lagged spot rate can outperform the lagged spot rate. The robustness of such results can never be taken for granted. Long data sets are needed for a definitive evaluation. Nevertheless, there is some reason to think that, notwithstanding puzzling short-run dynamics that are observed in the foreign exchange markets, the models win out in the end.[29]

(3) As explained in Section 1.2.2, unexpected changes in monetary policy do in fact frequently cause movements in the exchange rate in the direction hypothesized by the sticky-price monetary model. For example, news of contractionary American monetary policy that raises interest rates is associated with dollar appreciation. There is some reason, however, to believe that the instantaneous reaction is less than the medium-term reaction, i.e. that the exchange rate tends subsequently to continue to move in the same direction, notwithstanding that this finding is inconsistent with rational expectations. For instance, Eichenbaum and Evans (1993) find that it takes an estimated two years for the exchange rate to undergo the full reaction to an unexpected change in monetary policy. Clarida and Gali (1994), also find a lag before the peak effect.

The Eichenbaum–Evans pattern, if it is confirmed in subsequent research, would explain the longstanding puzzle regarding the forward discount bias, the first item listed above: the dollar appreciates gradually in the aftermath of an increase in the interest differential, rather than contemporaneously as the rational-expectations form of the overshooting model (or of any other model) says it should. An interval during which the interest differential is high is thus an interval during which the currency is likely to be appreciating, rather than depreciating. This would explain why the interest differential or forward discount on average points in the wrong direction. The question then becomes: Why does the currency appreciate gradually, rather than suddenly?

The rudiments of a theory of endogenous speculative bubbles, and therefore an answer to the question, may lie in the microstructure of the foreign exchange markets.

---

[29]There is an analogy with the tests of the proposition whether the real exchange rate follows a random walk, against the alternative of a slow return toward a long-run equilibrium. It is by now widely accepted that the slow return to equilibrium is there, but the power of unit root tests in twenty years of data is very low and so one needs a century of data to find it (or a cross-section).

Such a theory must contain three elements: (i) a role for fundamentals that puts an eventual limit on the extent to which a speculative bubble can carry the market away from equilibrium, so that fundamentals win out in the long run, (ii) something like a combination of risk-aversion and model uncertainty (as suggested by the existing heterogeneity of forecasting techniques) that in the short-run is capable of breaking the usual rational-expectations arbitrage that links the exchange rate to its long-run equilibrium, and (iii) some short-run dynamics that arise from the trading process itself (e.g. noise trading that generates volatility which swamps macro fundamentals on a short-term basis). These three elements could be described, respectively, as (i) the eventual bursting of speculative bubbles, (ii) the potential for speculative bubbles, (iii) the endogenous genesis and prolongation of speculative bubbles. We are hopeful that more will be accomplished on these research frontiers soon.

References

Allen, H. and M. Taylor (1989), "Chartists, noise and fundamentals: A study of the London foreign exchange market", Center for Economic Policy Research Working Paper No. 341.

Allen, P. and P. Kenen (1980), Asset markets, exchange rates, and economic integration (Cambridge University Press, New York).

Backus, D. (1984), "Empirical models of the exchange rate: Separating the wheat from the chaff", Canadian Journal of Economics 17:824–846.

Baillie, R. and T. Bollerslev (1989), "Common stochastic trends in a system of exchange rates", Journal of Finance 44:167–181.

Baillie, R. and T. Bollerslev (1991), "Intra-day and inter-market volatility in foreign exchange rates", Review of Economic Studies 58:565–585.

Batten, J. and R. Bhar (1993), "Volume and price volatility in yen futures markets: Within and across three different exchanges", Centre for Japanese Economic Studies Working Paper No. 93-15, Macquarie University, Sydney.

Baxter, M. (1994), "Real exchange rates and real interest rates: Have we missed the business-cycle relationship?", Journal of Monetary Economics 33:5–38.

Baxter, M. and A.C. Stockman (1989), "Business cycles and the exchange rate system", Journal of Monetary Economics 23:377–400.

Beck, S. (1993), "The Ricardian equivalence proposition: Evidence from foreign exchange markets", Journal of International Money and Finance 12:154–169.

Bessembinder, H. (1993), "Bid–ask spreads in the interbank foreign exchange markets", Journal of Financial Economics, forthcoming.

Bilson, J. (1978), "The monetary approach to the exchange rate: Some empirical evidence", International Monetary Fund Staff Papers 25:48–75.

Black, S. (1973), "International money markets and flexible exchange rates", Studies in International Finance 25, Princeton University, Princeton, NJ.

Black, S. and M. Salemi (1988), "FIML estimation of the dollar–Deutschemark risk premium in a portfolio model", Journal of International Economics 25:205–224.

Blanchard, O. (1979), "Speculative bubbles, crashes and rational expectations", Economic Letters, 387–389.

Blanco, H. and P.M. Garber (1986), "Recurrent devaluations and speculative attacks on the Mexican peso", Journal of Political Economy 94:148–166.

Blake, D., M. Beenstock, and V. Brasse (1986), "The performance of UK exchange rate forecasters", The Economic Journal 96:986–999.

Blundell-Wignall, A. and F. Browne (1991), "Increasing financial market integration: Real exchange rates and macroeconomic adjustment", working paper, OECD.

Bollerslev, T., R. Chou, and K. Kroner (1992), "ARCH modeling in finance", Journal of Econometrics 52:5–59.

Bollerslev, T. and I. Domowitz (1993), "Trading patterns and prices in the interbank foreign exchange market", Journal of Finance 48:1421–1443.

Bollerslev, T. and M. Melvin (1994), "Bid-ask spreads and volatility in the foreign exchange market: An empirical analysis", Journal of International Economics 36:355–372.

Boothe, P. (1988), "Exchange rate risk and the bid–ask spread: A seven-country comparison", Economic Inquiry 26:485–492.

Boothe, P. and D. Glassman (1987), "The statistical distribution of exchange rates", Journal of International Economics 22:153–167.

Boughton, J. (1988), "The monetary approach to exchange rates: What now remains?", Essays in International Finance 171, Princeton University, Princeton, NJ.

Bovenberg, A.L. (1989), "The effects of capital income taxation on international competitiveness and trade flows", American Economic Review 79:1045–1064.

Branson, W. (1977), "Asset markets and relative prices in exchange rate determination", Sozialwissenschaftliche Annalen 1:69–89.

Branson, W. (1983), "Macroeconomic determinants of real exchange risks", in: R.J. Herring, ed., Managing foreign exchange risk (Cambridge University Press, Cambridge, UK).

Branson, W. and D. Henderson (1985), "International asset markets: Specification and influence", in: R. Jones and P. Kenen, eds., Handbook of international economics, vol. 2 (North-Holland, Amsterdam).

Branson, W., H. Halttunen, and P. Masson (1977), "Exchange rates in the short-run: The dollar-Deutschemark rate", European Economic Review 10:303–324.

Branson, W., H. Halttunen, and P. Masson (1979), "Exchange rates in the short-run: Some further Results", European Economic Review 12:395–402.

Buiter, W. and M. Miller (1982), "Real exchange rate overshooting and the output cost of bringing down inflation", European Economic Review 18:85–123.

Calvo, G. and C. Rodriguez (1977), "A model of exchange rate determination under currency substitution and rational expectations", Journal of Political Economy 85:617–626.

Campbell, J. and R. Clarida (1987), "The dollar and real interest rates", Carnegie–Rochester Conference on Public Policy 27.

Casella, A. (1989), "Testing for rational bubbles with exogenous or endogenous fundamentals: The German hyperinflation once more", Journal of Monetary Economics 24:109–122.

Catte, P., G. Galli, and S. Rebecchini (1994), "Concerted interventions and the dollar: An analysis of daily data", in: P. Kenan, F. Papadia and F. Saccomani, eds., The international monetary system in crisis and reform: Essays in memory of Rinaldo Ossola (Cambridge University Press, Cambridge).

Cavaglia, S., F. Nieuwland, W. Verschoor, and C. Wolff (1994), "On the biasedness of forward foreign exchange rates: Irrationality or risk premia?", Limburg Institute of Financial Economics, The Netherlands; Journal of Business, forthcoming.

Cavaglia, S., W. Verschoor, and C. Wolff (1993a), "Asian exchange rate expectations", Journal of the Japanese and International Economies 7:57–77.

Cavaglia, S., W. Verschoor, and C. Wolff (1993b), "Further evidence on exchange rate expectations", Journal of International Money and Finance 12:78–98.

Chen, Z. (1992), "Cointegration and exchange rate forecasting: A state space model", London School of Economics, United Kingdom.

Chinn, M. (1991), "Some linear and nonlinear thoughts on exchange rates", Journal of International Money and Finance 10:214–230.

Chinn, M. and J. Frankel (1994), "Patterns in exchange rate forecasts for 25 currencies", Journal of Money, Credit and Banking 26.

Chinn, M. and R.A. Meese (1994), "Banking on currency forecasts", Journal of International Economics, vol. 38, no. 1/2. February 1995: 161–178.

Clarida, R. and J. Galli (1994), "Sources of real exchange rate fluctuations: How important are nominal shocks?", National Bureau of Economic Research Working Paper No. 4658; and in: Carnegie–Rochester Conference on Public Policy, forthcoming.

Copeland, L. (1989), "Exchange rates and news: A vector autoregression approach", in: R. MacDonald and M. Taylor, eds., Exchange rates and open economy macroeconomics (Basil Blackwell, Oxford, UK and Cambridge, MA) 218–238.

Cornell, B. (1982), "Money supply announcements, interest rates, and foreign exchange", Journal of International Money and Finance 1:201–208.

Cutler, D., J. Poterba and L. Summers (1991), "Speculative dynamics", Review of Economics Studies, 58, May, 529–546.

Davutyan, N. and J. Pippenger (1985), "Purchasing power parity did not collapse during the 1970s", American Economic Review 75:1151–1158.

De Grauwe, P. and D. Decupere (1992), "Psychological barriers in the foreign exchange market", Centre for Economic Policy Research Discussion Paper No. 621.

DeGrauwe, P. and H. Dewachter (1990), "A chaotic monetary model of the exchange rate", Centre for Economic Policy Research Discussion Paper No. 466.

De Long, J.B., A. Shleifer, L. Summers, and R. Waldmann (1990), "Noise trader risk in financial markets", Journal of Political Economy 98-4:703–738.

Diebold, F.X. and J. Nason (1990), "Nonlinear Exchange Rate Prediction?", Journal of International Economics 28:315–332.

Diebold, F.X., S. Husted, and M. Rush (1991), "Real exchange rates under the gold standard", Journal of Political Economy 99:1252–1271.

Diebold, F.X., J. Gardeazabal, and K. Yilmaz (1994), "On co-integration and exchange rate dynamics", Journal of Finance 49:727–735.

Dominguez, K. (1986), "Are foreign exchange forecasts rational?", New evidence from survey data, Economic Letters 21:277–282.

Dominguez, K. (1990), "Market responses to coordinated central bank intervention", Carnegie–Rochester Series on Public Policy 32:121–163.

Dominguez, K. (1992), "The informational role of official foreign exchange intervention operations: The signalling hypothesis", in: K. Dominguez, Exchange rate efficiency and the behavior of international asset markets (Garland Publishing Company, New York).

Dominguez, K.M. and J.A. Frankel (1993a), "Does foreign exchange intervention matter? Disentangling the portfolio and expectation effects", National Bureau of Economic Research Working Paper No. 3299; abridged versions in: American Economic Review 83, December 1993, and in: J. Frankel, On exchange rates (MIT Press, Cambridge, MA).

Dominguez, K.M. and J.A. Frankel (1993b), Does foreign exchange intervention work? (Institute for International Economics, Washington, DC).

Dooley, M. and P. Isard (1982a), "A portfolio-balance rational-expectations model of the dollar-mark rate", Journal of International Economics 12:257–276.

Dooley, M. and P. Isard (1982b), "The role of the current account in exchange rate determination: A comment on Rodriguez", Journal of Political Economy 90:1291–1294.

Dooley, M. and P. Isard (1983), "The portfolio-balance model of exchange rates and some structural estimates of the risk premium", International Monetary Fund Staff Papers 30:683–702.

Dooley, M. and P. Isard (1987), "Country preferences, currency values and policy issues", Journal of Policy Modeling 9:65–81.

Dooley, M. and P. Isard (1991), "A note on fiscal policy, investment location decisions, and exchange rates", Journal of International Money and Finance 10:161–168.

Dooley, M., P. Isard, and M. Taylor (1992), "Exchange rates, country preferences, and gold", National Bureau of Economic Research Working Paper No. 4183.

Dornbusch, R. (1976a), "Expectations and exchange rate dynamics", Journal of Political Economy 84:1161–1176.

Dornbusch, R. (1976b), "The theory of flexible exchange rate regimes and macroeconomic policy", Scandinavian Journal of Economics 78:255–275.

Dornbusch, R. (1978), "Monetary policy under exchange rate flexibility", in: Managed exchange rate flexibility, Federal Reserve Bank of Boston Conference Series.

Dornbusch, R. (1980), "Exchange rate economics: Where do we stand?", Brookings Papers on Economic Activity 1:143–194.

Dornbusch, R. (1982), "Equilibrium and disequilibrium exchange rates", Zeitschrift für Wirtschafts- und Sozialwissenschaften 102:573–799; reprinted in: R. Dornbusch, Dollars, debts, and deficits (MIT Press, Cambridge, MA).

Dornbusch, R. (1987), "Flexible exchange rates 1986", Economic Journal 1:1–18.

Driskill, R. (1981), "Exchange rate dynamics: An empirical investigation", Journal of Political Economy 89:357–371.

Driskill, R., N. Mark, and S. Sheffrin (1992), "Some evidence in favor of a monetary rational expectations model with imperfect capital substitutability", International Economic Review 33:223–238.

Edison, H. (1993), The effectiveness of central bank intervention: A survey of the post-1982 literature, Essays in International Finance (Princeton University, Princeton, NJ).

Edison, H. and B.D. Pauls (1993), "A re-assessment of the relationship between real exchange rates and real interest rates: 1974–1990", Journal of Monetary Economics 31:165–187.

Edwards, S. (1982), "Exchange rates and news: A multi-currency approach", Journal of International Money and Finance 1:211–224.

Edwards, S. (1983), "Floating exchange rates, expectations and new information", Journal of Monetary Economics 11:321–336.

Eichenbaum, M. and C. Evans (1993), "Some empirical evidence on the effects of monetary policy shocks on exchange rates", National Bureau of Economic Research Working Paper No. 4271.

Eichengreen, B. (1988), "Real exchange rate behavior under alternative international monetary regimes: Interwar evidence", European Economic Review 32:363–371.

Eijffinger, S.C.W. and N.P.D. Gruijters (1991), "On the effectiveness of daily interventions by the Deutsche Bundesbank and the Federal Reserve system in the U.S. dollar/Deutschemark exchange market", Tilburg University Research Memorandum FEW394, Tilburg 1989.

Engel, C. M. (1992), "Can the Markov switching model forecast exchange rates?", National Bureau of Economic Research Working Paper No. 4210.

Engel, C.M. and J. Frankel (1984a), "Why interest rates react to money announcements: An answer from the foreign exchange market", Journal of Monetary Economics 13:31–39.

Engel, C.M. and J. Frankel (1984b), "The secular inflation term in open-economy Phillips curves: A comment on Flood", European Economic Review 24:161–164.

Engel, C.M. and J.D. Hamilton (1990), "Long swings in the dollar", American Economic Review 80:689–713.

Engel, C.M. and A. Rodrigues (1989), "Tests of international CAPM with time-varying covariances", Journal of Applied Econometrics 4:119–138.

Engle, R., T. Ito, and W.-L. Lin (1990), "Meteor showers or heat waves? Heteroskedastic intra-daily volatility in the foreign exchange market", Econometrica 58:525–542.

Engle, R., T. Ito, and W.-L. Lin (1992), "Where does the meteor shower come from? The role of stochastic policy coordination", Journal of International Economics 32:221–240.

Evans, G.W. (1986), "A test for speculative bubbles in the sterling-dollar exchange rate", American Economic Review 76:621–636.

Evans, M. and K. Lewis (1992), "Peso problems and heterogeneous trading: Evidence from excess returns in foreign exchange and euromarkets", National Bureau of Economic Research Working Paper No. 4003, 16–19.

Fieleke, N. (1981), "Foreign-currency positioning by U.S. firms: Some new evidence", Review of Economics and Statistics 63:35–42.

Finn, M.G. (1986), "Forecasting the exchange rate", Journal of International Money and Finance 5:181–193.

Flood, R.A. and P. Garber (1980), "Market fundamentals versus price-level bubbles: The first tests", Journal of Political Economy 88:745–770.

Flood, R.A. and P. Garber (1983), "A model of stochastic process switching", Econometrica 51:537–552.

Flood, R.A. and P. Garber (1991), "The linkage between speculative attack and target zone models of exchange rates", Quarterly Journal of Economics 106:1367–1372.

Flood, R.A. and R.J. Hodrick (1990), "On testing for speculative bubbles", The Journal of Economic Perspectives 4:85–101.

Flood, R.A., and A.K. Rose (1993), "Fixing exchange rates", National Bureau of Economic Research Working Paper No. 4503.

Flood, R.A., A.K. Rose, and D.J. Mathieson (1991), "An empirical exploration of exchange rate target zones", Carnegie–Rochester Conference Series on Public Policy 35:7–65.

Frankel, J.A. (1979), "On the mark: A theory of floating exchange rates based on real interest differentials", American Economic Review 69:601–622.

Frankel, J.A. (1982), "In search of the exchange risk premium: A six-currency test assuming mean-variance optimization", Journal of International Money and Finance 1:255–274.

Frankel, J.A. (1988), "Recent estimates of time-variation in the conditional variance and in the exchange risk premium", Journal of International Money and Finance 7:115–125.

Frankel, J.A. (1993), "Monetary and portfolio-balance models of the determination of exchange rates", in: J. Frankel, On exchange rates (MIT Press, Cambridge, MA).

Frankel, J. and M. Chinn (1993), "Exchange rate expectations and the risk premium: Tests for a cross-section of 17 currencies", Review of International Economics 1:136–144.

Frankel, J. and K.A. Froot (1986), "Understanding the U.S. dollar in the eighties: The expectations of chartists and fundamentalists", Economic Record 1986 Supplement, 24–38.

Frankel, J. and K.A. Froot (1987a), "Short-term and long-term expectations of the yen/dollar exchange rate: Evidence from survey data", Journal of the Japanese and International Economies 1:249–274.

Frankel, J. and K.A. Froot (1987b), "Using survey data to test standard propositions regarding exchange rate expectations", American Economic Review 77:133–153.

Frankel, J. and K.A. Froot (1990a), "Chartists, fundamentalists, and the demand for dollars", in: A. Courakis and M. Taylor, eds., Private behavior and government policy in interdependent economies (Clarendon Press, Oxford).

Frankel, J. and K.A. Froot (1990b), "Exchange rate forecasting techniques, survey data, and implications for the foreign exchange market", National Bureau of Economic Research Working Paper No. 3470.

Frankel, J. and G. Hardouvelis (1985), "Commodity prices, money surprises, and Fed credibility", Journal of Money, Credit and Banking 17:427–438.

Frankel, J. and R.A. Meese (1987), "Are exchange rates excessively variable?", National Bureau of Economic Research Macroeconomics Annual 2:117–153.

Frenkel, J.A. (1976), "A monetary approach to the exchange rate: Doctrinal aspects and empirical evidence", Scandinavian Journal of Economics 78:200–224.

Frenkel, J.A. (1980), "Exchange rates, prices and money: Lessons from the 1920s", American Economic Review 70:235–342.

Frenkel, J.A. (1981), "Flexible exchange rates, prices and the role of 'news'", Journal of Political Economy 89:665–705.

Frenkel, J.A. and H.G. Johnson (1978), eds., The economics of exchange rates (Addison–Wesley, Reading, MA).

Friedman, M. (1953), "The case for flexible exchange rates", in: Essays in positive economics (University of Chicago, Chicago).

Froot, K. and J. Frankel (1989), "Forward discount bias: Is it an exchange risk premium?", Quarterly Journal of Economics 104:139–161.

Froot, K.A. and T. Ito (1989), "On the consistency of short-run and long-run exchange rate expectations", Journal of International Money and Finance 8:487–510.

Froot, K.A. and R. Thaler (1990), "Anomalies: Foreign exchange", Journal of Economic Perspectives 4:179–192.

Froot, K.A. and M. Obstfeld (1991), "Exchange-rate dynamics under stochastic regime shifts", Journal of International Economics 31:203–229.

Garber, P. and M. Spencer "Dynamic hedging and the interest rate defense", in J. Frankel, G. Galli, and A. Giovannini, eds., The microstructure of foreign exchange markets (University of Chicago Press, Chicago), forthcoming.

Girton, L. and D. Henderson (1977), "Central bank operations in foreign and domestic assets under fixed and flexible exchange rates", in: P. Clark, D. Logue, and R. Sweeney, eds., The effects of exchange rate adjustment (Department of the Treasury, Washington, D.C.) 151–179.

Glassman, D. (1987), "Exchange rate risk and transactions costs: Evidence from bid–ask spreads", Journal of International Money and Finance 6:479–490.

Goldberg, M. and R. Frydman (1993a), "Theories, consistent expectations and exchange rate dynamics", in: H. Frisch and A. Wörgötter, eds., Open-economy macroeconomics (Macmillan Publishing, London).

Goldberg, M., and R. Frydman (1993b), "Qualitative rationality and behavior in the foreign exchange market", mimeo, New York University Economics Department.

Golub, S. (1989), "Foreign-currency government debt, asset markets, and the balance of payments", Journal of International Money and Finance 8:285–294.

Goodhart, C. (1988), "The foreign exchange market: A random walk with a dragging anchor", Economica 55:437–460.

Goodhart, C. and A. Demos (1990), "Reuters screen images of the foreign exchange market: The Deutschemark/dollar spot rate", Journal of International Securities Markets 4:333–348.

Goodhart, C. and L. Figliuoli (1991), "Every minute counts in financial markets", Journal of International Money and Finance 10:23–52.

Goodhart, C. and M. Giugale (1993), "From hour to hour in the foreign exchange market", The Manchester School 61:1–34.

Goodhart, C., T. Ito, and R. Payne (1994), "One day in June 1993: A study of the working of Reuters 2000-2 electronic foreign exchange trading system (Bank of Italy, Perugia, Italy)", in: J. Frankel, G. Galli, and A. Giovannini, eds., The microstructure of foreign exchange markets (University of Chicago Press, Chicago), forthcoming.

Goodman, S. (1979), "Foreign exchange forecasting techniques: Implications for business and policy", Journal of Finance 34:415–427.

Grilli, V. and N. Roubini (1993), "Liquidity and exchange rates: Puzzling evidence from the G-7 countries", mimeo, Yale University.

Hansen, L.P. and R.J. Hodrick (1980), "Forward exchange rates as optimal predictors of future spot rates", Journal of Political Economy 88:829–853.

Hardouvelis, G. (1988), "Economic news, exchange rates, and interest rates", Journal of International Money and Finance 7:23–25.

Haynes, S. and J. Stone (1981), "On the mark: Comment", American Economic Review 71:1060–1067.

Henderson, D. and S. Sampson (1983), "Intervention in foreign exchange markets: A summary of ten staff studies", Federal Reserve Bulletin 69:830–836.

Henderson, D. (1984), "Exchange market intervention operations: Their role in financial policy and their effects", in: J. Bilson and R. Marston, eds., Exchange rate theory and practice (University of Chicago Press, Chicago).

Henderson, D., D. Danker, R. Haas, S. Symansky, and R. Tryon (1987), "Small empirical models of exchange market intervention: Applications to Germany, Japan and Canada", Journal of Policy Modeling 9:143–173.

Hodrick, R. (1978), "An empirical analysis of the monetary approach to the determination of the exchange rate", in: J. Frenkel and H.G. Johnson, eds., The economics of exchange rates (Addison–Wesley, Reading, MA) 97–116.

Hodrick, R. (1988), "The empirical evidence on the efficiency of forward and futures foreign exchange markets", in: Fundamentals of pure and applied economics (Harwood Academic Publishers, Chur, Switzerland).

Hogan, K., M. Melvin, and D. Roberts (1991), "Trade balance news and exchange rates: Is there a policy signal?", Journal of International Money and Finance 10:S90–S99.

Hsieh, D. (1989), "Testing for nonlinear dependence in daily foreign exchange rates", Journal of Business 62:339–368.

Hsieh, D. and A. Kleidon (1994), "Bid–ask spreads in foreign exchange markets: implications for models of asymmetric information" (Bank of Italy, Perugia, Italy), in: J. Frankel, G. Galle, and A. Giovannini, eds., The microstructure of foreign exchange markets (University of Chicago Press, Chicago), forthcoming.

Isard, P. (1983), "An accounting framework and some issues for modeling how exchange rates respond to the news", in J. Frenkel, ed., Exchange rates and international macroeconomics (University of Chicago Press, Chicago).

Ito, T. (1990), "Foreign exchange rate expectations: Micro survey data", American Economic Review 80:434–449.

Ito, T. (1994), "Short-run and long-run expectations of the yen/dollar exchange rate", Journal of the Japanese and International Economies 8:119–143.

Ito, T. and V.V. Roley (1987), "News from the U.S. and Japan: Which moves the yen/dollar exchange rate", Journal of Monetary Economics 19:255–277.

Ito, T. and V.V. Roley (1990), "Intraday yen/dollar exchange rate movements: news or noise?", Journal of International Financial Markets, Institutions and Money 1:1–31.

Jones, R. and P.B. Kenen (1985), Handbook of international economics, vol. 2 (North-Holland, Amsterdam).

Jorion, P. (1994), "Risk and turnover in the foreign exchange market", (Bank of Italy, Perugia, Italy), in: J. Frankel, G. Galli, and A. Giovannini, eds., The microstructure of foreign exchange markets (University of Chicago Press, Chicago), forthcoming.

Kaminsky, G. and K. Lewis (1993), "Does foreign exchange intervention signal future monetary policy?", National Bureau of Economic Research Working Paper No. 4298.

Kenen, P. (1988), Managing exchange rates (The Royal Institute of International Affairs, Council on Foreign Relations Press, New York).

Klein, M. (1993), "The accuracy of reports of foreign exchange intervention", Journal of International Money and Finance 12:644–653.

Klein, M. and E. Rosengren (1991), "What do we learn from foreign exchange intervention?", working paper, Tufts University.

Kouri, P. (1976), "The exchange rate and the balance of payments in the short run and in the long run: A monetary approach", Scandinavian Journal of Economics 78:280–304.

Krugman, P.R. (1978), "Purchasing power parity and exchange rates: Another look at the evidence", Journal of International Economics 8:397–407.

Krugman, P.R. (1979), "A model of balance of payments crises", Journal of Money, Credit and Banking 11:311–325. Reprinted in: Currencies and crises (MIT Press, Cambridge, MA, 1992) 61–76.

Krugman, P.R. (1985), "Is the strong dollar sustainable?", in: The U.S. dollar – Recent developments, outlook and policy options (Federal Reserve Bank, Kansas City) 103–133.

Krugman, P.R. (1991), "Target zones and exchange rate dynamics", Quarterly Journal of Economics 116:669–682.

Krugman, P.R. (1993), "Recent thinking about exchange rate determination and policy", in: A. Blundell-Wignall, ed., The exchange rate and the balance of payments (Reserve Bank of Australia, Sydney) 6–22.

Krugman, P.R. and M. Miller, eds., (1991), Exchange rate targets and currency bands (Cambridge University Press, Cambridge).

Krugman, P.R. and M. Miller (1993), "Why have a target zone?", Carnegie–Rochester Conference Series on Public Policy 38:279–314.

Lee, T.-H. (1994), "Spread and volatility in spot and forward exchange rates", Journal of International Money and Finance 13:375–383.

Levich, R. and L. Thomas (1993), "The significance of technical trading-rule profits in the foreign exchange market: A bootstrap approach", Journal of International Money and Finance 12:563–586.

Lewis, K.K. (1988), "Testing the portfolio balance model: A multi-lateral approach", Journal of International Economics 7:273–288.

Lewis, K.K. (1989), "Changing beliefs and systematic forecast errors", American Economic Review 79:621–636.

Lewis, K.K. (1990), "Occasional interventions to target rates", National Bureau of Economic Research Working Paper No. 3398.

Lewis, K.K. (1993), "Are foreign exchange intervention and monetary policy related and does it really matter?", National Bureau of Economic Research Working Paper No. 4377.

Liu, P. and G.S. Maddala (1992), "Rationality of survey data and tests for market efficiency in the foreign exchange markets", Journal of International Money and Finance 11:366–381.

Lucas, R.E. Jr. (1982), "Interest rates and currency prices in a two-country world", Journal of Monetary Economics 10:335–360.

Lyons, R. (1991), "Information intermediation in the microstructure of the foreign exchange market", revised version of National Bureau of Economic Research Working Paper No. 3889.

Lyons, R. (1993), "Tests of microstructural hypotheses in the foreign exchange market", National Bureau of Economic Research Working Paper No. 4471.

Lyons, R. (1994), "Foreign exchange volume: Sound and fury signifying nothing?", (Bank of Italy, Perugia, Italy), in: J. Frankel, G. Galli, and A. Giovannini, eds., The microstructure of foreign exchange markets (University of Chicago Press, Chicago), forthcoming.

MacDonald, R. (1983), "Some tests of the rational expectations hypothesis in the foreign exchange markets", Scottish Journal of Political Economy 30:235–250.

MacDonald, R. (1990a), "Are exchange market forecasters 'rational': Some survey-based tests", The Manchester School of Economic and Social Studies 58:229–241.

MacDonald, R. (1990b), "Exchange rate economics: An empirical perspective", in: G. Bird, ed., The international financial regime (Academic Press Ltd., London and San Diego) 91–144.

MacDonald, R. (1992), "Exchange rate survey data: A disaggregated G-7 perspective", mimeo, University of Dundee.

MacDonald, R. and M.P. Taylor (1989), "Economic analysis of foreign exchange markets: An expository survey", in: R. MacDonald and M.P. Taylor, eds., Exchange rates and open economy macroeconomics (Basil Blackwell, Oxford, UK and Cambridge, MA) 1–108.

MacDonald, R. and M.P. Taylor (1992), "Exchange rate economics", International Monetary Fund Staff Papers 39:1–57.

MacDonald, R. and M.P. Taylor (1993a), "The monetary approach to the exchange rate: Rational expectations, long-run equilibrium, and forecasting", International Monetary Fund Staff Papers 40:89–107.

MacDonald, R. and M.P. Taylor (1993b), "Exchange rate behavior under alternative exchange rate arrangements", mimeo, International Monetary Fund.

MacDonald, R. and M.P. Taylor (1994), "The monetary model of the exchange rate: long-run relationships, short run dynamics, and how to beat a random walk", Journal of International Money and Finance 13:276–290.

MacDonald, R. and T.S. Torrance (1988a), "Exchange rates and the news: Some evidence using UK survey data", The Manchester School 56:69–76.

MacDonald, R. and T.S. Torrance (1988b), "On risk, rationality and excessive speculation in the Deutschemark–US dollar exchange market: Some evidence using survey data", Oxford Bulletin of Economics and Statistics 50:107–123.

MacDonald, R. and T.S. Torrance (1990), "Expectations formation and risk in four foreign exchange markets", Oxford Economic Papers 42:544–561.

Mark, N.C. (1990), "Real and nominal exchange rates in the long run", Journal of International Economics 28:115–136.

Mark, N.C. (1994), "Exchange rates and fundamentals: Evidence on long-horizon predictability", American Economic Review 84.

McKinnon, R. (1976), "Floating exchange rates 1973–74: The emperor's new clothes", in: K. Brunner and A. Meltzer, eds., Institutional arrangements and the inflation problem. Carnegie–Rochester Series on Public Policy 3:79–114.

McKinnon, R. (1988), "Monetary and exchange rate policies for international financial stability: A proposal", Journal of Economic Perspectives 2:83–103.

Meese, R.A. (1986), "Testing for bubbles in exchange markets", Journal of Political Economy 94:345–373.

Meese, R.A. (1990), "Currency fluctuations in the post-Bretton Woods era", Journal of Economic Perspectives 4:117–134.

Meese, R.A. and K. Rogoff (1983a), "Empirical exchange rate models of the seventies", Journal of International Economics 14:3–24.

Meese, R.A. and K. Rogoff (1983b), "The out-of-sample failure of empirical exchange rate models", in: J. Frenkel, ed., Exchange rates and international macroeconomics (University of Chicago Press, Chicago).

Meese, R.A. and K. Rogoff (1988), "Was it real? The exchange rate – interest differential relationship over the modern floating-rate period", Journal of Finance 43:933–948.

Meese, R.A. and A.K. Rose (1991), "An empirical assessment of non-linearities in models of exchange rate determination", Review of Economic Studies 58:603–619.

Meese, R.A. and K. Singleton (1982), "On unit roots and the empirical modeling of exchange rates", Journal of Finance 37:1029–1035.

Miller, M. and P. Weller (1991), "Exchange rates bands with price inertia", Economic Journal 101:1380–1399.

Mundell, R. (1964), "Exchange rate margins and economic policy", in: J. Carter Murphy, ed., Money in the international order (Southern Methodist University Press, Dallas).

Mussa, M. (1976), "The exchange rate, the balance of payments, and monetary and fiscal policy under a regime of controlled floating", Scandinavian Journal of Economics 78:229–248.

Mussa, M. (1979), "Empirical regularities in the behavior of exchange rates and theories of the foreign exchange market", in: K. Brunner and A.H. Meltzer, eds., Policies for employment, prices, and exchange rates (North-Holland, New York) 9–57.

Mussa, M. (1981), The role of official intervention, Group of thirty occasional papers, No. 6 (Group of Thirty, New York).

Mussa, M. (1986), "Nominal exchange rate regimes and the behavior of the real exchange rate", in: K. Brunner and A.H. Meltzer, eds., Real business cycles, real exchange rates and actual policies (North-Holland, New York) 117–213.

Mussa, M. (1990), Exchange rates in theory and in reality, Essays in International Finance No. 179 (Princeton University, Princeton, NJ).

Niehans, J. (1975), "Some doubts about the efficacy of monetary policy under flexible exchange rates", Journal of International Economics 5:225–281.

Obstfeld, M. (1986), "Balance of payments crises and devaluation", American Economic Review 76:72–81.

Obstfeld, M. (1990), "The effectiveness of foreign-exchange intervention: Recent experience: 1985–1988", in: W. Branson, J. Frenkel, and M. Goldstein, eds., International policy coordination and exchange rate fluctuations (University of Chicago Press, Chicago).

Obstfeld, M. and K. Rogoff (1983), "Speculative hyperinflations in maximizing models: Can we rule them out?", Journal of Political Economy 91:675–687.

Obstfeld, M. and K. Rogoff (1984), "Exchange rate dynamics with sluggish prices under alternative price-adjustment rules", International Economic Review 25:159–174.

Obstfeld, M. and A. Stockman (1985), "Exchange rate dynamics", in: R. Jones and P. Kenen, eds., Handbook of international economics, vol. 2 (North-Holland, Amsterdam).

Papell, D. (1988), "Expectations and exchange rate dynamics after a decade of floating", Journal of International Economics 25:303–317.

Papell, D. (1989), "Monetary policy in the United States under flexible exchange rates", American Economic Review 79:1106–1116.

Papell, D. (1993), "Cointegration and exchange rate dynamics", mimeo, University of Houston.

Rodriguez, C. (1980), "The role of trade flows in exchange rate determination: A rational expectations approach", Journal of Political Economy 88:1148–1158.

Rogoff, K. (1984), "On the effects of sterilized intervention: An analysis of weekly data", Journal of Monetary Economics 14:133–150.

Rogoff, K. (1985), "Can exchange rate predictability be achieved without monetary convergence? Evidence from the EMS", European Economic Review 28:93–115.

Rose, A. (1994), "Exchange rate volatility, monetary policy, and capital mobility: Empirical evidence on the Holy Trinity", National Bureau of Economic Research Working Paper No. 4630, January.

Schinasi, G. and P.A.V.B. Swamy (1989), "The out-of-sample forecasting performance of exchange rate models when coefficients are allowed to change", Journal of International Money and Finance 8:375–390.

Schulmeister, S. (1987), "An essay on exchange rate dynamics", Research Unit Labor Market and Employment Discussion Paper No. 87-8 (Wissenschaftzentrum Berlin für Sozialforschung, Berlin).

Schulmeister, S. (1988), "Currency speculation and dollar fluctuations", Banca Nazionale del Lavoro Quarterly Review 167:343–365.

Schulmeister, S. and M. Goldberg (1989), "Noise trading and the efficiency of financial markets", in: G. Luciani, ed., The American financial system: Between euphoria and crisis (Quaderni della Fondazione Adriano Olivetti, Rome) 117–153.

Somanath, V.S. (1986), "Efficient exchange rate forecasts", Journal of International Money and Finance 5:195–220.

Stockman, A. (1980), "A theory of exchange rate determination", Journal of Political Economy 88:673–698.

Stockman, A. (1987), "The equilibrium approach to exchange rates", Federal Reserve Bank of Richmond Economic Review 73:12–30.

Stockman, A. (1988), "Real exchange-rate flexibility under pegged and floating exchange-rate systems", Carnegie–Rochester Conference Series on Public Policy 29:259–294.

Svensson, L.E.O. (1992), "An interpretation of recent research on exchange rate target zone", Journal of Economic Perspectives 6:103–118.

Svensson, L.E.O. (1993), "Assessing target zone credibility", European Economic Review 37:763–793.

Takagi, S. (1991), "Exchange rate expectations: A survey of survey studies", International Monetary Fund Staff Papers 38:156–183.

Tandon, K., and T. Urich (1987), "International market response to announcements of U.S. macroeconomic data", Journal of International Money and Finance 6:71–83.

Taylor, M. and H. Allen (1992), "The use of technical analysis in the foreign exchange market", Journal of International Money and Finance 11:304–314.

Throop, A. (1993), "A generalized uncovered interest parity model of exchange rates", Federal Reserve Bank of San Francisco Economic Review 2:3–16.

Tryon, R. (1983), "Small empirical models of exchange market intervention: A review of the literature", Staff Studies No. 134 (Board of Governors of the Federal Reserve System, Washington, DC).

Wei, S.-J. (1994), "Anticipations of foreign exchange volatility and bid–ask spreads", National Bureau of Economic Research Working Paper No. 4737.

Whitt, J. (1992), "Nominal exchange rates and unit roots: A reconsideration", Journal of International Money and Finance 11:539–511.

Williamson, J. (1985), The exchange rate system, Policy Analyses in International Economics No. 5 (Institute for International Economics, Washington DC).

Williamson, J. (1987), "Exchange rate management: The role of target zones", American Economic Review 77:200–204.

Williamson, J. and M. Miller (1987), Targets and indicators: A blueprint for the international coordination of economic policy, Policy Analyses in International Economics No. 22 (Institute for International Economics, Washington, DC).

Wolff, C. (1987), "Time-varying parameters and the out-of-sample forecasting performance of structural exchange rate models", Journal of Business and Economic Statistics 5:87–97.

Woo, W.T. (1985), "The monetary approach to exchange rate determination under rational expectations", Journal of International Economics 18:1–16.

Woo, W.T. (1987), "Some evidence of speculative bubbles in the foreign exchange markets", Journal of Money, Credit, and Banking 19:499–514.

Chapter 34

THE INTERTEMPORAL APPROACH TO THE CURRENT ACCOUNT

MAURICE OBSTFELD

University of California, Berkeley

and

KENNETH ROGOFF*

Princeton University

Contents

*We thank Geun Mee Ahn, Harald Hau, Matthew Jones, Giovanni Olivei, and Clara Wang for excellent research assistance and the National Science Foundation, the German Marshall Fund of the United States, and the Ford Foundation for financial support. Helpful suggestions were made by David Backus, Richard Clarida, Jon Faust, Kiminori Matsuyama, Cedric Tille, and participants in the March 1994 conference for the Handbook at Princeton University.

Handbook of International Economics, vol. III, Edited by G. Grossman and K. Rogoff
© *Elsevier Science B.V., 1995*

1. Introduction

The intertemporal approach views the current-account balance as the outcome of forward-looking dynamic saving and investment decisions. Intertemporal analyses of the current account became common in the early 1980s as a result of papers by Buiter (1981), Obstfeld (1982), Sachs (1981), Svensson and Razin (1983), and many others, although the approach had explicit precursors in work on trade and growth by Bardhan (1967), Bruno (1970), and Hamada (1969).[1] As usual, this new focus in open-economy macroeconomics resulted both from theoretical advances in other parts of economics and from economic events that existing open-economy models seemed ill equipped to examine.

Lucas's (1976) influential critique of econometric policy evaluation was one important theoretical motivation for an intertemporal approach. His insistence on grounding policy analysis in the actual forward-looking decision rules of economic agents suggested that open-economy models might yield more reliable policy conclusions if demand and supply functions were derived from the optimization problems of households and firms rather than specified to match reduced-form estimates based on ad hoc econometric specifications.

Further impetus to develop an intertemporal approach came from events in the world capital market, especially the substantial current-account imbalances that followed the sharp world oil-price increases of 1973–74 and 1979–80. The divergent patterns of current-account adjustment by industrialized and developing countries raised the inherently intertemporal problem of characterizing the optimal dynamic response to external shocks. Neither the classical monetary models nor the Keynesian models in vogue at the time offered reliable guidance on this question. Similarly, the explosion in recycled bank lending to developing countries after the first oil shock sparked fears that borrowers' external debt levels might become unsustainable. The need to evaluate developing-country debt levels again led naturally to the notion of an intertemporally optimal current-account deficit.

This chapter surveys the theory and empirical work on the intertemporal approach to the current account as it has developed since the early 1980s.[2] Recently, some researchers have studied dynamic stochastic international models with complete Arrow–Debreu forward markets for uncertain consumption. This particular offshoot of the intertemporal approach is the "complete-markets"

---

[1] A number of studies published in the early 1980s based exchange-rate or balance-of-payments models on intertemporal foundations. These contributions are surveyed in the chapter by Maurice Obstfeld and Alan C. Stockman in volume 2 of this Handbook (Obstfeld and Stockman 1985).

[2] For a complementary survey, see Razin (1995).

model. Because complete-markets models fit more naturally into Marianne Baxter's chapter in this Handbook, they are summarized only briefly here. We reserve the term "intertemporal approach" – as well as the bulk of our discussion – for models with international borrowing and lending but not necessarily with complete international markets in state-contingent claims.

The chapter begins with an introductory section, Section 2, that explores the concept of the current account, its behavior in recent history, and the conceptual adequacy of measures of the current account as reported by government agencies.

Section 3 lays out basic intertemporal models of the current account, starting with the deterministic case and then exploring stochastic models. Section 4 shows how stochastic models can be used to devise tests of the intertemporal approach, and goes on to evaluate the resulting evidence.

Much of the discussion through Section 4 of this chapter focuses on *positive* predictions of the intertemporal approach. A major advantage of the approach, however, is its relevance to *normative* questions. Section 5 therefore takes up the reasons why an intertermporal approach to the current account is essential for sound policy formulation.

Finally, we note that, given the extensive recent literature this chapter aspires to encompass, there are several instances where space permits us only to sketch algebraic derivations. We try to alert the reader whenever intermediate algebra has been pruned especially severely, so that he or she will not become bogged down during a first reading. Space limits likewise allow us to provide only an illustrative rather than an exhaustive set of references.

2. The current account: Basic concepts and historical overview

A country's current-account balance over any time period is the increase in residents' claims on foreign incomes or outputs, less the increase in similar foreign-owned claims on home income or output. Thus, in theory, the current account includes not only exports less imports (broadly defined to include all the income on and payouts on cross-border assets: dividends, interest payments, insurance premia and payments, etc.), but also net capital gains on existing foreign assets. From the close of World War I until relatively recently, most countries' holdings of foreign assets had been limited both in quantity and scope, so the latter consideration was secondary. A focus on the current account as the net export balance led some economic thinkers to view relative international prices as its central determinant. Thus was born the "elasticities approach" to the current account, under which the determinants of international expenditure levels and incomes are held fixed in the background while static price elasticities of demand and supply determine the net international flow of capital.

As undergraduate macroeconomics texts demonstrate, however, the current account also is national saving less domestic investment. If saving falls short of desired investment, for example, foreigners must take up the balance, acquiring as a result claims on domestic income or output. This alternative viewpoint, which led to the absorption approach, stresses how macroeconomic factors must ultimately determine international borrowing or lending patterns [Alexander (1952)].

The intertemporal approach to current-account analysis extends the absorption approach through its recognition that private saving and investment decisions, and sometimes even government decisions, result from forward-looking calculations based on expectations of future productivity growth, government spending demands, real interest rates, and so on. The intertemporal approach achieves a synthesis of the absorption and elasticities view, however, by accounting for the macroeconomic determinants of relative prices and by analyzing the impact of current and future prices on saving and investment.

International capital flows, in the form of trade credits and commercial traffic in such assets as jewels and precious metals, were already common by biblical times. By the early fourteenth century, Italian banks spanning western Europe and the Levant had become large-scale lenders to sovereigns such as King Edward III of England, whose invasion of France in 1340, aided by foreign finance, initiated the Hundred Years War. The two most powerful Florentine banking houses, those of the Bardi and the Peruzzi, were bankrupted along with many lesser banks in 1343 when Edward proved unable to meet his obligations. But as Europe recovered from this early banking crisis and from the subsequent Black Death (1348), international financial linkages grew strong once again. The Catholic church, through its usury doctrine, unwittingly promoted the internationalization of banking in this period. While domestic loans for interest were prohibited, there was no definitive ban on exchanges of bills payable in different countries and currencies, even when the terms negotiated included implicit interest charges [de Roover (1966)]. Theological constraints thus led the largest banks to maintain extensive systems of foreign branches.

The expulsion of the Jews from the Iberian peninsula at the end of the fifteenth century, followed by widespread and continuing persecutions of Protestants after the Reformation, created networks of refugee communities with both the motivation and connections to move capital between countries. During European wars of the seventeenth and eighteenth centuries, international capital markets developed further as some governments turned to large-scale debt sales to foreigners. [See Neal (1990).] By the early nineteenth century at the latest, the outlines of modern international capital markets are visible in investors' search for profit opportunities on distant shores.

The era of the classical international gold standard, spanning the late nineteenth and early twentieth centuries, is often held up as a benchmark case of unfettered capital mobility between nations. Figure 2.1 shows data on saving, investment, and their difference, the current account, for a dozen countries over 1885–1913. (All data are nominal flows divided by a nominal income or output measure.)[3] The graphs indeed show several examples of large and protracted current-account imbalances, indicators of extensive trade across time. Canada ran persistent deficits which, by the eve of World War I, exceeded 15 percent of gross national product (GNP). These large flows were undoubtedly promoted by Canada's close political and cultural links with the United Kingdom, the largest lender. But even countries without such close ties to potential lenders were able to draw extensively on international capital markets. Japan ran an external deficit of 10 percent of national expenditure in financing its 1904–1905 war with Russia. During World War I, the country ran a comparable surplus to help finance its financially beleaguered allies.[4]

Data from the interwar period, shown in Figure 2.2, reveal a partial resurgence of net international borrowing and lending as postwar reconstruction progresses, but this process comes to a sudden halt as restrictions on international payments proliferate after the onset of the Great Depression.[5] Post-1945 data disclose a reverse evolution. Initially, current-account imbalances were slight because of official restrictions on international capital movements, with most industrial-country currencies being inconvertible through 1959. After the early 1970s (see Figure 2.3), net international capital flows expanded as a result of petrodollar recycling, the removal of many industrial-country restrictions on international payments following the adoption of floating exchange rates, and technological evolution in the financial industry. By the 1980s, the largest industrial countries, Germany, Japan, and the United States, were showing substantial external imbalances. At the same time many developing countries, caught in a debt crisis brought on in part by vigorous borrowing in the 1970s, found themselves denied access to resource inflows. Only in the early 1990s did this stark borrowing constraint begin to ease.

Unfortunately, the saving and investment flows reported in national income and product accounts (NIPA) and shown in Figures 2.1 through 2.3 don't always conform closely to theoretically correct concepts of saving and investment, particularly when international capital mobility is extensive. One especially serious defect is the failure of NIPA national income measures fully to reflect capital gains and losses on net foreign assets. During 1991, for example, the NIPA mea-

---

[3]These data, as well as those shown in Figure 2.2 below, are from Jones and Obstfeld (1994). Finland was actually a possession of Russia during the 1885–1913 period, but it was afforded a fair amount of administrative autonomy.

[4]For a discussion of wars and the Japanese current account during the first part of the twentieth century, see Obstfeld and Rogoff (1996), ch. 1.

[5]See Eichengreen (1990) for further discussion.

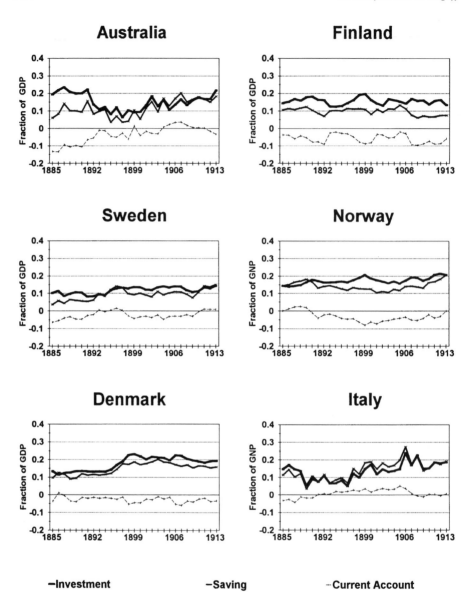

Figure 2.1. Saving, investment, and the current account: Classical gold standard, 1885–1913.

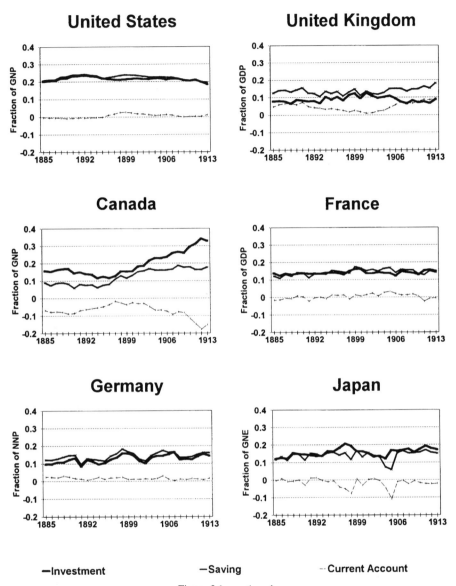

Figure 2.1. *continued.*

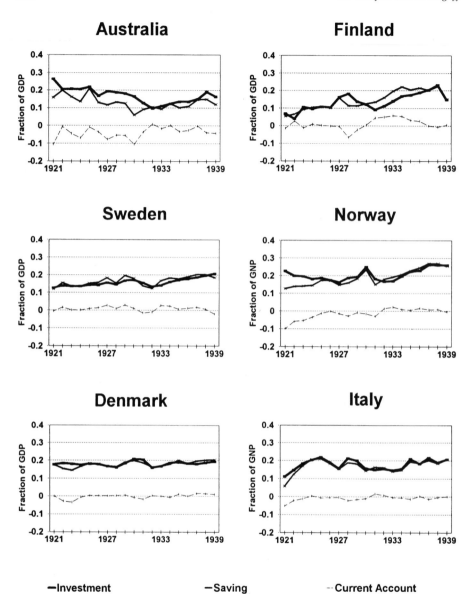

Figure 2.2. Saving, investment, and the current account: Inter-war era, 1921–1939.

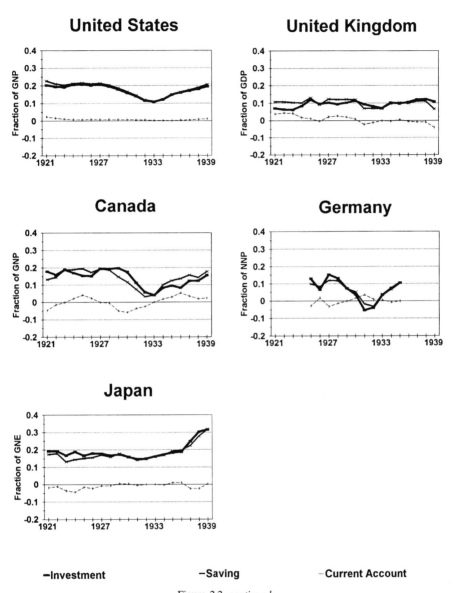

Figure 2.2. *continued.*

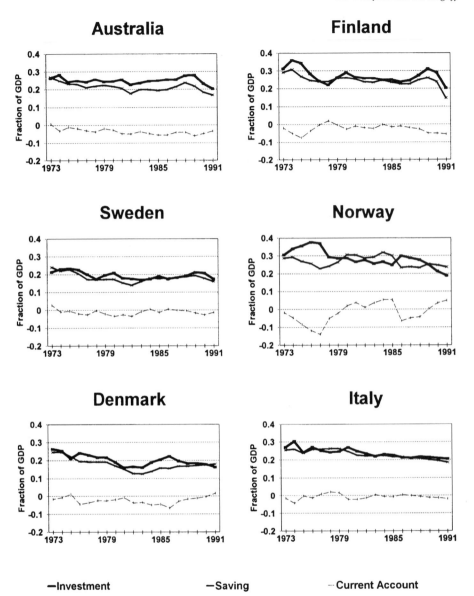

Figure 2.3. Saving, investment, and the current account: Post-Bretton Woods era, 1973–1991.

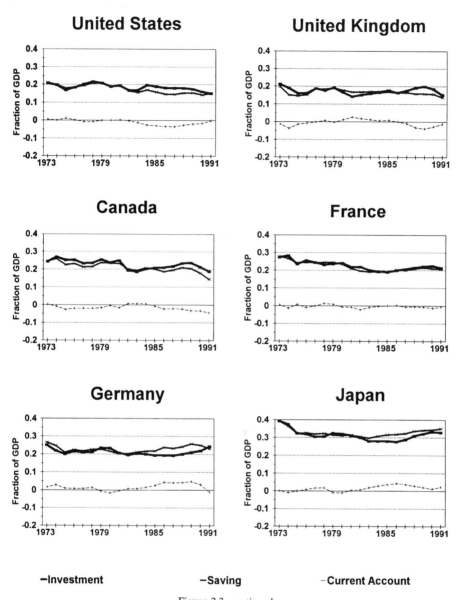

−Investment   −Saving   ‑‑Current Account

Figure 2.3. *continued.*

sure of saving less investment for the United States, the current account, was reported by the U.S. Department of Commerce as −$3.7 billion. The Department of Commerce also calculated, however, that on a market-value basis, U.S. assets held abroad at the end of 1990 appreciated in dollar value by $67.8 billion (more than the entire 1991 purchases of foreign assets by U.S. residents, $62.2 billion). At the same time, the dollar value of foreign claims on the U.S. at the end of 1990 rose by $172.8 billion (more than 2.5 times as large as the 1991 foreign purchases of U.S. assets, $67.0 billion).[6] In economic terms, the true dollar U.S. current-account deficit for 1991 is probably much closer to −$3.7 billion + $67.8 billion − $172.8 = −$108.7 billion than to its simple NIPA measure. And even this figure reflects only partial coverage of international asset holdings.

The numbers in Figures 2.1 through 2.3 are misleading for another reason. As Section 3 shows, it is changes in *real*, not nominal, asset holdings that matter for a country's welfare. Thus, NIPA measures of the current account, even if corrected to include nominal capital gains and losses, must be adjusted as well to correct for the inflationary erosion of foreign assets' real values.

These problems plague all of the empirical literature discussed in Section 4, although it would be possible to remedy them somewhat for a few industrial countries. In empirically evaluating theories it is obviously crucial to achieve the best possible match between the conceptual framework and the data brought to bear in testing it.

3. Intertemporal approaches to the current account

A realistic economic model incorporating all elements relevant to the typical country's current account would be hopelessly complex. Instead of attempting to construct such a comprehensive model, we turn in this section to a succession of models that illustrate what we believe to be the key elements influencing saving–investment balances in the world economy. In following this strategy, we largely parallel the development of theoretical thinking on the current account over the past fifteen years An important set of insights can be derived even from deterministic models; this is our first order of business. We then introduce uncertainty about the economic environment and deduce a number of essential modifications of the preceding nonstochastic framework. The introduction of uncertainty is, of course, a prerequisite for the empirical analysis of the intertemporal approach that we discuss in Section 4.

---

[6]The United States capital-account surplus, equal to $67.0 billion − $62.2 billion = $4.8 billion, differs from the recorded current-account deficit by a statistical discrepancy of −$1.1 billion.

3.1. Deterministic models of the current account

The first broad class of models to be described assumes that individual decision makers have perfect foresight and complete information about their economic environment. While these models lack realism along some dimensions, they serve at least two very useful purposes. First, they elucidate a number of questions for which uncertainty is of secondary importance, and second, they provide a benchmark against which to measure the predictions of richer stochastic models. As we shall see later, stochastic models in which real bonds are the only assets countries trade imply responses to shocks similar to the impulse responses of deterministic models.

3.1.1. A one-good model with representative national residents

Consider a small open economy that produces and consumes a single composite good and trades freely with the rest of the world. Free trade includes the international exchange of assets. We assume that the only traded asset is a consumption-indexed bond with fixed face value that pays net interest at the rate r_t between periods $t-1$ and t. Importantly, labor is internationally immobile. In per capita terms, let A_{t+1} denote the economy's stock of net foreign claims at the end of period t, Y_t net domestic product or output in period t, C_t private consumption, G_t government consumption, and I_t net investment.[7] Then the identity linking net foreign asset accumulation – that is, the current account, CA_t – to the saving-investment balance is:

$$CA_t = A_{t+1} - A_t = r_t A_t + Y_t - C_t - G_t - I_t \tag{3.1}$$

Define the market discount factor for date s consumption by

$$R_{t,s} = \frac{1}{\prod_{v=t+1}^{s}(1+r_v)} \tag{3.2}$$

(where $R_{t,t} = 1$). Forward iteration of eq. (3.1) leads to

$$(1+r_t)A_t = \sum_{s=t}^{\infty} R_{t,s}(C_s + G_s + I_s - Y_s) + \lim_{s \to \infty} R_{t,s} A_{s+1}$$

Because foreign lenders will not allow the economy to roll over a debt indefinitely through unlimited borrowing, the condition $\lim_{s \to \infty} R_{t,s} A_{s+1} \geq 0$ applies above. The resulting *intertemporal budget constraint* for the economy is thus:

$$\sum_{s=t}^{\infty} R_{t,s}(C_s + G_s + I_s) \leq (1+r_t)A_t + \sum_{s=t}^{\infty} R_{t,s} Y_s \tag{3.3}$$

In the models we survey no resources are willingly forgone, so (3.3) always holds

---

[7] We will assume for simplicity that capital does not depreciate.

with equality. In that case, (3.3) states that the present value of the economy's expenditures must equal its initial net foreign wealth plus the present value of domestic production.

The intertemporal budget constraint delimits the feasible choices of the economy. To describe the circumstances in which current-account imbalances will arise, however, one must specify how the components of expenditure and output are determined. We assume that the representative consumer maximizes the time-separable function

$$U_t = \sum_{s=t}^{\infty} \beta^{s-t} u(C_s) \tag{3.4}$$

where $\beta \in (0, 1)$, $u'(C) > 0$, $u''(C) < 0$.

The strong intertemporal separability of utility assumed in (3.4) will form the backbone of our formal analysis. Before going further, it is worthwhile to offer some justification for this decision.

(1) One might wish to start with a very general intertemporally nonseparable utility function of the form $U_t = U(C_t, C_{t+1}, ...)$. But this would yield few concrete and testable behavioral predictions. Instead we prefer to begin with a tractable basic setup like eq. (3.4) with strong implications. Preferences then can be generalized if the basic setup seems to be leading us astray.[8]

(2) Aggregation, across both goods and individuals, may cause intertemporal dependencies approximately to cancel out at the level of total per capita consumption.

(3) At the levels of time aggregation common in macroeconomic models, the assumption of intertemporal separability is not implausible. In any event, while empirical research on data at these frequencies has raised interesting questions about the time-separable utility model, it does not clearly point to a superior nonseparable alternative.

Having defended our choice of intertemporally additive utility functions, we now begin to pursue their implications. Let V_t be the real value of domestic firms at the end of period $t-1$ (after period $t-1$ dividends have been paid), B_t the stock of interest-earning claims owned by the domestic private sector at the end of $t-1$, w_t the real wage in period t, L_t the per capita supply of labor, and T_t lump-sum taxes levied by the home government. Then the intertemporal budget constraint of the representative consumer is[9]

---

[8]Plausible non-time-separable alternatives to (3.4) can be analyzed; [see, for example, Devereux and Shi (1991), Obstfeld (1982), Shi and Epstein (1993), and Svensson and Razin (1983)].

[9]Strictly speaking, the way the next constraint is expressed assumes perfect foresight between dates $t-1$ and t, so that a rate of return of r_t actually is earned on shares ex post. This assumption is made only to avoid cluttering the notation, and is not imposed in what follows. A more general formulation simply would replace $(1 + r_t)V_t$ by the ex post value (inclusive of dividends) of shares bought on date $t-1$.

$$\sum_{s=t}^{\infty} R_{t,s} C_s = (1 + r_t)(V_t + B_t) + \sum_{s=t}^{\infty} R_{t,s}(w_s L_s - T_s) \tag{3.5}$$

When (3.4) is maximized subject to (3.5), consumption necessarily follows the intertemporal Euler equation

$$u'(C_t) = \beta(1 + r_{t+1})u'(C_{t+1}) \tag{3.6}$$

This optimality condition, stressed long ago by Irving Fisher (1930), equates the marginal rate of substitution of present for future consumption, which is just $\beta u'(C_{t+1})/u'(C_t)$, to the price of future consumption in terms of present consumption, $1/(1 + r_{t+1})$. An implication is that, leaving aside discrepancies between β and $1/(1+r_{t+1})$, optimized consumption will follow a smooth, constant path (recall that $u(C)$ is strictly concave). A convenient closed-form description of the current account is obtained by specializing further to the case in which $u(C)$ takes the isoelastic form

$$u(C) = \frac{c^{1-1/\sigma} - 1}{1 - 1/\sigma}$$

with $\sigma > 0$ the elasticity of intertemporal substitution. In this case (3.6) implies that optimal consumption growth obeys

$$C_{t+1} = \beta^{\sigma}(1 + r_{t+1})^{\sigma} C_t \tag{3.7}$$

The consumption path described above must satisfy the economy's intertemporal constraint; using (3.7) to eliminate C_s ($s > t$) from (3.3) shows that the economy's date t consumption will be:

$$C_t = \frac{(1 + r_t)A_t + \sum_{s=t}^{\infty} R_{t,s}(Y_s - G_s - I_s)}{\sum_{s=t}^{\infty} R_{t,s}(\beta^{s-t}/R_{t,s})^{\sigma}} \tag{3.8}$$

Equation (3.8) leads to an illuminating general characterization of the current account. Define the "permanent" level of variable X on date t, $\tilde{X}_t$, by

$$\tilde{X}_t \equiv \frac{\sum_{s=t}^{\infty} R_{t,s} X_s}{\sum_{s=t}^{\infty} R_{t,s}}$$

and define $(\widetilde{\beta/R})^{\sigma}$ as the following weighted average of ratios of $(s - t)$-period subjective and market discount factors raised to the power σ:

$$(\widetilde{\beta/R})^{\sigma} \equiv \frac{\sum_{s=t}^{\infty} R_{t,s}(\beta^{s-t}/R_{t,s})^{\sigma}}{\sum_{s=t}^{\infty} R_{t,s}}$$

Then, *after many steps,* eqs. (3.1) and (3.8) show the current account surplus on date t to be:

$$CA_t = (r_t - \tilde{r}_t)A_t + (Y_t - \tilde{Y}_t) - (G_t - \tilde{G}_t)$$

$$-(I_t - \tilde{I}_t) + \left[1 - \frac{1}{(\widetilde{\beta/R})^\sigma}\right](\tilde{r}_t A_t + \tilde{Y}_t - \tilde{G}_t - \tilde{I}_t) \qquad (3.9)$$

(As we alluded in the introduction, there are several places where we advise the reader to consider holding off on reproducing a result until a later reading; this is the first.) Equation (3.9) yields a number of important predictions (each of which requires a ceteris paribus clause):[10]

(1) If the economy is a net foreign claimant and the world interest rate is above its permanent average, then the current account will be in greater surplus as people smooth consumption in the face of temporarily high foreign interest income. If the economy is a net foreign debtor, temporarily high interest rates will have an opposite current-account effect.

(2) Output above its permanent level will contribute to a higher current-account surplus, again due to consumption smoothing. Similarly, the private sector will use foreign borrowing to cushion its consumption from abnormally high government consumption and investment needs.

(3) The last term in (3.9) reflects consumption *tilting* due to divergences in the current and future periods between world real interest rates and the domestic rate of time preference, $(1 - \beta)/\beta$. When the home country is on average more impatient than the rest of the world, β is lower than future world interest rates will tend to be, resulting in $(\widetilde{\beta/R})^\sigma < 1$. There will then be a secular tendency toward current-account deficits, and thus toward secularly increasing foreign debt and declining consumption. When it is foreigners on the other hand who are (on average) more impatient, so that $(\widetilde{\beta/R})^\sigma > 1$, consumption's time path will have an upward tilt. The tilting effect is proportional to the economy's "permanent" resources. Also, the tilting effect is stronger the higher is the ease of intertemporal substitution in consumption, measured by σ.

---

[10] A less general version of eq. (3.9) is presented by Sachs (1982). To derive the first entry on the right-hand side of (3.9), observe that

$$\frac{1 + r_t}{\sum_{s=t}^{\infty} R_{t,s}} = \frac{r_t + \sum_{s=t+1}^{\infty} R_{t,s} r_s}{\sum_{s=t}^{\infty} R_{t,s}} = \frac{\sum_{s=t}^{\infty} R_{t,s} r_s}{\sum_{s=t}^{\infty} R_{t,s}} = \tilde{r}_t.$$

where we have made use of the fact that

$$\sum_{s=t+1}^{\infty} R_{t,s} r_s = 1$$

The rest is straightforward; for details, see Obstfeld and Rogoff (1996), ch. 2.

Before exploring the short-run implications of eq. (3.9), it is useful to consider some of the model's predictions for steady-state current-account behavior in a growing economy. As we shall see, a growing economy can run a current-account deficit indefinitely.

Incorporating the investment effects of growth forces one to model explicitly the linkage between capital accumulation and production. Assume that the production function for a small economy is Cobb–Douglas:

$$Y_t = \theta_t K_t^\alpha L^{1-\alpha}$$

($\alpha < 1$), where K_t is the end of period $t-1$ capital stock (available for production in period t), L is the constant labor force (which we will normalize to 1 for convenience), and the productivity coefficient θ grows so that

$$\theta_{t+1} = (1+g)^{1-\alpha}\theta_t$$

with $g > 0$. Assume also that the capital stock can adjust in a period, without installation costs. In the absence of unanticipated shocks, the marginal product of capital, $\alpha\theta_t K_t^{\alpha-1}$, thus must equal r, the constant world interest rate; $r > g$ by assumption.[11] Then, in a steady-state equilibrium, investment is easily shown to be

$$I_t = K_{t+1} - K_t = g\left(\frac{\alpha\theta_t}{r}\right)^{1/(1-\alpha)} = \left(\frac{\alpha g}{r}\right) Y_t$$

Output and investment therefore both grow at rate g. If government spending is zero, then one can use (3.9) to show that the optimal current account is given by

$$CA_t = A_{t+1} - A_t = -[1 - (1+r)^\sigma \beta^\sigma]A_t - \frac{1+g-(1+r)^\sigma\beta^\sigma}{r-g}\left(1 - \frac{\alpha g}{r}\right)Y_t$$

Division by Y_t yields a difference equation in A/Y,

$$\frac{A_{t+1}}{Y_{t+1}} = \left(\frac{(1+r)^\sigma\beta^\sigma}{1+g}\right)\frac{A_t}{Y_t} - \frac{1+g-(1+r)^\sigma\beta^\sigma}{(1+g)(r-g)}\left(1-\frac{\alpha g}{r}\right)$$

Provided $(1+r)^\sigma\beta^\sigma < 1+g$, the steady state is stable; it is the negative number

$$\overline{A/Y} = -\frac{1-(\alpha g/r)}{(r-g)}. \tag{3.10}$$

Notice that, because $\alpha g/r = I/Y$, the long-run ratio of foreign debt to output equals the ratio to current output of the *entire present value* of future output net of investment.

---

[11] For the world economy as a whole, the assumption that the growth rate does not exceed the interest rate can be justified using the standard Cass-Koopmans general equilibrium growth model.

What size debt-output ratio does eq. (3.10) imply? Suppose the world real interest rate r is 8 percent per year, g is 4 percent per year, and $\alpha = 0.4$. Then $\overline{A/Y} = -20$, and the economy's trade balance surplus each period must be $-(r-g)\overline{A/Y} = 80$ percent of GDP!

Such large debt levels and debt burdens are never observed in practice: economies that must borrow at market interest rates rarely have debts as great as a single year's GDP. The anomalous prediction points to some shortcomings of the model. With finite lifetimes, individuals currently alive wouldn't be able to borrow against the entire present value of the economy's output. There is no allowance in the model for sovereign risk. Finally, we note that the world interest rate r is determined by the rest of the world's growth rate. In this example, however, the world growth rate must equal $(1+r)^\sigma \beta^\sigma$ [see Obstfeld and Rogoff (1996), ch. 2], which is less than $1+g$ by assumption. But if a small economy were to grow faster than the world for a sufficiently long period, it would cease being small and the fixed interest rate assumption would be violated. If, on the other hand, the country's growth rate eventually converges to the world growth rate, the country's ability and desire to borrow from world capital markets are reduced.

3.1.2. The role of comparative advantage

The theory of international trade offers a useful perspective on these results. The reason is that foreign borrowing and lending can be viewed as *intertemporal trade*, that is, as the exchange of consumption available on different dates. The principle of comparative advantage thus applies.

Imagine that the home country faces a constant world interest rate equal to $1+r = 1/\beta$ and that $Y_t > Y_s$ for $s > t$. Equation (3.9) predicts that (absent other current-permanent differences) the country will have a current-account surplus. The principle of comparative advantage makes the same prediction. In the absence of trade, the country's autarky interest rates, equal to $u'(Y_t)/\beta^{s-t}u'(Y_s)$, lie below the corresponding world interest rates, $(1+r)^{s-t}$. It therefore pays for the representative resident to export present consumption by lending abroad, since present consumption is comparatively cheap at home, and to import future consumption by receiving repayment for the loans at a later date.

Similarly, temporarily high investment needs can raise a country's autarky interest rate above the world level, making it an importer of present consumption, that is, an external borrower.

This perspective makes clear that it is only the country-specific or idiosyncratic components of shocks that result in current-account imbalances. The global components of shocks, in contrast, affect all countries similarly and thus open up no new opportunities for gains through intertemporal trade. Countries cannot all smooth consumption perfectly in the face of a shock that temporarily depresses world output, for example. Instead, the world real interest rate is bid up and all countries tilt their consumption paths upward.

3.1.3. Modeling output fluctuations and investment

Our earlier investment example assumed that a nation's capital stock can be adjusted without cost to equate capital's marginal product to the world interest rate. Empirical observation makes this assumption difficult to swallow: even at the industry level, we simply do not observe large discrete changes in stocks of capital over very short periods. If there are costs to installing capital, however, capital stocks will move more sluggishly and protracted deviations of capital's marginal product from r are possible. A simple model illustrates how costly investment affects current-account dynamics.[12]

Assume that final output is produced according to the standard homogeneous and concave production function $\theta_t F(K_t, L_t)$, where, as before, θ_t captures shifts in total factor productivity, and where K_t is given by past investment decisions. A firm making decisions on date t maximizes the present discounted value of its profits (which equal the dividends shareholders receive):

$$\sum_{s=t}^{\infty} R_{t,s} \left[\theta_s F(K_s, L_s) - w_s L_s - I_s - \frac{a I_s^2}{2 K_s} \right] \tag{3.11}$$

Above, $\frac{a}{2}(I_t^2/K_t)$ is the deadweight output cost of installing

$$K_{t+1} - K_t = I_t \tag{3.12}$$

units of capital, where $a > 0$ is an adjustment-cost parameter. According to (3.11), the efficiency of investment in producing installed capital declines at an increasing rate as the ratio of investment to installed capital rises. Given (3.11), the economy's net output on date t is $Y_t = \theta_t F(K_t, L_t) - \frac{a}{2}(I_t^2/K_t)$.

The conditions for maximizing profits (3.11) subject to (3.12) include

$$I_t = \frac{q_t - 1}{a} K_t \tag{3.13}$$

and the investment Euler equation

$$q_t = \frac{\theta_{t+1} F_K(K_{t+1}, L_{t+1}) + \frac{a}{2}(I_{t+1}/K_{t+1})^2 + q_{t+1}}{1 + r_{t+1}} \tag{3.14}$$

---

[12]Matsuyama (1987) develops an open-economy model with costly investment. The effects of residential investment are studied in Matsuyama (1990).

where q_t (Tobin's q) is the Lagrange multiplier on constraint (3.12) and has the usual interpretation as the shadow price of installed capital.

Forward iteration on (3.14) shows that

$$q_t = \sum_{s=t+1}^{\infty} R_{t,s} \left[\theta_s F_K(K_s, L_s) + \frac{a}{2}(I_s/K_s)^2 \right] \tag{3.15}$$

(we have excluded bubbles in the price of capital). Equation (3.15) states that q_t, the *ex dividend* shadow price of a unit of capital at the end of period t, equals the present value of its future marginal products plus the present value of its future contributions to lowering the costs of investment.[13]

Multiply eq. (3.14) by K_{t+1} and use eq. (3.12) to express it as

$$q_t K_{t+1} = \frac{\theta_{t+1} F_K(K_{t+1}, L_{t+1}) K_{t+1} + \frac{a}{2}(I_{t+1}^2/K_{t+1}) + q_{t+1}(K_{t+2} - I_{t+1})}{1 + r_{t+1}}$$

Because the production function is homogeneous of degree one and $q_{t+1} = 1 + a(I_{t+1}/K_{t+1})$ [recall eq. (3.13)], the foregoing relationship, iterated forward successively to eliminate terms of form $q_s K_{s+1}$, implies that

$$q_t K_{t+1} = \sum_{s=t+1}^{\infty} R_{t,s} \left[\theta_s F(K_s, L_s) - w_s L_s - I_s - \frac{a I_s^2}{2 K_s} \right] \equiv V_{t+1} \tag{3.16}$$

Thus, the optimizing firm's *ex dividend* market value at the end of period t, V_{t+1}, is the same as the shadow value of its installed capital: in Hayashi's (1982) terminology, average q equals marginal q.[14]

To see some of the model's predictions for current account and investment dynamics, let us simplify by assuming that r, θ, and L are constant and consider a situation in which the capital stock K is initially below its steady state level. Thus the marginal product of capital, $\theta F_K(K_t, L)$ exceeds r, $q > 1$, and both K and Y are expected to rise over time. As the capital stock rises toward its steady-state level, $\bar{K}$, where $\theta F_K(\bar{K}, L) = r$, q falls to one.[15] According to (3.9) the current account (abstracting from government-spending changes, and assuming the economy consists of a representative firm owned by a representative agent)

[13] Equation (3.15) defines the *ex dividend* shadow price on date t because it does not include the profit earned on that date and paid out to shareholders as dividends.

[14] As Hayashi shows, this equality is due to the homogeneity of degree one of the production and installation-cost functions.

[15] For discussions of these dynamics, see Abel (1982) and Summers (1981).

is given by

$$
CA_t = \left\{ \left[\theta F(K_t, L) - \frac{aI_t^2}{2K_t} \right] - \frac{r}{1+r} \sum_{s=t}^{\infty} \left(\frac{1}{1+r} \right)^{s-t} \left[\theta F(K_s, L) - \frac{aI_s^2}{2K_s} \right] \right\}
$$
$$
- \left[\frac{q_t - 1}{a} K_t - \frac{r}{1+r} \sum_{s=t}^{\infty} \left(\frac{1}{1+r} \right)^{s-t} \frac{q_s - 1}{a} K_s \right]
$$

Since K is rising over time, final output is rising over time as well. Since investment also is falling,[16] date t installation costs exceed their permanent level. Thus, $Y_t = \theta F(K_t, L) - \frac{a}{2}(I_t^2/K_t)$ falls short of its permanent level, contributing a negative component to the current account. The fact that investment also is above its permanent level contributes a second negative component to the current account.

Suppose K initially lies below its long-run steady-state value because the economy has just experienced an unanticipated permanent increase in factor productivity, θ. We can see from the preceding analysis that the economy runs a current-account deficit. A classical example of this dynamic is Norway in the 1970s (Figure 2.3), which borrowed extensively to build up its North Sea oil production following the first oil-price shock.

Note that an unanticipated permanent rise in θ not only leads to a current account deficit but causes an immediate rise in output as well. Therefore, with productivity shocks the model can in principle explain the well-documented countercyclical behavior of the current account.[17] Of course, this result rests on the assumption that the rise in θ is permanent. Imagine, in contrast, an unexpected rise in θ_t lasting only a single period. This change will not affect investment plans for future dates, and so the only effect is a level of output temporarily above the permanent level. Equation (3.9) shows that a current account surplus will arise on date t. Productivity shocks with greater persistence cause some investment and hence smaller initial current-account surpluses, and, if persistent enough, they can produce an initial deficit, as in the permanent case.

---

[16] Investment equals $(q-1)K/a$, but with q falling while K is rising, it may not be obvious that I falls over time. The assertion in the text is always true in the neighborhood of the steady state. To see why, observe that

$$
\begin{aligned}
I_{t+1} - I_t &= K_t \left[\frac{(q_{t+1} - q_t)}{a} + \frac{(q_{t+1} - 1)(q_t - 1)}{a^2} \right] \\
&\doteq \bar{K} \left(\frac{q_{t+1} - q_t}{a} \right)
\end{aligned}
$$

to a first-order approximation.

[17] See the article by Morris Goldstein and Mohsin S. Khan in volume 2 of this Handbook (Goldstein and Khan 1985).

The reader should note that in the present one-good small-economy model, changes in investment can affect consumption, but investment itself is determined by elements that are *independent* of consumption preferences. Investment decisions are made to maximize the present discounted value of the country's output, evaluated at the world interest rate. The country's saving behavior is irrelevant. This independence of investment from consumption preferences need not hold if the economy uses capital to produce nontraded goods and services as well as tradeables; it can also break down if there is a nontraded input in production, such as labor. Introducing nontraded goods and services leads to a number of other modifications of our basic one-good model's results, as we shall see in the next section.

3.1.4. Nontradeables, consumption, and investment

An economy that consumes and produces nontradeables as well as tradeables may behave quite differently from the one examined so far. We begin by seeing how nontradeables can affect consumption decisions.

In this section, it will be convenient to reinterpret C as a composite *index* of the representative individual's consumption of tradeables and nontradeables, C_T and C_N, but retain the assumption that the period utility function $u(C)$ is isoelastic with intertemporal substitution elasticity σ. Assume, moreover, that composite consumption C has the CES form:

$$C = \left[\alpha^{1/\rho} C_T^{(\rho-1)/\rho} + (1-\alpha)^{1/\rho} C_N^{(\rho-1)/\rho} \right]^{\rho/(\rho-1)} \tag{3.17}$$

Here, ρ is the (intratemporal) substitution elasticity between tradeables and nontradeables. Take tradeables as the numeraire commodity and let p be the price of nontradeables in terms of tradeables. Then, as one can easily show, the exact consumer-price index (CPI) in tradeables, defined as the minimal cost in tradeables of a unit of subutility C, is given by

$$P = \left[\alpha + (1-\alpha)p^{1-\rho} \right]^{1/(1-\rho)} \tag{3.18}$$

For the special case $\rho = 1$ (Cobb–Douglas preferences), $P = p^{1-\alpha}$. These same calculations reveal that, given C, the optimal consumption levels for tradeables and nontradeables are:

$$C_T = \alpha \left(\frac{1}{P} \right)^{-\rho} C, \qquad C_N = (1-\alpha) \left(\frac{p}{P} \right)^{-\rho} C \tag{3.19}$$

Given the intratemporal allocation rules in (3.19), the consumer's *intertemporal* decision problem can be analyzed entirely in terms of composite consumption C and the price index P. The consumer maximizes (3.4) subject to the budget constraint corresponding to (3.5) but written in terms of expenditure on C:

$$\sum_{s=t}^{\infty} R_{t,s} P_s C_s = (1 + r_t)(V_t + B_t) + \sum_{s=t}^{\infty} R_{t,s}(w_s L_s - T_s)$$

(Above, asset stocks, wages, and taxes still are expressed in units of tradeables). The intertemporal Euler equation for the consumption index C is now

$$C_{t+1} = \beta^{\sigma}(1 + r_{t+1})^{\sigma} \left(\frac{P_t}{P_{t+1}}\right)^{\sigma} C_t \tag{3.20}$$

This relationship is analogous to Euler eq. (3.7), except that overall consumption growth depends on the utility-based real interest factor $(1 + r_{t+1})(P_t/P_{t+1})$, and not simply on the relative intertemporal price of tradeables $1 + r_{t+1}$. [Dornbusch (1983) stresses this point.] Combining eqs. (3.19) and (3.20) shows that the Euler equation for *tradeables* expenditure, C_T, is

$$C_{Tt+1} = \beta^{\sigma}(1 + r_{t+1})^{\sigma} \left(\frac{P_t}{P_{t+1}}\right)^{\sigma - \rho} C_{Tt} \tag{3.21}$$

Equations (3.20) and (3.21) show, in particular, that consumption need no longer be intertemporally smoothed when the time-preference rate and world tradeable goods interest rate coincide. For example, if the CPI, P, is rising over time, the real interest rate will be below the own interest rate on tradeables, r. So total consumption expenditure *measured in tradeables, PC*, will fall over time if $\sigma > 1$ and rise over time if $\sigma < 1$. Similarly, while a rising path of P tilts that of C downward with an elasticity σ, the price changes cause C_T to rise relative to C with elasticity ρ [see eq. (3.19)]. If $\rho > \sigma$ and $\beta(1 + r) = 1$, for example, consumption of tradeables will rise over time if P is rising.[18]

Some general-equilibrium implications of these points can be illustrated by a simple model in which the economy's output of nontradeables, Y_N, is exogenous. If we assume (for simplicity) that neither the government nor the domestic investment process uses up nontradeables, then the condition of equilibrium in the nontradeable sector is simply $C_N = Y_N$, and by (3.19) the equilibrium relative price of nontradeables is

$$p = \left[\frac{(1 - \alpha)C_T}{\alpha Y_N}\right]^{1/\rho}$$

In the Cobb–Douglas case $\rho = 1$, and it is simple to write down the equilibrium growth process for tradeables consumption by combining the preceding expression with eq. (3.21):

$$C_{Tt+1} = \beta^{\frac{\sigma}{\sigma - \alpha(\sigma - 1)}} (1 + r_{t+1})^{\frac{\sigma}{\sigma - \alpha(\sigma - 1)}} \left(\frac{Y_{Nt+1}}{Y_{Nt}}\right)^{\frac{(1-\alpha)(\sigma-1)}{\sigma - \alpha(\sigma-1)}} C_{Tt} \tag{3.22}$$

---

[18]For a panel of 13 developing countries, Ostry and Reinhart (1992) present Euler-equation estimates of $\sigma = 1.27$ or 1.22 and $\rho = 0.38$ or 0.50 (depending on the instrumental variables used in estimation). These results indicate that the case $\sigma > \rho$ may be relevant.

Notice that even when nontradeables output is constant, the growth of tradeables consumption usually reflects the presence of nontradeables in the consumption basket. The reason: growth in C_T affects p and thus the domestic real interest rate.

A fundamental implication of these results is that empirical studies of the intertemporal approach should distinguish carefully between fluctuations in traded and nontraded outputs. As an example, suppose that the path of traded output is flat, that $\beta(1 + r) = 1$, and that $Y_{Nt} < Y_{Nt+1}$. According to eq. (3.22), consumption of tradeables will be rising if $\sigma > 1$ and falling if $\sigma < 1$. Because the current account surplus is the difference between the economy's endowment of tradeables and its absorption of tradeables, even the sign of the current account balance may not be related in a simple way to the time path of the economy's total real output.

One can add a labor-leisure tradeoff to the intertemporal model by viewing leisure as a nontradeable (assuming there is no international migration). In this context the real wage plays the role that the relative price of nontradeables p played above.[19]

Also, as we suggested at the end of the preceding section, the presence of a sector producing nontradeables permits domestic consumption preferences to affect the economy's investment behavior. A shift in preferences toward nontradeables, for instance, will reduce investment if the nontradeables sector is the relatively labor-intensive one.[20]

Allowing for nontradeables is an important step towards having a more realistic model of current account behavior. In the next section we consider another important modification.

3.1.5. Consumer durables and the current account

Eighteen percent of 1993 United States consumption spending was devoted to durables (including clothing and shoes). But the theory we have developed thus far does not capture the possibility that consumer purchases in one period may yield utility over several periods. We now illustrate how the presence of durables can alter current account responses.

In this subsection, let C stand for the individual's consumption of nondurables and let D be the stock of durables he or she owns; all goods can be traded. A stock D of durables yields a proportional service flow each period, including the period in which it is acquired. The consumer in a small country maximizes

$$U_t = \sum_{s=t}^{\infty} \beta^{s-t} [\alpha \log C_s + (1 - \alpha) \log D_s]$$

---

[19] For an early analysis of the effects of introducing nontraded labor on current account dynamics, see Bean (1986).

[20] See, for example, Murphy (1986) and Engel and Kletzer (1989).

subject to the finance constraints

$$A_{t+1} - A_t = rA_t + Y_t - C_t - G_t - (K_{t+1} - K_t) - p_t[D_t - (1-\delta)D_{t-1}]$$

and a solvency condition. Here, D_t is the stock of durables (including newly purchased durables) held over period t, p_t is their price in terms of nondurables, δ is their depreciation rate, and r, the world interest rate, is constant. Note that A, Y, C, G, and K are measured in nondurables. Durability implies $\delta < 1$.

In addition to the usual intertemporal Euler equation for nondurables consumption, the individual's first-order conditions include

$$\frac{(1-\alpha)C_t}{\alpha D_t} = p_t - \frac{1-\delta}{1+r}p_{t+1} \equiv \iota_t,$$

which equates the marginal rate of substitution of nondurables for the services of durables to the *user cost* or rental price of durables.

Assuming $\beta = 1/(1+r)$, consumption of nondurables is

$$C_t = \frac{\alpha r}{1+r}\left[(1+r)A_t + (1-\delta)p_t D_{t-1} + \sum_{s=t}^{\infty}\left(\frac{1}{1+r}\right)^{s-t}(Y_s - I_s - G_s)\right]$$

while consumption of durables' services is

$$D_t = \frac{(1-\alpha)r}{\iota_t(1+r)}\left[(1+r)A_t + (1-\delta)p_t D_{t-1} + \sum_{s=t}^{\infty}\left(\frac{1}{1+r}\right)^{s-t}(Y_s - I_s - G_s)\right].$$

Let's suppose for simplicity that, p_t and, hence, the user cost, ι_t, are constant. The last equations then imply that the consumer smooths, not the path of expenditures $p[D_t - (1-\delta)D_{t-1}]$ on durables, but the *service* flow from durables, which is proportional to D_t. With durables, the current account is the same as implied by (3.9) (assuming, as we have here, that $r = (1-\beta)/\beta$), but with an additional term that depends on new durables purchases (*we omit the derivation*):

$$CA_t = \left\{(Y_t - \tilde{Y}_t) - (G_t - \tilde{G}_t) - (I_t - \tilde{I}_t)\right\} + (\iota - p)\Delta D_t \tag{3.23}$$

Noting that the price of purchasing a durable outright, p, must be greater Than the one-period user cost ι, we see that the introduction of durables necessarily increases the volatility of current-account responses to unexpected income changes.

3.1.6. The terms of trade and the transfer problem

One of the earliest problems motivating the intertemporal approach was the need to understand how changes in the terms of trade – the price of a country's exports in terms of its imports – affect saving and the current account. Early applications of Keynesian models by Harberger (1950) and Laursen and Metzler (1950) had modeled adverse terms-of-trade shocks as real income-reductions that reduce saving and the external surplus in proportion to Keynes's marginal propensity to save. Instead, the intertemporal approach emphasized the response of forward-looking individuals to the changes in lifetime consumption possibilities that terms-of-trade movements cause.

The simplest case is of a specialized economy with an exogenous endowment Y of its export good, but which also consumes imports. As in the model with nontradeables, we again assume an isoelastic period utility function defined over a CES index C; here it depends on the individual's consumptions C_M of imports and C_X of exports:

$$C = \left[\alpha^{1/\rho} C_M^{(\rho-1)/\rho} + (1-\alpha)^{1/\rho} C_X^{(\rho-1)/\rho}\right]^{\rho/(\rho-1)}$$

Let p now denote the price of exports in terms of imports, which is determined exogenously in the world market. The consumption-based price level in terms of imports is again denoted by P and given by formula (3.18).

The natural benchmark case, assumed by Svensson and Razin (1983), supposes that intertemporal trade is done through bonds indexed to the consumption index, C. In this case r is the own rate of interest on the consumption index, and the budget constraint corresponding to (3.3) in the present setup (abstracting from investment and government) is

$$\sum_{s=t}^{\infty} R_{t,s} C_s = (1+r_t)A_t + \sum_{s=t}^{\infty} R_{t,s} \left(\frac{p_s Y_s}{P_s}\right)$$

The Euler equation for the consumption index is again (3.7), implying the consumption function corresponding to (3.8), which has $I = G = 0$ and pY/P in place of Y. To focus on the terms of trade, it is helpful to assume that $r = (1-\beta)/\beta$ and Y are constant, in which case the consumption function reduces to:

$$C_t = rA_t + \frac{r}{1+r} \sum_{s=t}^{\infty} \left(\frac{1}{1+r}\right)^{s-t} \left(\frac{p_s Y}{P_s}\right)$$

A fall in the terms of trade lowers p (the relative price of exports in terms of imports) relative to P (the overall CPI in terms of imports). Thus, fluctuations in the terms of trade affect the consumption index and the current account (which here is measured in consumption-index units) exactly like fluctuations in GDP at constant terms of trade. In particular, a temporary terms-of-trade setback causes a current-account deficit, whereas a permanent setback causes an immediate shift to the new, lower consumption level consistent with external

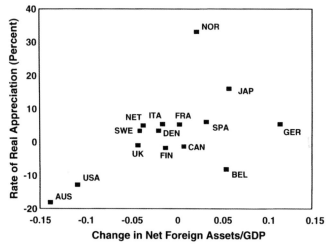

Figure 3.1. Real currency appreciation versus the change in foreign assets, 1981–1990.

balance. Obstfeld (1982) and Svensson and Razin (1983) illustrate how this latter result depends on the strong intertemporal separability of utility. [21]

This subsection has, thus far, focused on the response of the current account to exogenous terms-of-trade changes. When countries have some monopoly power in trade, however, shifts in their current accounts may influence terms of trade by redistributing wealth internationally.

The impact of international wealth transfers on the terms of trade is a classic problem of international finance. In the 1920s, Keynes and Ohlin disagreed on the price effects of German reparations; in the 1990s, observers of the protracted United States external deficits have debated the need for a fall in the relative price of American exports.[22]

For a cross-section of 15 OECD countries, Figure 3.1 plots the percent change in the trade-weighted WPI real exchange rate (a terms-of-trade proxy) against the change in the ratio of net foreign assets to output. The net foreign asset series attempt to account not only for measured current account flows, but for

[21] Ostry (1988) and Edwards (1989) study interactions between the terms of trade and the relative price of nontradeables. Gavin (1990) considers the terms of trade in a richer dynamic setting. For developing countries, it may be natural to assume that bonds are indexed to imports (e.g. "dollars"). In that case the intertemporal budget constraint differs from the one we have analyzed, so that the Euler equation for C is formally the same as (3.20). If the world bond rate is constant, expected terms of trade movements therefore have consumption-tilting effects through the consumption-based real interest rate.

[22] See, for example, the papers in Bergsten (1991).

capital gains and losses.[23] The changes are calculated as the 1986–1990 average less the 1981–1985 average.

The figure shows a distinct positive relationship – an increase in a country's net foreign assets appears to be associated with an improvement in its terms of trade. The least-squares regression line is

$$\Delta \log(p_j) = 0.039 + 1.042 \Delta(A/Y)_j + u_j; R^2 = 0.31$$
$$\quad\quad\quad (0.027)\quad (0.433)$$

implying a statistically significant relationship. According to the regression, an increase of 1 percent in the ratio of net foreign assets to output is associated with a 1 percent improvement in the terms of trade.

Obviously, this regression provides only a nonstructural correlation. To assess accurately the consequences of an exogenous wealth transfer would require a full econometric structural model. Given the perennial importance of the transfer effect in policy discussions, the development of empirical intertemporal models that can explain its magnitude is a research priority.

Theoretically, the transfer effect can operate through several channels in a general-equilibrium setting. Two potential mechanisms are home preference for domestic exports [see, for example, Buiter (1989)] and the presence of a non-tradeables sector that competes for resources with the exportable sector. A special case of the latter mechanism is due to the effect of a wealth change on labor supply and, hence, on the supply of exportables.

A simple two-country model exhibits the labor-supply channel for the transfer effect. Assume that the home country specializes in producing good X and the foreign country good M. Moreover, assume that in both countries ρ, the elasticity of substitution in demand between the two produced goods, equals 1. Let the period utility function, common to the home and foreign countries, be an isoelastic function of an index that depends on both consumption and leisure,

$$C^\xi (H - L)^{1-\xi} = \left(C_M^\alpha C_X^{1-\alpha} \right)^\xi (H - L)^{1-\xi}$$

where $0 < \xi < 1$, H is an individual's endowment of time, and L his or her labor supply. Let home output be produced according to the production function $Y = \omega L$ and foreign output according to $Y^* = \omega^* L^*$. Let P once again denote

---

[23] Real exchange rate data come from International Monetary Fund, *International Financial Statistics*. Net foreign asset positions come from *OECD Economic Outlook* 55 (June 1994), p. A54. The country sample is Australia (for which the CPI was used), Belgium–Luxembourg, Canada, Denmark, Finland, France, Germany, Italy, Japan, Netherlands, Norway, Spain, Sweden, the United States, and the United Kingdom. We are skeptical that the real appreciation of 33 percent that the IMF reports for Norway is accurate. (The IMF reports a similar number based on CPIs.) OECD data place Norway's real appreciation over 1981–1990 closer to 15 percent. However, the observation on Norway is not driving the regression results reported below.

the price of the index C in terms of home imports, and assume bonds are indexed to C. The home country's net external assets are A, and the foreign country's, therefore, are $-A$. Using the steady-state consumption functions to solve for demand and supply in either of the goods markets, one can show (*after many steps*) that the equilibrium terms of trade satisfy the condition

$$\frac{p\alpha\omega H}{P} - \frac{(1-\alpha)\omega^* H^*}{P} = \frac{(1-\xi)(1-\beta)}{\xi\beta}A$$

From this implicit terms-of-trade equation one can easily see the effect of an exogenous shift in net external assets from the foreign to the home country (that is, of a rise in A). An absolute rise in p, the relative price of home exports, raises p relative to P, and P itself rises absolutely. If A rises, a rise in p therefore maintains equilibrium. The intuition why a wealth transfer to the home country improves its terms of trade is simple. If home residents receive a financial windfall, they spend some of it on leisure. Output of the home good thus falls and its relative price must rise.

3.1.7. Demographic structure, fiscal policy, and the current account

The single representative agent paradigm followed so far in this chapter may furnish misleading predictions about the current account when the economy consists instead of heterogeneous families born on different dates and unconnected by altruistic links. A model based on the overlapping-generations structure in Weil (1989) illustrates some possible implications of allowing for demographic complexity.[24]

We will identify the economy's total population with its labor supply, L_t, which grows at rate n: $L_{t+1} = (1+n)L_t$, with L_0 normalized to 1. This labor force, however, consists of immortal unconnected individuals (or dynasties) born on successive dates. A representative from the generation born on date v (the generation's "vintage") maximizes $U_{v,t} = \sum_{s=t}^{\infty} \beta^{s-t} u(C_{v,s})$ subject to

$$\sum_{s=t}^{\infty} R_{t,s} C_{v,s} = (1+r_t)(V_{v,t} + B_{v,t}) + \sum_{s=t}^{\infty} R_{t,s}(w_s - T_s)$$

(where $B_{v,t}$ denotes vintage v's bond holdings and each individual supplies one unit of labor per period). Notice that consumption and wealth are vintage-specific, whereas all people face the same wage, interest rates, and (by assumption) lump-sum taxes. A key assumption is that $V_{v,v} = B_{v,v} = 0$: vintages are born with no financial wealth, only with a lifetime endowment equal to the

---

[24] For alternative open-economy models with overlapping generations, see Buiter (1981, 1989), Blanchard (1985), Persson (1985), Frenkel and Razin (1987), and Eaton (1988).

present value of after-tax labor income. (One can think of the model as one in which primogeniture governs the bequest of family wealth.) Investment can be modeled exactly as in Section 3.1.3. The only difference is that a growing labor force requires positive steady-state investment.

To make the main points it suffices to work with the special case in which the interest rate is constant at r and the period utility function is $u(C) = \log(C)$.[25] In this case,

$$C_{v,t} = (1 - \beta) \left[(1 + r)(V_{v,t} + B_{v,t}) + \sum_{s=t}^{\infty} \left(\frac{1}{1+r} \right)^{s-t} (w_s - T_s) \right] \qquad (3.24)$$

is the consumption function.

In investigating the economy's aggregate behavior, it is helpful to work with per capita aggregate measures of macro-variables such as consumption and wealth. Assume that the economy starts on date 0. Let $X_{v,t}$ be the vintage-specific value of variable X on date t. Observe that the size of generation $v = 0$ is 1, that of generation 1 is $(1 + n) - 1 = n$, that of generation 2 is $(1 + n)^2 - (1 + n) = n(1 + n)$, and so on up through vintage t, which is of size $n(1 + n)^{t-1}$. Thus the per capita average value of X on date t is:

$$X_t = \frac{X_{0,t} + nX_{1,t} + n(1 + n)X_{2,t} + \cdots + n(1 + n)^{t-1}X_{t,t}}{(1 + n)^t} \qquad (3.25)$$

To compute aggregate per capita consumption, observe that V_t, defined as in the last equation, is the average per capita value of claims to domestic firms at the end of period $t - 1$ and is still given by (3.11) if the quantities in that equation are interpreted as per capita aggregates. Equations (3.11), (3.24), and (3.25) thus imply[26]

$$C_t = (1 - \beta) \left[(1 + r)B_t + \sum_{s=t}^{\infty} \left(\frac{1}{1+r} \right)^{s-t} (Y_s - T_s - I_s) \right] \qquad (3.26)$$

Above, consumption has been expressed as a function of the time path of taxes. To understand the role of taxation, however, we must for the first time in this chapter explicitly consider exactly how the domestic government coordinates the time paths of public expenditures and taxes.

Let D_t now denote the government's per capita debt at the end of date $t-1$. Then if G_t denotes per capita government consumption, the intertemporal public-sector budget constraint on date t is

---

[25] This case corresponds to isoelastic preferences with $\sigma = 1$.

[26] To derive this equation, we assume perfect foresight between dates $t-1$ and t, so that $(1+r)V_t = Y_t - w_t - I_t + V_{t+1}$. The next equation holds, however, even without the perfect foresight assumption, as can be seen by modifying consumers' intertemporal budget constraints as explained in the footnote preceding eq. (3.5) above. In deriving (3.26), we have made use of the fact that the production function is homogenous of degree one.

$$(1+r)(1+n)^t D_t + \sum_{s=t}^{\infty} \left(\frac{1}{1+r}\right)^{s-t} (1+n)^s G_s = \sum_{s=t}^{\infty} \left(\frac{1}{1+r}\right)^{s-t} (1+n)^s T_s$$

This constraint equates the present value of tax revenues to the present value of spending plus initial debt. If $r \le n$ neither the government's revenue nor its spending has a finite present value, so we assume $r > n$. Division of the preceding constraint by $(1+n)^t$ renders it in per capita terms as:

$$(1+r)D_t + \sum_{s=t}^{\infty} \left(\frac{1+n}{1+r}\right)^{s-t} G_s = \sum_{s=t}^{\infty} \left(\frac{1+n}{1+r}\right)^{s-t} T_s$$

To see what this constraint implies for private consumption, lead it one period and observe that

$$D_{t+1} = \frac{(1+r)D_t + G_t - T_t}{1+n} \tag{3.27}$$

Solving eq. (3.27) for T_t and taking present values, we obtain

$$\sum_{s=t}^{\infty} \left(\frac{1}{1+r}\right)^{s-t} T_s = (1+r)D_t - \sum_{s=t+1}^{\infty} \left(\frac{1}{1+r}\right)^{s-t-1} nD_s + \sum_{s=t}^{\infty} \left(\frac{1}{1+r}\right)^{s-t} G_s$$

which, after rearranging, can be expressed in the form:

$$\sum_{s=t}^{\infty} \left(\frac{1}{1+r}\right)^{s-t} T_s = \sum_{s=t}^{\infty} \left(\frac{1}{1+r}\right)^{s-t} G_s + (1+r)\left(1 - \frac{n}{r}\right) D_t$$

$$- \sum_{s=t}^{\infty} \left(\frac{1}{1+r}\right)^{s-t} \left(\frac{1+r}{r}\right) n(D_{s+1} - D_s) \tag{3.28}$$

Expression (3.28) shows that in the overlapping-generations economy, government debt is net wealth to the private sector and higher future government deficits *lower* the present value of taxes for those currently alive, holding the path of government consumption constant. Why is this so? Equation (3.27) shows that if D_t were a unit higher the government would have to raise taxes in all future periods by only $r - n$ to keep the per capita public debt constant. Thus, an extra unit of government bonds in the hands of someone alive at the start of date t raises his or her discounted stream of tax liabilities by only

$$\sum_{s=t}^{\infty} \left(\frac{1}{1+r}\right)^{s-t} (r - n) = (1+r)\left(1 - \frac{n}{r}\right)$$

How do current and future government deficits alter the tax bill of current generations? Let the government cut per capita taxes by $1 + n$ units in period t and finance this tax cut by issuing enough additional debt to make D_{t+1} one unit higher [see eq. (3.27)]. If the government is to maintain this new higher per capita debt level, it must raise taxes by $r - n$ per capita from date $t + 1$ on. Thus, for someone alive on date t, the net effect of a deficit-financed tax cut is to lower the present value of taxes by

$$1 + n - \sum_{s=t+1}^{\infty} \left(\frac{1}{1+r}\right)^{s-t} (r - n) = \left(\frac{1+r}{r}\right) n$$

Deficit-financed tax cuts in periods after t have a corresponding discounted effect on the tax liabilities of those alive on date t.

The mechanism underlying these results is well known: the more debt the government issues, the more taxes can be shifted onto future generations yet unborn. Severing altruistic links between those alive today and some of those who will be alive tomorrow creates a situation in which current generations do not fully internalize the future tax liabilities arising from government debt issue. If, in contrast, $n = 0$, there are no future entrants to the economy to be taxed and, as (3.28) shows, the time profile of government debt no longer matters to economic agents. In this case, government debt is not net wealth and the Ricardian equivalence of deficit- and tax-financed government expenditure holds. In the representative-agent economy considered earlier, government borrowing has no influence on the current account.

This is not the case here. Because the economy's overall net foreign assets are $A_t = B_t - D_t$, substitution of (3.28) into consumption function (3.26) shows that

$$C_t = (1 - \beta) \left\{ \frac{n}{r} D_t + \sum_{s=t}^{\infty} \left(\frac{1}{1+r}\right)^{s-t} \left(\frac{1+r}{r}\right) n(D_{s+1} - D_s) \right.$$
$$\left. + (1+r)A_t + \sum_{s=t}^{\infty} \left(\frac{1}{1+r}\right)^{s-t} (Y_s - I_s - G_s) \right\}$$

In per capita terms, the date-t current account is $(1+n)A_{t+1} - A_t = rA_t + Y_t - C_t - I_t - G_t$, so, other things equal, a higher current level of government debt or a higher trajectory for future government deficits will raise current consumption and the economy's foreign borrowing.

Despite some notable episodes, it has proven difficult to verify a strong statistical correlation between budget and current-account deficits. Below we present cross-section regressions for industrialized countries over five-year subsamples of 1976–1990.[27] Each subsample cross-section observation is formed by aver-

---

[27] The sample consists of the OECD countries as of 1994, except for Belgium, Luxembourg and Turkey. The data for current-account deficits and central government budget deficits relative to GDP come from International Monetary Fund, *International Financial Statistics*. Due to lack of data, Switzerland is omitted from the 1981–1985 regression and Canada, New Zealand, and Switzerland are omitted from the 1986–90 regression. Regressions based on general government deficits yield similar results [see Obstfeld and Rogoff (1996), ch. 3].

aging a country's annual current-account surplus ratio to GDP and its central government deficit ratio to GDP.

$$1976-1980$$
$$(CA/Y)_j = -0.208 - 0.406 \ (\Delta D/Y)_j + u_j; R^2 = 0.23$$
$$(0.907) \quad (0.171)$$

$$1981-1985$$
$$(CA/Y)_j = 0.995 - 0.506 \ (\Delta D/Y)_j + u_j; R^2 = 0.32$$
$$(1.206) \quad (0.173)$$

$$1986-1990$$
$$(CA/Y)_j = -0.881 - 0.016 \ (\Delta D/Y)_j + u_j; R^2 = 0.00$$
$$(0.707) \quad (0.114)$$

Over the first two subsamples there is a strong negative correlation between budget deficits and the current-account surplus, as the overlapping-generations model would suggest.[28] During the most recent subsample, however, the correlation evaporates. The last result suggests that factors other than government budgets dominated several countries' current accounts over 1986–1990. If one runs the same regression on a sample that includes non-industrialized countries, the results are weaker. Beware: these simple correlations are merely suggestive and have no structural interpretation. In particular, they cannot tell us the effect of an exogenous increase in a government's budget deficit on the current account. Another serious issue is to choose the appropriate measure of the intergenerational incidence of budget policies. For example, even if the social security account of the budget is balanced, it represents a huge transfer from young to old. Clearly, a better understanding of the "twin deficits" will require structural models and careful attention to intergenerational distribution.

Models incorporating more complex demographics have important implications aside from their predictions about government financial imbalances. Consider, for example, the implications of expected productivity growth. In a representative-agent framework, higher productivity growth will tend to weaken the current account as people borrow today against higher future income. (Investment effects would strengthen this result.) In a life-cycle setting the implications of higher productivity growth are less clear. If each individual benefits identically from the change regardless of his or her age, the results are much the same as in a representative-agent model. But suppose that productivity growth raises the labor incomes of young workers but does not affect the labor incomes of older workers. Because young savers will count more heavily in aggregate saving than old dissavers, saving will tend to rise and the current account to

---

[28] In a sample including four industrialized countries and Mexico, Bernheim (1988) finds a similar correlation between budget deficits and current-account deficits over 1976–1985.

improve. Deaton (1992) discusses how life-cycle theories might explain the observed tendency for national saving and growth rates to be positively correlated in cross sections.

An important property of overlapping-generations models is that they permit a steady-state with positive consumption for a small open economy, even if individuals have fixed time-preference rates different from the world interest rate. In the Weil (1989) model just sketched, for example, the small economy can reach a steady state even if individual cohorts' consumption levels are rising or falling over time; what is needed is that the birth rate of new individuals be large enough to offset the discrepancy between $\beta(1 + r)$ and 1. If $\beta(1 + r) < 1$, $n > 0$ guarantees this outcome; if $\beta(1 + r) > 1$, the inequality $\beta(1 + r) < 1 + n$ is necessary.

3.2. Stochastic models of the current account

A theory of current-account determination that makes no allowance for the uncertainty about the future underlying consumption and investment decisions cannot be fully satisfactory. Unfortunately, however, the introduction of stochastic elements can raise the technical difficulty of writing down solutions to individuals' maximization problems by an order of magnitude. Below we review the predictions of some leading stochastic models. A key theme emerging from the discussion is that the current-account response to various shocks depends on whether markets exist for insuring against the shocks' effects. This theme leads us, at the section's end, to consider a model in which the extent to which shocks are insurable is endogenous.

3.2.1. Complete markets

The most tractable case of uncertainty is that in which insurance markets exist for *all* future contingencies, with outcomes fully verifiable and contracts fully enforceable. In the classic Arrow–Debreu world of complete markets, equilibrium resource allocations are efficient and, from a formal point of view, the economy can be analyzed as if perfect certainty applied. There are simply many more commodities, commodities now being indexed by the state of nature in which they are demanded and supplied.[29]

---

[29] International models with complete markets are analyzed by Lucas (1982), Stockman (1988a), Stulz (1988), Cole and Obstfeld (1991), Stockman and Tesar (1995), Backus, Kehoe, and Kydland (1992), and Baxter and Crucini (1993a), among many others. Lucas's (1982) model does not actually assume complete markets, and in fact can contain far more states of nature than assets. However, other special assumptions made by Lucas result in an allocation the same as the one complete markets would produce.

Except for certain special cases, market completeness requires that people be able to trade as many independent assets as there are prospective states of nature. Equivalently, they must be able to trade a complete set of Arrow–Debreu securities, each of which pays off only in one state. The result of this trade is that individuals everywhere in the world equalize their marginal rates of substitution of present for future state-contingent consumption to the same Arrow–Debreu prices, so that for all countries i and j, and all dates t,

$$\frac{u'(C^i_{t+1})}{u'(C^i_t)} = \frac{u'(C^j_{t+1})}{u'(C^j_t)} \tag{3.29}$$

given shared rates of time preference (that is, the βs cancel). Condition (3.29) precludes further mutual gains, on any date or in any state, from inter-consumer risk pooling. Investment decisions are made to maximize the present value of profits evaluated at state-contingent output prices.

When all people throughout the world trade prospective risks in insurance markets, some local economic shocks effectively become global shocks and their current account effects are diminished or even eliminated. Consider, for instance, a pure exchange economy that experiences a temporary idiosyncratic positive output shock. Absent insurance markets, the country would run a current-account surplus, accumulating some foreign assets so as to smooth the benefits of the shock over all future periods. Under complete markets, however, the home economy has already traded much of its output risk to foreigners and purchased, in turn, claims on their risky output processes. Thus, the home economy's positive output shock will cause a small synchronized increase in every country's consumption under complete markets. But it will also cause a shift in every country's *income* as "dividend" payments flow from the home country to its foreign shareholders. With internationally identical isoelastic preferences, no current-account imbalances result. Indeed, in that case, there are never unanticipated current account movements. (Regardless of the utility function, differences in time preference can generate predictable nonzero current accounts under complete markets.)

If period utility is not isoelastic and identical across countries, world output shocks will, in general, cause current-account imbalances. Even in this case, shocks that affect the distribution of output across countries, but leave world output unchanged, have no current-account implications.

Returning to the case of internationally identical isoelastic utility but introducing production, a positive shock to the productivity of domestic investment causes a current-account deficit, as in our earlier perfect-foresight models. But that deficit will reflect only an influx of savings from abroad to share in ownership of the incremental investment. (Indeed, the existing capital of firms will already have a globally dispersed ownership.) The deficit does not reflect consumption-smoothing effects, because all countries' income profiles are rising in proportion. Despite the deficit – indeed, because of it – the international wealth distribution is constant.

Under literally complete markets, risks due to changes in government consumption also would be perfectly pooled among nations. An exogenous unexpected rise in United States spending on highway repairs due, say, to bad weather, would be financed mostly by contingent-contract payments from foreigners to the United States. The obvious adverse incentives introduced by such contracts illustrate why, in practice, asset markets are hardly complete. If a country's residents have sold most of domestic firms' future earnings on forward markets, its government has every incentive to raise corporate taxes sharply after the fact. More generally, under asymmetric information, moral hazards affecting private as well as government behavior impede complete risk sharing. Informal observation and statistical evidence both confirm that even in a domestic context, risks are far from being pooled as the complete-markets paradigm would predict. In the international context, sovereign risk and distance, together with cultural and legal differences, greatly magnify the difficulties.[30]

3.2.2. Bonds as the only asset

Let us look instead at the opposite extreme, that in which the only asset nations trade is a one-period bond indexed to tradeable consumption goods and offering a certain one-period return. This restriction on the menu of assets is too severe to furnish a completely realistic model, but it does serve to produce a model quite comparable to the deterministic one studied earlier. Later on we discuss hybrid models in which there are markets for some, but not all, risks.

For simplicity, we again choose as our framework a representative-agent economy in which all goods are traded. Now the individual maximizes the conditional expectation

$$U_t = E_t \left\{ \sum_{s=t}^{\infty} \beta^{s-t} u(C_s) \right\} \tag{3.30}$$

subject to a budget constraint like (3.5) equating the present value of consumption to initial financial wealth plus the present value of after-tax labor income. The consumption levels in (3.30) are contingency plans for consumption that depend on the individual's history through the date the plan is implemented. The budget constraint depends on stochastic future earnings, taxes, and interest rates. The sequence of contingent consumption plans the consumer chooses on

---

[30] See Obstfeld (1995) for a survey of evidence. The limited extent of international risk sharing has prompted Shiller (1993) to propose creating international markets in GDP futures.

date t must satisfy the budget constraint for every prospective history of the economy.

The intertemporal Euler equation derived in the certainty case now holds in expectation [cf. eq. (3.6)]:

$$u'(C_t) = \beta(1 + r_{t+1})E_t \{u'(C_{t+1})\} \tag{3.31}$$

To obtain closed-form consumer decision rules, we approximate $u(C)$ by the quadratic function

$$u(C) = C - \frac{h}{2} C^2$$

With this approximation (3.31) becomes

$$E_t C_{t+1} = \frac{1}{\beta(1 + r_{t+1})} C_t + \frac{1}{h} \left(1 - \frac{1}{\beta(1 + r_{t+1})}\right)$$

Here we see that the relation between β and the gross world interest rate induces a tilt in expected consumption growth as was also true in Subsection 3.1[31].

To simplify further, assume temporarily that the interest rate is constant at r, with $\beta(1 + r) = 1$; the result is the "random walk" prediction for consumption derived by Hall (1978):

$$E_t C_{t+1} = C_t \tag{3.32}$$

In equilibrium, the economy's intertemporal budget constraint, eq. (3.3), must hold for every possible sequence of outcomes when its elements are random. Applying the date-t expectations operator to both sides of (3.3) and using (3.32), we have the certainty-equivalence consumption function:

$$C_t = \frac{r}{1 + r} E_t \left\{ (1 + r)A_t + \sum_{s=t}^{\infty} \left(\frac{1}{1 + r}\right)^{s-t} (Y_s - G_s - I_s) \right\} \tag{3.33}$$

Equation (3.33) yields predictions for current accounts qualitatively similar to those of the deterministic consumption function (3.8) developed earlier. As a result, this equation and its relatives provide the leading vehicles for empirical studies of current-account determination. The linear-quadratic formulation has, however, at least three conceptual drawbacks:

---

[31] In the preceding equation the ratio of the gross interest rate to $1/\beta$ enters both in the slope and in the intercept, with opposite effects on expected date-$(t + 1)$ consumption. The quadratic utility specification makes sense, however, only so long as $C < 1/h$, ensuring that the marginal utility of consumption is positive. Under this assumption, it is clear that the intercept effect dominates: lowering β, for example, lowers expected date-$(t + 1)$ consumption in the last equation.

(1) Under quadratic utility $u'''(C) = 0$, so there is no precautionary saving. When, instead, $u'''(C) > 0$, marginal utility $u'(C)$ is a convex function. This convexity implies that an increase in uncertainty over future consumption raises its expected marginal utility and, thus, saving.[32]

(2) In both estimating and simulating intertemporal models, it is frequently convenient to be able to linearize or log-linearize first-order Euler conditions. Assuming quadratic period utility is really just another way of linearizing. The basic problem with this approach is that a linearized model will be very inaccurate far away from the point of approximation. Yet if the linearization implies, as in (3.32), that consumption follows a random walk, consumption will eventually drift arbitrarily far from any initial level. As Obstfeld (1982) and Svensson and Razin (1983) showed, one way to avoid a unit root in consumption is to assume an endogenous, rather than fixed, rate of time preference. If the rate of impatience rises with the level of consumption, a stationary consumption distribution is possible. Under uncertainty, precautionary saving can mimic this behavior (even with a fixed time-preference rate) because consumers save less at higher wealth levels. [See Carroll (1992) and Deaton (1992).] Another solution is to assume overlapping cohorts of finite-lived agents who leave no bequests. Unfortunately, no alternative can match the linear-quadratic infinite-lifetime framework for easy empirical implementation. Ultimately the justification for using the latter setup must rest on the presumption that it yields a reasonable approximation to behavior away from boundaries. More research proving or disproving this presumption would be useful.[33]

(3) The consumption function (3.33) does not necessarily constrain consumption to be non-negative in all states of the world. If negative levels of consumption are ruled out, consumption cannot literally follow a random walk as in (3.32).[34]

We turn next to investigating how, when bonds are the only internationally traded asset, the separation between domestic investment and consumption implied by complete markets can break down.

It is natural to assume again that the domestic firm makes its investment decision on date t to maximize the present discounted value of profits. But with uncertainty, it is no longer obvious what discount rate should be used to value the risky stream of dividends the firm issues to shareholders. With population normalized to 1, the firm's *ex dividend* value, V_{t+1}, is the price of a per capita

---

[32] On precautionary saving behavior, see Leland (1968).

[33] Clarida (1990) develops an exact general-equilibrium model of international borrowing and lending under endowment uncertainty, heterogenous fixed discount rates, and lower limits on individual assets. He finds that when there is no aggregate output uncertainty, there is a stationary distribution of wealth and consumption levels in which some households are borrowing-constrained.

[34] The problem of nonnegativity constraints afflicts the commonly used consumption functions derived in continuous-time models by stochastic dynamic programming. See Cox and Huang (1989).

share in the firm in date t asset trading. Using dynamic programming (*the details are omitted here*), one can show that V_{t+1} follows a stochastic process such that the following Euler equation holds:

$$V_{t+1}u'(C_t) = \beta E_t\{[\theta_{t+1}F(K_{t+1}, L_{t+1}) - w_{t+1}L_{t+1} \\ -I_{t+1} - aI_{t+1}^2/2K_{t+1} + V_{t+2}]u'(C_{t+1})\}$$

Iterated forward substitutions for V yield a stochastic version of (3.16),

$$V_{t+1} = E_t\left\{\sum_{s=t+1}^{\infty} \beta^{s-t}\frac{u'(C_s)}{u'(C_t)}\left[\theta_s F(K_s, L_s) - w_s L_s - I_s - \frac{aI_s^2}{2K_s}\right]\right\} \qquad (3.34)$$

Given that the firm is owned entirely by domestic residents, the present value of a claim to its future dividends in any particular state of nature depends on *domestic* consumer's marginal utility in that state of nature relative to current marginal utility.

We can decompose (3.34) further as[35]

$$V_{t+1} = \sum_{s=t+1}^{\infty} E_t\left\{\beta^{s-t}\frac{u'(C_s)}{u'(C_t)}\right\}E_t\left\{\theta_s F(K_s, L_s) - w_s L_s - I_s - \frac{aI_s^2}{2K_s}\right\}$$

$$+ \sum_{s=t+1}^{\infty} \beta^{s-t}\text{Cov}_t\left\{\frac{u'(C_s)}{u'(C_t)}, \theta_s F(K_s, L_s) - w_s L_s - I_s - \frac{aI_s^2}{2K_s}\right\}$$

Define $R_{t,s}^L$ to be the market discount factor between periods t and s, that is, the price of sure (that is, noncontingent) date s consumption in terms of date t consumption. Of course, $R_{t,t+1}^L$ is simply the inverse of the gross short rate, $1 + r_{t+1}$.[36] The $(s - t)$-period analog of eq. (3.31) is

$$u'(C_t) = \left(\beta^{s-t}/R_{t,s}^L\right)E_t\{u'(C_s)\}$$

so the previous equation can be written as

$$V_{t+1} = \sum_{s=t+1}^{\infty} R_{t,s}^L E_t\left\{\theta_s F(K_s, L_s) - w_s L_s - I_s - \frac{aI_s^2}{2K_s}\right\}$$

$$+ \sum_{s=t+1}^{\infty} \beta^{s-t}\text{Cov}_t\left\{\frac{u'(C_s)}{u'(C_t)}, \theta_s F(K_s, L_s) - w_s L_s - I_s - \frac{aI_s^2}{2K_s}\right\} \qquad (3.35)$$

[35]The result below uses the fact that if X and X' are two random variables, $E(XX') = E(X)E(X') + \text{Cov}(X, X')$.

[36]In a deterministic model, $R_{t,s}^L = R_{t,s}$ as defined in eq. (3.2). The equality breaks down here because future short rates are stochastic, whereas $R_{t,s}^L$ is known on date t.

Equation (3.35) shows that the firm's value is the conventional present value of dividends plus a *risk premium*: the firm is valued more highly if it pays out unexpectedly high dividends when the marginal utility of owners' consumption is unexpectedly high. The presence of a risk premium introduces an additional channel through which shifts in consumption preferences can influence investment behavior.

The firm's investment behavior can be characterized by maximizing the sum of current profits and (3.34) subject to (3.12). As in the deterministic case current investment is governed by (3.13), where $q_t = V_{t+1}/K_{t+1}$ and V_{t+1} is given by (3.34). The result is a richer q model of investment with current-account predictions similar to those of Section 3.1.[37]

3.2.3. Partially complete markets

In reality countries trade not only bonds but a rich menu of assets, including equity shares, currency-denominated instruments, and other securities with state-contingent payoffs. This trade ensures that some, if not all, consumption risks can be pooled and that the current-account effects arising in the last set of models will be muted.

Equation (3.31) implies that whenever there is free trade in noncontingent bonds between two countries i and j, the expected growth rates of their residents' marginal utilities from consumption are equal, assuming a common rate of time preference. Thus,

$$E_t \left\{ \frac{u'(C_{t+1}^i)}{u'(C_t^i)} \right\} = E_t \left\{ \frac{u'(C_{t+1}^j)}{u'(C_t^j)} \right\} \tag{3.36}$$

Under complete markets [see eq. (3.29)], this equation holds ex post, not just in expectation. When only (3.36) holds, however, differences in marginal rates of intertemporal substitution can occur after the fact.

When some, but not all, risks can be traded between countries, consumption behavior will be intermediate between the predictions of (3.29) and (3.36). Specifically, (3.29) predicts that marginal rate of intertemporal substitution differences do not arise, while (3.36) predicts these differences can arise unexpectedly. In the intermediate case, the ex post difference

$$\frac{u'(C_{t+1}^i)}{u'(C_t^i)} - \frac{u'(C_{t+1}^j)}{u'(C_t^j)}$$

will be conditionally uncorrelated with any date-$(t+1)$ random variable on which

---

[37] See, for example, Baxter and Crucini (1993b) and Glick and Rogoff (1995).

contingent contractual payments can be conditioned. Thus, if X_{t+1} is a random variable on which contracts can be written prior to date $t + 1$,

$$
\text{Cov}_t \left\{ \frac{u'(C^i_{t+1})}{u'(C^i_t)} - \frac{u'(C^j_{t+1})}{u'(C^j_t)}, X_{t+1} \right\} = 0 \tag{3.37}
$$

For example, if people in different countries can effectively pool the idiosyncratic consumption risks due to nominal exchange-rate fluctuations through foreign exchange market deals, then realized exchange rate fluctuations will be statistically unrelated to international differences in the growth of $u'(C)$.[38] Because it is only partial, however, such insurance clearly leaves scope for unexpected current-account movements.

Svensson (1988) develops a two-period model in which period 1 asset trading serves to pool consumption risks for period 2. Svensson shows that the usual logic of trade theory can be extended to analyze not only the current account under uncertainty, but also the asset composition of gross capital flows between countries. He develops a two-period pure exchange model of international trade in a possibly incomplete set of risky assets. In that model, a multi-commodity comparative advantage principle applies [see Dixit and Norman (1980), p. 95]: the inner product of a country's net asset import vector with the vector of home *minus* foreign autarky asset prices is positive.

When countries trade equity shares as well as noncontingent bonds, the separation between domestic investment and consumption may still obtain even though asset markets are incomplete. As (3.37) shows, domestic and foreign residents must attach the same values to the state-contingent profits of a firm that they trade. A sufficient condition for the separation property to hold is that investment decisions themselves do not change these common valuations [see Ekern and Wilson (1974)].

3.2.4. Endogenous market incompleteness

We have seen that some of the model's predictions concerning current account behavior depend critically on the structure of asset markets and in particular the degree to which complete markets prevail. We have argued that the complete markets model is inadequate empirically, but if so it would be helpful to have a deeper understanding of the frictions that impinge on market completeness, rather than just assuming market limitations exogenously.

In this section we present an example, drawn from Gertler and Rogoff (1990), of how international capital flows behave in the presence of moral hazard deriving from asymmetric information at the microeconomic level. A key insight

---

[38] For a formal derivation, see Obstfeld (1994).

from the model, which carries over to other settings, is that international asset markets can bring the global allocation of resources part of the way, but only part of the way, toward the full-information optimum. Thus, the intertemporal approach, as sketched above, may well get the *directions* of net international capital flows right while overstating magnitudes.

We now adopt a two-period, single good setup in which each of the numerous atomistic residents of a small country maximizes

$$u(C_1, C_2) = C_2 \tag{3.38}$$

given exogenous endowments E_1 of the consumption good in period 1 and E_2 in period 2. The utility function (3.38) is obviously very special (clearly $C_1 = 0$ is optimal) but it allows us to simplify the analysis while still making our main points. The focus, instead, is on investment. Each resident has two ways to transform E_1 into future consumption. He or she may lend in the world capital market and earn a riskless net rate of return r. Alternatively, current resources can be invested in a risky domestic project. If a resident invests K in period 1, then the project's stochastic payoff in period 2 is Y, where

$$Y = \begin{cases} \phi > 0 & \text{with probability } \pi(K) \\ 0 & \text{with probability } 1 - \pi(K) \end{cases}$$

Above, $\pi(K)$ is increasing, strictly concave, and twice continuously differentiable, with $\pi(0) = 0$, $\pi(\infty) = 1$, and $1 + r < \phi \pi'(0) < \infty$. These assumptions ensure that higher investment increases the likelihood of a successful outcome (but at a diminishing rate) and that the prospect of success would justify nonzero investment under symmetric information. Every individual has one potential investment project and different individuals' investment outcomes are statistically independent.

In this model, the optimal full-information investment level is K^*, defined by

$$\pi'(K^*)\phi = 1 + r \tag{3.39}$$

At this point, the marginal return to investing equals the return that can be earned through lending abroad. Let us assume that

$$E_1 + \frac{E_2}{1 + r} < K^*$$

This inequality implies that each resident needs to borrow a positive amount from foreigners to be able to invest optimally. Furthermore, the condition is equivalent to the inequality $E_2 < (1 + r)(K^* - E_1)$, which states that it is infeasible for lenders to finance the investment level K^* through a risk-free loan. If an investment project fails, even the borrower's entire period 2 endowment is insufficient to repay lenders $(1 + r)(K^* - E_1)$. Thus, loan contracts take the following, state-contingent, form: in return for a loan of size L in period 1, the borrower promises to repay Z^g in period 2 in the event his or her investment is successful and $Z^b < Z^g$ in the event it fails. Lenders are competitive and do not offer a loan contract unless its expected gross return equals $1 + r$:

$$\pi(K)Z^g + [1 - \pi(K)]Z^b = (1 + r)L \tag{3.40}$$

The provisions of loan contracts are assumed to be fully enforceable.

The moral hazard problem underlying the model arises from its information structure. Lenders observe a borrower's endowments and the output of the investment project (that is, whether the project is successful or not); of course, they also know the size of the loan. They *cannot*, however, verify the level of investment, K. Thus, borrowers cannot commit themselves to any specific level of investment by writing promises about K into the loan contract. For example, there is no way lenders can prevent borrowers from investing nothing at all and instead secretly placing all of their resources, borrowed as well as nonborrowed, in foreign assets (an action reminiscent of "capital flight"). But if borrowers do so, there is no chance their projects will succeed. The informational asymmetry allowing this kind of behavior leads to inefficient investment and borrowing levels, as we now show.[39]

Given the available loan contract, a typical borrower maximizes expected second period consumption

$$E\{C_2\} = \pi(K)(\phi - Z^g) - [1 - \pi(K)]Z^b + (1 + r)(E_1 + L - K) + E_2 \tag{3.41}$$

subject to the constraint

$$E_1 + L \geq K \tag{3.42}$$

Constraint (3.42) does not bind when the borrower is secretly investing resources abroad rather than at home. The necessary Kuhn–Tucker conditions for a maximum are:

$$\pi'(K)[\phi - (Z^g - Z^b)] = 1 + r + \lambda \tag{3.43}$$

$$\lambda \geq 0, \quad \lambda(E_1 + L - K) = 0 \tag{3.44}$$

Conditions (3.43) and (3.44) imply that even a borrower with access to a loan L large enough to permit the desired investment level (so that $\lambda = 0$) picks a K that satisfies

---

[39] If borrowers could commit to invest K^*, lenders would break even by lending them $L = K^* - E_1$ and setting $Z^b = E_2$, $Z^g = (1 + r)[K^* - E_1 - (1 - \pi(K^*))E_2]/\pi(K^*)$. [Because $\pi(K)$ is strictly concave and $\pi(0) = 0$, $Z^g < \phi + E_2$.] In this model, there is an implicit assumption that foreign direct investment cannot substitute perfectly for lending; that is, foreigners cannot circumvent the agency problem by purchasing investment opportunities in the borrowing country and exploiting them optimally themselves. This assumption could be justified by a threat of nationalization, or simply by a comparative informational advantage of local residents in finding suppliers, monitoring workers, greasing the collective palm of local officialdom, etc.

$$\pi'(K)[\phi - (Z^g - Z^b)] = 1 + r \tag{3.45}$$

and, thus, is strictly *below* the full-information optimum level described by eq. (3.39). The reason is that the change in payoff to the borrower when a project succeeds is

$$\phi - Z^g - (-Z^b) = \phi - (Z^g - Z^b) < \phi$$

Although lenders cannot observe K directly, they have rational expectations and thus can figure out the level of K borrowers will choose for a given loan contract. They therefore offer a loan contract such that the K the borrower chooses, given L, Z^g, and Z^b, satisfies the required rate of return condition (3.40). Competition among lenders ensures that this contract is optimal for the borrower, subject to the constraints mentioned. Formally, the optimal incentive-compatible contract (L, Z^g, Z^b) maximizes $E\{C_2\}$ subject to (3.40), (3.42), (3.45), and the inequality $Z^b \leq E_2$.

The optimal contract satisfies $Z^b = E_2$ (so as to minimize the gap $\check{Z} \equiv Z^g - Z^b$ and, thus, the gap between K and K^*).[40] Furthermore, the contract satisfies (3.42) with equality: increasing L above $K - E_1$ would force a rise in Z^g and, with it, a worsening in investment incentives. Combining these facts with the incentive-compatibility constraint (3.45) and the lenders' zero-profit condition (3.40), we see that the optimal contract is the solution to the three-equation system

$$\pi'(K)(\phi - \check{Z}) = 1 + r$$

$$\check{Z} = (1 + r)\left(K - E_1 - \frac{E_2}{1 + r}\right)/\pi(K)$$

$$L = K - E_1.$$

This solution has a number of important implications:

(1) The incentive-compatible investment level is below the full-information optimum of (3.39). Accordingly, period 1 capital inflows are below the level a full-information model would predict.

(2) An increase in the productivity parameter ϕ increases the period 1 capital inflow and investment level, but it also widens the spread $\check{Z}$ between the good- and bad-outcome loan payments. Thus, (under mild restrictions on $\pi(K)$) the resulting capital inflow is less than in the full-information case.

(3) The expected marginal product of capital, $\pi'(K)\phi$, exceeds the world (and domestic) riskless interest rate, $1 + r$.

(4) An increase in either endowment, E_1 or E_2, raises investment by lowering $\check{Z}$. In the first case this effect is due to a lesser reliance on external funds, in

---

[40] See Gertler and Rogoff (1990) for details.

the second to the possibility of a larger loan payment in the bad-outcome state. The invariance of investment with respect to intertemporal preferences that characterized the single-sector models described earlier need not hold when investment is subject to moral hazard.[41]

In a two-country general equilibrium version of the model, one can show that endogenous differences in capital market imperfections can dramatically reduce the flow of capital from rich to poor countries, and even reverse it [see Gertler and Rogoff (1990)].

The preceding model has abstracted both from the consumption smoothing motive behind the current account and from the borrowers' desire to engage in asset trades that reduce the uncertainty of second-period consumption. It is straightforward to add second-period risk aversion to the model by assuming that (3.38) is replaced by

$$u(C_1, C_2) = C_2 - \frac{h}{2} C_2^2$$

In order to focus on the new issues that arise, it is convenient to suppose that $E_1 \geq K^*$. In this case, domestic residents' endowment is large enough so that they have no need to borrow to finance investment, and their only motive for tapping the international capital market is to insure period 2 consumption. Here again we have a moral hazard problem because nonverifiable investment decisions affect the probability distribution of second-period output. It can be shown that under the optimal incentive-compatible contract, consumption insurance will be partial and K will be below K^*.[42]

The general conclusion is that asymmetric information need not cause financial markets to break down entirely. Instead, financial markets may do only partially the job they could do in a world of full information. Note also that in thinking about the incompleteness of markets, it may be misleading to think of risks as being either insurable or noninsurable. In many cases, through what is basically a coinsurance mechanism, *some* gains from trade across states of nature will be realized even under moral hazard.[43] The same point applies to trade across time.

We have focused on capital-market imperfections arising from asymmetric information at the micro level. Another very important cause of international capital-market imperfection is sovereign default risk at the macro level. Sovereign risk need not be related to asymmetric information, but can have qualita-

---

[41] It is again easy to see that $Z^g < \phi + E_2$.

[42] See Obstfeld and Rogoff (1996), ch. 6.

[43] The implications of adverse selection problems can be quite different, although we do not consider them here. Atkeson and Lucas (1992) study a different moral hazard problem, one in which people (or countries) wish to insure against preference shocks. They find that under optimal incentive-compatible arrangements, the degree of consumption inequality in the world increases continually.

tively similar implications.[44] Jonathan Eaton and Raquel Fernandez present a detailed analysis of the effects of sovereign risk in their chapter in this Handbook. A common theme in sovereign-risk models is that the consumption-smoothing and risk-sharing roles of international capital markets still operate, but are tempered by default risk.

4. Empirical evidence on the intertemporal approach

The intertemporal approach to the current account has been subjected to extensive formal testing; much of the methodology used grows out of Hall's (1978) seminal work on the implications of the rational-expectations assumption for forward looking consumption theories. A less formal empirical methodology, pioneered by Feldstein and Horioka (1980), has been used to argue that the close relationship between national saving and investment rates in post-World War II data furnishes a *prima facie* case against the practical relevance of the intertemporal approach. These two research avenues are closely intertwined, as any attempt to reconcile the Feldstein–Horioka findings with the intertemporal approach rests on the validity of models such as those surveyed in Section 3.[45]

4.1. The relationship between national saving and domestic investment rates

In a closed economy, national saving equals domestic investment and the current account is always zero. Furthermore, any observed increase in national saving will automatically be accompanied by an equal rise in domestic investment. A basic premise of the intertemporal approach is that capital is to some degree internationally mobile, so that current account imbalances are a possibility. Given this premise, the intertemporal approach predicts a number of situations in which divergences between saving and investment will arise. An empirical finding that national saving rates affect domestic investment rates with unit coefficients would therefore appear to be strong evidence against the applicability of the intertemporal approach.

Feldstein and Horioka (1980), in the first of a series of related papers by Feldstein and coauthors, argued that capital mobility is sufficiently limited, at

---

[44] Atkeson (1991) presents an interesting analysis incorporating both asymmetric information and sovereign risk.

[45] We do not survey the methodology of calibrating open-economy models with incomplete markets so as to match moments of actual aggregate data. Interesting recent work along this line, exemplified by Baxter and Crucini (1993b) and Kollmann (1992), is discussed in Marianne Baxter's chapter in this Handbook. We also refrain from more than a brief and highly selective account of the copious literature on measuring international capital mobility. See Frankel (1993) and Obstfeld (1995) for recent surveys.

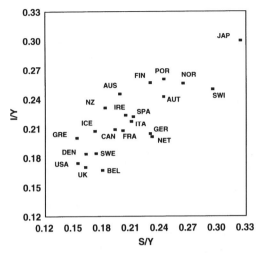

Figure 4.1. Saving and investment averages, 1982–1991 (as a fraction of GDP).

least over long horizons, that changes in national saving rates ultimately feed through fully to domestic investment rates. As evidence, they reported cross-sectional regressions of gross domestic investment rate averages (I/Y) on gross national saving rate averages (S/Y). These ratios of nominal flows, of course, suffer from all the conceptual deficiencies discussed at the end of Section 2. For a sample of 16 OECD countries over 1960–74, Feldstein and Horioka found that:

$$(I/Y)_j = \underset{(0.018)}{0.035} + \underset{(0.074)}{0.887}(S/Y)_j + u_j; R^2 = 0.91$$

Feldstein and Bacchetta (1991) report similar results for a 1974–86 sample of 23 OECD members. Figure 4.1 shows the cross-sectional saving-investment association in the OECD sample over the decade 1982–91, with Luxembourg, which is an outlier, omitted. The estimation result for this sample, leaving out developing Turkey, is:

$$(I/Y)_j = \underset{(0.020)}{0.088} + \underset{(0.094)}{0.622}(S/Y)_j + u_j; R^2 = 0.69$$

This equation shows a weakening, but still very significant, positive association.
   Feldstein and his collaborators argue that if capital indeed were highly mobile among countries, slope coefficients like the one above should be much smaller than 1, as a country's savings would then be free to seek out the most productive investment opportunities worldwide. Although the intertemporal approach is consistent with a world in which changes in saving behavior impinge on do-

mestic investment, it certainly does not support the policy conclusion, preferred by Feldstein, that government measures to raise a country's saving rate will automatically cause a long-run pari passu increase in its investment rate.

If capital is truly immobile and the intertemporal approach irrelevant, however, then the time-series relationship between individual countries' saving and investment rates, like the cross-sectional relationship among long saving and investment averages, also should be close. We can think of the time-series relationship among contemporaneous detrended saving and investment rates as capturing the coherence of high-frequency changes, while the Feldstein–Horioka regression captures the association between low-frequency or "sustained" changes. Indeed, it is hard to see how capital could be truly immobile in the long run but not in the short run, since the long run is just a succession of short runs. And even if international trade in long-term instruments or long-lived assets were highly limited – a hypothesis that the data do not support – short-term instruments can be rolled over.

The time-series and cross-section aspects of the saving–investment relationship are quite distinct: the time-series relationship could be close and the cross-section relationship not, or vice versa. An example is provided by the United Kingdom during the pre-World War I gold standard (Figure 2.1). It is apparent that the short-run saving–investment correlation is very close.[46] Nonetheless, the U.K. ran current-account surpluses approaching 10 percent of GDP in this same period.

It is a "stylized fact", somewhat sensitive to the detrending method adopted, that the time-series saving-investment correlation is fairly strong in recent data. (See Figure 2.3 for some industrial-country data, but there are exceptions, the most glaring of which is Norway with its highly negatively correlated saving and investment rates.) For the OECD countries including Luxembourg but excluding Turkey, the average correlation between saving and investment rates is 0.495 over 1974–90 after linear time detrending. The correlation is 0.512 when the data are first-differenced to remove trend.

Even in a world of complete capital mobility though, such correlations are not necessarily surprising and can easily be explained on the basis of the intertemporal approach. For example, the discussion of gradual capital–stock adjustment in Section 3 implies that a shock to total factor productivity, if short-lived but not completely transitory, raises saving as well as investment. Baxter and Crucini (1993a,b) and Mendoza (1991) (the latter in a small-country setting, the former in a global-economy setting) have shown that intertemporal mobile-capital models based on investment-adjustment costs can easily produce time-series saving-investment correlations at least as large as those in the data. Part of the mechanism underlying the Baxter–Crucini findings is allowance for global

---

[46] See Obstfeld (1986) for a more detailed statistical analysis of the U.K. data.

economic shocks, which obviously will induce positive saving-investment correlations.

We have been focusing on time-series evidence, but Feldstein and Horioka's cross-sectional findings can also be rationalized by the presence of common factors that might simultaneously influence countries' saving and investment rates.

It seems likely that of the many potential explanations of the Feldstein–Horioka results, no single one fully explains the behavior of all countries. Taken together, however, and combined with other evidence indicating substantial international mobility of capital, the arguments below suggest that the Feldstein–Horioka finding provides no basis at all for dismissing the basic premises of the intertemporal approach:

(1) Even post-1973, governments have sometimes adjusted fiscal or monetary policies to avoid large and protracted current-account imbalances. The evidence on this current-account targeting hypothesis is mostly anecdotal, however, and there are of course prominent instances (like the United States in the 1980s) in which macroeconomic policies have instigated major external imbalances.[47]

(2) OECD countries may be sufficiently well endowed with capital to have reached stochastic steady states for their external debt or asset levels. In this situation the intertemporal budget constraint of the economy would imply that long averages of saving-investment differences are small. Developing countries, which presumably could realize greater gains from intertemporal trade through borrowing for investment purposes, are likely to be more distant from a stationary distribution of foreign debt. This interpretation seems borne out by the cross-sectional results for developing countries prior to the onset of their debt crisis in 1982. For this sample, the cross-sectional saving-investment association is much looser than for the OECD sample.[48]

(3) The Gertler–Rogoff investment model discussed in Section 3 shows why investment may respond positively to higher retained earnings, that is, to higher corporate saving. Thus, it seems plausible that in countries with higher saving rates, the cost of capital will be lower and investment higher. A main prediction of the moral-hazard model is that risk-free interest rates are equalized among countries – as indeed they mostly are in the industrialized world (Obstfeld 1995) – whereas the marginal product of capital is high in countries with low corporate wealth. Although there is some evidence in favor of this hypothesis, an account of how corporate saving and investment are related need not have strong implications for the relationship between total saving and investment. For example, private domestic owners of firms may pierce the corporate veil

---

[47]The fragility of the econometric evidence is illustrated by Feldstein and Bacchetta's (1991) reinterpretation of the regressions Summers (1988) offers as evidence of current-account targeting.

[48]See Fieleke (1982), Dooley, Frankel, and Mathieson (1987), and Summers (1988).

and offset corporate saving decisions through their own consumption. To the extent that the investing firms are owned by foreigners, their decision to retain earnings increases foreign rather than domestic saving, other things equal.

(4) In a Heckscher–Ohlin framework, a nonspecialized economy experiencing a rise in saving can absorb more capital without a fall in capital's domestic rate of return. Alternative explanations of the saving-investment association based on this observation are suggested by Fukao and Hamada (1994) and Obstfeld (1995).

(5) In the life-cycle theory of consumption, sustained demographic or productivity changes that increase a country's long-term investment rate also may increase its saving rate. Section 3.1.7's discussion of overlapping-generations models provides a leading example: higher productivity growth that affects most strongly the incomes of young workers will cause saving as well as investment to rise. Feldstein and Bacchetta (1991) and Summers (1988) have dismissed this line of explanation, notwithstanding some supportive evidence offered by Tesar (1991). In a more recent contribution, however, Taylor (1994) revisits the Feldstein–Horioka equation, controlling for (a) measures of domestic relative prices, (b) the age-structure of the population, and (c) the interaction of the age structure with the growth rate of domestic output. He finds that for a number of country samples the cross-sectional saving-investment association disappears.

Far from showing the irrelevance of the intertemporal approach, the large literature spawned by Feldstein and Horioka's (1980) nonstructural exploration suggests to us that models like those reviewed in Section 3 capture key elements behind the cross-sectional and time-series regularities governing saving and investment rates. The further empirical challenge for the intertemporal approach is to show that structural forward-looking models of the current account are not grossly incompatible with actual experience. We turn next to tests of such models.

4.2. Tests of intertemporal current-account models

Most structural time-series studies of the intertemporal approach to the current account essentially test versions of eq. (3.9), according to which the current account depends on deviations of interest rates, output, government spending, and investment from "permanent" levels. Indeed, most (but not, as we shall see, all) of these studies focus on the special case of (3.9) with a constant real interest rate $r = (1 - \beta)/\beta$

$$CA_t = (Y_t - \tilde{Y}_t) - (G_t - \tilde{G}_t) - (I_t - \tilde{I}_t) \tag{4.46}$$

Though less general than eq. (3.9), eq. (4.46) embodies many central elements of the intertemporal approach. It therefore is reasonable to ask whether there is any evidence in favor of (4.46) before turning to more complex models. For example, do temporary rises in government spending cause current-account deficits? Questions like this one seem simple enough, but a number of empirical subtleties arise in answering them.

4.2.1. Measuring permanent values: A digression

Even before turning to the econometric studies, it is useful to address what is perhaps the most problematic issue of all, the construction of the expected permanent values $\tilde{Y}$, $\tilde{G}$, and $\tilde{I}$.

A first difficulty is that it is not obvious what real interest rate to use to discount expected future output flows.[49] Most of the studies surveyed below use fairly low discount rates, in the range of 2 to 4 percent per year. These numbers correspond roughly to average ex post real returns on U.S. Treasury bills post-World War II. But is a (nominally) riskless rate the appropriate one for discounting very risky future output flows? For the United States, the mean rate of return on risky assets has historically been much higher than that on bonds [Mehra and Prescott (1985)], at least since the late nineteenth century. To the extent data are available, a similar result seems to hold for a number of other countries. Bernanke (1985) argues that an annual real interest rate as high as 14 percent is needed to rationalize U.S. consumption–income relationships in a related closed-economy setting.

A second difficulty concerns the sensitivity of empirical measures of $\tilde{Y}$, $\tilde{G}$, and $\tilde{I}$ to apparently benign differences in the time series process generating the underlying values of Y, I, and G. This problem interacts with the previous one, because the sensitivity to the data-generating process is especially acute under a low interest rate.[50] Consider the following example, in which output (expressed as a deviation from mean output) is generated by the process

$$Y_t = \rho Y_{t-1} + v_t \tag{4.47}$$

with $0 \le \rho \le 1$, v_t a white-noise error, and time measured in years. If a low real interest rate is used to construct permanent output

$$\tilde{Y}_t = \frac{r}{1+r}\left[Y_t + \frac{\mathrm{E}_t\, Y_{t+1}}{1+r} + \frac{\mathrm{E}_t\, Y_{t+2}}{(1+r)^2} + \dots\right] \tag{4.48}$$

distant future incomes will have relatively large weights. When $r = 0.03$, $\mathrm{E}_t\, Y_{t+20}$, for example, though discounted, still has a weight more than half that of current output, Y_t. This means that when r is low, estimates of $\tilde{Y}_t$ may be very sensitive to the serial-correlation parameter ρ, especially in the neighborhood of $\rho = 1$. Noting that under eq. (4.47) $\mathrm{E}_t\, Y_{t+k} = \rho^k Y_t$, one sees that eq. (4.48) implies:

---

[49]Sometimes this issue can be finessed [see the discussion of Glick and Rogoff (1995) below.]
[50]This discussion draws on Glick and Rogoff (1995).

$$\tilde{Y}_t = \frac{r}{1 + r - \rho} Y_t \equiv \mu Y_t \tag{4.49}$$

When $\rho = 1$, $\mu = 1$ and so $\tilde{Y}_t = Y_t$, regardless of the value of r. But when $r = 0.03$ and $\rho = 0.97$ (a value differing from 1 by an amount generally too small to detect empirically), μ drops to only 0.5: permanent output is half of current output. As ρ becomes small this hypersensitivity abates. In practice, unfortunately, ρ tends to be quite close to 1, so that the presence of a unit root is difficult to reject. It should be clear that estimates of $\tilde{Y}_t$ can be similarly sensitive to estimates of time trends.[51]

The present-value calculations are less sensitive to ρ when the real interest rate is higher. How high must real interest rates be? With $r = 0.14$ (the value mentioned by Bernanke) and $\rho = 0.97$ in eq. (4.49), $\mu = 0.824$. With $r = 0.5$, $\mu = 0.943$. Real interest rates high enough to make μ insensitive to ρ in the vicinity of a unit root appear implausible.

With these cautions in mind we proceed to look at the literature.

4.2.2. Early tests

Early econometric tests of the intertemporal approach as represented by eq. (4.46) include Ahmed (1986, 1987), Hercowitz (1986), and Johnson (1986). Hercowitz, who looks at Israeli data over 1950–1981, presents some support for an intertemporal model but also finds that the model exaggerates the current account's response to output fluctuations. Johnson focuses on Canada over 1952–1976. He rejects Ricardian equivalence, but concludes that Canada's private sector can plausibly be modeled in line with a version of the intertemporal approach that allows for some liquidity-constrained consumers.[52]

Ahmed's papers are distinctive in their use of long historical data series on government expenditures from the United Kingdom. In the 1986 paper, Ahmed looks at annual 1908–80 data to gauge the impact of U.K. government spending on the current account (actually, the trade balance, TB). The 1987 paper analyzes a pre-World War I sample on public military spending and trade balances running from 1732 to 1913. Ahmed argues that the expenditures accompanying Britain's wars were largely exogenous and were almost certainly viewed as temporary by the public. Thus, on the basis of the intertemporal approach, one

---

[51] The same problems arise in the macroeconomic literature on estimating consumption functions. Deaton (1987), for example, argues that if income is stationary in growth rates (a hypothesis that is difficult statistically to reject given the limited post-WWII time series), then consumption should move *more* than one-for-one with income innovations. There is, on the other hand, no "Deaton's paradox" if income is highly serially correlated but still stationary.

[52] Roubini (1988) combines the intertemporal approach with the tax-smoothing theory of government deficits, finding mixed results for a sample of OECD countries.

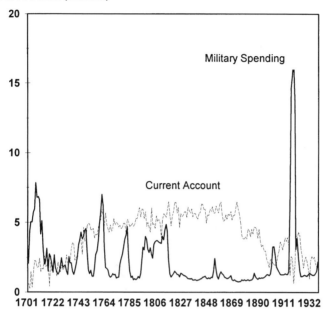

1854 Pounds (Millions)

Figure 4.2. United Kingdom: Military spending and current account, 1701–1938 (detrended annual data).

might expect Britain to have been running external deficits during wars.[53] In the twentieth century, swings in British government spending have been dominated by the two world wars, both of which were accompanied by large current-account deficits. Figure 4.2 uses data from Ahmed's papers to graph military spending against the current account over 1701–1938.[54] This 238-year sample provides a more demanding testing ground than the twentieth century alone, as the period is punctuated by many wars.[55]

A negative correlation between surges in government spending and the cur-

[53] The result that temporary war-time increases in public spending should lead to an external deficit does not necessarily hold if the *whole world* is at war. In an all-encompassing global war, higher government spending everywhere would push up world interest rates with current account implications that would depend mostly on countries' net external asset holdings. This point illustrates the distinction between global and country-specific shocks emphasized in Section 3 above.

[54] Both series have had a 2 percent annual growth trend removed, as in Ahmed (1987). The current account has been constructed from Ahmed's trade balance data using a 3 percent per annum sterling rate of return on foreign assets starting from an assumed zero net foreign asset position in 1701. We thank Shaghil Ahmed for providing us with the data from his papers.

[55] The possible gain or loss of colonial territories and privileges, which was the motive for much warfare before World War I, naturally could be expected to exert an additional wealth effect on the current account. Ideally, this effect should be controlled for in estimation.

rent account is fully consistent with theories other than the intertemporal approach, for example, a Keynesian multiplier model. To reduce the set of alternative theories consistent with the data, Ahmed explores formal econometric tests. A representative result from Ahmed (1986) is

$$TB_t = -0.21 \, (G_t - \tilde{G}_t) - 0.44 \ \ \tilde{G}_t + \varepsilon_t; \ R^2 = 0.28, \ \text{D.W.} = 2.32$$
$$\quad \ \ (0.05) \qquad\qquad (0.85)$$

which is estimated over 1908–80.[56] This regression shows that the temporary component of government spending has a significant negative influence on the current account, whereas the permanent component itself does not, consistent with (4.46). Unfortunately, the regression's specification leaves open the possibility that G_t is the *only* significant determinant of the current account and that $\tilde{G}_t$ plays no role at all – as an atemporal Keynesian model would predict.

Using our estimated current account in place of the trade balance, we have run a similar regression on the 1701–1938 data, but while keeping $G_t - \tilde{G}_t$ in the regression we replace $\tilde{G}_t$ by G_t so as to encompass transparently the intertemporal and Keynesian alternatives within a single test.[57] The resulting regression, run using a Cochrane–Orcutt correction for first-order serial correlation is[58]

$$CA_t = -0.016 \, (G_t - \tilde{G}_t) - 0.028 \ \ G_t + \varepsilon_t; \ \ \rho = 0.907$$
$$\quad \ \ (0.013) \qquad\qquad (0.093) \qquad\qquad\ (0.027)$$

In this specification, neither current nor permanent government spending is individually significant. As usual, it is unclear whether the intertemporal approach is simply false, or whether the many extraneous simplifications and maintained hypotheses imposed by the econometrician are to blame. It is therefore useful to turn to a newer empirical approach based on a less restrictive framework.

4.2.3. Present-value models of the current account

Ghosh (1995), Otto (1992), and Sheffrin and Woo (1990) apply an alternative methodology that makes use of the information embodied in past current accounts to make more accurate predictions of $\tilde{Y}$, $\tilde{G}$, and $\tilde{I}$. These studies build on the methodology developed by Campbell (1987) and by Campbell and Shiller (1987).[59]

[56] See Table 1, regression I (with $\rho = 0.02$) on p. 211.

[57] To form $\tilde{G}$ we used an autoregressive forecasting model of detrended government spending.

[58] Similar results are obtained when we use the trade balance in place of the current account, as Ahmed (1987) does.

[59] Campbell's (1987) study of private U.S. saving is especially relevant to the current-account studies we are about to discuss. Comparison with Campbell's results is difficult, however, because he examines a different question, the accumulation of private wealth of all kinds in response to fluctuations in after-tax labor income.

Define

$$Q \equiv Y - G - I$$

The starting point for the present-value methodology is again eq. (4.46), expressed in the form

$$CA_t = Q_t - \tilde{Q}_t \tag{4.50}$$

The new variable Q can be thought of as the net private noninterest cash flow. Although the main innovation of the Campbell–Shiller approach does not really require it, Ghosh, Sheffrin–Woo, and Otto all follow Campbell and Shiller in rewriting eq. (4.50) as

$$CA_t = -E_t \left\{ \sum_{s=t+1}^{\infty} \left(\frac{1}{1+r} \right)^{s-t} \Delta Q_s \right\} \tag{4.51}$$

where $\Delta Q_t = Q_t - Q_{t-1}$ is the *difference* of the cash flow variable. Equation (4.51) says that the current account balance tends to be negative when net cash flow is expected to rise, and positive when net cash flow is expected to fall. Conditional expectations are assumed to be linear projections on available information.

What advantage is there to estimating eq. (4.51), where Q_t enters in differenced form, rather than eq. (4.50), where its level enters? The differenced version is appropriate if one is concerned that there is a unit root in Q_t, so that removal of a time trend is not sufficient for stationarity.[60] If Q_t is indeed $I(1)$ (has a unit root), then, as Campbell and Shiller have emphasized, eq. (4.51) allows one to use the stationary variable ΔQ_t as a regressor without having to difference *both* CA and Q, which is inefficient in the likely event that CA is stationary.[61]

The fundamental difference between the Ghosh, Sheffrin–Woo, and Otto approach and earlier studies concerns how one proxies for private agents' expectations of future values of Q. The basic insight of the Campbell–Shiller methodology is that as long the information set used by the econometrician does not contain all the information available to private agents, then past values of CA contain information useful in constructing estimates of agents' expectations of future values of Q. Obviously, incorporating this insight doesn't actually require using first differences, as in eq. (4.51), rather than levels, as in eq. (4.50).

Suppose, for example, that one forms expectations of future values of ΔQ_t by first estimating a first-order VAR (the generalization to higher-order VARs is straightforward)

[60] Ghosh (1995) cannot reject the hypothesis of a unit root in Q_t for his sample. Sheffrin and Woo (1990) and Otto (1992) report similar results.

[61] Trehan and Walsh (1991) discuss conditions under which stationarity of CA is necessary for a country's intertemporal budget balance.

$$\begin{bmatrix} \Delta Q_t \\ CA_t \end{bmatrix} = \begin{bmatrix} \psi_1 & \psi_2 \\ \psi_3 & \psi_4 \end{bmatrix} \begin{bmatrix} \Delta Q_{t-1} \\ CA_{t-1} \end{bmatrix} + \begin{bmatrix} \varepsilon_{1t} \\ \varepsilon_{2t} \end{bmatrix} \tag{4.52}$$

and then makes use of its implication that

$$E_t \begin{bmatrix} \Delta Q_{t+k} \\ CA_{t+k} \end{bmatrix} = \begin{bmatrix} \psi_1 & \psi_2 \\ \psi_3 & \psi_4 \end{bmatrix}^k \begin{bmatrix} \Delta Q_t \\ CA_t \end{bmatrix} \tag{4.53}$$

to form an estimated current account, $\widehat{CA_t}$.[62] If I is the 2×2 identity matrix and Ψ the matrix of the ψs, then eqs. (4.51) and (4.53) imply that

$$\widehat{CA_t} = -\begin{bmatrix} 1 & 0 \end{bmatrix} \begin{bmatrix} (1+r)^{-1}\Psi \end{bmatrix} \begin{bmatrix} I - (1+r)^{-1}\Psi \end{bmatrix}^{-1} \begin{bmatrix} \Delta Q_t \\ CA_t \end{bmatrix}$$

$$\equiv \begin{bmatrix} \Phi_{\Delta Q} & \Phi_{CA} \end{bmatrix} \begin{bmatrix} \Delta Q_t \\ CA_t \end{bmatrix} \tag{4.54}$$

If the version of the intertemporal approach embodied in (4.51) is true, then the theoretically predicted value of $\begin{bmatrix} \Phi_{\Delta Q} & \Phi_{CA} \end{bmatrix}$ in (4.54) is simply $\begin{bmatrix} 0 & 1 \end{bmatrix}$! The reason this restriction emerges is obvious when the VAR captures *all* information people use to forecast future cash flow. The same restriction also holds true, however, when the VAR captures only a subset of that information. The reason is that $-CA_t$ captures the representative consumer's best estimate of the present value of future cash-flow changes, *regardless* of what other information he or she has.

Applying the above approach, Sheffrin and Woo find that the restriction $\widehat{CA_t} = CA_t$ is rejected for Canada, Denmark, and the U.K. in their 1955–85 sample, although it is not rejected for Belgium. Ghosh, whose sample period is 1960–88, finds that the restriction is not rejected for the U.S., but that it fails for Canada, Germany, Japan, and the United Kingdom.

Equation (4.54) leads to a stringent test of the model, but a number of more general tests less sensitive to maintained hypothesis could be applied. One basic implication of the model is that CA_t should Granger-cause ΔQ_t. Ghosh finds that in his full sample, even this weaker test still is passed only by the United States data. Sheffrin and Woo arrive at more positive results. Another approach is adopted by Otto (1992), who tests the restriction that

$$E_{t-1}\{CA_t - \Delta Q_t - (1+r)CA_{t-1}\} = 0$$

which follows straightforwardly from eq. (4.51). Otto rejects the present-value model for Canada and the U.S. after finding that lagged variables help in predicting $CA_t - \Delta Q_t - (1+r)CA_{t-1}$.

---

[62] Once again, this requires a choice of the constant real risk-free interest rate r.

While the formal evidence therefore is very mixed,[63] Ghosh, Sheffrin and Woo, and Otto all stress that the informal evidence obtained by simply lining up actual current accounts with the model's predictions can be quite impressive. This perspective is useful, because no empirical model is likely to be literally true. In Figure 4.3, we graph two illustrative cases, Sweden and the United Kingdom, using post war data; both figures are based on a first-order VAR with ΔQ and CA as discussed above. The model performs very well for Sweden, but poorly for the United Kingdom. One problem might be that the model does not explicitly incorporate the effects of oil prices changes, which have been important for Britain in recent years.

Indeed, if one extends the data on Great Britain over a longer historical period, the model's performance looks much better. For annual British data over the period 1870–1991, a first-order VAR for ΔQ and CA yields[64]

$$\begin{bmatrix} \Delta Q_t \\ CA_t \end{bmatrix} = \begin{bmatrix} 0.24 & -0.14 \\ -0.11 & 0.84 \end{bmatrix} \begin{bmatrix} \Delta Q_{t-1} \\ CA_{t-1} \end{bmatrix}$$

Figure 4.4 is constructed using the above estimates and assuming a real interest rate of 4 percent per annum. Extending the data set yields a dramatically better fit than when one estimates the model over post-World War II data alone. Though the visual evidence is fairly striking, the model still fails a formal test of the restriction embodied in eq. (4.54). From the above VAR estimates, one obtains $[\widehat{\Phi}_{\Delta Q} \quad \widehat{\Phi}_{CA}] = [-0.26 \quad 0.54]$, which differs significantly from the null hypothesis value of $[0 \quad 1]$.

A common theme in the graphical evidence presented by Ghosh, Sheffrin–Woo, and Otto is that the actual current account is often far more volatile than the predicted current account. This seems to contradict the Feldstein–Horioka conclusion that current account movements are relatively small compared to what one would expect in theory. Ghosh formally compares the variances of the predicted and actual current account series and finds that, except in the U.S. case (where he cannot reject equality of the variances), the variance of the *actual* series is higher. Otto similarly finds that Canada's current account is six times as volatile as the predicted series.[65] Ghosh interprets his finding as evidence of "too

---

[63] Ghosh and Ostry (1995) apply the present-value approach to developing countries and argue that, if anything, it performs better than for industrialized countries. They find that across a large sample of developing countries, the level and volatility of net capital movements predicted by their consumption-smoothing model closely parallels those in the data. This finding is puzzling – developing countries' capital markets tend to be less open than those of the industrialized countries – but one possible explanation relies on the distinction between global and country-specific shocks that we make below. Plausibly, developing countries are relatively more susceptible to country-specific as opposed to global shocks, so that the present-value model, which assumes a given and constant real interest rate, does somewhat better.

[64] Historical data are from Feinstein (1972) and Maddison (1991).

[65] Sheffrin and Woo's data (which they generously supplied to us) yield similar results.

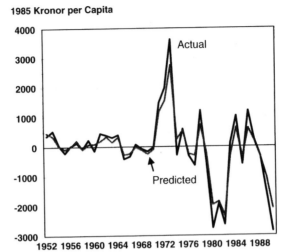

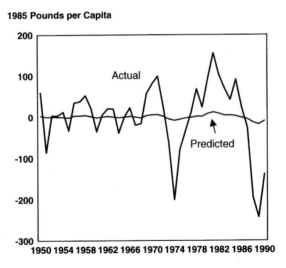

Figure 4.3. Sweden: Actual and predicted current account balance (annual data).

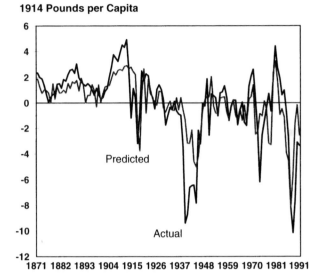

Figure 4.4. United Kingdom: Actual and predicted current account balance (annual data).

much" capital mobility, in contrast to the Feldstein–Horioka claim of too little. One possible explanation of the Ghosh–Otto findings is to view them as related to Deaton's paradox of excessive consumption smoothness. The Deaton paradox can be resolved by stipulating that income, though highly serially correlated, does not literally contain a unit root. (When income is stationary in growth rates rather than in levels, a small change in current income can imply a very large change in permanent income and, hence, in predicted consumption.) Just as the assumption of a unit root in income can lead to the conclusion that consumption is too smooth, it can also produce the result that saving or the current account is too volatile. This may help explain the Ghosh–Otto volatility results, though further investigation is required.

4.2.4. Global versus country-specific shocks and the current account

One shortcoming of the studies considered so far is their implicit assumption that all shocks to cash flow are purely idiosyncratic.[66] In reality, even a small country's output growth or investment may be highly correlated with that in the rest of the world. Output shocks which identically impact all countries should, however, express themselves primarily through the global interest rate, and not

---

[66]This criticism, of course, applies with equal force to much of the macroeconometric literature on consumption.

in individual countries' current accounts. Glick and Rogoff (1995) argue that this issue is empirically important and try to confront it. Their model also attempts to trace shocks to output and investment back to changes in factor productivity, allowing for more structure than the empirical studies just discussed.[67] A simpler version of the Glick–Rogoff framework suffices to illustrate their main points.

Let's label the country-specific component of cash flow Q^c and the global component Q^w, so that

$$\Delta Q = \Delta Q^c + \Delta Q^w$$

The global component is the part of Q that is perfectly correlated with average world Q. Then, assuming that Q^c is $I(1)$, and that initial net foreign asset positions are zero, one can (*after many steps*) show that eq. (4.51) is replaced by the approximate current-account equation[68]

$$CA_t = -E_t \left\{ \sum_{s=t+1}^{\infty} \left(\frac{1}{1+r} \right)^{s-t} \Delta Q_s^c \right\} \tag{4.55}$$

where the interest rate used is that prevailing along an initial steady-state path. According to (4.55), only country-specific shocks affect current accounts.[69]

To separate Q^c from Q^w, Glick and Rogoff consider annual data for the G-7 countries over 1960–90, treating these countries as the world (which, in terms of economic size, isn't a bad approximation for most of their sample period). They consider two alternative methods of separating shocks into local and global components. The simplest is to form Q^c as $Q - Q^w$, where Q^w is taken to be a mean-GNP weighted average for the entire group. The more sophisticated approach is to regress each country's ΔQ on an index of the remaining countries' cash flows, defining Q^c as the regression residual. Glick and Rogoff find that the two approaches yield similar results for their ultimate current-account and investment equations. Overall, global shocks appear to account for a very significant portion of total productivity shocks in the G-7 countries, roughly 50 percent.[70] Glick and Rogoff find that the global versus country-specific distinction greatly improves the ability of the intertemporal approach to explain

---

[67] Leiderman and Razin (1991) develop a model similar to Glick and Rogoff's, although they do not distinguish between global and country-specific shocks.

[68] The derivation of equation (4.55) requires that the variances of the underlying productivity shocks be constant. The global component of the shock, Q^w, affects world interest rates but not the current account.

[69] If initial net foreign asset positions are not zero, the interest-rate effects of global shocks can redistribute income from debtors to creditors in a way that alters current accounts. [Recall eq. (3.9) above.] Glick and Rogoff show that this effect is empirically small.

[70] Costello (1993) and Stockman (1988) have found, for slightly different country samples and industry-level data, that global productivity or output shocks seem to be less correlated between similar manufacturing industries in different countries than between different industries in the same country. That evidence apparently points to a greater role for country-specific shocks, and it remains to reconcile it with the results discussed in the text.

actual current accounts: the coefficients on the global shocks are invariably much smaller than those on the country-specific shocks, and are usually insignificant.

4.2.5. Extensions

The empirical consumption-smoothing models discussed so far all ignore the precautionary motive for saving, as was remarked earlier. Caballero (1990) has shown, however, that under specified assumptions one can obtain closed-form consumption functions based on the period utility function $u(C) = -\exp(-\nu C)$, where ν is the coefficient of absolute risk aversion. Thus, there is no need to rely exclusively on a linear-quadratic formulation for closed-form solutions. Ghosh and Ostry (1992, 1994) apply Caballero's results to add a precautionary saving effect to the present-value model of the current account.[71] The key new parameter appearing in their extended framework is $\sigma_\xi^2 = \mathrm{Var}(\xi)$, where

$$\xi_t = \tilde{Q}_t - \mathrm{E}_{t-1}\tilde{Q}_t$$

is the date-t innovation to expected permanent private cash flow. Ghosh and Ostry (1992) look at quarterly 1955–90 time-series data for Canada, Japan, the United Kingdom, and the United States. Because they are looking at time-series rather than cross-section data, they must negotiate the difficult issue of time variation in σ_ξ^2, which is a conditional variance in a dynamic setting. Long enough intervals must be allowed for accurate measures of σ_ξ^2, but intervals should not be so long as to preclude enough data points for meaningful time-series regressions.[72] Using two- to five-year intervals to measure σ_ξ^2, Ghosh and Ostry find that their precautionary variable usually enters significantly and with the correct sign in present-value current account regressions. Ghosh and Ostry (1994) find similarly positive results for developing countries. Their point estimates suggest that precautionary savings are of the order of magnitude of 5 percent of imports for the African region, 4 percent for commodity exporters, and 14 percent for fuel exporters.

None of the empirical studies discussed thus far distinguishes between durables and nondurables or between tradeables and nontradeables. As we emphasized in our theoretical discussion, both distinctions can be important for the current account. Burda and Gerlach (1993) argue that, in theory, durable-goods imports are much more sensitive to expected movements in the real exchange rate (because of the resulting expectations of capital gain or loss) than are nondurables imports. Estimating their model poses a number of difficulties: in particular, the theory calls for a measure of the stock of consumer durables, but this is difficult to obtain in practice. Using a vector error-correction time-

---

[71] An alternative theoretical treatment is Rodriguez (1993).
[72] An alternative approach would be to adopt an explicit parameterization of $\mathrm{Var}_{t-1}(\xi_t)$.

series specification including quarterly data on the current account, expected permanent net income, the relative price of durables in terms of nondurables, and a variable capturing expected changes in that price, Burda and Gerlach find that the expected price changes have a significant correlation with the U.S. current account over 1970–88. This finding, they argue, provides support for the empirical role of the durables versus nondurables distinction. It is difficult to compare these results with those of the empirical models discussed earlier because the Burda–Gerlach setup, with its very general lag structure, imposes much less theoretical structure. It would be interesting to pursue an alternative approach based on eq. (3.23).[73]

Rogoff (1992) incorporates nontraded goods into an empirical intertemporal model, although his primary focus is on explaining the well-documented near random-walk behavior of real exchange rates. His main result is that intertemporal consumption smoothing in traded goods might account for the persistence of innovations in real exchange rates. In the simplest case, assume exogenous output of tradeables and nontradeables, a Cobb–Douglas period utility function [$\rho = 1$ in eq. (3.17)], and an intertemporal substitution elasticity, σ, of 1. In this case, as we saw earlier, people smooth their consumption of tradeables independently of the evolution of their nontradeables consumption. As above, the real exchange rate, the relative price of nontradeables on date t, depends on C_{Tt}, Y_{Nt}, and consumers' expenditure shares. A permanent shock to tradeables output raises C_T permanently and thereby permanently raises the relative price of nontradeables. But even a *temporary* rise in traded-goods output raises C_T permanently because of consumption smoothing. The model thus can explain why the persistence in real exchange rate movements might be much greater than that of the underlying exogenous shocks. A country's ability to borrow and lend in international markets is the key to this result: it would not obtain absent international capital mobility. Rogoff (1992) applies his model to data for Japan and the United States, finding some support, though further testing is required.

5. How useful is the theory?

Even in its most rudimentary forms, the intertemporal approach to the current account has proved valuable for analyzing a host of important problems. Without an intertemporal approach, it would be hard to analyze or evaluate the current-account patterns that followed the two oil shocks of the 1970s. The dynamic budget constraints emphasized throughout this chapter are also essential in analyzing episodes of capital-market disruption, such as the developing-country debt crisis of the 1980s. True, the standard intertemporal models must

---

[73] For some preliminary empirical results, see Obstfeld and Rogoff (1996), ch. 2.

be extended to take account of default risk but, as we have seen, the main qualitative insights do not change. More generally, models that fail to integrate investment, saving, and growth make it virtually impossible to understand why some countries have persistent current account imbalances. Why, for example, are Canada's and Australia's current accounts perennially in deficit, and Japan's in surplus, despite wide swings in their currencies' real exchange rates? Overlapping-generations variants of the intertemporal model are indispensable for thinking about how, say, the aging of Japan's population could eventually lead to a fall in Japan's persistent trade surpluses.

As positive descriptions of the current account, the simple intertemporal theories are not without their limitations. As we saw above, simple time-series models based on consumption smoothing seem to work fairly well for some countries (for example, Sweden) but, in other cases, clearly miss much of the action. Further research allowing for time-varying interest rates, multiple goods, durables, nominal price rigidities, and some liquidity-constrained consumers may lead to better descriptive power. If the simplest infinitely-lived representative agent models are to be believed, then it is a puzzle that ratios of foreign debt to output seldom exceed 1:1 when plausible parameter estimates suggest that ratios of 5:1 or 10:1 could easily be sustainable and even optimal.

Observed debt-GDP ratios are easier to rationalize in economies with finite-lived dynasties, but such models, while capable of embracing a wider set of empirical phenomena, also pose empirical puzzles. A fairly robust implication is that government deficits lead to current-account deficits, but the empirical evidence supporting this prediction, while suggestive, is hardly a basis for strong conclusions. The striking industrial-country correlation observed over 1976–1985 is not clearly evident later on. Promising directions for future investigation include models with more detailed intergenerational structures and a more comprehensive accounting of the intergenerational transfers implied by fiscal and social insurance policies.

The models we have discussed in this chapter provide only a starting point. Obviously, the task of building and empirically applying richer and more realistic intertemporal models will not be an easy one. But there is no avoiding this challenge, since the two leading alternatives to the intertemporal model are seriously flawed.

One alternative that has been explored extensively in recent research is the complete markets model, in which country-specific shocks of all types – to human as well as financial wealth, to personal as well as corporate taxes – can be insured internationally. If this approach is correct, of course, then the current account is little more than an accounting convention without major significance even for a country's relative wealth position. (See the discussion in Section 3.2.1.) We have argued that real-world international capital markets are very far from the frictionless, full-information, complete-markets ideal. Factors inhibiting complete domestic capital markets include moral hazard problems in lending at the microeconomic level, finite lifetimes, and difficulties in insuring labor income. In international markets, these problems are compounded by sovereign default risk, difficulties in insuring national government spending shocks, and cultural and institutional differences. Of course, it would be vastly preferable to model explicitly these capital-market imperfections rather than simply to assume limited asset trade, especially for understanding the impact of government policy. We have discussed some work along these lines and presented a simple example. Until these models have been more fully developed, however, the intertemporal model seems to provide a much closer description of reality than does the complete markets model.

Complete-market models represent an extreme alternative to the intertemporal approach. At the opposite pole are variants of the open-economy IS–LM model due to Mundell (1968) and Fleming (1962). This approach, which ignores intertemporal choice and even intertemporal budget constraints, remains overwhelmingly dominant in policy circles. But as a framework for addressing fundamentally dynamic phenomena such as the current account and government debt, the Mundell–Fleming paradigm, even when jerry-rigged with dynamic add-ons, is fatally handicapped.

The Mundell–Fleming approach offers no valid benchmark for evaluating external balance. In practice, policymakers often strive to avoid a negative current account. Just as efficient international trade generally requires unbalanced trade across commodity groups, however, efficient trade across time often calls for an unbalanced current account. The intertemporal approach identifies circumstances, for example, a transitory fall in output or a rise in domestic investment productivity, that justify a current account deficit. On these issues, the Mundell–Fleming approach has nothing to say.

Evaluating the real exchange rate consistent with full employment and external balance is another prime concern of policy: intervention or realignment decisions may hinge on the determination that a currency's value is "misaligned". Since the Mundell–Fleming approach has nothing to say about external balance, it is, a fortiori, unable to address the possibility of misalignment.

Because it lacks microfoundations or even the most basic intertemporal budget constraints, the Mundell–Fleming approach provides no grounds for normative judgments on current accounts or international macroeconomic policies. No economist would take seriously an assessment of tax, trade, or regulatory policy based on a model with these shortcomings. The intertemporal approach to the current account offers a viable framework for assessing macroeconomic policy, one that must supplant the Mundell–Fleming framework for normative questions.

It is hard to portray Mundell–Fleming as a successful positive current-account theory, either. Without denying the theory's empirical appeal in capturing short-run macroeconomic developments over some episodes, the core model has no clear, much less testable, predictions about current-account dynamics. Again, as intertemporal models become more tractable and enjoy wider empirical testing, it seems to us that they must ultimately come to supplant modified Mundell–Fleming models for positive as well as normative questions.

References

Abel, A.B. (1982), "Dynamic effects of permanent and temporary tax policies in a q model of investment", Journal of Monetary Economics 9:353–373.

Ahmed, S. (1986), "Temporary and permanent government spending in an open economy: Some evidence for the United Kingdom", Journal of Monetary Economics 17:197–224.

Ahmed, S. (1987), "Government spending, the balance of trade and the terms of trade in British history", Journal of Monetary Economics 20, 195–220.

Alexander, S.S. (1952), "Effects of a devaluation on a trade balance", International Monetary Fund Staff Papers 2:263–278.

Atkeson, A. (1991), "International lending with moral hazard and risk of repudiation", Econometrica 59:1069–1089.

Atkeson, A. and R.E. Lucas, Jr. (1992), "On efficient distribution with private information", Review of Economic Studies 59:427–453.

Backus, D.K., P.J. Kehoe, and F.E. Kydland (1992), "International real business cycles", Journal of Political Economy 100:745–775.

Bardhan, P.K. (1967), "Optimum foreign borrowing", in: K. Shell, ed., Essays in the theory of optimal economic growth (MIT Press, Cambridge, MA).

Baxter, M. and M.J. Crucini (1993a), "Explaining saving-investment correlations", American Economic Review 83:416–436.

Baxter, M. and M.J. Crucini (1993b), "Business cycles and the asset structure of foreign trade", Working Paper, University of Rochester.

Bean, C.R. (1986), "The terms of trade, labour supply and the current account", Economic Journal 96:38–46.

Bergsten, C.F., ed. (1991), International adjustment and financing: The lessons of 1985–1991 (Institute for International Economics, Washington, DC).

Bernanke, B. (1985), "Adjustment costs, durables, and aggregate consumption", Journal of Monetary Economics 15:41–68.

Bernheim, B.D. (1988), "Budget deficits and the balance of trade", in: L. Summers, ed., Tax policy and the economy, vol. 2 (MIT Press, Cambridge, MA).

Blanchard, O.J. (1985), "Debt, deficits, and finite horizons", Journal of Political Economy 93:223–247.

Bruno, M. (1970), "Trade, growth and capital", Working Paper, MIT Press, Cambridge, MA.

Buiter, W.H. (1981), "Time preference and international lending and borrowing in an overlapping-generations model", Journal of Political Economy 89:769–797.

Buiter, W.H. (1989), Budgetary policy, international and intertemporal trade in the global economy (North-Holland, Amsterdam).

Burda, M. and S. Gerlach (1992), "Intertemporal prices and the U.S. trade balance", American Economic Review 82:1235–1253.

Caballero, R. (1990), Consumption puzzles and precautionary savings, Journal of Monetary Economics 25:113–136.

Campbell, J.Y. (1987), "Does saving anticipate declining labor income? An alternative test of the permanent income hypothesis", Econometrica 55:1249–1274.

Campbell, J.Y. and R.J. Shiller (1987), "Cointegration and tests of present value models", Journal of Political Economy 95:1062–1088.

Carroll, C.D. (1992), "The buffer-stock theory of saving: Some macroeconomic evidence", Brookings Papers on Economic Activity 2:61–135.

Clarida, R.H. (1990), "International lending and borrowing in a stochastic stationary equilibrium", International Economic Review 31:543–558.

Cole, H.L. and M. Obstfeld (1991), "Commodity trade and international risk sharing: How much do financial markets matter?", Journal of Monetary Economics 28:3–24.

Costello, D.M. (1993), "A cross-country, cross-industry comparison of productivity growth", Journal of Political Economy 101:207–222.

Cox, J.C. and C. Huang (1989), "Optimal consumption and portfolio policies when asset prices follow a diffusion process", Journal of Economic Theory 49:33–83.

Deaton, A. (1987), "Life cycle models of consumption: Is the evidence consistent with the theory?", in: T.F. Bewley, ed., Advances in econometrics: Fifth world congress, vol. 2 (Cambridge University Press, Cambridge, UK).

Deaton, A. (1992), Understanding consumption (Clarendon Press, Oxford, UK).

de Roover, R. (1966), The rise and decline of the Medici bank, 1397–1494 (W.W. Norton, New York).

Devereux, M.B. and S. Shi (1991), "Capital accumulation and the current account in a two-country model", Journal of International Economics 30:1–25.

Dixit, A.K. and V. Norman (1980), Theory of international trade: A dual, general equilibrium approach (James Nisbet & Co. Ltd. and Cambridge University Press, Welwyn and Cambridge, UK).

Dooley, M., J. Frankel, and D.J. Mathieson (1987), "International capital mobility: What do saving–investment correlations tell us?", International Monetary Fund Staff Papers 34:503–530.

Dornbusch, R. (1983), "Real interest rates, home goods, and optimal external borrowing", Journal of Political Economy 91:141–153.

Eaton, J. (1988), "Foreign-owned land", American Economic Review 78:76–88.

Edwards, S. (1989), Real exchange rates, devaluation, and adjustment (MIT Press, Cambridge, MA).

Eichengreen, B. (1990), "Trends and cycles in foreign lending", in: H. Siebert, ed., Capital flows in the world economy (J.C.B. Mohr, Tubingen).

Ekern, S. and R. Wilson (1974), "On the theory of the firm in an economy with incomplete markets", Bell Journal of Economics and Management Science 5:171–180.

Engel, C. and K. Kletzer (1989), "Saving and investment in an open economy with non-traded goods", International Economic Review 30:735–752.

Feinstein, C.H. (1972), National income, expenditure, and output of the United Kingdom, 1855–1965 (Cambridge University Press, Cambridge, UK).

Feldstein, M. and P. Bacchetta (1991), "National saving and international investment", in: B.D. Bernheim and J.B. Shoven, eds., National saving and economic performance (University of Chicago Press, Chicago, IL).

Feldstein, M. and C. Horioka (1980), "Domestic saving and international capital flows", Economic Journal 90:314–329.

Fieleke, N.S. (1982), "National saving and international investment", in: Saving and government policy (Federal Reserve Bank of Boston, Boston, MA).

Fisher, I. (1930), The theory of interest (Macmillan, New York).

Fleming, J.M. (1962), "Domestic financial policies under fixed and under floating exchange rates", International Monetary Fund Staff Papers 9:369–379.

Frankel, J.A. (1993), "Quantifying international capital mobility in the 1980s", in: On exchange rates (MIT Press, Cambridge, MA).

Frenkel, J.A. and A. Razin (1987), Fiscal policies and the world economy: An intertemporal approach (MIT Press, Cambridge, MA).

Fukao, K. and K. Hamada (1994), "International trade and investment under different rates of time preference", Journal of the Japanese and International Economies 8:22–52.

Gavin, M. (1990), "Structural adjustment to a terms of trade disturbance: The role of relative prices", Journal of International Economics 28:217–243.

Gertler, M. and K. Rogoff (1990), "North-South lending and endogenous domestic capital market inefficiencies", Journal of Monetary Economics 26:245–266.

Ghosh, A. (1995), "Capital mobility amongst the major industrialized countries: Too little or too much?", Economic Journal 105:107–128.

Ghosh, A. and J. Ostry (1992), "Macroeconomic uncertainty, precautionary savings, and the current account", Working Paper, International Monetary Fund.

Ghosh, A. and J. Ostry (1994), "Export instability and the external balance in developing countries", International Monetary Fund Staff Papers 41:214–235.

Ghosh, A. and J. Ostry (1995). "The current account in developing countries: A perspective from the consumption-smoothing approach", World Bank Economic Review 9.

Glick, R. and K. Rogoff (1995), "Global versus country-specific productivity shocks and the current account", Journal of Monetary Economics 35:159–192.

Goldstein, M. and M.S. Khan (1985), "Income and price effects in foreign trade", in R.W. Jones and P.B. Kenen, eds., Handbook of international economics, vol. 2 (North-Holland, Amsterdam).

Hall, R.E. (1978), "Stochastic implications of the life cycle-permanent income hypothesis: Theory and evidence", Journal of Political Economy 86:971–987.

Hamada, K. (1969), "Optimal capital accumulation by an economy facing an international capital market", Journal of Political Economy 77:684–697.

Harberger, A.C. (1950), "Currency depreciation, income and the balance of trade", Journal of Political Economy 58:47–60.

Hayashi, F. (1982), "Tobin's marginal q and average q: A neoclassical interpretation", Econometrica 50:213–224.

Hercowitz, Z. (1986), "On the determination of the external debt: The case of Israel", Journal of International Money and Finance 5:315–334.

Johnson, D. (1986), "Consumption, permanent income, and financial wealth in Canada: Empirical evidence on the intertemporal approach to the current account", Canadian Journal of Economics 19:189–206.

Jones, M.T. and M. Obstfeld (1994), "Saving and investment under the gold standard", Working Paper, University of California at Berkeley.

Kollmann, R. (1992), "Incomplete asset markets and international real business cycles", Working Paper, University of Montreal.

Laursen, S. and L.A. Metzler (1950), "Flexible exchange rates and the theory of employment", Review of Economics and Statistics 32:281–299.

Leiderman, L. and A. Razin (1991), "Determinants of external imbalances: The role of taxes, government spending, and productivity", Journal of the Japanese and International Economies 5:421–450.

Leland, H.E. (1968), "Savings and uncertainty: The precautionary demand for savings", Quarterly Journal of Economics 82:465–473.

Lucas, R.E., Jr. (1976), "Econometric policy evaluation: A critique", Carnegie–Rochester Conference Series on Public Policy 1:19–46.

Lucas, R.E., Jr. (1982), "Interest rates and currency prices in a two-country world", Journal of Monetary Economics 10:335–359.

Maddison, A. (1991), Dynamic forces in capitalist development (Oxford University Press, Oxford).

Matsuyama, K. (1987), "Current account dynamics in a finite horizon model", Journal of International Economics 23:299–313.

Matsuyama, K. (1990), "Residential investment and the current account", Journal of International Economics 28:137–153.

Mehra, R. and E.C. Prescott (1985), "The equity premium: A puzzle", Journal of Monetary Economics 15:145–161.

Mendoza, E.G. (1991), "Real business cycles in a small open economy", American Economic Review 81:797–818.

Mundell, R.A. (1968), International economics (Macmillan, New York).

Murphy, R.G. (1986), "Productivity shocks, non-traded goods and optimal capital accumulation", European Economic Review 30:1081–1095.

Neal, L. (1990), The rise of financial capitalism: International capital markets in the age of reason (Cambridge University Press, Cambridge, UK).

Obstfeld, M. (1982), "Aggregate spending and the terms of trade: Is there a Laursen–Metzler effect?", Quarterly Journal of Economics 97:251–270.

Obstfeld, M. (1986), Capital mobility in the world economy: Theory and measurement", Carnegie–Rochester Conference Series on Public Policy 24:55–103.

Obstfeld, M. (1994), "Are industrial-country consumption risks globally diversified?", in: L. Leiderman and A. Razin, eds., Capital mobility (Cambridge University Press, Cambridge, UK).

Obstfeld, M. (1995), "International capital mobility in the 1990s", in: P.B. Kenen, ed., Understanding interdependence: The macroeconomics of the open economy (Princeton University Press, Princeton, NJ).

Obstfeld, M. and K. Rogoff (1996), Foundations of international macroeconomics, (MIT Press, Cambridge, MA).

Obstfeld, M. and A.C. Stockman (1985), "Exchange-rate dynamics", in: R.W. Jones and P.B. Kenen, eds., Handbook of international economics, vol. 2 (North-Holland, Amsterdam).

Ostry, J.D. (1988), "The balance of trade, terms of trade, and real exchange rate", International Monetary Fund Staff Papers 35:541–573.

Ostry, J.D. and C.M. Reinhart (1992), "Private saving and terms of trade shocks", International Monetary Fund Staff Papers 39:495–517.

Otto, G. (1992), "Testing a present-value model of the current account: Evidence from US and Canadian time series", Journal of International Money and Finance 11:414–430.

Persson, T. (1985), "Deficits and intergenerational welfare in open economies", Journal of International Economics 19:1–19.

Razin, A. (1995), "The dynamic optimizing approach to the current account: Theory and evidence", in: P.B. Kenen, ed., Understanding interdependence: The macroeconomics of the open economy (Princeton University Press, Princeton, NJ).

Rodriguez, A. (1993), "Precautionary saving and the Laursen–Metzler effect", Journal of International Money and Finance 12:332–343.

Rogoff, K. (1992), "Traded goods consumption smoothing and the random walk behavior of the real exchange rate", Bank of Japan Monetary and Economic Studies 10:1–29.

Roubini, N. (1988), "Current accounts and budget deficits in an intertemporal model of consumption and taxation smoothing", National Bureau of Economic Research Working Paper No. 2773.

Sachs, J.D. (1981), "The current account and macroeconomic adjustment in the 1970s", Brookings Papers on Economic Activity 1:201–268.

Sachs, J.D. (1982), "The current account in the macroeconomic adjustment process", Scandinavian Journal of Economics 84:147–159.

Sheffrin, S.M. and W.T. Woo (1990), "Present value tests of an intertemporal model of the current account", Journal of International Economics 29:237–253.

Shi, S. and L.G. Epstein (1993), "Habits and time preference", International Economic Review 34:61–84

Shiller, R.J. (1993), Macro markets: Creating institutions for managing society's largest economic risks (Clarendon Press, Oxford, UK).

Stockman, A.C. (1988a), "Fiscal policies and international financial markets", in: J.A. Frenkel, ed., International aspects of fiscal policies (University of Chicago Press, Chicago, IL).

Stockman, A.C. (1988b), "Sectoral and national aggregate disturbances to industrial output in seven European countries", Journal of Monetary Economics 21:387–409.

Stockman, A.C. and L.L. Tesar (1995), "Tastes and technology in a two-country model of the business cycle: Explaining international comovements", American Economic Review 85:168–185.

Stulz, R. (1988), "Capital mobility and the current account", Journal of International Money and Finance 7:167–180.

Summers, L.H. (1981), "Taxation and corporate investment: A q-theory approach", Brookings Papers on Economic Activity, 67–127.

Summers, L.H. (1988), "Tax policy and international competitiveness", in: J.A. Frenkel, ed., International aspects of fiscal policies (University of Chicago Press, Chicago, IL).

Svensson, L.E.O. (1988), "Trade in risky assets", American Economic Review 78:375–394.

Svensson, L.E.O. and A. Razin (1983), "The terms of trade and the current account: The Harberger–Laursen–Metzler effect", Journal of Political Economy 91:97–125.

Taylor, A.M. (1994), "Domestic saving and international capital flows reconsidered", National Bureau of Economic Research Working Paper No. 4892.

Tesar, L.L. (1991), "Savings, investment, and international capital flows", Journal of International Economics 31:55–78.

Trehan, B. and C.E. Walsh (1991), "Testing intertemporal budget constraints: Theory and applications to U.S. federal budget and current account deficits", Journal of Money, Credit and Banking 23:206–223.

Weil, P. (1989), "Overlapping families of infinitely-lived agents", Journal of Public Economics 38:183–198.

Chapter 35

INTERNATIONAL TRADE AND BUSINESS CYCLES

MARIANNE BAXTER[*]

University of Virginia

Contents

[*]I would like to thank, without implicating, the following individuals who have provided very helpful comments and suggestions: David Backus, Mario Crucini, Atish Ghosh, Urban Jermann, Patrick Kehoe, Robert King, Michael Kouparitsas, Maurice Obstfeld, Kenneth Rogoff, Kei-Mu Yi, and Alex Wolman.

Handbook of International Economics, vol. III, Edited by G. Grossman and K. Rogoff
© Elsevier Science B.V., 1995

1. Introduction

Virtually all economies experience recurrent fluctuations in economic activity that persist for periods of several quarters to several years. Further, there is a definite tendency for the business cycles of developed countries to move together – there is a world component to business cycles. The challenge to theory is to develop a consistent explanation for these phenomena. This chapter summarizes the contributions of a particular branch of the literature on open economy macroeconomics. This research has stressed the importance of general equilibrium considerations for understanding business cycles – even in small economies. Further, this research program has stressed the importance of modeling the dynamics of capital accumulation together with the consumption/saving/labor supply decisions of individuals. As we shall see, there have been some notable early successes of this approach, yet much work remains to be done. Thus, the goals of this chapter are threefold. First, we review the empirical motivation for this approach and evaluate the successes and failures of the early models in capturing the main features of international business cycles. Second, we explore in detail the predictions of this approach for the business-cycle response of home and foreign economies to shocks to domestic fiscal variables and to technology. Third, we describe current research which extends the basic model in several directions, and outline some directions for future research.

This chapter is structured as follows. Section 2 investigates the empirical determinants of the current account, and finds that flows of durable goods are an important determinant of current account movements. In particular, since investment is a highly volatile macroeconomic aggregate, movements in investment play a dominant role in fluctuations in the current account at business-cycle frequencies. Section 3 presents the basic two-country model. This is a general equilibrium model of two countries producing a single consumption-investment good, with frictionless trade in goods. Despite the model's simplicity, it contains the three most important elements for thinking about the determinants of business cycles and the current account in general equilibrium: intertemporal optimization by consumers, optimal investment decisions by producers, and endogenous determination of the interest rate. This section also discusses alternative assumptions regarding the degree of market completeness, and specifies how the model may be closed under each set of assumptions. Section 4 addresses the issues associated with solving and simulating dynamic equilibrium models. This section also discusses the literature on the measurement of productivity.

Section 5 studies the business cycle and current account dynamics in the basic model, when the economy is subject to stochastic disturbances to total factor productivity. The key finding is that asset market restrictions are more likely to be important (i) the more persistent is the shock; and (ii) the less rapidly the shock is transmitted abroad. When there are important differences across asset structures, these stem from differences in the wealth effects, and not from differences in substitutions associated with variations in interest rates and wage rates. Section 6 studies the business-cycle implications of the one-good model. The main finding here is that the basic model does an adequate job of replicating many of the main features of within-country business cycles, but three main puzzles remain. This section also explores the relationship between country size and the volatility of the current account and national business cycles.

In Section 7, we study the effects of shocks to government spending and tax rates. We examine how the effects of a fiscal shock depends on the source of the shock and its expected duration, and use our model to discuss the link between fiscal deficits and interest rates, and also investigate its predictions for the "twin deficits" phenomenon.

Section 8 reviews the literature on multi-good models of international business cycle. We begin by reviewing the recent literature on the "J-curve"; we then discuss the extent to which the multi-good model overcomes the problems inherent in the one-good model, and conclude with a discussion of related literature. Section 9 concludes with a brief summary and a discussion of potential directions for future research.

2. Business cycles and the current account in open economies

This section reviews the salient features of international business cycles and current account fluctuations. These features of the data will guide the quantitative theory which is the subject of the remainder of the chapter.

2.1. Filtering issues

Since many macroeconomic time series are nonstationary, computation of moments requires that the data be transformed to remove the nonstationarity. A commonly used transformation is the linear filter advocated by Hodrick and Prescott (1980).[1] The important properties of this filter are the following: (i) the filter will render stationary any time series that is integrated of order four or less; and (ii) when applied to quarterly data, the filter acts as a reasonable approximation to a high-pass filter that passes cycles of frequency eight years or less with the customary value of $\lambda = 1600$ for the smoothing parameter. Al-

---

[1] The properties of this filter have been extensively studied: see, for example, King and Rebelo (1993).

ternative approaches to filtering are application of the first-difference filter, and removal of deterministic trends.

Recently, Baxter and King (1994) proposed a method for measuring business cycle components of models and data through the application of an approximate band-pass filter. The basic idea is to follow Burns and Mitchell (1946) and current NBER practice in defining a "business cycle" as those components of the data with periodicity between six and thirty-two quarters. For quarterly data, the approximate band-pass filter and the Hodrick–Prescott filter generally yield similar results.[2]

2.2. Open economy business cycles

A large and growing literature on the statistical properties of international business cycles finds that fluctuations across countries and across time periods display a remarkable consistency in the key stylized facts.[3] Within countries, consumption and investment tend to be strongly procyclical, with consumption less volatile than output and investment more volatile. Net exports are countercyclical. Across countries, cyclic movements in output tend to be positively correlated, as are cyclic movements in consumption, investment, and labor input. Table 2.1 details the key business-cycle statistics for ten industrialized countries. We present results for the following macroeconomic aggregates: real output, real consumption purchases (including durables), real investment, employment, government purchases, and net exports as a fraction of output.[4]

2.2.1. Within-country business cycles

The first panel of Table 2.1 presents volatility statistics, defined as the standard deviation of each aggregate, measured as percent per quarter (except for net

---

[2] At other data frequencies, the correspondence between the Hodrick–Prescott filter and the business-cycle filter will not be close, unless the researcher correctly sets the value of the Hodrick–Prescott "smoothing parameter", commonly denoted λ. With annual data, for example, current practice is to set $\lambda = 100$ or $\lambda = 400$. However, the value of λ required to approximate the business-cycle filter in annual data is $\lambda = 10$. Higher values of λ pass through too much of the low-frequency variation in a series, compared with the ideal filter; [see Baxter and King (1994) for more details].

[3] Several papers in the literature compare business cycles across countries; [see for example, papers by Backus, Kehoe, and Kydland (1992a,b), and Blackburn and Ravn (1991)]. There is also a growing literature on business-cycle stylized facts within specific countries: [see, for example, Blackburn and Ravn (1992), Brandner and Neusser (1992), Correia, Neves, and Rebelo (1992), Englund, Persson, and Svensson (1990), and Kim, Buckle, and Hall (1992)].

[4] The data are originally from the OECD and the IMF, and were assembled and provided by David Backus, Patrick Kehoe, and Finn Kydland. The time period covered is 1970–1990. The logarithms of all variables (except net exports, which is left in level form) were filtered with the $BP_{12}(6, 32)$ filter defined by Baxter and King (1994).

Table 2.1
Business cycles in 10 OECD countries

	US	Australia	Austria	Canada	France	Germany	Italy	Japan	Switzerland	UK
A. Volatility (% per quarter)										
Output	2.00	1.48	1.26	1.60	0.96	1.46	1.80	1.32	2.06	1.56
Consumption	1.43	0.87	1.18	1.37	0.92	1.12	1.41	1.45	1.33	1.78
Investment	6.70	4.06	3.05	4.45	2.83	3.61	3.59	3.37	4.20	3.66
Employment	1.24	0.51	1.65	1.39	0.56	0.94	0.55	0.47	1.40	1.19
Gov't purchases	1.36	1.38	0.47	0.88	0.67	1.00	0.41	0.82	0.81	0.98
Net exports	0.51	1.23	0.99	0.75	0.85	0.82	1.45	0.93	1.47	1.16
B. Volatility relative to own-country output										
Output	1.00	1.00	1.00	1.00	1.00	1.00	1.00	1.00	1.00	1.00
Consumption	0.71	0.59	0.94	0.86	0.95	0.77	0.78	1.10	0.65	1.14
Investment	3.35	2.75	2.43	2.78	2.94	2.48	1.99	2.56	2.04	2.35
Employment	0.62	0.34	1.31	0.87	0.58	0.64	0.31	0.36	0.68	0.77
Gov't purchases	0.68	0.93	0.38	0.55	0.70	0.69	0.23	0.62	0.39	0.63
Net exports	0.25	0.83	0.78	0.47	0.88	0.56	0.80	0.71	0.72	0.74
C. Correlation with own-country output										
Output	1.00	1.00	1.00	1.00	1.00	1.00	1.00	1.00	1.00	1.00
Consumption	0.82	0.61	0.74	0.88	0.67	0.69	0.86	0.79	0.85	0.85
Investment	0.97	0.79	0.79	0.57	0.83	0.88	0.86	0.93	0.84	0.68
Employment	0.91	0.09	0.62	0.75	0.90	0.63	0.54	0.80	0.84	0.54
Gov't purchases	0.01	0.22	-0.36	-0.32	0.18	0.17	0.21	-0.12	0.16	0.04
Net exports	-0.37	-0.05	-0.63	-0.35	-0.33	-0.21	-0.73	-0.32	-0.66	-0.40
D. Cross-correlation with same U.S. variable										
Output	1.00	0.60	0.54	0.81	0.46	0.85	0.49	0.66	0.48	0.64
Consumption	1.00	-0.13	0.45	0.46	0.42	0.64	0.04	0.49	0.48	0.42
Investment	1.00	0.21	0.57	0.00	0.22	0.66	0.39	0.59	0.38	0.46
Employment	1.00	-0.17	0.58	0.50	0.36	0.60	0.11	0.48	0.43	0.68
Gov't purchases	1.00	0.46	0.31	0.08	-0.18	0.40	0.23	0.06	-0.01	-0.10
Net exports	1.00	0.03	0.29	-0.10	-0.25	-0.23	-0.28	-0.59	-0.10	-0.11

Data source: OECD and IMF, provided by David Backus; sample period is 1970:1–1990:1. All variables except net exports are in logarithms; all variables filtered with the $BP_{12}(6, 32)$ approximate band-pass filter described in Baxter and King (1994).

exports); panel B reports the volatility (standard deviation) of the macro aggregates relative to own-country output. The volatility of output ranges between about one and two percent, while consumption is generally slightly less volatile than output, with investment being about two to three times more volatile than output. The relative volatility of employment ranges from a low of about 0.35 (Italy and Japan) to a high of 1.31 in Austria. Government purchases of goods and services also display a wide range of relative variation, as do net exports. With regard to net exports, the U.S. is the outlier (0.25). In the other countries considered, net exports are substantially more volatile relative to output, with relative volatility statistics in the range 0.50 to 0.90. Panel C of Table 2.1 summarizes the patterns of within-country comovement at business cycle frequencies. Consumption, investment, and employment are all strongly procyclical. Government purchases, by contrast, appear largely acyclic. Finally, net exports are uniformly countercyclical.

2.2.2. Cross-country business cycles

Panel D of Table 2.1 shows the pattern of international comovement in macro aggregates. Specifically, this table gives the correlation of each macro aggregate with the corresponding U.S. aggregate. Here we observe the tendency for outputs of developed countries to move together: the correlation of every country's output with that of the U.S. is positive and in fact is quite substantial for several of the countries. Consumption also tends to be positively correlated across countries, but here the correlations are smaller. In fact, there is no country in our sample for which the consumption correlation exceeds the output correlation. Investment also tends to be positively correlated across countries, as do employment and government purchases. Net exports, by contrast, exhibit much lower correlation across countries, with most countries showing a negative correlation between their net exports and those of the United States. (As a group, of course, the rest of the world must have net exports that are negatively correlated with those of the U.S.)

2.3. The current account

The current account – defined as the difference between national saving and national investment – is heavily scrutinized by policymakers and economists alike as an important barometer of a country's health. Because a current account deficit corresponds to domestic dissaving (or accumulation of debt), news of these deficits is typically received with alarm. Since the current account occupies such a prominent position in policy debates, we devote this sub-section to exploring the important empirical determinants of fluctuations in the net exports and the current account.

2.3.1. Cyclic fluctuations in net exports and the current account

For several reasons, it is useful to consider decomposing fluctuations in the current account into trend and business-cycle components. First, the models developed in the rest of this chapter focus primarily on the business-cycle fluctuations in the current account and macroeconomic activity. Second, to the extent that movements in the current account diverge from movements in net exports, these are likely to be due to divergences in interest payments on the national debt, which change slowly over time. In the U.S., for example, the stock of national debt is large relative to the quarter-to-quarter *changes* in the stock. Thus the aggregate debt stock changes slowly, so that the difference between net exports and the current account also changes slowly, unless interest rates are exceptionally volatile. That is, the difference between net exports and the current account is concentrated in the low-frequency components of these time series.

To see this effect graphically, Figure 2.1 plots net exports and the current account for the U.S., together with the cyclic fluctuations in these variables, where the cyclic components are extracted using the $BP_{12}(6, 32)$ filter. Although the levels of net exports and the current account can (and do) diverge from each other for sustained periods of time, their business-cycle components covary quite strongly. In fact, there is a strong correspondence between the business cycle fluctuations in the trade and current accounts for most countries, even during the period of high and volatile interest rates that occurred in the late 1970's–early 1980's (detailed results are not reported here due to space constraints).

2.3.2. Components of the current account

The share of durable goods in U.S. net exports has averaged about 50–60 percent over the past 30 years. While durable goods account for a large fraction of international trade, they are even more important in terms of *fluctuations* in the trade and current account balances. The economic mechanism is easy to understand – investment is a volatile time series, thus international flows of investment goods are likely to dominate fluctuations in the trade account. The top two panels of Figure 2.2 plot real exports and imports for the U.S. together with their durable goods and capital goods components. The lower panels plot the cyclic components of these variables. This figure shows strikingly that the cyclic fluctuations in both exports and imports are almost exclusively due to fluctuations in durable goods. In fact, the fluctuations in durable goods trade are primarily the result of fluctuations in just one category of durable goods – the category labeled "capital goods".[5]

---

[5]This category includes aircraft, ships, tanks, engines, construction and mining equipment, a variety of types of industrial machinery, computer and office equipment, refrigeration and heating

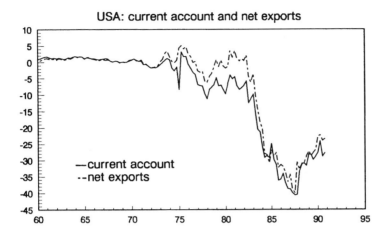

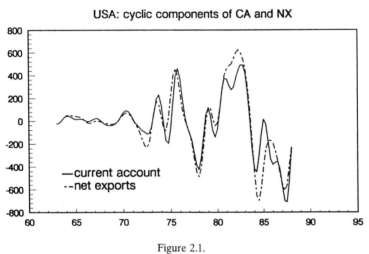

Figure 2.1.

2.3.3. The current account and investment

The summary statistics presented in Table 2.1 suggested a negative correlation between the level of national investment and the surplus on the current account or net exports, i.e. investment is positively correlated with output, while net exports are negatively correlated with output. This correlation is, in fact,

equipment, electrical equipment, and railroad equipment. Burda and Gerlach (1992) have emphasized the importance of durable goods for recent fluctuations in the U.S. trade balance; [see also related work by Sadka and Yi (1994).]

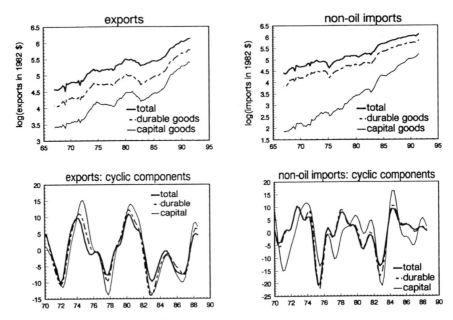

Figure 2.2. The composition of exports and imports.

negative for each of the countries studied, with the exception of Japan (these statistics are not reported in the table). The relationship between the current account and investment has also been the subject of regression analyses. In an early contribution, Sachs (1981) regressed the current account ratio on the GNP gap and the investment ratio for 14 countries, and found that current account deficits were associated with investment booms, and that this effect was stronger for smaller countries. More recently, Glick and Rogoff (1995) have found that investment booms were associated with current account deficits.[6]

Overall, on the basis of this look at the data, we have an emerging picture of the economic factors that are important for open economy business cycles and fluctuations in net exports and the current account. At the center of the picture are investment dynamics – the high volatility of investment is a central feature of national business cycles, and there is strong evidence that investment booms tend to be accompanied by a deficit in the current account. These factors have played a major role in the development of equilibrium models of international business cycles.

[6]However, Penati and Dooley (1984) and Tesar (1991) have shown that this relationship may not be robust over all countries and all time periods.

3. The basic model

This section develops a two-country version of the standard one-sector stochastic growth model. There is a single final good produced in each of the two countries: this good is used both for consumption and for investment. In this single-good model, international trade takes place both to smooth consumption and to equalize the cross-country after-tax returns to capital. Despite the model's simplicity, it contains the three most important elements for thinking about the determinants of the trade and current accounts in general equilibrium: intertemporal optimization by consumers, optimal investment decisions by producers, and endogenous determination of the interest rate. These elements form the basis for the general principles that determine the economy's responses to shocks; these principles are discussed in detail below.

The world comprises two countries: the home country and the foreign country. This model is described by the equations below.[7] The foreign country is distinguished from the home country by means of a star. Where stars are absent from foreign-country equations, the variable, parameter, or function in question is assumed to be identical across countries. The model is discussed in terms of the home country alone when there is no danger of confusion; all variables are expressed in per capita terms unless otherwise stated.

3.1. Preferences

Residents of each country value leisure and consumption of the single produced good – labor is immobile across countries. Specifically, consumers in each country choose leisure L_t, and consumption, C_t, to maximize

$$E \sum_{t=0}^{\infty} \beta^t U(C_t, L_t) ; \text{ home country };$$

$$E \sum_{t=0}^{\infty} \beta^t U(C_t^*, L_t^*) ; \text{ foreign country }.$$

where β denotes the individual's subjective discount factor. The period utility function, U, is specialized to a constant-relative-risk-aversion form, so that trend growth in wages does not lead to trend growth in leisure [see the discussion in King, Plosser, and Rebelo (1988) and also principle #5 below]:

$$U(C_t, L_t) = (1 - \sigma)^{-1} \left(C_t^\theta L_t^{1-\theta} \right)^{1-\sigma} . \tag{3.1}$$

[7] This presentation of the basic model draws on material in Rebelo (1987), Baxter and Crucini (1993a,b), and Crucini (1993a).

For the purpose of our analysis, we further specialize period utility by setting $\sigma = 1$, so that we are in the familiar case of logarithmic utility:[8]

$$U(C_t, L_t) = \theta \ln C_t + (1 - \theta) \ln L_t .$$ (3.2)

This specification of utility implies that consumption and leisure choice will be governed by five main principles, as follows.

Principle #1: Holding fixed the level of labor input, wealth is the primary determinant of the level of consumption.

Principle #2: Holding fixed the level of labor input, consumption growth is determined by the real interest rate. That is,

$$\log \frac{c_{t+1}}{c_t} = \frac{1}{\sigma}(r_t - \bar{r})$$

where $(r_t - \bar{r})$ denotes the deviation of the interest rate from its steady state level.

These first two principles are important for the consumption-savings decisions by households, and are exploited repeatedly by Obstfeld and Rogoff (this volume) in their analysis of the current account. In the presence of variable labor, there are three additional principles, the first two of which parallel those for consumption above:

Principle #3: Wealth is an important determinant of the level of leisure, i.e. it is an important determinant of labor supply.

Principle #4: Labor is intertemporally reallocated in response to changes in interest rates.

Principle #5: The real wage, and expectations concerning its future path, are important determinants of the level of labor supply. In particular, with the CRRA specification of utility, there is no labor supply response to a permanent increase in the level of the real wage. However, there are important labor supply responses to temporary changes in the real wage rate, since temporary changes in the wage rate induce intertemporal substitution.

Finally, individuals face the constraint that time devoted to market work plus leisure cannot exceed the time endowment, normalized to one unit in each country:

$$1 - L_t - N_t \geq 0; \text{ home country}$$ (3.3)

$$1 - L_t^* - N_t^* \geq 0; \text{ foreign country} .$$ (3.4)

---

[8]We adopt the log specification for period utility because it simplifies some aspects of our analysis. Much of the literature uses the specification (3.1) with $1 < \sigma < 5$. This alteration of preferences is not quantitatively important for the analysis of this paper.

3.2. Technology

There is a representative firm operating in each country, whose goal is to maximize the present discounted value of cash flow. For the home country firm, the goal is to maximize $\sum_{t=0}^{\infty} P_t^d d_t$, where d_t is the firm's cash flow in period t, and P_t^d is the discount factor applied to cash flows in period t (there is an analogous expression for the foreign firm). The home firm's cash flow is given by

$$d_t \equiv Y_t - I_t - w_t N_t \, ,$$

where Y_t denotes gross output, I_t is investment, N_t is labor input, and w_t is the real wage. Output in each country is produced via constant-returns-to-scale production functions. Production is subject to exogenous shocks to total factor productivity, which may be partly country-specific in origin:

$$Y_t = F_t(K_t, N_t) = A_t K_t^{1-\alpha}(X_t N_t)^\alpha; \text{ home country} \tag{3.5}$$

$$Y_t^* = F_t(K_t^*, N_t^*) = A_t^*(K_t^*)^{1-\alpha^*}(X_t^* N_t^*)^{\alpha^*}; \text{ foreign country} , \tag{3.6}$$

where K_t and K_t^* denote the capital stocks utilized by the home and foreign firms, respectively. In general, K_t does not correspond to capital owned by residents of the home country since individuals may be permitted to rent capital to firms in either country; similarly, K_t^* does not necessarily correspond to foreign-owned capital. The variables X_t and X_t^* represent labor-augmenting technical change, and are assumed to grow at the common, constant (gross) rate γ_X. A_t and A_t^* are the stochastic components of the productivity variables.

Capital accumulates over time according to

$$K_{t+1} = (1 - \delta)K_t + \phi(I_t/K_t)K_t; \text{ home country} \tag{3.7}$$

$$K_{t+1}^* = (1 - \delta)K_t^* + \phi(I_t^*/K_t^*)K_t^*; \text{ foreign country} \tag{3.8}$$

where δ is the depreciation rate of capital, and the function ϕ controls the number of units of output which must be foregone to increase the capital stock in a particular location by one unit, as in Hayashi (1982). We assume that $\phi > 0$, $\phi' > 0$, and $\phi'' < 0$. Capital adjustment costs have been incorporated to mitigate the response of investment to location-specific shocks. With a single good produced in each of two countries, capital owners have a strong incentive to shift the location of their capital in response to persistent movements in productivity. Without some friction in the capital adjustment process, the model would display excessive volatility of investment.

In parallel with the principles governing the consumption and labor responses to shocks, there are several principles stemming from this specification of technology.

Principle #6: The magnitude of the (worldwide) wealth effect on consumption and labor increases with the persistence of the shocks to wage and non-wage income. For a shock of given size – for example, a positive productivity shock in one country – the magnitude of the wealth effect will be larger, the more protracted is the positive shift in productivity. The way in which this wealth effect is shared internationally will depend on the market structure, as discussed below.

Principle #7: Labor demand by firms depends positively on the level of the capital stock and on the level of productivity. As we shall see in Section 5 below, there are important dynamic interactions of labor and capital in response to shocks.

Principle #8: Investment depends positively on Tobin's "q"—the value of existing capital relative to new capital. Tobin's "q", in turn, depends positively on the marginal product of capital, which increases with labor input and the level of technology, and decreases with the level of the capital stock. Finally, Tobin's "q" (and thus investment) depends negatively on the real interest rate. The response of investment to each of these variables is larger, in absolute value, the more persistent is the expected deviation from steady state levels.

3.3. Government

We assume that the government of the home country taxes national output at the rate τ_t (yielding tax revenues of $\tau_t Y_t$), purchases and disposes of goods in the amount G_t, and transfers goods to private individuals in the amount T_t. In the foreign country, the tax rate is τ_t^*, government purchases are denoted G_t^*, and transfers are T_t^*. In both countries, variations in tax revenues stemming from variations in national outputs are offset either through variations in transfer payments, or through issuance of debt that will be repaid by increases in lump-sum taxes (decreases in transfers). Thus the flow budget constraints for the two governments are:

$$G_t + T_t = \tau_t Y_t; \text{ home country} \tag{3.9}$$

$$G_t^* + T_t^* = \tau_t^* Y_t^*; \text{ foreign country .} \tag{3.10}$$

Ricardian equivalence obtains in this economy because of the infinite horizon of the representative individuals. That is, there is an equivalence between financing current government expenditures with lump-sum taxes, or financing them with debt which will be retired in the future by increasing lump-sum taxes. In Section 7 below, we explore the model's implications for the domestic and international effects of disturbances to government purchases and tax rates.

3.4. Market structure

To close the model, we must specify the structure of markets available to individuals. We assume that there is frictionless international trade in output, so that there is a unified world resource constraint for the single produced good:

$$\pi(Y_t - C_t - I_t - G_t) + (1 - \pi)(Y_t^* - C_t^* - I_t^* - G_t^*) \geq 0. \tag{3.11}$$

In addition to the market for final goods, nations are also linked by financial markets. Since there is cross-country heterogeneity in the shocks to productivity, government expenditure and taxation, the extent of international financial linkages is likely to be important for the extent of consumption-smoothing and risk-pooling that individuals can achieve. By consumption smoothing, we mean the simple transfer of a unit of the consumption good from one date to another. By risk-pooling, we mean the transfer of consumption from one state of nature to another.

For the most part, the general equilibrium, open economy business cycle literature has studied models in which asset markets are assumed to be complete: individuals may trade any contingent claims they wish [see, for example, Backus, Kehoe, and Kydland (1992a) and Baxter and Crucini (1993a)]. In equilibrium, individuals attain the optimal degree of consumption smoothing, and pool all idiosyncratic risks. By contrast, the small open economy literature [see, for example, Mendoza (1991), Cardia (1992), and Correia, Neves, and Rebelo (1994)] as well as the "intertemporal approach to the current account" [as exposited, for example, by Frenkel and Razin (1987)] typically assume that the only financial asset available to individuals is a risk-free real bond. That is, individuals can engage in consumption-smoothing, but not risk-pooling.

Below, we investigate the extent to which financial linkages are likely to be important for business cycles and the behavior of the current account. At this point, we simply set up some additional notation necessary for discussing the economy in which financial trade is limited to a non-contingent real bond. For simplicity (but without loss of generality) we consider only one-period real discount bonds. Let B_t denote the per capita quantity of these discount bonds purchased by the home country, which mature in period $t + 1$. Let r_t denote the world rate of return on these risk-free securities, and let $P_t^B \equiv (1 + r_t)^{-1}$ denote the price of a discount bond purchased in period t.

The flow budget constraints for the economy whose financial trade is limited to the real bond are given by:

$$P_t^B B_{t+1} + C_t + I_t = Y_t + B_t; \text{ home country} \tag{3.12}$$

$$P_t^B B_{t+1}^* + C_t^* + I_t^* = Y_t^* + B_t^*; \text{ foreign country}. \tag{3.13}$$

We assume that bonds are in zero net supply in the world. Letting π denote the fraction of the world population that lives in the home country, the world market-clearing condition for bonds is:

$$\pi B_t + (1 - \pi)B_t^* = 0. \tag{3.14}$$

There is one last principle related to the extent of international financial market linkages:

Principle #9: The magnitude of a country's wealth effect depends on the market structure, since this governs the extent to which a country's risks can be diversified internationally.

4. Model solution, measurement, and calibration

The model described in the preceding section does not have an analytic solution, except in a small number of special cases.[9] Because of the dynamic interactions of the labor/leisure choice with optimal capital accumulation, the equilibrium decision rules are generally not simple functions of the exogenous shocks. Thus our analysis of the model's predictions must necessarily involve studying approximate solutions to a particular, parameterized version of the model. This section describes the central issues involved in approximating and parameterizing the model.

4.1. The Euler equation approach to model solution

A great deal of research effort has recently been devoted to seeking fast, accurate solution methods for application to dynamic equilibrium models. In many models of interest, competitive equilibrium and Pareto optimum do not coincide (due, for example, to the presence of distortionary taxation or market incompleteness); thus, standard solution techniques cannot be used. Most of the methods currently in use begin from the observation that the system of first-order necessary conditions obtained from the model implicitly defines the equilibrium prices and quantities as nonlinear functions of the model's state variables (e.g. the capital stock and the exogenous shocks to productivity and government policies).[10] A variety of methods have been proposed for solving this nonlinear system of equations to obtain the equilibrium decision rules.[11] One particular application of this general strategy is to take a log-linear approximation to the system of Euler equations, and then use standard linear systems procedures for solving this linear system of equations. We use the specific implementation of the procedure developed by King, Plosser, and Rebelo (1987); this method has

---

[9]For example, one special case which admits an analytic solution is logarithmic utility, fixed labor input, and a 100 percent rate of depreciation of capital, as in Long and Plosser (1983). See Cantor and Mark (1987, 1988) and Dellas (1986) for analyses of open economy real business cycle models which incorporate these assumptions and thus possess analytic solutions. Another case with an analytic solution has log utility and fixed labor input, but specifies capital accumulation as $K_{t+1} = BK_t^{1-\delta}I_t^{\delta}$, with $0 < \delta \leq 1$.

[10]Baxter (1991) describes this general approach in more detail.

[11]See, for example, the survey paper by Taylor and Uhlig (1990) and the papers cited therein, as well as Judd (1990).

been shown to be quite accurate for the one-sector neoclassical model when shocks to the economy are of realistic size [see, for example, Dotsey and Mao (1992)].

4.2. Measurement and estimation of the productivity process

A crucial element of the analysis is the measurement and estimation of the exogenous shocks to total factor productivity – the so-called "Solow residuals". These are defined as the residuals from the production functions, as follows:

$$\log A_t = \log Y_t - (1 - \alpha) \log K_t - \alpha \log N_t; \text{ home country}$$

$$\log A_t^* = \log Y_t^* - (1 - \alpha^*) \log K_t^* - \alpha \log N_t^*; \text{ foreign country}.$$

Typically, researchers find that the following is an adequate representation of the joint stochastic process for productivity (constants and trends are suppressed):

$$\begin{bmatrix} \log A_t \\ \log A_t^* \end{bmatrix} = \begin{bmatrix} \rho & v^* \\ v & \rho^* \end{bmatrix} \begin{bmatrix} \log A_{t-1} \\ \log A_{t-1}^* \end{bmatrix} + \begin{bmatrix} \varepsilon_t \\ \varepsilon_t^* \end{bmatrix} \tag{4.1}$$

where $E(\varepsilon_t) = E(\varepsilon_t^*) = 0$. Under this specification, innovations to productivity which originate in one country (ε_t or ε_t^*) are transmitted to the other country via the "diffusion" parameters, v and v^*. The "persistence" parameters, ρ and ρ^*, are important for the serial correlation of the technology variable within a country. The variance–covariance matrix for the innovations to the productivity process is:

$$E(\varepsilon_t, \varepsilon_t^*)(\varepsilon_t, \varepsilon_t^*)' = \begin{bmatrix} \sigma_\varepsilon^2 & \psi \\ \psi & \sigma_\varepsilon^2 \end{bmatrix}. \tag{4.2}$$

Direct estimation of the parameters of the productivity process has been hindered by the poor quality of international data on capital and labor input. For example, Backus, Kehoe, and Kydland (1992a) measure the productivity shocks as residuals from an aggregate production function, where labor input is measured as employment, and without a measure of capital input. More recently, Reynolds (1993) has constructed measures of aggregate Solow residuals for several pairs of countries, using several different measures of labor and capital.[12] Both sets of researchers find that movements in productivity are highly persistent ($\rho, \rho^* > 0$) (in fact, they are typically close to 1); and that innovations to productivity are positively correlated across countries ($\psi > 0$). The evidence on spillovers is mixed, with the Backus et al. (1992) estimates suggesting important spillovers ($v, v^* > 0$), especially from the U.S. to other countries, but with

---

[12] See Costello (1993) for a study of the properties of growth rates of cross-country, cross-industry Solow residuals.

Reynolds' estimates suggesting a much less important role for spillover effects. Although Backus et al. and Reynolds both obtain point estimates that suggest the productivity shocks are trend-stationary, it is not possible to reject the null hypothesis of a unit root without spillovers at standard significance levels [see Baxter and Crucini (1993b)]. Overall, Reynolds stresses that a substantial degree of uncertainty remains regarding the parameters of the productivity shock process.

4.3. Comparing models with data

A central component of the analysis is comparison of the model's predictions with the data, in order to evaluate the extent to which the model captures key features of the data, and to learn about aspects of the model that require further improvement. Since these highly restricted, small-scale equilibrium models cannot possibly beat an unrestricted VAR in a horse race of explanatory power, researchers in this area have tended not to use formal statistical methods to evaluate whether the models can be rejected by the data. Instead, a more informal approach to model evaluation has been pursued, in which the model's central moment predictions are compared with corresponding moments computed from the data. This section briefly reviews the issues involved in making this comparison.[13]

A natural question arises as to when to filter in order to produce a stationary model. For example, should the productivity shock be rendered stationary before simulating the model? Or should the model be simulated with the "raw" productivity shock process, and *then* filtered? The correct procedure is the following. First, the researcher must estimate the forcing process (for productivity, government policy, terms of trade shocks, preference shocks) as best he can. There will generally be some form of nonstationarity, and it may be difficult to tell whether the productivity data are I(1) or just a near-unit-root trend-stationary process. The model should then be simulated with the estimated shock process.[14] This approach will, of course, generally produce nonstationary model outcomes. For comparison with the data, both model and data should be filtered with the same filter. If we think of a business-cycle filter as the approximate band-pass described above, then this procedure compares the "business cycle components" of the model and the data in a way that is sensible.

The reason that it is incorrect to pre-filter productivity series to obtain a sta-

---

[13]See King (1995) for discussion of the relationship between the evaluation methods of "real business cycle" analysis and those of traditional econometrics.

[14]The method of King, Plosser, and Rebelo (1987) will work even when the shocks are I(1) processes as long as they are not more explosive than $\sqrt{1/\beta}$, where β is the subjective discount factor.

tionary forcing process is that the low-frequency and nonstationary components of the shock process will generally have implications for the behavior of the endogenous macro variables *at all frequencies* – including business-cycle frequencies. Thus we do not want to filter out the low-frequency and nonstationary components of the shock before simulating the model, because we may well have removed components of the shock process that are important for the way the model behaves at business-cycle frequencies.

Finally, it is important to note that pre-filtering to produce a stationary forcing process does not guarantee that the model will produce stationary outcomes. As stressed by Baxter and Crucini (1993b), and also present in the analyses of Rogoff (1992) and Sen and Turnovsky (1990), when international contingent claims markets are less than complete, exogenous shocks generally cause international wealth redistributions, which induce unit-root components into national consumptions, outputs, investments, labor inputs and net exports.

4.4. Calibration

In most of the equilibrium open economy business cycle literature, the approach taken to obtaining a parameterized model is generally the so-called "calibration approach" advocated by Kydland and Prescott (1982). Under this approach, certain parameters of the model are chosen so that the model matches certain long-run properties of the data. For example, the model's parameters are set so that the model's steady state is consistent with the long-run experience of the U.S. economy with respect to growth rates, factor shares, proportion of time devoted to market activities, the average level of the real interest rate, and the rate of depreciation of capital.[15] The parameterization of the shock process is estimated from the data (see Section 4.2 above).

We parameterize our baseline model following King, Plosser, and Rebelo (1988); see their paper for more discussion of the parameterization. Under this parameterization, the steady state share of time devoted to market work is 0.20; the representative agent's discount factor, β, is 0.9875; the growth rate of labor-augmenting technical change, γ_X, is 1.004; capital depreciates at the rate of 2.5 percent per quarter; and labor income as a fraction of GNP is 0.58. The steady state share of government expenditures as a fraction of GNP is set at its approximate post-war US average of 20 percent, and taxes as a fraction of GNP are set equal to their approximate current level of 30 percent.

---

[15] More recently, some researchers have advocated GMM estimation of selected parameters; [see, for example, Christiano and Eichenbaum (1992)]. Under this approach, the estimate of (say) share parameters will be the same as under the calibration approach, since each will select the historical mean as the best estimate of the parameter. However, the GMM approach produces standard errors while the calibration approach does not.

This model differs from most closed-economy real business cycle models in that we impose costs of adjustment in capital. Our near-steady-state analysis does not require that we specify a functional form for the adjustment cost function, ϕ. We need only specify three parameters which describe the behavior of ϕ near the steady state. The first two of these parameters govern (i) the steady state value of Tobin's "q", and (ii) the steady state share of investment in national product. Effectively, these amount to specifying $\phi(I/K)$ and $\phi'(I/K)$ at the steady state. We set these parameters so that the model with adjustment costs has the same steady state as the model without adjustment costs. Thus the steady state Tobin's "q" is one, and the steady state share of investment is the same as in the model without adjustment costs. A third parameter which must be specified is the elasticity of the marginal adjustment cost function, η, which governs the response of (I/K) to movements in "q". Since previous empirical studies have not estimated a cost of adjustment parameter for an open economy model such as ours, we use data on investment volatility to restrict this parameter, setting $\eta = 15$ as in Baxter and Crucini (1993a,b).

Relative country size plays an important role in our analysis. In the context of our model, as in Crucini (1993a), country size is captured by population size. We have not incorporated cross-country differences in the central parameters of preferences or technology; nor have we introduced cross-country differences in per capita income, by making smaller countries systematically richer (per capita) or poorer than larger countries. This permits us to isolate the source of any differences in equilibrium outcomes in small versus large economies arising from country size, per se. For application to particular countries, one would of course wish to calibrate the two countries differently, so that each matched the long-run features of a specific economy.

5. Business cycle and current account dynamics in the basic model: Productivity shocks

This section studies the business-cycle and current account responses to shocks to total factor productivity. We compare the domestic and international responses under alternative assumptions for the stochastic process governing productivity, and under alternative assumptions regarding the degree of asset market completeness.[16] Our approach is to study a sequence of economies, beginning with the prototypical small open economy facing a fixed world interest rate, and working toward analysis of a large economy (an economy which can

---

[16]For related analyses of general equilibrium models with incomplete markets, see Conze, Lasry, and Scheinkman (1990), and Kollman (1992).

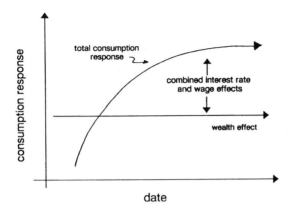

Figure 5.1. The Hicksian decomposition.

affect the world interest rate) with variable labor input. In this progression, we will encounter the principles enumerated in Section 3 above.

As is usual in general equilibrium analyses, shocks induce both wealth and substitution effects, which in non-quantitative models often results in an overall response of indeterminate sign. A benefit of our quantitative approach is that we can evaluate the relative importance of these effects in determining the overall response of an economy to a particular shock. Our method for decomposing the effects of shocks is described in the first sub-section below.

5.1. Hicksian decompositions

Economists have long found it useful to decompose the response of individuals to a shock into responses due to variations in wealth or income, and responses due to variation in prices. One particular decomposition, due to Sir John Hicks (1939) has long been used in comparative statics analyses. A version of this decomposition for dynamic models has been developed by King (1990). These "Hicksian decompositions" are very useful for understanding the equilibrium response of a dynamic economy to shocks of various sorts, and we shall use them extensively throughout this chapter. This sub-section describes in an intuitive way how these decompositions work.

Consider an economy in which the time path of consumption has been disturbed by a shock. In particular, suppose that the shock has caused consumption and labor input to deviate from their prior steady-state paths as illustrated in Figure 5.1. In general equilibrium, the shock will typically cause disturbances to the path of real wages and also to the path of interest rates. Further, the shock will have an effect on the individual's wealth as measured by the present value of lifetime expected utility.

Following Hicks, the wealth effect is measured as follows. Compute the change in lifetime expected utility which occurs because of the displacement of consumption and leisure from their steady state paths. Next, compute the constant changes in consumption and leisure which produce the same change in lifetime utility, while preserving the intratemporal efficiency condition for consumption and leisure. We will call this constant amount the "wealth effect" of the shock, the consumption component of which is sketched in Figure 5.1. At each point, the difference between the actual value of consumption or leisure and the amount due to the wealth effect is due to substitution effects associated with variations in the wage rate and the interest rate. To compute the wage rate effect of a shock, imagine holding individuals' wealth levels fixed at their initial, steady-state level, and imagine that the interest rate is also at its steady state level. Now, ask the consumer how his consumption and leisure choices would be altered if he were faced with the alteration in the time path of wages induced by the shock. These alterations in consumption and leisure are the wage rate effects of the shock. The interest rate effects are computed in a similar fashion, by tracing out the effects on consumption and leisure of the interest rate response, holding wages and wealth fixed at initial steady-state levels.

5.2. Dynamic response to a permanent productivity shock

To begin our analysis of the general equilibrium effects of shifts in total factor productivity, we consider an unanticipated, permanent increase in the level of total factor productivity in the home country. We will develop our understanding of the importance of endogenous interest rate determination, variable labor, and the effect of country size by studying a sequence of economies, as follows. The first sub-section below considers an economy with fixed labor input and which is sufficiently small that the effect on the world interest rate of country-specific shocks is negligible. The next sub-section considers the same small open economy, but with variable labor. The third sub-section studies a "large" country – a country whose GDP is half the world's GDP – with variable labor input. This example allows us to study the importance of interest rate effects in the overall dynamic response to the productivity shock.

5.2.1. A small open economy with fixed labor input

A natural starting point is a small open economy with fixed labor input. In this economy, there will be only wealth effects of shocks: interest rate effects will be

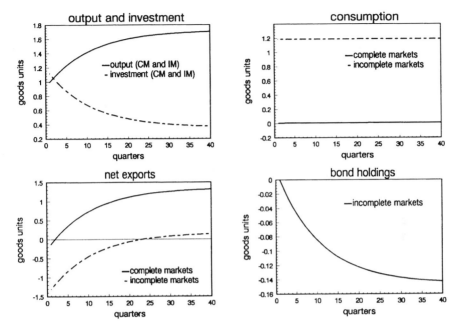

Figure 5.2. Permanent productivity shock in a small open economy with fixed labor input.

absent because of the small country assumption, and wage effects will be absent because labor input is fixed. Consider an unanticipated, permanent increase of 1 percent in the country's level of total factor productivity. The country represents only 1 percent of world GDP, so that the effect of country-specific shocks on world aggregates is essentially zero. The response of domestic macroeconomic aggregates are plotted in Figure 5.2. Solid lines denote the response of the country when it has access to complete contingent-claims markets; dashed lines denote the response of the economy when its financial trade is limited to a non-contingent real bond. Units of output are chosen so that the direct effect of the 1 percent increase in productivity is a one-unit increase in output.

Output and investment. The permanent increase in the level of productivity stimulates an investment boom and a rising path for output. This is an application of principle #8: investment depends positively on the marginal product of capital. The long-run effect on output is 1.72 goods units.[17] The response of

---

[17] The one-unit increase in output on impact is due to the productivity shock alone, since capital is predetermined and labor input does not change. The long-run effect can be derived from the steady state condition that $\partial F/\partial K = r + \delta$. Differentiating this, and using eqn. (3.5) yields $dA/A = \alpha(dK/K)$, or $dK/K = (1/\alpha)dA/A$. Thus $dY/Y = dA/A + (1 - \alpha)dK/K$ or, substituting, for dK/K and setting $\alpha = 0.58$ (this is labor's share), we have $dY/Y = (1/\alpha)dA/A = 1.72dA/A$.

output and investment is the same across asset structures because labor input is assumed to be fixed. That is, the only determinant of investment and output dynamics is the physical product of capital which, due to the fixity of labor, is the same across asset structures.

Consumption. The consumption response, in contrast to output and investment, is sensitive to the asset structure. Under complete markets, individuals pool all idiosyncratic risks; in the "bond economy" they simply use the non-contingent real bond to effect consumption-smoothing in response to idiosyncratic wealth shocks. Since the world wealth effect of a permanent productivity shock in the small economy is approximately zero, under complete markets the consumption response in the home (small) country is also approximately zero. However, the productivity shock represents a significant alteration in home country wealth, and in the bond economy the wealth effect of the shock is concentrated on the home country. That is, absent risk-pooling, a permanent increase in productivity represents a significant, positive wealth shock to the home country, and consumption correspondingly rises. These implications reflect principles #1 and #9: consumption depends on wealth, and the wealth effect of a shock depends on the asset structure.

Notice, in particular, that consumption rises on impact by more than the output. Since output continues to rise after the impact period, permanent income theory predicts that consumption should rise by more than output.[18] Further, the predicted response of consumption is flat after the first period since the interest rate is unaffected by the shock. Because this economy is too small to affect interest rates and because labor input is fixed, there is only a wealth effect on consumption.

Net exports and the current account. Finally, we consider the response of net exports of goods as well as the response of the current account. Net exports are defined in the context of our model as $Y - C - I - G$, where our output measure is GDP. The current account adds to net exports net interest payments on domestic debt held abroad and other net transfers. In the bond economy, it is straightforward to compute the current account in a way that is consistent with NIPA practice. However, many researchers have noted that current NIPA practice produces a less-than-ideal measure of the current account, since it fails to incorporate shifts in net foreign asset holdings that occur (for example) due to unrealized capital gains or losses on foreign assets [see, for example, Baxter and

---

[18]Recall that capital is predetermined and labor is fixed, so that the impact effect on output is simply due to the direct productivity effect. Further, the presence of adjustment costs is responsible for the upward slope to the dynamic response of output: absent adjustment costs, output would jump to its new steady state level in period 2.

Crucini (1993a), Obstfeld (1986), and Stockman and Svensson (1987)]. In the complete markets economy, however, measuring the current account is further complicated by the fact that there are a variety of ways to decentralize the equilibrium (by trading insurance claims, in essence) and current NIPA practice would not necessarily appropriately capture all of these. We choose to avoid this issue entirely by just reporting net exports when discussing the complete markets economy.

Turning, then, to the behavior of net exports (which we will also refer to as the "trade account") we see that there is a trade deficit on impact under both complete and incomplete markets structures. In the complete markets economy, the transfer of goods from the foreign country in the impact period is necessary so that investment can rise by the socially optimal amount in response to the shock (recall that investment increased by more than output on impact). In subsequent periods output exceeds investment, and the excess is shared equally as an increase among all individuals in the world. Although the world is so large that the resulting increase in consumption is small for each individual, in the home country the effect is a significant trade surplus from period 2 onward. However, there is no accompanying increase in foreign indebtedness to the small country – the trade surplus may be viewed as representing payments in fulfillment of a contingent-claims contract that specified these payments in the event that the home country experienced an increase in productivity.

In the bond economy, net exports move to a deficit position on impact, and remains in deficit for the first five years of the transition period (20 quarters). This is due to the larger increase in consumption in the bond economy relative to the complete markets economy; recall that the output and investment responses were the same across market structures. Absent complete markets, however, the trade deficit implies that the home country is selling bonds to the foreign country to finance the rise in consumption. Thus, beginning in period 2, the home country will be paying interest on their foreign debt in addition to running a trade deficit, so that the current account is in deficit along the entire transition to the new steady state.

Investment, net exports, and the current account. Finally, consider the relationship between investment and the current account in the bond economy. Investment increases on impact by 1.11 goods units, while net exports fall on impact by 1.30 goods units. As Glick and Rogoff (1995) have noted, permanent increases in productivity lead to the implication that the current account should respond by more than investment in a small open economy with fixed labor and a constant interest rate. However, Glick and Rogoff provide empirical evidence that current account responses are typically smaller in magnitude than investment responses. We return to this puzzle in Section 5.2.3 below.

5.2.2. A small open economy with variable labor input

Having studied the response of the prototypical small open economy with fixed interest rates and fixed labor input, we turn next to the question of how variable labor input affects the dynamic response to productivity shocks. Variable labor is important for two reasons. First, variations in the quantity of labor input alter the marginal product of capital and hence affect investment (principle #8). Prior work by Baxter and King (1993) and others have stressed that the dynamic interactions of capital and labor are important for understanding the dynamic response of economies to a variety of shocks. Second, variable labor input will lead to important differences across asset structures in the responses of investment and output, compared with the economy studied above in which labor input was fixed. We shall see that alterations in asset structure can lead to significant alterations in the response of labor and hence in the response of investment and output. These effects arise because the wealth effect of shocks is sensitive to asset structure and, as we demonstrate below, because the wealth effect on labor input is predicted by these models to be empirically quite important,

Output, investment, consumption, and labor input. The top panels of Figure 5.3 plot the response of macroeconomic aggregates to the same unexpected, 1 percent increase in productivity studied in the previous section. Beginning with analysis of the complete markets economy, we see that labor input rises on impact and continues to rise toward the new steady state, as does output. Investment also rises on impact, but declines toward the new steady state. Comparing the magnitudes of the investment and output responses to those of the fixed-labor economy studied above, we find that investment increases on impact by more than three times as much in the variable-labor economy (3.4 goods units, compared with 1.1 with fixed labor), while the complete markets output response is almost twice as large with variable labor. In the new steady state, the change in output in the variable-labor economy is nearly five times higher, compared with the fixed-labor economy.

What are the economic mechanisms leading to such a strong response in the variable-labor economy, under complete markets? Clearly, it cannot be substitution effects induced by variation in the real interest rate, since these have been ruled out by the small country assumption. The lower panels of Figure 5.3 plot the Hicksian decompositions of the response of consumption and labor. This figure shows that, under complete markets, the wealth and wage effects on consumption are approximately equal and of opposite sign, so that the overall consumption effect is approximately zero. Under incomplete markets, both the wealth and wage effect on consumption are positive. Adding variable labor has incorporated dynamics associated with principle #5: labor input (and thus income and consumption) are affected by temporary variations in wage rates.

Turning to the behavior of labor input, we see that there is a substantial wealth effect operating under complete markets, in accordance with principle #3. That is, the negative wealth effect associated with complete markets is translated into a substantial increase in labor input arising from this channel. On impact, there is a mitigating effect of the wage rate, although the wage effect on labor input becomes positive as well once the capital stock has accumulated sufficiently. In the bond economy (the incomplete-markets economy) the wealth effect on labor input is negative (i.e. individuals are wealthier, so they choose to work less hard). Although the wage effect is positive, the net effect on impact is a decline in labor input. However, the wage effect rises through time and in the new steady state, labor input has risen.

To be more specific about the way that wealth effects operate in this economy, it is useful to consider the type of state-contingent contracts that could support the social optimum of complete risk-pooling. The optimal response

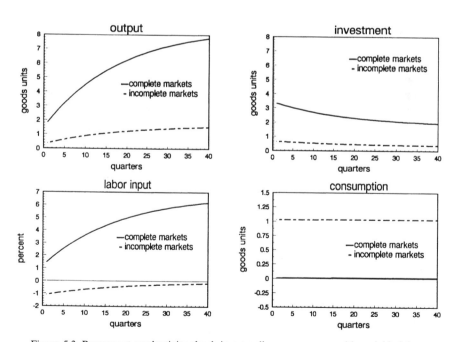

Figure 5.3. Permanent productivity shock in a small open economy with variable labor.

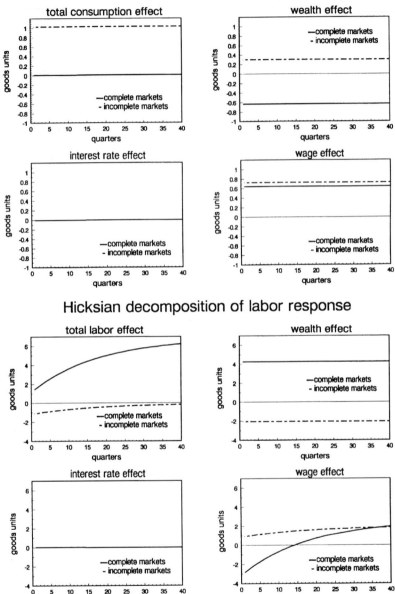

Figure 5.3. *continued*

to a country-specific productivity shock is for residents of that country to work much harder in response to the shock, in order to take advantage of the increase in productivity (recall that labor is assumed to be immobile across countries). The increase in the available supply of consumption goods produced by this additional labor input is then shared equally across all individuals in the world, regardless of nationality. Since the originating country is so small, the increase in consumption involved is negligible, while the increase in work effort in the home country is substantial. Overall, the level of utility enjoyed by residents of the home country falls when they experience a positive productivity shock, since they work much harder and consume only a little bit more. Put differently, individuals in the home country experience a negative wealth shock as a consequence of the positive home country productivity shock. The negative wealth shock is the main force behind the stronger response of labor input and hence, investment and output, compared with the complete markets model with fixed labor input.[19]

Returning to Figure 5.3, we see that the responses of investment and output are different across asset structures when labor input is variable, in contrast to the predictions of the fixed-labor model studied earlier. The central reason for these differences is differences in the wealth effects of the productivity shock across asset structures. In particular, in the bond economy an increase in home country productivity leads to a positive wealth effect in that country. Since individuals value both consumption and leisure, they respond to a positive productivity shock (a positive wealth shock) by increasing consumption and decreasing labor supply. This explains the decline in labor supply in the home country on impact. The rising path of labor input over time is due to the rising path of wages; as capital is accumulated the marginal product of labor rises, making it more profitable for individuals to work more. The smaller response of labor in the bond economy explains why investment and, hence output responses are also smaller than in the complete markets economy. In fact, the investment and output responses are smaller in the variable-labor bond economy than they were in the fixed-labor economy studied in the subsection above. This is due to the fact that, with fixed labor, the positive wealth effect of the shock does not cause labor input to decline, as it does in the current experiment.

Net exports and the current account. The responses of net exports and the current account in the variable-labor economy are surprisingly similar to those in the fixed-labor economy studied above (these are not plotted in Figure 5.3). In

---

[19] If consumption and leisure enter non-separably in the period utility function, consumption rises by more under complete markets in the economy experiencing the shock. This is necessary to satisfy the intra-temporal efficiency condition for consumption and leisure. However, the effect is not large enough to overturn the implication that the wealth effect of a positive productivity shock is negative under complete markets.

particular, the trade account moves into deficit on impact under both market structures, but rapidly moves into surplus in the complete-markets structure as the home economy begins to transfer goods abroad as part of the risk-pooling agreement. The current account is unaffected in the complete-markets economy for reasons described above, while it registers a deficit throughout the transition period in the bond economy.

5.2.3. A large economy with fixed labor

In a large economy with fixed labor, there are both wealth and interest rate effects of shocks, but no wage effect. In the small open economy with fixed labor input, there were only wealth effects. The addition of interest rate effects changes the response only slightly, compared with that case. Investment and output responses continue to be invariant to asset structure, while consumption rises by more under incomplete markets. The addition of the interest rate effect means that the consumption response displays an upward slope over time, reflecting the fact that the interest rate rises in response to the shock and then falls back toward the initial steady state level.

However, there is one point of special interest that arises in this case. With fixed labor supply (or simply if labor supply is very inelastic), on impact the current account registers a deficit that is *smaller* in absolute value than the increase in investment. This is an important result, because it shows that current account movements can be smaller than investment responses, as Glick and Rogoff (1995) find in the data. That is, with endogenous interest rates, it is no longer necessarily the case that the response of the current account to a permanent productivity shock is larger in absolute value than the response of investment.

5.2.4. A large country with variable labor

Finally, we consider the effect of a permanent productivity shock on a large country with variable labor. This experiment combines all the important elements of our general equilibrium framework: endogenous interest rate determination, dynamic interactions of capital and labor, and significant effects of country size. In particular, it adds interest rate effects (associated with principles #2 and #4) to the dynamic effects operating in the small economy with variable labor.

Figure 5.4 plots the response of macroeconomic aggregates in the home and foreign country to the same permanent, unanticipated 1 percent increase in home country productivity. In many respects, the effects of allowing variable labor in the large economy are similar to the effects described above for the small economy with variable labor. Specifically, the variable-labor economy displays

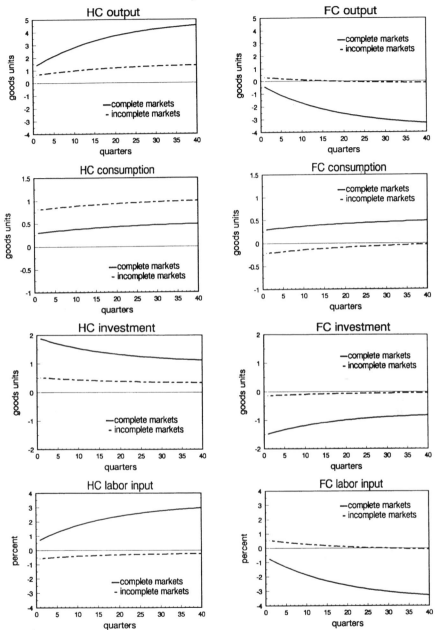

Figure 5.4. Permanent productivity shock in a large economy with variable labor.

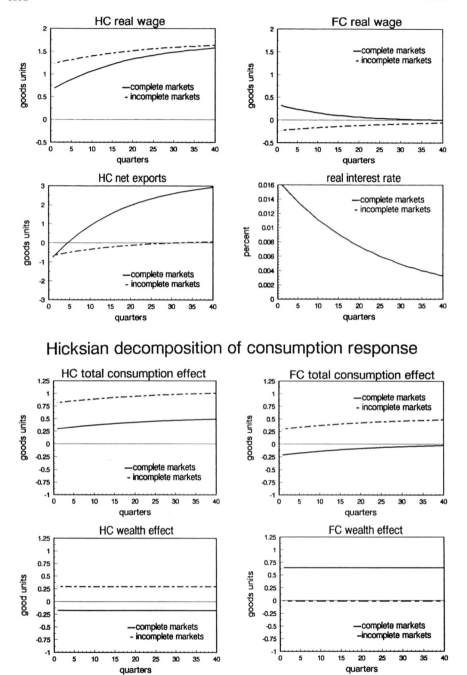

Figure 5.4. *continued*

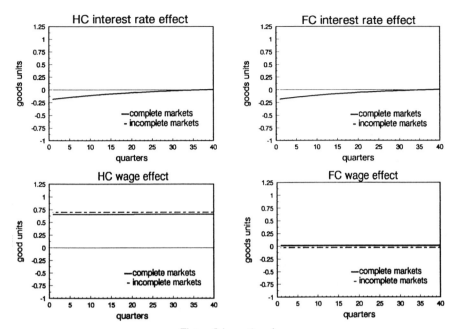

Figure 5.4. *continued*

investment and output responses that depend on asset structure. The reason is that the wealth effects of the shock on labor input differ markedly across asset structures. Under complete markets the positive productivity shock represents a negative wealth shock; in the bond economy, the shock produces a positive wealth effect. Labor input consequently increases in the complete markets economy, but falls in the bond economy.

Figure 5.4 sheds more light on the various components of the responses by plotting the associated Hicksian decompositions. The addition of variable labor to the large economy induces wage effects on consumption which this figure shows are very important to the overall response. In the complete markets economy, the wage effect on consumption is positive – sufficiently so that it outweighs the depressing effect of the wealth and interest rate effects. In the bond economy, the positive wage effect reinforces the positive wealth effect in leading to a stronger overall effect on consumption. In terms of the labor response, the wage effects are of similar magnitude to the wealth effects, and under both asset structures the wage and wealth effects are of opposite sign. These effects are then combined with the interest rate effect, which is positive under both asset structures. The net effect on the bond economy is one in which the wealth effect dominates: labor input initially falls in response to the shocks.

We can gauge the effect of country size and interest rate variation by comparing the responses of the small and the large countries (Figures 5.3 and 5.4). Compared with the small country, the large country's investment response is smaller, because the large-country productivity shock drives up the world interest rate. The initial increase in consumption is also smaller in the large country, as the increase in the interest rate induces individuals to postpone consumption. However, the net effect on net exports and the current account of incorporating variable labor is minimal, as it was in the small economy.

5.3. *Dynamic response to temporary productivity shocks*

In the preceding section we studied the response of a sequence of model economies to an unexpected, permanent increase in productivity. While it is natural to think of technical innovation as something that is permanent, the innovation process may be trend-stationary rather than difference-stationary, as assumed above. In fact, empirical investigations of the stochastic process for productivity typically generate point estimates that suggest trend-stationarity, although the null hypothesis of a unit root cannot usually be rejected. This subsection investigates how our predictions for the response to productivity shocks is altered when the shocks are assumed to be trend-stationary.

5.3.1. *Trend-stationary shocks with spillovers*

Backus, Kehoe, and Kydland (1992a) estimated a productivity process for the U.S. vs. six OECD countries, using quarterly post-war data on output and labor input. Their "symmetrized" version of their preferred estimate for the log of productivity is given by the process below (omitting constants and trend terms):

$$\begin{bmatrix} \log A_t \\ \log A_t^* \end{bmatrix} = \begin{bmatrix} 0.906 & 0.088 \\ 0.088 & 0.906 \end{bmatrix} \begin{bmatrix} \log A_{t-1} \\ \log A_{t-1}^* \end{bmatrix} + \begin{bmatrix} \varepsilon_t \\ \varepsilon_t^* \end{bmatrix}.$$

The estimate of the contemporaneous correlation of the innovations to the productivity process was $\psi = 0.258$. Under this specification, shocks to productivity are highly persistent, and shocks originating in one country are transmitted to the other country at the rate of 8.8 percent per quarter. The shocks are trend-stationary, however, since the largest eigenvalue of the matrix multiplying lagged productivity is $\rho + \nu = 0.906 + 0.088 = 0.994$.

Consider the version of the model with two equally-sized countries and variable labor, in which there is a 1 percent shock to total factor productivity which originates in the home country. The response of both countries is plotted in Figure 5.5. The most striking impression from this figure is how similar the responses are between the complete markets and bond economies. In the case of

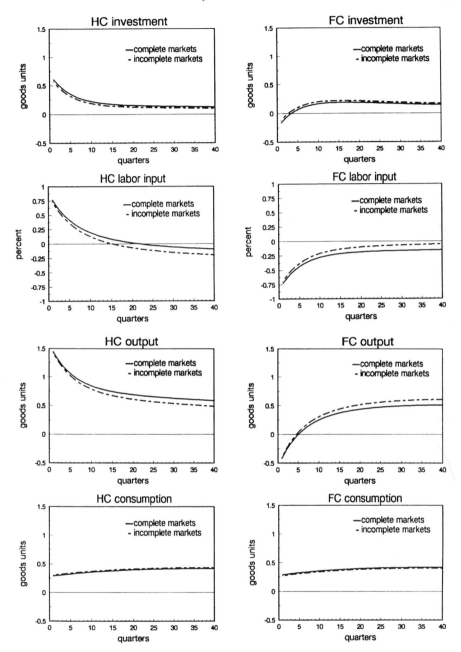

Figure 5.5. Trend stationary shocks with spillovers

permanent shocks, there were important differences in the wealth effects across asset structures, as illustrated by the Hicksian decompositions. These differential wealth effects were responsible for very different responses of labor input, investment, output, and consumption across asset structures. In the present example, the extreme similarity of the responses across asset structures can be traced to the same reason: the wealth effect of the shock is nearly identical across the two asset structures. That is, a shock that originates in the home country is transmitted to the foreign country rapidly enough that the foreign country can sustain a consumption path nearly as high as that obtained under complete risk-pooling. The only financial asset needed by the foreign country is a risk-free real bond, which allows residents of the foreign country to borrow for the purpose of consumption while waiting for the positive productivity shock to be transmitted to their country. Since this is the single financial asset provided in the "bond economy", restrictions on other types of asset trade have minimal effect![20]

Net exports and the current account. Finally, we turn to the behavior of net exports and the current account. In contrast to a permanent shock, the trend-stationary-with-spillover shock leads to surpluses in both the trade and current accounts for the country in which the shock originates (these are not plotted). This effect is easy to understand, once we recall that the shock leads foreigners to decumulate bonds to sustain consumption while waiting for the shock to arrive. Thus the foreign current account deficit must be offset by a current account surplus in the home country. However, the implication that output and investment booms are associated with current account surpluses runs counter to the empirical findings of Sachs (1981) and, more recently, Glick and Rogoff (1995). Even without transmission, the productivity shock must have its largest autoregressive root larger than about 0.99 to generate a current account deficit in response to an unexpected increase in productivity.

Compared with permanent shocks, temporary shocks generate a smaller wealth effect together with increased opportunities for intertemporal substitution (principles #2, #4, and #6). This is most evident in the response of home country labor input which, under incomplete markets, rises in response to the shock (recall that it fell in the case of a permanent shock). Labor input rises in this case for two reasons: first, the substitutions associated with wages are stronger, as the productivity shock is not expected to last forever; and second, the wealth effect which depresses labor input is smaller, the less persistent is the shock. Further, the higher are spillovers, the higher is the common wealth effect of the shock across countries in the absence of any risk-sharing. In conclusion, we find that closing asset markets, with the resulting alteration of relative

---

[20] For further discussion, see Baxter and Crucini (1993b).

wealth effects, is less important (i) the less persistent are shocks; and (ii) the more rapid is the international transmission of shocks.

5.3.2. Permanent effects of temporary shocks

An important feature of the two-country general equilibrium model is that temporary shocks generally have permanent effects on macroeconomic quantities when countries do not have access to complete contingent-claim markets. This is in sharp contrast to the standard, closed-economy "real business cycle" model such as that of King, Plosser, and Rebelo (1988) which was carefully constructed so that trend growth in real wages would not lead to trend growth in labor input (because of exactly-offsetting income and substitution effects on labor input). In the complete-markets version of our two-country model, the resulting risk-pooling means that there are no ex post wealth redistributions, which preserves the result that steady-state labor input is invariant to temporary shocks to technology. When asset trade is restricted, however, international wealth redistributions arise whenever a shock has a country-specific component, and the resulting alteration in relative wealth levels leads to permanent shifts in labor input in both countries.

The intuition is easily developed with reference to the standard, permanent-income theory of consumption, as in Hall (1978). When a permanent-income consumer is faced with a change in the present value of his income, whether it be due to a temporary or a permanent shock, he responds by permanently changing his level of consumption. If the individual values both consumption and leisure, both respond in a permanent way to changes in wealth. In the context of this model, even temporary changes in productivity affect relative wealth levels in the bond economy and, hence, even temporary productivity shocks have permanent effects on labor input, investment, output, consumption, and net exports.

This implication is important, since most macroeconomists believe that macroeconomic quantity variables contain stochastic trends. Our analysis has shown that, so long as asset markets are less than perfectly complete, even temporary shocks will be sufficient to induce stochastic trends in endogenous quantity variables. In particular, it is not necessary that the forcing process have a unit root in order for shocks to that process to produce unit roots in macroeconomic time series.

6. Business-cycle implications of the one-good model

This section explores the extent to which the one-good model matches the salient features of international business cycles. The first of the three main sections below compares the predictions of the model to the stylized facts presented in Section 2. The second sub-section addresses the model's predictions for differential response in small vs. large countries. From this analysis, three main puzzles will arise which are addressed in the last sub-section.

6.1. How well does the model match empirical business cycles?

To put more structure on this question, we ask how well the one-good model matches empirical business cycles when driven by productivity shocks alone. The estimation of the productivity shock process was discussed in Section 4.2 above, and the main finding was that shocks to productivity are highly persistent, are correlated across countries, and show some weak evidence of transmission from one country to another. Estimates of the persistence of shocks are generally quite high, especially for shocks originating in the U.S. and, as noted earlier, the null hypothesis of a unit root cannot be rejected. We therefore take as our benchmark case the following parameterization of the productivity process (4.1): $\rho = \rho^* = 0.995$, $\nu = \nu^* = 0.0$.[21] The variance-covariance structure of the error terms is (4.2), with $\sigma_\varepsilon^2 = 0.73$, and $\psi = 0.19$.[22]

The results of the simulations for the benchmark economy are reported in Table 6.1A; the country is assumed to represent one-half of the world ($\pi = 1/2$). Since the model was parameterized to match the U.S. economy, the within-country statistics should resemble the U.S. statistics from Table 2.1.[23] Results are reported for two market structures: the complete markets economy, denoted "CM" in the table, and for the incomplete markets economy, denoted "IM," in which only goods and noncontingent real bonds are internationally traded.

Within-country business cycles. Output is more volatile in the complete markets economy (with a standard deviation of 1.69 percent per quarter) compared with the incomplete markets economy (1.04 percent), although neither model replicates the level of volatility found in the post-1970 data – the corresponding statistic for U.S. output is 2.00 percent. The higher volatility of the complete markets economy derives from the substantially larger labor supply responses in that economy, as discussed in Section 5 above. The higher labor volatility

---

[21] This specification is in the range generated by prior researchers, with a largest eigenvalue of 0.995 approximately equal to the eigenvalue of 0.994 implied by the symmetrized parameterization of Backus et al. (1992). However, Reynolds (1993) finds little statistical support for international "spillovers" of technology, so we set these equal to zero (i.e. $\nu = \nu^* = 0$).

[22] These are the estimates of the variances and covariance estimated by Backus, Kehoe, and Kydland (1992a) in their "symmetrized" case; they are also in the range found by Reynolds (1993) for a variety of approaches to measuring the Solow residuals.

[23] The moments reported in Table 6.1 were obtained after applying the same band-pass filter that was used to filter the data for Table 2.1.

Table 6.1
Model predictions

	Standard deviation		Relative std. dev.		Persistence		Corr w/output, lag 0			Other correlations	
	CM	IM	CM	IM	CM	IM	CM	IM		CM	IM
A. Benchmark case: Trend-stationary shocks with correlated innovations											
Output	1.69	1.04	1.00	1.00	0.93	0.92	1.00	1.00	y,y^*	−0.55	0.20
Consumption	0.79	1.06	0.47	1.02	0.91	0.90	0.48	0.94	c,c^*	1.00	0.11
Investment	9.14	4.09	5.41	3.93	0.90	0.90	0.73	0.76	i,i^*	−0.93	−0.67
Labor	1.19	0.30	0.70	0.29	0.94	0.94	0.88	0.13	N,N^*	−0.99	−0.92
Net exports	1.23	0.76	0.73	0.73	0.94	0.91	0.06	−0.25	s,i	0.76	0.45

CM: results for complete markets economy; IM: results for economy trading noncontingent bonds and goods only. Parameterization of this case is: $\rho = \rho^* = 0.995, \nu = \nu^* = 0, \mathrm{corr}(\varepsilon,\varepsilon^*) = 0.258, \mathrm{var}(\varepsilon) = \mathrm{var}(\varepsilon^*) = 0.73$.

	Standard deviation		Relative std. dev.		Persistence		Corr w/output, lag 0			Other correlations	
	CM	IM	CM	IM	CM	IM	CM	IM		CM	IM
B. Trend-stationary shocks with large spillovers: The BKK parameterization											
Output	1.32	1.31	1.00	1.00	0.89	0.89	1.00	1.00	y,y^*	−0.25	−0.24
Consumption	0.78	0.78	0.59	0.60	0.91	0.91	0.61	0.65	c,c^*	1.00	1.00
Investment	2.68	2.52	2.02	1.93	0.89	0.89	0.98	0.97	i,i^*	−0.20	−0.10
Labor	0.84	0.80	0.63	0.61	0.88	0.88	0.81	0.80	N,N^*	−0.99	−0.99
Net exports	0.64	0.64	0.48	0.49	0.89	0.89	0.78	0.78	s,i	0.92	0.90

CM: results for complete markets economy; IM: results for economy trading noncontingent bonds and goods only. Parameterization of this case is: $\rho = \rho^* = 0.906, \nu = \nu^* = 0.088, \mathrm{corr}(\varepsilon,\varepsilon^*) = 0.258, \mathrm{var}(\varepsilon) = \mathrm{var}(\varepsilon^*) = 0.73$.

naturally induces higher investment volatility, and the combination of the two factors makes output much more volatile under complete markets.

In terms of *relative* volatility, consumption is smoother in the complete markets economy, while investment is more volatile for the reasons outlined above. Interestingly, the relative volatility of net exports is unaffected by market structure. Similarly, the persistence of the macro aggregates (measured as autocorrelation at lag 1) is largely unaffected by market structure.

By contrast, the pattern of within-country comovement is affected by market completeness. Because of the insurance characteristics of the complete markets equilibrium, consumption is much less correlated with output under that structure than with incomplete markets (under complete markets, the correlation is too low relative to the data presented in Table 2.1). But labor is more highly correlated with output under complete markets – again, as a result of the optimal risk-sharing character of that equilibrium (comparison with the data here is problematic, since the data measure employment and the model's predictions are for total hours worked). Finally, we note that net exports are roughly uncorrelated with output under complete markets, but are negatively correlated (as in the data) under incomplete markets. We conclude from this that the model does a reasonable job of replicating the within-country character of business cycles, with the incomplete markets version of the model performing somewhat better along several dimensions.[24]

Cross-country business cycles. We turn next to the model's predictions for cross-country business-cycle statistics. Several of the key statistics are presented in the last two columns of Table 6.1A: these are the international correlations of output; consumption; investment; and labor input, as well as the saving–investment correlation. The complete markets model predicts output correlations that are too low, relative to the data, together with consumption correlations that are much too high. The incomplete markets model does much better, predicting positive correlations of both outputs and consumptions, but with consumption correlations that are lower than output correlations (although both appear somewhat too low, relative to the data). Both market structures predict negative international correlation of investment and labor input and both predict substantial positive correlation between national saving and investment. Each of these findings represents a puzzle, and we return to these puzzles in Section 6.2 below.

The effect of "spillovers". To investigate the importance of international "technology spillovers" for business cycles, panel B of Table 6.1 simulates the model using the symmetrized parameterization of Backus, Kehoe, and Kydland (1993).

---

[24] However, van Wincoop (1993) finds that the standard real business cycle model cannot produce enough volatility in the real interest rate, compared with the data.

Under this parameterization, $\rho = \rho^* = 0.906$ and $\nu = \nu^* = 0.088$, with the variance-covariance matrix as in the benchmark case. Inspection of this panel shows that there are few differences between the complete and incomplete market economies. Apparently, the spillovers of technology are strong enough that virtually all shocks are common shocks, so that there are very limited opportunities for international risk-sharing. The only difference between the two countries is that one country experiences the shock before the other, so that one country dissaves (decumulates debt) while waiting for the shock to arrive. The single financial instrument in the economy – the noncontingent bond – is the perfect vehicle for this consumption-smoothing.

Overall, this version of the model performs more poorly than our benchmark version along two key dimensions. First, net exports are positively correlated with output, while these are negative in the data. Second, cross-country output correlations are negative, while consumption correlations are 1.00 (even with incomplete markets). This analysis suggests that common shocks are more likely to be the reason for observed international comovement, rather than transmission of shocks over time.

6.2. Business cycles in small vs. large countries

This model predicts a natural link between country size and the volatility of macroeconomic aggregates, which stems from the endogenous response of the interest rate to disturbances originating in large economies. Specifically, positive productivity shocks increase the marginal product of capital and stimulate investment. At the same time, however, the shock drives up world interest rates and crowds out investment. This effect is stronger, the larger is the country in question. As a result, the model predicts that investment should be more volatile in smaller countries because smaller countries effectively face a flatter supply curve for capital (i.e. they can import a great deal of capital without significantly affecting the world interest rate). Second, current accounts should be more volatile in smaller economies due to higher investment volatility, combined with the fact that a greater share of investment is financed abroad.

The empirical relationship between economic size and business cycle characteristics has been studied by Crucini (1992), Head (1992) and Zimmerman (1991). These studies find that larger countries, such as the members of the G-7, have less volatility in investment, consumption, and the trade balance compared with smaller countries. Further, the G-7 countries have larger correlations between savings rates and investment rates, with smaller countries having a stronger tendency for investment booms to be associated with declines in the trade balance. The standard, one-sector open economy model predicts these findings.

Other quantitative-theoretic analyses of small open economies subject to a variety of shocks have recently been carried out by Mendoza (1991), Cardia (1992), and Correia, Neves, and Rebelo (1994). Leiderman and Razin (1991) construct an optimizing model of the current account that is similar to the models developed in the rest of the literature, but they estimate the decision rules of their model using two-stage least squares. Gaudin and Yi (1993) explore the empirical importance of the real interest rate for trade balances of small open economies. They find that a sustained, one-percent increase in interest rates raises the trade balance by about 0.40 percent, which suggests that interest rate shocks are an important source of fluctuations in the trade balance for small economies.

6.3. Three puzzles

Our analysis of the business-cycle predictions of the one-good model has uncovered three puzzles which are worth further discussion.

6.3.1. The saving-investment puzzle

Many authors, notably Obstfeld (1986) and Tesar (1991), have documented the strong time-series correlation between national savings and national investment. It would be natural to conclude from this that international financial markets must not be sufficiently open to allow individuals to separate consumption decisions from investment decisions. However, Sachs (1981) found that current account deficits tended to be associated with investment booms, suggesting that international financial markets are sufficiently open to allow flexible foreign financing of investment; this finding was recently confirmed by the analysis of Glick and Rogoff (1995). The apparent puzzle was resolved by Baxter and Crucini (1993a) who showed that substantial, positive saving-investment correlations are a robust implication of the basic model, even with complete contingent-claims markets. Further, the model rationalizes the Sachs findings. These results show that the time-series saving-investment correlation is not an informative statistic concerning the degree of international financial integration.[25]

6.3.2. The consumption correlation puzzle

The second puzzle is that international consumption correlations are lower than international output correlations, but that the complete markets model (and the

---

[25]Many other authors have also shown, in the context of non-quantitative models, that saving and investment can be positively correlated without restrictions on asset markets; [see, for example, Engel and Kletzer (1989), and Finn (1990)].

model with spillovers, regardless of asset structure) predicts that consumption correlations should exceed output correlations. To appreciate how odd the observed pattern of correlations really is, consider two extreme cases: the first being complete risk-pooling, and the second being the Keynesian consumption function, $C = \alpha Y$. Under complete risk-pooling, as we have seen, consumptions are perfectly correlated (or nearly so) as individuals diversify away all idiosyncratic variation in consumption. But even with the Keynesian consumption function, the cross-country correlation of consumption should be exactly the same as the cross-country correlation of output. It is particularly striking, then, that our benchmark model with incomplete markets can rationalize output correlations that exceed consumption correlations. Several other authors have also provided examples of economies which can replicate observed consumption–output correlations: [see, for example, Reynolds (1992) and Devereaux, Gregory, and Smith (1992)].

Lewis (1993) undertakes an empirical investigation of the forces behind the low international correlation of consumption. She analyzes the Euler equation for efficient consumption choice, and investigates whether modification of the model in terms of (i) variable leisure; (ii) addition of consumer durables and nontraded goods; and (iii) capital market restrictions are important for explaining the low international correlation of consumption. She finds that variable leisure is not important for resolving the puzzle, but that adding durables and nontradeables go a long way toward producing the finding that there is international risk-pooling in tradeable goods. Further, the evidence for risk-pooling is substantially stronger in countries without restrictions on international capital movements. In related work, Atkeson and Bayoumi (1991), Crucini (1993), and van Wincoop (1992a,b) find that risk pooling tends to be stronger across regions within countries than across national boundaries.

6.3.3. The international comovement puzzle

The third puzzle is that our basic model consistently predicts that investment is negatively correlated across countries, and also predicts negative cross-country correlation of labor input. However, these correlations are positive in the data. The one-good character of the model, combined with the international mobility of physical capital, leads to a strong tendency to move capital to its most productive location in response to persistent productivity shocks. Given that capital moves to the more-productive location, the returns to labor rise sharply in the country experiencing the investment boom, while they are (relatively) low in the other country. In an early analysis of the "comovement problem", Rebelo (1987) showed that labor input in different locations would be negatively correlated unless the correlation of the innovations to the location-specific shocks exceeded about 0.95. Although the innovations to Solow residuals are positively correlated across countries, this correlation is not strong enough to overcome the natural mechanisms leading to negative comovement.

For a model to generate realistic international comovement of labor and investment, it seems necessary to develop a model with multiple goods and important linkages between the goods, either on the consumption or the production side. We return to this topic in Section 8 below.

7. Fiscal shocks

This section studies the business cycle and current account responses to fiscal shocks. In particular, we study the responses to unanticipated variations in government purchases and tax rates, under alternative asset market structures. We investigate whether the model lends support to the view that government budget deficits lead to trade and current account deficits, and use our model to interpret the results of the large empirical literatures on the "twin deficits" and the deficit-interest rate link.[26]

7.1. Government purchases

This sub-section studies the dynamic response of both small and large countries to alterations in government purchases. Shocks to government purchases historically have had both temporary and permanent components, with the most significant movements in the temporary components associated with wartime periods. We will confine our attention to analysis of government purchases which do not directly affect private productive opportunities and which do not alter the marginal utility of consumption of privately-produced goods.[27]

7.1.1. Permanent shocks

As a first experiment, consider an unanticipated, permanent increase in government purchases which occurs in a small open economy with fixed labor input. The increase in government purchases represents a pure wealth shock. Throughout, we assume that variations in government purchases are financed by changes

---

[26] This section draws heavily on Baxter (1993).

[27] Baxter and King (1993) use a one-sector model of a closed economy to study shocks to government purchases which are valued in consumption; which increase the private marginal product of capital; and which augment the stock of government-provided capital. They found that these modifications were of minor quantitative importance, except for government capital. Additions to the government capital stocks can be quantitatively important if the government capital stock is under-provided, as has been argued by Aschauer (1989).

in government debt which will ultimately be repaid by increases in lump-sum taxes (decreases in transfers). We call this debt "Ricardian debt" because Ricardian equivalence holds in this model.[28] Since the country is very small, the shock to world wealth is approximately zero. Under complete markets, therefore, there will be approximately zero change in consumption, both at home and in the foreign country. When markets are incomplete, so that the small country can trade a risk-free bond but cannot trade securities with contingent payouts, the country bears the entire wealth effect itself. In this case, private consumption falls immediately by the amount of the increase in government spending, in accordance with principle #1 (see Section 3). Investment, output, and the current account are unaffected by the shock.

Next, consider the response of a large economy with variable labor. Because of the country's size, the increase in government purchases will drive up the world interest rate, providing another channel by which the shock affects consumption and labor input (principles #2 and #4), consequently affecting investment and output as well. The complete markets model predicts that both countries increase labor effort and decrease consumption by the same amount, due to the complete risk-pooling and the fact that variations in government purchases have no direct incentive effects in the originating country. Consequently, the responses of investment and output are identical across countries.

Under incomplete markets, since the home country bears the entire wealth shock, the responses differ across countries, as plotted in Figure 7.1. The negative wealth shock in the home country leads to an increase in labor input. The interest rate also rises in response to the shock (not plotted): this is a secondary force leading to an increase in labor input in the home country, and also explains the rise in foreign labor input. Output and investment rise in the home country, and remain permanently above the original steady state. Foreign output rises initially with the increase in foreign labor input, although foreign investment falls. The home country experiences current account and net export deficits on impact. In the new steady state, the foreign country holds a higher stock of claims on the home country, and finances part of its consumption from interest receipts. Thus the new steady state involves lower labor input and higher consumption in the foreign country, compared with the initial steady state. In the home country, by contrast, the new steady state is characterized by lower consumption and higher labor input. Finally, we note that in the large coun-

---

[28] Arvanitis (1994) and Dotsey and Mao (1993) develop alternative approaches to modeling the financing decision of the government. Each of these contributions specifies particular rules for retiring the debt, which may involve future increases in taxes or future cuts in government purchases. Both find that the form of the rule can have important effects on current responses to fiscal shocks. In the present context, we abstract from these interesting and potentially important effects, in order to focus on the direct effects of the policy shock alone.

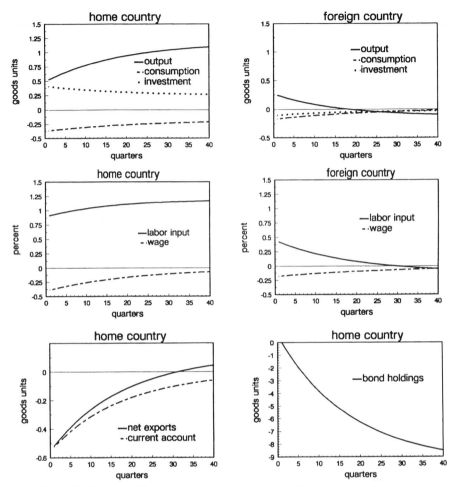

Figure 7.1. Permanent increase in government purchases: Incomplete markets case.

try case, there continues to be a predicted link between government spending, investment booms, and current account deficits.

7.1.2. Temporary shocks

Temporary variations in government purchases have potentially very different effects from permanent changes, since temporary changes offer much greater possibilities for intertemporal substitution. In particular, the more temporary is

Table 7.1
Wealth and substitution effects of fiscal shocks

A. Increase in government purchases

ρ_g	Consumption response (goods units)				Labor response (percent)			
	Total	Wealth	Interest rate	Wage rate	Total	Wealth	Interest rate	Wage rate
0	−0.0787	−0.0028	−0.073	0.0028	0.1979	0.0188	0.4925	−0.3134
0.4	−0.088	−0.0046	−0.0789	−0.0045	0.2213	0.0308	0.5321	−0.3416
0.8	−0.1248	−0.0127	−0.1012	−0.0109	0.3140	0.0856	0.6825	−0.4540
0.95	−0.2046	−0.0399	−0.1412	−0.0236	0.5148	0.2690	0.9517	−0.7060
0.975	−0.2474	−0.0642	−0.1542	−0.0291	0.6224	0.4325	1.0397	−0.8498
1	−0.3620	−0.1827	−0.1827	−0.0366	0.9107	1.2318	0.9623	−1.2833

B. Decrease in tax rate

ρ_t	Consumption response (goods units)				Labor response (percent)			
	Total	Wealth	Interest rate	Wage rate	Total	Wealth	Interest rate	Wage rate
0	0.0610	0.0002	0.0111	0.0497	0.4861	−0.0015	−0.0747	0.5623
0.4	0.0609	0.0004	0.0101	0.0504	0.4865	−0.0026	−0.0682	0.5572
0.8	0.0614	0.0014	0.0057	0.0543	0.4852	−0.0096	−0.0383	0.5331
0.95	0.0720	0.0069	−0.0089	0.0740	0.4586	−0.0464	0.0599	0.4452
0.975	0.0873	0.0130	−0.0216	0.0958	0.4201	−0.0880	0.1457	0.3624
1	0.1817	0.0475	−0.0828	0.2171	0.1825	−0.3199	0.5580	−0.0556

the shock, the smaller is the wealth effect and the larger are the substitution effects associated with changes in wage rates and interest rates. We illustrate these effects using the following stochastic process for temporary government spending shocks, where $\overline{G}$ is the average or "trend" level of purchases:

$$G_t = (1 - \rho_G)\overline{G} + \rho_G G_{t-1} + \varepsilon_{Gt} .$$

Table 7.1A shows how the wealth effect and initial-period wage and interest rate effects of the one-unit increase in government purchases depend on the persistence of the shock to government purchases, ρ_G. Results are presented for the incomplete-markets economy only. Looking first at the wealth effect on consumption and labor input, we see that these are small until the shocks become very persistent, with ρ_G greater than 0.95. The wealth effect is larger in magnitude under incomplete markets – about twice as large, since the economy in question represents half of world GDP – but the effect is nevertheless small unless the shock is very persistent. The relative importance of the wage and interest rate effects is therefore greater for shocks with lower persistence. Under both asset structures, the consumption response is dominated by the interest rate effect until the shock is extremely persistent. That is, the decline of consumption on impact is largely due to the effect of a temporary increase in the interest rate caused by the expansion of government purchases.

Turning next to the response of labor input, we find that both the interest rate and the wage rate are quantitatively important, but of opposite sign. The temporarily low real wage induces declines in labor input, while the temporary rise in the interest rate stimulates labor input. The two effects are predicted to be of roughly equal and opposite sign, so that they approximately cancel each other out. In the end, the response of labor input is roughly determined by the size of the wealth effect. Many economists are concerned that labor input may not respond to variations in intertemporal prices (interest rates) as predicted by this model. It is interesting to note, therefore, that – absent the interest rate effect – labor input would decline in response to government purchases shocks, since the wage effect dominates the wealth effect under either asset structure.

7.2. Shocks to tax rates

This section briefly considers the domestic and international implications of shocks to tax rates. Our model considers only a distorting tax on total output or, equivalently, identical taxes on capital and labor.[29] To facilitate comparison of these experiments with the one-unit increase in the level of government purchases studied above, we consider a *decrease* in the distorting tax rate in an amount that would lead to a one-unit increase in the government fiscal deficit if there were no response of labor input. As before, we assume that the tax cut is financed by "Ricardian debt".

7.2.1. Permanent shocks

Figure 7.2 plots the incomplete-markets (bond) economy's response to this permanent, unanticipated, decline in the tax rate. This shock differs importantly from the government purchases shock studied earlier, since the decline in the tax rate generates a positive wealth effect, whereas the purchases shock led to a negative wealth effect. As with the government purchases shock, domestic labor input rises in response to the shock. However, in the case of the tax cut, the increase in domestic labor input is due to a positive wage effect (the tax cut raises the marginal product of labor) combined with the interest rate effect (the interest rate rises with the tax cut). These two substitution effects are strong enough to overcome the wealth effect, which by itself would lead to a decrease in domestic labor input in response to the tax cut. Given the rise in labor input, domestic investment rises as well, as does domestic output. Domestic consumption also rises, because of the positive wealth effect of the shock.

---

[29]For a more complete analysis of the open economy implications of a rich menu of tax shocks, both anticipated and unanticipated, [see Arvanitis (1994)].

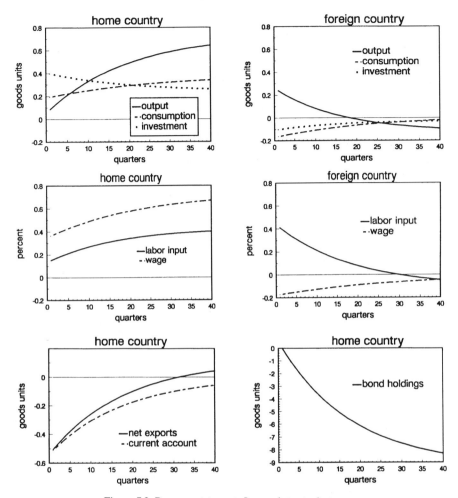

Figure 7.2. Permanent tax cut: Incomplete markets case.

In the foreign country, labor input initially rises due to the interest rate effect. Foreign output rises on impact, but falls over time. Investment falls in the foreign country, as capital owners locate new investment goods in the now-more-productive home country. The home country experiences initial current account and net export deficits, which improve over time. In the new steady state, as in the case of an increase in government purchases, the foreign country holds a larger stock of bonds, and finances part of its consumption from interest payments. However, the economic mechanisms leading to this shift in bond holdings differs importantly between the two experiments. In the case of a shock to government purchases, residents of the home country decumulate bonds to smooth their consumption path in response to the negative wealth shock. In the case of the permanent home country tax cut, the foreign country is permanently a lower-marginal-product place to work, and foreign residents find it advantageous (compared with the initial steady state) to support relatively more of their consumption from interest on debt, rather than by working.

7.2.2. Temporary shocks

Since the tax distorts private decisions, variations in the tax rate affect private incentives directly. Thus the analysis of tax shocks is more complicated than our earlier analysis of shocks to government purchases, which had only a direct wealth effect. Table 7.1B summarizes the wealth and substitution effects on consumption of variations in tax rates of differing degrees of persistence, where we have assumed a stochastic process for taxes of the form:

$$\tau_t = (1 - \rho_\tau)\bar{\tau} + \rho_\tau \tau_{t-1} + \varepsilon_{\tau t} \ .$$

As before, we only consider the incomplete markets economy. For both the consumption and labor responses, the wage effect is the dominant influence under both asset structures until the shock becomes very highly persistent. When the tax cut becomes close to permanent (ρ_τ close to 1) the wealth effect begins to be important. Finally, we note that the sign of the interest rate effect depends on the degree of persistence of the tax shock – we provide an explanation for this phenomenon in Section 7.3.2 below.

7.3. The twin deficits

Many economists have noted an apparent link between fiscal deficits and current account deficits, with the link appearing especially strong since about the mid-1970's. At the same time, fiscal deficits are thought to crowd out private economic activity through increases in interest rates. This sub-section explores the model's implications for these phenomena.

7.3.1. Government purchases

Table 7.2A shows the incomplete markets model's predictions for the effect of an unanticipated increase in government purchases on the current account deficit, interest rates, and the fiscal deficit in the bond economy. We assume here that the increase in purchases is financed on impact by an increase in debt

Table 7.2
International effects of fiscal shocks
A. Impact effect of one-unit increase in government purchases

ρ_g	Fiscal deficit	Trade deficit	CA deficit	Interest rate*
0.000	0.97	0.50	0.51	47.5
0.200	0.97	0.50	0.51	38.0
0.400	0.97	0.50	0.51	28.5
0.600	0.96	0.50	0.51	19.2
0.800	0.95	0.50	0.51	10.2
0.900	0.94	0.50	0.50	6.3
0.950	0.92	0.50	0.50	5.0
0.975	0.90	0.49	0.50	4.7
1.000	0.84	0.48	0.49	5.1

B. Impact effect of decrease in tax rate (one-unit decline in revenue)

ρ_t	Fiscal deficit	Trade deficit	CA deficit	Interest rate*
0.000	0.92	−0.13	−0.13	−12.4
0.200	0.92	−0.12	−0.12	−9.0
0.400	0.92	−0.10	−0.10	−5.5
0.600	0.92	−0.07	−0.07	−2.1
0.800	0.92	0.00	0.00	1.3
0.900	0.92	0.10	0.11	3.1
0.950	0.92	0.21	0.22	4.0
0.975	0.93	0.31	0.31	4.5
1.000	0.97	0.47	0.48	5.0

*Annualized basis points.

as described above, so that the increase in purchases leads to an increase (on impact) in the fiscal deficit. This table shows that there is a robust relationship between the fiscal deficit and the current account deficit and, in particular, the impact effect of purchases shocks on the current account are largely insensitive to the persistence of the shock.[30] The interest rate effect, on the other hand, is very sensitive to persistence. For purely temporary shocks ($\rho_G = 0$) the one-unit increase in purchases leads to an increase in interest rates of about 50 basis points. When the shock is permanent, the interest rate effect is negligible – only about 5 basis points.

This analysis suggests one potential reason why the large empirical literature on the relationship between fiscal deficits and interest rates has not found a robust relationship between fiscal deficits and interest rates. The effects are simply

[30] Ahmed (1987) studies a related model but without variable labor; his model predicts that the current account effect should be larger for temporary shocks. He presents some empirical evidence to support this prediction.

not very large when the variations in government purchases are highly persistent. One empirical study which does find a significant relationship is Barro's (1987) analysis of wartime experiences in Great Britain. Our analysis predicts that it should be exactly this type of large, temporary increase in purchases which would have the largest effect on world interest rates. Yi (1993) also finds that government purchases play a role in explaining recent U.S. net export deficits.

7.3.2. Taxes

As with government purchases, we investigate whether this model predicts a "twin deficits" phenomenon in response to decreases in distortionary taxation. Table 7.2B shows the impact effect of the tax cut on the fiscal deficit, the trade deficit, and the interest rate for the bond economy. We note first that the sign of the interest rate effect depends on the persistence of the tax cut. For extremely short-lived tax cuts (low values of ρ_τ) individuals would prefer to work harder while the tax cut is in effect, and smooth consumption over the infinite future by saving in the current period. The investment effect of a very short-lived tax cut is, however, expected to be minimal. In the extreme case of $\rho_\tau = 0$, there is no direct incentive to alter investment since the tax cut will have disappeared by the time the new capital is in place. Hence, in order to balance saving and investment, the interest rate must fall to partially discourage saving. However, there is still a current account surplus as individuals purchase bonds from foreigners to partially smooth consumption in response to the temporary tax cut.

As the tax cut becomes more persistent, the intertemporal substitution effects associated with labor input become relatively less important and the investment effects become relatively more important. Once ρ_τ exceeds about 0.80, the investment response is sufficiently strong that the interest rate must rise to equate world saving and world investment. As a consequence of the strong investment response, the home country experiences a current account deficit for very persistent decreases in the tax rate.

These results suggest an explanation for why empirical investigations of the "twin deficits" phenomenon have had mixed results. Our model predicts that temporary decreases in taxes should lead to current account surpluses, while more persistent tax cuts should lead to current account deficits. Empirical work which does not attempt to stratify the source of the fiscal deficit by separating government purchase shocks from tax shocks, and which does not separate permanent shocks from temporary shocks, is unlikely to uncover a robust relationship. A similar argument applies to empirical analyses of the relationship between deficits and interest rates – the model predicts very different effects depending on the source of the deficit shock and its persistence. In recent work, Kollman (1994) constructs a two-country real business cycle model, and finds that the model with incomplete markets can explain much of the recent variation in the U.S. trade balance, when driven by measured shocks to technology, taxes, and government purchases.[31]

8. Multi-good models

The single-good model, with its nine principles arising from intertemporal trade and the dynamics of capital accumulation, has taken us a long way toward understanding the transmission and propagation of business cycles across countries. Nevertheless, it is too limited a vehicle for addressing many questions at the heart of international trade and finance. This section summarizes the recent literature on multi-good models of international business cycles. These models have been generally developed to address two sets of questions left unanswered by the single-good model.

The first question concerns the behavior of the terms of trade and its relation to the trade balance and aggregate activity. While this linkage is likely important for understanding international business cycles, the single-good model obviously is silent on questions involving the terms of trade or the real exchange rate. Second, there is the "comovement problem": the single-good model, when driven by empirically reasonable shock processes, cannot generate macro aggregates that exhibit the strong, positive, international comovement observed in the data. The comovement problem may be overcome in a multi-good setting with interdependencies in production and/or consumption. We summarize the literature on each of these questions in the following two sub-sections, and conclude with a discussion of other studies involving models with multiple goods.

8.1. The terms of trade and the "J-curve"

The relationship between the terms of trade and the balance of trade has long received a great deal of attention, both from policy makers, and also from academic economists. In particular, there is substantial interest in the so-called "J-curve" which describes a situation in which a deterioration in the terms of trade is associated with an initial worsening of the trade balance that subsequently improves (i.e. moves toward surplus). Early contributors to this literature include Junz and Rhomberg (1973) and Magee (1973); see also Meade (1988). More recently, Rose and Yellen (1989) use modern time-series methods to in-

---

[31] In related work, Devereux and Shi (1991) study the relationship between international debt and capital accumulation in a two-country model with endogenous time preference. They find that more-patient countries, or those with larger government sectors or lower productivity should be long-run creditors. They also find that it is possible for external asset accumulation to display "overshooting" behavior.

vestigate whether a J-curve can be detected in the past 25 years of U.S. data. Their findings are quite negative: they find little statistical evidence of a stable J-curve in U.S. data.

On the theoretical side, a large literature has developed models that explored the conditions under which a deterioration in the terms of trade would lead to an improvement in the trade balance.[32] Arvanitis and Mikkola (1994) and Backus, Kehoe, and Kydland (1994) have recently constructed two-good dynamic models of international trade which they use to explore the relationship between the terms of trade and the balance of trade. Figure 8.1 shows the cross-correlation functions for cyclic fluctuations in the terms of trade and net exports for eight countries. This figure shows that the contemporaneous correlation (lag 0) between net exports and the terms of trade is negative, but a rising correlation between the terms of trade and future net exports (i.e. the correlation rises with the lead, k). The correlation between the terms of trade and lagged net exports tends to be negative. It is this cross-correlation function, which Backus et al. (1994) term the "S-curve", that the model will try to replicate. Note that the "S-curve", which is a description of unconditional cross-correlations between the two variables, is not the same thing as the "J-curve", which describes the conditional dynamic response of one variable following a shock to the other. Thus it is possible to find an "S-curve" in the data, even absent a detectable "J-curve".

Each of these investigations specifies the following structure for the world economy; this presentation draws heavily on that of Arvanitis and Mikkola (1994). There are two goods produced in a two-country world – one good is produced by each country. The goods are both tradeable, and each good is used both as consumption and as investment in each country.

Preferences. Consumers in each country choose leisure, L, and consumption of the domestic good, C_x and of the foreign good, C_y, to maximize expected lifetime utility. Thus, residents of the home country maximize

$$E_0 \sum_{t=0}^{\infty} \beta^t U(C_{xt}, C_{yt}, L_t)$$

with momentary utility specialized to the following:

$$U(C_{xt}, C_{yt}, L_t) = \frac{1}{1-\sigma} \left\{ \left[\left(\eta_c C_{xt}^{-\mu} + (1 - \eta_c) C_{yt}^{-\mu} \right)^{-1/\mu} \right]^{\vartheta} L_t^{1-\vartheta} \right\}^{1-\sigma}.$$

Residents of the foreign country maximize

---

[32]For a review of the early literature on the Harberger–Laursen–Metzler effect and a modern critique based on the intertemporal approach to the current account, see Persson and Svensson (1985).

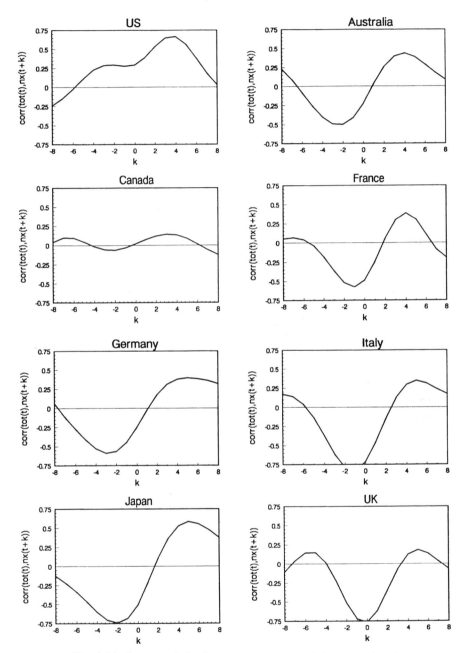

Figure 8.1. Cross-correlation between net exports and the terms of trade

$$E_0 \sum_{t=0}^{\infty} \beta^t U(C_{xt}^*, C_{yt}^*, L_t^*)$$

where momentary utility, $U(.)$, is given by:

$$U(C_{xt}^*, C_{yt}^*, L_t^*) = \frac{1}{1-\sigma}$$
$$\times \left\{ \left[(1 - \eta_c)(C_{xt}^*)^{-\mu} + \eta_c(C_{yt}^*)^{-\mu} \right)^{-1/\mu} \right]^{\vartheta} (L_t^*)^{1-\vartheta} \right\}^{1-\sigma}.$$

The two countries' utility functions are parameterized symmetrically: note each country prefers the consumption of its own good (the relative shares are governed by the parameter η_c, so a preference for one's own good means $\eta_c > 0.50$). The elasticity of substitution between consumptions of the two goods is $\zeta \equiv (1 + \mu)^{-1}$.

Production. Each country specializes in the production of a single good. The home country produces X while the foreign country produces Y: both production technologies use domestic labor together with domestic and foreign capital, as follows:

$$X_t = A_t \left[\left(\eta_p K_{xt}^{-\mu} + (1 - \eta_p) K_{yt}^{-\mu} \right)^{-1/\mu} \right]^{1-\alpha} (X_t N)_t^{\alpha}; \tag{8.1}$$

$$Y_t = A_t^* \left[\left((1 - \eta_p)(K_{xt}^*)^{-\mu} + \eta_p(K_{yt}^*)^{-\mu} \right)^{-1/\mu} \right]^{1-\alpha} (X_t^* N_t^*)^{\alpha}$$

where, as before, X_t and X_t^* capture deterministic trend growth in labor-augmenting technical change, and A_t and A_t^* represent total-factor-augmenting shocks to productivity, which are assumed to follow a vector-Markov process. Capital accumulation in the Arvanitis–Mikkola model is subject to small, convex costs of adjustment. Backus et al., employ a time-to-build technology, but also explore a variant they call "time-to-ship".

Calibration. The model is calibrated in the standard way to replicate long-run shares, with curvature parameters taken from existing statistical studies. The Solow residual process is the one discussed earlier. As both sets of authors note, the results are extremely sensitive to the parameter $\zeta \equiv (1 + \mu)^{-1}$, yet little is known about the value of this parameter. The benchmark value of ζ used by Backus et al. (1994) is $\zeta = 1.5$. The assumption that the critical parameter, μ, is the same in both production and consumption permits a convenient aggregation of consumptions, investments, and government purchases, which they note is common in the computational-general-equilibrium trade literature; [see for example, Whalley (1985)].

Market structure. Backus et al. (1994) assume that there are complete contingent-claim markets available to all individuals. Arvanitis and Mikkola (1994) also study the complete markets economy, as well as a case that allows international trade only in physical goods and a noncontingent real bond.

Results. Backus et al. (1994) find that this model generates an "*S*-curve" for reasonable parameter values. In fact, the model also generates a "*J*-curve", in which the trade balance initially deteriorates following a positive productivity shock. That is, the positive productivity shock leads to a deterioration in the terms of trade, since the price of the domestic good falls. At the same time, the higher productivity draws capital from abroad, leading to a trade deficit. As the investment boom slows down and as domestic output and saving rise, the trade balance improves. Clearly, the dynamics of capital accumulation are central to the model's ability to generate the "*J*-curve" and also the "*S*-curve."

Backus et al. (1994) provide a compelling illustration of the importance of capital by exhibiting the results for an economy with variable labor but without capital. In this case, consumption smoothing is the dominant force behind the trade balance, and the positive productivity shock leads to increased saving, i.e. a trade surplus. Neither a "*J*-curve" nor an "*S*-curve" is observed in this case. Further, neither effect is observed when the shock is to government spending, even with capital.

Although this model replicates the "*S*-curve" and possesses a "*J*-curve", the economic forces behind these effects are not those stressed in the older literature. That is, the "*J*-curve" does not arise because quantities of exports and imports are slow to adjust to terms-of-trade changes, although the relative price changes themselves are passed through relatively quickly. Rather, the "*J*-curve" is a consequence of the dynamics of capital accumulation. Finally, the two-good model does not deliver enough volatility in the terms of trade or in the trade balance. For the benchmark parameterization of Backus et al. (1994), the volatility of net exports is about one-third that found in the data, while the model's predicted volatility for the terms of trade is about one-tenth that found in the data. Arvanitis and Mikkola (1994) experiment with allowing the elasticity of substitution in consumption to differ from that in production. The intuition is that a low elasticity of substitution in consumption will help produce volatility in the trade balance, while a high elasticity of substitution in production will help produce volatility in the terms of trade. They find that this alteration improves the model's predictions for volatility of the terms of trade and the trade balance, but that the model still falls short along this dimension.

Related literature. Praschnik (1993) studies a multi-sector model of a developing economy, and finds that relative price shocks are important for output volatility, but that productivity shocks are important for generating cyclic comovement of macroeconomic aggregates. Mendoza (1995) develops a three-sector model of a country facing a fixed world interest rate, and finds that terms-of-trade shocks account for a significant fraction of GDP variability, when the model is calibrated to mimic the G-7 countries. Macklem (1993) studies the relationship between terms-of-trade disturbances and fiscal policy in a small open economy calibrated to Canadian data. Schmitt-Grohe (1994) examines the extent to which the terms of trade transmit business cycles between the U.S. and Canada.

8.2. Comovement

In Section 6.3.3 we described the "comovement problem" as one of the central problems with the one-good dynamic equilibrium trade model. The most widely-discussed feature of this problem is the consumption–output puzzle. There is a growing literature in which model variants are developed that successfully resolve this problem. A non-exhaustive list includes contributions by Devereaux, Gregory, and Smith (1992) which retains the complete-markets setup but alters the form of momentary utility; Reynolds (1992) which studies a two-good, two-country model similar to this one; and Stockman and Tesar (1995), who incorporate nontraded goods, but fail to resolve the consumption–output puzzle in the absence of preference shocks. In terms of the two-good model described above, the complete-markets version of the model continues to exhibit output correlations that are too low and consumption correlations are too high, with negative international correlation of labor inputs and investments. Arvanitis and Mikkola (1994) find that restricting asset trade to bonds alone helps to resolve this problem, if the productivity shocks are sufficiently persistent. Specifically, they generate output and consumption correlations that are both positive, but with the output correlation larger than the consumption correlations. These findings are consistent with results obtained by Baxter and Crucini (1993b), as well as the results from our benchmark case: see Table 6.1.

However, there is another part of the puzzle, which is that all the models discussed so far tend to predict substantial, negative international comovement of labor inputs and investments so long as investment goods are traded internationally. Specifically, the two-good models of Arvanitis and Mikkola (1994), Backus et al. (1994), and Reynolds (1992, 1993) all predict substantial, negative international correlations of investments and labor inputs, regardless of market structure. This is somewhat surprising, as these models incorporate international linkages on both the consumption and production side, so that there is a mechanism by which expansion of output in one country leads to a desire for more of the other country's good (as a complementary consumption good, or as complementary capital). Nevertheless, the overriding force behind investment dynamics in these two-good models is still the one that was at work in the one-good model. That is, investment flows to the more productive location, and labor input falls in the location with low investment.

8.3. Other contributions

In addition to the two topics reviewed above, there are several intriguing new developments in the general area of multi-good models. Canova and Dellas (1993) investigated whether trade interdependence could account for international comovement. Their results are mixed, and their overall conclusion is that the role of trade interdependencies in economic fluctuations is moderate. In related work, however, Costello and Praschnik (1993) study the interrelationships of macroeconomic aggregates across industrialized and developing economies. They find that output in the U.S. and Japan Granger-causes output in developing countries, and that variation in output in the U.S. and Japan accounts for a large fraction of the variation of output in developing countries.

Canova (1993) develops a three good, three country model characterized by complete markets. Each country produces only one good although production in each country requires output of all three countries as capital input. Further, individuals value consumption of all three goods. Canova studies several parametric cases in an effort to determine whether the common international component of national business cycles is due to common shocks or to transmission. He finds that production interdependencies determine the characteristics of the propagation of technology shocks, while consumption interdependencies are responsible for the transmission of government spending shocks.

9. New directions

This chapter has summarized the large and growing literature on the quantitative equilibrium approach to modeling the dynamic interactions of trading economies. This approach has met with success in capturing many of the salient features of open economy business cycles, yet many puzzles remain. This section briefly outlines those areas in which new research is likely to be most productive.

Comovement. The standard, one-good model could not replicate the observed, strong positive international comovements in macroeconomic aggregates. It has proved particularly difficult to write down plausibly-parameterized models which can generate positive comovement of labor and investment across countries. The two-good models reviewed in Section 8 did not fare better than the one-good model along this dimension. Thus a major challenge to the theory is to develop a model which can explain international comovement in labor input and investment. A natural direction to pursue is to incorporate intermediate goods in an effort to strengthen the intersectoral (and, thus, international) linkages on the supply side. Current work by Canova (1992), Costello and Praschnik (1993) and Kouparitsas (1994a) has made a start in this direction.

Volatility of net exports and the terms of trade. A second challenge to existing theory is the volatility of net exports and the terms of trade. The standard two-good model misses badly along this dimension, as it substantially underpredicts the volatility of these variables. Recent work by Kouparitsas (1994b) has found that the volatility both net exports is linked to the industrial structure of an economy, and in particular is linked to the composition of the traded goods. For example, countries whose export bases are not well-diversified, or in which exports are confined to high-volatility industries (such as primary materials) have more volatile business cycles and higher net export volatility. In a companion paper, Kouparitsas (1994c) finds that terms of trade volatility is also closely related to trade structure. In particular, he finds that countries in which the composition of exports differs importantly from the composition of imports also have highly volatile terms of trade. That is, he finds that terms of trade fluctuations mainly reflect movements in relative goods prices, rather than movements in relative country price levels or exchange rates. These findings suggest that models incorporating a richer industrial structure, with important roles for intermediate goods and the resulting intersectoral linkages, may be central to explaining the observed volatility of net exports and the terms of trade.

Measurement. As we develop richer models of intersectoral and international linkages, our data requirements will grow as well. It will become essential to have international data at the sectoral level for use in calibrating and estimating our models. Further work in assembling and interpreting sectoral international data is very desirable.

Applications. The modeling approach surveyed in this paper has developed to the point where these models have useful and important insights to offer in particular applied contexts. That is, it is feasible, and desirable, to construct particular versions of these models for application to particular countries or economic events. Canova (1993), for example, has constructed a three-region world which he has parameterized to correspond to the U.S., Germany, and Japan. His focus was on understanding the mechanisms by which various shocks are transmitted across countries.

Kouparitsas (1994a) constructs a two-region world, in which one region, the North, imports raw materials and exports manufactured goods. The second region, the South, exports raw materials and imports manufactures. The North is parameterized to resemble major industrialized countries, while the South is parameterized to correspond to non-oil, commodity-exporting, developing countries. Using this framework, Kouparitsas examines the extent to which fluctuations in the Northern economy cause fluctuations in the terms of trade and induce business cycles in the Southern economy.

In conclusion, recent work in dynamic open economy macroeconomics has laid the foundations for studying the equilibrium relationship between international trade and business cycles. There is much more work to be done, as suggested above, with many exciting challenges ahead of us.

References

Ahmed, S. (1987), "Government spending, the balance of trade, and the terms of trade in British history", Journal of Monetary Economics 20:195–220.

Arvanitis, A.V. (1994), "Financial market linkages, fiscal policies, and international business cycles", Ph.D. dissertation, University of Rochester.

Arvanitis, A.V. and A. Mikkola (1994), "Asset market structure and international trade dynamics", manuscript, University of Rochester.

Aschauer, D. (1989), "Is public expenditure productive?", Journal of Monetary Economics 23:177–200.

Atkeson, A. and T. Bayoumi (1991), "Do private capital markets insure against risk in a common currency area: Evidence from the US", manuscript, International Monetary Fund.

Backus, D., P. Kehoe and F. Kydland (1992a), "International real business cycles", Journal of Political Economy 101:745–775.

Backus, D. and P. Kehoe (1992b), "International evidence on the historical properties of business cycles", American Economic Review 82:864–888.

Backus, D., P. Kehoe and F. Kydland (1994), "Dynamics of the trade balance and the terms of trade: The J-curve", American Economic Review 84:84–103.

Barro, R.J. (1987), "Government spending, interest rates, prices, and budget deficits in the United Kingdom, 1701–1918", Journal of Monetary Economics 20:221–248.

Baxter, M. (1991), "Approximating suboptimal dynamic equilibria: An Euler equation approach", Journal of Monetary Economics 27:173–200.

Baxter, M. (1993), "Financial market linkages and the international transmission of fiscal policy", manuscript, University of Virginia.

Baxter, M. and M.J. Crucini (1993a), "Explaining saving–investment correlations", American Economic Review 83:416–436.

Baxter, M. and M.J. Crucini (1993b), "Business cycles and the asset structure of foreign trade", manuscript, University of Virginia.

Baxter, M. and R.G. King (1993), "Fiscal policy in general equilibrium", American Economic Review 83:315–334.

Baxter, M. and R.G. King (1994), "Measuring business cycles: Approximate band-pass filters for economic time series", manuscript, University of Virginia.

Blackburn, K. and M.P. Ravn (1991), "Contemporary macroeconomic fluctuations: An international perspective", University of Southampton Discussion Paper No. 9106.

Blackburn, K. and M.P. Ravn (1992), "Business cycles in the U.K.: Facts and fictions", Economica 59:383–401.

Brandner, P. and K. Neusser (1992), "Business cycles in open economies: Stylized facts for Austria and Germany", Weltwirtschaftliches Archiv 128:67–87.

Burda, M.C. and S. Gerlach (1992), "Intertemporal prices and the U.S. trade balance", American Economic Review 82:1234–1253.

Burns, A.M. and W.C. Mitchell (1946), Measuring business cycles (National Bureau of Economic Research, New York).

Canova, F. (1992), "Sources and propagation of international business cycles: Common shocks or transmission?", manuscript, European University Institute.

Canova, F. and H. Dellas (1993), "Trade interdependence and the international business cycle", Journal of International Economics 34:23–47.

Cantor, R. and N. Mark (1987), "International debt and world business fluctuations", Journal of International Money and Finance 6:153–165.

Cantor, R. and N. Mark (1988), "The international transmission of real business cycles", International Economic Review 29:493–507.

Cardia, E. (1992), "The dynamics of a small open economy in response to monetary, fiscal, and productivity shocks", Journal of Monetary Economics 28:411–434.

Christiano, L. and M. Eichenbaum (1992), "Current real-business-cycle theories and aggregate labor-market fluctuations", American Economic Review 82:430–450.

Conze, A., J.-M. Lasry, and J. Scheinkman (1990), "Borrowing constraints and international co-movements", manuscript, University of Chicago.

Correia, I., J. Neves and S. Rebelo (1992), "Business cycles in Portugal: Theory and evidence", in: Amaral, Lucena, and Mello, eds., Portugal toward 1992 (Kluwer Academic Publishers, Boston, MA).

Correia, I., J. Neves and S. Rebelo (1994), "Business cycles in a small open economy", European Economic Review, forthcoming.

Costello, D.M. (1993), "A cross-country, cross-industry comparison of productivity growth", Journal of Political Economy 101:207–222.

Costello, D.M. and J. Praschnik (1993), "Intermediate goods and the transmission of international business cycles", manuscript, University of Western Ontario.

Crucini, M.J. (1993a), "Country size and economic fluctuations", manuscript, Ohio State University.

Crucini, M.J. (1993), "International risk-sharing: A simple comparative test", manuscript, Ohio State University.

Dellas, H. (1986), "A real model of the world business cycle", Journal of International Money and Finance 5:381–394.

Devereux, M.B. and S. Shi (1991), "Capital accumulation and the current account in a two-country model", Journal of International Economics 30:1–25.

Devereux, M.B., A. Gregory, and G. Smith (1992), "Realistic cross-country consumption correlations in a two-country, equilibrium, business-cycle model", Journal of International Money and Finance 11:3–16.

Dotsey, M. and C.-S. Mao (1992), "How well do approximation methods work?", Journal of Monetary Economics 29:25–58.

Dotsey, M. and C.-S. Mao (1994), "The effects of fiscal policies in the neoclassical growth model", Federal Reserve Bank of Richmond Working Paper No. 94–3.

Engel, C. and K. Kletzer (1989), "Saving and investment in an open economy with non-traded goods", International Economic Review 30:735–752.

Englund, P., T. Persson, and L. Svensson (1990), "Swedish business cycles: 1861–1988", manuscript, Stockholm University.

Finn, M. (1990), "On savings and investment dynamics in a small open economy", Journal of International Economics 29:1–21.

Frenkel, J. and A. Razin (1987), Fiscal policies and the world economy: An intertemporal approach (MIT Press, Cambridge, MA).

Gaudin, S. and K.-M. Yi (1993), "The role of real interest rates in explaining trade balance movements in small open economies", manuscript, Rice University.

Glick, R. and K. Rogoff (1995), "Global versus country-specific productivity shocks and the current account", Journal of Monetary Economics 35:159–192.

Hall, R. (1978), "Stochastic implications of the life cycle-permanent income hypothesis: Theory and evidence", Journal of Political Economy 86:971–987.

Hayashi, F. (1982), "Tobin's marginal q and average q: A neoclassical interpretation", Econometrica 50:213–224.

Head, A. (1992), "Country size, international risk sharing, and business cycles: Theory and evidence", manuscript, Queen's University.

Hicks, J.P. (1939), Value and capital (Oxford University Press, Oxford).

Hodrick, R. and E. Prescott (1980), "Post-war U.S. business cycles: An empirical investigation", manuscript, Carnegie Mellon University.

Judd, K. (1990), "Minimum weighted residual methods for solving dynamic economic models", manuscript, Hoover Institution.

Junz, H. and R. Rhomberg (1973), "Price competitiveness in export trade among industrial countries", American Economic Review 63:412–418.

Kim, K., R.A. Buckle, and V.B. Hall (1992), "Key features of New Zealand business cycles", manuscript, Victoria University of Wellington; and Economic Record, forthcoming.

King, R.G. (1990), "Value and capital in the equilibrium business cycle program", in: L. McKenzie and S. Zamagni, eds., Value and capital: Fifty years later (Macmillan, London).

King, R.G. (1995), "Quantitative theory and econometrics", Federal Reserve Bank of Richmond Economic Quarterly Bulletin, forthcoming, Summer 1995.

King, R.G., C.I. Plosser and S.T. Rebelo (1987), "Technical Appendix to: Production, growth, and business cycles", working paper, Rochester Center for Economic Research.

King, R.G., C.I. Plosser and S.T. Rebelo (1988), "Production, growth, and business cycles I: The basic neoclassical model", Journal of Monetary Economics 21:195–232.

King, R.G. and S.T. Rebelo (1993), "Low frequency filtering and real business cycles", Journal of Economic Dynamics and Control 17:207–231.

Kollman, R. (1992), "Incomplete asset markets and international real business cycles", manuscript, University of Montreal.

Kollman, R. (1993), "Fiscal policy, technology shocks, and the US trade balance deficit", manuscript, University of Montreal.

Kouparitsas, M. (1994a), "North–South business cycles", manuscript, University of Virginia.

Kouparitsas, M. (1994b), "The relationship between business cycle volatility and export diversification", manuscript, University of Virginia.

Kouparitsas, M. (1994c), "Relative prices and the terms of trade", manuscript, University of Virginia.

Kydland, F. and E. Prescott (1982), "Time to build and aggregate fluctuations", Econometrica 50:1345–1370.

Leiderman, L. and A. Razin (1991), "Determinants of external imbalances: The role of taxes, government spending, and productivity", Journal of the Japanese and International Economies 5:421–450.

Lewis, K.K. (1993), "What can explain the apparent lack of international consumption risk sharing?", manuscript, Wharton School of the University of Pennsylvania.

Long, J. and C. Plosser (1983), "Real business cycles", Journal of Political Economy 91:1345–1370.

Macklem, R.T. (1993), "Terms-of-trade disturbances and fiscal policy in a small open economy", Economic Journal 103:916–936.

Magee, S. (1973), "Currency contracts, pass-through, and devaluation", Brookings Papers on Economic Activity 1973:1:303–323.

Meade, E. (1988), "Exchange rates, adjustment, and the *J*-curve", Federal Reserve Bulletin 74:633–644.

Mendoza, E.G. (1991), Real business cycles in a small open economy, American Economic Review 81:797–818.

Mendoza, E.G. (1995), "The terms of trade, the real exchange rate, and economic fluctuations", International Economic Review, 36:101–137.

Obstfeld, M. (1986), "Capital mobility in the world economy: Theory and measurement", Carnegie–Rochester Conference Series on Public Policy 24:55–103.

Obstfeld, M. and K. Rogoff (1995), "The intertemporal approach to the current account", in: G. Grossman and K. Rogoff, eds., Handbook of international economics, vol. 3 (North-Holland, Amsterdam).

Penati, A. and M. Dooley (1984), "Current account imbalances and capital formation in industrial countries, 1949–1981", IMF Staff Papers 31:1–24.

Persson, T. and L. Svensson (1985), "Current account dynamics and the terms of trade: Harberger–Laursen–Metzler two generations later", Journal of Political Economy 93:43–65.

Praschnik, J. (1993), "The importance of input price shocks for business cycles in developing economies", manuscript, University of Western Ontario.

Prescott, E. (1986), "Theory ahead of business-cycle measurement", Carnegie–Rochester Conference Series on Public Policy 24:11–44.

Rebelo, S.T. (1987), "Tractable heterogeneity and near-steady-state dynamics", manuscript, Northwestern University.

Razin, A. (1993), "The dynamic-optimizing approach to the current account: Theory and evidence", National Bureau of Economic Research Working Paper No. 4334.

Reynolds, P. (1992), "International comovements in production and consumption: Theory and evidence", manuscript, University of Southern California.

Reynolds, P. (1993), "International comovements in aggregate productivity: An empirical analysis", manuscript, University of Southern California.

Rogoff, K. (1992), "Traded goods consumption smoothing and the random walk behavior of the real exchange rate", Bank of Japan Monetary and Economic Studies 10:1–29.

Rose, A. and J. Yellen (1989), "Is there a *J*-curve?", Journal of Monetary Economics 24:53–68.

Sachs, J.D. (1981), "The current account and macroeconomic adjustment in the 1970's", Brookings Papers on Economic Activity 1981:1:201–268.

Sadka, J. and K.-M. Yi (1994), "Consumer durables, permanent terms of trade shocks, and the recent U.S. trade deficits", manuscript, Rice University.

Schmitt-Grohe, S. (1994), "The international transmission of economic fluctuations: Effects of U.S. business cycles on the Canadian economy", manuscript, University of Chicago.

Sen, P. and S. Turnovsky (1990), "Investment tax credit in an open economy", Journal of Public Economics 42:277–299.

Stockman, A.C. and L.E.O. Svensson (1987), "Capital flows, investment, and exchange rates", Journal of Monetary Economics 19:171–201.

Stockman, A.C. and L.L. Tesar (1995), "Tastes and technology in a two-country model of the business cycle: Explaining international comovements", American Economic Review, 85:168–185.

Taylor, J. and H. Uhlig (1990), "Solving nonlinear stochastic growth models: A comparison of alternative solution methods", Journal of Business and Economic Statistics 8:1–18.

Tesar, L.L. (1991), "Savings, investment, and international capital flows", Journal of International Economics 31:55–78.

Whalley, J. (1985), Trade liberalization among major trading areas, (MIT Press, Cambridge, MA).

van Wincoop, E. (1992a), "International risk-sharing", manuscript, Boston University.

van Wincoop, E. (1992b), "Regional risk-sharing", manuscript, Boston University.

van Wincoop, E. (1993), "Real interest rates in a global bond economy", manuscript, IGIER, Milan, Italy.

Yi, K.-M. (1993), "Can government purchases explain recent U.S. net export deficits?", Journal of International Economics 35:201–255.

Zimmerman, C. (1991), International real business cycles among large and small countries, manuscript, Carnegie Mellon University.

Chapter 36

THE OPERATION AND COLLAPSE OF FIXED EXCHANGE RATE REGIMES

PETER M. GARBER

Brown University and NBER

and

LARS E.O. SVENSSON*

IIES, Stockholm University; CEPR; and NBER

Contents

*We thank the discussants Peter Kenen and Andrew Rose, the editor Kenneth Rogoff, and other conference participants for comments.

Handbook of International Economics, vol. III, Edited by G. Grossman and K. Rogoff
© *Elsevier Science B.V., 1995*

1. Introduction

Since the end of the Bretton Woods system in 1973, the exchange rates of the three major currencies have not been officially pegged. These twenty-one years are the longest period in modern economic history during which the values of major currencies have been allowed to float. Nevertheless, even in this era of floating exchange rates, most of the smaller central banks have maintained policies of pegging their exchange rates to the major currencies. Alternatively, as in the European Exchange Rate Mechanism, an individual central bank in a group of central banks may peg its currency to a weighted average of the values of the group's currencies. Even the major currency central banks frequently intervene in exchange markets to prevent the values of their currencies from moving excessively. Occasionally, they agree to impose informal upper and lower bounds on exchange rates.

Because of the still dominant position of fixed exchange rates in central bank operating policies, it is important to understand how fixed exchange rate systems operate and how they come to an end. In this chapter, we will report on recent research contributions to our understanding of the dynamics of a fixed exchange rate system. These contributions can be placed readily into two categories – research on target zones and research on speculative attacks on fixed exchange rate regimes. We will also briefly discuss the various rationales for selecting a fixed exchange rate system over a floating exchange rate regime. Our focus, however, will be almost entirely on the positive economics of fixed exchange rates. This focus is consistent with most of the research in the past decade: that is, given that a target zone or fixed exchange rate system is chosen, researchers have concentrated mainly on determining its dynamic development. Although, as we will report, much empirical research has been done to examine the theoretical models, the recent literature is, in a sense, primarily a theoretical one. Most research in this area is based on the simple monetary model of the exchange rate, which, as shown in the chapter by Frankel and Rose, does not perform well empirically in the short run. Nevertheless, this literature has had great influence in central banks, given the background of the existence of important target zone systems and of major exchange rate crises in the past decade.

2. The choice of a fixed exchange rate regime

Several explanations have been advanced for the existence of fixed exchange rate regimes. First, under some conditions, a fixed exchange rate may minimize instabilities in real economic activity, so that on a macroeconomic level the fixed exchange rate would be the preferable policy regime. Second, because of a past inability to control itself from launching inflationist policies, a country's central bank may lack credibility with the public, which expects an inflationary policy. In an attempt to acquire credibility, the central bank may fix the exchange rate of its currency to that of a more disciplined central bank. Third, disruptions of the exchange rate may arise from bubbles generated by a speculative financial system. A fixed exchange rate would muffle such extraneous disturbances and insulate the real economy from them. Finally, on a microeconomic level, a country with poorly developed or illiquid money markets, may fix the exchange rate to provide its residents with a synthetic money market with the liquidity of the markets of the country that provides the vehicle currency.

In an influential article Poole (1970) discussed in an IS–LM framework the choice between a monetary policy aimed at stabilizing the interest rate and one aimed at stabilizing the money supply. He showed that the choice depends on the nature of the shocks to the economy, especially whether the shocks are real or monetary in origin. Poole's approach has since been extended to open economies and to the choice of the exchange rate regime depending upon the nature of the shocks that hit the open economy. Starting with Turnovsky (1976), Boyer (1978), and Parkin (1978), a very large literature has developed. An excellent survey is available in Genberg (1989).

This literature lays out a model of a small open economy that is hit by real and monetary domestic and foreign shocks. The problem is to choose the optimal monetary regime, and hence exchange rate regime, from a short-run stabilization point of view. The information set is incomplete and the underlying shocks – disturbances to the LM and IS functions – are unobservable. Policy rules contingent upon the available information are chosen to minimize a weighted sum of output and inflation variances.

The results of this type of model can be summarized as follows: If the variance of the LM shock is sufficiently large relative to the variance of the IS shock, a fixed exchange rate will be better than a floating exchange rate. In the reverse case, a freely floating exchange rate will be better than a fixed exchange rate. In the general case, when neither IS nor LM shocks dominate, a managed float will be the best policy.

When an aggregate supply function and wage indexation are added, the implications of the relative variance of the IS and LM shocks for the choice of exchange rate regime still hold. When there are only LM shocks, a fixed exchange rate is still optimal. When there are only IS shocks, however, the optimal policy is not a free float, and the policy depends on the degree of wage indexation. In the general case with both kind of shocks, the optimal policy is still a managed float that depends in a complicated way on the nature of the shocks and the structure of the economy.

As Genberg (1989) points out, the general result in this kind of work is that the optimal exchange rate regime is neither a fixed exchange rate nor a freely floating rate, but instead a managed float monetary rule, where money supply reacts to exchange rates, interest rates and other indicators that convey information about the shocks that hit the economy. The optimal monetary rule depends, however, in an exceedingly complicated way on the nature of the shocks and the structure of the economy. The ranking of the restricted simple monetary rules, fixed and floating exchange rates, varies from case to case. The information requirement for choosing the optimal rule, or for ranking the simple regimes, is simply overwhelming. Therefore, there seem to be no operationally useful results.

In the mid-1980's, a class of models was developed that explained the choice of particular policy rules as a means of avoiding the social losses that might emerge in the presence of a central bank with complete discretion to set the monetary variables. As extensions of Kydland and Prescott's (1977) results, the literature on rules versus discretion was developed mainly in the context of a closed economy but has been extended to the choice of exchange rate regime. Persson and Tabellini's chapter in this volume provides an extensive development of these models.

The intuition behind the rules vs. discretion models is relatively straightforward in the context of a one-shot game between the central bank and the public, but also emerges in a repeated interaction. The monetary authority has the dual objective of raising output above a natural rate that is considered too low and of reducing the deviation of inflation from some target. Weighted to coincide with social preferences, these objectives are combined to form both the social and the monetary authority's objective function. Output can move away from the natural rate through monetary intervention only if the public's expectation of inflation is incorrect. Thus, the monetary authority can affect output only through acting contrary to the public's expectations. Knowing that the monetary authority will seek to increase inflation above their expectations, the public will increase its expected rate of inflation. In reaction, the monetary authority will have to increase inflation yet more, but as the realized inflation moves away from the target, further efforts to affect output become ever more costly in terms of social welfare. The equilibrium of this one-shot game emerges when the public's expectations of inflation coincide with realized inflation. The equilibrium, however, is sub-optimal: inflation is higher than the target, and since the public is correct in its expectations there is no movement of output away from the natural rate.

As one means of implementing a lower inflation, Rogoff (1985) suggests appointing an independent central banker known to have a greater aversion to inflation than the general public, thereby generating a lower equilibrium inflation rate. As an alternative to finding its own reputed anti-inflationist, a central bank may piggy-back on the reputation of any already established conservative central banker by implementing a fixed exchange rate. For example, it is often argued [Giavazzi and Pagano (1988), Giavazzi and Giovannini (1989, Chapter 5), Currie (1992)] that the countries in the European Monetary System with a reputation for relatively high inflation were able to employ the tough reputation of the Bundesbank to buy some credibility for the disinflationary programs of the 1980's, thereby reducing the severity of the potential associated recessions. Of course, a self-imposed fixed exchange rate can be ephemeral and is often a fig-leaf for an inveterately inflationary government. Acting in a manner that forces the abandonment of a fixed exchange rate regime does impose some direct costs on a central bank in the form of lost reserves of potentially large magnitude if the central bank suffers a speculative attack, and this potential loss may buy some credibility. Even this loss is limited, however. First, the public does not know how much of its reserves the central bank will use to defend the currency. Second, if it ceases to intervene while it still has positive net reserves, the central bank will realize a capital gain in the ensuing devaluation. Also, abandonment of a fixed exchange rate is immediately obvious, so a switch to discretionary policy cannot be obfuscated.

A fixed exchange rate arranged cooperatively with other countries should be more conducive to discipline than a unilateral system because domestic policies that tend to force its abandonment would incur additional costs in the form of a loss of face with other sovereign monetary authorities. Cooperation in defending the multilateral system against speculative attack may also increase its viability relative to that of a unilateral system.

In their chapter in this volume, Frankel and Rose show that the movement of floating exchange rates cannot be readily explained from the movements of standard measures of market fundamentals. They explore the possibility that speculative bubbles drive exchange rates. If speculators generate extraneous volatility in exchange rates and if such volatility has a real impact, then it may be desirable to fix exchange rates. If speculation is self-driven, official intervention to fix rates may short circuit the dynamic of expectations of exchange rate movements and eliminate this source of volatility at little cost. As will be shown in the discussion of the speculative attack literature, however, a fixed exchange rate system can itself generate a set of beliefs that can lead to a speculative attack and collapse of the system.

As indicated by our description, none of these normative approaches is a generally satisfactory explanation of the prevalence or even the existence of fixed exchange rates. The normative issues of fixed exchange rate regimes remain an open area for future research.

3. Exchange rate target zones

3.1. Introduction

Fixed exchange rate regimes used to be modelled in the literature as having a constant fixed exchange rate, with occasional discrete jumps, or realignments. However, fixed exchange rate regimes in the real world typically have explicit finite *bands* within which exchange rates are allowed to fluctuate. For instance, before their widening in August 1993 to ± 15 percent the bands within the exchange rate mechanism of the European Monetary System (ERM) were ±2.25 percent around a central parity (Portugal and Spain had ± 6 percent bands). The bands within the Bretton Woods System were ± 1 percent around dollar parities.

For concreteness, Figure 3.1a shows a typical exchange rate band. The curve shows the logarithm of the French franc/Deutschemark exchange rate from the start of the ERM in March 1973 through March 1992. The ± 2.25 percent band around the central parity is shown as the thin horizontal lines. The central parity (not shown) is in the center of the band. The vertical axis measures percentage deviation from the initial March 1973 central parity. Realignments, shifts in the central parity, took place in September 1979, October 1981, June 1982, March 1983, April 1986 and January 1987. On all these occasions the franc was devalued against the mark, that is, the FF/DM exchange rate (the number of francs per mark) increased. Figure 3.1b, which we shall refer to below, shows a 3-month FF/DM Euro interest rate differential, that is, the difference between a franc interest rate and a mark interest rate on the Euromarket for deposits with 3-month maturity.

The existence of such exchange rate bands raises two main questions, one positive and one normative. The first, positive, question is: how do exchange rate bands work compared to completely fixed rates; or, more precisely, what are the dynamics of exchange rates, interest rates and central bank interventions within exchange rate bands? The second, normative, question is: does the difference between bands and completely fixed exchange rates matter and, if so, which of the two arrangements is best; or, more precisely, what are the tradeoffs that determine the optimal bandwidth?

Exchange rate target zones – which has become the name given to fixed exchange rates regimes with bands – have been the subject of intensive research in recent years. This research has by now dealt fairly thoroughly with the first, positive question, whereas the second, normative question has hardly yet been touched upon. This section will present an interpretation of some selected recent theoretical and empirical research on exchange rate target zones, with emphasis on main ideas and results and without technical detail. The section is selective

(a)

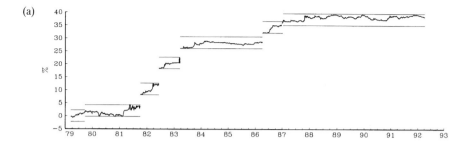

(b)

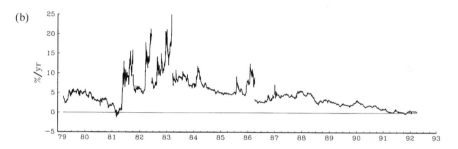

Figure 3.1. (a) Log FF/DM exchange rate; (b) FF/DM 3-month interest rate differential.

and not a survey of the literature. Bertola (1994) gives a comprehensive and detailed survey with an extensive bibliography.[1]

3.2. The Krugman target zone model

After some earlier work on exchange rate target zones [for instance, Williamson (1985), Frenkel and Goldstein (1986), Williamson and Miller (1987), and Dumas (1992)][2] the recent work took off with Paul Krugman's elegant target zone

[1]The section builds upon Svensson (1992b).

[2]Williamson (1985) and Williamson and Miller (1987) advocated a rather wide target zone for *real* exchange rates as a method for international economic policy coordination, without using an explicit target zone model. Williamson-type target zones are quite different from the narrow *nominal* exchange rate bands that are the focus of this article and it is perhaps confusing that the same name is used for both. Dumas (1992), in a remarkable paper first presented and circulated under a different title in the summer of 1987, developed a general equilibrium model of an endogenous target zone for the real exchange rate, which contained most of the ingredients in the later work on nominal exchange rate target zones. A parallel literature on real investment under uncertainty, especially contributions by Avinash Dixit, was the source of many of the techniques used in the target zone literature [see Dixit (1992) for a survey].

model [Krugman (1991)]. This paper, first circulated in 1988, presented what has become the standard target zone model and the starting point for almost all the research that followed.[3]

Krugman started from the presumption that the exchange rate, like any other asset price, depends on both some current fundamentals and expectations of future values of the exchange rate. In order to simplify, the log exchange rate at time t, s_t, is assumed to depend linearly on an aggregate "fundamental" at time t, f_t, incorporating the different fundamental determinants of the exchange rate (like domestic output and money supply; foreign interest rate, money supply, price level, etc.) and the instantaneous expected rate of exchange rate depreciation, $E_t[ds_t]/dt$, according to the "exchange rate equation"[4]

$$s_t = f_t + \alpha \frac{E_t[ds_t]}{dt}.$$ (3.1)

The fundamental is assumed to consist of two components,

$$f_t = v_t + m_t.$$ (3.2)

One component, "(the log of) velocity" v_t, is exogenous to the central bank and stochastic; the other component, "(the log of) money supply" m_t, is controlled by the central bank and changed by "interventions". By controlling the money supply, the central bank can control the aggregate fundamental, and thus the exchange rate. In an exchange rate target zone, the central bank controls the money supply to keep the exchange rate within a specified band around a specified central parity, for example ± 2.25 percent for most of the EMS bands before August 1993.[5] We denote this band by

$$\underline{s} \le s_t \le \overline{s},$$ (3.3)

where $\underline{s}$ and $\overline{s}$ are the lower and upper edges of the exchange rate band.

---

[3] A forerunner, Krugman (1987), was circulated in the late fall of 1987. It used a discrete-time model and did not resolve all technical difficulties.

[4] The positive constant α is the semi-elasticity of the exchange rate with respect to the instantaneous expected rate of currency depreciation. The instantaneous expected rate of currency depreciation is the limit of $E_t[s_{t+\Delta t} - s_t]/\Delta t = E_t[\ln(S_{t+\Delta t}/S_t)]/\Delta t$ when Δt approaches zero, where E_t denotes expectations conditional upon information available at time t, and S_t is the exchange rate expressed in units of domestic currency per unit foreign currency at time t. This model was used by Flood and Garber (1983) in studying endogenously-timed policy regime switches in foreign exchange markets.

The model can be derived from the so-called monetary model of exchange rate determination. That model has a poor empirical record. (See Frankel and Rose's chapter in this volume for details.) However, the simple linear structure allows a convenient closed form solution, whereas the general results are likely to be robust to the inclusions of sticky prices and other factors that would make the model more realistic [cf. Sutherland (1994)].

[5] It does not matter precisely how the central bank implements its monetary policy, for instance whether it is using the interest rate or the money supply as an instrument. Here for concreteness we consider money supply to be the instrument.

The Krugman model has two crucial assumptions. First, the exchange rate target zone is perfectly credible, in the sense that market agents believe that the lower and upper edges of the band will remain fixed forever, and that the exchange rate will forever stay within the band.[6] Second, the target zone is defended with "marginal" interventions only. That is, the money supply is held constant and no interventions at all occur as long as the exchange rate is in the interior of the exchange rate band. When the exchange rate reaches the weak edge of the band, the money supply is reduced (by an infinitesimal amount) to prevent the currency from weakening further; vice versa when the exchange rate reaches the strong edge of the band. Both these crucial assumptions are counter to empirical facts, something that we shall return to below.

For an explicit solution to the model, the stochastic process for the exogenous component of the fundamental, velocity, must also be specified. A very convenient assumption is that velocity is a Brownian motion with drift μ and rate of variance σ^2,

$$\mathrm{d}f_t = \mu\,\mathrm{d}t + \sigma\,\mathrm{d}W_t, \tag{3.4}$$

where $\mathrm{d}W_t$ is the increment of a Wiener process.[7]

The assumption of a Brownian motion for velocity is attractive, because it implies that the free-float exchange rate will also be a Brownian motion, which matches the empirical observations that free-float exchange rates seem to behave like random walks [Meese and Rogoff (1983)]. Let a free-float exchange rate regime be characterized by no interventions, that is, a constant money supply. Then it is easy to see that the free-float exchange rate is given by

$$s_t = \alpha\mu + f_t. \tag{3.5}$$

The two crucial assumptions mentioned above for the target zone, together with the Brownian motion assumption about velocity, allow the target zone exchange rate to be expressed as a function of the aggregate fundamental, the "target zone exchange rate function" $s_t = S(f_t)$, where the fundamental is restricted to a band that corresponds to the exchange rate band,

$$\underline{f} \le f_t \le \overline{f}, \tag{3.6}$$

---

[6]The crucial restriction is actually that the target zone is perfectly credible when the exchange rate is in the *interior* of the band. Krugman discussed the possibility of a collapse to a free float the first time the exchange rate reaches the *edge* of the band.

[7]Krugman actually assumed that the fundamental is a Brownian motion without drift, that is, with $\mu = 0$, the continuous-time analog of a random walk. The intricacy of Brownian motions is a frequent stumbling block for new students of the target zone literature. However, for the purpose of the present discussion, the reader needs to know only two things about a variable that follows a Brownian motion drift: its realized sample paths are continuous over time and do not include discrete jumps; and changes in the variable over any fixed time interval t, $f_t - f_o$, are distributed as a normal random variable with mean μt and variance $\sigma^2 t$, which hence are proportional to the time interval's length.

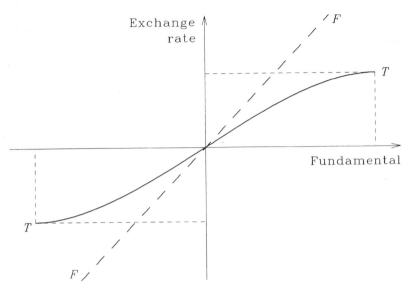

Figure 3.2. The Krugman model.

where the lower and upper edges of the fundamental band fulfill $\underline{s} = S(\underline{f})$ and $\overline{s} = S(\overline{f})$.

Figure 3.2 shows the relation between the exchange rate and the fundamental, both for the free float and the target zone, for the simplest case when the drift μ is zero. The fundamental is measured along the horizontal axis, the exchange rate along the vertical axis. The free-float relation is simply the 45-degree dashed line FF; the exchange rate is simply equal to the fundamental. The target zone exchange rate function is the S-shaped solid curve TT. The horizontal dashed lines show the edges of the exchange rate band.

In order to derive the exchange rate function, the expected exchange rate depreciation on the right-hand side of (3.1) is rewritten with the help of Ito's Lemma. This results in a second-order differential equation for the exchange rate as a function of the fundamental, the general solution to which is

$$s_t = \alpha\mu + f_t + A_1\,e^{\lambda_1 f_t} + A_2\,e^{\lambda_2 f_t}, \tag{3.7}$$

where $\lambda_1 = -\mu/\sigma^2 + \sqrt{\mu/\sigma^2 + 2/(\alpha\sigma^2)}$ and $\lambda_2 = -\mu/\sigma^2 - \sqrt{\mu/\sigma^2 + 2/(\alpha\sigma^2)}$, and where A_1 and A_2 are constants.[8] The constants are determined by the

---

[8] By Ito's Lemma we have $E_t\,ds_t = S_f E_t\,df_t + (1/2)S_{ff}E\,df_t^2$, where S_f and S_{ff} denote the first and second derivative of the exchange rate function. By the property of Brownian motions, $E_t\,df_t = \mu\,dt$ and $E_t\,df_t^2 = \sigma^2\,dt$. Substitution into (3.1) results in the second-order ordinary differential equation

$$S_{ff}(f) + \frac{2\mu}{\sigma^2}S_f(f) - \frac{2}{\alpha\sigma^2}S(f) + \frac{2}{\alpha\sigma^2}f = 0.$$

conditions that the exchange rate function is flat at the edges of the fundamental band,

$$S_f(\underline{f}) = S_f(\overline{f}) = 0. \tag{3.8}$$

(where subscript denotes derivative).

These conditions are generally called "smooth pasting" conditions, a concept known in option-pricing theory [see Dixit (1992)]. The intuition for the smooth-pasting conditions is far from easy, and another frequent stumbling block for new students of the target zone literature. The smooth pasting conditions mean that at the boundary of the exchange rate band, the exchange rate is completely insensitive to the fundamental. Why might this be so? It is easy to understand in the case when the drift of the fundamental is zero. Then, first we note that there is a clear jump, a discontinuity, in the expected change of the fundamental at the edge of the band. In the interior of the band, the fundamental is a Brownian motion, without drift, so its expected change is zero. At the edges of the band, the fundamental can either remain at the edge or drift back into the band, so its expected rate of change is suddenly *not* zero; at the upper edge it is negative, at the lower edge it is positive. Second, there can be no jump or discontinuity in the expected change of the exchange rate at the edge. To see this, recall that the exchange rate is a linear function of the fundamental and the expected change in the exchange rate. Now, there can be no jump in the exchange rate at the edge of the band, otherwise there would be a safe arbitrage (a one-sided bet) since it could only jump one way, into the exchange rate band. Furthermore, the fundamental is continuous and does not jump.[9] Therefore, the expected change in the exchange rate must also be continuous and not take a jump. Third, if the expected change in the fundamental takes a jump, but the expected change in the exchange rate does not, the exchange rate must be completely insensitive to the fundamental at that point.[10]

There are two main results in the Krugman model. These results follow from the shape of the exchange rate function *TT*.

The first main result is that the slope of the S-shaped curve is less than one at all times. This result is sometimes called the "honeymoon" effect, from a reference in Krugman (1987) to a "target zone honeymoon". The intuition behind the honeymoon effect is straightforward enough. When the exchange rate is higher (the currency is weaker) and closer to the upper (weak) edge of the exchange rate band, the probability that it will, within a given finite time, reach the upper edge is higher. As a result, the probability of a future intervention

---

[9]The velocity component is continuous since it is a Brownian motion. The money supply component is constant except at the edge where it moves infinitesimally just enough to prevent the fundamental from going further in the "wrong" direction.

[10]By Ito's Lemma we have $E_t \, ds_t = S_f E_t \, df_t + (1/2) S_{ff} E_t \, df_t^2$, where $E_t \, df_t^2 = \sigma^2 \, dt$. Now, if $E_t \, df_t$ is discontinuous at the edges, but $E_t \, ds_t$ is not, the first derivative must be zero at the edges, $S_f = 0$.

to reduce the money supply and strengthen the currency is higher. This means that a future currency appreciation is expected, which the market turns into an immediate appreciation and a lower exchange rate. In this case, the exchange rate is less than the rate predicted by the current fundamental alone, because an expected currency appreciation is being taken into account. In other words, the target zone exchange rate is less than the free-float exchange rate, for a given level of the fundamental. Symmetrically, when the exchange rate is stronger and closer to the lower (strong) edge of the band, a future currency depreciation is expected, implying that the exchange rate is higher (the currency is stronger) than the free-float exchange rate, for a given level of the fundamental.

The honeymoon effect leads to the important insight that a perfectly credible target zone is inherently stabilizing: the expectations of future interventions to stabilize the exchange rate makes the exchange rate more stable than the underlying fundamental. Put differently, a target zone means stabilizing the fundamentals (between the vertical dashed lines in Figure 3.2), but the exchange rate stabilizes even more (between the horizontal dashed lines in Figure 3.2).

The second main result is the smooth-pasting property mentioned above. This property has received considerable theoretical interest. Besides being a neat result, it also has more practical implications. It means that the exchange rate should rather be a nonlinear function of the underlying fundamentals. This could perhaps partially explain why existing linear exchange rate models behaved so badly empirically [Meese and Rogoff (1983), see also Frankel and Rose's chapter in this volume]. The theory of exchange rate target zones actually to a large extent became identified with smooth pasting and marginal interventions. Soon after, several researchers clarified and extended the Krugman results, and also confronted the model's implications with data. That confrontation was close to calamitous.

3.3. Empirical tests of the Krugman model

The Krugman model has clear empirical implications for exchange rates and interest rate differentials. It also has empirical implications for the aggregate fundamental, which is not directly observable but can be estimated from the observed variables. These empirical implications have been tested extensively on data from the ERM, the Nordic countries (especially Sweden), the Bretton Woods system and the Gold Standard. These tests have consistently rejected the model.

3.3.1. Exchange rates

The Krugman model implies numerous predictions about the behavior of exchange rates. One implication is that the distribution of the exchange rate within the band must be U-shaped – that is, the exchange rate must spend most of the time near the edges of the band. To understand this implication, recall the S-shape of the exchange rate function and the "smooth pasting" at the edges of the band, which implies that the exchange rate is very insensitive to the fundamental near the edges of the band. Hence the exchange rate will move slowly near the edges of the band; where the exchange rate moves slowly, it will appear often. The fundamental, in contrast, moves with a constant speed between its bounds, hence its distribution is uniform.

The U-shape of the exchange rate's density is clearly rejected by the data. The data shows that the distribution is hump-shaped, with most of the probability mass in the interior of the band and very little near the edges of the band [Bertola and Caballero (1992), Flood, Rose and Mathieson (1991), Lindberg and Söderlind (1994)]. This is, for instance, the case for the FF/DM exchange rate in Figure 3.1a, which spends most of the time well into the interior of the exchange rate band.

3.3.2. Interest rate differentials

The Krugman model has specific predictions also for interest rate differentials between domestic and foreign currency interest rates. These predictions are particularly specific under the assumption of uncovered interest parity, that the interest rate differential between the domestic and foreign currency interest rates equal the expected rate of currency depreciation,

$$i_t - i_t^* = \frac{E_t[ds_t]}{dt},$$ (3.9)

where i_t and i_t^* are the domestic and foreign-currency interest rates.[11]

We define the (log) exchange rate within the band, x_t, as the deviation of the log exchange rate from the log central parity,

$$x_t \equiv s_t - c_t.$$ (3.10)

It follows that the expected rate of currency depreciation can be written

$$\frac{E_t \, ds_t}{dt} \equiv \frac{E_t \, dx_t}{dt} + \frac{E_t \, dc_t}{dt};$$ (3.11)

the sum of what we shall call the expected rate of currency depreciation within the band and the expected rate of realignment (the expected rate of change in the central parity). Under the assumption of perfect credibility (one of the

---

[11] Uncovered interest parity is equivalent to a zero (nominal) foreign exchange risk premium, the difference between the expected domestic currency rate of return on a foreign currency investment and the expected rate of return on a domestic currency investment. For floating exchange rates, uncovered interest parity is usually strongly rejected by the data, [see Froot and Thaler (1990)]. For exchange rate target zones, Svensson (1992a) argues that the foreign exchange risk premium is likely to be small, and that hence uncovered interest parity should be a good approximation.

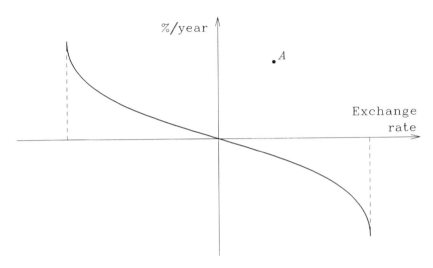

Figure 3.3. The expected rate of currency depreciation within the band.

two main assumptions of the Krugman model), no realignments are expected to occur, and the expected rate of currency depreciation is the same thing as the expected rate of currency depreciation within the band. Then we can write

$$i_t - i_t^* = \frac{E_t \, dx_t}{dt}. \tag{3.12}$$

The expected rate of currency depreciation within the band is in the Krugman model negatively-related to the exchange rate as shown by the negatively sloped curve in Figure 3.3. The intuition behind the negative slope is easy (in order to save space, we will skip explaining the particular nonlinear shape). When the exchange rate is high and at the upper edge of the exchange rate band, the currency is weak and cannot depreciate further. The exchange rate can either remain at the weak edge or drift back towards the interior of the band, in which case the currency appreciates. There is an expected currency appreciation: the expected rate of currency depreciation is negative. Analogously, when the exchange rate is at the lower edge of the band, the expected rate of currency depreciation is positive.

The negative relation between the expected rate of currency depreciation within the band and the exchange rate within the band implies that the exchange rate within the band displays *mean reversion*, that is, the expected future exchange rate within the band is closer to the long-run mean of the exchange rate within the band the further away in time it is. This mean reversion is an important general property of target zone exchange rates that is independent of the validity of the specific Krugman model, and it will be important in the discussion of extensions of the model below.

Now, under the two assumptions of uncovered interest parity and perfect credibility, the interest rate differential should equal the expected rate of currency depreciation within the band. Then the Krugman model predicts a negative deterministic relation between the interest rate differential and the exchange rate, and the correlation between the two should be strongly negative (the correlation need not be −1 since the relationship is a bit nonlinear).

However, this deterministic relationship is rejected by the data. Plots of interest rate differentials against exchange rates result in wide scatters of observations. The correlations between exchange rates and interest rate differentials are often positive or zero, and only occasionally negative, depending upon the sample and the sample period [Svensson (1991c), Flood, Rose and Mathieson (1991), Lindberg and Söderlind (1994)]. It is not difficult to see that a plot of interest rate differentials in Figure 3.1b against the deviations between the exchange rates and the central parity (the centre of the band) in Figure 3.1a results in anything but a negative deterministic relation!

3.3.3. Testing the crucial assumptions directly

The crucial assumptions of the Krugman model, perfect credibility and only marginal interventions, can be tested separately. Perfect credibility seems unrealistic given the frequency of realignments that have actually occurred, for instance for the FF/DM exchange rate in Figure 3.1a. Furthermore, there is clear direct evidence, for instance in Figure 3.1b, of many of these realignments having been anticipated. The large interest rate differentials observed immediately before some of the realignments must be interpreted as investors demanding very high franc interests as compensation for an anticipated devaluation of the franc. The easiest way of testing the credibility assumption more formally is the "simplest test" described in Svensson (1991a); it consists of examining whether forward exchange rates for different maturities fall outside the exchange rate band. If forward exchange rates fall outside the exchange rate band for some maturity, under the maintained assumption of international capital mobility the exchange rate target zone cannot be perfectly credible; if it were perfectly credible, unexploited profit opportunities would exist on the forward foreign exchange market. The assumption of perfect credibility is clearly rejected for most exchange rate target zones and most sample periods [Svensson (1991a), Flood, Rose and Mathieson (1991)].

Tests of the other crucial assumption, that the central bank undertakes only marginal interventions, require data on (or indications of) central banks' actions. Where those are available, the assumption is clearly rejected. In fact, interventions that occur in the interior of the exchange rate band, "intra-marginal" interventions, are the rule rather than the exception [Giavazzi and Giovannini (1989), Mundaca (1990), Dominguez and Kenen (1992), Edison and Kaminsky (1991), Lindberg and Söderlind (1995)].

In summary, the Krugman model with its assumptions of perfect credibility and only marginal intervention has been overwhelmingly rejected by the data. The experience may seem an excellent example of "the great tragedy of Science – the slaying of a beautiful hypothesis by an ugly fact" (T.H. Huxley). We think it is fair to state that some of the many researchers who had enthusiastically embraced the theory felt some embarrassment and even pessimism because of the glaring mismatch with the data. Nevertheless, the empirical rejection stimulated researchers to get back to the drawing board. It soon appeared that two extensions of the Krugman model seemed to resolve the empirical difficulties. These extensions, examined in Sections 3.4 and 3.5, involve removing the two crucial assumptions by incorporating imperfect credibility and intra-marginal interventions.

3.4. Extension 1: Imperfect credibility

Clearly, as Figure 3.1a demonstrates, exchange rate bands are sometimes shifted, realigned. Then the central parity – the centre of the band – takes a jump to a new level. If the change in the central parity is so large that the new exchange rate band does not overlap with the old, as in October 1981, the exchange rate must jump as well. If the new band does overlap with the old band, as in September 1979, the exchange rate may or may not jump. Furthermore, the realignments seem, at least to some extent, to be anticipated, as indicated in Figure 3.1b by the large interest rate differentials observed shortly before some of the realignments. One obvious extension of the Krugman model is, therefore, to incorporate time-varying realignment risk. We shall begin by discussing how the theory can be modified, then consider the empirical implications of doing so.[12]

3.4.1. Time-varying realignment risk

Let us now consider the situation where the exchange rate band can move. The central parity jumps at realignments and remains constant between re-

---

[12]Bertola and Svensson (1993) presented the first target zone model with time-varying realignment risk. Several papers in the literature [including Krugman (1991)] had previously considered imperfect credibility in the form of possible realignments at the edges of the band but not inside the band. Empirically, perfect credibility has been rejected in periods when the exchange rates have been far from the edges of the band. Actual realignments have occurred both when exchange rates have been near as well as further away from the edges (cf. June 1982 and April 1986 in Figure 3.1a). This supports the presumption that realignment risk is relevant also when exchange rates are away from the edges of the band.

alignments. Investors are uncertain as to when realignments will occur and how large they will be, and they form expectations of realignments given the available information. This means that we can express the expected rate of (total) currency depreciation as the sum of two components as in (3.11), the expected rate of depreciation within the band and the expected rate of realignment. The latter component should be interpreted as the product of two factors, the first being the probability per unit of time of a realignment, the other being the expected size of a realignment if it occurs. Consider the simplest case when the expected rate of realignment is exogenous and does not directly depend on the exchange rates.

Substitution of (3.11) into (3.1) and some rewriting results in the modified exchange rate equation

$$x_t = h_t + \alpha \frac{E_t \, dx_t}{dt}, \tag{3.13}$$

where a new composite fundamental h_t is defined as

$$h_t \equiv f_t - c_t + \alpha \frac{E_t \, dc_t}{dt}, \tag{3.14}$$

the sum of the old aggregate fundamental (less the central parity) and the product of α and the expected rate of realignment.

The new linear relation between the exchange rate within the band, the new composite fundamental and the expected rate of currency depreciation within the band is formally identical to the old linear relation between the exchange rate, the old aggregate fundamental and the expected rate of (total) currency depreciation. This implies that there may exist a relation, an exchange rate function, between the exchange rate within the band and the new composite fundamental that is similar to the relation between the exchange rate and the old fundamental in the Krugman model, the relation displayed in Figure 3.2. (In fact, in the special case in which the expected rate of realignment is perceived to be an exogenous Brownian motion, the new exchange rate function is of exactly the same form as the solution to the Krugman model.)

Despite the similarity with the Krugman model, behind the new composite fundamental there are now *two* fundamentals, the old aggregate fundamental, f_t, and the expected rate of realignment, $E_t \, dc_t/dt$, (which in turn may depend on additional variables). It no longer makes sense to plot the exchange rate against only one of the state variables – the old aggregate fundamental – since it omits the expected rate of realignment, which is another state variable.

The introduction of time-varying realignment risk has important consequences for how interest rate differentials are determined, and how plots of interest rate differentials against exchange rate should be interpreted. Under the assumption of uncovered interest parity, the interest rate differential equals the expected (total) rate of currency depreciation, eq. (3.15), but this is now equal to the sum of the expected rate of currency depreciation within the band and the new term, the expected rate of realignment,

$$i_t - i_t^* = \frac{E_t \, dx_t}{dt} + \frac{E_t \, dc_t}{dt}. \tag{3.15}$$

Hence, for an observation of the interest rate differential and exchange rate within the band, such as point A in Figure 3.3, the vertical difference between point A and the downward-sloping curve (the expected rate of currency depreciation within the band) is explained by the expected rate of realignment. Including time-varying realignment expectations hence offers a reason why there need not be a deterministic relation between interest rate differentials and exchange rates. Even though the expected rate of currency depreciation within the band is negatively correlated with the exchange rate within the band, depending upon how the expected rate of realignment fluctuates over time and is correlated with the exchange rate, any correlation pattern between the interest rate differential and exchange rate is possible.

3.4.2. The "drift-adjustment" method to estimate realignment expectations

The credibility, or rather the lack thereof, of exchange rate target zones is always an issue of great interest, not only for the central bankers and finance ministers directly involved, but also for investors and economics journalists. The approach to determine interest rate differentials presented above has led to a new method to measure realignment expectations and evaluate the credibility of exchange rate target zones. This method has much better precision than the "simplest test" of target zone credibility referred to above.

From (3.15) we can write

$$\frac{E_t \, dc_t}{dt} = i_t - i_t^* - \frac{E_t \, dx_t}{dt} \tag{3.16}$$

the expected rate of realignment equals the difference between the interest rate differential and the expected rate of currency depreciation within the band. From this two things follow: First, unless the expected rate of currency depreciation within the band is negligible, the interest rate differential is a misleading indicator of realignment expectations. Second, a direct estimate of the expected rate of realignment results if an estimate of the expected rate of currency depreciation within the band is constructed and this estimate is subtracted from the interest rate differential. This method can be called the "drift-adjustment" method to estimate realignment expectations, since the interest rate differential is adjusted by the "drift" of the exchange rate within the band.[13]

The difficulty with the method lies in estimating the expected rate of future currency depreciation within the band, that is, to predict the expected future exchange rate within the band. For floating exchange rates, predicting future exchange rate is usually considered a futile exercise, and a simple random walk usually out performs other forecasting models [Meese and Rogoff (1983)]. However, what is at stake here is predicting the expected future exchange rate *within the band*; that is, the future exchange rate's expected deviation from the future central parity. Predicting this has turned out to be much more fruitful than predicting (total) future exchange rates, since – unlike floating exchange rates – exchange rates within the band, both theoretically (see above) and empirically, display strong mean-reversion. In practice, a simple linear regression of future exchange rates within the band on the current exchange rate within the band and current domestic and foreign interest rates seems to predict quite well. This way of estimating the expected rate of realignment has the great advantage that it does not depend on any specific theory of exchange rates; nor does it matter whether expected rates of realignments are exogenous or endogenous (for instance, whether or not they are influenced by the exchange rate's position within the band).

Estimates of expected rates of currency depreciation within the band done for ERM exchange rates and Nordic exchange rates indicate that for time horizons up to one year, the estimates are often of the same order of magnitude as the interest rate differentials (up to 2–3 percent per year). Therefore, the use of interest rate differentials as indicators of target zone credibility, without adjusting for expected rates of depreciation within the band, is potentially misleading for horizons up to one year.

Estimating the confidence intervals for expected rates of depreciation within the band results in confidence intervals for expected rates of realignments. These can be used for statistical inference and hypothesis tests. For short horizons, the drift-adjustment method seems to have much better precision and power than the "simplest test". In many cases, with the drift-adjustment method the hypothesis that expected rates of realignment are zero can be rejected also for short horizons down to one month, whereas the "simplest test" is usually inconclusive for short horizons [Lindberg, Söderlind and Svensson (1993)]. Typically, estimated expected rates of realignment vary quite a bit over time, and they vary more than the interest rate differentials. EMS expected rates of realignment are smaller in later years than in earlier ones, showing an increase over

---

[13] The drift-adjustment method was suggested by Bertola and Svensson (1993) and is empirically implemented in Rose and Svensson (1995), Lindberg, Söderlind and Svensson (1993), and Svensson (1993).

time in the system's credibility, except shortly before the September 1992 crisis [Svensson (1993), Rose and Svensson (1994)].[14]

3.5. Extension 2: Intra-marginal interventions

The earlier discussion pointed out that empirical distributions of exchange rates within the band are hump-shaped, with most of the observations in the middle of the exchange rate band, in contrast to the U-shape predicted by the Krugman model, where most of the observations would occur near the edges of the band. The most obvious explanation for this hump-shape is that the exchange rate is kept in the middle of the band by intra-marginal interventions, that is, central bank interventions that occur in the interior of the exchange rate band.[15]

In the real world, central banks' intervention behavior is by all accounts both complicated and shifting over time. A first approximation to this complicated behavior is to propose that in addition to marginal interventions at the edges of the band there are intra-marginal "leaning-against-the-wind" interventions, that is, interventions that aim at returning the exchange rate to a specified target level within the band. A simple way to model such interventions, in terms of the target zone model with imperfect credibility described in the previous section, is to specify that the intra-marginal interventions result in the expected rate of change (the drift) of the composite fundamental towards central parity is proportional to the distance to central parity, that is,

$$\frac{E_t \, dh_t}{dt} = -\rho h_t, \tag{3.17}$$

where ρ, the rate of mean reversion, is a positive constant.[16]

The result of this modification is illustrated in Figure 3.4. The dashed 45-degree line marked *FF* again corresponds to the free-float exchange rate regime,

[14]When estimation is done for a particular finite maturity or time horizon $\Delta t > 0$, interest rate differentials of that maturity are adjusted by estimates of the expected rate of depreciation within the band over the same horizon, $E_t[x_{t+\Delta t} - x_t]/\Delta t$. The estimated expected rate of realignment $E_t[c_{t+\Delta t} - c_t]/\Delta t$ can then be interpreted in the following way. Suppose the time horizon is 3 months, and that an estimated expected rate of realignment is 12 percent per year. Conditional upon a given expected size of the realignment if it occurs, the expected conditional realignment size, a probability of a realignment within the time horizon can be constructed. Suppose the expected conditional realignment size is 5 percent. Then the expected "frequency", probability per unit of time, of realignment is the expected rate of realignment divided by the expected conditional realignment size, that is, in our case 2.4 per year. Per 3 months, this is 1/4 of 2.4, that is, 0.6. Hence, the market expects a realignment to occur within 3 months with probability 60 percent, conditional upon the realignment size 5 percent.

[15]Mean-reversion of the fundamental in the Krugman model was first discussed by Froot and Obstfeld (1991) and Delgado and Dumas (1991). Its practical and empirical importance was established by Lindberg and Söderlind (1995). See also Lewis (1993).

[16]Realignments, which were discussed in the previous section, can be seen as another kind of intervention.

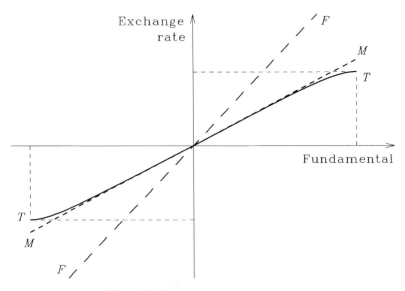

Figure 3.4. Intra-marginal interventions.

when no interventions are undertaken. Let us then first consider a "managed-float" exchange rate regime, when interventions are mean-reverting towards a central parity, but there is no specified band and no marginal interventions. The result will be the dashed line *MM* in Figure 3.4, which is less sloped than the free-float line. The equation for the *MM* line is

$$x_t = \frac{h_t}{1 + \alpha\rho}. \tag{3.18}$$

In other words, a honeymoon effect operates in the managed-float regime even without an exchange rate band. This effect results in the exchange rate fluctuating less than in the free-float regime, for given fluctuations in the composite fundamental. This is because the mean-reverting interventions imply that when the exchange rate is above the central parity (the currency is weak) the currency is expected to appreciate, which by itself reduces the exchange rate.

Now add an explicit target zone regime to the intra-marginal interventions, which means specifying a band and marginal interventions in case the exchange rate reaches the edge of this band. The resulting exchange rate function is plotted as the solid curve *TT* in Figure 3.4. The curve is close to the *MM* line corresponding to the managed float, except that it has a slight S-shape and smooth pasting at the edges of the band. As drawn here, there is an additional honeymoon effect relative to the managed float, but it is much smaller than the honeymoon effect in the managed float relative to the free float. For the same parameters and a significant degree of mean-reversion, the S-shape is much less pronounced than in the Krugman model of Figure 3.2.

Why is it plausible that the S-shape is less pronounced than in the Krugman model? And why is the exchange rate function so close to that in a managed float?

When the exchange rate is above the central parity (the currency is weak) the currency is expected to appreciate for two reasons. One reason is expected intra-marginal interventions to appreciate the currency towards the central parity. This reason is present also in a managed float. The other reason is expected future marginal interventions to prevent the exchange rate moving outside the band, in the event that the future exchange rate reaches the upper edge of the band. That reason is only present in the target zone regime. However, the probability of the future exchange rate ever reaching the edges of the band is smaller with mean-reverting interventions than in the Krugman model. The expected currency appreciation caused by the second reason is therefore smaller than that caused by the first reason.

In a target zone with mean-reverting interventions, the unconditional distribution of the composite fundamental is hump-shaped [Lindberg and Söderlind (1995) show that it is actually a truncated normal distribution]. With sufficiently strong mean-reverting interventions added, the exchange rate function is almost linear and very close to the exchange rate function for a managed float. As a consequence, the unconditional distribution of the exchange rate will be hump-shaped (with possibly some small extra probability mass at the edges of the band).

These predictions square well with the empirical hump-shaped exchange rate distributions. That the exchange rate function may be almost linear is consistent with the difficulty of finding empirical evidence of nonlinearities. In a structural estimation of a target zone model with mean-reverting interventions for the Swedish krona, Lindberg and Söderlind (1995) find reasonable parameter values, fairly strong mean-reversion, and that the overall fit of the model is quite good, much better than the Krugman model.

This analysis leads to the conjecture that the initial emphasis in target zone models on nonlinearities, smooth pasting and infrequent marginal interventions was misplaced. Target zones are better described as similar to managed floats with intra-marginal mean-reverting interventions, with additional marginal interventions defending the target zone in the rare cases when the exchange rate reaches the edge of the band. The honeymoon effect is probably important, whereas smooth pasting and nonlinearities seem empirically insignificant. An official exchange rate band should consequently not be seen as a commitment to mostly marginal interventions, but as a practical way of expressing a verifiable general commitment to limit exchange rate variability with intra-marginal interventions. After all, it would be impractical and unverifiable to announce a commitment to stabilize exchange rates in terms of a degree of mean-reversion or in terms of a standard deviation.

That the Krugman model has turned out to be misleading as a model of real world exchange rate bands should not detract from Krugman's important *technical* contribution, namely how to analyze how expectations of *future* infrequent intervention (rather than current continuous intervention) matter for current asset prices.

3.6. Why exchange rate bands?

The issues we have discussed so far all concern the first, positive, question that was mentioned above: what are the dynamics of exchange rates, interest rates and central bank interventions in exchange rate target zones? Let us now turn to the second, normative, question: are exchange rate bands optimal?

Let us first narrow down the normative question. It can be separated into three consecutive questions: First, when is a fixed exchange rate regime better than floating, where a fixed exchange rate regime in practice means a more or less narrow band around a central parity with possible occasional realignments of the central parity? Second, how often (if ever) and by how much should the central parity be realigned? Third, how narrow should the band be? The first and second questions have been extensively discussed in the traditional literature on exchange rate regimes [see Genberg (1989) for a recent survey] and in the recent literature on macroeconomic policy and credibility [see Persson and Tabellini (1990) for a survey]. They are discussed in Section 2 of the chapter and in Persson and Tabellini's chapter of this volume. Here we shall briefly discuss the third question, which has received very little attention in the literature.[17]

Why have a nonzero band instead of just a zero band, since the latter seems simpler?[18] One reason for a nonzero band that was emphasized by Keynes (1930, pp. 319–331) is that it allows some degree of national monetary independence, so that monetary policy can to some extent be used for domestic stabilization. That monetary independence can arise in a fixed exchange rate regime with free capital mobility may be a surprise to many readers, given the standard textbook result that a fixed exchange rate and free capital mobility implies a complete loss

---

[17] Cukierman, Kiguel, and Leiderman (1994) develop a positive theory of when a central bank chooses an exchange rate band, how wide the band is, and when it will be realigned. This is done in a setup where the central bank can make a commitment to a band and faces a given cost if it reneges on the commitment. Their paper is hence related to the literature on escape clauses and monetary policy, for instance, Flood and Isard (1989) and Lohmann (1992).

[18] For simplicity we disregard that for technical reasons the minimum bandwidth is not exactly equal to zero but a small positive number, since the bandwidth must exceed the normal interbank bid–asked spread for exchange rates if the central bank does not want to take over all currency trade. The normal spread is very small, though, say around 0.04 percent.

of monetary independence, in the sense that the central bank cannot then set the domestic interest rate at a level different from the foreign interest rate. Let us first explain the textbook result, then show how it is modified with nonzero exchange rate bands.

Recall the assumption that investors, in order to invest in both domestic and foreign currency, demand that the interest rate differential between the domestic and foreign interest rate equals the sum of the expected rate of realignment and the expected rate of currency depreciation within the band, [eq. (3.15)]. With a zero band, the last term is equal to zero and the interest rate differential is simply equal to the expected rate of realignment,

$$i_t - i_t^* = \frac{E_t \, dc_t}{dt} \tag{3.19}$$

The domestic central bank has then no choice but to let the domestic interest rate fulfill this condition. If it tries to set a lower domestic interest rate there will be a capital outflow because investors shift their investment to the foreign currency, and a loss of foreign exchange reserves will force the central bank to raise the interest rate. If it tries to set a higher domestic interest rate, there will be a capital inflow because international investors shift their investment to the domestic currency, and an increase in foreign exchange reserves will increase liquidity in the economy and force the domestic interest rate down. This is the textbook case of a complete loss in monetary autonomy.[19]

With a nonzero band, the expected rate of currency depreciation within the band is no longer always zero. Now the central bank can control the domestic interest rate via control over the expected rate of currency depreciation within the band in eq. (3.15). The way to control the expected rate of currency depreciation within the band is to exploit the mean reversion of the exchange rate within the band. If the central bank increases the exchange rate above its mean within the band, the exchange rate is expected to fall in the future towards the mean. That is, an expected currency appreciation within the band is created, which will reduce the domestic interest rate. Similarly, reducing the exchange rate below its mean generates an expected currency depreciation within the band, which increases the domestic interest rate.

This monetary independence allows the central bank some freedom to adjust the domestic interest rates to local conditions, for instance lowering the interest rate in a recession and increasing it during a boom. We believe this degree of monetary independence is the best explanation of why fixed exchange rate regimes have nonzero bands. Put differently, governments and central banks prefer to have some monetary independence; they therefore prefer nonzero

---

[19]Strictly speaking, the domestic interest rate equals the foreign interest rate only if the expected rate of realignment is zero, that is, if the exchange rate regime is completely credible. Also, technically the central bank can still control the domestic interest rate if it can somehow manipulate the expected rate of realignment, but that is not usually considered an example of monetary independence.

bands in fixed exchange rate regimes.[20] However, even if bands result in some monetary independence, it does not follow that this monetary independence in a fixed exchange rate regime is sufficiently large to matter, in the sense of having significant effects on output or inflation.[21, 22]

The optimality of exchange rate bands in fixed exchange rate regimes remains an under-researched area. With the improved understanding of the positive questions of how the exchange rate target zones actually work, it should now be possible to deal with the normative issue of their optimality.[23]

---

[20] Another reason for nonzero bands, discussed in De Grauwe (1992, pp. 103–107), is that sufficiently wide bands (and sufficiently small realignments) allow the new and old bands to overlap at realignments. This way realignments are possible without discrete jumps in exchange rates, that is, realignments need not imply one-sided bets on which way the exchange rate will move. This should reduce the amount of speculation and interest rate movements before each realignment. In Figure 3.1, at the two realignments with overlapping bands (September 1979 and January 1987) it appears that the interest rate differential was indeed less volatile than at the other realignments.

[21] Note that this monetary independence is limited to interest rates of short maturities, say less than one year. The reason is that the expected rate of currency depreciation within the band over a longer maturity is by necessity small: the amount of currency depreciation is bounded by the bandwidth, and it is divided by a long maturity in order to be expressed as a rate. Furthermore, the control is only temporary, in the sense that the average expected rate of currency depreciation within the band must be zero since on average the exchange rate within the band cannot deviate from its mean. Thus, the average interest rate differential over a longer period must still equal the average expected rate of realignment. Temporarily, expected rates of depreciation within the band can clearly be sizeable, though: If the exchange rate is 1 percent above the central parity, still far from the the upper edge of an ERM ±2.25 percent band, and is expected to reach the center of the band in 6 months, the expected rate of appreciation within the band is 2 percent per year, which is a sizeable reduction of the 6-month domestic interest rate. The control over the domestic interest rate is limited even in the short run if the expected rate of realignment is sensitive to exchange rate movements within the band: suppose an increase in the exchange rate above central parity (weakening of currency) leads to an increase in the expected rate of realignment. This by itself increases the domestic interest rates and counters the decrease because of an expected currency appreciation within the band.

[22] The monetary independence can be exploited in order to smooth domestic interest rates, a behavior often attributed to central banks (Goodfriend, 1991). When there is an increase in the the domestic interest rate, say because the foreign interest rate or the expected rate of realignment increases, the central bank can dampen the effect on the domestic interest rate by increasing the exchange rate and creating an expected currency appreciation within the band. A tradeoff between domestic interest rate variability and the exchange rate band results. Svensson (1994b) uses Swedish krona data to quantify this tradeoff, as a measure of the amount of monetary independence in an exchange rate band. The amount of monetary independence then appears to be sizeable in some instances: An increase in the exchange rate band from zero to ± 2 percent allows the standard deviation of the 1-month domestic interest rate to be reduced by a half.

[23] Williamson (1985, 1989) advocates a target zone for the real value of the dollar. He argues that floating exchange rates are subject to irrational destabilizing speculation which leads to excessive volatility and "misaligned" real exchange rates. A target zone would remedy this, but it should be fairly wide (say ± 10 percent) to allow sufficient latitude for monetary policy, for changes in the central rate without discontinuous changes in exchange rates, and for uncertainty about the correct level of target rate. Recently Corbae, Ingram, and Mondino (1990) and Krugman and Miller (1992) have expressed this excess-volatility case for target zones in formal models. Although the excess-volatility argument is sometimes used in general support of fixed exchange rates rather than floating exchange rates, it does not seem to be very relevant for the choice of bandwidth for ERM-type narrow nominal exchange rate bands. As discussed by Krugman and Miller (1992), the excess-volatility argument may however be important in understanding the G-3 (Germany, Japan, and the United States) Louvre agreement in 1987 to stabilize the dollar.

3.7. Conclusion

In summary, the recent work on exchange rate target zones took off in 1988 with Krugman (1991). The Krugman model employs two crucial assumptions: perfect credibility of the target zone and exclusively marginal central bank interventions to defend it. Two main results follow: the "honeymoon effect", that target zones are inherently stabilizing, and "smooth pasting", that the exchange rate is a nonlinear function of its fundamental determinants and insensitive to these fundamentals at the edge of the exchange rate band. The Krugman model has very specific empirical implications. These have been consistently rejected by the data, as have the two crucial assumptions. New work by several researchers has extended the Krugman model by removing the two crucial assumptions, which has made the theory fit the data very well.[24]

Allowing for realignment expectations can explain observed correlations between exchange rates and interest rate differentials, and has led to a new method to empirically estimate realignment expectations, the "drift-adjustment" method. Allowing for intra-marginal interventions can explain the fact that exchange rate observations tend to cluster in the center of the bands. Such interventions also imply a strong honeymoon effect but insignificant non-linearities and smooth pasting. A target zone then appears very similar to a "managed float" with a target central parity but without an explicit band.

From this it appears that the initial emphasis in the target zone literature on exclusively marginal interventions, nonlinearities and smooth pasting was largely misplaced. Real world exchange rate target zones are in practice better understood as managed floats with a target exchange rate level which is mainly defended by frequent mean-reverting intra-marginal interventions, and in addition infrequently supported by marginal interventions at the edges of the band in the very rare cases when the exchange rate actually reaches the edges of the band. The official bands are then best seen as a practical and verifiable way of expressing a general commitment to stabilize exchange rates relative to a central parity (and definitely not as a commitment to marginal interventions only). With this much improved understanding of the actual working of exchange rate target zones, it should be possible to direct future research more towards the under-researched normative issue of the optimality of exchange rate bands.

Much work remains to be done. The models are still extremely simplified, and would surely be more realistic with more state variables, sticky prices, and real effects [perhaps along the lines of Miller and Weller (1991a,b), Klein (1990), and Beetsma and van der Ploeg (1994)]. There is certainly room for more realistic intervention policies – for instance, explicit smoothing of exchange rates and

---

[24]On the other hand, the fact that the theory more easily encompasses different constellations of data means that it is more difficult to test, since some strong, testable implications have been removed.

interest rates – and for attempts to estimate changes in the intervention policy. The theory for multilateral target zones, as opposed to unilateral and bilateral target zones, is not yet worked out.[25] We suspect there is more to be said on the role of exchange rate uncertainty inside the band, the foreign exchange risk premium, and the degree of substitutability between domestic- and foreign-currency denominated assets. The amount of monetary independence that arises in an exchange rate band, and whether it has significant real effects, certainly needs to be clarified further.

The period from the Fall 1992 to the Fall 1993 has been a dramatic period for fixed exchange rate regimes, with intensive speculative attacks against both ERM currencies and Nordic currencies. At the time of writing (August 1994), Italy and the United Kingdom have left the ERM and allowed their currencies to float. The bands for the other ERM currencies have been widened to ± 15 percent, except for the Dutch guilder and the Deutschemark which remain in the narrow band. Finland, Sweden and Norway have one after the other abandoned their unilateral fixed exchange rate regimes for flexible rate regimes.

A view that is expressed with increasing frequency is that with free international capital mobility only the extreme regimes of either a common currency or floating separate currencies are viable, whereas the intermediate one of fixed exchange rates between separate currencies are not. This view is contradicted by the experience so far of Europe's hard currency bloc: Germany, Holland and Austria, where the latter two countries clearly seem able to maintain their fixed rates against the Deutschemark. The specific reasons why some countries can maintain credible fixed exchange rates should be a fruitful area for further research.

Recent events have led to renewed interest in the literature on speculative attacks and regime collapses. This literature is covered in the next section of our paper.

4. Speculative attacks on fixed exchange rate regimes

4.1. Introduction

A salient feature of fixed exchange rate regimes is their inevitable collapse into some other policy regime. The collapse is frequently spectacular – extraordinarily large interventions into foreign exchange markets and losses by central banks, large jumps in short term interest rates aimed at squeezing short positions in the attacked currency, remarkable widening of spreads in financial markets, impositions of capital controls, large and discontinuous shifts in the

---

[25] See Jørgenson and Mikkelsen (1993) for a discussion of a trilateral target zone model.

value of the exchange rate, and a period of turbulent floating in a transition to the new regime. Such events obviate comparisons of the exchange rate volatility under a floating rate regime to that under a fixed rate regime. Rather, the relative merits of a fixed exchange rate regime must be judged on the basis of the reduced exchange rate volatility while the regime lasts together with the extreme turbulence of the collapse and transition to a new regime. Making such a comparison requires a model in which the timing and magnitude of balance of payments crises emerge endogenously. In this section, we will describe the features of the basic speculative attack models and show that it and its extensions form a template for a typical speculative attack, such as the attacks on the European Exchange Rate Mechanism. Our intent is to present a schematic flavor of how the model operates. For a more extensive review of the speculative attack literature, the reader is referred to Agenor, Bhandari, and Flood (1992).

Modern models of speculative attacks on fixed exchange rates are driven by a presumption that the adherence to a fixed exchange rate is a secondary policy – it is to be maintained only as long as it is compatible with policies that have priority. This is true of models both in which the primary policy is pursued while the fixed exchange rate is in effect and in which the primary policy is implemented only after the collapse of the fixed exchange rate as in the models with multiple equilibria described below. Because a central bank can always preserve a fixed exchange rate through a sustained high interest rate or, equivalently, through a sufficiently drastic contraction in monetary base, the presumption of priority of other goals is an obvious starting point. Primary policy goals may include the maintenance of stability of some other prices such as government securities or stock market prices, the maintenance of economic stability through activist monetary policy, the maintenance of price level stability, the preservation of solvency of a banking system, or even the support of real estate prices. Typically, the priority of these other policies is expressed in speculative attack models as an exogenous growth in domestic credit that eventually leads to the collapse of the fixed exchange rate, though other forces such as a shift in real exchange rates or real money demand may also lead to an attack.

The speculative attack literature is an offshoot of the general area of regime switches that emerged through the development of forward looking macroeconomic models in the 1970's, of which Sargent and Wallace's (1973) article on shifts in money creation regimes is most relevant. In this model, Sargent and Wallace presume a shift from an inflationist to a zero money growth regime at a known future time and solve for the current value of the price level prior to the regime shift. The solution methodology requires the determination of the post-reform price level and the principle of price level continuity at the moment of the regime shift. Price level continuity establishes a boundary condition, which, when the law of motion of the price level is solved backwards, uniquely determines the current price level.

The methods of the policy-switching approach achieved popularity because they permitted investigators studying macroeconomic data to come to grips with the "peculiar" behavior that surrounds crises and other discrete events. As one of its most valuable products, the approach has allowed economists to combine economic behavior in times of crisis with behavior during more normal times in a continuous series of observations. This approach has been most fruitful when applied to speculative attacks on asset price fixing schemes.

The seminal articles in the speculative attack literature were Salant and Henderson's (1978) study of attacks on buffer stocks held to peg the real price of gold and Krugman's (1979) study of attacks on fixed exchange rate regimes. Salant and Henderson postulated a model of a fixed world supply of bullion, a growing demand for gold for industrial and consumption purposes, and a buffer stock held by an authority that would be sold at a fixed real price. Eventually, rising demand would have to exhaust the buffer stock of gold, so there would be a switch in regime from a fixed real price to a rising price. The departure in Salant and Henderson from the previous exogenous regime switching models lay in their realization that the timing of the regime switch was endogenous and that the buffer stock would not drop continuously to zero at the time of the switch but would be attacked and forced discontinuously to zero. At the time of the switch in regime, there would be a jump in the continuous rate of capital gains on holding gold – the rate of change of the real gold price would jump from zero to a positive value. This would now make it worthwhile for private speculators to hold gold bullion, and they would move to acquire the gold left in the buffer stocks. If there were no gold left in the buffer stock at this moment, the increased demand for gold would cause a discontinuous jump in the real price of gold. The principle of ruling out such unusual anticipated capital gains was carried over from the previous regime switching literature. Thus, the attack must come when the buffer stock still has gold holdings – indeed, the attack should occur at exactly the moment that the transfer of the remaining stock into private hands would satisfy speculative demand without a price jump.

These principles – no anticipated asset price discontinuities, endogenous timing of attack on a buffer stock, a discontinuity between pre-attack and post-attack rates of capital gain, and the attack's occurring when a finite buffer stock was still in the hands of the authorities – were the concepts that Krugman applied to attacks on fixed exchange rate regimes. Krugman's model simultaneously studied the dynamics of an endogenous exchange rate and an endogenous real income, however, so it did not lend itself readily to determining explicitly the timing and magnitude of a speculative attack. Most further developments of the Krugman crisis model avoided two dimensional dynamics for expositional ease. In the examples that follow, therefore, we will use a log-linear version of the one-dimensional, special case of fixed real income developed by Flood and

Garber (1984b), which has been the basis of several of the further developments in the literature.

4.2. A basic model of speculative attacks

In the basic speculative attack model, the central bank of a small country fixes the exchange rate of its currency relative to that of a large country whose logarithmic price level and interest rate, p^* and i^*, respectively, are treated as parameters. The model is summarized in equations (4.1) through (4.5):

$$m_t - p_t = -\alpha i_t, \tag{4.1}$$

$$m_t = \ln(D_t + R_t), \tag{4.2}$$

$$\frac{\mathrm{d}D_t}{\mathrm{d}t} = \mu D_t, \tag{4.3}$$

$$p_t = p^* + s_t, \tag{4.4}$$

$$i_t = i^* + \frac{\mathrm{d}s_t}{\mathrm{d}t}. \tag{4.5}$$

The variables m_t, p_t, i_t, D_t, and R_t are the logarithm of the domestic money base, the logarithm of the price level, the instantaneous domestic interest rate, domestic credit assets at the central bank, and the book value of net foreign reserves of the central bank, respectively. Equation (4.1) is a money market equilibrium condition, where the real money demand depends negatively on the instantaneous domestic interest rate. Equation (4.2) is an accounting identity in logarithmic form from the central bank's balance sheet: the monetary base equals central bank domestic credit assets plus net foreign reserves. Equation (4.3) reflects the presumption that the fixed exchange rate policy is secondary – primary policy goals dictate that domestic credit is programmed to grow at the constant rate μ. Equations (4.4) and (4.5) reflect assumptions of purchasing power parity and open interest rate parity, respectively.

From this model, the operating properties of both a floating exchange rate and a fixed exchange rate regime can be determined. Substituting for p_t and i_t in eq. (4.1) from eqs. (4.4) and (4.5) yields the law of motion of the exchange rate:

$$s_t = -\beta + m_t + \alpha \frac{\mathrm{d}s_t}{\mathrm{d}t}, \tag{4.6}$$

where $\beta = p^* - \alpha i^*$.

If the exchange rate is fixed at $\bar{s}$, the anticipated rate of change of the exchange rate is zero, $\mathrm{d}s_t/\mathrm{d}t = 0$, so m_t is constant and increases in domestic credit must be exactly balanced by declines in reserves. The continual growth in domestic credit will cause reserves to decline steadily as the central bank intervenes in foreign exchange markets to maintain the fixed exchange rate. The fixed exchange rate policy will eventually be terminated if the central bank will not permit net reserves to fall below some minimum value, and in this basic model it is assumed that a permanent floating exchange rate regime will ensue. The minimum level of reserves may be negative, reflecting foreign exchange denominated borrowing on the part of the central bank. Establishing a minimum reserve level reflects either a desire on the part of the central bank to limit its risk of foreign exchange losses from an excessively unbalanced position or credit line limits imposed by potential lenders. Both constraints are important factors in speculative attacks. For expositional purposes, we will assume that the minimum reserve level is zero.

The determination of the time that the fixed exchange rate terminates proceeds in two steps. First, from the law of motion of the exchange rate, solve for the floating exchange rate given the current level of domestic credit and contingent on net reserves being at the minimum level of zero. This contingent exchange rate is known as the *shadow floating exchange rate, $\tilde{s}_t$* – it will not be the exchange rate in effect prior to the collapse of the fixed exchange rate, but afterwards it will be identical to the value of the floating exchange rate. Second, find the time T that the shadow exchange rate equals the fixed exchange rate $\bar{s}$. Invoking the principle of the continuity of the exchange rate at the time of the collapse, this must be the time of the collapse.

It can be verified that in the floating regime, after the collapse of the fixed exchange rate, $ds_t/dt = dm_t/dt = dd_t/dt = \mu$, since money supply m_t is identical to $d_t = \ln D_t$. By substitution in (4.6) the solution for the floating exchange rate is

$$s_t = \tilde{s}_t = \alpha\mu - \beta + m_t = \alpha\mu - \beta + d_t. \tag{4.7}$$

So at the time T of the collapse, the exchange rate fulfills

$$\bar{s} = \tilde{s}_T = \alpha\mu - \beta + d_T. \tag{4.8}$$

Finally, since $d_T = d_0 + \mu T$, the time of the collapse can be determined as

$$T = [\bar{s} + \beta - d_0]/\mu - \alpha = [m_0 - d_0]/\mu - \alpha = \ln(1 + R_0/D_0)/\mu - \alpha. \tag{4.9}$$

The time of the collapse can be delayed by increasing the initial level of net reserves relative to domestic credit and advanced if the rate of change of domestic credit increases. Note that even a large current fractional foreign reserve backing of the domestic money stock will not preclude a collapse.

Why do reserves jump downward discontinuously in an attack? The intuition for this result can be derived by considering the money market equilibrium in

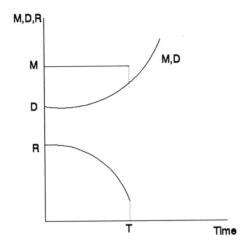

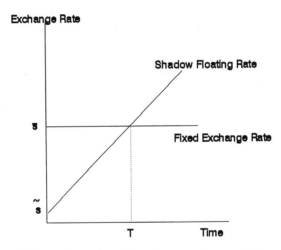

Figure 4.1. Money, domestic credit, and reserves in a speculative attack.

the moment before and the moment after the collapse. Before the collapse, anticipated depreciation is zero, so the demand for domestic money evaluated in foreign currency is $m - \bar{s} = \beta$. Immediately after the collapse anticipated depreciation jumps up discontinuously because the steady growth in domestic credit then translates into a steady growth of money during the floating rate regime. Since the exchange rate is continuous at the collapse, there is a downward jump in demand for domestic nominal money, and this can be satisfied by exchanging domestic currency at the central bank's foreign exchange window for the remaining reserves. Figure 4.1 depicts the movements of the money stock, domestic credit and reserves before and after the attack. Prior to the attack, the exchange rate is fixed with no anticipated depreciation, so nominal money demand and supply are constant. Nevertheless, domestic credit is continually rising, and this is matched by a mirror-image fall in reserves. At the time of the attack, nominal money demand falls discontinuously to D_T; and the supply is reduced accordingly through an attack that drives reserves discontinuously to zero. From T onward, the money stock is identical to and grows with domestic credit.

4.3. Extensions of the basic model

Although they are closely related in content and technique, the literatures on target zones and on speculative attacks experienced remarkably different paths of development. Krugman's (1991) initial paper on target zones was released in different forms in two working papers distributed in 1987 and 1988. These led to such an immediate explosion of jointly evolving theoretical and empirical studies that by the time the initial paper was published, the field was already mature. In contrast, the development of the speculative attack literature was initially very slow. After Krugman's (1979) publication, nothing further was published until 1984, though, of course, papers incorporating Krugman's technique were under development in the early 1980's. It was only in the last half of the 1980's that the literature was substantially filled out. More importantly, relatively few empirical studies were undertaken to test the speculative attack theory, and these generally were calibrations that ratified the predictions of the speculative attack model.

4.3.1. Random timing of attacks

The speculative attack model lends itself easily to further development. For example, in the basic model, the domestic instantaneous interest rate will not deviate from the foreign rate during the fixed exchange rate regime. Empirically, however, overnight interest rates of countries maintaining fixed exchange rates have deviated substantially from foreign interest rates. This has arisen because there is always some possibility that the fixed exchange rate system may not be continued, even on a day-to-day basis. Also, countries have intervened strenuously to defend their exchange rates by operating an interest rate defense in which the domestic rate is purposely raised to high levels to squeeze sellers of the currency. This drawback of the basic model arises from the assumption of perfect foresight about the timing and magnitude of the attack. In further developments, the perfect foresight assumption has usually been dropped by making the domestic credit process random or by making the minimum reserve level of the central bank uncertain. Krugman (1979) originally argued that uncertainty about the reserves available for intervention would affect the dynamics of attacks on the exchange rate, leading to recurring periods of attacks on the fixed rate. Flood and Garber (1984b) added randomness to the domestic credit variable in a discrete time version of the model. The operating principles of the altered models are the same as for the basic model except that the requirement of asset price continuity is replaced by a requirement that there be no expected price discontinuity – that is, no forseeable opportunity to make abnormal profits – at any given time.

4.3.2. Alternative post-attack regimes

To gain additional realism, the assumption that the fixed exchange rate collapses into a permanent floating rate can be altered to include a collapse followed by a temporary period of floating that leads to a new, devalued fixed exchange rate, as in Obstfeld (1984). Under a temporary floating regime, the principle of continuity between the fixed exchange rate and the shadow floating exchange rate at the time of the attack remains. However, the law of motion of the post-attack floating exchange rate is driven in part by the future fixing of the exchange rate, which implies that the solution to the differential eq. (4.6) will combine the particular solution (4.7) and a homogeneous solution. Alternatively, the attack on the fixed exchange rate may lead immediately to a devaluation, to a new fixed exchange rate, or the pre-attack regime may be a crawling peg rather than a pure fixed exchange rate, as in Connolly and Taylor (1984).

4.3.3. Empirical applications

Attacks on fixed exchange rates. Addressing the post-attack exchange rate policy more realistically has been motivated by efforts to breathe empirical life into the speculative attack model. For instance, Blanco and Garber (1986) adapted the model to a regime of recurring discontinuous devaluations to interpret dynamics of the Mexican exchange rate in quarterly data from 1973 through 1982. In this period, there were two major devaluations – in 1976 and 1982. Blanco and Garber noted that the permanent shadow floating exchange rate is the minimum exchange rate that can emerge after an attack. For a policy of devaluation to a new fixed exchange rate to be viable requires that the new exchange rate exceeds the shadow floating rate. Blanco and Garber modeled the difference between the new fixed rate and the shadow floating rate as a policy rule: a policy constant multiplied by a positive, random disturbance. Given the parameters of money demand, the domestic credit creation policy, the minimum reserves of the central bank, and real income, all the variables that drive the shadow floating exchange rate can be aggregated into a single, hybrid forcing variable whose law of motion can be estimated. Using this law of motion and the devaluation rule, together with a distributional assumption for the disturbances of the model, it is possible to compute theoretical one-quarter ahead expected exchange rates and probabilities of devaluation. Blanco and Garber then estimated the value of the fixed minimum reserve level and the parameter governing the devaluation policy rule by minimizing the deviations of the theoretical one-quarter ahead expected exchange rates from observed forward exchange rates. They found that the estimated probabilities of devaluations one-quarter ahead, jumped to peaks of 20 percent just prior to the major devaluations of 1976 and 1982 and fell to low levels immediately after devaluations. Also, the theoretical exchange rates contingent on devaluation were within a 95 percent confidence interval, albeit quite wide, of the exchange rates that actually emerged in the two large devaluations.

Attacks on crawling pegs. Cumby and van Wijnbergen (1989) applied the speculative attack model to the Argentine crawling peg of 1979–1981. Connolly (1986) also studied this episode. Under a crawling peg, the central bank will sell foreign exchange at an announced exchange rate that depreciates at a predetermined rate. The principle for determining the time of attack on this regime is the same as in a fixed exchange rate regime: when the shadow exchange rate exceeds the official exchange rate, speculators will attack. Instead of a comparison of the shadow floating exchange rate with a fixed, official exchange rate, the shadow floating exchange rate is compared with an official exchange rate that moves deterministically with time. An attack might lead to a floating exchange rate, a crawling peg with an increased rate of depreciation, or a devaluation. As empirical departures, Cumby and van Wijnbergen estimated the stochastic processes of each of the forcing variables separately, rather than as an arbitrarily constructed aggregate as in Blanco and Garber. Also, they assumed that the minimum level of reserves was not known to the public; rather, they assumed that it was a random variable drawn by the central bank and unknown to the public. Cumby and van Wijnbergen found that the probability of attack was driven primarily by domestic credit creation and that it reached its highest level of about 80 percent just prior to the attack that led to the abandonment of the Argentine policy.

Goldberg (1994) used Mexican data from 1980 through 1986 to study the effects of both fiscal and monetary shocks on attacks on the peso in both the fixed exchange rate period studied by Blanco and Garber and in the ensuing crawling peg regime. Connolly and Fernandez (1987) also studied the Mexican data for this period. Goldberg added to the list of forcing variables of the exchange rate by explicitly modelling real exchange rate movements and foreign credit disturbances. Also, rather than take a stand on the minimum reserve level, she estimated the model for a range of minimum reserves. The criteria for judging the model are to compare the step-ahead (one month) probabilities that the shadow exchange rate exceeds official rates with periods of exchange rate crises and to compare computed shadow exchange rates with official rates. Goldberg finds that the step ahead probabilities generally reach levels of 100 percent in the period before a crisis and that at such times the realized shadow exchange rates exceed the official rates. She also finds that domestic credit creation, not external credit disturbances, drove the timing of speculative attacks.

Government finance constraints and the creation of domestic credit. For pedagogical ease, the basic speculative attack model is typically driven by exogenously expanding domestic credit, which inevitably leads to the collapse of the system. It is natural to inquire about the source of this domestic credit expansion, and researchers generally presume that it funds exigent government deficits. In the context of the attacks on the United States gold standard during the 1890's, Garber and Grilli (1986) discuss the legally imposed borrowing constraints faced by the U.S. Secretary of the Treasury in trying to fund a deficit and show that they forced the circulation of a silver-backed (i.e. domestic credit) money that undermined the gold standard. The efforts of the Treasury Secretary to preserve the gold standard and satisfy legal constraints on his borrowing authority led to the Belmont–Morgan contract, under which a syndicate underwrote a Treasury bond issue and undertook the responsibility for intervening in the foreign exchange markets to preserve the gold standard, effectively providing a short term credit line to the Treasury. These services were paid for by what was at the time regarded as an excessively large spread between the issue price and immediate market price. Grilli (1990) estimated the parameters of money demand and forcing variables of domestic credit to compute the step-ahead probability of attack on the gold standard. He then examined how these probabilities were affected by the provisions of the Belmont–Morgan contract. Using results from the optimal contracting literature, he concluded that the Treasury Secretary had acted to establish that contract within his legal authority and within the cost that he was willing to pay minimized the probability of attack.

Multiple equilibria. The choice of a fixed exchange rate regime is often motivated from a desire to establish a nominal anchor for monetary policy – in the absence of the requirement to maintain the fixed rate, monetary policy may become inflationary. Under this motivation, the assumption of an exogenous domestic credit policy is not tenable. Rather, in further developments of the basic model, it has been assumed that the domestic credit policy is endogenous: while the fixed exchange rate is maintained, domestic credit growth is strictly in accord with the indefinite existence of the regime, i.e. $\mu = 0$; but contingent on the fixed exchange rate regime's collapse, the loss of discipline will cause domestic credit growth to increase, i.e. $\mu > 0$. Flood and Garber (1984a) and Obstfeld (1986) showed that such endogeneity of the domestic credit forcing variable can lead to multiple equilibria exchange rate dynamics in models of speculative attacks. The fixed exchange rate can last indefinitely if speculators believe that there will be no collapse. If speculators believe that a collapse will occur, however, the attack on reserves will terminate the fixed exchange rate regime, trigger the contingent jump in domestic credit growth, and ratify the attack. Thus, speculators' beliefs about the viability of the regime become the key to the dynamics. In the context of the basic model, suppose that $\mu = 0$ during the fixed exchange rate regime. From the solution for the time of the attack, $T = \infty$, so the fundamentals are correct for the indefinite survival of the regime. Now suppose that contingent on a collapse of the regime $\mu > 0$ and that $\ln(1 + R_0/D_0)/\mu < \alpha$. Then a sudden attack will be justified – the post-attack solution for the floating exchange rate will jump upward, or at least start depreciating sufficiently rapidly to ratify the sudden reduction in the domestic money supply.

More than a technical curiosum, the possibility of multiple equilibria has been invoked as an explanation for some of the speculative attacks that occurred during the collapse of the narrow bands of the European Exchange Rate Mechanism. For example, Goldstein et al. (1993) and Svensson (1994a) discuss the the scenario in their study of the ERM crisis, and Eichengreen and Wyplosz (1993) argue strongly that the emergence of multiple equilbria was a principal cause of attacks on some countries' adherence to the system. Obstfeld (1994) has extended his results by examining in more detail the exigencies that drive government finance into post-attack domestic credit expansions.

Prior to the attacks on the European Exchange Rate Mechanism, the literature on speculative attacks could have been characterized as a mature literature – that is, one in which most of the interesting questions had been asked and addressed. A review of the references indicates that most of the literature on speculative attacks was published in the mid- to late 1980's. The few articles published in the 1990's were already circulating in unpublished form by the end of the 1980's.

The huge scale of the attacks on the European Exchange Rate Mechanism, together with the financial tools in the hands of speculators, has been interpreted as a shift in the balance of power between central banks and market forces. The perception of this shift, in turn, has led to a revived interest in the multiple equilibrium versions of the speculative attack models described in Section 4.3 of this chapter. It is widely understood, however, that it is difficult to distinguish between situations in which multiple equilibria may be present and situations in which exogenous policies inevitably lead to a collapse of a fixed exchange rate. The development of methods to distinguish between these two models of speculative attacks in the data is an important open issue in the field.

4.4. Conclusion

The theoretical bases of research on exchange rate target zones and speculative attacks on fixed exchange rates are remarkably similar. Both areas rely on
the same basic monetary model of exchange rates for ease of describing exchange rate dynamics, and both rely on similar boundary events to determine
the dynamic path of the exchange rates.

The development of the two areas, however, proceeded in remarkably different ways. The study of target zones attracted a large research effort that
was driven by empirical results; and research interest in it waxed, matured, and
waned quickly – five years being an unusually rapid period for an important
area of economic study. The study of speculative attacks proceeded at a much
more leisurely pace; and the theoretical development, which centered on the extension of the results to the innumerable possible pre- and post- attack regimes,
was far less influenced by empirical results. Also, empirical results have tended
to be supportive of the theory.

These differences in the influence of empirical research emanate from the
demands being made of the data and from the data available. Target zone
models – at least the simple ones – make strong statements about exchange rate
dynamics within the band and the relation between interest rates and exchange
rates that can be tested because of the availability of long time series of financial
variables. The large data sets have power to reject the strong implications of
the model. Speculative attack models have little to say about the dynamics of
exchange rates, except that fixed exchange rates will collapse, which is indeed
an important empirical regularity. The only test of the model, given available
data, is to determine whether the timing of the attack is consistent with the
dynamics of the post-attack exchange rate. Because there are usually only a
few attacks on a given currency, each episode is almost a single event, so data
analysis becomes an exercise in description because of the researcher's freedom
to postulate a post-attack regime and an unobservable minimum reserve level
that imply the observed timing of the attack.

Box: The mechanics of speculative attacks. Perfect foresight models of speculative attacks involve a sudden, discontinuous collapse of the money supply; but
since they abstract away from the banking system they are generally silent about
the financial transactions that transmit the attack to the central bank and they
generally ignore defensive measures taken by central banks at the time of an
attack. Models with uncertainty about the magnitude of intervention or disturbances to the fundamentals of the shadow exchange rate are more forthcoming
about phenomena at the time of an attack: they imply a rise in interest rates as
a devaluation becomes possible and they admit a decline in the domestic money
supply as the uncertainty about devaluation evolves.

In this section, we will explore the mechanism that transmits the attack to the central bank. Specifically, we will outline the instruments normally used by speculators, show how the banking system operates to transmit the attack, and describe the interaction between central bank foreign exchange interventions and the simultaneous central bank support for other markets through the discount window. Finally, we will consider post-collapse central bank operations aimed at recovering losses suffered in the attack. For a more detailed description of the micro-finance of a speculative attack, see Goldstein et al. (1993), Annex IV, on which this box is based. Purely for illustration, we will presume that the pound is the currency under attack and that the pound is fixed against the Deutschemark.

Forward contracts that settle in one or more months are the instrument of choice of non-bank sellers of currency in a foreign exchange crisis. Forward contracts allow sellers to lock in financing at the relatively low rates prevailing prior to an attack for a protracted period. Typically, a seller can obtain a forward contract from a bank with a margin deposit of ten percent of the face value of the contract. Thus, a relatively small amount of capital can be leveraged into a large foreign exchange sale.

The bank on the other side of this contract finds itself in a long position in pounds – the forward contract commits it to receive pounds and deliver some other currency, e.g. Deutschemarks – and it immediately seeks to balance the position through a sale of pounds. The standard wholesale method through which banks rebalance their currency positions is to use a combination of spot currency sales and currency swaps – specifically, they engage in a spot sale of pounds; and in the swap they deliver DM for pounds spot and pounds for DM forward.

Figure 4.2 illustrates how the receipts and payments associated with these transactions rebalance the bank's position. Suppose that the fixed spot exchange rate is DM3/pound. In the first step, the forward contract commits the bank to receive 100 pounds and pay 300 DM in one month, thereby generating a currency mismatch. In the second step, a spot sale of pounds for DM balances the currency position of the bank but creates a maturity mismatch. Specifically, a long position in one-month pounds is funded with rollover pounds, and a long position in rollover DM is funded with one-month DM. The purpose of the currency swap is to eliminate this maturity mismatch, as seen in step 3. Note that a forward sale of a currency quickly generates a spot sale of the currency.

If a non-bank buyer of pounds simultaneously arrives at another bank in the world, the opposite positions will be arranged by the selling bank, so on net the banking system will rebalance its pound position. In a crisis, however, non-bank position-taking in pounds will be one-way, so the global banking system can remain balanced in pounds only by borrowing from and trading spot with the Bank of England or with the alliance of central banks involved in defending the

Step 1. Forward Contract = Currency Mismatch

Receipt			Payment
Pounds in one month	100	300	DM in one month

Step 2. Forward Contract + Spot Sale = Maturity Mismatch

Receipt			Payment
Pounds in one month (Forward)	100	100	Pounds in two days (Spot)
DM in two days (Spot)	300	300	DM in one month (Forward)

Step 3. Forward + Spot + Swap = Balanced Position

Receipt			Payment
Pounds in one month (Forward)	100	100	Pounds in one month (Swap)
Pounds in two days (Swap)	100	100	Pounds in two days (Spot)
DM in one month (Swap)	300	300	DM in one month (Forward)
DM in two days (spot)	300	300	DM in two days (Swap)

Figure 4.2. Receipts and payments from forward contract operations.

pound parity. If the Bank of England intervenes by buying pounds forward from a bank, usually one of the UK clearing banks, a further and opposite round of balancing currency swaps and spot purchases of pounds will ensue to allow the UK bank to rebalance its position. Globally, the banking system does not take a position in currencies or maturities and operates only as a market maker transmitting the attack from the non-banks to the Bank of England. Alternatively stated, the global banking system will take its profits from a speculative attack in the form of increased volume and bid–offer spreads in the markets for all foreign exchange products and short-term credit.

While central banks intervene massively in forward markets, there is a limit on the extent of their intervention. One source of limitation is self-imposed – central banks themselves are reluctant to assume an excessively short position in foreign currencies because their capital might be wiped out in the event of a devaluation, thereby forcing them to approach the government for a capital injection and risking their independence. Thus, many central banks will buy in their currency through forward contracts only to the extent that the contracts are covered by holdings of foreign exchange. Indeed, this central bank aversion to capital losses on own account validates the assumption generally made in the speculative attack literature that the central bank under attack will cease intervening when its net reserves reach zero. A second source of limitation arises from the prudential credit line limits imposed by the banking system on any single borrower. The domestic banks, e.g. the UK clearing banks, would not impose a limit on their own central bank, but they, in turn, will face a credit limit cap vis-à-vis the positions they assume with other banks in covering their positions.

If the central bank does not assume the role of the residual buyer of its currency on forward markets, the balancing operations of the banking system will force the central bank to intervene in spot exchange markets and to provide domestic credit through the discount window to fund the attack. Since the forward sales of the currency trigger an equal net spot sale, the central bank's intervention on the spot market will equal the net forward sales to the banking system plus the net spot sales. In the swap leg of the banking system's balancing operation, however, a counterparty must deliver spot pounds, which are then absorbed by the central bank in the spot exchange intervention. The spot pounds for delivery in the swap contract are acquired by discounting eligible paper at the central bank's discount facility, which in most countries is available without limit at an interest rate that is usually above interbank rates. In an exchange crisis, however, the discount rate becomes the market rate, and the central bank provides the credit in domestic currency needed by short sellers of the currency.

That the central bank continues to fuel the attack against itself rather than to raise the interest rate to extreme levels is another manifestation of the dual goals of the central bank – it wants the fixed exchange rate, but it also wants to put a floor under the value of those assets eligible for discount. It can always defeat that attack by setting a high enough interest rate and avoiding the sterilization through the discount window of the reserve outflow. Its refusal to do so signals that it prefers to stabilize domestic asset prices rather than to stabilize the foreign exchange rate.

5. Suggestions for further reading

5.1. Exchange rate target zones

Bertola (1994) provides a comprehensive and more technical survey of the recent target zone research, including an extensive bibliography.

Froot and Obstfeld (1991) give a rigorous presentation of the Krugman model, with several extensions and a treatment of regime shifts. The Krugman model is critically evaluated in Krugman and Miller (1992). Miller and Weller (1991a,b) present an important variant of the Krugman model with sticky prices and real effects. Further extensions along this line are provided by Klein (1990) and Beetsma and van der Ploeg (1994). Flood and Garber (1991) extend the Krugman model to include finite interventions inside the band, Perraudin (1990) extends it to include discrete jumps in the fundamental. Svensson (1991b) derives empirical implications of the Krugman model for exchange rates and interest rate differentials; Svensson (1991c) derives and tests implications for the term structure of interest rate differentials. Extensive empirical tests of the Krugman model are presented in Flood, Rose, and Mathieson (1991), Smith and Spencer (1991), and Lindberg and Söderlind (1994). Pessach and Razin (1994) estimate a Krugman model on Israeli data.

The extension to time-varying realignment risk is made in Bertola and Svensson (1993). The drift-adjustment method is empirically implemented in Rose and Svensson (1995), Svensson (1993), Frankel and Phillips (1992) and Lindberg, Söderlind, and Svensson (1993). An alternative model with realignment risk at the edge of the band that can explain the hump-shaped unconditional exchange rate distribution is presented in Bertola and Caballero (1992) and further extended by Bertola and Caballero (1991) and Bartolini and Bodnar (1992).

The extension to intra-marginal mean-reverting interventions is presented in Froot and Obstfeld (1991), Delgado and Dumas (1991), and Pesenti (1990). Lewis (1993) develops a model with occasional intra-marginal intervention. Intra-marginal interventions are documented in Mundaca (1990), Dominguez and Kenen (1991), Edison and Kaminsky (1991), and Lindberg and Söderlind (1995); the latter contains a structural estimation on Swedish data of an extended target zone model that incorporates both intra-marginal interventions and time-varying realignment risk.

A sizeable part of the literature has dealt with regime shifts and regime collapses, the role of reserves, and the problem of bubbles. This includes Froot and Obstfeld (1991), Bertola and Caballero (1992), Krugman and Rotemberg (1991), Delgado and Dumas (1991, 1992), Miller and Sutherland (1991), Buiter and Grilli (1991), Buiter and Pesenti (1990), and Dumas and Svensson (1994). Klein and Lewis (1993) estimate learning about, and shifts in, an implicit dollar/Deutschemark and dollar/yen exchange rate target zone between the Plaza agreement 1985 and the stockmarket crash 1987.

The excessive-volatility argument for a target zone is developed by Williamson (1985, 1989), Corbae, Ingram, and Mondino (1990), and Krugman and Miller (1992). The amount of monetary independence in an exchange rate band, which was discussed already by Keynes (1930, pp. 319–331), is examined again in Svensson (1994b).

The techniques used, notably stochastic calculus, are discussed, in order of increasing difficulty, in Dixit (1992), Dixit (1991), Bertola (1994), Harrison (1985), and Karatzas and Shreve (1988).

5.2. Speculative attacks on fixed exchange rate regimes

Agénor, Bhandari, and Flood (1992) provide a more extensive review of the speculative attack literature.

While the basic speculative attack models are based on behavioral rules for the public or the authorities, several models have been constructed with optimizing behavior for the authorities or the public. These include models analyzed by Obstfeld (1986a), Claessens (1988, 1991), and Penati and Penacchi (1989).

The standard speculative attack models assume that capital is perfectly mobile and implicitly assume that credit in domestic currency is readily available for foreign exchange speculation. As an alternative that is more realistic for many countries, Wyplosz (1986), Bachetta (1990), Dellas and Stockman (1993) have developed models of speculative attack on fixed exchange rates in the presence of capital controls.

For ease of analysis, speculative attack models almost always are based on an assumption of price flexibility so that real variables are exogenous to the exchange rate. Flood and Hodrick (1986), Willman (1988), and Krugman (1979) provide models in which exchange rate movements are jointly determined with real variables.

Except for a few papers, little consideration has been given to the relation between government financing requirements and the creation of domestic credit. Buiter (1987) and van Wijnbergen (1991) study this relationship.

Though it is well-known that the real exchange rate is driven by the nominal exchange rate, speculative attack models generally assume a constant or/and exogenous real exchange rate. Connolly and Taylor (1984) and Connolly (1986) study cases in which the real exchange rate is affected by anticipated speculative attacks on the fixed rate.

Rather than a situation in which a fixed exchange rate collapses into a floating exchange rate, there are many cases of countries with floating rates that suddenly fixed their exchange rates. The anticipation of a future fixing of the exchange rate will affect the dynamics of the floating exchange rate in a manner that is studied by Flood and Garber (1983, 1984b), Djajic (1989), Froot and Obstfeld (1991), Smith and Smith (1990), and Smith (1991).

Grilli (1986) has considered in a model of uncertain domestic credit growth the timing of speculative attacks on a country that maintains a fixed exchange rate as long as reserves neither fall below a minimum value nor rise above a maximum value. Once it leaves the fixed exchange rate, however, it does not return.

References

Agénor, P.-R., J.S. Bhandari, and R.P. Flood (1992), "Speculative attacks and models of balance of payments crises", International Monetary Fund Staff Papers 39:357–394.

Bacchetta, P. (1990), "Temporary capital controls in a balance-of-payments crisis", Journal of International Money and Finance 9:246–257.

Bartolini, L. and G. Bodnar (1992), "Target zones and forward rates in a model with repeated realignments", Journal of Monetary Economics 30:373–408.

Beetsma, R.M.W.J. and F. van der Ploeg (1994), "Intra-marginal interventions, bands and the pattern EMS exchange rate distributions", International Economic Review 35:583–602.

Bertola, G. (1994), "Continuous-time models of exchange rates and intervention", in: F. van der Ploeg, ed., Handbook of international economics (Basil Blackwell, London).

Bertola, G. and R.J. Caballero (1992), "Target zones and realignments", American Economic Review 82:520–536.

Bertola, G. and R.J. Caballero (1991), "Sustainable intervention policies and exchange rate dynamics", in: P. Krugman and M. Miller, eds., Exchange rate targets and currency bands (Cambridge University Press, Cambridge, UK) 186–206.

Bertola, G. and L.E.O. Svensson (1993), "Stochastic devaluation risk and the empirical fit of target zone models", Review of Economic Studies 60:689–712.

Blanco, H. and P.M. Garber (1986), "Recurrent devaluation and speculative attacks on the Mexican peso", Journal of Political Economy 94:148–166.

Buiter, W.H. (1987), "Borrowing to defend the exchange rate and the timing of and magnitude of speculative attacks", Journal of International Economics 23:221–239.

Buiter, W.H. and V. Grilli (1991), "Anomalous speculative attacks on fixed exchange rate regimes: Possible resolutions of the 'gold standard paradox'", in: P. Krugman and M. Miller, eds., Exchange rate targets and currency bands (Cambridge University Press, Cambridge, UK) 140–176.

Buiter, W.H. and P.A. Pesenti (1990), "Rational speculative bubbles in an exchange rate target zone", Centre for Economic Policy Research Discussion Paper No. 479.

Claessens, S. (1988), "Balance of payments crises in a perfect foresight optimizing model", Journal of International Money and Finance 7:363–372.

Claessens, S. (1991), "Balance of payments crises in an optimal portfolio model", European Economic Review 35:81–101.

Connolly, M.B. (1986), "The speculative attack on the peso and the real exchange rate: Argentina, 1979–81", Journal of International Money and Finance 5:117–130.

Connolly, M.B. and A. Fernandez (1987), "Speculation against the pre-announced exchange rate in Mexico: January 1983 to June 1985", in: M. Connolly and C. Gonzalez, eds., Economic reform and stabilization in Latin America (Praeger Publishers, New York).

Connolly, M.B. and D. Taylor (1984), "The exact timing of the collapse of an exchange rate regime and its impact on the relative price of traded goods", Journal of Money, Credit, and Banking 16:194–207.

Corbae, D., B. Ingram and G. Mondino (1990), "On the optimality of exchange rate band policies", working paper, University of Iowa.

Cukierman, A., M.A. Kiguel, and L. Leiderman (1994), "The choice of exchange rate bands: Balancing credibility and flexibility", in: L. Leiderman and A. Razin, eds., Capital mobility: The impact on consumption, investment and growth (Cambridge University Press, Cambridge, UK).

Cumby, R.E. and S. van Wijnbergen (1989), "Financial policy and speculative runs with a crawling peg: Argentina 1979–81", Journal of International Economics 27:111–127.

Currie, D. (1992), "Hard ERM, hard ecu, and European monetary union", in: M. Canzoneri, V. Grilli and P. Masson, eds., Establishing a central bank: Issues in Europe and lessons from the US (Cambridge University Press, Cambridge, UK).

De Grauwe, P. (1992), The economics of monetary integration (Oxford University Press, Oxford).

Delgado, F. and B. Dumas (1992), "Monetary contracting between central banks and the design of sustainable exchange rate zones", Journal of International Economics 34:201–224.

Delgado, F. and B. Dumas (1991), "Target zones, broad and narrow", in: P. Krugman and M. Miller, eds., Exchange rate targets and currency bands (Cambridge University Press, Cambridge, UK) 35–56.

Dellas H. and A. Stockman (1993), "Self-fulfilling expectations, speculative attacks and capital controls", Journal of Money Credit and Banking 25:721–730.

Dixit, A.K. (1991), "A simplified treatment of the theory of optimal control of Brownian motion", Journal of Economic Dynamics and Control 15:657–673.

Dixit, A.K. (1992), "Investment and hysteresis", Journal of Economic Perspectives 6:107–132.

Djajic, S. (1989), "Dynamics of the exchange rate in anticipation of pegging", Journal of International Money and Finance 8:559–571.

Dominguez, K.M. and P. Kenen (1992), "Intra-marginal intervention in the EMS and the target-zone model of exchange-rate behavior", European Economic Review 36:1523–1532.

Dumas, B. (1992), "Dynamic equilibrium and the real exchange rate in a spatially separated world", Review of Financial Studies 5:153–180.

Dumas, B. and L.E.O. Svensson (1994), "How long do unilateral target zones last?", Journal of International Economics 36:467–481.

Edison, H. and G. Kaminsky (1991), "Target zones, intervention, and exchange rate volatility: France 1979–1990", working paper, Federal Board of Governors. Washington, DC.

Eichengreen, B. and C. Wyplosz (1993), "The unstable EMS", Brookings Papers on Economic Analysis 1:51–124.

Flood, R.P. and P. Garber (1983), "A model of stochastic process switching", Econometrica 51:537–552.

Flood, R.P. and P. Garber (1984a), "Gold monetization and gold discipline", Journal of Political Economy 92:90–107.

Flood, R.P. and P. Garber (1984b), "Collapsing exchange rate regimes: Some linear examples", Journal of International Economics 17:1–13.

Flood, R.P. and P. Garber (1991), "The linkage between speculative attack and target zone models of exchange rates", Quarterly Journal of Economics 106:1367–1372.

Flood, R.P. and R. Hodrick (1986), "Real aspects of exchange rate regime choice with collapsing fixed rates", Journal of International Economics 21:215–232.

Flood, R.P. and P. Isard (1989), "Monetary policy strategies", International Monetary Fund Staff Papers 36:612–632.

Flood, R.P., A.K. Rose, and D.J. Mathieson (1991), "An empirical exploration of exchange-rate target-zones", Carnegie–Rochester Series on Public Policy 35:7–65.

Frankel, J.A. and S. Phillips (1992), "The European monetary system: Credible at last?", Oxford Economic Papers 44:791–816.

Frankel, J.A. and M. Goldstein (1986), "A guide to target zones", International Monetary Fund Staff Papers 33:633–673.

Froot, K. and M. Obstfeld (1991), "Stochastic process switching: Some simple solutions", Econometrica 59:241–250.

Froot, K.A. and M. Obstfeld (1991), "Exchange-rate dynamics under stochastic regime shifts: A unified approach", Journal of International Economics 31:203–229.

Froot, K.A. and R.H. Thaler (1990), "Anomalies: Foreign exchange", Journal of Economic Perspectives 4:179–192.

Garber, P. and V. Grilli (1986), "The Belmont–Morgan Syndicate as an optimal investment banking contract", European Economic Review 30:649–677.

Genberg, H. (1989), "Exchange rate management and macroeconomic policy: A national perspective", Scandinavian Journal of Economics 91:439–469.

Giavazzi, F. and A. Giovannini (1989), Limiting exchange rate flexibility: The European monetary system (MIT Press, Cambridge, MA).

Giavazzi, F. and M. Pagano (1988), "The advantages of tying one's hands", European Economic Review 32:1055–1082.

Goldberg, L.S. (1994), "Predicting exchange rate crises: Mexico revisited", Journal of International Economics 36:413–430.

Goldstein, M., D. Folkerts-Landau, P. Garber, L. Rojas-Suarez, and M. Spencer (1993), Exchange rate management and international capital flows, International capital markets, Part I (International Monetary Fund, Washington, DC).

Goodfriend, M. (1991), "Interest rates and the conduct of monetary policy", Carnegie–Rochester Conference Series on Public Policy 34:7–30.

Grilli, V. (1986), "Buying and selling attacks on fixed exchange rate systems", Journal of International Economics 20:143–156.

Grilli, V. (1990), "Managing exchange rate crises: Evidence from the 1890's", Journal of International Money and Finance 9:258–275.

Harrison, M. (1985), Brownian motion and stochastic flow systems (Wiley, New York).

Jørgenson, B.N. and H.O.E. Mikkelsen (1993), "An arbitrage-free trilateral target zone model", working paper, Northwestern University.

Karatzas, I. and S.E. Shreve (1988), Brownian motion and stochastic calculus (Springer-Verlag, New York).

Keynes, J.M. (1930), A treatise on money, Vol. II: The applied theory of money (Macmillan, London).

Klein, M.W. (1990), "Playing with the band: Dynamic effects of target zones in an open economy", International Economic Review 31:757–772.

Klein, M.W. and K.K. Lewis (1993), "Learning about intervention target zones", Journal of International Economics 35:275–295.

Krugman, P. (1979), "A model of balance of payments crises", Journal of Money Credit and Banking 11:311–325.

Krugman, P. (1987), "Trigger strategies and price dynamics in equity and foreign exchange markets", National Bureau of Economic Research Working Paper No. 2459.

Krugman, P. (1991), "Target zones and exchange rate dynamics", Quarterly Journal of Economics 106:669–682.

Krugman, P. and M. Miller (1991), Exchange rate targets and currency bands (Cambridge University Press, Cambridge, UK).

Krugman, P. and M. Miller (1993), "Why have a target zone?", Carnegie–Rochester Conference Series on Public Policy 38:279–314.

Krugman, P. and J. Rotemberg (1991), "Speculative attacks on target zones", in: P. Krugman and M. Miller, eds., Exchange rate targets and currency bands (Cambridge University Press, Cambridge, UK) 117–132.

Lewis, K.K. (1993), "Occasional interventions to target rates with a foreign exchange application", working paper, University of Pennsylvania.

Lindberg, H. and P. Söderlind (1994), "Testing the basic target zone model on Swedish data: 1982–1990", European Economic Review, 38:1441–1469.

Lindberg, H. and P. Söderlind (1995), "Intervention policy and mean reversion in exchange rate target zones: The Swedish case", Scandinavian Journal of Economics, 96:499–513.

Lindberg, H., P. Söderlind, and L.E.O. Svensson (199), "Devaluation expectations: The Swedish krona 1982–1991", Economic Journal 103:1170–1179.

Lohmann, S. (1992), "Optimal commitment in monetary policy: Credibility versus flexibility", American Economic Review 82:273–286.

Meese, R.A. and K. Rogoff (1983), "Empirical exchange rate models of the seventies: Do they fit out of sample?", Journal of International Economics 14:3–24.

Meese, R. A. and A. K. Rose (1990), Nonlinear, nonparameter nonessential exchange rate estimation", American Economic Review 80:192–196.

Miller, M. and A. Sutherland (1991), "Britain's return to gold and entry into the EMS: Joining conditions and credibility", in: P. Krugman and M. Miller, eds., Exchange rate targets and currency bands (Cambridge University Press, Cambridge, UK) 82–106.

Miller, M. and P. Weller (1991a), "Currency bands, target zones, and price flexibility", International Monetary Fund Staff Papers 38:184–215.

Miller, M. and P. Weller (1991b), "Exchange rate bands with price inertia", Economic Journal 101:1380–1399.

Mundaca, G.B. (1990), "Intervention decisions and exchange rate volatility in a target zone", working paper, Norges Bank.

Obstfeld, M. (1984), "Balance of payments crises and devaluation", Journal of Money, Credit and Banking 16:208–217.

Obstfeld, M. (1986a), "Rational and self-fulfilling balance of payments crises", American Economic Review 76:72–81.

Obstfeld, M. (1986b), "Speculative attack and the external constraint in a maximizing model of the balance of payments", Canadian Journal of Economics 19:1–22.

Penati, A. and G. Pennacchi (1989), "Optimal portfolio choice and the collapse of a fixed exchange rate regime", Journal of International Economics 27:1–24.

Perraudin, W.R.M. (1990), "Exchange rate bands with point process fundamentals", working paper, International Monetary Fund.

Persson, T. and G. Tabellini (1990), Macroeconomic policy, credibility and politics (Harwood, London).

Pesenti, P.A. (1990), "Perforate and imperforate currency bands: Exchange rate management and the term structure of interest rate differentials", working paper, Yale University.

Pessach, S. and A. Razin (1994), "Targeting the exchange rate under inflation", Review of International Economics 2:40–49.

Rose, A.K. and L.E.O. Svensson (1994), "European exchange rate credibility before the fall", European Economic Review 38:1185–1216.

Rose, A.K. and L.E.O. Svensson (1995), "Expected and predicted realignments: The FF/DM exchange rate during the EMS", Scandinavian Journal of Economics, 97:173–200.

Salant, S.W. and D.W. Henderson (1978), "Market anticipation of government gold policies and the price of gold", Journal of Political Economy 86:627–648.

Sargent, T. and N. Wallace (1973), "The stability of models of money and growth with perfect foresight", Econometrica 41:1043–1048.

Smith, G.W. (1991), "Solution to a problem of stochastic process switching", Econometrica 59:241–250.

Smith, G.W. and R.T. Smith (1990), "Stochastic process switching and the return to gold (1925)", Economic Journal 100:164–175.

Smith, G.W. and M.G. Spencer (1991), "Estimation and testing in models of exchange rate target zones and process switching", in: P. Krugman and M. Miller, eds., Exchange rate targets and currency bands (Cambridge University Press, Cambridge, UK) 211–239.

Sutherland, A. (1994), "Target zone models with price inertia: Solutions and testable implications", Economic Journal 104:96–112.

Svensson, L.E.O. (1991a), "The simplest test of target zone credibility", International Monetary Fund Staff Papers 38:655–665.

Svensson, L.E.O. (1991b), "Target zones and interest rate variability", Journal of International Economics 31:27–54.

Svensson, L.E.O. (1991c), "The term structure of interest rates in a target zone: Theory and Swedish data", Journal of Monetary Economics 28:87–116.

Svensson, L.E.O. (1992a), "The foreign exchange risk premium in a target zone with devaluation risk", Journal of International Economics 33:21–40.

Svensson, L.E.O. (1992b), "An interpretation of recent research on exchange rate target zones", Journal of Economic Perspectives" 6:119–144.

Svensson, L.E.O. (1993), "Assessing target zone credibility: mean reversion and devaluation expectations in the EMS 1973–1992", European Economic Review 37:763–802.

Svensson, L.E.O. (1994a), "Fixed exchange rates as a means to price stability: What have we learned?", European Economic Review 38:447–468.

Svensson, L.E.O. (1994b), "Why exchange rate bands? Monetary independence in spite of fixed exchange rates", Journal of Monetary Economics 33:157–199.

van Wijnbergen, S. (1991), "Fiscal deficits, exchange rate crises, and inflation", Review of Economic Studies 58:81–92.

Williamson, J. (1985), The exchange rate system (Institute for International Economics, Washington, DC).

Williamson, J. and M.H. Miller (1987), Targets and indicators: A blueprint for the international coordination of economic policy (Institute for International Economics, Washington, DC).

Williamson, J. (1989), "The case for roughly stabilizing the real value of the dollar", American Economic Review 79:41–45.

Willman, A. (1989), "The collapse of the fixed exchange rate regime with sticky wages and imperfect substitutability between domestic and foreign bonds", European Economic Review 32:1817–1838.

Wyplosz, C. (1986), "Capital controls and balance of payments crises", Journal of International Money and Finance 5:167–179.

Chapter 37

PUZZLES IN INTERNATIONAL FINANCIAL MARKETS

KAREN K. LEWIS*

University of Pennsylvania

Contents

*I am grateful for comments from Greg Bauer, Geert Bekaert, Charles Engel, Ken Froot, Bob Hodrick, Urban Jermann, Dick Marston, Maury Obstfeld, Ken Rogoff, Lars Svensson, Ingrid Werner, and participants at the Handbook of International Economics Conference at Princeton University. Any errors are mine alone.

Handbook of International Economics, vol. III, Edited by G. Grossman and K. Rogoff
© *Elsevier Science B.V., 1995*

0. Introduction

International financial markets have undergone tremendous growth over the last decade. During this period, foreign exchange and equity markets have attained record-breaking volumes. Furthermore, moves toward liberalizing capital markets around the world are likely to continue to fuel this growth in the future.

This growth experience has highlighted important issues concerning the function of international capital markets. At least two of these issues focus upon key ingredients of models used in the field of international macroeconomics and finance. First, an important building block to many models, including topics covered elsewhere in this book, is the assumption of uncovered interest parity. According to the Fisher (1930) interest parity condition, the expected returns in one country should be equalized through speculation to the returns in another country once converted to the same currency. Thus, the ex ante expected home currency returns on foreign deposits in excess of domestic deposits should be zero. Despite this theoretical prediction, the behavior of domestic relative to foreign returns has decisively rejected this assumption over the floating rate period.[1] This rejection clearly leads to the question: What can explain the behavior of domestic relative to foreign returns and can these explanations suggest ways in which models of the rest of the economy are either succeeding or failing?

A second issue raised by the growth in international financial trade corresponds to the decisions of domestic investors. An implicit assumption behind many economic models is that investors will take advantage of potential gains in returns and risk-sharing through integrated capital markets. At the same time, recent evidence shows that domestic investors continue to hold almost all of their wealth in domestic assets. This evidence leads to other important questions. Why do domestic investors appear to ignore potential gains to foreign investment opportunities and does the answer imply necessary modifications to our views about international capital market equilibrium?

In this chapter, I address each of these two general questions by evaluating the research surrounding them.[2] While the evidence to date has helped clarify the set of possible answers, complete explanations continue to be elusive. For this reason, the two questions could be restated as two puzzles in international finance.

The first puzzle concerns explanations for deviations from uncovered interest parity

---

[1] For early evidence of this rejection, see Cumby and Obstfeld (1981, 1984).

[2] As such, the intention of this investigation is not to comprehensively survey the literature in international finance, but to critically evaluate various explanations for these two outstanding puzzles. Comprehensive surveys on certain aspects of this chapter can be found elsewhere. In particular, Hodrick (1987) surveys the empirical methods in international finance, while Adler and Dumas (1983), Stulz (1994), and Dumas (1994) survey the literature on international portfolio choice.

or, equivalently, excess returns on foreign relative to domestic deposits. Explaining this puzzle has been made more difficult by an important observation made by Fama (1984). In a simple regression test, he showed that, not only are excess returns predictable ex ante, but the variance of these predictable returns is greater than the variance of the expected change in the exchange rate itself. Thus, theoretical models of the excess returns across countries must explain, not only their presence, but their high variation. This behavior I call the "predictable excess return puzzle".

In Section 1, I consider various explanations for the puzzle. First, under standard assumptions about rational expectations, *ex post* excess returns just equal the market's true expected excess returns plus a forecast error that is unpredictable ex ante. Under this assumption, predictable excess returns must be identically equal to the foreign exchange risk premium. I consider two standard risk premium models, one based upon a static capital-asset-pricing model (CAPM) and the other based upon a dynamic general equilibrium model. While these models can explain non-zero excess returns, they cannot explain the high degree of variation in returns. In essence, the factors that should theoretically determine the risk premium do not display sufficient variability to explain the puzzle.

I then consider explanations based upon forecast errors. Froot and Frankel (1989) have shown with survey measures of expected exchange rates that excess returns through the mid-1980s were largely driven by systematic forecast errors, not by risk premia. Explanations of this phenomenon can be broken into two groups. First, market forecasts are irrational. Second, the market is rational but the distribution of economic disturbances perceived by traders is different than the one measured by researchers. While no formal testable model of the former explanation has yet been proposed, evidence from the latter explanation provides some insights. Evans and Lewis (1995) provide evidence that systematic forecast errors can explain some of the predictable excess return puzzle. However, a substantial amount of variability in these returns remains unexplained. I conclude the section with conjectures about how this puzzle may be resolved in the future.

Section 1 also describes a related issue, central bank intervention. The presence of systematic deviations from uncovered interest parity has been used as an explanation for why central bank interventions may be able to affect the exchange rate. I summarize this argument and its relationship to the evidence on the foreign exchange risk premium.

Section 2 introduces the second puzzle called "home bias", the phenomenon that domestic investors hold too little of their portfolios in foreign assets. I consider this puzzle with the two models used to examine the foreign exchange risk premium. Both models suggest that domestic investors hold too little of their wealth in the form of foreign assets. The first type of model, based upon CAPM, implies that domestic investors should hold foreign assets in their portfolio in a fraction that depends upon their degree of risk aversion, among other variables. While plausible levels of risk aversion suggest that U.S. investors in the 1980s should have held over one half of their wealth in foreign equities, evidence suggests that they held less than 10 percent in these securities.

The second type of model, based upon complete markets, gives predictions about consumption risk-sharing. If investors have allocated their portfolios optimally, they will perfectly pool their risks and will hold the same international portfolio shares as do foreigners. As a result, consumption growth rates will be equal across countries except for measurement errors and taste shocks. Despite this prediction, the evidence implies that country-specific output risk is not diversified away.

Thus, whether from a partial or general equilibrium point of view, the "home bias" puzzle appears significant. I consider some potential explanations for this puzzle, such as the presence of non-traded goods. Even after accounting for these modifications, however, the puzzle seems to remain. I conclude by pointing to implied directions for future research.

1. The behavior of excess foreign exchange returns

The behavior of the excess return on foreign pure discount bonds relative to their domestic counterparts has been an important variable in the study of international financial markets. A higher expected return on foreign relative to domestic deposits with equivalent default risk and maturity implies that the currency composition of the deposits is significant in determining the relative returns. If so, then an important task is to understand why.

For this purpose, note that "covered interest parity (CIP)" is:[3]

$$i_t - i_t^* = f_t - s_t .$$ (1.1)

where i_t and i_t^* are the interest rates on domestic and foreign deposits, respectively, s_t is the logarithm of the domestic currency price of foreign currency at time t, and f_t is the logarithm of the forward rate, the time t domestic currency price of foreign currency delivered at time $t + 1$.

Holding a foreign deposit will give the investor the foreign interest rate return plus the capital gain on foreign currency, $i_t^* + s_{t+1} - s_t$. If the investor borrowed in dollars to obtain the funds for this investment, the excess return on foreign currency would

---

[3]With continuous compounding, the cost of borrowing in domestic currency, $\exp(i_t)$, must through arbitrage be equal to the return from taking one unit of domestic currency and buying spot $1/S_t$ units of foreign currency, where S_t is the level of the exchange rate, investing it at the rate $\exp(i_t^*)$, and selling the returns forward at F_t, the level of the forward rate. Thus, CIP says: $\exp(i_t) = \exp(i_t^*)(F_t/S_t)$. Taking the logarithm of this expression and rearranging gives eq. (1.1). Alternatively, (1.1) can be derived as a logarithmic approximation when the interest rates are not continuously compounded. Following the same logic as above, CIP says: $(1 + i_t) = (1 + i_t^*)(F_t/S_t)$. Taking the logarithm and using the approximation that $\log(1 + i_t) \approx i_t$ gives eq. (1.1).

be:

$$er_{t+1} \equiv i_t^* + s_{t+1} - s_t - i_t . \tag{1.2}$$

Substituting covered interest parity (1.1) into (1.2) gives:

$$er_{t+1} \equiv s_{t+1} - f_t . \tag{1.3}$$

Both forms of excess returns will be used below.

Since the excess return is not known at the time of taking out the contract, t, analyzing any behavioral aspects of these returns depends upon measures of expected excess returns. One such measure is the statistically predicted value of the excess return based upon time t information:

$$per_t \equiv E_t(er_{t+1}) = E_t \Delta s_{t+1} - (f_t - s_t), \tag{1.4}$$

where $E_t(\cdot)$ is the statistical expectations operator conditional on time t information. Thus,

$$er_{t+1} = per_t + \varepsilon_{t+1}, \tag{1.5}$$

where the last term is the statistical forecast error, $\varepsilon_{t+1} \equiv s_{t+1} - E_t s_{t+1}$.

1.1. Some empirical regularities

Much of the early research on excess returns asked whether the predictable component of these returns were equal to zero. Under the assumption that the market forms expectations by linear statistical prediction, then predicted excess returns will equal zero if uncovered interest parity holds. To see why, note that uncovered interest parity says:[4]

$$i_t - i_t^* = E_t^m s_{t+1} - s_t \tag{1.6}$$

where $E_t^m(\cdot)$ is the market's expectation conditional upon current information. Note that this expectation is not necessarily the statistical expectation, $E_t(\cdot)$. Below I will discuss some of the literature in which the market's expectation does not equal the statistical expectation conditional upon current information, so that $E_t(\cdot) \neq E_t^m(\cdot)$.

Thus, uncovered interest parity in (1.6) says that the returns on a unit of domestic currency invested in a domestic deposit equals the expected returns from converting the domestic currency into the foreign currency, investing it in a foreign deposit and then converting the proceeds back into domestic currency at the future realized exchange rate. If uncovered interest parity holds and furthermore the market's

---

[4]This expression can be derived in logarithmic form following similar steps to the covered interest parity condition in footnote 3.

expectation equals the statistical prediction of the exchange rate, then predictable excess returns must be equal to 0, since in this case, $per_t \equiv i_t^* + E_t^m s_{t+1} - s_t - i_t = 0$.

Figure 1.1 plots estimates of the predictable excess annualized monthly returns for the dollar/DM and dollar/yen rate from the beginning of 1975 to the end of 1989.[5] The figure graphs the predicted excess returns given current information as measured by the forward premium. These predicted returns are the actual returns regressed upon the forward premium, $f_t - s_t$, according to the linear projection equation given in Panel A of Table 1.1:[6,7]

$$er_{t+1} = b_0 + b_1(f_t - s_t) + u_{t+1}. \tag{1.7}$$

The dashed lines represent the two standard error confidence bands around the predicted values.

Three features of the predicted returns stand out from this analysis. First, the predicted returns are significantly different from zero over some periods in the sample. Second, the returns change sign during the sample. The predictable excess returns on holding DM or yen deposits was significantly negative during part of the early 1980s and was significantly positive in the late 1980s. Therefore, explanations of excess foreign bond returns must explain not only why these returns are not zero, but also why they are sometimes negative and at other times positive. Third, the predictable returns display considerable variability. The DM returns range from 20 percent to -30 percent per annum, while the yen returns vary from over 32 percent to -30 percent.

This last feature of predictable returns is the most difficult to reconcile with standard models. Fama (1984) emphasized it dramatically with the decomposition described next.

1.1.1. The Fama result

Fama (1984) illustrated the degree of predictable excess return variability using a simple regression test. This simple test has produced a challenge for researchers in international finance. I will therefore use this basic result as a benchmark for

---

[5]These data are from Citibase and were kindly provided by Geert Bekaert. In constructing the spot and forward rates, I took the average of the bid and ask rates. While averaging in this way introduces measurement error, Bekaert and Hodrick (1993) find that the biases introduced by the measurement error are small.

[6]Bilson (1981) estimated this regression and found that uncovered interest parity does not hold. A subsequent literature has verified this finding over other sample periods and currencies.

[7]In principle, this regression could be run on any variables that help explain excess returns. A number of authors have found that these returns can be explained by lagged excess returns [Hansen and Hodrick (1983)], lagged stock returns [Giovannini and Jorion (1987a)], the spread between long and short interest rates in different currencies [Campbell and Clarida (1987)], and industrial production [Cumby (1988)], to name a few. This regression was run for parsimony and because it relates to the Fama (1984) regression described below.

A. DM Returns

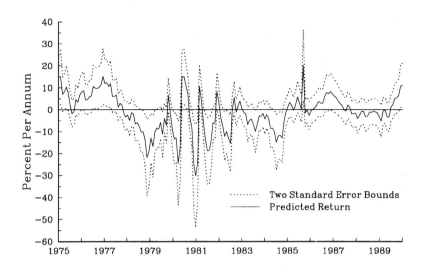

B. Yen Returns

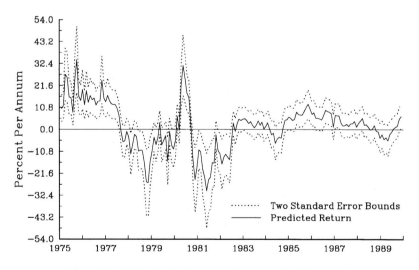

Figure 1.1. Predictable foreign returns in excess of dollar returns.

Table 1.1
The Fama regression and the foreign excess return puzzle

A. The Fama regression: full sample

$$\Delta s_{t+1} = \beta_0 + \beta_1 (f_t - s_t) + u_{t+1}$$

Exchange Rate	β_0 (St. Err)	β_1 (St. Err)	MSL Ho: $\beta_1 = 1/2$	MSL Ho: $\beta_1 = 1$
$/DM	−13.70** (5.81)	−3.33** (1.60)	.004	.009
$/£	7.95** (3.48)	−2.31** (0.79)	<.001	<.001
$/¥	−12.87** (3.61)	−2.28** (0.83)	<.001	<.001

B. Summary statistics

Exchange Rate	Mean$(s_{t+1} - f_t)$ (St. Dev$(s_{t+1} - f_t)$)	Var$(f_t - s_t)$	Var$(E_t \Delta s_{t+1})$	Var(per_{t+1})
$/DM	1.4 (41.3)	4.1	44.9	75.9
$/£	0.1 (41.9)	11.3	60.0	123.4
$/£	−1.6 (40.8)	12.0	62.3	128.9

C. Fama regression: Subsamples

Exchange Rate	1975–79 β_1 (St. Err) (MSL: $\beta_1 = 1/2$)	1980–84 β_1 (St. Err.) (MSL: $\beta_1 = 1/2$)	1984–89 β_1 (St. Err) (MSL: $\beta_1 = 1/2$)
$/DM	1.06 (2.67) (.58)	−1.32 (2.34) (.22)	−12.05** (4.13) (.10)
$/£	0.92 (1.50) (.61)	−2.91** (1.10) (.001)	−9.70* (4.90) (.02)
$/¥	−1.33 (1.14) (.06)	−2.07 (1.51) (.05)	−11.39** (3.76) (.001)

Notes: β_1 is the estimates of the regression of the exchange rate change on the forward premium. Exchange rate changes are annualized monthly rates.
* indicates significantly different than zero at the 10 percent marginal significance level.
** indicates significantly different than zero at the 5 percent marginal significance level.

discussing various theoretical explanations for the behavior of predictable returns below.[8]

The test regresses the change in the exchange rate on the forward premium:

$$\Delta s_{t+1} = \beta_0 + \beta_1(f_t - s_t) + u_{t+1}, \tag{1.8}$$

where Δ is the backward difference operator and u_{t+1} is an error term. Note that this regression is equivalent to eq. (1.7) where $\beta_1 = 1 + b_1$ and $\beta_0 = b_0$. If predictable excess returns are zero, then $E_t s_{t+1} = f_t$ and $\beta_1 = 1$ or, equivalently, $b_1 = 0$ in (1.7).

Table 1.1, Panel A shows the results of this regression using the dollar exchange rates against the DM, British pound and Japanese yen over the period from 1975 to 1989. As the table shows, the estimate of β_1 are all significantly less than one. In fact, they are even significantly negative! This result is typical of many other studies examining the same relationship.[9]

When $\beta_1 < \frac{1}{2}$, this coefficient can convey information about the variability in the expected change in the exchange rate relative to the predictable component of excess returns.[10] To see why, note that the probability limit of the OLS coefficient β_1 is:

$$\begin{aligned}
\beta_1 &= \mathrm{Cov}(\Delta s_{t+1}, f_t - s_t)/\mathrm{Var}(f_t - s_t) \\
&= [\mathrm{Cov}(E_t \Delta s_{t+1}, f_t - s_t) + \mathrm{Cov}(\varepsilon_{t+1}, f_t - s_t)]/\mathrm{Var}(f_t - s_t) \\
&= \mathrm{Cov}(E_t \Delta s_{t+1}, f_t - s_t)/\mathrm{Var}(f_t - s_t),
\end{aligned} \tag{1.9}$$

where the last equality follows because $\mathrm{Cov}(\varepsilon_{t+1}, f_t - s_t) = 0$ by construction.

In this case, a finding of $\beta_1 < \frac{1}{2}$ as in Table 1.1 implies that the variance of the predictable component of excess returns exceeds the variance of the linear prediction of the exchange rate change. In other words,

$$\mathrm{Var}(per_t) > \mathrm{Var}(E_t(\Delta s_{t+1})). \tag{1.10}$$

To see why, note that the variance of (1.4) can be written:

$$\mathrm{Var}(per_t) = \mathrm{Var}(E_t \Delta s_{t+1}) - 2\,\mathrm{Cov}(f_t - s_t, E_t \Delta s_{t+1}) + \mathrm{Var}(f_t - s_t). \tag{1.11}$$

Substituting (1.11) and then (1.9) for the left-hand side of (1.10) implies that the

---

[8]This regression test is only one of many tests that have been applied to excess foreign currency returns as described in Hodrick (1987). I emphasize the Fama result only as a useful discussion point for later analysis.

[9]This result is less apparent for some of the cross exchange rates within the European Monetary System. For example, Bossaerts and Hillion (1991) find positive estimates of β_1 for most currencies against the French franc. On the other hand, Bekaert and Hodrick (1993) have examined the same relationship using other non-dollar cross rates and found similar relationships to those against the dollar, as in Table 1.1.

[10]The following discussion modifies the Fama (1984) result more generally to describe predictable excess returns without making any assumption about expectations. Later, I will discuss the relationship actually described by Fama concerning the variance of the foreign exchange risk premium.

inequality will hold if:

$$\text{Cov}(f_t - s_t, E_t \Delta s_{t+1}) / \text{Var}(f_t - s_t) = \beta_1 < \tfrac{1}{2} . \tag{1.12}$$

This relationship can also be seen using the estimates in Table 1.1. As shown in Panel B, the standard deviations of predicted excess returns are roughly twice the corresponding standard deviations of the predicted values from regressions of the change in the exchange rate on the forward premium.

Therefore, the striking conclusion from Table 1.1 is that, not only are excess returns non-zero and predictable given current information, their variance is quite large relative to expected exchange rate changes.

1.1.2. Potential explanations

What explains these results? This is an important issue that has been the focus of a great deal of research over the past decade. Generally, the explanations can be classified into two groups: (a) the foreign exchange risk premium, or (b) expectational errors. To see how explanations fall into these two groups, it is useful to decompose the Fama regression coefficient further.

For this purpose, define the risk premium on the position with the return in (1.3) as:

$$rp_t \equiv E_t^m s_{t+1} - f_t = E_t^m \Delta s_{t+1} - (f_t - s_t) \tag{1.13}$$

Equation (1.13) says that the market's expected return for holding foreign deposits is an equilibrium premium paid for taking more risk. The market's forecast error is:

$$\Delta s_{t+1} - E_t^m \Delta s_{t+1} = \eta_{t+1} . \tag{1.14}$$

Thus, the excess return can be written as:

$$er_{t+1} = rp_t + \eta_{t+1} . \tag{1.15}$$

Consider first the notion that the behavior of predictable returns found above was due to the risk premium, the interpretation given by Fama (1984). According to this view, expectations are rational and the statistical distribution of the economy is known to the market. In this case, $\varepsilon_{t+1} = \eta_{t+1}$ so that the predictable part of excess returns, per_t, is just equal to the risk premium, rp_t. The evidence in Table 1.1 then implies that the variance of the risk premium exceeds the variance of the market's expectations of exchange rate changes.

Consider next the opposite extreme. Suppose that the risk premium were constant and equal to rp_0 so that $er_{t+1} = rp_0 + \eta_{t+1}$. In this case, the high variation in predictable excess returns found in Table 1.1 must arise from variation in the component of the forecast error that is correlated with lagged information.

Of course, time-varying risk premia and systematic forecast errors are not mutually exclusive and the behavior of predictable excess returns could result from a combination of these two factors.

Below, I will describe explanations for the behavior of excess returns based upon these two broad classifications. First, the predicted returns may be the outcome of an equilibrium process. According to this explanation, the returns were positive to investors with an open position in non-dollar bonds during the late 1980s and negative during the early 1980s because the market as a whole was compensating investors for taking this position. Under this explanation, the predictable returns are a "foreign exchange risk premium".

Second, the predicted returns may result from systematic forecast errors. These systematic forecast errors could arise from two different types of sources. One source is the presence of some irrational traders in the market. For example, traders buying yen forward during the late 1980s may not have used all information efficiently, and expected to make profits even though they were systematically wrong.

A second source of systematic forecast errors arises from difficulties in measuring expectations of predictable returns. According to this explanation, the regression equations used to measure expectations as in Figure 1.1 may not accurately reflect the market's expectation of returns. For example, traders buying yen forward in the late 1980s may have placed some probability on the likelihood that the dollar would rebound significantly. This event would introduce a so-called "peso problem" in measuring the expected returns in the standard ways described above. I discuss each of these explanations below.

1.2. The foreign exchange risk premium

One explanation for predictable excess returns is that domestic investors who are willing to hold foreign bonds and then convert the returns back into domestic currency at the future prevailing exchange rate must be compensated for the foreign exchange risk. According to this explanation, expectations are rational so that $E_t = E_t^m$ always. Since this assumption applies to all of the risk premium models, I will simply write the market's expectations in this section as E_t.

Why might non-zero predictable excess returns be the result of an equilibrium process? I will describe two types of risk premium models. The first set of models is static in nature and treats the processes followed by exchange rates, interest rates, and inflation rates as exogenous. As such, the models in this group are partial equilibrium.

The second set of models I will present below focuses upon intertemporal investment decisions and also allows the exchange rate, interest rate, and inflation processes to emerge endogenously from underlying technology and monetary processes. According to these models, the foreign exchange risk premium is determined together with the other variables.

In the context of these models, a useful way to summarize the variability puzzle in excess returns found above is the Hansen and Jaganathan (1991) bound. This measure gives a lower bound to the risk premium implied by financial returns in general. Estimates of these lower bounds are quite difficult to reconcile with implied risk premia from the theoretical models, as will be demonstrated below.[11]

1.2.1. The risk premium based upon partial equilibrium CAPM

The first efforts toward understanding the foreign exchange risk premium followed as natural extensions of the static version of the "capital asset pricing model".[12] The international version of the model involves all wealth including equity.[13] However, to focus upon the foreign exchange risk premium as well as the implications for central bank intervention, I will delay incorporating equity into the analysis until Section 2.

I begin with the simplest version of this model. I treat this model in discrete time and use logarithmic approximations. While this simplification greatly streamlines the analysis, it ignores a potentially important component to the risk premium arising from Jensen's Inequality. I will return to introduce this component following the basic analysis below.

Suppose there are two representative agents in each of two countries. They each want to maximize end-of-period wealth. If real wealth for the home investor at the end of time t is defined as W_t, then his real wealth in the next period is defined as:

$$W_{t+1} = W_t(1 + r_{p,t+1}), \quad W^*_{t+1} = W^*_t(1 + r^*_{p,t+1}) \tag{1.16}$$

where $r_{p,t+1}$ is the real return on the home portfolio from t to $t+1$. To consider this portfolio return more carefully, suppose that the home and foreign investors can hold only a home and a foreign asset. I will first describe the portfolio decision on the part of the home investor. The portfolio decision for the foreign investor is completely symmetric.

The real return on the home portfolio is:

$$r_{p,t+1} = x_t r^*_{t+1} + (1 - x_t)r_{t+1} \tag{1.17}$$

where x_t is the share of W_t held in the foreign asset, r^*_{t+1} is the return on the foreign asset and r_{t+1} is the return on the domestic asset both realized at $t+1$.

To write these real returns in terms of observables, their nominal returns in each

---

[11]The puzzle posed by the high variability of the estimated H–J bounds implied by foreign exchange returns relative to theoretical models is similar to that posed by other markets such as equity returns. However, the degree of risk aversion required to reconcile theory with the empirical bounds appears to be exceptionally high for foreign exchange returns.

[12]See Sharpe (1964), Lintner (1965), and Mossin (1966).

[13]See the development of this model in Solnik (1974a).

currency are deflated by exchange rate and price level changes:

$$1 + r_{t+1}^* \equiv (1 + i_t^*)(S_{t+1} P_t / S_t P_{t+1}) \approx 1 + i_t^* + \Delta s_{t+1} - \pi_{t+1},$$
$$1 + r_{t+1} \equiv (1 + i_t)(P_t / P_{t+1}) \approx 1 + i_t - \pi_{t+1}, \qquad (1.18)$$

where P_t is the domestic price level at time t, i_t and i_t^* are the nominal returns on assets held from time t to $t+1$. For simplicity, this real return is approximated using the nominal rates less the domestic inflation rate defined as π_{t+1}. It is therefore convenient to rewrite the real return on the portfolio in terms of the nominal return:

$$i_{p,t+1} \equiv x_t(i_t^* + \Delta s_{t+1}) + (1 - x_t)i_t \qquad (1.19)$$

so that $r_{p,t+1} = i_{p,t+1} - \pi_{t+1}$.

As with the domestic CAPM, the investor is assumed to choose x_t to maximize an objective function that is increasing in the mean but decreasing in the variance of end-of-period wealth, denoted $\mathrm{Var}_t(W_{t+1})$, where Var_t is the variance conditional upon information known at time t. Thus, the objective function is:

$$V = V(E_t(W_{t+1}), \mathrm{Var}_t(W_{t+1})), \quad V_1 > 0, V_2 < 0. \qquad (1.20)$$

Solving the model requires calculating the mean and variance of wealth in terms of the observables. The conditional mean and variance can be rewritten by substituting (1.18) into (1.17).

$$E_t W_{t+1} = W_t + W_t E_t(x_t er_{t+1} + r_{t+1})$$
$$\mathrm{Var}_t W_{t+1} = W_t^2 \, \mathrm{Var}_t(x_t er_{t+1} + r_{t+1}). \qquad (1.21)$$

Deriving the first-order conditions of (1.20) with respect to x_t, substituting (1.21) into the result and defining the measure of relative risk aversion as $\rho \equiv -2V_2 W_t / V_1$ where V_i are the partial derivatives of V with respect to the ith argument, gives:[14]

$$per_{t+1} = \rho \, \mathrm{Cov}_t(er_{t+1}, i_{p,t+1}) - \rho \, \mathrm{Cov}_t(er_{t+1}, \pi_{t+1}). \qquad (1.22)$$

This first-order condition is the basic CAPM relationship that holds if the home investor were (counterfactually) to comprise the entire market.

Adler and Dumas (1983) describe the intuition behind this model. The more risk averse are investors, the greater their aversion to variance and the higher is ρ. Furthermore, as (1.22) shows, given the price of risk, the expected excess return increases with the covariance between the excess return and the nominal return on wealth, $i_{p,t+1}$. If the excess return has a high covariance with the overall portfolio, the

---

[14]This measure of relative risk aversion is approximately the Arrow–Pratt measure: $-U''W/U'$, where $U(W)$ is the utility function. Taking a Taylor-series expansion of $E(U(W))$ and differentiating with respect to $E(W)$ and $\mathrm{Var}(W)$ shows that ρ as defined in the text is the same as the Arrow–Pratt measure.

predictable excess return must be correspondingly high to compensate the investor for risk.

The last term reflects the degree to which the foreign asset provides a hedge against inflation. Since the value of wealth falls with inflation, a higher covariance of returns with inflation increases the hedging properties of the foreign asset. Therefore, the required excess return decreases with this term.

This basic equation underlies the choice of equity as well as deposits across countries, as I will return to discuss more fully in Section 2. However, since I am focusing upon the foreign exchange risk premium in this section, I will now use the fact that the domestic and foreign assets are risk-free bonds in their respective currencies. Also, in order for aggregate outside bonds to be considered net wealth, Ricardian equivalence must not hold. In this case, the conditional covariance between excess returns arises solely from the conditional covariance between exchange rates.[15] Therefore, eq. (1.22) can be written as:

$$per_{t+1} = \rho x_t \, \text{Var}_t(\Delta s_{t+1}) - \rho \, \text{Cov}_t(\Delta s_{t+1}, \pi_{t+1}) . \tag{1.23}$$

Thus, the first-order conditions depend only upon the variability of exchange rates and inflation.

Determining (1.23) as a world market equilibrium requires solving the problem from the foreign investor's point of view and summing demand functions across domestic and foreign residents. Following the same steps as above for the foreign investor implies the equilibrium relationship,[16]

$$
\begin{aligned}
per_{t+1} = \rho[x_t w_t - (1 - x_t^*)w_t^*] \, \text{Var}_t(\Delta s) \\
- \rho[w_t \, \text{Cov}_t(\Delta s_{t+1}, \pi_{t+1}) + w_t^* \, \text{Cov}_t(\Delta s_{t+1}, \pi_{t+1}^f)]
\end{aligned}
\tag{1.24}
$$

where x_t^* is the share of foreigner's wealth that they hold in their own assets, where ρ^f is the foreign inflation rate, and where w_t and w_t^* are the shares of the world wealth held by home and foreign residents, respectively, so that $w_t + w_t^* = 1$.

Equation (1.24) has an intuitive interpretation. Suppose first that inflation were perfectly forecastable. In this case, the covariance terms are zero and the sign of the risk premium would depend upon the difference between $x_t w_t$ and $(1 - x_t^*)w_t^*$, or the difference between domestic holdings of foreign bonds and foreign holdings of domestic bonds. When domestic residents are net creditors so that $x_t w_t > (1 - x_t^*)w_t^*$, then the overall effect on the risk premium is to compensate domestic investors for

[15]Using the definition of er and i_p in (1.19), $\text{Cov}(er_{t+1}, i_{p,t+1}) = \text{Var}(\Delta s_{t+1})x_t$ and $\text{Cov}(er_{t+1}, \pi_{t+1}) = \text{Cov}(\Delta s_{t+1}, \pi_{t+1})$.

[16]Following these steps, the first-order conditions for the foreign investor is: $per_{t+1} = \rho x_t^* \, \text{Var}(\Delta s_{t+1}) + \rho \, \text{Cov}(er_{t+1}, \pi_{t+1}^*)$ where π_{t+1}^* is the foreign inflation measured in terms of the domestic currency. Solving this condition with respect to x^*, summing demand equations $x_t W_t + x_t^* W_t^*$, and setting the aggregated demand equal to the given supply of foreign bonds, the equilibrium expected excess return can be written as in eq. (1.24).

net holdings of foreign deposits. Next, consider the effects of uncertain inflation. In this case, holdings of deposits in the other country can provide a hedge against inflation depending upon the covariance between own inflation and the exchange rate.

Equation (1.24) examines only two risk-free bonds and two investors in order to demonstrate the intuition simply. More generally, the portfolio should include all possible assets available to the investor. Similarly, the inflation hedges should be aggregated over all countries in the world. Adler and Dumas (1983) show how this model generalizes allowing for many countries. In this case, the exchange rate variance in (1.24) becomes a variance-covariance matrix across currencies, and the inflation hedge component depends upon the covariance matrix of exchange rates and inflation rates across countries.

1.2.1.1. The Jensen's inequality term

In continuous time, the predictable excess returns also depend upon a term arising from Jensen's inequality.[17] Instead of eq. (1.22), the expression for predictable excess returns is:

$$per_t = \rho \, \text{Cov}_t(er_{t+1}, i_{p,t+1}) + (1 - \rho) \, \text{Cov}_t(er_{t+1}, \pi_{t+1}). \qquad (1.25)$$

The presence of this term implies that (1.23) becomes:

$$per_t = \rho x_t \, \text{Var}_t(\Delta s_{t+1}) + (1 - \rho) \, \text{Cov}_t(\Delta s_{t+1}, \pi_{t+1}). \qquad (1.26)$$

Thus, even when expectations are rational and investors are risk neutral so that $\rho = 0$, predictable excess returns are non-zero and equal to $\text{Cov}_t(\Delta s_{t+1}, \pi_{t+1})$. For this reason, Frenkel and Razin (1980) and Engel (1984) pointed out that due to this Jensen's inequality term, predictable excess returns are not zero even when investors are risk averse and expectations are statistically unbiased. Since predictable excess returns are not zero even in the absence of risk aversion, it may be argued that these returns should not be called a "risk premium".

How important is this Jensen's inequality term? Clearly this depends upon the importance of the covariance between the exchange rate and inflation. Empirically, the covariance between exchange rates and inflation is quite small and near zero as will be shown in Section 2. In fact, a number of authors including Engel (1984) and Cumby (1988) have found that the behavior of excess returns measured in real terms and in nominal terms do not behave very differently. Therefore, it seems unlikely that this term can help explain an important fraction of excess return behavior.

1.2.1.2. Empirical evidence: What is wrong with the model?

A number of authors have examined the implied behavior of the foreign exchange risk premium based upon the model above. The general finding is that estimates of

---

[17]See the derivation in Adler and Dumas (1983), for example.

the parameter of risk aversion are large but insignificantly different than zero and that the restrictions of the model are rejected.[18]

Why doesn't this model seem to explain the foreign exchange risk premium? Recall the results found in the Fama regression in Table 1.1 and consider them in light of eq. (1.24). The Fama result implies that the model must explain a very high degree of variability in the risk premium, with a standard deviation of between 9 and 11 percent for the dollar against the DM, pound, and yen. Equation (1.24) shows that this variability must come from either the asset shares across countries, the wealth shares, or the conditional variances and covariances.

However, the standard deviation of measures of outside bonds and relative wealth positions, as measured by current account changes, is only about 1 to 3 percent per annum.[19] As for volatility arising from movements in conditional variances, Engel and Rodrigues (1989) found that the largest period of variation in conditional variances was in 1979. During this period, conditional variances moved over a range of about .3 percent per annum, with these ranges much lower over other periods.[20] Overall, these variables do not exhibit sufficient variation to be able to explain the variance in predictable returns.

Recall also that predictable excess returns change sign frequently, even over short periods, as depicted in Figure 1.1. However, the model predicts that these changes in sign will take place only when countries change from net debtor to creditor positions or when conditional variances change sufficiently. The infrequent shifts between net debtor to creditor positions and the lack of variability in conditional variances suggest that this model cannot explain the changes in sign in predictable returns either.

From a theoretical point of view, this model suffers from other problems as well. First, the optimization problem faced by the representative investor is a static one. Second, the model is partial equilibrium in nature. The exchange rate and interest rate processes are exogenous to the model so these variables cannot depend jointly upon the risk premium. These issues are directly addressed in the general equilibrium framework described next.

1.2.2. The risk premium in general equilibrium

1.2.2.1. A stylized model
Given the theoretical difficulties with the static CAPM risk premium model, much of the subsequent analysis of the foreign exchange risk premium has been developed

---

[18]Frankel (1982) used a version of this model to estimate the measure of risk aversion assuming purchasing power parity and constant variances of returns. Lewis (1988b) relaxed the assumption of purchasing power parity by estimating the model using direct measures of the covariance between inflation and exchange rates. Engel and Rodrigues (1989) allowed variances to be time-varying. Despite these and other refinements in the literature, the model is typically rejected.

[19]These variances were measured using historical data on outside bonds as constructed in Lewis (1988a).

[20]On the plausibility of the conditional variance explaining the risk premium, see the discussion among Frankel (1986), Pagan (1986), and Giovannini and Jorion (1987a,b).

using general equilibrium pricing conditions. Basic relationships among asset pricing variables were motivated by the two-country complete markets model of Lucas (1982). Although this model is too stylized to explain the empirical behavior of the exchange rate itself, the intuition from this model has motivated various tests of relationships that are more general than this model. For this reason, I will review the model briefly before considering these general relationships.

In the Lucas model, there are representative agents with identical preferences in each of two countries. They seek to maximize the expected infinite life-time utility function:

$$E_0\left\{\sum_{t=0}^{\infty} \beta^t U(C_t^i, C_t^{*i})\right\} \tag{1.27}$$

for residents of country i where C_t^i and C_t^{*i} are the domestic and foreign produced goods, respectively, consumed by the resident of country i at time t.

Consumers in each country can buy goods produced in the other country. To keep the production side of the economy simple, suppose that goods are produced exogenously with outputs each period defined as the vector: $\psi_t = (Y_t, Y_t^*)$. Every period, the home consumer receives the output of the home good, Y_t, and endowments of money, M_t, while the foreign consumer receives the current output of the foreign good, Y_t^*, as well as foreign money, M_t^*. To buy goods, however, each consumer must buy the domestic good with domestic money at price $P_{y,t}$, and the foreign good with the foreign money at price $P_{y*,t}$. This restriction and the assumption that consumers know their current endowments before buying goods imply a cash-in-advance constraint,

$$P_{y,t} = M_t/2Y_t \quad \text{and} \quad P_{y*,t} = M_t^*/2Y_t^* . \tag{1.28}$$

As Lucas (1978) has shown, it is possible to price any asset from a basic general equilibrium model with complete markets. Hodrick and Srivastava (1986), Domowitz and Hakkio (1985), and Engel (1992a) examine the implications of the foreign exchange risk premium in this model.[21] To find the risk premium, recall that: $rp_t \equiv s_{t+1} - f_t \approx (E_t(S_{t+1}) - F_t)/S_t$, where $F_t = \exp(f_t)$ and $S_t = \exp(s_t)$. Therefore, solving for the risk premium requires solving for the spot and forward exchange rates.

To solve for the spot exchange rate, notice first that the relative price of good Y^* in terms of good Y, defined as p, is given by:

$$p_t = U_{c*}(\psi_t)/U_c(\psi_t), \tag{1.29}$$

where U_c and U_{c*} are the marginal utilities with respect to C and C^*, respectively.

---

[21]Engel (1992a) shows how the risk premium in this model requires dependence between monetary and real disturbances. He shows that the assumption of monetary and real independence in the applications by Hodrick and Srivastava (1986) and Domowitz and Hakkio (1985) imply that the risk premium would be zero.

According to the law of one price, the nominal exchange rate and this relative price are related according to:

$$p_t = S_t P_{y*,t}/P_{y,t} \,. \tag{1.30}$$

Using eqs. (1.28), (1.29), and (1.30), the nominal exchange rate can alternatively be rewritten:

$$S_t = p_t P_{y,t}/P_{y*,t} = [U_{c*}(\psi_t)/U_c(\psi_t)]P_{y,t}/P_{y*,t}$$
$$= [U_{c*}(\psi_t)/U_c(\psi_t)][M_t Y_t^*/M_t^* Y_t] \,. \tag{1.31}$$

The nominal exchange rate is the contemporaneous marginal rate of substitution in utility between holdings of domestic money M and foreign money $M*$.[22] Using this specification of the spot exchange rate together with covered interest parity, the model can be solved for the forward rate, and thus the risk premium, as will be shown below in general settings.

As eq. (1.31) shows, the Lucas model allows an exact calculation of the determinants of the spot exchange rate by defining the components of the nominal marginal rates of substitution in consumption in each country. However, the basic intuition obtained from the first-order conditions of this model holds in much more general settings described next.

1.2.2.2. First-order conditions and the risk premium

Consider now the foreign exchange risk premium in a more general setting in which the investor maximizes utility by choosing consumption and investments over time with a utility function such as in (1.27). The relationship between spot and forward rates is determined by domestic and foreign interest rates through covered interest parity. The price of a deposit paying one unit of each currency at time $t + 1$ is given by:

$$1/R_{t+1}^{rf} = E_t\{\beta U_c(\psi_{t+1})P_{y,t}/U_c(\psi_t)P_{y,t+1}\} \equiv E_t(Q_{t+1})$$
$$1/R_{t+1}^{rf*} = E_t\{\beta U_{c*}(\psi_{t+1})P_{y*,t}/U_{c*}(\psi_t)P_{y*,t+1}\} \equiv E_t(Q_{t+1}^*) \tag{1.32}$$

where R_{t+1}^{rf} and R_{t+1}^{rf*} are the nominal interest rates on a risk-free deposit paying one unit of M and $M*$, respectively, in period $t + 1$.[23] Q_{t+1} is defined as the intertemporal marginal rate of substitution of one unit of domestic currency between period t and

---

[22]This model implies that the exchange rate depends only upon contemporaneous variables, and is therefore not forward-looking. Svensson (1985a,b) assumes a different timing to the cash-in-advance constraint which implies a precautionary motive for holding money, making the exchange rate depend upon expected future values. Engel (1992b) derives the risk premium implications of this model. Bekaert (1992) introduces a transactions technology for money holdings and provides a richer production economy.

[23]These rates are related to the earlier definition of interest rates according to: $R_{t+1}^{rf} \equiv (1 + i_t)$ and $R_{t+1}^{rf*} \equiv (1 + i_t^*)$.

period $t + 1$, while Q^*_{t+1} is the counterpart in foreign currency. Below, I will call Q_{t+1} and Q^*_{t+1}, respectively, the domestic and foreign nominal intertemporal rates of substitution.

The relationship in eq. (1.32) holds for any economy in which no arbitrage opportunities are present.[24] As described by Telmer (1993), this relationship also holds in settings where investors cannot fully insure all possible states of the world because markets are incomplete.

The spot exchange rate is simply the contemporaneous ratio of nominal rates of substitution in consumption. Therefore, using the definitions for Q and Q^*, the ratio of future to current exchange rates can be written:

$$(S_{t+1}/S_t) = (Q^*_{t+1}/Q_{t+1}) \, . \tag{1.33}$$

Equation (1.29) from the Lucas model provides a specific example of this general relationship.

Covered interest parity and (1.32) imply:

$$F_t = S_t R^{rf}_{t+1}/R^{rf*}_{t+1} = S_t E_t(Q^*_{t+1})/E_t(Q_{t+1}) \, . \tag{1.34}$$

Note that the relationship between the forward rate and spot rate in (1.34) is quite general. To solve for the forward rate using the specific form of the Lucas model requires only substituting the solution for the spot rate in (1.31).

These relationships may now be stated in the form of the Fama result. Recall that Table 1.1 showed that $\text{Var}(rp_t)$ is greater than $\text{Var}(E_t \Delta s_{t+1})$, where $rp_t \equiv E_t s_{t+1} - f_t \approx (E_t S_{t+1} - F_t)/S_t$ and $E_t \Delta s_{t+1} \approx (E_t S_{t+1} - S_t)/S_t$. Using the expressions for the spot rate in (1.33) and the forward rate in (1.34), the Fama result says that: $\text{Var}(rp_t) > \text{Var}(E_t \Delta s_{t+1})$ or that,

$$\text{Var}\{E_t(Q^*_{t+1}/Q_{t+1}) - [E_t(Q^*_{t+1})/E_t(Q_{t+1})]\} > \text{Var}\{E_t(Q^*_{t+1}/Q_{t+1})\} \, . \tag{1.35}$$

In other words, the risk premium is the difference between the ratio of expected marginal rates of substitution in consumption and the expectation of this ratio. The variance of this difference exceeds the variance of the expected ratio of marginal rates of substitution alone.

The generality of the intertemporal relationships between the marginal rates of substitution and the interest rates in (1.32) suggests that testing these relationships are natural first steps.[25] Mark (1985) tests the intertemporal restrictions with consumption for a consumer with constant relative risk aversion utility. He estimates the parameter of risk aversion to be quite large, generally in a range of 12 to 50 for most sets of instrumental variables. As suggested by the large variability of the predictable excess

---

[24]The generality of this relationship has stimulated a large literature on consumption smoothing behavior. See for example Hall (1978) and papers in the survey in Hall (1989).

[25]Indeed, the relationships are so general that they must hold for domestic assets, as well as foreign currency returns as will be described in more detail below.

returns, large amounts of risk aversion are required to reconcile the variability of the predictable returns to the risk premium model. While Mark finds that the over-identifying restrictions of the model are not rejected for some instruments, the relative risk aversion parameter is estimated quite imprecisely, so that the hypothesis that the parameter of risk aversion is zero cannot be rejected.

Such parametric tests are useful for understanding how particular utility functions must behave to produce the behavior of excess returns given by the data. However, to relax the assumption of particular utility functions, more general tests have been developed to investigate the relationship across all asset returns. Below, I describe two types of these general tests: latent variable models and Hansen–Jaganathan bounds.

1.2.2.3. Latent variable model

The latent variable test was pioneered in foreign exchange studies by Hansen and Hodrick (1983) and was developed independently for application in a standard CAPM environment by Gibbons and Ferson (1985).

To understand the basic intuition behind this test, note that the first order condition of intertemporal maximization underlying (1.32) implies that the following relation-ship holds:[26]

$$E_t(Q_{t+1}R^j_{t+1}) = 1 \quad \forall j . \tag{1.36}$$

As before, Q_{t+1} is the intertemporal marginal rate of substitution in consumption and R^j_{t+1} is the gross rate of return on any asset j realized at time $t + 1$. For now, I will treat consumption as a single domestic good, C, although this framework could be modified to include a composite good.[27] Since relation (1.36) holds for any asset with return j, it also holds for the risk-free rate.

$$E_t\{Q_{t+1}(R^j_{t+1} - R^{rf}_{t+1})\} = E_t\{Q_{t+1}er^j_{t+1}\} = 0 \tag{1.37}$$

where $er^j_{t+1} \equiv R^j_{t+1} - R^{rf}_{t+1}$ is the excess return on asset j over the risk free rate. Since the conditional expectation of the risk-free rate is known at time t, eq. (1.37) for this rate can be rewritten as in (1.32). Using the definition of covariances and (1.32), eq. (1.37) can be rewritten as:[28]

$$E_t(er^j_{t+1}) = -\text{Cov}_t(R^j_{t+1}, Q_{t+1})R^{rf}_{t+1} . \tag{1.38}$$

Since (1.38) holds for any asset, we may substitute out the risk-free rate with any

---

[26]The intertemporal first order condition for an asset with any nominal payoff R^j_{t+1} is: $U_c(\psi_t)(1/P_{y,t}) = E_t(U_c(\psi_{t+1})(1/P_{y,t+1})R^j_{t+1})$. Dividing both sides by the left-hand side expression and using the definition of Q gives eq. (1.36).

[27]Adler and Dumas (1983) consider such an extension for the CAPM in their appendix.

[28]In other words, the fact that $E(XY) = E(X)E(Y) + \text{Cov}(X, Y)$ for any X and Y.

asset b to get:

$$E_t(er^j_{t+1}) = [\text{Cov}_t(R^j_{t+1}, Q_{t+1})/\text{Cov}_t(R^b_{t+1}, Q_{t+1})]E_t(er^b_{t+1}).$$ (1.39)

Since all returns depend upon their conditional covariances with the marginal rate of substitution in consumption, they must move in proportion to each other according to the ratios of these conditional covariances.

In order to test this restriction, Hansen and Hodrick (1983) as well as many subsequent researchers assume that the conditional covariances between returns and the marginal rate of substitution in consumption move in proportion across assets over time. Under this assumption, the ratios of covariances in (1.39) are constant. Generally, the studies find that the over-identifying restrictions implied by returns moving in proportion are not rejected for low frequencies such as quarterly returns, but are strongly rejected for high frequency data, such as weekly.[29]

Cumby (1988, 1990) and Lewis (1991) question whether the rejections come from the auxiliary assumption that covariances move in proportion to each other. Consistent with the pattern of rejection in the latent variable tests, Lewis (1991) finds that the ratios of covariances in (1.39) appear to move in proportion only over longer holding periods. However, the question remains whether this tendency not to reject over longer horizons is a matter of low power.

Bekaert and Hodrick (1992) indirectly consider this possibility by using the one step ahead information in a VAR of foreign exchange and equity returns to test the latent variable restrictions. They find that a single factor model as implied by (1.39) is rejected, although a two factor model appears to fit the data better.

The main contribution of this literature testing for latent variable relationships seems to be its characterization of the behavior of excess returns. This literature shows that some factors, or comovements, help explain returns. A single factor model could be the result of a general equilibrium pricing relationship, but it could also be due to any model that suggests a proportional relationship between returns. Therefore, the latent variable test appears too general to draw any implications for the validity of general equilibrium pricing models.

1.2.2.4. Hansen–Jaganathan bounds

A useful way to compare the variability of predictable excess returns with the implications of any one model has been provided in the pioneering work of Hansen

---

[29]Hansen and Hodrick (1983) tested these restrictions using monthly excess foreign returns across six currencies, rejecting this restriction with marginal significance levels near 5 percent. Hodrick and Srivastava (1984) expanded the sample period and rejected the model. Giovannini and Jorion (1987a) examined weekly returns and used returns from the stock market, finding the restrictions to be rejected. Campbell and Clarida (1987) used three month returns across the Eurocurrency term structure as well as the foreign exchange market. Lewis (1990) surveyed this literature and found that the rejection of the latent variable restrictions is sensitive only to the holding period, not the inclusion of term structure rather than equity returns. Considering a number of combinations of returns and holding periods, that study found that the shorter the holding period, the more likely the restrictions are to reject.

and Jaganathan (1991), originally applied to US T-Bill rates. Since the basic framework holds for *all* returns, it clearly has implications for the foreign exchange risk premium.

The Hansen–Jaganathan (H–J) bounds use combinations of excess returns to provide a lower bound on the volatility of the intertemporal marginal rate of substitution in consumption, Q_{t+1}. This lower bound is a powerful empirical tool since it must hold for any model and, as such, is free of parameters. To see how this relationship is derived, consider again eq. (1.37) using the Law of Iterated Expectations and subsuming the superscript j:

$$E(Q_{t+1}er_{t+1}) = 0. \tag{1.37'}$$

Suppose that the intertemporal marginal rate of substitution can be written as a linear projection on er_{t+1}.

$$Q_{t+1} = \delta_0 + \delta'er_{t+1} + e_{t+1}, \tag{1.40}$$

where e_{t+1} is the projection error. Then by OLS, the parameter vector δ can be written:

$$\begin{aligned} \delta &= \sum{}^{-1} [E(Q_{t+1}er_{t+1}) - E(Q_{t+1})E(er_{t+1})] \\ &= -\sum{}^{-1} E(Q_{t+1})E(er_{t+1}), \end{aligned} \tag{1.41}$$

where Σ is the variance of er_{t+1} (when er is a vector, Σ is the variance-covariance matrix) and where the second equality follows by eq. (1.37'). Substituting (1.41) into (1.40) above and noting that the variance of e_t is positive, we have:

$$\sigma^2(Q_{t+1}) > [E(Q_{t+1})]^2 E(er_{t+1})' \sum{}^{-1} E(er_{t+1}) \tag{1.42}$$

or,

$$\sigma(Q_{t+1})/[E(Q_{t+1})] > \left[E(er_{t+1})' \sum{}^{-1} E(er_{t+1}) \right]^{1/2}. \tag{1.42'}$$

Bekaert and Hodrick (1992) estimate H–J bounds as in (1.42') using different measures of returns. For a combination of equity and foreign exchange returns in the US, Japan, UK, and Germany, they find that the bounds are in the vicinity of 0.6 to 0.7. However, Bekaert (1994) calculated the ratio of the $\sigma(Q)/E(Q)$ for an extension of the Lucas (1982) model to be 0.01 assuming a relative risk aversion parameter of 2. To obtain bounds near the Bekaert and Hodrick (1992) estimates, this risk aversion coefficient must be over 140!

1.2.3. Foreign exchange intervention and the risk premium

The foreign exchange risk premium has also been used to explain the popularity of foreign exchange intervention by central bankers. To illustrate some recent foreign exchange activity, Figures 1.2 depict intervention by the US authorities during 1985 to 1990 against the DM/$ and ¥/$ exchange rates, respectively.[30] While the US went through periods such as 1986 in which no intervention was undertaken, other periods such as 1988 were marked by frequent intervention. Other major central banks such as the Bank of Japan and the Bundesbank, the German central bank, were even more actively involved in intervention during this period. Roughly speaking, interventions to sell dollars appeared to take place when the dollar was relatively strong such as in late 1985 and in 1989, while dollar purchases took place when the dollar was weaker such as in 1987 and early 1988.

Whether these interventions affect the exchange rate or not remains an issue of active empirical research.[31] Nevertheless, it is clear that central bankers continue to intervene. This obvious fact has led researchers to search for reasons why intervention may be effective in changing the exchange rate. One explanation depends upon the presence of a risk premium.

Before describing how a risk premium can provide a rationale for intervention, it is important to first understand why the effectiveness of intervention appears so puzzling to researchers. For this purpose, consider a typical foreign exchange intervention operation. Suppose that the U.S. authorities would like to support the dollar against the yen. In this case, they would conduct dollar purchasing operations. These operations can be understood as a two step procedure. First, they would buy dollars and sell yen reserves in the foreign exchange market. If the authorities took no further action, then the US high-powered money supply would decline by the amount of the dollar purchases. For this reason, they would then undertake a second step to "sterilize" the effects upon the money supply. That is, they would offset the decline in the money supply by buying T-Bills through open-market operations. This sterilization procedure is carried out through monetary policy targeting in the United States, Germany and other countries.

This sterilization practice produces a challenge for explaining how intervention can affect the exchange rate. Conventional demand and supply intuition suggests that a decline in the US money supply leads to an appreciation in the dollar since the exchange rate is the relative price of monies. However, the second step of "sterilization" implies that the money supplies are not affected. Therefore, how can

---

[30]The intervention series was supplied by the Federal Reserve Board of Governors and the exchange rate series is the Wednesday rate reported in the Federal Reserve Bulletin.
[31]For a recent survey, see Edison (1993).

A. Against the DM

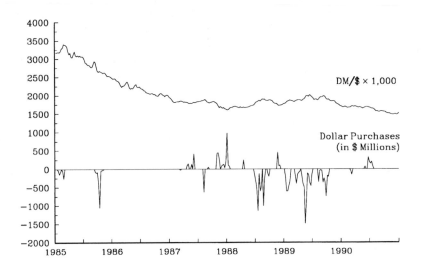

B. Against the Yen

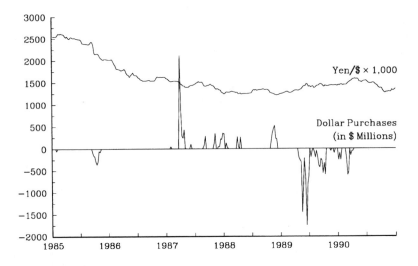

Figure 1.2. US foreign exchange intervention against the DM and yen.

the intervention process possibly affect the exchange rate? The proposed answer: the "portfolio balance" effect through a risk premium.[32]

The "portfolio balance" explanation is straightforward.[33] It is true that money supplies are not affected under sterilized intervention, it is argued, but relative supplies of interest-bearing assets are. After the sterilized intervention described above, the private sector is left holding less US T-Bills and more yen interest-bearing assets. Unless the private sector is indifferent to the currency denomination of its portfolio, the relative return on these assets must change. Specifically, the intervention creates an excess supply of yen bonds and an excess demand for dollar bonds at the previous relative rate of return. One way to attain this equilibrium is for the dollar to appreciate so that both the value of and rate of return on dollar bonds is now higher relative to yen bonds than before the intervention.

The strength of this channel therefore depends upon how much intervention affects the relative price of bonds. Consider this relative expected rate of return in the context of the partial equilibrium model described in Section 1.2. Recall that this return was written as:

$$i_t^* - i_t + E_t \, \Delta s_{t+1} = \rho x_t \, \text{Var}(\Delta s) - \rho \, \text{Cov}(\Delta s, \pi) . \tag{1.23}$$

Now suppose central bankers intervene by purchasing dollars. In this case, x_t will increase since the private sector will be left holding relatively more foreign bonds and less dollar bonds. Therefore, the expected excess return on foreign bonds must increase.

Sterilization is intended to keep the money supply and, hence, the interest rates constant. For this reason, the interest rates, i_t and i_t^*, are typically assumed to be constant following the intervention. An increase in x_t then requires an increase in $E_t \, \Delta s_{t+1}$ in order to clear the financial market.[34] The expected future exchange rate is assumed to be constant so that the intervention requires that the spot rate, s_t, declines and the dollar appreciates.[35]

The plausibility of this channel clearly depends upon how much the exchange rate must respond in order to maintain portfolio balance. If investors are relatively

[32] An alternative explanation is the "signalling" story. This story, articulated by Mussa (1981), suggests that current sterilized intervention is correlated with future changes in the money supply. Therefore, even though current money supplies are not altered through intervention, traders believe that future money will change, inducing an immediate response in exchange rates. For a discussion of this literature, see the chapter by Frankel and Rose (1995) in this volume.

[33] The portfolio balance approach was developed by Kouri (1976), Branson (1977), and Girton and Henderson (1977), among others. For a discussion, see Branson and Henderson (1984).

[34] Changes in the current spot rate can also offset the increase in foreign bond portfolio shares directly since these shares are measured in units of domestic currency. For more on this relationship, see Branson and Henderson (1984).

[35] This assumption is stronger than needed. As long as the expected future exchange rate does not increase sufficiently so that the current spot rate increases, the basic argument of the portfolio balance model will hold.

risk-neutral so that $\rho \approx 0$, they will consider bonds close substitutes and the expected relative rate of return will be close to zero. In this case, large changes in intervention through asset shares x will have little effect upon the exchange rate. While the specifics of the CAPM model provide the motivation for these effects, it is also clear that any portfolio model in which investors consider bonds denominated in different currencies to be highly substitutable will yield the same prediction that intervention is relatively ineffective. Thus, the plausibility of the portfolio balance channel hinges upon whether changes in the currency denomination of the portfolio affect the equilibrium relative returns of assets.

The empirical studies that examine this issue fall into two basic groups. The first set of studies estimate portfolios of bond demand equations that are not restricted to follow the CAPM restrictions in (1.23'). Rogoff (1984) and Lewis (1988a) find no evidence that bond demands are sufficiently inelastic that intervention would affect expected real rates of return. A second set of studies uses the CAPM restrictions to examine this relationship. Clearly, this set includes all studies of the static international CAPM, considered in Section 1.2, even though intervention may not have been the focus of the study. As described there, this literature has been summarily unsuccessful in relating bond supplies to a measure of the foreign exchange risk premium. However, Dominguez and Frankel (1993) use survey data as a measure of expectations as well as intervention as a measure of bonds. They find some support for the hypothesis that intervention affects the expected relative rates of return. Since the forecasts captured in survey measures are irrational, as will be described below, more research must be done to understand how intervention affects expectations before monetary authorities could potentially use intervention policy in a predictable fashion.

The portfolio balance story typically ignores the effects of expectations in the general equilibrium of the economy. Backus and Kehoe (1989) show that this omission can be quite important. They show that government debt instruments can be manipulated as in a sterilized intervention without affecting exchange rates at all. Furthermore, sterilized interventions to support the dollar may be correlated with dollar appreciations, depreciations, or not at all.

1.2.4. Empirical conclusions

Whether from a partial or general equilibrium point of view, explaining the foreign exchange risk premium requires a high degree of implied variability in predictable excess returns. Observable ingredients in the risk premium models do not vary sufficiently to explain this behavior on their own. In the static CAPM, bond supplies and conditional variances do not fluctuate sufficiently. In general equilibrium, the relatively low degree of variability in consumption is inconsistent with the high degree of variability in asset returns. Thus, unless risk aversion is extremely high, neither the static CAPM nor the general equilibrium relationships can explain the risk premium.

The high variability in excess returns relative to predictions of theoretical models is a problem that plagues other markets as well.[36] One direction that has been pursued to explain risk premia in markets such as equity is to depart from the standard time-separable iso-elastic utility function. Backus, Gregory and Telmer (1993) examine the theoretical implications of risk premia based upon non-standard utility preferences, particularly habit-persistence.[37] They find that habit-persistence raises the variability of the intertemporal marginal rate of substitution, but does not explain other features of the model. Bekaert, Hodrick, and Marshall (1994) consider utility functions that allow for first-order risk aversion as opposed to the second-order risk aversion implied by standard utility functions. Based upon a class of utility functions related to Epstein and Zin (1990), they find that the variability of the risk premium increases. However, they are not able to match the risk premium on the foreign exchange, equity and bond markets of the US and Japan. While these seem important directions to pursue, there appears to remain a discrepancy between the actual and theoretical variability in excess returns.

This discrepancy has led some to argue that the anomalous behavior of predictable returns may be due to systematic expectational errors. In this case, expectational errors may contribute to the high degree of variability in predictable excess returns.

There are two basic groups of explanations for these expectational errors. First, forecast errors may be systematic because some agents in the market are not rational. The "market's forecast" is really a composite of a heterogeneous group of traders. Since some of these traders are irrational, measures of the market's expectations will not be rational. The second explanation for systematic expectational errors arises from statistical problems with measuring expectations. I next describe each of these two explanations.

1.3. Market inefficiencies and rational expectations

Understanding the behavior of predictable excess returns requires an identifying decomposition between the forecast error component and the risk premium component. The analysis above used the standard decomposition that forecast errors are conditionally uncorrelated with past information so that all predictable excess returns must equal the foreign exchange risk premia. If this assumption is violated, however, then predictable excess returns confound risk premia and forecast errors.

Froot and Frankel (1989) provide a decomposition of each component of

---

[36]For example, Mehra and Prescott (1985) show that the US equity premium, the return on stocks in excess of the risk free rate, requires high variability in the marginal rate of substitution in consumption, implying an implausibly high risk aversion parameter.

[37]For more on habit-persistence utility functions, see Constantanides (1990) and Abel (1990).

predictable excess returns. The behavior of these returns can be conveniently summarized in the Fama (1984) regression of excess returns on forward premia described previously in Section 1.1.1. Since the change in the exchange rate equals the market's expected future exchange rate plus a forecast error, $\Delta s_{t+1} = E_t^m \Delta s_{t+1} + \eta_{t+1}$, the regression coefficient can also be written as:

$$\beta_1 = [\text{Cov}(E_t^m \Delta s_{t+1}, f_t + s_t) + \text{Cov}(\eta_{t+1}, f_t - s_t)]/\text{Var}(f_t - s_t). \qquad (1.43)$$

Rewriting the forward premium, $f - s$, in (1.43) in terms of its identity with the risk premium in (1.13), the probability limit of β_1 is:

$$\beta_1 = 1 - \beta_{rp} - \beta_{re}$$

where

$$\beta_{rp} = [\text{Var}(rp_t) - \text{Cov}(E_t^m \Delta s_{t+1}, rp_t)]/\text{Var}(f_t - s_t),$$
$$\beta_{re} = -\text{Cov}(\eta_{t+1}, f_t - s_t)/\text{Var}(f_t - s_t). \qquad (1.44)$$

This equation shows that if $\beta_1 \neq 1$, then either (a) the risk premium is time-varying, or else (b) the market's forecast error is correlated with the forward premium, or (c) some combination of the two.

Fama interpreted the finding of $\beta_1 \neq 1$ as the result of a risk premium, since under standard rational expectations assumptions $E_t s_{t+1} = E_t^m s_{t+1}$ and $\text{Cov}(\eta_{t+1}, f_t - s_t) = 0$. In this case, $\beta_{re} = 0$ and $\beta_1 = 1 - \beta_{rp}$. Under this assumption, the variance of the risk premium exceeds the variance of the market's expectations of exchange rate changes, an implication difficult to explain with conventional risk premium models.

If instead, the risk premium were constant, then $\beta_1 = 1 - \beta_{re}$. A finding that $\beta_1 < 1$ implies that $\text{Cov}(\eta_{t+1}, f_t - s_t) < 0$, or that the forecast error is negatively correlated with the forward premium. In this case, the forward rate systematically predicts exchange rate movements in the opposite direction from their subsequent movement.

Determining which component, β_{re} or β_{rp}, is most important requires some measure of expectations. Froot and Frankel (1989) examine this decomposition using exchange rate forecasts from surveys conducted by financial firms.[38] They identify the median forecast across traders surveyed at each period t as a measure of the market's expected future spot rate, $E_t^m s_{t+1}$. They combine this measure of expectations with the forward rate to identify the risk premium.

With this identification, Froot and Frankel (1989) decompose the Fama coefficient into the component due to the risk premium, rp_t, and the component due to the forecast error, η_{t+1}. Table 1.2 shows the results of calculating β_1, β_{rp}, and β_{re} using

---

[38]They combine surveys from three different sources: the MMS, the Economist, and the AMEX. The sample periods as well as sampling procedures differ across these surveys. See Frankel and Froot (1987) and Froot and Frankel (1989) for a more detailed description.

Table 1.2
Components of the Fama regression coefficient

Date set	Dates	(1) β_1	(2) β_{rp}	(3) β_{re}
Economist	6/81–12/85	−0.57	0.08	1.49
3 month	''	−1.21	−0.30	2.51
6 month	''	−1.98	−0.00	2.99
12 month	''	0.29	0.19	0.52
MMS 1 month	11/82–1/88	−1.74	−2.07	4.81
MMS 3 month	1/83–10/84	−6.25	1.18	6.07
AMEX	1/76–7/85	−2.21	−0.03	3.25
6 month	''	−2.42	−0.22	3.63
12 month	1/76–7/84	−2.14	0.03	3.11

Notes: From Froot and Frankel (1989).

their data set. Over the different time periods of the various survey measures, the coefficient estimates in the column labeled β_1 are typically negative, similar to the results found in Table 1.1.

The contribution of the risk premium is given in column (2). From eq. (1.44), note that for time-varying risk premia to explain the negative estimates of β_1, it must be true that $\beta_{rp} > 1$. However, column (2) shows that all but one of the estimates of β_{rp} are less than one. Only the MMS 3 month survey gives an estimate of $\beta_{rp} > 1$, but in this case the estimate of β_1 exceeds −6! Thus, even in this case, the risk premium does not explain an important fraction of the variation of the predictable excess return. For the other samples, the estimates of β_{rp} are frequently close to zero, implying that the variance of the risk premium is small compared to that of the forecast error.

On the other hand, the contribution of the forecast error is considerable as shown in column (3) of Table 1.2. Recall that for the correlation between forecast errors and forward premia to explain the negative estimates of β_1, it must be true that $\beta_{re} > 1$. For every case in which $\beta_1 < 0$, column (3) shows that $\beta_{re} > 1$. Thus, the important component in the variability of predictable returns appears to be the forecast error, and not the risk premium.

1.3.1. Interpretation

The results in Table 1.2 clearly contradict the standard interpretation of rational expectations. Forecast errors appear to be significantly correlated with the lagged forward premium, a variable readily observable to traders. Where does this correlation come from?

There are two general ways in which this question has been answered. First, the aggregated expectations of the market may be irrational. Frankel and Froot (1987) use the same survey measure of expectations to determine how expectations depend upon lagged information. Consistent with the evidence in Table 1.2 they find that these expectations are significantly different from the *ex post* realized exchange rate, so that expectations appear irrational. They also find that exchange rate expectations take the form of a distributed lag of past exchange rates, that these expectations are stabilizing and that they are not driven by destabilizing bandwagon effects.

This irrationality may arise from the presence of heterogeneous traders in the market. Though not specifically related to the foreign exchange market, De Long, Shleifer, Summers, and Waldmann (1990) show that the presence of irrational traders can affect prices and that these traders can even earn higher expected returns than their rational counterparts. Intuitively, the unpredictability of irrational traders' beliefs creates a risk in asset prices that deters rational traders from aggressively betting against them. Bearing a disproportionate amount of risk, the irrational traders can earn a higher expected return and therefore rational agents do not necessarily compete them out of the market.

Models of heterogeneous agents have been developed to evaluate the foreign exchange market more directly, as well. Frankel and Froot (1988) present a model of two types of traders, "chartists" and "fundamentalists" who have different horizons for holding assets. They show that this model is capable of explaining some of the myopic expectations apparent from survey data. Froot and Thaler (1990) argue that the Fama result is consistent with the market waiting one period before reacting to new information. To date, however, heterogeneous agent models have yet to be developed in a testable way to provide evidence of their effects upon excess foreign exchange returns.[39]

A second general answer to the question posed above comes from statistical difficulties with measuring the market's forecasts under rational expectations that depend upon the sample. These difficulties arise when the distribution of shocks that affect the economy undergo infrequent shifts.[40] Examples of these types of shifts may be as obvious as monetary policy regime changes, oil price shocks, and natural disasters, or they may be more subtle such as a shift in the trend of the exchange rate. In any case, when rational economic agents incorporate into their forecasts uncertainty about shifts in the distribution of economic shocks, the forecast errors may be serially correlated for periods of time. The length of this time period depends upon the infrequency and therefore the likelihood of the shift occurring. I describe these issues next.

---

[39] An important step in this direction is the recent work by Lyons (1993). He develops a market microstructure model of the behavior of traders. Based upon trade-by-trade data from an individual trader, he is able to test some implications of his model. The relationship between this microstructure model and the equilibrium behavior of returns remains an important direction for future research.

[40] Strictly speaking, the issue arises whenever the number of shifts in the sample is unrepresentative of the underlying distribution. Therefore, the shifts may in fact be too frequent in the sample. Since the examples considered below and in the literature involve too few rather than too many shifts in the sample, I will discuss only this case in the text.

1.4. Rational systematic forecast errors

The problem that shifts in a given sample may be unrepresentative of the underlying distribution is clearly a problem endemic to all measurements of expectations. This problem can therefore affect all areas of economics in which expectations are important. However, the problem in international finance has been understood for some time in the context of infrequent exchange rate realignments.[41] This intuition has natural extensions for floating exchange rates.

The problem can be loosely grouped into two categories: learning about a possible past shift in the economic distribution; and expectations about a future shift in the economic distribution. For simplicity, I will discuss each case separately. I will then finish the section by discussing how both features are likely to be present in excess return behavior.

1.4.1. Learning

To understand the effects of rational learning, consider an extreme case when there is a potential once-and-for-all shift in the underlying distribution of the economy. Examples of such shifts could be a change in monetary operating procedures, a shift from an expansionary to contractionary monetary policy regime, or a change in fiscal policy such as a change in taxes with unknown future effects.

To help fix ideas, suppose that the shift would imply a stronger value of the domestic currency, such as a tightening in domestic monetary policy, for example. Define the expected future exchange rate conditional upon the old regime as $E_t(s_{t+1}|O)$ and the expectation conditional upon the new regime as $E_t(s_{t+1}|N)$, where $E_t(s_{t+1}|O) > E_t(s_{t+1}|N)$. This inequality can also be written as $E_t(\Delta s_{t+1}|O) > E_t(\Delta s_{t+1}|N)$ since the current spot rate is in the time t information set. The expected future exchange rate at time t will be a probability-weighted average of the two expected values:

$$E_t s_{t+1} = (1 - \lambda_t)E_t(s_{t+1}|N) + \lambda_t E_t(s_{t+1}|O) \tag{1.45}$$

where λ_t is the market's assessed probability at time t that monetary policy is based upon the old regime.

The evolution of the market's probability of the old regime is based upon a rational learning process. In particular, suppose that traders know that if a change in policy occurred, it happened a time $\tau < t$. Then, traders will update their probabilities that the regime is new by subsequent observations of the exchange rate according to

---

[41]Rogoff (1980) first wrote about this problem in the Mexican peso futures market. Krasker (1980) developed a parametric hyperinflation example to quantify the potential size distortions in market efficiency tests arising from the peso problem.

Bayes' law:

$$\lambda_t = \frac{\lambda_{t-1}L(\Delta s_t, \Delta s_{t-1}, \ldots, \Delta s_{\tau+1} \mid O)}{(1 - \lambda_{t-1})L(\Delta s_t, \Delta s_{t-1}, \ldots, \Delta s_{\tau+1} \mid N) + \lambda_{t-1}L(\Delta s_t, \Delta s_{t-1}, \ldots, \Delta s_{\tau+1} \mid O)}$$

(1.46)

where $L(\cdot \mid O)$ and $L(\cdot \mid N)$ is the likelihood of the observation given the regime is old and new, respectively. Suppose that the regime actually changed at time τ.[42] Then since $E_t(\Delta s_{t+1} \mid N) < E_t(\Delta s_{t+1} \mid O)$, the actual observations of the exchange rate will tend to decrease over time, thereby increasing the likelihood of the New regime, relative to the old regime so that λ_t will decrease over time. As the number of observations grows large,

$$\plim_{t \to \infty} \lambda_t = 0.$$

(1.47)

Thus, as the number of observations increases, the market learns about the new regime.

Consider the behavior of forecast errors during this learning period, however. For expositional simplicity, suppose that the process is in fact "new". Subtracting the realized exchange rate from the expectation in eq. (1.45) gives:

$$s_{t+1}^N - E_t s_{t+1} \equiv \eta_{t+1} = [s_{t+1}^N - E_t(s_{t+1} \mid N)] - \lambda_t[E_t(s_{t+1} \mid O) - E_t(s_{t+1} \mid N)],$$

$$= \eta_{t+1}^N - \lambda_t \nabla s_{t+1}$$

(1.48)

where s_{t+1}^N indicates a realization of the exchange rate from process N, $\eta_{t+1}^N \equiv s_{t+1}^N - E_t(s_{t+1} \mid N)$ and $\nabla s \equiv E_t(\Delta s_{t+1} \mid O) - E_t(\Delta s_{t+1} \mid N)$, the difference between the expected future exchange rate changes conditional upon each regime. Note that η_{t+1}^N is the forecast error conditional upon the true regime and is therefore uncorrelated with time t information. However, as long as the market believes the old regime is possible so that $\lambda_t \neq 0$, then the difference between expected exchange rates in each regime, ∇s, will introduce a potential for the mean to be non-zero.

To see how learning may affect the behavior of predictable excess returns described in Table 1.1 and Figure 1.1, recall the definition of excess returns: $er_{t+1} = rp_t + (s_{t+1} - E_t s_{t+1})$. Suppose now that the variability of the risk premium is small, as suggested by the survey data. In order to focus upon the behavior of forecast errors in this discussion, I will assume for now that the risk premium is zero but will reintroduce it below. In this extreme assumption, the behavior of forecast errors can be identified solely with the behavior of excess returns.

Consider first the mean of excess returns. The mean of excess returns in a sample

---

[42]Even if the change did not occur, learning implies that the forecast errors will be serially correlated with a non-zero mean as well as other features to be described below. [See Lewis (1989a,b)].

of size T is the sample mean of the forecast errors:

$$\text{Mean}(er_t) = \frac{\sum_{t=\tau}^{T}(s_{t+1} - E_t s_{t+1})}{T} = -\frac{\sum_{t=\tau}^{T} \lambda_t \nabla s_{t+1}}{T} \tag{1.49}$$

where the last equality follows since $E(\sum_{t=\tau}^{T} \eta_t^N / T) = 0$.

Now notice the systematic tendency of forecast errors during learning. If $E_t(s_{t+1} | N) < E_t(s_{t+1} | O)$ so that $\nabla s > 0$, then the mean of η_t will be negative as long as $\lambda_t > 0$. The intuition behind this result is straightforward. As long as the market is not sure if a shift has occurred, by (1.45) they will place a probability weight of λ_t on the possibility that the old regime is in place. However, since the domestic currency is expected to be weaker in this regime, the market will be systematically surprised at the strength of the domestic currency. Over time, however, $\lambda \rightarrow 0$ and the mean of excess returns in (1.49) equals zero.

Now consider the Fama regression of excess returns on the forward premium during learning. In the extreme case when the risk premium is zero, the coefficient on the forward premium is $\beta_1 = 1 - \beta_{re}$, where:

$$\beta_{re} = -\frac{\text{Cov}(\eta_{t+1}, f_t - s_t)}{\text{Var}(f_t - s_t)} = -\frac{\text{Cov}(\eta_{t+1}, E_t s_{t+1} - s_t)}{\text{Var}(E_t s_{t+1} - s_t)}. \tag{1.50}$$

Since $\beta_1 < 1$, the covariance between the forecast error and the expected exchange rate change must be negative in order for learning to explain the Fama result.

While β_{re} must go to zero as the sample size gets large, the covariance between the forecast error and the forward premium can be negative if the market places a sufficient amount of probability on the old regime. To illustrate this possibility, I will assume that the forecasts conditional upon each regime are uncorrelated. In this case, the numerator of (1.50) is:

$$\text{Cov}(\eta_{t+1}, E_t \Delta s_{t+1}) = \lambda_t[(1 - \lambda_t) \text{Var}(E_t \Delta s_{t+1}^N) - \lambda_t \text{Var}(E_t \Delta s_{t+1}^O)]. \tag{1.51}$$

The covariance between forecast errors and the expected change in the exchange rate can thus be negative when the probability-weighted variance of the exchange rate in the old regime exceeds its counterpart in the new regime. If the probability of the old regime is sufficiently large, the covariance will be negative. As λ goes to zero over time, this covariance also goes to zero.

To emphasize the role played by the probability, suppose that the variance of the exchange rate in the two regimes were the same. In this case, the covariance in (1.51) can be rewritten:

$$\text{Cov}(\eta_{t+1}, E_t \Delta s_{t+1}) = \lambda_t(1 - 2\lambda_t) \text{Var}(E_t \Delta s_{t+1}^i), \quad \text{for } i = O, N. \tag{1.52}$$

In this simple case, the covariance is negative whenever the probability of the old regime exceeds one-half. During such a period, $\beta_{re} > 0$ contributing to the finding that $\beta_1 < 1$.

The intuition behind this result is straightforward. During learning, the market expects a weaker domestic currency than is realized *ex post*. The forward premium reflects the expected change in the exchange rate that in turn depends upon the probability of the old regime in which the exchange rate depreciates. However, since the regime is in fact new, the forecast errors tend to reflect unexpected systematic appreciations in the domestic currency. This interaction generates a negative covariation between the forecast error and the forward premium when the probability of the old regime is considered high by the market. As the market believes the old regime less likely, the negative covariance between forecast errors and forward premium disappears.

Lewis (1989b) uses a model in which the exchange rate depends upon US monetary policy to examine the potential effects of learning about contractionary shifts in the US money market during the early 1980s. Based upon conservative parameter values, this paper finds that learning explained about half of the behavior of excess returns. As shown in Figure 1.1, the mean of excess returns on holding open dollar positions during this period were substantially larger than for the entire sample period. Thus, learning about shifts in policies may have important effects upon exchange rate forecast errors.

On the other hand, Panel C of Table 1.1 points to a difficulty with explaining the Fama result entirely with learning. As the market learns, the probability of the old regime must go to zero and, with no risk premium, the Fama coefficient should converge to one. If learning about tight US monetary policy during the early 1980s were driving all of the Fama result, subsample estimates should therefore find that β_1 is closer to one by the late 1980s. Panel C reports estimates of the Fama regression breaking the sample into thirds. While the coefficients tend to be closer to one during the 1970s, the estimates are significantly negative with larger absolute values in the late 1980s.[43] Clearly, the Fama finding is not the result of a particular period in history for dollar exchange rates.

Of course, the market may have believed that they were learning about a different shift in the late 1980s. In other words, the distribution of economic shocks could potentially be subject to multiple shifts. If so, then rational traders should incorporate the possibility that the exchange rate process may shift in the future. I discuss this possibility next.

1.4.2. Peso problems

A "peso problem" arises when market participants anticipate a future discrete shift in policy that is not materialized within the sample period examined. Milton Friedman

---

[43]Additional evidence is provided in Bekaert and Hodrick (1993) who find significant negative coefficients for the Fama regression using cross exchange rates that do not include the dollar.

allegedly first used this term to explain why Mexican peso deposit rates during the early 1970s remained substantially higher than U.S. dollar interest rates even though the exchange rate had been fixed for a decade. As Friedman argued, the market expected a devaluation of the peso, so that higher Mexican peso interest rates reflected a weaker peso at the forward rate implied through covered interest parity. This conjecture was subsequently justified when the Mexican peso was devalued in the late 1970s.[44]

The first written discussion of the "peso problem" appears in Rogoff (1980). He considers a regression of the Mexican peso/US dollar exchange rate on the futures rate. He argues that a reason for rejecting the hypothesis that the coefficient equals one may have been the market's anticipation of a devaluation in the peso.

Under floating exchange rates, Evans and Lewis (1995) examine potential "peso problem" effects upon various features of excess return behavior, including the Fama result. This investigation was motivated by the observation in Engel and Hamilton (1990) and Kaminsky (1993) that the dollar exchange rate appears to have undergone appreciating and then depreciating regimes. Additional evidence of the markets beliefs about jumps in the exchange rate resulting from these shifts come from option pricing. Bates (1994) finds that the risk of a significant change in the dollar exchange rate was priced into foreign exchange options during the period.

To see the potential effects of anticipated future changes in exchange rate regimes, consider the expected future exchange rate based upon the current regime, C, and an alternative regime, A, that may be realized in the future:

$$E_t s_{t+1} = (1 - \ell_t) E_t(s_{t+1} \mid C) + \ell_t E_t(s_{t+1} \mid A) \tag{1.53}$$

where ℓ_t is the probability that the exchange rate regime will shift from the current regime to an alternative regime, A. In contrast to eq. (1.45), note that eq. (1.53) depends only upon the expected *future* change in regime, not learning about a past change.

As long as the shift in regime does not materialize, then the exchange rate will be generated by the current regime, C. Therefore, the forecast error will be:

$$s_{t+1}^C - E_t s_{t+1} \equiv \eta_{t+1} = (s_{t+1}^C - E_t(s_{t+1} \mid C)) + \ell_t(E_t(s_{t+1} \mid C) - E_t(s_{t+1} \mid A))$$
$$= \eta_{t+1}^C + \ell_t \nabla s_{t+1} \tag{1.54}$$

where now η_{t+1}^C is the forecast error conditional upon C, and $\nabla s_{t+1} \equiv E_t(s_{t+1} \mid C) - E_t(s_{t+1} \mid A)$.

Substituting this definition for η_t into the sample mean in (1.48) and (1.49) into the regression coefficient in (1.50) shows that, by replacing λ with ℓ, the same relationships hold for the peso problem as they do for learning.

---

[44]Lizondo (1983) provides a discussion and a theoretical model of the Mexican peso futures market in anticipation of a devaluation.

The difference between future anticipated shifts in the exchange rate process and learning about a past change is that a shift will eventually materialize if the market is rational. Thus, the appropriate measure of β_1 should be based upon the number of shifts in regime that take place in a typical sample. Evans and Lewis (1995) consider this possibility by first estimating a model of regime switching in the dollar–yen, dollar–DM and dollar–pound exchange rates during the floating rate sample. Based upon rational expectations of a shift in regimes, they then generate the empirical distributions of the Fama regression coefficient.

Table 1.3 shows how the standard Fama results are affected when traders expect the exchange rate to switch regimes. Panels A and B report the effects upon estimates based upon, respectively, monthly and quarterly returns using the same data as in Table 1.1. Column (1) gives the marginal significance levels based upon standard distribution theory for the hypothesis that the estimate equals one. The hypothesis is rejected with marginal significance levels less than one percent in all cases, as found in Table 1.1.

Columns (2) and (3) demonstrate the effects of peso problems. Column (2) reports the mean bias given by the difference between the estimated β_1 and the true β_1^* from the switching model in Evans and Lewis (1995). In all cases, the Fama coefficient is biased downward as a result of the peso problem. Column (3) gives the ratio of the estimated standard deviation of the risk premium over the true standard deviation of the risk premium. For all currencies and both frequencies, the standard deviation of the measured risk premium exceeds that of the true risk premium from the model. For

Table 1.3
The Fama result and the peso problem

Exchange Rate	(1) Asymptotic p-value for Ho: $\beta_1 = 1$	(2) Bias in coefficient	(3) Bias in variance
	A. Monthly returns		
$/BP	<.001	−0.726	1.222
$/DM	.001	−1.068	1.237
$/¥	<.001	−0.107	1.035
	B. Quarterly returns		
$/BP	.001	−0.724	1.216
$/DM	.0045	−0.720	1.162
$/¥	<.001	−0.124	1.031

Notes: Column (1) gives the p-values based upon standard asymptotics of the hypothesis that the coefficient (β_1) in regressions of exchange rate changes on the forward premium are equal to one. Estimates are based upon data used in Table 1.1. Columns (2) and (3) are based upon the exchange rate switching model in Evans and Lewis (1995) using the same data. Column (2) reports the mean bias in the coefficient due to the peso problem when traders anticipate shifts in the exchange rate. Column (3) gives the mean of the estimate of the standard deviation in the risk premium based upon standard inferences divided by the true standard deviation from the model.

the pound and the DM, the standard deviations of the measured risk premium are about 20 percent higher than the actual standard deviation. This evidence suggests that standard inference techniques based upon assuming zero covariance between the forecast error and the forward premium can be misleading in the Fama regression. Potentially, an important component of the deviations from one may be introduced by peso problems.

At the same time, the evidence in Table 1.3 shows that peso problems alone cannot explain all of the behavior of predictable excess returns. Even after adjusting for the peso problem bias in coefficients and variances, the remaining component of predictable returns remains sizeable. Similarly, when Bates (1994) tests for whether expected jumps can fully explain the deviations from uncovered interest parity, he finds that the test is rejected. However, Table 1.3 also indicates that the bias introduced by peso problems can be economically significant.

This discussion suggests that, when the economic environment changes discretely, forecast errors are likely to be serially correlated in small samples. Whether a sample is small or not depends upon the infrequency of shifts in the distribution. For example, Engel and Hamilton (1990) and Evans and Lewis (1995) find that the dollar appeared to go through roughly 3 appreciating and 2 depreciating regimes against the DM from 1975 to 1989. If traders are making their forecasts on the potential for these regimes to change, then it would take many such shifts to give mean zero, serially correlated forecast errors.

1.5. Risk premia, market inefficiencies, learning, or peso problems?

To this point, I have described research investigating the source of foreign currency excess returns. Researchers who believe that forecast errors must be uncorrelated with everything in the lagged information set are forced to accept the view that these predictable excess returns are the result of an equilibrium risk premium model. However, no risk premium model with believable measures of risk aversion has yet been able to generate the variability in predictable excess returns that are observed in the data.

On the other hand, survey measures of expectations suggest that most of the action in predictable excess returns comes from forecast errors that are correlated with lagged information. While considering heterogeneous trader models appears to be an important direction for future research, no such model has yet been provided to explain the behavior of excess returns.

In the meantime, I have shown that discrete changes in the economic environment can help explain serially correlated forecast errors as well as the high variance of predictable excess returns, even within the context of a representative agent framework. When once-and-for-all shifts in the economic distribution occur, forecast errors are likely to covary in the opposite direction from the forward premium, potentially generating a downward bias in the Fama coefficient. However, learning about a single past change in the economic environment can only explain particular time periods such as the early 1980s and cannot explain the persistence of the high variation in predictable excess returns.

I also showed that anticipated future changes in the exchange rate regime could produce behavior similar to that of learning. While serially correlated errors disappear in sample sizes that include many regime shifts, the average length of a cycle of appreciation and then depreciation in the dollar/DM rate found in Evans and Lewis (1995) has been about $7\frac{1}{2}$ years. At this rate, it would be about 225 years before a sample of 30 of these events would be observed.

Examining each of these explanations in isolation might lead to the conclusion that predictable excess returns remain a complete mystery. However, each of these explanations have ignored the other explanations. It seems likely that if there are shifts in regimes, then anticipations of these shifts will affect the market's assessment of risk and therefore the foreign exchange risk premium. Heterogeneous views toward this risk may be compounded into an aggregate measure of the risk premium that exceeds the measures in conventional studies. Thus, a difficult but important direction for future research will be to integrate the various explanations for the behavior of excess returns.

2. International portfolio allocation

Another empirical puzzle that has attracted the attention of international finance researchers concerns the choice of international assets by domestic investors. Domestic residents tend to hold a very large proportion of their wealth in domestic assets alone. The magnitude of this investment in domestic relative to foreign equities is difficult to reconcile with standard portfolio arguments.[45]

This issue has recently been emphasized by French and Poterba (1991) and Tesar and Werner (1992). Table 2.1, Panel A gives the measure of the U.S. equity portfolio shares decomposed into source of equity by country using numbers taken from French and Poterba (1991).[46] As the column under "actual share" shows, about 94 percent of the US investor's wealth was held in domestic equity.

To evaluate whether this large proportion of holdings in domestic assets is surprising requires an international investment model. For this purpose, I will use the same models described in Section 2. Therefore, I will only briefly review them in this section. Section 2.1 reviews the partial equilibrium CAPM model. This model suggests that the optimal holding of domestic US assets is less than 50 percent. From

---

[45]The relatively low degree of domestic relative to foreign holdings of equities has been recognized at least since Levy and Sarnat (1970).

[46]These data are adjusted from the U.S. Treasury Bulletin and Howell and Cozini (1990) and correspond to June 1990 values. French and Poterba (1991) also consider British equities.

Table 2.1
The "home bias" puzzle for the US

A. Multilateral

Country	Actual share	Implied model share				
		$\rho = 1$	$\rho = 2$	$\rho = 3$	$\rho = 6$	$\rho = 10$
US	.936	.465	.464	.463	.458	.453
Japan	.032	.442	.440	.438	.432	.425
Germany	.005	.092	.096	.099	.109	.123

B. Summary statistics for excess equity returns

Country	Mean(i)	Std. dev(i)	Cov(i, π)*
US	9.96	52.90	–
Japan	17.15	74.80	−0.01
Germany	11.46	81.89	0.10

Note: Optimal shares calculated as: (2.5) $\underline{\chi}_i = \rho^{-1} E_i \underline{r}_{t+1} \text{Var}(\underline{r}_{t+1})^{-1}$ derived in text.
* Covariance estimates calculated as the covariance between exchange rate changes and U.S. inflation.

this perspective, the evidence in Table 2.1 that more than 90 percent of US holdings are in domestic assets is indeed surprising.

Section 2.2 considers the portfolio holdings suggested by a general equilibrium model. If preferences are iso-elastic and goods are tradeable, then countries should share equally in each other's stockmarkets. This implication is also clearly inconsistent with the numbers in Table 2.1. Since this result depends upon the utility function, I also examine a more general framework that provides predictions for consumption in the presence of risk-sharing under complete markets. These predictions give similar implications for the home bias puzzle. In particular, domestic consumption is significantly correlated with idiosyncratic income shocks, in contrast to the implications of optimal international risk-sharing.[47]

The pervasiveness of the home bias puzzle both in terms of foreign equity holdings and international consumption patterns suggests that investors are either prevented from arbitraging differences or that the gains from doing so may not be large enough. In Section 2.3, I will consider these possibilities.

2.1. "Home bias" based upon partial equilibrium

What pattern of equity holdings should we expect to find from a partial equilibrium point of view? To see the basic intuition, it is useful to contrast the implied behavior of returns with the CAPM model based upon deposits discussed in Section 1.2. That model gave the following general relationship for returns on foreign relative to

[47]The implications of international risk sharing were pointed out in Scheinkman (1984) and Leme (1984).

domestic deposits:

$$per_{t+1} = \rho \, \text{Cov}_t(er_{t+1}, i_{p,t+1}) - \rho \, \text{Cov}_t(er_{t+1}, \pi_{t+1}).$$ (1.22)

Required returns on foreign relative to domestic deposits depend positively upon the measure of relative risk-aversion, ρ, and the variability of returns captured by the covariance between excess returns and the return on the portfolio. The returns depend negatively upon the covariance between returns and inflation.

2.1.1. Optimal portfolio shares of foreign assets

I will now focus upon equity holdings at home and abroad, but will show that the expected returns on these assets take a similar form as those of foreign currency deposits. Suppose first that there are only two assets, domestic equity and foreign equity. Define the vector of portfolio weights, $\chi_t = (\chi_t^h, \chi_t^f)'$, where χ_t^h is the share in the home stock and χ_t^f is the share in the foreign stock, respectively. Furthermore, define the vector of real returns as $\underline{r}_{t+1} = (r_{t+1}^h, r_{t+1}^f)'$. Now consider the investor's decision. He chooses the vector of portfolio weights, χ, to maximize an objective function that is increasing in expected wealth, but decreasing in the variance of wealth, as in eq. (1.20). Expected wealth can now be written:

$$E_t W_{t+1} = W_t + W_t \chi_t' E_t \underline{r}_{t+1}.$$ (2.1)

And the variance of wealth becomes:

$$\text{Var}_t(W_{t+1}) = W_t^2 \, \text{Var}_t(\chi_t' \underline{r}_{t+1}) = W_t^2 \chi_t' \, \text{Var}_t(\underline{r}_{t+1}) \chi_t$$ (2.2)

where $\text{Var}_t(\underline{r})$ is the conditional variance-covariance matrix of the vector $\underline{r}$.

Substituting (2.1) and (2.2) into (1.20) and maximizing with respect to χ gives the first-order conditions:

$$E_t \underline{r}_{t+1}' = \rho \chi_t' \, \text{Var}_t(\underline{r}_{t+1}).$$ (2.3)

Note that by decomposing the equity portfolio in terms of nominal returns, $\underline{r}_{t+1} \equiv \underline{i}_{t+1} - \pi_{t+1} \iota$ where ι is a 2×1 vector of ones, and noting that the portfolio return is $r_{p,t+1} = \chi_t' \underline{r}_{t+1}$, the first order conditions can be rewritten:

$$E_t \underline{r}_{t+1} = \rho \, \text{Cov}_t(\underline{r}_{t+1}, i_{p,t+1}) - \rho \, \text{Cov}_t(\underline{r}_{t+1}, \pi_{t+1}).$$ (2.4)

Note that these equilibrium returns have the same form and, hence, intuition as the foreign exchange returns in (1.23). As the covariance of returns with the portfolio increases, the required return of each asset increases according to the portfolio weights of the asset. The required return also increases with the covariance between the domestic and foreign assets since a higher covariance increases the over-all risk of the portfolio. Finally, required returns decrease with the covariance between returns and inflation since the higher this covariance, the better the hedge of equity returns against inflation. The returns depend upon these variances and covariances according to the risk aversion parameter, ρ.

To see what this model implies about portfolio holdings, solve (2.3) in terms of the domestic asset demand equations.[48]

$$\underline{\chi}_t = \rho^{-1} E_t \underline{r}_{t+1} \operatorname{Var}_t(\underline{r}_{t+1})^{-1}. \tag{2.5}$$

Thus, the share of holdings in each asset depends inversely upon the measure of relative risk aversion, ρ, and the variability of returns. However, it depends positively upon the expected returns.[49] To examine returns in a multiple country setting, it is straightforward to extend (2.5) to the case of N different countries. In this case, $\underline{r}$ is the $N \times 1$ vector of equity returns in each of N countries and $\underline{\chi}$ is the vector of portfolio shares in each country.

This framework can be used to evaluate how closely the model's implied portfolio shares match the actual shares in Table 2.1. For this purpose, Panel A of Table 2.1 reports the implied portfolio shares using (2.5) based upon unconditional variances and data from monthly observations of country stock indexes and exchange rates from the *London Financial Times* over the period from January 1976 to February 1992. The covariance between returns and inflation is proxied by the covariance between exchange rates and inflation.

As this analysis shows, US investors have a much stronger preference for domestic equity holdings than is suggested by the CAPM model. This behavior is not particular to Americans. French and Poterba (1991) show that this behavior also holds for Japanese, German, British, and French residents. Therefore, "home bias" appears to be a general phenomenon.

2.1.2. Empirical tests: How good is the model?

One explanation for the evidence might simply be that the CAPM model is not a very good description of the world. I described evidence above showing that this model did not help describe the foreign exchange risk premium very well, but how does it do as an empirical characterization of stock returns?

Early empirical research on the international CAPM such as Solnik (1974b) and Stehle (1977) looked at the relationship in (2.4) based upon unconditional returns,

---

[48] Solnik (1974a) was the first to derive international equilibrium rates of return where consumers differ in their consumption prices. Stulz (1981a) shows how the consumption-based CAPM with i.i.d. shocks can be analyzed in a multi-country setting without assuming PPP. In this case, the equilibrium returns depend upon asset demand functions similar to (2.5) that are aggregated over investors of all countries. [See also Hodrick (1981)].

[49] As explained in Adler and Dumas (1983), the second term depends upon the minimum variance portfolio. Thus, even a risk-neutral investor with $\rho = 0$ would hold this portfolio since it provides an optimal hedge against inflation, in the absence of a real risk-free bond.

finding mixed results. These studies tested for the pricing relationship between returns rather than using measures of asset shares. More recently, Dumas and Solnik (1993) have estimated a conditional version of the model using returns in both equities and deposits allowing for time-varying covariances.[50] They find that the hypothesis of zero price on exchange rate risk is rejected, so that exchange rate variability appears to have explanatory power for equity returns. They also find that the international partial equilibrium CAPM is not rejected by the data.

Engel (1993), Engel and Rodrigues (1993), and Thomas and Wickens (1993) use asset share data to estimate models similar to (2.4). These studies reject the over-identifying restrictions of the model. Similar to Dumas and Solnik (1993), however, Engel (1993) finds that the model helps explain excess returns.

Other studies have used the CAPM as a benchmark to examine the factor relationships between equity returns in different countries. Harvey (1991) considers whether the behavior of equity returns for seventeen markets can be explained according to their covariance with the world equity return, consistent with the CAPM model. Assuming purchasing power parity, he finds that for most countries except Japan the model appears to explain country returns relatively well. Ferson and Harvey (1993) examine the predictability of a single beta asset pricing model for equity returns in eighteen countries also assuming purchasing power parity and no exchange rate risk. As in Harvey (1991), they find that the model has explanatory power for returns. However, they also find that these returns are better explained by multiple beta models that incorporate factors intended to capture exchange rate and other local sources of risk. Despite these other risk sources, the greatest source of risk priced in their model appears to be a global equity market risk component. Campbell and Hamao (1992) test a single factor latent variable restrictions across the US and Japan and find that they are rejected, although domestic equity returns and interest rates appear to be important predictors of foreign equity returns. They interpret their findings as evidence for market integration.

Overall, the evidence appears to be mixed. Tests of the international CAPM based upon asset share data tend to reject the model, while tests based upon relationships among returns tend to find more support in the form of explanatory power, particularly when account is taken of exchange rate risk. Whether the restrictions of the model are rejected or not, it appears to have some predictive content for international equity returns.

2.1.3. Is the international risk diversifiable with domestic assets?

Since the evidence suggests that the international CAPM relationships cannot be completely dismissed and therefore the home bias puzzle remains open, the next step

---

[50]They use the method described in Harvey (1991). This framework assumes that conditional variances are a linear function of a set of information variables.

is to consider possible explanations within these relationships. The analysis described above focuses upon the risk associated with international equity and, potentially, bond returns. However, it seems possible that the risk measured by the returns on international assets might be captured by returns on some domestic assets. If so, then, domestic residents may hold a disproportionately large component of domestic assets simply because they can gain the same diversification benefits with particular domestic securities as foreign assets.

One possible group of domestic returns that may be correlated with foreign returns corresponds to the equity of domestic multinational corporations. Since much of their earnings come from abroad, it might seem that their returns more closely match the returns on foreign stock markets than do other domestic companies. Jacquillat and Solnik (1978) ask whether the stocks of domestic multi-national firms have this diversification potential by regressing the returns of their stocks on the returns of stock indexes for a set of countries. They find that the coefficients on their own domestic stock index (the traditional market "betas") are close to one. Therefore, domestic multinational stocks are not much different in their diversification benefits than holding the domestic market portfolio.

Another approach would be to argue that the benefits of diversification come from industry-specific risk and not country-specific risk. Roll (1992) argued that industry-specific sources of risk explain international stock market indexes. However, Heston and Rouwenhoerst (forthcoming) and Solnik and de Freitas (1988) find that the primary sources of risk are in fact country-specific.[51]

This evidence suggests that the home bias puzzle is not explainable by the fact that domestic sources of risk can substitute perfectly for foreign risk factors.

2.2. "Home bias" based upon general equilibrium

The partial equilibrium nature of the CAPM treats equity returns as exogenous to the model and focuses upon the investor's static portfolio decision. On the other hand, general equilibrium pricing models simultaneously solve for the equity returns together with the intertemporal asset allocation decision. To illustrate this joint solution, I will return to the general equilibrium framework examined in Section 1.2 to show how international equity returns are determined in this context.

The implications of this model for the "home bias" puzzle are not as straightforward as in the static CAPM described above. In general, it is not possible to determine what should be the optimal portfolio holdings. Under additional assumptions, however, there are at least two basic implications of the model that may be compared with empirical observations on home bias. First, if the utility function is

---

[51]These papers use an arbitrage pricing theory (APT) approach to finding the factors of risk that determine stock prices. On the APT, see also Solnik (1983), and Bansal, Hsieh, and Viswanathan (1993).

iso-elastic, then portfolio holdings should be identical for all countries. This assumption is clearly at variance with the evidence in Table 2.1. Second, even if the utility function is not iso-elastic but markets are complete, then the intertemporal marginal rates of substitution in consumption should be equalized across countries. If, further, utility is iso-elastic, then complete markets imply that consumption growth rates should also be equalized across countries. As will be shown below, this prediction is also contrary to the evidence in the data.

2.2.1. International equity markets

To see the implications of general equilibrium for the absence of "home bias", consider again the framework described in Section 1.2. As there, it is expositionally useful to consider an endowment economy with one tradeable, non-durable good. Suppose there are j countries, each producing endowments of the good in the amount of Y_t^j for country j at time t. The stream of payments of these endowments can be purchased by buying a share of equity in country j at price z_t^j. This equity pays out endowments as dividends.

2.2.1.1. The closed economy prices
For later discussion, it is useful to first consider the price of these stocks in the absence of trade in world markets. For country j, the domestic investor's decision is restricted to buying shares in domestic equity or other domestic assets. Maximizing the expected present value of utility,

$$E_0 \sum_{t=0}^{\infty} \beta^t U(C_t^j)$$

with respect to consumption of the good, defined as C, and the share of domestic equity gives the first-order condition:[52]

$$U'(C_t^j)z_t^j = \beta E_t\{U'(C_{t+1}^j)[Y_{t+1}^j + z_{t+1}^j]\} \qquad (2.6)$$

or, solving (2.6) in terms of z, the domestic equity price is:

$$z_t^j = E_t \sum_{\tau=1}^{\infty} q_{t+\tau} Y_{t+\tau}^j \qquad (2.7)$$

where $q_{t+1} \equiv \{\beta U'(C_{t+1}^j)/U'(C_t^j)\}$. Note that q_t is the real intertemporal marginal rate of substitution in consumption while Q_t, defined in Section 1.2, is the nominal marginal rate of substitution.

The first order condition given in (2.6) is quite general and does not depend upon the specific assumptions of this model. The real stock price is the sum of the expected

---

[52]This first-order condition can be found by maximizing the lifetime utility over the shares of domestic equities, θ_t, subject to the constraint that $C_t^j + \theta_t z_t^j \leq \theta_{t-1} Y_t^j + \theta_{t-1} z_t^j$.

intertemporal marginal rates of substitution in consumption arising from the future dividend payments. Due to the generality of this first-order condition, this stock price formulation underlies many studies of equity markets.[53]

Under the specific assumptions of the endowment economy, the price can be further solved in terms of the production state. In equilibrium, the quantity of shares must equal one and, in the absence of investment, consumption equals production: $C_t^j = Y_t^j$. Therefore, in equilibrium, $q_{t+1} = \{\beta U'(Y_{t+1}^j)/U'(Y_t^j)\}$. In the absence of trade in international equity markets, each country will hold all of the stock of its own country and will consume its own output.

2.2.1.2. The integrated world market equilibrium

Now consider the price determined by perfectly integrated world capital markets. In this case, investors in country j may choose among foreign assets, determining a portfolio share for equity holdings in countries $i = 1, \ldots, N$. The stock of each country i has a price in the world stock market of $\underline{z}_t^i$. In this case, as long as countries have the same iso-elastic utility function, then they will all hold the same portfolio.[54] This result is general and does not depend upon the completeness of markets nor the endowment nature of the economy. The common portfolio can be characterized as a world mutual fund.

Determining the actual portfolio holdings as well as the consumption levels requires solving for the wealth levels and, hence, the stock prices of each country. First, defining the price of the world mutual fund as $\underline{z}_t$ and its dividend stream as $\underline{Y}_t = \sum_{j=1}^{N} Y_t^j$, the same steps may be followed as for the closed economy case to yield the mutual fund price:

$$\underline{z}_t = E_t \sum_{\tau=1}^{\infty} \underline{q}_{t+\tau} \underline{Y}_{t+\tau} \tag{2.8}$$

where now $\underline{q}_{t+1} \equiv \{\beta U'(\underline{Y}_{t+1}^j)/U'(\underline{Y}_t^j)\}$. Similarly, the price of each country's stock on world markets is:

$$\underline{z}_t^i = E_t \sum_{\tau=1}^{\infty} \underline{q}_{t+\tau} Y_{t+\tau}^j . \tag{2.9}$$

Each country j will sell its endowment stream on world markets and receive z^j. Country j will in turn buy shares θ^j in the mutual fund at price $\underline{z}$. Therefore, country j will hold shares equal to $\theta^j = (z^j/\underline{z})$. Consumption for country j will correspondingly be given by: $C_t^j = \theta^j \underline{Y}_t$. Each country shares in world consumption according to its share of wealth as valued according to the world stock market.

This result leads to a second implication for integrated stock markets under

---

[53] For example, Hansen and Singleton (1983) and Shiller (1981) test restrictions implied by this pricing relationship using US stock returns.
[54] See the discussion in Ingersoll (1987) and the references therein.

iso-elastic utility: countries share in the world consumption growth rate and therefore have the same consumption growth rates. As described in the chapter by Baxter (1995), this result depends only upon complete asset markets and does not depend upon the endowment assumptions in this discussion.[55]

2.2.1.3. Theoretical implications of no ''home bias'' relative to the evidence

Above, we showed that in the absence of ''home bias'', general equilibrium relationships based upon iso-elastic utility and complete markets would imply that two variables would be the same for all countries in the world: first, portfolio shares; and second, consumption growth rates.

As shown above, US as well as German, British, Japanese and French residents hold most of their equity holdings in their own countries. Therefore, they clearly do not hold the same portfolio shares. Furthermore, Tesar and Werner (1992) show that around the world foreigners hold a small fraction of the domestic stock markets. It is clear that this implication of the general equilibrium framework is rejected by casual data.

As for the implied common movement in consumption growth rates, this implication requires that no country-specific component should explain domestic consumption growth.[56] Since consumption data are often plagued by measurement error, one way to examine this issue is to run a cross-sectional regression of consumption growth on output growth and a constant to capture the common component across countries. This regression may be written as:

$$\ln(C^j_{t+1}/C^j_t) = b_0 + b_1 \ln(Y^j_{t+1}/Y^j_t) + \zeta^j_{t+1} \tag{2.10}$$

where $b_0 \equiv \ln(\underline{C}_{t+1}/\underline{C}_t)$, the aggregate consumption growth rate, is a constant across countries at each point in time, Y^j_t is the output level in country j at time t, b_i are parameters, and ζ^j_{t+1} is a residual including the measurement error.

Complete markets and optimal risk-sharing imply that $b_1 = 0$. In other words, consumption should vary with the common component of international consumption captured by the constant and should be independent of any country specific disturbances. In particular, it should be independent of output.

Table 2.2 reports the results of estimates of eq. (2.10) for 72 countries in the Penn World Tables over five year intervals. As the numbers show, the coefficient b_1 is significantly positive in all cases. This result implies that countries consume more in

---

[55]In business cycle models with complete markets, intertemporal marginal rates of substitution in consumption are equalized across countries. To see that markets are complete in the example above, note that the only sources of uncertainty are the endowment realizations across countries. As a result, the set of possible states is spanned by holdings of equities so that markets are complete.

[56]This implication derives from the implicit assumption above that consumption is separable in the utility function from other goods such as leisure. If this assumption does not hold, then the following test may be amended with similar conclusions. See Lewis (1993).

Table 2.2
Home bias puzzle and international consumption patterns

A. Cross-sectional regressions of consumption growth on income growth

Growth rate year pairs	Coeff. b_1 (Std. error)
1951–50	0.87** (.09)
1956–55	1.07** (.09)
1961–60	1.26** (.11)
1966–65	0.92** (.16)
1971–70	1.40** (.11)
1976–75	1.04** (.19)
1981–80	0.83** (.11)
1986–85	1.06** (.16)

B. Domestic relative to foreign turnover of stock ownership

Country	Domestic ratio	Foreign equity held by dom. res.	Domestic equity held by for. res.
Canada	0.61	7.7	2.2
UK	0.77	NA	1.4
US	1.07	2.5	1.6

Notes: Cross-sectional regression in Panel A use top 72 countries in Penn World Tables by data quality. Panel B from Tesar and Werner (1992).

response to country-specific increases in income than the aggregated world consumption growth rate.[57] These findings are consistent with the view that domestic residents hold a suboptimally high proportion of their wealth in domestic equities, as we have found to be true above.

2.2.2. Empirical evidence: How good are the pricing relationships?

Note that the first-order conditions for equity pricing in eq. (2.6) can be written in the general form $E_t(q_{t+1} r^j_{t+1}) = 1$, where $r^j_{t+1} \equiv [Y^j_{t+1} + z^j_{t+1}]/z^j_t$. When prices and dividends are in nominal terms, then this first-order condition can be written as the product of the nominal intertemporal marginal rate of substitution in consumption and

---

[57]Lewis (1994) considers a related regression using panel estimation. Obstfeld (1989, 1994c) finds similar results in time series regressions of the industrialized countries. See Baxter (1995) for more discussion.

the stock returns given in (1.36): $E_t(Q_{t+1}R^j_{t+1}) = 1.$[58] Therefore, all of the evidence on latent variable models and Hansen–Jagannathan bounds described for excess foreign exchange returns are equally applicable to equity returns as well.

Cumby (1990) tested for a single latent variable among stock returns across a set of countries and found that the restrictions were rejected. Campbell and Hamao (1992) found that the US and Japanese stocks helped forecast each other. A single latent variable model was rejected for the 1970s, but not the 1980s. Other studies have tested the relationship using both foreign exchange returns and stock returns, generally rejecting the restrictions.[59] Bekaert and Hodrick (1992) also calculate the Hansen–Jagannathan bounds using both stock and foreign exchange returns, finding that these lower bounds on the intertemporal marginal rate of substitution in consumption are much larger than could be derived from standard theoretical models.

Essentially, the evidence based upon first-order conditions in general equilibrium equity pricing relationships across countries provide the same inconsistencies as do foreign exchange returns. First, latent variable comovements do not necessarily provide evidence for general equilibrium pricing relationships, even if they exist. A number of studies have found common transmission effects among stock markets without reference to general equilibrium pricing effects.[60]

The variability of the equity premium implied by the data is much larger than the variability implied by theory. As before, this discrepancy leaves open the question of whether other utility functions or modifications of the model's assumptions will ultimately provide more evidence for the model. Therefore, other studies have asked whether modifications of the basic model might help explain ''home bias''.

2.2.3. Are non-traded goods responsible for the ''home bias''?

The basic model considered above assumes that residents of all countries consume a single tradeable good. Stockman and Dellas (1989) point out that if investors consume non-traded goods in addition to traded goods, then domestic investors will hold all of the equities with payouts in domestic non-traded goods and will share equally in the world equity market in traded goods when their wealth levels are equal. Since domestic residents hold all of the non-traded goods equities, the domestic

---

[58]That is, defining Z as the nominal stock price and e as the nominal endowment,

$$Z^j_t = E_t \sum_{\tau=1}^{\infty} Q_{t+\tau} e^j_{t+\tau}.$$

[59]See, for example, Bekaert and Hodrick (1992), Giovannini and Jorion (1987a) and Lewis (1990).

[60]For example, see Eun and Shim (1989). King and Wadhwani (1990) find international transmission effects between equity markets following the October 1987 crash and argue that these effects result from traders with imperfect information rationally trying to learn the true equity values.

residents' total holdings of traded and non-traded equities will be biased toward home equities.[61]

Stockman and Dellas (1989) assume that non-traded goods are separable from tradeable goods in utility. However, Baxter, Jermann, and King (1994) show that the Stockman-Dellas result is sensitive to the assumption that utility is separable between traded and non-traded goods. Depending upon the degree of substitutability between tradeables and non-tradeables and the level of risk aversion, domestic residents may want to hold less than 100 percent of domestic non-traded good equities and may even want to short it.[62]

Non-traded goods can also help explain the bias in consumption growth rates toward domestic country disturbances, as found in Table 2.2. Tesar (1993) and Stockman and Tesar (1995) show theoretically and empirically that the presence of non-traded goods can lower the implied correlation between consumption growth rates. For a panel data set of 72 countries, Lewis (1993) shows that non-traded goods can explain less than one percent of the variance in idiosyncratic component of consumption growth rates, leaving much of the idiosyncratic movements unexplained.[63]

In sum, the presence of non-traded goods may theoretically explain the home bias puzzle as reflected in portfolio holdings as well as consumption comovements. However, a clear relationship between portfolio holdings and non-traded goods depends upon particular values to parameters in the utility function. It has yet to be determined whether these values are plausible enough to explain the home bias puzzle. In terms of consumption co-movements, non-tradeables alone do not appear to be able to explain empirically the idiosyncratic movements in consumption growth rates across countries. Overall, the presence of non-traded goods moves in the direction of explaining the home bias puzzle, but leaves open the question of whether it can explain the puzzle.

[61] This explanation is related to an argument in several earlier papers based upon partial equilibrium analysis. Hedging domestic price uncertainty could result in home bias, it was argued, when domestic residents consume a higher share of domestic goods than foreigners. Branson and Henderson (1984) survey this literature and show that the relationship is ambiguous. Eldor, Pines, and Schwartz (1988) present sufficient conditions for home bias based upon this relationship using a general equilibrium model.

[62] The effects of non-separabilities in utility are also considered in Pesenti and van Wincoop (1994) and Tesar (forthcoming). These papers assume that domestic residents are restricted from holding foreign non-traded goods equities, and derive conditions under which an investor would find it optimal to be biased toward domestic traded goods equities. Baxter, Jermann, and King (1994) show that as long as investors are able to hold foreign non-traded goods equities, domestic investors will never choose to bias their portfolio holdings toward domestic traded goods equities.

[63] Baxter (1995) provides a discussion of the larger literature in this area as well as the related issue of non-traded factors in production.

2.3. Restrictions and frictions in international equity market transactions

The low degree of risk-sharing whether viewed from a partial equilibrium or a general equilibrium point of view currently remains a puzzle in international finance. Since home bias does not seem readily explainable by modifications to the standard models described above, the search for an explanation leads naturally to questions about basic underlying assumptions of the models. Both the partial and general equilibrium frameworks assume that markets are perfectly integrated without any government restrictions or other impediments. They also assume that investors are rationally informed about the potential gains of diversifying into foreign stock markets and, implicitly, that these gains are large enough to offset any transactions costs from acquiring foreign equities.[64] Any of these assumptions may be invalidated and, if so, may help explain the puzzle. I describe evidence concerning these explanations next.

2.3.1. Segmented equity markets and government restrictions

One explanation for the puzzle may be that domestic investors face barriers to acquiring foreign equities. The inability to obtain or hold foreign equities at the same cost as foreign residents may be the result of government restrictions such as taxes or may reflect more subtle constraints. In the extreme case of complete capital market immobility, countries may be forced to hold only their own equities as in the example described in Section 2.2. More realistically, countries are likely to face some restrictions that potentially impede capital flows, with the likely outcome that portfolios of domestic residents are biased toward domestic equities.

General recognition that international capital market restrictions exist has led to studies concerning the theoretical effects and empirical evidence of segmented markets. Stulz (1981b) analyzes the effects of taxes on gross holdings of foreign assets, finding that some foreign assets will not be held by domestic residents in equilibrium.[65] Errunza and Losq (1985) develop and test a restricted version of the Stulz (1981b) model in which domestic investors cannot hold foreign equities but foreign investors can hold both domestic and foreign equities. They apply this model to U.S. (domestic) relative to developing country (foreign) markets and find that parameter restrictions implied by the hypothesis of mild segmentation are not rejected. Errunza and Losq (1989) theoretically consider the effects of capital flow restrictions on the holdings of equity positions and their welfare implications.

Since market segmentation seems most likely to exist between the developed

---

[64]Obstfeld (1994a) provides a useful survey of the issues behind capital market movements as well as measures of capital immobility.

[65]Black (1974) examines the effects of proportional taxes on net holdings of risky foreign assets. In this model, sufficiently high barriers to investment induce large short holdings of foreign assets but not an equilibrium in which foreign assets are not held at all by domestic residents.

countries and developing or emerging markets, recent research has examined the behavior of equities in these markets. Bonser-Neal, Brauer, Neal, and Wheatley (1990) analyze the effects of government liberalizations on the pricing of "country funds", mutual funds comprised of the assets in specific countries. For five developing countries with foreign investment restrictions, they consider the ratios between the price of the funds in the international market relative to the net asset values (NAVs) of their underlying component equities within the country. Bonser-Neal, et al. find that the price–NAV ratios fall significantly either in anticipation or following liberalizations of investment restrictions. They interpret this evidence as demonstrating that government-imposed barriers have been effective in segmenting international capital markets. Hardouvelis, La Porta, and Wizman (1993) also find that cross-border investment restrictions are significant in explaining the difference between prices and NAVs of country funds.

Harvey (1993) provides a broad empirical examination of returns in twenty emerging markets. He finds that standard international asset pricing models based upon integrated capital markets fail to explain the returns and predictability of country returns, concluding that models based upon market segmentation seem more likely to explain these returns. Similarly, Claessens and Rhee (1993) investigate the stock performance in emerging markets in relation to their accessibility by foreign investors, finding that they reject market integration.

As described in Section 2.2 above, home bias in portfolio holdings is linked in general equilibrium models to country-specific effects on domestic consumption. Using a panel data set of capital market restrictions for 72 countries, Lewis (1993) finds that the country-specific bias in domestic consumption is significantly larger for countries with capital market restrictions than those without any restrictions.

Taken together, the evidence suggests that government restrictions can be important for explaining why the portfolios of domestic residents in developing, relatively unrestricted countries may be biased away from holdings of equities in emerging markets. On the other hand, this argument is more difficult to make for the developed countries that do not face these restrictions. As we have seen, the US demonstrates a strong "home bias" in equity holdings with developed countries yet it does not impose significant restrictions of capital account movements.

Additional evidence of this implausibility is provided in Tesar and Werner (1992). They calculate the turnover rate on foreign equity held by domestic residents as well as the turnover rate on domestic equity held by foreign residents. Panel B of Table 2.2 reports their results together with the total turnover. While the total turnover rate averages less than one, the turnover rates for international equity flows is *higher*. Therefore, the flows of capital on international equity transactions tend to be higher than those on domestic flows. Significant restrictions on international transactions would suggest the opposite pattern. Although this evidence does not provide any standard errors and therefore should be interpreted with caution, it suggests that international equity transactions are not significantly impeded among these countries.

2.3.2. Market frictions: How big are the gains?

Behind the home bias puzzle is the presumption that investors would benefit sufficiently from acquiring foreign equities in order to offset any transactions costs. However, acquisition of foreign securities is not costless, even in ideal circumstances. With fully integrated capital markets, there are at least brokerage costs and perhaps the costs of getting information about foreign countries and companies. While these costs may be arguably small, they must be compared with the potential gains from diversifying. On this issue, studies based upon the partial equilibrium CAPM and the general equilibrium approach appear to give quite different answers.

Based upon the partial equilibrium CAPM, the portfolio improvement from diversifying into foreign securities has been recognized since at least Levy and Sarnat (1970). More recently, Grauer and Hakansson (1987) show that the gains to a US investor from diversifying into 14 non-US equity and bond markets is quite large. For example, relative to the US S&P 500 index with a mean of 10 percent and a standard deviation of 17.3 percent, portfolios including foreign assets could dominate with means of 13 percent or more and standard deviations of 16 percent or less.

On the other hand, general equilibrium models suggest that gains to international diversification can be quite small.[66] Cole and Obstfeld (1991) calculated the gains from diversifying in a two-country general equilibrium model without growth. They found that the gains from moving from an autarkic equilibrium without trade in financial markets to one in which investors optimally hold foreign securities are miniscule, between 0.1 percent to 0.2 percent of annual consumption. On the other hand, Obstfeld (1994b) finds that the gains from diversification can be much larger when growth is incorporated into the analysis.

The distinct approaches used in these two literatures obscure an important empirical difference that may help explain the striking contrasts between their implied gains to risk sharing. That is, general equilibrium models tend to base their calculations of welfare gains on consumption data while the partial equilibrium calculations come from equity return data. As described above with respect to Hansen–Jagannathan bounds, consumption-based models have been unsuccessful in generating sufficient variability in theoretical returns to be able to explain equity and foreign exchange premia. Lewis (1994) shows that this discrepancy is important. When the variability in equity returns from a general equilibrium approach is matched with the actual equity return volatility instead of consumption volatility, then general equilibrium models also generate significant welfare costs, even in the absence of growth.

While this evidence is preliminary, it suggests that the same problems in explaining risk premia volatility may also plague unified attempts to calculate welfare costs of insufficient risk sharing.

[66]Tesar (forthcoming) surveys this literature.

2.3.3. Market inefficiencies

Another explanation for home bias is simply that the market is inefficient and investors do not recognize the potential gains to their portfolio performance. In this vein, French and Poterba (1991) have argued that the home bias in portfolio holdings can be explained by the fact that domestic investors are overly optimistic about the returns in the home market. Using the model in Section 2.1, they calculate the degree to which domestic expected returns would have to exceed actual returns in order to justify the large share of domestic wealth held in domestic assets. They find that the "optimism" on U.S. equity was about 4 percent. Also, the expected returns on foreign stocks should have been 1 percent to 7 percent lower than they actually were.

Baxter and Jermann (1993) take this argument a step farther by considering human capital as part of wealth. They argue that domestic wealth is comprised of, not only financial wealth, but also human capital. Since their measured U.S. returns on human capital are positively correlated with U.S. equities, and since human capital is non-tradeable, the domestic investor should take short positions in the domestic financial market. They calculate the degree of "optimism" as in French and Poterba and find results similar to theirs.

Therefore, one answer to the home bias puzzle is that domestic investors are simply uninformed or irrational about foreign relative to domestic returns. If so, this answer leads to questions similar to those raised about irrational forecast errors in Section 1. Where does the irrational domestic optimism or foreign pessimism come from? Can it be explained by heterogeneous agent models? Are there testable implications of this explanation? So far, theoretical models and tests based upon this explanation have yet to be produced.

2.4. The future of the "home bias" puzzle

This section has reviewed arguments to explain the bias by domestic residents toward holdings of domestic assets in their portfolios. I have showed the presence of this bias based upon both partial and general equilibrium models, as well as attempts to modify the standard models to explain the results. While modifications, such as the presence of non-traded goods, move in the direction of lessening the puzzle, the evidence so far suggests that these modifications are unlikely to fully resolve the issue.

Other evidence suggests that restrictions in capital markets might help explain the home bias by developed countries away from developing country equities. Among the well integrated markets of many developed countries, this explanation seems unlikely to be an important explanation, however. Whether the potential gains to investors are large enough to warrant international diversification remains an open question – calculations based upon stock returns tend to find that the gains are large, while those based upon consumption find that the gains are tiny. Although unpalatable to most economists, a final possibility is simply that investors are uninformed about foreign diversification, although testable models based upon this argument have not been provided.

An important development in the last decade has been the increased accessibility of domestic residents to foreign markets through international mutual funds as well as more open capital markets. While acquiring individual foreign stocks may be costly through either informational difficulties arising from different languages, accounting systems, or legal risks, mutual funds that hold foreign securities readily provide the domestic investor with the gains of international diversification. These mutual funds typically do not cost much more than the domestic funds. Anecdotal evidence during the early 1990s from newspapers suggested that American investors were acquiring foreign securities and mutual funds in record numbers. Therefore, it remains to be seen whether the home bias puzzle will disappear as foreign securities become easier to purchase by domestic residents.

References

Abel, A. (1990), "Asset prices under habit formation and catching up with the Joneses", American Economic Review 80:38–42.

Adler, M. and B. Dumas (1983), "International portfolio choice and corporate finance: A synthesis", Journal of Finance 38:925–984.

Backus, D.K., A.W. Gregory, and C.I. Telmer (1993), "Accounting for forward rates in markets for foreign currency", Journal of Finance 48:1887–1908.

Backus, D.K. and P.J. Kehoe (1989), "On the denomination of government debt: A critique of the portfolio balance approach", Journal of Monetary Economics 23:359–376.

Bansal, R., D.A. Hsieh, and S. Viswanathan (1993), "A new approach to international arbitrage pricing", Journal of Finance 48:1719–1747.

Bates, D.S. (1994), "Dollar jump fears: 1984–1992", working paper, University of Pennsylvania.

Baxter, M. (1995), "International business cycles", in: G. Grossman and K. Rogoff, eds., Handbook of international economics, vol. 3 (North-Holland, Amsterdam).

Baxter, M. and U.J. Jermann (1993), "The international diversification puzzle is worse than you think", Rochester Center for Economic Research Working Paper No. 350.

Baxter, M., U.J. Jermann, and R.G. King (1994), "Non-traded goods, non-traded factors, and international non-diversification", working paper, University of Virginia.

Bekaert, G. (1992), "The time-variation in risk and return in foreign exchange markets: A general equilibrium approach", Stanford University Working Paper Series, No. 1276.

Bekaert, G. (1994), "Exchange rate volatility and deviations from unbiasedness in a cash-in-advance model", Journal of International Economics 36:29–52.

Bekaert, G. and R.J. Hodrick (1992), "Characterizing predictable components in excess returns on equity and foreign exchange markets", Journal of Finance 47:467–510.

Bekaert, G. and R.J. Hodrick (1993), "On biases in the measurement of foreign exchange risk premiums", Journal of International Money and Finance 12:115–138.

Bekaert, G., R.J. Hodrick, and D. Marshall (1994), "The implications of first-order risk aversion for asset market premiums", National Bureau of Economic Research Working Paper No. 4624.

Black, F. (1974), "International capital market equilibrium with investment barriers", Journal of Financial Economics 1:337–352.

Bilson, J.F.O. (1981), "The 'speculative efficiency' hypothesis", Journal of Business 54:435–452.

Bonser-Neal, C., G. Brauer, R. Neal, and S. Wheatley (1990), "International investment restrictions and closed-end country fund prices", Journal of Finance 45:523–548.

Bossearts, P. and P. Hillion (1991), "Market microstructure effects of government intervention in the foreign exchange market", Review of Financial Studies 4:513–541.

Branson, W. (1977), "Asset markets and relative prices in exchange rate determination", Sozialwissenschaftliche Annalen 1:69–89.

Branson, W. and D. Henderson (1984), "The specification and influence of asset markets", in: R.W. Jones and P.B. Kenen, eds., Handbook of international economics, vol. 1 (North-Holland, Amsterdam).

Campbell, J.Y. and R.H. Clarida (1987), "The term structure of Euromarket interest rates: An empirical investigation", Journal of Monetary Economics 19:25–44.

Campbell, J.Y. and Y. Hamao (1992), "Predictable stock returns in the United States and Japan: A study of long-term capital market integration", Journal of Finance 47:43–70.

Claessens, S. and M. Rhee (1993), "The effects of equity barriers on foreign investment in developing countries", National Bureau of Economic Research Working Paper No. 4579.

Cole, H.L., and M. Obstfeld, (1991), "Commodity trade and international risk sharing: How much do financial markets matter?", Journal of Monetary Economics 28:3–24.

Constantinides, G. (1990), "Habit formation: A resolution of the equity premium puzzle", Journal of Political Economy 98:519–543.

Cumby, R.E. (1988), "Is it risk? Explaining deviations from uncovered interest parity", Journal of Monetary Economics 22:279–300.

Cumby, R.E. (1990), "Consumption risk and international equity returns: Some empirical evidence", Journal of International Money and Finance 9:181–192.

Cumby, R.E. and M. Obstfeld (1981), "A note on exchange-rate expectations and nominal interest differentials: A test of the Fisher hypothesis", Journal of Finance 36:697–703.

Cumby, R.E. and M. Obstfeld (1984), "International interest rate and price level linkages under flexible exchange rates: A review of recent evidence", in: J.F.O. Bilson and R.C. Marston, eds., Exchange rate theory and practice (University of Chicago Press, Chicago).

De Long, J.B., A. Shleifer, L.H. Summers, and R.J. Waldmann (1990), "Noise trader risk in financial markets", Journal of Political Economy 98:703–738.

Dominguez, K. and J. Frankel (1993), "Does foreign exchange intervention matter? The portfolio effect", American Economic Review 83:1356–1369.

Domowitz, I. and C. Hakkio (1985), "Conditional variance and the risk premium in the foreign exchange market", Journal of International Economics 19:47–66.

Dumas, B. (1994), "Partial-equilibrium vs general-equilibrium models of international capital market equilibrium", in: R. van der Ploeg, ed., Handbook of international macroeconomics (Basil Blackwell, Oxford).

Dumas, B. and B. Solnik (1993), "The world price of exchange rate risk, working paper", Hautes Etudes Commerciales School of Management.

Edison, H.J. (1993), "The effectiveness of central-bank intervention: A survey of the literature after 1982", Special Papers in International Economics No. 18, Princeton University Printing Services, Princeton, NJ.

Eldor, R., D. Pines, and A. Schwartz (1988), "Home asset preferences and productivity shocks", Journal of International Economics 25:165–176.

Engel, C.M. (1984), "Testing for the absence of expected real profits from forward market speculation", Journal of International Economics 17:299–308.

Engel, C.M. (1992a), "On the foreign exchange risk premium in a general equilibrium model", Journal of International Economics 32:305–319.

Engel, C.M. (1992b), "The risk premium and the liquidity premium in foreign exchange markets", International Economic Review 33:871–879.

Engel, C.M. (1993), "Tests of CAPM on an international portfolio of bonds and stocks", National Bureau of Economic Research Working Paper No. 4598.

Engel, C.M. and J.D. Hamilton (1990), "Long swings in the dollar: Are they in the data and do the markets know it?", American Economic Review 80:689–713.

Engel, C.M. and A.P. Rodrigues (1989), "Tests of international CAPM with time-varying covariances", Journal of Applied Econometrics 4:119–138.

Engel, C.M. and A.P. Rodrigues (1993), "Tests of mean-variance efficiency of international equity markets", Oxford Economic Papers 45:403–421.

Epstein, L. and S. Zin (1990), "'First order' risk aversion and the equity premium puzzle", Journal of Monetary Economics 26:387–407.

Errunza, V. and E. Losq (1985), "International asset pricing under mild segmentation: Theory and evidence", Journal of Finance 40:105–124.

Errunza, V. and E. Losq (1989), "Capital flow controls, international asset pricing, and investor's welfare: A multi-country framework", Journal of Finance 44:1025–1037.

Eun, C.S. and S. Shim (1989), "International transmission of stock market movements", Journal of Financial and Quantitative Analysis 24:241–256.

Evans, M.D.D. and K.K. Lewis (1995), "Do long-term swings in the dollar affect estimates of the risk premium?", Review of Financial Studies, forthcoming.

Fama, E. (1984), "Forward and spot exchange rates", Journal of Monetary Economics 14:319–338.

Ferson, W.E. and C.R. Harvey (1993), "The risk and predictability of international equity returns", Review of Financial Studies 6:527–566.

Fisher, I. (1930), The theory of interest (Macmillan, New York).

Frankel, J.A. (1982), "In search of the exchange risk premium: A six-currency test assuming mean-variance optimization", Journal of International Money and Finance 1:255–274.

Frankel, J.A. (1986), "The implications of mean-variance optimization for four questions in international macroeconomics", Journal of International Money and Finance 5 (Supplement):S53–S75.

Frankel, J.A. and K.A. Froot (1987), "Using survey data to test standard propositions regarding exchange rate expectations", American Economic Review 77:133–153.

Frankel, J.A. and K.A. Froot (1988), "Explaining the demand for dollars: International rates of return and the expectations of chartists and fundamentalists", in: R. Chambers and P. Paarlberg, eds., Agriculture, macroeconomics and the exchange rate (Westview Press, Boulder, CO).

Frankel, J.A. and A. Rose (1995), "An empirical characterization of nominal exchange rates", in: K. Rogoff and G. Grossman, eds., Handbook of international economics (North Holland, Amsterdam).

French, K. and J. Poterba (1991), "International diversification and international equity markets", American Economic Review 81:222–226.

Frenkel, J.A. and A. Razin (1980), "Stochastic prices and tests of efficiency of foreign exchange markets", Economic Letters 6:165–170.

Froot, K.A. and J.A. Frankel (1989), "Forward discount bias: Is it an exchange risk premium?", The Quarterly Journal of Economics 104:139–161.

Froot, K.A. and R. Thaler (1990), "Anomalies: Foreign exchange", Journal of Economic Perspectives 4:179–192.

Gibbons, M. and W.E. Ferson (1985), "Testing asset pricing models with changing expectations and an unobservable market portfolio", Journal of Financial Economics 14:217–236.

Giovannini, A. and P. Jorion (1987a), "Interest rates and risk premia in the stock market and in the foreign exchange market", Journal of International Money and Finance 6:107–124.

Giovannini, A. and P. Jorion (1987b), "Foreign-exchange risk premia volatility once again", Journal of International Money and Finance 7:111–114.

Girton, A. and D. Henderson (1977), "Central bank operations in foreign and domestic assets under fixed and flexible exchange rates", in: P. Clark, D. Logue, and R. Sweeney, eds., The effects of exchange rate adjustment (US Treasury, Washington, DC).

Grauer, R.R. and N.H. Hakansson (1987), "Gains from international diversification: 1968–85 returns on portfolios of stocks and bonds", Journal of Finance 42:721–739.

Hall, R.E. (1978), "Stochastic implications of the life cycle-permanent income hypothesis: Theory and evidence", Journal of Political Economy 86:971–987.

Hall, R.E. (1989), "Consumption", in: R.J. Barro, ed., Modern business cycle theory (Harvard University Press, Cambridge, MA).

Hansen, L.P. and R.J. Hodrick (1983), "Risk averse speculation in the forward foreign exchange market: An econometric analysis of linear models", in: J.A. Frenkel, ed., Exchange rates and international macroeconomics (University of Chicago Press, Chicago).

Hansen, L.P. and R. Jagannathan (1991), "Implications of security market data for models of dynamic economies", Journal of Political Economy 99:225–262.

Hansen, L.P. and K.J. Singleton (1983), "Stochastic consumption, risk aversion, and the temporal behavior of asset returns", Journal of Political Economy 91': 249–265.

Hardouvelis, G.A., R. La Porta, and T.A. Wizman (1993), "What moves the discount on country equity funds"? National Bureau of Economic Research Working Paper No. 4571.

Harvey, C. (1991), "The world price of covariance risk", Journal of Finance 46:111–158.

Harvey, C. (1993), "Predictable risk and returns in emerging markets, working paper", Duke University.

Heston, S.L. and K.G. Roewenhorst (1994), "Industrial structure explains the benefits of international diversification?", Journal of Financial Economics 36:3–27.

Hodrick, R.J. (1981), "International asset pricing with time-varying risk premia", Journal of International Economics 11:573–587.

Hodrick, R.J. (1987), The empirical evidence on the efficiency of forward and futures foreign exchange markets (Harwood Academic Publishers, Chur, Switzerland).

Hodrick, R.J. and S. Srivastava (1984), "An investigation of risk and return in forward foreign exchange", Journal of International Money and Finance 3:5–29.

Hodrick, R.J. and S. Srivastava (1986), "The covariation of risk premiums and expected future spot exchange rates", Journal of International Money and Finance 5 (Supplement):S5–S21.

Howell, M. and A. Cozzini (1990), International equity flows – 1990 edition (Salomon Brothers European Equity Research, London, UK).

Ingersoll, J.E., Jr. (1987), "Portfolio Separation Theorems", in: Theory of financial decision making (Rowman and Littlefield, Savage, MD).

Jacquillat, B. and B. Solnik (1978), "Multinationals are poor tools for diversification", Journal of Portfolio Management 4:3–12.

Kaminsky, G.L. (1993), "Is there a peso-problem? Evidence from the dollar/pound exchange rate 1976–1987", American Economic Review 83:450–472.

King, M.A. and S. Wadhwani (1990), "Transmission of volatility between stock markets", Review of Financial Studies 3:5–33.

Kouri, P. (1976), "The exchange rate and the balance of payments in the short run and in the long run: A monetary approach", Scandinavian Journal of Economics 78:280–308.

Krasker, W. (1980), "The 'peso problem' in testing the efficiency of forward exchange markets", Journal of Monetary Economics 6:269–276.

Leme, P. (1984), "Integration of international capital markets", working paper, University of Chicago.

Levy, H. and M. Sarnat (1970), "International diversification of investment portfolios", American Economic Review 60:668–675.

Lewis, K.K. (1988a), "Testing the portfolio balance model: A multi-lateral approach", Journal of International Economics 24:109–127.

Lewis, K.K. (1988b), "Inflation risk and asset market disturbances: The mean-variance model revisited", Journal of International Money and Finance 7:273–288.

Lewis, K.K. (1989a), "Can learning affect exchange rate behavior? The case of the dollar in the early 1980's", Journal of Monetary Economics 23:79–100.

Lewis, K.K. (1989b), "Changing beliefs and systematic rational forecast errors with evidence from foreign exchange", American Economic Review 79:621–636.

Lewis, K.K. (1990), "The behavior of Eurocurrency returns across different holding periods and monetary regimes", Journal of Finance 45:1211–1236.

Lewis, K.K. (1991), "Should the holding period matter for the intertemporal consumption-based CAPM?", Journal of Monetary Economics 28:365–389.

Lewis, K.K. (1993), "What can explain the apparent lack of international consumption risk-sharing?", working paper, University of Pennsylvania.

Lewis, K.K. (1994), "Why do consumption and stock returns suggest such different costs of imperfect risk-sharing?", working paper, University of Pennsylvania.

Lintner, J. (1965), "The valuation of risky assets and the selection of risky investment in stock portfolios and capital budgets", Review of Economics and Statistics 47:13–37.

Lizondo, J.S. (1983), "Foreign exchange futures prices under fixed exchange rates", Journal of International Economics 14:69–84.

Lucas, R.E., Jr. (1978), "Asset prices in an exchange economy", Econometrica 46:1429–1445.

Lucas, R.E., Jr. (1982), "Interest rates and currency prices in a two-country world", Journal of Monetary Economics 10:336–360.

Lyons, R.K. (1993), "Tests of microstructural hypotheses in the foreign exchange market", National Bureau of Economic Research Working Paper No. 4471.

Mark, N. (1985), "On time-varying risk premia in the foreign exchange market", Journal of Monetary Economics 16:3–18.

Mehra, R. and E.C. Prescott (1985), "The equity premium: A puzzle", Journal of Monetary Economics 15:145–162.

Mossin, J. (1966), "Equilibrium in a capital asset market", Econometrica 34:768–783.

Mussa, M. (1981), "The role of official intervention", Group of Thirty Occasional Papers, No. 6, Group of Thirty, New York.

Obstfeld, M. (1989), "How integrated are world capital markets? Some new tests", in: G. Calvo, R. Findlay, J. de Macedo, eds., Debt, stabilization and development: Essays in memory of Carlos Diaz-Alejandro (Basil Blackwell, Oxford).

Obstfeld, M. (1994a), "International capital market mobility in the 1990s", in: P.B. Kenen, ed., Understanding interdependence: The macroeconomics of the open economy (Princeton University Press, Princeton, NJ).

Obstfeld, M. (1994b), "Risk-taking, global diversification, and growth", American Economic Review 84:1310–1329.

Obstfeld, M. (1994c), "Are industrial-country consumption risks globally diversified?", in: L. Liederman and A. Razin, eds., Capital mobility: The impact on consumption, investment, and growth (Cambridge University Press, Cambridge).

Pagan, A. (1986), "A note on the magnitude of risk premia", Journal of International Money and Finance 7:109–110.

Pesenti, P. and E. van Wincoop (1994), "International portfolio diversification and non-traded goods", working paper, Princeton University.

Rogoff, K. (1980), "Tests of the martingale model for foreign exchange futures markets", in Essays on expectations and exchange rate volatility, Ph.D. dissertation, Massachusetts Institute of Technology, Cambridge, MA.

Rogoff, K. (1984), "On the effects of sterilized intervention: An analysis of weekly data", Journal of Monetary Economics 14:133–159.

Roll, R. (1992), "Industrial structure and the comparative behavior of international stock market indexes", Journal of Finance 47:3–41.

Scheinkman, J.A. (1984), "General equilibrium models of economic fluctuations: A survey of theory", working paper, University of Chicago.

Sharpe, W. (1964), "Capital asset prices: A theory of market equilibrium under conditions of risk", Journal of Finance 19:425–442.

Shiller, R.J. (1981), "Do stock prices move too much to be justified by subsequent changes in dividends?", American Economic Review 71:421–436.

Solnik, B. (1974a), "An equilibrium model of the international capital market", Journal of Economic Theory 8:500–524.

Solnik, B. (1974b), "The international pricing of risk: An empirical investigation of the world capital market structure", Journal of Finance 29:365–378.

Solnik, B. (1983), "International arbitrage pricing theory", Journal of Finance 38:449–457.

Solnik, B. and A. de Freitas (1988), "International factors of stock price behaviour", in: S. Khoury and A. Ghosh, eds., Recent developments in international finance and banking (Lexington Books, Lexington, MA).

Stehle, R. (1977), "An empirical test of the alternative hypotheses of national and international pricing of risky assets", Journal of Finance 32:493–502.

Stockman, A.C. and H. Dellas (1989), "International portfolio nondiversification and exchange rate variability", Journal of International Economics 26:271–290.

Stockman, A.C. and L. Tesar (1995), "Tastes and technology in a two-country models of the business-cycle: Explaining international comovements", American Economic Review, 85:168–185.

Stulz, R.M. (1981a), "A model of international asset pricing", Journal of Financial Economics 9:383–406.

Stulz, R.M. (1981b), "On the effects of barriers to international investment", Journal of Finance 36:923–934.

Stulz, R.M. (1994), "International portfolio choice and asset pricing: An integrative survey", in: R.

Jarrow, V. Maksimovic, and W.T. Ziemba, eds., Finance, in: Series of handbooks in operations research and management science (North-Holland, Amsterdam).

Svensson, L.E.O. (1985a), "Currency prices, terms of trade and interest rates: A general equilibrium asset-pricing cash-in-advance approach", Journal of International Economics 18:17–42.

Svensson, L.E.O. (1985b), "Money and asset prices in a cash-in-advance economy", Journal of Political Economy 93:919–944.

Telmer, C.I. (1993), "Asset pricing puzzles and incomplete markets", Journal of Finance 48:1803–1832.

Tesar, L. (1993), "International risk sharing and non-traded goods", Journal of International Economics 35:69–89.

Tesar, L. (1995), "Evaluating the gains from international risk-sharing", in: A. Meltzer and C. Plosser, eds., Carnegie-Rochester conference series on public policy, forthcoming.

Tesar, L.L. and I.M. Werner (1992), "Home bias and the globalization of securities markets", National Bureau of Economic Research Working Paper No. 4218.

Thomas, S.H. and M.R. Wickens (1993), "An international CAPM for bonds and equities", Journal of International Money and Finance 12:390–412.

Chapter 38

DOUBLE-EDGED INCENTIVES:
INSTITUTIONS AND POLICY COORDINATION*

TORSTEN PERSSON

IIES, Stockholm University

and

GUIDO TABELLINI

Bocconi University, and IGIER, Milano

Contents

*We are very grateful to Fabio Ghironi for his research assistance and to Kerstin Blomquist for her secretarial assistance. Thanks also to Barry Eichengreen, Raquel Fernandez, Fabio Ghironi, Rex Ghosh, Dale Henderson, Peter Kenen, Maury Obstfeld, and Ken Rogoff for discussions and seminar participants at Princeton University and the Board of Governors for comments on an earlier draft. Finally, we thank the Bank of Sweden Tercentenary Foundation and the C.N.R. for financial support.

Handbook of Development Economics, vol. III, Edited by G. Grossman and K. Rogoff
© *Elsevier Science B.V., 1995*

1. General introduction

A large portion of international macroeconomics deals with the international transmission of national macroeconomic policies. Such spillovers naturally raise the possibility of inefficiencies: national policymakers who set their fiscal and monetary policies to maximize a domestic objective, but ignoring the externalities they impose on other countries, may find themselves in equilibria that entail collective irrationality. This well-known insight from simple game theory has formed the basis for a large literature on "international policy coordination" or "cooperation". The literature was started by the insightful work of Hamada in the mid 1970s [Hamada (1974, 1976, 1979)]. For the most part, he dealt with fixed exchange rate regimes, following the monetary approach to the balance of payments in the pre-rational expectations tradition. Nevertheless, he used modern game theory to illustrate how decentralized non-cooperative policymaking would result in suboptimal outcomes. When Cooper (1985) published his survey of strategic interdependence and policy coordination, the next wave of work was only beginning to form. This wave grew progressively stronger in the eighties; it reflected methodological advances – like the rational expectations revolution and the time consistency debate – as well as real world events – like the two oil shocks and the transition to floating exchange rates. Canzoneri and Henderson, who were themselves key contributors to this second wave of research, present many of the central arguments in their recent book [Canzoneri and Henderson (1991)].

In this chapter, we attempt to take stock of the literature in the last ten years and make some suggestions on how it may proceed in the future. We illustrate some of the most important insights of this literature, by help of a few core two-country models, which we extend in various directions. We start with fiscal policy. Our illustrations revolve around two types of externalities: one tied to international redistribution via the intertemporal terms of trade, the other to a fiscal externality in capital taxation, when capital is mobile between countries. Our fiscal-policy models are simple but fully specified two-period general equilibrium models with articulated micro foundations. In monetary policy we instead consider externalities arising from static terms of trade effects. The analysis here does not rest on explicit micro foundations, but on quadratic payoff functions and linear and static macroeconomic models.

Two main themes emerge from the analysis. First, that the analysis of international policy interactions is enriched by taking the incentives in the domestic policy process into account. These domestic incentives can either be tied to credibility issues or to political institutions. At a general level, we identify a two-way interaction: the incentives in the domestic policy process spill over into the international arena, and the international strategic considerations partly shape domestic policy. This two-way interaction has been stressed in the recent, unformalized, research in political science, triggered off by an influential article by Putnam (1988). In his critical discussion of the concrete attempts to coordinate macroeconomic policy in the 1980s, Feldstein (1988) raises similar issues.

The second central theme is our focus on the institutions that can enforce cooperation. Here we borrow from the recent microeconomic literature on principal-agent relations and contracts. This approach is particularly fruitful in understanding the role of delegation in the policy process. In domestic policy formation, voters delegate the choice of fiscal policy to the legislature. The legislature or the executive in turn often delegates the choice of monetary policy to the central bank. Such domestic delegation can go a long way towards reducing the inefficiencies of noncooperative policymaking, both in fiscal policy and in monetary policy. A hierarchical principal-agent approach can also be helpful in analyzing international arrangements, both for fiscal and monetary policy. Motivated largely by the current process of European integration, the arrangements we study range from ad hoc arrangements to substantial economic and political integration. We discuss alternative task assignments between member countries and the central policymaking level, and alternative processes for collective decision making. The design of international institutions shapes the policy outcomes and the distribution of the gains from coordination, particularly if countries are asymmetric.

The chapter is organized in two related but self contained parts. Part A deals with fiscal policy, Part B with monetary policy. A separate introduction to each part gives a more detailed road map to what we do. There are several reasons for studying these two policy areas separately. One is analytical convenience. We now have fairly complete, yet simple, work-horse general equilibrium models for fiscal policy, whereas no such simple model is available for monetary policy (a recent promising framework, however, is provided by Obstfeld and Rogoff (1994)). Hence, we follow most of the existing tradition of studying fiscal and monetary policy separately. A second reason for separating the analysis of fiscal and monetary policy is that the real world institutions – domestic and international – governing policy formation are very different in the two areas. With regard to domestic institutions, fiscal policy choices result from collective decisions of politically motivated representatives; monetary policy on the other hand is typically implemented by a singleminded independent agency. With regard to international institutions, monetary policy cooperation has generally taken the form of exchange rate agreements. For fiscal policy instead there are few examples of institutions enforcing tight international cooperation. There is one exception: federal structures can be thought of as performing this task for different regions within a single country.

Space constraints and a desire to keep our analysis simple and self contained prevent us from doing full justice to all branches of the policy coordination literature. Our focus is really on incentives and enforcement, rather than on details of the policy spillovers between different economies. Therefore, we do not cover at all the large, theoretical and empirical, literature that deals with the transmission of macroeconomic policy in the world economy. In particular, we do not cover the attempts to quantify the gains (or losses) from policy coordination on the basis of simulations with large scale econometric models. This kind of work is presented, for instance, in Bryant et al. (1988). In earlier work, Oudiz and Sachs (1984) had found that the gains from policy coordinations were likely to be small. Neither do we cover the work on the dynamics of policy coordination like the dynamic-game simulation approach to policy coordination that stemmed from the contributions in Buiter and Marston (1985). An up-to-date survey of the subsequent literature is found in Currie and Levine (1993).

When dealing with enforcement of cooperative outcomes, our focus is on institutional mechanisms. A branch of the literature, which we do not cover here, instead suggests reputational mechanisms, which rely on well-known insights from the theory of repeated games. A comprehensive treatment of this approach to reputation in policy coordination can be found in the recent book by Canzoneri and Henderson (1991). Even though we stress the difference between institutional and reputational mechanisms, the distinction may not be all that sharp, after all. Specifically, there is a literature that emphasizes how certain institutions may strengthen the scope for reputational enforcement by, for instance, facilitating monitoring or coordinating punishments of players that deviate from cooperative behavior [see Schotter (1981)]. This is the approach taken by Robert Staiger when discussing the role of international institutions in his chapter on trade policy institutions in this volume.

An interesting branch of the literature studies policy coordination in the context of policymaker uncertainty about policy goals, model parameters, and so on. We only touch tangentially on these issues, which are well summarized in the recent book by Ghosh and Masson (1994). By focusing on two-country models only, we are unable to deal with some interesting issues related to multilateralism, such as how European monetary integration would affect US–Europe interactions; an example of a study of these issues is Cohen and Wyplosz (1989). Finally, we cover neither the interaction between monetary and fiscal policy in an international strategic context [for instance, Jensen (1992), Sibert (1991), van der Ploeg (1989)], nor the recent interesting work on the politics of monetary policy cooperation [Eichengreen and Frieden (1994)].

PART A. FISCAL POLICY

How are policies transmitted from one country to the next? This is the first question addressed by any paper on international policy coordination. One purpose of this part is to illustrate the international transmission of fiscal policies, using a simple general equilibrium model with microfoundations. We focus on two transmission mechanisms. One is changes in the terms of trade (i.e. in some world market prices). The other is changes in the net of tax return available to internationally mobile capital in different localities.[1]

Rational governments typically exploit these international spillovers for their own benefit, or for the benefit of their own citizens. Cooperation means abstaining from this individualistic behavior, so as not to harm foreign citizens. A second purpose of this part is to illustrate the prospective gains from international cooperation. When countries cooperate with each other, welfare maximizing governments set fiscal policy according to some versions of a Ramsey Rule of optimal taxation. Without cooperation, on the other hand, both countries depart from Ramsey Rule in order to exploit the international spillovers for their own benefit. Thus, they both attempt to turn the terms of trade in their favor, or they both attempt to attract foreign capital. However, these attempts are self-defeating: both countries end up in an inferior equilibrium, in which policies do not obey Ramsey Rule. This is why international cooperation may be welfare improving.

An important step in this argument, though, is to postulate that governments indeed maximize social welfare. If they don't, for political or other reasons, policies do not obey Ramsey Rule anyway, and we are in the world of the third best. The question then is whether the absence of cooperation exacerbates or weakens the other domestic policy distortions. One reason why it may go the wrong way has been suggested by Vaubel (1985). If governments have a private agenda (be it re-election or a partisan ideological platform), then it may be better to have them compete rather than collude. That is, cooperation may enable the domestic and foreign incumbent to collude at the voters' expense. A second idea, due to Rogoff (1985), is that cooperation may harm credibility because it may weaken the government's resolve to fight inflation. This idea is discussed at length in Part B, with regard to monetary policy, but it has an analogue in tax policy. Tax competition may be desirable, because it reduces the government temptation to confiscate wealth or to over-tax capital: if governments do not cooperate internationally, overtaxed investors can flee the country.

The final general question addressed in the literature is how to enforce cooperation, given that it is not a best response. There are two ways to answer this question. One, stressed in much of the literature on monetary policy coordination, is "Reputation" – for references see Part B. The other, to which we devote more attention, is through institution design. Policymakers do not operate in a vacuum. Their incentives are at least partly governed by domestic and international institutions. What features of domestic institutions are more likely to encourage cooperative behavior? How is conflict resolved within international institutions when countries differ or their

---

[1] There is a large literature on the international transmission of fiscal policy through terms of trade effects or tax competition. The books by Frenkel and Razin (1987) and by Frenkel, Razin, and Sadka (1991) contain a complete theoretical discussion of both issues respectively. The challenges posed by the international mobility of tax bases have also been extensively studied at a more applied level and with more institutional detail [see for instance the contributions collected in Giovannini, Hubbard, and Slemrod (1993) and, with reference to European integration, Keen (1993)].

interests diverge? The last two sections of this part discuss some recent attempt to answer these questions, borrowing from the work of political scientists [Putnam (1988)] and from some recent literature on fiscal federalism.

2. Terms of trade effects

The purpose of this section is to illustrate a typical externality in fiscal policy, namely changes in the *terms of trade*. When countries are not atomistic relative to the rest of the world, changes in their government spending or distorting taxes affect world market prices, and thus have welfare effects abroad. This creates a motive for international policy coordination. A coordinated policy internalizes the welfare effects of the domestic policy on the rest of the world.

In this section we focus on intertemporal terms of trade effects. Larger government surpluses increase the world real interest rate via distorting taxation; the welfare effect is positive on net creditors and negative on net debtors. Thus, net creditor countries have an incentive to expand budget surpluses beyond what is dictated by their domestic objectives, to exploit the terms of trade effect; the opposite is true for net debtor countries. Naturally, for the world as a whole the welfare effects of changes in the terms of trade wash out: what one country gains, the other loses. Hence policy coordination calls for neglecting the terms of trade effects and paying attention only to the internal objectives.

In models with more than one commodity, fiscal policy also changes the relative price of exportables versus importables. In this case too, policy coordination amounts to neglecting (i.e. abstaining from exploiting) the terms of trade effects. In fact, our discussion of international spillovers of monetary policy in Part B will largely revolve around such atemporal terms of trade effects.

The analysis of policy induced terms of trade effects dates back at least to Nurkse's (1945) study of competitive depreciations. Johnson's (1965) seminal contribution on trade wars was probably the first to study the strategic implications of a conflict over the terms of trade.

2.1. The model

The world is made up of two countries, each inhabited by a representative consumer. There are two periods, and one (traded) commodity. Public consumption, g, is exogenous and only takes place in the second period. Consider the home country first. Consumer preferences are defined over private consumption, c, and leisure, x:

$$u = U(c_1) + c_2 + V(x_1) + V(x_2),$$ (2.1)

where U and V are well behaved concave utility functions. Output is non-storable and is produced with only one input, labor, denoted l. The real wage is unity, and the government can only tax labor income. Hence we can write the consumer budget constraints in periods 1 and 2 respectively as:

$$l_1(1 - \tau_1) \geq c_1 + qa$$
$$l_2(1 - \tau_2) + a \geq c_2,$$

(2.2)

where τ is the tax rate on labor income, and a denotes the assets (or liabilities if negative) acquired by the consumer in the first period, at the world market price q. Thus, a denotes a claim to one unit of period-2 output, and q is the price of future goods, the inverse of the (gross) world real interest rate.

In line with the assumption that government spending takes place in period 2 only, we can write the government budget constraints in the two periods as:

$$\tau_1 l_1 \geq qb$$
$$\tau_2 l_2 + b \geq g,$$

(2.3)

where a positive value of b denotes the assets accumulated by the public sector, whereas a negative value denotes public debt. Implicitly, it is assumed that b and a are perfect substitutes, and thus have the same world price q.

Together, these budget constraints imply a resource constraint for the country as a whole: the present discounted value of net exports must sum to zero:

$$z_1 + qz_2 = 0$$

(2.4)

where net exports are $z_1 = l_1 - c_1$ and $z_2 = l_2 - c_2 - g$ in periods 1 and 2 respectively. The foreign country is identical in all these respects. Foreign country variables are denoted with a ''*''.

For intertemporal terms of trade effects to play a role, the two countries must have a net external position different from zero. Therefore we assume that labor is more productive in period 1 than in period 2 in the home country, while the opposite is true in the foreign country. Specifically, the home consumer can split its effective time endowments between leisure and labor in the two periods according to the following constraints:

$$1 + e \geq x_1 + l_1$$
$$1 - e \geq x_2 + l_2$$

(2.5)

where $e > 0$ is a measure of the higher period-1 productivity of labor (or equivalently of the more abundant effective time endowment). The foreign consumer faces the same constraints, except that e enters with the opposite sign in both expressions. Under this assumption, the home country is a net external creditor, and the foreign country a net debtor.

The equilibrium condition in period 1 output markets (or equivalently in the world financial markets) closes the model:

$$z_1 + z_1^* = 0 . \tag{2.6}$$

Going through the private optimality conditions, it is easy to show that first period net exports in the home country can be written as a function $z_1 = Z(q, b)$, decreasing in both arguments. Intuitively, larger public assets (a higher value of b) require a higher labor tax rate in period 1 (see the government budget constraint), and thus smaller labor and output supplies in period 1. And a higher market price q of future goods (a lower interest rate) reduces net exports for three reinforcing reasons: (i) it increases consumption of the cheaper period 1 good; (ii) it discourages period 1 labor supply via an intertemporal substitution effect; (iii) it forces the government to increase the labor income tax, so as to buy the same amount b of public assets, and this further discourages period 1 labor supply. Exactly the same arguments apply to the foreign country.[2]

The equilibrium condition (2.6) thus defines the equilibrium market price as a function of public assets in both countries, $q = Q(b, b^*)$. Applying the implicit function theorem to (2.6), it is easy to show that the function Q is decreasing in both arguments: a greater accumulation of public assets in either country (a larger budget surplus) brings about a smaller equilibrium value of q, and thus a higher world real interest rate.

It may seem counter intuitive that budget surpluses raise world real interest rates. In this model the budget effect operates entirely via distorting taxes and the supply side of the economy. A larger period-1 budget surplus corresponds to a higher labor income tax which reduces period-1 labor supply in the country where it originates, and thus creates a world wide excess demand for period 1 goods.[3] To restore equilibrium, an increase in the real interest rate is needed. Naturally, this result is not general, and in other models the link between budget surpluses and the real interest rate would be reversed. What is important is that unilateral changes in fiscal policy generally affect the world real interest rate, and that this creates a motive for international policy coordination.

---

[2] Because of the linearity of period 2 consumption in the utility function, all income effects are absorbed by c_2. Points (i) and (ii) in the text thus reflect only the substitution effects induced by a change in q.

[3] Remember that all income effects here are absorbed by c_2.

2.2. Coordinated versus non-coordinated policies

We now turn to the welfare effects of alternative economic policies. There is one independent policy instrument in each country in the first period. We take it to be b.[4] It is convenient to work with the consumer indirect utility function, defined over the relative price q and the policy variable:

$$u = J(b, g, q).\tag{2.7}$$

This function thus summarizes all the welfare effects of the domestic economic policies and of world prices on the home consumer. A similar function is defined for the foreign consumer.[5]

In the absence of international coordination, a benevolent home government sets economic policy to maximize (2.7), taking foreign policy as given and realizing that the world price obeys the equilibrium function $q = Q(b, b^*)$. The foreign government behaves symmetrically. A policy equilibrium without international coordination is thus a Nash equilibrium between the two governments.

Letting a subscript denote a partial derivative, we can write the reaction function of the home government in period 1 as:

$$J_b = J_q Q_b = 0.\tag{2.8}$$

A similar expression holds for the foreign country. The first term on the left hand side captures the domestic effects of a larger government surplus. Since g is held constant, this term reflects tax smoothing considerations: when $J_b = 0$, the policy

---

[4]Public consumption is given, so there is nothing to choose in period 2. In period 1, the government budget constraint and the consumer first-order conditions define a one to one mapping between b and τ_1. Despite this equivalence, the choice of the policy instruments here could make a difference. The reason is that, as shown below, in the absence of policy coordination the two governments behave as Nash players. If the slope of their reaction functions is affected by which instrument is set, then the choice of instruments makes a difference, like in Bertrand versus Cournot equilibria in oligopoly.

[5]The indirect utility function is a function, say $I(\tau_1, \tau_2, q)$, defined over the relative prices τ_1, τ_2, and q. By the government budget constraints, moreover, the tax rates τ_1 and τ_2 can be written as $\tau_1 = T_1(q, b)$ and $\tau_2 = T_2(q, b)$. Thus the indirect utility function $J(b, g, q)$ is defined as

$$J(b, g, q) = I(T_1(q, b), T_2(q, b), q).$$

Later on, we will be interested in the partial derivative J_q, which can be obtained as follows. First note that $J_q = I_{\tau 1} T_{1q} + I_q$. By the envelope theorem, $I_{\tau 1} = -l_1/q$ and $I_q = -a/q$. Moreover, (2.3) and the private sector first-order conditions imply

$$T_{1q} = (b - \tau_1 L_{1q})/(l_1 + \tau_1 L_{1\tau} b) = (\tau_1 - \varepsilon_1/(1 + \varepsilon_1))/q > 0,$$

where $L_{1\tau}$ and L_{1q} are the partials of the first-period labor supply function and $\varepsilon_1 = \tau_1 L_{1\tau}/l_1 < 0$ is the labor supply elasticity with respect to the tax rate. Combining these expressions and simplifying, we obtain

$$J_q = (z_2 + \varepsilon_1 l_1/q(1 + \varepsilon_1))/q.$$

satisfies the intertemporal Ramsey rule of optimal taxation. Moreover, as shown in Footnote 5, $J_q = (z_2 + \varepsilon_1 l_1 / q(1 + \varepsilon_1))/q$, where $-1 < \varepsilon_1 < 0$ is the elasticity of first-period labor supply with respect to the tax rate. Hence (2.8) can be rewritten as:

$$J_b + Q_b l_1 \varepsilon_1 / q(1 + \varepsilon_1) = -z_2 Q_b / q . \tag{2.9}$$

The left-hand side is a "modified" Ramsey Rule for optimal taxation, consisting of two terms. J_b is the marginal welfare effect of the government surplus, due to the tax distortions in labor supply. The second term reflects the fact that higher interest rates redistribute away from the home private sector towards the government (who is a net creditor). With distorting taxes this redistribution is welfare improving and creates an additional reason for having a surplus; recall that $Q_b < 0$. The right-hand side captures instead the international redistribution due to higher interest rates – a strategic terms-of-trade effect. Equation (2.9) thus says that, in a Nash equilibrium, the home country deviates from the modified Ramsey rule by running a larger government surplus ($J_b < 0$) if it is a net creditor (if $z_2 < 0$). Moreover, the deviation from Ramsey rule is larger when the net, foreign position is larger and the interest rate is more sensitive to domestic policies. A similar argument holds for the foreign country. As illustrated by (2.9), the reason for this behavior is the incentive to exploit the intertemporal terms of trade effects of fiscal policies.

Under our assumptions in eq. (2.5), the home country is a net creditor while the foreign country is a net debtor. Thus the home government has a bias in favor of large budget surpluses, while the opposite is true abroad. These two biases tend to offset each other, so that in the Nash equilibrium the real interest rate is not very different from what it would be if both countries abstained from exploiting the terms of trade and only obeyed the modified Ramsey Rule.

To show that policy coordination implies exactly that, let us define policy coordination as a cooperative equilibrium, namely a regime in which the two governments set their policies to maximize worldwide welfare, defined as the sum of domestic and foreign consumers indirect utilities. The corresponding first-order condition for the home government is:

$$J_b + (J_q + J_q^*)Q_b = 0 . \tag{2.10}$$

A similar condition holds for foreign policy. By the argument in Footnote 5 and by $z_2 + z_2^* = 0$, we have

$$J_q + J_q^* = (\varepsilon_1 l_1 / (1 + \varepsilon_1) + \varepsilon_1^* l_1^* / (1 + \varepsilon_1^*))/q^2$$

Hence, equation (2.10) can be rewritten as a new "modified" Ramsey rule.

$$J_b + Q_b l_1 \varepsilon_1 / q(1 + \varepsilon_1) = -Q_b l_1^* \varepsilon_1^* / q(1 + \varepsilon_1^*) .$$

The right-hand side now represents the additional benefit of a larger domestic surplus, accruing to the foreign government, due to the higher world interest rate. This term is always positive (for both countries). Thus, cooperation calls for a larger surplus than non-cooperative policymaking. Not surprisingly, policy cooperation leaves both countries better off. Because cooperation is not a Nash equilibrium, however, both countries have an incentive to unilaterally deviate to their Nash strategies. How, then, can policy coordination be sustained? The answer can take one of two forms. Policy coordination can be sustained either by long term relationships between countries that create "reputational" incentives, or by institutions that enforce policy commitments. In this chapter, we mainly address the second possibility and in this fiscal policy part it is addressed in Sections 5 and 6.

We close the subsection with two remarks. One concerns the set of policy instruments. We have followed the literature in taking it to be exogenously determined. This is unsatisfactory for two reasons. First, in this model a more efficient instrument for affecting the terms of trade is a capital export tax (for the creditor country), or an import tax (for the debtor country).[6] Second, if policy coordination is not self-enforcing, then any international agreement concerning specific policy instruments can be side-stepped by means of other instruments, not covered by the agreement. This problem arises in many other areas of policy analysis – see for instance the chapter by Rodrik in this volume – and unfortunately there is no easy way around it.

The other remark concerns our definition of cooperation as the maximization of worldwide welfare. This definition becomes problematic if there are relevant asymmetries, so that the two countries not necessarily enter with equal weights in the world social welfare function. In this case, implementation of efficient equilibria may require lump-sum side payments. If side payments are ruled out, an additional constraint must be imposed on the cooperative outcome. This point is addressed in Chari and Kehoe (1990) and is further discussed in Section 6 below.

2.3. Notes on the literature

Frenkel and Razin (1985), (1987), and van Wijnbergen (1986), discuss the international transmission of fiscal policies in a similar but more general intertemporal model without capital. Devereux (1987) describes a model where the benefits of cooperation derive from terms of trade effects similar to those of this section. Similar issues arise also in overlapping generations models. See, in particular, Persson (1985), Buiter (1987) and Chang (1988).

---

[6]Naturally, policy coordination would remain welfare improving in this case too.

3. Cooperation among politically motivated governments

A central assumption in Section 2 is that governments act as benevolent social planners. If governments are politically motivated – by a desire to be reappointed or to implement a partisan policy platform – international policy cooperation is not always welfare improving. Intuitively, international cooperation may enable the incumbent governments at home and abroad to collude at the expense of voters or of political opponents. If economic policies are distorted by political incentive constraints, international competition, rather than cooperation, may be desirable, as it may relax or offset the domestic incentive constraints. We illustrate this point, by an extension of our previous model.

3.1. Political instability and government myopia

Let public consumption in the second period be a choice variable of the government, alongside with public assets, b. Moreover, and more importantly, assume that consumers in both countries are heterogeneous in their evaluations of public consumption. Specifically, suppose that the ith consumer's preferences in the home country are given by the following utility function

$$u^i = U(c_1) + c_2 + V(x_1) + V(x_2) + \alpha^i H(g), \tag{3.1}$$

where the notation is as in the previous section, H is a concave and well behaved utility function, and consumers differ in the weight α^i assigned to public consumption. Policy decisions are taken sequentially over time by majority vote. In period 1 there is a majority vote, in each country, on the budget surplus, b and b^* respectively. And in period 2 there is another vote on g and g^*. In all other respects the model is identical to that of Section 1.

As all the voters have the same preferences, except for the linear parameter α^i, their preferences are single peaked and the median voter result holds [see Grandmont (1978)]. The political equilibrium – defined as a policy that cannot be beaten under majority rule in a pair-wise comparison – coincides with the policy preferred by the median voter. The key political feature emphasized in this section is that the identity of the median voter may change over time. Because political decisions are taken sequentially, shocks to the participation rate or changes in the eligibility of the voters can bring about changes in the identity of the median voter.

This political instability distorts the intertemporal preferences of the legislator, giving rise to excessive myopia or farsightedness, depending on the circumstances.

Specifically, let α_t^m be the weight assigned to public consumption by the home median voter in period t, for $t = 1, 2$. We want to allow for $\alpha_1^m \neq \alpha_2^m$ in both countries. We refer to an individual with a large α as a ''liberal'', and one with a small α as a "conservative". For simplicity (but with no loss of generality) we assume that α_2^m is known with certainty in period 1.

Consider how the size of public consumption is chosen in period 2, given b and b^*. As argued in the previous section, there are no policy spillovers across countries in period 2. Thus the equilibrium policy is chosen independently in each country. At home, public consumption is set by the home median to maximize his indirect utility function. This indirect utility function is ex post, in the sense that b is predetermined and q does not enter any of the relevant (period 2) budget constraints [see (2.2) and (2.3) above]. Thus it can be written as:

$$\hat{u}_2^m = \hat{J}(b, g) + \alpha_2^m H(g). \tag{3.2}$$

The equilibrium policy maximizes (3.2), and must satisfy the first order condition:

$$\hat{J}_g + \alpha_2^m H_g = 0. \tag{3.3}$$

Equation (3.3) implicitly defines equilibrium public consumption: $g = G(b, \alpha_2^m)$. It is easy to show that G is increasing in both arguments. Thus, a more liberal median voter spends more. Larger inherited public assets also imply more public spending, as the marginal cost of distorting taxation is smaller. An analogous result holds for the foreign country.[7]

Next, turn to period 1, and suppose initially that there is no international policy coordination. The home median voter chooses b to maximize his ex ante indirect utility function, taking into account the effect of his choices on the world interest rate through the function $Q(\cdot)$, as well as the incentive constraint that public consumption is chosen by the second period median voter through the function $G(\cdot)$. The corresponding first order condition for b is:

$$J_b = J_q Q_b + G_b(J_g + \alpha_1^m H_g) = 0. \tag{3.4}$$

The first term on the left hand side of (3.4) is the usual optimal taxation effect. The second term is the terms of trade effect discussed in the previous section. The last term captures the political incentive constraint. Public consumption will be set next period by a legislator with different policy preferences. The optimal budget surplus thus takes into account the effect on future public spending. In other words, the budget surplus is set strategically, to influence future domestic policies. An analogous first order condition holds for the foreign country.

Equation (3.4) can be simplified further, recalling the expression for J_q in Footnote

---

[7] The result that $G_b > 0$ follows by applying the implicit function theorem to 3.3, and noting that $\hat{J}_{gb} = -\hat{J}_{gg} > 0$.

5, and noting that $J_g = \hat{J}_g$, to obtain:[8]

$$J_b + Q_b l_1 \varepsilon_1 / q(1 + \varepsilon_1) = -z_2 Q_b / q + (\alpha_2^m - \alpha_1^m) G_b H_g . \tag{3.5}$$

Equation (3.5) is identical to the reaction function (2.9) derived in Section 2, except that on the right hand side there is one more term capturing the political incentive constraint. As $H_g > 0$ and $G_b > 0$, this term has the same sign as $(\alpha_2^m - \alpha_1^m)$. Thus, the political incentive constraint can reinforce or weaken the bias in favor of large budget surpluses. If the first period legislator is more conservative than its successor $(\alpha_2^m > \alpha_1^m)$, there is a political bias in favor of small budget surpluses. The reason is that small budget surpluses – larger deficits – are used strategically to force a spending cut on the future legislator. The opposite is true if the first period legislator is more liberal than its successor $(\alpha_2^m < \alpha_1^m)$.

3.2. The benefits of cooperation reconsidered

Suppose now that the home and foreign legislators cooperate with each other. That is, suppose that, once the identity of the current and future majorities are publicly known, the current majorities in the two countries are allowed to strike a deal. The deal says that fiscal policies are set to maximize the sum of the home and foreign median voters welfare. This arrangement can be thought of as either cooperation among two governments (elected by the corresponding median voters), or as cooperation among the two legislatures.

Repeating the same steps as above and as in Section 2, it is easy to verify that the cooperative policy must satisfy an expression identical to (3.5), except that z_2 on the right-hand side is replaced by $\varepsilon_1^* l_1^* / (1 + \varepsilon_1^*)$, as in Section 2.2. Under international coordination the two countries thus again abstain from exploiting the terms of trade effects of fiscal policy and internalize the benefits of higher interest rates, accruing to the foreign government. But now, with politically motivated governments, there are two domestic considerations: the Ramsey rule, and the domestic political distortion. If the international terms of trade effects and the political effects offset each other, the Ramsey optimum is closer to the non-cooperative than to the cooperative equilibrium. This can happen if the net debtor country is run by a more liberal policymaker in period 1, or if the net creditor country is run by a more conservative policymaker in period 1. In other words, if the home country is a net creditor, cooperation could generate an outcome further away from Ramsey rule if $\alpha_2^m > \alpha_1^m$, whereas the reverse holds abroad.

---

[8] $J_g = \hat{J}_g$ follows from the linearity of consumer preferences in c_2, and from the fact that J_g is a partial derivative, which *is* taken holding b and q fixed.

Can we say that in this case cooperation is counterproductive, in that it decreases welfare of both countries? Clearly this is not literally true of the period 1 median voters in both countries. They are better off with cooperation than without it, since they are more able to reach their domestic objectives. But these domestic objectives are distorted by a political incentive constraint (the strategic effect of budget surpluses). In the presence of these constraints, a correct comparison evaluates ex ante welfare with and without cooperation. Specifically, assume that individuals know their own preferences (their α^i parameter), but don't know the other voters preferences. In particular, assume they don't know the identity of the period-1 and period-2 majorities in both countries. It can be shown that in this case the Ramsey rule is optimal for every voter irrespective of her α^i parameter. In this sense, cooperation is indeed counterproductive whenever it takes equilibrium policies further away from the Ramsey rule.

3.3. Notes on the literature

The idea that international policy cooperation may be counterproductive because it enables collusion among politically motivated governments is found in Vaubel (1985), without reference to a specific model. Putnam (1989) also discusses it at length with reference to specific real world episodes. Edwards and Keen (1993) make essentially the same point in a model of tax competition where governments destroy resources for their own private benefit. The result that political instability may lead to excessive budget deficits is discussed at length in Persson and Tabellini (1990), who in turn summarize earlier work by Persson and Svensson (1989), Alesina and Tabellini (1990), Tabellini and Alesina (1990). The analysis of international policy coordination with a political bias towards budget deficits is due to Tabellini (1990), who focuses on a slightly different economic model. Finally, the result of this section can also be interpreted as saying that cooperation among a subset of players may be counterproductive, an interpretation stressed by Canzoneri and Henderson (1991) in a nonpolitical model of monetary policy. (See further Part B, below.)

4. Tax competition

A second important externality in fiscal policy arises if tax bases are internationally mobile. In this section we consider a typical example, namely capital taxation. With internationally mobile capital, governments have an incentive to keep taxes low, to attract capital from abroad. As both governments do that, capital does not move in a (symmetric) Nash equilibrium, but taxes are inefficiently low. Cooperation calls for raising taxes on capital in both countries.

4.1. The model

The model is similar to that of Sections 2 and 3, except that the tax base is capital rather than labor. Again we assume two identical representative consumers, two periods and a single commodity. Public consumption takes place in the second period. Consumer preferences in the home country are:

$$u = U(c_1) + c_2 + H(g), \tag{4.1}$$

where the notation is the same as above.

In the first period the consumer receives an exogenous endowment e, that can be consumed or invested at home or abroad. The investment technology is identical in the two countries: One unit invested today yields one unit tomorrow, gross of taxes. Foreign investment, however, carries some "mobility costs", meant to capture the extra transaction and information costs associated with foreign investment. For simplicity, these costs are borne in the second period, when the fruits of investment mature. Capital invested at home is taxed at the domestic rate θ, whereas capital invested abroad is taxed at the foreign rate θ^*. Under these assumptions, we can write the consumer budget constraints as:

$$e \geq c_1 + k + f \equiv c_1 + s$$
$$c \leq (1 - \theta)k + (1 - \theta^*)f - M(f) \tag{4.2}$$
$$\equiv (1 - \theta)s + (\theta - \theta^*)f - M(f)$$

where k and f denote domestic and foreign investment of the home country $s \equiv k + f$ denotes savings, and $M(f)$ is a function capturing the mobility costs of foreign investment. We assume that $M(0) = 0$, $M_f > 0$ if $f > 0$, and $M_{ff} > 0$.

Finally, the government budget constraint in the second period is:

$$g \leq \theta k + \theta f^* \equiv \theta(s - f + f^*) \tag{4.3}$$

where an $*$ denotes a foreign variable. Implicit in (4.2) and (4.3) is thus the assumption that capital is taxed according to the source principle, and not the residence principle, and that the same rate applies irrespective of who owns the capital.[9]

By the private optimality conditions, in an interior optimum, savings are a function of the domestic tax rate, $s = S(\theta) \equiv 1 - U_c^{-1}(1 - \theta)$, with $S_\theta < 0$. Moreover, investment abroad is a function $f = F(\theta, \theta^*)$, with $F_\theta = -F_\theta^* > 0$. Thus, a unilaterally higher capital tax rate at home encourages capital flight, and vice versa if the foreign tax rate rises. Finally, domestic investment at home can be written as: $k = K(\theta, \theta^*)$

---

[9]This assumption is appropriate in the case of industrial capital and foreign direct investments. Even in the case of financial capital, it may not be too far fetched if there are enforcement problems.

$= S(\theta) - F(\theta, \theta^*)$. Thus, a higher capital tax rate in the home country discourages home investment in two ways: it reduces savings and induces capital flight by home citizens. The foreign country is identical in all respects. In particular, $F_{\theta*}^* = F_{\theta}$ and $F_{\theta}^* = F_{\theta*}$.

4.2. Equilibrium policies with and without cooperation

Consider first the cooperative equilibrium as defined in the previous section, namely as the pair of policies that maximize world wide welfare. The timing of events is as follows. (1) In period 1 governments choose tax policy; (2) Having observed the policy, consumers choose how much to save and where to invest; (3) In period 2 no new decision is made, and the budget constraints dictate how much private and public consumption is feasible, given the period 1 choices. Thus, we remain in the typical framework of optimal taxation theory and abstract from any credibility problem vis-à-vis private investors. This assumption is removed in the next section.

To compute the optimal tax rates, use the previous notation to write the home consumer indirect utility function as:

$$v(\theta, \theta^*) \equiv U(1 - s(\theta)) + (1 - \theta)s(\theta) + (\theta - \theta^*)F(\theta, \theta^*)$$
$$- M(F(\theta, \theta^*) + H[\theta(s(\theta) - F(\theta, \theta^*) + F(\theta, \theta^*))]).$$

The foreign consumer indirect utility function, $v(\theta, \theta^*)$, is analogously defined. Optimal tax rates maximize $[v(\theta, \theta^*) + v^*(\theta, \theta^*)]$.

Appealing to the envelope theorem and going through this optimal taxation exercise, one can pin down the equilibrium tax rate in the home country by the following optimality condition (a similar condition holds for the foreign country).[10]

$$H_g = \frac{1}{1 - \eta^C}. \tag{4.4}$$

In (4.4) $\eta^C > 0$ denotes the elasticity of the relevant tax bases (k and f^*) for the home government with respect to the domestic tax rate, in a cooperative equilibrium. The left hand side of (4.4) is the marginal benefit of public consumption. The right hand side is the marginal cost of higher taxes, which also reflects the tax distortion on investment decisions. The higher is the elasticity η^C, the greater is the distortion and

---

[10]Equation (4.4) is obtained from the problem of maximizing the sum of the welfare of both consumers, domestic and foreign, with respect to home policies. By symmetry, the first order condition of this problem with respect to θ simplifies to

$$-S + F - F^* + (S - F + F^* + \theta S_\theta)H_g = 0,$$

from which (4.4) and (4.5) follow.

hence the lower is the optimal tax rate (because $H(\cdot)$ is concave and the left hand side is decreasing in g and hence in θ).

The key determinant of the equilibrium tax rate is thus the elasticity η^C. In a cooperative equilibrium, this elasticity can be written as:

$$\eta^C = -S_\theta \theta / s . \tag{4.5}$$

Note that the elasticity η^C only reflects the savings elasticity and it neglects the investment elasticity due to the international movements of capital. The reason is that when the two governments cooperate they refrain from exploiting international capital mobility for their own benefit.

This does not happen with non-cooperative policymaking. Specifically, consider the Nash equilibrium, in which both governments maximize the welfare of their own citizens, taking the tax rate in the other country as given. Thus the home government maximizes $v(\theta, \theta^*)$ defined above, given θ^*. Its reaction function is defined by a condition similar to (4.4), except that the elasticity η^c on the right hand side is now replaced by the following elasticity

$$\eta^N = -(S_\theta + 2F_\theta^*)\theta / S , \tag{4.6}$$

where the N superscript is a reminder that the elasticity is computed in the Nash equilibrium.[11]

Contrasting (4.5) and (4.6) and recalling that $F_\theta^* < 0$, it follows immediately that $\eta^N > \eta^C$. By (4.4), then, the equilibrium tax rate is higher with cooperation than without it. The intuition is straightforward. In the absence of cooperation, both governments face an incentive to unilaterally reduce taxes, to attract foreign capital and to keep domestic capital within their borders. This incentive is larger the greater is international capital mobility (i.e. the more negative is F_θ^*).

Like in Section 2, lack of cooperation reduces worldwide welfare. In the Nash equilibrium, there is no capital flight from either country. Tax competition does not pay: it simply distorts governments' incentives. In both countries, Nash equilibrium public consumption is too low and private savings too high compared with the (second-best) optimal taxation rule. This distortion is greater (and so is the benefit from cooperation) the larger is international capital mobility. In the limit, if capital is

---

[11]Equation 4.6 is derived from the problem of maximizing the consumer indirect utility function, subject to the government budget constraint and taking the foreign tax rate as given. The first order condition for that problem with respect to θ turns out to be:

$$-S + F + (S - F + F^* + \theta S_\theta - \theta F_\theta + \theta F_\theta^*)H_g = 0$$

which, after some rewriting yields 4.4. To derive 4.6, we have relied on two simplifications. First, by symmetry both governments choose the same equilibrium tax rate. Hence in equilibrium $F = F^* = 0$. Second, by the private optimality conditions discussed in the previous subsection $K_\theta = S_\theta - F_\theta$ and $-F_\theta = F_\theta^* < 0$.

perfectly mobile across countries (if $F_\theta = \infty$), the only Nash equilibrium has zero tax rates and zero public consumption in both countries.

4.3. Credibility and cooperation

In Section 3 we saw that international cooperation can reduce social welfare in the presence of political distortions, even though it is desirable for the incumbent. We now show that there is another domestic incentive constraint that can make cooperation counterproductive. If the government lacks credibility, then it matters whether cooperation makes government policy more or less credible. Note that here the government maximizes social welfare. Thus, cooperation can be undesirable for society as a whole, as well as for the government that engages in cooperation.

To illustrate this point, suppose that we change the timing of events in the model of the previous section as follows. (1) In period 1 individuals save; (2) In period 2 the governments of both countries choose economic policy; (3) Finally, individuals choose the location of their investment. Thus, savings and investment are temporally separated or, equivalently, capital can be moved across countries after policy choices have been made.

Under this timing, the savings decision anticipates the forthcoming equilibrium tax policy. But when taxes are set, savings are predetermined and thus the perceived elasticity of savings with respect to the tax rate is zero. In this case case tax policy suffers from a credibility problem. Governments cannot credibly convince savers that taxes will be low, because they have ex post incentives to tax savings a lot. Cooperation can make things worse, because it effectively removes the only remaining check on high capital taxation, namely international mobility.

To make the argument more precise, remove the term S_θ from the elasticities expressions (4.5) and (4.6). With cooperation, the elasticity of the tax base becomes zero, $\eta^C = 0$. In the Nash equilibrium the elasticity η^N remains positive in absolute value, but it is a smaller number than in the previous subsection (because in (4.6) both S_θ and $F_\theta^* < 0$). By (4.4) it then follows that the equilibrium tax rate is higher, both in the non-cooperative and the cooperative regime, when credibility problems are present. Summarizing, lack of credibility always increases the equilibrium tax rate. When there is international cooperation, the equilibrium tax rate is so high that the marginal utility of public spending equals that of private consumption. That is, the governments do not perceive capital taxation to be distorting at all. Without cooperation, the tax competition effect is still operative so that taxes remain lower than with cooperation, even though they are higher than in the Nash equilibrium of the previous section. Tax competition can therefore be socially desirable, by giving credibility to a policy of low capital taxes.

The general insight is similar to that of Section 3. Policy coordination can be counterproductive when the international and the domestic incentive constraints pull the equilibrium policy in opposite directions. Tax competition by itself pulls the tax rate below the Ramsey optimum, but lack of credibility pulls it above. Hence the equilibrium in which both incentive constraints are binding may be superior to that in which only one of them is binding. The same idea also applies to monetary policy, as will be discussed in Part B.

4.4. Notes on the literature

Optimal taxation when tax bases are internationally mobile has been extensively studied. A general analysis can be found in Gordon (1983) and in Razin and Sadka (1991). The book by Frankel, Razin and Sadka (1991) provides a comprehensive summary. Wilson (1987) adds endogenous wage rates to a model similar to that of this section. The idea that lack of credibility can make policy coordination counterproductive is due to Rogoff (1985), who introduced it in the case of monetary policy. Kehoe (1989) has extended it to the capital taxation model of this section. Tax competition has also been studied with much more emphasis or institutional detail. See, for instance, Giovannini, Hubbard, and Slemrod (1993) and, with reference to European integration, Keen (1993) and Sørensen (1992).

5. Domestic institutions in fiscal policy

So far we have discussed whether or not there are *prospective* gains from international cooperation in fiscal policy. But how can cooperative outcomes be implemented? This question is very important, given that each country has incentives to unilaterally deviate from the cooperative equilibrium unless some mechanism enforces it.

In Sections 6 and 10 below we study international institutions, with different degrees of centralization, that enforce fiscal and monetary policy cooperation. In this section, and in Section 9, we show that appropriate domestic political institutions can go some way towards implementing the cooperative outcome. This result is of interest because it demonstrates that better outcomes may be achievable, without any need to enforce international agreements.

To make this point, we once again abandon the world of social planners and representative consumers. The general theme is familiar from Section 3 and has also been studied in recent work in political science on two-stage games [Putnam (1988)]. When individual citizens are heterogeneous and governments politically motivated, there are more than just two players besides the home and foreign government: there are different domestic policymakers or political actors within each country. In Section 3 we viewed international policy coordination as collusion between two incumbents, at the expense of future policymakers, and we argued that cooperation could be socially undesirable. In this section we focus instead on the relationship between voters – the principals – and governments – the agents – in a representative democracy. This relationship is not fixed, but reflects the international policy regime. If international policy spillovers are important, voters elect a government that is fit to "play" the international policy game. Thus, on the one hand, international policy spillovers have domestic political repercussions. On the other hand, domestic politics plays a role in the international policy equilibrium. In the specific model of this section domestic politics mitigates the adverse consequences of tax competition, and reduces the need for international policy coordination, even though this is not always the case.

The model is identical to that of Section 4.1, except that individuals differ in the weight they attach to the utility of public consumption. Specifically, the preferences of individual i at home are still given by (4.1), except that the term $H(g)$ is replaced by $\alpha^i H(g)$, where the weight α^i differs across individuals and is distributed in the population with mean and median both equal to unity – this implies that the median voter optimum coincides with the utilitarian optimum. To preserve symmetry, the distribution is the same in the two countries.

The sequence of events is as follows: (1) Elections are held simultaneously in both countries; (2) The elected governments simultaneously and non-cooperatively choose tax policy; (3) Savings and investment decisions are made. Thus, we assume away all credibility problems in capital taxation and any international institution enforcing international agreement. An equilibrium is defined by two conditions (in addition to the optimal economic behavior of individuals). It must be a Nash equilibrium among the elected policymakers, who choose the optimal tax rate given foreign policy. It must also be a political equilibrium. That is, the elected policymakers are preferred to any other candidate by a majority of the voters in their own country, given the outcome of foreign elections and given how the policymakers behave once in office.

This definition makes clear that elections are partly driven by a strategic motive. A successful candidate is one who can yield a favorable Nash equilibrium in the subsequent policy game. Thus there is an agency problem. Policymakers behave as Nash players with respect to each other, once in office. But voters do not take the foreign tax rate as given when comparing different candidates, they only take the foreign electoral outcome as given. As shown below, this makes voters wish to elect a policymaker who does not share their own preferences.

5.1. Nash equilibrium of the policy game

Suppose that policymakers of type α^p and α^{*p*} have been elected in the home and foreign country respectively. The Nash equilibrium among them is obtained exactly like in Section 4.2 above. The optimal tax rate for the home policymaker is therefore defined by a condition like (4.4) (reproduced here for convenience):

$$\alpha^{P}H_{g} = \frac{1}{1-\eta^{N}}.$$

(5.1)

A similar condition holds in the foreign country. The elasticity η^{N} is still given by (4.6). Equations (5.1) and (4.6) implicitly define the reaction function of the home policymaker, namely a function $\theta = T^{P}(\theta^{*})$, and similarly for the foreign policymaker. These reaction functions are illustrated in Figure 5.1. Their slope is ambiguous and turns out to depend on the concavity of the utility function $H(g)$. We assume that H is not very concave, in which case the reaction functions are upward sloping. Their position depends on the government type, as captured by the parameters α^{P} and $\alpha^{*P^{*}}$. A higher value of α^{P} (i.e. more weight given to public consumption) induces higher tax rates and hence shifts the domestic reaction function to the right, towards the dotted line, while a similar argument holds for the foreign government.[12] Intuitively, a larger α^{P} implies a higher marginal benefit from public consumption. The elected policymaker at home is thus more willing to raise capital taxes for any foreign tax rate. Because the best response of the foreign government is

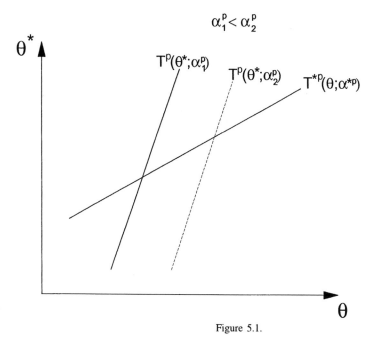

Figure 5.1.

[12]These results can be derived by applying the implicit function theorem to the equation in Footnote 11 above, except that on the left hand side of the term H_{g} is remultiplied by α^{P}.

to raise θ^*, the equilibrium tax rates in *both* countries go up as α^P rises. The same argument holds with respect to α^{*P^*}.

In summary, the equilibrium tax rate in each country is an increasing function of the policymaker weights α^P and α^{*P^*}. It is through this feature of the equilibrium that elections matter for the equilibrium outcome.

5.2. Political equilibrium

With this result in mind, let us now turn to stage (1) of the game, when policymakers are elected. Because the voters' preferences are single peaked, the elections are won by the candidate preferred by the median voter. But under the timing spelled out above, the median voters in both countries prefer a candidate other than themselves. They realize that tax competition in the subsequent stage of the game will force the elected governments to keep taxes inefficiently low. By electing a ''liberal'' policymaker, who is willing to tax and spend a lot ex post, the home median voter can induce the *foreign* policymaker to increase his equilibrium tax rate, and this has a positive spillover effect at home. The same argument applies in the foreign country. Hence, in both countries elections are won by a candidate more liberal than the median voter, and the resulting equilibrium policy entails correspondingly higher tax rates.

To illustrate this point more formally, let us compute the tax rate θ that the home median voter would wish to see implemented at home. Under the assumed timing, the home median voter does not take the foreign rate θ^* as given. He instead realizes that the foreign tax rate is determined by the foreign reaction function, $\theta^* = T^{*P}(\theta)$, with a^{*P} taken as given. The home median therefore maximizes his own preferences, subject to the usual government budget constraint and to the additional incentive constraint: $\theta^* = T^{*P}(\theta)$.

The tax rate solving this optimization problem must satisfy the usual optimality condition,

$$H_g = \frac{1}{1 - \hat{\eta}^{NR}}. \tag{5.2}$$

Since by assumption the median value of α is 1, the left hand side captures the marginal benefit of public consumption for the median voter. The elasticity η^{NR} is now given by the expression:

$$\eta^{NR} = -(S_\theta + 2F_\theta^*(1 - T_\theta^*))\theta/S. \tag{5.3}$$

Comparing this new elasticity with the corresponding expression in (4.6), we see that $\eta^{NR} < \eta^N$, because $1 > T_\theta^* > 0$. Hence, at the election stage, the home median voter prefers a higher tax rate than the one that he himself would implement in a Nash equilibrium, but not as high as in the cooperative equilibrium. The reason has been mentioned above. When voting, the median voter does not take the foreign tax rate as given; instead he takes the foreign policymaker and thus the foreign reaction function as given. He thus realizes that the foreign policymaker reacts to a higher tax rate θ (implemented by a more liberal policymaker type) by raising $\theta*$. This reduces the perceived elasticity of the capital tax base, because it reduces the danger of capital flight following the election of a liberal government type. The median voter implements his preferred tax rate by electing a more liberal type than himself.[13]

Two general lessons can be drawn from this example. First, political delegation may help relax the international incentive constraint. The political equilibrium tax rates are higher than in the Nash equilibrium of Section 4. Tax competition is therefore less damaging than in that simpler model and the benefits of international policy cooperation for the median voters less stark. By delegating policy to a more liberal type, voters manage to raise the equilibrium tax rate even without any international cooperation. Second, domestic politics and international policy spillovers are closely intertwined. The tax competition externality favors left-wing candidates in the political race, because they yield a better international policy equilibrium.

These results, however, are not general, and rely on strategic complimentarity of the policy instruments. If the function H is very concave, then it could happen that the reaction functions are negatively sloped (i.e. we have strategic substitutability). In this case political delegation could make things worse, in that the political equilibrium tax rate would be even lower than in the simple Nash equilibrium. Moreover, the elected government would be more to the right, rather than to the left, of the respective median voters.

5.3. Notes on the literature

Putnam (1989) and the contributions in Evans, Jacobsen and Putnam (1993) view international negotiations as a two-stage game between voters and politicians. Strategic delegation has been studied, among others, by Vickers (1985) with regard to managers and shareholders in oligopolistic firms, and by Fershtman, Judd, and Kalai (1991) in a more abstract setting. The model and the results in this section are reminiscent of those in Persson and Tabellini (1992), even though their model has heterogenous endowments rather than heterogenous preferences.

---

[13]This can be verified by comparing eqs. (5.1) and (5.2), together with $\eta^{NR} < \eta^{N}$.

6. International institutions in fiscal policy

For some macroeconomic policies, international institutions may sustain commitments to a cooperative outcome. Examples include the European Union, international tax treaties, exchange rate agreements. What are the important features of these institutions? If countries differ from each other, how is disagreement resolved within different institutions? These questions have received more attention in the literature on local public finance than in the literature of international macroeconomics. But some insights concerning federal fiscal institutions are also relevant for the implementation of international policy cooperation. This section highlights some results of the literature on fiscal federalism in the context of the tax competition model of the previous section. We abstract from credibility problems and assume that savings decisions are taken after the policy is in place. We retain the assumption of Section 5, that different voters evaluate public consumption with different weights α^i. However, we only consider voting equilibria over policies, not over people.

6.1. Tax harmonization

Consider first the case discussed in Section 5, of two identical economies. Then everyone agrees that the optimal policy, for both countries, is the cooperative outcome defined implicitly by (4.4) and (4.5). Implementing this outcome requires a commitment to refrain from unilaterally reducing taxes in one country. A simple institution that can provide this commitment is an agreement to harmonize taxes, that is, to set $\theta = \theta^*$. Since the two countries are identical, there is no conflict of interest and this agreement can be sustained under a variety of essentially equivalent institutions.

One such institution is full centralization of the policy decision. Concretely, let the equilibrium tax rate be chosen under majority rule with the citizens of both countries eligible to vote, under the constraint that the same tax rate applies in both countries. It is easy to show that, by symmetry, the cooperative outcome of Section 4 is the political equilibrium.

But the same outcome can also be implemented under a more decentralized institutional environment. Suppose that, after the "world wide" vote – but before the savings decision – citizens in each country are called to "ratify" the previous common decision, again by majority rule. If both countries ratify the common tax rate, then that rate gets implemented. If one country rejects ratification, then both countries are allowed to reoptimize and select any tax rate they wish, acting non-cooperatively.

To see that cooperation remains an equilibrium, suppose that the cooperative tax rate has been selected by a majority of the voters at stage (1). Then, at the ratification stage (2), the voters essentially have to choose between the cooperative policy in both countries, or the Nash equilibrium policy *in both countries*. Clearly, cooperation is preferred, and the tax harmonization decision ratified. But then, the cooperative tax rate indeed becomes the equilibrium policy selected at stage (1).

The key to this argument is related to that of the previous section. The international institution successfully implements cooperation because it forces the voters to choose *among equilibria*, not among policies. And since the two countries are identical, a majority in both countries agrees that the cooperative equilibrium dominates the non-cooperative one.

If the two countries differ, however, the previous argument can break down, because cooperation is no more uniquely defined and a majority of the voters in one country may prefer the non-cooperative outcome. Specifically, suppose that voters in the home country typically assign a larger weight α^i to public consumption than in the foreign country. In particular, the weight assigned by the domestic median voter is larger than that of the foreign median: $\alpha^m > \alpha^{*m}$. In this case the two medians prefer different common tax rates, and the details of how that common rate is chosen become important. If it is chosen by a "world wide" vote, then the political equilibrium is a tax rate in between those preferred by the home and foreign medians, exactly where depends on the shape of the α distributions. Ratification now potentially matters because it imposes a *participation constraint* on the political equilibrium: not every outcome of the first-stage vote is ratified, but only those that are superior to the Nash equilibrium for a majority of voters in both countries. Clearly, in an equilibrium only outcomes that will subsequently be ratified are candidates for approval at stage (1). Thus, when the participation constraint binds, a common tax rate is still implemented. But this tax rate is now defined by the condition that the median voter in one of the two countries is indifferent between that common rate and the Nash equilibrium. The more qualified is the majority required to approve ratification, the more the participation constraint is likely to bind.

6.2. Bargaining

An alternative procedure for selecting the cooperative policy when countries differ is through bargaining. Ratification implies that reversion to Nash is a natural threat point. We thus consider Nash bargaining among the two median voters, with the non-cooperative Nash equilibrium as the threat point.[14] The bargaining outcome is very different, depending on whether the international institution allows side payments or not.

If side payments are ruled out, the equilibrium is less efficient: cooperation cannot avoid $\theta \neq \theta^*$, and costly international capital movements take place. It is easy to

[14]Naturally there is an issue of strategic delegation here too, similar to that of Subsection 5.2. We abstract from it for simplicity (but see the Notes on the Literature section for references).

show that the home (high α^m) country sets a higher tax rate: $\theta > \theta*$, and thus loses capital to the foreign country.

Side payments increase efficiency because they allow government spending to differ in the two countries, even though their tax rates are equal. Side payments may not be relevant if we consider coordination in a single issue. But they may be highly relevant when the coordinating countries are integrated also in other areas of policy, as in Europe today. We therefore consider side payments in more detail. Let t denote a transfer from the foreign to the home government (a negative value of t denotes a transfer in the opposite direction). The indirect utility function of the home median voter now becomes:

$$v(\theta, \theta*, t) \equiv U(1 - S(\theta)) + (1 - \theta)S(\theta) + (\theta - \theta*)F(\theta, \theta*) - M(F(\theta, \theta*))$$
$$+ \alpha^m H[t + \theta(S(\theta) - F(\theta, \theta*) + F*(\theta, \theta*))] . \qquad (6.1)$$

The foreign median voter's indirect utility function, $v*(\theta, \theta*, t)$, is similarly defined, except that t enters with the opposite sign. Efficient equilibria with side payments solve the following optimization problem:

$$\max_{\theta,\theta*t} [v(\theta, \theta*, t) + \delta v*(\theta, \theta*, t)]$$

for arbitrary values of δ. Going through this optimization problem reveals that, for any δ, $\theta = \theta*$ must satisfy the optimality conditions previously obtained for a cooperative equilibrium (4.4) and (4.5). Thus, there are no inefficient international capital movements. In addition, the first order condition for t implies:

$$\alpha^m H_g = \delta \alpha*^m H_g^* . \qquad (6.2)$$

Thus, if the two countries are weighted equally (if $\delta = 1$), the marginal utility of public spending must be equal for the two median voters. By assumption, however, $\alpha^m > \alpha*^m$. Hence (6.2) with $\delta = 1$ implies $H_g < H_g^*$: public spending is larger in the home (high α^m) country. Since $\theta = \theta*$, this requires $t > 0$: the home country receives a lump sum transfer from abroad. This makes intuitive sense. Efficiency requires $\theta = \theta*$. But since the home country values public consumption more, taxes collected abroad also finance some of its public spending. Naturally, as δ increases above unity (as the foreign country is weighted more), the equilibrium value of t diminishes until it becomes negative. The equilibrium values of θ and $\theta*$ change with δ, but the equality $\theta = \theta*$ still holds.

In a Nash bargaining equilibrium, δ is not unity, but reflects the relative bargaining power of the two countries. Specifically, a Nash bargaining equilibrium solves

$$\max_{v,v*} (v - v^N)(v* - v*^N) \qquad (6.3)$$

subject to being on the Pareto frontier (i.e. subject to $v + \delta v*$ constant), where v^N and $v*^N$ denote welfare in the non-cooperative equilibrium for the home and foreign medians. The first-order conditions for this optimization problem imply that the equilibrium value of δ satisfies:

$$\delta = \frac{v - v^N}{v^* - v^{*N}}.$$ (6.4)

The right-hand side of (6.4) can be shown to exceed unity. Thus, the foreign (low α^{*m}) country has more bargaining power and receives a larger weight. Intuitively, in the non-cooperative equilibrium the home (high α^m) country is forced to set $\theta > \theta^*$. It thus loses capital to the foreign country, with adverse consequences on its tax revenues. Cooperation is therefore more valuable to the home country and it loses bargaining power. We cannot tell, however, in which direction the equilibrium side payments go: even though, $\delta > 1$, the equilibrium sign of t can be positive or negative, depending on the properties of the utility functions and on the cost $M(\cdot)$ of capital flight.

Summarizing, when the two countries are equal, cooperation can be enforced by a variety of international institutions. The relevant feature of these institutions is to force policy makers to choose among equilibria rather than among policies. When the countries differ, on the other hand, enforcement is more problematic because the countries disagree over which efficient policy to implement. Disagreement can be resolved in a variety of non-equivalent ways. If a common policy is chosen by majority vote, ratification serves the important role of imposing a participation constraint. If instead a common policy is chosen by bargaining, efficiency requires compensating side payments. Naturally, the equilibrium tax rates implemented under voting *cum* ratification and under bargaining can be very different from each other, since they reflect very different parameters.

6.3. Notes on the literature

The idea that ratification, or rather secession, may impose a relevant constraint in fiscal policy formation originates in local public finance; see for instance Buchanan and Faith (1987) or Bolton and Roland (1992). Piketty (1993) explores a similar idea to the ratification equilibrium above in a model of capital taxation. Tax harmonization in the EEC has been studied by Sinn (1990). Bargaining equilibria have seldom been discussed with reference to international policy coordination. Important exceptions are Chari and Kehoe (1990), who illustrate the relevance of side payments when countries differ, and Ghosh and Masson (1994), who discuss private information and the incentives for policymakers to misrepresent information so as to get a more favorable outcome; see also Hughes-Hallet (1986) and Chang (1993). Persson and Tabellini (1994a,b,c) contrast alternative procedures for resolving disagreement over fiscal policy, among different regions of a federal state. They focus precisely on the difference between centralized voting and bargaining, but consider international risk-sharing rather than capital taxation.

PART B. MONETARY POLICY

Below we survey the literature since the mid seventies on strategic interactions in monetary policy. Our selective survey highlights the same main themes as in Part A. In Section 7 we formulate a "generic" two country macroeconomic model which we use throughout this part. The model focuses on international spillovers via the real exchange rate and is consistent with the reduced form of the models in Rogoff (1985) and Canzoneri and Henderson (1988, 1991), among others. In Section 8, we illustrate a main theme in the literature: if the two countries do not cooperate, the monetary response to an adverse symmetric shock, like an oil shock, may be too contractionary. A permanent conflict of interest over the terms of trade, as in Part A (Section 2) generates similar inefficiencies.

Frankel (1988) listed three difficulties in sustaining a coordinated monetary policy outcome in order to eliminate such inefficiencies. One problem pointed out by Rogoff (1985) is that, monetary policy coordination may be counterproductive if governments lack credibility. Subsection 8.3 presents Rogoff's argument, appealing to the same kind of second-best reasoning as in Section 3. The second problem listed by Frankel is uncertainty about initial positions, objective functions, or policy multipliers. This important topic has received considerable attention in the literature. We only deal with it tangentially, and refer the reader to the recent book by Ghosh and Masson (1994) for an exhaustive treatment of policy coordination under uncertainty. Finally, Frankel discussed the difficulty of enforcing cooperation, given the incentives for individual countries to unilaterally deviate. The literature has stressed that reputation may relax these incentives when policymakers interact repeatedly over time. The general argument is well known, and its specific application to monetary policy coordination well summarized in Canzoneri and Henderson (1991, chs. 4–5), and in Ghosh and Masson (1994, ch. 8). Hence, we don't deal with it here. Instead, we follow the approach of Part A, namely to highlight the role of institutions in supporting cooperation. Section 9 starts by discussing domestic institutions, while Section 10 turns to international institutions. Here the institutions take the form of fixed exchange rate arrangements like the Bretton Woods agreement or the EMS. These institutional arrangements may be interpreted as contracts that implement desirable policy outcomes by strategic delegation.

7. A common framework

The fiscal-policy analysis in Part A rested on simple, yet fully specified, general equilibrium models with choice-theoretic foundations both on the economic and the political side. Our analysis of monetary policy in this part instead relies on social welfare functions defined directly over macroeconomic outcomes and on reduced-form relations between macroeconomic outcomes and policy instruments. This lack of explicit microeconomic underpinnings reflects the state of the art in much of the literature, which relies on linear versions of the Mundell–Fleming model. Working with reduced forms, enables us to avoid the taxonomy of different model specifications that would be necessary to fully capture the argument in each individual contribution.

7.1. A simple model

As before, there are two countries: the home and the foreign country. Each country specializes in the production of a national good, but consumes both goods. The policymaker in the home country has access to a single policy instrument, m, which we identify with money growth. He evaluates the effects of monetary policy according to the following "welfare" function defined over macroeconomic outcomes:

$$W(p, x, z; \theta, \varepsilon). \tag{7.1}$$

In (7.1), $W(\cdot)$ is a concave function, defined over CPI-inflation, p, output (measured as a deviation from the natural rate) x, and the rate of change of the real exchange rate, z, defined as the relative price of foreign goods in terms of home goods. If z enters the payoff function directly, it is because of real income concerns. As for θ and ε, they are symmetrically distributed shocks that may affect macroeconomic outcomes. These shocks enter the payoff function because they may also alter the way the policymaker evaluates specific macroeconomic outcomes, by modifying the partial derivatives W_p, W_x, or W_z. We generally assume that there is a well-defined inflation target, normalized to zero:

$$W_p \gtreqless 0 \quad \text{as} \quad p \lesseqgtr 0. \tag{7.2}$$

The sign patterns of the other partials W_x and W_z will vary somewhat in the different specifications below. Throughout, we assume that the $W(\cdot)$ function is quadratic and separable in the macroeconomic outcomes: the partials in p, x, and z, when non-zero, are linear in these variables and the cross-partials W_{ij} for i, $j = p$, x, z are zero. However, we maintain the general functional form in (7.1), rather than going to a parametric example, to facilitate the interpretation of the results.

The distinction between θ-shocks and ε-shocks has to do with information availability. We follow the literature in assuming that private agents sign nominal contracts for wages (or prices). The policymaker knows the realization of both types of shocks when setting m, but private agents only have information about the θ-shocks. The policymaker's superior information with regard to ε-shocks may either reflect a genuine information advantage, or else the relative costs of decision making: monetary policy can be altered at very short notice, whereas wage contracts cannot. This private information over the ε shock provides a role for stabilization policies, as in Fischer (1977).

Following much of the literature, the real exchange rate, z, is the only source of spillovers across countries. Defined as the rate of change in the relative price of foreign goods, we can write z as:

$$z = s + q^* - q, \tag{7.3}$$

where s is the change in the nominal exchange rate and $q(q^*)$ is the own-currency change in the price of home (foreign) country goods. Thus a positive value of z reflects a real depreciation. We represent the macroeconomic outcomes by the following semi-reduced forms:

$$p = P(\underset{+}{m}, \underset{+}{z}; \theta, \varepsilon) \tag{7.4}$$

$$x = X(\underset{+}{m - m^e}, z; \theta, \varepsilon) \tag{7.5}$$

$$z = Z(\underset{+}{m - m^e}, \underset{+}{m^* - m^{*e}}; \theta, \varepsilon, \theta^*, \varepsilon^*), \tag{7.6}$$

where the e superscript denotes private expectations, conditional on θ, and where an asterisk "$*$" denotes a foreign variable. A sign under a variable denotes an assumption about the corresponding partial derivative that will be maintained throughout.

The CPI-inflation rate p in (7.4) increases with money growth, as well as with a real depreciation. This reduced form follows from (i) the definition of CPI-inflation

$$p = P(q, z), \tag{7.7}$$

where $P(\cdot)$ is increasing in both arguments, and (ii) an assumption that the rise in home-goods prices depends on θ-shocks and ε-shocks and is an increasing function of domestic money growth:

$$q = Q(m; \theta, \varepsilon). \tag{7.8}$$

In keeping with the rational-expectations surprise-supply literature, domestic output (employment) x is only affected by monetary surprises. The $Z(\cdot)$ function can be thought of as the inverse of a relative demand function, where the relative demand for home goods, $d - d^*$, is a decreasing function of the relative price of foreign goods: $D(z; \theta, \theta^*, \varepsilon, \varepsilon^*)$ with $D_z(\cdot) > 0$. If so, we can write the equilibrium condition $(d - d^*) = (x - x^*)$ as $z = D^{-1}((x - x^*); \theta, \theta^*, \varepsilon, \varepsilon^*)$, which together with (7.5) and its foreign counterpart defines (7.6).

We normalize the model by assuming

$$p = 0 \quad \text{when} \quad m = m^e = z = \theta = \varepsilon = 0,$$

$$x = 0 \quad \text{when} \quad m = m^e, \text{ and } z = \theta = \varepsilon = 0, \tag{7.9}$$

$$z = 0 \quad \text{when} \quad m = m^e, m^* = m^{*e}, \text{ and } \theta = \varepsilon = \theta^* = \varepsilon^* = 0.$$

The policy objective and macroeconomic outcomes of the foreign country are specified in a completely analogous way. Finally, we assume that all the macro-economic outcome functions are linear in their arguments, but, again, maintain the general form for ease of interpretation. Together with the assumption that objective functions are quadratic, this makes our model a linear-quadratic one.

Unless we make explicit assumptions to the contrary, we assume the following timing: (1) The values of θ and θ^* are observed by everyone; (2) Private agents form expectations: m^e and m^{*e}; (3) The values of ε and ε^* are observed by the policymakers; (4) Money growth rates, m and m^*, are chosen simultaneously; (5) Macroeconomic outcomes are realized. That is, we study a "discretionary" policy environment, where there is some scope for stabilization policy due to the policy-makers' information advantage.

The major contributions that we survey below can each be described within this common framework, or slight variant with alternative assumptions about the signs of partials in the objective function (7.1) and the reduced forms (7.4)–(7.6).

7.2. Notes on the literature

The model in this section is essentially the reduced form of the static models in Canzoneri and Henderson (1988, 1991). It also encompasses other models, like those in Canzoneri and Gray (1985) and Rogoff (1985), among others.

8. International externalities and domestic incentives

8.1. Conflict over stabilization

After the experience of the two oil shocks, the literature in the early to mid eighties focused on a particular aspect of decentralized and uncoordinated policymaking: inefficiencies may arise because individual countries try – in vain – to export some of the necessary adjustment to a common stagflationary shock to other countries. We illustrate the main idea in a first specialized version of our common framework, which is essentially the one suggested by Canzoneri and Henderson (1988).

In this version the two countries are completely symmetric. Neither the objective functions nor the output levels are directly affected by the real exchange rate which, however, directly affects CPI-inflation through import prices. Thus we assume:

$$W_z = W_z^* = X_z = X_z^* = 0 . \tag{8.1}$$

Further, policymakers evaluate output realizations according to

$$W_x, W_x^* \gtreqless 0 \quad \text{as} \quad x, x^* \lesseqgtr 0 . \tag{8.2}$$

Thus, there are no shocks of the common-information type giving rise to domestic incentive problems:

$$\theta = \theta^* = 0 . \tag{8.3}$$

The remaining shock is common to both countries:

$$\varepsilon = \varepsilon^* , \tag{8.4}$$

and has the character of a supply shock, in that

$$X_\varepsilon = X_\varepsilon^* < 0, P_\varepsilon = P_\varepsilon^* > 0, \quad \text{and} \quad Z_\varepsilon = 0 . \tag{8.5}$$

Cooperative policy. What would happen in a cooperative equilibrium? As usual, we assume in this regime that the two countries choose monetary policies so as to maximize the sum of their objective functions. For any ε, the optimal value for home money growth must satisfy the first-order condition:

$$W_p P_m + W_x X_m + (W_p P_z - W_{p*}^* P_z) Z_m = W_p P_m + W_x X_m = 0 , \tag{8.6}$$

where the first equality follows from the symmetry of the model (which makes $P_z^* = -P_z$). Taking expectations of (8.6) over ε, we can solve for equilibrium expectations, m^e. Plugging m^e back into (8.6), we obtain the cooperative equilibrium value of m, conditional on ε. We label this value $m^C = M^C(\varepsilon, \varepsilon^*)$. By symmetry of structure and shocks, we have $m^{*C} = m^C = M^C(\varepsilon, \varepsilon)$.

We make four observations about the cooperative equilibrium defined by (8.6): First, if there is no supply shock, so that $\varepsilon = 0$, each country reaches its first-best macroeconomic outcome at $m^C = M^C(0, 0) = 0$. (This follows by P_m and X_m both being positive and by $W_p = W_x = p = x = z$ 0 at $m = m^e = m^* = m^{*e} = 0$.) Second, at non-zero values of ε, higher output has to be optimally traded off against higher inflation. [By (7.3) and (8.1), $sgn[x] = -sgn[p]$ at $m = m^e = 0$ for $\varepsilon \neq 0$; it follows that $sgn[W_p] = -sgn[W_x]$ at $M^C(\varepsilon, \varepsilon)$.] Whether the home policymaker in fact chooses to expand or contract money growth depends on the relative weight he imposes on inflation relative to output and on the properties of the $P(\cdot)$ and $X(\cdot)$ functions. Hence, $M^C(\varepsilon, \varepsilon)$ can be positive or negative. Third, the effects of monetary policy that go through the real exchange rate are effectively ignored in the optimum solution. This is because the indirect effects of home monetary policy on the foreign inflation rate are internalized, and because of the symmetry – both in shocks and economic structure;

formally, the third term in the leftmost expression in (8.2) is equal to zero. This is, of course, a precise analog to the results on intertemporal terms of trade effects in fiscal policy of Section 2. Finally, due to the symmetry, the implied equilibrium real exchange rate change is independent of ε: $z = Z^C(\varepsilon, \varepsilon) = 0$ all ε.

Non-cooperative policy. Suppose that the two policymakers instead make decentralized and independent monetary policy decisions. As in Part A, we study the Nash equilibrium associated with such non-cooperative behavior. The home country's policymaker thus sets m to maximize his objective, taking m^*, as well as m^e and m^{*e}, as given. This yields the first-order condition:

$$W_p P_m + W_x X_m = -W_p P_z Z_m \,. \tag{8.7}$$

Taking expectations of (8.7) over ε defines equilibrium expectations, m^e. Inserting them back into (8.7) yields the state-dependent non-cooperative equilibrium policy, $m^N = M^N(\varepsilon, \varepsilon^*)$.

How does this solution compare to the cooperative optimum? When there is no supply shock, $\varepsilon = 0$, m^N like m^C implements the first best at $m = m^e = 0$. (The P, X and Z-partials are all non zero, whereas $W_p = W_x = p = x = 0$ at this point.) But when a non-zero symmetric supply shock is realized m^N is different from m^C. As can be seen from (8.6) and (8.7), the difference between the policies is proportional to $-W_p P_z Z_m$, an expression which has the same sign as ε at the cooperative optimum (as W_p has the opposite sign of ε and $P_z Z_m$ is always positive). Because the left-hand side of (8.6) and (8.7) is decreasing in m by concavity, we have

$$M^N(\varepsilon, \varepsilon) \gtreqless M^C(\varepsilon, \varepsilon) \text{ as } \varepsilon \lesseqgtr 0 \,. \tag{8.8}$$

In other words, monetary policy is distorted in the absence of cooperation: here it is too contractionary when there is a stagflationary shock ($\varepsilon > 0$), and too expansionary in the opposite case.

To see the intuition, consider a positive realization of ε. The home policymaker, who is optimally trading off high CPI-inflation against low output, has an additional incentive to contract money growth: to generate a negative value of z real appreciation, so as to lower CPI inflation via lower prices of imported goods. Hence, m^N is lower than m^C. But because the foreign policymaker has an analogous incentive, and because of symmetry, the effect on the real exchange rate is nullified in equilibrium. That is to say, $Z^N(\varepsilon, \varepsilon) = Z^C(\varepsilon, \varepsilon) = 0$. All that remains relative to the cooperative optimum is a contractionary bias in both countries. If both countries jointly expanded their money growth rates from m^N, their payoffs would improve: by (8.7) the increase in m would, by itself, have a zero (first-order) effect on W, but the accompanying increase in m^* would raise W by preventing a real depreciation and thereby limit the increase in home inflation. With a favorable supply shock, ($\varepsilon < 0$), the non-cooperative equilibrium instead has an expansionary bias. The general result in this version of the model is thus that non-cooperative policymaking induces "overactivism" by policymakers.

How the bias depends on the supply shock is clearly affected by the specification of the macroeconomic model. Canzoneri and Gray (1985) also discuss policy coordination in the context of supply shocks in a similar symmetric two-country world. But (in one version) their model has $P_z = 0$, $X_z > 0$. This leads to an expansionary bias as $\varepsilon > 0$. Policymaking is thus still distorted, albeit in a different direction.

8.2. Conflict over real income

The international conflict in the previous section is only temporary. We have already seen that the cooperative and non-cooperative solutions coincide if $\varepsilon = 0$. A temporary supply shock thus causes only a temporary conflict over stabilization. In a richer, dynamic model the conflict would still only be temporary, even if the ε-shock was permanent. The policymaker's *incentive* to export inflation to the foreign country, by decreasing domestic output via a surprise monetary contraction, would certainly remain. But his *ability* to do so goes away once the original wage contracts are rewritten (formally, the ε-shock would become a θ-shock). Suppose, however, that we amend the model in Section 8.1 with real income objectives for policymakers. That is, the model is exactly the same except that the home country policymaker values an improvement in its terms of trade, a decrease in z

$$W_z = -W_z^* < 0. \tag{8.9}$$

This adds a permanent source of conflict between the countries, which is really the same as in Section 2 above.

Cooperative policy. The first-order condition for home money growth in this amended version of the model becomes:

$$
\begin{aligned}
W_p P_m &+ W_x X_m + [(W_p - W_{p*}^*)P_z + (W_z + W_z^*)]Z_m \\
&= W_p P_m + W_x X_m = 0,
\end{aligned} \tag{8.10}
$$

where we have used (8.9) to arrive at the second equality. Comparing (8.10) and (8.6), the optimal cooperative policy is exactly as before. This is a pretty obvious result: internalizing the spill-over effects on the foreign country in a symmetric model is effectively identical to removing the international real income conflict.

Non-cooperative policy. With non-cooperative monetary policymaking, the corresponding first-order condition is

$$W_p P_m + W_x X_m = -(W_p P_z + W_z)Z_m .$$ (8.11)

The home country policymaker now has an incentive to improve the terms of trade via contractionary monetary policy once wage contracts have been written. This incentive is captured by the new term $-W_z Z_m$ on the right hand side of (8.11). This term is always positive, independently of ε, which adds a permanent contractionary bias to monetary policy. But this incentive will be frustrated in equilibrium; by a similar contractionary incentive abroad, we still have $Z^N(\varepsilon, \varepsilon) = 0$.

We can make two observations about the associated non-cooperative equilibrium: Unlike in the stabilization example, non-cooperative policy no longer corroborates the cooperative optimum in the absence of supply shocks. This, of course, reflects the presence of a permanent conflict over the terms of trade. Also, the conflict over real income may either reinforce or weaken the conflict over stabilization. If we have an adverse supply shock, $\varepsilon > 0$, the stabilization and real income incentives pull in the same direction, namely towards a more contractionary policy than in the cooperative optimum ($W_p P_z$ and W_z have the same sign). But when $\varepsilon < 0$, they pull in different directions. Indeed, by continuity (of P_ε and W_p), there must be a negative value of ε such that the non-cooperative and cooperative policies coincide (for this value, W_p is precisely equal to $-P_z/W_z$, at the point $M^C(\varepsilon, \varepsilon)$).

8.3. Domestic credibility problems

In the two examples above, the only prospective source of inefficiency is the lack of cooperation between the two governments. To say this in another way: the cooperative optimum is an ex post Pareto optimal outcome from the viewpoint of the two policymakers. But as we have already seen in the analysis of Part A, the result changes when we add binding domestic incentive constraints. The recent macro-economic literature has stressed how lack of commitment in monetary policy may generate an inflation bias. In a perceptive and early contribution, Rogoff (1985) pointed out how such domestic incentive problems may render international coopera-tion undesirable. We now illustrate his argument in a specialized version of the model. The thrust of the analysis closely resembles our treatment of credibility problems in capital taxation in Section 4.

We go back to the setup of Section 3.1 above, where there are no direct effects of the real exchange rate on policy objectives or outputs, so that (8.2) holds.[15] To

---

[15]Rogoff's model actually has the property that the real exchange rate depreciation has a negative effect on output: $X_z, X_z^* < 0$. This may be because nominal wages are (partly) indexed to the CPI, or because domestic production requires foreign intermediate inputs. None of our qualitative results below however, hinge on ignoring this effect.

simplify the argument, we initially assume that there are no ε-shocks. On the other hand, there is a common θ-shock. We let θ measure the distance between the home policymaker's preferred level of output and the natural rate.[16] All realizations of θ are assumed to be positive. In summary, we thus make the following assumptions:

$$W_z = W_z^* = X_z = X_z^* = 0, \tag{8.12}$$

$$W_x, W_{x*}^* \gtreqless 0 \text{ as } x, x^* \lesseqgtr \theta, \tag{8.13}$$

$$W_{x\theta} > 0, \tag{8.14}$$

$$\theta = \theta^*, \tag{8.15}$$

$$\varepsilon = \varepsilon^* = 0. \tag{8.16}$$

We continue to assume that the two countries are symmetric also in all other respects.

Cooperative policy. Assume as before that the two policymakers agree to set their money growth rates so as to maximize the sum of their objectives, given the realization of θ and the private expectations $m^e(\theta, \theta)$ and $m^{*e}(\theta, \theta)$. The optimum condition for m becomes

$$W_p P_m + W_x X_m + (W_p P_z - W_{p*}^* P_z)Z_m = W_p P_m + W_x X_m = 0. \tag{8.17}$$

This first-order condition is identical to (8.6), with which it shares the property that the real exchange rate effect of domestic monetary expansion is effectively ignored in the cooperative optimum. Yet it does not produce the same solution. Consider the hypothetical solution $m = m^e = 0$ which would produce $p = x = 0$. Whereas the marginal cost of inflation W_p is zero at that point, by (7.2), the marginal benefit of output W_x is positive, by (8.13). There is evidently an incentive to expand monetary policy, given that X_m is positive. This incentive keeps on biting up to the point where W_p has become sufficiently negative to deter further expansion. How far m and p have to rise depends on θ. We thus have $M^C(\theta, \theta) > 0$, with $M_\theta^C > 0$. But because θ is public information (and there are no other shocks), the policy is completely anticipated, so that $m^e(\theta, \theta) = M^C(\theta, \theta)$.

To summarize, we end up with positive inflation $p > 0$, but with output at the natural rate, $x = 0$. The policymaker would like to announce the policy $m = 0$ ex ante. In the absence of a commitment technology such an announcement is not credible, however, because it is not incentive compatible ex post. Of course, this is nothing but the well known Kydland–Prescott *cum* Barro–Gordon inflation bias as it appears in

---

[16]We could think about this shock either as fluctuations in the natural rate for a given target level of output, or as fluctuations in the policy objective for a given natural rate. As it stands, our model has the latter interpretation, in that we keep the natural rate of output fixed at zero, but this is really only a matter of normalization.

our particular model. Since monetary policies are perfectly anticipated, the real exchange rate is equal to its natural value $Z(\theta, \theta) = 0$, for all θ.

Non-cooperative policy. In the absence of cooperation, policymakers no longer ignore the real exchange rate effects of monetary policy. Equilibrium monetary policy in the home country has to satisfy the same condition as in Section 8.1, which we can rewrite as

$$W_p(P_m + P_z Z_m) + W_x X_m = 0 . \tag{8.18}$$

The equilibrium choice of m still involves trading off the marginal cost of higher inflation against the marginal benefit of higher output. Hence, n continues to be an increasing function of θ, $M^N(\theta, \theta)$. But the policymaker now perceives an additional marginal cost when considering an expansion of m: for given foreign monetary policy, an expansion generates a real depreciation, whereby higher prices of imported goods add further to CPI-inflation (this corresponds to the term $W_p P_z Z_m$ on the left-hand side of (8.18)). Clearly then, $M^N(\theta, \theta) < M^C(\theta, \theta)$ for any θ. Again, policy is perfectly anticipated such that $m^e(\theta, \theta) = M^N(\theta, \theta)$, and $x = 0$, for all θ. And, again, we have an identical outcome in the foreign country, such that the equilibrium has $z = 0$. Clearly then p is always higher in the cooperative regime, which makes the outcome strictly worse than in the noncooperative regime.

Perceived exchange rate effects thus provide a disincentive to inflate, which by itself creates a contractionary bias in monetary policy. This contractionary bias is a vice in a setup with only international conflict – as in Sections 8.2–8.3. But it becomes a virtue when coupled with a domestic incentive problem, which tends to give too much rationally expected inflation without any gains in employment. The parallels with the second-best arguments in Sections 3 and 4 should be obvious.

If we reintroduce the supply shocks from Sections 3.1–3.2, we clearly get a tradeoff: cooperation is helpful in promoting more efficient stabilization, but unhelpful in not putting a check on the domestic incentive problem. Whether the benefits outweigh the cost depends on whether the coordination problem is more serious than the credibility problem. An ex ante assessment of which regime would be preferable would have to rely on comparing the expected value of the objective (2.1) under specific assumptions about the distributions for θ and ε. Rogoff takes this to imply that gains form cooperation can be ensured only when appropriate domestic institutions are in place. We leave the discussion of this and other institutional issues to Section 9 below.

Discussion. The second-best logic of two incentive constraints pulling in different directions also helps to understand other "paradoxes" in the literature on monetary policy coordination. One example is the result due to Oudiz and Sachs (1985), who showed that when policymakers do not cooperate, having access to commitment in monetary policy may reduce each country's payoff. A similar result holds with regard to the exchange of information. The informal literature often argues that the international exchange of information always produces better outcomes, even in the absence of joint policy choice. But, drawing on the IO-literature on information sharing, Ghosh and Masson show (1994, ch. 7), that information exchange can sometimes produce worse outcomes. The reason, in their model, is that policymakers who ignore the realization of foreign shocks pursue underactivist policies. Exchange of information may or may not lead to better outcome, depending on whether there is underactivism or overactivism in the Nash equilibrium without information exchange.[17]

When discussing Rogoff's paradoxical result, Canzoneri and Henderson (1988) stress an interpretation in terms of coalitions: cooperation between a subset of the players in a game (here, the two governments, but not private agents forming expectations) does not necessarily produce better outcomes for these players, even though cooperation by the grand coalition of all the players would. The same logic helps understand why, as in Canzoneri and Henderson (1991, ch. 3), cooperation by two countries separately in a three-country world may actually reduce the equilibrium payoff to the cooperating countries.

8.4. Notes on the literature

Several of the papers in Bryant et al. (1988) discuss the empirical importance of international policy spillovers. Horne and Masson (1988) and Fischer (1988) survey a number of studies that attempt to measure empirically the gains from coordination. Most studies seem to find relatively modest gains from coordination, a fact that Canzoneri and Henderson (1991) attribute to the nature of the exercise: the studies allow for gains from joint stabilization, but not from eliminating permanent conflicts. Perhaps one may speculate that allowing in empirical studies for domestic incentive problems may give rise to larger prospective gains from coordination, but only to the extent that coordination serves to eliminate first-order losses due to these domestic incentive problems.

Miller and Salmon (1985) derived a Rogoff-type result in a dynamic policy game, based on a two-country version of the sticky-price Dornbusch overshooting model, whereas van der Ploeg (1988) demonstrated it in a model where the private sector in each country is modeled as a forward-looking and intertemporally maximizing representative agent. A related paradox can be found in Frenkel and Rockett (1989),

---

[17]Canzoneri and Edison (1990) also distinguish between cooperation and coordination and conclude that information exchange (i.e. cooperation) generally helps. Their argument is different, however, and relies on the insight that policy coordination games often have multiple equilibria, because of multiple instruments, or reputational effects, for instance. Then communication, may allow the countries to coordinate on a favorable Nash equilibrium, which could produce gains without any need for outside enforcement.

who demonstrate that coordination of monetary policies may lead to worse outcomes if policymaker's disagree over how the world economy works. The Oudiz–Sachs result mentioned in the text relies on a truly forward looking private sector; it is exposited in a two-period model by Canzoneri and Henderson (1991, ch. 5). Similar results can also be found in Levine and Currie (1987) and in Currie, Levine, and Vidalis (1987).

9. Domestic institutions in monetary policy

Suppose the international environment indeed implies important international spill-over effects in monetary policy. So far, we have only discussed prospective gains from policy cooperation, arising from the joint choice of policy instruments to maximize the worldwide payoff. Which mechanisms can decentralize the cooperative outcome to policymakers who set their policy instruments to maximize their individual payoffs? One answer in the literature is that cooperative outcomes in a non-cooperative setting can be enforced by "reputational mechanisms" when policymakers interact repeatedly over time. We do not pursue that line of argument here. The main reason is that it is already well-known: applications of the "folk theorem" of repeated games abound in many branches of the recent economics literature dealing with strategic interaction. All the drawbacks of the argument – like its lack of predictive power because of multiple equilibria – are well known, too. The recent book by Canzoneri and Henderson (1991, chs. 4–5) discusses reputational forces in a strategic international monetary setting at length.

Instead, we discuss implementation by contractual mechanism. Specifically, we borrow freely from the microeconomic literature on contracts and principal-agent relations. In our view, the role that central banks play in the design of monetary policy throughout the developed world supports the idea that an analysis of optimal delegation can yield important insights. This is the approach taken by Persson and Tabellini (1993) and Walsh (1995), who have studied how to tackle domestic incentive problems in monetary policy by institution design. As we shall see, a contractual approach can also be used to reinterpret some of the existing literature on institutions and international policy cooperation. In this section we look at decentral-ized policymaking without any international institutional arrangements in place. But in the next section we introduce more centralized arrangements, to end up in full monetary union with centralized policymaking.

9.1. One-sided exchange rate pegs

The paper by Canzoneri and Gray (1985) also studies a fixed exchange rate regime in the context of international conflict over stabilization. In their perceptive approach, a fixed exchange rate regime is modeled as a particular non-cooperative game, where one country makes a one-sided commitment to a specific monetary policy "reaction function", while the other country chooses its policy freely. This regime implements the cooperative optimum in a symmetric setting like the one in Section 8 above. In this subsection we first demonstrate how the Canzoneri–Gray result can be interpreted as a contractual arrangement. But we also show that the result is not robust and discuss its underpinnings.

General setting. In one of the countries – the home country for concreteness – we now distinguish explicitly between two public authorities: "society" (that is, a benevolent government or a social planner) is the principal that delegates the conduct of monetary policy to its agent, "the central bank". Society has the objective function identified by (7.2) and writes a "performance contract" with its home central bank. The central bank shares society's overall objective, but also cares about a transfer, T, provided under the contract. This transfer can be thought of either as direct performance related pay, or as indirect rewards and punishments. The central bank thus maximizes $(W + T)$. Unlike in the literature on contracts and regulatory design, we assume that the transfer is not costly to the principal, because the budgetary or non-pecuniary consequences of the transfer to the central bank are likely to be negligible relative to the macroeconomic outcomes at stake. However, we do assume the agent requires a specific minimum (and positive) expected payoff to participate in the game.

Symmetric shocks. Consider the symmetric supply shock model of Section 8.1. Before any other event takes place, the home country imposes a non-linear performance contract on its central bank. The contract is defined over the change in the nominal exchange rate, s:

$$T^s(s; \varepsilon, \varepsilon^*) = \begin{cases} \alpha & \text{if } s = 0 \\ \alpha - c & \text{otherwise}, \end{cases} \tag{9.1}$$

where c is a positive number and α is chosen so as to fulfill the agent's participation constraint. Thus, if the home central bank abandons the pegged exchange rate, it faces a prohibitive cost, provided that c is high enough (it exceeds the value of W for all realizations of policies and shocks).[18] The rest of the model is as before, except that we adopt the following timing: (1) Society commits to a contract in the home country; (2) Expectations m^e and m^{*e} are formed; (3) The shock ε is realized; (4)

---

[18]This way of modeling a fixed exchange rate regime is related to the approach in Obstfeld (1992), who does not use the contractual language explicitly, but nevertheless assumes that a central bank faces a lump sum cost for breaking its promise to peg the exchange rate. The structure of the game is also somewhat reminiscent of the setup studied in Lohman (1992) where a central banker is chosen ex ante together with a lump-sum penalty to society for firing him ex post.

The foreign policymaker chooses $m*$; (5) The home central bank chooses m; (6) Macroeconomic outcomes are realized.

Clearly, this performance contract will make the home central bank choose the same money growth as the foreign policymaker, to keep the exchange rate fixed. This follows, because the nominal exchange rate change

$$s = z + q - q*,$$

is zero if and only if $m = m*$, given that the equilibrium in this regime will again have the property that $m^e = m*^e = 0$.[19] Faced with this reaction function, when choosing $m*$ at stage (4), the foreign policymaker realizes that $z = 0$ whichever policy he sets. His optimal policy choice therefore ignores any effects on z and is thus defined by the first-order condition:

$$W^*_{p*} P^*_{m*} + W^*_{x*} X^*_{m*} = 0. \tag{9.2}$$

But this, as we know, is exactly the condition that produces the cooperative optimum. Thus, we have a Nash equilibrium which implements the cooperative solution with $m = m* = M^C(\varepsilon, \varepsilon)$.

The lesson is thus that, in this symmetric setting, there is no need for any cooperative agreement. The cooperative solution can be self-enforced in a decentralized non-cooperative setting by a one-sided exchange rate peg. What is necessary is that the home government's contract with its central bank includes strong enough sanctions for giving up the fixed exchange rate. Notice also that this arrangement presupposes a certain independence of the central bank in the pegging country, such that a de facto delegation of monetary policy is feasible. It is tempting to think of the examples of the successful one-sided peg of the Austrian schilling against the Deutschmark during the last ten to fifteen years along these lines. The Austrian central bank has a very independent position by its statute from 1984, and an explicit legislated target to protect the internal and external value of the schilling. Also, the Austrian and German economies are integrated enough that the symmetry assumption seems to make sense.

Asymmetric shocks. Clearly, the result that a contract inducing the home country policymaker to keep the exchange rate fixed is not robust to natural extensions of the model. An important proviso is the symmetry assumption. Specifically, when the two countries have asymmetric economic structures or face less than perfectly positively

---

[19]Using 7.1 we can write s as:

$$s = Z(m - m^e, m* - m*^e; \varepsilon, \varepsilon) + Q(m; \varepsilon) - Q*(m*; \varepsilon*).$$

From $m^e = m*^e = 0$, and symmetry plus linearity of the reduced forms, it follows that s is zero if and only if $m = m*$.

correlated shocks, the cooperative optimum entails an asymmetric policy response. To fix ideas, consider the opposite case of perfectly negatively correlated shocks

$$\varepsilon^* = -\varepsilon. \tag{9.3}$$

so that

$$X_\varepsilon = -X_\varepsilon^* < 0, P_\varepsilon = -P_\varepsilon^* > 0, \text{ and } Z_\varepsilon < 0. \tag{9.4}$$

In this case the *cooperative* optimum policies (under hypothetical joint decision making) will be mirror images of each other. The two policies have to satisfy

$$W_p P_m + W_x X_m = -2W_p P_z Z_m, \tag{9.5}$$

$$W_{p^*}^* P_{m^*}^* + W_{x^*}^* X_{*} = -2W_p^* P_z^* Z_{m^*}^* = 2W_p P_z Z_m, \tag{9.6}$$

where we have used the fact that $W_p = -W_p^*$ by $\varepsilon^* = -\varepsilon$, and that $P_z = -P_z^*$, and $Z_m = -Z_{m^*}^*$ by symmetry. From (9.4) it follows that $M^C(\varepsilon, -\varepsilon) = -M^{*C}(\varepsilon, -\varepsilon)$. The equilibrium real exchange rate change has the opposite sign of ε in this cooperative optimum

$$\text{sgn}[Z^C(\varepsilon, -\varepsilon)] = -\text{sgn}[\varepsilon]. \tag{9.7}$$

In words, a negative supply shock at home together with a positive supply shock abroad calls for a real appreciation of the home currency under the assumptions of the model.

It is easy to show that the bias in the *non-cooperative* simultaneous move equilibrium goes in the opposite direction to the symmetric-shock case. For example, if $\varepsilon = -\varepsilon^* > 0$, the home country expands its money growth rate too much if it fails to internalize that the foreign country – having suffered a positive supply shock – desires higher inflation, something which would be helped by a further fall in z.

Suppose that the home country government has written a performance contract with its central bank, which like (9.1) penalizes any failure to keep the exchange rate fixed. If the penalty is stiff enough, so that the home central bank complies for all realizations $(\varepsilon, \varepsilon^*)$, then the resulting policy is not only worse than the cooperative optimum, but even worse than the simultaneous move non-cooperative equilibrium. The reason is that, given $\varepsilon = -\varepsilon^*$, there is only one difference $m - m^*$ that keeps s constant at 0. Thus, the home central bank still reacts one-for-one to changes in m^*.[20] This means that the foreign policymaker again effectively ignores the effect of his

---

[20]The reaction function for the home central bank can be found from the requirement that $s = z + q - q^*$ is kept constant, which implies

$$dm/dm^* = (Q_{m^*}^* - Z_{m^*})/(Q_m + Z_m) = 1,$$

where the last equality follows from symmetry.

policy on z, and sets policy so as to fulfill (9.2). But as we have seen, in (9.4), the cooperative optimum requires not only that he take this effect into account, but that he give it double weight!

Discussion. A fixed exchange rate contract is thus only beneficial for both countries in the case of extreme symmetry. Suppose we are willing to make the symmetry assumption. Two further problems with the Canzoneri–Gray result are revealed by thinking about it in contracting terms. One is the rationale for the fixed exchange rate contract. So far we have taken the existence and form of the contract as exogenous. In the contracting framework it becomes natural to ask whether it is indeed in the interest of the central bank's principal – society – to write the contract in this particular way. The solution is admittedly Pareto optimal, but if the principal has the ability to impose a binding contract on its agent, it can likely achieve a strategic advantage by giving contractual incentives to its central bank to act in a more aggressive way, so as to impose a larger burden of the adjustment on the foreign country. Put differently, if we endogenize contract formation in the framework of this section, the fixed exchange rate contract is unlikely to be credible in the sense that it survives as a subgame perfect equilibrium.[21] A related problem is the asymmetric roles of the two countries. The home country can commit to a contract, whereas the foreign country cannot. But the foreign central bank can commit to a policy, whereas the home central bank cannot. The result would perhaps be more convincing if the roles of the two countries were more symmetric.

The next section shows that these difficulties are not necessarily insurmountable. There we study a different, and more symmetric institutional setup, where the cooperative optimum can be implemented as a subgame perfect equilibrium with decentralized delegation of monetary policy and endogenous contract formation in both countries, even with asymmetries in shocks or structure.

9.2. Decentralized contracting and policymaking

Suppose now that the government in each of the two countries delegates monetary policy to its central bank in the same stabilization context as above. As before this is done by a state-dependent non-linear performance contract, which is written before anything else happens. Importantly, both contracts are publicly observable. Under these conditions, the general results on delegation games in Fershtman, Judd and Kalai (1991) apply, which means that the cooperative optimum is indeed a subgame perfect equilibrium. As far as we know, this recent idea has not yet been applied to international policy coordination. We argue below that the underlying logic may have

---

[21] See Giavazzi and Giovannini (1989) for a discussion about how such incentives may break up a fixed exchange rate arrangement.

particular appeal in the case at hand, even though it cannot handle interesting extensions.

Implementation. The underlying economic assumptions are as in Section 4.1, but the supply shocks can have any correlation structure. The timing instead is more symmetric, namely: (1) The two governments simultaneously impose performance contracts on their central banks, which are observed by everyone; (2) Expectations are formed; (3) Supply shocks are realized; (4) The two central bankers simultaneously choose monetary policies; (5) Macroeconomic outcomes are realized.

Suppose that at stage (1) the home government writes a contract with its central bank of the following form

$$
T^W(W, W^*; \varepsilon, \varepsilon^*)
$$
$$
= \begin{cases} \alpha & \text{if } W(m, m^*; \varepsilon, \varepsilon^*), W^*(m^*, m; \varepsilon, \varepsilon^*) \geq W^C(\varepsilon, \varepsilon^*), W^{*C}(\varepsilon, \varepsilon^*) \\ \alpha - c & \text{otherwise} \end{cases}
$$

$$(9.8)$$

and that the foreign government writes an analogous contract. $W(m, m^*; \varepsilon, \varepsilon^*)$ is the reduced form expression for the home government's payoff given m and m^* and $W^C(\varepsilon, \varepsilon^*)$ is the home country's payoff at the cooperative optimum in state $\varepsilon, \varepsilon^*$. The contract in (9.8) – and its foreign counterpart – is again on target compensation form. But rather than over the exchange rate, it is defined directly over government payoffs, and hence indirectly over monetary policies. Note that the *home* contract is contingent on the payoff of *both* countries. The home central banker is rewarded if the cooperative payoffs are reached by both countries, but not otherwise.

Key to the implementation result is that the strategy of each central banker is made conditional on the contracts in both countries. Specifically, assume that the home central bank's strategy is:

$$
m(\varepsilon, \varepsilon^*)
$$
$$
= \begin{cases} M^C(\varepsilon, \varepsilon^*) & \text{iff } [T^W(W, W^*; \varepsilon, \varepsilon^*), T^{*W}(W^*, W; \varepsilon, \varepsilon^*)] \geq (\alpha, \alpha) \\ M^N(\varepsilon, \varepsilon^*) & \text{otherwise} \end{cases}
$$

$$(9.9)$$

and that the foreign central bank chooses $m^*(\varepsilon, \varepsilon^*)$ in an analogous way.

The strategies specified in (9.8)–(9.9) constitute a subgame perfect equilibrium that implements the cooperative optimum policies for each realization of $(\varepsilon, \varepsilon^*)$. Clearly, once the performance contracts (9.8) are in place, it becomes optimal for the central banks to respond with the cooperative policies.[22] What about the incentives for

---

[22]This is not the only equilibrium: (M^N, M^{*N}) is also an equilibrium of the agents' game. Fershtman, Judd, and Kalai (1991) discuss how to redefine the delegation game so as to get rid of equilibria that are Pareto dominated for both agents. When the agents are communicating, as is certainly the case in international policy coordination, Pareto dominated equilibria are clearly implausible. See also the distinction in footnote 16 between cooperation and coordination.

the two societies to write the contracts in this way? Suppose home society contemplates a deviation. Because the suggested equilibrium is ex post Pareto optimal, writing another contract that alters the home central bank's policy must either lower the home country's payoff, which can never be optimal, or else increase its payoff at the expense of the foreign country. But in the latter case the foreign central bank can not achieve the target payoff prescribed in its contract. Consequently it chooses the policy $M^{*N}(\varepsilon, \varepsilon^*)$, to which the home central bank optimally responds by setting $M^N(\varepsilon, \varepsilon^*)$. This is clearly worse than achieving the cooperative outcome in both countries. Note that an important role of the contract in each country is to induce good behavior of the central bank *abroad*. This is a nice analog to our earlier delegation result in Section 5, where the median voter in each country had incentives to elect a policymaker with distorted preferences precisely to induce a better tax policy abroad.

This is not the unique subgame perfect equilibrium contract implementing the optimum: any payoff for cooperative behavior for the agents that satisfy their participation constraints will do the same trick. However, these equilibria are all equivalent in policy outcomes. If the transfers were indeed costly to the two principals, setting the rewards such that each agent received a net payoff that just satisfied his participation constraint would be the unique subgame perfect equilibrium – see however footnote.

Discussion. Applying the Fershtman–Judd–Kalai argument to policy coordination games may seem a little contrived to some readers. We will spell out some of the obvious weaknesses below, but we still think there are some interesting insights. One is that the implementation here is entirely decentralized and does not require any international agreements. The government in each country de facto commits to following the cooperative monetary policies, but only through the contracts with their own central banks. Implementation, of course, requires that these rather elaborate domestic contracts are enforceable. At a general level, however, an ability to commit through *domestic* institutional arrangements seems eminently more plausible than being able to commit to an international contract, at least if we think of the suggested cooperation as applying to discretionary deals in response to ongoing shocks in the world economy. We basically agree with Feldstein's (1988) claim that it is probably unrealistic to expect real-world policymakers to pursue policies that run against their domestic interests. Therefore, it is interesting that strong domestic institutions may lead to internationally cooperative outcomes purely as a result of self interested choices.

But the implementation scheme we have studied also has severe drawbacks. One is that it relies heavily on the very sharp "take-it-or-leave-it" incentives embodied in our non-linear and state-dependent contracts. A second drawback is that the contracts are defined over payoffs, rather than over policies that may be easier to observe. And a third is that ex post Pareto optimality of the underlying cooperative policies is a necessary condition for the scheme to work. This means that the argument can be extended to policy environments with a permanent conflict over the terms of trade, as in Section 8.2. But it need not apply to a policy environment with domestic incentive problems, such as the credibility problems studied in Section 8.3. Some of these drawbacks are addressed in the next section which deals with a contractual approach to rule-based prospective cooperation within the context of institutionalized and multilateral international monetary arrangements.

9.3. Notes on the literature

After Canzoneri and Gray, several authors have studied how alternative rules – like policy assignments to central banks might help improve on non-cooperative equilibria. Giavazzi and Giovannini (1989) study exchange rate arrangements and show that it makes a difference whether the pegging country's policy instrument is the exchange rate rather than the money supply. Frankel (1991) considers a more symmetric arrangement and argues that symmetric nominal income targeting may overcome some of the obstacles to policy coordination.

The analogy between the central banks as agents to their political principals and managers as agents to their firms' owners, or natural monopolies as agents to their government regulators has been noted for a long time, but it is only recently that it has entered the formalized literature. Dolado, Griffiths, and Padilla (1994) study how strategic non-cooperative delegation of monetary policy to "conservative central bankers" may either improve or worsen policy outcomes, depending on the direction of international spillover effects. Vickers (1985) is an early contribution to the industrial organization literature on strategic vertical delegation, which is usefully surveyed by Caillaud and Rey (1995). The central reference to the modern literature on regulation and contracts is Laffont and Tirole (1993).

10. International institutions in monetary policy

10.1. Multilateral pegs

We remain in the stabilization model of Sections 8–9 without a direct conflict over the terms of trade. However, we now allow for both ex ante observable (to wage setters) θ-shocks and unobservable ε-shocks, and for an arbitrary correlation structure between these shocks. As before, the countries are completely symmetric in all other respects. We now show that international institutions may help resolve credibility problems, as well as international coordination problems. This result squares with the observation that many countries seem reluctant to find domestic solutions to their credibility problems and resort instead to international arrangements.

To get some perspective on this question, we first consider a single *international* principal trying to provide the two central banks with the appropriate incentives for their decentralized policymaking via a pair of contracts. These contracts can be thought of as being written at an initial "institution design stage", when negotiators from the two symmetric countries get together and form a binding international agreement. At this point in time the objective function is the sum of the two countries expected payoffs:

$$E[W(p, x, z; \theta, \varepsilon) + W^*(p^*, x^*, z; \theta^*, \varepsilon^*)], \tag{10.1}$$

where E denotes the unconditional expectations operator, taken over $(\theta, \theta^*, \varepsilon, \varepsilon^*)$.

We assume the following sequence of events: (1) An international principal imposes a performance contract on each central bank, observed by everyone; (2) θ and θ^* are realized; (3) Expectations about m^e and m^{*e} are formed; (4) ε and ε^* are realized; (5) The two central banks simultaneously choose monetary policies; (6) Macroeconomic outcomes are realized.

To get a handle on what contracts the principal would like to write, consider the hypothetical problem of finding the state-contingent policies $m(\theta, \theta^*, \varepsilon, \varepsilon^*)$ and $m^*(\theta, \theta^*, \varepsilon, \varepsilon^*)$ that maximize 10.1, under the constraint that private expectations are formed rationally:

$$m^e(\theta, \theta^*) = E_{\varepsilon, \varepsilon^*}[m(\theta, \theta^*, \varepsilon, \varepsilon^*)], m^{*e}(\theta, \theta^*) = E_{\varepsilon, \varepsilon^*}[m^*(\theta, \theta^*, \varepsilon, \varepsilon^*)]. \tag{10.2}$$

Here, $E_{\varepsilon, \varepsilon^*}$ denotes the conditional expectations operator, that is, the expectation taken over $(\varepsilon, \varepsilon^*)$, given the realization (θ, θ^*). The solution to this problem gives the ex ante optimal policies from the point of view of the international principal.

Eliminating the multipliers on the constraints in 10.2, and exploiting symmetry, the first-order conditions for the optimal choices of $m(\theta, \theta^*, \varepsilon, \varepsilon^*)$ and $m^*(\theta, \theta^*, \varepsilon, \varepsilon^*)$ can be written as:

$$W_p P_m + (W_x - E_{\varepsilon, \varepsilon^*} W_x) \cdot X_m + (W_p - W_{p^*}^*) \cdot P_z Z_m = 0, \tag{10.3}$$

$$W_{p^*}^* P_m + (W_{x^*}^* - E_{\varepsilon, \varepsilon^*} W_{x^*}^*) \cdot X_m - (W_{p^*}^* - W_p) \cdot P_z Z_m = 0. \tag{10.4}$$

Recall that the derivatives of W and W^* are linear in the macroeconomic outcomes, which themselves are linear functions of m, m^*, m^e, and m^{*e}. For each state, these two conditions are therefore linear functions of $m(\theta, \theta^*, \varepsilon, \varepsilon^*)$, $m^*(\theta, \theta^*, \varepsilon, \varepsilon^*)$ and of the expectations $m^e(\theta, \theta^*)$ and $m^{*e}(\theta, \theta^*)$. We can find the latter by taking expectations (over ε and ε^*) of (10.3) and (10.4). Plugging the resulting expressions into (10.3) and (10.4), we have two equations in two unknowns and we can solve for the ex ante optimal state-contingent policies under cooperation.

The tradeoffs expressed in (10.3) involve terms that are all familiar from the above analysis, with one exception. The third term in (10.3), $-E_{\varepsilon, \varepsilon^*} W_x X_m$, measures the marginal cost of higher expected money growth (inflation), which it is appropriate to internalize at stage (1), before private agents have formed their expectations. Note that this term depends on θ, because W_x is increasing in θ, but not on θ^*. Similarly, the third term in (10.4), $-E_{\varepsilon,\varepsilon^*}W_x^*X_m$, depends on θ^* but not on θ. For future reference, we note an important property of the optimal state-contingent policies: it is possible to show that they are not dependent on the realizations of θ and θ^*. The optimal policies under hypothetical commitment thus do not respond to observable shocks. Intuitively, this is because (i) agents have rational expectations, (ii) real variables are only affected by monetary surprises, and (iii) the cost of expected inflation does not depend directly on θ and θ^*. We refer to the resulting policies as $M^{CC}(\varepsilon, \varepsilon^*)$ and $M^{*CC}(\varepsilon, \varepsilon^*)$, where CC stands for cooperation and (hypothetical) commitment.

We now show that the central-bank contracts can be structured to implement the ex ante *cooperative* optimum. Consider the incentives faced by the home central bank when it chooses policy ex post and in a decentralized fashion, without any contracts in place at stage (3). The partial derivatives of W and W^* with respect to m and m^*, taking $m^e(\theta, \theta^*)$ and $m^{*e}(\theta, \theta^*)$ as given, are:

$$\partial W/\partial m = W_p P_m + W_x X_m + W_p P_z Z_m . \tag{10.5}$$

$$\partial W^*/\partial m^* = W_p^* P_{m^*} + W_p^* X_{m^*} - W_p^* P_z Z_m . \tag{10.6}$$

Compared to the expressions in (10.3) and (10.4), two terms are missing from each expression. The missing terms reflect the incentive constraints faced by the individual agents setting policy ex post at stage (3), namely credibility and individual, rather than joint, optimality. Unlike the common international principal setting policy ex ante at stage (1), the two central banks take expectations as given, and thus neglect the effect of equilibrium policy on expectations – the third term in (10.3) and (10.4). Similarly, they neglect the spillover effects of domestic policy on inflation abroad – the fifth term in (10.3) and (10.4). The role of a useful contract is thus to implement the policies $M^{CC}(\varepsilon, \varepsilon^*)$ and $M^{*CC}(\varepsilon, \varepsilon^*)$, by making the central banks at stage (3) internalize the effects of policy on expectations and foreign payoffs, and hence correct the distortions induced by ex post, decentralized policymaking. (As we have seen in Section 8.3, these two incentive constraints may well pull in opposite directions, so it is unclear exactly how distorted equilibrium outcomes would be.)

Optimal contracts. In the model at hand, there are multiple performance contracts the principal could impose on the two central banks at stage (1), to implement $M^{CC}(\varepsilon, \varepsilon^*)$ and $M^{*CC}(\varepsilon, \varepsilon^*)$ at stage (3). By assumption, the change in the nominal exchange rate s and the two CPI's p and p^* are linear functions of m and m^*. This means that the right incentives can be embodied in performance contracts over any combinations of these variables, provided that state-contingent contracts can be written. In particular, a feasible way to implement the optimum is a policy assignment where – say – the foreign country's central bank has a performance contract tied to

m^* (or p^*), whereas the home central bank has an exchange-rate contract tied to s. These contracts could clearly be written on the same non-linear, take-it-or-leave-it form as in Section 9. But the principal could also impose the right marginal incentives for $M^{CC}(\varepsilon, \varepsilon^*)$ and $M^{*CC}(\varepsilon, \varepsilon^*)$ by two *linear* performance contracts, in close analogy with the linear contracts in the closed economy models of Persson and Tabellini (1993) and Walsh (1994). Such linear performance contracts embody less stark and perhaps more intuitive incentive mechanisms. In particular, the following pair of contracts would work:

$$T^s(s; \theta, \varepsilon, \varepsilon^*) = \alpha - t^s(\theta, \varepsilon, \varepsilon^*) \cdot s \qquad (10.7)$$

$$T^m*(m^*; \theta^*, \varepsilon, \varepsilon^*) = \alpha - t^m*(\theta^*, \varepsilon, \varepsilon^*) \cdot m^* . \qquad (10.8)$$

Thus, both central banks face performance contracts that are linear in the exchange rate and the money growth rate, respectively. The state-contingent slope coefficients are given by $t^s(\theta, \varepsilon, \varepsilon^*) \equiv (E_{\varepsilon, \varepsilon^*} W_x X_m + W_p^* P_z Z_m)/(Z_m + Q_m)$ and $t^{m*}(\theta^*, \varepsilon, \varepsilon^*) \equiv E_{\varepsilon, \varepsilon^*} W_{x^*}^* X_m - W_p P_z Z_m$, where it is understood that the derivatives are evaluated at the ex ante optimal policies $M^{CC}(\varepsilon, \varepsilon^*)$ and $M^{*CC}(\varepsilon, \varepsilon^*)$.

The contract for the foreign central bank is easiest to interpret. As is apparent from (10.4), (10.6) and (10.8), the contract confronts the foreign central bank with the appropriate corrective incentives. First, it makes the foreign central bank internalize the costs of higher money growth in terms of higher expected inflation; because the ex post incentive to inflate depends on θ^*, the optimal contract has to be stiffer – the slope coefficient larger – the higher is θ^*. Second, it makes the foreign central bank internalize the spillover effect on inflation in the home country, via the real exchange rate; the importance of this effect is governed by ε and θ^*. The exchange rate contract faced by the home central bank has a similar interpretation, except for the denominator, which is there because the contract is a performance contract in the exchange rate. Hence, it controls the incentives to set m only indirectly, via s: at stage (3) the marginal effect of m on T is given by, $T_s S_m = -t^s(\theta, \varepsilon, \varepsilon^*) \cdot (Z_m + Q_m)$, as $s = z + q - q^*$.

The international principal can thus implement the ex ante cooperative optimum by a careful choice of linear contracts. The proviso is that the slope coefficients have to be state contingent, in θ and θ^* to relax the credibility constraints, and in ε and ε^* to relax the individual optimality constraints.

Multilateral exchange rate regimes. The theoretical framework sketched above clearly bears some resemblance to the history and operation of the most important international exchange-rate arrangements of the post-war period. Both the Bretton Woods system and the EMS did indeed grow out of an initial and lengthy period of multilateral negotiations – like the institution design stage of the model. Also, both arrangements had a codified set of prospective rewards and sanctions tied to the behavior of central banks – like the contractual transfers in the model.[23] Finally, both arrangements amounted – like in the model – to an explicit or implicit policy assignment among the member countries. The US Fed and the German Bundesbank would direct their policies towards a domestic monetary target providing a nominal anchor to the system. The other central banks instead would have an adjustable exchange rate target vis-à-vis the central currency, whereby they would capture some credibility from the anchor country.

But why would these real-world international monetary arrangements involve the exchange rate as a key intermediate target, rather than a more symmetric arrangement? Some would argue that the exchange rate is used as a target because it is so easy to monitor. It is also hard to find an analog to the explicit state-contingency of the contractual mechanism supporting the optimal policy in the model. The reason may be that it is very difficult to foresee, monitor and verify the macroeconomic events that would potentially trigger state-contingent international sanctions or rewards for specific monetary policies. Allowing only non-state contingent contracts, we would have to insist on the slope coefficients in (10.7) and (10.8) being constant, which would clearly induce some inefficiency.[24]

In fact, the Bretton Woods system and the EMS – together with the domestic monetary institutions in the central currency country – are perhaps best described as mechanisms for implementing a simple rule with an ''escape clause'': in normal circumstances the central-currency country would pursue a restrictive monetary policy and the exchange rate against the central currency would remain pegged. But temporary slippage of the monetary anchor and realignments would be allowed under exceptional circumstances.[25] In the model above, at stage (1), the international principal could implement such an escape-clause equilibrium by replacing the contracts in (10.7) and (10.8) by a pair of non-linear, state-independent contracts. Deviations from a fixed exchange rate and a specific foreign money growth rate $m*$ would be punished by a pair of non-contingent negative transfers (c^s, c^m). How often the escape clause would be triggered would depend on (c^s, c^m): the lower their value, the more realizations of θ, $\theta*$, ε, and $\varepsilon*$ would induce the central banks at stage (3) to break the contract and pursue a decentralized, discretionary policy.

Such a multilateral peg system would also be suboptimal, relative to the hypothetical benchmark of the ex ante cooperative optimum. Just how suboptimal

---

[23]Examples were the obligation to inform and consult with the IMF or with other countries before exchange rate changes; the conditional rights to draw on SDR's to finance balance of payments deficits and the possibility of IMF conditionality in the case of the Bretton Woods system; the short-run credit facilities, the ties to other EC institutions like the CAP, and the practice not to allow full restoration to parity of overvalued currencies at realignments, in the case of the EMS.

[24]Ghosh and Masson (1994, ch. 9) discuss the incentives for policymakers to actively distort information to gain a strategic advantage in international coordination games.

[25]The classic formulation in Article IV of the Bretton Woods agreement about allowing devaluations only in situations of ''fundamental disequilibrium'' reminds precisely about the notion of a rule with an escape clause.

depends on the properties of the shocks. Frequent realizations of high values of θ and θ^* and low or negative correlation between ε and ε^* would lead to frequent breach of the simple rule. But with limited credibility problems of monetary policy – or a central country with a great deal of credibility – and relatively parallel macroeconomic development in the participating countries, the incentives to deviate from the simple rule would be small. Perhaps it is not too far-fetched to describe the fifties and (most of) the sixties under the Bretton Woods system, as well as the eighties under the EMS, just in those terms.

As we have seen in Section 9.2, however, in the wake of asymmetric ε-shocks it is worse to have a monetary arrangement that creates strong incentives for convergent monetary policies than to have no arrangement at all. Asymmetric shocks are therefore especially likely to put strain on the simple rule and potentially on the whole mechanism. It is interesting to note that the eventual breakdown of the Bretton Woods system and the EMS were indeed both preceded by asymmetric shocks to the central currency country: the US fiscal shock in connection with the Vietnam war and Johnson's great society program, and German unification respectively.

10.2. Monetary union

The complete form of monetary policy cooperation would be full monetary union, with a single money managed by a *single* central bank. The previous discussion suggests that full monetary union would be a suboptimal arrangement if there are asymmetric shocks. But if the cooperative optimum under commitment is infeasible, we face a second-best institution design problem, namely a choice between different suboptimal alternatives. Furthermore, our simple model abstracts from a number of complicating factors. For one, it has no room for speculative attacks, or more generally, speculation-induced volatility of capital movements and asset prices. The 1992–1994 turmoil in world asset markets, with the effective breakup of the EMS, suggests that the relevant choice may be between floating rates (and appropriate domestic institutions) versus full monetary union.[26] Moreover, we have confined our analysis to stabilization policies. But other prospective gains, such as savings on transactions costs [Casella (1992)] or microeconomic benefits in other areas of integration [Basevi, Delbono, and Denicolo (1992)], may only be reaped with full monetary union.

Whatever its motivation, monetary union raises several interesting questions. First, under which circumstances should a single country join a monetary union? To the list that starts with Mundell's (1961) high factor mobility, and includes the predominant type of macroeconomic shocks, the recent literature on "optimum currency areas"

---

[26]Peter Garber and Lars E.O. Svensson's chapter in this volume discusses the literature on speculative attacks.

has added large domestic incentive problems in monetary policy. But there is also an interesting systemic question: how does the design of the common central bank resolve conflicting interests of member countries and shape the union's monetary policy? Keeping with our approach in this chapter, these positive and normative questions could be productively analyzed, by drawing on principal-agent theory and contract theory. A common central bank is an instance of common agency: this common agent serves multiple principals (the member countries) with partly common, partly conflicting interests.[27] The themes would be the same as in our analysis of fiscal policy: participation constraints have to be respected, particularly with asymmetric countries, and the specific collective decision-making mechanism shapes the policy outcome, as well as the distributions of costs and benefits. Even though they use a different language, the recent papers by Casella and Feinstein (1989), Alesina and Grilli (1992) and Von Hagen and Süppel (1994) effectively address these problems. They all suggest that one cannot analyze the question of how to design a common central bank without paying close attention to the broader political and institutional framework in which the member countries interact.

An interesting issue for further work would be how alternative international monetary arrangements could handle the incentives for individual policymakers to conceal or distort information about the state of their economies. The contract theory approach would seemingly be very valuable here, given that it has essentially been developed to deal with incentive problems and conflicting interests in the presence of asymmetric information.

10.3. Notes on the literature

The literature on the Bretton Woods system is too voluminous to be surveyed here. The recent volume edited by Bordo and Eichengreen (1993) contains many useful studies, analytical as well as descriptive. Likewise there is a large literature on the EMS and on monetary union in Europe. Useful collections of articles can be found in de Cecco (1989) and Canzoneri, Grilli and Masson (1992). Martin (1992) compares optimal monetary policy delegation in monetary union and under flexible exchange rates. Giavazzi and Pagano (1988) discuss the EMS and the incentives created by the practice of not allowing full compensation of inflation differentials at EMS realignments. Cohen and Wyplosz (1989) specifically emphasize the role of the EMS as a coordination device.

---

[27]Bernheim and Whinston (1986) formulate a general model of common agency. This approach has recently been applied to the study of trade policy by Grossman and Helpman. [See their (1994) paper, and Dani Rodrik's chapter in this volume.]

References

Alesina, A. and V. Grilli (1992), "The European central bank: Reshaping monetary policies in Europe", in: M. Canzoneri, V. Grilli, and P. Masson (eds.) Establishing a central bank: Issues in Europe and lessons from the U.S. (Cambridge University Press, Cambridge, UK).

Alesina, A. and G. Tabellini (1990), "A positive theory of fiscal deficits and government debt", Review of Economic Studies 57:403–414.

Basevi, G., F. Delbono, and V. Delnicolo (1990), "International monetary cooperation under tariff threat", Journal of International Economics 28:1–23.

Bernheim, D. and M. Whinston (1986), "Menu auctions, resource allocation and economic influence", Quarterly Journal of Economics 101:131.

Bolton, P. and G. Roland (1992), "The break-up of nations: A political economy approach", manuscript, University of Brussels.

Bordo, M. and B. Eichengreen (1993), A retrospective on the Bretton Woods system (University of Chicago Press, Chicago).

Bryant, R., D. Henderson, G. Holtham, P. Hooper, and S. Symansky (1988), Empirical macroeconomics for interdependent economies (Brookings Institution, Washington, D.C.).

Buchanan, J. and R. Faith (1987), "Secessions and the limits of taxation: Toward a theory of internal exit", American Economic Review 77:1023–1031.

Buiter, W. (1987), "Fiscal policy in open interdependent economies", in: J. Frenkel and A. Razin, eds., Economic policy in theory and practice (Macmillan, London) 101–144.

Buiter, W. and R. Marston (1985), International economic policy coordination (Cambridge University Press, Cambridge, UK).

Caillaud, B. and P. Rey (1995), "Strategic aspects of delegation", European Economic Review, forthcoming.

Canzoneri, M. and Edison, H. (1990), "A new interpretation of the coordination problem and its empirical significance", in: P. Hooper et al. eds., Financial sectors in open economies: Empirical analysis and policy issues (Board of Governors of the Federal Reserve System, Washington).

Canzoneri, M. and J. Gray (1985), "Monetary policy games and the consequences of noncooperative behavior", International Economic Review 26:547–564.

Canzoneri, M., V. Grilli, and P. Masson (1992), eds., Establishing a central bank: Issues in Europe and lessons from the U.S. (Cambridge University Press, Cambridge, UK).

Canzoneri, M. and D. Henderson (1988), "Is sovereign policymaking bad?", Carnegie–Rochester Conference Series 28:93–140.

Canzoneri, M. and D. Henderson (1991), Monetary policy in interdependent economies: A game-theoretic approach (MIT Press, Cambridge, MA).

Carraro, C. and F. Giavazzi (1989), "Can international policy coordination really be counterproductive", National Bureau of Economic Research Working Paper No. 2669.

Casella, A. (1992), "Participation in a currency union", American Economic Review 82:847–863.

Casella, A. and J. Feinstein (1989), "Management of a common currency", in: M. de Cecco and A. Giovannini, eds., A European central bank? (Cambridge University Press, Cambridge, UK).

Chang, R. (1989), "International coordination of fiscal deficits?", Journal of Monetary Economics 25:347–366.

Chang, R. (1993), "Bargaining in a monetary union", manuscript, New York University.

Chari, V. and P. Kehoe (1990), "International coordination of fiscal policy in limiting economies", Journal of Political Economy 98:617–636.

Cohen, D. and C. Wyploz (1989), "European monetary union: An agnostic evaluation", in: R. Bryant et al. eds., Macroeconomic policies in an interdependent world (Brookings Institution, Washington, D.C.).

Cooper, R. (1985), "Economic interdependence and coordination of economic policies", in: R. Jones and P. Kenen, eds., Handbook of international economics, vol. 2 (North-Holland, Amsterdam).

Currie, D. and P. Levine (1993), Rules, reputation, and macroeconomic policy coordination (Cambridge University Press, Cambridge, UK).

Currie, D., P. Levine, and N. Vidalis (1987), "International cooperation and reputation in an empirical two-bloc model", in: R. Bryant and R. Portes, eds., Global macroeconomics: Policy conflict and cooperation (Macmillan Press, London).

de Cecco, M. and A. Giovannini (1989), eds., A European central bank? (Cambridge University Press, Cambridge, UK).

Devereux, M. (1987), "Fiscal spending, the terms of trade, and real interest rates", Journal of International Economics 22:1–23.

Dolado, J., M. Griffiths, and J. Padilla (1994), "Delegation in international monetary policy games", European Economic Review 38:1057–1069.

Edwards, J. and M. Keen (1993), "Tax competition and Leviathan", manuscript, University of Essex.

Eichengreen, B. and J. Frieden (1994), The political economy of European monetary unification (Westview, Boulder, CO).

Evans, P., H. Jacobson, and R. Putnam (1993), "Double-edged diplomacy", International bargaining and domestic policies (University of California Press, Berkeley).

Feldstein, M. (1988), "Distinguished lecture on economics in government: Thinking about international economic coordination", Journal of Economic Perspectives 2:3–13.

Fershtman, C, K. Judd and E. Kalai (1991), "Observable contracts: Strategic delegation and cooperation", International Economic Review 32:551–559.

Fischer, S. (1977), "Long-term contracts, rational expectations and the optimal money supply rule", Journal of Political Economy 85:191–205.

Fischer, S. (1988), "International macroeconomic policy coordination", in: M. Feldstein, ed., International Economic Cooperation (University of Chicago Press, Chicago).

Frankel, J. (1988), "Obstacles to international macroeconomic policy coordination", International Finance Section paper, Princeton University.

Frankel, J. and K. Rocket (1988), "International macroeconomic policy coordination when policy-makers disagree on the model", American Economic Review 78:318–340.

Frankel, J. (1991), "The obstacles to macroeconomic policy coordination in the 1990s and an analysis of international nominal targeting", manuscript, University of California, Berkeley.

Frenkel, J., A. Razin, and E. Sadka (1991), International taxation in an integrated world (MIT Press, Cambridge, MA).

Frenkel, J. and A. Razin (1985), "Fiscal expenditures and international economic interdependence", in: W. Buiter and R. Marston, eds., International economic policy coordination (Cambridge University Press, Cambridge, UK) 37–72.

Ghosh, A. and P. Masson (1994), Economic cooperation in an uncertain world (Blackwells, Oxford).

Giavazzi, F. and M. Pagano (1988), "The advantage of tying one's hands: EMS discipline and central bank credibility", European Economic Review 32:1055–1082.

Giavazzi, F. and A. Giovannini (1989), "Monetary policy interactions under managed exchange rates", Economica 56:199–214.

Giovannini, A., G. Hubbard, and J. Slemrod (1993), Studies in international taxation (University of Chicago Press, Chicago and London).

Gordon, R. (1983), "An optimal taxation approach to fiscal federalism", Quarterly Journal of Economics 98:567–586.

Grandmont, J.-M. (1978), "Intermediate preferences and the majority rule", Econometrica 46:317–330.

Grilli, V., D. Masciandaro, and G. Tabellini (1991), "Political and monetary institutions and public financial policies in the industrial countries", Economic Policy 13:342–392.

Grossman, G. and E. Helpman (1994), "Protection for sale", American Economic Review 84:833–850.

Hamada, K. (1974), "Alternative exchange rate systems and the interdependence of monetary policies", in: R. Aliber, ed., National monetary policies and the international financial system (University of Chicago Press, Chicago).

Hamada, K. (1976), "A strategic analysis of monetary interdependence", Journal of Political Economy 84:677–700.

Hamada, K. (1979), "Macroeconomic strategy and coordination under alternative exchange rates", in: R. Dornbusch and J. Frenkel, eds., International economic policy (Johns Hopkins University Press, Baltimore).

Horne, J. and P. Masson (1988), "Scope and limits of international economic cooperation and policy coordination", International Monetary Fund Staff Papers 35:259–296.

Hughes-Hallet, A. (1987), "International policy design and the sustainability of policy bargains", Journal of Economic Dynamics and Control 10:467–494.

Jensen, H. (1992), "The advantage of international fiscal cooperation under alternative monetary regimes", manuscript, University of Aarhus.

Johnson, H. (1965), "An economic theory of protectionism, tariff bargaining, and the formation of customs unions", Journal of Political Economy 73:256–283.

Keen, M. (1993), "Structure of the fiscal and social changes according to their degree of mobility", manuscript, University of Essex.

Kehoe, P. (1989), "Policy cooperation among benevolent governments may be undesirable", Review of Economic Studies 56:289–296.

Laffont, J.-J. and J. Tirole (1993), A theory of incentives and procurement in regulation (MIT Press, Cambridge, MA).

Levine, P. and D. Currie (1987), "Does international macroeconomic policy coordination pay and is it sustainable?: A two country analysis", Oxford Economic Papers 39:38–74.

Lohman, S. (1992), "The optimal degree of commitment: Credibility versus flexibility", American Economic Review 82:273–286.

Martin, P. (1992), "Choosing central bankers in Europe", Graduate Institute of International Studies.

Miller, M. and M. Salmon (1985), "Policy coordination and dynamic games", in: W. Buiter and R. Marston, eds., International economic policy coordination (Cambridge University Press, Cambridge, UK).

Mundell, R. (1961), "A theory of optimum currency areas", American Economic Review 51:657–665.

Nurkse, R. (1945), "Conditions of international monetary equilibrium", Essays in international finance, No. 4, Princeton University.

Obstfeld, M. (1992), "Destabilizing effects of exchange-rate escape clauses", manuscript, University of California, Berkeley.

Obstfeld, M. and K. Rogoff (1994), "Exchange rate dynamics redux", manuscript, University of California, Berkeley and Princeton University.

Oudiz, G. and J. Sachs (1984), "Macroeconomic policy coordination among the industrial economies", Brookings Papers on Economic Activity 1:1–64.

Oudiz, G. and J. Sachs (1985), "International policy coordination in dynamic macroeconomic models", in: W. Buiter and R. Marston, eds., International economic policy coordination (Cambridge University Press, Cambridge, UK).

Persson, T. (1985), "Deficits and welfare in open economies", Journal of International Economics 19:67–84.

Persson, T. and L. Svensson (1989), "Why a stubborn conservative would run a deficit: Policy with time inconsistent preferences", Quarterly Journal of Economics 104:325–345.

Persson, T. and G. Tabellini (1990), Macroeconomic policy, credibility and politics (Harwood Academic Publishers, London).

Persson, T. and G. Tabellini (1992), "The politics of 1992: Fiscal policy and European integration", Review of Economic Studies 59:689–701.

Persson, T. and G. Tabellini (1993), "Designing institutions for monetary stability", Carnegie–Rochester Conference Series, Fall.

Persson, T. and G. Tabellini, (1994a), "Does centralization increase the size of government?", European Economic Review 38:765–773.

Persson, T. and G. Tabellini (1994b), "Federal fiscal constitutions: Risk sharing and moral hazard", manuscript, Stockholm University forthcoming in Econometrica.

Persson, T. and G. Tabellini (1994c), "Federal fiscal constitutions: Risk sharing and redistribution", Innocenzo Gasparini Institute for Economic Research Working Paper No. 61.

Piketty, T. (1993), A federal voting mechanism to solve the fiscal-externality problem, manuscript, DELTA.

Putnam, R. (1988), "Diplomacy and domestic politics: The logic of two-level games", International Organization 42:427–460.

Razin, A. and E. Sadka (1991), "International fiscal policy coordination and competition: An exposition", National Bureau of Economic Research Working Paper No. 3779.

Rogoff, K. (1985), "Can international monetary policy coordination be counterproductive?", Journal of International Economics 18:199–217.

Schotter, A. (1981), The economic theory of social institutions (Cambridge University Press, Cambridge, UK).

Sibert, A. (1991), "Public finance and coordination problems in a common currency area", Federal Reserve Bank of Kansas City Research Working Paper No. 91/06.

Sinn, H.-W. (1990), "Tax harmonization and tax competition", European Economic Review 34:489–504.

Sørensen, P.B. (1991), "Coordination of capital income taxes and monetary union: What needs to be done", Institute of Economics, Copenhagen, Working Paper No. 21.

Tabellini, G. (1990), "Domestic policies and the international coordination of fiscal policies", Journal of International Economics 28:245–265.

Tabellini, G. and A. Alesina (1990), "Voting on the budget deficit", American Economic Review 80:37–49.

Van der Ploeg, F. (1989), "Fiscal aspects of monetary integration in Europe", Centre for Economic Policy Research, Discussion Paper No. 340.

Van Wijnbergen, S. (1986), "On fiscal deficits, the real exchange rate and the world rate of interest", European Economic Review 30:1013–1023.

Vaubel, R. (1985), "International collusion or competition for macroeconomic policy coordination", Recherches Economiques de Louvain 51:223–240.

Vickers, J. (1984), "Delegation and the theory of the firm", Economic Journal (Supplement) 95:138–147.

Von Hagen, J. and R. Süppel (1994), "Central bank constitutions for federal monetary unions", European Economic Review 38:774–782.

Walsh, C. (1995), "Optimal contracts for central bankers", American Economic Review 85:150–167.

Wilson, J. (1987), "Trade, capital mobility and tax competition", Journal of Political Economy 95:835–856.

Chapter 39

SOVEREIGN DEBT

JONATHAN EATON and RAQUEL FERNANDEZ*

Boston University

Contents

*We thank Andrew G. Atkeson, Torsten Persson and Ken Rogoff for their comments.

Handbook of International Economics, vol. III, Edited by G. Grossman and K. Rogoff
© *Elsevier Science B.V., 1995*

1. Introduction

As the 1980's experience with sovereign debt made clear, international lending differs greatly from domestic lending and even more so from the textbook representation of a perfectly competitive, full information, loan market in which debt contracts are always honored. As Carlos F. Diaz-Alejandro remarked at the onset of the period, "we're not in Kansas anymore".[1] Repudiation, renegotiation, and reputation, are all words that quickly reentered the international lexicon as theoretical work strove to keep up with unfolding events. Much interesting work was generated as a consequence and it would be hard for any chapter of reasonable length to do this area full justice. Instead, we focus on a few key questions and papers to organize thinking about the literature and the issues, rather than attempt to be all-encompassing.

The focus of this chapter is on specific problems posed by sovereign debt, that is, debt incurred by governments, typically those of developing countries, to foreign investors seeking a competitive return.[2] Most recently sovereign debt has taken the form primarily of loans from commercial banks, although in earlier periods governments raised funds abroad mainly through bonds issued in foreign capital markets. Whatever form it has taken, three broad facts have characterized sovereign debt: (1) Governments have at times been able to borrow substantial amounts. (2) Much of what they borrow they eventually repay. (3) Repayment is often complicated, involving delay, renegotiation, public intervention, and default.[3] The literature we survey here is meant to provide an understanding of these facts.

We organize the literature around three central questions. The first, addressed in Section 2, is why countries ever choose to repay their debts. This question forced the literature to confront the strategic nature of sovereign lending and led to the development of relatively sophisticated models which identify various motives for repayment. These models yield different predictions about the quantity that will be lent and the behavior that will ensue.[4] The second question, the topic of Section 3, is

---

[1]Diaz-Alejandro (1984).

[2]We do not survey work on government debt to public institutions, on private borrowing in international capital markets, or on direct foreign investment, although much of the literature that we survey contains lessons for these phenomena as well.

[3]For example, a number of middle-income developing countries began to receive substantial net resource transfers from private creditors in the early 1970s. For the largest debtors, those classified by the World Bank as "severely indebted middle-income countries", such transfers constituted nearly 2 percent of GNP at their peak in 1976. The direction of these transfers was reversed in 1983. For the remainder of the decade these countries made net resource transfers to their private creditors, which peaked in 1986 at over 2 percent of GDP. Sovereign debt for this group constituted over 30 percent of GDP at its maximum in 1986. (World Bank (1993).)

[4]There is little empirical work on this question. Exceptions are Eichengreen and Portes (1986), Lindert and Morton (1988), and Ozler (1991, 1993), who examine how the debt repayment in the 1930s differed from that of the 1980s, and whether subsequent credit terms differed for countries that had defaulted.

what can go wrong. The literature has identified problems that can emerge at various stages in the relationship between creditors and debtors which can generate inefficient outcomes. The focus is on inefficiencies that can arise both in the lending stage and in the debtor's subsequent investment and consumption behavior. The last question, the concern of Section 4, is what can be done to correct these problems. The literature here, both theoretical and empirical, examines the effects of debt overhang, the potential benefits of debt buybacks to creditors and debtors, the role of third parties, and the functioning of secondary markets more generally. We conclude in Section 5 with a discussion of some insights the literature may provide for alternative forms of international finance.

2. Repayment incentives

Why do sovereign debtors ever repay their debts? The search for an answer to this question has motivated much of the research in this field. Our understanding of the conditions necessary to support repayment (and therefore lending in the first place) has been much advanced as a consequence. To avoid some of the (often terminological) confusion that emerged, we focus on a few key issues rather than take a chronological approach to the literature.

To begin with, sovereign debt differs from private debt in two important respects. First, there is often little that a sovereign entity can use as collateral to guarantee the value of a loan. Second, the ability of a court to force a sovereign entity to comply with its wishes is extremely limited. An immediate implication is that the country's desire to avoid some sanction if it fails to repay, or to obtain some reward if it repays, must be central.

The fact that debt repayment cannot be enforced automatically meant that the challenge, especially early in this literature, was not so much to produce a model consistent with some set of "stylized facts", but rather to explain the phenomenon of sovereign lending in the first place. In fact, much of the literature can be viewed as an attempt to clarify the role played by different benefits or penalties, for example, exclusion from future credit markets, inability to conduct trade, difficulties in borrowing in the domestic credit market, or a loss of output. The dichotomy between benefits and penalties is artificial, depending solely on what initial state is identified with the status quo.[5] A critical difference, however, between types of penalties is whether creditors possess the ability to commit to penalizing a debtor that is in default and, if so, whether penalization takes the form of a commitment to a given level of punishment or to a particular punitive instrument. Assumptions about the existence of this technology are very often made implicitly in this literature. Another

---

[5]So, for example, the failure to repay leading to exclusion from future credit markets is a penalty, but it can also be recast as a benefit, i.e. the ability to access credit markets upon repayment.

feature critical to understanding the efficacy of sanctions is the debtor's environment, i.e. the alternatives open to a defaulting country. This issue attracted more attention.

This section starts out first by examining, in a variety of environments, the ability of a particular penalty – the exclusion from credit markets – to support repayment. We choose to focus on this sanction in particular both because of its prominence in the literature and because, unlike in simple penalty models, while commitment to this punishment is assumed, the value of the penalty (i.e. the disutility derived from it) is generally determined by the country's actions. The assumption that creditors can commit to a penalty is then dropped and the efficacy and consequences of various other proposed penalties is examined in the context of sovereign-debt renegotiation.

2.1. Can exclusion from future credit markets support repayment?

This question has motivated much of the literature within this field. Often, and perhaps unfortunately, it has been couched in terms of "reputation". That is, as asking whether a country will repay its debt in order to maintain a "good" reputation for repayment. While the desire to maintain a reputation can be interpreted as different from the desire to avoid a penalty or to reap a reward, the two are often confused. The exclusion of a country from future lending is, of course, a penalty. Hence, one question is whether the sole penalty of exclusion from credit markets in the future is sufficient incentive for a country to repay its debts. The answer, not surprisingly, depends on the alternatives open to the country in a sense that will be made specific further on. We now review some of the major insights generated in this area.

An early model here is that of Eaton and Gersovitz (1981). In this model, the desire to maintain future access to credit markets provides an incentive to repay, although in general the first best amount of lending (i.e. the amount of lending that would be done in the absence of the relevant incentive compatibility constraints) is not sustainable. We now turn to a simple framework in which to review their arguments.

Consider a country that faces a gross world interest rate $r > 1$, and has a discount factor $\beta < 1/r$. The country seeks to maximize at time t an intertemporal utility function given by $U_t = \sum_{\tau=t}^{\infty} \beta^{\tau} u(c_{\tau})$. For simplicity, suppose that this country's output y_t is exogenous and deterministic and that there is no storage technology. Its debt evolves according to $D_{t+1} = (D_t - p_t)r$, where $p_t = y_t - c_t$ is the payment made by the country to its creditors at time t. Note that p_t negative simply indicates a payment from the creditors to the country.

Were the country able credibly to promise to repay its debt, it would face a maximization problem given by:

$$\max_{c_t} U = \sum_{t=0}^{\infty} \beta^t u(c_t) \text{ s.t. } \sum_{t=0}^{\infty} \frac{c_t}{r^t} \leq \sum_{t=0}^{\infty} \frac{y_t}{r^t} \qquad (2.1)$$

where the constraint in eq. (2.1) is a simple feasibility constraint requiring that the present discounted value of consumption not exceed the present discounted value of output. Note that under financial autarky this constraint would imply $c_t = y_t, \forall t$. The first-order condition for the above maximization problem is:

$$(r\beta)^t u'(c_t) = \lambda \quad \forall t \tag{2.2}$$

where λ is the Lagrange multiplier associated with the feasibility constraint in eq. (2.1).

Let the country's utility function be given by $u(c_t) = \log(c_t)$. Furthermore, assume that y_t can take on only two values: y_H in odd periods and y_L in even ones, with $y_H > y_L \geq 0$.

To solve for the country's optimal consumption path, note that, starting from a period in which the value of output is low, the present value of the country's future resources is given by:

$$V_0 = \frac{r[ry_L + y_H]}{r^2 - 1}. \tag{2.3}$$

Thus, were the country able to commit to debt repayment, its optimal consumption path would satisfy,

$$c_t^* = [r\beta]^t (1 - \beta) V_0 \tag{2.4}$$

where * denotes the optimal choice of the variable.

Let us now drop the assumption that the country can commit to the repayment of its debt. Then in addition to the feasibility constraint, the maximization problem of (2.1) must also respect an incentive compatibility constraint of the form:

$$\tilde{W}_t = \sum_{\tau=t}^{\infty} \beta^\tau u(\tilde{c}_\tau) \geq V_t = \sum_{\tau=t}^{\infty} \beta^\tau u(y_\tau) \quad \forall t \tag{2.5}$$

where $\sim$ denotes the value of the variable given that the country is following some specified repayment path. Equation (2.5) expresses the requirement that the country be at least as well off, at each and every moment, repaying its debt according to some given repayment path, as it would be by defaulting on repayment and consuming its autarkic output thereafter. Note that, among other things, this restriction implies that there can be no time s such that for all $t > s$ the country is making non-negative payments.

It is easy to see that the consumption path implied by the solution to eq. (2.4) is strictly decreasing over time (since $\beta r < 1$) and that, in the limit as $t \to \infty$, $c^* \to 0$. That is, under full commitment the country would borrow in order to increase its consumption at first and then slowly lower its consumption to zero, fully repaying its debt over time. An immediate consequence of dispensing with the commitment technology, therefore, is that it is no longer possible for the country's borrowing path to support its optimal consumption path since after some time τ this path would have the country consume an amount strictly smaller than y_L. This would violate the incentive compatibility constraint expressed in (2.5), since once the country's consumption drops below y_L, it can do strictly better by reneging on its debt and consuming its autarkic output thereafter. This is a general message that emerges from the debt literature: the existence of incentive compatibility constraints in addition to feasibility implies that the first-best allocation is rarely attainable.

Having established that the optimal consumption path cannot be supported in the absence of a commitment technology, it remains to be asked whether the threat of financial autarky is sufficient to support any borrowing at all. In order for this question to be answered affirmatively, there must exist a borrowing–repayment path such that (2.5) is always respected. To show how this can come about, we examine a stationary path in which the amount x is borrowed in low-output periods and the amount rx is repaid in high-output periods and solve for the optimal consumption path under this rule.

A necessary condition for repayment is first that there exist the desire to smooth consumption in the manner specified above. From (2.2), the condition for this is $r\beta y_H > y_L$. Note, however, that this condition is not sufficient since it does not address the country's temptation to renege on its repayment in a high-output period. In order to find a necessary and sufficient condition we rewrite the constraint in (2.5) more explicitly for the specific utility function and endowment paths assumed. Since the problem is stationary, we can write the constraint as:

$$\log(y_H - rx) + \beta \log(y_L + x) > \log(y_H) + \beta \log(y_L). \tag{2.6}$$

Since the two sides of the inequality are equal at $x = 0$, a necessary and sufficient condition for a stationary path with positive lending to be sustained is that the derivative of the left hand side is positive when evaluated at $x = 0$. Taking the appropriate derivative yields:

$$\beta y_H > r y_L \tag{2.7}$$

as the required condition. Note that this condition is indeed more restrictive than that needed to ensure the desirability of consumption smoothing. The reason for this is straightforward. Whereas the desire to smooth consumption requires the country to be willing to forego rx *next period* in exchange for x this period, the incentive-compatibility constraint requires the country to be willing to forego rx *this period* in exchange for merely x next period. It is easy to show that if (2.7) is satisfied, the country's optimal stationary borrowing is given by $x = [\beta y_H - ry_L]/[r(1 + \beta)]$.

Other papers that examine the same motivation to repay include Atkeson (1991), Cole, Dow, and English (1995), Grossman and van Huyck (1989), and Manuelli (1986). An important assumption made throughout, however, either explicitly or implicitly, is that the country is unable to enter into another financial agreement (e.g., an investment or insurance contract) after it reneges on its debt. We now turn to an examination of the consequences of relaxing this assumption.

2.2. The debtor's environment

Several later papers in the literature changed the focus of the question from the nature of the mechanism that might support sovereign lending to the type of environment that might destroy it. An influential paper in this vein is Bulow and Rogoff (1989b).

In "LDC debt: Is to forgive to forget", Bulow and Rogoff argue that if a country is able to enter into a particular type of contract *irrespective of its behavior regarding its debt contract*, then the sole threat of exclusion from future borrowing is unable to sustain positive lending. Before reviewing their argument in a general framework with uncertainty, it is instructive to show how allowing the economy described in the previous section (i.e. a pure endowment economy) to invest or open an account in which it earns the capital market's rate of return destroys its ability to borrow.

Consider, therefore, a non-stochastic endowment economy with access to a storage technology (or independent bank account) whose proceeds are not seizable by creditors and which provides a rate of return equal to that demanded by creditors, i.e. r. Assume that the value of all future output discounted to any time t is bounded. Then there necessarily must exist an upper bound, say $M > 0$, which creditors will not allow the country's debt to exceed. We will show that as long as M is strictly positive, the country's ability to invest or to make payments and withdrawals that earn it the market rate of return will lead it to renege on its debt. This ability consequently destroys the country's access to funds.

Let s be the period in which the country's debt equals M and let variables with a ~ indicate the values that those variables take when the country follows a given repayment path.[6] Furthermore, let A_t be the country's investment in period t in the account that earns the (gross) market rate of return r, and let G_t be its return in period t. Note that A_t is the total amount held by the country in its account during period t. Since this account is self-financed, A_t must be non-negative. We next show that for any path of $\tilde{A}_t, \tilde{p}_t$ with positive debt, there always exists a deviation such that the country reneges on its debt and is made strictly better off.

Consider the following deviation from the strategy of following the repayment path as of period s. Let the country take the payment that it was called upon to make that period, $\tilde{p}_s$, and instead invest it in the alternative account, together with any other additional investment it would have made that period, i.e. $\tilde{A}_s$. Note that since $\tilde{D}_s = M$ and $\tilde{D}_{s+1} = r(\tilde{D}_s - \tilde{p}_s) \le M$, it follows that $\tilde{p}_s \ge rM/(r - 1) > 0$. That is, the country invests a strictly positive amount in its account. The following period the country

---

[6] For simplicity of exposition we assume that the upper bound is attained; it is easy to see how the argument should be modified otherwise.

obtains $G_{s+1} = r(\tilde{A}_s + \tilde{p}_s) = \tilde{G}_{s+1} + r\tilde{p}_s$. To reduce notation denote $r\tilde{p}_s$ by g_{s+1}. The country continues with the modification of its original strategy by making an additional investment of $\tilde{p}_{s+1}$ into the account, so that $A_{s+1} = \tilde{A}_{s+1} + g_{s+1} + \tilde{p}_{s+1}$. Note that A_{s+1} is strictly positive since $\tilde{A}_{s+1}$ is non-negative and $g_{s+1} + \tilde{p}_{s+1} = rM - (\tilde{D}_{s+1} - \tilde{p}_{s+1}) \geq rM - (M/r) > 0$. Thus, $\tilde{p}_{s+1}$ can be negative (in which case the country is making itself a payment from its account). It is easy to show that by continuing to invest $\tilde{A}_t + g_t + \tilde{p}_t$ in every period following s, the country's consumption path is unchanged from what it was under the $\sim$ plan and its savings τ periods after s is no smaller than $\tilde{A}_{s+\tau} + Mr^\tau - (M/r)$, i.e. it exceeds the original savings by a strictly positive amount. It follows that in any period after s, the country can increase its consumption above the amount called for by its repayment program by using some of these additional savings (but leaving itself with at least an additional amount M/r in its account). Thus, this strategy leaves the country strictly better off than following its repayment plan. Consequently, the only M that can be maintained as an upper bound in equilibrium is $M = 0$, i.e. there can be no positive lending.

The intuition behind the argument given above is straightforward. Once the value (appropriately discounted) of the country's debt is sufficiently high, it has an incentive to default with probability one if it can obtain the market rate of return by opening an account or making an investment. This must be true once the value of the debt has reached its maximum since the amount paid out by the country from that time period on to each and every other future time period has a positive present discounted value.[7] This implies that as of time period s, and following the allocation rule $\sim$, there is no period in which the bank is lending the country an amount that the country could not have self-financed solely by accumulating its payments as of period s in an interest-bearing account. This alternative is naturally preferable since in addition it allows the country to default on the outstanding debt. Of course, the country's ability to pursue this strategy only makes it worse off, since it implies that no loans will be made in the first place.

Rosenthal (1991) shows that the argument given above can be generalized to the case of a concave storage technology or investment function (e.g., a production function in which the rate of return is a decreasing function of the capital invested) where the motivation to borrow is that, at least initially, the rate of return on the country's investment project exceeds that of the world capital market. Although the argument is more complex, the basic intuition underlying this result is similar to that above. That is, once the value of the country's future net payments is sufficiently high, the country is better off making use solely of its own technology and defaulting on its debt.

We now turn to a more general version of the first argument as made by Bulow and Rogoff, which allows for uncertainty but which, as a result, also requires stronger assumptions.

---

[7] If it didn't, then the value of the outstanding debt under the plan $\sim$ would, as of that period, exceed M.

We consider an economy whose production function is given by $Y_t = f(\bar{I}_{t-1}, \bar{\theta}_t)$ where $\bar{I}_{t-1} \equiv (I_{t-1}, I_{t-2}, \ldots)$ and I_t is investment in period t and $\bar{\theta}_t \equiv (\theta_t, \theta_{t-1}, \ldots)$. The θ_i's are assumed to be exogenous and serially independent shocks. Both $\bar{I}_t$ and $\bar{\theta}_t$ are assumed to be observable and verifiable. At the beginning of each period the shock is realized and observed and then the country makes its allocation decisions for that period.

Consider a debt contract that specifies, for every verifiable state of nature $\bar{\theta}_t$ and for every time period t, a payment $p_t(\bar{\theta}_t)$. Note that, as before, p_t may be positive or negative depending on whether a payment from the country to its creditors or its reverse is indicated. The contract can be implicit or explicit (in any case, as before, creditors are assumed to have the power to commit to making any positive payments called upon by the contract). Lastly, as before, any default by the country excludes it from all future debt contracts; there is no other penalty.

Before proceeding with the argument we introduce some useful definitions. Define,

$$\tilde{W}_t(\bar{\theta}_t) = E_t \sum_{s=t}^{\infty} \tilde{y}_s / (r-1)^{s-t} \tag{2.8}$$

where the $\sim$ denotes a particular allocation path and $\tilde{y}_s = \tilde{Y}_s - \tilde{I}_s \geq 0$ and $\tilde{W}_t < \infty \; \forall t$. Equation (2.8), therefore, gives the expected market value of a claim to the country's entire future income as of period t (given that the country follows the allocation path $\sim$). Furthermore, define

$$\tilde{D}_t(\bar{\theta}_t) = E_t \sum_{s=t}^{\infty} \tilde{p}_s / (r-1)^{s-t} \tag{2.9}$$

as the country's expected present discounted value of its future repayments (again following the allocation path $\sim$). Clearly, in order for the debt to be payable according to this path, it must be that $\tilde{D}_t(\bar{\theta}_t) \leq \tilde{W}_t(\bar{\theta}_t)$ for all t and all $\bar{\theta}_t$. That is, the value of the debt must not exceed the value to a claim to the country's entire future output stream. Lastly we define k as the smallest k' such that for all t,

$$\tilde{D}_t(\bar{\theta}_t) \leq k' \tilde{W}_t(\bar{\theta}_t) \quad \forall \bar{\theta}_t. \tag{2.10}$$

Note that,

$$E_t \tilde{W}_{t+1} = r(\tilde{W}_t - \tilde{y}_t) \tag{2.11}$$

and that

$$E_t \tilde{D}_{t+1} = r(\tilde{D}_t - \tilde{p}_t) \tag{2.12}$$

where $\bar{\theta}_t$ is suppressed (here and henceforth) unless required for clarity.

In addition to debt contracts, the country is also able to enter into cash-in-advance type contracts (for simplicity assumed to be of one period). In such a contract the country, by paying an amount A_t at the end of period t (i.e. after θ_t has been observed), receives in exchange $G(\bar{\theta}_{t+1})$ in period $t+1$. This contract must satisfy two requirements:

(i) $E_t[G_{t+1}(\bar{\theta}_{t+1})] = rA_t$ and

(ii) $G_{t+1}(\bar{\theta}_{t+1}) \geq 0 \quad \forall \bar{\theta}_{t+1}$.

The first condition states that the country should obtain in expected value terms the market rate of return the following period, where r continues to be the (gross) world risk-free interest rate. If we assume that the country is small in international capital markets, i.e. unable to affect this rate, then this condition would follow from the existence of a perfectly competitive "cash-in-advance market" with risk-neutral lenders. The second condition indicates that a one-period contract at time t cannot be designed to require a strictly positive payment from the country at time $t+1$ (since the country would have no incentive to repay it). Note that the assumption of competitive markets implies that the country can write the cash-in-advance contract in any way it wishes as long as it respects the two requirements above. That is, we are assuming in particular that this contract can be made contingent on the same variables as the debt contract.

We now show that if the country can enter into the type of contract specified above, then this possibility destroys all equilibria with positive debt since there will always exist a state in which the country will be able to do better by reneging on its debt contract.

Consider a time period s and a history of shocks $\bar{\theta}_s$ such that $\tilde{D}_s \geq k(\tilde{W}_s - \tilde{y}_s) > 0$ (note that by eq. 2.10 this state must exist). Without loss of generality in what follows we normalize all cash-in-advance contracts made under the repayment plan $\sim$ to zero in this and in every succeeding period. We now show that the country can as of this period make itself strictly better off by reneging on all future payments and following the strategy described below. This strategy will allow the country to maintain the same investment path as under the debt contract and strictly increase its consumption in some time periods without decreasing it in any other period.

Thus, instead of making its called upon payment of $\tilde{p}_s$ that period, let the country invest the amount $A_s = \tilde{p}_s + k(\tilde{W}_s - \tilde{y}_s) - \tilde{D}_s \leq \tilde{p}_s$. Note that $\tilde{p}_s \geq 0$ since otherwise, by (2.11) and (2.12), we would have $\tilde{D}_{t+1} > k\tilde{W}_{t+1}$ which is ruled out by definition of k. The same reasoning yields $A_s \geq 0$.

In every subsequent period $t > s$, let the country invest $A_t = G_t + \tilde{p}_t - k\tilde{y}_t$ in return for $G_{t+1}(\bar{\theta}_{t+1}) = k\tilde{W}_{t+1}(\bar{\theta}_{t+1}) - \tilde{D}_{t+1}(\bar{\theta}_{t+1}) \geq 0$. Note that this cash-in-advance contract fulfills both requirements stipulated previously since, by (2.11) and (2.12), $E_t G_{t+1}(\bar{\theta}_{t+1}) = kE_t \tilde{W}_{t+1}(\bar{\theta}_{t=1}) - E_t \tilde{D}_{t+1}(\bar{\theta}_{t+1}) = r[k(\tilde{W}_t(\bar{\theta}_t) - \tilde{y}_t) - (\tilde{D}_t(\bar{\theta}_t) - \tilde{p}_t)] = r[G_t + \tilde{p}_t - k\tilde{y}_t] = rA_t \geq 0$. In any time period t in which $\tilde{p}_t$ would take a negative value (i.e. the country would have received a further loan from the banks) the country is simply making this payment to itself from G_t. The accumulated funds are always sufficient for it to be able to do so since $A_t = G_t + \tilde{p}_t - k\tilde{y}_t = k(\tilde{W}_t - \tilde{y}_t) - (\tilde{D}_t - \tilde{p}_t) = [kE_t\tilde{W}(\bar{\theta}_{t+1}) - E_t\tilde{D}_{t+1}(\bar{\theta}_{t+1}0)]/r \geq 0$.

Note that by following the strategy outlined above the country is in each period making zero debt repayments and instead is making an additional cash-in-advance contract of $\tilde{p}_t - k\tilde{y}_t \leq \tilde{p}_t$, i.e. no greater than the payment that it would have made to its creditors in that period. This implies that the country can increase its consumption by the amount $k\tilde{y}_t \geq 0$ in each period. Furthermore, note that in at least one of the periods following s the expected value of this consumption increase must be strictly positive. Otherwise, $\tilde{y}_t$ would equal zero in all time periods after s, which would imply that no payments were expected as of period s. But that would require that the value of the debt at time s be zero or negative, contradicting our initial assumption.

Summing up, the point of the Bulow and Rogoff argument is that if cash-in-advance contracts, fully indexed to the same states of nature as the debt contract, are available to a debtor that reneges on its debts, then the exclusion from future debt contracts is insufficient motivation for a country to repay its debt.

Does this imply that one must look elsewhere than exclusion from future credit markets to explain sovereign lending? There are several assumptions in the model above that are unlikely to correspond fully with reality. First, it may be costly for a country to obtain cash-in-advance contracts, or the rate of return on these may be smaller than the return required by the country's creditors. While either possibility may permit positive lending to be sustained in equilibrium, the maximum amount of debt that could be supported by these costs would be precisely the amount that would make the country indifferent between switching to the cash-in-advance contract strategy and staying with its debt arrangement.

Alternatively, the creditor-debtor relationship may be special in that not all states of nature nor all actions taken by the country may be observable or verifiable outside it. Or, they may be observable and verifiable only at a large cost to outsiders who are less likely to have the expertise and on-going relationship with the country as a large commercial bank. This factor likewise would make it costly to switch to a cash-in-advance contract. How much debt these costs could support is an empirical question that needs to be addressed.

Second, the argument assumes that the insuring party can itself commit not to renege on its commitment to pay the amount stipulated by the contract. That is, while the initial creditor has a problem getting the initial debtor (i.e. the country) to repay, a debtor in default is assumed not to have this problem with its own debtors. This assumption may need justification. While it is relatively easy to believe that reputational considerations (e.g., their business with other clients) may usually be a sufficient incentive to impede the insuring party from reneging on its contractual commitments, these same considerations may not apply toward clients that are themselves in bad standing. Alternatively, these transactions may themselves be ruled out if the creditors possess the authority and means to seize any payments made to the reneging debtor.

In light of the above comments, Kletzer and Wright (1990) model a situation in which two agents, one a risk-neutral creditor and the other a risk-averse borrower with a fluctuating endowment, have no external mechanism to enforce contracts with each other, i.e. no party has the ability to enforce contracts in a unilateral fashion. Nevertheless, there exist subgame perfect equilibria in which the risk-neutral agent provides some insurance to the risk-averse agent. If the two agents have equal discount factors then, as that discount factor approaches one, full insurance of the risk-averse agent is attained. If the risk-averse agent has a lower discount factor, however, then typically only partial insurance is achievable.

2.3. Reputational considerations

Does the existence of cash-in-advance contracts rule out other mechanisms in which "reputation" plays a role? The answer is a qualified no and it is here that the terminology becomes confusing. If the question is whether it is possible for the exclusion from debt contracts to be a sufficient penalty to induce repayment, then one way to read the Bulow and Rogoff paper is that it provides a set of sufficient conditions for this punishment to be unable to support positive lending. If, on the other hand, the question is understood to mean will the country ever repay its debts in order to gain a reputation for doing so, then the question of "reputation" should be divorced from the cost of being excluded from capital markets (although this additional cost will only make the country more willing to gain this "reputation"). We now turn to a few examples that develop the reputational argument further.

Consider the possibility that a country's default on its debt obligation triggers an adverse reaction in some other relationship (or game) in which the country is involved. Why might this adverse reaction occur? One possibility is that it is part of a trigger strategy in a supergame. In such a scenario the country would be involved in an infinitely repeated game with either the same or with another party. The equilibrium of the one-shot version of that game should yield both parties a lower payoff than "cooperation", the term we will give to a particular pair of one-shot strategies that are not sustainable as equilibrium strategies in a finite horizon or one-shot game. The cooperative outcome, however, would be sustainable when the game is infinitely repeated, supported, for example, by the "grim" threat of forever playing the one-shot equilibrium strategies should one of the players ever defect from its cooperative strategy. (Of course, one may also construct strategies that are "renegotiation proof" to support this outcome by penalizing players that defect through the temporary play of the one-shot strategies). In addition, however, the strategies would specify that should the country at any moment default on its debt obligations (i.e. its other relationship), then this would also trigger the grim one-shot equilibrium strategies forever thereafter. As long as the benefits from maintaining this cooperative relationship outweighed the gains from defaulting on its debt, the country should be willing to repay its debts in order to maintain a reputation for repayment. Note, however, that it is the cost of the benefits foregone in the other relationship that make this behavior feasible.

The mechanism specified above allows positive lending to be sustained but it also has some unappealing properties. In particular, while feasible, it is not compelling that the strategies in the second game depend on the actions of the debtor in the debt game. More appealing would be the possibility that some information would be revealed were the country to default. It is difficult to think of natural relationships in which this would be the case, however. It would require the existence of some characteristic which is private information that would affect both a country's willingness to pay *and* the action that another player would want to take in some other game.

Cole and Kehoe (1992) provide an example of the above situation in a finite horizon game with two types of government: One is the usual type with the kind of utility function that we have previously specified and the other, called ''honest'', by assumption incurs a large disutility cost from defaulting on any contract. The government, aside from its debt contract, also enters every period into a contract with a union which it promises to pay at the end of every period after that period's work is performed. Were the type of government common knowledge, then the sole subgame-perfect equilibrium in the game between workers and the regular government is the one-shot equilibrium of zero debt and no union contract, since in the last period of the game the government will renege on its payment to the union, thus unraveling all possibility of cooperation in any other period. If these preferences are private information, however, then the regular type government can attempt to gain a reputation for honesty, a la Kreps–Wilson (1982) and Milgrom–Roberts (1982), by repaying for some period of time. In such an equilibrium, for a long enough time horizon, even a small probability that the government is honest will allow some positive lending. How satisfactory it is to assume that this type of government (the ''honest'' type) exists is less clear.

The Kletzer and Wright (1990) paper previously discussed can also be read as an example in which reputation in the sense indicated above can sustain positive lending. Without automatic enforcement by either party, the only equilibrium in any finite relationship is autarky. If their interaction is indefinite, however, then there are subgame-perfect equilibria that sustain positive lending.

2.4. Carrots and sticks

The earliest literature in this field studied the implications of various models in which creditors are able to penalize a debtor country by some amount P if the latter does not repay its debt. This literature took as its starting point the notion that if $U_p \geq U_d$, where U_p stands for the country's utility from repayment and U_d stands for its utility from default, then the country would be willing to repay its debt (ignoring solvency problems). The implications of these models for how much debt the country repays are rather trivial; the interesting issues that arise instead are, for example, the importance of seniority clauses, possible inefficiencies in investment behavior, and the effects of various policies, all discussed in Section 3. Instead, we turn to an issue that arises less prominently when examining reputational considerations for repayment but that is central when one considers the possibility of costly penalties.

2.5. Sovereign-debt renegotiations

It would seem impossible to go wrong by saying, as above, that a country will repay its debt if its utility from doing so is greater than its utility from non-repayment. In the absence of a commitment technology on the part of the creditors (either to withholding the carrot or to applying the stick), however, the validity of this statement depends on the precise strategic environment. Once loans have been extended to the country, the relationship between creditor and debtor is one of bilateral monopoly. If penalizing the country is at all costly, then the implicit commitment assumed by much of the earlier literature is questionable. Formally, the question arises as to whether the strategies are subgame perfect, i.e. in the absence of commitment would the creditors really find it in their interest to apply the penalties were they called upon to do so. Furthermore, even if the strategies are subgame perfect, it is also questionable whether the strategy space is rich enough. For example, a creditor that must incur a cost c in order to penalize a debtor by the amount P (with $c < P$) may be unable to resort credibly to this punishment if the debtor is allowed to offer it a payment of $P - c$. Thus, whether the situation is modeled in such a way so as to allow the country the option of making this offer becomes critical.

A natural way to deal with the concerns raised above is to allow the relevant parties to bargain or to renegotiate their original debt contract. One of the first papers to allow for this possibility is Bulow and Rogoff (1989a). They use an infinite horizon, small country (unable to affect interest rates or the world prices of traded goods) model. The country's output is exogenously determined. The country obtains utility from consumption of both domestic (h) and foreign (f) goods and this is assumed to be linear in both goods (which allows the bargaining game to be easily solved), with a rate of time preference given by δ, i.e.

$$U = \sum_{\tau = t}^{\infty} (c_\tau^h + c_\tau^f)/(1 + \delta). \tag{2.13}$$

In each period the country produces Y units of the domestic good. These can be consumed, stored or traded for foreign goods. Should the country store its goods, the next period the amount left over is reduced by the fraction γ. The authors assume that q, the relative price of the domestic good in terms of the foreign good, is greater than one. This ensures that the country would, everything else equal, prefer to trade its domestic goods for foreign ones.

The country can borrow abroad at the gross world interest rate of $r > 1$. Creditors can, should the country fail to pay its debt (renegotiated or otherwise), seize a portion of its exports. The net benefit to them from doing so is assumed to be a fraction α of the country's exports. The country, should it attempt to trade when it has not repaid its (renegotiated or not) debt, obtains only a fraction $1 - \beta$ of what it would have obtained were it in compliance with its creditors. It is assumed that $0 < \alpha \le \beta \le 1$ and, to ensure that the country would wish to borrow, it is also assumed that $\delta > r - 1$.

In order to determine the maximum quantity that creditors would be willing to lend a country under this scenario we proceed in three steps. First, note that if the country could commit to debt repayment, it would borrow and consume in the first period $qY/(r - 1)$ of the foreign good, and thereafter dedicate itself to repaying its debt.

Second, we drop the commitment assumption and examine the amount of debt that can be supported by the creditor's ability to impose a penalty on the debtor. The creditor's sole threat against the debtor is its ability to seize the country's goods should the latter attempt to trade without an agreement. Thus the country should be willing to pay the difference between what it would obtain were its trade unimpeded and what it would obtain should it trade without reaching an agreement, i.e. $\beta qY/(r - 1)$. Since the country always has the option of not trading and instead consuming its domestic output, however, lenders will only be able to obtain the minimum between the country's gains from unimpeded trade and what the country could obtain by not trading at all, i.e.

$$\min \left[\beta, (q - 1)/q \right] qY/(r - 1). \tag{2.14}$$

The problem with this solution, however, is that it assumes that the creditor has all the bargaining power in the game, i.e. that it is up to the creditor to leave the debtor indifferent rather than, for example, vice-versa.

Third, therefore, we can allow, as do Bulow and Rogoff, for the country and its lenders to bargain á la Rubinstein (1982). In this bargaining game players take turns making offers to one another, the game ending when an offer is accepted. In order to avoid supergame equilibria, the authors assume that after some date T in the future, the country's output falls to zero (they then take the limit as $T \to \infty$). By solving for the Rubinstein bargaining solution as of period T for a pie that is shrinking by a proportion γ each period and then using backwards induction to find the outcome of the bargaining game as of the first period, it is possible to establish the outcome of the entire game.

Since the details of the calculation are not particularly illuminating, we shall omit them here. Suffice it to note that, as in a regular Rubinstein bargaining game, the solution is efficient with agreement reached in the first period. The creditors obtain a share that depends inversely on the interest rate (since that makes the bank more impatient) and is proportional to δ (since that makes the country more impatient). If, however, the share obtained by the country should yield it less than its implied share in (2.14), then the bargaining solution must be modified to yield the country its maximum "outside offer", i.e. the maximum of the shares $1 - \beta$ and $1/q$.

While bargaining is one way in which to deal with the problem of renegotiation, it is well known that bargaining models are quite sensitive to the exact specification of the bargaining game.[8] Furthermore, too much emphasis may be given in these models to the ability of parties to talk – to make offers and counteroffers – rather than to other actions agents may be able to take. In light of this, Fernandez and Rosenthal (1990) construct a model that examines the bilateral monopoly question without introducing bargaining in the form of an offer-counteroffer model. Instead the authors allow the parties to take actions which strategically determine the strength of the two parties. Their result lends support to models that have assumed that all the bargaining power lies with the banks since they obtain this same result in an explicitly strategic model.

The motivation for repayment in Fernandez and Rosenthal is of the "carrot" variety. The country's economy is specified as in a one-sector growth model. The country starts the game with a given amount of debt in place which grows according to a specified gross interest rate r. The game is one of alternating moves: in each period the creditor first decides how much, if any, of the debt it wishes to forgive, and then the debtor makes its consumption, investment and repayment decision for that period. The game ends (it can go on indefinitely) whenever the outstanding debt is repaid, whereupon the country automatically receives a "bonus" the following period. The "bonus" is not paid by the creditors. It can be interpreted as improved access to international capital markets, better ability to conduct trade, etc. The bonus function is assumed to be a continuous, increasing function of the capital stock that the country ends the game with, equaling zero if the country ends the game with zero capital.

A few definitions are helpful. Let

$$v(K) = \max_{0 \leq c \leq g(K)} (u(c) + \beta v(g(K) - c)) \qquad (2.15)$$

and

$$w(K, D) = \max_{c + p \leq g(K)} (u(c) + \beta w(g(K) - c - p, r(D - p)))$$

$$w(K, 0) = \max_{c \leq g(K)} (u(c) + \beta Z(g(K) - c)) \qquad (2.16)$$

where $v(K)$ is the value to the debtor of maximizing utility under the assumption that it will never repay its debt (and therefore never obtain the corresponding bonus) and that it starts out with an initial capital stock of K. Thus, (2.15) is simply the

---

[8]See Gale and Hellwig (1989) for an example of a renegotiation game with private information and multiple equilibria.

intertemporal optimization problem faced by an economy under financial autarky, and we refer to it as the country's stand alone program. Note that $K_{t+1} = g(K_t) - c_t - p_t$. The function $w(K, D)$, on the other hand, is the value to the debtor of pursuing an optimal plan (i.e. choosing consumption, investment, and repayments over time that are utility maximizing) for repaying its debt given that it starts out with a debt of D and a capital stock K and given that it assumes that in the future it will not obtain any debt forgiveness. Similarly, $w(K, 0)$ is the value to the debtor of having zero debt and obtaining the bonus $Z(g(K) - c)$ the following period given that it has a capital stock of K in this period. Z is assumed to be an increasing and continuous function of K_{T+1} with $Z(0) = v(0)$ and bounded below by the function v.

Lastly, define φ as the non-negative value of debt forgiveness, f, such that $w(K, D - \varphi) = v(K)$, i.e. this is the value of debt forgiveness such that the debtor is indifferent between two options: pursuing an optimal repayment strategy given that it expects no future forgiveness, and following the optimal growth strategy with no repayment ever of the debt, and therefore no access to bonus. Note that if $w(K, D) \geq v(K)$, then φ is defined to be equal to zero and that the evolution of the country's debt is given by $D_{t+1} = r(D_t - p_t - f_t)$.

The authors show that the unique subgame-perfect equilibrium has the creditor in each period setting $f = \varphi$. This amount of forgiveness ensures that the debtor is indifferent between repaying the remaining debt over time and following its stand alone program. Thus, in equilibrium the creditor forgives all the necessary debt in the first period and thereafter the debtor repays its debt optimally over time. Note that the equilibrium is efficient.

The above result is rather surprising. It is natural to ask why the debtor cannot distort its investment path in such a way as to make the creditor worse off and extract more concessions. The important thing to note is that, while indeed the debtor can extract further reductions in its level of debt from the creditor by deviating from the $w(\cdot)$ plan, and in so doing make the creditor worse off, it has no incentive to do so given the creditor's strategy: Starting from any point at which $v(K) = w(K, D)$, any deviation on its part that results in $v(K') < w(K', D')$ will generate another forgiveness such that $v(K') = w(K', D - f)$ (where $K' = g(K) - c$), but $v(K) = \max [u(c) + \beta v(g(K) - c)] \geq u(\tilde{c}) + \beta v(g(K) - \tilde{c}) \ \forall c, \ 0 \leq \tilde{c} \leq g(K)$. Therefore, the debtor is in fact not making itself better off by pursuing this deviation and consequently has no incentive to do so. It is more complicated to show that the equilibrium payoffs to this game are unique and thus that the creditors must end up with all the "surplus" in the game. The authors demonstrate that any forgiveness which yields the debtor more utility than $v(K)$ can be decreased by some $\varepsilon > 0$ without any adverse consequence to the creditor (indeed with net positive benefit), thus establishing payoff uniqueness.

Debt repayments and renegotiation have not shown the smoothness that the models discussed above predict. While it is probably possible to generate multiple periods of renegotiation and debt rescheduling by introducing uncertainty and shocks over time, there are two important ingredients left out of these models that undoubtedly play an important role in reality: (i) disagreement among creditors, and, interacting with the first, (ii) expectations about third party intervention. The next section discusses these and other factors that contributed to the problems encountered during the period of the debt crisis.

3. What can go wrong?

A message of the previous section is that a sovereign country may lack the incentive to repay the amount of debt that it needs to finance its optimal investment and consumption program. We now turn to the distortions created by the inadequacy of these incentives. The literature suggests situations in which: (1) Sovereign countries borrow too much or too little. (2) Default leads to the suffering of sanctions that are a deadweight loss, such as a trade or credit embargo that leaves socially efficient intratemporal and intertemporal exchanges unexploited. (3) Debt obligations distort government policy in debtor countries. (4) The fiscal burden imposed by sovereign debt leads to capital flight and the abandonment of profitable investment opportunities.[9]

These various distortions emerge at different stages in the relationship between borrowers and lenders: (1) when creditors originally make the loans, (2) when debtors face the burden of repaying debt, and (3) when the lending community reacts to those burdens. This section considers what can go wrong with the original contracts and how they can distort behavior in borrowing countries. Section 4 turns to the restructuring of loan contracts in response to these problems.

3.1. The loan contracts: Underborrowing and overborrowing

If a sovereign debtor has limited incentive to repay its debts, the lending community faces at least two problems in making efficient lending arrangements. One is monitoring and controlling the amount that the country has borrowed in the first place. The second is getting the country to pay.

We illustrate each of these problems, and how they can lead to an inefficient amount of borrowing, with the following simple framework. We consider a country with a gross payoff of $W(L)$ from borrowing an amount L, where W is differentiable and increasing and concave in the amount borrowed. The country's net payoff is its

---

[9]The history of sovereign debt provides episodes in which each kind of event apparently occurred. Problems have been sufficiently dire to lead observers to invoke the term "debt crisis", as during the 1930s and 1980s.

gross payoff less its repayment of principal and interest along with any harm H that it suffers for nonpayment.

Potential creditors have access to an international capital market in which they can borrow and lend at a safe gross interest rate r. They are competitive and risk neutral, so that any loans that they extend to this country must offer an expected return r. In the absence of an enforcement constraint, then, the country would want to borrow an amount L^* that equates the marginal gross benefit of borrowing $W'(L^*)$ to the cost of capital r. This is the efficient loan amount with perfect enforcement. It ensures the country a net payoff $W(L^*) - rL^*$, the maximum possible with competitive lending. As we show below, imperfections created by imperfect enforcement can reduce the country's net payoff, both by leading to loan amounts either below or above the efficient level, and by forcing the country to suffer the penalty of default.

Following much of the literature, we assume that the cost to the borrower of not meeting its debt service obligations is an amount H, where H may not be known at the time the loan amount L is extended. Rather, it is drawn from a distribution $F(H)$ that has mean $\bar{H}$. Its actual value is learned, at least by the borrower, before it decides how much to pay its creditors.

While this two-period formulation masks much of the complex dynamics of the interaction between creditors and debtors discussed in the previous discussion, it captures the essential problem raised by sovereign debt: The borrower must receive the loan before it experiences the cost either of repaying or of failing to repay.

Two key issues are the following: (1) Can creditors control the total amount that the country borrows? (2) If the debtor pays less than it owes does it actually suffer the penalty of default?

3.1.1. Seniority

To illustrate how these two problems can distort allocations, we begin by considering a situation in which creditors: (a) collect debt according to seniority and (b) use the threat of the penalty to collect as much as they can (up to what is owed), never actually imposing the penalty. The domestic legal system typically gives loan contracts these features. We show that, under appropriate restrictions on the distribution of the cost of default, they provide the borrower the same net payoff that it would obtain if enforcement were perfect, even though lenders may not collect all that they are owed.

Consider a debtor that has borrowed L. We order its debt according to seniority using as an index points in the interval $[0, L]$: A loan amount with a lower value of this index is senior to a loan with a higher value. The contracted gross interest rate on a loan with seniority l is $R(l)$. We denote the amount owed on all loans senior to it as $\Gamma(l) = \int_0^l R(j)\,dj$. Loans are repaid according to their seniority. The debtor's total debt service obligations are $\Gamma(L)$. If H exceeds this amount then the debtor pays all its debts. Otherwise, it pays what it owes up to the amount H according to seniority and defaults on the rest.[10] There is no further penalty. Competition among lenders ensures that:

$$R(l)\{1 - F[\Gamma(l)]\} = r \tag{3.1}$$

for all $l \in [0, L]$. The left-hand side of this expression is the expected payment to the lender who makes a loan with seniority l, which is the contracted payment times the probability that the cost of default exceeds the amount to be repaid on senior loans. The right-hand side is the market interest rate.

Loan Supply: Integrating (3.1) from 0 to any total loan amount L by parts indicates that competitive lenders governed by seniority can extend loans up to an amount $\bar{L} = \bar{H}/r$ and still satisfy the zero-profit constraint on each loan. Loans above this amount cannot satisfy the zero-profit condition given that senior loans do.

Loan Demand: The debtor's net payoff is:

$$W(L) - \Gamma(L)\{1 - F[\Gamma(L)]\} - \int_0^{\Gamma(L)} H \, dF(H) = W(L) - rL. \tag{3.2}$$

Maximizing this expression with respect to the total loan amount L and the zero-profit condition (3.1) implies that the borrower's net payoff is highest at $L = L^*$, $W(L^*) - rL^*$.

If $L^* > \bar{L}$ then the borrower will be constrained to borrow $\bar{L}$. It would like to borrow more but will find additional lenders unwilling to extend it loans under any terms whatsoever. If $L^* < \bar{L}$ then it will borrow L^* and achieve the same payoff that it would under perfect enforcement.[11]

Hence, as long as the expected penalty exceeds rL^*, seniority with potential partial repayment allows competitive lenders to provide the borrower the same amount of capital and the same net payoff that it would receive if they could enforce repayment perfectly. The loan schedule is upward-sloping in the amount borrowed, with junior debt demanding a higher nominal interest payment. However, the expected interest cost to the debtor is the safe world interest rate, so that it borrows up to the point at

---

[10]Note that we abstract from any problems associated with a country's insolvency, or "inability" to pay.

[11]To say more, we make specific assumptions about the distribution $F(H)$. The Pareto distribution:

$$F(H) = 1 - \left(\frac{\underline{H}}{H}\right)^{\theta}, \theta > 0, H \geq \underline{H}$$

$$F(H) = 0, H < \underline{H}$$

turns out to be especially convenient. If the penalty has this distribution, then the interest function that solves the zero-profit condition is:

$$R(l) = r, L \leq \underline{H}/r$$

$$R(l) = r[(1 - \theta)(rL/\underline{H}) + \theta]^{\theta/(1-\theta)}, L \geq \underline{H}/r$$

if $\theta < 1$. Note that the interest rate is increasing in L once rL exceeds $\underline{H}$. If $\theta \geq 1$ then any loan amount above $\underline{H}$ will yield an expected loss. No lending above $\underline{H}/r$ occurs.

which the marginal benefit of borrowing equals the safe rate. The borrower sometimes defaults upon junior loans, but never suffers the default penalty. Creditors use the threat of default to collect payments up to the amount that corresponds to the penalty of default.[12] What is collected is distributed among creditors according to their seniority.

With seniority imposed by the legal system, individual creditors do not need to ration credit to ensure an efficient outcome. They do, however, have to know the debtor country's indebtedness at the time that they lend.

3.1.2. Credit rationing with shared debt forgiveness

While public lending institutions such as the World Bank and IMF regard their loans as senior to those of private lenders, seniority provisions have not been a typical feature of sovereign debt to private creditors.[13] In place of seniority provisions, debt contracts have typically included pari passu clauses that require the debtor to treat all creditors as equals, giving any individual creditor the right to its pro rata share of any payment made to another creditor.

As we demonstrate here, however, the outcome can still be efficient, but efficiency requires credit rationing.

Loan Supply: If all loans have equal footing then, with partial repayment, the creditor can expect to receive an amount:

$$R[1 - F(D)] - \frac{1}{L} \int_0^D H \, dF(H) \tag{3.3}$$

for each unit lent, where R is the contractual interest rate, L the amount lent, and $D = RL$ total contractual obligations. Competition among risk-neutral lenders will equate this amount to the safe world interest rate r. The implied loan supply schedule has slope:

$$R'(L) = \frac{r - R[1 - F(D)]}{L[1 - F(D)]} \tag{3.4}$$

---

[12] We discussed negotiations between a debtor and its creditors in Section 2. The outcome we consider here is a special one. It would emerge, for example, if creditors could make a take it or leave it offer, with no possible renegotiation. Refusal by the debtor would lead to its automatic penalization.

[13] See, for example, the discussions in Alexander (1987) and Detragiache (1993). One reason for their absence is that, as discussed in Section 2, a potential cost of default is exclusion from future participation in international capital markets. Enforcing a credit embargo requires the solidarity of the creditors, which seniority is likely to undermine. If partial repayment occurs, junior creditors bear the entire cost of forgiveness but must desist from interfering with the debtor's future credit activity. Another reason is that, as we discuss below, situations can arise in which individual lenders find it in their interest to extend new loans to finance a current payment shortfall. Any creditor who extends new money ex post subordinates its debt to a creditor who does not, even if the creditor extending new debt is legally senior in terms of the original debt. In this context the seniority of the original debt has little meaning. What matters is the relative incentives of the creditors to provide new finance.

which is necessarily positive. The zero-profit condition again implies that the maximum that creditors will lend is $\bar{L} = \bar{H}/r$.

Loan Demand: The competitive outcome will be an R and L on this schedule that maximizes the borrower's net payoff:

$$W(L) - D[1 - F(D)] - \int_0^D H \, dF(H) . \tag{3.5}$$

Maximizing this amount with respect to L again implies a loan demand of L^*.

Just as with seniority, the country borrows the minimum of L^* and $\bar{L}$.[14]

As Kletzer (1984) emphasizes, either outcome requires that lenders set not only the interest rate, but the total amount of indebtedness. Given the contractual interest rate R, the borrower would typically want to borrow more than would be compatible with the zero-profit condition. To avoid making losses lenders cannot lend more than the appropriate L. Hence the market cannot achieve this first-best equilibrium if lenders cannot ration credit, as we show in the next section.[15]

3.1.3. Potential overborrowing

To see what difference rationing makes, now assume that competitive lenders can set the contractual interest rate on what they lend, but cannot control how much is borrowed overall. If any borrowing can occur at all, the zero-profit condition and loan supply schedule remain as in the constrained case. However, given the lenders' choice of R, the borrower maximizes its expected net payoff, *taking R as given.* Knowing in advance that the borrower will borrow as much as it wants once they have set R, the competitive lenders will set R to be consistent with zero profits. The first-order condition for a maximum, incorporating the zero-profit condition, is then:

$$W'(L) = r - \frac{1}{L} \int_0^D H \, dF(H) . \tag{3.6}$$

The marginal benefit of the loan is strictly below the world cost of capital: The debtor borrows *more* than it would with seniority or rationing, and more than the efficient

---

[14]For the case in which $F(H)$ is Pareto, the zero-profit condition implies the loan supply schedule:

$$R = (\underline{H}/L)[\theta + (1 - \theta)(rL/\underline{H})]^{1/(1-\theta)} .$$

[15]In fact, in the early years of large-scale commercial bank lending to developing countries, lenders did not seem to have access to good information on countries' total indebtedness. To the extent that lenders did have information, they did not appear to be coordinating their lending decisions. The World Bank and Bank for International Settlements established reporting systems to address the need for better information, but each system had holes that were filled only after some countries had already run up sizable debts. More recently, banks and official lending institutions seem to have been much better informed about total indebtedness, and to be coordinating their lending more carefully.

amount of borrowing with perfect enforcement. The reason is that each increment borrowed increases the probability of default on existing loans, increasing the interest rate that lenders must charge to earn a zero profit. Since lenders have already set the interest rate when the borrower decides how much to borrow, the borrower does not take into account the effect of its amount of borrowing on credit terms. This externality leads to "too much" borrowing. The borrower suffers from its creditors' inability to ration credit to it, however. While it borrows more, the terms on which it borrows deteriorate to the point that it is worse off. The debtor would benefit from an ability to precommit to a lower level of debt.[16]

3.1.4. Rationing with potential penalization

So far we have assumed that lenders can use the *threat* of the default penalty to collect the maximum that the borrower would be willing to pay in order to avoid the penalty. The penalty itself is never invoked. In the context of sovereign debt, however, collecting partial payment can be difficult. One reason is that individual lenders may not control the penalties associated with default. If the cost of not repaying debt is a general loss of creditworthiness, then the market as a whole participates in invoking the penalty. Even if lenders do control the penalty, they may not know the borrower's cost of default when trying to extract payment. At the time that payment was due, the borrower would try to claim that the cost of default was the lowest possible realization, and offer to pay no more. If the lender cannot ascertain the borrower's cost of default then the ex ante optimal debt contract would make no provision for renegotiation.[17] One reason that sovereign debt contracts have been difficult to renegotiate is that the pari passu provisions of the debt contracts require that all of a sovereign debtor's creditors agree to any renegotiation of debts. This requirement may make renegotiation difficult because of the free-rider problems that we discuss in Section 4.[18]

Suppose that debt cannot be renegotiated, so that failure to live up to the original loan contract causes the borrower to suffer the default penalty. In the simplest formulation of this problem the borrower suffers the penalty if it pays anything less than the full amount. There is consequently no point in paying anything at all if it

---

[16]For the case in which $F(H)$ is Pareto, the lenders' zero-profit condition again requires $\theta < 1$ for any lending to occur at all. The first-order condition for an interior maximum is that

$W'(L) = r[1 - \theta(1 - \underline{H}/rL)].$

[17]This argument assumes, however, that lenders cannot control the imposition of the penalty. If they can, then by applying it with appropriate probability in response to the amount lent, they might be able to extract partial payment from a debtor unwilling to pay all that it owed. Diamond (1984) and Gale and Hellwig (1989) discuss the use of penalties in extracting debt repayment and renegotiation. Hellwig (1977) models the time-inconsistency problem facing a lender whose debtor is not paying all that it owes on schedule.

[18]Fernandez and Ozler (1991) have written on the divergent interests of large and small banks in such negotiations.

does not pay all that it owes. In this case lenders either recover the full amount that they are owed, or nothing.

Continuing to denote the contractual interest rate as R, the expected repayment on a loan to a country that has borrowed L is just $R[1 - F(D)]$. What debtors can expect to get is $Y = [1 - F(D)]D$, which increases or decreases with contractual obligations D depending on the sign of $1 - F(D) - DF'(D)$.[19]

A possibility is that an increase in contractual debt, even though it increases what is paid if repayment occurs, also increases the probability of default to the extent that expected payment falls. A situation in which at some point more debt strictly reduces the total amount that creditors can hope to get has sometimes been called a "debt Laffer curve", although the term is more commonly applied to situations, which we discuss below, in which higher debt obligations reduce payment by distorting decisions in debtor countries.[20] If a country is on the "wrong" (downward) sloping side of this relationship then creditors can increase their expected receipts by forgiving debt.

If competitive lenders can ration credit, a borrower's indebtedness should never leave the debtor on the wrong side of the Laffer curve. An alternative debt contract that offered the same loan amount at a lower cost would leave the debtor better off at no expense to creditors. Competition among potential creditors would eliminate such dominated contracts.

If lenders ration credit they will choose R and L to maximize the debtor's expected net payoff subject to this zero-profit condition. The first-order condition for a maximum, *taking into account the effect of borrowing on the interest rate*, is:

$$W'(L) = r\left[\frac{1 - F(D)}{1 - F(D) - DF'(D)}\right]. \tag{3.7}$$

The equilibrium loan is less than the amount that equates the marginal value of the loan to safe world interest rate. With potential default and credit rationing, there is *less* lending than would occur with perfect enforcement.[21]

So far, we have shown that with credit rationing with potential default leads to *less* lending than would occur with perfect enforcement, while unconstrained lending with potential partial payment leads to *more* lending than with perfect enforcement. What happens if credit markets are subject to both phenomena?

3.1.5. Unconstrained borrowing with potential penalization

Say that lenders cannot monitor and control the borrower's total indebtedness, and cannot collect partial payment if repayment incentives are inadequate to enforce full

---

[19] Eaton and Gersovitz (1994) discuss the sign of this term.

[20] The term is due to Krugman (1989). Sachs (1990), Kenen (1990), Bulow and Rogoff (1990) and Eaton (1990a) discuss the term and its relationship to debt restructuring.

[21] When $F(H)$ is Pareto, the loan supply schedule is $R(L) = [r(L/\underline{H})^\theta]^{1/(1-\theta)}$ and the equilibrium loan amount satisfies $W'(L) = r/(1 - \theta)$. As before, any lending at all beyond $\underline{H}/r$ requires that $\theta < 1$.

payment. The zero-profit condition and loan supply schedule remain as in the previous section. The difference, as in the case of partial payment, is that now lenders control the contractual interest rate but not total lending. Once they set the interest rate, then the borrower can borrow all that it wants at this rate. Its optimal indebtedness, *taking the interest rate as given*, satisfies, upon substitution of the zero-profit condition:

$$W'(L) = r .$$ (3.8)

While unconstrained borrowing by itself leads to more borrowing than would occur with perfect enforcement, and potential default leads to less, together the two effects cancel, and the same amount is borrowed as would be the case if enforcement were perfect.

The borrower is less well off, however, since it suffers the penalty of default with positive probability. The borrower is even worse off than if credit were rationed. With rationing the borrower is at its highest possible net welfare given the loan supply schedule Without rationing it remains on this schedule, but borrows more at a higher contractual interest rate.

3.1.6. A digression: Sovereign debt and the social cost of capital

The cases discussed indicate how problems associated with sovereign debt can cause the marginal product of capital, and hence the social cost of capital, to diverge from the world cost of capital. The direction of the divergence is ambiguous, however. Potential repudiation acts to make the marginal product of capital exceed the world interest rate, while lenders' inability to subordinate junior debts or to ration credit has the opposite effect.

Moreover, there is no clear relationship between the contractual interest rate and the social cost of capital. Consider the case with credit rationing and potential penalization If the default penalty follows a Pareto distribution with parameter $\theta = 1/2$ and lower bound $\underline{H}$ then the marginal product of capital will equal twice the world interest rate, or $2r$. The contractual interest rate is then lower than the marginal product of capital if $rL < 2\underline{H}$ but exceeds it once the relationship equality is reversed. Thus, in economies where capital is highly productive (as measured by the amount of borrowing that equates the marginal product to $2r$) relative to the incentive to repay debt (as measured by $\underline{H}$), the contractual interest rate will overstate the contribution of an additional unit of capital. In economies that have less ability to use capital relative to their incentive to repay the contractual interest rate understates the marginal product of capital.

3.1.7. Do creditors penalize default?

When countries fail to repay, do they suffer? The evidence is ambiguous. Eichengreen (1989) and Lindert and Morton (1989) find that defaulting in the 1930s did not hurt a country's credit terms in the 1970's. Ozler (1991), however, finds that this result is sensitive to these authors' inclusion of countries that did not exist in the 1930s in their analysis. Within a fixed sample of countries, those that defaulted did worse than those that did not. Countries that came into being only after the 1930s were treated more like defaulters from the earlier period than like repayers from that period, suggesting that countries earn better credit terms by repaying previous loans rather than suffer worse credit terms as a consequence of defaulting on previous loans.[22]

Cohen (1992) examines the growth experience of debtor countries in the 1980s. While these countries all suffered a slowdown in growth, he concludes that repaying debt or failing to repay debt had little effect on growth once factors like the terms of trade and domestic investment are taken into account.

3.2. Debt and domestic distortions

One concern raised by sovereign debt is that the debt itself might distort the incentives of borrowing country governments in a way that is detrimental to their own or to their creditors' welfare. As discussed in Section 2, a common assumption has been that the incentive to repay increases with the debtor's output at the time that debt repayment is due. Steps that the borrower takes to increase its future output then increase what it is expected to pay. Debt thus acts as a marginal tax on the return to investment, giving debtor countries greater incentive to consume rather than to invest available resources.[23]

Another assumption is that default disrupts the debtor's trade. Hence, by allocating resources to reduce the gains from trade, such as investing in import-competing rather than export activities, a debtor reduces its vulnerability to trade disruption and its incentive to repay debt.[24] In fact, a common observation has been that large debtor's focused their investments in import-competing and nontraded goods sectors rather than in export sectors.[25]

We extend the analysis above to demonstrate how foreign debt can distort a debtor's behavior. For concreteness we consider the case in which lenders can ration credit and collect the most that the debtor is willing to repay. A key issue is the timing of decisions, in particular, whether the debtor acts before or after it borrows.

We now allow the debtor's payoff gross of debt repayment and default costs to

---

[22]Eaton (1990b) develops a model with this implication for the evolution of credit terms.

[23]Sachs and Cohen (1985) provide an early statement of the proposition that debt provides an incentive to use resources for current consumption rather than for investment.

[24]Goldberg and Spiegel (1992) develop a two-sector model of borrowing and repayment. Creditors can seize the output of one sector but not the other. Having borrowed, the sovereign has an incentive to shift investment toward the sector that is out of the creditors' reach.

[25]See, for example, Diaz-Alejandro (1985).

depend not only on the amount that it borrows, but upon some action γ over which it has control. This action, for example, could be overall investment, or the share of investment devoted to the export sector. Hence the borrower's gross payoff is now $W(L, \gamma)$, which is differentiable, increasing and concave in the loan amount L, and concave in the action γ. We assume that γ achieves an interior maximum γ^*, which is the level that the borrower would choose in the absence of debt considerations, or with perfect enforcement.

We also allow γ to affect repayment incentives, however. The distribution of the cost of default H is now $F(H, \gamma)$. We assume that F is decreasing in γ, meaning that this action increases the likelihood that high values of the default penalty will be realized. Hence, other things equal, a debtor that chooses a higher level of γ has a greater incentive to repay.

The borrower's net payoff is now:

$$W(L, \gamma) - D[1 - F(D, \gamma)] - \int_0^D H F_H(H, \gamma)\, dH , \tag{3.9}$$

where $D = RL$ is the debtor's contractual debt obligations. The lender's zero-profit condition becomes:

$$R[1 - F(D, \gamma)] + \frac{1}{L} \int_0^D H F_H(H, \gamma)\, dH = r . \tag{3.10}$$

Differentiating this expression with respect to γ and integrating by parts yields:

$$R_\gamma = \frac{\int_0^D F_\gamma(H, \gamma)\, dH}{1 - F(D, \gamma)} , \tag{3.11}$$

which falls as γ rises. Hence, not surprisingly, the debtor improves its credit terms by taking an action that increases the cost of default.

3.2.1. Commitment to policies

Say that the borrower can decide about γ before lenders determine their credit terms. It will then take into account the effect of its choice on the credit terms that it will then get. If the loans are demand determined, so that $W'(L) = r$, then the debtor has no incentive to modify its choice of policy to affect credit terms, so will continue to set $\gamma = \gamma^*$.

If, however, loans are supply constrained at $\bar{L} = \bar{H}/r$ then the optimal choice of γ is determined by the condition:

$$W_\gamma(L, \gamma) = [W_L(L, \gamma) - r] \frac{\int_0^\infty F_\gamma(H, \gamma)\, dH}{r} . \tag{3.12}$$

Since higher values of γ shift the distribution of the default penalty upward, the term on the right of this expression is negative, implying that the optimal value of γ exceeds what it would be with perfect enforcement. If the borrower can commit to an action that influences its cost of default before credit terms are set, it should modify its action to increase its expected cost of default. It will benefit by improving its credit terms.[26]

3.2.2. Lack of commitment

Say instead that the borrower can decide on γ only after it has taken out loans. At that point its interest rate R and loan amount L are given. Hence the borrower ignores the impact that γ would have on them, even though creditors may have correctly anticipated its choice of γ when setting loan terms.

The borrower's first-order condition for an optimal choice of γ is now:

$$W\gamma = -\int_0^D F_\gamma(H, \gamma) \, \mathrm{d}H \ . \tag{3.13}$$

The term on the right is now positive. Since a lower choice of γ reduces what debtor can expect to pay, it sets γ below γ^*. Hence, if the borrower takes an action that influences its cost of default only after credit terms are established, then it will modify its action to reduce its expected cost of default.

To summarize, a debtor has reason to modify its actions to increase its incentive to repay if it can commit to taking these actions before credit terms are established. Once credit terms are set, however, the direction of the incentive is reversed: The debtor has an incentive to modify its actions to reduce its incentive to repay.[27]

3.2.3. Was there a debt Laffer curve?

The "debt Laffer curve" argument holds that debt distorts decisions in debtor countries so much that a reduction in contractual debt can increase what creditors can hope to receive. The question remains as to why so much was lent in the first place.

Cohen (1990) uses the secondary market price of debt to estimate the relationship between the market value and nominal value of debt for 16 highly indebted countries. A "debt Laffer curve" would imply that, at some point, an increase in the value of nominal debt would be associated with a decrease in the market value of the debt. He

---

[26]If the borrower cannot be rationed or suffers the default penalty rather than making partial payment, it has further incentive to try to commit to policies that improve its credit terms. These cases are left as exercises for the interested reader.

[27]One interpretation of the conditionality that the IMF imposes on borrowers is a means of enforcing borrowers' commitments to actions that improve their credit terms with private lenders. By borrowing from the IMF, a country exposes itself to punishment should it not take these actions, enhancing its commitment to taking them.

could not reject the hypothesis that the relationship between nominal and market value was positive in the relevant range for all countries in the sample.[28]

3.3. The fiscal problem

Most of the debt that developing countries ran up during the 1970s and 1980s was incurred or guaranteed by the governments of these countries. One reason for the prominent role of the government might have been creditors' suspicions about the local judicial system's ability or willingness to enforce a loan contract with a private debtor. Even in cases where debt was initially nonguaranteed, private creditors turned to the government to make good on loans that went sour.[29]

An implication of the government's role as primary debtor, or as implicit or explicit guarantor of private debt, is that debt came to represent a significant potential tax burden on the economy. One impact that this burden might have had is to discourage subsequent investment and output.

3.3.1. Government debt and the strategic complementarity of private investment

Eaton and Gersovitz (1988) develop a model to show how government debt incurred to finance public investment can harm credit terms and potentially discourage private investment. An implication is that, by increasing the potential tax burden on private investment domestically, government debt can discourage private investment and give rise to capital flight abroad.

In their model the government must borrow to invest in infrastructure, and uses revenue from taxes on income from subsequent production to finance repayment. If there is a large amount of domestic investment then the tax base suffices to finance repayment and provide investors a return that is competitive with that abroad. But if the amount of investment is too small then the government must tax what investment there is at such a high rate that the after-tax domestic return is no longer competitive.

There can be two locally stable equilibria. In one the level of investment is sufficient to allow the government to finance its debt burden and still provide private investors a competitive rate of return. The government fully repays its debt. The other equilibrium is one in which private investment is zero, and the domestic rate of return

---

[28] A possible explanation is that the markets foresaw subsequent debt reductions in cases where the relationship between nominal and market values became negative. This explanation would imply, of course, that markets expected an efficient outcome.

[29] Diaz-Alejandro (1985) recounts the Chilean government's experience with foreign commercial banks that held it accountable for loans to local private banks that went bankrupt. The foreign banks demanded that the government assume the debts or face worsened credit terms itself. The Chilean government acquiesced and assumed the debts in question. Hence the creditors acted as if a government guarantee was implicit in their lending to private parties.

on domestic investment is strictly less than the world interest rate. The government can repay only a part of its debt.

The reason for the multiplicity of equilibria is that the tax burden on capital implied by the government debt creates a "strategic complementarity" among private investors. Over a range, an increase in investment by any single investor increases the after-tax return to other private investors by reducing their tax burden.[30]

3.3.2. Debt guarantees and moral hazard

Eaton (1987) extends the analysis to show that explicit or implicit government guarantees of loans to private entities can lead to overborrowing and encourage the flight of nationally-owned capital abroad. Again, crucial assumptions are that at least part of the burden of financing debt service will fall on domestic investment, and that domestic capital, by fleeing abroad, escapes taxation at home.

Say that the economy has a large number n of domestic investment projects, each one associated with a risk-neutral entrepreneur. For simplicity, assume that the projects and entrepreneurs are identical. Conditional upon an investment level k and its entrepreneur putting in effort, each project yields an amount $f(k)$ with probability λ and 0 with remaining probability. If the entrepreneur does not put in effort then output is 0 for sure. Putting in effort costs the entrepreneur an amount β in terms of income. The entrepreneur owns capital in amount $\bar{k}$ and borrows an additional amount l at rate R. If the project succeeds the entrepreneur pays back debt, pays a tax t, and keeps the rest. If the project fails the entrepreneur goes bankrupt, and pays neither debt nor taxes.

The entrepreneur can also invest his or her own capital abroad, escape taxation, and earn a return r' which might, because of evasion costs, fall short of the safe world borrowing rate r. However, as long as:

$$\lambda[f(\bar{k} + l) - Rl - t] - \beta > r'\bar{k} \tag{3.14}$$

it will pay the entrepreneur to invest in the domestic project and put in effort to ensure its success. Otherwise, the entrepreneur is better off investing abroad and not bothering to put in effort on the project. Foreign lending occurs before entrepreneurs decide where to invest their own capital and how much effort to put into their projects.

In the absence of any loan guarantees or taxes, competitive foreign lenders will be willing to lend at rate r/λ if they expect that the entrepreneur has an incentive to put in effort. The entrepreneur has this incentive as long as the above condition holds at this rate and at a zero tax.

---

[30]Dooley and Kletzer (1994) provide a very general model relating capital flight to external debt and tax policies in debtor countries.

Say, however, that foreign lenders require a loan guarantee from the local government. One reason to do so is their inability, relative to the government, to distinguish failed projects from successful ones whose owners are feigning failure to keep the total return for themselves. These guarantees are financed by a tax on successful projects. Let m denote the number of projects whose entrepreneurs invest abroad and fail to put in effort. Financing failed projects thus requires a tax:

$$t = \frac{m + (1 - \lambda)(n - m)}{\lambda(n - m)} R\bar{l} \tag{3.15}$$

on each successful project, where $\bar{l}$ is the loan to the average entrepreneur.

Again, there can be two equilibria. In one, all entrepreneurs put effort into their projects and invest domestically. The tax rate is $(1 - \lambda)/\lambda$. Output is $\lambda n f(\bar{k} + l)$. All lenders are repaid, by the entrepreneur if his project succeeded, or by the government if it failed. In the other, entrepreneurs invest abroad and do not put effort into their projects. The government reneges on its loan guarantees. Lenders are not repaid. Output collapses.

Say that the high-output equilibrium occurs with probability ω. With loan guarantees, risk-neutral lenders will charge an interest rate r/ω, since the risk that they now face is not the failure of a specific project but the realization of the bad equilibrium. Facing this interest rate, entrepreneurs will borrow to satisfy the first-order condition:[31]

$$\omega f'(\bar{k} + l) = r. \tag{3.16}$$

While these models are extreme in their assumptions and implications, they illustrate how a government role as a debtor, or guarantor of private debt, can create interdependence in lending and investment behavior. An outcome can emerge in which the potential tax obligations implied by the debt discourage entrepreneurial activity and lead to capital flight.

4. What can be done?

Having discussed various problems that sovereign debt can create, we now turn to policies that have been proposed and, on occasion, implemented to alleviate these problems. Since the latter part of the 1980s and 1990s have been periods in which the

---

[31] Note that this condition implies more borrowing than the level that maximizes national income, which equates the expected marginal product to the world interest rate, or: $\omega \lambda f'(\bar{k} + l) = r$. The reason for the discrepancy is that, with loan guarantees, an individual borrower does not bear the full cost of his loan. More borrowing generates a negative externality on other borrowers who must make good on the guarantee if the entrepreneur's own project goes bad. Since credit terms no longer reflect the possibility of failure of the individual project, there is again an incentive to "overborrow".

major debtor countries have been making net transfers to their private creditors, the focus of much of the more recent literature has been on the disposition of outstanding debt rather than on why the loans were ever made in the first place. In this section we consider means of alleviating existing debt problems, grouping proposed solutions into three categories: those initiated by private creditors, those initiated by the debtors, and those initiated by the international public sector. In the concluding section we turn to the nature of debt contracts themselves, and discuss the extent to which alternative institutional arrangements for providing developing countries access to international capital markets might have avoided the problems that emerged.

4.1. Creditor initiatives

Consider the options facing a creditor in dealing with a debtor that is not paying all that it owes. There are four basic choices that can be applied separately or in combination:

1. Seeking legal remedy. The debtor could appeal to the judicial system to declare the debtor in default. Such a declaration would give the creditor the right to any assets of the debtor within the jurisdiction of the legal system. This claim would not only transfer existing assets to the creditor, but would impede subsequent transactions between the debtor country and agents in the jurisdiction of the creditor.

The first consequence harms the debtor and benefits the creditor only to the extent that the debtor has assets abroad. To the extent that the debtor is a net debtor, these assets will not suffice to cover the claims against it. The second consequence is more likely to discourage the debtor from engaging in intertemporal and intratemporal trade than to result in any transfer to the creditor. Unlike the transfer of assets to the creditor, this second consequence is likely to constitute a deadweight loss.

Hence the creditor's limited ability to seize the debtor's assets renders the legal remedies available to creditors much less effective than in a domestic context. In fact, the creditors of sovereign debtors have rarely turned to their judicial system for redress. They have typically pursued the other options discussed below. Nevertheless, creditors' ability to pursue legal remedies, and thereby impose significant costs on the debtor, has undoubtedly had a significant effect on debtor behavior.[32]

2. Lending the difference. The creditor can lend the debtor the difference between what it owes and how much it is willing to pay. Formally, lending could mean making new loans, often called, in the context of the debt crisis, "new money", rescheduling payments on existing loans, or tolerating arrears.

Obviously this option only postpones ultimately dealing with the debtor's payment

---

[32]Kaletsky (1985) and Alexander (1987) discuss legal remedies in the case of sovereign default. Bulow and Rogoff (1989a) model the implications of these remedies for loan market equilibrium.

problems.[33] It makes sense if the creditor thinks that the debtor's repayment prospects will improve in the future. It also makes sense if the creditor thinks that pursuing one of the other options may be more fruitful later on.

3. Forgiving the difference. The lender can forgive the debtor the difference between what it owes and how much it is willing to pay. This option makes sense if the creditor thinks that the borrower is unlikely ever to pay the amount forgiven and that forgiving some debt increases the prospects for repayment of what remains.

4. Getting someone else to lend the difference. It would seem unlikely that other lenders would find additional lending more attractive than the initial lender. In fact, the initial lender may have reason to lend to keep alive its hope of repayment on its initial debt. Other lenders do not have this reason to lend. As we discuss in Section 4.3, however, in the context of sovereign debt official lending institutions may have an incentive to assume debts in order to avoid the cost that default might impose upon the world economy as a whole.

We adopt the framework we developed in Section 3 to illustrate the creditors' options. We expand the repayment period to two periods in order to illustrate the relevant dynamics, and ignore the initial lending decision, which at this point is a bygone. Consider the situation of a debtor that currently owes its private creditors an amount D_0 but is willing to pay at most $H_0 < D_0$. In a subsequent period, period 1, it is willing to pay, up to what it owes, an amount H which is currently unknown by anyone, but is expected to be drawn from a distribution $F(H, \gamma)$, where γ is a decision made by the creditor in the current period. Again, we assume that larger values of γ increase the likelihood of repayment, so that $F_\gamma < 0$. The debtor's payoff each period i is a function $U^i(T_i, \gamma)$ of its net transfer to the creditor that period, T_i and its choice of γ. At the beginning of period 0 the creditor owes D_1 in period 1.

4.1.1. A single creditor

To illustrate the first three options we initially assume that there is a single creditor (or a unified consortium of creditors). Its objective is to maximize the discounted value of what the debtor transfers to it over two periods, or $T_0 + \beta^c T_1$, where β^c is the creditor's discount factor. We turn to the problems raised by multiple creditors in the next section.

Seeking a legal remedy will be worthwhile only if the creditor's expected net benefit from the anticipated remedy exceeds H_0. For reasons that we have discussed, in the case of sovereign debt this may be unlikely.

Consider now the second and third options. Denote the amount of any new lending in period 0 by N and the amount of debt forgiven in period i by F_i. By definition, the

[33]Unless the lender intends always to roll over debts in the future, in which case it is really forgiving the debt (option 3).

difference between what the debtor owes and what it pays in period 0 is either rolled over or forgiven, so that $D_0 - T_0 = N + F_0$. Let R denote the gross interest rate on new lending. Period 1 debt becomes $D = D_1 - F_1 + RN$.

All that matters to either party is the actual amount transferred in period 0, $T_0 = D_0 - F_0 - N$, and what happens to debt outstanding at the beginning of the next period, $D = D_1 - F_1 + RN$. Depending on the credit terms that apply to new loans, the same levels of T_0 and D can be achieved with many different combinations of refinance and forgiveness. We can state the problem, then, in terms of these magnitudes. The debtor's expected welfare is:

$$\max_\gamma \; U^0(D_0 - T_0, \gamma) + \beta^D \left\{ [1 - F(D, \gamma)]U^1(D, \gamma) + \int_0^D U^1(H, \gamma)F_H(H, \gamma)\,dH \right\}$$

(4.1)

while the creditor's payoff is:

$$T_0 + \beta^C \left\{ [1 - F(D, \gamma)]D + \int_0^D PF_H(H, \gamma)\,dH \right\}.$$

(4.2)

The creditor, then, wants to restructure debt so that the consequent current net transfer T_0 and payment the next period maximize its payoff subject to the constraint that $T_0 \leq H_0$.

If T_0 and D have no bearing on the debtor's choice of γ then the creditor does best by setting $T_0 = H_0$ and D as high as possible. The literature, however, has focused on the role of debt in distorting the debtor's incentives to undertake policies conducive to repayment. First-order conditions for an interior maximum are then:

$$\frac{dY}{dT_0} = 1 - \beta^C \int_0^D F_\gamma(H, \gamma)\,dH \frac{d\gamma}{dT_0} = 0$$

(4.3)

$$\frac{dY}{dD} = \beta^C \left\{ [1 - F(D, \gamma)] - \int_0^D F_\gamma(H, \gamma)\,dH \frac{d\gamma}{dD} \right\} = 0.$$

(4.4)

Hence the creditor will want to modify its choices to try to encourage the debtor to choose a higher value of γ.

How do credit terms affect the debtor's choice of γ? Differentiating the debtor's first-order condition for its best choice of γ, and invoking the second-order condition, indicates that $d\gamma/dT_0$ has the same sign as $U^0_{T\gamma}(T_0, \gamma)$, and that $d\gamma/dD$ has the same sign as:

$$-F\gamma(D, \gamma)U^1_T(D, \gamma) + [1 - F(D, \gamma)]U^1_{T\gamma}(D, \gamma).$$

(4.5)

The first result simply means that the creditor has an incentive to reduce its demand for current payment if paying less now raises the debtor's utility from taking an action that increases its repayment prospects in the future.

The implications of the second result are more complicated. The first term is necessarily negative: Higher debt gives the debtor less incentive to reform by reducing its utility in situations where it pays everything. The sign of the second term is that of the cross-partial $U^1_{T\gamma}(D, \gamma)$, which is positive if paying less in the future raises the debtor's utility from reforming, and negative if paying less in the future lowers its utility from reforming. The typical assumption in the literature is that creditors "tax" a portion of any of the benefits of reform, so that the target's incentive to reform diminishes as its debt increases.[34]

But simple and plausible alternatives yield different conclusions. Continuing the example introduced in Section 3, let $F(H, \gamma)$ have the Pareto distribution:

$$F(H, \gamma) = 1 - \left(\frac{\gamma \underline{H}}{H}\right)^{\theta} \quad \theta \in (0, 1). \tag{4.6}$$

Say that the borrower's utility each period is an increasing, concave function of output less transfer payments to creditors less reform effort γ. Output in the earlier period is given at y_0 while output in the later period is an increasing, concave function of γ, $y(\gamma)$. The borrower's expected payoff over the two periods is then:

$$\max_{\gamma} \ u(y_0 - \gamma - T_0) + \beta^D \left\{ [u(y(\gamma)) - D] \left(\frac{\gamma \underline{H}}{D}\right)^{\theta} \right.$$
$$\left. + \int_{\gamma \underline{H}}^{D} [u(y(\gamma)) - H] \theta (\gamma \underline{H})^{\theta} H^{-\theta - 1} \, \mathrm{d}H \right\}. \tag{4.7}$$

In this case a reduction in the transfer demanded in period 0 definitely increases the borrower's incentive to reform. The reason is that reforming uses up current resources, raising the marginal utility of current relative to future consumption. Lowering current debt-service obligations, by lowering the marginal utility of period 0 consumption, increases the incentive to undertake reform.

The effect of lowering *future* debt service obligations depends upon the sign of the expression:

$$\frac{\sigma \gamma y'(\gamma)}{y(\gamma) - D} - \theta \tag{4.8}$$

where $\sigma = -u''(y(\gamma) - D)(y(\gamma) - D)/u'(y(\gamma) - D)$, the elasticity of the marginal utility of period 1 income. If reform lowers period 1 output ($y'(\gamma)$ negative), then reducing debt again necessarily increases the incentive to reform. If reform raises later output, however, then *increasing* debt raises the incentive to reform if the utility function is highly concave (σ large) and output highly responsive to reforms. The

---

[34]See, for example, Sachs (1984), Krugman (1988), Froot (1989), and Claessens and Diwan (1990).

reason is that higher debt acts to raise the marginal utility of consumption in the later period, increasing the incentive to undertake reforms that transfer income to the later period.[35]

It might seem that competition among lenders would prevent initial creditors from refinancing at terms that yield supernormal profits on the additional funds. However, the original loan contracts typically prohibit the debtor from borrowing from outside creditors, giving the initial creditors a monopoly on any further lending to the borrower.[36]

To summarize, a creditor's best response to a shortfall in debt service depends upon the implications of a larger future debt burden for repayment prospects. As long as the debtor remains on the upward sloping part of its "debt Laffer curve" in future periods then the creditor should refinance at the highest possible terms. These terms could even yield supernormal returns if the original creditor can bar other creditors from lending to the distressed debtor. If the debtor is near the peak of the curve in future periods, however, then the creditor would do better to provide additional finance at concessionary terms. If the debtor is already over the top then the creditor should simply forgive the current shortfall and reduce future debt as well.

4.1.2. Multiple creditors

So far, the discussion has assumed a single creditor or a group of creditors who can act in concert. Much of the concern about creditors' response to debt problems derives from the potential inability of a diffuse and diverse set of lenders to reach an agreement about restructuring debt. One concern is that individual lenders, even if they have similar characteristics, will be unable to coordinate an efficient response. Another is that their interests might diverge, preventing them from reaching an agreement. We treat each in turn.

The coordination problem

The following example illustrates the problem of coordinating the refinance of a payments shortfall among multiple lenders, even when they are identical in terms of their preferences and exposure.[37] As before, we consider a borrower who currently owes an amount D_0 but is willing to pay only H_0. What it is willing to pay subsequently is drawn from a distribution $F(H)$, and what it currently owes that

---

[35]Corden (1989) points out the generally ambiguous relationship between the level of debt and the incentive to undertake reforms that increase the probability of paying off the debt.

[36]The expected benefit of future monopoly power over the creditor should have been reflected in the terms of the initial loans. Ozler (1989) finds that reschedulings during the 1970s were typically associated with an appreciation of the equity value of the creditor banks involved, suggesting that the banks were using the debtors' payment problems to exploit their monopoly position during this period. During the 1980s, however, reschedulings had the opposite effect on the equity value of the banks.

[37]Cooper and Sachs (1985), Krugman (1988), Detragiache and Garella (1993), and Spiegel (1993a) model the public goods problem posed by debt forgiveness.

period is D_1. Assume now, however, that there are N creditors who happen to have the same level of initial exposure.

In period 0, then, each creditor j receives an amount H_0/N and must decide what interest rate R_j to charge on what it must refinance, which is $(D_0 - H_0)/N$.[38] To introduce a "debt Laffer curve" in its simplest form assume that repayment in the second period is an all or nothing event, so that if the debtor is unwilling to pay all that it owes it pays nothing and suffers the consequence of default. In this case, what an individual creditor can expect to receive next period, as a function of its own and other lenders' finance terms, is:

$$Y_i = \left[1 - F\left(D_1 + \frac{D_0 - H_0}{N} \sum_{j=1}^{N} R_j \right) \right] \frac{D_1 + (D_0 - H_0)R_i}{N}. \tag{4.9}$$

An interior Nash equilibrium in refinance terms (if it exists) is one in which each lender chooses a refinance rate R that satisfies the first-order condition:

$$[1 - F(D)] - F'(D)D/N = 0 \tag{4.10}$$

where $D = D_1 + (D_0 - H_0)R$, the total amount owed in period 1. Ultimate period 1 indebtedness thus increases with the number of creditors, and exceeds the amount of debt that maximizes expected repayment unless $N = 1$. As N approaches infinity the equilibrium amount of debt implies almost certain default. Hence uncoordinated refinancing necessarily puts the debtor over the top of the debt Laffer curve, if it has a top. The reason is that higher interest costs impose a negative externality on other creditors by increasing the likelihood of default on their loans. The result relates to that on the potential for overborrowing when uncoordinated lenders cannot ration credit or impose seniority.

If the penalty of default is uniformly distributed on the interval $[0, \bar{H}]$, for example, then the "debt Laffer curve" peaks at a period 1 debt of $\bar{H}/2$. The Nash equilibrium in credit terms leaves the debtor a total period 1 debt of $N\bar{H}/(N+1)$. Expected total repayment is $N\bar{H}/(N+1)^2$.[39]

Secondary debt markets, which we discuss in greater detail in Section 4.2, provide a natural coordination mechanism. Diffusely held, the debt in our example is worth only $N\bar{H}/(N+1)^2$. If a consolidator could buy it up at this price and reduce its nominal level to the peak of the "debt Laffer curve" the expected yield would be $(N-1)^2\bar{H}/[4(N+1)^2]$. A reason given for the failure of this mechanism is the incentive for an individual investor to hold on to its own claim and demand a higher

---

[38]Note that this choice encompasses both refinance at competitive terms and total forgiveness of the current shortfall. Denoting a creditor i's choice by R_i, for example, full forgiveness implies $R_i = 0$ while R_i negative implies not only full forgiveness of the current shortfall and relief of future debt as well.

[39]The Pareto distribution fails to illustrate this result. The reason is that, with this distribution, expected repayment is monotonically increasing or decreasing in the amount owed; there is no nondegenerate "debt Laffer curve".

price, dissipating the consolidator's return. Various methods of purchase might still allow a potential debt consolidator to achieve a gain. One mechanism is to make any purchase contingent on participation by a broad range of creditors. By holding out, then, an individual creditor would kill the whole deal. In fact, a number of the debt restructuring schemes contain such "participation clauses" to avoid free riding on the consolidator.

The heterogeneity problem

Things can get even worse if lenders have different attributes. Differences that have received attention are those between large and small lenders (Spiegel, 1992; Fernandez and Ozler, 1991) and sound and unsound lenders (Demirguc-Kunt, Diwan, and Spiegel, 1993). We discuss the implications of each in turn.

Consider the Nash equilibrium in refinancing above. Assume, however, that creditors differ according to their initial exposure. Small lenders have greater incentive to free ride, so will refinance at a higher rate (or, equivalently, forgive a smaller share) than large lenders. Moreover, their superior ability to free ride means that small lenders do better in the Nash equilibrium than their share of exposure would imply. A consequence is that in any negotiations between large and small lenders about refinancing the debt, small lenders might successfully demand more than what their share of exposure would indicate. Similarly, they might demand a higher price per unit of their debt. Descriptions of loan restructurings indicate that small lenders did indeed tend to take a much harder line than large lenders.

Fernandez and Kaaret (1992) formally analyze the potential inefficiencies that the coexistence of large and small creditors can introduce. They examine negotiations between a sovereign debtor and its large creditors to restructure debt.[40] The debtor does not know how much the large banks can pressure the country's small creditors into reaching an agreement. They show how this informational asymmetry, for the reasons given in Kreps and Wilson (1982), can delay any agreement between the debtor and the large creditors, possibly for many periods.[41]

Fernandez and Ozler (1991) model bargaining between a debtor and large and small creditor banks. Only large banks have the ability to punish a recalcitrant debtor, but at a cost borne only by them. Since the benefits of repayment are distributed pro rata, the maximum penalty that the lenders can credibly threaten collectively increases ceteris paribus with the concentration of debt in the hands of the large banks. Their empirical analysis confirms that the secondary market price of a country's debt is positively correlated with the proportion of the country's debt held by big banks.

Some of the banks involved in sovereign lending have had solvency problems of

---

[40]Normally, the syndicate of lenders was represented by the largest creditors at debt negotiations, but final agreement required the assent of all.

[41]Armendariz de Aghion (1990) uses a similar model to explain why only major debtors received new loans following the onset of the debt problems of the 1980s.

their own. For reasons explained by Stiglitz and Weiss (1981), the prospect of bankruptcy creates an incentive to take greater risk. This incentive has implications for how risky lenders might restructure debt. Consider again the problem of restructuring debt to provide the debtor country the incentive to undertake policies that improve prospects for repayment, assuming now that the creditor can get whatever the debtor is willing to pay. Say, however, that the creditor itself will go bankrupt if the debtor pays less than some minimum amount $\underline{T}$. The creditor does not care about repayment amounts less than this since it won't be around to collect. It will want to set repayment terms to satisfy the first-order conditions:

$$\frac{\mathrm{d}Y}{\mathrm{d}T_0} = 1 - \beta^C \int_{\underline{T}}^{D} F_\gamma(H, \gamma) \, \mathrm{d}H \, \frac{\mathrm{d}\gamma}{\mathrm{d}T_0} = 0 \tag{4.11}$$

$$\frac{\mathrm{d}Y}{\mathrm{d}D} = \beta^C \left\{ [1 - F(D, \gamma)] - \int_{\underline{T}}^{D} F_\gamma(H, \gamma) \, \mathrm{d}H \, \frac{\mathrm{d}\gamma}{\mathrm{d}D} \right\} = 0 . \tag{4.12}$$

Comparing these with the incentives facing a sound lender, the risky lender has less incentive to reduce obligations to encourage reform. The reason is that it does not benefit from reform at low levels of payment.

This argument suggests why banks in precarious positions have less incentive to restructure debt than sound banks, and why risky banks might hold on to sovereign loans while sounder banks are unloading them. It also indicates why unsound banks might take a harder line in negotiations among lenders to restructure debt. Finally, it suggests why it might be hard for an individual creditor to consolidate debt if it does not know the relevant characteristics of the current creditors. They would have an incentive to overstate their valuation of the debt in order to get a higher price.

4.2. Debtor initiatives

Another approach to solving debt problems has been to allow the debtor to take the initiative in restructuring its debt by buying it back on the secondary market.[42] Buybacks have taken numerous forms, depending on how they are financed. In their purest form, the debtor government buys back the debt with its own foreign exchange. In other cases foreign donors have provided the resources. In "swap" arrangements the debtor government has exchanged domestic currency for debt at some specified price. The use of this currency has usually been tied to some particular

---

[42]The original loan agreements typically prohibited debt buybacks. Hence, to be legal, buybacks require waivers from creditors. In many cases waivers have been granted. In other cases debtors may have bought back debt surreptitiously, through third parties, for example. A reason for the original restrictions might have been a fear that the debtor would take actions to manipulate the price of its debt, and then buy it back at depressed prices. A similar logic lies behind the prohibition on insider trading.

purpose, such as direct foreign investment (debt-equity swaps) or environmental protection (debt-for-nature swaps). These swap arrangements can be thought of as a combination of a pure buyback in combination with a subsidy to direct foreign investment or environmental protection, with the amount of the subsidy depending upon both the price of the debt and the exchange rate.

We focus here on the buyback component of these schemes. One question that has generated a great deal of controversy is the division of any gains from a buyback between a debtor and its creditors. Bulow and Rogoff (1988a), for example, argue that buybacks financed out of the debtor's own resources at market prices benefit creditors at the expense of the debtor. Whether this is the case or not turns out to depend on two key magnitudes: (1) the extent to which creditors can collect the maximum that the debtor is willing to pay rather than to impose penalties for nonpayment and (2) how much current spending on buybacks reduces resources available for future repayment. We parameterize these magnitudes as follows: (1) In the event that the debtor lacks the incentive to pay all that it owes, it pays the most that it is willing, thus avoiding the cost of default, with probability π, and pays nothing, suffering the penalty of default, with remaining probability. (2) Each dollar of debtor resources used for current buybacks reduces what's available for future repayment by λ dollars.

Average vs. marginal debt

To analyze buybacks we need to consider the price at which buybacks occur. The price should reflect what creditors expect to get paid. In terms of the two-period model developed in the previous section, the total value of outstanding debt to creditors amounts to:

$$V^C(D) = \pi \int_0^D H \, dF(H) + [1 - F(D)]D . \qquad (4.13)$$

Given the absence of seniority, the market price q should equal the value per unit, or the average value of debt to the creditor:

$$q = \frac{V^C(D)}{D} = \pi \int_0^D \frac{H}{D} \, dF(H) + [1 - F(D)] . \qquad (4.14)$$

What does the debtor gain by reducing its debt by one unit? Its total expected repayment plus expected harm from the cost of default is:

$$V^D(D) = \int_0^D H \, dF(H) + [1 - F(D)]D . \qquad (4.15)$$

Differentiating with respect to D gives the marginal cost of debt to the debtor, which is just $[1 - F(D)]$, just the probability of full repayment. Except in the extreme case in which partial repayment never occurs ($\pi = 0$) the value to the debtor of reducing debt by one unit is strictly less than the market price of debt.

Buying back a unit of debt lowers what the debtor is willing to pay the next period by λq, and lowers its contractual obligations by one. The first magnitude constrains what the debtor pays with probability $F(D)$ and the second magnitude constrains what it pays with remaining probability. Hence the debtor's expected payments fall by $1 - F(D) - F(D)\lambda q$. What matters to the debtor, then, is how this magnitude compares with what the borrower pays to buy back a unit of debt, or q.

If $\lambda = 0$, meaning that the loss of resources for the current buyback does not reduce future willingness to pay, then the buyback is at the debtor's expense. At the other extreme, if $\lambda = 1$, meaning that resources used now reduce what the debtor is willing to pay in the future dollar for dollar, then the debtor benefits from the buyback. What happens to the creditor depends on the likelihood of efficient renegotiation. If $\pi = 1$, as Bulow and Rogoff (1988a) assume, then the benefits to the two parties sum to zero: If the debtor loses then the creditor benefits and vice versa. If $\pi < 1$, however, then it is possible for both parties to benefit. A buyback, by reducing the possibility of default, reduces the likelihood that the debtor will experience the cost of default.

Buybacks and the price of debt
How does a buyback affect the price of debt? Differentiating the expression for the price with respect to a buyback in amount B, and evaluating the result at $B = 0$, gives an expression with the sign of:

$$q - 1 + F(D) - \pi\lambda F(D) + (1 - \lambda)(1 - \pi)F'(D)D . \tag{4.16}$$

How does this magnitude relate to the effect of the buyback on the creditor's and debtor's situation? This expression has the same sign as the effect of the buyback on the total resources captured by the creditor: If the price goes up after a buyback then creditors benefit from the buyback, while if it falls they lose. As we showed in the previous section, however, if there is some chance that the debtor will experience default penalties, then an improvement in the creditor's situation does not necessarily come at the expense of the debtor. Both could gain.[43]

---

[43] A number of papers provide scenarios in which debt buybacks could benefit a debtor. Costa-Cabral (1993) provides a very general model of debt buybacks which incorporates a domestic investment decision, showing that a buyback can lead to more investment. Goldberg and Spiegel (1992) show that buybacks can help a debtor country by eliminating its incentive to direct investment away from sectors whose output is subject to seizure by disgruntled creditors. Detragiache (1993a) shows that the fiscal burden imposed by future debt can make buybacks desirable. Acharya (1991) provides a model in which buybacks signal a willingness to undertake investments that will increase repayment in the future. To support this hypothesis he provides evidence that: (1) creditors are more likely to provide debt relief to countries with buyback programs; (2) buybacks lead to higher secondary market prices of debt; and (3) a country's willingness to engage in buybacks is correlated with other measures of its creditworthiness.

Secondary market prices: Bolivian and other experiences

A buyback that received particular attention from academics was undertaken by Bolivia. Bulow and Rogoff (1988a) report that when the possibility of the buyback was first discussed in September 1986. Bolivia's private bank debt traded at 6 cents on the dollar, so that its nominal debt of $670 million had a market value of just $40.2 million. In March 1988, with donated funds, Bolivia bought back $308 million in nominal debt for $34 million (at a price of around 11 cents on the dollar). After the buyback the price of the remaining $362 million in debt outstanding remained at 11 cents on the dollar, so that it had a market value of $39.8 million. Since the market value of the debt presumably affects what creditors hope to collect, an implication is that the buyback had no effect on what creditors expected Bolivia to pay subsequent to the buyback. In other words, the resources captured by the creditors in the buyback itself was pure gravy.[44] Whether the banks' gain was Bolivia's loss depends on the extent to which a reduction in debt led to any efficiency gain. The likelihood that potential efficiency gains were worth the cost of the buyback has been hotly debated.

More recently, Dooley, Fernandez-Arias, and Kletzer (1994) have undertaken a more comprehensive econometric analysis of secondary market prices with a panel of 21 developing countries during 1986–1992. They conclude that the dominant factor governing price movements was the international interest rate, rather than conditions or policies in the countries themselves.[45]

4.3. Public initiatives

The argument that the private sector cannot restructure sovereign debt efficiently has led to proposals for government intervention. Kenen (1990) and Sachs (1990), among others, propose that a public institution buy up debt from private creditors and restructure it. The argument is that it would overcome the coordination problem facing private creditors discussed in Section 4.1.2. At issue is whether the institution would finance itself. Proponents argue that problem debtors are indeed on the downward sloping parts of their ''debt Laffer curves''. Hence a public institution, by consolidating and reducing debt, would collect more than private debtholders could expect to receive.

Another form of public involvement is through participation in negotiations between private creditors and sovereign debtors. Recently this has taken the form of what are called ''Brady plans'' in which private creditors are asked to refinance debt,

---

[44]Sachs (1988), however, argued why troubled banks might nonetheless oppose buybacks. They had been carrying debt on their books at face rather than at market value. Selling the loans at the market price would force them to write down the value of their assets, possibly forcing liquidation.

[45]Other contributions to the literature on secondary market prices are Dooley (1988), Claessens, van Wijnbergen, and Pennachi (1992), Cohen and Portes (1992), and Dooley and Stone (1993).

usually given the choice between providing new loans at fixed rates or accepting "exit bonds" with reduced principal and interest. In exchange for refinancing, public lending institutions have provided a partial guarantee of what is refinanced. This procedure makes creditors who refinance under the plan effectively senior to those who do not. How much these schemes will ultimately cost the public depends upon the extent to which the guarantees are called upon.[46]

Most discussion of either type of public involvement has taken the existence of the outstanding loans as given. At issue, however, is the extent to which private lenders and borrowers anticipate the possibility of subsequent public involvement when the loans are made initially. Even though public intervention may be optimal ex post, i.e. once loans have been made, its anticipation could lead creditors initially to lend more than is efficient, so that, ex ante, public involvement makes things worse.

Bulow and Rogoff (1988b) demonstrate this possibility in a model of trilateral debt renegotiation among a sovereign debtor, its private creditors, and official institutions. If the negotiations fail, private creditors will seek legal remedies which benefit them but which harm the debtor and the world economy as a whole. To avoid a breakdown in the negotiations the official institutions provide a transfer to the debtor to help it repay its private creditors. The original loan contracts reflect anticipated public involvement down the road.[47]

5. Conclusion

As stated in the introduction, the literature on sovereign debt that we survey here was motivated by the wave of commercial bank lending to developing-country governments during the 1970s and 1980s. As international credit markets evolve, an outstanding research issue is to identify how alternative modes of finance could avoid the potential market failures that this work points to. One issue is the extent to which other forms of finance would add to the fiscal burden of the recipient country.[48] Another is how alternative forms would allocate exogenous risks between debtors and

---

[46]Spiegel (1993b) models burden sharing between private and official lenders in the presence of deposit insurance. A reason to give banks a "menu" of options is to overcome the heterogeneity problem discussed in Section 4.1.2. Weaker banks, for example, might prefer to provide new money rather than to accept exit bonds since these have a higher option value. Demirguc-Kunt, Diwan, and Spiegel (1993) find that this is exactly what happened in the Brazilian debt reduction deal of 1988. Claessens, Oks, and van Wijnbergen (1992) analyze the Mexican experience after its Brady deal.

[47]Wells (1993) models how changes in IMF lending procedures can influence the incentive of private creditors to restructure debt.

[48]For example, direct foreign investment and equity investment do not add directly to the tax obligations of the borrowing country government. Nevertheless, one lesson of the debt literature is that foreign investors may force a government to assume the obligations of its private nationals. The potential for multiplicity of equilibria and capital flight remain unless the government can credibly desist from serving as the implicit guarantor of foreign private investment of any form.

creditors.[49] Third, and most problematic, is the extent to which governments of borrowing countries would be committed to protecting the interests of foreign investors under alternative regimes.[50] A lesson of the debt literature is that the incentive for a sovereign government to honor external liabilities is subtle, and highly sensitive to the overall environment provided by the international financial system.

References

Acharya, S. (1991), "Debt buybacks signal sovereign countries' creditworthiness: theory and tests", Finance and Economics Discussion Series Paper No. 180, Board of Governors of the Federal Reserve System.

Armendariz de Aghion, B. (1990), "International debt: An explanation of the commercial banks' lending behavior after 1982", Journal of International Economics 28:173–186.

Alexander, L.S. (1987), "Three essays on sovereign default and international lending", Ph.D. dissertation, Yale University.

Atkeson, A. (1991), "International lending with moral hazard and risk of repudiation", Econometrica 59:1069–1090.

Bhattacharya, S. and E. Detragiache (1993), "The role of multinational institutions in the market for sovereign debt", Innocenzo Gasparini Institute for Economic Research Working Paper No. 39.

Bulow, J. and K. Rogoff (1988a), "The buy back boondoggle", Brookings Papers on Economic Activity 2:675–704.

Bulow, J. and K. Rogoff (1988b), "Multilateral negotiations for rescheduling developing country debt", International Monetary Fund Staff Papers 35:644–657.

Bulow, J. and K. Rogoff (1989a), "A constant recontracting model of sovereign debt", Journal of Political Economy 97:155–178.

Bulow, J. and K. Rogoff (1989b), "LDC debt: Is to forgive to forget?", American Economic Review 79:43–50.

Bulow, J. and K. Rogoff (1990), "Cleaning up third world debt without getting taken to the cleaners", Journal of Economic Perspectives, 4:31–42.

Bulow, J. and K. Rogoff (1991), "Sovereign debt repurchases: No cure for overhang", Quarterly Journal of Economics 427:1219–1235.

Chang, R. (1991), "Private investment and sovereign debt negotiations", C.V. Starr Research Report 91-47, New York University.

Claessens, S. (1995), "Symposium on emerging capital markets", World Bank Economic Review, 9:1–174.

[49]On the face of it, debt finance leaves the country bearing the full burden of domestic shocks. As Grossman and van Huyck (1988) argue, however, the opportunity to renegotiate syndicated bank loans implicitly allows a country to "default excusably" when it faces especially adverse circumstances. The greater dispersion of creditors in the case of bond finance might suggest that bonds would allow for much less flexibility in resetting terms in response to bad outcomes. Nevertheless, Eichengreen and Portes (1989) claim that the terms of bond issues were often renegotiated when the borrowing country ran into trouble. Conditions in international credit markets pose another source of risk. Detragiache (1992) compares the risk-sharing properties of floating and fixed rate contracts. Worrall (1990) and Atkeson (1991) analyze the risk-sharing characteristics of sovereign debt contracts in general equilibrium settings.

[50]While sovereign debt is subject to default risk, direct foreign investment and equity investment are subject to the risk not only of expropriation, but of other government actions, such as changes in tax laws and regulations, that shift profits away from investors. The literature on expropriation includes papers by Eaton and Gersovitz (1984) and Cole and English (1988). Claessens (1995) provides a set of papers analyzing emerging equity markets in developing countries.

Claessens, S. and I. Diwan (1990), "Investment incentives: New money, debt relief, and the critical role of conditionality in the debt crisis", The World Bank Economic Review 4:21–41.

Claessens, S., I. Diwan, and D. Oks (1992), "Interest rates, growth, and external debt: The macroeconomic impact of Mexico's Brady deal", manuscript, The World Bank.

Claessons, S., D. Oks, and S. van Wijnbergen (1993), "Interest rates, growth, and external debt: The macroeconomic impact of Mexico's Brady deal", manuscript, The World Bank.

Claessons, S., S. van Wijnbergen, and G. Pennachi (1992), "Deriving developing country repayment capacity from the market prices of sovereign debt", World Bank Policy Research Paper No. WPS/1043.

Cohen, D. (1990), "Debt relief: Implications of secondary market discount and debt overhangs", The World Bank Economic Review 4:43–53.

Cohen, D. (1991), Private lending to sovereign states: A theoretical autopsy (MIT Press, Cambridge, MA).

Cohen, D. (1992), "The debt crisis: A postmortem", National Bureau of Economic Research Macroeconomics Annual 7:65–105.

Cohen, D. (1993), "Low investment and large LDC debt in the 1980s", American Economic Review 83:437–449.

Cohen, D. and R. Portes (1990), "The price of LDC dept", CEPR Discussion Paper No. 459.

Cohen, D. and J. Sachs (1986), "Growth and external debt under risk of debt repudiation", European Economic Review 30:579–590.

Cole, H.L., J. Dow, and W.B. English (1995), "Default, settlement and signaling: Lending resumption in a reputation model of sovereign debt", International Economic Review, 36:365–386.

Cole, H. and W.B. English (1988), "Expropriation and direct investment", International Economics Research Center, University of Pennsylvania.

Cole, H.L. and P.J. Kehoe (1992), "Reputation spillover across relationships with enduring and transient benefits: Reviving reputation models of debt", working paper, Federal Reserve Bank of Minneapolis.

Cooper, R.N. and J. Sachs (1985), "Borrowing abroad: The debtor's perspective", in: G.W. Smith and J.T. Cuddington, eds., International debt and the developing countries (World Bank, Washington, D.C.).

Corden, W.M. (1989), "Debt relief and adjustment incentives: A theoretical exploration", in: J. Frenkel, M. Dooley, and P. Wickham, eds., Analytical issues in debt (International Monetary Fund, Washington, D.C.).

Costa-Cabral, C. (1993), "Evaluating debt repurchases: What are the alternatives to investment?" Universidad Carlos III de Madrid Working Paper 93-43.

Demirguc-Kunt, A. and E. Detragiache (1992), "Interest rates, official lending, and the debt crisis: A reassessment", Debt and International Finance Working Paper No. 932, The World Bank.

Demirguc-Kunt, A., I. Diwan, and M.M. Spiegel (1993), "Heterogeneity in bank valuation of LDC debt: Evidence from the 1988 Brazilian debt-reduction program", manuscript, The World Bank and New York University.

Demirguc-Kunt, A. and E. Fernandez-Arias (1992), "Burden sharing among official and private creditors", World Bank Working Paper No. 943.

Detragiache, E. (1992), "Optimal loan contracts and floating-rate debt in international lending to LDCs", European Economic Review 36:1241–1261.

Detragiache, E. (1993a), "Sensible buybacks of sovereign debt", Journal of Development Economics, forthcoming.

Detragiache, E. (1993b), "Fiscal adjustment and official reserves in sovereign debt negotiations", manuscript, Johns Hopkins University.

Detragiache, E. and P.G. Garella (1993), "Debt restructuring with multiple creditors: A public good approach", Innocenzo Gasparini Institute for Economic Research Working Paper No. 47.

Diamond, D. (1984), "Financial intermediation and delegated monitoring", Review of Economic Studies 51:393–414.

Diaz-Alejandro, C.F. (1984), "Latin American debt: I don't think we are in Kansas anymore", Brookings Papers on Economic Activity, 2:335–389.

Diaz-Alejandro, C.F. (1985), "Good-bye financial repression, hello financial crash", Journal of Development Economics 19:1–24.

Diwan, I. and S. Claessens (1989a), "Market based debt reductions", in: I. Hussain and I. Diwan, eds., Dealing with the debt crisis.

Diwan, I. and S. Claessens (1989b), "An analysis of debt-reduction schemes initiated by debtor countries", Debt and International Finance Working Paper No. 153, The World Bank.

Diwan, I. and K. Kletzer (1992), "Voluntary choices in concerted deals: The menu approach to debt reduction in developing countries", The World Bank Economic Review 6:91–108.

Diwan, I. and D. Rodrik (1992), "External debt, adjustment, and burden sharing: A unified framework", Princeton Studies in International Finance 73.

Diwan, I. and M.M. Spiegel (1993), "Are buybacks back?: Menu-driven debt reduction schemes with heterogeneous creditors", manuscript, The World Bank and New York University.

Dooley, M. (1988), "Buybacks and the market valuation of external debt", International Monetary Fund Staff Papers 35:215–229.

Dooley, M.P., E. Fernandez-Arias, and K.M. Kletzer (1994), "Recent private capital flows to developing countries: Is the debt crisis history?", National Bureau of Economic Research Working Paper No. 4792.

Dooley, M. and K.M. Kletzer (1994), "Capital flight, external debt, and domestic fiscal policies", National Bureau of Economic Research Working Paper No. 4793.

Dooley, M. and M. Stone (1993), "Endogenous creditor seniority and external debt values", IMF Staff Papers, 40: 395–413.

Eaton, J. (1987), "Public debt guarantees and private capital flight", World Bank Economic Review 7:377–396.

Eaton, J. (1990a), "Debt relief and the international enforcement of loan contracts", Journal of Economic Perspectives 4:43–56.

Eaton, J. (1990b), "Sovereign debt, reputation, and credit terms", National Bureau of Economic Research Working Paper No. 3424.

Eaton, J. and M. Gersovitz (1981), "Debt with potential repudiation: Theoretical and empirical analysis", Review of Economic Studies 48:289–309.

Eaton, J. and M. Gersovitz (1984), "A theory of expropriation and deviations from perfect capital mobility", Economic Journal 94:16–40.

Eaton, J. and M. Gersovitz (1988) "Country risk and the organization of international capital transfer", in J.B. de Macedo and R. Findlay, eds., Debt growth and stabilization. Essays in memory of Carlos F. Diaz-Alejandro (Basil Blackwell, Oxford).

Eaton, J. and M. Gersovitz (1994), "Some curious properties of a familiar model of debt and default", Economic Letters, forthcoming.

Eaton, J., M. Gersovitz, and J. Stiglitz (1986), "The pure theory of country risk", European Economic Review 30:481–513.

Edwards, S. (1984), "LDC's foreign borrowing and default risk: An empirical investigation", American Economic Review 74:726–734.

Eichengreen, B. and R. Portes (1986), "Debt and default in the 1930s: Causes and consequences", European Economic Review 30:599–640.

Eichengreen, B. and R. Portes (1989), "Settling defaults in the era of bond finance", World Bank Economic Review 3:211–240.

Fernandez, R. and J. Glazer (1990), "The scope for collusive behavior among debtor countries", Journal of Development Economics 32:297–313.

Fernandez, R. and D. Kaaret (1992), "Bank heterogeneity, reputation, and debt renegotiation", International Economic Review 33:61–78.

Fernandez, R. and S. Ozler (1991), "Debt concentration and secondary market prices: A theoretical and empirical analysis", National Bureau of Economic Research Working Paper 3654.

Fernandez, R. and R. Rosenthal (1990), "Sovereign debt renegotiations: A strategic analysis", Review of Economic Studies 57:331–350.

Froot, K. (1989), "Buy-backs, exit-bonds, and the optimality of debt and liquidity relief", International Economic Review 30:45–70.

Gale, D. and M. Hellwig (1989), "Repudiation and renegotiation: The case of sovereign debt", International Economic Review 30:3–31.

Gersovitz, M. (1983), "Trade, capital mobility and sovereign immunity", Research Program in Development Studies Paper No. 108, Princeton University.

Goldberg, L. and M.M. Spiegel (1992), "Debt write downs and debt-equity swaps in a two-sector model", Journal of International Economics 33:267–283.

Grossman, H.I. and J.B. van Huyck (1988), "Sovereign debt as a contingent claim: excusable default, repudiation and reputation", American Economic Review 78:1088–1097.

Hellwig, M. (1977), "A model of borrowing and lending with bankruptcy", Econometrica 45:1879–1906.

Helpman, E. (1989), "Voluntary debt reduction", International Monetary Fund Staff Papers 36:580–611.

Helpman, E. (1990), "The simple analytics of debt equity swaps", American Economic Review 79:440–451.

Jaffee, D. and F. Modigliani (1969), "A theory of credit rationing", American Economic Review 59:850–872.

Kahn, R.B. (1984), "External borrowing and the commons nature of foreign exchange", unpublished manuscript, Board of Governors of the Federal Reserve System.

Kaletsky, A. (1985), The costs of default, Twentieth century fund (Priority Press, New York).

Kaneko, M. and J. Prokop (1993), "A game-theoretic to the international debt overhang", Journal of Economics 1:1–24.

Kenen, P.B. (1990), "Organizing debt relief: The need for a new institution", Journal of Economic Perspectives, 4:7–18.

Keynes, J.M. (1924), "Foreign investment and national advantage", The Nation and Atheneum, 584–587.

Kletzer, K.M. (1984), "Asymmetries of information and LDC borrowing with sovereign risk", Economic Journal 94:287–307.

Kletzer, K.M. and B. Wright (1990), "Sovereign debt renegotiations in a consumption-smoothing model", manuscript, University of California at Santa Cruz.

Kreps, D.M. and R. Wilson (1982), "Reputation and imperfect information", Journal of Economic Theory 27:253–279.

Krugman, P. (1988), "Financing vs. forgiving a debt overhang: Some analytic notes", Journal of Development Economics 29:253–268.

Lindert, P. and P. Morton (1989), "How sovereign debt has worked", in: J. Sachs, ed., Developing country debt and economic performance (University of Chicago Press, Chicago).

Manuelli, R. (1986), "A general equilibrium model of international credit markets", manuscript, Stanford University.

Milgrom, P. and J. Roberts (1982), "Predation, reputation, and entry deterrence", Journal of Economic Theory 27:280–312.

Ozler, S. (1989), "On the relation between reschedulings and bank value", American Economic Review 79:1117–1135.

Ozler, S. (1991), "Evolution of commercial credit terms: An empirical study of commercial bank lending to developing countries", Journal of Development Economics 38:79–97.

Ozler, S. (1993), "Have commercial banks ignored history?", American Economic Review 83:608–620.

Rosenthal, R. (1991), "On the incentives associated with foreign debt", Journal of International Economics 30:167–176.

Rubinstein, A. (1982), "Perfect equilibrium in a bargaining model", Econometrica 50:97–109.

Sachs, J. (1984), "Theoretical issues in international borrowing", Princeton Studies in International Finance No. 54.

Sachs, J. (1988), "The debt overhang of developing countries", in J.B. de Macedo and R. Findlay, eds., Debt stabilization, and growth essays in memory of Carlos F. Diaz-Alejandro (Basil Blackwell, Oxford).

Sachs, J. (1990), "A strategy for efficient debt reduction", Journal of Economic Perspectives 4:19–29.

Sachs, J. and D. Cohen (1985), "LDC borrowing with default risk", Kredit und Kapital 8:211–235.

Spiegel, M.M. (1992), "Concerted lending: Did large banks bear the burden?", Journal of Money, Credit, and Banking 24:465–481.

Spiegel, M.M. (1993a), "Fixed premium deposit insurance and collective action problems among banks", manuscript, New York University.

Spiegel, M.M. (1993b), "Burden-sharing in sovereign debt renegotiations", manuscript, New York University.

Stiglitz, J.E. and A. Weiss (1981), "Credit rationing in markets with imperfect information", American Economic Review 71:393–410.

Wells, R. (1993), "Tolerance of arrearages: How IMF loan policy can effect debt reduction", American Economic Review 71:621–633.

World Bank (1993), World debt tables.

Worrall, T. (1990), "Debt with potential repudiation", European Economic Review 34:1099–1109.

INDEX